Programming with MFC

Microsoft® Visual C++™

**Development System for Windows® 95 and Windows NT™
Version 4**

Microsoft Corporation

PUBLISHED BY
Microsoft Press
A Division of Microsoft Corporation
One Microsoft Way
Redmond, Washington 98052-6399

Library of Congress Cataloging-in-Publication Data
Microsoft Visual C++ programmer's references / Microsoft Corporation.
   -- 2nd ed.
       p.   cm.
   Includes index.
     v. 1. Microsoft Visual C++ user's guide -- v. 2. Programming with
MFC -- v. 3. Microsoft foundation class library reference, part 1 --
v. 4. Microsoft foundation class library reference, part 2 -- v.
5. Microsoft Visual C++ run-time library reference -- v.
6. Microsoft Visual C/C++ language reference.
     ISBN 1-55615-915-3 (v. 1). -- ISBN 1-55615-921-8 (v. 2). -- ISBN
1-55615-922-6 (v. 3). -- ISBN 1-55615-923-4 (v. 4). -- ISBN
1-55615-924-2 (v. 5). -- ISBN 1-55615-925-0 (v. 6)
     1. C++ (Computer program language) 2. Microsoft Visual C++.
I. Microsoft Corporation.
QA76.73.C153M53   1995
005.13'3--dc20   95-35604
                                                            CIP

Printed and bound in the United States of America.

1 2 3 4 5 6 7 8 9   QMQM   0 9 8 7 6 5

Distributed to the book trade in Canada by Macmillan of Canada, a division of
Canada Publishing Corporation.

A CIP catalogue record for this book is available from the British Library.

Microsoft Press books are available through booksellers and distributors worldwide. For further
information about international editions, contact your local Microsoft Corporation office. Or
contact Microsoft Press International directly at fax (206) 936-7329.

Acquisitions Editor: Eric Stroo
Project Editor: Brenda L. Matteson

Contents

Figures and Tables

Tables

Contents

Introduction

This book contains information on programming with the Microsoft® Foundation Class Library (MFC). The class library is a set of C++ classes that encapsulate the functionality of applications written for the Microsoft Windows® operating system. This version of MFC supports programming for Win32® platforms, including Microsoft Windows NT™ and Windows 95.

Part 1, meant to be read sequentially, is an overview of the class library, designed to help you understand the major components of an MFC application and how they work together. Part 1 explains the following topics:

- The key components of an MFC application:
  - An application object, which represents your application
  - Document template objects, which create document, frame window, and view objects
  - Document objects, which store data and serialize it to persistent storage
  - View objects, which display a document's data and manage the user's interaction with the data
  - Frame window objects, which contain views
  - Thread objects, which let you program multiple threads of execution using MFC classes
- Dialog boxes, controls, and control bars, such as toolbars and status bars.
- OLE visual editing and OLE Automation.
- OLE controls and the classes and tools used to develop them.
- Database support using Open Database Connectivity (ODBC) and Data Access Objects (DAO).
- Useful general-purpose classes, such as strings, collections, exceptions, and date/time objects.

Part 2, designed for random access, presents an encyclopedia—an alphabetical collection of articles on programming with MFC. You can use these articles to follow many different threads of information. For an overview of how the articles work with each other, see the first article Using the Encyclopedia. Articles that begin particularly important threads include:

- MFC
- OLE Overview
- Database Overview
- OLE Controls

Document Conventions

This book uses the following typographic conventions:

Example	Description
STDIO.H	Uppercase letters indicate filenames, registers, and terms used at the operating-system command level
char, _setcolor, __far	Bold type indicates C and C++ keywords, operators, and library routines. Within discussions of syntax, bold type indicates that the text must be entered exactly as shown.
	Many constants, functions, and keywords begin with either a single or double underscore. These are required as part of the name. For example, the compiler recognizes the **__cplusplus** manifest constant only when the leading double underscore is included.
expression	Words in italics indicate placeholders for information you must supply, such as a filename. Italic type is also used occasionally for emphasis in the text.
⟦option⟧	Items inside double square brackets are optional.
#pragma pack {1 | 2}	Braces and a vertical bar indicate a choice among two or more items. You must choose one of these items unless double square brackets (⟦ ⟧) surround the braces.
`#include <io.h>`	This font is used for examples, user input, program output, and error messages in text.
CL ⟦option...⟧ file...	Three dots (an ellipsis) following an item indicate that more items having the same form may appear.

`while()`
`{`
`  .`
`  .`
`  .`
`}`
	A column or row of three dots tells you that part of an example program has been intentionally omitted.

Example	Description
CTRL+ENTER	Small capital letters are used to indicate the names of keys on the keyboard. When you see a plus sign (+) between two key names, you should hold down the first key while pressing the second.
	The carriage-return key, sometimes marked as a bent arrow on the keyboard, is called ENTER.
"argument"	Quotation marks enclose a new term the first time it is defined in text.
"C string"	Some C constructs, such as strings, require quotation marks. Quotation marks required by the language have the form " " and ' ' rather than " " and ' '.
Dynamic-Link Library (DLL)	The first time an acronym is used, it is usually spelled out.
Microsoft Specific →	Some features documented in this book have special usage constraints. A heading identifying the nature of the exception, followed by an arrow, marks the beginning of these exception features.
END Microsoft Specific	**END** followed by the exception heading marks the end of text about a feature which has a usage constraint.

Overview of the MFC Library

Using the Classes to Write Applications for Windows

Taken together, the classes in the Microsoft Foundation Class Library (MFC) make up an "application framework"—the framework on which you build an application for Windows. At a very general level, the framework defines the skeleton of an application and supplies standard user-interface implementations that can be placed onto the skeleton. Your job as programmer is to fill in the rest of the skeleton—those things that are specific to your application. You can get a head start by using AppWizard to create the files for a very thorough starter application. You use the Microsoft Visual C++™ resource editors to design your user-interface elements visually, ClassWizard to connect those elements to code, and the class library to implement your application-specific logic.

Version 3.0 and later of the MFC framework supports 32-bit programming for Win32 platforms, including Microsoft Windows 95 and Microsoft Windows NT version 3.51 and later. MFC Win32 support includes multithreading.

This chapter presents a broad overview of the application framework. It also explores the major objects that make up your application and how they are created. Among the topics covered in this chapter are the following:

- The framework
- Division of labor between the framework and your code
- The application class, which encapsulates application-level functionality
- How document templates create and manage documents and their associated views and frame windows
- Class **CWnd**, the root base class of all windows
- Graphic objects, such as pens and brushes

Subsequent chapters continue the framework story, covering:

- Chapter 2, Working with Messages and Commands
- Chapter 3, Working with Frame Windows, Documents, and Views
- Chapter 4, Working with Dialog Boxes, Controls, and Control Bars
- Chapter 5, Working with OLE

Besides giving you a considerable head start in writing applications for Windows, MFC also makes it much easier to write applications that specifically use OLE. You can make your application an OLE Visual Editing container, an OLE Visual Editing server, or both, and you can add OLE Automation so that other applications can use objects from your application or even drive it remotely.

- Chapter 6, Developing OLE Controls

  The OLE control development kit (CDK) is now fully integrated with the framework. This chapter supplies an overview of OLE control development with MFC.

- Chapter 7, Working with Databases

  MFC also supplies a set of database classes that simplify writing data-access applications. Using the database classes, you can connect to databases via an Open Database Connectivity (ODBC) driver, select records from tables, and display record information in an on-screen form.

- Chapter 8, Using the General-Purpose Classes

  In addition, MFC is fully enabled for writing applications that use Unicode™ and multibyte character sets (MBCS), specifically double-byte character sets (DBCS).

For a step-by-step tutorial in which you build an application with the framework, read *Tutorials*, Chapters 2 through 11. The following table directs you to other documents:

Table 1.1 Where to Find More Information

Topic	Book	Chapters
Classes mentioned in this book	*Class Library Reference*	Alphabetic reference
AppWizard	*Visual C++ User's Guide*	Chapter 1
ClassWizard and WizardBar	*Visual C++ User's Guide*	Chapter 14
Development environment	*Visual C++ User's Guide*	Chapters 1–22
Tutorials	*Tutorials*	Chapters 2–35
Diagnostics, exceptions	*Programming with MFC* (this book)	Part 2 (see Diagnostics and Exceptions)
Macros and globals	*Class Library Reference*	Alphabetic reference
Resources	*Visual C++ User's Guide*	Chapters 5–12
OLE programming	*Programming with MFC*	Chapter 5 and Part 2 (see OLE Overview)
OLE controls programming	*Programming with MFC*	Chapter 6 and Part 2 (see OLE Controls)
Database programming (ODBC and DAO)	*Programming with MFC*	Chapter 7 and Part 2 (see Database Overview)

The Framework

Your work with the framework is based largely on a few major classes and several Visual C++ tools. Some of the classes encapsulate a large portion of the Win32 application programming interface (API). Other classes encapsulate application concepts such as documents, views, and the application itself. Still others encapsulate OLE features and ODBC and DAO data-access functionality.

SDI and MDI

MFC makes it easy to work with both single document interface (SDI) and multiple document interface (MDI) applications.

SDI applications allow only one open document frame window at a time. MDI applications allow multiple document frame windows to be open in the same instance of an application. An MDI application has a window within which multiple MDI child windows, which are frame windows themselves, can be opened, each containing a separate document. In some applications, the child windows can be of different types, such as chart windows and spreadsheet windows. In that case, the menu bar can change as MDI child windows of different types are activated.

Note Under Windows 95, applications will increasingly be SDI as the operating system moves towards a "document-centered" view.

Documents, Views, and the Framework

At the heart of the framework are the concepts of document and view. A document is a data object with which the user interacts in an editing session. It is created by the New or Open command on the File menu and is typically saved in a file. A view is a window object through which the user interacts with a document.

The key objects in a running application are:

- The document(s)

  Your document class (derived from **CDocument**) specifies your application's data.

  If you want OLE functionality in your application, derive your document class from **COleDocument** or one of its derived classes, depending on the type of functionality you need.

- The view(s)

  Your view class (derived from **CView**) is the user's "window on the data." The view class specifies how the user sees your document's data and interacts with it. In some cases, you may want a document to have multiple views of the data.

  If you need scrolling, derive from **CScrollView**. If your view has a user interface that is laid out in a dialog-template resource, derive from **CFormView**. For simple text data, use or derive from **CEditView**. For a form-based data-access application, such as a data-entry program, derive from **CRecordView** (for ODBC) or **CDaoRecordView** (for DAO). Also available are classes **CTreeView**, **CListView**, and **CRichEditView**.

- The frame windows

  Views are displayed inside "document frame windows." In an SDI application, the document frame window is also the "main frame window" for the application. In an MDI application, document windows are child windows displayed inside a main frame window. Your derived main frame-window class specifies the styles and other characteristics of the frame windows that contain your views. Derive from **CFrameWnd** to customize the document frame window for SDI applications. Derive from **CMDIFrameWnd** to customize the main frame window for MDI applications. Also derive a class from **CMDIChildWnd** to customize each of the distinct kinds of MDI document frame windows that your application supports.

- The document template(s)

  A document template orchestrates the creation of documents, views, and frame windows. A particular document-template class, derived from class **CDocTemplate**, creates and manages all open documents of one type. Applications that support more than one type of document have multiple document templates. Use class **CSingleDocTemplate** for SDI applications, or use class **CMultiDocTemplate** for MDI applications.

- The application object

  Your application class (derived from **CWinApp**) controls all of the objects above and specifies application behavior such as initialization and cleanup. The application's one and only application object creates and manages the document templates for any document types the application supports.

- Thread objects

  If your application creates separate threads of execution—for example, to perform calculations in the background—you'll use classes derived from **CWinThread**. **CWinApp** itself is derived from **CWinThread** and represents the primary thread of execution (or the main process) in your application. You can also use MFC in secondary threads.

In a running application, these objects cooperatively respond to user actions, bound together by commands and other messages. A single application object manages one or more document templates. Each document template creates and manages one or more documents (depending on whether the application is SDI or MDI). The user views and manipulates a document through a view contained inside a frame window. Figure 1.1 shows the relationships among these objects for an SDI application.

Figure 1.1   Objects in a Running SDI Application

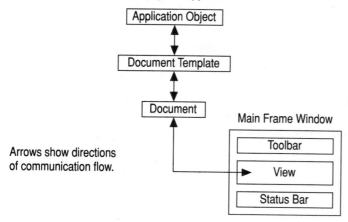

The rest of this chapter explains how the framework tools, AppWizard, ClassWizard, WizardBar, and the resource editors, create these objects, how they work together, and how you use them in your programming. Documents, views, and frame windows are discussed in more detail in Chapter 3, Working with Frame Windows, Documents, and Views.

AppWizard, ClassWizard, and the Resource Editors

Visual C++ includes two wizards and the WizardBar for use in MFC programming, along with many integrated resource editors. For OLE controls programming, the ControlWizard serves a purpose much like that of AppWizard. While you can write MFC applications without most of these tools, the tools greatly simplify and speed your work.

Use AppWizard to Create an MFC Application

Use AppWizard to create an MFC project in Visual C++—which can include OLE and database support. Files in the project contain your application, document, view, and frame-window classes; standard resources, including menus and an optional toolbar; other required Windows files; and optional .RTF files containing standard Windows Help topics.

Use ClassWizard to Manage Classes and Windows Messages

ClassWizard helps you create handler functions for Windows messages and commands; create and manage classes; create class member variables; create OLE Automation methods and properties; create database classes; and more.

Tip ClassWizard also helps you to override virtual functions in the MFC classes. Select the class and select the virtual function to override. The rest of the process is similar to message handling, as described in the following paragraphs.

Applications running under Windows are "message driven." User actions and other events that occur in the running program cause Windows to send messages to the windows in the program. For example, if the user clicks the mouse in a window, Windows sends a **WM_LBUTTONDOWN** message when the left mouse button is pressed and a **WM_LBUTTONUP** message when the button is released. Windows also sends **WM_COMMAND** messages when the user selects commands from the menu bar.

In the framework, various objects—documents, views, frame windows, document templates, the application object—can "handle" messages. Such an object provides a "handler function" as one of its member functions, and the framework maps the incoming message to its handler.

A large part of your programming task is choosing which messages to map to which objects and then implementing that mapping. To do so, you use ClassWizard.

ClassWizard will create empty message-handler member functions, and you use the source code editor to implement the body of the handler.

Quick access to frequently used features of ClassWizard are available at the top of your source code files in the WizardBar, built into the frame window that displays your source code file.

Use the Resource Editors to Create and Edit Resources

Use the Visual C++ resource editors to create and edit menus, dialog boxes, custom controls, accelerator keys, bitmaps, icons, cursors, strings, and version resources. ClassWizard works with the editors: for example, when you create a dialog-template resource, you can run ClassWizard to connect the resource to a dialog class. As of Visual C++ version 4.0, a toolbar editor makes creating toolbars much easier.

To help you even more, the Microsoft Foundation Class Library provides a file called COMMON.RES, which contains "clip art" resources that you can copy from COMMON.RES and paste into your own resource file. COMMON.RES includes toolbar buttons, common cursors, icons, and more. You can use, modify, and redistribute these resources in your application. For more information about COMMON.RES, see the article COMMON.RES Sample Resources.

For more information about the tools and how they work together, see the article Tools for MFC Programming.

Building on the Framework

Your role in configuring an application with the framework is to supply the application-specific source code and to connect the components by defining what messages and commands they respond to. You use the C++ language and standard C++ techniques to derive your own application-specific classes from those supplied by the class library and to override and augment the base class's behavior.

Table 1.2 shows what you do in relation to what the framework does. Table 1.3 shows your role and the framework's role in creating OLE applications. Table 1.4 shows your role and the framework's role in creating OLE controls. Table 1.5 shows the same kind of information for working with databases. For the most part, you can follow these tables as a sequence of steps for creating an MFC application, although some of the steps are alternative options. For example, most applications use one type of view class from the several types available.

Table 1.2   Sequence for Building an Application with the Framework

Task	You do	The framework does
Create a skeleton application.	Run AppWizard. Specify the options you want in the options pages. Options include making the application an OLE server, container, or both; adding OLE Automation; and making the application database-aware.	AppWizard creates the files for a skeleton application, including source files for your application, document, view, and frame windows; a resource file; a project file (.MAK); and others—all tailored to your specifications.
See what the framework and AppWizard offer without adding a line of your own code.	Build the skeleton application and run it in Visual C++.	The running skeleton application derives many standard File, Edit, View, and Help menu commands from the framework. For MDI applications, you also get a fully functional Window menu, and the framework manages creation, arrangement, and destruction of MDI child windows.

Table 1.2 Sequence for Building an Application with the Framework *(cont.)*

Task	You do	The framework does
Construct your application's user interface.	Use the Visual C++ resource editors to visually edit the a7 Create menus. Define accelerators. Create dialog boxes. Create and edit bitmaps, icons, and cursors. Edit the toolbar created for you by AppWizard. Create and edit other resources. You can also test the dialog boxes in the dialog editor.	The default resource file created by AppWizard supplies many of the resources you need. Visual C++ lets you edit existing resources and add new resources, easily and visually.
Map menus to handler functions.	Use ClassWizard or WizardBar to connect menus and accelerators to handler functions in your code.	ClassWizard or WizardBar inserts message-map entries and empty function templates in the source files you specify and manages many manual coding tasks.
Write your handler code.	Use ClassWizard or the Class View in the Project Workspace window to jump directly to the code in the source code editor. Fill in the code for your handler functions.	ClassWizard brings up the editor, scrolls to the empty function template, and positions the cursor for you.
Map toolbar buttons to commands.	Map each button on your toolbar to a menu or accelerator command by assigning the button the appropriate command ID.	The framework controls the drawing, enabling, disabling, checking, and other visual aspects of the toolbar buttons.
Test your handler functions.	Rebuild the program and use the built-in debugging tools to test that your handlers work correctly.	You can step or trace through the code to see how your handlers are called. If you've filled out the handler code, the handlers carry out commands. The framework will automatically disable menu items and toolbar buttons that are not handled.

Table 1.2   Sequence for Building an Application with the Framework *(cont.)*

Task	You do	The framework does
	Design dialog-template resources with the dialog editor. Then use ClassWizard to create a dialog class and the code that handles the dialog box.	The framework manages the dialog box and facilitates retrieving information entered by the user.
Initialize, validate, and retrieve dialog-box data.	You can also define how the dialog box's controls are to be initialized and validated. Use ClassWizard to add member variables to the dialog class and map them to dialog controls. Specify validation rules to be applied to each control as the user enters data. Provide your own custom validations if you wish.	The framework manages dialog-box initialization and validation. If the user enters invalid information, the framework displays a message box and lets the user reenter the data.
Create additional classes.	Use ClassWizard to create additional document, view, and frame-window classes beyond those created automatically by AppWizard. You can create additional database recordset classes, dialog classes, and so on.	ClassWizard adds these classes to your source files and helps you define their connections to any commands they handle.
Add ready-to-use components to your application.	Use Component Gallery to add a variety of components.	These components are easy to integrate into your application and save you a great deal of work.
Implement your document class.	Implement your application-specific document class(es). Add member variables to hold data structures. Add member functions to provide an interface to the data.	The framework already knows how to interact with document data files. It can open and close document files, read and write the document's data, and handle other user interfaces. You can focus on how the document's data is manipulated.
Implement Open, Save, and Save As commands.	Write code for the document's `Serialize` member function.	The framework displays dialog boxes for the Open, Save, and Save As commands on the File menu. It writes and reads back a document using the data format specified in your `Serialize` member function.

Table 1.2 Sequence for Building an Application with the Framework *(cont.)*

Task	You do	The framework does
Implement your view class.	Implement one or more view classes corresponding to your documents. Implement the view's member functions that you mapped to the user interface with ClassWizard. A variety of **CView**-derived classes are available, including **CListView** and **CTreeView**.	The framework manages most of the relationship between a document and its view. The view's member functions access the view's document to render its image on the screen or printed page and to update the document's data structures in response to user editing commands.
Enhance default printing.	If you need to support multipage printing, override view member functions.	The framework supports the Print, Print Setup, and Print Preview commands on the File menu. You must tell it how to break your document into multiple pages.
Add scrolling.	If you need to support scrolling, derive your view class(es) from **CScrollView**.	The view automatically adds scroll bars when the view window becomes too small.
Create form views.	If you want to base your views on dialog-template resources, derive your view class(es) from **CFormView**.	The view uses the dialog-template resource to display controls. The user can tab from control to control in the view.
Create database forms.	If you want a form-based data-access application, derive your view class from **CRecordView** (for ODBC programming) or **CDaoRecordView** (for DAO programming).	The view works like a form view, but its controls are connected to the fields of a **CRecordset** or **CDaoRecordset** object representing a database table. MFC moves data between the controls and the recordset for you.
Create a simple text editor.	If you want your view to be a simple text editor, derive your view class(es) from **CEditView**.	The view provides editing functions, Clipboard support, and file input/output.

Table 1.2   Sequence for Building an Application with the Framework *(cont.)*

Task	You do	The framework does
Add splitter windows.	If you want to support window splitting, add a **CSplitterWnd** object to your SDI frame window or MDI child window and hook it up in the window's **OnCreateClient** member function.	The framework supplies splitter-box controls next to the scroll bars and manages splitting your view into multiple panes. If the user splits a window, the framework creates and attaches additional view objects to the document.
Build, test, and debug your application.	Use the facilities of Visual C++ to build, test, and debug your application.	Visual C++ lets you adjust compile, link, and other options. And it lets you browse your source code and class structure.

Table 1.3 shows your role and the framework's role in creating OLE applications. These represent options available rather than a sequence of steps to perform.

Table 1.3   Creating OLE Applications

Task	You do	The framework does
Create an OLE server.	Run AppWizard. Choose OLE Full Server or OLE Mini-server in the OLE options. (From an existing application, emulate Step 7 in the Scribble tutorial.)	The framework generates a skeleton application with OLE server capability enabled. All of the OLE capability can be transferred to your existing application with only slight modification.
Create an OLE container application from scratch.	Run AppWizard. Choose OLE Container in the OLE options. In ClassWizard, jump to the source code editor. Fill in code for your OLE handler functions.	The framework generates a skeleton application that can insert OLE objects created by OLE server applications.
Create an application that supports OLE Automation from scratch.	Run AppWizard. Choose Automation Support in the OLE options. Use ClassWizard to expose methods and properties in your application for automation.	The framework generates a skeleton application that can be activated and automated by other applications.

Table 1.4 shows your role and the framework's role in creating OLE controls.

Table 1.4 Creating OLE Controls

Task	You do	The framework does
Create an OLE control framework.	Run a custom AppWizard, called OLE ControlWizard, to create your control. Specify the options you want in the options pages. Options include number of controls in the project, licensing, subclassing, and an 'About Box' method.	AppWizard creates the files for an OLE control with basic functionality, including source files for your application, control, and property page(s); a resource file; a project file (.MAK); and others—all tailored to your specifications.
See what the control and OLE ControlWizard offer without adding a line of your own code.	Build the OLE control and test it with Test Container.	The running control has the ability to be resized and moved. It also has an About Box method (if chosen) that can be invoked.
Implement the control's methods and properties.	Implement your control-specific methods and properties by adding member functions to provide an exposed interface to the control's data. Add member variables to hold data structures and use event handlers to fire events when you determine.	The framework has already defined a map to support the control's events, properties, and methods, leaving you to focus on how the properties and methods are implemented. The default property page is viewable and a default About Box method is supplied.
Construct the control's property page(s).	Use the Visual C++ resource editors to visually edit the control's property page interface: Create additional property pages. Create and edit bitmaps, icons, and cursors. You can also test the property page(s) in the dialog editor.	The default resource file created by AppWizard supplies many of the resources you need. Visual C++ lets you edit existing resources and add new resources, easily and visually.
Test the control's events, methods, and properties.	Rebuild the control and use Test Container to test that your handlers work correctly.	You can invoke the control's methods and manipulate its properties through the property page interface or through Test Container. In addition, use Test Container to track events fired from the control and notifications received by the control's container.

Table 1.5 shows your role and the framework's role in writing database applications.

Table 1.5   Creating Database Applications

Task	You do	The framework does
Decide whether to use the MFC DAO classes or the MFC ODBC classes.	See DAO or ODBC in *Programming with MFC*. For general information, see the article Database Overview.	The framework supplies two sets of database classes, one based on Data Access Objects (DAO) and the Microsoft Jet database engine, and the other based on ODBC.
Create your skeleton application with database options.	Run AppWizard. Select options on the database options page. If you choose one of the options that creates a record view, also specify a data source and table name(s) and/or query name(s).	AppWizard creates files and specifies the necessary includes. Depending on whether you specify DAO or ODBC and which other options you specify, the files can include a recordset class.
Design your database form(s).	Use the Visual C++ dialog editor to place controls on the dialog template resources for your record view classes.	AppWizard creates an empty dialog template resource for you to fill in.
Create additional record view and recordset classes as needed.	Use ClassWizard to create the classes and the dialog editor to design the views.	ClassWizard creates additional files for your new classes.
Create recordset objects as needed in your code. Use each recordset to manipulate records.	Your recordsets are based on the classes derived from **CRecordset** or **CDaoRecordset** with the wizards. If you're using DAO, you can also use **CDaoRecordset** objects without deriving a class of your own.	The framework uses record field exchange (DFX for DAO, RFX for ODBC) to exchange data between the database and your recordset's field data members. If you're using a record view, dialog data exchange (DDX) exchanges data between the recordset and the controls on the record view.
Or create an explicit **CDatabase** or **CDaoDatabase** object in your code for each database you want to open.	Base your recordset objects on the database objects.	The database object provides an interface to the data source.

Table 1.5 Creating Database Applications *(cont.)*

Task	You do	The framework does
In DAO, access a "workspace."	Use a **CDaoWorkspace** object to: access DAO's default workspace. manage a separate transaction space. access the Microsoft Jet database engine.	The workspace lets you manage one or more open databases in a single transaction space.
In DAO, work with tables and perform data definition language (DDL) tasks.	Use a **CDaoTableDef** object to: create a recordset. add a table. attach to an external data source, such as ODBC. examine table structure. add or delete fields and indexes and set other table properties.	
In DAO, work with stored queries.	Use a **CDaoQueryDef** object to: create a recordset. store a query. execute an action query or an SQL pass-through query.	
Bind data columns to your recordset dynamically.	In DAO, use a **CDaoRecordset** object directly to set or get field and parameter values. See the article DAO Recordset: Binding Records Dynamically. In ODBC, add code to your derived recordset class to manage the binding. See the article Recordset: Dynamically Binding Data Columns (ODBC).	

Table 1.5   Creating Database Applications *(cont.)*

Task	You do	The framework does
Work with data in external data sources, such as ODBC data sources (for which you need an ODBC driver, under either ODBC or DAO). A non-external data source is one you can open directly with the Microsoft Jet database engine.	In most cases with DAO, use **CDaoTableDef** objects to attach tables from the external data source rather than opening the data source directly.	

As you can see, AppWizard, the Visual C++ resource editors, ClassWizard, WizardBar and the framework do a lot of work for you and make managing your code much easier. The bulk of your application-specific code is in your document and view classes. For a tour of this process with real applications, see *Tutorials*:

- Chapters 2 through 11 show you how to use the basic MFC framework.
- Chapters 12 through 19 teach OLE programming techniques.
- Chapters 20 through 29 explain OLE control development.
- Chapters 30 through 33 explain ODBC database programming techniques.
- Chapter 34 explains DAO database programming.
- Chapter 35 explains how to obtain the Windows 95 logo.

While it is possible to do these tasks by hand or using other tools, your savings in time, energy, and errors suggest that using the tools and framework is greatly to your benefit.

How the Framework Calls Your Code

It is crucial to understand the relationship between your source code and the code in the framework. When your application runs, most of the flow of control resides in the framework's code. The framework manages the message loop that gets messages from Windows as the user chooses commands and edits data in a view. Events that the framework can handle by itself don't rely on your code at all. For example, the framework knows how to close windows and how to exit the application in response to user commands. As it handles these tasks, the framework uses message handlers and C++ virtual functions to give you opportunities to respond to these events as well. But your code is not in the driver's seat, the framework is.

Your code is called by the framework for application-specific events. For example, when the user chooses a menu command, the framework routes the command along a sequence of C++ objects: the current view and frame window, the document associated with the view, the document's document template, and the application object. If one of these objects can handle the command, it does so, calling the appropriate message-handler function. For any given command, the code called may be yours or it may be the framework's.

This arrangement is somewhat familiar to programmers experienced with traditional programming for Windows or event-driven programming.

In the next few topics, you'll see what the framework does as it initializes and runs the application and then cleans up as the application terminates. You'll also get a clearer picture of where the code you write fits in.

CWinApp: The Application Class

The main application class encapsulates the initialization, running, and termination of an application for Windows. An application built on the framework must have one (and only one) object of a class derived from **CWinApp**. This object is constructed before windows are created.

Note Your application class constitutes your application's primary thread of execution. Using Win32 API functions, you can also create secondary threads of execution. These threads can use the MFC library. For more information, see the article Multithreading.

Like any program for Windows, your framework application has a **WinMain** function. In a framework application, however, you don't write **WinMain**. It is supplied by the class library and is called when the application starts up. **WinMain** performs standard services such as registering window classes. Then it calls member functions of the application object to initialize and run the application.

To initialize the application, **WinMain** calls your application object's InitApplication and InitInstance member functions. To run the application's message loop, **WinMain** calls the **Run** member function. On termination, **WinMain** calls the application object's ExitInstance member function. Figure 1.2 shows the sequence of execution in a framework application.

Figure 1.2 Sequence of Execution

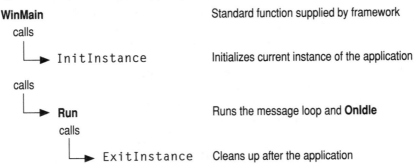

WinMain	Standard function supplied by framework
calls	
InitInstance	Initializes current instance of the application
calls	
Run	Runs the message loop and **OnIdle**
calls	
ExitInstance	Cleans up after the application

Note   Names shown in **bold** type indicate elements supplied by the Microsoft Foundation Class Library and Visual C++. Names shown in `monospaced` type indicate elements that you create or override.

CWinApp and AppWizard

When it creates a skeleton application, AppWizard declares an application class derived from **CWinApp**. AppWizard also generates an implementation file that contains the following items:

- A message map for the application class
- An empty class constructor
- A variable that declares the one and only object of the class
- A standard implementation of your `InitInstance` member function

The application class is placed in the project header and main source files. The names of the class and files created are based on the project name you supply in AppWizard. The easiest way to view the code for these classes is through the Class View in the Project Workspace window.

The standard implementations and message map supplied are adequate for many purposes, but you can modify them as needed. The most interesting of these implementations is the `InitInstance` member function. Typically you will add code to the skeletal implementation of `InitInstance`.

Overridable CWinApp Member Functions

CWinApp provides several key overridable member functions:

- **InitInstance**
- **Run**
- **ExitInstance**
- **OnIdle**

The only **CWinApp** member function that you must override is **InitInstance**.

InitInstance Member Function

Windows allows you to run more than one copy, or "instance," of the same application. **WinMain** calls **InitInstance** every time a new instance of the application starts.

The standard `InitInstance` implementation created by AppWizard performs the following tasks:

- As its central action, creates the document templates that, in turn, create documents, views, and frame windows. For a description of this process, see Document Templates.

- Loads standard file options from an .INI file or the Windows registry, including the names of the most recently used files.

- Registers one or more document templates.

- For an MDI application, creates a main frame window.

- Processes the command line to open a document specified on the command line or to open a new, empty document.

You can add your own initialization code or modify the code written by the wizard.

Run Member Function

A framework application spends most of its time in the **Run** member function of class **CWinApp**. After initialization, **WinMain** calls **Run** to process the message loop.

Run cycles through a message loop, checking the message queue for available messages. If a message is available, **Run** dispatches it for action. If no messages are available—often the case—**Run** calls **OnIdle** to do any idle-time processing that you or the framework may need done. If there are no messages and no idle processing to do, the application waits until something happens. When the application terminates, **Run** calls **ExitInstance**. Figure 1.3 shows the sequence of actions in the message loop.

Message dispatching depends on the kind of message. For more information, see Chapter 2, Working with Messages and Commands.

ExitInstance Member Function

The **ExitInstance** member function of class **CWinApp** is called each time a copy of your application terminates, usually as a result of the user quitting the application. Override **ExitInstance** if you need special cleanup processing, such as freeing graphics device interface (GDI) resources or deallocating memory used during program execution. Cleanup of standard items such as documents and views, however, is provided by the framework, with other overridable functions for doing special cleanup specific to those objects.

OnIdle Member Function

When no Windows messages are being processed, the framework calls the **CWinApp** member function **OnIdle** (described in the *Class Library Reference*). Override **OnIdle** to perform background tasks. The default version updates the state of user-interface objects such as toolbar buttons and performs cleanup of temporary objects created by the framework in the course of its operations. Figure 1.3 illustrates how the message loop calls **OnIdle** when there are no messages in the queue.

Figure 1.3   The Message Loop

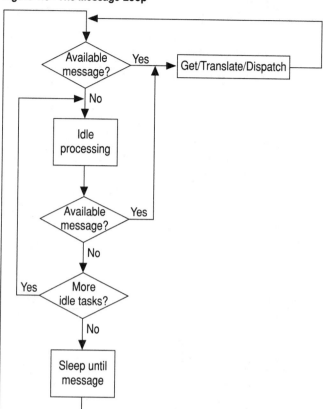

Special CWinApp Services

Besides running the message loop and giving you an opportunity to initialize the application and clean up after it, **CWinApp** provides several other services.

Shell Registration

By default, AppWizard makes it possible for the user to open data files that your application has created by double-clicking them in the Windows File Manager. If your application is an MDI application and you specify an extension for the files your application creates, AppWizard adds calls to the **EnableShellOpen** and **RegisterShellFileTypes** member functions of **CWinApp** to the InitInstance override that it writes for you.

RegisterShellFileTypes registers your application's document types with File Manager. The function adds entries to the registration database that Windows maintains. The entries register each document type, associate a file extension with the file type, specify a command line to open the application, and specify a dynamic data exchange (DDE) command to open a document of that type.

EnableShellOpen completes the process by allowing your application to receive DDE commands from File Manager to open the file chosen by the user.

This automatic registration support in **CWinApp** eliminates the need to ship an .REG file with your application or to do special installation work.

File Manager Drag and Drop

Windows versions 3.1 and later allow the user to drag filenames from the file view window in the File Manager and drop them into a window in your application. You might, for example, allow the user to drag one or more filenames into an MDI application's main window, where the application could retrieve the filenames and open MDI child windows for those files.

To enable file drag and drop in your application, AppWizard writes a call to the **CWnd** member function **DragAcceptFiles** for your main frame window in your InitInstance. You can remove that call if you do not want to implement the drag-and-drop feature.

Note You can also implement more general drag-and-drop capabilities—dragging data between or within documents—using OLE. For information, see the article Drag and Drop (OLE).

Keeping Track of the Most Recently Used Documents

As the user opens and closes files, the application object keeps track of the four most recently used files. The names of these files are added to the File menu and updated when they change. The framework stores these filenames in an .INI file with the same name as your project and reads them from the file when your application starts up. The InitInstance override that AppWizard creates for you includes a call to the **CWinApp** member function **LoadStdProfileSettings**, which loads information from the .INI file, including the most recently used filenames.

Document Templates

To manage the complex process of creating documents with their associated views and frame windows, the framework uses two document template classes: **CSingleDocTemplate** for SDI applications and **CMultiDocTemplate** for MDI applications. A **CSingleDocTemplate** can create and store one document of one type at a time. A **CMultiDocTemplate** keeps a list of many open documents of one type.

Some applications support multiple document types. For example, an application might support text documents and graphics documents. In such an application, when the user chooses the New command on the File menu, a dialog box shows a list of possible new document types to open. For each supported document type, the application uses a distinct document template object. Figure 1.4 illustrates the configuration of an MDI application that supports two document types. The figure shows several open documents.

Figure 1.4   An MDI Application with Two Document Types

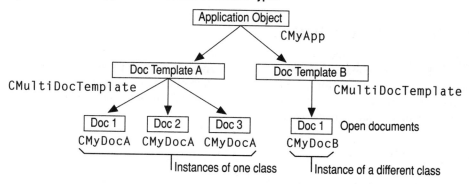

Document templates are created and maintained by the application object. One of the key tasks performed during your application's InitInstance function is to construct one or more document templates of the appropriate kind. This feature is described in Document Template Creation. The application object stores a pointer to each document template in its template list and provides an interface for adding document templates.

If you need to support two or more document types, you must add an extra call to **AddDocTemplate** for each document type.

Document Template Creation

While creating a new document in response to a New or Open command from the File menu, the document template also creates a new frame window through which to view the document.

The document-template constructor specifies what types of documents, windows, and views the template will be able to create. This is determined by the arguments you pass to the document-template constructor. The following code illustrates creation of a **CMultiDocTemplate** for a sample application:

```
AddDocTemplate( new CMultiDocTemplate( IDR_SCRIBTYPE,
        RUNTIME_CLASS( CScribDoc ),
        RUNTIME_CLASS( CMDIChildWnd ),
        RUNTIME_CLASS( CScribView ) ) );
```

The pointer to a new **CMultiDocTemplate** object is used as an argument to **AddDocTemplate**. Arguments to the **CMultiDocTemplate** constructor include the resource ID associated with the document type's menus and accelerators, and three uses of the **RUNTIME_CLASS** macro. **RUNTIME_CLASS** returns the **CRuntimeClass** object for the C++ class named as its argument. The three

CRuntimeClass objects passed to the document-template constructor supply the information needed to create new objects of the specified classes during the document creation process. The example shows creation of a document template that creates CScribDoc objects with CScribView objects attached. The views are framed by standard MDI child frame windows.

Document/View Creation

The framework supplies implementations of the New and Open commands (among others) on the File menu. Creation of a new document and its associated view and frame window is a cooperative effort among the application object, a document template, the newly created document, and the newly created frame window. Table 1.6 summarizes which objects create what.

Table 1.6 Object Creators

Creator	Creates
Application object	Document template
Document template	Document
Document template	Frame window
Frame window	View

Relationships Among MFC Objects

To help put the document/view creation process in perspective, first consider a running program: a document, the frame window used to contain the view, and the view associated with the document.

- A document keeps a list of the views of that document and a pointer to the document template that created the document.

- A view keeps a pointer to its document and is a child of its parent frame window.

- A document frame window keeps a pointer to its current active view.

- A document template keeps a list of its open documents.

- The application keeps a list of its document templates.

- Windows keeps track of all open windows so it can send messages to them.

These relationships are established during document/view creation. Table 1.7 shows how objects in a running program can access other objects. Any object can obtain a pointer to the application object by calling the global function **AfxGetApp**.

Table 1.7   Gaining Access to Other Objects in Your Application

From object	How to access other objects
Document	Use **GetFirstViewPosition** and **GetNextView** to access the document's view list.
	Call **GetDocTemplate** to get the document template.
View	Call **GetDocument** to get the document.
	Call **GetParentFrame** to get the frame window.
Document frame window	Call **GetActiveView** to get the current view.
	Call **GetActiveDocument** to get the document attached to the current view.
MDI frame window	Call **MDIGetActive** to get the currently active **CMDIChildWnd**.

Typically, a frame window has one view, but sometimes, as in splitter windows, the same frame window contains multiple views. The frame window keeps a pointer to the currently active view; the pointer is updated any time another view is activated.

Note   A pointer to the main frame window is stored in the **m_pMainWnd** member variable of the application object. A call to **OnFileNew** in your override of the **InitInstance** member function of **CWinApp** sets **m_pMainWnd** for you. If you don't call **OnFileNew**, you must set the variable's value in **InitInstance** yourself. (SDI OLE server applications may not set the variable if /Embedding is on the command line.) Note that **m_pMainWnd** is now a member of class **CWinThread** rather than **CWinApp**.

Creating New Documents, Windows, and Views

Figures 1.5, 1.6, and 1.7 give an overview of the creation process for documents, views, and frame windows. Later chapters that focus on the participating objects provide further details.

Upon completion of this process, the cooperating objects exist and store pointers to each other. Figures 1.5, 1.6, and 1.7 show the sequence in which objects are created. You can follow the sequence from figure to figure.

Figure 1.5 Sequence in Creating a Document

Application

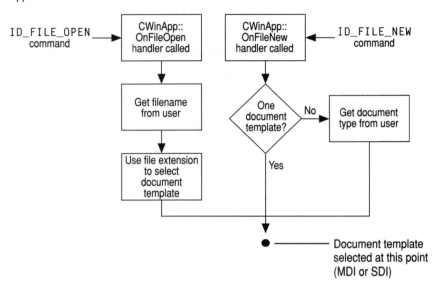

Figure 1.6   Sequence in Creating a Frame Window

Document Template: OpenDocumentFile

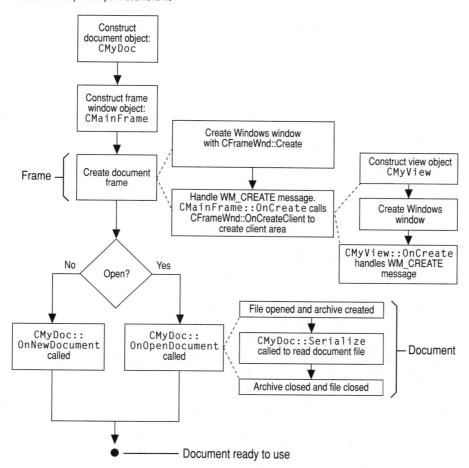

Document ready to use

Figure 1.7 Sequence in Creating a View

View

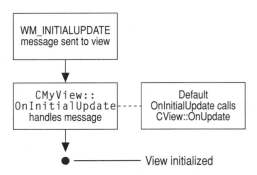

For information about how the framework initializes the new document, view, and frame-window objects, see classes **CDocument**, **CView**, **CFrameWnd**, **CMDIFrameWnd**, and **CMDIChildWnd** in the *Class Library Reference*. Also see Technical Note 22 under MFC Technical Notes in Visual C++ Books Online, which explains the creation and initialization processes further under its discussion of the framework's standard commands for the New and Open items on the File menu.

Initializing Your Own Additions to These Classes

Figures 1.5, 1.6, and 1.7 also suggest the points at which you can override member functions to initialize your application's objects. An override of **OnInitialUpdate** in your view class is the best place to initialize the view. The **OnInitialUpdate** call occurs immediately after the frame window is created and the view within the frame window is attached to its document. For example, if your view is a scroll view (derived from **CScrollView** rather than **CView**), you should set the view size based on the document size in your OnInitialUpdate override. (This process is described in the description of class **CScrollView**.) You can override the **CDocument** member functions **OnNewDocument** and **OnOpenDocument** to provide application-specific initialization of the document. Typically, you must override both since a document can be created in two ways.

In most cases, your override should call the base class version. For more information, see the named member functions of classes **CDocument**, **CView**, **CFrameWnd**, and **CWinApp** in the *Class Library Reference*.

Windows of Your Own with CWnd

Although the framework provides windows on your documents, you may at times want to create your own windows, particularly child windows. Keeping in mind how much the framework does for you, the present discussion focuses on windows in a more general way, with particular emphasis on creating windows of your own. For more information about the frame windows that the framework creates, see Chapter 3, Working with Frame Windows, Documents, and Views.

In MFC, all windows are ultimately derived from class **CWnd**. This includes dialog boxes, controls, control bars, and views as well as frame windows and your own child windows, as shown in the MFC hierarchy diagram in the *Class Library Reference*.

Window Objects

A C++ window *object* (whether for a frame window or some other kind of window) is distinct from its corresponding Windows window (the **HWND**), but the two are tightly linked. A good understanding of this relationship is crucial for effective programming with MFC.

The window *object* is an object of the C++ **CWnd** class (or a derived class) that your program creates directly. It comes and goes in response to your program's constructor and destructor calls. The Windows *window*, on the other hand, is an opaque handle to an internal Windows data structure that corresponds to a window and consumes system resources when present. A Windows window is identified by a "window handle" (**HWND**) and is created after the **CWnd** object is created by a call to the **Create** member function of class **CWnd**. The window may be destroyed either by a program call or by a user's action. The window handle is stored in the window object's **m_hWnd** member variable. Figure 1.8 shows the relationship between the C++ window object and the Windows window. Creating windows is discussed in Creating Windows. Destroying windows is discussed in Destroying Window Objects.

Figure 1.8 Window Object and Windows Window

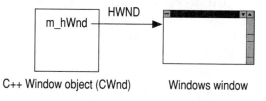

C++ Window object (CWnd)   Windows window

CWnd and its derived classes provide constructors, destructors, and member functions to initialize the object, create the underlying Windows structures, and access the encapsulated **HWND**. **CWnd** also provides member functions that encapsulate Windows APIs for sending messages, accessing the window's state, converting coordinates, updating, scrolling, accessing the Clipboard, and many other tasks. Most Windows window-management APIs that take an **HWND** argument are encapsulated as member functions of **CWnd**. The names of the functions and their parameters are preserved in the **CWnd** member function. For details about the Windows APIs encapsulated by **CWnd**, see class **CWnd** in the *Class Library Reference*.

The general literature on programming for Windows is a good resource for learning how to use the **CWnd** member functions, which typically encapsulate the **HWND**

APIs. For example, see Charles Petzold's *Programming Windows 3.1*, third edition, and Jeffrey Richter's *Advanced Windows NT*.

One of the primary purposes of **CWnd** is to provide an interface for handling Windows messages, such as **WM_PAINT** or **WM_MOUSEMOVE**. Many of the member functions of **CWnd** are handlers for standard messages—those beginning with the identifier **afx_msg** and the prefix "On," such as **OnPaint** and **OnMouseMove**. Chapter 2, Working with Messages and Commands, covers messages and message handling in detail. The information there applies equally to the framework's windows and those that you create yourself for special purposes.

Derived Window Classes

Although you can create windows directly from **CWnd**, or derive new window classes from **CWnd**, most windows used in a framework program are instead created from one of the **CWnd**-derived frame-window classes supplied by MFC:

CFrameWnd   Used for SDI frame windows that frame a single document and its view. The frame window is both the main frame window for the application and the frame window for the current document.

CMDIFrameWnd   Used as the main frame window for MDI applications. The main frame window is a container for all MDI document windows and shares its menu bar with them. An MDI frame window is a top-level window that appears on the desktop.

CMDIChildWnd   Used for individual documents opened in an MDI main frame window. Each document and its view are framed by an MDI child frame window contained by the MDI main frame window. An MDI child window looks much like a typical frame window but is contained inside an MDI frame window instead of sitting on the desktop. However, the MDI child window lacks a menu bar of its own and must share the menu bar of the MDI frame window that contains it.

In addition to frame windows, several other major categories of windows are derived from **CWnd**:

Views   Views are created using the **CWnd**-derived class **CView** (or one of its derived classes). A view is attached to a document and acts as an intermediary between the document and the user. A view is a child window (not an MDI child) that typically fills the client area of an SDI frame window or an MDI child frame window (or that portion of the client area not covered by a toolbar and/or a status bar).

Dialog Boxes   Dialog boxes are created using the **CWnd**-derived class **CDialog**.

Forms   Form views based on dialog-template resources, like dialog boxes, are created using classes **CFormView**, **CRecordView**, or **CDaoRecordView**.

Controls   Controls such as buttons, list boxes, and combo boxes are created using other classes derived from **CWnd**.

Control Bars   Child windows that contain controls. Examples include toolbars and status bars.

Refer again to the MFC hierarchy diagram in the *Class Library Reference*. Views are explained in Chapter 3, Working with Frame Windows, Documents, and Views. Dialog boxes, controls, and control bars are explained in Chapter 4, Working with Dialog Boxes, Controls, and Control Bars.

In addition to the window classes provided by the class library, you may need special-purpose child windows. To create such a window, write your own **CWnd**-derived class and make it a child window of a frame or view. Bear in mind that the framework manages the extent of the client area of a document frame window. Most of the client area is managed by a view, but other windows, such as control bars or your own custom windows, may share the space with the view. You may need to interact with the mechanisms in classes **CView** and **CControlBar** for positioning child windows in a frame window's client area.

Note As of MFC version 4.0, toolbars and status bars are based on the toolbar and status bar controls supplied by Windows 95 or Windows NT 3.51. However, the older mechanisms are preserved. See the article Toolbars: Using Your Old Toolbars.

Creating Windows discusses creation of window objects and the Windows windows they manage.

Creating Windows

Most of the windows you need in a framework program are created automatically by the framework. You have already seen how the framework creates the frame windows associated with documents and views. But you can create your own windows—in addition to the windows supplied by the framework—for special purposes.

Registering Window "Classes"

In a traditional program for Windows, you process all messages to a window in its "window procedure" or "**WndProc**." A **WndProc** is associated with a window by means of a "window class registration" process. The main window is registered in the **WinMain** function, but other classes of windows can be registered anywhere in the application. Registration depends on a structure that contains a pointer to the **WndProc** function together with specifications for the cursor, background brush, and so forth. The structure is passed as a parameter, along with the string name of the class, in a prior call to the **RegisterClass** function. Thus a registration class can be shared by multiple windows.

In contrast, most window class registration activity is done automatically in a framework program. If you are using MFC, you typically derive a C++ window class from an existing library class using the normal C++ syntax for class inheritance. The framework still uses traditional "registration classes," and it provides several standard ones, registered for you in the standard application initialization function. You can register additional registration classes by calling the **AfxRegisterWndClass** global function and then pass the registered class to the **Create** member function of

CWnd. As described here, the traditional "registration class" in Windows is not to be confused with a C++ class.

For more information, see Technical Note 1 under MFC in Books Online.

General Creation Sequence

If you are creating a window of your own, such as a child window, this section describes what you need to know. The framework uses much the same process to create windows for your documents as that described earlier in the chapter.

All the window classes provided by MFC employ two-phase construction. That is, during an invocation of the C++ **new** operator, the constructor allocates and initializes a C++ object but does not create a corresponding Windows window. That is done afterwards by calling the **Create** member function of the window object.

The **Create** member function makes the Windows window and stores its **HWND** in the C++ object's public data member **m_hWnd**. **Create** gives complete flexibility over the creation parameters. Before calling **Create**, you may want to register a window class with **AfxRegisterWndClass** in order to set the icon and class styles for the frame.

For frame windows, you can use the **LoadFrame** member function instead of **Create**. **LoadFrame** makes the Windows window using fewer parameters. It gets many default values from resources, including the frame's caption, icon, accelerator table, and menu.

Note Your icon, accelerator table, and menu resources must have a common resource ID, such as **IDR_MAINFRAME**.

Destroying Window Objects

Care must be taken with your own child windows to destroy the C++ window object when the user is finished with the window. If these objects are not destroyed, your application will not recover their memory. Fortunately, the framework manages window destruction as well as creation for frame windows, views, and dialog boxes. If you create additional windows, you are responsible for destroying them.

In the framework, when the user closes the frame window, the window's default **OnClose** handler calls **DestroyWindow**. The last member function called when the Windows window is destroyed is **OnNcDestroy**, which does some cleanup, calls the **Default** member function to perform Windows cleanup, and lastly calls the virtual member function **PostNcDestroy**. The **CFrameWnd** implementation of **PostNcDestroy** deletes the C++ window object.

Do not use the C++ **delete** operator to destroy a frame window or view. Instead, call the **CWnd** member function **DestroyWindow**. Frame windows, therefore, should be allocated on the heap with operator **new**. Care must be taken when allocating frame windows on the stack frame or globally. Other windows should be allocated on the stack frame whenever possible.

If you need to circumvent the object-**HWND** relationship, MFC provides another **CWnd** member function, **Detach**, which disconnects the C++ window object from the Windows window. This prevents the destructor from destroying the Windows window when the object is destroyed.

Working with Window Objects

Working with windows calls for two kinds of activity:

- Handling Windows messages
- Drawing in the window

To handle Windows messages in any window, including your own child windows, use ClassWizard to map the messages to your window class. Then write message-handler member functions in your class. Chapter 2, Working with Messages and Commands, details message handling.

Most drawing in a framework application occurs in the view, whose OnDraw member function is called whenever the window's contents must be drawn. If your window is a child of the view, you might delegate some of the view's drawing to your child window by having OnDraw call one of your window's member functions.

In any case, you will need a device context for drawing.

Device Contexts

A device context is a Windows data structure that contains information about the drawing attributes of a device such as a display or a printer. All drawing calls are made through a device-context object, which encapsulates the Windows APIs for drawing lines, shapes, and text. Device contexts allow device-independent drawing in Windows. Device contexts can be used to draw to the screen, to the printer, or to a metafile.

CPaintDC objects encapsulate the common idiom of Windows, calling the **BeginPaint** function, then drawing in the device context, then calling the **EndPaint** function. The **CPaintDC** constructor calls **BeginPaint** for you, and the destructor calls **EndPaint**. The simplified process is to create the **CDC** object, draw, and destroy the **CDC** object. In the framework, much of even this process is automated. In particular, your OnDraw function is passed a **CPaintDC** already prepared (via **OnPrepareDC**), and you simply draw into it. It is destroyed by the framework and the underlying device context is released to Windows upon return from the call to your OnDraw function.

CClientDC objects encapsulate working with a device context that represents only the client area of a window. The **CClientDC** constructor calls the **GetDC** function, and the destructor calls the **ReleaseDC** function. **CWindowDC** objects encapsulate a device context that represents the whole window, including its frame.

CMetaFileDC objects encapsulate drawing into a Windows metafile. In contrast to the **CPaintDC** passed to OnDraw, you must in this case call **OnPrepareDC** yourself. For more information about these classes, see the *Class Library Reference*.

Drawing is discussed in greater detail in Chapter 3, Working with Frame Windows, Documents, and Views.

Although most drawing—and thus most device-context work—in a framework program is done in the view's OnDraw member function, as described in Chapter 3, you can still use device-context objects for other purposes. For example, to provide tracking feedback for mouse movement in a view, you need to draw directly into the view without waiting for OnDraw to be called.

In such a case, you can use a **CClientDC** device-context object to draw directly into the view. For more information about mouse drawing, see Interpreting User Input Through a View in Chapter 3.

Graphic Objects

Windows provides a variety of drawing tools to use in device contexts. It provides pens to draw lines, brushes to fill interiors, and fonts to draw text. MFC provides graphic-object classes equivalent to the drawing tools in Windows. Table 1.8 shows the available classes and the equivalent Windows GDI handle types.

The general literature on programming for the Windows GDI applies to the Microsoft Foundation classes that encapsulate GDI graphic objects. This section explains the use of these graphic-object classes:

Table 1.8 Classes for Windows GDI Objects

Class	Windows handle type
CPen	**HPEN**
CBrush	**HBRUSH**
CFont	**HFONT**
CBitmap	**HBITMAP**
CPalette	**HPALETTE**
CRgn	**HRGN**

Each of the graphic-object classes in the class library has a constructor that allows you to create graphic objects of that class, which you must then initialize with the appropriate create function, such as **CreatePen**.

The following four steps are typically used when you need a graphic object for a drawing operation:

1. Define a graphic object on the stack frame. Initialize the object with the type-specific create function, such as **CreatePen**. Alternatively, initialize the object in the constructor. See the discussion of one-stage and two-stage creation below.

2. Select the object into the current device context, saving the old graphic object that was selected before.

3. When done with the current graphic object, select the old graphic object back into the device context to restore its state.

4. Allow the frame-allocated graphic object to be deleted automatically when the scope is exited.

Note   If you will be using a graphic object repeatedly, you can allocate it once and select it into a device context each time it is needed. Be sure to delete such an object when you no longer need it.

You have a choice between two techniques for creating graphic objects:

• One-stage construction: Construct and initialize the object in one stage, all with the constructor.

• Two-stage construction: Construct and initialize the object in two separate stages. The constructor creates the object and an initialization function initializes it.

Two-stage construction is always safer. In one-stage construction, the constructor could throw an exception if you provide incorrect arguments or memory allocation fails. That problem is avoided by two-stage construction, although you do have to check for failure. In either case, destroying the object is the same process.

The following brief example shows both methods of constructing a pen object:

```
void CMyView::OnDraw( CDC* pDC )
{
    CPen myPen1( PS_DOT, 5, RGB(0,0,0) );    // One-stage
    // Two-stage: first construct the pen
    CPen myPen2;
    // Then initialize it
    if( myPen2.CreatePen( PS_DOT, 5, RGB(0,0,0) ) )
        // Use the pen
}
```

After you create a drawing object, you must select it into the device context in place of the default pen stored there:

```
void CMyView::OnDraw( CDC* pDC )
{
    CPen penBlack;  // Construct it, then initialize
    if( newPen.CreatePen( PS_SOLID, 2, RGB(0,0,0) ) )
    {
        // Select it into the device context
        // Save the old pen at the same time
        CPen* pOldPen = pDC->SelectObject( &penBlack );

        // Draw with the pen
        pDC->MoveTo(...);
        pDC->LineTo(...);

        // Restore the old pen to the device context
        pDC->SelectObject( pOldPen );
    }
    else
    {
        // Alert the user that resources are low
    }
}
```

The graphic object returned by **SelectObject** is a "temporary" object. That is, it will be deleted by the **OnIdle** member function of class **CWinApp** the next time the program gets idle time. As long as you use the object returned by **SelectObject** in a single function without returning control to the main message loop, you will have no problem.

CHAPTER 2

Working with Messages and Commands

Chapter 1 introduced the major objects in a running framework application written with the Microsoft Foundation Class Library (MFC). This chapter describes how messages and commands are processed by the framework and how you connect them to their handler functions using the ClassWizard tool. Topics covered include:

- Messages and commands
- Message categories
- How the framework calls a message handler
- Message maps
- Managing messages and commands with ClassWizard
- Dynamic update of user-interface objects
- Dynamic display of command information in the status bar

Messages and Commands in the Framework

Applications written for Microsoft Windows are "message driven." In response to events such as mouse clicks, keystrokes, window movements, and so on, Windows sends messages to the proper window. Framework applications process Windows messages like any other application for Windows. But the framework also provides some enhancements that make processing messages easier, more maintainable, and better encapsulated.

The following topics introduce the key terms used in the rest of the chapter to discuss messages and commands:

- Messages
- Message handlers
- Message categories

- Windows messages and control-notification messages
- Command messages
- Message maps
- User-interface objects and command IDs
- Command targets

Messages

The message loop in the **Run** member function of class **CWinApp** retrieves queued messages generated by various events. For example, when the user clicks the mouse, Windows sends several mouse-related messages, such as **WM_LBUTTONDOWN** when the left mouse button is pressed and **WM_LBUTTONUP** when the left mouse button is released. The framework's implementation of the application message loop dispatches the message to the appropriate window.

The important categories of messages are described in Message Categories.

Message Handlers

In MFC, a dedicated *handler* function processes each separate message. Message-handler functions are member functions of a class. This book uses the terms *message-handler member function*, *message-handler function*, *message handler*, and *handler* interchangeably. Some kinds of message handlers are also called "command handlers."

Writing message handlers accounts for a large proportion of your work in writing a framework application. This chapter describes how the message-processing mechanism works.

What does the handler for a message do? The answer is that it does whatever you want done in response to that message. ClassWizard will create the handlers for you and allow you to implement them. You can jump directly from ClassWizard to the handler function's definition in your source files and fill in the handler's code using the Visual C++ source code editor. Or you can create all of your handlers with ClassWizard, then move to the editor to fill in all functions at once. For details on using ClassWizard, see How to Manage Commands and Messages with ClassWizard.

You can use all of the facilities of Microsoft Visual C++ and MFC to write your handlers. For a list of all classes, see About the Microsoft Foundation Classes in the *Class Library Reference*.

Message Categories

What kinds of messages do you write handlers for? There are three main categories:

1. Windows messages

This includes primarily those messages beginning with the **WM_** prefix, except for **WM_COMMAND**. Windows messages are handled by windows and views. These messages often have parameters that are used in determining how to handle the message.

2. Control notifications

This includes **WM_COMMAND** notification messages from controls and other child windows to their parent windows. For example, an edit control sends its parent a **WM_COMMAND** message containing the **EN_CHANGE** control-notification code when the user has taken an action that may have altered text in the edit control. The window's handler for the message responds to the notification message in some appropriate way, such as retrieving the text in the control.

The framework routes control-notification messages like other **WM_** messages. One exception, however, is the **BN_CLICKED** control-notification message sent by buttons when the user clicks them. This message is treated specially as a command message and routed like other commands.

3. Command messages

This includes **WM_COMMAND** notification messages from user-interface objects: menus, toolbar buttons, and accelerator keys. The framework processes commands differently from other messages, and they can be handled by more kinds of objects, as explained below.

Windows Messages and Control-Notification Messages

Messages in categories 1 and 2—Windows messages and control notifications—are handled by windows: objects of classes derived from class **CWnd**. This includes **CFrameWnd**, **CMDIFrameWnd**, **CMDIChildWnd**, **CView**, **CDialog**, and your own classes derived from these base classes. Such objects encapsulate an **HWND**, a handle to a Windows window.

Command Messages

Messages in category 3—commands—can be handled by a wider variety of objects: documents, document templates, and the application object itself in addition to windows and views. When a command directly affects some particular object, it makes sense to have that object handle the command. For example, the Open command on the File menu is logically associated with the application: the application opens a specified document upon receiving the command. So the handler for the Open command is a member function of the application class. For more about commands and how they are routed to objects, see How the Framework Calls a Handler.

Mapping Messages

Each framework class that can receive messages or commands has its own "message map." The framework uses message maps to connect messages and commands to their handler functions. Any class derived from class **CCmdTarget** can have a message map. Later topics of this chapter explain message maps in detail and describe how to use them.

In spite of the name "message map," message maps handle both messages and commands—all three categories of messages listed in Message Categories.

User-Interface Objects and Command IDs

Menu items, toolbar buttons, and accelerator keys are "user-interface objects" capable of generating commands. Each such user-interface object has an ID. You associate a user-interface object with a command by assigning the same ID to the object and the command. As explained in Messages, commands are implemented as special messages. Figure 2.1 shows how the framework manages commands. When a user-interface object generates a command, such as ID_EDIT_CLEAR_ALL, one of the objects in your application handles the command—in the figure, the document object's OnEditClearAll function is called via the document's message map.

Figure 2.1 Commands in the Framework

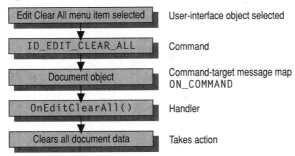

Edit Clear All menu item selected	User-interface object selected
ID_EDIT_CLEAR_ALL	Command
Document object	Command-target message map ON_COMMAND
OnEditClearAll()	Handler
Clears all document data	Takes action

Figure 2.2 shows how MFC updates user-interface objects such as menu items and toolbar buttons. Before a menu drops down, or during the idle loop in the case of toolbar buttons, MFC routes an update command. In the figure, the document object calls its update command handler, OnUpdateEditClearAll, to enable or disable the user-interface object.

Figure 2.2   Command Updating in the Framework

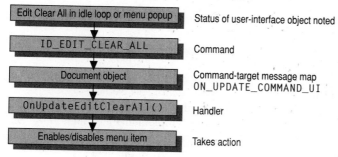

Edit Clear All in idle loop or menu popup	Status of user-interface object noted
ID_EDIT_CLEAR_ALL	Command
Document object	Command-target message map ON_UPDATE_COMMAND_UI
OnUpdateEditClearAll()	Handler
Enables/disables menu item	Takes action

Command IDs

A command is fully described by its command ID alone (encoded in the **WM_COMMAND** message). This ID is assigned to the user-interface object that generates the command. Typically, IDs are named for the functionality of the user-interface object they are assigned to.

For example, a Clear All item in the Edit menu might be assigned an ID such as **ID_EDIT_CLEAR_ALL**. The class library predefines some IDs, particularly for commands that the framework handles itself, such as **ID_EDIT_CLEAR_ALL** or **ID_FILE_OPEN**. You will create other command IDs yourself.

When you create your own menus in the Visual C++ menu editor, it is a good idea to follow the class library's naming convention as illustrated by **ID_FILE_OPEN**. Standard Commands explains the standard commands defined by the class library.

Standard Commands

The framework defines many standard command messages. The IDs for these commands typically take the form:

ID_*Source_Item*

where *Source* is usually a menu name and *Item* is a menu item. For example, the command ID for the New command on the File menu is **ID_FILE_NEW**. Standard command IDs are shown in bold type in the documentation. Programmer-defined IDs are shown in a font that is different from the surrounding text.

The following is a list of some of the most important commands supported:

File Menu Commands   New, Open, Close, Save, Save As, Page Setup, Print Setup, Print, Print Preview, Exit, and most-recently-used files.

Edit Menu Commands   Clear, Clear All, Copy, Cut, Find, Paste, Repeat, Replace, Select All, Undo, and Redo.

View Menu Commands   Toolbar and Status Bar.

Window Menu Commands   New, Arrange, Cascade, Tile Horizontal, Tile Vertical, and Split.

Help Menu Commands   Index, Using Help, and About.

OLE Commands (Edit Menu)   Insert New Object, Edit Links, Paste Link, Paste Special, and *typename* Object (verb commands).

The framework provides varying levels of support for these commands. Some commands are supported only as defined command IDs, while others are supported with thorough implementations. For example, the framework implements the Open command on the File menu by creating a new document object, displaying an Open dialog box, and opening and reading the file. In contrast, you must implement commands on the Edit menu yourself, since commands like **ID_EDIT_COPY** depend on the nature of the data you are copying.

For more information about the commands supported and the level of implementation provided, see Technical Note 22 under MFC Technical Notes in Books Online. The standard commands are defined in the file AFXRES.H.

Command Targets

Figure 2.1 shows the connection between a user-interface object, such as a menu item, and the handler function that the framework calls to carry out the resulting command when the object is clicked.

Windows sends messages that are not command messages directly to a window whose handler for the message is then called. However, the framework routes commands to a number of candidate objects—called "command targets"—one of which normally invokes a handler for the command. The handler functions work the same way for both commands and standard Windows messages, but the mechanism by which they are called is different, as explained in How the Framework Calls a Handler.

How the Framework Calls a Handler

The following topics first examine how the framework routes commands, then examine how other messages and control notifications are sent to windows:

- Message sending and receiving
- How noncommand messages reach their handlers
- Command routing

Message Sending and Receiving

Consider the sending part of the process and how the framework responds.

Most messages result from user interaction with the program. Commands are generated by mouse clicks in menu items or toolbar buttons or by accelerator keystrokes. The user also generates Windows messages by, for example, moving or resizing a window. Other Windows messages are sent when events such as program startup or termination occur, as windows get or lose the focus, and so on. Control-notification messages are generated by mouse clicks or other user interactions with a control, such as a button or list-box control in a dialog box.

The **Run** member function of class **CWinApp** retrieves messages and dispatches them to the appropriate window. Most command messages are sent to the main frame window of the application. The **WindowProc** predefined by the class library gets the messages and routes them differently, depending on the category of message received.

Now consider the receiving part of the process.

The initial receiver of a message must be a window object. Windows messages are usually handled directly by that window object. Command messages, usually originating in the application's main frame window, get routed to the command-target chain described in Command Routing.

Each object capable of receiving messages or commands has its own message map that pairs a message or command with the name of its handler.

When a command-target object receives a message or command, it searches its message map for a match. If it finds a handler for the message, it calls the handler. For more information about how message maps are searched, see How the Framework Searches Message Maps. Refer again to Figure 2.1.

How Noncommand Messages Reach Their Handlers

Unlike commands, standard Windows messages do not get routed through a chain of command targets but are usually handled by the window to which Windows sends the message. The window might be a main frame window, an MDI child window, a standard control, a dialog box, a view, or some other kind of child window.

At run time, each Windows window is attached to a window object (derived directly or indirectly from **CWnd**) that has its own associated message map and handler functions. The framework uses the message map—as for a command—to map incoming messages to handlers.

Command Routing

Your responsibility in working with commands is limited to making message-map connections between commands and their handler functions, a task for which you use ClassWizard. You must also write most command handlers.

All messages are usually sent to the main frame window, but command messages are then routed to other objects. The framework routes commands through a standard sequence of command-target objects, one of which is expected to have a handler for the command. Each command-target object checks its message map to see if it can handle the incoming message.

Different command-target classes check their own message maps at different times. Typically, a class routes the command to certain other objects to give them first chance at the command. If none of those objects handles the command, the original class checks its own message map. Then, if it can't supply a handler itself, it may route the command to yet more command targets. Table 2.1 shows how each of the classes structures this sequence. The general order in which a command target routes a command is:

1. To its currently active child command-target object.

2. To itself.

3. To other command targets.

How expensive is this routing mechanism? Compared to what your handler does in response to a command, the cost of the routing is low. Bear in mind that the framework generates commands only when the user interacts with a user-interface object.

Table 2.1 Standard Command Route

When an object of this type receives a command . . .	It gives itself and other command-target objects a chance to handle the command in this order:
MDI frame window (**CMDIFrameWnd**)	1. Active **CMDIChildWnd** 2. This frame window 3. Application (**CWinApp** object)
Document frame window (**CFrameWnd**, **CMDIChildWnd**)	1. Active view 2. This frame window 3. Application (**CWinApp** object)
View	1. This view 2. Document attached to the view
Document	1. This document 2. Document template attached to the document
Dialog box	1. This dialog box 2. Window that owns the dialog box 3. Application (**CWinApp** object)

Where numbered entries in the second column of Table 2.1 mention other objects, such as a document, see the corresponding item in the first column. For instance, when you read in the second column that the view forwards a command to its document, see the "Document" entry in the first column to follow the routing further.

An Example

To illustrate, consider a command message from a Clear All menu item in an MDI application's Edit menu. Suppose the handler function for this command happens to be a member function of the application's document class. Here's how that command reaches its handler after the user chooses the menu item:

1. The main frame window receives the command message first.

2. The main MDI frame window gives the currently active MDI child window a chance to handle the command.

3. The standard routing of an MDI child frame window gives its view a chance at the command before checking its own message map.

4. The view checks its own message map first and, finding no handler, next routes the command to its associated document.

5. The document checks its message map and finds a handler. This document member function is called and the routing stops.

If the document did not have a handler, it would next route the command to its document template. Then the command would return to the view and then the frame window. Finally, the frame window would check its message map. If that check failed as well, the command would be routed back to the main MDI frame window and then to the application object—the ultimate destination of unhandled commands.

OnCmdMsg

To accomplish this routing of commands, each command target calls the **OnCmdMsg** member function of the next command target in the sequence. Command targets use **OnCmdMsg** to determine whether they can handle a command and to route it to another command target if they cannot handle it.

Each command-target class may override the **OnCmdMsg** member function. The overrides let each class route commands to a particular next target. A frame window, for example, always routes commands to its current child window or view, as shown in Table 2.1.

The default **CCmdTarget** implementation of **OnCmdMsg** uses the message map of the command-target class to search for a handler function for each command message it receives—in the same way that standard messages are searched. If it finds a match, it calls the handler. Message-map searching is explained in How the Framework Searches Message Maps.

Overriding the Standard Routing

In rare cases when you must implement some variation of the standard framework routing, you can override it. The idea is to change the routing in one or more classes by overriding **OnCmdMsg** in those classes. Do so:

- In the class that breaks the order to pass to a nondefault object.

- In the new nondefault object or in command targets it might in turn pass commands to.

If you insert some new object into the routing, its class must be a command-target class. In your overriding versions of **OnCmdMsg**, be sure to call the version that you're overriding. See the **OnCmdMsg** member function of class **CCmdTarget** in the *Class Library Reference* and the versions in such classes as **CView** and **CDocument** in the supplied source code for examples.

How the Framework Searches Message Maps

The framework searches the message-map table for matches with incoming messages. Once you use ClassWizard to write a message-map entry for each message you want a class to handle and to write the corresponding handlers, the framework calls your handlers automatically. The following topics explain message-map searching:

- Where to find message maps
- Derived message maps

Where to Find Message Maps

When you create a new skeleton application with AppWizard, AppWizard writes a message map for each command-target class it creates for you. This includes your derived application, document, view, and frame-window classes. Some of these message maps already have AppWizard-supplied entries for certain messages and predefined commands, and some are just placeholders for handlers that you will add.

A class's message map is located in the .CPP file for the class. Working with the basic message maps that AppWizard creates, you use ClassWizard to add entries for the messages and commands that each class will handle. A typical message map might look like the following after you add some entries:

```
BEGIN_MESSAGE_MAP(CMyView, CView)
    //{{AFX_MSG_MAP(CMyView)
    ON_WM_MOUSEACTIVATE()
    ON_COMMAND(ID_EDIT_CLEAR_ALL, OnEditClearAll)
    ON_UPDATE_COMMAND_UI(ID_EDIT_CLEAR_ALL, OnUpdateEditClearAll)
    ON_BN_CLICKED(ID_MY_BUTTON, OnMyButton)
    //}}AFX_MSG_MAP
END_MESSAGE_MAP()
```

The message map consists of a collection of macros. Two macros, **BEGIN_MESSAGE_MAP** and **END_MESSAGE_MAP**, bracket the message map. Other macros, such as **ON_COMMAND**, fill in the message map's contents. These macros are explained later in this chapter.

Note The message-map macros are not followed by semicolons.

The message map also includes comments of the form

```
//{{AFX_MSG_MAP(CMyView)
//}}AFX_MSG_MAP
```

that bracket many of the entries (but not necessarily all of them). ClassWizard uses these special comments when it writes entries for you. All ClassWizard entries go between the comment lines.

When you use ClassWizard to create a new class, it provides a message map for the class. Alternatively, you can create a message map manually using the source code editor.

Derived Message Maps

During message handling, checking a class's own message map is not the end of the message-map story. What happens if class CMyView (derived from **CView**) has no matching entry for a message?

Keep in mind that **CView**, the base class of CMyView, is derived in turn from **CWnd**. Thus CMyView *is* a **CView** and *is* a **CWnd**. Each of those classes has its own message map. Figure 2.3 shows the hierarchical relationship of the classes, but keep in mind that a CMyView object is a single object that has the characteristics of all three classes.

Figure 2.3   A View Hierarchy

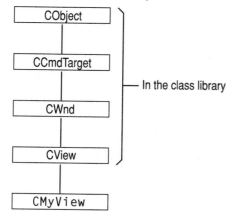

So if a message can't be matched in class CMyView's message map, the framework also searches the message map of its immediate base class. The **BEGIN_MESSAGE_MAP** macro at the start of the message map specifies two class names as its arguments:

```
BEGIN_MESSAGE_MAP(CMyView, CView)
```

The first argument names the class to which the message map belongs. The second argument provides a connection with the immediate base class—**CView** here—so the framework can search its message map, too.

The message handlers provided in a base class are thus inherited by the derived class. This is very similar to normal virtual member functions without needing to make all handler member functions virtual.

If no handler is found in any of the base-class message maps, default processing of the message is performed. If the message is a command, the framework routes it to the next command target. If it is a standard Windows message, the message is passed to the appropriate default window procedure.

To speed message-map matching, the framework caches recent matches on the likelihood that it will receive the same message again. One consequence of this is that the framework processes unhandled messages quite efficiently. Message maps are also more space-efficient than implementations that use virtual functions.

Message-Map Structure

In your source files, a message map consists of a sequence of predefined macros. The macros inside the message map are called "entry macros." The entry macros used in a message map depend upon the category of the message to be handled. The following sample shows a message map with several common entries (given in the same order as the items in Table 2.2:

```
BEGIN_MESSAGE_MAP(CMyView, CView)
    //{{AFX_MSG_MAP(CMyView)
    ON_WM_MOUSEACTIVATE()
    ON_COMMAND(ID_EDIT_CLEAR_ALL, OnEditClearAll)
    ON_UPDATE_COMMAND_UI(ID_EDIT_CLEAR_ALL, OnUpdateEditClearAll)
    ON_BN_CLICKED(ID_MY_BUTTON, OnMyButton)
    ON_MESSAGE(WM_MYMESSAGE, OnMyMessage)
    ON_REGISTERED_MESSAGE(WM_FIND, OnFind)
    //}}AFX_MSG_MAP
END_MESSAGE_MAP()
```

Table 2.2 summarizes the various kinds of entries. Each entry consists of a macro with zero or more arguments. The macros are predefined by the class library. For examples of the macros, see the message map above.

Table 2.2 Message-Map Entry Macros

Message type	Macro form	Arguments
Predefined Windows messages	**ON_WM_XXXX**	None
Commands	**ON_COMMAND**	Command ID, Handler name
Update commands	**ON_UPDATE_COMMAND_UI**	Command ID, Handler name
Control notifications	**ON_XXXX**	Control ID, Handler name

Table 2.2   Message-Map Entry Macros *(cont.)*

Message type	Macro form	Arguments
User-defined message	**ON_MESSAGE**	User-defined message ID, Handler name (see Technical Note 6 under MFC Technical Notes in Books Online)
Registered Windows message	**ON_REGISTERED_MESSAGE**	Registered message ID variable, Handler name (see Technical Note 6 under MFC Technical Notes in Books Online)
A range of command IDs	**ON_COMMAND_RANGE**	Start and end of a contiguous range of command IDs. See Message-Map Ranges.
A range of command IDs for updating	**ON_UPDATE_COMMAND_UI_RANGE**	Start and end of a contiguous range of command IDs. See Message-Map Ranges.
A range of control IDs	**ON_CONTROL_RANGE**	A control-notification code and the start and end of a contiguous range of command IDs. See Message-Map Ranges.

Names in the table with the notation **_XXX** represent groups of messages whose names are based on standard message names or control-notification codes in Windows. For example: **ON_WM_PAINT**, **ON_WM_LBUTTONDOWN**, **ON_EN_CHANGE**, **ON_LB_GETSEL**. Even though the **ON_WM_XXX** macros take no arguments, the corresponding handler functions often do take arguments, passed to them by the framework.

Message-Map Ranges

MFC also supports mapping ranges of messages to a single message-handler function. You can map:

- Ranges of command IDs to:
  - A command handler function.
  - A command update handler function.
- A control-notification message for a range of control IDs to a message-handler function.

Mapping a range of messages is useful in a variety of situations. For example, to handle the "zoom" command in the MFC OLE sample HIERSVR, a range of menu command IDs is mapped to a single handler function. You might also map a range of command IDs to a single update handler function so that all of the commands are either enabled or disabled together. (Update handlers are explained in How to Update User-Interface Objects.)

Note ClassWizard does not support message-map ranges. You must write these message-map entries yourself.

For more information about message-map ranges, see the article Message Map: Ranges of Messages.

Declaring Handler Functions

Certain rules and conventions govern the names of your message-handler functions. These depend on the message category, as described in the following topics:

- Standard Windows messages
- Commands and control notifications

Standard Windows Messages

Default handlers for standard Windows messages (**WM_**) are predefined in class **CWnd**. The class library bases names for these handlers on the message name. For example, the handler for the **WM_PAINT** message is declared in **CWnd** as:

```
afx_msg void OnPaint();
```

The **afx_msg** keyword suggests the effect of the C++ **virtual** keyword by distinguishing the handlers from other **CWnd** member functions. Note, however, that these functions are not actually virtual; they are instead implemented through message maps. Message maps depend solely on standard preprocessor macros, not on any extensions to the C++ language. The **afx_msg** keyword resolves to white space after preprocessing.

To override a handler defined in a base class, simply use ClassWizard to define a function with the same prototype in your derived class and to make a message-map entry for the handler. Your handler "overrides" any handler of the same name in any of your class's base classes.

In some cases, your handler should call the overridden handler in the base class so the base class(es) and Windows can operate on the message. Where you call the base-class handler in your override depends on the circumstances. Sometimes you must call the base-class handler first and sometimes last. Sometimes you call the base-class handler conditionally, if you choose not to handle the message yourself. Sometimes you should call the base-class handler, then conditionally execute your own handler code, depending on the value or state returned by the base-class handler.

Important It is not safe to modify the arguments passed into a handler if you intend to pass them to a base-class handler. For example, you might be tempted to modify the *nChar* argument of the OnChar handler (to convert to uppercase, for example). This behavior is fairly obscure, but if you need to accomplish this effect, use the **CWnd** member function **SendMessage** instead.

How do you determine the proper way to override a given message? ClassWizard helps with this decision. When ClassWizard writes the skeleton of the handler function for a given message—an `OnCreate` handler for **WM_CREATE**, for example—it sketches in the form of the recommended overridden member function. The following example recommends that the handler first call the base-class handler and proceed only on condition that it does not return –1.

```
int CMyView::OnCreate(LPCREATESTRUCT lpCreateStruct)
{
    if (CView::OnCreate(lpCreateStruct) == -1)
        return -1;
    // TODO: Add your specialized creation code here
    return 0;
}
```

By convention, the names of these handlers begin with the prefix "On." Some of these handlers take no arguments, while others take several. Some also have a return type other than **void**. The default handlers for all **WM_** messages are documented in the *Class Library Reference* as member functions of class **CWnd** whose names begin with "On." The member function declarations in **CWnd** are prefixed with **afx_msg**.

Commands and Control Notifications

There are no default handlers for commands or control-notification messages. Therefore, you are bound only by convention in naming your handlers for these categories of messages. When you map the command or control notification to a handler, ClassWizard proposes a name based on the command ID or control-notification code. You can accept the proposed name, change it, or replace it.

Convention suggests that you name handlers in both categories for the user-interface object they represent. Thus a handler for the Cut command on the Edit menu might be named

```
afx_msg void OnEditCut();
```

Because the Cut command is so commonly implemented in applications, the framework predefines the command ID for the Cut command as **ID_EDIT_CUT**. For a list of all predefined command IDs, see the file AFXRES.H. For more information, see Standard Commands.

In addition, convention suggests a handler for the **BN_CLICKED** notification message from a button labeled "Use As Default" might be named

```
afx_msg void OnClickedUseAsDefault();
```

You might assign this command an ID of `IDC_USE_AS_DEFAULT` since it is equivalent to an application-specific user-interface object.

Both categories of messages take no arguments and return no value.

How to Manage Commands and Messages with ClassWizard

ClassWizard is a tool is designed specifically to connect Windows messages and user-interface objects such as menus to their handlers.

The typical development scenarios are as follows:

- You determine that one of your classes must handle a certain Windows message, so you run ClassWizard and make the connection.

- You create a menu or accelerator resource, then invoke ClassWizard to connect the command associated with that object to a handler.

As you work with the framework, you'll find that ClassWizard greatly simplifies your message-management tasks.

ClassWizard writes the following information to your source files:

- The appropriate message-map entry for the connection

- A declaration of the handler as a member function of the class

- An empty function template for you to fill in with the handler's code

For detailed information about using ClassWizard to connect messages to handlers, see Chapter 14, Working with Classes, in the *Visual C++ User's Guide*. For examples, see Chapter 7, Binding Visual Objects to Code Using WizardBar, and Chapter 8, Adding a Dialog Box, in *Tutorials*.

Important Use ClassWizard to create and edit all message-map entries. If you add them manually, you may not be able to edit them with ClassWizard later. If you add them outside the bracketing comments, `//{{AFX_MSG_MAP(classname)` and `//}}AFX_MSG_MAP`, ClassWizard cannot edit them at all. Note that by the same token ClassWizard will not touch any entries you add outside the comments, so feel free to add messages outside the comments if you do not want them to be modified. Some messages, such as message-map ranges, must be added outside the comments.

How to Update User-Interface Objects

Typically, menu items and toolbar buttons have more than one state. For example, a menu item is grayed (dimmed) if it is unavailable in the present context. Menu items can also be checked or unchecked. A toolbar button can also be disabled if unavailable, or it can be checked.

Who updates the state of these items as program conditions change? Logically, if a menu item generates a command that is handled by, say, a document, it makes sense to have the document update the menu item. The document probably contains the information on which the update is based.

If a command has multiple user-interface objects (perhaps a menu item and a toolbar button), both are routed to the same handler function. This encapsulates your user-interface update code for all of the equivalent user-interface objects in a single place.

The framework provides a convenient interface for automatically updating user-interface objects. You can choose to do the updating in some other way, but the interface provided is efficient and easy to use.

The following topics explain the use of update handlers:

- When update handlers are called
- The **ON_UPDATE_COMMAND_UI** macro
- The **CCmdUI** class

When Update Handlers Are Called

Suppose the user clicks the mouse in the File menu, which generates a **WM_INITMENUPOPUP** message. The framework's update mechanism collectively updates all items on the File menu before the menu drops down so the user can see it.

To do this, the framework routes update commands for all menu items in the pop-up menu along the standard command routing. Command targets on the routing have an opportunity to update any menu items by matching the update command with an appropriate message-map entry (of the form **ON_UPDATE_COMMAND_UI**) and calling an "update handler" function. Thus, for a menu with six menu items, six update commands are sent out. If an update handler exists for the command ID of the menu item, it is called to do the updating. If not, the framework checks for the existence of a handler for that command ID and enables or disables the menu item as appropriate.

If the framework does not find an **ON_UPDATE_COMMAND_UI** entry during command routing, it automatically enables the user-interface object if there is an **ON_COMMAND** entry somewhere with the same command ID. Otherwise, it disables the user-interface object. Therefore, to ensure that a user-interface object is enabled, supply a handler for the command the object generates or supply an update handler for it. See Figure 2.2.

It is possible to disable the default disabling of user-interface objects. For more information, see the **m_bAutoMenuEnable** member of class **CFrameWnd** in the *Class Library Reference*.

Menu initialization is automatic in the framework, occurring when the application receives a **WM_INITMENUPOPUP** message. During the idle loop, the framework searches the command routing for button update handlers in much the same way as it does for menus.

The ON_UPDATE_COMMAND_UI Macro

Use ClassWizard to connect a user-interface object to a command-update handler in a command-target object. It will automatically connect the user-interface object's ID to the **ON_UPDATE_COMMAND_UI** macro and create a handler in the object that will handle the update.

For example, the Scribble tutorial in *Tutorials* updates a Clear All command in its Edit menu. In the tutorial, ClassWizard adds a message-map entry in the chosen class, a function declaration for a command-update handler called OnUpdateEditClearAll in the class declaration, and an empty function template in the class's implementation file. The function prototype looks like this:

```
afx_msg void OnUpdateEditClearAll( CCmdUI* pCmdUI );
```

Like all handlers, the function shows the **afx_msg** keyword. Like all update handlers, it takes one argument, a pointer to a **CCmdUI** object.

The CCmdUI Class

When it routes the update command to the handler, the framework passes the handler a pointer to a **CCmdUI** object (or to an object of a **CCmdUI**-derived class). This object represents the menu item or toolbar button or other user-interface object that generated the command. The update handler calls member functions of the **CCmdUI** structure through the pointer to update the user-interface object. For example, here is an update handler for the Clear All menu item:

```
void CMyClass::OnUpdateToolsMyTool( CCmdUI* pCmdUI )
{
    if( ToolAvailable() )
        pCmdUI->Enable( TRUE );
}
```

This handler calls the **Enable** member function of an object with access to the menu item. **Enable** makes the item available for use.

How to Display Command Information in the Status Bar

When you run AppWizard to create the skeleton of your application, you can easily support a toolbar and a status bar. A single option in AppWizard supports both. When a status bar is present, the framework automatically gives helpful feedback as the user of your application moves the mouse through items in the menus. The framework automatically displays a prompt string in the status bar when the menu item is being selected. For example, when the user drags the mouse over the Cut item on the Edit menu, the framework might display "Cut the selection and put it on the Clipboard" in the message area of the status bar. The prompt helps the user grasp the menu item's purpose. This also works when the user clicks a toolbar button.

You can easily add to this status-bar help by defining prompt strings for the menu items that you add to the program. To do so, provide the prompt strings when you edit the properties of the menu item in the menu editor. The strings you define this way are stored in your application's resource file; they have the same IDs as the commands they explain.

By default, AppWizard adds the ID for a standard prompt, "Ready," which is displayed when the program is waiting for new messages. If you specify the Context-Sensitive Help option in AppWizard, the ID for a help prompt, "For Help, press F1," is added to your application. This ID is **AFX_IDS_IDLEMESSAGE**.

Working with Frame Windows, Documents, and Views

Previous chapters introduced the primary objects in an application built upon the framework of the Microsoft Foundation Class Library (MFC) and showed how these objects communicate via messages and commands.

This chapter takes you deeper into three of the most important objects in a framework application:

- Frame windows, which contain and manage your views
- Documents, which define your application's data
- Views, which display your documents and manage user interaction with them

The chapter also explains how the framework manages printing and print preview since printing functionality is intimately tied to the view.

One of the most important features of the framework is the division of labor among frame windows, documents, and views. The document manages your data. The view displays it and takes user input. And the frame window puts a frame around the view. Code that defines and manipulates data resides in the document class. Code that displays the data and interprets user input resides in the view class.

Frame Windows

When an application runs under Microsoft Windows, the user interacts with documents displayed in frame windows. A document frame window has two major components: the frame and the contents that it frames. A document frame window can be a single document interface (SDI) frame window or a multiple document interface (MDI) child window. Windows manages most of the user's interaction with the frame window: moving and resizing the window, closing it, and minimizing and maximizing it. You manage the contents inside the frame.

The framework uses frame windows to contain views. The two components—frame and contents—are represented and managed by two different classes in MFC. A frame-window class manages the frame, and a view class manages the contents. The view window is a child of the frame window. Drawing and other user interaction with the document take place in the view's client area, not the frame window's client area. The frame window provides a visible frame around a view, complete with a caption bar and standard window controls such as a control menu, buttons to minimize and maximize the window, and controls for resizing the window. The "contents" consist of the window's client area, which is fully occupied by a child window—the view. Figure 3.1 shows the relationship between a frame window and a view.

Figure 3.1 Frame Window and View

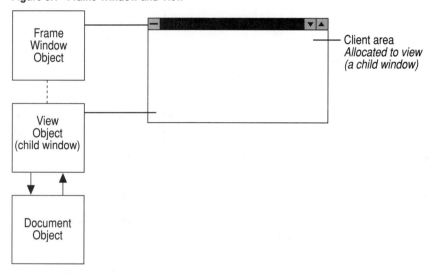

This chapter also discusses splitter windows. In a splitter window, the frame window's client area is occupied by a splitter window, which in turn has multiple child windows, called panes, which are views.

The following topics explain about frame windows:

- Window classes
- The frame-window classes created by AppWizard
- Managing child windows
- Managing the current view
- Managing menus, control bars, and accelerators
- Working with the File Manager
- Orchestrating other window actions

Window Classes

Each application has one "main frame window," a desktop window that usually has the application name in its caption. Each document usually has one "document frame window." A document frame window contains at least one view, which presents the document's data. For an SDI application, there is one frame window derived from class **CFrameWnd**. This window is both the main frame window and the document frame window. For an MDI application, the main frame window is derived from class **CMDIFrameWnd**, and the document frame windows, which are MDI child windows, are derived from class **CMDIChildWnd**.

These classes provide most of the frame-window functionality you need for your applications. Under normal circumstances, the default behavior and appearance they provide will suit your needs. If you need additional functionality, derive from these classes.

The Frame-Window Classes Created by AppWizard

When you use AppWizard to create a skeleton application, in addition to application, document, and view classes, AppWizard creates a derived frame-window class for your application's main frame window. The class is called CMainFrame by default, and the files that contain it are named MAINFRM.H and MAINFRM.CPP.

If your application is SDI, your CMainFrame class is derived from class **CFrameWnd**. If your application is MDI, CMainFrame is derived from class **CMDIFrameWnd**. If you choose to support a toolbar, the class also has member variables of type **CToolBar** and **CStatusBar** and an OnCreate message-handler function to initialize the two control bars.

If your application is MDI, AppWizard does not derive a new document frame-window class for you. Instead, it uses the default implementation in **CMDIChildWnd**. Later on, if you need to customize your document frame window, you can use ClassWizard to create a new document frame-window class.

These frame-window classes work as created, but to enhance their functionality, you must add member variables and member functions. You may also want to have your window classes handle other Windows messages.

Using Frame Windows

The framework creates document frame windows—and their views and documents—as part of its implementation of the New and Open commands on the File menu. Because the framework does most of the frame-window work for you, you play only a small role in creating, using, and destroying those windows. You can, however, explicitly create your own frame windows and child windows for special purposes.

Creating Document Frame Windows

As you saw in Document/View Creation, the **CDocTemplate** object orchestrates creating the frame window, document, and view and connecting them all together. Three **CRuntimeClass** arguments to the **CDocTemplate** constructor specify the frame window, document, and view classes that the document template creates dynamically in response to user commands such as the New command on the File menu or the New Window command on an MDI Window menu. The document template stores this information for later use when it creates a frame window for a view and document.

In order for the **RUNTIME_CLASS** mechanism to work correctly, your derived frame-window classes must be declared with the **DECLARE_DYNCREATE** macro. This is because the framework needs to create document frame windows using the dynamic construction mechanism of class **CObject**. For details about **DECLARE_DYNCREATE**, see the article CObject Class: Deriving a Class from CObject and the Macros and Globals section in the *Class Library Reference*.

When the user chooses a command that creates a document, the framework calls upon the document template to create the document object, its view, and the frame window that will display the view. Chapter 1, Using the Classes to Write Applications for Windows, describes this creation process. When it creates the document frame window, the document template creates an object of the appropriate class—a class derived from **CFrameWnd** for an SDI application or from **CMDIChildWnd** for an MDI application. The framework then calls the frame-window object's **LoadFrame** member function to get creation information from resources and to create the Windows window. The framework attaches the window handle to the frame-window object. Then it creates the view as a child window of the document frame window.

Note You cannot create your own child windows or call any Windows API functions in the constructor of a **CWnd**-derived object. This is because the **HWND** for the **CWnd** object has not been created yet. Most Windows-specific initialization, such as adding child windows, must be done in an **OnCreate** message handler.

Destroying Frame Windows

The framework manages window destruction as well as creation for those windows associated with framework documents and views. If you create additional windows, you are responsible for destroying them.

In the framework, when the user closes the frame window, the window's default **OnClose** handler calls **DestroyWindow**. The last member function called when the Windows window is destroyed is **OnNcDestroy**, which does some cleanup, calls the **Default** member function to perform Windows cleanup, and lastly calls the virtual member function **PostNcDestroy**. The **CFrameWnd** implementation of **PostNcDestroy** deletes the C++ window object. You should never use the C++ **delete** operator on a frame window. Use **DestroyWindow** instead.

When the main window closes, the application closes. If there are modified unsaved documents, the framework displays a message box to ask if the documents should be saved and ensures that the appropriate documents are saved if necessary.

What Frame Windows Do

Besides simply framing a view, frame windows are responsible for numerous tasks involved in coordinating the frame with its view and with the application. **CMDIFrameWnd** and **CMDIChildWnd** inherit from **CFrameWnd**, so they have **CFrameWnd** capabilities as well as new capabilities that they add. Examples of child windows include views, controls such as buttons and list boxes, and control bars, including toolbars, status bars, and dialog bars. The frame window is responsible for managing the layout of its child windows. In the framework, a frame window positions any control bars, views, and other child windows inside its client area. The frame window also forwards commands to its views and can respond to notification messages from control windows. Chapter 1, Using the Classes to Write Applications for Windows, shows how commands are routed from the frame window to its view and other command targets.

Managing Child Windows

MDI main frame windows (one per application) contain a special child window called the **MDICLIENT** window. The **MDICLIENT** window manages the client area of the main frame window, and itself has child windows: the document windows, derived from **CMDIChildWnd**. Because the document windows are frame windows themselves (MDI child windows), they can also have their own children. In all of these cases, the parent window manages its child windows and forwards some commands to them.

In an MDI frame window, the frame window manages the **MDICLIENT** window, repositioning it in conjunction with control bars. The **MDICLIENT** window, in turn, manages all MDI child frame windows. Figure 3.2 shows the relationship between an MDI frame window, its **MDICLIENT** window, and its child document frame windows.

Figure 3.2   MDI Frame Windows and Children

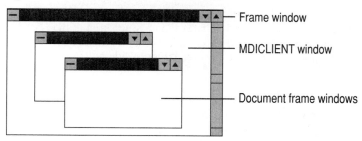

An MDI frame window also works in conjunction with the current MDI child window, if there is one. The MDI frame window delegates command messages to the MDI child before it tries to handle them itself.

Managing the Current View

As part of the default implementation of frame windows, a frame window keeps track of a currently active view. If the frame window contains more than one view, as for example in a splitter window, the current view is the most recent view in use. The active view is independent of the active window in Windows or the current input focus.

When the active view changes, the framework notifies the current view by calling its **OnActivateView** member function. You can tell whether the view is being activated or deactivated by examining **OnActivateView**'s *bActivate* parameter. By default, **OnActivateView** sets the focus to the current view on activation. You can override **OnActivateView** to perform any special processing when the view is deactivated or reactivated. For example, you might want to provide special visual cues to distinguish the active view from other, inactive views. For more information, see the **OnActivateView** member function of class **CView** in the *Class Library Reference*.

A frame window forwards commands to its current (active) view, as described in Chapter 1, Using the Classes to Write Applications for Windows, as part of the standard command routing.

Managing Menus, Control Bars, and Accelerators

The frame window manages updating user-interface objects, including menus, toolbar buttons, and the status bar. It also manages sharing the menu bar in MDI applications.

The frame window participates in updating user-interface items using the **ON_UPDATE_COMMAND_UI** mechanism described in How to Update User-Interface Objects. Buttons on toolbars and other control bars are updated during the idle loop. Menu items in drop-down menus on the menu bar are updated just before the menu drops down.

The frame window also positions the status bar within its client area and manages the status bar's indicators. The frame window clears and updates the message area in the status bar as needed and displays prompt strings as the user selects menu items or toolbar buttons, as described in Chapter 2, in How to Display Command Information in the Status Bar.

For MDI applications, the MDI frame window manages the menu bar and caption. An MDI frame window owns one default menu that is used as the menu bar when there are no active MDI child windows. When there are active children, the MDI frame window's menu bar is taken over by the menu for the active MDI child window. If an MDI application supports multiple document types, such as chart and worksheet documents, each type puts its own menus into the menu bar and changes the main frame window's caption.

CMDIFrameWnd provides default implementations for the standard commands on the Window menu that appears for MDI applications. In particular, the New Window command (**ID_WINDOW_NEW**) is implemented to create a new frame window and view on the current document. You need to override these implementations only if you need advanced customization.

Multiple MDI child windows of the same document type share menu resources. If several MDI child windows are created by the same document template, they can all use the same menu resource, saving on system resources in Windows.

Each frame window maintains an optional accelerator table that does keyboard accelerator translation for you automatically. This mechanism makes it easy to define accelerator keys (also called shortcut keys) that invoke menu commands.

Frame-Window Styles

The frame windows you get with the framework are suitable for most programs, but you can gain additional flexibility by using the advanced functions **PreCreateWindow** and **AfxRegisterWindowClass**. **PreCreateWindow** is a member function of **CWnd**. **AfxRegisterWindowClass** is a global function documented in Macros and Globals in the *Class Library Reference*.

If you apply the **WS_HSCROLL** and **WS_VSCROLL** styles to the main frame window, they are instead applied to the **MDICLIENT** window so users can scroll the **MDICLIENT** area.

If the window's **FWS_ADDTOTITLE** style bit is set (which it is by default), the view tells the frame window what title to display in the window's title bar based on the view's document name.

Working with the File Manager

The frame window manages a relationship with the Windows File Manager.

By adding a few initializing calls in your override of the **CWinApp** member function **InitInstance**, as described in Chapter 1, in CWinApp: The Application Class, you can have your frame window indirectly open files dragged from the Windows File Manager and dropped in the frame window. See File Manager Drag and Drop.

The frame window can also respond to dynamic data exchange (DDE) requests to open files from the File Manager (if the file extension is registered or associated with the application). See Shell Registration.

Orchestrating Other Window Actions

The frame window orchestrates semimodal states such as context-sensitive help and print preview. The framework's role in managing context-sensitive help is described in the article Help. For a description of the frame window's role in print preview, see Printing and Print Preview.

Documents and Views

The parts of the framework most visible both to the user and to you, the programmer, are the document and view. Most of your work in developing an application with the framework goes into writing your document and view classes. This section describes:

- The purposes of documents and views and how they interact in the framework.
- What you must do to implement them.

The **CDocument** class provides the basic functionality for programmer-defined document classes. A document represents the unit of data that the user typically opens with the Open command on the File menu and saves with the Save command on the File menu.

The **CView** class provides the basic functionality for programmer-defined view classes. A view is attached to a document and acts as an intermediary between the document and the user: the view renders an image of the document on the screen and interprets user input as operations upon the document. The view also renders the image for both printing and print preview.

Figure 3.3 shows the relationship between a document and its view.

Figure 3.3 Document and View

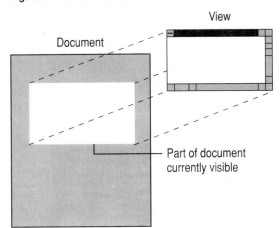

The document/view implementation in the class library separates the data itself from its display and from user operations on the data. All changes to the data are managed through the document class. The view calls this interface to access and update the data.

Documents, their associated views, and the frame windows that frame the views are created by a document template, as described in Document/View Creation. The document template is responsible for creating and managing all documents of one document type.

Document and View Classes Created by AppWizard

AppWizard gives you a head start on your program development by creating skeletal document and view classes for you. You can then use ClassWizard to map commands and messages to these classes and the Visual C++ source code editor to write their member functions.

The document class created by AppWizard is derived from class **CDocument**. The view class is derived from **CView**. The names that AppWizard gives these classes and the files that contain them are based on the project name you supply in the AppWizard dialog box. From AppWizard, you can use the Classes dialog box to alter the default names.

Some applications might need more than one document class, view class, or frame-window class. For more information, see Multiple Document Types, Views, and Frame Windows.

Using Documents and Views

Working together, documents and views:

- Contain, manage, and display your application-specific data.
- Provide an interface for manipulating the data.
- Participate in writing and reading files.
- Participate in printing.
- Handle most of your application's commands and messages.

Managing Data

Documents contain and manage your application's data. To use the AppWizard-supplied document class, you must do the following:

- Derive a class from **CDocument** for each type of document.
- Add member variables to store each document's data.
- Override **CDocument**'s **Serialize** member function in your document class. **Serialize** writes and reads the document's data to and from disk.

You may also want to override other **CDocument** member functions. In particular, you will often need to override **OnNewDocument** and **OnOpenDocument** to initialize the document's data members and **DeleteContents** to destroy dynamically allocated data. For information about overridable members, see class **CDocument** in the *Class Library Reference*.

Document Data Variables

Implement your document's data as member variables of your document class. For example, the Scribble tutorial program declares a data member of type **CObList**—a linked list that stores pointers to **CObject** objects. This list is used to store arrays of points that make up a freehand line drawing.

How you implement your document's member data depends on the nature of your application. To help you out, MFC supplies a group of "collection classes"—arrays, lists, and maps (dictionaries), including collections based on C++ templates—along with classes that encapsulate a variety of common data types such as **CString**, **CRect**, **CPoint**, **CSize**, and **CTime**. For more information about these classes, see the Class Library Overview in the *Class Library Reference*.

When you define your document's member data, you will usually add member functions to the document class to set and get data items and perform other useful operations on them.

Your views access the document object by using the view's pointer to the document, installed in the view at creation time. You can retrieve this pointer in a view's member functions by calling the **CView** member function **GetDocument**. Be sure to cast this pointer to your own document type. Then you can access public document members through the pointer.

If frequent data transfer requires direct access, or you wish to use the nonpublic members of the document class, you may want to make your view class a friend (in C++ terms) of the document class.

Serializing Data to and from Files

The basic idea of persistence is that an object should be able to write its current state, indicated by the values of its member variables, to persistent storage. Later, the object can be re-created by reading, or "deserializing," the object's state from persistent storage. A key point here is that the object itself is responsible for reading and writing its own state. Thus, for a class to be persistent, it must implement the basic serialization operations.

The framework provides a default implementation for saving documents to disk files in response to the Save and Save As commands on the File menu and for loading documents from disk files in response to the Open command. With very little work, you can implement a document's ability to write and read its data to and from a file. The main thing you must do is override **CDocument**'s **Serialize** member function in your document class.

AppWizard places a skeletal override of the **CDocument** member function **Serialize** in the document class it creates for you. After you have implemented your application's member variables, you can fill in your Serialize override with code that sends the data to an "archive object" connected to a file. A **CArchive** object is similar to the **cin** and **cout** input/output objects from the C++ iostream library. However, **CArchive** writes and reads binary format, not formatted text.

The Document's Role

The framework responds automatically to the File menu's Open, Save, and Save As commands by calling the document's `Serialize` member function if it is implemented. An **ID_FILE_OPEN** command, for example, calls a handler function in the application object. During this process, the user sees and responds to the File Open dialog box and the framework obtains the filename the user chooses. The framework creates a **CArchive** object set up for loading data into the document and passes the archive to `Serialize`. The framework has already opened the file. The code in your document's `Serialize` member function reads the data in through the archive, reconstructing data objects as needed. For more information about serialization, see the article Serialization (Object Persistence).

The Data's Role

In general, class-type data should be able to serialize itself. That is, when you pass an object to an archive, the object should know how to write itself to the archive and how to read itself from the archive. MFC provides support for making classes serializable in this way. If you design a class to define a data type and you intend to serialize data of that type, design for serialization.

Bypassing the Archive Mechanism

As you have seen, the framework provides a default way to read and write data to and from files. Serializing through an archive object suits the needs of a great many applications. Such an application reads a file entirely into memory, lets the user update the file, and then writes the updated version to disk again.

However, some applications operate on data very differently, and for these applications serialization through an archive is not suitable. Examples include database programs, programs that edit only parts of large files, programs that write text-only files, and programs that share data files.

In these cases, you can override the **Serialize** member function of **CDocument** in a different way to mediate file actions through a **CFile** object rather than a **CArchive** object.

You can use the **Open**, **Read**, **Write**, **Close**, and **Seek** member functions of class **CFile** to open a file, move the file pointer (seek) to a specific point in the file, read a record (a specified number of bytes) at that point, let the user update the record, then seek to the same point again and write the record back to the file. The framework will open the file for you, and you can use the **GetFile** member function of class **CArchive** to obtain a pointer to the **CFile** object. For even more sophisticated and flexible use, you can override the **OnOpenDocument** and **OnSaveDocument** member functions of class **CWinApp**. For more information, see class **CFile** in the *Class Library Reference*.

In this scenario, your `Serialize` override does nothing, unless, for example, you want to have it read and write a file header to keep it up to date when the document closes.

For an example of such nonarchived processing, see the MFC Advanced Concepts sample CHKBOOK.

Handling Commands in the Document

Your document class may also handle certain commands generated by menu items, toolbar buttons, or accelerator keys. By default, **CDocument** handles the Save and Save As commands on the File menu, using serialization. Other commands that affect the data may also be handled by member functions of your document. For example, in the Scribble tutorial program, class `CScribDoc` provides a handler for the Edit Clear All command, which deletes all of the data currently stored in the document. Unlike views, documents cannot handle standard Windows messages.

Displaying Data in a View and Interacting with the User

The view's responsibilities are to display the document's data graphically to the user and to accept and interpret user input as operations on the document. Your tasks in writing your view class are to:

- Write your view class's `OnDraw` member function, which renders the document's data.

- Connect appropriate Windows messages and user-interface objects such as menu items to message-handler member functions in the view class.

- Implement those handlers to interpret user input.

In addition, you may need to override other **CView** member functions in your derived view class. In particular, you may want to override **OnInitialUpdate** to perform special initialization for the view and **OnUpdate** to do any special processing needed just before the view redraws itself. For multipage documents, you also must override **OnPreparePrinting** to initialize the Print dialog box with the number of pages to print and other information. For more information on overriding **CView** member functions, see class **CView** in the *Class Library Reference*.

The Microsoft Foundation Class Library also provides several derived view classes for special purposes:

- **CScrollView**, which provides automatic scrolling and view scaling.

- **CFormView**, which provides a scrollable view useful for displaying a form made up of dialog controls. A **CFormView** object is created from a dialog-template resource.

- **CRecordView** and **CDaoRecordView**, which are form views whose controls are connected to the fields of a **CRecordset** or **CDaoRecordset** object, respectively, representing a database table.

- **CEditView**, which provides a view with the characteristics of an editable-text control with enhanced editing features. You can use a **CEditView** object to implement a simple text editor. Note that as of MFC version 4.0, **CEditView** has a new base class, called **CCtrlView**.

The following table shows **CCtrlView** and other new view classes:

Table 3.1 New View Classes

Class	Description
CCtrlView	Base class of **CTreeView**, **CListView**, **CEditView**, and **CRichEditView**. These classes let you use document/view architecture with the indicated Windows common controls.
CDaoRecordView	A form view that fills its controls from a **CDaoRecordset** object. This class is analogous to **CRecordView**.
CListView	A view containing a **CListCtrl** object.
CRichEditView	A view containing a **CRichEditCtrl** object. This class is analogous to **CEditView**, but unlike **CEditView**, **CRichEditView** handles formatted text.
CTreeView	A view containing a **CTreeCtrl** object, for views that resemble the Workspace window in Visual C++.

To take advantage of these special classes, derive your view classes from them. For more information, see Scrolling and Scaling Views and Special View Classes. For more information on the database classes, see Chapter 7, Working with Databases.

Drawing in a View

Nearly all drawing in your application occurs in the view's OnDraw member function, which you must override in your view class. (The exception is mouse drawing, discussed in Interpreting User Input Through a View.) Your OnDraw override:

1. Gets data by calling the document member functions you provide.

2. Displays the data by calling member functions of a device-context object that the framework passes to OnDraw.

When a document's data changes in some way, the view must be redrawn to reflect the changes. Typically, this happens when the user makes a change through a view on the document. In this case, the view calls the document's **UpdateAllViews** member function to notify all views on the same document to update themselves. **UpdateAllViews** calls each view's **OnUpdate** member function. The default implementation of **OnUpdate** invalidates the view's entire client area. You can override it to invalidate only those regions of the client area that map to the modified portions of the document.

The **UpdateAllViews** member function of class **CDocument** and the **OnUpdate** member function of class **CView** let you pass information describing what parts of the document were modified. This "hint" mechanism lets you limit the area that the view must redraw. **OnUpdate** takes two "hint" arguments. The first, *lHint*, of type **LPARAM**, lets you pass any data you like, while the second, *pHint*, of type **CObject***, lets you pass a pointer to any object derived from **CObject**.

When a view becomes invalid, Windows sends it a **WM_PAINT** message. The view's **OnPaint** handler function responds to the message by creating a device-context object of class **CPaintDC** and calls your view's OnDraw member function. You do not normally have to write an overriding OnPaint handler function.

Recall from Chapter 1 that a device context is a Windows data structure that contains information about the drawing attributes of a device such as a display or a printer. All drawing calls are made through a device-context object. For drawing on the screen, OnDraw is passed a **CPaintDC** object. For drawing on a printer, it is passed a **CDC** object set up for the current printer.

Your code for drawing in the view first retrieves a pointer to the document, then makes drawing calls through the device context. The following simple OnDraw example illustrates the process:

```
void CMyView::OnDraw( CDC* pDC )
{
    CMyDoc* pDoc = GetDocument();
    CString s = pDoc->GetData();   // Returns a CString
    CRect rect;

    GetClientRect( &rect );
    pDC->SetTextAlign( TA_BASELINE | TA_CENTER );
    pDC->TextOut( rect.right / 2, rect.bottom / 2,
                  s, s.GetLength() );
}
```

In this example, you would define the GetData function as a member of your derived document class.

The example prints whatever string it gets from the document, centered in the view. If the OnDraw call is for screen drawing, the **CDC** object passed in *pDC* is a **CPaintDC** whose constructor has already called **BeginPaint**. Calls to drawing functions are made through the device-context pointer. For information about device contexts and drawing calls, see class **CDC** in the *Class Library Reference* and Working with Window Objects.

For more examples of how to write OnDraw, see the MFC Samples, which you can access under Samples in Books Online.

Interpreting User Input Through a View

Other member functions of the view handle and interpret all user input. You will usually define message-handler member functions in your view class to process:

- Windows messages generated by mouse and keyboard actions.

- Commands from menus, toolbar buttons, and accelerator keys.

These message-handler member functions interpret the following actions as data input, selection, or editing, including moving data to and from the Clipboard:

- Mouse movements and clicks, drags, and double-clicks

- Keystrokes

- Menu commands

Which Windows messages your view handles depends on your application's needs.

You saw earlier, in Messages and Commands in the Framework, how to assign menu items and other user-interface objects to commands and how to bind the commands to handler functions with ClassWizard. You have also seen how the framework routes such commands and sends standard Windows messages to the objects that contain handlers for them.

For example, your application might need to implement direct mouse drawing in the view. The Scribble tutorial example shows how to handle the **WM_LBUTTONDOWN, WM_MOUSEMOVE**, and **WM_LBUTTONUP** messages respectively to begin, continue, and end the drawing of a line segment. On the other hand, you might sometimes need to interpret a mouse click in your view as a selection. Your view's `OnLButtonDown` handler function would determine whether the user was drawing or selecting. If selecting, the handler would determine whether the click was within the bounds of some object in the view and, if so, alter the display to show the object as selected.

Your view might also handle certain menu commands, such as those from the Edit menu to cut, copy, paste, or delete selected data using the Clipboard. Such a handler would call some of the Clipboard-related member functions of class **CWnd** to transfer a selected data item to or from the Clipboard.

Printing and the View

Your view also plays two important roles in printing its associated document.

The view:

- Uses the same `OnDraw` code to draw on the printer as to draw on the screen.

- Manages dividing the document into pages for printing.

For more information about printing and about the view's role in printing, see Printing and Print Preview.

Scrolling and Scaling Views

MFC supports views that scroll and views that are automatically scaled to the size of the frame window that displays them. Class **CScrollView** supports both kinds of views.

For more information about scrolling and scaling, see class **CScrollView** in the *Class Library Reference*. For a scrolling example, see Chapter 9, Enhancing Views, in *Tutorials*.

Scrolling

Frequently the size of a document is greater than the size its view can display. This may occur because the document's data increases or the user shrinks the window that frames the view. In such cases, the view must support scrolling.

Any view can handle scroll-bar messages in its **OnHScroll** and **OnVScroll** member functions. You can either implement scroll-bar message handling in these functions, doing all the work yourself, or you can use the **CScrollView** class to handle scrolling for you.

CScrollView does the following:

- Manages window and viewport sizes and mapping modes
- Scrolls automatically in response to scroll-bar messages

You can specify how much to scroll for a "page" (when the user clicks in a scroll-bar shaft) and a "line" (when the user clicks in a scroll arrow). Plan these values to suit the nature of your view. For example, you might want to scroll in 1-pixel increments for a graphics view but in increments based on the line height in text documents.

Scaling

When you want the view to automatically fit the size of its frame window, you can use **CScrollView** for scaling instead of scrolling. The logical view is stretched or shrunk to fit the window's client area exactly. A scaled view has no scroll bars.

Multiple Document Types, Views, and Frame Windows

The standard relationship among a document, its view, and its frame window is described in Document/View Creation. Many applications support a single document type (but possibly multiple open documents of that type) with a single view on the document and only one frame window per document. But some applications may need to alter one or more of those defaults.

Multiple Document Types

AppWizard creates a single document class for you. In some cases, though, you may need to support more than one document type. For example, your application may need worksheet and chart documents. Each document type is represented by its own document class and probably by its own view class as well. When the user chooses the File New command, the framework displays a dialog box that lists the supported document types. Then it creates a document of the type that the user chooses. Each document type is managed by its own document-template object.

To create extra document classes, use the Add Class button in the ClassWizard dialog box. Choose **CDocument** as the Class Type to derive from and supply the requested document information. Then implement the new class's data.

To let the framework know about your extra document class, you must add a second call to **AddDocTemplate** in your application class's InitInstance override. For more information, see Document Templates.

Multiple Views

Many documents require only a single view, but it is possible to support more than one view of a single document. To help you implement multiple views, a document object keeps a list of its views, provides member functions for adding and removing views, and supplies the **UpdateAllViews** member function for letting multiple views know when the document's data has changed.

MFC supports three common user interfaces requiring multiple views on the same document. These models are:

- View objects of the same class, each in a separate MDI document frame window.

  You might want to support creating a second frame window on a document. The user could choose a New Window command to open a second frame with a view of the same document and then use the two frames to view different portions of the document simultaneously. The framework supports the New Window command on the Window menu for MDI applications by duplicating the initial frame window and view attached to the document.

- View objects of the same class in the same document frame window.

  Splitter windows split the view space of a single document window into multiple separate views of the document. The framework creates multiple view objects from the same view class. For more information, see Splitter Windows.

- View objects of different classes in a single frame window.

  In this model, a variation of the splitter window, multiple views share a single frame window. The views are constructed from different classes, each view providing a different way to view the same document. For example, one view might show a word-processing document in normal mode while the other view shows it in outline mode. A splitter control allows the user to adjust the relative sizes of the views.

Figure 3.4 shows the three user-interface models in the order presented above.

Figure 3.4 Multiple-View User Interfaces

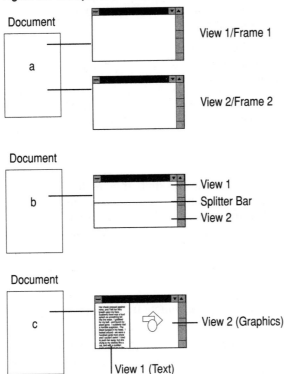

The framework provides these models by implementing the New Window command and by providing class **CSplitterWnd**, as discussed in Splitter Windows. You can implement other models using these as your starting point. For sample programs that illustrate different configurations of views, frame windows, and splitters, see MFC Samples under Samples in Books Online.

For more information about **UpdateAllViews**, see class **CView** in the *Class Library Reference* and Chapter 9, Enhancing Views, in *Tutorials*.

Splitter Windows

In a splitter window, the window is, or can be, split into two or more scrollable panes. A splitter control (or "split box") in the window frame next to the scroll bars allows the user to adjust the relative sizes of the panes. Each pane is a view on the same document. In "dynamic" splitters, the views are of the same class, as shown in Figure 3.4(b). In "static" splitters, the views can be of different classes. Splitter windows of both kinds are supported by class **CSplitterWnd**.

Dynamic splitter windows, with views of the same class, allow the user to split a window into multiple panes at will and then scroll different panes to see different parts of the document. The user can also unsplit the window to remove the additional views. The splitter windows added to the Scribble application in Chapter 9 of *Tutorials* are an example. That chapter describes the technique for creating dynamic splitter windows. A dynamic splitter window is shown in Figure 3.4(b).

Static splitter windows, with views of different classes, start with the window split into multiple panes, each with a different purpose. For example, in the Visual C++ bitmap editor, the image window shows two panes side by side. The left-hand pane displays a life-sized image of the bitmap. The right-hand pane displays a zoomed or magnified image of the same bitmap. The panes are separated by a "splitter bar" that the user can drag to change the relative sizes of the panes. A static splitter window is shown in Figure 3.4(c).

For more information, see class **CSplitterWnd** in the *Class Library Reference* and MFC Samples under Samples in Books Online.

Initializing and Cleaning Up Documents and Views

Use the following guidelines for initializing and cleaning up after your documents and views:

- The framework initializes documents and views; you initialize any data you add to them.

- The framework cleans up as documents and views close; you must deallocate any memory that you allocated on the heap from within the member functions of those documents and views.

Note   Recall that initialization for the whole application is best done in your override of the **InitInstance** member function of class **CWinApp**, and cleanup for the whole application is best done in your override of the **CWinApp** member function **ExitInstance**.

The life cycle of a document (and its frame window and view or views) in an MDI application is as follows:

1. During dynamic creation, the document constructor is called.

2. For each new document, the document's **OnNewDocument** or **OnOpenDocument** is called.

3. The user interacts with the document throughout its lifetime.

4. The framework calls **DeleteContents** to delete data specific to a document.

5. The document's destructor is called.

In an SDI application, step 1 is performed once, when the document is first created. Then steps 2 through 4 are performed repeatedly each time a new document is opened. The new document reuses the existing document object. Finally, step 5 is performed when the application ends.

Initializing

Documents are created in two different ways, so your document class must support both ways. First, the user can create a new, empty document with the File New command. In that case, initialize the document in your override of the **OnNewDocument** member function of class **CDocument**. Second, the user can use the Open command on the File menu to create a new document whose contents are read from a file. In that case, initialize the document in your override of the **OnOpenDocument** member function of class **CDocument**. If both initializations are the same, you can call a common member function from both overrides, or **OnOpenDocument** can call **OnNewDocument** to initialize a clean document and then finish the open operation.

Views are created after their documents are created. The best time to initialize a view is after the framework has finished creating the document, frame window, and view. You can initialize your view by overriding the **OnInitialUpdate** member function of **CView**. If you need to reinitialize or adjust anything each time the document changes, you can override **OnUpdate**.

Cleaning Up

When a document is closing, the framework first calls its **DeleteContents** member function. If you allocated any memory on the heap during the course of the document's operation, **DeleteContents** is the best place to deallocate it.

Note You should not deallocate document data in the document's destructor. In the case of an SDI application, the document object might be reused.

You can override a view's destructor to deallocate any memory you allocated on the heap.

Special View Classes

Besides **CScrollView**, the Microsoft Foundation Class Library provides three other classes derived from **CView**:

- **CFormView**, a view with attributes of a dialog box and a scrolling view. A **CFormView** is created from a dialog-template resource. You can create the dialog-template resource with the Visual C++ dialog editor.

- **CRecordView** or **CDaoRecordView**, a form view whose controls are connected to fields of a **CRecordset** or **CDaoRecordset** object that represents a database table.

- **CEditView**, a view that uses the Windows edit control as a simple multiline text editor. You can use a **CEditView** as the view on a document.

About CFormView

CFormView provides a view based on a dialog-template resource. You can use it to create formlike views with edit boxes and other dialog controls. The user can scroll

the form view and tab among its controls. Form views support scrolling using the
CScrollView functionality. For more information, see class **CFormView** in the *Class Library Reference*.

About CRecordView and CDaoRecordView

CRecordView provides database forms for applications that use the MFC ODBC classes. Similarly, **CDaoRecordView** provides database forms for applications that use the MFC DAO classes. You can use AppWizard or ClassWizard to create a form whose controls exchange data directly with the fields data members of a **CRecordset** or **CDaoRecordset** object. The recordset object selects data for a "current record" in an associated table in a database. For more information, see classes **CRecordView**, **CDaoRecordView**, **CRecordset**, and **CDaoRecordset** in the *Class Library Reference* and Chapter 7, Working with Databases.

About CEditView

CEditView provides the functionality of a **CEdit** control with enhanced editing features: printing; find and replace; cut, copy, paste, clear, and undo commands; and File Save and File Open commands. You can use a **CEditView** to implement a simple text-editor view. See classes **CEditView** and **CEdit** in the *Class Library Reference*.

Printing and Print Preview

Microsoft Windows implements device-independent display. This means that the same drawing calls, made through a device context passed to your view's OnDraw member function, are used to draw on the screen and on other devices, such as printers. You use the device context to call graphics device interface (GDI) functions, and the device driver associated with the particular device translates the calls into calls that the device can understand.

When your framework document prints, OnDraw receives a different kind of device-context object as its argument; instead of a **CPaintDC** object, it gets a **CDC** object associated with the current printer. OnDraw makes exactly the same calls through the device context as it does for rendering your document on the screen.

The framework also provides an implementation of the File Print Preview command as described in Previewing the Printed Document.

The article Printing describes in detail the partnership between you and the framework during printing and print preview. In particular, see Figure 1 in the article. Chapter 10, Enhancing Printing, in*Tutorials* provides an example.

Printing the Document

To print, the framework calls member functions of the view object to set up the Print dialog box, allocate fonts and other resources needed, set the printer mode for a given page, print a given page, and deallocate resources. Once the document as a whole is set up, the process iteratively prints each page. When all pages have been printed, the framework cleans up and deallocates resources. You can, and sometimes must, override some view member functions to facilitate printing. For information, see class **CView** in the *Class Library Reference*.

When the view's **OnPrint** member function is called, it must calculate what part of the document image to draw for the given page number. Typically, **OnPrint** adjusts the viewport origin or the clipping region of the device context to specify what should be drawn. Then **OnPrint** calls the view's **OnDraw** member function to draw that portion of the image.

Previewing the Printed Document

The framework also implements print-preview functionality and makes it easy for you to use this functionality in your applications. Print preview shows a reduced image of either one or two pages of the document as it would appear when printed. The implementation also provides controls for printing the displayed page(s), moving to the next or the previous page, toggling the display between one and two pages, zooming the display in and out to view it at different sizes, and closing the display. If the framework knows how long the document is, it can also display a scroll bar for moving from page to page.

To implement print preview, instead of directly drawing an image on a device, the framework must simulate the printer using the screen. To do this, MFC implements the **CPreviewDC** class, which is used in conjunction with the implementation class **CPreviewView**. All **CDC** objects contain two device contexts. In a **CPreviewDC** object, the first device context represents the printer being simulated; the second represents the screen on which output is actually displayed.

In response to a Print Preview command from the File menu, the framework creates a **CPreviewDC** object. Then when your application performs an operation that sets a characteristic of the printer device context, the framework performs a similar operation on the screen device context. For example, if your application selects a font for printing, the framework selects a font for screen display that simulates the printer font. When your application sends output that would go to the printer, the framework instead sends it to the screen.

The order and manner in which pages of a document are displayed are also different for print preview. Instead of printing a range of pages from start to finish, print preview displays one or two pages at a time and waits for a cue from the user before it displays different pages.

You are not required to do anything to provide print preview, other than to make sure the Print Preview command is in the File menu for your application. However, if you choose, you can modify the behavior of print preview in a number of ways. For more information about making such modifications to print preview in your application, see Technical Note 30 under MFC Technical Notes in Books Online.

Working with Dialog Boxes, Controls, and Control Bars

The previous chapter explained windows, particularly the frame windows used to display views of documents. As you saw briefly in that chapter, class **CWnd** is the base class of many other window classes besides the frame windows.

This chapter covers the following topics, including several additional categories of window classes:

- Dialog boxes
- Control windows
- Control bars

Dialog boxes are used to retrieve input from the user. Inside a dialog box, the user interacts with controls, such as buttons, list boxes, combo boxes, and edit boxes. You can also place controls in a frame window, a view, or a control bar. Using "property sheets," your MFC dialog boxes can also use the "tab dialog box" look used in many dialog boxes in Microsoft Word, Excel, and Visual C++ itself.

A toolbar is a control bar that contains bitmapped buttons; these buttons can be configured to appear and behave as pushbuttons, radio buttons, or check boxes. An MFC toolbar can "dock" to any side of its parent window or float in its own mini-frame window. A toolbar can also "float" over the application's windows, and you can change its size. A status bar is a control bar that contains text-output panes, or "indicators." A dialog bar is a control bar based on a dialog-template resource; as in a dialog box, the user can tab among the controls.

Dialog Boxes

Applications for Windows frequently communicate with the user through dialog boxes. Class **CDialog** provides an interface for managing dialog boxes, the Visual C++ dialog editor makes it easy to design dialog boxes and create their dialog-template resources, and ClassWizard simplifies the process of initializing and validating the controls in a dialog box and of gathering the values entered by the user.

The following topics provide details about dialog boxes:

- Dialog components
- Modal and modeless dialog boxes
- Property sheets and property pages in a dialog box
- Creating a dialog resource template
- The life cycle of a dialog box
- Dialog data exchange and validation
- Type-safe access to controls in a dialog box
- Mapping Windows messages to your class
- Common dialog classes

Dialog-Box Components in the Framework

In the framework, a dialog box has two components:

- A dialog-template resource that specifies the dialog box's controls and their placement.

  The dialog resource stores a dialog template from which Windows creates the dialog window and displays it. The template specifies the dialog box's characteristics, including its size, location, style, and the types and positions of the dialog box's controls. You will usually use a dialog template stored as a resource, but you can also create your own template in memory.

- A dialog class, derived from **CDialog**, to provide a programmatic interface for managing the dialog box.

  A dialog box is a window and will be attached to a Windows window when visible. When the dialog window is created, the dialog-template resource is used as a template for creating child window controls for the dialog box.

Modal and Modeless Dialog Boxes

You can use class **CDialog** to manage two kinds of dialog boxes:

- Modal dialog boxes, which require the user to respond before continuing the program
- Modeless dialog boxes, which stay on the screen and are available for use at any time but permit other user activities

The resource editing and ClassWizard procedures for creating a dialog template are the same for modal and modeless dialog boxes.

Creating a dialog box for your program requires the following steps:

1. Use the dialog editor to design the dialog box and create its dialog-template resource.

2. Use ClassWizard to create a dialog class.

3. Connect the dialog resource's controls to message handlers in the dialog class.

4. Use ClassWizard to add data members associated with the dialog box's controls and to specify dialog data exchange and dialog data validations for the controls.

Property Sheets and Property Pages

An MFC dialog box can take on a "tab dialog" look by incorporating property sheets and property pages. Called a "property sheet" in MFC, this kind of dialog box, similar to many dialog boxes in Microsoft Word, Excel, and Visual C++, appears to contain a stack of tabbed sheets, much like a stack of file folders seen from front to back, or a group of cascaded windows. Controls on the front tab are visible; only the labeled tab is visible on the rear tabs. Property sheets are particularly useful for managing large numbers of properties or settings that fall fairly neatly into several groups. Typically, one property sheet can simplify a user interface by replacing several separate dialog boxes.

As of MFC version 4.0, property sheets and property pages are implemented using the common controls that come with Windows 95 and Windows NT version 3.51 and later.

Property sheets are implemented with classes **CPropertySheet** and **CPropertyPage** (described in the *Class Library Reference*). **CPropertySheet** defines the overall dialog box, which can contain multiple "pages" based on **CPropertyPage**.

For information on creating and working with property sheets, see the article Property Sheets.

Creating the Dialog Resource

To design the dialog box and create the dialog resource, you use the Visual C++ dialog editor. In the dialog editor, you can:

- Adjust the size and location your dialog box will have when it appears.

- Drag various kinds of controls from a controls palette and drop them where you want them in the dialog box.

- Position the controls with alignment buttons on the toolbar.

- Test your dialog box by simulating the appearance and behavior it will have in your program. In Test mode, you can manipulate the dialog box's controls by typing text in text boxes, clicking pushbuttons, and so on.

When you finish, your dialog-template resource is stored in your application's resource script file. You can edit it later if needed. For a full description of how to create and edit dialog resources, see Chapter 6, Using the Dialog Editor, in the *Visual*

C++ User's Guide. This technique is also used to create the dialog-template resources for **CFormView** and **CRecordView** classes.

When the dialog box's appearance suits you, use ClassWizard to create a dialog class and map its messages, as discussed in Creating a Dialog Class with ClassWizard.

Creating a Dialog Class with ClassWizard

Table 4.1 lists dialog-related tasks that ClassWizard helps you manage.

Table 4.1   Dialog-Related Tasks

Task	Apply to . . .
Create a new **CDialog**-derived class to manage your dialog box.	Each dialog box.
Map Windows messages to your dialog class.	Each message you want handled.
Declare class member variables to represent the controls in the dialog box.	Each control that yields a text or numeric value you want to access from your program.
Specify how data is to be exchanged between the controls and the member variables.	Each control you want to access from your program.
Specify validation rules for the member variables.	Each control that yields a text or numeric value, if desired.

Mapping dialog-class member variables to dialog-box controls and specifying data exchange and validation are explained in Dialog Data Exchange and Validation.

Creating Your Dialog Class

For each dialog box in your program, create a new dialog class to work with the dialog resource.

Chapter 14, Working with Classes, in the *Visual C++ User's Guide* explains how to create a new dialog class. When you create a dialog class with ClassWizard, ClassWizard writes the following items in the .H and .CPP files you specify:

In the .H file:

- A class declaration for the dialog class. The class is derived from **CDialog**.

In the .CPP file:

- A message map for the class.
- A standard constructor for the dialog box.
- An override of the **DoDataExchange** member function. Edit this function with ClassWizard. It is used for dialog data exchange and validation capabilities as described later in this chapter.

Life Cycle of a Dialog Box

During the life cycle of a dialog box, the user invokes the dialog box, typically inside a command handler that creates and initializes the dialog object; the user interacts with the dialog box; and the dialog box closes.

For modal dialog boxes, your handler gathers any data the user entered once the dialog box closes. Since the dialog object exists after its dialog window has closed, you can simply use the member variables of your dialog class to extract the data.

For modeless dialog boxes, you may often extract data from the dialog object while the dialog box is still visible. At some point, the dialog object is destroyed; when this happens depends on your code.

Creating and Displaying Dialog Boxes

Creating a dialog object is a two-phase operation. First, construct the dialog object. Then create the dialog window. Modal and modeless dialog boxes differ somewhat in the process used to create and display them. Table 4.2 lists how modal and modeless dialog boxes are normally constructed and displayed.

Table 4.2 Dialog Creation

Dialog type	How to create it
Modeless	Construct **CDialog**, then call **Create** member function.
Modal	Construct **CDialog**, then call **DoModal** member function.

Creating Modal Dialog Boxes

To create a modal dialog box, call either of the two public constructors declared in **CDialog** and then call the dialog object's **DoModal** member function to display the dialog box and manage interaction with it until the user chooses OK or Cancel. This management by **DoModal** is what makes the dialog box "modal." For modal dialog boxes, **DoModal** loads the dialog resource.

Creating Modeless Dialog Boxes

For a modeless dialog box, you must provide your own public constructor in your dialog class. To create a modeless dialog box, call your public constructor and then call the dialog object's **Create** member function to load the dialog resource. You can call **Create** either during or after the constructor call. If the dialog resource has the property **WS_VISIBLE**, the dialog box appears immediately. If not, you must call its **ShowWindow** member function.

Using a Dialog Template in Memory

Instead of using the methods given in Table 4.2, you can create either kind of dialog box indirectly from a dialog template in memory. For more information, see class **CDialog** in the *Class Library Reference*.

Setting the Dialog Box's Background Color

You can set the background color of your dialog boxes by calling the **CWinApp** member function **SetDialogBkColor** in your InitInstance override. The color you set is used for all dialog boxes and message boxes.

Initializing the Dialog Box

After the dialog box and all of its controls are created but just before the dialog box (of either type) appears on the screen, the dialog object's **OnInitDialog** member function is called. For a modal dialog box, this occurs during the **DoModal** call. For a modeless dialog box, **OnInitDialog** is called when **Create** is called. You typically override **OnInitDialog** to initialize the dialog box's controls, such as setting the initial text of an edit box. You must call the **OnInitDialog** member function of the base class, **CDialog**, from your OnInitDialog override.

Handling Windows Messages

Dialog boxes are windows, so they can handle Windows messages if you supply the appropriate handler functions.

Retrieving Data from the Dialog Object

The framework provides an easy way to initialize the values of controls in a dialog box and to retrieve values from the controls. The more laborious manual approach is to call functions such as the **SetDlgItemText** and **GetDlgItemText** member functions of class **CWnd**, which apply to control windows. With these functions, you access each control individually to set or get its value, calling functions such as **SetWindowText** and **GetWindowText**. The framework's approach automates both initialization and retrieval.

Dialog data exchange (DDX) lets you exchange data between the controls in the dialog box and member variables in the dialog object more easily. This exchange works both ways. To initialize the controls in the dialog box, you can set the values of data members in the dialog object, and the framework will transfer the values to the controls before the dialog box is displayed. Then you can at any time update the dialog data members with data entered by the user. At that point, you can use the data by referring to the data member variables.

You can also arrange for the values of dialog controls to be validated automatically with dialog data validation (DDV).

Use ClassWizard to add DDX and DDV capabilities to a dialog class. DDX and DDV are explained in more detail in Dialog Data Exchange and Validation.

For a modal dialog box, you can retrieve any data the user entered when **DoModal** returns **IDOK** but before the dialog object is destroyed. For a modeless dialog box, you can retrieve data from the dialog object at any time by calling **UpdateData** with the argument **TRUE** and then accessing dialog class member variables. This subject is discussed in more detail in Dialog Data Exchange and Validation.

Closing the Dialog Box

A modal dialog box closes when the user chooses one of its buttons, typically the OK button or the Cancel button. Choosing the OK or Cancel button causes Windows to send the dialog object a **BN_CLICKED** control-notification message with the button's ID, either **IDOK** or **IDCANCEL**. **CDialog** provides default handler functions for these messages: **OnOK** and **OnCancel**. The default handlers call the **EndDialog** member function to close the dialog window. You can also call **EndDialog** from your own code. For more information, see the **EndDialog** member function of class **CDialog** in the *Class Library Reference*.

To arrange for closing and deleting a modeless dialog box, override **PostNcDestroy** and invoke the **delete** operator on the **this** pointer. Destroying the Dialog Box explains what happens next.

Destroying the Dialog Box

Modal dialog boxes are normally created on the stack frame and destroyed when the function that created them ends. The dialog object's destructor is called when the object goes out of scope.

Modeless dialog boxes are normally created and "owned" by a parent view or frame window—the application's main frame window or a document frame window. The default **OnClose** handler calls **DestroyWindow**, which destroys the dialog-box window. If the dialog box stands alone, with no pointers to it or other special ownership semantics, you should override **PostNcDestroy** to destroy the C++ dialog object. You should also override **OnCancel** and call **DestroyWindow** from within it. If not, the "owner" of the dialog box should destroy the C++ object when it is no longer necessary.

Dialog Data Exchange and Validation

Dialog data exchange (DDX) is an easy way to initialize the controls in your dialog box and to gather data input by the user. Dialog data validation (DDV) is an easy way to validate data entry in a dialog box. To take advantage of DDX and DDV in your dialog boxes, use ClassWizard to create the data members and set their data types and specify validation rules. For additional information about DDX/DDV and for examples, see Chapter 14, Working with Classes, in the *Visual C++ User's Guide* and Chapter 8, Adding a Dialog Box, in *Tutorials*.

Data Exchange

If you use the DDX mechanism, you set the initial values of the dialog object's member variables, typically in your **OnInitDialog** handler or the dialog constructor. Immediately before the dialog is displayed, the framework's DDX mechanism transfers the values of the member variables to the controls in the dialog box, where they appear when the dialog box itself appears in response to **DoModal** or **Create**. The default implementation of **OnInitDialog** in **CDialog** calls the **UpdateData** member function of class **CWnd** to initialize the controls in the dialog box.

The same mechanism transfers values from the controls to the member variables when the user clicks the OK button (or whenever you call the **UpdateData** member function with the argument **TRUE**). The dialog data validation mechanism validates any data items for which you specified validation rules.

Figure 4.1 illustrates dialog data exchange.

Figure 4.1 Dialog Data Exchange

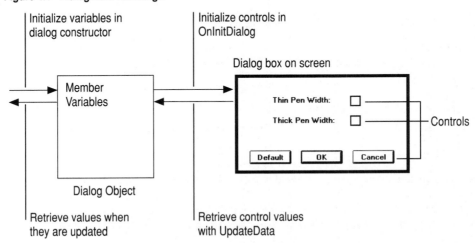

UpdateData works in both directions, as specified by the **BOOL** parameter passed to it. To carry out the exchange, **UpdateData** sets up a **CDataExchange** object and calls your dialog class's override of **CDialog**'s **DoDataExchange** member function. **DoDataExchange** takes an argument of type **CDataExchange**. The **CDataExchange** object passed to **UpdateData** represents the context of the exchange, defining such information as the direction of the exchange.

When you (or ClassWizard) override **DoDataExchange**, you specify a call to one DDX function per data member (control). Each DDX function knows how to exchange data in both directions based on the context supplied by the **CDataExchange** argument passed to your DoDataExchange by **UpdateData**.

MFC provides many DDX functions for different kinds of exchange. The following example shows a DoDataExchange override in which two DDX functions and one DDV function are called:

```
void CMyDialog::DoDataExchange(CDataExchange* pDX)
{
    CDialog::DoDataExchange(pDX);      // Call base class version
    //{{AFX_DATA_MAP(CMyDialog)
    DDX_Check(pDX, IDC_MY_CHECKBOX, m_bVar);
    DDX_Text(pDX, IDC_MY_TEXTBOX, m_strName);
    DDV_MaxChars(pDX, IDC_MY_TEXTBOX, m_strName, 20);
    //}}AFX_DATA_MAP
}
```

The DDX_ and DDV_ lines between the //{{AFX_DATA_MAP and //}}AFX_DATA_MAP delimiters are a "data map." The sample DDX and DDV functions shown are for a check-box control and an edit-box control, respectively.

If the user cancels a modal dialog box, the **OnCancel** member function terminates the dialog box and **DoModal** returns the value **IDCANCEL**. In that case, no data is exchanged between the dialog box and the dialog object.

Data Validation

You can specify validation in addition to data exchange by calling DDV functions, as shown in the example in Data Exchange. The **DDV_MaxChars** call in the example validates that the string entered in the text-box control is not longer than 20 characters. The DDV function typically alerts the user with a message box if the validation fails and puts the focus on the offending control so the user can reenter the data. A DDV function for a given control must be called immediately after the DDX function for the same control.

You can also define your own custom DDX and DDV routines. For details on this and other aspects of DDX and DDV, see Technical Note 26 under MFC Technical Notes in Books Online.

ClassWizard will write all of the DDX and DDV calls in the data map for you. Do not manually edit the lines in the data map between the delimiting comments.

Type-Safe Access to Controls in a Dialog Box

The controls in a dialog box can use the interfaces of MFC control classes such as **CListBox** and **CEdit**. You can create a control object and attach it to a dialog control. Then you can access the control through its class interface, calling member functions to operate on the control, as shown below. The methods described here are designed to give you type-safe access to a control. This is especially useful for controls such as edit boxes and list boxes.

There are two approaches to making a connection between a control in a dialog box and a C++ control member variable in a **CDialog**-derived class.

Without ClassWizard

The first approach uses an inline member function to cast the return type of class **CWnd**'s **GetDlgItem** member function to the appropriate C++ control type, as in this example:

```
// Declared inline in class CMyDialog
CButton* GetMyCheckbox()
{
    return (CButton*)GetDlgItem(ID_MYCHECKBOX);
}
```

You can then use this member function to access the control in a type-safe manner with code similar to the following:

```
GetMyCheckbox()->SetState(TRUE);
```

With ClassWizard

However, there is a much easier way to accomplish the same effect if you are familiar with the DDX features. You can use the Control property in ClassWizard.

If you simply want access to a control's value, DDX provides it. If you want to do more than access a control's value, use ClassWizard to add a member variable of the appropriate class to your dialog class. Attach this member variable to the Control property.

Member variables can have a Control property instead of a Value property. The Value property refers to the type of data returned from the control, such as **CString** or **int**. The Control property enables direct access to the control through a data member whose type is one of the control classes in MFC, such as **CButton** or **CEdit**.

Note For a given control, you can, if you wish, have multiple member variables with the Value property and at most one member variable with the Control property. You can have only one MFC object mapped to a control because multiple objects attached to a control, or any other window, would lead to an ambiguity in the message map.

You can use this object to call any member functions for the control object. Such calls affect the control in the dialog box. For example, for a check-box control represented by a variable m_checkboxDefault, of type **CButton**, you could call:

```
m_checkboxDefault.SetState(TRUE);
```

Here the member variable m_checkboxDefault serves the same purpose as the member function GetMyCheckbox shown earlier in the "Without ClassWizard" discussion. If the check box is not an auto check box, you would still need a handler in your dialog class for the **BN_CLICKED** control-notification message when the button is clicked.

For more information about controls, see Controls.

Mapping Windows Messages to Your Class

If you need your dialog box to handle Windows messages, override the appropriate handler functions. To do so, use ClassWizard to map the messages to the dialog class. This writes a message-map entry for each message and adds the message-handler member functions to the class. Use the Visual C++ source code editor to write code in the message handlers. Chapter 2, Working with Messages and Commands, describes message maps and message-handler functions in detail.

Commonly Overridden Member Functions

Table 4.3 lists the most likely member functions to override in your **CDialog**-derived class.

Table 4.3   Commonly Overridden Member Functions of Class CDialog

Member function	Message it responds to	Purpose of the override
OnInitDialog	**WM_INITDIALOG**	Initialize the dialog box's controls.
OnOK	**BN_CLICKED** for button **IDOK**	Respond when the user clicks the OK button.
OnCancel	**BN_CLICKED** for button **IDCANCEL**	Respond when the user clicks the Cancel button.

OnInitDialog, **OnOK**, and **OnCancel** are virtual functions. To override them, you declare an overriding function in your derived dialog class using ClassWizard; in these cases, ClassWizard will not add any message-map entries because they are not necessary.

OnInitDialog is called just before the dialog box is displayed. You must call the default **OnInitDialog** handler from your override—usually as the first action in the handler. By default, **OnInitDialog** returns **TRUE** to indicate that the focus should be set to the first control in the dialog box.

OnOK is typically overridden for modeless but not modal dialog boxes. If you override this handler for a modal dialog box, call the base class version from your override—to ensure that **EndDialog** is called—or call **EndDialog** yourself.

OnCancel is usually overridden for modeless dialog boxes.

For more information about these member functions, see class **CDialog** in the *Class Library Reference* and the discussion on Life Cycle of a Dialog Box.

Commonly Added Member Functions

If your dialog box contains pushbuttons other than OK or Cancel, you need to write message-handler member functions in your dialog class to respond to the control-notification messages they generate. For an example, see Chapter 8, Adding a Dialog Box, in *Tutorials*. You can also handle control-notification messages from other controls in your dialog box.

Common Dialog Classes

In addition to class **CDialog**, MFC supplies several classes derived from **CDialog** that encapsulate commonly used dialog boxes, as shown in Table 4.4. The dialog boxes encapsulated are called the "common dialog boxes" and are part of the Windows common dialog library (COMMDLG.DLL). The dialog-template resources and code for these classes are provided in the Windows common dialog boxes that are part of Windows versions 3.1 and later.

Table 4.4 Common Dialog Classes

Derived dialog class	Purpose
CColorDialog	Lets user select colors.
CFileDialog	Lets user select a filename to open or to save.
CFindReplaceDialog	Lets user initiate a find or replace operation in a text file.
CFontDialog	Lets user specify a font.
CPrintDialog	Lets user specify information for a print job.

For more information about the common dialog classes, see the individual class names in the *Class Library Reference*. MFC also supplies a number of standard dialog classes used for OLE. For information about these classes, see the base class, **COleDialog**, in the *Class Library Reference*.

Three other classes in MFC have dialog-like characteristics. For information about classes **CFormView** and **CRecordView**, see About CFormView and About CRecordView and CDaoRecordView. For information about class **CDialogBar**, see Control Bars.

Controls

MFC supplies a set of classes that correspond to the standard control windows provided by Windows. These include buttons of several kinds, static- and editable-text controls, scroll bars, list boxes, and combo boxes. Table 4.5 lists the classes and the corresponding standard controls. Additional Controls describes new kinds of controls.

Table 4.5 Standard Control Window Classes

Class	Windows control
CStatic	Static-text control
CButton	Button control: pushbutton, check box, radio button, or group-box control
CListBox	List-box control
CComboBox	Combo-box control
CEdit	Edit control
CScrollBar	Scroll-bar control

Each control class encapsulates a Windows control and provides a member-function user interface to the underlying control. Using a control object's member functions, you can get and set the value or state of the control and respond to various standard messages sent by the control to its parent window (usually a dialog box). For additional control classes, see Additional Controls.

You can create control objects in a window or dialog box. You can also use a control class as an interface to a control created in a dialog box from a dialog-template resource.

Additional Controls

In addition to the standard Windows controls, MFC provides several other control classes. These provide buttons labeled with bitmaps instead of text, control bars, and splitter-window controls. Splitter windows are discussed in Chapter 3, Working with Frame Windows, Documents, and Views.

Table 4.6 lists the the additional classes and their purposes.

Table 4.6   Additional Control Classes

Class	Purpose
CBitmapButton	Button labeled with a bitmap instead of text
CToolBar	Toolbar arranged along a border of a frame window and containing other controls
CStatusBar	Status bar arranged along a border of a frame window and containing panes, or indicators
CDialogBar	Control bar created from a dialog-template resource and arranged along a border of a frame window

Note   VBX controls are not supported in 32-bit versions of Visual C++.

Control bars, including toolbars, status bars, and dialog bars, are discussed in Control Bars.

Bitmap Buttons

Class **CBitmapButton** allows you to have button controls labeled with bitmaps instead of text. An object of this class stores four **CBitmap** objects that represent various states of the button: up (active), down (pushed), focused, and disabled. Bitmap buttons can be used in dialog boxes. For more information, see class **CBitmapButton** in the *Class Library Reference*. Figure 4.2 shows bitmap buttons in a dialog box.

Figure 4.2 Bitmap Buttons

Controls and Dialog Boxes

Normally the controls in a dialog box are created from the dialog template at the time the dialog box is created. Use ClassWizard to manage the controls in your dialog box. For details, see Dialog Data Exchange and Validation, Type-Safe Access to Controls in a Dialog Box, and Mapping Windows Messages to Your Class.

Making and Using Controls

You make most controls for dialog boxes in the Visual C++ dialog editor. But you can also create controls in any dialog box or window. The following topics explain how to add controls to a dialog box:

- Using the dialog editor.
- By hand.
- Deriving control classes from existing MFC control classes.

Using the Dialog Editor to Add Controls

When you create your dialog-template resource with the dialog editor, you drag controls from a controls palette and drop them into the dialog box. This adds the specifications for that control type to the dialog-template resource. When you construct a dialog object and call its **Create** or **DoModal** member function, the framework creates a Windows control and places it in the dialog window on screen.

Adding Controls By Hand

To create a control object yourself, you will usually embed the C++ control object in a C++ dialog or frame-window object. Like many other objects in the framework, controls require two-stage construction. You should call the control's **Create** member function as part of creating the parent dialog box or frame window. For dialog boxes, this is usually done in **OnInitDialog**, and for frame windows, in **OnCreate**.

The following example shows how you might declare a **CEdit** object in the class declaration of a derived dialog class and then call the **Create** member function in **OnInitDialog**. Because the **CEdit** object is declared as an embedded object, it is automatically constructed when the dialog object is constructed, but it must still be initialized with its own **Create** member function.

```
class CMyDialog : public CDialog
{
protected:
    CEdit m_edit;    // Embedded edit object
public:
    virtual BOOL OnInitDialog();
};
```

The following `OnInitDialog` function sets up a rectangle, then calls **Create** to create the Windows edit control and attach it to the uninitialized **CEdit** object.

```
BOOL CMyDialog::OnInitDialog()
{
    CDialog::OnInitDialog();
    CRect rect(85, 110, 180, 210);

    m_edit.Create(WS_CHILD | WS_VISIBLE | WS_TABSTOP |
            ES_AUTOHSCROLL | WS_BORDER, rect, this, ID_EXTRA_EDIT);
    m_edit.SetFocus();
    return FALSE;
}
```

After creating the edit object, you can also set the input focus to the control by calling the **SetFocus** member function. Finally, you return 0 from **OnInitDialog** to show that you set the focus. If you return a nonzero value, the dialog manager sets the focus to the first control item in the dialog item list. In most cases, you'll want to add controls to your dialog boxes with the dialog editor.

Deriving Controls from a Standard Control

As with any **CWnd**-derived class, you can modify a control's behavior by deriving a new class from an existing control class.

To create a derived control class, follow these steps:

1. Derive your class from an existing control class and optionally override the **Create** member function so that it provides the necessary arguments to the base-class **Create** function.

2. Use ClassWizard to provide message-handler member functions and message-map entries to modify the control's behavior in response to specific Windows messages.

3. Provide new member functions to extend the functionality of the control (optional).

Using a derived control in a dialog box requires extra work. The types and positions of controls in a dialog box are normally specified in a dialog-template resource. If you create a derived control class, you cannot specify it in a dialog template since the resource compiler knows nothing about your derived class. To place your derived control in a dialog box, follow these steps:

1. Embed an object of the derived control class in the declaration of your derived dialog class.

2. Override the **OnInitDialog** member function in your dialog class to call the **SubclassDlgItem** member function for the derived control.

SubclassDlgItem "dynamically subclasses" a control created from a dialog template. When a control is dynamically subclassed, you hook into Windows, process some messages within your own application, then pass the remaining messages on to Windows. For more information, see the **SubclassDlgItem** member function of class **CWnd** in the *Class Library Reference*. The following example shows how you might write an override of **OnInitDialog** to call **SubclassDlgItem**:

```
BOOL CMyDialog::OnInitDialog()
{
    CDialog::OnInitDialog();
    m_wndMyBtn.SubclassDlgItem(IDC_MYBTN, this);
    return TRUE;
}
```

Because the derived control is embedded in the dialog class, it will be constructed when the dialog box is constructed, and it will be destroyed when the dialog box is destroyed. Compare this code to the example in Adding Controls By Hand.

Control Bars

Control bars greatly enhance a program's usability by providing quick, one-step command actions. Control bars include toolbars, status bars, and dialog bars. The base class of all control bars is **CControlBar**.

- A toolbar is a control bar that displays a row of bitmapped buttons that activate commands. Pressing a toolbar button is similar to choosing a menu item. The buttons can act like pushbuttons, check boxes, or radio buttons. A toolbar is usually aligned to the top of a frame window, but an MFC toolbar can also be dragged and "docked" to any other side of its parent window, and it can be "floated"—placed in a floating mini-frame window. When it is floating, the user can resize the toolbar. A toolbar can also display "tool tips" as the user moves the mouse over the toolbar's buttons. A tool tip is a tiny popup window that presents a short description of the button's purpose.

- A status bar is a control bar with a row of text output panes, or "indicators." The output panes are commonly used as message lines and as status indicators. Examples include the command help-message lines that briefly explain the selected menu or toolbar command and the indicators that indicate the status of the SCROLL LOCK, NUM LOCK, and other keys. Status bars are usually aligned to the bottom of a frame window.

- A dialog bar is a control bar with the functionality of a modeless dialog box. Dialog bars are created from dialog templates and can contain any Windows control. Dialog bars support tabbing among controls and can be aligned to the top, bottom, left, or right side of a frame window.

The basic functionality of all three control-bar types is similar. The base class, **CControlBar**, provides the functionality for positioning the control bar in its parent frame window. Because a control bar is usually a child window of a parent frame window, it is a "sibling" to the client view or MDI client of the frame window. A control-bar object uses information about its parent window's client rectangle to position itself. Then it alters the parent's remaining client-window rectangle so that the client view or MDI client window fills the rest of the client window.

Note   If a button on the control bar doesn't have a **COMMAND** or **UPDATE_COMMAND_UI** handler, the button is automatically disabled by the framework.

As of MFC version 4.0, toolbars, status bars, and tool tips are implemented using Windows 95 functionality instead of the previous implementation specific to MFC.

Toolbars — An Overview

Toolbars display a collection of easy-to-use buttons that represent commands. AppWizard makes it easy to add a toolbar to your application. Moreover, the toolbar can:

- Remain stationary along one side of its parent window.
- Be dragged and "docked" by the user on any side or sides of the parent window you specify.
- Be "floated" in its own mini-frame window so the user can move it around to any convenient position.
- Be resized while floating.

Note   As of MFC version 4.0, toolbars and tool tips are implemented using Windows 95 functionality instead of the previous implementation specific to MFC. For more information, see the article Toolbars.

For backward compatibility, MFC retains the older toolbar implementation in class **COldToolBar**. The documentation for earlier versions of MFC describe **COldToolBar** under **CToolBar**.

MFC toolbars can also be made to display "tool tips"—tiny popup windows containing a short text description of a toolbar button's purpose. As the user moves the mouse over a toolbar button, the tool tip window pops up to offer a hint.

For more information about "dockable" toolbars, see the article Toolbars: Docking and Floating. For more information about tool tips, see the article Toolbars: Tool Tips. For additional information about how toolbars have been reimplemented using the **CToolBarCtrl** class, and how that affects you, see the article Toolbars.

The buttons in a toolbar are analogous to the items in a menu. Both kinds of user-interface objects generate commands, which your program handles by providing handler functions. Often toolbar buttons duplicate the functionality of menu commands, providing an alternative user interface to the same functionality. Such duplication is arranged by giving the button and the menu item the same ID.

Once constructed, a **CToolBar** object creates the toolbar image by loading a single bitmap that contains one image for each button. AppWizard creates a standard toolbar bitmap that you can customize with the Visual C++ toolbar editor.

You can make the buttons in a toolbar appear and behave as pushbuttons, check boxes, or radio buttons.

For more information, see class **CToolBar** in the *Class Library Reference*. Also see the articles Toolbars, Toolbars: Docking and Floating, Toolbars: Tool Tips, Status Bars, Control Bars, Dialog Bars.

Status Bars

A **CStatusBar** object is a control bar with a row of text output panes, or "indicators." The output panes commonly are used as message lines and as status indicators. Examples include the menu help-message lines that briefly explain the selected menu command and the indicators that show the status of the SCROLL LOCK, NUM LOCK, and other keys.

As of MFC version 4.0, status bars are implemented using class **CStatusBarCtrl**, which encapsulates a Windows 95 status bar control. For backward compatibility, MFC retains the older status bar implementation in class **COldStatusBar**. The documentation for earlier versions of MFC describe **COldStatusBar** under **CStatusBar**.

CStatusBar::GetStatusBarCtrl, a member function new to MFC 4.0, allows you to take advantage of the Windows common control's support for status bar customization and additional functionality. **CStatusBar** member functions give you most of the functionality of the Windows common controls; however, when you call **GetStatusBarCtrl**, you can give your status bars even more of the characteristics of a Windows 95 status bar. When you call **GetStatusBarCtrl**, it will return a reference to a **CStatusBarCtrl** object. You can use that reference to manipulate the status bar control.

Figure 4.3 shows a status bar that displays several indicators.

Figure 4.3 A Status Bar

Save the active document	CAP NUM SCRL

Like the toolbar, the status-bar object is embedded in its parent frame window and is constructed automatically when the frame window is constructed. The status bar, like all control bars, is destroyed automatically as well.

For an example of using a status bar, see the Scribble tutorial program in *Tutorials*. For more information, see class **CStatusBar** in the *Class Library Reference*. Also see the articles Toolbars, Dialog Bars, Control Bars.

Dialog Bars

Because it has the characteristics of a modeless dialog box, a **CDialogBar** object provides a more powerful toolbar. There are several key differences between a toolbar and a **CDialogBar** object. A **CDialogBar** object is created from a dialog-template resource, which you can create with the Visual C++ dialog editor and which can contain any kind of Windows control. The user can tab from control to control. And you can specify an alignment style to align the dialog bar with any part of the parent frame window or even to leave it in place if the parent is resized. Figure 4.4 shows a dialog bar with a variety of controls.

Figure 4.4   A Dialog Bar

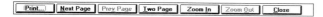

In other respects, working with a **CDialogBar** object is like working with a modeless dialog box. Use the dialog editor to design and create the dialog resource.

One of the virtues of dialog bars is that they can include controls other than buttons.

While it is normal to derive your own dialog classes from **CDialog**, you do not typically derive your own class for a dialog bar. Dialog bars are extensions to a main window and any dialog-bar control-notification messages, such as **BN_CLICKED** or **EN_CHANGE**, will be sent to the parent of the dialog bar—the main window.

For more information about dialog bars, see class **CDialogBar** in the *Class Library Reference*.

Working with OLE

The OLE classes of the Microsoft Foundation Class Library (MFC) are a set of C++ classes that provide an object-oriented interface to the OLE application programming interface (API). These OLE classes leverage the class library framework, making it easy to use OLE with the remainder of the class library, although you can use portions of the OLE classes without using all of the class library. With Visual C++ version 2.0, the OLE classes were ported to Win32.

The OLE classes add the following components to the class library:

- C++ classes that provide an object-oriented interface to the OLE API.
- Extensions to the document/view architecture to support OLE.
- Extensions to AppWizard for creating programs that use OLE.
- Extensions to ClassWizard for creating and editing automation classes.
- Sample programs that illustrate use of the classes and wizards.
- Online documentation that includes overview, tutorials, encyclopedia articles on programming topics, and class reference materials.

In this chapter, you'll find information on:

- Overview of OLE
- Features of the OLE classes
- Requirements for using the OLE classes
- Distributing your application
- Getting started with the OLE classes

Overview of OLE

OLE is a technology that allows applications to transfer and share information.

A History of OLE

Originally, OLE was synonymous with the term "compound document" and "OLE" was an acronym for the phrase "Object Linking and Embedding." OLE (version 1) was a mechanism for applications that did not have specific knowledge about one another to work together to create compound documents, embedding objects created by one application within a document created by another application.

Today, OLE is much more. So much more, in fact, that OLE is no longer an abbreviation; it is simply the name applied to this communication technology. In addition to supporting compound documents, OLE supports automation and OLE controls. There are also significant improvements to compound documents, now sometimes called "OLE documents."

OLE Features

OLE is an extensible technology. It currently supports OLE documents, OLE Automation, and OLE controls. Without adversely affecting any current features supported by OLE, new features can seamlessly be added.

OLE documents support more than simply linking and embedding; for example, in-place activation (visual editing), drag-and-drop editing, and short-cut menus (context-sensitive menus accessed by the right mouse button). For more information, see the articles Servers, Containers, and Drag and Drop (OLE).

OLE Automation supports one application exposing objects to be programmatically manipulated by another application. For example, Microsoft Excel can expose spreadsheet and chart objects that can be manipulated by a program written using Visual Basic or Visual C++. For more information, see the articles Automation Servers and Automation Clients.

OLE and COM

OLE is built upon the Component Object Model (COM), which is a communications protocol. COM describes manipulating interfaces, reporting status, and the use of the Registry to resolve universally unique identifiers.

COM is built around interfaces. A COM interface is a specification for interaction between COM objects. It is a list of semantically related functions (or methods) for the COM object, each with a known parameter profile and a return type. Once an interface is defined, it cannot change; any reference to the interface must conform to that definition. If you use MFC to create your OLE applications, the application framework will negotiate the OLE interfaces for you. You will only need to supply application-specific functionality for methods provided by these interfaces. For more information, see Interfaces in *OLE 2 Programmer's Reference, Volume 1*.

Many of the functions described in OLE interfaces return status code (SCODE) values. An SCODE is a 32-bit value containing a severity flag, a facility code, and an informational code. For more information, see Structure of OLE Error Codes in *OLE 2 Programmer's Reference, Volume 1*.

Each interface and each type of COM object is accessed by a universally unique identifier (UUID). A UUID is a 128-bit value that is used to uniquely identify an entity within COM/OLE. These are also known as globally unique identifiers (GUIDs). Two of the most important kinds of UUIDs are interface identifiers (IIDs) and class identifiers (CLSIDs).

OLE defines an interface identifier for each interface. The IID is used when manipulating interfaces. For more information, see **IUnknown::QueryInterface** in *OLE 2 Programmer's Reference, Volume 1*.

A class identifier is associated with each class (type) of OLE object (component). The CLSID is used in creating objects of a given class. For more information, see The CLSID Key and Subkeys in *OLE 2 Programmer's Reference, Volume 1*.

Features of the OLE Classes

The MFC OLE classes supply the following features:

- They are integrated with other parts of MFC.

- They encapsulate much of the complexity of the OLE API in a small set of C++ classes that provide a higher-level interface to OLE.

- They allow you to call OLE API functions directly wherever the OLE classes don't meet your needs.

The OLE classes support containers, servers, drag and drop, automation, message filters, compound files, and automatic registration. Explanations of these terms can be found in the article OLE Overview. If you need access to other portions of the OLE API, you can work with it directly. A number of tools and sample applications are also available to help you test your OLE applications. For more information, see the article Debugging OLE Applications: Tools.

Visual C++ combines key OLE components, including the required header files, libraries, DLLs, tools, and documentation. A number of sample programs are also included for testing your applications.

Requirements for Using the OLE Classes

This product assumes that you are familiar with C++. It is also helpful if you are familiar with writing applications for Windows and know how to use the Microsoft Foundation Class Library. Some understanding of OLE architecture will help, but is not required; for any OLE information you do need, Visual C++ provides OLE documentation in the WIN32 Software Development Kit (SDK). Additional information about OLE is available in Kraig Brockschmidt's book *Inside OLE 2* (Microsoft Press, 1994).

Distributing Your OLE Application

When you write an application with the OLE classes and distribute it to your customers, you may also need to distribute some DLL components of the OLE SDK —and MFC. Which DLLs are required depends on how you write your application with the class library.

Distributable Components

Your Visual C++ license authorizes you to freely distribute the release mode OLE and MFC DLLs that are needed to support an OLE application developed using Visual C++. Both the license and the file \REDIST\REDISTRB.WRI on the Visual C++ CD-ROM disc list the files that are redistributable. Should there be a discrepancy between these two lists, assume that the list in REDISTRB.WRI is correct.

Getting Started with the MFC OLE Classes

The best place to begin reading about the OLE classes is the article OLE Overview. OLE Overview introduces the classes and points to related articles about the concepts, components, and procedures of the OLE classes. For information about how the articles are structured and how to get the most from them, see the first article, Using the Encyclopedia.

For hands-on experience, see the three tutorials for the OLE classes:

- OLE Server Tutorial, which builds a new "Step 7" onto the Scribble tutorial.presented in Chapters 2 through 11 in *Tutorials*. The server tutorial begins in Chapter 12, Creating an OLE Server.

  Note The OLE server tutorial is a continuation of the general MFC tutorial, called Scribble. If you are familiar with MFC programming already, you can begin the server tutorial based on the Scribble Step 6 files. See the tutorial for details.

- OLE Container Tutorial, which builds CONTAINER, an OLE container application.

- OLE Automation Server Tutorial, which creates AUTOCLIK, an OLE automation server, that is an application that can be driven by other applications.

The Class Library Overview of the *Class Library Reference* lists MFC classes by category, including OLE classes, with brief descriptions designed to help you locate the class you need.

Note   The OLE documentation refers to embedded and linked items as "objects" and refers to types of items as "classes." To avoid confusion with C++ terminology, the Visual C++ *Class Library Reference* uses the term "item" to distinguish the OLE entity from the corresponding C++ object, and the term "type" to distinguish the OLE category from the C++ class.

CHAPTER 6

Developing OLE Controls

The OLE control classes in the Microsoft Foundation Class Library (MFC) are a set of C++ classes that you use, in combination with a specialized tool set, to develop OLE controls. The OLE control classes create a framework that supports OLE functionality, such as in-place activation, OLE automation, and drag and drop, to create small, powerful custom controls that are also very portable. OLE controls are used by specialized OLE control containers in current versions of Visual C++, Visual Basic, and other products. For more information on fundamental OLE control concepts, see the article OLE Controls.

OLE controls are reusable software components with features that make them an attractive solution for unique problems such as monitoring a specific aspect of an application or displaying data values as a pie chart. Important features include:

- Event firing

    OLE controls notify a control container of important actions, such as mouse clicks and data input, by firing events. OLE controls can implement stock events, such as Click, or custom events unique to a control.

- OLE Automation

    OLE controls support OLE Automation by implementing a set of methods and properties. These methods and properties control the appearance and characteristics of the control and are accessible to any OLE control container.

- Persistence

    OLE controls can save the state of properties and methods to a stream or file. This state can be used to initialize a new instance of the control or to restore the control to its previous state.

- Portability between OLE control containers

    OLE controls, because they incorporate OLE functionality, can usually be placed into any OLE control container and work correctly.

In this chapter, you'll find information on:

- Implementing an OLE control
- Installing the OLE control classes and tools
- Getting started with OLE controls

Implementing an OLE Control

An OLE control is implemented as an OLE document object that supports visual editing. OLE controls have capabilities beyond those of ordinary OLE objects, such as the ability to fire events.

Frequently, OLE objects require substantial effort to implement. MFC provides a large part of the required implementation for an OLE control—you need provide only the implementation code for the control's interfaces and events. You determine:

- How the control is displayed and painted

  You determine how the container draws your control when it is active (full interaction with its container) or inactive (limited interaction with its container). You also control the appearance when your control is printed or rendered into a metafile.

- Control properties

  A container can access a control's properties through the control's automation interface. Your application defines what happens when these properties are changed. You can also design a user interface, called a property page, to allow the user to access your control's properties at run time.

- Control events

  You can assign arguments to control events and define their names. You can also determine when an event should be fired.

- Control methods

  Methods are operations, such as Refresh and DoClick, that can be invoked by the control's user. You define the arguments and return type for methods supported by the control.

- Which property states of your control need to be persistent

  Persistent properties allow the control's state to be saved to permanent storage. OLE controls provide functions to serialize any type of control property.

When you write an OLE control, your project produces an OLE control file, which is a dynamic link library (DLL) with an .OCX extension. This file can contain the implementation of one or more controls and, when registered and loaded, defines the controls that can be accessed by the user. You can distribute OLE controls that you develop to other developers and users. For more information, see the article OLE Controls: Distributing OLE Controls.

Installing OLE Control Classes and Tools

When you install Visual C++, the MFC OLE control classes and retail and debug OLE control run-time DLLs are automatically installed if OLE Controls are selected in setup. To install the OLE control development tools, REGSVR32, and Test Container during Setup, select the Tools button to enable the Details button. Choose Details and check the OLE Development Tools checkbox. For more information on Test Container, see the article Test Container.

By default, the OLE control classes and tools are installed in the following subdirectories:

- **BIN**

  Contains the executables for Test Container and REGSVR32.

- **BIN\IDE**

  Contains the executable for ControlWizard.

- **HELP**

  Contains the Help files for the OLE control development tools.

- **MFC\INCLUDE**

  Contains the include files required to develop OLE controls.

- **MFC\SRC**

  Contains the source code for specific OLE control classes in the class library.

- **MFC\LIB**

  Contains the libraries required to develop OLE controls.

- **SAMPLES\MFC\CONTROLS**

  Contains a set of OLE control samples.

Getting Started with OLE Controls

The best place to begin reading about OLE controls is the article OLE Controls. This article introduces the OLE control classes and points to related articles about the concepts, components, and procedures for developing OLE controls. For information about how the articles are structured and how to get the most from them, see the first article, Using the Encyclopedia.

For hands-on experience, see the Circle Tutorial in *Tutorials*. This tutorial describes the typical development cycle of an OLE control. It includes steps on adding events, methods and properties, property pages, and using fonts and pictures. The Circle tutorial begins in Chapter 20.

Working with Databases

The Microsoft Foundation Class Library (MFC) supplies two distinct sets of database classes. These sets of classes are for:

- Programming with Data Access Objects (DAO).

- Programming with Open Database Connectivity (ODBC).

Database Class Components

Both sets of classes provide a high-level application programming interface (API) for access to databases from C++ and Microsoft Windows. Although you can use the database classes without some parts of the class library application framework, such as documents and views, in most cases you'll probably want to take advantage of the full class library.

The database classes add the following components to the class library:

- C++ database classes that supply a high-level API for accessing databases through either DAO or ODBC.

- Extensions to AppWizard and ClassWizard for creating application-specific database classes.

- Sample programs that illustrate use of the classes and the wizards.

- Online documentation that includes overviews, tutorials, encyclopedia articles on programming topics, and class reference materials.

To locate these components, see the encyclopedia articles Database Overview, DAO and MFC, and ODBC and MFC.

What This Database Chapter Contains

In this chapter, you'll find information on:

- When you might want to use a database with your application.

- What the MFC database classes are.

- Whether you should use the DAO classes or the ODBC classes.

- Information about installing either or both.

When Should You Use the Database Classes?

Many applications require data storage in a database, and many other applications could benefit from using a database. A database gives you a flexible data repository that can be accessed, in many cases, by multiple users and multiple applications. Databases can store large amounts of data and provide fast access to the data for queries and updates.

What Are the Database Classes?

Both sets of MFC database classes supply high-level abstractions that make database programming easier. You could choose to use DAO or ODBC directly, but writing to their APIs is considerably more complex and challenging than using the MFC classes. This is especially true if you are writing small, relatively simple applications. Ideally, you might wish for the ease of Microsoft Visual Basic or Microsoft Access Basic without losing the power and flexibility of C++.

Both sets of MFC classes supply a database programming model very similar to the model used in Microsoft Visual Basic and Microsoft Access Basic. You work with familiar objects that encapsulate and simplify a great deal of the underlying functionality, hiding much of the complexity (unless you need it, in which case you can still use the APIs directly). For example, to create a simple form-based application for viewing records or data entry, you use a database object to manage your connection to a database management system (DBMS). And you use one or more recordset objects to run queries and manage the resulting sets of records.

For more information, see the encyclopedia article Database Overview and its companion articles DAO and MFC and ODBC and MFC. The article DAO: Writing a Database Application might be useful as well, even if you are using the ODBC classes.

Which Classes: DAO or ODBC?

Whether you use the DAO classes or the ODBC classes depends on your needs. Generally speaking, the DAO classes provide more extensive support than the ODBC classes, including the ability to manipulate the structure of your databases directly from the MFC classes rather than calling the underlying implementation (DAO or ODBC).

However, if you're working entirely with ODBC data sources, especially in client/server situations, the ODBC classes might be more appropriate for your needs.

MFC still supports the ODBC classes, which are designed for a different set of needs, but you can also access ODBC data sources via the DAO classes in addition to taking advantage of the Microsoft Jet database engine. If you don't require the extra functionality of the DAO classes, you can continue to use the ODBC classes.

The two sets of classes present a sufficiently similar interface that porting from one to the other is relatively easy.

Note   The MFC DAO classes and DAO require additional space on your hard disk.

For additional guidelines, see the encyclopedia article Database Overview.

Installing MFC Database Support

When you run Setup for Visual C++, you can choose to install database components or not.

If you do choose database components, you can select any ODBC drivers you need. Note that you might need ODBC drivers regardless of whether you plan to use DAO or ODBC, if you are working with ODBC data sources. If you select any drivers, they are installed on your hard disk, along with the ODBC driver manager and the ODBC administrator program.

In addition, Setup installs necessary components from the DAO and ODBC software development kits (SDKs).

ODBC Drivers Installed

If you select a Typical Installation, Setup installs the following ODBC drivers:

- Microsoft FoxPro
- Microsoft Access
- dBASE
- Microsoft SQL Server

If you select a Custom Installation, you can also install the following additional ODBC drivers:

- Text files
- Paradox
- Microsoft Excel

See the article ODBC Driver List for a list of ODBC drivers included in this version of Visual C++ and for information about obtaining additional drivers.

DAO SDK Components Installed

The following components of the DAO SDK are installed by default:

- Microsoft Jet (3.x MDB)
- Microsoft Jet (1.x, 2.x)
- All of the database formats listed under Databases You Can Access with DAO in the article Database Overview

If you wish to install other DAO SDK components, such as the DAO SDK C++ classes, example files, or the Windows Help version of the DAO Help file, run SETUP.EXE from the \DAOSDK directory of the Visual C++ CD-ROM disc.

ODBC SDK Components Installed

Visual C++ version 4.0 includes many key ODBC components, including the required header files, libraries, DLLs, and tools. These include the ODBC Administrator control panel application, which you use to configure ODBC data sources, and the ODBC Driver Manager. Also included are ODBC drivers for many popular DBMSs, as listed in ODBC Drivers Installed.

Visual C++ also includes the full ODBC SDK, which gives you additional information and tools for writing and testing ODBC drivers.

Using the General-Purpose Classes

This chapter summarizes the use of the general-purpose classes in the Microsoft Foundation Class Library (MFC). These classes provide useful services, including:

- Services provided by deriving your classes from class **CObject**
- File input/output with class **CFile**
- Collection classes for storing aggregate data
- Strings
- Time and date
- Diagnostic services
- Exception handling

CObject Services

The **CObject** base class provides the following services to objects of its derived classes:

- Object diagnostics
- Run-time class information
- Object persistence

Some of these services are available only if you use certain macros in derived class declarations and implementations. To make use of the services listed above and explained in the following topics, you should seriously consider deriving most of your nontrivial classes from **CObject**. Many of the MFC classes are so derived, including almost all of the application architecture classes that make up the framework. (The various categories of classes that make up the framework are listed in the MFC hierarchy diagrams.)

Object Diagnostics

MFC provides many diagnostic features. Some object diagnostics include diagnostic dump context and supplied by the **CObject** class. For global diagnostic features, see Memory Diagnostics.

Diagnostic Dump Context

The **CDumpContext** class works in conjunction with the **Dump** member function of the **CObject** class to provide formatted diagnostic printing of internal object data. **CDumpContext** provides an insertion (<<) operator that accepts, among other types, **CObject** pointers; standard types, such as **BYTE** and **WORD**; and **CString** and **CTime** objects.

A predefined **CDumpContext** object, **afxDump**, is available in the Debug version of the Microsoft Foundation classes (**#define_DEBUG** is required in your source code). The **afxDump** object allows you to send **CDumpContext** information to the debugger output window or to a debug terminal. For more information about **afxDump**, see Macros and Globals in the *Class Library Reference*, and Technical Note 12 under MFC Technical Notes in Books Online.

Object Validity Checking

You override the base class **AssertValid** member function in your derived class to perform a specific test of your object's internal consistency. Call the **ASSERT_VALID** macro, passing it a pointer to any **CObject**, to call that object's AssertValid function. The implementation of an AssertValid function usually includes calls to the **ASSERT** macro. For more information about **AssertValid**, see the article Diagnostics.

Run-Time Class Information

MFC offers the developer some optional features that make it possible to do run-time type checking.

Note For related information on Run-Time Type Information support in the C++ language, see Run-Time Type Information in the *C++ Language Reference*. However, MFC does not use the C++ run-time type information (RTTI) mechanism.

If you derive a class from **CObject** and include one of three macros (**IMPLEMENT_DYNAMIC, IMPLEMENT_DYNCREATE,** or **IMPLEMENT_SERIAL**), you can use member functions to:

- Access the class name at run time.

- Safely cast a generic **CObject** pointer to a derived class pointer.

Run-time class information is particularly valuable in the Debug environment because it can be used to detect incorrect casts and to produce object dumps with class names included. For more information, see the article CObject Class: Accessing Run-Time Class Information.

Note To access run-time type information, you must use the **DECLARE_DYNAMIC**, **DECLARE_DYNCREATE**, or **DECLARE_SERIAL** macro in your class declaration, and you must use the corresponding **IMPLEMENT_DYNAMIC**, **IMPLEMENT_DYNCREATE**, or **IMPLEMENT_SERIAL** macro in your class implementation.

Run-time class information is, of course, available in the Release environment. During serialization, the run-time class information is used to store the object's type with the object data.

Run-time class testing is not meant to be a substitute for using virtual functions added in a common base class. Use the run-time type information only when virtual functions are not appropriate.

Object Persistence

Class **CObject**, in conjunction with class **CArchive**, supports "object persistence" through a process called serialization. Object persistence allows you to save a complex network of objects in a permanent binary form (usually disk storage) that persists after those objects are deleted from memory. Later you can load the objects from persistent storage and reconstruct them in memory. Loading and saving serializable data is mediated by an "archive" object of class **CArchive**.

To create your own serializable **CObject**-derived class, you must use the **DECLARE_SERIAL** macro in the class declaration, and you must use the corresponding **IMPLEMENT_SERIAL** macro in the class implementation. If you have added new data members in your derived class, you must override the base class **Serialize** member function to store object data to the archive object and load object data from it. Once you have a serializable class, you can serialize objects of that class to and from a file via a **CArchive** object.

A **CArchive** object provides a type-safe buffering mechanism for writing or reading serializable objects to or from a **CFile** object. Usually the **CFile** object represents a disk file; however, it can be also be a memory file (**CMemFile** object), perhaps representing the Clipboard. A given **CArchive** object either stores (writes, serializes) data or loads (reads, deserializes) data, but never both. Thus two successively created **CArchive** objects are required to serialize data to a file and then deserialize it back from the file. The life of a **CArchive** object is limited to one pass—either writing an object to a file or reading an object from a file.

When storing an object to a file, an archive attaches the **CRuntimeClass** name to the object. Then, when another archive loads the object from a file, the archive uses the **CRuntimeClass** name of the object to dynamically reconstruct the object in memory. A given object may be referenced more than once as it is written to the file by the storing archive. The loading archive, however, will reconstruct the object only once. The details about how an archive attaches **CRuntimeClass** information to objects and reconstructs objects, taking into account possible multiple references, are described in Technical Note 2 under MFC Technical Notes in Books Online.

As you serialize data to an archive, the archive accumulates the data until its buffer is full. When the buffer is full, the archive then writes its buffer to the **CFile** object pointed to by the **CArchive** object. Similarly, as you read data from an archive, the archive reads data from the file to its buffer, and then from the buffer to your deserialized object. This buffering reduces the number of times a hard disk is physically read, thus improving your application's performance.

There are two ways to create a **CArchive** object. The most common way, and the easiest, is to let the framework create one for your document on behalf of the Save, Save As, and Open commands on the File menu. The other way is to explicitly create the **CArchive** object yourself.

To let the framework create the **CArchive** object for your document, simply implement the document's Serialize function, which writes and reads to and from the archive. You also have to implement Serialize for any **CObject**-derived objects that the document's Serialize function in turn serializes directly or indirectly.

There are other occasions besides serializing a document via the framework when you may need a **CArchive** object. For example, you might want to serialize data to and from the Clipboard, represented by a **CMemFile** object. Or, you might want to develop a user interface for saving files that is different from the one offered by the framework. In this case, you can explicitly create a **CArchive** object. You do this the same way the framework does. For more detailed information, see the articles Files and Serialization (Object Persistence).

The File Classes

The **CFile** family of classes provides a C++ programming interface to files. The **CFile** class itself gives access to low-level binary files, and the **CStdioFile** class gives access to buffered "standard I/O" files. **CStdioFile** files are often processed in "text mode," which means that newline characters are converted to carriage return–linefeed pairs on output.

New **CFile** and its derived classes now make the filename available. See the **GetFileName** member function.

CMemFile supports "in-memory files." The files behave like disk files except that bytes are stored in RAM. An in-memory file is a useful means of transferring raw bytes or serialized objects between independent processes.

Because **CFile** is the base class for all file classes, it provides a polymorphic programming interface. If a **CStdioFile** file is opened, for example, its object pointer can be used by the virtual **Read** and **Write** member functions defined for the **CFile** class. The **CDumpContext** and **CArchive** classes, described previously, depend on the **CFile** class for input and output. For more information, see the article Files.

The Collection Classes

MFC contains a number of ready-to-use lists, arrays, and maps that are referred to as "collection classes." A collection is a very useful programming idiom for holding and processing groups of class objects or groups of standard types. A collection object appears as a single object. Class member functions can operate on all elements of the collection.

MFC supplies two kinds of collection classes:

- Collection templates
- Nontemplate collections

The collection template classes are based on C++ templates, but the original collection classes released with MFC version 1.0—not based on templates—are still available.

Most collections can be archived or sent to a dump context. The **Dump** and **Serialize** member functions for **CObject** pointer collections call the corresponding functions for each of their elements. Some collections cannot be archived—for example, pointer collections.

Note   The collection classes **CObArray**, **CObList**, **CMapStringToOb**, and **CMapWordToOb** accept **CObject** pointer elements and thus are useful for storing collections of objects of **CObject**-derived classes. If such a collection is archived or sent to a diagnostic dump context, then the element objects are automatically archived or dumped as well. For more about collection classes, including details about which classes can be serialized and dumped, see the article Collections: Choosing a Collection Class.

When you program with the application framework, the collection classes will be especially useful for implementing data structures in your document class. For an example, see the document implementation in the Scribble tutorial contained in *Tutorials*.

Lists

In addition to "list" class templates, MFC supplies predefined list classes for **CString** objects, **CObject** pointers, and void pointers. A list is an ordered grouping of elements. New elements can be added at the head or tail of the list, or before or after a specified element. The list can be traversed in forward or reverse sequence, and elements can be retrieved or removed during the traversal.

Arrays

In addition to "array" class templates, MFC supplies predefined array classes for bytes, words, doublewords, **CString** objects, **CObject** pointers, and void pointers. An array implemented this way is a dynamically sized grouping of elements that is directly accessible through a zero-based integer subscript. The subscript ([ ]) operator can be used to set or retrieve array elements. If an element above the current array bound is to be set, you can specify whether the array is to grow automatically. When growing is not required, array collection access is as fast as standard C array access.

Maps

A "map" is a dictionary that maps keys to values. In addition to map class templates, predefined map classes support **CString** objects, words, **CObject** pointers, and void pointers. Consider the **CMapWordToOb** class as an example. A **WORD** variable is used as a key to find the corresponding **CObject** pointer. Duplicate key values are not allowed. A key-pointer pair can be inserted only if the key is not already contained in the map. Key lookups are fast because they rely on a hashing technique.

The CString Class

The **CString** class supports dynamic character strings. **CString** objects can grow and shrink automatically, and they can be serialized. Member functions and overloaded operators add Basic-like string-processing capability. These features make **CString** objects easier to use than C-style fixed-length character arrays. Conversion functions allow **CString** objects to be used interchangeably with C-style strings. Thus a **CString** object can be passed to a function that expects a pointer to a constant string (**const char***) parameter.

As of MFC version 4.0, **CString** uses reference counting for efficient return-by-value and pass-by-value. For more information, see the article Strings.

CString is enabled for both multibyte character sets (MBCS, also known as double-byte character sets, DBCS) and Unicode. **CString** now also supplies functionality similar to **sprintf** with the **Format** member function and supports reducing string storage overhead with the **FreeExtra** member function.

Note Class **CString** is not derived from class **CObject**.

Like other Microsoft Foundation classes, the **CString** class allocates memory on the heap. You must be sure that **CString** destructors are called at appropriate times to free unneeded memory. There is no automatic "garbage collection" as there is in Basic. For more information about **CString**, see the *Class Library Reference* and the article Strings.

The CTime and CTimeSpan Classes

In addition to the **CTime** and **CTimeSpan** classes, which have been part of MFC from version 1.0, as of version 4.0 you can also use class **COleDateTime**. You will probably want to use the new class for most purposes.

The **CTime** class encapsulates the run-time **time_t** data type. Thus it represents absolute time values in the range 1970 to 2036, approximately. There are member functions that convert a time value to years, months, days, hours, minutes, and seconds. The class has overloaded insertion and extraction operators for archiving and for diagnostic dumping. For Win32 support, there are also **CTime** constructors based on the Win32 **SYSTEMTIME** and **FILETIME** structures. The **SYSTEMTIME**-based constructor is the most convenient to use with Win32.

The **CTimeSpan** class extends **time_t** by representing relative time values. When one **CTime** object is subtracted from another one, the result is a **CTimeSpan** object. A **CTimeSpan** object can be added to or subtracted from a **CTime** object. A **CTimeSpan** value is limited to the range of $\pm$ 68 years, approximately. For more information about **CTime** and **CTimeSpan**, see the *Class Library Reference* and the article Date and Time.

Note   Classes **CTime** and **CTimeSpan** are not derived from class **CObject**.

Diagnostic Services in MFC

The Microsoft Foundation Class Library provides diagnostic services that make it easier to debug your programs. These services include macros and global functions that allow you to trace your program's memory allocations, dump the contents of objects during run time, and print debugging messages during run time. Most of these services require the Debug version of the library and thus should not be used in released applications. For a detailed description of the functions and macros available, see the article Diagnostics and the overview of Macros and Globals in the *Class Library Reference*.

Diagnostics for Memory

Many applications use the C++ **new** operator to allocate memory on the heap. MFC provides a special Debug version of **new** that inserts extra control bytes in allocated memory blocks. These control bytes, together with the run-time class information that results from **CObject** derivation, allow you to analyze memory-allocation statistics and detect memory-block bounds violations. A memory dump can include the source filename and the line number of the allocated memory and, in the case of objects from **CObject**-derived classes, the name of the class and the output from its **Dump** function. For more information, see Memory Diagnostics in the article Diagnostics: Detecting Memory Leaks.

Important   As of MFC version 4.0, MFC uses the same debug heap as the C run-time library. For more information, see Chapter 4, Debug Version of the C Run-Time Library in the *Run-Time Library Reference*.

Tip   You can activate the debug version of **new** on a per-CPP file basis by #defining **DEBUG_NEW**.

Diagnostic Output

Many programmers want diagnostic output statements in their programs, particularly during the early stages of development. The **TRACE** statement acts like **printf** except that the **TRACE** code is not generated by the compiler with the Release version of the library. In the Windows environment, debugging output goes to the debugger if it is present.

Important For important information on using **TRACE**, see the Macros and Globals section of the *Class Library Reference* and Technical Note 7 under MFC Technical Notes in Books Online.

You can use the **afxDump** dump context object for stream-style dumping of standard types as well as MFC objects. If you use **afxDump**, be sure to bracket references with **#ifdef _DEBUG** and **#endif** statements. For more information on **afxDump**, see the article Diagnostics: Dumping Object Contents.

Assertions

In the Debug environment, the **ASSERT** macro evaluates a specified condition. If the condition is false, the macro displays a message in a message box that gives the source filename and the line number and then terminates the program. In the Release environment, the **ASSERT** statement has no effect.

VERIFY, a companion macro, evaluates the condition in both the Debug and Release environments. It prints and terminates only in the Debug environment.

Classes derived from **CObject**, directly or indirectly, can also override the **AssertValid** member function to test the internal validity of objects of the class. For an example, see Object Validity Checking.

Note As of version 4.0, MFC uses the C run-time library for assertions, which results in some changes to assertion message formatting. Assertion message boxes now include the application (.EXE) name, the filename, and the line number.

Handling Exceptions

MFC uses C++ exceptions as proposed by the ANSI C++ standard. The MFC exception macros used in previous versions of MFC are provided for backward compatibility with existing MFC applications. You can choose to use either C++ exceptions or the original MFC exception mechanism. These macros allow you to deal with abnormal conditions that are outside the program's control. Abnormal conditions include low memory, I/O errors, and attempted use of an unsupported feature. They do not include programming errors or normally expected conditions such as an end-of-file condition. In general, you can consider an uncaught exception to be a bug that remains in your program after shipping.

In most cases, you should use the C++ exception mechanism rather than MFC's original macro-based mechanism. If you are programming for Windows NT, you should use C++ exceptions instead of Windows NT structured exceptions (SEH).

Exception handling in MFC relies on "exception objects" and uses standard C++ exceptions. The process starts with the interruption of normal program execution in response to a **throw** expression. Execution resumes at the appropriate **catch** statement leading into code that presumably deals with the abnormal condition. Exception objects can include standard C++ data types as well as objects of classes derived from **CException**. **CException**-based exception objects differentiate the various kinds of exceptions and are used for communication.

Note   MFC now supports C++ exceptions and the **try**, **catch**, and **throw** keywords. For more information, see the article Exceptions.

This exception-handling scheme eliminates the need for extensive error testing after every library function call. If, for example, you enclose your entire program in an exception-handling block, then you don't have to test for low memory after each statement that contains the **new** operator.

If you don't provide **try** and **catch** exception-processing code in your classes, exceptions will be caught in the Microsoft Foundation code. This results in termination of the program through the global function **AfxTerminate**, which normally calls the run-time function **abort**. However, if you use the **AfxSetTerminate** function, the effect of **AfxTerminate** is changed. When programming for Windows, it is important to remember that exceptions cannot cross the boundary of a "callback." In other words, if an exception occurs within the scope of a message or command handler, it must be caught there, before the next message is processed. If you do not catch an exception, the **CWinApp** member function **ProcessWndProcException** is called as a last resort. This function displays an error message and then continues processing. You can customize the default handling of uncaught exceptions by overriding **CWinApp::ProcessWndProcException**.

For exception-processing examples and a more detailed explanation of error categories, see the article Exceptions. For a detailed description of the MFC-specific functions and macros available, see the Macros and Globals section in the *Class Library Reference*. For a general discussion of C++ exception handling, see Chapter 7, C++ Exception Handling, in *Programming Techniques*.

MFC Encyclopedia

Using the Encyclopedia

The programming articles show you how to accomplish specific tasks and explain important topics in more detail than is possible in the reference or the tutorial. The articles are available both online and in print. Online, they are linked with the reference and with each other, to make browsing easy and to let you find your own path through the topics. In print, the articles are cross-referenced in the index.

This article explains:

- How the articles are structured
- What the articles contain
- Where to begin

How the Articles Are Structured

The encyclopedia is hierarchical, with the following structure:

- At the top level, there are main articles arranged in alphabetical order.
- Below most of the main articles are clusters of related "child" articles. Child articles are arranged logically—following their main article—rather than alphabetically.

The title of each child article begins with the name of its parent main article so you can always find your way back. For example, the article ClassWizard: OLE Support is a child article of a main ClassWizard article.

Articles also have the following helpful navigation features:

- Each main article usually ends with a list of its child articles.

  Online, these are "jumps" for easy access to the articles.
- Most articles contain numerous cross-references to other articles and to related information in the reference.
- Books Online provides scrollbars and browse buttons so you can easily read an article or group of articles straight through.

What the Articles Contain

Article content is of two types:

- Architectural information
- Procedural information

Architectural articles explain how some part of the class library works. Each article covers a conceptual topic, such as "how documents and views are created," "how

OLE servers and containers interact," or "how database updates work." Conceptual articles give you a foundation as you work out your own solution using the many facilities of the Microsoft Foundation Class Library.

Procedural articles detail the steps for performing a task. Each article explains starting conditions, steps to follow, and the results you can expect at the end. Procedural articles mark out the "beaten path"—the common tasks that most programmers will need to perform. Most such tasks are of a beginning or intermediate level of difficulty.

Where to Begin

If you are primarily interested in:

This topic...	Begin with the article...
Database topics, including both Open Database Connectivity (ODBC) and Data Access Objects (DAO)	Database Overview (under "D")
Debugging and diagnostics	Debugging
MFC in general, 32-bit programming, or porting to 32 bit	MFC
OLE topics	OLE Overview
OLE controls	OLE Controls
Windows Sockets programming	Windows Sockets in MFC: Overview

For other MFC programming topics, look up the topic you are interested in. For example, if you are interested in how to use ClassWizard, begin with the article titled ClassWizard.

Activation

This article explains the role of "activation" in the visual editing of OLE items. After a user has embedded an OLE item in a container document, it may need to be used. To do this, the user double-clicks the item, which activates that item. The most frequent activity for activation is editing. Many current OLE items, when activated for editing, cause the menus and toolbars in the current frame window to change to reflect those belonging to the server application that created this item. This behavior, known as "in-place activation," allows the user to edit any embedded item in a compound document without leaving the container document's window.

It is also possible to edit embedded OLE items in a separate window. This will happen if either the container or server application does not support in-place activation. In this case, when the user double-clicks an embedded item, the server application is launched in a separate window and the embedded item appears as its own document. The user edits the item in this window. When editing is complete, the user closes the server application and returns to the container application.

As an alternative, the user can choose "open editing" with the *<object>* Open command on the Edit menu. This opens the object in a separate window.

Note Editing embedded items in a separate window is standard behavior in version 1 of OLE, and some OLE applications may support only this style of editing.

In-place activation promotes a "document-centric" approach to document creation. The user can treat a compound document as a single entity, working on it without switching between applications. However, in-place activation is used only for embedded items, not for linked items: they must be edited in a separate window. This is because a linked item is actually stored in a different place. The editing of a linked item takes place within the actual context of the data, that is where the data is stored. Editing a linked item in a separate window reminds the user that the data belongs to another document.

See Also Containers, Servers

Activation: Verbs

This article explains the role primary and secondary verbs play in OLE activation.

Usually, double-clicking an embedded item allows the user to edit it. However, certain items don't behave this way. For example, double-clicking an item created with the Sound Recorder application does not open the server in a separate window; instead, it plays the sound.

The reason for this behavior difference is that Sound Recorder items have a different "primary verb." The primary verb is the action performed when the user double-clicks an OLE item. For most types of OLE items, the primary verb is Edit, which launches the server that created the item. For some types of items, such as Sound Recorder items, the primary verb is Play.

Many types of OLE items support only one verb, and Edit is the most common one. However, some types of items support multiple verbs. For example, Sound Recorder items support Edit as a secondary verb.

Another verb used frequently is Open. The Open verb is identical to Edit, except the server application is launched in a separate window. This verb should be used when either the container application or the server application does not support in-place activation.

Any verbs other than the primary verb must be invoked through a submenu command when the item is selected. This submenu contains all the verbs supported by the item and is usually reached by the *typename* Object command on the Edit menu. For information on the *typename* Object command, see the article Menus and Resources: Container Additions.

The verbs a server application supports are listed in the Windows registration database. If your server application is written with the Microsoft Foundation Class Library, it will automatically register all verbs when the server is started. If not, you should register them during the server application's initialization phase. For more information, see the article Registration.

See Also   Activation, Containers, Servers

Administrator, ODBC

See the articles Data Source: Managing Connections (ODBC) and ODBC Administrator.

Application Framework

The Microsoft Foundation Class Library (MFC). For more information, see the article MFC.

AppWizard

AppWizard lets you configure the skeleton of a new C++ application that uses the Microsoft Foundation Class Library (MFC).

To run AppWizard, choose the New command from the File menu in Visual C++. In the New dialog box, select the file type "Project Workspace." In the New Project Workspace dialog box, choose MFC AppWizard (exe) in the Type box. (If you're building an MFC extension DLL, choose MFC AppWizard (dll) instead.) You can also use AppWizard to insert a new project within your project workspace. From the Insert menu, choose Project. Then select one of the AppWizard types from the Insert Project dialog box.

For general information about using AppWizard, see Chapter 1, Creating Applications Using AppWizard in the *Visual C++ User's Guide*.

Custom AppWizards

As of Visual C++ version 4.0, you can build your own custom versions of AppWizard. This lets you create wizards specialized to create the features you need. For details, see Creating Custom AppWizards in Chapter 25 of the *Visual C++ User's Guide*.

AppWizard Features

AppWizard lets you configure the skeleton application with the following options:

- Specify a Visual C++ project name and directory.

- Specify a project type. You can create a project for an executable application (.EXE) or for a dynamic link library (.DLL).

  AppWizard supports the new DLL model in MFC, and you can create a regular DLL or an MFC extension DLL. Your regular DLL can use MFC either statically or shared. See the article Dynamic-Link Libraries (DLLs).

- Specify an application type: single document interface (SDI), multiple document interface (MDI), or dialog-based. The dialog-based option lets you easily use a dialog box as your application's user interface.

- Specify a language (locale) for your resources. The default is U.S. English.

New Feature
- Specify database options, either ODBC-based or DAO-based. You can:

  - Specify minimal support by including the correct header files and link libraries, or you can derive your view class from **CRecordView** (ODBC) or **CDaoRecordView** (DAO) for a form-based application.

  - Provide a user interface for opening and saving disk files in addition to accessing a database from the same application.

  - Specify a data source to connect to and which tables you want to access.

- Specify OLE options: your application can be a container, a mini-server, a full server, or both a container and a server, and it can have OLE Automation support.

  Tip To get an OLE in-proc server, choose OLE Automation support for your DLL project (which must be a regular DLL; it can link statically or dynamically to MFC). Automating an MFC extension DLL mainly provides only an .ODL file.

New Feature
- Specify support for OLE compound files.

New Feature
- Specify support for OLE controls. See the article OLE Control Containers: Manually Enabling OLE Control Containment.

- Specify whether you want:

  - A toolbar or a status bar. By default, the toolbar is an MFC "dockable" toolbar, a new feature in MFC version 3.0.

  - An About dialog box (in dialog-based applications).

  - Support for printing and print preview.

  - Support for context-sensitive help. This support has been updated for Windows 95.

  - Support for 3D controls.

  - Helpful source-file comments to guide where you add your own code.

New Feature

- Specify whether you want support for Windows Open System Architecture (WOSA) components: MAPI or Windows Sockets. Windows Sockets and OLE Automation are available in DLLs as well as executable applications.

- Specify which styles and captions you want for the main frame and child window.

- Specify document template strings.

- Specify whether you want splitter window support.

- Specify the number of files listed in the most-recently-used (MRU) file list on the File menu.

- Specify whether you want to link with the MFC libraries statically or dynamically. Linking dynamically with AFXDLL (MFC in a DLL) reduces the size of your executable file and lets several applications share a single copy of MFC at run time. By default, AppWizard provides the dynamic linking support.

- Specify the names of your application's classes and what class you derive your view class from. New view classes are available, including **CTreeView**, **CListView**, **CRichEditView**, and **CDaoRecordView**.

  Tip To select **CRichEditView**, your application must be an OLE container. If you didn't select the Container option, or Both Container and Server, on the OLE options page in AppWizard, the wizard makes that change for you when you select **CRichEditView** as your base view class.

For a description of the most commonly used AppWizard features, see Chapter 1, Creating Applications Using AppWizard, in the *Visual C++ User's Guide*.

The following articles explain other aspects of using AppWizard, including database and OLE support:

- AppWizard: Files Created

- AppWizard: Database Support

- AppWizard: OLE Support

AppWizard: Files Created

This article describes the files that AppWizard creates for you, depending on which options you've chosen.

The article first describes the core files common to all AppWizard-created applications and then describes files that are added when you select toolbar and Help support. Topics include:

- File and class naming conventions
- Standard AppWizard files
- Precompiled header files
- Context-sensitive help files
- AppWizard files added by options

Tip You'll undoubtedly want to examine the source code files you created. To orient you, AppWizard also creates a text file, README.TXT, in your new application directory. This file explains the contents and uses of the other new files created by AppWizard for *your* application, reflecting *your* option choices.

File and Class Naming Conventions

In the rest of this article, filenames and class names that AppWizard creates based on the project name you supply are shown as:

PROJNAMExxx.eee

CProjnameXxx

where *xxx* is the word View, Doc, Set, and so on, and *eee* is the filename extension. AppWizard no longer truncates the project name, so you get whatever you entered as a project name in full. Support for long filenames in Windows 95 and Windows NT eliminates the need for truncated names.

Standard AppWizard Files

The following categories of standard files created by AppWizard are described in this article:

- Project files and makefiles
- Application source and header files
- Resource files

Other files created include:

- Precompiled header files
- Context-sensitive help files
- AppWizard files added by options

Project Files and Makefiles

PRJNAME.MAK   This is the project file for your MFC project. It is also an NMAKE-compatible file.

PRJNAME.CLW   This file contains information used by ClassWizard to edit existing classes or add new classes. ClassWizard also uses this file to store information needed to create and edit message maps and dialog data maps, and to create prototype member functions.

Application Source and Header Files

Depending on the type of application—single document, multiple document, or dialog-based—AppWizard creates some of the following application source and header files:

PRJNAME.H   This is the main include file for the application. It contains all global symbols and **#include** directives for other header files.

PRJNAME.CPP   This file is the main application source file. It creates one object of the class `CPrjnameApp` (which is derived from **CWinApp**) and overrides the **InitInstance** member function.

    `CPrjnameApp::InitInstance` does several things. It registers document templates, which serve as a connection between documents and views, creates a main frame window, and creates an empty document (or opens a document if one is specified as a command-line argument to the application).

IPFRAME.CPP, IPFRAME.H   These files are created if the Mini-Server or Full-Server option is selected in AppWizard's OLE Options page (step 3 of 6). The files derive and implement the in-place frame window class, named **CInPlaceFrame**, used when the server is in-place activated by an OLE container application.

MAINFRM.CPP, MAINFRM.H   These files derive the **CMainFrame** class from either **CFrameWnd** (for SDI applications) or **CMDIFrameWnd** (for MDI applications). The **CMainFrame** class handles the creation of toolbar buttons and the status bar, if the corresponding options are selected in AppWizard's Application Options page (step 4 of 6).

CHILDFRM.CPP, CHILDFRM.H   These files derive the **CChildFrame** class from **CMDIChildWnd**. The **CChildFrame** class is used for MDI document frame windows. These files are always created if you select the MDI option.

*PROJNAME*DLG.CPP, *PROJNAME*DLG.H   These files are created if you choose a dialog-based application. The files derive and implement the dialog class, named `CProjnameDlg`, and include skeleton member functions to initialize a dialog and perform dialog data exchange (DDX). Your About dialog class is also placed in these files instead of in *PROJNAME*.CPP.

*PROJNAME*DOC.CPP, *PROJNAME*DOC.H   These files derive and implement the document class, named `CProjnameDoc`, and include skeleton member functions to initialize a document, serialize (save and load) a document, and implement debugging diagnostics.

*PROJNAME*VIEW.CPP, *PROJNAME*VIEW.H   These files derive and implement the view class, named `CProjnameView`, that is used to display and print the document data. The `CProjnameView` class is derived from **CEditView**, **CFormView**, **CRecordView**, **CDaoRecordView**, **CTreeView**, **CListView**, **CRichEditView**, **CScrollView**, or **CView** and has skeleton member functions to draw the view and implement debugging diagnostics. If you have enabled support for printing, message-map entries are added for print, print setup, and print preview command messages. These entries call the corresponding member functions in the base view class.

Resource Files

AppWizard creates a number of resource-related files. If the project is for a DLL, the wizard also creates a .DEF file, which is available for your list of exports.

PROJNAME.RC, RESOURCE.H   This is the resource file for the project and its header file. The resource file contains the default menu definition and accelerator and string tables for a generic MFC application. It also specifies a default About box and an icon file (RES*PROJNAME*.ICO). The resource file includes the file AFXRES.RC for standard Microsoft Foundation class resources. If toolbar support has been specified as an option, it also specifies the toolbar bitmap file (RES\TOOLBAR.EPS).

RES*PROJNAME*.ICO   This is the icon file for the generic MFC application. This icon appears when the application is minimized and is also used in the About box.

RES\TOOLBAR.BMP   This bitmap file is used to create tiled images for the toolbar. The initial toolbar and status bar are constructed in the **CMainFrame** class.

Precompiled Header Files

STDAFX.CPP, STDAFX.H   These files are used to build a precompiled header file *PROJNAME*.PCH and a precompiled types file STDAFX.OBJ.

Context-Sensitive Help Files

MAKEHELP.BAT   This batch file can be used to build the Help file for your application.

PROJNAME.HPJ   This is the Help project file used by the help compiler to create your application's help file.

HLP\AFXCORE.RTF   This is the template help file for document-based (MDI/SDI) applications.

HLP\AFXPRINT.RTF   This file, created if printing support is selected (which it is by default), describes the printing commands and dialog boxes.

HLP*PROJNAME*.CNT   This file provides the structure for the Contents window in Windows Help.

Other .RTF files are created if you choose OLE or database options. See README.TXT in your project directory for a description of these files.

AppWizard Files Added by Options

Most of the options you can choose in AppWizard use the standard files to implement their features. This section describes additional nonstandard files created to support certain options.

Note   For information about the files created when you choose database options, see the article AppWizard: Database Source Files and Resources. For information about the files created when you choose OLE options, see the article describing the option. For example, for files related to an OLE server application, see the articles on OLE servers.

PROJNAME.ODL   This file is created if you have selected OLE Automation support. You can use this file as input to the Make Type Library utility, which creates a corresponding type library (.TLB) file.

PROJNAME.REG   This file is created in two cases. (1) You have selected any OLE server option or OLE Automation option. (2) You have selected a document file extension (one of the options available in the Advanced Options dialog box). The file demonstrates the kind of registration settings the framework will set for you.

RES\TOOLBAR.BMP   This file is created only if you have chosen any OLE server support and have also chosen the Dockable Toolbar option. The file contains tiled images for the toolbar when the server application is in-place activated inside a container application. The file is similar to the standard RES\TOOLBAR.BMP except that many nonserver commands are removed.

See Also   AppWizard: Database Source Files and Resources

AppWizard: Database Support

When you set options for your new skeleton application in AppWizard, you can specify database options in addition to the general AppWizard options. You can set database options from AppWizard's Database Options page (step 2 of 6) for a document-based application (MDI/SDI). This article explains the database options you can set for:

- Open Database Connectivity (ODBC)

  – or–

- Data Access Objects (DAO)

DAO support is new for MFC version 4.0. For information on both ODBC and DAO support, see the article Database Overview.

Figure 1 shows the AppWizard Database options page.

Figure 1. AppWizard's Database Options

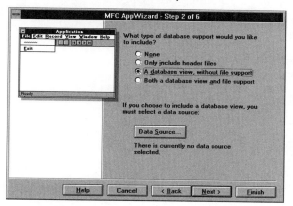

Important If you are using the MFC ODBC classes, or if you are using ODBC data sources through DAO, you must have the Microsoft Open Database Connectivity (ODBC) software installed on your machine with at least one configured data source and the appropriate ODBC driver for that data source in order to use the database classes. Visual C++ Setup installs the ODBC software, including the drivers you select.

If you want database support in your application, use the following procedure. The procedure assumes you have read the introductory material on AppWizard in Chapter 1, Creating Applications Using AppWizard, in the *Visual C++ User's Guide*.

▶ **To create an application with database support**

1 Create an MFC AppWizard project.

Tip You might want to consider creating a single document interface (SDI) application. A data-entry application, for example, probably doesn't require more than one view of the database.

2 On AppWizard's Database Options page (step 2 of 6), choose your database support option. The options are described in the article AppWizard: Database Options.

3 If you chose either A Database View, Without File Support or Both a Database View and File Support in step 2 of this procedure, a Data Source button is enabled. Choose Data Source.

– or –

If you chose Only Include Header Files, choose Next and continue with step 6 of this procedure. You will have to create your recordset classes later with ClassWizard.

4 In the Database Options dialog box, select either ODBC or DAO.

If you choose ODBC in step 4 of this procedure, complete your choices as described in Choosing ODBC Options. If you choose DAO in step 4 of this procedure, complete your choices as described in Choosing DAO Options.

5 After completing the actions described in step 4 of this procedure, choose Next and complete your nondatabase AppWizard selections. When you finish, choose the Finish button, then OK.

AppWizard creates files for your project.

Tip In the procedures Choosing ODBC Options and Choosing DAO Options, you can select multiple tables in the Select Database Tables dialog box.

Choosing ODBC Options

Follow the steps listed here to complete your ODBC database selections in AppWizard. Then return to step 5 in the procedure To Create An Application With Database Support.

▶ To complete your ODBC options

1 In the Database Options dialog box, after selecting ODBC, select an ODBC data source from the drop-down list box, which contains the names of data sources already registered on your machine through the ODBC Administrator tool described in the article ODBC Administrator.

2 Select other available options in the Database Options dialog box.

Some options may not be available. For explanations of these options, click the Help button in the dialog box.

3 Click OK.

4 In the Select Database Tables dialog box, select the names of one or more tables in the data source whose columns you want to bind to your recordset.

For some ODBC drivers, queries can be used as the source, but the wizards don't detect this.

5 Click OK.

6 Return to step 5 in the procedure To Create An Application With Database Support.

Choosing DAO Options

Follow these steps to complete your DAO database selections in AppWizard. Then return to step 5 in the procedure To Create An Application With Database Support.

▶ To complete your DAO options

1 In the Database Options dialog box, after selecting DAO, click the Browse button next to the edit control to display an Open dialog box.

2 In the Open dialog box, browse for a database file to open.

3 Select other available options in the Database Options dialog box.

Some options may not be available. For explanations of these options, click the Help button in the dialog box.

4 Click OK.

5 In the Select Database Tables dialog box, select the names of one or more tables in your chosen database whose columns you want to bind to your recordset.

6 Click OK.

7 Return to step 5 in the procedure To Create An Application With Database Support.

See Also AppWizard: Database Options, AppWizard: Database Source Files and Resources, Database Overview

AppWizard: Database Options

This article describes the MFC database options available in AppWizard. These options include:

- None
- Only include header files
- A database view, without file support
- Both a database view and file support

A record view—derived from class **CRecordView** (for ODBC) or class **CDaoRecordView** (for DAO)—is a form view, based on a dialog template resource, that uses dialog data exchange (DDX) to exchange data between the view's controls and a **CRecordset**-derived object (for ODBC) or a **CDaoRecordset**-derived object (for DAO). You can map the form's controls to data members of a recordset. For more information about record views, see the article Record Views. For more information about recordsets, see the article Recordset (ODBC) or the article DAO Recordset.

No Database Support

AppWizard defaults to this option ("None" in the AppWizard dialog box) and adds no database support to your application.

Only Include Header Files

Choose this option for the minimum database support. AppWizard adds an **#include** directive for the header file that defines the database classes. The file AFXDB.H (for ODBC) and the file AFXDAO.H (for DAO) are included in STDAFX.H.

Note that if you do choose a database view with AppWizard, you will only be given the single **#include** that corresponds to your choice of ODBC or DAO. Your application probably won't need access to both. When you don't choose a database view, however, AppWizard can't anticipate which you prefer, so it provides both.

With this support, you can use any of the database classes, related macros and global functions, and other items defined in the appropriate include file. AppWizard creates no database-related classes for you except for a view class and a recordset class if you choose one of the Database View options; you can create what you need later with ClassWizard.

AppWizard no longer explicitly adds libraries to the link line. The libraries are automatically included by special **#pragma** directives scattered throughout the MFC header files. You don't need to worry about library names.

A Database View, Without File Support

Choose this option when you want an application with the following characteristics:

- A view class derived from **CRecordView** or **CDaoRecordView** rather than **CView**.

  This view class makes your application form-based. AppWizard creates an empty dialog template resource to which you must later add dialog controls with the Visual C++ dialog editor.

- A class derived from **CRecordset** or **CDaoRecordset**.

  The record view class contains a pointer to a recordset object based on this class. Record view controls are mapped to recordset field data members via dialog data exchange (DDX).

- No disk-file user interface and serialization.

  A database application usually manages data record-by-record, interacting with the database, rather than managing whole data files.

- No document-related File-menu commands.

  This option also creates a menu resource whose File menu lacks document-related commands: New, Open, Save, and Save As. Without serialization, you probably don't need these commands.

Note Choosing this option makes the application single document interface (SDI). Choosing file support allows either SDI or MDI (multiple document interface).

This option creates a **CDocument**-derived class. In general, you'll use this class to store a **CRecordset** object, or a pointer to one. For more information on how to use this document class, see the article MFC: Using Database Classes Without Documents and Views. The article discusses various document/view configurations, including applications with no document or view.

For more information about the files and resources AppWizard creates under this option, see the article AppWizard: Database Source Files and Resources.

Both a Database View and File Support

Choose this option when you want an application with the following characteristics:

- A view class derived from **CRecordView** or **CDaoRecordView** rather than **CView**.

  This view class makes your application form-based. AppWizard creates an empty dialog template resource to which you must later add dialog controls with the Visual C++ dialog editor.

- A class derived from **CRecordset** or **CDaoRecordset**.

  The record view class contains a pointer to a recordset object based on this class. Record view controls are mapped to recordset field data members via dialog data exchange (DDX).

- A disk-file interface in addition to a record view on the database.

  This application opens a disk file in addition to a database. The disk file might store, for example, "style sheet" information, so the user can configure, save, and quickly restore alternative views of the database.

The document class that AppWizard creates under this option supports serialization, and the application includes support for document-related commands on the File menu: New, Open, Save, and Save As. For more information on how to use this document class, see the article MFC: Using Database Classes Without Documents and Views.

Note For the last two options, AppWizard binds all columns of the table(s) you select to the recordset. If you don't want all the columns, you can remove some of them later with ClassWizard. See the article ClassWizard: Binding Recordset Fields to Table Columns.

For more details about using AppWizard, see Chapter 1, Creating Applications Using AppWizard, in the *Visual C++ User's Guide*.

The following article explains the files and resources that AppWizard creates, depending on the database options you select:

- AppWizard: Database Source Files and Resources

See Also ClassWizard

AppWizard: Database Source Files and Resources

This article explains:

- The database-related classes and files that AppWizard creates.
- The resources that AppWizard creates.

This article applies to both the MFC ODBC classes and the MFC DAO classes.

For information about the files and resources that AppWizard creates besides those for database options, see the article AppWizard: Files Created.

Database Classes and Files

The classes and files that AppWizard creates depend on which option you choose. For details on the database options, see the article AppWizard: Database Options.

If you choose the None or Only include header files option, AppWizard creates no special classes or files for database support.

If you choose the option A database view, without file support or the option Both a database view and file support, AppWizard creates the following classes and files:

Classes Created by AppWizard

AppWizard creates application, frame-window, document, and view classes. The view class is derived from **CRecordView** (for ODBC) or **CDaoRecordView** (for DAO). It also creates a **CRecordset**-derived class (for ODBC) or a **CDaoRecordset**-derived class (for DAO) associated with the record view class.

Class Names Assigned by AppWizard

AppWizard names the record view class and its associated recordset class as follows:

Record View Class Name   AppWizard names the record view class based on the name of your Visual C++ project, denoted here by *Projname*. This name has the form "C*Projname*View". By default, the name ends in "View," but you can change the default name offered. If you change the default class name offered, the class is given the name you specify.

Recordset Class Name   The recordset class is named "C*Projname*Set" or the base name you gave for the project with "Set" appended. By default, the name ends in "Set", but you can change the default name offered. If you change the default class name offered, the class is given the name you specify.

Filenames Created by AppWizard

As with other files created by AppWizard, the filenames for the record view class are based on the name of your Visual C++ project. AppWizard writes the view class in files *PRJONAME*VIEW.H/.CPP. The wizard writes the recordset class in files *PROJNAME*SET.H/.CPP. The project name is no longer truncated.

Database Resources

If you choose the A database view, without file Support option or the Both a database view and file support option, AppWizard creates not only the classes described above under Database Classes and Files, but also the following resources:

- A dialog template resource whose resource ID is **IDD_*PROJNAME*_FORM**, where *PROJNAME* is based on your project name.

- A menu resource that includes commands for moving from record to record in the record view. AppWizard also creates command-handler functions and user-interface update handlers in the **CRecordView**-derived or **CDaoRecordView**-derived class for these commands.

If you choose Both a database view and file support, the menu resource includes document-related commands on the File menu: New, Open, Save, and Save As.

If you choose A database view, without file support, the document-related File menu commands are omitted. General commands, such as Exit, remain on the menu.

If the application is single document interface (SDI), the menu's resource ID is **IDR_MAINFRAME**. For a multiple document interface (MDI) application, AppWizard uses the document's menu resource, whose ID is **IDR_***DOCNAME***TYPE**, where *DOCNAME* is the document's type string.

Note   Choosing the option "A database view, without file support" makes the application SDI. Choosing file support allows either SDI or MDI.

- A set of toolbar buttons for the navigational commands (if you choose the Dockable Toolbar option as well as a Database Support option).

Important   The dialog template resource that AppWizard creates contains only the static text string "TODO: Place form controls on this dialog." You must use the Visual C++ dialog editor to delete the string and add controls that will map to your recordset data members. See the article ClassWizard: Creating a Database Form.

See Also   ClassWizard

AppWizard: OLE Support

AppWizard supports the following OLE features:

- OLE visual editing

AppWizard creates an entire project, including implementation and header files, that supports a variety of OLE visual editing application types. These types include different styles of container applications such as visual editing container/servers and simple container applications. You can also create visual editing mini-servers and full-servers. For more information on OLE options, see the article AppWizard: Creating an OLE Visual Editing Application.

- Ability to support Automation in your classes

Check the Automation support option if you want your application to have OLE Automation support. This means that your document class is exposed as a programmable object that can be used by any Automation client. You can also expose other classes you create as OLE Automation programmable objects. For more information on Automation, see the articles ClassWizard: OLE Automation Support, Automation Clients, and Automation Servers.

For general information about using AppWizard, see Chapter 1, Creating Applications Using AppWizard, in the *Visual C++ User's Guide*.

See Also   OLE Overview

In the *Class Library Reference*: **COleServerDoc**, **COleDocument**, **COleServerItem**, **COleClientItem**, **COleIPFrameWnd**

AppWizard: Creating an OLE Visual Editing Application

This article explains:

- The purpose of the OLE Options page.
- The creation of an OLE visual editing application.
- Classes and resources created by AppWizard.
- Filenames suggested by AppWizard.

The OLE Options Page

AppWizard's OLE Options page (step 3 of 6) allows you to access the many features of OLE that are implemented by the MFC OLE classes. These features include visual editing, OLE Automation, OLE compound files, and OLE controls. You access these features by choosing the visual editing options that your application will support, creating an application of one of the following OLE visual editing types:

- Container
- Mini-Server
- Full-Server
- Both Container and Server

Creating an OLE Visual Editing Application

▶ **To create an OLE visual editing application**

1 Create a new MFC AppWizard project and specify the project name, the project path and drive, and the name of the subdirectory for project files.

– or–

Add a subproject to your existing project. To add a subproject, choose Project from the Insert menu. Specify the name of the subproject. It will be created in a subdirectory named for your subproject.

2 Use the AppWizard OLE Options page (step 3 of 6).

3 Choose the form of OLE visual editing you want in your application:

- None: Select if you do not want visual editing support. This is the default setting.

- Container: Select if you want your application to visually contain OLE objects. For more information on containers, see the article Containers.

- Mini-Server: Select if you want your application to be visually embedded inside an OLE container. Note that mini-servers cannot run as stand-alone applications, and only support embedded items. For more information on servers, see the article Servers.

- Full-Server: Select if you want your application to be visually embedded inside an OLE container. Full-servers are able to run as stand-alone applications, and support both linked and embedded items. For more information on servers, see the article "Servers."

- Both container and server: Select if you want your application to be both a visual editing container and a server.

4 Repeatedly choose Next to move to the next AppWizard Options page and set other options for your application.

5 When you have finished setting options, choose Finish. This displays your choices.

6 Click OK to confirm your choices.

AppWizard creates files for your classes in the directory you specified and opens the project. For more information, see Classes and Resources Created and Filenames Suggested below.

Classes and Resources Created

AppWizard creates application, document, view, and frame-window classes. The exact classes created will differ depending on which visual editing option you chose from the OLE Options page.

All document-based (non-dialog based) applications created with AppWizard, regardless of the type of OLE support, have an application class derived from **CWinApp**, an About dialog class created from **CDialog**, a view class derived from **CView** (or from one of its derived classes), and one or two frame-window classes. If your application uses a multiple document interface, your frame-window classes are derived from **CMDIFrameWnd** and **CMDIChildWnd**. If your application uses a single document interface, your frame-window class is derived from **CFrameWnd**.

The class from which your application's document class is derived will vary depending on the visual editing options you selected. For non-visual editing applications, the class is derived from **CDocument**. For mini-, full-, and container-servers, the class is derived from **COleServerDoc**. For containers, the class is derived from **COleDocument**.

In addition to the above-mentioned classes, servers will have two additional classes: an in-place frame-window class derived from **COleFrameWnd** and a server item class derived from **COleServerItem**.

Containers will have a container class derived from **COleClientItem**.

Filenames Suggested

As with other files created by AppWizard, the suggested filenames for the document, view, frame window, server item, and container classes are based on the name of your Visual C++ project. For example, AppWizard writes the view class in files *PROJNAME*VIEW.H/.CPP and the document class is found in files *PROJNAME*DOC.H/.CPP. AppWizard no longer truncates long filenames. You can change the suggested filenames if you like. For a complete description of the project created by AppWizard, see the file README.TXT created by AppWizard with the rest of your project, found in your project directory, and see the article AppWizard: Files Created.

Asynchronous Access

See classes **CDatabase** and **CRecordset** in the *Class Library Reference*.

Automation

OLE Automation makes it possible for one application to manipulate objects implemented in another application, or to "expose" objects so they can be manipulated.

An "automation client" is an application that can manipulate exposed objects belonging to another application. This is also called an "automation controller."

An "automation server" is an application that exposes programmable objects to other applications. This is sometimes also called an "automation component."

The server application exposes OLE automation objects. These automation objects have properties and methods as their external interface. Properties are named attributes of the automation object. Properties are like the data members of a C++ class. Methods are functions that work on an automation object. Methods are like the public member functions of a C++ class.

Note Properties can have member functions that access them. A Get/Set function pair typically access a property of the object.

Passing Parameters in OLE Automation

One of the difficulties in creating automation methods is providing a uniform "safe" mechanism to pass data between between automation servers and clients. OLE automation uses the **VARIANT** type to pass data. The **VARIANT** type is a tagged union. It has a data member for the value, this is an anonymous C++ union, and a data member indicating the type of information stored in the union. The **VARIANT** type supports a number of standard data types: 2- and 4-byte integers, 4- and 8-byte floating point numbers, strings, and Boolean values. In addition, it supports the **HRESULT** (OLE error codes), **CURRENCY** (a fixed-point numeric type), and

DATE (absolute date and time) types, as well as pointers to **IUnknown** and **IDispatch** interfaces.

The **VARIANT** type is encapsulated in the **COleVariant** class. The supporting **CURRENCY** and **DATE** classes are encapsulated in the **COleCurrency** and **COleDateTime** classes.

See Also Automation Clients, Automation Servers

Automation Clients

OLE Automation makes it possible for your application to manipulate objects implemented in another application, or to "expose" objects so they can be manipulated. An "automation client" is an application that can manipulate exposed objects belonging to another application. The application that exposes the objects is called the "OLE Automation server." The client manipulates the server application's objects by accessing those objects' properties and functions.

There are two types of OLE Automation clients:

- Clients that dynamically (at run time) acquire information about the properties and operations of the server.

- Clients that possess static information (provided at compile time) that specifies the properties and operations of the server.

Clients of the first kind acquire information about the server's methods and properties by means of queries to the OLE system's **IDispatch** mechanism. Although it is adequate to use for dynamic clients, **IDispatch** is difficult to use for static clients, where the objects being driven must be known at compile time. For static bound clients, the Microsoft Foundation classes provide the **COleDispatchDriver** class along with ClassWizard support.

Static bound clients use a "proxy class" that is statically linked with the client application. This class provides a type-safe C++ encapsulation of the server application's properties and operations.

The class **COleDispatchDriver** provides the principal support for the client side of OLE Automation. Using ClassWizard, you create a class derived from **COleDispatchDriver**.

You then specify the type-library file describing the properties and functions of the server application's object. ClassWizard reads this file and creates the **COleDispatchDriver**-derived class, with member functions that your application can call to access the server application's objects in C++ in a type-safe manner. Additional functionality inherited from **COleDispatchDriver** simplifies the process of calling the proper OLE Automation server.

See Also   Automation Clients: Using Type Libraries, AppWizard: OLE Support, ClassWizard: OLE Automation Support, ClassWizard: Adding Automation Properties and Methods

Automation Clients: Using Type Libraries

Automation clients must have information about server objects' properties and methods if the clients are to manipulate the servers' objects. Properties have data types; methods often return values and accept parameters. The client requires information about the data types of all of these in order to statically bind to the server object type.

This type information can be made known in several ways. The recommended way is to create a "type library."

For information on Microsoft Object Description Language (ODL) and **MkTypLib**, see Chapters 2 and 9 of *OLE Programmer's Reference, Volume 2*.

ClassWizard can read a type-library file and create a "dispatch class" derived from **COleDispatchDriver**. An object of that class has properties and operations duplicating those of the server object. Your application calls this object's properties and operations, and functionality inherited from **COleDispatchDriver** routes these calls to the OLE system, which in turn routes them to the server object.

ClassWizard automatically maintains this type-library file for you if you chose to include OLE Automation when the project was created. As part of each build, the .TLB file will be built with **MkTypLib**.

▶ **To create a dispatch class from a type-library (.TLB) file**

1 In ClassWizard, click the Add Class button. The Add Class button appears on each page of ClassWizard.

   The Add Class menu appears.

2 From the Add Class menu, choose From An OLE TypeLib.

   An Open dialog box appears.

3 Use the Open dialog box to select the .TLB file.

   Tip   Some type library information is stored in files with .DLL, .OCX, or .OLB file extensions.

4 Click the OK button.

   The Confirm Classes dialog box appears. The list box lists the external names of the classes described in the type-library file. Other controls in the Confirm Classes dialog box show the proposed names for the dispatch classes and for the header and implementation files for those classes. As you select a class in the list box, the Class Name box shows the name for the corresponding class.

You can use the Browse buttons to select other files, if you prefer to have the header and implementation information written in existing files or in a directory other than the project directory.

5 In the Confirm Classes dialog box, edit the names of the new dispatch classes and their files.

6 Choose OK to close the Confirm Classes dialog box.

The Type Library Tool writes header and implementation code for your dispatch class, using the class names and filenames you have supplied, and adds the .CPP file to your project.

See Also   ClassWizard: Adding Automation Properties and Methods

Automation Servers

OLE Automation makes it possible for your application to manipulate objects implemented in another application, or to "expose" objects so they can be manipulated. An automation server is an application that exposes programmable objects to other applications, which are called "automation clients." Exposing programmable objects enables clients to "automate" certain procedures by directly accessing the objects and functionality the server makes available.

Exposing objects in this way is beneficial when applications provide functionality that is useful for other applications. For example, a word processor might expose its spell-checking functionality so that other programs can use it. Exposure of objects thus enables vendors to improve their applications' functionality by using the "ready-made" functionality of other applications.

By exposing application functionality through a common, well-defined interface, OLE Automation makes it possible to build applications in a single general programming language like Microsoft Visual Basic instead of in diverse application-specific macro languages.

Support for Automation Servers

ClassWizard, AppWizard, and the framework all provide extensive support for automation servers. They handle much of the overhead involved in making an automation server, so you can focus your efforts on the functionality of your application.

The framework's principal mechanism for supporting OLE Automation is the dispatch map, a set of macros that expands into the declarations and calls needed to expose methods and properties for OLE. A typical dispatch map looks like this:

```
BEGIN_DISPATCH_MAP(CMyServerDoc, COleServerDoc)
    //{{AFX_DISPATCH_MAP(CMyServerDoc)
    DISP_PROPERTY(CMyServerDoc, "Msg", m_strMsg, VT_BSTR)
    DISP_FUNCTION(CMyServerDoc, "SetDirty", SetDirty, VT_EMPTY, VTS_I4)
    //}}AFX_DISPATCH_MAP
END_DISPATCH_MAP()
```

ClassWizard assists in maintaining dispatch maps. When you add a new method or property to a class, ClassWizard adds a corresponding DISP_FUNCTION or DISP_PROPERTY macro with parameters indicating the class name, external and internal names of the method or property, and data types.

ClassWizard also simplifies the declaration of OLE Automation classes and the management of their properties and operations. When you use ClassWizard to add a class to your project, you specify its base class. If the base class allows automation, ClassWizard displays controls you use to specify whether the new class should support OLE Automation, whether it is "OLE Createable" (that is, whether objects of the class can be created on a request from an OLE client), and the external name for the OLE client to use.

ClassWizard then creates a class declaration, including the appropriate macros for the OLE features you have specified. ClassWizard also adds the skeleton code for implementation of your class's member functions.

AppWizard simplifies the steps involved in getting your automation server application off the ground. If you select Automation support in AppWizard's OLE Options page, AppWizard adds to your application's **InitInstance** function the calls required to register your automation objects and run your application as an OLE Automation server.

See Also AppWizard: OLE Support, Automation Clients, ClassWizard: OLE Automation Support

In *Tutorials*: Chapter 16, Creating an OLE Automation Server

In the *Class Library Reference*: **CCmdTarget**, **COleDispatchDriver**

Automation Servers: Object-Lifetime Issues

When an automation client creates or activates an OLE item, the server passes the client a pointer to that object. The client establishes a reference to the object through a call to the OLE function **IUnknown::AddRef**. This reference is in effect until the client calls **IUnknown::Release**. (Client applications written with the Microsoft Foundation Class Library's OLE classes need not make these calls; the framework does so.) The OLE system and the server itself may establish references to the object. A server should not destroy an object as long as external references to the object remain in effect.

The framework maintains an internal count of the number of references to any server object derived from **CCmdTarget**. This count is updated when an automation client or other entity adds or releases a reference to the object.

When the reference count becomes 0, the framework calls the virtual function **CCmdTarget::OnFinalRelease**. The default implementation of this function calls the **delete** operator to delete this object.

The Microsoft Foundation Class Library provides additional facilities for controlling application behavior when external clients have references to the application's objects. Besides maintaining a count of references to each object, servers also maintain a global count of active objects. The global functions **AfxOleLockApp** and **AfxOleUnlockApp** update the application's count of active objects. If this count is nonzero, the application does not terminate when the user chooses Close from the system menu or Exit from the File menu. Instead, the application's main window is hidden (but not destroyed) until all pending client requests have been completed. Typically, **AfxOleLockApp** and **AfxOleUnlockApp** are called in the constructors and destructors, respectively, of classes that support OLE Automation.

Sometimes circumstances force the server to terminate while a client still has a reference to an object. For example, a resource on which the server depends may become unavailable, causing the server to encounter an error. Or the user may close a server document that contains objects to which other applications have references.

See Also   In the *Class Library Reference*: **AfxOleLockApp**, **AfxOleUnlockApp**, **AfxOleCanExitApp**

In the *OLE 2 Programmer's Reference, Volume 1*: **IUnknown::AddRef**, **IUnknown::Release**

Binary Large Object

See the article Recordset: Working with Large Data Items (ODBC).

BLOB

See the article Recordset: Working with Large Data Items (ODBC).

Catalog Information

Information about the tables in a data source can include the names of tables and the columns in them, table privileges, names of primary and foreign keys, information about predefined queries or stored procedures, information about indexes on tables, and statistics about tables.

See the article Data Source: Determining the Schema of the Data Source (ODBC).

See also information about the ODBC "catalog functions" in the ODBC SDK *Programmer's Reference* and the MFC Database sample program CATALOG.

Note In the MFC DAO classes, you can get catalog information as follows: Use **CDaoDatabase::GetTableDefCount** and **CDaoDatabase::GetTableDefInfo** to enumerate the tables in the database and obtain information for each table in a **CDaoTableDefInfo** structure. For more information, see the article DAO: Obtaining Information About DAO Objects.

ClassWizard

ClassWizard helps you create additional classes beyond those you create with AppWizard. ClassWizard also lets you browse and edit your classes.

To run ClassWizard, choose the ClassWizard command from the View menu in Visual C++.

Introducing WizardBar

In Visual C++ version 4.0, considerable ClassWizard functionality is available in the new WizardBar that appears at the top of your source-code windows. For more information about WizardBar, see Using WizardBar in Chapter 14 of the *Visual C++ User's Guide*.

ClassWizard Features

ClassWizard supports the following features:

New and Updated Features

- Support for creating and managing new classes derived from most of the MFC classes.

  For example, ClassWizard makes it easy to create classes for your owner-draw list boxes and other controls.

  Other categories of new base classes include new view classes and classes for DAO database support. For a full list of classes you can derive from with ClassWizard, see Classes Offered by ClassWizard in Chapter 14 of the *Visual C++ User's Guide*.

- The Add Class feature is easier to use. Class creation options include creating the new class from scratch, from a file (formerly called importing a class), or from an OLE type library (formerly on the OLE Automation tab). You can also include your class in Component Gallery.

- Support for working with classes in multiple projects and in multiple directories.

- Support for using OLE controls (control containment). You can use ClassWizard to:

  - Map a member variable of your dialog class to an OLE control in the dialog box. The procedure is the same as for mapping Windows controls.

  - Handle events fired by an OLE control using member functions of the dialog class for the dialog box that contains the control. The procedure is the same as for mapping Windows messages and commands.

- Support for database access, using either Open Database Connectivity (ODBC) or Data Access Objects (DAO). You can:

  - Create classes derived from **CRecordset** (for ODBC) or **CDaoRecordset** (for DAO).

  - Specify a data source, tables, and columns for a recordset.

  - Create database form classes derived from **CRecordView** (for ODBC) or **CDaoRecordView** (for DAO).

  - Map controls of a record view database form to the fields of a recordset object.

- Support for "reflected messages." For more information, see Message Reflection in the article MFC: Changes from MFC Versions 3.0 and 3.1.

Existing Features

- Support for mapping dialog controls to class member variables.

  This helps you enable dialog data exchange (DDX) and dialog data validation (DDV) for the controls in your dialog boxes. DDX exchanges data between dialog controls and their corresponding member variables in a dialog class. DDV validates this data.

- Support for message maps. You can use ClassWizard to:

  - Map Windows messages to message-handler functions in your classes.

  - Map command messages from menu items, toolbar buttons, and accelerators to handler functions in your classes.

  - Map control-notification messages from dialog controls to your classes.

  - Provide "update handlers" to enable or disable user-interface objects, such as menus and toolbar buttons.

  - Jump from ClassWizard to the handler function for a particular message or command.

- Specify a "filter" that determines which categories of Windows messages ClassWizard offers to map to handlers in your class.
- Support for OLE Automation. You can use ClassWizard to:
  - Add classes that support OLE Automation.
  - Add properties and methods to your classes that support OLE Automation.
  - Create a C++ class for an existing OLE Automation object on your system, such as Microsoft Excel.
- Support for developing OLE Controls. You can use ClassWizard to:
  - Specify properties and methods for OLE Controls.
  - Specify the events your OLE Control can fire.

  For more information, see the article OLE Controls. The OLE Control Development Kit (CDK) is now fully integrated with MFC.
- Support for overriding many MFC virtual member functions. You can use ClassWizard to:
  - Browse virtual functions provided by MFC and choose the ones you want to override.
  - Jump to the code for editing.
- Foreign classes.

  Just as you can map dialog box controls to dialog class data members, you can map window controls to data members of class **CRecordset** for ODBC or **CDaoRecordset** for DAO (called a "foreign class" in this context). For more information, see the article ClassWizard: Foreign Objects.

For More Information
For general information about using ClassWizard, see Chapter 14, Working with Classes, in the *Visual C++ User's Guide*.

The following articles describe ClassWizard tips and techniques:

- ClassWizard: Tips and Troubleshooting
- ClassWizard: Database Support
- ClassWizard: OLE Automation Support

See Also   AppWizard

ClassWizard: Special-Format Comment Sections

This article explains where and how ClassWizard edits your source files.

When you add a new class using ClassWizard, special-format comments are placed in your code to mark the sections of the header and implementation files that ClassWizard edits. ClassWizard never modifies code that is outside these commented sections.

Message-Map Comments

For most classes, there are two related sections of code that ClassWizard edits: the member-function definitions in the class header file and the message-map entries in the class implementation file.

The ClassWizard comments in the header file look like this:

```
//{{AFX_MSG(<classname>)
    afx_msg void OnAppAbout();
//}}AFX_MSG
```

The ClassWizard section in the implementation file is set off with comments that look like this:

```
//{{AFX_MSG_MAP(<classname>)
    ON_COMMAND(ID_APP_ABOUT, OnAppAbout)
//}}AFX_MSG_MAP
```

The notes in the ClassWizard section act as placeholders. ClassWizard removes the note from any ClassWizard section in which it writes code.

Virtual Function Comments

As with message handlers, ClassWizard writes code to two locations when you use it to override a virtual function in one of your classes.

The ClassWizard comments in the header file look like the following example for virtual function overrides:

```
//{{AFX_VIRTUAL(<classname>)
    virtual BOOL InitInstance();
//}}AFX_VIRTUAL
```

The ClassWizard section in the implementation file has no special comments. Virtual function definitions in the .CPP file look like other function definitions.

Data Map Comments

For dialog boxes, form views, and record views, ClassWizard creates and edits three other sections that are marked with special format comments:

- Member variable declarations in the class header file:

```
//{{AFX_DATA
..
//}}AFX_DATA
```

- Member variable initialization in the class implementation file:

```
//{{AFX_DATA_INIT
..
//}}AFX_DATA_INIT
```

- Data-exchange macros in the implementation file:

```
//{{AFX_DATA_MAP
..
//}}AFX_DATA_MAP
```

Field Map Comments

For record field exchange, ClassWizard creates and edits three other sections that are marked with special format comments:

- Member variable declarations in the class header file:

```
//{{AFX_FIELD
..
//}}AFX_FIELD
```

- Record exchange function calls in the implementation file:

```
//{{AFX_FIELD_MAP
..
//}}AFX_FIELD_MAP
```

- Member variable initializations in the class header file:

```
//{{AFX_FIELD_INIT
..
//}}AFX_FIELD_INIT
```

OLE Dispatch Map Comments

For OLE method dispatch, ClassWizard creates and edits four other sections that are marked with special format comments:

- OLE events in the class header file:

```
//{{AFX_EVENT
..
//}}AFX_EVENT
```

- OLE events in the class implementation file:

```
//{{AFX_EVENT_MAP
..
//}}AFX_EVENT_MAP
```

- OLE Automation declarations in the class header file:

```
//{{AFX_DISP
..
//}}AFX_DISP
```

- OLE Automation mapping in the class implementation file:

```
//{{AFX_DISP_MAP
..
//}}AFX_DISP_MAP
```

For more information see Working with Dialog Box Data in Chapter 14 of the *Visual C++ User's Guide*.

ClassWizard: Tips and Troubleshooting

This article summarizes key tips and troubleshooting advice for using ClassWizard effectively. The following topics are covered:

- Using ClassWizard tab dialogs
- Adding functions with ClassWizard
- Adding variables with ClassWizard
- Adding code from ClassWizard
- Importing classes from other projects
- Opening your .RC file

Using ClassWizard Tab Dialogs

ClassWizard has a "tab dialog" user interface: the ClassWizard dialog box contains "tabs" that resemble the tabs on a group of file folders. Each tab's label shows what kind of functionality you can edit on that tab. To select a tab, click its label. Use the following tips:

- Use the Message Maps tab to browse the messages that a class can handle or to create, edit, or delete the member functions mapped to the messages. Use the Edit Code button to jump to a message handler function's code in the Visual C++ source code editor.

- Use the Member Variables tab to bind member variables to dialog, form view, or record view controls. You can also bind record view member variables both to record view controls and to the columns of a table in your data source.

- Use the OLE Automation tab to create and edit the OLE Automation capabilities of your application. For example, you can create Automation properties and methods.

- Use the OLE Events tab to specify actions that will cause your OLE control to fire events. For example, you can specify that a mouse click on your control fires a particular event that the control's container responds to with a handler. Note that this tab is for OLE control developers. If you are using an OLE control in your dialog box and want to handle events, use the Message Maps tab just as you would for handling messages.

- Use the Class Info tab to browse and set general class options. You can set a class's message filter to determine what messages ClassWizard offers to map to handlers in your class. You can also view or set a "foreign object" associated with your dialog form view or record view class. For information about foreign objects, see the article ClassWizard: Foreign Objects.

Adding Functions with ClassWizard

ClassWizard lets you create handler functions and connect them to the menu items, toolbar buttons, and accelerators whose commands they respond to. Use the following tips:

- To connect a dialog box or other user-interface object to a menu command or toolbar button with ClassWizard, you must first create the dialog box, menu entry, or toolbar button and its object ID using the appropriate Visual C++ resource editor.

- You can bind more than one user-interface object to a single function. You can bind both a menu command and a toolbar button to a single function, for instance. In this case, selecting either object in your application causes the same action.

- If you delete a member function in the ClassWizard dialog box, the declaration is deleted from the class in the header file, and the message-map entry is deleted from the implementation file. But you must delete the function code and any cross-references to the function manually. Use the browser to help you locate these references.

- To add a function and edit its related code, you should make your selections in this order on the ClassWizard Message Maps tab:

  1. Select a project.

  2. Select the project that contains the class you want to edit.

  3. Select a class name.

  4. Select an Object ID.

  5. Select a Message.

  You can then select an associated function to edit or delete, or click the Add Function button to add a member function to the class.

  By convention, the names of all message-handling functions begin with the prefix **On**.

- Override virtual functions in much the same way, also on the Message Maps tab:

  1. Select a class name.

  2. In the Object IDs box, select the class name again.

  3. In the Messages box, select a virtual function to override.

  4. Choose Add Function.

Adding Variables with ClassWizard

ClassWizard lets you add member variables to some classes. For example, you can add member variables to a dialog class to represent the dialog box's controls. Use the following tips:

- Edit Variables is available in the ClassWizard dialog box only in classes with a data map. This includes dialog, form view, and record view classes. Neither ClassWizard nor AppWizard make changes to your code outside the data map.

- By convention, the names of all member variables begin with the prefix **m_**.

- By using ClassWizard to map a dialog control to a dialog-class member variable with the Value property (the default), you can use dialog data exchange (DDX) and dialog data validation (DDV). This eliminates the need to move data between the control and the member variable yourself. It also allows you to specify validation rules for the data. For more information about DDX and DDV, see Dialog Data Exchange in Chapter 14 of the *Visual C++ User's Guide* and Dialog Data Exchange and Validation in Chapter 1 of *Programming with MFC*.

- You can also map a dialog control to a dialog-class member variable with the Control property. This creates a member variable of an appropriate class, such as **CEdit**. You can then call the member functions of the control object through this variable.

Adding Code from ClassWizard

After you've added a new member function in the ClassWizard dialog box, choose Edit Code to add the implementation code for the function. A Visual C++ source code editor window opens with the file containing the class for the member function. A highlighted comment indicates where to add your code. Use the following tip:

- You can select a function in ClassWizard's Message Maps tab and then click Edit Code to locate and examine code quickly.

Importing Classes from Other Projects

Classes you created for another programming project can sometimes be reused in new projects. For information about how to "import" these classes into your new project so that ClassWizard is aware of them, see Importing a Class in Chapter 14 of the *Visual C++ User's Guide*. Also use the following tip:

- If you are importing several message-handling classes from another project, you can save time by rebuilding the ClassWizard information file (project .CLW) rather than importing each class separately in the Add Class dialog box. You can completely rebuild the .CLW file by deleting the project's .CLW file and then opening ClassWizard. Answer Yes when asked if you want to rebuild the .CLW file. Then use the Select Source Files dialog box to provide ClassWizard with a list of files in your project.

Note The .H and .CPP files for the classes you import must have special-format comments, as described in the article ClassWizard: Special-Format Comment Sections.

Opening Your .RC File

Visual C++ lets you open resources in two ways. You can open individual resources (in compiled form) in the Visual C++ resource editors. Or you can open the .RC file to edit it directly as a text file. Use the following tip:

• To open the .RC file as text, choose the Open command on the File menu and select the Open As option to Text.

ClassWizard: Database Support

You can use ClassWizard to work with two main database classes for Open Database Connectivity (ODBC) or two main classes for Data Access Objects (DAO):

• **CRecordset** (for ODBC) or **CDaoRecordset** (for DAO)   Represents a set of records selected from a data source.

• **CRecordView** (for ODBC) or **CDaoRecordView** (for DAO)   Supplies a database form, based on a dialog resource template, whose controls map to the field data members of an associated recordset object.

DDX and Foreign Object Support

When you create a record view class, you associate it with a particular **CRecordset**-derived or **CDaoRecordset**-derived class and map the record view's controls to field data members of the recordset class.

This close association between a record view and a recordset takes advantage of another feature you can use in ClassWizard: "foreign objects." Dialog data exchange (DDX) lets you simplify data transfer between the controls in a dialog box or form view and the data members in a corresponding class. With foreign objects, you can exchange data between the controls and the data members of a separate object—in this case, between the controls of a record view and the data members of a recordset.

When you specify the **CRecordset**-derived class or **CDaoRecordset**-derived class to associate with a **CRecordView**-derived class or **CDaoRecordView**-derived class, you can name an existing recordset class or create a new one. ClassWizard adds a member variable to the record view class named, by default, **m_pSet**. The data type of this variable is the recordset class. Figure 1 shows the relationships between a record view on the screen, a record view object, and a recordset object. The recordset is the foreign object. ClassWizard creates the record view and recordset classes and maps record view controls to recordset data members via **m_pSet**.

Figure 1 DDX and Foreign Objects

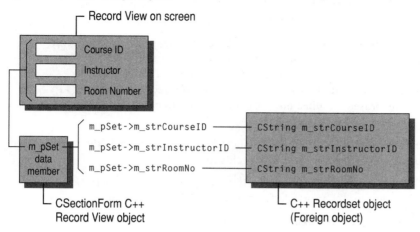

Database Source Files

When you create a **CRecordset/CDaoRecordset** or
CRecordView/CDaoRecordView class with ClassWizard, the wizard creates the
classes in the files you specify in the Add Class dialog box. The default filenames are
based on the class name you enter. You can modify the default names, place the
recordset and record view in the same files, or consolidate all recordsets in one set of
files.

Browsing and Editing Database Classes

You can also browse and edit existing classes with ClassWizard. When you edit an
existing recordset class, ClassWizard provides a dialog box that you can use to update
the table columns bound to the recordset if the table's schema has changed since you
created the class. You can also, with a little extra work, use this mechanism to specify
the columns of additional tables for a join of tables. For more information about joins
in ODBC, see the article Recordset: Performing a Join (ODBC). Performing a join
with DAO is similar.

The following articles explain the details of using ClassWizard's database support:

- ClassWizard: Creating a Recordset Class
- ClassWizard: Binding Recordset Fields to Table Columns
- ClassWizard: Creating a Database Form
- ClassWizard: Mapping Form Controls to Recordset Fields
- ClassWizard: Foreign Objects

See Also ClassWizard: Creating a Recordset Class, AppWizard, Database Overview

ClassWizard: Creating a Recordset Class

This article explains how to create a recordset class with ClassWizard.

You'll need a new **CRecordset**-derived class (for ODBC) or **CDaoRecordset**-derived class (for DAO) for each table, join of tables, or predefined query you work with in your program. Each recordset class specifies its own set of columns and may also specify parameters. For information about the structure of your recordset class and its uses, see the article Recordset: Architecture (ODBC) or DAO Recordset: Architecture.

For information about mapping recordset field data members to columns in the table, see the article ClassWizard: Binding Recordset Fields to Table Columns.

For information about using a **CRecordset** (ODBC) for a join of tables, see the article Recordset: Performing a Join (ODBC). (Performing a join with DAO is similar.)

For information about using a **CRecordset** for a predefined query, see the article Recordset: Declaring a Class for a Predefined Query (ODBC). For information about predefined ("saved") queries in DAO, see the article DAO Querydef.

Table 1 shows the major steps in creating a recordset class.

Table 1   Recordset Class Creation Summary

To	Do this
Create the class	Use the Add Class dialog box in ClassWizard.
Select a data source and database table for the class	Select options in the Database Options dialog box. These include a data source, possibly a recordset type, and possibly some advanced options. Then specify details about the data source in the Select Database dialog box (for ODBC) or the Open dialog box (for DAO). Next, use the Select Database Tables dialog box to select tables from those available on the data source.
Remove any column mappings you don't want. By default, AppWizard and ClassWizard bind all columns in the table to recordset field data members	Select a column name on the Member Variables tab and choose Delete Variable.
Optionally parameterize the underlying SQL statements	Manually add parameter data members, or, in DAO, base your recordset on a parameterized a querydef object.
Optionally use dialog data exchange (DDX) to map recordset data members to controls in a record view	See the article Record Views.

For more information about parameterizing your class, see the article Recordset: Parameterizing a Recordset (ODBC) or the article DAO Queries: Filtering and Parameterizing Queries. For information about using DDX between record view controls and recordset data members, see the article ClassWizard: Mapping Form Controls to Recordset Fields.

Creating the Recordset Class

You can add a new class derived from class **CRecordset** or **CDaoRecordset** in ClassWizard's Add Class dialog box. This dialog box is available from any tab in ClassWizard. (All figures follow the procedure below.)

▶ **To create the recordset class**

1 Run ClassWizard.

2 Choose the Add Class button to open the Add Class dialog box (Figure 1).

3 If you're using the MFC ODBC classes, select **CRecordset** as the base-class type of the new class. If you're using the MFC DAO classes, select **CDaoRecordset**.

4 In the Create New Class dialog box, enter a name for the class and filenames for its .H and .CPP files.

5 Choose the Create button.

The Database Options dialog box (Figure 2) opens.

6 Choose ODBC or DAO. Then select a data source:

- For ODBC, select from the drop-down list. Depending on what you choose, you might need to make a further selection in an Open dialog box. If the data source is on a server, you might be prompted to log in to the server.

- For DAO, click the browse button beside the DAO edit control. Then, in the Open dialog box, navigate to the database file you want to use. (By default, the dialog box displays only Microsoft Jet databases, .MDB, but you can open any database that the Microsoft Jet database engine can read. For information, see the article Database Overview.

7 Click OK.

8 In the Select Database Tables dialog box (shown in Figure 3), select the name(s) of the table(s) you want.

On ClassWizard's Member Variables tab, notice that ClassWizard binds all of the table's columns to recordset field data members. For information about removing bindings you don't want, see the article ClassWizard: Binding Recordset Fields to Table Columns.

9 When you finish, choose OK to close ClassWizard. ClassWizard writes your class files in the specified directory and adds them to your project.

Figure 1   Specifying Information for a New Class

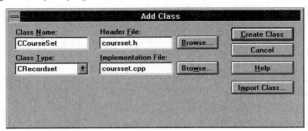

Figure 2   Selecting a Data Source in ClassWizard

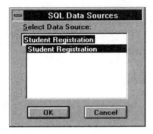

Figure 3   Selecting a Database Table in ClassWizard

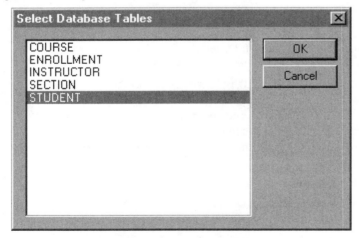

See Also   ClassWizard: Database Support, ClassWizard: Binding Recordset Fields to Table Columns

ClassWizard: Binding Recordset Fields to Table Columns

Both AppWizard and ClassWizard bind all columns of your selected tables to the recordset. This article applies to both the MFC ODBC classes and the MFC DAO classes. The article explains how to:

- Remove data members for any columns you don't want in the recordset.

  If you want only a subset of the columns bound by the wizards, use ClassWizard to remove the field data members for any columns you don't want.

- Select table columns and map them to recordset field data members.

  If you subsequently remove any of the bindings the wizards made, you can later rebind them with ClassWizard.

- Update columns in your recordset to reflect new columns in the table on the data source.

This and related articles use the terms "column" and "field" interchangably when referring to recordset fields.

Removing Columns from Your Recordset

You might sometimes need to remove columns from a recordset. Both AppWizard and ClassWizard automatically bind all table columns to the recordset. If you want only a subset of the columns, use the following procedure.

▶ **To remove a column from a recordset**

1 In ClassWizard, choose the Member Variables tab.

2 Select a member variable name in the Members column of the Column Names box.

3 Choose Delete Variable.

  The member variable is removed from your recordset class. (The column in the data source to which the member variable was bound is not deleted.)

Warning Be careful not to remove any columns that are part of the table's primary key. In some tables, the primary key is a single column; in others, it's composed of two or more columns taken together. Removing these columns could damage your data on the data source.

Adding Columns to Your Recordset

Once you select a table, ClassWizard displays a list of all columns in the table. You can remove column bindings, and you can later rebind columns whose bindings have been removed. The following procedure explains how to bind an unbound column.

▶ To add a column to the recordset

1 Create the recordset class and associate it with one or more database tables.

If you create the class with ClassWizard, follow the procedure To create the recordset class in this article.

If you create the class with AppWizard, follow the procedure in the article AppWizard: Database Support.

2 In ClassWizard, on the Member Variables tab, select the recordset class name in the Class Name box if it is not already selected.

3 Select a column in the Column Names box.

4 Choose the Add Variable button to open the Add Member Variable dialog box.

5 Type a name for the recordset data member that will represent the selected column.

ClassWizard supplies a standard data member prefix, m_, for the name. Append the rest of the name to this prefix or type over it.

The variable's property and data type are already specified in the dialog box. The property for these variables is always "Value." The data type is based on the data type of the column on the data source.

6 Choose OK to close the Add Member Variable dialog box.

7 Choose OK to close ClassWizard.

ClassWizard writes your class files to the specified directory and adds them to your project.

Tip Rather than binding columns to data members one at a time, you can choose the Bind All button to bind all columns. ClassWizard gives the data members default names based on the column names. Binding columns one at a time gives you more control over the columns bound and how they're named, but Bind All is quick and easy.

Figure 1 shows the Member Variables tab with a data member added for one of the available columns.

Figure 1   Adding a Data Member to the Recordset

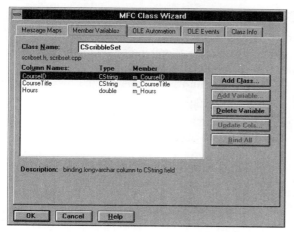

Updating Your Recordset's Columns

Tables in a data source sometimes change—in particular, columns may be added to a table. To bring your recordset class up to date with respect to these changes, use the Update Columns button.

▶ **To update the columns in your recordset**

1 On ClassWizard's Member Variables tab, select your recordset class.

2 Choose the Update Columns button.

Any new columns are shown in the list but not yet bound to recordset field data members. To bind them, see the procedure To add a column to the recordset in Adding Columns to Your Recordset.

When you use Update Columns, columns you've previously bound to recordset data members are left alone; to unbind a column, delete its data member. Any columns in the table that aren't bound to the recordset disappear from the refreshed recordset.

See Also   ClassWizard: Creating a Database Form, ClassWizard: Creating a Recordset Class, AppWizard

ClassWizard: Creating a Database Form

The Microsoft Foundation Class Library database classes supply class **CRecordView** (for ODBC) and class **CDaoRecordView** (for DAO) for implementing database forms with controls in which to display record fields. This article explains how to create a record view class with ClassWizard and associate it with a recordset class.

Important   To use the MFC database classes, you must have specified at least minimum database support ("Only include header files") in AppWizard. If you didn't, open file STDAFX.H and add an **#include** directive for AFXDB.H (if you're using the MFC ODBC classes) or AFXDAO.H (if you're using the MFC DAO classes).

The purpose of a record view class is to provide a form view whose controls are mapped directly to the field data members of a recordset object (and indirectly to the corresponding columns in a table on the data source). Setting up this mapping enables dialog data exchange (DDX) directly between the form's controls and the recordset's field data members. This article explains how to make the association.

Tip The easiest way to use a record view as your application's main view is to do so when you initially run AppWizard. See the article AppWizard: Database Support.

The following procedure begins the process.

▶ **To create a record view associated with a recordset**

1 Create the recordset class.

See the article ClassWizard: Creating a Recordset Class.

2 Create a dialog-template resource.

See Chapter 6, Using the Dialog Editor, in the *Visual C++ User's Guide*.

In the Styles and More Styles property pages of your dialog template, set the following properties, as you would for a **CFormView** object:

- In the Style box, select Child (**WS_CHILD** on).
- In the Border box, select None (**WS_BORDER** off).
- Clear the Visible check box (**WS_VISIBLE** off).
- Clear the Titlebar check box (**WS_CAPTION** off).

Tip As you place controls on your dialog template, you can help ClassWizard be smarter. See the tips in the article ClassWizard: Mapping Form Controls to Recordset Fields.

To continue from step 2, see the following procedure.

▶ **To create the record view class**

1 Run ClassWizard with the Visual C++ dialog editor open on your dialog-template resource.

2 In the Adding a Class dialog box, choose Create a New Class (unless you are importing or using an existing class). For more information, see Adding a Class in Chapter 14 of the *Visual C++ User's Guide*.

3 In the Create New Class dialog box, specify **CRecordView** (for ODBC) or **CDaoRecordView** (for DAO) as the base class for the new class.

4 Enter a name for the class and filenames for its .H and .CPP files and select any other options you need, such as OLE Automation.

5 Choose the Create button.

6 In the Select a Recordset dialog box, select the recordset class you created in step 1 of the procedure To create a record view associated with a recordset.

–or–

Choose New to create a new recordset class. In this case, select a data source and table for the recordset as prompted. Close the Select a Record Set dialog box. On returning to the Member Variables tab, select your new recordset class.

7 Bind columns to recordset field data members. See the article ClassWizard: Binding Recordset Fields to Table Columns.

Note If you next choose the Class Info tab, you'll see your recordset class listed in the Foreign Class box. For more information about "foreign" classes, see the article ClassWizard: Foreign Objects.

8 Choose OK to exit ClassWizard.

For information about binding your record view controls to the recordset, see the article ClassWizard: Mapping Form Controls to Recordset Fields.

See Also ClassWizard: Database Support, ClassWizard: Creating a Recordset Class, ClassWizard: Binding Recordset Fields to Table Columns

ClassWizard: Mapping Form Controls to Recordset Fields

A database form based on class **CRecordView** (for the MFC ODBC classes) or **CDaoRecordView** (for the MFC DAO classes) uses dialog data exchange (DDX) to exchange data between the form's controls and the field data members of the form's associated recordset object. This article explains how to use ClassWizard to set up the DDX connection between the controls and the recordset.

This connection is different from the normal use of DDX, which connects the controls in a dialog box directly to the data members of the associated dialog class. DDX for a record view object is indirect. The connection goes from form controls through the record view object to the field data members of the associated recordset object. For more information, see the articles Record Views and ClassWizard: Foreign Objects. Table 1 summarizes the mapping process.

Table 1 Mapping Record View Controls to a Recordset

To	Do this
Specify the form control	Select the record view class on ClassWizard's Member Variables tab and select one of the form's control IDs
Specify the recordset data member to connect it to	Use the Add Variable dialog box to select a recordset data member indirectly

The following procedure assumes you have already followed the procedures in the article ClassWizard: Creating a Database Form. Specifically, you've created a **CRecordset**-derived or **CDaoRecordset**-derived class and added some field data members to it, created a dialog-template resource, created a **CRecordView**-derived or **CDaoRecordView**-derived class, and associated the record view class with the recordset class. Your record view class is associated with the dialog-template resource, to which you've added controls with the Visual C++ dialog editor.

▶ **To map the form controls to the recordset**

1 Choose ClassWizard's Member Variables tab.

2 In the Class Name box, select the name of your record view class.

3 In the Control IDs box, select a control ID.

4 Choose the Add Variable button to name a variable associated with the control.

5 In the Add Member Variable dialog box, choose a variable name by selecting a recordset data member in the Member Variable Name drop-down list box.

Important Use the drop-down list box to select a data member name from the associated recordset (a foreign object). The names that appear are of the form m_pSet->m_recordsetVarName. You can type the name instead, but selecting from the drop-down list is faster and more accurate.

All variables of the recordset class appear in the box, not just variables of the currently selected data type.

6 Choose OK to close the Add Member Variable dialog box.

7 Repeat steps 3 through 6 for each control in the record view that you want to map to a recordset field data member.

8 Choose OK to close ClassWizard.

By selecting a name from the drop-down list, you specify a connection that passes through the record view object to a field data member of its associated recordset object.

Tip If you're running ClassWizard with the Visual C++ dialog editor open, the following shortcut is available. Choose a control on the form; then press CTRL and double-click the mouse. This opens ClassWizard's Add Member Variables dialog box, where you can bind a recordset field data member to the control. (If you use this shortcut before a class has been created for the dialog template, ClassWizard opens and displays its Add Class dialog box.)

If you follow a simple rule when placing controls on your record view form, ClassWizard is able to preselect the most likely recordset member in the dialog box. The rule is to place the static text label for the control ahead of the corresponding control in the tab order.

Tip You can use CTRL+Double-click for pushbuttons too. In these cases, ClassWizard creates a message handler function for the **BN_CLICKED** notification message in your record view class. You can edit its code to specify the button's action.

See Also   ClassWizard: Foreign Objects

ClassWizard: Foreign Objects

ClassWizard extends dialog data exchange (DDX) by allowing you to map controls on a form or dialog box indirectly to a "foreign object"—a **CRecordset** or **CDaoRecordset** object. This article explains:

- What foreign objects are.
- How to use foreign objects.

Foreign Objects

The best way to understand foreign objects is to consider DDX for a dialog box or form view and then see how it is extended. This discussion considers a form view, based on class **CFormView**.

DDX maps the controls in a form view to data members of the **CFormView**-derived class associated with the dialog-template resource. Controls in a form view correspond one-to-one with form view class data members. Two entities are connected: the form view on the screen and the form view class. (Dialog boxes work this way too.)

DDX for foreign objects connects not two entities but three. Figure 1 shows this connection, with a record view on screen at one end, a **CRecordView** class in the middle, and a third object—the foreign object—at the other end: a **CRecordset** object. (These could be a **CDaoRecordView** and a **CDaoRecordset**.)

Figure 1   DDX for Foreign Objects

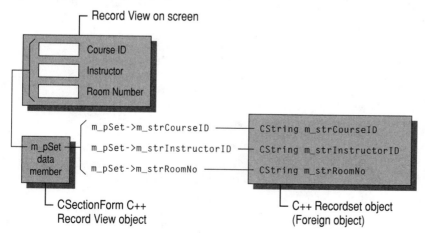

The record view class in Figure 1 contains a member variable, a pointer whose type matches the class of the foreign object. The DDX mapping is from three record view controls to members of the foreign object through the pointer, as illustrated by the following **DoDataExchange** function:

```
void CSectionForm::DoDataExchange(CDataExchange* pDX)
{
  CRecordView::DoDataExchange(pDX);
  //{{AFX_DATA_MAP(CSectionForm)
  DDX_FieldText(pDX, IDC_COURSE,
    m_pSet->m_strCourseID, m_pSet);
  DDX_FieldText(pDX, IDC_INSTRUCTOR,
    m_pSet->m_strInstructor, m_pSet);
  DDX_FieldText(pDX, IDC_ROOMNO,
    m_pSet->m_strRoomNo, m_pSet);
  //}}AFX_DATA_MAP
}
```

Notice the indirect reference to recordset fields, through the m_pSet pointer to a CSections recordset object:

```
m_pSet->m_strCourseID
```

Also notice that m_pSet is repeated as the fourth argument in each **DDX_FieldText** call.

ClassWizard and Foreign Objects

You set the foreign class and object on ClassWizard's Class Info tab. The Foreign Class box names the class of the foreign object (**CRecordset** for ODBC or **CDaoRecordset** for DAO). The Foreign Object box names the pointer variable that points to an object of that class. (You can specify only one foreign object per class.)

If you select a class based on a dialog-template resource on ClassWizard's Member Variables tab, ClassWizard locates the appropriate pointer variable in the class and puts its type into the Foreign Class box. It also puts the variable name into the Foreign Object box. You can change these values if you wish.

If you create a **CRecordView** or **CDaoRecordView** class with AppWizard and then use ClassWizard to specify the DDX connections, ClassWizard automatically notes the presence in the view class of a pointer to a **CRecordset**-derived or **CDaoRecordset**-derived object. ClassWizard sets this as the value in the Foreign Class box. It puts the name of the pointer variable into the Foreign Object box.

See Also   ClassWizard: Mapping Form Controls to Recordset Fields

ClassWizard: OLE Automation Support

ClassWizard supports the following OLE Automation features:

- Add classes that support OLE Automation. This makes your application an OLE Automation server. These classes will be exposed to OLE Automation clients such as Microsoft Visual Basic or Microsoft Excel.

- Add methods and properties to your classes that support OLE Automation.

- Create a C++ class for another OLE Automation object on your system, such as Microsoft Excel. This makes your application an OLE automation client.

  You must call **AfxOleInit** in **InitInstance** to initialize OLE for your application.

  For more information, see the article ClassWizard: Accessing Automation Servers.

An OLE Automation class has a programming interface that other applications use to manipulate objects that your application implements. This is referred to as a "dispatch interface." For more information about dispatch interfaces, see the *OLE Programmer's Reference, Volume 2*.

ClassWizard's Add Class button now allows you to create classes supporting OLE Automation. Click this button on the OLE Automation tab to display a dialog box in which you can choose to create a new class or import an existing class. The Create New Class dialog box appears if you create a new class so you can specify the name of your class, the base class, the filenames in which your class is implemented, and and the dialog display resource for the base class, if necessary. You can also choose whether your class supports OLE Automation, and whether to add the new class to Component Gallery.

▶ To add an OLE Automation class

1 Run ClassWizard from the View menu.

2 Click the Add Class button. The Add Class menu appears.

3 From the Add Class menu, select New. The Create New Class dialog box appears.

4 Type a name for the class.

5 Select a base class. Typically, new automation classes are derived from **CCmdTarget**.

6 If you do not like the filenames specified by ClassWizard, click the Change button. The Change Files dialog appears.

  Enter new names for the .H and .CPP files. Alternately, you can use the Browse buttons to select files. Then click OK to return to the Create New Class dialog box.

7 Choose the OLE Automation option to expose this class to OLE Automation clients. If you choose Creatable By Type ID, you can specify a Type ID for this automation object. The automation client will create an object of this class using the Type ID.

8 Set the Add Component To Gallery option if you want to add your new class to Component Gallery after it is created.

9 When you have entered all the necessary information, click the Create button to create the necessary code and add it to your project.

To continue defining the dispatch interface for your OLE Automation class, see the article ClassWizard: Adding Automation Properties and Methods.

A class that is OLE Creatable allows other applications to create a stand-alone object of the class, for example by using the Visual Basic function **CreateObject**, and to incorporate that automation object into their application. In general, you should make only your top-level classes, such as documents, creatable from other OLE applications. Classes that are parts of these top-level classes are usually not OLE Creatable and are instead accessed from a member function in the top-level class.

For example, consider a list document, which contains a list of items. It's a good idea to make the top-level document class OLE Creatable, because this allows other applications to create a list from nothing. You then add/enumerate the items in the list, but you cannot create them as stand-alone objects because they depend on their position inside the list. For this reason, only stand-alone objects should be OLE Creatable. Note that if you selected Creatable By Type ID in AppWizard your document class is OLE Creatable. In other words, it can be accessed by automation clients.

Note OLE insertable items are made possible by class **COleTemplateServer**. When you choose OLE support in AppWizard, a **COleTemplateServer** object manages your documents. Such documents can be created by OLE Automation.

The following articles explain the details of using ClassWizard's OLE support:

- ClassWizard: Adding Automation Properties and Methods
- ClassWizard: Accessing Automation Servers

ClassWizard: Adding Automation Properties and Methods

This article explains how to use ClassWizard to add OLE Automation properties and methods to an OLE Automation class. Topics include:

- Adding a member variable property to your class
- Adding a Get/Set Methods property to your class
- Adding a method to your class

A class that supports OLE Automation exposes a set of functions (known as methods) and properties—the dispatch interface—for use by other applications. ClassWizard offers a simple, quick way to implement this ability in your classes.

Member-Variable Properties

Use member variable properties if you need to allocate storage for the values. The most common case for member variables is when there is no user interface to be updated when changes occur.

▶ **To add a member variable property to your OLE automation class**

1 In ClassWizard, choose the OLE Automation tab.

2 Select a class name that supports OLE automation. Your document class supports OLE automation if you checked the OLE automation check box in AppWizard. Notice that the Add Property and Add Method buttons are unavailable for classes that do not support OLE automation.

3 Click the Add Property button and supply the following information:

- External Name: Name that automation clients use to refer to this property.
- Type: Any of the choices found in the list box.
- Implementation: Choose Member Variable.
- Variable Name: Name of the C++ class data member.

Tip You can also supply the name of a notification function that is called when the variable changes.

4 Click OK to close ClassWizard.

Get/Set Properties

Use Get/Set Methods properties if you are dealing with calculated properties. The most common use of Get/Set properties is to reflect changes in a user interface for calculated properties or items that are updated.

▶ **To add a Get/Set Methods property to your OLE automation class**

1 In ClassWizard, choose the OLE Automation tab.

2 Select a class name that supports OLE automation. You can also select the name of your document class if you checked the OLE Automation check box in AppWizard. Notice that the Add Property and Add Method buttons are unavailable for classes that do not support OLE automation.

3 Click the Add Property button and supply the following information:

- External Name: Name that automation clients use to refer to this property.
- Type: Any of the choices found in the list box.
- Implementation: Choose Get/Set Methods.
- Get Function: The name of the member function used to get the property value.
- Set Function: The name of the member function used to set the property value. This function can include special processing for when the property value is changed.

4 Add any method parameters you need, using the grid control:

- Double-click in the first empty row under the Name label to activate an edit control; then enter the parameter name.
- Double-click the row under the Type label to activate a drop-down list; then select the parameter's type.

Continue this procedure until you have entered all the parameters you need. To delete a parameter, delete its row by clicking once in the row and pressing the DELETE key or the BACKSPACE key.

5 Choose OK to create the necessary code.

Tip To create a read-only property, delete the name of the Set Function.

▶ To add a method to your OLE automation class

1 In ClassWizard, choose the OLE Automation tab.

2 Select a class name that supports OLE automation. You can also select the name of your document class if you checked the OLE Automation check box in AppWizard. Notice that the Add Property and Add Method buttons are unavailable for classes that do not support OLE automation.

3 Open the Add Method dialog box and supply the following information:

- External Name: Name that automation clients use to refer to this method.
- Internal Name: Name of the C++ member function to add to the class.
- Return Type: Any choice found in the list box.

4 Add any method parameters you need, using the grid control:

- Double-click in the first empty row under the Name label to activate an edit control; then enter the parameter name.
- Double-click the row under the Type label to activate a drop-down list; then select the parameter's type.

  Continue this procedure until you have entered all the parameters you need. To delete a parameter, delete its row by clicking once in the row and pressing the DELETE key or the BACKSPACE key.

5 Choose OK in the Add Method dialog box to create the member function.

See Also ClassWizard: Accessing Automation Servers

ClassWizard: Accessing Automation Servers

OLE automation allows other applications to expose objects and their interfaces to your application. You can make use of this feature by writing automation clients in C++, as well as in Visual Basic and other interpreted languages that support automation.

For information and a procedure, see the article Automation Clients: Using Type Libraries.

Client, OLE Automation

See the article Automation Clients.

Clipboard

The Clipboard is the standard Windows method of transferring data between a source and a destination. It can also be very useful in OLE operations. With the advent of OLE, there are two Clipboard mechanisms in Windows. The standard Windows Clipboard API is still available, but it has been implemented by the OLE data transfer mechanism. OLE uniform data transfer (UDT) supports Cut, Copy, and Paste with the Clipboard and drag-and-drop. This article describes:

- When to use the OLE Clipboard mechanism and when to use the standard Clipboard mechanism.

- Using the OLE Clipboard mechanism.

The Clipboard is a system service shared by the entire Windows session, so it does not have a handle or class of its own. You manage the Clipboard through member functions of class **CWnd**.

For a brief introduction to the standard Windows Clipboard API, see the article Clipboard: Using the Windows Clipboard.

When to Use Each Mechanism

Follow these guidelines in using the Clipboard:

- Use the OLE Clipboard mechanism now to enable new capabilities in the future. While the standard Clipboard API will be maintained, the OLE mechanism is the future of data transfer.

- Use the OLE Clipboard mechanism if you are writing an OLE application or you want any of the OLE features, such as drag and drop.

- Use the OLE Clipboard mechanism if you are providing OLE formats.

Using the OLE Clipboard Mechanism

OLE uses standard formats and some OLE-specific formats for transferring data through the Clipboard.

When you cut or copy data from an application, the data is stored on the Clipboard to be used later in paste operations. This data is in a variety of formats. When a user chooses to paste data from the Clipboard, the application can choose which of these formats to use. The application should be written to choose the format that provides the most information, unless the user specifically asks for a certain format, using Paste Special. Before continuing, you may want to read the Data Objects and Data Sources (OLE) family of articles. They describe the fundamentals of how data transfers work, and how to implement them in your applications.

Windows defines a number of standard formats that can be used for transferring data through the Clipboard. These include metafiles, text, bitmaps, and others. OLE defines a number of OLE-specific formats, as well. It is a good idea for applications that need more detail than given by these standard formats to register their own custom Clipboard formats. Use the **RegisterClipboardFormat** function to do this.

For example, Microsoft Excel registers a custom format for spreadsheets. This format carries much more information than, for example, a bitmap does. When this data is pasted into an application that supports the spreadsheet format, all the formulas and values from the spreadsheet are retained and can be updated if necessary. Microsoft Excel also put data on the Clipboard in formats so that it can be pasted as an OLE item. Any OLE document container can paste this information in as an embedded item. This embedded item can be changed using Microsoft Excel. The Clipboard also contains a simple bitmap of the image of the selected range on the spreadsheet. This can also be pasted into OLE document containers or into bitmap editors, like Paint. In the case of a bitmap, however, there is no way to manipuate the data as a spreadsheet.

To retrieve the maximum amount of information from the Clipboard, applications should check for these custom formats before pasting data from the Clipboard.

For example, to enable the Copy command, you might write a handler something like the following:

```
void CMyView::OnEditCopy()
{
  // Create an OLE data source on the heap
  COleDataSource* pData = new COleDataSource;
  // ...
  // Get the currently selected data
  // ...
  // For the appropriate data formats...
  pData->CacheData( CF_??, hData );
  // ...
  // The Clipboard now owns the allocated memory
  // and will delete this data object
  // when new data is put on the Clipboard
  pData->SetClipboard();
}
```

For more detailed information, see the following articles:

- Clipboard: Copying and Pasting Data
- Clipboard: Adding Other Formats
- Clipboard: Using the Windows Clipboard

See Also Clipboard: Copying and Pasting Data, OLE Overview, Data Objects and Data Sources (OLE), Clipboard: Using the Windows Clipboard

Clipboard: Using the Windows Clipboard

This article describes how to use the standard Windows Clipboard API within your MFC application.

Most applications for Windows support cutting or copying data to the Windows Clipboard and pasting data from the Clipboard. The Clipboard data formats vary among applications. The framework supports only a limited number of Clipboard formats for a limited number of classes. You will normally implement the Clipboard-related commands—Cut, Copy, and Paste—on the Edit menu for your view. The class library defines the command IDs for these commands: **ID_EDIT_CUT**, **ID_EDIT_COPY**, and **ID_EDIT_PASTE**. Their message-line prompts are also defined.

Chapter 2, Working with Messages and Commands, explains how to handle menu commands in your application by mapping the menu command to a handler function. As long as your application does not define handler functions for the Clipboard commands on the Edit menu, they remain disabled. To write handler functions for the Cut and Copy commands, implement selection in your application. To write a handler function for the Paste command, query the Clipboard to see whether it contains data in a format your application can accept. For example, to enable the Copy command, you might write a handler something like the following:

```
void CMyView::OnEditCopy()
{
  if ( !OpenClipboard() )
  {
    AfxMessageBox( "Cannot open the Clipboard" );
    return;
  }
  // Remove the current Clipboard contents
  if( EmptyClipboard() )
  {
    AfxMessageBox( "Cannot empty the Clipboard" );
    return;
  }
  // ...
  // Get the currently selected data
  // ...
  // For the appropriate data formats...
  if ( ::SetClipboardData( CF_??, hData ) == NULL )
  {
    AfxMessageBox( "Unable to set Clipboard data" );
    CloseClipboard();
    return;
  }
  // ...
  CloseClipboard();
}
```

The Cut, Copy, and Paste commands are only meaningful in certain contexts. The Cut and Copy commands should be enabled only when something is selected, and the Paste command only when something is in the Clipboard. You can provide this behavior by defining update handler functions that enable or disable these commands depending on the context. For more information, see How to Update User-Interface Objects in Chapter 2.

The Microsoft Foundation Class Library does provide Clipboard support for text editing with the **CEdit** and **CEditView** classes. The OLE classes also simplify implementing Clipboard operations that involve OLE items. For more information on the OLE classes, see Using the OLE Clipboard Mechanism in the article Clipboard.

Implementing other Edit menu commands, such as Undo (**ID_EDIT_UNDO**) and Redo (**ID_EDIT_REDO**), is also left to you. If your application does not support these commands, you can easily delete them from your resource file using the Visual C++ resource editors.

See Also   Clipboard: Copying and Pasting Data

Clipboard: Copying and Pasting Data

This article describes the minimum work necessary to implement copying to and pasting from the Clipboard in your OLE application. It is recommended that you read the Data Objects and Data Sources (OLE) family of articles before proceeding.

Before you can implement either copying or pasting, you must first provide functions to handle the Copy, Cut, and Paste options on the Edit menu.

Copying Data

▶ **To copy data to the Clipboard**

1 Determine whether the data to be copied is native data or is an embedded or linked item.

- If the data is embedded or linked, obtain a pointer to the **COleClientItem** object that has been selected.

- If the data is native and the application is a server, create a new object derived from **COleServerItem** containing the selected data. Otherwise, create a **COleDataSource** object for the data.

2 Call the selected item's **CopyToClipboard** member function.

3 If the user chose a Cut operation instead of a Copy operation, delete the selected data from your application.

To see an example of this sequence, see the **OnEditCut** and **OnEditCopy** functions in the MFC OLE sample programs OCLIENT and HIERSVR. Note that these samples maintain a pointer to the currently selected data, so step 1 is already complete.

Pasting Data

Pasting data is more complicated than copying it because you need to choose the format to use in pasting the data into your application.

▶ **To paste data from the Clipboard**

1 In your view class, implement **OnEditPaste** to handle users choosing the Paste option from the Edit menu.

2 In the **OnEditPaste** function, create a **COleDataObject** object and call its **AttachClipboard** member function to link this object to the data on the Clipboard.

3 Call **COleDataObject::IsDataAvailable** to check whether a particular format is available.

Alternately, you can use **COleDataObject::BeginEnumFormats** to look for other formats until you find one most suited to your application.

4 Perform the paste of the format.

For an example of how this works, see the implementation of the **OnEditPaste** member functions in the view classes defined in the MFC OLE sample programs OCLIENT and HIERSVR.

Tip The main benefit of separating the paste operation into its own function is that the same paste code can be used when data is dropped in your application during a drag-and-drop operation. As in OCLIENT and HIERSVR, your **OnDrop** function can also call **DoPasteItem**, reusing the code written to implement Paste operations.

To handle the Paste Special option on the Edit menu, see the article Dialog Boxes in OLE.

See Also Clipboard: Adding Other Formats, Data Objects and Data Sources: Creation and Destruction, OLE Overview

Clipboard: Adding Other Formats

This article explains how to expand the list of supported formats, particularly for OLE support. The article Clipboard: Copying and Pasting Data describes the minimum implementation necessary to support copying and pasting from the Clipboard. If this is all you implement, the only formats placed on the Clipboard are **CF_METAFILEPICT**, **CF_EMBEDSOURCE**, **CF_OBJECTDESCRIPTOR**, and possibly **CF_LINKSOURCE**. Most applications will need more formats on the Clipboard than these three.

Registering Custom Formats

To create your own custom formats, follow the same procedure you would use when registering any custom Clipboard format: pass the name of the format to the **RegisterClipboardFormat** function and use its return value as the format ID.

Placing Formats on the Clipboard

To add more formats to those placed on the Clipboard, you must override the **OnGetClipboardData** function in the class you derived from either **COleClientItem** or **COleServerItem** (depending on whether the data to be copied is native). In this function, you should use the following procedure.

▶ **To place formats on the Clipboard**

1 Create a **COleDataSource** object.

2 Pass this data source to a function that adds your native data formats to the list of supported formats by calling **COleDataSource::CacheGlobalData**.

3 Add standard formats by calling **COleDataSource::CacheGlobalData** for each standard format you want to support.

This technique is used in the MFC OLE sample program HIERSVR (examine the **OnGetClipboardData** member function of the **CServerItem** class). The only difference in this sample is that step three is not implemented because HIERSVR supports no other standard formats.

See Also   Data Objects and Data Sources: Manipulation

CObject Class

CObject is the root base class for most of the Microsoft Foundation Class Library (MFC). The **CObject** class contains many useful features that you may want to incorporate into your own program objects, including serialization support, run-time class information, and object diagnostic output. If you derive your class from **CObject**, your class can exploit these **CObject** features.

The cost of deriving your class from **CObject** is minimal. Your derived class will have the overhead of four virtual functions and a single **CRuntimeClass** object.

The following articles explain how to derive a class from **CObject** and how to access run-time class information using **CObject**:

- CObject Class: Deriving a Class from CObject
- CObject Class: Specifying Levels of Functionality
- CObject Class: Accessing Run-Time Class Information
- CObject Class: Dynamic Object Creation

See Also   Files, Serialization (Object Persistence)

CObject Class: Deriving a Class from CObject

This article describes the minimum steps necessary to derive a class from **CObject**. Other CObject Class articles describe the steps needed to take advantage of specific **CObject** features, such as serialization and diagnostic debugging support.

In the discussions of **CObject**, the terms "interface file" and "implementation file" are used frequently. The interface file (often called the header file, or .H file) contains the class declaration and any other information needed to use the class. The implementation file (or .CPP file) contains the class definition as well the code that implements the class member functions. For example, for a class named `CPerson`, you would typically create an interface file named PERSON.H and an implementation file named PERSON.CPP. However, for some small classes that will not be shared among applications, it is sometimes easier to combine the interface and implementation into a single .CPP file.

You can choose from four levels of functionality when deriving a class from **CObject**:

- Basic functionality: No support for run-time class information or serialization but includes diagnostic memory management.
- Basic functionality plus support for run-time class information.
- Basic functionality plus support for run-time class information and dynamic creation.
- Basic functionality plus support for run-time class information, dynamic creation, and serialization.

Classes designed for reuse (those that will later serve as base classes) should at least include run-time class support and serialization support, if any future serialization need is anticipated.

You choose the level of functionality by using specific declaration and implementation macros in the declaration and implementation of the classes you derive from **CObject**.

Table 1 shows the relationship among the macros used to support serialization and run-time information.

Table 1   Macros Used for Serialization and Run-Time Information

Macro used	CObject::IsKindOf	CRuntimeClass::CreateObject	CArchive::operator>> CArchive::operator<<
Basic **CObject** functionality	No	No	No
DECLARE_DYNAMIC	Yes	No	No
DECLARE_DYNCREATE	Yes	Yes	No
DECLARE_SERIAL	Yes	Yes	Yes

▶ **To use basic CObject functionality**

- Use the normal C++ syntax to derive your class from **CObject** (or from a class derived from **CObject**).

  The following example shows the simplest case, the derivation of a class from **CObject**:

```
class CPerson : public CObject
{
    // add CPerson-specific members and functions...
}
```

Normally, however, you may want to override some of **CObject**'s member functions to handle the specifics of your new class. For example, you may usually want to override the **Dump** function of **CObject** to provide debugging output for the contents of your class. For details on how to override **Dump**, see the article Diagnostics: Dumping Object Contents. You may also want to override the **AssertValid** function of **CObject** to provide customized testing to validate the consistency of the data members of class objects. For a description of how to override **AssertValid**, see Overriding the AssertValid Function in the article Diagnostics: Checking Object Validity.

The article CObject Class: Specifying Levels of Functionality describes how to specify other levels of functionality, including run-time class information, dynamic object creation, and serialization.

CObject Class: Specifying Levels of Functionality

This article describes how to add the following levels of functionality to your **CObject**-derived class:

- Run-time class information
- Dynamic creation support
- Serialization support

For a general description of **CObject** functionality, see the article CObject Class: Deriving a Class from CObject.

▶ To add run-time class information

CObject supports run-time class information through the **IsKindOf** function, which allows you to determine if an object belongs to or is derived from a specified class. For more detailed information, see the articles Files and Serialization (Object Persistence). This capability is not supported directly by the C++ language. The **IsKindOf** function permits you to do a type-safe cast down to a derived class.

Use the following steps to access run-time class information:

1. Derive your class from **CObject**, as described in the CObject Class: Deriving a Class from CObject article.

2. Use the **DECLARE_DYNAMIC** macro in your class declaration, as shown here:

```
class CPerson : public CObject
{
    DECLARE_DYNAMIC( CPerson )

    // rest of class declaration follows...
};
```

3. Use the **IMPLEMENT_DYNAMIC** macro in the implementation file (.CPP) of your class. This macro takes as arguments the name of the class and its base class, as follows:

```
IMPLEMENT_DYNAMIC( CPerson, CObject )
```

Note Always put **IMPLEMENT_DYNAMIC** in the implementation file (.CPP) for your class. The **IMPLEMENT_DYNAMIC** macro should be evaluated only once during a compilation and therefore should not be used in an interface file (.H) that could potentially be included in more than one file.

▶ **To add dynamic creation support**

CObject also supports dynamic creation, which is the process of creating an object of a specific class at run time. The object is created by the **CreateObject** member function of **CRuntimeClass.** Your document, view, and frame class should support dynamic creation because the framework (through the **CDocTemplate** class) needs to create them dynamically. Dynamic creation is not supported directly by the C++ language. To add dynamic creation, you must do the following:

1 Derive your class from **CObject**.

2 Use the **DECLARE_DYNCREATE** macro in the class declaration.

3 Define a constructor with no arguments (a default constructor).

4 Use the **IMPLEMENT_DYNCREATE** macro in the class implementation file.

▶ **To add serialization support**

"Serialization" is the process of writing or reading the contents of an object to and from a file. The Microsoft Foundation Class Library uses an object of the **CArchive** class as an intermediary between the object to be serialized and the storage medium. The **CArchive** object uses overloaded insertion (<<) and extraction (>>) operators to perform writing and reading operations.

The following steps are required to support serialization in your classes:

1 Derive your class from **CObject**.

2 Override the **Serialize** member function.

Note If you call **Serialize** directly, that is, you do not want to serialize the object through a polymorphic pointer, omit steps 3 through 5.

3 Use the **DECLARE_SERIAL** macro in the class declaration.

4 Define a constructor with no arguments (a default constructor).

5 Use the **IMPLEMENT_SERIAL** macro in the class implementation file.

Note A "polymorphic pointer" points to an object of a class (call it A) or to an object of any class derived from A (say, B). To serialize through a polymorphic pointer, the framework must determine the run-time class of the object it is serializing (B), since it might be an object of any class derived from some base class (A).

For more details on how to enable serialization when you derive your class from **CObject**, see the articles Files and Serialization (Object Persistence).

See Also CObject Class: Accessing Run-Time Class Information

CObject Class: Accessing Run-Time Class Information

This article explains how to access information about the class of an object at run time.

Note MFC does not use the Run-Time Type Information (RTTI) support introduced in Visual C++ 4.0. For more information about RTTI, see Run-Time Type Information in the *C++ Language Reference*.

If you have derived your class from **CObject** and used the **DECLARE_DYNAMIC** and **IMPLEMENT_DYNAMIC**, the **DECLARE_DYNCREATE** and **IMPLEMENT_DYNCREATE**, or the **DECLARE_SERIAL** and **IMPLEMENT_SERIAL** macros explained in the article, CObject Class: Deriving a Class from CObject, the **CObject** class has the ability to determine the exact class of an object at run time.

The ability to determine the class of an object at run time is most useful when extra type checking of function arguments is needed and when you must write special-purpose code based on the class of an object. However, this practice is not usually recommended because it duplicates the functionality of virtual functions.

The **CObject** member function **IsKindOf** can be used to determine if a particular object belongs to a specified class or if it is derived from a specific class. The argument to **IsKindOf** is a **CRuntimeClass** object, which you can get using the **RUNTIME_CLASS** macro with the name of the class. The use of the **RUNTIME_CLASS** macro is shown in this article.

▶ **To use the RUNTIME_CLASS macro**

- Use **RUNTIME_CLASS** with the name of the class, as shown here for the class **CObject**:

```
CRuntimeClass* pClass = RUNTIME_CLASS( CObject );
```

You will rarely need to access the run-time class object directly. A more common use is to pass the run-time class object to the **IsKindOf** function, as shown in the next procedure. The **IsKindOf** function tests an object to see if it belongs to a particular class.

▶ **To use the IsKindOf function**

1 Make sure the class has run-time class support. That is, the class must have been derived directly or indirectly from **CObject** and used the **DECLARE_DYNAMIC** and **IMPLEMENT_DYNAMIC**, the **DECLARE_DYNCREATE** and **IMPLEMENT_DYNCREATE**, or the **DECLARE_SERIAL** and **IMPLEMENT_SERIAL** macros explained in the article CObject Class: Deriving a Class from CObject.

2 Call the **IsKindOf** member function for objects of that class, using the **RUNTIME_CLASS** macro to generate the **CRuntimeClass** argument, as shown here:

```
// in .H file
class CPerson : public CObject
{
    DECLARE_DYNAMIC( CPerson )
public:
    CPerson(){};

    // other declaration
};

// in .CPP file
IMPLEMENT_DYNAMIC( CPerson, CObject )

CObject* pMyObject = new CPerson;

if( myObject->IsKindOf( RUNTIME_CLASS( CPerson ) ) )
{
    //if IsKindOf is true, then cast is all right
    CPerson* pmyPerson = (CPerson*) pmyObject;
}
```

Note IsKindOf returns **TRUE** if the object is a member of the specified class or of a class derived from the specified class. **IsKindOf** does not support multiple inheritance or virtual base classes, although you can use multiple inheritance for your derived Microsoft Foundation classes if necessary.

One use of run-time class information is in the dynamic creation of objects. This process is discussed in the article CObject Class: Dynamic Object Creation.

For more detailed information on serialization and run-time class information, see the articles Files and Serialization (Object Persistence).

CObject Class: Dynamic Object Creation

This article explains how to create an object dynamically at run time. The procedure uses run-time class information, as discussed in the article CObject Class: Accessing Run-Time Class Information.

▶ **To dynamically create an object given its run-time class**

- Use the following code to dynamically create an object by using the **CreateObject** function of the **CRuntimeClass**. Note that on failure, **CreateObject** returns **NULL** instead of raising an exception:

```
CRuntimeClass* pRuntimeClass = RUNTIME_CLASS( CMyClass );
CObject* pObject = pRuntimeClass->CreateObject();
ASSERT( pObject->IsKindOf( RUNTIME_CLASS( CMyClass ) ) );
```

Collections

This group of articles explains the MFC collection classes.

The Microsoft Foundation Class Library provides collection classes to manage groups of objects. These classes are of two types:

- Collection classes created from C++ templates
- Collection classes not created from templates

Other topics covered in this article include:

- Collection shapes
- Further reading about collections

Tip The nontemplate collection classes have been provided by MFC beginning with MFC version 1.0. If your code already uses these classes, you can continue to use them. If you write new type-safe collection classes for your own data types, consider using the newer template-based classes.

Collection Shapes

A collection class is characterized by its "shape" and by the types of its elements. The shape refers to the way the objects are organized and stored by the collection. MFC provides three basic collection shapes: lists, arrays, and maps (also known as dictionaries). You can pick the collection shape most suited to your particular programming problem.

Each of the three provided collection shapes is described briefly below. Table 1 in the article Collections: Choosing a Collection Class compares the features of the shapes to help you decide which is best for your program.

- List

The list class provides an ordered, nonindexed list of elements, implemented as a doubly linked list. A list has a "head" and a "tail," and adding or removing elements from the head or tail, or inserting or deleting elements in the middle, is very fast.

- Array

  The array class provides a dynamically sized, ordered, and integer-indexed array of objects.

- Map (also known as a dictionary)

  A map is a collection that associates a key object with a value object.

The Template-Based Collection Classes

The easiest way to implement a type-safe collection that contains objects of any type is to use one of the MFC template-based classes. For examples of these classes, see the MFC Advanced Concepts sample COLLECT.

Table 1 lists the MFC template-based collection classes.

Table 1 Collection Template Classes

Collection contents	Arrays	Lists	Maps
Collections of objects of any type	CArray	CList	CMap
Collections of pointers to objects of any type	CTypedPtrArray	CTypedPtrList	CTypedPtrMap

The Collection Classes Not Based on Templates

If your application already uses MFC nontemplate classes, you can continue to use them, although for new collections you should consider using the template-based classes. Table 2 lists the MFC collection classes not based on templates.

Table 2 Nontemplate Collection Classes

Arrays	Lists	Maps
CObArray	CObList	CMapPtrToWord
CByteArray	CPtrList	CMapPtrToPtr
CDWordArray	CStringList	CMapStringToOb
CPtrArray		CMapStringToPtr
CStringArray		CMapStringToString
CWordArray		CMapWordToOb
CUIntArray		CMapWordToPtr

Table 2 in the article Collections: Choosing a Collection Class describes the MFC collection classes in terms of their characteristics (other than shape):

- Whether the class uses C++ templates
- Whether the elements stored in the collection can be serialized
- Whether the elements stored in the collection can be dumped for diagnostics
- Whether the collection is type-safe

Further Reading About Collections

The following articles describe how to use the collection classes to make type-safe collections and how to perform a number of other operations using collections:

- Collections: Choosing a Collection Class
- Collections: Template-Based Classes
- Collections: How to Make a Type-Safe Collection
- Collections: Accessing All Members of a Collection
- Collections: Deleting All Objects in a CObject Collection
- Collections: Creating Stack and Queue Collections

Collections: Choosing a Collection Class

This article contains detailed information designed to help you choose a collection class for your particular application needs.

Your choice of a collection class depends on a number of factors, including:

- The features of the class shape: order, indexing, and performance, as shown in Table 1
- Whether the class uses C++ templates
- Whether the elements stored in the collection can be serialized
- Whether the elements stored in the collection can be dumped for diagnostics
- Whether the collection is type-safe

Table 1 summarizes the characteristics of the available collection shapes.

- Columns 2 and 3 describe each shape's ordering and access characteristics. In the table, the term "ordered" means that the order in which items are inserted and deleted determines their order in the collection; it does not mean the items are sorted on their contents. The term "indexed" means that the items in the collection can be retrieved by an integer index, much like items in a typical array.
- Columns 4 and 5 describe each shape's performance. In applications that require many insertions into the collection, insertion speed might be especially important; for other applications, lookup speed may be more important.
- Column 6 describes whether each shape allows duplicate elements.

Table 1 Collection Shape Features

Shape	Ordered?	Indexed?	Insert an element	Search for specified element	Duplicate elements?
List	Yes	No	Fast	Slow	Yes
Array	Yes	By int	Slow	Slow	Yes
Map	No	By key	Fast	Fast	No (keys) Yes (values)

Table 2 summarizes other important characteristics of specific MFC collection classes as a guide to selection. Your choice may depend on whether the class is based on C++ templates, whether its elements can be serialized via MFC's document serialization mechanism, whether its elements can be dumped via MFC's diagnostic dumping mechanism, or whether the class is type-safe—that is, whether you can guarantee the type of elements stored in and retrieved from a collection based on the class.

Table 2 Characteristics of MFC Collection Classes

Class	Uses C++ templates	Can be serialized	Can be dumped	Is type-safe
CArray	Yes	Yes [1]	Yes [1]	No
CTypedPtrArray	Yes	Depends [2]	Yes	Yes
CByteArray	No	Yes	Yes	Yes [3]
CDWordArray	No	Yes	Yes	Yes [3]
CObArray	No	Yes	Yes	No
CPtrArray	No	No	Yes	No
CStringArray	No	Yes	Yes	Yes [3]
CWordArray	No	Yes	Yes	Yes [3]
CUIntArray	No	No	Yes	Yes [3]
CList	Yes	Yes [1]	Yes [1]	No
CTypedPtrList	Yes	Depends [2]	Yes	Yes
CObList	No	Yes	Yes	No
CPtrList	No	No	Yes	No
CStringList	No	Yes	Yes	Yes [3]
CMap	Yes	Yes [1]	Yes [1]	No
CTypedPtrMap	Yes	Depends [2]	Yes	Yes
CMapPtrToWord	No	No	Yes	No
CMapPtrToPtr	No	No	Yes	No
CMapStringToOb	No	Yes	Yes	No
CMapStringToPtr	No	No	Yes	No
CMapStringToString	No	Yes	Yes	Yes [3]

Table 2   Characteristics of MFC Collection Classes *(cont.)*

Class	Uses C++ templates	Can be serialized	Can be dumped	Is type-safe
CMapWordToOb	No	Yes	Yes	No
CMapWordToPtr	No	No	Yes	No

1   To serialize, you must explicitly call the collection object's **Serialize** function; to dump, you must explicitly call its **Dump** function. You cannot use the form ar << collObj to serialize or the form dmp << collObj to dump.

2   Serializability depends on the underlying collection type. For example, if a typed pointer array is based on **CObArray**, it is serializable; if based on **CPtrArray**, it is not serializable. In general, the "Ptr" classes cannot be serialized.

3   If marked Yes in this column, a nontemplate collection class is type-safe provided you use it as intended. That is, for example, if you store bytes in a **CByteArray**, the array is type-safe. But if you use it to store characters, its type safety is less certain.

See Also   Collections: Template-Based Classes, Collections: How to Make a Type-Safe Collection, Collections: Accessing All Members of a Collection

Collections: Template-Based Classes

This article explains the type-safe template-based collection classes in MFC version 3.0 and later. Using these templates to create type-safe collections is more convenient and provides better type safety than using the collection classes not based on templates.

MFC predefines two categories of template-based collections:

- Simple array, list, and map classes

  CArray, **CList**, **CMap**

- Arrays, lists, and maps of typed pointers

  CTypedPtrArray, **CTypedPtrList**, **CTypedPtrMap**

The simple collection classes are all derived from class **CObject**, so they inherit the serialization, dynamic creation, and other properties of **CObject**. The typed pointer collection classes require you to specify the class you derive from—which must be one of the nontemplate pointer collections predefined by MFC, such as **CPtrList** or **CPtrArray**. Your new collection class inherits from the specified base class, and the new class's member functions use encapsulated calls to the base class members to enforce type safety.

For more information about Visual C++ templates, see Chapter 6, Templates, in *Programming Techniques*.

Using Simple Array, List, and Map Templates

To use the simple collection templates, you need to know what kind of data you can store in these collections and what parameters to use in your collection declarations.

Simple Array and List Usage

The simple array and list classes, **CArray** and **CList**, take two parameters: *TYPE* and *ARG_TYPE*. These classes can store any data type, which you specify in the *TYPE* parameter:

- Fundamental C++ data types, such as **int**, **char**, and **float**

- C++ structures and classes

- Other types that you define

For convenience and efficiency, you can use the *ARG_TYPE* parameter to specify the type of function arguments. Typically, you specify *ARG_TYPE* as a reference to the type you named in the *TYPE* parameter. For example:

```
CArray<int, int> myArray;
CList<CPerson, CPerson&> myList;
```

The first example declares an array collection, `myArray`, that contains **int**s. The second example declares a list collection, `myList`, that stores `CPerson` objects. Certain member functions of the collection classes take arguments whose type is specified by the *ARG_TYPE* template parameter. For example, the **Add** member function of class **CArray** takes an *ARG_TYPE* argument:

```
CArray<CPerson, CPerson&> myArray;
CPerson person;
myArray->Add( person );
```

Simple Map Usage

The simple map class, **CMap**, takes four parameters: *KEY*, *ARG_KEY*, *VALUE*, and *ARG_VALUE*. Like the array and list classes, the map classes can store any data type. Unlike arrays and lists, which index and order the data they store, maps associate keys and values: you access a value stored in a map by specifying the value's associated key. The *KEY* parameter specifies the data type of the keys used to access data stored in the map. If the type of *KEY* is a structure or class, the *ARG_KEY* parameter is typically a reference to the type specified in *KEY*. The *VALUE* parameter specifies the type of the items stored in the map. If the type of *ARG_VALUE* is a structure or class, the *ARG_VALUE* parameter is typically a reference to the type specified in *VALUE*. For example:

```
CMap< int, int, MY_STRUCT, MY_STRUCT& > myMap1;
CMap< CString, LPCSTR, CPerson, CPerson& > myMap2;
```

The first example stores `MY_STRUCT` values, accesses them by **int** keys, and returns accessed `MY_STRUCT` items by reference. The second example stores `CPerson` values, accesses them by **CString** keys, and returns references to accessed items. This example might represent a simple address book, in which you look up persons by last name.

Because the *KEY* parameter is of type **CString** and the *KEY_TYPE* parameter is of type **LPCSTR**, the keys are stored in the map as items of type **CString** but are referenced in functions such as **SetAt** through pointers of type **LPCSTR**. For example:

```
CMap< CString, LPCSTR, CPerson, CPerson& > myMap2;
CPerson person;
LPCSTR lpstrName = "Jones";
myMap2->SetAt( lpstrName, person );
```

Using Typed-Pointer Collection Templates

To use the typed-pointer collection templates, you need to know what kinds of data you can store in these collections and what parameters to use in your collection declarations.

Typed-Pointer Array and List Usage

The typed-pointer array and list classes, **CTypedPtrArray** and **CTypedPtrList**, take two parameters: *BASE_CLASS* and *TYPE*. These classes can store any data type, which you specify in the *TYPE* parameter. They are derived from one of the nontemplate collection classes that stores pointers; you specify this base class in *BASE_CLASS*. For arrays, use either **CObArray** or **CPtrArray**. For lists, use either **CObList** or **CPtrList**.

In effect, when you declare a collection based on, say **CObList**, the new class not only inherits the members of its base class, but it also declares a number of additional type-safe member functions and operators that provide type safety by encapsulating calls to the base class members. These encapsulations manage all necessary type conversion.

For example:

```
CTypedPtrArray<CObArray, CPerson*> myArray;
CTypedPtrList<CPtrList, MY_STRUCT*> myList;
```

The first example declares a typed-pointer array, myArray, derived from **CObArray**. The array stores and returns pointers to CPerson objects (where CPerson is a class derived from **CObject**). You can call any **CObArray** member function, or you can call the new type-safe **GetAt** and **ElementAt** functions or use the type-safe **[ ]** operator.

The second example declares a typed-pointer list, myList, derived from **CPtrList**. The list stores and returns pointers to MY_STRUCT objects. A class based on **CPtrList** is used for storing pointers to objects not derived from **CObject**. **CTypedPtrList** has a number of type-safe member functions: **GetHead**, **GetTail**, **RemoveHead**, **RemoveTail**, **GetNext**, **GetPrev**, and **GetAt**.

Typed-Pointer Map Usage

The typed-pointer map class, **CTypedPtrMap**, takes three parameters: *BASE_CLASS*, *KEY*, and *VALUE*. The *BASE_CLASS* parameter specifies the class from which to derive the new class: **CMapPtrToWord**, **CMapPtrToPtr**, **CMapStringToPtr**, **CMapWordToPtr**, **CMapStringToOb**, and so on. *KEY* is analogous to *KEY* in **CMap**: it specifies the type of the key used for lookups. *VALUE* is analogous to *VALUE* in **CMap**: it specifies the type of object stored in the map.

For example:

```
CTypedPtrMap<CMapPtrToPtr, CString, MY_STRUCT*> myPtrMap;
CTypedPtrMap<CMapStringToOb, CString, CMyObject*> myObjectMap;
```

The first example is a map based on **CMapPtrToPtr**—it uses **CString** keys mapped to pointers to MY_STRUCT. You can look up a stored pointer by calling a type-safe **Lookup** member function. You can use the **[ ]** operator to look up a stored pointer and add it if not found. And you can iterate the map using the type-safe **GetNextAssoc** function. You can also call other member functions of class **CMapPtrToPtr**.

The second example is a map based on **CMapStringToOb**—it uses string keys mapped to stored pointers to CMyObject objects. You can use the same type-safe members described in the previous paragraph, or you can call members of class **CMapStringToOb**.

Note If you specify a **class** or **struct** type for the *VALUE* parameter, rather than a pointer or reference to the type, the class or structure must have a copy constructor.

See Also Collections: How to Make a Type-Safe Collection

In the *Class Library Reference*: **CArray**, **CList**, **CMap**, **CTypedPtrArray**, **CTypedPtrList**, **CTypedPtrMap**

Collections: How to Make a Type-Safe Collection

This article explains how to make type-safe collections for your own data types. Topics include:

- Using template-based classes for type-safety
- Implementing helper functions
- Using nontemplate collection classes

The Microsoft Foundation Class Library provides predefined type-safe collections based on C++ templates. Because they are templates, these classes provide type safety and ease of use without the type-casting and other extra work involved in using a nontemplate class for this purpose. The MFC Advanced Concepts sample COLLECT demonstrates the use of template-based collection classes in an MFC application. In general, use these classes any time you write new collections code.

Using Template-Based Classes for Type-Safety

▶ **To use template-based classes**

1 Declare a variable of the collection class type. For example:

```
CList<int, int> m_intList;
```

2 Call the member functions of the collection object. For example:

```
m_intList.AddTail( 100 );
m_intList.RemoveAll( );
```

3 If necessary, implement the helper functions **SerializeElements**, **ConstructElements**, and **DestructElements**. For information on implementing these functions, see Implementing Helper Functions.

This example shows the declaration of a list of integers. The first parameter in step 1 is the type of data stored as elements of the list. The second parameter specifies how the data is to be passed to and returned from member functions of the collection class, such as **Add** and **GetAt**.

Implementing Helper Functions

The template-based collection classes **CArray**, **CList**, and **CMap** use six global helper functions that you can customize as needed for your derived collection class. For information on these helper functions, see Collection Class Helpers in the *Class Library Reference*. Three of these helper functions are used in constructing, destructing, and serializing collection elements; implementations of these functions are necessary for most uses of the template-based collection classes.

Construction and Destruction

The helper functions **ConstructElements** and **DestructElements** are called by members that respectively add and remove elements from a collection.

Helper	Called directly by	Called indirectly by
ConstructElements	**CArray::SetSize** **CArray::InsertAt**	**CList::AddHead** **CList::AddTail** **CList::InsertBefore** **CList::InsertAfter** **CMap::operator [ ]**
DestructElements	**CArray::SetSize** **CArray::RemoveAt** **CList::RemoveAll** **CMap::RemoveAll**	**CList::RemoveHead** **CList::RemoveTail** **CList::RemoveAt** **CMap::RemoveKey**

You should override these functions if their default action is not suitable for your collection class. The default implementation of **ConstructElements** sets to 0 the memory that is allocated for new elements of the collection; no constructors are called. The default implementation of **DestructElements** does nothing.

In general, overriding **ConstructElements** is necessary whenever the collection stores objects that require a call to a constructor (or other initializing function), or when the objects have members requiring such calls. Overriding **DestructElements** is necessary when an object requires special action, such as the freeing of memory allocated from the heap, when the object is destroyed.

For example, you might override **ConstructElements** for an array of **CPerson** objects as follows:

```
CPerson : public CObject { . . . };
CArray< CPerson, CPerson& > personArray;

void ConstructElements( CPerson* pNewPersons, int nCount )
{
    for ( int i = 0; i < nCount; i++, pNewPersons++ )
    {
        // call CPerson default constructor directly
        new( pNewPersons )CPerson;
    }
}
```

This override iterates through the new **CPerson** objects, calling each object's constructor. The special **new** operator used here constructs a new **CPerson** object in place rather than allocating memory from the heap.

Serializing Elements

The **CArray**, **CList**, and **CMap** classes call **SerializeElements** to store collection elements to or read them from an archive.

The default implementation of the **SerializeElements** helper function does a bitwise write from the objects to the archive, or a bitwise read from the archive to the objects, depending on whether the objects are being stored in or retrieved from the archive. Override **SerializeElements** if this action is not appropriate.

If your collection stores objects derived from **CObject** and you use the **IMPLEMENT_SERIAL** macro in the implementation of the collection element class, you can take advantage of the serialization functionality built into **CArchive** and **CObject**:

```
CPerson : public CObject { . . . };
CArray< CPerson, CPerson& > personArray;

void SerializeElements( CArchive& ar, CPerson* pNewPersons, int nCount )
{
    for ( int i = 0; i < nCount; i++, pNewPersons++ )
    {
        // Serialize each CPerson object
        pNewPersons->Serialize( ar );
    }
}
```

The overloaded insertion operators for **CArchive** call **CObject::Serialize** (or an override of that function) for each **CPerson** object.

Using Nontemplate Collection Classes

MFC also supports the collection classes introduced with MFC version 1.0. These classes are not based on templates. They can be used to contain data of the supported types **CObject***, **UINT**, **DWORD**, and **CString**. You can use these predefined collections (such as **CObList**) to hold collections of any objects derived from **CObject**. MFC also provides other predefined collections to hold primitive types such as **UINT** and void pointers (**void***). In general, however, it is often useful to define your own type-safe collections to hold objects of a more specific class and its derivatives. Note that doing so with the collection classes not based on templates is more work than using the template-based classes.

There are two ways to create type-safe collections with the nontemplate collections:

1. Use the nontemplate collections, with type casting if necessary. This is the easiest approach.

2. Derive from and extend a nontemplate type-safe collection.

▶ **To use the nontemplate collections with type casting.**

- Use one of the nontemplate classes, such as **CWordArray**, directly.

  For example, you can create a **CWordArray** and add any 32-bit values to it, then retrieve them. There is nothing more to do. You just use the predefined functionality.

  You can also use a predefined collection, such as **CObList**, to hold any objects derived from **CObject**. A **CObList** collection is defined to hold pointers to **CObject**. When you retrieve an object from the list, you may have to cast the result to the proper type since the **CObList** functions return pointers to **CObject**. For example, if you store `CPerson` objects in a **CObList** collection, you have to cast a retrieved element to be a pointer to a `CPerson` object. The following example uses a **CObList** collection to hold `CPerson` objects:

```
class CPerson : public CObject {...};

CPerson* p1 = new CPerson(...);
CObList myList;

myList.AddHead( p1 );    // No cast needed
CPerson* p2 = ( CPerson* )myList.GetHead();
```

This technique of using a predefined collection type and casting as necessary may be adequate for many of your collection needs. If you need further functionality or more type safety, use a template-based class, or read the next procedure.

▶ **To derive and extend a nontemplate type-safe collection**

- Derive your own collection class from one of the predefined nontemplate classes.

  When you derive your class, you can add type-safe wrapper functions to provide a type-safe interface to existing functions.

For example, if you derived a list from **CObList** to hold `CPerson` objects, you might add the wrapper functions `AddHeadPerson` and `GetHeadPerson`, as shown below.

```
class CPersonList : public CObList
{
public:
    void AddHeadPerson( CPerson* person )
        {AddHead( person );}

    const CPerson* GetHeadPerson()
        {return (CPerson*)GetHead();}
};
```

These wrapper functions provide a type-safe way to add and retrieve `CPerson` objects from the derived list. You can see that for the `GetHeadPerson` function, you are simply encapsulating the type casting.

You can also add new functionality by defining new functions that extend the capabilities of the collection rather than just wrapping existing functionality in type-safe wrappers. For example, the article Collections: Deleting All Objects in a CObject Collection describes a function to delete all the objects contained in a list. This function could be added to the derived class as a member function.

See Also Collections: Accessing All Members of a Collection, Technical Note 4

Collections: Accessing All Members of a Collection

The MFC array collection classes—both template-based and not—use indexes to access their elements. The MFC list and map collection classes—both template-based and not—use an indicator of type **POSITION** to describe a given position within the collection. To access one or more members of these collections, you first initialize the position indicator and then repeatedly pass that position to the collection and ask it to return the next element. The collection is not responsible for maintaining state information about the progress of the iteration. That information is kept in the position indicator. But, given a particular position, the collection is responsible for returning the next element.

The following procedures show how to iterate over the three main types of collections provided with MFC:

- Iterating an array
- Iterating a list
- Iterating a map

▶ **To iterate an array**

- Use sequential index numbers with the **GetAt** member function:

```
CTypedPtrArray<CObArray, CPerson*> myArray;

for( int i = 0; i < myArray.GetSize();i++ )
{
    CPerson* thePerson = myArray.GetAt( i );
    ...
}
```

This example uses a typed pointer array that contains pointers to CPerson objects. The array is derived from class **CObArray**, one of the nontemplate predefined classes. **GetAt** returns a pointer to a CPerson object. For typed pointer collection classes—arrays or lists—the first parameter specifies the base class; the second parameter specifies the type to store.

The **CTypedPtrArray** class also overloads the [ ] operator so that you can use the customary array-subscript syntax to access elements of an array. An alternative to the statement in the body of the for loop above is

```
CPerson* thePerson = myArray[ i ];
```

This operator exists in both **const** and non-**const** versions. The **const** version, which is invoked for **const** arrays, can appear only on the right side of an assignment statement.

▶ **To iterate a list**

- Use the member functions **GetHeadPosition** and **GetNext** to work your way through the list:

```
CTypedPtrList<CObList, CPerson*> myList;

POSITION pos = myList.GetHeadPosition();
while( pos != NULL )
{
    CPerson* thePerson = myList.GetNext( pos );
    ...
}
```

This example uses a typed pointer list to contain pointers to CPerson objects. The list declaration resembles the one for the array in the procedure "To iterate an array" (above) but is derived from class **CObList**. **GetNext** returns a pointer to a CPerson object.

▶ **To iterate a map**

- Use **GetStartPosition** to get to the beginning of the map and **GetNextAssoc** to repeatedly get the next key and value from the map, as shown by the following example:

```
CMap<CString, LPCTSTR, CPerson*, CPerson*> myMap;

POSITION pos = myMap.GetStartPosition();
```

```
while( pos != NULL )
{
    CPerson* pPerson;
    CString string;
    // Get key ( string ) and value ( pPerson )
    myMap.GetNextAssoc( pos, string, pPerson );
    // Use string and pPerson
}
```

This example uses a simple map template (rather than a typed pointer collection) that uses **CString** keys and stores pointers to CPerson objects. When you use access functions such as **GetNextAssoc**, the class provides pointers to CPerson objects. If you use one of the nontemplate map collections instead, you must cast the returned **CObject** pointer to a pointer to a CPerson.

Note For nontemplate maps, the compiler requires a reference to a **CObject** pointer in the last parameter to **GetNextAssoc**. On input, you must cast your pointers to that type, as shown in the next example.

The template solution is cleaner and provides better type safety. The nontemplate code is more complicated, as you can see here:

```
CMapStringToOb myMap;    // A nontemplate collection class

POSITION pos = myMap.GetStartPosition( );
while( pos != NULL )
{
    CPerson* pPerson;
    CString string;
    // Gets key (string) and value (pPerson)
    myMap.GetNextAssoc( pos, string,
                        (CObject*&)pPerson );
    ASSERT( pPerson->IsKindOf(
                RUNTIME_CLASS( CPerson ) ) );
    // Use string and pPerson
}
```

See Also Collections: Deleting All Objects in a CObject Collection

Collections: Deleting All Objects in a CObject Collection

This article explains how to delete all objects in a collection (without deleting the collection object itself).

To delete all the objects in a collection of **CObject**s (or of objects derived from **CObject**), you use one of the iteration techniques described in the article Collections: Accessing All Members of a Collection to delete each object in turn.

Caution Objects in collections can be shared. That is, the collection keeps a pointer to the object, but other parts of the program may also have pointers to the same object. You must be careful not to delete an object that is shared until all the parts have finished using the object.

This article shows you how to delete the objects in:

- A list
- An array
- A map

▶ **To delete all objects in a list of pointers to CObject**

1 Use **GetHeadPosition** and **GetNext** to iterate through the list.

2 Use the **delete** operator to delete each object as it is encountered in the iteration.

3 Call the **RemoveAll** function to remove all elements from the list after the objects associated with those elements have been deleted.

The preceding technique deletes all objects in a list.

The following example shows how to delete all objects from a list of CPerson objects. Each object in the list is a pointer to a CPerson object that was originally allocated on the heap.

```
CTypedPtrList<CObList, CPerson*> myList;
POSITION pos = myList.GetHeadPosition();

while( pos != NULL )
{
    delete myList.GetNext( pos );
}
myList.RemoveAll();
```

The last function call, **RemoveAll**, is a list member function that removes all elements from the list. The member function **RemoveAt** removes a single element.

Notice the difference between deleting an element's object and removing the element itself. Removing an element from the list merely removes the list's reference to the object. The object still exists in memory. When you delete an object, it ceases to exist and its memory is reclaimed. Thus, it is important to remove an element immediately after the element's object has been deleted so that the list won't try to access objects that no longer exist.

▶ **To delete all elements in an array**

1 Use **GetSize** and integer index values to iterate through the array.

2 Use the **delete** operator to delete each element as it is encountered in the iteration.

3 Call the **RemoveAll** function to remove all elements from the array after they have been deleted.

The code for deleting all elements of an array is as follows:

```
CArray<CPerson*, CPerson*> myArray;

int i = 0;
while (i < myArray.GetSize() )
{
    delete myArray.GetAt( i++ );
}

myArray.RemoveAll();
```

Like the list example above, you can call **RemoveAll** to remove all elements in an array or **RemoveAt** to remove an individual element.

► **To delete all elements in a map**

1 Use **GetStartPosition** and **GetNextAssoc** to iterate through the array.

2 Use the **delete** operator to delete the key and/or value for each map element as it is encountered in the iteration.

3 Call the **RemoveAll** function to remove all elements from the map after they have been deleted.

The code for deleting all elements of a **CMap** collection is as follows. Each element in the map has a string as the key and a CPerson object (derived from **CObject**) as the value.

```
CMap<CString, LPCSTR, CPerson*, CPerson*> myMap;
// ... Add some key-value elements ...
// Now delete the elements
POSITION pos = myMap.GetStartPosition();
while( pos != NULL )
{
    CPerson* pPerson;
    CString string;
    // Gets key (string) and value (pPerson)
    myMap.GetNextAssoc( pos, string, pPerson );
    delete pPerson;
}
// RemoveAll deletes the keys
myMap.RemoveAll();
```

You can call **RemoveAll** to remove all elements in a map or **RemoveKey** to remove an individual element with the specified key.

See Also   Collections: Creating Stack and Queue Collections

Collections: Creating Stack and Queue Collections

This article explains how to create other data structures, such as stacks and queues, from MFC list classes. The examples use classes derived from **CList**, but you can use **CList** directly unless you need to add functionality.

Stacks

Because the standard list collection has both a head and a tail, it is easy to create a derived list collection that mimics the behavior of a last-in-first-out stack. A stack is like a stack of trays in a cafeteria. As trays are added to the stack, they go on top of the stack. The last tray added is the first to be removed. The list collection member functions **AddHead** and **RemoveHead** can be used to add and remove elements specifically from the head of the list; thus the most recently added element is the first to be removed.

▶ To create a stack collection

- Derive a new list class from one of the existing MFC list classes and add more member functions to support the functionality of stack operations.

  The following example shows how to add member functions to push elements on to the stack, peek at the top element of the stack, and pop the top element from the stack:

```
class CTray : public CObject { ... };

class CStack : public CTypedPtrList< CObList, CTray* >
{
public:
    // Add element to top of stack
    void Push( CTray* newTray )
        { AddHead( newTray ); }

    // Peek at top element of stack
    CTray* Peek()
        { return IsEmpty() ? NULL : GetHead(); }

    // Pop top element off stack
    CTray* Pop()
        { return RemoveHead(); }
};
```

Note that this approach exposes the underlying **CObList** class. The user can call any **CObList** member function, whether it makes sense for a stack or not.

Queues

Because the standard list collection has both a head and a tail, it is also easy to create a derived list collection that mimics the behavior of a first-in-first-out queue. A queue is like a line of people in a cafeteria. The first person in line is the first to be served.

As more people come, they go to the end of the line to wait their turn. The list collection member functions **AddTail** and **RemoveHead** can be used to add and remove elements specifically from the head or tail of the list; thus the most recently added element is always the last to be removed.

▶ **To create a queue collection**

• Derive a new list class from one of the predefined list classes provided with the MFC Library and add more member functions to support the semantics of queue operations.

The following example shows how you can append member functions to add an element to the end of the queue and get the element from the front of the queue.

```
class CPerson : public CObject { ... };

class CQueue : public CTypedPtrList< CObList, CPerson* >
{
public:
    // Go to the end of the line
    void AddToEnd( CPerson* newPerson )
        { AddTail( newPerson ); }           // End of the queue

    // Get first element in line
    CPerson* GetFromFront()
        { return IsEmpty() ? NULL : RemoveHead(); }
};
```

Column

A column is a field in a table. For example, the first field in all the records in a table constitutes a vertical column in the table.

If you're using the MFC ODBC classes, see the article Recordset (ODBC). If you're using the MFC DAO classes, see the article DAO Workspace: Managing Transactions.

Commit

Completing an update to the data source.

If you're using the MFC ODBC classes, see the article Transaction (ODBC). If you're using the MFC DAO classes, see the article DAO Workspace: Managing Transactions.

COMMON.RES Sample Resources

Visual C++ includes sample resources that you can use in your own application. These include:

- A large number of icons that represent common business and data-processing tasks.
- Several commonly used cursors that are not included as predefined Windows resources.
- A selection of toolbar-button bitmaps.

These resources are located in a file called COMMON.RES in the MFC General sample CLIPART on the Visual C++ CD-ROM. Additional sample resources can be found in this directory.

▶ **To copy resources from COMMON.RES to your own resource script file**

1 Use the Visual C++ File menu to open both your .RC file and COMMON.RES at the same time.

2 Hold down the CTRL key and drag the resources you want from the COMMON.RES resource browser window to the resource browser window of your own application.

For more information about browsing and editing resources with Visual C++, see Chapter 5, Working with Resources, in the *Visual C++ User's Guide*.

Connection Points

This article explains how to implement OLE connection points using **CCmdTarget** and **CConnectionPoint**.

In the past, OLE's Component Object Model (COM) defined a general mechanism (**IUnknown::QueryInterface**) that allowed objects to implement and expose functionality in interfaces. However, a corresponding mechanism that allowed objects to expose their capability to call specific interfaces was not defined. That is, COM defined how incoming pointers to objects (pointers to that object's interfaces) were handled, but it did not have an explicit model for outgoing interfaces (pointers the object holds to other objects' interfaces). COM now has a model, called "connection points," that supports this functionality.

A connection has two parts: the object calling the interface, called the "source," and the object implementing the interface, called the "sink." A connection point is the interface exposed by the source. By exposing a connection point, a source allows sinks to establish connections to itself (the source). Through the connection point mechanism (the **IConnectionPoint** interface), a pointer to the sink interface is passed to the source object. This pointer provides the source with access to the sink's implementation of a set of member functions. For example, to fire an event implemented by the sink, the source can call the appropriate method of the sink's implementation. Figure 1 demonstrates the connection point just described.

Figure 1 An Implemented Connection Point

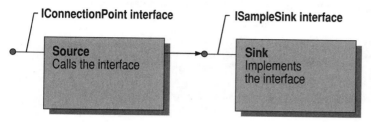

MFC implements this model in the **CConnectionPoint** and **CCmdTarget** classes. Classes derived from **CConnectionPoint** implement the **IConnectionPoint** interface, used to expose connection points to other OLE objects. Classes derived from **CCmdTarget** implement the **IConnectionPointContainer** interface, which can enumerate all of an object's available connection points or find a specific connection point.

For each connection point implemented in your class, you must declare a "connection part" that implements the connection point. If you implement one or more connection points, you must also declare a single "connection map" in your class. A connection map is a table of connection points supported by the OLE control.

The following examples demonstrate a simple connection map and one connection point. The first example declares the connection map and point; the second example implements the map and point. Note that CMyClass must be a **CCmdTarget**-derived class. In the first example, code is inserted in the class declaration, under the **protected** section:

```
class CMyClass : public CCmdTarget
{
 ...
 protected:
// Connection point for ISample interface
    BEGIN_CONNECTION_PART(CMyClass, SampleConnPt)
        CONNECTION_IID(IID_ISampleSink)
    END_CONNECTION_PART(SampleConnPt)

    DECLARE_CONNECTION_MAP()

};
```

The **BEGIN_CONNECTION_PART** and **END_CONNECTION_PART** macros declare an embedded class, XSampleConnPt (derived from **CConnectionPoint**) that implements this particular connection point. If you want to override any

CConnectionPoint member functions or add member functions of your own, declare them between these two macros. For example, the **CONNECTION_IID** macro overrides the **CConnectionPoint::GetIID** member function when placed between these two macros.

In the second example, code is inserted in the control's implementation file (.CPP). This code implements the connection map, which includes the connection point, `SampleConnPt`:

```
BEGIN_CONNECTION_MAP(CMyClass, CMyBaseClass)
    CONNECTION_PART(CMyClass, IID_ISampleSink, SampleConnPt)
END_CONNECTION_MAP()
```

If your class has more than one connection point, insert additional **CONNECTION_PART** macros between the **BEGIN_CONNECTION_MAP** and **END_CONNECTION_MAP** macros.

Finally, add a call to **EnableConnections** in the class's constructor. For example:

```
CMyClass::CMyClass()
{
EnableConnections();
...
}
```

Once this code has been inserted, your **CCmdTarget**-derived class exposes a connection point for the **ISampleSink** interface. Figure 2 illustrates this example.

Figure 2   A Connection Point Implemented with MFC

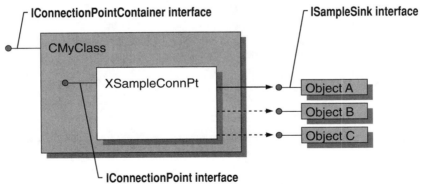

CMyClass is derived from CCmdTarget.
XSampleConnPt is derived from CConnectionPoint.

Usually, connection points support "multicasting"–the ability to broadcast to multiple sinks connected to the same interface. The following example fragment demonstrates how to multicast by iterating through each sink on a connection point:

```
void CMyClass::CallSinkFunc()
{
    const CPtrArray* pConnections = m_xSampleConnPt.GetConnections();
    ASSERT(pConnections != NULL);

    int cConnections = pConnections->GetSize();
    ISampleSink* pSampleSink;
    for (int i = 0; i < cConnections; i++)
    {
        pSampleSink = (ISampleSink*)(pConnections->GetAt(i));
        ASSERT(pSampleSink != NULL);
        pSampleSink->SinkFunc();
    }
}
```

This example retrieves the current set of connections on the SampleConnPt connection point with a call to **CConnectionPoint::GetConnections**. It then iterates through the connections and calls **ISampleSink::SinkFunc** on every active connection.

Connect String

A string containing the necessary information to connect to an Open Database Connectivity (ODBC) data source. Connect strings are used with ODBC data sources whether you are working with MFC's ODBC classes, including **CDatabase**, or with MFC's Data Access Object (DAO) classes, including **CDaoDatabase**.

See **CDaoDatabase::Open**, **CDatabase::Open**, and **CRecordset::GetDefaultConnect** in the *Class Library Reference*.

Containers

A "container application" is an application that can incorporate embedded or linked items into its own documents. The documents managed by a container application must be able to store and display OLE document components as well as data created by the application itself. A container application must also allow users to insert new items or edit existing items. Chapters 13 through 15 in *Tutorials* take you through the process of creating a container application. You should complete that tutorial before reading this family of articles.

The following articles detail various issues you must address when writing container applications:

- Containers: Implementing a Container
- Containers: Client Items
- Containers: Compound Files

- Containers: User-Interface Issues
- Containers: Advanced Features

See Also Servers, Activation, Menus and Resources

Containers: Implementing a Container

Chapters 13 through 15 in *Tutorials* describe the implementation of a simple visual editing container, CONTAINER, explaining each step in detail. This article summarizes the tutorial procedure and points you to other articles that provide more detailed explanations of the various facets of implementing containers. It also lists some optional OLE features you may want to implement and the articles describing these features.

▶ **To prepare your CWinApp-derived class**

1 Initialize the OLE libraries by calling **AfxOleInit** in the **InitInstance** member function.

2 Call **CDocTemplate::SetContainerInfo** in **InitInstance** to assign the menu and accelerator resources used when an embedded item is activated in-place. For more information on this topic, see the Activation article.

These features are provided for you automatically when you use AppWizard to create a container application. See the article AppWizard: OLE Support.

▶ **To prepare your view class**

1 Keep track of selected items by maintaining a pointer, or list of pointers if you support multiple selection, to the selected items. Your **OnDraw** function must draw all OLE items.

2 Override **IsSelected** to check whether the item passed to it is currently selected.

3 Implement an **OnInsertObject** message handler to display the Insert Object dialog box.

4 Implement an **OnSetFocus** message handler to transfer focus from the view to an in-place active OLE embedded item.

5 Implement an **OnSize** message handler to inform an OLE embedded item that it needs to change its rectangle to reflect the change in size of its containing view.

Because the implementation of these features varies dramatically from one application to the next, AppWizard provides only a basic implementation. You will likely have to customize these functions to get your application to function properly. For a more detailed explanation and an example of this, see Chapter 15 of *Tutorials* and the MFC Tutorial sample CONTAINER. For information about MFC samples, see MFC Samples under Samples in Books Online.

▶ **To handle embedded and linked items**

1 Derive a class from **COleClientItem**. Objects of this class represent items that have been embedded in or linked to your OLE document.

2 Override **OnChange**, **OnChangeItemPosition**, and **OnGetItemPosition**. These functions handle sizing, positioning, and modifying embedded and linked items.

AppWizard will derive the class for you, but you will likely need to override **OnChange** and the other functions listed with it in step 2 in the preceding procedure. The skeleton implementations need to be customized for most applications, because these functions are implemented differently from one application to the next. For more information about this, see step 2 of the CONTAINER tutorial in *Tutorials* and the MFC OLE sample DRAWCLI. For information about MFC samples, see Samples in Books Online.

You must add a number of items to the container application's menu structure to support OLE. For more information on these, see the article Menus and Resources: Container Additions.

You may also want to support some of the following features in your container application:

- In-place activation when editing an embedded item.

  For more information, see the article Activation.

- Creation of OLE items by dragging and dropping a selection from a server application.

  For more information, see the article Drag and Drop.

- Links to embedded objects or combination container/server applications.

  For more information, see the article Containers: Advanced Features.

See Also Containers: Client Items

Containers: Client Items

This article explains what client items are and from what classes your application should derive its client items.

"Client items" are data items belonging to another application that are either contained in or referenced by a container application's document. Client items whose data is contained within the document are "embedded;" those whose data is stored in another location referenced by the container document are "linked."

The document class in an OLE application is derived from the class **COleDocument** rather than **CDocument**. The **COleDocument** class inherits from **CDocument** all of the functionality necessary for using the document/view architecture on which MFC applications are based. **COleDocument** also defines an interface that treats a document as a collection of **CDocItem** objects. Several **COleDocument** member functions are provided for adding, retrieving, and deleting elements of that collection.

Every container application should derive at least one class from **COleClientItem**. Objects of this class represent items, embedded or linked, in the OLE document. These objects exist for the life of the document containing them, unless they are deleted from the document.

CDocItem is the base class for **COleClientItem** and **COleServerItem**. Objects of classes derived from these two act as intermediaries between the OLE item and the client and server applications, respectively. Each time a new OLE item is added to the document, the framework adds a new object of your client application's **COleClientItem**-derived class to the document's collection of **CDocItem** objects.

See Also Containers: Compound Files, Containers: User-Interface Issues, Containers: Advanced Features

In the *Class Library Reference*: **COleClientItem**, **COleServerItem**

Containers: Client-Item Notifications

This article discusses the overridable functions that the framework calls when server applications modify items in your client application's document.

COleClientItem defines several overridable functions that are called in response to requests from the component application, which is also called the "server application." These overridables usually act as notifications. They inform the container application of various events, such as scrolling, activation, or a change of position, and of changes that the user makes when editing or otherwise manipulating the item.

The framework notifies your container application of changes through a call to **COleClientItem::OnChange**, an overridable function whose implementation is required. This protected function receives two arguments. The first specifies the reason the server changed the item:

Notification	Meaning
OLE_CHANGED	The OLE item's appearance has changed.
OLE_SAVED	The OLE item has been saved.
OLE_CLOSED	The OLE item has been closed.
OLE_RENAMED	The server document containing the OLE item has been renamed.
OLE_CHANGED_STATE	The OLE item has changed from one state to another.
OLE_CHANGED_ASPECT	The OLE item's draw aspect has been changed by the framework.

These values are from the **OLE_NOTIFICATION** enumeration, which is defined in AFXOLE.H.

The second argument to this function specifies how the item has changed or what state it has entered:

When first argument is	Second argument
OLE_SAVED or **OLE_CLOSED**	Is not used.
OLE_CHANGED	Specifies the aspect of the OLE item that has changed.
OLE_CHANGED_STATE	Describes the state being entered (**emptyState**, **loadedState**, **openState**, **activeState**, or **activeUIState**).

For further information about the states a client item can assume, see the article Containers: Client-Item States.

The framework calls **COleClientItem::OnGetItemPosition** when an item is being activated for in-place editing. Implementation is required for applications that support in-place editing. AppWizard provides a basic implementation, which assigns the item's coordinates to the **CRect** object that is passed as an argument to **OnGetItemPosition**.

If an OLE item's position or size changes during in-place editing, the container's information about the item's position and clipping rectangles must be updated and the server must receive information about the changes. The framework calls **COleClientItem::OnChangeItemPosition** for this purpose. AppWizard provides an override that calls the base class's function. You should edit the function AppWizard writes for your **COleClientItem**-derived class so that the function updates any information retained by your client-item object.

See Also   Containers: Client-Item States

In the *Class Library Reference*: **COleClientItem::OnChangeItemPosition**

Containers: Client-Item States

This article explains the different states a client item passes through in its lifetime.

A client item passes through several states as it is created, activated, modified, and saved. Each time the item's state changes, the framework calls **COleClientItem::OnChange** with the **OLE_CHANGED_STATE** notification. The second parameter is a value from the **COleClientItem::ItemState** enumeration. It can be one of the following:

- **COleClientItem::emptyState**
- **COleClientItem::loadedState**
- **COleClientItem::openState**
- **COleClientItem::activeState**
- **COleClientItem::activeUIState**

In the "empty" state, a client item is not yet completely an item. Memory has been allocated for it, but it has not yet been initialized with the OLE item's data. This is the state a client item is in when it has been created through a call to **new** but has not yet undergone the second step of the typical two-step creation.

In the second step, performed through a call to **COleClientItem::CreateFromFile** or another **CreateFrom***xxxx* function, the item is completely created. The OLE data (from a file or some other source, such as the Clipboard) has been associated with the **COleClientItem**-derived object. Now the item is in the "loaded" state.

When an item has been opened in the server's window rather than opened in place in the container's document, it is in the "open" (or "fully open") state. In this state, a cross-hatch usually is drawn over the representation of the item in the container's window to indicate that the item is active elsewhere.

When an item has been activated in place, it passes, usually only briefly, through the "active" state. It then enters the "UI active" state, in which the server has merged its menus, toolbars, and other user-interface components with those of the container. The presence of these user-interface components distinguishes the UI active state from the active state. Otherwise, the active state resembles the UI active state. If the server supports Undo, the server is required to retain the OLE item's undo-state information until it reaches the loaded or open state.

See Also   Activation, Containers: Client-Item Notifications, Trackers

In the *Class Library Reference*: **CRectTracker**

Containers: Compound Files

This article explains the components and implementation of compound files and the advantages and disadvantages of using compound files in your OLE applications.

Compound files are an integral part of OLE. They are used to facilitate data transfer and OLE document storage. Compound files are an implementation of the structured storage model. Consistent interfaces exist that support serialization to a "storage," a "stream," or a file object. Compound files are supported in the Microsoft Foundation Class Library by the classes **COleStreamFile** and **COleDocument**.

Note   Using a compound file does not imply that the information comes from an OLE document or a compound document. Compound files are just one of the ways to store compound documents, OLE documents, and other data.

Components of a Compound File

OLE's implementation of compound files uses three object types: stream objects, storage objects, and **ILockBytes** objects. These objects are similar to the components of a standard file system in the following manner:

- Stream objects, like files, store data of any type.

- Storage objects, like directories, can contain other storage and stream objects.

- **LockBytes** objects represent the interface between the storage objects and the physical hardware. They determine how the actual bytes are written to whatever storage device the **LockBytes** object is accessing, such as a hard drive or an area of global memory. For more information about **LockBytes** objects and the **ILockBytes** OLE interface, see Chapter 6 in the *OLE 2 Programmer's Reference, Volume 1.*

Advantages and Disadvantages of Compound Files

Compound files provide benefits not available with earlier methods of file storage. They include:

- Incremental file accessing

- File access modes

- Standardization of file structure

The potential disadvantages of compound files—large size and performance issues relating to storage on floppy disks—should be considered when deciding whether to use them in your application.

Incremental Access to Files

Incremental access to files is an automatic benefit of using compound files. Because a compound file can be viewed as a "file system within a file," individual object types, such as stream or storage, can be accessed without the need to load the entire file. This can drastically decrease the time an application needs to access new objects for editing by the user. Incremental updating, based on the same concept, offers similar benefits. Instead of saving the entire file just to save the changes made to one object, OLE saves only the stream or storage object edited by the user.

File Access Modes

Being able to determine when changes to objects in a compound file are committed to disk is another benefit of using compound files. The mode in which files are accessed, either transacted or direct, determines when changes are committed.

- Transacted mode uses a two-phase commit operation to make changes to objects in a compound file, thereby keeping both the old and the new copies of the document available until the user chooses to either save or undo the changes.

- Direct mode incorporates changes to the document as they are made, without the ability to later undo them.

For more information on access modes, see the *OLE 2 Programmer's Reference, Volume 1.*

Standardization

The standardized structure of compound files allows different OLE applications to browse through compound files created by your OLE application with no knowledge of the application that actually created the file.

Size and Performance Considerations

Due to the complexity of the compound file storage structure and the ability to save data incrementally, files using this format tend to be larger than other files using unstructured or "flat file" storage. If your application frequently loads and saves files, using compound files can cause the file size to increase much more quickly. Because compound files can get large, the access time for files stored on and loaded from floppy disks can also be affected, resulting in slower access to files.

Another issue that affects performance is compound-file fragmentation. The size of a compound file is determined by the difference between the first and last disk sectors used by the file. A fragmented file can contain many areas of free space that do not contain data, but are counted when calculating the size. During the lifetime of a compound file, these areas are created by the insertion or deletion of storage objects.

Using Compound Files Format for Your Data

After creating an application that has a **COleDocument**-derived document class, ensure that your main document constructor calls **EnableCompoundFile**. When AppWizard creates OLE container applications, it inserts this call.

See Also Containers: User-Interface Issues

In the *Class Library Reference*: **COleStreamFile**, **COleDocument**

In the *OLE 2 Programmer's Reference, Volume 1*: **IStream**, **IStorage**, **ILockBytes**

Containers: User-Interface Issues

You must add a number of features to a container application's user interface to adequately manage linked and embedded items. These features involve changes to the menu structure and to the events that the application handles. For detailed information about them, see the following articles:

For information on	See
Menu additions for containers	Menus and Resources: Container Additions
Additional resources for containers	Menus and Resources: Container Additions
Painting linked or embedded items	*Tutorials*, Container Tutorial, Chapter 13
New dialog boxes for containers	Dialog Boxes in OLE

See Also Containers: Advanced Features, Menus and Resources

Containers: Advanced Features

This article describes the steps necessary to incorporate optional advanced features into existing container applications. These features are:

- An application that is both a container and a server
- An OLE link to an embedded object

Creating a Container/Server Application

A container/server application is an application that acts as both a container and a server. Microsoft Word for Windows is an example of this. You can embed Word for Windows documents in other applications, and you can also embed items in Word for Windows documents. The process for modifying your container application to be both a container and a full-server (you can't create a combination container/mini-server application) is similar to the process for creating a full-server.

The article Servers: Implementing a Server lists a number of tasks required to implement a server application. If you convert a container application to a container/server application, you'll need to perform some of those same tasks, adding code to the container. The following lists the important things to consider:

- The container code created by AppWizard already initializes the OLE subsystem. You won't need to change or add anything for that support.

- Wherever the base class of a document class is **COleDocument**, change the base class to **COleServerDoc**.

- Override **COleClientItem::CanActivate** to avoid editing items in place while the server itself is being used to edit in place.

  For example: the MFC OLE sample OCLIENT has embedded an item created by your container/server application. You open the OCLIENT application and in-place edit the item created by your container/server application. While editing your application's item, you decide you want to embed an item created by the MFC OLE sample HIERSVR. To do this, you cannot use in-place activation. You must fully open HIERSVR to activate this item. Because the Microsoft Foundation Class Library does not support this OLE feature, overriding **COleClientItem::CanActivate** allows you to check for this situation and prevent a possible run-time error in your application.

If you are creating a new application and want it to function as a container/server application, choose that option in the OLE Options dialog box in AppWizard and this support will be created automatically. For more information, see the article AppWizard: Creating an OLE Visual Editing Application. For information about MFC samples, see Samples in Books Online.

Links to Embedded Objects

The Links to Embedded Objects feature enables a user to create a document with an OLE link to an embedded object inside your container application. For example, create a document in a word processor containing an embedded spreadsheet. If your application supports links to embedded objects, it could paste a link to the spreadsheet contained in the word processor's document. This feature allows your application to use the information contained in the spreadsheet without knowing where the word processor originally got it.

▶ **To link to embedded objects in your application**

1 Derive your document class from **COleLinkingDoc** instead of **COleDocument**.

2 Create an OLE class ID (**CLSID**) for your application by using the Class ID Generator included with the OLE Development Tools.

3 Register the application with OLE.

4 Create a **COleTemplateServer** object as a member of your application class.

5 In your application class's **InitInstance** member function, do the following:

- Connect your **COleTemplateServer** object to your document templates by calling the object's **ConnectTemplate** member function.

- Call the **COleTemplateServer::RegisterAll** member function to register all class objects with the OLE system.

- Call **COleTemplateServer::UpdateRegistry**. The only parameter to **UpdateRegistry** should be **OAT_CONTAINER** if the application is not launched with the "/Embedded" switch. This registers the application as a container that can support links to embedded objects.

  If the application is launched with the "/Embedded" switch, it should not show its main window, similar to a server application.

The MFC OLE sample OCLIENT implements this feature. For an example of how this is done, see the **InitInstance** function in the OCLIENT.CPP file of this sample application.

See Also   Servers

Current Record

The current record is the record currently stored in the field data members of a recordset.

If you're using the MFC ODBC classes, see the article Recordset (ODBC). If you're using the MFC DAO classes, see the article DAO Recordset.

DAO and MFC

This article describes MFC's implementation of Microsoft Data Access Objects (DAO). Topics covered include:

- How MFC Encapsulates DAO
- Mapping of DAO objects to MFC classes
- Key differences between MFC and DAO
- Further reading about the MFC DAO classes

Note Whether you use the MFC DAO classes or the MFC ODBC classes depends on your situation and your needs. For a discussion of the differences between the two and guidance on choosing one, see the article Database Overview.

How MFC Encapsulates DAO

The MFC DAO classes treat DAO much as the MFC classes for programming Windows treat the Windows API: MFC encapsulates, or "wraps," DAO functionality in a number of classes that correspond closely to DAO objects. Class **CDaoWorkspace** encapsulates the DAO workspace object, class **CDaoRecordset** encapsulates the DAO recordset object, class **CDaoDatabase** encapsulates the DAO database object, and so on.

MFC's encapsulation of DAO is thorough, but it is not completely one-for-one. Most major DAO objects do correspond to an MFC class, and the classes supply generally thorough access to the underlying DAO object's properties and methods. But some DAO objects, including fields, indexes, parameters, and relations, do not. Instead, the appropriate MFC class provides an interface, via member functions, through which you can access, for example:

- The fields of a recordset object
- The indexes or fields of a table
- The parameters of a querydef
- The relations defined between tables in a database

Mapping of DAO Objects to MFC Classes

The following tables show how DAO objects correspond to MFC objects. Table 1 shows the MFC classes and the DAO objects they encapsulate. Table 2 shows how MFC deals with DAO objects that do not map directly to an MFC class.

Table 1   MFC Classes and Corresponding DAO Objects

Class	DAO object	Remarks
CDaoWorkspace	Workspace	Manages a transaction space and provides access to the database engine.
CDaoDatabase	Database	Represents a connection to a database.
CDaoTableDef	Tabledef	Used to examine and manipulate the structure of a table.
CDaoQueryDef	Querydef	Used to store queries in a database. You can create recordsets from a querydef or use it to execute action or SQL pass-through queries.
CDaoRecordset	Recordset	Used to manage a result set, a set of records based on a table or selected by a query.
CDaoException	Error	MFC responds to all DAO errors by throwing exceptions of this type.
CDaoFieldExchange	None	Manages exchange of data between a record in the database and the field data members of a recordset.

Table 2   How MFC Manages DAO Objects Not Mapped to Classes

DAO object	How MFC manages it
Field	Objects of classes **CDaoTableDef** and **CDaoRecordset** encapsulate fields and supply member functions for adding them, deleting them, and examining them.
Index	Objects of classes **CDaoTableDef** and **CDaoRecordset** encapsulate indexes and supply member functions for managing them. Tabledefs can add, delete, and examine indexes. Tabledefs and recordsets can set or get the currently active index.
Parameter	Objects of class **CDaoQueryDef** encapsulate parameters and supply member functions for adding them, deleting them, examining them, and getting and setting their values.
Relation	Objects of class **CDaoDatabase** encapsulate relations and supply member functions for adding them, deleting them, and examining them.

DAO Objects Not Exposed in MFC

MFC and DAO do not supply abstractions for some objects used within Microsoft Access: Application, Container, Control, Debug, Document, Form, Module, Report, Screen, and Section. If you create a Microsoft Access database and manipulate it from an MFC application, you can't access those objects through code.

MFC doesn't supply classes or interfaces to the DAO group and user objects — to work with DAO security, you must write your own code.

MFC also doesn't encapsulate DAO property objects, except that the MFC DAO classes do give you access to the properties of all exposed objects.

MFC does give you access to DAO's DBEngine object, through class **CDaoWorkspace**.

Accessing the Unexposed DAO Objects

The unexposed objects listed above can be accessed in two ways:

Outside the MFC classes by using the non-MFC C++ classes provided in the DAO SDK. The SDK is located in the DAOSDK directory on the Visual C++ CD-ROM.

Inside the MFC classes by calling DAO directly through a DAO interface pointer supplied by one of the MFC classes. For information, see Technical Note 54. Technical notes are available under MFC Technical Notes, under MFC in Books Online.

Key Differences Between MFC and DAO

MFC's version of data access objects differs from the underlying structure of DAO in some ways.

How MFC Accesses the Database Engine

DAO has a DBEngine object that represents the Microsoft Jet database engine. The DBEngine object provides properties and methods you can use to configure the database engine.

In MFC, there is no DBEngine object. Access to important properties of the database engine is supplied via class **CDaoWorkspace**. To set or get these properties, call any of the static member functions of **CDaoWorkspace**. For more information, see the articles DAO Workspace: The Database Engine and DAO Workspace: Accessing Properties of the Database Engine.

MFC Flattening of the DAO Object Hierarchy

Because MFC doesn't supply a class for every DAO object, the effect is that the DAO object hierarchy is somewhat "flattened" in MFC. The main examples of this flattening are:

- Putting access to the database engine in class **CDaoWorkspace** rather than in a database engine class.

- Encapsulating DAO field, index, parameter, and relation objects inside the classes that represent their owning objects. For example, access to fields is encapsulated in classes **CDaoTableDef** and **CDaoRecordset**. For information, see Table 2, How MFC Manages DAO Objects Not Mapped to Classes.

MFC and DAO Security

MFC does not encapsulate the DAO user and group objects in any way, which means that MFC doesn't provide DAO's security functionality.

You can still use DAO security from your MFC applications, but you will have to call DAO directly, using the **m_pDAOWorkspace** data member of class **CDaoWorkspace**. That member is a pointer to an OLE interface that gives access to a DAO workspace object's methods and properties. For information about calling

DAO directly, see Technical Note 54. Technical notes are available under MFC Technical Notes, under MFC in Books Online.

Tip The DAO Software Development Kit (SDK) supplies its own set of C++ classes (not compatible with MFC) for working with DAO. You can use these classes, if you wish, by installing the DAO SDK from the \DAOSDK directory on your Visual C++ CD-ROM. These classes are also an additional source of examples for using DAO from C++.

MFC does allow password protection via various MFC classes. For example, when you create a **CDaoWorkspace** object, you can specify a password to protect the database(s) that the workspace contains. To use this functionality, a SYSTEM.MDA file must be available to the database engine on the machine running your application. If no SYSTEM.MDA file is available to the database engine, your application cannot use any of the security features. For information about the SYSTEM.MDA file, see the topic Permissions Property in DAO Help.

Further Reading About the MFC DAO Classes

To learn more about using the MFC DAO classes, see the following articles (in the order recommended here):

- DAO: Writing a Database Application
- DAO: Database Tasks
- DAO: Creating, Opening, and Closing DAO Objects
- DAO Workspace
- DAO Database
- DAO Database: Using Workspaces and Databases
- DAO Recordset
- DAO Record Field Exchange (DFX)
- DAO Querydef
- DAO Tabledef
- DAO Workspace: Managing Transactions
- DAO Collections
- DAO External: Working with External Data Sources (primarily ODBC)
- DAO Workspace: The Database Engine
- AppWizard: Database Support
- ClassWizard: Database Support
- Exceptions: Database Exceptions
- Record Views

Tip From any of the MFC help topics in this documentation set, you can get to a topic called DAO: Where Is..., which helps you navigate online to the topics that you need. The topic is always available via the See Also button in the topic window.

See Also DAO: Where Is...

Data Access Objects (DAO)

Data Access Objects (DAO) provide a framework for using code to create and manipulate databases. DAO supplies a hierarchical set of objects that use the Microsoft Jet database engine to access data and database structure in:

- Microsoft Jet (.MDB) databases

- ODBC data sources, using an ODBC driver

- Installable ISAM databases, such as dBASE®, Paradox™, Microsoft FoxPro, and Btrieve®, which the database engine can read directly

To begin learning about the DAO technology, see the topic Data Access Objects Overview in DAO Help.

For information about the MFC classes that encapsulate DAO, begin with the articles Database Overview and DAO and MFC.

Tip From any of the MFC help topics in this documentation set, you can get to a topic called DAO: Where Is..., which helps you navigate online to the topics that you need. The topic is always available via the See Also button in the topic window.

See Also DAO: Where Is...

DAO: Where Is...

This article will help you locate topics of interest in the MFC DAO documentation and in the DAO Help topics. The article, which is always available via the See Also button in the topic window, is organized into the following categories:

- DAO Overviews

- DAO Objects

- Information By Topic

- Key DAO Help Topics

Documentation for the MFC DAO classes consists of two components:

- MFC-specific: MFC classes in the *Class Library Reference* and MFC encyclopedia articles in *Programming with MFC*. The articles all begin with the "DAO" prefix.

- DAO-specific: Topics from the DAO Help files shipped with products such as Microsoft Office. These topics have been incorporated into Visual C++ Books

Online, but note that they are oriented toward the Basic programming language. They are included to provide DAO-specific details in areas where MFC neither modifies nor adds to DAO functionality.

DAO Overviews

For overviews and general information about MFC DAO, see:

- Database Overview
- DAO and MFC
- Data Access Objects (DAO)
- DAO: Writing a Database Application
- DAO: Database Tasks

DAO Objects

Table 1   Where to find information about DAO objects

DAO Help topics	MFC class	MFC topics
Database Object	**CDaoDatabase**	DAO Database
Error Object	**CDaoException**	CDaoException
Querydef Object	**CDaoQueryDef**	DAO Querydef
Recordset Object	**CDaoRecordset**	DAO Recordset
Tabledef Object	**CDaoTableDef**	DAO Tabledef
Workspace Object	**CDaoWorkspace**	DAO Workspace

See Also   DAO Database: Using Workspaces and Databases, DAO: Creating, Opening, and Closing DAO Objects, DAO: Accessing Implicit MFC DAO Objects, DAO External: Working with External Data Sources, DAO Queries, DAO Record Field Exchange (DFX), Database Overview, DAO and MFC

Information By Topic

Table 2   Where to look for...

Topic	Location
Action queries	DAO Querydef: Action Queries and SQL Pass-Through Queries
Adding records	DAO Recordset: Recordset Operations
Application design options	DAO: Writing a Database Application
Attaching tables	DAO External: Working with External Data Sources
Buffering records	DAO Record Field Exchange: Double Buffering Records
Calling DAO directly	Database Overview

Table 2   Where to look for... *(cont.)*

Topic	Location
CDao*X*Info structures	DAO Collections: Obtaining Information About DAO Objects
Closing DAO objects	DAO: Creating, Opening, and Closing DAO Objects
Collections in DAO	DAO Collections
Console applications and DAO	DAO: Database Application Design Options
Creating DAO objects	DAO: Creating, Opening, and Closing DAO Objects
DAO objects not mapped to classes	DAO and MFC
DAO vs. ODBC	Chapter 7, Working with Databases Database Overview
Data definition language (DDL)	Database Overview
Database engine (Jet)	DAO Workspace: The Database Engine
Data types	DFX Data Types in DAO Record Field Exchange: Using the DFX Functions
DBMS targets	DAO: Writing a Database Application Database Overview
Default workspace	DAO Workspace: Explicitly Opening the Default Workspace
Definition of DAO	Database Overview
DLLs, DAO in	DAO: Database Application Design Options
Document/view architecture	DAO: Writing a Database Application
Documentation	Database Overview
Double buffering records	DAO Record Field Exchange: Double Buffering Records
Engine initialization	DAO Workspace: The Database Engine
External data sources, list	DAO: Working with External Data Sources
Filtering recordsets	DAO Queries: Filtering and Parameterizing Queries
Finding	DAO Recordset: Recordset Navigation
Forms	Record Views
How MFC encapsulates DAO	DAO and MFC
Installing DAO	Chapter 7, Working with Databases
ISAM databases, list	Database Overview
Jet database engine	DAO Workspace: The Database Engine
Multithreading and DAO	DAO: Database Application Design Options
Navigating in a recordset	DAO Recordset: Recordset Navigation
ODBC data sources	DAO: Working with External Data Sources
ODBC drivers	ODBC Driver List

Table 2   Where to look for... *(cont.)*

Topic	Location
ODBC vs. DAO	Chapter 7, Working with Databases Database Overview
OLE controls, DAO in	DAO: Database Application Design Options
Opening DAO objects	DAO: Creating, Opening, and Closing DAO Objects
Parameterizing queries	DAO Queries: Filtering and Parameterizing Queries
Pass-through queries	DAO Querydef: Action Queries and SQL Pass-Through Queries
Performance	DAO External: Improving Performance with External Data Sources
Programming model	Database Overview
Queries	DAO Queries
Querydefs	DAO Querydef
Record Field Exchange (DFX)	DAO Record Field Exchange (DFX)
Recordsets	DAO Recordset
Scrolling	DAO Recordset: Recordset Navigation
Security	DAO and MFC
Seeking	DAO Recordset: Recordset Navigation
SQL	DAO Queries: SQL for DAO
Tabledefs	DAO Tabledef
Task-oriented topics	DAO: Database Tasks
Transactions	DAO Workspace: Managing Transactions
Updating data	DAO Recordset: Recordset Operations
Views of DAO data	DAO: Writing a Database Application
When to use database classes	Chapter 7, Working with Databases
Workspace, typical scenario	DAO Database: Using Workspaces and Databases
Writing a database application	DAO: Writing a Database Application

See Also   DAO Database: Using Workspaces and Databases, DAO: Creating, Opening, and Closing DAO Objects, DAO: Accessing Implicit MFC DAO Objects, DAO External: Working with External Data Sources, DAO Queries, DAO Record Field Exchange (DFX), Database Overview, DAO and MFC

Key DAO Help Topics

The following topics are part of DAO Help and are not MFC-specific:

- Data Access Object Hierarchy
- Data Access Objects and Collections Reference
- Using Data Access

- Trappable Data Access Errors
- Microsoft Jet Database Engine SQL Data Types
- SQL Reserved Words
- Equivalent ANSI SQL Data Types
- SQL Aggregate Functions

DAO: Writing a Database Application

This family of articles discusses writing database applications with the MFC DAO classes. Other articles focus on various parts of the process; this article looks at using DAO from an application design standpoint.

In This Article

This article considers:

- What is a database application?
- First steps in writing your MFC DAO application
- Data viewing choices
- Documents and views with DAO
- DBMS choices

More Articles on the Process

The following additional articles discuss parts of the design and development process (in recommended reading order):

- DAO: Database Application Design Options
- DAO: Steps in Writing MFC DAO Applications

What Is a Database Application?

Of course, there is no one kind of database application. Such applications range from simple data entry or data viewing applications to complex client/server applications to applications of any sort that happen to use a database rather than disk-based files for input/output. In any case, the MFC DAO classes supply abstractions that you can use to accomplish your goals.

First Steps in Writing Your MFC DAO Application

To begin, you must make two fundamental decisions:

- How do you want to display data in your application: in a form, as a list, some other way, or not at all.
- What database management system(s) (DBMSs) do you intend to target?

Your decisions determine how your application fits into MFC's document/view architecture and how appropriate the DAO classes are for your application. Your answers also help determine the selections you make when you run AppWizard to begin constructing your application.

Data Viewing Choices

MFC supplies varying degrees of support for different viewing choices:

- Displaying one record at a time in a form.

  AppWizard will create a **CDaoRecordView**-derived class for you and connect it to a **CDaoRecordset** based on a table you specify. This makes it easy to create simple form-based applications.

- Displaying multiple records at a time.

  While AppWizard doesn't give any special help for this option, you can fairly easily hook a **CDaoRecordset** up to a **CListView** or **CTreeView**. For examples, see the MFC Database sample DAOVIEW.

- You can also use multiple views of the data simultaneously, either in separate windows or in panes of a splitter window.

Documents and Views with DAO

Do you need the MFC document/view architecture? The simplest architecture for MFC applications is to manage your data within an MFC document object and manage displaying that data separately in a view object. You aren't limited to this structure, though —other options include:

- Using a view object but treating the document as an unused appendage.

  You can make your data structures —mainly your **CDaoDatabase** and **CDaoRecordset** objects —members of your **CView**-derived class rather than of a **CDocument**-derived class. Database applications typically don't need MFC's serialization mechanism, which is the primary feature of **CDocument**.

  A particularly strong argument for using MFC's document/view architecture is the ability to manage multiple views of your data through the document. **CDocument** has an **UpdateAllViews** member function that you can call to synchronize your views as data displayed in them changes. This is as useful in database applications as in any other kind of application.

- Drawing your data directly into the client area of a **CFrameWnd**-derived class.

  You can handle Windows messages in the frame window and thus dispense with the view and the document. If you use a view, you can't just strip the document code from your application, but if you use neither view nor document, you can remove (or ignore) both. In this case, you can store your **CDaoDatabase** and **CDaoRecordset** objects in the frame window class.

- Basing your application on a dialog box.

AppWizard supports this approach, and you can store your **CDaoDatabase** object(s) as members of your **CDialog**-derived class.

For related information, see the articles MFC: Using Database Classes with Documents and Views and MFC: Using Database Classes Without Documents and Views

DBMS Choices

DAO is based on the Microsoft Jet database engine. This means DAO is optimally suited for working with Microsoft Jet (.MDB) databases. DAO also supports accessing external databases, including certain installable ISAM databases (which the database engine can read directly) and ODBC data sources. This means you can write DBMS-independent applications with DAO, targeting any data source that the Microsoft Jet database engine can read directly or for which your users will have the appropriate ODBC driver.

Note, however, that in general it is more efficient, with DAO, to attach ODBC data source tables to a Microsoft Jet database than it is to access the external data source directly. If your application is essentially targeted on an external data source such as Microsoft SQL Server or Oracle, you might want to consider using the MFC ODBC classes instead of DAO.

For related information, see the articles Database Overview and DAO External: Working with External Data Sources.

See Also   DAO: Where Is..., DAO: Database Tasks, DAO: Database Application Design Options, DAO: Steps in Writing MFC DAO Applications, MFC: Using Database Classes with Documents and Views, MFC: Using Database Classes Without Documents and Views.

DAO: Database Application Design Options

This article continues the discussion begun in the article DAO: Writing a Database Application. The article DAO: Steps in Writing MFC DAO Applications completes the discussion. Those articles discuss the decisions you need to make before you run AppWizard and the steps involved in creating your starter application.

Topics covered include:

- Application design examples
- DAO in DLLs, multithreaded applications, and OLE controls

Application Design Examples

This article gives examples to suggest some of the ways you might organize your application. Sample applications mentioned in the list are available under MFC Samples, under Samples in Books Online.

Examples:

- An application that uses a single form to view one record at a time.

  This approach might be suitable for simple data entry or data viewing applications.

  Let AppWizard create the **CDaoRecordView** and **CDaoRecordset** classes for you. Then design the form in the Visual C++ dialog editor.

  In this scenario, a single **CDaoRecordset** object persists for a session, and it uses an implicitly created **CDaoDatabase** object. The recordset, a data member of the **CDaoRecordView** class called **m_pSet**, contains all records in a table or all records returned by a query. The view lets the user scroll through the records one at a time.

  For an example, see Step 1 of the MFC Database sample DAOENROL.

- A similar single-form application that displays one record at a time but also uses a second recordset to fill a list box or combo box.

  Let AppWizard create the **CDaoRecordView** and a **CDaoRecordset** to control which record is currently displayed in the form's general controls.

  Use ClassWizard to create a second **CDaoRecordset** based on the table or query that fills the list or combo box.

  For a view of how this works, see the MFC Database sample ENROLL for the MFC ODBC classes. You'll have to translate some of the code, but the model is the same in DAO, and most of the code is very similar as well.

  Create additional recordsets to fill more list or combo boxes as needed.

- An application based on multiple forms.

  Perhaps the forms appear in separate windows or as panes in a splitter window. Let AppWizard create the first **CDaoRecordView** and **CDaoRecordset**. Then use ClassWizard to add more of each.

- A bulk data processing application, where no view is required.

  In AppWizard, select basic database support, without a view. A dialog-based application might be appropriate for this need.

  Use ClassWizard to create a **CDaoRecordset** class for each end of the migration. Then write code to use one recordset for input and the other for output. Perform any necessary data manipulation between the two recordsets. Note that you can use the MFC DAO classes in console applications. For more information, see DAO in DLLs, Multithreaded Applications, and OLE Controls.

- An application that displays multiple records at a time, perhaps in a **CListView** or a **CTreeView**.

  Use AppWizard to specify the view class on which to base your application-specific view. You can also use multiple views, perhaps displayed as panes of a splitter window.

  For an example, see the MFC Database sample DAOVIEW.

For information about splitter windows, see Chapter 9, Enhancing Views, in *Tutorials*. For information about using multiple views in general, see Multiple Document Types, Views, and Frame Windows in Chapter 3.

DAO in DLLs, Multithreaded Applications, and OLE Controls

This topic discusses the MFC DAO classes with respect to support for using the MFC DAO classes:

- In dynamic link libraries (DLLs)

- In OLE controls

- In multithreaded applications

- In console applications

- In applications built for Unicode or double-byte character systems (DBCS)

You can use the MFC DAO classes in any DLL. This means you can also use the classes in OLE controls.

DAO itself is not multithreaded, so you can't use the MFC DAO classes in multiple threads. Confine your DAO code to a single thread of execution.

Depending on what MFC functionality you call, you should be able to use the MFC DAO classes in console applications as well. Make sure the application uses no graphical user-interface elements. For example, if you're using an ODBC data source and you supply incomplete connection information, ODBC attempts to display a dialog box for the missing information. Avoid this situation in your console applications.

The MFC DAO classes are fully enabled for Unicode and DBCS.

See Also   DAO: Where Is..., DAO: Database Tasks, DAO: Writing a Database Application, DAO: Steps in Writing MFC DAO Applications, MFC: Using Database Classes with Documents and Views, MFC: Using Database Classes Without Documents and Views.

DAO: Steps in Writing MFC DAO Applications

This article continues the discussion begun in the articles DAO: Writing a Database Application and DAO: Database Application Design Options. Those articles describe application design choices. This article explains the steps you take to develop your application.

Once you've made your initial design decisions, follow these general steps:

1. Run AppWizard to create a skeleton application.

On the databases page, select the database options you want. It is at this stage that you specify a **CDaoRecordView** if you want a form-based application.

When you open the Database Options dialog box, select DAO rather than ODBC. The result is an application with the right include directives and libraries for using the DAO classes. The wizard prompts you to specify the name of a Microsoft Jet (.MDB) database.

2. If needed, add a **CDaoDatabase** object for each database your application can open simultaneously.

   If these objects need to persist for long periods, declare them as data members of one of your classes — the document is a good choice — that point to **CDaoDatabase** objects you create on the heap.

   If they are to persist for long, create the objects with the **new** operator, perhaps in your document's **OnNewDocument** member function or in a command-handler function for a menu command.

3. Use your **CDaoDatabase** object(s) to create **CDaoRecordset** objects that represent queries.

   If you prefer to create your recordsets on the fly, you can omit the **CDaoDatabase** object(s). MFC will implicitly create a **CDaoDatabase** object if you don't supply a pointer to one in the recordset's **Open** call.

   You can create your recordsets on the heap, or you can create them as local variables in a function.

See Also   DAO: Where Is..., DAO Recordset, Record Views, DAO: Database Tasks, DAO: Database Application Design Options, MFC: Using Database Classes with Documents and Views, MFC: Using Database Classes Without Documents and Views

DAO: Database Tasks

This article points you to other articles about performing common database tasks. Table 1 lists the tasks and articles.

Table 1   Articles About Common Database Tasks

	For information about...	See...
Applications	Writing a database application	DAO: Writing a Database Application
	Accessing the database engine	DAO Workspace: Accessing Properties of the Database Engine DAO Workspace: The Database Engine
Creating Objects	Creating DAO objects	DAO: Creating, Opening, and Closing DAO Objects

Table 1   Articles About Common Database Tasks *(cont.)*

	For information about...	See...
Opening Objects	Opening DAO objects	DAO: Creating, Opening, and Closing DAO Objects
Closing Objects	Closing DAO objects	DAO: Creating, Opening, and Closing DAO Objects
Collections (DAO)	Accessing collections	DAO Collections
	Obtaining information about objects in collections	DAO: Obtaining Information About DAO Objects
Databases	Creating an .MDB database	DAO Database
	Examining the schema of a database	DAO Tabledef DAO Tabledef: Examining a Database Schema at Run Time
	Working with multiple databases	DAO Workspace
ODBC	Working with ODBC data sources	DAO External: Working with External Data Sources
Queries Recordsets	Selecting records	DAO Queries DAO Recordset DAO Recordset: Creating Recordsets DAO Queries: Filtering and Parameterizing Queries
	Binding records dynamically	DAO Recordset: Binding Records Dynamically
	Updating records	DAO Recordset: Recordset Operations
	Defining stored queries	DAO Querydef
	Navigating in a recordset	DAO Recordset: Recordset Navigation
Record Field Exchange	Using DFX to exchange data between the database and a recordset's field data members	DAO Record Field Exchange (DFX)
	Moving data between a recordset and the controls on a form	Dialog Data Exchange and Validation
SQL	Using SQL with DAO	DAO Queries: SQL for DAO
Tables	Adding or deleting a table	DAO Tabledef: Using Tabledefs
	Adding or deleting a table field	DAO Tabledef: Using Tabledefs
	Adding or deleting a table index	DAO Tabledef: Using Tabledefs
Transactions	Managing database transactions	DAO Workspace: Managing Transactions DAO Workspace: Opening a Separate Transaction Space

See Also DAO: Where Is...

DAO: Creating, Opening, and Closing DAO Objects

This family of articles explains what it means to "open" or "create" an MFC DAO object and what it means to "close" the object when you finish with it.

This article discusses how MFC objects are constructed and points to related general articles. The following additional articles discuss the Create, Open, and Close actions:

- DAO: Creating DAO Objects
- DAO: Opening DAO Objects
- DAO: Closing DAO Objects

Two-Stage Construction of MFC DAO Objects

As with most MFC objects, you use a two-stage process to create the MFC object and put it into an open state.

Creating a New Object

▶ **To create a new MFC DAO object**

1 Construct the object (on the stack; or on the heap, using the **new** operator).

2 Call the object's **Create** member function.

3 In some cases, then call the **Append** member function to add the object to the appropriate DAO collection.

- Database objects are appended to the collection automatically upon creation. **CDaoDatabase** has no **Append** member function.

- Workspace and querydef objects can be created as temporary objects. To learn how to create a temporary object, see its class overview. Temporary objects are not appended.

- Objects that you want to persist between database engine sessions should be appended.

For details, see each class constructor in the *Class Library Reference*.

Opening an Existing Object

▶ **To construct and open an MFC DAO Object**

1 Construct the object (on the stack; or on the heap, using the **new** operator).

2 Call the object's **Open** member function.

Before you call **Open**, the object is typically uninitialized and unusable (for exceptions, see **CDaoWorkspace::Open**). This example shows how to construct and open a **CDaoRecordset** object:

```
// CDelinquentSet is derived from CDaoRecordset
// Construct the recordset using the default database
CDelinquentSet rsDelinquentAccts;

// Set the object's properties as needed, then...
rsDelinquentAccts.Open( );  // Using default parameters
```

Related Articles on Creating, Opening, and Closing Objects

For related information, see the following articles:

- DAO: Accessing Implicit MFC DAO Objects
- DAO Workspace: Explicitly Opening the Default Workspace
- DAO Workspace: Opening a Separate Transaction Space
- DAO Workspace: Accessing Properties of the Database Engine

See Also   In the *Class Library Reference*: **CDaoWorkspace::Open**, **CDaoWorkspace::Close**, **CDaoDatabase::Open**, **CDaoDatabase::Close**, **CDaoTableDef::Open**, **CDaoTableDef::Close**, **CDaoQueryDef::Open**, **CDaoQueryDef::Close**, **CDaoRecordset::Open**, **CDaoRecordset::Close**, **CDaoDatabase::Create**, **CDaoQueryDef::Create**, **CDaoTableDef::Create**, **CDaoWorkspace::Create**

DAO: Creating DAO Objects

All of the MFC DAO classes, except **CDaoRecordset**, have member functions for creating new objects. Creation means somewhat different things for different DAO objects. Topics covered include:

- Create member functions
- Meaning of the Create action for different DAO objects

Create Member Functions

The following objects have **Create** member functions:

- **CDaoWorkspace::Create**
- **CDaoDatabase::Create**
- **CDaoQueryDef::Create**
- **DaoTableDef::Create**

In addition, some objects supply member functions for creating subordinate objects, as shown in Table 1. MFC does not supply classes for these subordinate objects; instead, it supplies access to them through member functions of the appropriate containing class.

Table 1   Creating DAO Objects without MFC Classes

Owning class	Creation functions
CDaoDatabase	**CreateRelation**
CDaoTableDef	**CreateField, CreateIndex**

Meaning of the Create Action for Different DAO Objects

The concept of "create" has different meanings for different MFC DAO objects, as shown in Table 2.

Table 2   Meaning of Create for DAO Objects

Object	Meaning
Database	Creates a new Microsoft Jet database; that is, creates the .MDB file on disk. This is the one object that is automatically appended to its collection upon creation.
Querydef	Creates a new DAO querydef object underlying the MFC querydef object. The object is not saved in the database until you call **CDaoQueryDef::Append**.
Recordset	No **Create** member function. Construct a recordset object (usually of a class derived from **CDaoRecordset** using the MFC wizards) and call its **Open** member function to run the query or open the table. This also creates a new DAO recordset object underlying the MFC recordset object.
Tabledef	Creates a new table in the specified database, and a DAO tabledef object to represent it. You must then add fields and possibly indexes to complete the table. The table is actually added to the database when you call **CDaoTableDef::Append**.
Workspace	Creates a new DAO workspace object underlying the MFC workspace object. The object is not appended to the Workspaces collection until you call **CDaoWorkspace::Append**.

See Also   In the *Class Library Reference*: **CDaoWorkspace::Open**, **CDaoWorkspace::Close, CDaoDatabase::Open, CDaoDatabase::Close, CDaoTableDef::Open, CDaoTableDef::Close, CDaoQueryDef::Open, CDaoQueryDef::Close, CDaoRecordset::Open, CDaoRecordset::Close, CDaoDatabase::Create, CDaoQueryDef::Create, CDaoTableDef::Create, CDaoWorkspace::Create**

DAO: Opening DAO Objects

Opening a DAO object implies that there is an existing object to be placed in an open state. This is distinct from creating a new object. In the typical case, the object to open is an element of the appropriate DAO collection, housed in some other DAO object.

An **Open** call puts the object into an open state, ready to be used. After using an object, you should explicitly close it.

Topics include:

- Open member functions
- Meaning of the Open action for different DAO objects

Open Member Functions

The following MFC DAO objects have **Open** member functions:

- **CDaoDatabase::Open**
- **CDaoRecordset::Open**
- **CDaoQueryDef::Open**
- **CDaoTableDef::Open**
- **CDaoWorkspace::Open**

Meaning of the Open Action for Different DAO Objects

The concept of "open" has somewhat different meanings for different MFC DAO objects, as shown in Table 1. Typically, the object is already an element of a DAO collection that belongs to some other object. For example, each database object has a TableDefs collection that contains all tabledef objects in the database. The one object for which **Open** has a radically different meaning is **CDaoDatabase**; opening the object appends it to the Databases collection of a workspace object.

Table 1   Meaning of Open for DAO Objects

Object	Meaning
Database	Opens an existing database—usually a Microsoft Jet (.MDB) database.
Querydef	Opens the specified existing querydef object in the QueryDefs collection of a database.
Recordset	Runs the query defined by the recordset's SQL statement or by an associated querydef; or opens the specified tabledef via a table-type recordset.
Tabledef	Opens the specified existing tabledef object in the TableDefs collection of a database.
Workspace	Opens the default workspace unless you give the name of a workspace previously created with **CDaoWorkspace::Create**.

See Also   In the *Class Library* Reference: CDaoWorkspace::**Open**, **CDaoWorkspace::Close**, **CDaoDatabase::Open**, **CDaoDatabase::Close**, **CDaoTableDef::Open**, **CDaoTableDef::Close**, **CDaoQueryDef::Open**, **CDaoQueryDef::Close**, **CDaoRecordset::Open**, **CDaoRecordset::Close**,

CDaoDatabase::Create, **CDaoQueryDef::Create**, **CDaoTableDef::Create**, **CDaoWorkspace::Create**

DAO: Closing DAO Objects

All MFC DAO objects have **Close** member functions. Calling **Close** typically closes any subordinate objects, such as the active recordsets in a database object, before closing the parent object. The following illustrates closing a database object:

```
// pdbAccounts is an open CDaoDatabase object
pdbAccounts->Close( );
```

Note It is considered good practice to explicitly close your objects rather than relying on containing objects to close them.

Meaning of the Close Action for Different DAO Objects

The concept of "close" is fairly similar for MFC DAO objects. Closing an object:

- Releases memory associated with the object, including buffers used to store recordset data.
- Releases the underlying DAO object.
- Does not remove the object from any collection it belongs to. The exceptions are the workspace and recordset objects, which don't persist between database engine sessions.

What Happens When You Close Objects

For details about what happens when you close an MFC DAO object, see the **Close** member function for that object's class:

- **CDaoDatabase::Close**
- **CDaoQueryDef::Close**
- **CDaoRecordset::Close**
- **CDaoTableDef::Close**
- **CDaoWorkspace::Close**

Calling **Close** does not destroy the MFC object; you must do that separately.

Tip It's considered good programming practice to explicitly close your objects before they go out of scope.

See Also In the *Class Library* Reference: **CDaoWorkspace::Open**, **CDaoWorkspace::Close**, **CDaoDatabase::Open**, **CDaoDatabase::Close**, **CDaoTableDef::Open**, **CDaoTableDef::Close**, **CDaoQueryDef::Open**, **CDaoQueryDef::Close**, **CDaoRecordset::Open**, **CDaoRecordset::Close**, **CDaoDatabase::Create**, **CDaoQueryDef::Create**, **CDaoTableDef::Create**, **CDaoWorkspace::Create**

DAO: Accessing Implicit MFC DAO Objects

This article describes how to access the implicit MFC DAO objects that MFC creates for you in certain situations. The classic example is the workspace object associated with an existing **CDaoDatabase** or **CDaoRecordset** object. Normally you don't need an explicit **CDaoWorkspace** object, so you let MFC implicitly provide one. For a discussion, see the article DAO Database: Using Workspaces and Databases.

The Most Likely Case

In the most likely case—that you already have a **CDaoDatabase** or a **CDaoRecordset** object associated with the workspace you want to access—you can use data members of these objects to obtain a pointer to the implicit **CDaoWorkspace** object that they belong to. There are two scenarios, based on whether you have a database object or a recordset object to work from.

Scenario 1. One Level of Indirection

You have a **CDaoDatabase** object based on the workspace. Access the **CDaoDatabase** object's **m_pWorkspace** data member to obtain a **CDaoWorkspace** pointer, like this:

```
// pdbAccounts is a pointer to a CDaoDatabase object
// for the Accounts database
CDaoWorkspace* pws = pdbAccounts->m_pWorkspace;
```

Or you might simply use the implicit workspace to call a **CDaoWorkspace** member function:

```
pdbAccounts->m_pWorkspace->BeginTrans( );
```

Calling transaction functions in this way is a common situation.

Scenario 2. Two Levels of Indirection

You have a **CDaoRecordset** object indirectly based on the workspace (through a **CDaoDatabase**). Follow these steps:

1. Access the **CDaoRecordset** object's **m_pDatabase** data member to obtain a **CDaoDatabase** pointer.

2. Then access the database object's **m_pWorkspace** data member to obtain a **CDaoWorkspace** pointer, like this:

```
// rsDelinquentAccts is an existing CDaoRecordset
// object based on the Accounts database
CDaoDatabase* pdbAccounts = rs.m_pDatabase;
CDaoWorkspace* pws = pdbAccounts->m_pWorkspace;
```

Or you might simply use the implicit workspace behind your recordset's implicit database to call a **CDaoWorkspace** member function:

```
pdbAccounts->m_pWorkspace->CommitTrans( );
```

Note This is the recommended method for accessing such functions because it doesn't create a copy of a pointer to an implicit object. Copies of such pointers can be dangerous.

Uses for the Workspace Pointer

You can use the workspace pointer obtained in this indirect way to access the Workspaces collection, access the Databases collection, access properties of the database engine, and so on. Note that in most cases the workspace accessed this way is DAO's default workspace.

Caution If you store a copy to one of these pointers, be careful not to use it after the original object goes out of scope or is otherwise destroyed.

See Also DAO: Where Is..., DAO: Creating, Opening, and Closing DAO Objects

DAO: General Performance Tips

This article offers tips for improving the performance of your MFC DAO applications. Use these tips as your starting point, and benchmark your changes. Keep in mind that these tips will often help, but there are no absolutes. Weigh everything in the context of your database and your application. Topics covered include:

- Best tip
- Recordset types
- Selecting records
- ODBC
- Caching and double buffering
- Opening databases
- Attached tables
- SQL
- Transactions
- Locating records
- Other tips

How you improve performance in a database application depends on what kind of performance improvement you need. You might need some of the following kinds of performance improvements more than others:

- Better query speed
- Faster record location
- Faster scrolling through records
- Up-to-date record content in multi-user environments
- Better performance with external databases, especially ODBC data sources

Best Tip

The design of your data is usually a bigger factor in performance than the design of your code:

- Use Microsoft Access to examine your database design, queries, and indexes. Run your queries in Access and use the results to adjust your table and index designs for better performance. Then save the queries in your database for use from your code.

- Normalize your database schema to avoid storing multiple copies of your data. Consult any standard database text, such as C.J. Date's *Introduction to Database Systems*, 10th edition (Addison-Wesley, 1995), or consult the Microsoft Access documentation.

Also:

- Store infrequently updated tables in your local Microsoft Jet (.MDB) database. If the data doesn't change often, you can keep a local copy for queries and avoid having to move the data across the network.

Recordset Types

- In general, use a table-type recordset rather than either a dynaset-type recordset or a snapshot-type recordset if possible.

- For remote data, use snapshot-type recordsets rather than dynaset-type recordsets. But beware of Memo fields, especially in ODBC data sources. If the data contains Memo fields, use a dynaset-type recordset instead if you won't be retrieving all the fields from all the rows. Dynaset-type recordsets are also better for OLE objects in ODBC data sources.

- For ODBC data with OLE objects or Memo fields, use dynaset-type recordsets instead of snapshot-type recordsets.

Selecting Records

- For dynaset-type recordsets and snapshot-type recordsets, select only the fields you need instead of all fields.

- For snapshot-type recordsets against ODBC data sources, use the **dbForwardOnly** option in your recordsets if you'll be making a single pass through your data.

- For dynaset-type recordsets against ODBC data sources, cache multiple records. See the article DAO Recordset: Caching Multiple Records for Performance.

- If you're adding records to a dynaset-type recordset, especially against an ODBC data source, use the **dbAppendOnly** option.

- Requery recordsets rather than reopening them. Note that you lose this advantage if you change filters or sorts before you requery.

- Parameterize queries instead of using dynamic SQL statements, especially against ODBC data sources.

- Store queries instead of using dynamic SQL statements, especially on machines with low memory.

- Refresh current field values by calling **Move** with a parameter of **AFX_MOVE_REFRESH** instead of calling **MoveNext** and **MovePrev**. (Calling **Move** with a parameter of 0 is equivalent.)

ODBC

- Attach ODBC tables to a local Microsoft Jet (.MDB) database rather than opening the ODBC data source directly.

- Reduce your ODBC timeouts for faster performance in failure cases.

- For ODBC data with OLE objects or Memo fields, use dynaset-type recordsets instead of snapshot-type recordsets.

- For snapshot-type recordsets against ODBC data sources, use the **dbForwardOnly** option in your recordsets.

- For dynaset-type recordsets against ODBC data sources, cache multiple records. See the article DAO Recordset: Caching Multiple Records for Performance.

- With ODBC SQL statements that don't retrieve data, use pass-through queries where possible. For related information, see the article DAO Querydef: Action Queries and SQL Pass-Through Queries.

- Speed ODBC finds by downloading to a local indexed table and seeking. If you will be making numerous finds in the data, copy it to a local Microsoft Jet database table and use **Seek** to locate information.

- On ODBC data, use **Find** only on indexed fields; otherwise, open a new recordset using an SQL statement with an appropriate **WHERE** clause.

For more information about working with ODBC data sources, see the articles Database Overview and DAO External: Working with External Data Sources.

Caching and Double Buffering

- For best performance, turn off MFC's double-buffering mechanism. However, the tradeoff is that you must write more code to update a field. For more information, see the article DAO Record Field Exchange: Double Buffering Records.

- Cache multiple records when you are using an ODBC data source. See the article DAO Recordset: Caching Multiple Records for Performance.

- Cache tabledef references if they will be used many times. Keep your **CDaoQueryDef** objects open and reuse them rather than recreating them.

Opening Databases

- Open databases for exclusive use if you are the only user. Open databases read-only if all users will be read-only.

- Use the **dbDenyWrite** option if nobody else will be writing to the database.

- Retrieve data from ODBC databases by attaching to a Microsoft Jet (.MDB) database instead of opening the ODBC database directly.

Attached Tables

- Attach ODBC tables to a local Microsoft Jet (.MDB) database rather than opening the ODBC data source directly.

- Open attached Microsoft Jet tables as table-type recordsets by parsing the tabledef connect string for the database name and then opening that database directly.

SQL

- With ODBC SQL statements that don't retrieve data, use pass-through queries where possible. For related information, see the article DAO Querydef: Action Queries and SQL Pass-Through Queries.

- Replace code loops that run a query again and again with the equivalent SQL statements to run the query once for the whole loop. For example, rather than doing 100 update calls, run one bulk query for all of the affected records.

- Replace repeated execution of the same dynamic SQL with a temporary query. (This applies only if you are using a querydef pointer in **CDaoRecordset::Open** to create your recordset.)

Transactions

- Always embed your MFC DAO code in transactions if you are performing multiple updates. Balance transaction sizes against the likely available memory. Don't try to do ten thousand large updates in a single transaction. Instead, break the work into smaller lots of, say, 500 records.

Locating Records

- Use **Seek** rather than **Find**. (**Seek** only works with table-type recordsets.)

- Return to a location in a recordset using bookmarks rather than **Find**. See the article DAO Recordset: Bookmarks and Record Positions.

- Speed ODBC finds by downloading to a local indexed table and seeking. If you will be making numerous finds in the data, copy it to a local Microsoft Jet database table and use **Seek** to locate information.

- On ODBC data, use **Find** only on indexed fields; otherwise, open a new recordset.

Other Tips

- Use the power of Microsoft Jet queries to save writing and debugging code. For example, the Microsoft Jet database engine allows you to update the results of join queries and automatically distributes the changes to the underlying tables.

- Replace short Memo fields with long text fields.

- Replace floating-point numbers with integers.

DAO Collections

This article explains how to access the "collections" in which DAO keeps active DAO objects at all levels of the DAO object hierarchy. The article also explains how the collections are exposed in MFC. Topics covered include:

- DAO collections: definitions
- How MFC exposes DAO collections
- The default object in a collection
- How to access a collection
- The information you obtain about objects in a collection
- Contents of MFC·DAO information structures
- Primary, Secondary, and All information
- Information about collections in DAO

DAO Collections: Definition

In DAO, each object in the object hierarchy maintains one or more "collections" of subordinate objects. For example, the Microsoft Jet database engine maintains a collection of open workspaces. Each workspace object maintains a collection of open databases (and other collections, related to security). And so on. For a list of the DAO objects and the collections they house, see the topic Data Access Objects and Collections Reference in DAO Help.

How MFC Exposes DAO Collections

In the MFC DAO classes, MFC doesn't maintain a collection (such as a **CObArray**) of C++ objects parallel to the underlying DAO collection. Rather, MFC supplies member functions and/or data members through which you can access the underlying collection itself in DAO, where the DAO collections are stored. For example, class **CDaoWorkspace** supplies the **GetWorkspaceCount** member function to determine how many workspaces are in the database engine's Workspaces collection and the **GetWorkspaceInfo** member function to examine information about any workspace in the collection.

In general, the MFC DAO classes supply similar functions for all relevant DAO collections. The one significant exception is the Recordsets collection of the database object. MFC does not supply **GetRecordsetCount** and **GetRecordsetInfo** member functions in class **CDaoDatabase**. When you work with recordsets, you always have an explicit MFC **CDaoRecordset** object in your application. It's up to you to keep track of which recordsets you have open.

The Default Object in a Collection

The first element in a DAO collection, at element 0, is the default element of the collection. In particular, DAO's default workspace is element 0 in the Workspaces collection. Collections are zero-based.

How to Access a Collection

The following procedure uses the TableDefs collection of a **CDaoDatabase** object to illustrate the general process for accessing objects in a DAO collection.

▶ **To access the TableDefs collection (for example)**

1 Construct a **CDaoDatabase** object, or get a pointer to one from a **CDaoRecordset** object.

2 Call the object's **Open** member function unless you have obtained a database pointer from a recordset.

3 Use the **GetTableDefCount** and **GetTableDefInfo** member functions of the object to determine how many tabledefs the collection contains and to loop through the collection, obtaining information about each tabledef object.

For an example, see the LISTVIEW.CPP file in the MFC Database sample DAOVIEW. For a procedure, see the article DAO: Obtaining Information About DAO Objects.

The Information You Obtain About Objects in a Collection

To obtain information about the objects in a collection, you call a *GetXInfo* member function of the appropriate class. This function returns an object of one of the *CDaoXInfo* structures listed in Table 2 in the article DAO: Obtaining Information About DAO Objects. In general, there is a *CDaoXInfo* structure associated with each DAO object. These structures are commonly referred to as the MFC DAO "information structures."

Contents of MFC DAO Information Structures

A typical information structure looks something like this:

```
struct CDaoDatabaseInfo
{
    CString m_strName;          // Primary
    BOOL m_bUpdatable;          // Primary
    BOOL m_bTransactions;       // Primary
    CString m_strVersion;       // Secondary
    long m_lCollatingOrder;     // Secondary
    short m_nQueryTimeout;      // Secondary
    CString m_strConnect;       // All
};
```

For detailed descriptions of the structure members, see the individual structure in the *Class Library Reference*. Structures are listed in Table 2 in the article DAO: Obtaining Information About DAO Objects.

Primary, Secondary, and All Information

The notations "Primary," "Secondary," and "All" indicate which MFC DAO structure members are filled when you call a function such as **GetDatabaseInfo**. You can specify that you want just primary information, both primary and secondary information, or all information. Some structures don't include anything under the All designation.

Caution Using the Secondary and All options can be slow. In general, Primary is faster than Secondary, and Secondary is faster than All. Don't use All unless you must.

For more information about using **GetTableDefCount**, **GetTableDefInfo**, and similar functions, see the article DAO: Obtaining Information About DAO Objects.

Information About Collections in DAO

For general information about the DAO collections, see the topic Data Access Objects and Collections Reference in DAO Help.

See Also DAO: Where Is..., DAO Collections: Obtaining Information About DAO Objects

DAO: Obtaining Information About DAO Objects

Objects of most of the MFC DAO classes contain "collections" of subordinate objects. For example, a **CDaoDatabase** object contains collections of tabledefs, querydefs, and relations. For an explanation of how these collections fit into the MFC implementation, see the article DAO Collections.

The present article explains how to obtain information about the objects in a collection. The example given uses the database object's QueryDefs collection, but the same mechanism applies to other collections throughout the MFC implementation of DAO.

Topics covered include:

- Functions for accessing DAO collections
- Information returned by the GetXInfo functions
- Example: Obtaining Information About Querydefs
- Constants for specifying the levels of information you want

Functions for Accessing DAO Collections

Access the objects in a DAO collection through the *GetXCount* and *GetXInfo* member functions of the appropriate class, where *X* stands for Database, Field, Index, Parameter, Query, Table, Relation, or Workspace. Table 1 lists the available collection-access functions for each MFC class:

Table 1 Class Member Functions for Accessing Collections

Class	Count objects in collection	Get information about a specified object
CDaoWorkspace	GetDatabaseCount, GetWorkspaceCount	GetDatabaseInfo, GetWorkspaceInfo
CDaoDatabase	GetTableDefCount, GetRelationCount, GetQueryDefCount	GetTableDefInfo, GetRelationInfo, GetQueryDefInfo
CDaoTableDef	GetFieldCount, GetIndexCount	GetFieldInfo, GetIndexInfo
CDaoQueryDef	GetFieldCount, GetParameterCount	GetFieldInfo, GetParameterInfo
CDaoRecordset	GetFieldCount, GetIndexCount	GetFieldInfo, GetIndexInfo

Information Returned by the *GetXInfo* Functions

In general, use *GetXCount* functions to determine the upper bound for looping through a collection. On each iteration of the loop, call *GetXInfo* functions to retrieve the information. The *GetXInfo* functions return a reference to an object of class *CDaoXInfo*, which you can examine. Each different *CDaoXInfo* class (technically a C++ structure) supplies different information. You pass an object of type *CDaoXInfo* in the second (*xinfo*) parameter.

Note DAO collections are zero-based. When you iterate a collection, begin with element 0.

Table 2 lists the *CDaoXInfo* classes; see the class for details about its members.

Table 2 Classes for Obtaining Information About Collections

Object	Class (structure)
Database	CDaoDatabaseInfo
Field	CDaoFieldInfo
Index	CDaoIndexInfo
Index Field (field that is part of an index object)	CDaoIndexFieldInfo
Parameter	CDaoParameterInfo
QueryDef	CDaoQueryDefInfo
Relation	CDaoRelationInfo

Table 2   Classes for Obtaining Information About Collections *(cont.)*

Object	Class (structure)
Relation Field (field that is part of a relation object)	**CDaoRelationFieldInfo**
TableDef	**CDaoTableDefInfo**
Workspace	**CDaoWorkspaceInfo**

One additional DAO object, the error object, is handled somewhat differently in MFC, so you don't use the technique described in this article to work with error objects. For information, see class **CDaoException** in the *Class Library Reference.*

Example: Obtaining Information About Querydefs

This example shows how to loop through the QueryDefs collection of a **CDaoDatabase** object and obtain information about the QueryDefs in the collection. The example searches the QueryDefs collection for a particular named query, called "Senior Students" so it can then extract other information about the query—such as its SQL string or query type.

```
// pDB is a pointer to a CDaoDatabase object
// Allocate a CDaoQueryDefInfo object to
// receive the information
CDaoQueryDefInfo queryinfo;
int nQueries = pDB->GetQueryDefCount( );
for ( int i = 0; i < nQueries; i++ )
{
    GetQueryDefInfo( i, queryinfo );
    if ( queryinfo.m_strName = "Senior Students" )
    {
        // Get other information about the query ...
        // ...
        break;
    }
}
```

The code iterates through the collection, retrieving information about each object until the desired named query is found. Note that DAO collections are zero-based.

Tip   Some MFC DAO class functions use *CDaoXInfo* structures for input parameters as well as for output parameters. In those cases, you assign values to a *CDaoXInfo* object, then pass the object to the function.

Constants for Specifying the Levels of Information You Want

The syntax of the **GetQueryDefInfo** member function used in the example under Example: Obtaining Information About Querydefs is:

void GetQueryDefInfo(int *nIndex,* **CDaoQueryDefInfo&** *queryinfo,* **DWORD** *dwInfoOptions =*
AFX_DAO_PRIMARY_INFO);

In the example, the *queryinfo* parameter returns a reference to a **CDaoQueryDefInfo**
object. The example accepts the default value, **AFX_DAO_PRIMARY_INFO**, for
the *dwInfoOptions* parameter, which specifies which information to return. Table 3
lists the options in this case.

Table 3 Constants for Specifying the Levels of Information You Want

Constant	Meaning
AFX_DAO_PRIMARY_INFO	Primary level of information; in the querydef case, this includes Name and Type.
AFX_DAO_SECONDARY_INFO	Primary information plus a secondary level of information; in the querydef case, this would include Date Created, Date of Last Update, Returns Records, and Updatable.
AFX_DAO_ALL_INFO	Primary and secondary information plus additional information: in the querydef case, this would include SQL, Connect, and ODBCTimeout.

The items listed in column 2 of Table 3 correspond to data members of the
appropriate *CDaoXInfo* structure and, beneath that, to DAO properties.

Notice that the levels of information are cumulative: if you specify a higher level,
such as secondary or all, you get the lower levels as well. For details about what
information you can obtain for each collection type, see the appropriate *GetXInfo*
functions. The functions are listed in Table 2.

Caution In many cases, the information obtained with the **AFX_DAO_ALL_INFO** option can
be time-consuming or otherwise costly to obtain. For example, getting a count of the records in
a recordset can be time-consuming. Use this option with care.

See Also DAO: Where Is..., DAO Collections

DAO Database

This article explains the role of **CDaoDatabase** objects in your application. For task-
oriented information about using "database" objects, see the article DAO Database:
Using Workspaces and Databases. For an understanding of the DAO database object
underlying each MFC **CDaoDatabase** object, see the following topics in DAO Help:

- Database Object
- Databases Collection

Topics covered in this article include:

- Database: Definition
- External databases
- Database collections
- Database roles
- Accessing database objects
- Database persistence
- Further reading about databases

Database: Definition

A DAO database object, represented in MFC by class **CDaoDatabase**, represents a connection to a database through which you can operate on the data. You can have one or more **CDaoDatabase** objects active at a time in a given "workspace," represented by a **CDaoWorkspace** object.

For information about database management systems (DBMSs) you can work with, see Databases You Can Access with DAO in the article Database Overview.

External Databases

Besides using **CDaoDatabase** to work with Microsoft Jet (.MDB) databases, you can also access "external" data sources, particularly Open Database Connectivity (ODBC) data sources. For a list of external data sources, see the topic External Data Source: Definition in the article DAO: Working with External Data Sources.

Database Collections

In DAO:

- Each workspace object contains a "collection" of open database objects, called the Databases collection.
- Each DAO database objects contains collections of tabledefs, querydefs, recordsets, and relations.

In MFC, access to a workspace's Databases collection is through member functions of class **CDaoWorkspace**. Access to a database object's collections is through member functions of class **CDaoDatabase**.

Note MFC exposes all of a database's collections via member functions except for the Recordsets collection. In MFC, you always have an explicit **CDaoRecordset** object for each recordset you create, and it is up to you to track these objects.

For more information about DAO collections in MFC, see the article DAO Collections. For related information, see the topic Databases Collection in DAO Help.

Database Roles

CDaoDatabase can play the following roles—it allows you to:

- Create new Microsoft Jet (.MDB) database files.
- Store tabledef objects that you can use to manipulate the structure of the database's tables.
- Store querydef objects so you can reuse the queries they represent later.
- View and manipulate data in the database's tables.
- Work with data in local or remote databases.
- Work with the database's collections.

Accessing Database Objects

When you open a **CDaoRecordset** object without specifying an open **CDaoDatabase** object, MFC implicitly creates a **CDaoDatabase** object, along with the **CDaoWorkspace** that contains the database and the underlying DAO database object. You can also create explicit **CDaoDatabase** objects.

See the article DAO: Accessing Implicit MFC DAO Objects for information on accessing:

- The **CDaoDatabase** object associated with a **CDaoRecordset** object.
- The **CDaoWorkspace** object associated with a **CDaoDatabase** object.

Database Persistence

Database objects exist in memory for the life of a database engine session. When that session terminates, the default workspace, the Workspaces collection, the Databases collection in each open workspace, and the database objects in the Databases collection(s) cease to exist (although the databases they represent do persist). These software objects are not stored on disk or in a database. When you begin a new database engine session and want to use the workspaces and databases you used in the last session, you must recreate any explicit workspace objects you need, and reopen any databases you were using in the workspace.

Tip Use a Windows registry entry to preserve a record of the workspaces and databases you had open during a database engine session.

Further Reading About Databases

For more information about databases in MFC, see the following articles (in recommended reading order):

- DAO Database: Using Workspaces and Databases
- DAO External: Working with External Data Sources

- DAO: Accessing Implicit MFC DAO Objects
- DAO Collections
- DAO Tabledef
- DAO Querydef
- DAO Recordset

See Also   DAO: Where Is..., DAO: Database Tasks

DAO Database: Using Workspaces and Databases

This article explains how to use **CDaoWorkspace** and **CDaoDatabase** objects. Topics covered include:

- A typical workspace scenario
- Transactions in the typical scenario
- Beyond the typical scenario

A Typical Workspace Scenario

In the majority of data access applications, you work less at the workspace level than at the database or even recordset level. It might seem the normal thing to construct an explicit **CDaoWorkspace** object, then from it construct a **CDaoDatabase** object and from that construct **CDaoRecordset**, **CDaoQueryDef**, and **CDaoTableDef** objects. But the more typical approach is one of the following:

- Construct a **CDaoDatabase** object, perhaps stored in your **CDocument**-derived class. Then from it construct the necessary recordsets and other objects. You're likely to do this if you want to maintain a connection to a single database for the life of your application, or at least the life of your document. For related information, see the articles MFC: Using Database Classes with Documents and Views, MFC: Using Database Classes Without Documents and Views, and DAO: Writing a Database Application.

- Construct recordsets as needed, relying on MFC to create the necessary **CDaoDatabase** and **CDaoWorkspace** objects behind the scenes. You're likely to do this if you prefer to construct recordsets within the scope of a function, for example to run a query based on a menu command.

  Note   This is inefficient if you are continually opening and closing the same database. In that case, create an explicit **CDaoDatabase** object and use it for the life of your application.

Transactions in the Typical Scenario

The primary action taken on a workspace object that might be called typical is to use the object for transactions against one or more databases. The transaction commands in MFC are members of class **CDaoWorkspace**.

To access transaction commands in the most typical case, you can use the implicit workspace that MFC creates behind **CDaoDatabase** and **CDaoRecordset** objects (one implicit workspace for multiple objects). To issue transaction commands, such as **BeginTrans**, **CommitTrans**, or **Rollback**, you can choose to call those member functions of **CDaoWorkspace** through the pointer stored in your **CDaoRecordset** or **CDaoDatabase** object. For details about accessing such pointers, see the article DAO: Accessing Implicit MFC DAO Objects.

For example, from a recordset object, you might call:

```
// prs is a pointer to an already opened
// CDaoRecordset object
prs->m_pDatabase->m_pWorkspace->BeginTrans( );
...
```

Beyond the Typical Scenario

The typical scenario is not enough in some fairly rare cases. For a discussion of when you might need an explicit **CDaoWorkspace** object, see the article DAO Workspace.

See Also   DAO: Where Is..., DAO Workspace: Managing Transactions, DAO Workspace, DAO Database, DAO: Creating, Opening, and Closing DAO Objects

DAO External: Working with External Data Sources

This article explains the best approaches to using the MFC DAO classes with external data sources, primarily Open Database Connectivity (ODBC) data sources.

Topics include:

- External data source: definition
- External data sources you can use
- External data access choices
- Performance considerations with external data
- When you might need to open an external table directly
- Other articles about accessing external data
- For more information about accessing external data

External Data Source: Definition

Aside from working with a Microsoft Jet (.MDB) database on your local machine, you can use the MFC DAO classes to access "external" data of several kinds. External data includes data in the following circumstances—the data is in:

- An ODBC data source, either local or on a network server.

- An ISAM database such as dBASE® or Microsoft FoxPro®, accessible through the Microsoft Jet database engine, either locally or on a network server.
- A Microsoft Jet (.MDB) database, created directly with Microsoft Access or created with DAO and stored either locally or on a network server, that contains tables you want to attach to a primary Microsoft Jet database.

External Data Sources You Can Use

The discussion in this and related articles applies to the following external data sources:

- Microsoft FoxPro®, versions 2.0, 2.5, and 2.6. Can import and export data to and from version 3.0 but can't create objects.
- dBASE III®, dBASE IV®, and dBASE 5.0®
- Paradox™, versions 3.x, 4.x, and 5.x
- Btrieve®, versions 5.1x and 6.0
- Databases using the Microsoft Jet database engine (Microsoft Access, Microsoft Visual Basic, and Microsoft Visual C++), versions 1.x, 2.x, and 3.0
- ODBC data sources, including but not limited to Microsoft SQL Server, SYBASE® SQL Server, and ORACLE® Server. An ODBC data source is any DBMS for which you have the appropriate ODBC driver. For Visual C++ versions 2.0 and later, you need 32-bit ODBC drivers (except on Win32s, where you need 16-bit ODBC drivers). See the article ODBC Driver List for a list of ODBC drivers included in this version of Visual C++ and for information about obtaining additional drivers.
- Microsoft Excel version 3.0, 4.0, 5.0, and 7.0 worksheets
- Lotus® WKS, WK1, WK3, WK4 spreadsheets
- Text files

External Data Access Choices

The MFC DAO classes give you two choices for accessing tables stored in external data sources. You can either:

- Attach the tables to a Microsoft Jet (.MDB) database

  –or–

- Open the external database directly.

Attaching Tables

When you attach a table, it is treated in most respects—except that you can't modify the table's schema or open a tabledef or table-type recordset on it—as if it were a Microsoft Jet database table in the current database. The connection information to the external data source is stored with the table definition, making it easy to open recordsets on the table. The data is still stored in the external data source, however. For information on attaching tables, see the article DAO External: Attaching External Tables.

Tip If you attach a table from within Microsoft Access, you can then use the table from MFC.

Opening External Databases Directly

When you open a table directly, you specify the connection information each time you open the external database. This can involve communication overhead. For information on opening tables directly, see the article DAO External: Opening External Databases Directly.

Important In most cases, attaching a table is a faster method for accessing external data than opening a table directly, especially when the table is in an ODBC data source. If possible, it's best to consider attaching external tables rather than opening them directly. If you do open a table in an ODBC data source directly, keep in mind that performance will be significantly slower.

To attach or open a data source on a network, you must have access to the server and share and to the external table as well as appropriate permissions for access to the data, if applicable.

Performance Considerations with External Data

Keep in mind that external tables are not actually in your Microsoft Jet database. Each time you view data in an external table, your program must retrieve records from another file. This can take time, particularly if the table is an ODBC data source.

ODBC performance is optimal if you attach tables instead of opening them directly, and if you retrieve and view only the data you need. Restrict your queries to limit results and avoid excessive scrolling through records. For more performance tips, see the article DAO External: Improving Performance with External Data Sources.

For a discussion of why performance suffers with external data sources, particularly ODBC data sources, see the topic Accessing External Databases with DAO in DAO Help.

When You Might Need to Open an External Table Directly

Attaching external tables to a Microsoft Jet database is generally more efficient than opening the external data source directly. However, there still might be circumstances under which you would prefer to open the external database directly. Reasons:

- Non-ODBC external data sources give faster performance if you open them directly. Only ODBC is slower when opened directly.

- You need to enumerate the tables in the external data source to find out the database structure at run time. Unless you know the table names, you can't attach them.

- You need to manipulate the table's structure. You can't modify the schema of an attached table.

Other Articles About Accessing External Data

For more information, including procedures, see the following articles (in the recommended reading order):

- DAO External: Attaching External Tables
- DAO External: Creating an External Table
- DAO External: Refreshing and Removing Links
- DAO External: Improving Performance with External Data Sources

For More Information About Accessing External Data

An additional source of information is the *Advanced Topics* book from the Microsoft Access Developer's Toolkit. You'll need to translate Microsoft Access Basic examples to MFC, but the chapter on Accessing External Data gives detailed advice on using external data sources such as Microsoft FoxPro, dBASE, Paradox, and Btrieve.

For related information, see the topic Accessing External Databases with DAO in DAO Help.

For information about accessing specific external data sources, see the following topics in DAO Help:

- Accessing Data in ODBC Databases with DAO
- Accessing Data in a Btrieve Database with DAO
- Accessing Data in a dBASE Database with DAO
- Accessing Data in a Microsoft Excel Worksheet or Workbook with DAO
- Accessing Data in a Microsoft FoxPro Database with DAO
- Accessing Data in a Lotus Spreadsheet with DAO
- Accessing Data in a Paradox Database with DAO
- Accessing Data in a Text Document with DAO
- Accessing Data on CD-ROM with DAO

See Also   DAO: Where Is...

DAO External: Attaching External Tables

This article explains how to attach a table from an external data source, such as an ODBC data source, to your current Microsoft Jet (.MDB) database. Attaching external tables is generally more efficient than opening them directly, as explained in the article DAO External: Working with External Data Sources.

Important   In general, it is best for performance reasons to attach tables in ODBC data sources rather than opening them directly. You can open non-ODBC external data sources directly if you like.

Tip   If you attach a table from within Microsoft Access, you can then use the table from MFC.

▶ To attach an external table using the MFC DAO classes

1 Open your Microsoft Jet (.MDB) database—the one to which you'll attach the external table:

Construct a **CDaoDatabase** object, or obtain a pointer to one (from an open recordset object, for example) and call the object's **Open** member function.

2 Using the **CDaoDatabase** object, create a new **CDaoTableDef** object. Construct the tabledef object, then call its **Create** member function.

In the **Create** call, you can specify the source table name and the connect string. Or you can accept the defaults in **Create** and separately call **SetConnect** and **SetSourceTableName** to specify the connect string and the name of the table as it appears on the data source. The example following this procedure calls **SetConnect** and **SetSourceTableName**.

3 Attach the external table by appending it to the **CDaoDatabase** object's TableDefs collection.

Call the tabledef object's **Append** member function.

4 Use the attached table as if it were actually a table in the Microsoft Jet database.

You can do the following, among other things:

- Use the table to create a recordset.

- Examine fields and indexes in the table.

- Get or set validation conditions for the table.

The following example illustrates how to attach an external table:

```
// Construct the database and the tabledef
CDaoDatabase db;
CDaoTableDef td( &db );
td.Create( "Preferred Customers", 0, "Customers", "ODBC:DSN=afx;UID=sa;PWD=Fred" );

// Attach the tabledef to the external data source
td.Append( );

// Use td ...
```

The parameters to create are the tabledef name, attributes, source table name, and connect string.

Your link to the attached table remains active unless you delete the tabledef object or move the source table. If you move the source table, you can refresh the link using the tabledef object's **RefreshLink** member function.

Note For the external indexed sequential access method (ISAM) databases, such as FoxPro and dBASE, specify the full path to the directory in which the database files are located when a database name is called for.

Tip Because a tabledef object name can be any valid Microsoft Access table name, you can give the attached table a more descriptive name than is often allowed in the external data source. For example, if you attach an external dBASE table named SLSDATA, you can rename the attached table as "Sales Data 1995 (from dBASE)." The code in the previous example provides an example of this.

See Also DAO: Where Is..., DAO External: Working with External Data Sources, DAO External: Opening External Databases Directly

DAO External: Opening External Databases Directly

This article explains how to open a table in an ODBC data source directly, rather than by attaching the table to a Microsoft Jet (.MDB) database. For a general discussion of external data sources, see the article DAO External: Working with External Data Sources.

Important If you are working with an ODBC data source, it is recommended that you attach the external table to your Microsoft Jet database instead of opening it directly as described in this article. With an attached table from an ODBC data source, performance is significantly better. For information about attaching tables, see the article DAO External: Attaching External Tables.

▶ **To open an external table directly using the MFC DAO classes**

1 Open the external data source.

Construct a **CDaoDatabase** object, or obtain a pointer to one (from an open recordset object, for example) and call the object's **Open** member function. Supply appropriate connection information for the data source.

2 Create a recordset for the external table.

Construct a **CDaoRecordset** object, basing the recordset on the **CDaoDatabase** object for the external table.

3 Work with the recordset as you would with any recordset. But note that if you are working with ODBC performance may not be as good as if you had attached the table instead.

Note Creating the recordset requires that you supply the external table name. Usually, you'll do this when you create your **CDaoRecordset**-derived class with either AppWizard or ClassWizard. The external table name is a table name, not a filename, so you don't use the filename extension. This is true for all external data sources, such as dBASE and FoxPro, in which tables are stored as individual disk files.

Important When you specify the recordset type (table-type, dynaset-type, or snapshot-type), be aware that you can't use a table-type recordset with ODBC data sources.

For information about the preferred alternative to this procedure, see the article DAO External: Attaching External Tables.

See Also DAO: Where Is..., DAO External: Working with External Data Sources, DAO External: Attaching External Tables

DAO External: Creating an External Table

This article explains how to create a new table, with the correct format, in an external data source. For general information about external data sources, see the article DAO External: Working with External Data Sources.

▶ **To create an external table**

1 Open the external database directly.

   Construct a **CDaoDatabase** object and call its **Open** member function. Pass the appropriate connection information.

   You can't manipulate the schema of an attached table, so you must open directly.

2 Create a tabledef for the new table.

   Construct a **CDaoTableDef** object based on the **CDaoDatabase** object. Call the tabledef object's **Create** member function, specifying connection information and the name of the source table on which the tabledef is based.

   As an alternative, you could accept the default parameter values in **Create**, then call **SetConnect** and **SetSourceTableName**.

3 Add fields to the new table.

   Call the tabledef object's **CreateField** member function. The new field is automatically appended to the underlying DAO tabledef object's Fields collection.

4 Create the external data file by appending the tabledef object to the **CDaoDatabase** object's TableDefs collection.

See Also DAO: Where Is..., DAO External: Working with External Data Sources, DAO External: Attaching External Tables, DAO External: Refreshing and Removing Links

DAO External: Refreshing and Removing Links

This article explains how to refresh or remove a link to an attached table when the table has moved. For background, see the article DAO External: Attaching External Tables.

▶ **To refresh a link**

1 Reset the table's connection information—that is, change the path to the external data source.

Call the **SetConnect** member function for the saved tabledef object representing the attached table.

2 Call the tabledef object's **RefreshLink** member function.

▶ **To remove a link to an attached table**

• In the **CDaoDatabase** object for your Microsoft Jet (.MDB) database, call the **DeleteTableDef** member function. Specify the name of the external table (the tabledef name).

Important When you delete an attached table, only the link is deleted. The external table itself is unaffected.

See Also DAO: Where Is..., DAO External: Working with External Data Sources, DAO External: Attaching External Tables, DAO External: Creating an External Table

DAO External: Improving Performance with External Data Sources

This article explains some things you can do to improve performance when you connect to external data sources, such as ODBC data sources. For general information about external data sources, see the article DAO External: Working with External Data Sources.

Improving Performance with ODBC Data Sources

If you're connecting to an ODBC data source, the following guidelines apply:

• Use attached tables instead of directly opened tables whenever possible.

See the article DAO External: Working with External Data Sources and the topic Accessing External Databases with DAO in DAO Help.

Important This recommendation has the most significant impact on performance of all the recommendations in this list.

• Retrieve and view only the data you need.

Use restricted queries to limit the number of records you retrieve, and select only the columns you need. This requires transferring less data across the network.

Don't use dynaset-type recordsets if you're not updating the data.

Use forward-scrolling snapshot-type recordsets if you're only scrolling forward. Don't scroll through records unnecessarily, and avoid jumping to the last record of a large table.

- Use caching.

  In class **CDaoRecordset**, MFC supports caching a specified number of records. Doing so takes longer initially, when the data is retrieved into the cache, but moving through the records in the cache is faster than retrieving each record as it is scrolled to.

- Turn off the double-buffering option in MFC **CDaoRecordset** objects.

  This is a general way to improve performance that applies as well to working with external data sources.

- For bulk operations, such as adding records in bulk, use an SQL pass-through query. Call **SetConnect** for the **CDaoDatabase** representing your .MDB database. Then call the database object's **Execute** member function, or create a recordset, with the **dbSQLPassThrough** option set. For more information about pass-through queries, see the article DAO Querydef: Action Queries and SQL Pass-Through Queries. (You only need to set the connection information once, if you are always performing your SQL pass-through queries through the same connection.)

- Avoid using queries that cause processing to be done locally.

  Don't use user-defined functions with remote column arguments. Use heterogeneous joins (joins on tables in two databases) only on indexed columns, and realize if you do this that some processing is done locally. When accessing external data, the Microsoft Jet database engine processes data locally only when the operation can't be performed by the external database. Query operations performed locally include:

  - **WHERE** clause restrictions on top of a query with a **DISTINCT** predicate.

  - **WHERE** clauses containing operations that can't be processed remotely, such as user-defined functions that involve remote columns. (Note that in this case only the parts of the **WHERE** clause that can't be processed remotely will be processed locally.)

  - Joins between tables from different data sources.

  Note Simply having joins between tables from different data sources doesn't mean that all of the processing occurs locally. If restrictions are sent to the server, only relevant rows are processed locally.

  - Joins over aggregation or the **DISTINCT** predicate.

  - Outer joins containing syntax not supported by the ODBC driver.

  - **DISTINCT** predicates containing operations that can't be processed remotely.

  - **ORDER BY** arguments (if the remote data source doesn't support them).

  - **ORDER BY** or **GROUP BY** arguments containing operations that can't be processed remotely.

- Multiple-level **GROUP BY** arguments, such as those used in reports with multiple grouping levels.
- **GROUP BY** arguments on top of a query with a **DISTINCT** option.
- Cross-tab queries that have more than one aggregate or that have an **ORDER BY** clause that matches the **GROUP BY** clause.
- **TOP** or **TOP PERCENT** predicate.

See Also   DAO: Where Is..., DAO External: Working with External Data Sources, DAO External: Attaching External Tables

DAO Queries

This article explains what a query is and how to create and run one using the MFC DAO classes. Topics include:

- Query: definition
- Querydefs and recordsets
- Creating a query with a querydef
- Creating a query with a recordset

Query: Definition

A query is a formalized instruction to a database to either return a set of records or perform a specified action on a set of records as specified in the query. For example, the following SQL query statement returns records:

```
SELECT [Company Name] FROM Publishers WHERE State = "NY"
```

You can create and run select, action, crosstab, parameter, and other queries using the MFC DAO classes. Queries are expressed with Structured Query Language (SQL) statements like the one shown above. The most common query type is the **SELECT** query. For a list of other query types, see the topic Type Property in DAO Help, under Settings and Return Values listed for querydef objects.

How to Write SQL Statements

For general information on writing SQL queries, see the following topics in DAO Help:

- Querying a Database with SQL in Code
- Building SQL Statements in Code

Syntax of SQL Used with DAO

For a description of the SQL syntax used by DAO, see the topic Comparison of Microsoft Jet Database Engine SQL and ANSI SQL in DAO Help. For SQL syntax specific to your target database, see the documentation for your DBMS. For a list of additional topics on SQL in DAO Help, see the article DAO Queries: SQL for DAO.

Querydefs and Recordsets

You can work with queries in two ways:

- Use a DAO querydef object—the corresponding MFC object is represented by class **CDaoQueryDef**.

- Use a DAO recordset object—the corresponding MFC object is represented by class **CDaoRecordset**.

A querydef is a query definition, which you can optionally save as a persistent object in the database. A recordset is an object that represents and gives access to a set of records returned by a query.

Creating a Query with a Querydef

Once you create a querydef object, based on **CDaoQueryDef**, you can do the following with it:

- Save the querydef object in the database, which lets you run its query again later.

- Create parameters for the querydef, so you can run parameterized queries with it.

- Create a recordset based on the querydef.

- Use the querydef's **Execute** member function to directly execute a query that doesn't return records, such as an action query or a SQL pass-through query.

▶ **To create a querydef**

- See the detailed instructions in the article DAO Querydef: Using Querydefs.

Creating a Query with a Recordset

You can create a query with a recordset, represented by **CDaoRecordset**, in three ways:

- First create or open a **CDaoQueryDef** object; then base a **CDaoRecordset** object on it, using the version of **CDaoRecordset::Open** that takes a pointer to a **CDaoQueryDef** object.

 −or−

- First create or open a **CDaoTableDef** object, then base a **CDaoRecordset** object on it, using the version of **CDaoRecordset::Open** that takes a pointer to a **CDaoTableDef** object.

 −or−

- Create a recordset, usually based on a class that you derive from **CDaoRecordset** using AppWizard or ClassWizard, and open the recordset. No querydef is required.

▶ **To create a recordset with or without a querydef or tabledef**

- See the article DAO Recordset: Creating Recordsets.

You'll most likely base your recordsets on querydefs when you have a saved querydef for a query that you run frequently, or when you have just created a querydef that you plan to save in the database for later reuse. Or you'll base recordsets on tabledefs when you have a tabledef and want to work with the data in the table that the tabledef represents. Otherwise, you'll simply create a recordset (without a querydef) whenever you need one.

For related information, see the following topics in DAO Help:

- QueryDef Object
- Recordset Object
- CreateQueryDef Method

See Also   DAO: Where Is..., DAO Querydef, DAO Recordset

DAO Queries: SQL for DAO

SQL stands for Structured Query Language, the industry standard way to communicate with relational databases.

For information about SQL, see the topic SQL Property in DAO Help. For information about the SQL syntax used by DAO, see the topic Comparison of Microsoft Jet Database Engine SQL and ANSI SQL in DAO Help.

See Also   DAO: Where Is..., DAO Querydef, DAO Recordset, DAO Queries

DAO Queries: Filtering and Parameterizing Queries

This article describes how to restrict the number of records that a query returns. Topics covered include:

- Filtering recordsets
- Parameterizing queries

One of the great keys to good database performance is to restrict how many records you select. In general, the more records you select, the greater the overhead and the slower the performance. DAO and MFC let you "filter" the records that a query selects, and you can specify filtering criteria at run time rather than design time. The mechanism works as follows:

- You specify a filter for your query that restricts records using an SQL **WHERE** clause. For example:

```
WHERE [State] = "NY"
```

- Parameterizing specifies named parameters in the filter to which you can assign values at run time, based on information you calculate or obtain from the end-user. For example, the filter shown above looks like this with a named parameter:

```
WHERE [State] = [State Code]
```

State Code is the parameter name.

Filtering DAO Recordsets

Filtering records by any of the approaches described below relies on the SQL **WHERE** clause. You can also use the **HAVING** clause if you are using **GROUP BY**. For information about these keywords, see the following topics in DAO Help:

- WHERE Clause (SQL)
- HAVING Clause (SQL)
- GROUP BY Clause (SQL)

And see the topic SELECT Statement (SQL) in DAO Help.

The MFC DAO classes let you filter a recordset in two ways:

- You can (a) specify an SQL statement for your recordset that lacks a **WHERE** clause, then (b) supply a value at run time to the **m_strFilter** data member of your **CDaoRecordset**-derived class.

  −or−

- You can specify an SQL statement that includes a **WHERE** clause. Then you don't use **m_strFilter**.

Tip These two approaches are equivalent in terms of performance. The only difference is whether you build the **WHERE** clause in the SQL string you use to create the recordset or you let MFC build the clause using a value you've supplied for **m_strFilter**.

Important You can't use **m_strFilter** (or its companion **m_strSort**, which specifies an SQL **ORDER BY** clause for sorting) if you create your recordset from a **CDaoTableDef** or **CDaoQueryDef** object.

Example with m_strFilter

The following example shows filtering with **m_strFilter** (the first approach above):

```
// Filter records with m_strFilter but no parameter
// strStudentID is a value probably obtained from
// the user
rsEnrollmentSet.m_strFilter = "[Student ID] = " + strStudentID;
try
{
    // Open the recordset using the filtered string
    rsEnrollmentSet.Open( );
    // ...
```

```
}
// ...
```

MFC appends the value of **m_strFilter** to the recordset's SQL as long as there is not already a **WHERE** clause in the SQL string.

Example with a Complete WHERE Clause

The following example shows filtering with a pre-specified **WHERE** clause (the second approach above):

```
// Filter records with the SQL keyword WHERE
CString strSQL = rsEnrollmentSet.GetDefautlSQL( ) +
            "WHERE [Student ID] = " + strStudentID;
try
{
    // Open the recordset using the filtered SQL string
    rsEnrollmentSet.Open( dbOpenDynaset, strSQL );
    // ...
}
// ...
```

The example calls **GetDefaultSQL** to obtain the SQL string defined for the recordset's class at design time, using ClassWizard or AppWizard. Then it concatenates a **WHERE** clause, part of which is based on run-time information in strStudentID.

In either case, the result is a recordset that contains a smaller number of records because of the filtering.

Note The filtering and sorting mechanisms described here are not available for table-type recordsets. To filter or sort records in a table-type recordset, you must call DAO directly. Set the Filter and Sort properties of the recordset. To specify which index (if any) is active for the recordset, call **CDaoRecordset::SetCurrentIndex**. For information about calling DAO directly, see Technical Note 54 under MFC Technical Notes, under MFC in Books Online.

Parameterizing DAO Queries

In situations where your application executes the same query repeatedly, it is more efficient to create a stored querydef object that contains the SQL statement. Queries stored in the database execute faster and can be used by anyone with access to the database.

If your application needs to alter **WHERE** clause arguments in a query, you can also add a **PARAMETERS** clause to your query that permits the Microsoft Jet database engine to substitute values into the query at run time. Before running parameter queries, your application must substitute values for each of the parameters as stored in the Parameters collection of the querydef.

In general, parameterizing queries improves performance. The parameterized SQL statement doesn't have to be recompiled each time you run the query.

▶ **To create a parameter query**

1 Create a **PARAMETERS** clause string that includes a parameter name and data type for each parameter. Don't use the field name alone as the parameter name, because duplicating it may cause problems. You can include the field name within the parameter name, however. The example calls the parameter "Student Ident" rather than "Student ID", the name of the field.

If you are working with a database accessed by Microsoft Access, the parameter name is used as a prompt string. Keep this in mind if you expect Microsoft Access users to use this query.

Shown below is a typical **PARAMETERS** clause:

```
CString strParam = "PARAMETERS [Student Ident] TEXT ";
```

The parameter name is enclosed in square brackets here because the name contains a space. Otherwise the brackets are unnecessary.

2 Create a **SELECT** statement that retrieves the needed fields and incorporates the named parameters into the **WHERE** clause. In the example below, the parameters are used to filter the query to return only selected students. Note that the parameter [Student Ident] is substituted by the database engine during execution of the query at run time.

```
strSQL = strParam + "SELECT * FROM Enrollment WHERE
Enrollment.[Student ID] = [Student Ident]";
```

3 Create a named querydef ("Find Enrollments") with your SQL statement.

```
CDaoQueryDef qd( m_dbStudentReg );
qd.Create( "Find Enrollments", strSQL );
qd.Append( );
```

4 Set the querydef parameters.

First, you need to gain access to the querydef. You can either use the querydef object just created, or reference the stored querydef object from the QueryDefs collection. The example shows using the querydef just created.

```
COleVariant varParamValue( strStudentID );
qd.SetParamValue( "[Student ID]", varParamValue );
```

5 Execute the procedure.

Because this query returns records, you need to create a recordset to capture the result set.

```
CEnrollmentSet rsEnrollmentSet( &m_dbStudentReg );
rsEnrollmentSet.Open( &qd, dbOpenDynaset );
```

The parameter is defined as part of the SQL statement and becomes part of a **PARAMETERS** clause. You set the value of the parameter, at run time, by calling the querydef object's **SetParamValue** member function. This function takes:

- A parameter name, which must match the name you specified in the SQL string ("Student Ident" in the example).

- A **COleVariant** object that contains the value. **COleVariant** makes it easy to use the **VARIANT** data type from OLE for a variety of different actual types. In the example, the actual type is a string.

For more information and a different example (presented in the Basic language rather than C++), see the topic Creating Parameter Queries with DAO in DAO Help.

In the *Class Library Reference*, see **CDaoQueryDef** and **CDaoRecordset**. In particular, see **CDaoQueryDef::SetParamValue** and **CDaoQueryDef::GetParamValue**.

See Also DAO: Where Is..., DAO Queries, DAO Querydef, DAO Recordset, DAO Queries: SQL for DAO

DAO Querydef

This article describes "querydefs" and the key features of the MFC **CDaoQueryDef** class. For task-oriented information, see the article DAO Querydef: Using Querydefs. For an understanding of the DAO querydef object underlying each MFC **CDaoQueryDef** object, see the topic QueryDef Object in DAO Help.

Topics covered include:

- Querydef: definition

- Querydef uses

- Querydef parameters

- Querydefs and DAO collections

- Further reading about querydefs

Querydef: Definition

A DAO querydef, represented in MFC by a **CDaoQueryDef** object, is a query definition. The object defines the SQL statement for a query and provides operations for executing the query, for saving it in the database for reuse, for parameterizing the query, and more.

For information about specifying a query with SQL, see the article DAO Queries.

Saved queries are advantageous because you can keep frequently used queries, especially complex ones, for easy reuse later. For information about saving querydefs in a database, see the article DAO Querydef: Using Querydefs.

Tip If you are working with Microsoft Jet (.MDB) databases, the easiest way to create a querydef is to do it in Microsoft Access. Open your target database, create querydefs, and save them in the database. Then you can use the querydefs in your code.

Querydef Uses

Querydef objects have two primary uses, corresponding to two ways to run the query:

- Creating recordsets, which you then open to run the query.
- Directly executing queries that don't return records. These include action queries and some SQL pass-through queries (those that return no records).

For information about these querydef uses, see the article DAO Querydef: Using Querydefs. For information about action queries and SQL pass-through queries, see the article DAO Querydef: Action Queries and SQL Pass-Through Queries.

QueryDef Parameters

Sometimes you'd like to be able to select records using information you've calculated or obtained from your user at run time. Parameterized queries let you pass such information at run time.

A query parameter is an element containing a value that you can change to affect the results of the query. For example, a query returning data about an employee might have a parameter for the employee's name. You can then use one querydef object to find data about any employee by setting the parameter to a specific name before running the query. This has two valuable effects:

- It can result in better execution speed, particularly on the second and subsequent requeries.
- It lets you build a query at run time, based on information not available to you at design time, such as information that you must obtain from the user or information that you must calculate.

Important In DAO, the parameter names are exposed rather than only the positions as in ODBC. While ODBC does allow named parameters, users of the MFC ODBC classes will be more familiar with using positional parameters.

For more information about DAO parameters, see the following topics in DAO Help:

- Parameter Object, Parameters Collection Summary
- Creating Parameter Queries
- PARAMETERS Declaration (SQL)

For more information about using parameterized queries, see the article DAO Queries: Filtering and Parameterizing Queries.

QueryDefs and DAO Collections

Each DAO database object maintains a QueryDefs collection—a collection of all saved querydefs in the database. Each querydef object maintains two collections of its own:

- Parameters   All defined parameters for the query.
- Fields   The fields in one or more tables that correspond to the parameters. For example, an Employee Name field corresponds to an Employee Name parameter.

MFC objects don't store a representation of a DAO collection. Instead, MFC accesses the collection through the underlying DAO object. For more information, see the article DAO Collections.

MFC also doesn't provide a C++ class to represent every DAO object. In particular, there is no MFC parameter object or field object. You work with a querydef's parameters and fields through member functions of class **CDaoQueryDef**. For more information, see the article DAO Queries: Filtering and Parameterizing Queries.

Further Reading About Querydefs

For more information about querydefs in MFC, see the following additional articles (in the recommended reading order):

- DAO Queries
- DAO Querydef: Using Querydefs
- DAO Queries: Filtering and Parameterizing Queries
- DAO Querydef: Action Queries and SQL Pass-Through Queries

See Also   DAO: Where Is..., DAO Recordset

DAO Querydef: Using Querydefs

This article explains how to use **CDaoQueryDef** objects. Topics covered include:

- Creating a querydef
- Saving a querydef (in Microsoft Jet (.MDB) databases only)
- Opening a previously saved querydef
- Using a temporary querydef
- Creating a recordset from a querydef
- Directly executing a query (an action query or an SQL pass-through query that doesn't return records)

For a general understanding of querydefs and their uses, see the topic QueryDef Object in DAO Help.

Creating a Querydef

Creating a querydef, whether you save it in the database or use it as a temporary object, requires specifying the SQL statement that defines the query and setting any needed properties of the querydef. If the querydef represents a parameterized query, you also need to create the parameters and their corresponding fields and later set their values.

Tip You can also set and get field values and parameter values (in a recordset) dynamically, without using a querydef. See the article DAO Recordset: Binding Records Dynamically.

Creating a new MFC **CDaoQueryDef** object creates the underlying DAO querydef object.

▶ **To create a querydef**

1 Construct a **CDaoQueryDef** object.

2 Call the querydef object's **Create** member function.

   In the **Create** call, pass a user-defined name for the querydef and a string that contains the SQL statement on which the querydef is based. While you can define the SQL string for a recordset with AppWizard or ClassWizard, you must write the SQL string for a querydef yourself. (You usually use class **CDaoQueryDef** directly rather than deriving your own querydef classes from it.)

3 Save the querydef object in the database by calling its **Append** member function, unless you want to work with a temporary (unsaved) querydef. (See Using a Temporary Querydef.)

4 Either create a recordset based on the querydef or call the querydef object's **Execute** member function.

Close the querydef when you finish with it: call its **Close** member function. For more information, see the detailed instructions under **CDaoQueryDef::Create** in the *Class Library Reference*.

Querydef objects have several properties you can set—primarily for querydefs to be used with ODBC data sources.

▶ **To set a querydef's properties (primarily for ODBC)**

1 Create the querydef, using a **CDaoQueryDef** object, as described above.

2 Call any of the following member functions: **SetConnect**, **SetODBCTimeout**, **SetReturnsRecords**, **SetName**, **SetSQL**.

3 Save the querydef in the QueryDefs collection by calling **Append**, unless you want to use the querydef as a temporary object. (See Using a Temporary Querydef.)

4 Use the querydef.

You can use **SetName** and **SetSQL** for a querydef based on any kind of database. You can call these member functions at any time to rename the querydef object or to respecify its SQL statement. **SetReturnsRecords** applies only to SQL pass-through queries. The other functions apply only to ODBC data sources.

After creating a querydef, you will usually want to save it in the database by appending it to the QueryDefs collection. See Saving a Querydef. The alternative is to use the querydef as a temporary object. See Using a Temporary Querydef. You can't use the querydef unless you correctly create it as a temporary querydef or you append it to the collection.

Once created, use the querydef to create recordsets or to execute action queries or SQL pass-through queries. For information about action queries and SQL pass-through queries, see the article DAO Querydef: Action Queries and SQL Pass-Through Queries.

Saving a Querydef

A saved querydef persists in its database (.MDB only), stored there along with the database's tables and data. You can think of a saved query as a compiled SQL statement—when you run the query, it executes faster than a standard new query because the database engine doesn't have to compile the SQL statement before executing it.

Tip   The easiest way to create a querydef is to do it in Microsoft Access. Open your target .MDB database, create querydefs, and save them in the database. Then you can use the querydefs in your code.

▶ **To save a querydef**

1 Create the querydef as described under Creating a Querydef.

2 Call **CDaoQueryDef::Append** for the object.

Appending the querydef object to the database's QueryDefs collection makes the object persistent between database engine sessions. You can open and run the query, or modify it, at any time. Other users of your database can use the querydef as well.

The alternative to saving a querydef is using it as a temporary object.

Opening a Previously Saved Querydef

Once you've saved a querydef in a database's QueryDefs collection, you can open it at any time and run its query, either by creating a recordset or by calling **Execute**.

▶ **To open a saved querydef**

1 Construct a **CDaoQueryDef** object.

2 Call its **Open** member function.

In the **Open** call, pass the user-defined name under which the querydef was stored.

Using a Temporary Querydef

A temporary querydef object has the following characteristics:

- It is never appended to the QueryDefs collection in the database, unlike a saved querydef.

- It is created by passing either **NULL** or an empty string for the querydef's name.

Note MFC differs from the underlying DAO implementation in the way querydefs are appended to the collection. In DAO, a newly created querydef (provided you give it a name) is automatically appended to the QueryDefs collection. In MFC, you must explicitly call **Append**.

Saved querydefs are accessible to other users of your database (who have the appropriate permissions, if security is in effect). Temporary querydefs are not accessible to other users. In some cases, you might want to create a querydef and use it without storing it. For example, you might want to use querydef parameters but not want to save the querydef for reuse.

Whether a querydef is temporary or not depends on what you pass in the *lpszName* parameter to **Create**. Querydefs can be in one of the states listed in Table 1:

Table 1 QueryDef States and Their Meanings

State	Meaning
Appended	You give the querydef a name when you create it. Then you call **Append**.
Unappended	You give the querydef a name but you haven't called **Append**. The querydef is unusable. This is not the same thing as a temporary querydef.
Temporary	You pass **NULL** or an empty string ("") for the querydef name when you create the querydef. You can't append a temporary querydef, because it has no name. But you can use it to create recordsets or to call the **Execute** member function.

▶ **To create a temporary querydef**

1 Construct a **CDaoQueryDef** object.

2 Call its **Create** member function, passing **NULL** or an empty string ("").

3 *Don't* call **CDaoQueryDef::Append**.

You can still use a temporary querydef to create recordsets or to execute action queries or SQL pass-through queries.

Creating a Recordset from a Querydef

The most common way to use a querydef is to base a recordset on it. The recordset inherits the querydef's SQL statement.

▶ **To create a recordset from a querydef**

1 Create a saved or temporary querydef as described in Creating a Querydef, or open a previously saved querydef.

2 Construct a **CDaoRecordset** object.

3 Call the recordset object's **Open** member function, passing a pointer to your querydef object.

Calling **Open** runs the query. For a more detailed discussion, see the article DAO Recordset: Creating Recordsets.

You can create any number of recordsets from the same querydef object. They will all have the same SQL statement unless you change the querydef's SQL statement between creating recordsets.

For related information, see the article DAO Queries.

Executing a Querydef

Not all queries return records. Queries that don't return records include:

- Action queries, which update data or alter the database's structure.
- SQL pass-through queries, which pass the SQL statement to the back-end DBMS without processing it in the Microsoft Jet database engine.

To execute such queries, you use a querydef rather than a recordset. For more information about action queries and SQL pass-through queries, see the article DAO Querydef: Action Queries and SQL Pass-Through Queries.

▶ **To directly execute a query that doesn't return records**

1 Create a saved or temporary querydef as described in Creating a Querydef.

2 Call the querydef's **Execute** member function.

For more information about executing queries, see **CDaoQueryDef::Execute** in the *Class Library Reference* and the topic Execute Method in DAO Help.

See Also   DAO: Where Is..., DAO Querydef, DAO Recordset, DAO Queries, DAO Querydef: Action Queries and SQL Pass-Through Queries

DAO Querydef: Action Queries and SQL Pass-Through Queries

This article tells you where to find information about action queries and SQL pass-through queries.

For information about action queries, including a definition, see the following topics in DAO Help:

- Action Query
- Querying a Database with SQL in Code

For information about SQL pass-through queries, including a definition, see the following topics in DAO Help:

- Using SQL PassThrough with DAO
- QueryDef Object

Quick SQL Pass-Through Queries

The fastest way to work with ODBC data sources is via attached tables. See the article DAO External: Working with External Data Sources. For doing bulk operations, the best, and often fastest, approach is to use an SQL pass-through query. It's possible to do a quick pass-through query using a recordset and without having to create a querydef, even a temporary one. This is also helpful if you're converting existing code that uses the **DB_SQLPASSTHROUGH** option in many places.

DAO's Connect property for databases normally doesn't have a value for Microsoft Jet (.MDB) databases. But you can assign an ODBC connect string to the property and use the **dbSQLPassthrough** option in a recordset. This means you don't have to open the ODBC data source directly to use SQL pass-through.

For example:

```
// pdb is a pointer to a CDaoDatabase object
// (an .MDB database)
// Set up the connect string
CString strConnect = "ODBC;DSN=ntstuff;UID=sa;PWD=Fred;APP=App
Name;WSID=MyComputer;DATABASE=pubs;TABLE=dbo.authors;";
pdb->SetConnect( strConnect );
// Use SQL pass-through in a recordset
// Set up the SQL and open the recordset
CString strSQL = "whatever";
CDaoRecordset rs( pdb );
try
{
    rs.Open( dbOpenSnapshot, strSQL, dbSQLPassThrough );
    // ...
}
// ...
```

See Also   DAO: Where Is..., DAO Querydef, DAO Querydef: Using Querydefs

In the *Class Library Reference*: **CDaoQueryDef::Execute**.

DAO Record Field Exchange (DFX)

The MFC DAO database classes automate moving data between the data source and a recordset using a mechanism called "DAO record field exchange" (DFX). DFX is similar to dialog data exchange (DDX) and, at the interface level, almost identical to record field exchange (RFX) for the MFC ODBC classes. If you understand RFX, you will find DFX easy to use.

Note The MFC DAO database classes are distinct from the MFC database classes based on ODBC. All DAO class names have the "CDao" prefix. Where the ODBC classes are based on Open Database Connectivity (ODBC), the DAO classes are based on Data Access Objects (DAO), which use the Microsoft Jet database engine. In general, the MFC DAO classes are more capable than the MFC ODBC classes. For more information, see the article DAO and MFC.

The DoFieldExchange Mechanism for DAO

Moving data between a data source and the field data members of a recordset requires multiple calls to the recordset's **DoFieldExchange** function and considerable interaction between the framework and DAO. The DFX mechanism is type-safe and saves you the work of allocating storage and binding data to it. Sometimes, however, there will be a performance penalty for this ease of use. (For more information about DDX, see Chapter 14, Working with Classes, in the *Visual C++ User's Guide*.)

Derived Recordset Classes for DAO

DFX is mostly transparent to you. If you declare your recordset classes with AppWizard or ClassWizard, DFX is built into them automatically. DAO recordset classes are normally derived from the base class **CDaoRecordset** supplied by the framework (but see Using CDaoRecordset Directly Instead of Deriving). AppWizard lets you create an initial recordset class. ClassWizard lets you add other recordset classes as you need them. You use ClassWizard to map recordset field data members to table columns on the data source. For more information and examples, see the article ClassWizard: Creating a Recordset Class.

You must manually add a small amount of DFX code in two cases—when you want to:

- Use parameterized queries. See the article DAO Queries: Filtering and Parameterizing Queries.
- Perform joins—using one recordset for columns from two or more tables, joined on a common field by a **WHERE** clause in the SQL statement such as:

```
WHERE Course.CourseID = Section.CourseID
```

Using CDaoRecordset Directly Instead of Deriving

There is an alternative to using DFX (and derived **CDaoRecordset** classes). You can use **CDaoRecordset** directly (without deriving from it) to bind a specified field in the current record dynamically. For more information, see the article DAO Recordset: Binding Records Dynamically.

More Information About DFX

If you need a more advanced understanding of DFX, see the article DAO Record Field Exchange: How DFX Works.

The following articles explain the details of using recordset objects:

- DAO Record Field Exchange: Using DFX
- DAO Record Field Exchange: Working with the Wizard Code
- DAO Record Field Exchange: Using the DFX Functions

In the *Class Library Reference*, see classes **CDaoRecordset** and **CDaoFieldExchange**.

See Also   DAO: Where Is..., DAO Recordset, ClassWizard: Creating a Recordset Class, AppWizard: Database Support

DAO Record Field Exchange: Using DFX

This article explains what you do to use DFX in relation to what the framework does. The related article, DAO Record Field Exchange: Working with the Wizard Code, continues the discussion. That article introduces the main components of DFX and explains the code that AppWizard and ClassWizard write to support DFX and how you might want to modify the wizard code.

Note   This article is about the DAO version of record field exchange. If you are using the MFC ODBC classes rather than the MFC DAO classes, see the article Record Field Exchange: Using RFX instead.

Writing calls to the DFX functions in your **DoFieldExchange** override is explained in the article DAO Record Field Exchange: Using the DFX Functions.

Table 1 shows your role in relation to what the framework does for you.

Table 1   Using DFX: You and the Framework

You...	The framework...
Declare your recordset classes with ClassWizard. Specify names and data types of field data members.	ClassWizard derives a **CDaoRecordset** class and writes a **DoFieldExchange** override for you, including a DFX function call for each field data member.

Table 1   Using DFX: You and the Framework *(cont.)*

You...	The framework...
(Optional) Manually add any needed parameter data members to the class. Manually add a DFX function call to **DoFieldExchange** for each parameter data member, add a call to **CDaoFieldExchange::SetFieldType** for the group of parameters, and specify the total number of parameters in **m_nParams**. (See DAO: Filtering and Parameterizing Queries for an alternative way to parameterize queries.)	
Construct an object of your recordset class. Then, before opening the object, set the values of its parameter data members, if any. (If you create your recordset from a querydef object, you can specify parameters in the querydef.)	For efficiency, the framework prebinds the parameters, using DAO. When you pass parameter values, the framework passes them to the DAO data source. Only the parameter values are sent for requeries, unless the sort and/or filter strings have changed.
Open a recordset object using **CDaoRecordset::Open**.	Executes the recordset's query, binds columns to field data members of the recordset, and calls **DoFieldExchange** to exchange data between the first selected record and the recordset's field data members.
Scroll in the recordset using **CDaoRecordset::Move** or a menu or toolbar command.	Calls **DoFieldExchange** to transfer data to the field data members from the new current record.
Add, update, and delete records.	Calls **DoFieldExchange** to transfer data to the database.

In the *Class Library Reference*, see **CDaoRecordset**, **CDaoFieldExchange**, and, under Macros and Globals, Record Field Exchange Functions.

See Also   DAO: Where Is..., DAO Record Field Exchange (DFX), DAO Record Field Exchange: Working with the Wizard Code, DAO Record Field Exchange: Using the DFX Functions, DAO Record Field Exchange: How DFX Works, DAO Recordset

DAO Record Field Exchange: Working with the Wizard Code

This article explains the code that AppWizard and ClassWizard write to support DFX and how you might want to alter that code.

Note This article is about the DAO version of record field exchange. If you are using the MFC ODBC classes rather than the MFC DAO classes, see the article Record Field Exchange: Working with the Wizard Code instead.

When you create a recordset class with ClassWizard (or with AppWizard), the wizard writes the following DFX-related elements for you, based on the data source, table, and column (field) choices you make in the wizard:

- Declarations of the recordset field data members

- An override of **CDaoRecordset::DoFieldExchange**

- Initialization of recordset field data members in the recordset class constructor

The Field Data Member Declarations for DAO

The wizards write a recordset class declaration in an .H file that resembles the following for a user-defined class called CSectionSet:

```
class CSectionSet : public CDaoRecordset
{
public:
    CSectionSet(CDaoDatabase* pDatabase = NULL);
    DECLARE_DYNAMIC(CSectionSet)

// Field/Param Data
    //{{AFX_FIELD(CSectionSet, CDaoRecordset)
    CString     m_CourseID;
    CString     m_SectionNo;
    CString     m_InstructorID;
    CString     m_RoomNo;
    CString     m_Schedule;
    int         m_Capacity;
    //}}AFX_FIELD

// Overrides
    // ClassWizard generated virtual function overrides
    //{{AFX_VIRTUAL(CSectionSet)
    public:
    virtual CString GetDefaultDBName();
    virtual CString GetDefaultSQL();
    virtual void DoFieldExchange(CDaoFieldExchange*
                                                pFX);

    //}}AFX_VIRTUAL

// Implementation
#ifdef _DEBUG
    virtual void AssertValid() const;
    virtual void Dump(CDumpContext& dc) const;
#endif

};
```

Notice the following key features about the class above:

- Special "//{{AFX_FIELD" comments that bracket the field data member declarations. ClassWizard uses these to update your source file.

- The wizard overrides several **CDaoRecordset** virtual functions. The most important of these is the **DoFieldExchange** member function.

Caution Never edit the code inside "//{{AFX" brackets. Always use ClassWizard. If you add parameter data members or new field data members that you bind yourself, add them outside the brackets.

The DoFieldExchange Override for DAO

DoFieldExchange is the heart of DFX. The framework calls **DoFieldExchange** any time it needs to move data either from data source to recordset or from recordset to data source. **DoFieldExchange** also supports obtaining information about field data members through the **IsFieldDirty** and **IsFieldNull** member functions.

The following **DoFieldExchange** override is for a user-defined CSectionSet class. ClassWizard writes the function in the .CPP file for your recordset class.

```
void CSectionSet::DoFieldExchange(CDaoFieldExchange* pFX)
{
    //{{AFX_FIELD_MAP(CSectionSet)
    pFX->SetFieldType(CDaoFieldExchange::outputColumn);
    DFX_Text(pFX, _T("CourseID"), m_CourseID);
    DFX_Text(pFX, _T("SectionNo"), m_SectionNo);
    DFX_Text(pFX, _T("InstructorID"), m_InstructorID);
    DFX_Text(pFX, _T("RoomNo"), m_RoomNo);
    DFX_Text(pFX, _T("Schedule"), m_Schedule);
    DFX_Short(pFX, _T("Capacity"), m_Capacity);
    //}}AFX_FIELD_MAP
}
```

Notice the following key features of the function:

- The special "//{{AFX_FIELD_MAP" comments. ClassWizard uses these to update your source file. This section of the function is called the "field map."

- A call to **CDaoFieldExchange::SetFieldType**, through the *pFX* pointer. This call specifies that all DFX function calls up to the end of **DoFieldExchange** or the next call to **SetFieldType** are "output columns." See **CDaoFieldExchange::SetFieldType** in the *Class Library Reference* for more information.

- Several calls to the **DFX_Text** and **DFX_Short** global functions—one per field data member. These calls specify the relationship between a column name on the data source and a field data member. The DFX functions do the actual data transfer. The class library supplies DFX functions for all of the common data types. For more information about DFX functions, see the article DAO Record Field Exchange: Using the DFX Functions and, in the *Class Library Reference* under Macros and Globals, Record Field Exchange Functions.

- The *pFX* pointer to a **CDaoFieldExchange** object that the framework passes when it calls **DoFieldExchange**. The **CDaoFieldExchange** object specifies the operation that **DoFieldExchange** is to perform, the direction of transfer, and other context information.

- The use of the **_T** macro for Unicode enabling. For more information, see the article Strings: Unicode and Multibyte Character Set (MBCS) Support.

The Recordset Constructor for DAO

The recordset constructor that the wizards write contains two things related to DFX:

- An initialization for each field data member

- An initialization for the **m_nFields** data member, which contains the number of field data members

The constructor for the CSectionSet recordset example looks like this:

```
CSectionSet::CSectionSet(CDaoDatabase* pdb)
    : CDaoRecordset(pdb)
{
    //{{AFX_FIELD_INIT(CSectionSet)
    m_CourseID = _T("");
    m_SectionNo = _T("");
    m_InstructorID = _T("");
    m_RoomNo = _T("");
    m_Schedule = _T("");
    m_Capacity = 0;
    m_nFields = 6;
    //}}AFX_FIELD_INIT
    m_nDefaultType = dbOpenDynaset;

    m_bCheckCacheForDirtyFields = TRUE;
}
```

This code initializes all of the field data members that require initialization and specifies how many field data members there are (in **m_nFields**). The code also sets the values of two special recordset data members:

- **m_nDefaultType** Set to the type of recordset you specify in the wizard. All recordsets created from this class default to the type set here, but you can override the default for any particular recordset object by specifying a new type when you call **CDaoRecordset::Open**.

- **m_bCheckCacheForDirtyFields** If set to **TRUE** (the default), the recordset uses a "double-buffering" mechanism to detect edits to fields by comparing them to a copy of the record. For more information, see the article DAO Record Field Exchange: Double Buffering Records.

Note The code above is enabled for Unicode.

Important If you add any field data members manually, you must increment **m_nFields**. Do so with another line of code outside the "//{{AFX_FIELD_INIT" brackets, such as:

```
m_nFields += 3;
```

This is the code for adding three new fields. If you add any parameter data members, you must initialize the **m_nParams** data member, which contains the number of parameter data members. Put the **m_nParams** initialization outside the brackets.

For more information about these special recordset data members, see the article DAO Recordset: Architecture.

See Also DAO: Where Is..., DAO Record Field Exchange (DFX), DAO Record Field Exchange: Using DFX, DAO Record Field Exchange: Using the DFX Functions, DAO Record Field Exchange: How DFX Works, DAO Recordset, DAO Queries: Filtering and Parameterizing Queries

DAO Record Field Exchange: Using the DFX Functions

This article explains how to use the DFX function calls that make up the body of your **DoFieldExchange** override.

Note This article is about the DAO version of record field exchange. If you are using the MFC ODBC classes rather than the MFC DAO classes, see the article Record Field Exchange: Using the RFX Functions instead.

The DFX global functions exchange data between columns (fields) on the data source and field data members in your recordset. Normally you use ClassWizard to write the DFX function calls in your recordset's **DoFieldExchange** member function. This article describes the functions briefly and shows the data types for which DFX functions are available. Technical Note 53 under MFC Technical Notes in Books Online describes how to write your own DFX functions for additional data types.

DFX Function Syntax

Each DFX function takes three parameters (and some take an optional fourth or fifth parameter):

- A pointer to a **CDaoFieldExchange** object. You simply pass along the *pFX* pointer passed to **DoFieldExchange**.
- The name of the column (field) as it appears in the data source. The names in your SQL statement must match those in the DFX call. Advanced programmers might want to qualify the column names, for example by adding aggregate functions or other SQL modifications. For general guidelines, see the article Recordset: Obtaining SUMs and Other Aggregate Results (ODBC) (the article is for the MFC

ODBC classes, but the general principles it illustrates apply as well to DAO). You can also add **GROUP BY** and other clauses to your SQL, either in the SQL statement or in the DFX function calls. The column (field) name, and any modifications to it, are used to build a query.

- The name of the corresponding field data member or parameter data member in the recordset class.

- (Optional) In some of the functions, which handle variable-length data, your specification of how much memory to preallocate for the data. For details, see **DFX_Binary**, **DFX_Text**, and **DFX_LongBinary**.

- (Optional) A flag that specifies whether the field is to be double buffered. For more information, see **DoFieldExchange** and the article DAO Record Field Exchange: Double Buffering Records.

For more information, see Record Field Exchange Functions under Macros and Globals in the *Class Library Reference*.

DFX Data Types

The class library supplies DFX functions for transferring many different data types between the data source and your recordsets. Table 1 summarizes the DFX functions by data type. In cases where you must write your own DFX function calls, select from these functions by data type.

Table 1   Data Types and DFX Functions

DFX function	C++ data type	DAO data type
DFX_Binary	**CByteArray**	**DAO_BYTES**
DFX_Bool	**BOOL**	**DAO_BOOL**
DFX_Byte	**BYTE**	**DAO_BYTES**
DFX_Currency	**COleCurrency**	**DAO_CURRENCY**
DFX_DateTime	**COleDateTime**	**DAO_DATE**
DFX_Double	**double**	**DAO_R8**
DFX_Long	**long**	**DAO_I4**
DFX_LongBinary	**CByteArray** or **CLongBinary***	**DAO_BYTES**
DFX_Short	**short**	**DAO_I2**
DFX_Single	**float**	**DAO_R4**
DFX_Text	**CString***	**DAO_CHAR**

Note Mapping long binary objects, such as pictures or OLE objects, to **CByteArray** is now preferred over mapping them to class **CLongBinary**. **DFX_Text** maps between **CString** and **DAO_WCHAR** if the symbol **_UNICODE** is defined. **CByteArray** gives you easier control over the contents of the long binary object.

Note You can use DFX to bring data of a DAO type into a variable of a different type as long as a conversion exists between the two. Take care, however, in cases such as converting a string to a date. If the string doesn't parse to a correct date format, an error will result.

For information about the DAO data types in the third column of Table 1, see the topic Type Property in DAO Help.

For more information about the DFX functions in the first column of Table 1, see Record Field Exchange Functions under Macros and Globals in the *Class Library Reference*. Also in the *Class Library Reference* see **CDaoRecordset** and **CDaoFieldExchange**.

See Also DAO: Where Is..., DAO Record Field Exchange (DFX), DAO Record Field Exchange: Using DFX, DAO Record Field Exchange: Working with the Wizard Code, DAO Record Field Exchange: Using the DFX Functions, DAO Record Field Exchange: How DFX Works, DAO Queries: Filtering and Parameterizing Queries, DAO Recordset

DAO Record Field Exchange: How DFX Works

This article explains the DFX process. This is a fairly advanced topic, covering:

- DFX and the recordset
- The DFX process

Note This article is about the DAO version of record field exchange. If you are using the MFC ODBC classes rather than the MFC DAO classes, see the article Record Field Exchange: How RFX Works instead.

DFX and the Recordset

The recordset object's field data members, taken together, constitute an "edit buffer" that holds the selected columns of one record. When the recordset is first opened and is about to read the first record, DFX binds (associates) each selected column to the address of the appropriate field data member. When the recordset updates a record, DFX calls DAO to send the appropriate commands to the database engine. DFX uses its knowledge of the field data members to specify the columns (fields) in the data source to write.

There are two ways of working with the edit buffer in a recordset:

- Use MFC's "double-buffering" mechanism.

  By default, your recordsets keep a second copy of the edit buffer for most data types (excluding the variable-length types, such as text and binary data). The copy is used for comparison with the edit buffer, to detect changes. You can choose to turn double buffering off, but keeping it turned on simplifies managing record field updates, adding and deleting records, and so on. For more information about double buffering, see the article DAO Record Field Exchange: Double Buffering Records.

- Don't use double buffering; instead, manage all field activity yourself.

  If you turn off the default double buffering, each time you edit a field you must call **SetFieldDirty** and **SetFieldNull** (passing the parameter **FALSE**). That is, you must take explicit actions so MFC does not have to compare the edit buffer with a copy to detect your changes. For more information, see the article DAO Record Field Exchange: Double Buffering Records.

If you have double buffering enabled (the default), the framework backs up the edit buffer at certain stages so it can restore its contents if necessary. With double buffering enabled, DFX backs up the edit buffer before adding a new record and before editing an existing record. It restores the edit buffer in some cases—for example, after an **Update** call following **AddNew**.

Besides exchanging data between the data source and the recordset's field data members, DFX manages binding parameters. When the recordset is opened, any parameter data members are bound in the order of the named parameters in the SQL statement that **CDaoRecordset::Open** receives or constructs. For more information, see the article DAO Queries: Filtering and Parameterizing Queries.

Your recordset class's override of **DoFieldExchange** does all the work, moving data in both directions. Like dialog data exchange (DDX), DFX needs information about the data members of your class. ClassWizard provides the necessary information by writing a recordset-specific implementation of **DoFieldExchange** for you, based on the field data member names and data types you specify with the wizard.

The DAO Record Field Exchange Process

This section describes the sequence of DFX events as a recordset object is opened and as you scroll and add, update, and delete records. Table 1 in the article DAO Record Field Exchange: Using DFX shows the process at a high level, illustrating operations as a recordset is opened. Table 1 and Table 2 in this article show the process as DFX processes a **Move** command in the recordset and as DFX manages an update. During these processes, **DoFieldExchange** is called to perform many different operations. The **m_nOperation** data member of the **CDaoFieldExchange** object determines which operation is requested.

DFX: Initial Binding of Columns and Parameters

The following DFX activities occur, in the order shown, when you call a recordset object's **Open** member function:

- If the recordset has parameter data members, the framework calls **DoFieldExchange** to "bind" the parameters to named parameters in the recordset's SQL statement.

- The framework calls **DoFieldExchange** a second time to bind the columns to corresponding field data members in the recordset. This establishes the recordset object as an edit buffer containing the columns of the first record.

- The recordset opens either a table-type recordset or an SQL-based recordset (dynaset or snapshot) and selects the first record. The record's columns are loaded into the recordset's field data members.

Table 1 shows the sequence of DFX operations when you open a recordset.

Table 1   Sequence of DFX Operations During Recordset Open

Your operation	DoFieldExchange operation	Database operation
1. Open the recordset.		
	2. Build an SQL statement. **DoFieldExchange** might have a querydef, a tabledef, or an SQL statement handed to it. If not, MFC builds the statement.	
		3. Open the querydef or tabledef, or create a temporary querydef (using either an SQL statement passed in or one built by MFC) and open it.
	4. Bind parameter data member(s).	
	5. Bind field data member(s) to column(s).	
		6. Create the recordset.
		7. DAO moves to the first record and fills in the data.
	8. Fix up the data for C++.	

DFX: Scrolling

When you scroll from one record to another, the framework calls **DoFieldExchange** to replace the values previously stored in the field data members with values for the new record.

Table 2 shows the sequence of DFX operations when the user moves from record to record.

Table 2   Sequence of DFX Operations During Scrolling

Your operation	DoFieldExchange operation	Database operation
1. Call **MoveNext** or one of the other Move functions.		
		2. DAO does the move and fills in the data.
	3. Fix up the data for C++.	

DFX: Adding New Records and Editing Existing Records

If you add a new record, the recordset operates as an edit buffer to build up the contents of the new record. As with adding records, editing records involves changing the values of the recordset's field data members. From the DFX perspective, the sequence is as follows:

1. If double buffering is on, your call to the recordset's **AddNew** or **Edit** member function causes DFX to store the current edit buffer so it can be restored later.

2. If double buffering is on, **AddNew** or **Edit** prepares the fields in the edit buffer so DFX can detect changed field data members. If double buffering is off for an **Edit** call, the fields are not prepared for detection (in this case, it's up to you to manage edits explicitly—see the article DAO Record Field Exchange: Double Buffering Records). The fields of a record prepared for **AddNew** are set to null whether double buffering is in effect or not.

   Since a new record has no previous values to compare new ones with, **AddNew** (with double buffering) sets the value of each field data member to a **PSEUDO_NULL** value. Later, when you call **Update**, DFX compares each data member's value with the **PSEUDO_NULL** value; if there's a difference, the data member has been set. (**PSEUDO_NULL** is not the same thing as a record column with a true Null value; nor is either the same as C++ **NULL**.)

   Note MFC does not use a **PSEUDO_NULL** value for **COleDateTime** or **COleCurrency** fields. Those data types have Nulls built in.

   Unlike the **Update** call for **AddNew**, the **Update** call for **Edit** compares updated values with previously stored values rather than using **PSEUDO_NULL**, if double buffering is on. If double buffering is off, you must call **SetFieldDirty** after an edit (and **SetFieldNull** if appropriate). The difference between **Edit** and **AddNew** is that **AddNew** has no previous stored values for comparison.

3. You directly set the values of field data members whose values you want to edit or that you want filled for a new record. (This can include calling **SetFieldNull**.)

4. If double buffering is on, your call to **Update** checks for changed field data members, as described in step 2 (see Table 2). If none have changed, **Update** returns 0. If some field data members have changed, **Update** propagates the changes to the database.

5. For **AddNew**, **Update** concludes by restoring the previously stored values of the record that was current before the **AddNew** call. For **Edit**, the new, edited values remain in place if double buffering is in effect.

Table 3 shows the sequence of DFX operations when you add a new record or edit an existing record.

Table 3   Sequence of DFX Operations During AddNew and Edit

Your operation	DoFieldExchange operation	Database operation
1. Call **AddNew** or **Edit**.		
	2. Back up the edit buffer if double buffering is on.	
	3. For **AddNew**, mark field data members as "clean" and Null. For **Edit**, call **Edit** in DAO.	
4. Assign values to recordset field data members.		
5. Call **Update**.		
	6. Check for changed fields if double buffering is on.	
		7. Progagate changes to the database. Call **Update** in DAO.
	8. For **AddNew**, restore the edit buffer to its backed-up contents if double buffering is on. If it is off, the values set for the new record remain in the recordset data members. For **Edit**, delete the backup if double buffering is on.	
9. If double buffering is off, you must refresh the current record after **AddNew**. Call **Move** with the **AFX_MOVE_REFRESH** parameter to restore the record that was previously current.		

DFX: Deleting Existing Records

When you delete a record, DFX sets all the fields to **NULL** as a reminder that the record is deleted and you must move off it. You won't need any other DFX sequence information.

In the *Class Library Reference* see **CDaoFieldExchange**, **CDaoRecordset::DoFieldExchange**, and, under Macros and Globals, Record Field Exchange Functions.

See Also   DAO: Where Is..., DAO Record Field Exchange (DFX), DAO Record Field Exchange: Using DFX, DAO Record Field Exchange: Working with the Wizard Code, DAO Record Field Exchange: Using the DFX Functions, ClassWizard

DAO Record Field Exchange: Double Buffering Records

This article explains the double buffering mechanism that MFC uses to detect changes to the current record in a recordset. Topics covered include:

- Double buffering: definition
- Using double buffering
- Effects of double buffering

In the DAO database classes, records are double buffered by default. For information about turning double buffering off, see Using Double Buffering.

Double Buffering: Definition

In MFC's **CDaoRecordset** class, double buffering is a mechanism that simplifies detecting when the current record in a recordset has changed. Using double buffering with your DAO recordsets reduces the amount of work you have to do when adding new records and editing existing records.

By default, your MFC DAO recordsets keep a second copy of the edit buffer (the field data members of the recordset class, taken collectively; DAO Help calls the corresponding buffer a "copy buffer"). As you make changes to the data members, MFC compares them to the copy (the "double buffer") to detect the changes.

Note   Not all fields are double buffered by default. Variable length fields, such as those containing binary data, are not. But you can choose to double buffer them if you wish. Note that this can affect performance if the binary data is large.

The alternative to double buffering—not keeping a copy of the data—requires you to make additional function calls when you edit a field of the current record.

For example, suppose your user changes the name of her contact person at company X. With double buffering, MFC detects the change for you. Without it, you must accompany the change with a call to **CDaoRecordset::SetFieldDirty** and a call to **SetFieldNull** (with a parameter of **FALSE**). If a field is supposed to be Null, you must explicitly call **SetFieldNull**. You must make these calls for every change to a record field.

In general, you get better performance with double buffering off, but double buffering is a considerable convenience when performance is not critical.

Using Double Buffering

Double buffering is the default for recordset fields of most data types, but not for the variable-length data types, such as text and binary. Because data of those types is potentially very large, storing a second copy of the data is not a good default. However, if you know your data will not be prohibitively large, you can turn double buffering on for these types as well. You can also choose to turn double buffering off. You can control double buffering for the whole recordset or on a field-by-field basis.

Overall double buffering is controlled by the **CDaoRecordset::m_bCheckCacheForDirtyFields** data member. Field-by-field double buffering is controlled by the *dwBindOptions* parameter to any of the DFX functions (**DFX_Text**, **DFX_Binary**, **DFX_Short**, and so on).

▶ **To turn double buffering on or off for the whole recordset**

- Set the value of **m_bCheckCacheForDirtyFields** to **AFX_DAO_ENABLE_FIELD_CACHE** (on) or **AFX_DAO_DISABLE_FIELD_CACHE** (off). A typical place to do this is in the recordset constructor.

Note If this data member is **TRUE** (the default), double buffering is on for all field data members except those of variable-length data type (binary, long binary, and text). If this data member is **FALSE**, double buffering is off for all fields, regardless of data type.

▶ **To turn double buffering on or off for a specific field in the recordset**

- In the DFX function call for the field, set the *dwBindOptions* parameter to **TRUE** (on) or **FALSE** (off).

DFX function calls are made in your recordset class's **DoFieldExchange** member function. See the article DAO Record Field Exchange: Working with the Wizard Code for a discussion of **DoFieldExchange**.

Possible values for *dwBindOptions* are:

- **AFX_DAO_ENABLE_FIELD_CACHE** (Default) Double buffering is on for the field.

- **AFX_DAO_DISABLE_FIELD_CACHE** Double buffering is off for the field.

In the following example, double buffering is on for the first field but explicitly turned off for the second field.

```
void CSections::DoFieldExchange(CDaoFieldExchange* pFX)
{
    //{{AFX_FIELD_MAP(CSections)
    pFX->SetFieldType(CDaoFieldExchange::outputColumn);
    DFX_Short(pFX, "Capacity", m_Capacity);
    DFX_Short(pFX, "Enrollment", m_Enrollment,
                   AFX_DAO_DISABLE_FIELD_CACHE);
    //}}AFX_FIELD_MAP
}
```

Effects of Double Buffering

If double buffering is on, as it is by default, record data is double buffered when:

- You call **CDaoRecordset::Edit** to edit the fields of the current record.
- You call **CDaoRecordset::AddNew** to add a new record to the recordset.

MFC copies the field data members of the recordset into a buffer (the "double buffer"). Then it uses the copy to detect changes to the original field data members in the recordset. For more discussion of how double buffering fits into the record updating process, see the article DAO Record Field Exchange: How DFX Works.

Tip To improve performance you might sometimes prefer to turn double buffering off. However, alternatives include:

- Creating queries that only return the fields and rows that you actually need.
- Specifying in your recordset only the fields that you will always use. Then you can supplement those fields by calling **CDaoRecordset::GetFieldValue** at appropriate times to retrieve the fields you need only occasionally. See the article DAO Recordset: Binding Records Dynamically.

In the *Class Library Reference*, see **CDaoRecordset::m_bCheckCacheForDirtyFields**.

See Also DAO: Where Is..., DAO Recordset, DAO Record Field Exchange (DFX), DAO Record Field Exchange: Working with the Wizard Code

DAO Recordset

This article describes the key features of the MFC **CDaoRecordset** class. Additional articles explain how to use recordsets. For task-oriented information, see the article DAO Recordset: Creating Recordsets. For an understanding of the DAO recordset object underlying each MFC **CDaoRecordset** object, see the topic Recordset Object in DAO Help.

Topics covered include:

- DAO recordset: definition
- DAO recordset types
- Derived DAO recordset classes
- DAO recordset operations
- Recordsets and querydefs
- Recordsets and tabledefs
- Recordsets and DAO Collections
- DAO recordset performance features
- Further reading about DAO recordsets

DAO Recordset: Definition

A DAO recordset, represented in MFC by a **CDaoRecordset** object, represents the records in a base table or the records that result from running a query. Recordsets are the principal way in which you work with data using the MFC DAO classes. For a description of the DAO recordset object underlying each **CDaoRecordset** object, see the topic Recordset Object in DAO Help.

A recordset represents, simultaneously:

- All of the records in a table or query—a set of records.
- The current record in that set, whose fields fill the recordset's field data members, if any. Scrolling to a different record in the set fills the recordset's field data members with new values.

For information about recordset features and capabilities, including searching, navigating, updating, bookmarking, and constraining which records are selected, see class **CDaoRecordset** in the *Class Library Reference*. Also see the list of additional recordset articles in Further Reading About DAO Recordsets.

DAO Recordset Types

You can create three kinds of **CDaoRecordset** objects:

- Table-type recordsets, representing a base table in a Microsoft Jet (.MDB) database
- Dynaset-type recordsets, which result from a query
- Snapshot-type recordsets, consisting of a static copy of a set of records

Table 1 summarizes the characteristics and purposes of the three recordset types.

Table 1   Characteristics of Recordset Types

Characteristic	Table-Type	Dynaset-Type	Snapshot-Type
Based On	A base table	A query	A query
Updatable	Yes	Yes	No
Dynamic	Yes	Yes	No
Best Uses	Working with a single table (in a non-ODBC database).	Working with records, possibly containing fields from one or more tables. Reflects changes by other users and is updatable.	Finding data or preparing reports. Reflects the state of the data at the time of the snapshot.
Limitations	Can use only with .MDB databases or ISAM tables opened directly.	Doesn't reflect new records that meet selection criteria after the recordset opens. See below.	Not updatable. The snapshot is not quite instantaneous. See below.

A table-type recordset is based directly on the table rather than on a query.

A "dynaset" is a recordset that reflects changes to the underlying records by other users of the database or by other recordsets. As your application scrolls to a changed record, a new copy is retrieved, bringing it up to date. This behavior is ideal for situations in which it is important to be completely up to date.

Note A dynaset is a dynamic *but fixed* set of records. New records that meet the selection criteria after the dynaset-type recordset has been created are not added to the recordset. This includes records that other users add.

A "snapshot" reflects the state of the data at a particular moment, the moment the snapshot is taken. This behavior is ideal for reporting.

Note Because it takes time to retrieve the records for a snapshot, the moment at which the snapshot occurs is not instantaneous.

Derived DAO Recordset Classes

Normally, you work with recordsets by deriving your own application-specific recordset classes from **CDaoRecordset**. You can create your recordset classes with AppWizard or ClassWizard (or by writing the same code yourself). When you use AppWizard or ClassWizard, the wizard prompts you to specify a database, a recordset type, and a table name on which to base the recordset. The wizard then lets you specify which columns to use in the recordset.

Recordset Features
The resulting recordset class has the following features:

- It contains a data member for each column (field) in the recordset.

- It has a member function you can use to get the name of the data source on which the recordset is based.

- It has a member function you can use to get the SQL string on which the recordset query is based. You indirectly define the SQL string with ClassWizard. The string might contain a table name (for a table-type recordset that selects all fields in each record) or an SQL **SELECT** statement.

- It has a member function, **DoFieldExchange**, that manages exchanging data between the data source and the recordset's data members (in both directions).

For more information about these features, see the article DAO Recordset: Architecture.

Binding Records Dynamically
You do not necessarily have to derive a recordset class. You can use **CDaoRecordset** objects directly, employing the **GetFieldValue** member function to retrieve individual columns (fields) of the current record immediately. For more information, see DAO Recordset: Binding Records Dynamically.

For information about using recordsets, see the article DAO Recordset: Creating Recordsets.

Recordsets and Querydefs

Besides constructing **CDaoRecordset**-based objects directly, you can create them indirectly from a **CDaoQueryDef** object. A querydef is a predefined query usually saved in a DAO database object's QueryDefs collection. Querydefs are a way to prepare frequently-used or complex queries and store them in a database for reuse. One version of the **CDaoRecordset::Open** member function is initialized by a pointer to a **CDaoQueryDef** object.

Tip For convenience, you can use Microsoft Access to create querydefs. Then you can use the querydefs in your MFC program.

For more information, see the articles DAO Recordset: Creating Recordsets and DAO Querydef.

Recordsets and Tabledefs

As with querydefs, you can construct a recordset from a **CDaoTableDef** object. A tabledef encapsulates the structure definition of a table. Tabledefs are saved in the database object's TableDefs collection. A version of **CDaoRecordset::Open** is initialized by a pointer to a **CDaoTableDef** object.

Tip For convenience, you can use Microsoft Access to create tabledefs. Then you can use the tabledefs in your MFC program.

For more information, see the articles DAO Recordset: Creating Recordsets and DAO Tabledef.

Recordsets and DAO Collections

DAO maintains a Recordsets collection, and each recordset maintains collections of DAO field objects and Index objects.

The Recordsets Collection

In DAO, the DAO database object maintains a Recordsets collection containing all active recordsets based on the database. When you open a DAO recordset it is appended to the collection.

MFC chooses not to expose the DAO Recordsets collection. In MFC, you have an explicit **CDaoRecordset** object in your program for each DAO recordset you create. It's up to you to keep track of the recordsets you open.

The Fields and Indexes Collections

In DAO, a recordset object maintains a collection of the fields in the recordset and a collection of the indexes in the underlying table.

MFC exposes each of these collections via member functions that let you get the number of objects in the collection and examine information about any of the objects. For more information about the **GetFieldCount**, **GetFieldInfo**, **GetIndexCount**, and **GetIndexInfo** member functions of **CDaoRecordset**, see the articles DAO: Obtaining Information About DAO Objects and DAO Collections.

DAO Recordset Performance Features

In MFC, you can:

- Cache multiple records from an ODBC data source in a configurable buffer.

  It takes longer to fill the buffer, but having multiple records in memory speeds searching and navigating in the recordset. Caching has no effect or benefit for non-ODBC data sources. For more information, see the article DAO Recordset: Caching Multiple Records.

- Use a double-buffering mechanism in which two copies are kept of the current record. Use the second copy to test whether fields in the first copy have changed.

  Double buffering saves you the work of calling member functions such as **SetFieldDirty** or **SetFieldNull** for a field being edited. The trade-off is storing two copies, which can be significant overhead for variable-length data types. For more information, see the article DAO Record Field Exchange: Double Buffering Records.

Further Reading About DAO Recordsets

For more information about recordsets, see the following articles. If you're new to recordsets, you might want to read the articles in the order listed.

Basic Recordset Operations

- DAO Recordset: Creating Recordsets
- DAO Queries
- DAO Queries: Filtering and Parameterizing Queries
- DAO Recordset: Recordset Operations
- DAO Workspace: Managing Transactions
- DAO Record Field Exchange (DFX)

Navigating in Recordsets

- DAO Recordset: Recordset Navigation
- DAO Recordset: Bookmarks and Record Positions
- DAO Recordset: Seeking and Finding

Advanced Recordset Operations

- DAO Recordset: Caching Multiple Records for Performance

- DAO Recordset: Binding Records Dynamically
- DAO Record Field Exchange: Double Buffering Records
- DAO Tabledef: Examining a Database Schema at Run Time

See Also   DAO: Where Is..., DAO Querydef, DAO Tabledef, DAO Workspace

DAO Recordset: Architecture

This article apples to the MFC DAO classes. For ODBC recordsets, see the article Recordset: Architecture (ODBC).

This article describes the data members that comprise the architecture of a recordset object:

- Field data members
- Parameter data members
- m_nFields and m_nParams data members

A Sample DAO Recordset Class

When you use ClassWizard to declare a recordset class derived from **CDaoRecordset**, the resulting class has the general structure shown in the following simple class:

```
class CCourseSet : public CDaoRecordset
{
public:
  CCourseSet(CDaoDatabase* pDatabase = NULL);
  DECLARE_DYNAMIC(CCourseSet)

// Field/Param Data
  //{{AFX_FIELD(CCourseSet, CDaoRecordset)
  CString m_CourseID;
  CString m_CourseTitle;
  //}}AFX_FIELD
  CString m_IDParam;

// Overrides
  // ClassWizard generated virtual function overrides
  //{{AFX_VIRTUAL(CCourseSet)
  public:
  virtual CString GetDefaultDBName( );
  virtual CString GetDefaultSQL( );
  virtual void DoFieldExchange(CDaoFieldExchange* pFX);
  //}}AFX_VIRTUAL

// Implementation
// ...

};
```

Near the beginning of the class, ClassWizard writes a set of field data members inside the //{{AFX_FIELD delimiters. When you create the class with ClassWizard, you must specify one or more field data members. If the class is parameterized, as the sample class is (with the data member m_strIDParam), you must manually add parameter data members. ClassWizard doesn't support adding parameters to a class.

DAO Field Data Members

The most important members of your recordset class are the field data members. For each column you select from the data source, the class contains a data member of the appropriate data type for that column. For example, the sample class shown at the beginning of this article has two field data members, both of type **CString**, called m_CourseID and m_CourseTitle.

When the recordset selects a set of records, the framework automatically "binds" the columns of the current record (after the **Open** call, the first record is current) to the field data members of the object. That is, the framework uses the appropriate field data member as a buffer in which to store the contents of a record column (field).

As the user scrolls to a new record, the framework uses the field data members to represent the current record. The framework refreshes the field data members, replacing the previous record's values. The field data members are also used for updating the current record and for adding new records. As part of the process of updating a record, you specify the update values by assigning values directly to the appropriate field data member(s).

DAO Parameter Data Members

If the class is "parameterized," it has one or more parameter data members. A parameterized class lets you base a recordset query on information obtained or calculated at run time. (For an alternative approach to parameterizing a recordset by using a querydef, see the article DAO Queries: Filtering and Parameterizing Queries.)

Note You must manually place these data members outside the //{{AFX_FIELD comment brackets.

Typically, the parameter helps narrow the selection, as in the following example. Based on the sample class at the beginning of this article, the recordset object might execute the following SQL statement:

```
SELECT CourseID, CourseTitle FROM Course WHERE CourseID = [Course Ident]
```

The [Course Ident] is a named parameter whose value you supply at run time. When you construct the recordset and set its m_strIDParam data member to "MATH101", the effective SQL statement for the recordset becomes:

```
SELECT CourseID, CourseTitle FROM Course WHERE CourseID = MATH101
```

Note This is the "effective" SQL, but the actual SQL works more efficiently. In particular, it does not do a simple text replacement.

The square brackets are only required if the column or parameter name contains spaces.

By defining parameter data members, you tell the framework about parameters in the SQL string. The framework binds the parameter, which lets DAO know where to get values to substitute for the parameter name. In the example, the resulting recordset contains only the record from the Course table with a CourseID column whose value is "MATH101". All specified columns of this record are selected. You can specify as many parameters (and named placeholders for them) as you need.

Note MFC does nothing itself with the parameters—in particular, it doesn't perform a text substitution. Instead, MFC gives the parameter values to DAO, which uses them.

Important The name of a parameter is important. For details about this and more information about parameters, see the article DAO Queries: Filtering and Parameterizing Queries.

Using m_nFields and m_nParams with DAO

When ClassWizard writes a constructor for your class, it also initializes the **m_nFields** data member, which specifies the number of field data members in the class. If you add any parameters to your class, you must also add an initialization for the **m_nParams** data member, which specifies the number of parameter data members. The framework uses these values to work with the data members.

For more information and examples, see the articles DAO Record Field Exchange (DFX) and DAO Queries: Filtering and Parameterizing Queries. For related information, see the following topics in DAO Help:

- Creating Parameter Queries with DAO
- PARAMETERS Declaration (DAO)

See Also DAO: Where Is..., DAO Recordset, DAO Queries, DAO Querydef

DAO Recordset: Creating Recordsets

This article explains the process of creating recordset objects based either on class **CDaoRecordset** itself or on a class derived from **CDaoRecordset**.

You can use recordset objects in two ways:

- Create recordsets directly from class **CDaoRecordset** and bind record fields dynamically.

  For information about why and how to bind records dynamically, see the article DAO Recordset: Binding Records Dynamically.

- Use AppWizard or ClassWizard to derive your own custom recordset class from **CDaoRecordset** and use DAO Record Field Exchange (DFX) to manage binding record data to recordset class field data members.

  For information about deriving recordset classes with the wizards, see the articles AppWizard: Database Support and ClassWizard: Creating a Recordset Class.

  For information about using DFX, see the article DAO Record Field Exchange (DFX).

In either case, you can base your recordset objects on a query defined by a **CDaoQueryDef** object or a **CDaoTableDef** object, or you can specify the recordset objects' SQL strings either at design time, when you create the class with a wizard, or at run time, when you pass a string containing an SQL statement to the **CDaoRecordset::Open** member function.

If you base your recordset on:

- A querydef

  The recordset inherits the querydef's SQL string.

- A tabledef

  The recordset (a table-type recordset) is based on the table. Creating a recordset from a tabledef is similar to creating one from a querydef. See the following procedure for creating from a querydef.

- The SQL string specified at design time, in the wizard

  The recordset uses the SQL string retrieved by calling its **GetDefaultSQL** member function. The wizard codes the string as the value returned by this function.

- An SQL string specified at run time, in the **Open** call

  The SQL string passed to **Open** overrides the SQL defined at design time.

The following procedure shows how to use a querydef as the basis for a recordset. Using a tabledef to create a recordset is similar.

▶ To create a recordset from a querydef

1 Create the querydef, as described in Creating a Query with a Querydef, or use an existing querydef object.

2 Construct a **CDaoRecordset** object.

3 Call the recordset object's **Open** member function, passing a pointer to the querydef object.

Opening the recordset runs the query, using the SQL statement defined by the querydef.

Note You can only create a dynaset-type or snapshot-type recordset from a querydef.

The following code shows the process of creating a recordset from a querydef:

```
// pdb is a pointer to an open CDaoDatabase object
try
{
    // Construct the querydef
    CDaoQueryDef qd( pdb );

    // Set up the SQL string and create the querydef
    CString strSQL =
      _T("SELECT [Company Name] FROM Publishers WHERE State = 'NY'");
    qd.Create( _T("My Querydef"), strSQL );

    // Construct a CDaoRecordset-derived object
    // and open it based on the querydef
    CPublisherSet rsPub( pdb );
    rsPub.Open( &qd );
}
catch( CDaoException* e )
// ...
```

▶ **To create a recordset without a querydef**

1 Construct a **CDaoRecordset** object.

2 Call the recordset object's **Open** member function. Specify an SQL string, or rely on the one that the wizard creates.

For an example in code, see the article DAO Recordset: Creating Recordsets.

The SQL statement for the recordset is one of the following:

- The default SQL string that you established when you created the recordset class using AppWizard or ClassWizard. If you pass **NULL** for the *lpszSQL* parameter to **Open**, the recordset uses the default SQL string. The recordset obtains the default SQL string by calling its own **GetDefaultSQL** member function. The default SQL string is coded as the value returned by that function rather than being stored in a data member.

- An SQL string that you pass in your call to **Open**. This string overrides the default SQL string defined in the recordset class.

In either case, your SQL string can consist of any of the following:

- A **SELECT** statement of the basic form:

```
SELECT column-list FROM table-list
```

- One or more tabledef and/or querydef names, separated by commas, which bases the query on tables and/or queries. This list is usually based on choices you made with one of the wizards. The query selects all columns (fields) in the tables/queries, unless you modify it.

For details, see **CDaoRecordset::Open**. For related information, see the topic Recordset Object in DAO Help.

For information about SQL, see the topic SQL Property in DAO Help.

For information about the SQL syntax used by DAO, see the topic Comparison of Microsoft Jet Database Engine SQL and ANSI SQL in DAO Help.

See Also   DAO: Where Is..., DAO Recordset, DAO Querydef, DAO Record Field Exchange (DFX), DAO Queries: SQL for DAO, DAO Queries

DAO Recordset: Recordset Navigation

This article explains how to move (scroll) from record to record in a recordset. It also tells you where to find more information about other recordset navigation mechanisms, such as **Seek**, **Find**, and bookmarks.

Topics covered include:

- Other navigation techniques
- Scrolling in DAO recordsets

For more information, see the topic Positioning the Current Record Pointer with DAO in DAO Help.

Other Navigation Techniques

Besides scrolling, discussed in Scrolling in DAO Recordsets, class **CDaoRecordset** supplies five other ways to navigate to a particular record or to a particular place in a recordset:

- **Seek**   See Using Seek in the article DAO Recordset: Seeking and Finding.
- **Find**   See Using Find in the article DAO Recordset: Seeking and Finding.
- **SetBookmark**   See Bookmarks in MFC in the article DAO Recordset: Bookmarks and Record Positions.
- **SetPercentPosition**   See Absolute and Percent Positions in MFC in the article DAO Recordset: Bookmarks and Record Positions.
- **SetAbsolutePosition**   See Absolute and Percent Positions in MFC in the article DAO Recordset: Bookmarks and Record Positions.

Scrolling in DAO Recordsets

Recordsets provide several member functions you can use to "scroll" or move from one record to the next, previous, first, or last record, or move n records relative to the current position. You can also test whether you have scrolled beyond the first or the last record.

To determine whether scrolling is possible in your recordset, call the **CanScroll** member function of class **CDaoRecordset**.

▶ **To scroll in DAO**

- Forward one record: call the **MoveNext** member function.

- Backward one record: call the **MovePrev** member function.

- To the first record in the recordset: call the **MoveFirst** member function.

- To the last record in the recordset: call the **MoveLast** member function.

- *N* records relative to the current position: call the **Move** member function. Specify the value of *N*, negative (for previous records) or positive (for later records), in your call.

▶ **To test for the end or the beginning of the recordset in DAO**

- Have you scrolled past the last record? Call the **IsEOF** member function.

- Have you scrolled past the first record (moving backward)? Call the **IsBOF** member function.

For example, the following code uses **IsBOF** and **IsEOF** to detect the limits of a recordset as the code scrolls through it in both directions.

```
// Open a snapshot; first record is current
CEnrollmentSet rsEnrollmentSet( NULL );
rsEnrollmentSet.Open( );

// Deal with empty recordset
if( rsEnrollmentSet.IsEOF( ) )
    return FALSE;

// Scroll to the end of the snapshot
while ( !rsEnrollmentSet.IsEOF( ) )
    rsEnrollmentSet.MoveNext( );

// Past last record, so no record is current
// Move to the last record
rsEnrollmentSet.MoveLast( );

// Scroll to beginning of the snapshot
while( !rsEnrollmentSet.IsBOF( ) )
    rsEnrollmentSet.MovePrev( );

// Past first record, so no record is current
rsEnrollmentSet.MoveFirst( );
// First record (if any) is current again
```

IsEOF returns a nonzero value if the recordset is positioned past the last record. **IsBOF** returns a nonzero value if the recordset is positioned before the first record. In either case, there is no current record to operate on. If you call **MovePrev** when **IsBOF** is already true, or call **MoveNext** when **IsEOF** is already true, the framework throws a **CDaoException**.

Tip In the general case, where records may be deleted by you or by other users (other recordsets), check that both **IsEOF** and **IsBOF** return a nonzero value to detect an empty recordset.

See Also DAO: Where Is..., DAO Recordset, DAO Recordset: Seeking and Finding, DAO Recordset: Bookmarks and Record Positions

DAO Recordset: Recordset Operations

This article discusses several key recordset operations, particularly those involving updating records. Topics covered include:

- Adding new records
- Editing existing records
- Deleting records
- Requerying recordsets

For related information about using recordsets, see the following articles:

- DAO Queries
- DAO: Creating, Opening, and Closing DAO Objects
- DAO Recordset: Creating Recordsets
- DAO Recordset: Recordset Navigation
- DAO Recordset: Bookmarks and Record Positions
- DAO Recordset: Seeking and Finding
- DAO Recordset: Binding Records Dynamically
- DAO Recordset: Caching Multiple Records for Performance
- DAO Record Field Exchange (DFX)

Important Your ability to update records requires that you have update permission for your database and that you have an updatable table-type or dynaset-type recordset. You can't update snapshot-type recordsets with the MFC DAO classes.

Adding New Records in DAO

For general information about adding records in DAO, see the following topics in DAO Help:

- Populating Recordsets and Counting Records with DAO
- AddNew Method
- Update Method

For information about where the new record appears and other considerations, see **CDaoRecordset::AddNew**. For information about the role of double buffering, see the article DAO Record Field Exchange: How DFX Works.

▶ **To add a new record to a recordset**

1 Determine whether your recordset is updatable.

Call the recordset's **CanUpdate** member function.

2 Call the recordset's **AddNew** member function.

The fields of the new recordset, represented by the recordset's edit buffer (the recordset's data members), are initially all Null. **AddNew** prepares the MFC recordset's edit buffer, which DAO calls the copy buffer. For more information about the edit buffer with **AddNew**, see the article DAO Record Field Exchange: How DFX Works.

3 Assign values to the new record's fields.

If you're using a **CDaoRecordset**-derived class with DFX, assign values to the fields. If you have double buffering turned off, make the following two calls for each field you assign a value to:

- **SetFieldDirty**
- **SetFieldNull** with the parameter **FALSE** (meaning "not Null").

Or, if you explicitly want the field to be Null, call only **SetFieldNull**, with the parameter **TRUE**.

4 Complete the process by calling the recordset's **Update** member function.

Update adds the record. If no transaction is in effect, the change takes place immediately. Otherwise, the change takes place when you call **CDaoWorkspace::CommitTrans**.

If you move to another record without calling **Update**, the change is lost. For more information, see **AddNew**.

Editing Existing Records in DAO

For general information about editing records in DAO, see the following topics in DAO Help:

- Edit Method
- Update Method

If you have double buffering turned on, MFC maintains a copy of the edit buffer so it can detect changes to the recordset fields for you. You don't have to call **SetFieldDirty** and **SetFieldNull** (passing **FALSE**) for each change. For more information, see the article DAO Record Field Exchange: Double Buffering Records.

For details about what **Edit** does and about the role of double buffering, see **CDaoRecordset::Edit** and the article DAO Record Field Exchange: How DFX Works.

▶ **To edit an existing record in a recordset**

1 Determine whether your recordset is updatable.

Call the recordset's **CanUpdate** member function.

2 Move to the record you want to edit.

Use any of the recordset's navigation mechanisms that take you to a specific record.

3 Call the recordset's **Edit** member function.

Edit prepares the recordset's edit buffer, which DAO calls the copy buffer. For more information about the edit buffer with **Edit**, see the article DAO Record Field Exchange: How DFX Works.

4 Assign values to the fields you want to change.

If you're using a **CDaoRecordset**-derived class with DFX, assign values to the fields. To give a field the value Null, call **SetFieldNull** (passing **TRUE**). If you have double buffering turned off, call **SetFieldDirty** and **SetFieldNull** (passing **FALSE**) for each field you assign a value to.

5 Complete the process by calling the recordset's **Update** member function.

Update changes the record in the database. If no transaction is in effect, the change takes place immediately. Otherwise, the change takes place when you call **CDaoWorkspace::CommitTrans**.

If you move to another record without calling **Update**, the change is lost. For more information, see **Edit**. For information about double buffering, see the article DAO Record Field Exchange: Double Buffering Records.

Deleting Records in DAO

For general information about deleting records in DAO, see the topic Delete Method in DAO Help.

▶ **To delete a record from a recordset**

1 Determine whether your recordset is updatable.

Call the recordset's **CanUpdate** member function.

2 Move to the record you want to edit.

Use any of the recordset's navigation mechanisms that take you to a specific record.

3 Call the recordset's **Delete** member function.

You don't call **Update** for a deletion.

4 Move to another record before you attempt any other recordset operations.

In table-type and dynaset-type recordset objects, **Delete** removes the current record and makes it inaccessible. Although you can't edit or use the deleted record, it remains current. Once you move to another record, however, you can't make the deleted record current again. Subsequent references to a deleted record in a recordset are invalid and cause an exception to be thrown. For more information, see **Delete**. You can tell whether you're on a deleted record by calling **IsDeleted**.

Requerying in DAO

If you need to re-run a recordset query, perhaps with new parameter values each time, you can do either of the following:

- Call **Close** to close the recordset, reset any parameters or other properties, and call **Open** again.

- Reset any parameters or other properties, then call **Requery**.

The purpose of either approach to requerying the recordset is to "refresh" the recordset by running its query again, perhaps with changed parameters or properties. You can also requery to refresh results in a multi-user environment (multiple users or recordsets modifying the same data). In general, **Requery** is somewhat more efficient than **Close** and **Open**, but see the Important note below.

This description of the use and behavior of **Requery** is exactly as in DAO. But MFC adds one feature: your ability to change the recordset's **m_strFilter** and/or **m_strSort** data members before you either call **Requery** or call **Open** again. If you do change either data member, MFC closes, then reopens the recordset.

Important   If you change **m_strFilter** or **m_strSort**, you lose the performance benefit of **Requery**. In this case, calling **Requery** performs no better than calling **Close** and **Open**.

For more information, see **Requery** in the *Class Library Reference*, and see the topic Requery Method in DAO Help.

See Also   DAO: Where Is..., DAO Recordset

DAO Recordset: Bookmarks and Record Positions

This article explains MFC's interfaces to:

- The Bookmark property in DAO recordsets.

- The AbsolutePosition and PercentPosition properties in DAO recordsets.

For details about these properties in DAO, see the following topics in DAO Help:

- Bookmark Property

- AbsolutePosition Property

- PercentPosition Property

- Positioning the Current Record Pointer with DAO

Those DAO Help topics explain the fundamentals of the properties. This article explains how MFC exposes them to you.

Bookmarks in MFC

Because records can be deleted from a recordset, you can't rely on the absolute position of a record within the recordset. The reliable way to keep track of the position of a particular record in your recordset is to use the record's bookmark.

Except for snapshot-type recordsets, each record has a unique bookmark from the time the recordset is created. In MFC, class **CDaoRecordset** supplies member functions for:

- Getting the bookmark of the current record, so you can save it in a variable.
- Moving quickly to a given record by specifying its bookmark, which you've saved earlier in a variable.

You can check whether a recordset supports bookmarks by calling **CDaoRecordset::CanBookmark**.

For example, suppose you want to mark the current record so you can later return to it easily. The following code does this:

```
// rs is a CDaoRecordset or
// CDaoRecordset-derived object

COleVariant varRecordToReturnTo;
varRecordToReturnTo = rs.GetBookmark( );

//...more code in which you move to other records
rs.GotoBookmark( varRecordToReturnTo );
```

There is no need to extract the underlying data type from the **COleVariant** object. Simply get it with **CDaoRecordset::GetBookmark** and return to that bookmark with **CDaoRecordset::SetBookmark**.

Absolute and Percent Positions in MFC

Besides bookmarks (and **Move**, **Seek**, and **Find**), DAO provides two other ways to position the current record in a recordset: percent positioning and absolute positioning.

Note Neither absolute nor percent positioning is recommended for moving the current record to a specific record. Use a bookmark instead. See Bookmarks in MFC.

Neither percent positioning nor absolute positioning is available for table-type recordsets.

Percent Positioning

You can set the current record to a position that follows a specified percentage of the records in a recordset, and you can get the percentage position of the current record. This is useful for setting scroll bars. That is, you can:

- Call **CDaoRecordset::GetPercentPosition** to determine the percentage position of the current record—what percentage of the records precede the current record.

- Call **CDaoRecordset::SetPercentPosition** to make the record at a specified percentage position in a recordset the current record. For example, you might make the record at 50% the current record—halfway through the recordset.

Keep in mind the following guidelines:

- Percent positioning is approximate, and the exact record that is set can be affected by deletion of records.

- If you call **SetPercentPosition** before the recordset is fully populated, the amount of movement is relative to the number of populated records. Records are populated as you move to them and they are retrieved from the database. You can determine the number of populated records by calling **GetRecordCount**. You can populate all records in the recordset by calling **MoveLast** (keep in mind that calling **MoveLast** can be slow for dynaset-type and snapshot-type recordsets).

For related information, see the topic PercentPosition Property in DAO Help.

Absolute Positioning

You can set or get the record number of the current record in a recordset. That is, you can:

- Call **CDaoRecordset::GetAbsolutePosition** to get the AbsolutePosition property of the recordset, which contains the ordinal position (zero-based) of the current record in a recordset.

- Call **CDaoRecordset::SetAbsolutePosition** to set the AbsolutePosition property. This makes the record at that ordinal position in the recordset the current record.

Important The absolute position of a record is potentially unreliable. If the user can delete records ahead of a position, the ordinal number of records following the deletion is decreased. Bookmarks are a more reliable method of working with record positions. See Bookmarks in MFC.

Keep in mind the following guideline:

- Setting a position greater than the number of populated records causes MFC to throw an exception. Records are populated as you move to them and they are retrieved from the database. You can determine the number of populated records by calling **GetRecordCount**.

For related information, see the topic AbsolutePosition Property in DAO Help.

See Also DAO: Where Is..., DAO Recordset, DAO Recordset: Recordset Navigation, DAO Recordset: Seeking and Finding

DAO Recordset: Seeking and Finding

This article explains how to use the **Seek** and **Find** member functions of class **CDaoRecordset**. Topics covered include:

- Using Seek
- Using Find

These two mechanisms for locating records that meet certain criteria are used in different situations, as described in Table 1.

Table 1 Using Seek vs. Using Find

Criterion	Seek	Find
Use In	Indexed table-type recordsets.	Dynaset-type or snapshot-type recordsets.
Limitations	Can't use on attached tables, but can use on installable ISAM databases.	Can't use on a forward-only scrolling snapshot-type recordset. Use with ODBC-based recordsets can be inefficient.
Call Before Seek/Find	**SetCurrentIndex**	
Call After Seek/Find	Check **Seek** or **Find** return value	Check **Seek** or **Find** return value

Seek and **Find** are not the only means of navigating in a recordset. You can also use:

- **Move**, **MoveFirst**, **MoveLast**, **MoveNext**, and **MovePrev**
- **GetBookmark**, **SetBookmark**
- **GetAbsolutePosition**, **SetAbsolutePosition**
- **GetPercentPosition**, **SetPercentPosition**

For more information, see each **CDaoRecordset** member function in the *Class Library Reference*.

Using Seek

The **CDaoRecordset::Seek** member function lets you search for a record in a table-type recordset based on a table index. Two versions of the function provide for seeking based on:

- Up to three specified keys, each of which represents a field that makes up part of the current index.

- An array of keys, for indexes with four or more fields. Each key represents one of the fields. The array must contain at least one and no more than 13 keys.

In both versions, the search is based on a string containing a relational operator, such as "=" or ">=", in the *lpszComparison* parameter and the **COleVariant** value specified in the first key.

For example, suppose the comparison operator is "=" and the first key is the value "Microsoft" (the first key being a Company Name field). Using the first version of **Seek**, you would find the first record that has a Company Name of "Microsoft". The found record becomes the current record. The following code illustrates how to use **Seek**:

```
// rs is a table-type recordset
try
{
    // Set current index for recordset and
    // save current position.
    rs.SetCurrentIndex( _T("PartNameIndex") );
    COleVariant varCurrentPos = rs.GetBookmark( );

    // Find first record whose Part Name
    // field is "Framis Lever".
    if ( rs.Seek( _T("="), _T("Framis Lever") ) )
        // Return to the saved position
        rs.GotoBookmark( varCurrentPos );
    else
        // Do something in response to Seek failure
}
catch( CDaoException* e )
{
    e->Delete( );
}
```

This code seeks the first record whose Part Name field (the first field in the PartNameIndex index) is "Framis Lever" (whatever a framis lever is).

For more information, see the **Seek** and **SetCurrentIndex** member functions in the *Class Library Reference*. For related information about the underlying DAO functionality, see the following topics in DAO Help:

- Seek Method
- NoMatch Property
- Index Object
- Index Property

Using Find

The **CDaoRecordset::Find** member function and its relatives, **FindNext**, **FindPrev**, **FindFirst**, and **FindLast**, let you search for a record in a dynaset-type or snapshot-type recordset. The Find member functions search from a location and in a direction as shown in Table 2:

Table 2 The Find Family of Functions

Find operation	Begin at	Search direction
FindFirst	Beginning of recordset	End of recordset
FindLast	End of recordset	Beginning of recordset
FindNext	Current record	End of recordset
FindPrev	Current record	Beginning of recordset

The basic **Find** function takes two parameters:

- The type of find: **AFX_DAO_NEXT**, **AFX_DAO_PREV**, **AFX_DAO_FIRST**, or **AFX_DAO_LAST**.

- A filter—a string expression like the **WHERE** clause in an SQL statement (without the keyword), that specifies the criterion for finding. The expression can be compound, using **AND**, **OR**, and so on.

Find is a virtual function. This means you can, if necessary, override it to provide your own implementation. The other **Find** functions are all based on **Find**, so they use whatever functionality you provide in your override. You shouldn't normally need to override **Find**, however.

For details not discussed here about the **Find** member functions, see the individual functions, starting with **Find**. For related information about the underlying DAO functionality, see the topic Positioning the Current Record Pointer with DAO in DAO Help:

For example, suppose you have a dynaset-type recordset in which you want to find the first record with a State code of "NY":

```
// rs is a dynaset-type recordset previously opened
CString strCriteria = _T("STATE = 'NY'");
try
{
    if ( rs.FindFirst( strCriteria ) )
        // Do something with the found record
    rs.FindNext( strCriteria );
    // ...
}
catch( CDaoException* e )
{
    e->Delete( );
}
```

This code finds the first record that matches the criterion, then finds the next record that matches the criterion.

See Also DAO: Where Is..., DAO Recordset, DAO Recordset: Recordset Navigation, DAO Recordset: Bookmarks and Record Positions

DAO Recordset: Binding Records Dynamically

This article explains how to use an object of class **CDaoRecordset** directly, without deriving your own recordset class. Topics covered include:

- The Standard Case: Using a Derived Recordset Class
- Binding records dynamically instead
- Dynamically setting and getting parameter values

As the MFC Database sample DAOVIEW shows, you can use dynamic binding to work with database schema information not known at design time. For related information on examining a database schema at run time, see the article DAO Tabledef: Examining a Database Schema at Run Time.

The Standard Case: Using a Derived Recordset Class

For many applications, you will prefer to create, at design time, a **CDaoRecordset**-derived class. Using AppWizard or ClassWizard, you can design a class that represents your table or query. You specify the database, the table, and the columns (fields). This information is then encapsulated in the class's connection information, its SQL string, and its data members. Records are statically bound to the recordset at run time via the **DoFieldExchange** mechanism. For more information, see the article DAO Recordset: Creating Recordsets.

The point is that to operate this way, you must know the database schema at design time so you can specify which table to use and which fields to use from that table. In many applications, this works well. If your database schema is relatively static and users are not constantly adding or deleting tables and table fields, you can design in this way.

Binding Records Dynamically Instead

If your database schema is relatively dynamic, or if you face a situation in which the schema is unknown at design time, dynamic binding could be the answer.

For dynamic binding, you don't need a derived **CDaoRecordset** class. Instead, you use **CDaoRecordset** directly. Here's the general process:

1. Construct a **CDaoRecordset** object.
2. Call its **Open** member function to connect to a specified database and run a query.
3. Navigate through the records, using the recordset's navigation member functions, such as **Move**.

4. Call the recordset's **GetFieldValue** member function to retrieve, immediately, the value of a specified field in the record. Or call **Edit**, then **SetFieldValue**, then **Update** to set the field in the database.

Binding dynamically in this way is flexible. You don't have to know the database schema at design time, and you can keep up with a changing schema. This mechanism doesn't use the **DoFieldExchange** mechanism.

You may get better performance with dynamic binding than with static binding via DAO record field exchange (DFX) if you don't need every field bound for every record retrieved. However, for applications in which the database schema is reasonably unchanging, binding via DFX is a good choice because DFX manages all of the recordset's fields for you, reducing the amount of code you must write to bind fields.

The following example, borrowed from the MFC Database sample DAOVIEW, illustrates dynamic binding. The code creates a table-type recordset, which is used to scroll through all records in a table, getting the values of fields in the current record and adding them to an MFC **CListCtrl** object.

```
// db is a pointer to a CDaoDatabase object.
// dbOpenTable specifies a table-type recordset.
// CCrack is a custom class used to get the actual
// type from a COleVariant object.
// nRecord is used for positioning in the list control.

CDaoRecordset rs( &db );
int nRecord = 0;

// Open MFC DAO objects in a try block to catch
// security violations when opening tables
try
{
    // Open the recordset, passing a table name
    // for the SQL
    rs.Open( dbOpenTable, strTableName );

    // Move through records
    while( !rs.IsEOF( ) )
    {
        COleVariant var;
        // Move through fields in current record
        int nFields = rs.GetFieldCount( );
        for ( int i=0; i < nFields; i++ )
        {
            var = rs.GetFieldValue( i );
            // Add field value to list control
            m_ctlList.AddItem( nRecord,i,
                        CCrack::strVARIANT( var ) );
        }
        nRecord++;
        rs.MoveNext( );
```

```
    }
}
catch( CDaoException* e )
{
    // Do nothing--used for security violations
    // when opening tables
    e->Delete( );
}
```

The key features in this example are:

- The direct use of **CDaoRecordset** rather than a class derived from **CDaoRecordset**. The example therefore doesn't use the DAO record field exchange (DFX) mechanism.

- The call to **GetFieldValue**, which returns a value of type **COleVariant** for a specified field in the current record. The field is specified as the index of the field in the recordset object's Fields collection.

Also of interest are:

- The user-defined class `CCrack`, which has members for extracting the actual data type from a **COleVariant** object. See the files CRACK.H and CRACK.CPP in the MFC Database sample DAOVIEW. `CCrack` is not an official MFC class.

- The use of an exception handler around the **CDaoRecordset::Open** call and the other recordset operations. Using a **try/catch** block is recommended, if only to catch security violations when you try to open a table.

Note In addition to binding recordset fields dynamically, you can also bind query parameters dynamically. If you base your **CDaoRecordset** on a **CDaoQueryDef** object that has parameters defined, you can get or set the values of the parameters by calling **CDaoQueryDef::GetParamValue** or **CDaoQueryDef::SetParamValue**. Set parameter values for the querydef, then open a recordset based on the querydef. This mechanism doesn't use DFX.

For other examples of dynamic binding, see the LISTVIEW.CPP file in the MFC Database sample DAOVIEW, and see the MFC Database sample DAOCTL, which illustrates a data-bound OLE control.

Dynamically Setting and Getting Parameter Values

If you create recordsets based on a querydef object, you can parameterize the querydef, then use it to create a recordset:

1. Use the **PARAMETERS** clause in the querydef's SQL statement to establish the parameters. For information, see the topics PARAMETERS Declaration (SQL) and Creating Parameter Queries with DAO in DAO Help. See also the article DAO Queries: Filtering and Parameterizing Queries.

2. Create the querydef based on that SQL statement. See the article DAO Querydef: Using Querydefs.

3. Set the values of the parameters by calling **CDaoQueryDef::SetParamValue** for each parameter.

4. Create and open a recordset based on the querydef. See the article DAO Recordset: Creating Recordsets.

If you want to examine the value of a querydef's parameter, call **CDaoQueryDef::GetParamValue**.

See Also   DAO: Where Is..., DAO Recordset, DAO Tabledef: Examining a Database Schema at Run Time

DAO Recordset: Caching Multiple Records for Performance

This article discusses the mechanism by which you can use a configurable buffer to cache multiple records in a recordset.

Note   The recordset caching mechanism described here applies only to ODBC data sources. It has no effect or benefit with non-ODBC databases.

Topics covered include:

• When should you use record caching?

• Configuring the record cache

• Filling the record cache

Normally, records are retrieved from the database one at a time. To improve the performance of operations such as seeking and scrolling in recordsets based on ODBC data sources, you can cause DAO to cache multiple records. When you request a record, the database engine looks for it first in the cache. If the record is not in the cache, the database engine gets the record from the server. This is marginally slower at the time the cache is filled, but faster for operations that navigate through the records later. Use of this mechanism is limited in several ways, however (besides its limitation to ODBC); see When Should You Use Record Caching?.

For an understanding of the DAO data caching mechanism that underlies MFC **CDaoRecordset** objects, see the following topics in DAO Help:

• CacheSize, CacheStart Properties

• FillCache Method

When Should You Use Record Caching?

Is record caching right for your application? This depends on several factors:

- Are you using a remote data source? Caching is really useful only for remote data—ODBC data sources.

- Are you using dynaset-type recordsets? Caching is for use with these recordsets only.

- What kind of performance do you need to optimize? If your application makes intensive use of scrolling, seeking, finding, or other methods of positioning the current record, you probably should cache records.

- Keep in mind that caching has storage overhead and that it can take extra time to fill the cache. Records retrieved from the cache also don't reflect changes made by other users in the database.

Configuring the Record Cache

To use MFC's record caching, you need to do two things:

- Set the record position at which the cache is to start.

  Specify the first of the records to be cached by giving its bookmark in a call to **CDaoRecordset::SetCacheStart**. You can obtain a record's bookmark by moving to the record and calling **CDaoRecordset::GetBookmark**. **GetBookmark** returns a **COleVariant** value that you can store in a variable. Use the variable in your **SetCacheStart** call.

- Set the size of the cache, in records.

  Call **CDaoRecordset::SetCacheSize** to specify how many records are to be cached.

How big should you make your cache? This depends on your needs and what you are optimizing for. If you expect your users to perform long scrolls or seeks, moving through many records at a time, you probably need a larger cache.

A typical case might be an application that, for example, displays 25 records at a time. For such an application, a cache of 75 records might be a good choice. This would allow quick response for both scrolling up and down and paging up and down.

Filling the Record Cache

DAO fills the cache as you request that records be retrieved from the data source. But you can explicitly fill all or part of the cache at any time by calling **CDaoRecordset::FillCache**.

When you call **FillCache**, you can specify either or both of the following:

- The bookmark of the record at which you want to start filling the cache. If you omit the *lBookmark* parameter to **FillCache**, the cache is filled starting with the record specified in DAO's CacheStart property. You can set that value with **CDaoRecordset::SetCacheStart**.

- The number of records you want to put into the cache. This can be less than the cache size you specified with a call to **CDaoRecordset::SetCacheSize**. If you omit the *lSize* parameter to **FillCache**, the number of records defaults to DAO's CacheSize property value, which you can set with **SetCacheSize**.

For more information, see the **CDaoRecordset::FillCache** member function in the *Class Library Reference*. For information about the DAO caching mechanism, see the following topics in DAO Help:

- CacheSize, CacheStart Properties
- FillCache Method

See Also   DAO: Where Is..., DAO Recordset

DAO Tabledef

This article describes "tabledefs" and the key features of the MFC **CDaoTableDef** class. Additional articles explain how to use tabledefs. For task-oriented information, see the article DAO Tabledef: Using Tabledefs. For an understanding of the DAO tabledef object underlying each MFC **CDaoTableDef** object, see the topic TableDef Object in DAO Help.

Topics covered include:

- Tabledef: definition
- Tabledef uses
- Tabledefs and DAO collections
- Further reading about tabledefs

Tabledef: Definition

A DAO tabledef, represented in MFC by a **CDaoTableDef** object, is an object that defines the structure of a base table or an attached table.

A base table is a table in a Microsoft Jet (.MDB) database. You can manipulate the structure of a base table using DAO objects or data definition language (DDL) SQL statements, and you can use recordsets and action queries to modify data in a base table.

An attached table is a table in another database linked to a Microsoft Jet (.MDB) database. Data for attached tables remains in the external database where it may be manipulated by other applications. You can't use the table-type recordset with attached tables, and you can't modify the schema of attached tables, but you can use dynaset-type and snapshot-type recordsets with attached tables.

Tabledef Uses

The main use for tabledef objects is to manipulate the structure of a table. You can:

- Base a recordset on a tabledef. The recordset is a table-type recordset. See **CDaoRecordset::Open** in the *Class Library Reference*.
- Examine the structure of local base tables, attached tables, and external tables. The structure of a table includes its fields and indexes.
- Add or delete fields and indexes in local base tables and external tables that you open directly rather than attaching.
- Set the connection information and the name of an attached table and refresh the link to an attached table.

- Determine whether the data in table fields is editable.

- Get or set a table's validation conditions.

You can use tables as the basis for opening recordsets in two ways. You can:

- Open a recordset based on a **CDaoTableDef** pointer.

- Create a table-type recordset based on the table, usually by using AppWizard or ClassWizard.

For a complete discussion of what you can do with tabledefs, see the topic TableDef Object in DAO Help.

Tabledefs and DAO Collections

Each DAO database object maintains a TableDefs collection—a collection of all saved table definitions in the database. The collection contains one tabledef for each table in the database. Each tabledef object maintains two collections of its own:

- Fields   All of the fields in the table definition—one for each field in the underlying table.

- Indexes   All of the indexes defined for the table.

MFC objects don't store a representation of a DAO collection. Instead, MFC accesses the collection through the underlying DAO object. For more information, see the article DAO Collections.

MFC also doesn't provide a C++ class to represent every DAO object. In particular, there is no MFC field object or index object. You work with a tabledef's fields and indexes through member functions of class **CDaoTableDef**.

Further Reading About Tabledefs

For more information about tabledefs in MFC, see the following additional articles (in the order recommended here):

General Tabledef Article

- DAO Tabledef: Using Tabledefs

- DAO Tabledef: Examining a Database Schema at Run Time

Tables in External Data Sources

- DAO External: Working with External Data Sources

- DAO External: Attaching External Tables

- DAO External: Opening External Databases Directly

- DAO External: Creating an External Table

- DAO External: Refreshing and Removing Links

- DAO External: Improving Performance with External Data Sources

See Also DAO: Where Is..., DAO Querydef, DAO Recordset, DAO Database

DAO Tabledef: Using Tabledefs

This article explains how to use **CDaoTableDef** objects. Topics covered include:

- Creating a tabledef
- Opening an existing tabledef
- Creating a table-type recordset

Creating a Tabledef

Creating a tabledef creates a new table in the target database. You create the tabledef and add fields (and possibly indexes) to it. The new table doesn't contain any data until you either add records from Microsoft Access (for a Microsoft Jet (.MDB) database) or create a recordset that adds records to the table.

Creating a new MFC **CDaoTableDef** object creates the underlying DAO tabledef object.

▶ **To create a tabledef**

1 Construct a **CDaoTableDef** object, supplying a pointer to the **CDaoDatabase** object to which the tabledef will belong.

2 Call the tabledef object's **Create** member function.

3 Set any of the tabledef object's properties that you want. Call the **SetAttributes**, **SetConnect**, **SetName**, **SetSourceTableName**, **SetValidationRule**, or **SetValidationText** member functions.

4 Call the tabledef object's **Append** member function to save the tabledef in the database's TableDefs collection. You can append before or after creating fields, as described in the next step.

5 Add fields to the tabledef by calling its **CreateField** member function for each field. (You can't modify the schema of an attached table, so this step applies only to local base tables and tables in external data sources that you open directly.)

6 Optionally add indexes to the tabledef by calling its **CreateIndex** member function for each index.

Tip The easiest way to create a tabledef is to create it in Microsoft Access. Open the target database, create tables, and save them in the database. Then you can use the tabledefs from your application's code.

Opening an Existing Tabledef

If you want to examine or manipulate the structure of an existing table, open an MFC tabledef object based on the DAO tabledef object stored in the database's TableDefs collection. Objects in the TableDefs collection are accessed by the user-defined name specified when the tabledef was created and appended to the collection.

▶ **To open a tabledef for an existing table**

1 Construct a **CDaoTableDef** object, passing a pointer to the **CDaoDatabase** object to which the tabledef belongs.

2 Call the tabledef object's **Open** member function, specifying the user-defined name of the tabledef saved in the TableDefs collection. The name may or may not be the same as the name of the underlying source table.

For examples, see the MFC Database sample DAOVIEW.

The following code from the LISTVIEW.CPP file in DAOVIEW illustrates opening a tabledef to get information about its fields and then add the field information to a list control:

```
// db is an open CDaoDatabase object
// strTableName is the user-defined name of the tabledef to open
CDaoTableDef td( &db );
try
{
    td.Open( strTableName );
    short nFields = td.GetFieldCount( );
    for( short i=0; i < nFields; i++ )
    {
        td.GetFieldInfo(i,fieldInfo);
        m_ctlList.AddColumn(fieldInfo.m_strName,i);
    }
}
catch( CDaoException* e )
{
    // Do nothing. Used to catch security violations opening tables.
    e->Delete( );
}
td.Close( );
```

Creating a Table-Type Recordset

Unless a table is in an external data source, you can create table-type recordsets based on the table, in two ways:

- Create a tabledef, then create a recordset from the tabledef.

- Create a recordset and specify **dbOpenTable** in the *nOpenType* parameter to **CDaoRecordset::Open**.

A table-type recordset represents a base table (a table in a Microsoft Jet (.MDB) database) in code. You can't open a table-type recordset on an ODBC database or on an attached table, but you can open one on an ISAM database opened directly, such as a FoxPro, dBASE, Paradox, or Btrieve database.

You can use a table-type recordset to examine, add, change, or delete records in a single base table. You can't use an SQL statement to filter or sort data as you can with dynaset-type and snapshot-type recordsets. This means you get all records, but table-type recordsets behave somewhat like dynaset-type recordsets in that only the current record is loaded into memory. When you move to a new record, it is loaded. Sorting is based on a predefined index. Table-type recordsets support bi-directional scrolling.

For more information, see class **CDaoRecordset** in the *Class Library Reference* and see the following topics in DAO Help:

- Recordset Object
- Table-Type Recordset Object

See Also   DAO: Where Is..., DAO Recordset, DAO External: Working with External Data Sources, DAO External: Creating an External Table

DAO Tabledef: Examining a Database Schema at Run Time

This article discusses how to examine the schema of a database—the structure of the database, as defined by its tables and their fields and indexes—at run time. While many applications are based on knowledge of the database schema at design time, there are situations in which you might need to determine the schema dynamically at run time:

- Your application is designed to work with arbitrary schemas.

  See the MFC Database sample DAOVIEW for an example of this.

- The schema of your target database tends to change.

  Perhaps users can add and delete tables and even alter the structure of tables by adding or deleting fields and indexes.

How Dynamic Examination of the Schema Works

Dynamic examination of the schema is based on the use of DAO collections. A DAO database object contains the following collections: TableDefs, QueryDefs, Recordsets, and Relations. MFC exposes all of these via **CDaoDatabase** member functions except for the Recordsets collection. For details about how MFC exposes collections, see the articles DAO Collections and DAO Collections: Obtaining Information About DAO Objects.

An Example of Dynamic Schema Examination

The following illustration uses the TableDefs collection, but the principles demonstrated apply equally to the other collections.

▶ **To enumerate the TableDefs collection for a CDaoDatabase object**

1 Get the number of tabledef objects in the underlying DAO collection by calling **CDaoDatabase::GetTableDefCount**.

2 In a loop from 0 to the number of tabledefs, call **CDaoDatabase::GetTableDefInfo** for each object in the collection.

3 For each tabledef object, examine the **CDaoTableDefInfo** object returned by **GetTableDefInfo**. From this object, you can get:

- The name of the tabledef object as well as the name of the ODBC source table that the tabledef represents.

- Whether the table schema is updatable.

- Tabledef attributes.

- The date the tabledef object was created and the date it was last updated.

- The ODBC connection information for the table.

- The validation rule and validation text for the tabledef, if any.

- The number of records in the underlying table (obtaining this count might take considerable time for a large table, and the count might be somewhat unreliable).

The MFC Database sample DAOVIEW performs these steps and lists the table names in a list control or a tree control. It then does the same thing for the fields and indexes in the tables and for the other collections in the database: QueryDefs and Relations.

See Also   DAO: Where Is..., DAO Recordset, DAO Recordset: Binding Records Dynamically

DAO Workspace

This article explains the role of **CDaoWorkspace** objects in your application. For task-oriented information about using workspaces, see the article DAO Database: Using Workspaces and Databases. For an understanding of the DAO workspace object underlying each MFC **CDaoWorkspace** object, see the topic Workspace Object in DAO Help.

Topics covered include:

- Workspace: definition

- MFC workspaces are transaction spaces

- Database engine access

- Workspace collections
- Default workspace
- Workspace roles
- Accessing workspace objects
- Workspace persistence
- Further reading about workspaces

Workspace: Definition

A DAO workspace, represented in MFC by class **CDaoWorkspace**, manages a session with the Microsoft Jet database engine. A workspace can contain one or more open DAO database objects, represented in your program, explicitly or implicitly, by **CDaoDatabase** objects. In DAO, workspaces manage a single transaction space in which any transaction applies to all open databases and recordsets. DAO workspaces also manage database security.

MFC Workspaces Are Transaction Spaces

In MFC, workspaces are primarily transaction spaces; MFC does not expose DAO's security features, although you can program them yourself by directly calling DAO. For more information, see Technical Note 54 under MFC Technical Notes, under MFC in Books Online.

Database Engine Access

In DAO, a separate DBEngine object manages the properties of the single instance of the Microsoft Jet database engine underlying multiple open workspaces. In MFC, access to the database engine's properties is through static member functions of class **CDaoWorkspace**. For more information, see the article DAO Workspace: The Database Engine.

Workspace Collections

In DAO:

- The DBEngine object contains a "collection" of open workspace objects, called the Workspaces collection.
- Each DAO workspace object in turn contains collections of open databases, active users, and active user groups.

In MFC, access to both the DBEngine's Workspaces collection and any workspace's Databases collection is through member functions of a **CDaoWorkspace** object. MFC does not provide direct access to the Users collection or the Groups collection, which are part of DAO's security support; MFC does not expose DAO security features. For information about DAO collections in MFC, see the article DAO Collections.

Default Workspace

In DAO, the first workspace in the Workspaces collection is called the default workspace. By default, if you open databases, they exist within the default workspace. In MFC, if you open a database object without specifying a workspace, or open a recordset object without specifying a database object, MFC implicitly uses DAO's underlying default workspace to manage transactions.

You seldom have to explicitly create a **CDaoWorkspace** object, but you can create explicit **CDaoWorkspace** objects if you need an explicit object for any of the activities described in Workspace Roles.

Information About Workspaces in DAO Help

For information about workspaces in DAO, see the topic Workspace Object in DAO Help. For more information about workspaces in MFC, see the rest of this article and the article DAO Database: Using Workspaces and Databases.

Workspace Roles

CDaoWorkspace can play the following roles:

- Provide explicit access to DAO's default workspace.

- Provide access to the Workspaces collection or the default workspace's Databases collection.

- Provide a separate transaction space if you need to separate the transactions on one database from those on another database.

- Provide access to the properties of the database engine.

Accessing Workspace Objects

MFC implicitly creates a **CDaoWorkspace** object, and its underlying DAO workspace, when you:

- Construct a **CDaoDatabase** object without specifying the workspace.

- Construct a **CDaoRecordset** object without specifying the database.

See the article DAO: Accessing Implicit MFC DAO Objects for information on accessing:

- The **CDaoWorkspace** object associated with a **CDaoDatabase** object

- The **CDaoWorkspace** object associated with the **CDaoDatabase** object associated with a **CDaoRecordset** object

Workspace Persistence

Workspaces exist in memory for the life of a database engine session. When that session terminates, the default workspace, the Workspaces collection, and the Databases collections of any workspaces cease to exist (the actual databases do persist). These software objects are not stored on disk or in a database. When you begin a new database engine session and want to use the workspaces and databases you used in the last session, you must recreate any explicit workspace objects you need and reopen any databases you want associated with a workspace.

Tip Use a Windows registry entry to preserve a record of the workspaces and databases you had open during a database engine session.

Further Reading About Workspaces

For more information about workspaces in MFC see the following articles (in the recommended order):

- DAO Database: Using Workspaces and Databases
- DAO Workspace: Explicitly Opening the Default Workspace
- DAO: Accessing Implicit MFC DAO Objects
- DAO Workspace: Opening a Separate Transaction Space
- DAO Workspace: Accessing Properties of the Database Engine
- DAO Collections

See Also DAO: Where Is..., DAO Database: Using Workspaces and Databases, DAO Workspace: The Database Engine, DAO Database, DAO: Creating, Opening, and Closing DAO Objects

DAO Workspace: Explicitly Opening the Default Workspace

Normally you don't need to refer explicitly to DAO's default workspace. MFC uses it automatically when you open new databases, recordsets, tabledefs, and querydefs. But sometimes you need explicit access to the default workspace—for example, to access the Workspaces collection or to set database engine properties. For that kind of access, you might need a **CDaoWorkspace** object.

The Most Likely Case

The most likely case is that you already have a **CDaoDatabase** object or a **CDaoRecordset** object based on the default workspace (or on an additional workspace). For those cases, see the article DAO: Accessing Implicit MFC DAO Objects. Otherwise, if you don't have a database or recordset object handy, you can still open the default workspace as follows:

▶ **To explicitly open the default workspace**

1 Construct a **CDaoWorkspace** object.

2 Call the object's **Open** member function. Specify **NULL** for the *lpszName* parameter.

3 Call other member functions or access data members.

Closing this **CDaoWorkspace** object has no effect on DAO's default workspace. That workspace is terminated when the database engine session terminates. For information on database engine termination, see the article DAO Workspace: The Database Engine.

See Also DAO: Where Is..., DAO: Accessing Implicit MFC DAO Objects, DAO Workspace, DAO: Creating, Opening, and Closing DAO Objects

DAO Workspace: The Database Engine

MFC and DAO use the Microsoft Jet database engine, currently version 3.0, to retrieve data from and store data in user and system databases. The Microsoft Jet database engine is the data manager component on which various implementations are built, such as the MFC DAO classes, Microsoft Access, and Microsoft Visual Basic, and the Microsoft Desktop Database Drivers (currently version 3.0).

This article explains how you interact with the database engine via MFC. Topics covered include:

- Data sources you can access
- How MFC exposes the database engine
- Database engine collections
- Initializing and uninitializing the database engine

Data Sources You Can Access

While the database engine is best suited for working with Microsoft Jet (.MDB) databases, you can access several ISAM databases and any database for which you have an ODBC driver, including remote databases such as Microsoft SQL Server or Oracle. For more information about these non-.MDB sources, see the article DAO External: Working with External Data Sources.

How MFC Exposes the Database Engine

In DAO, the database engine is represented by a DBEngine object. This object sits at the top of the DAO object hierarchy and contains all of the other objects, such as workspaces and databases. For detailed information about this DAO object, see the topic DBEngine Object in DAO Help. To view the DAO object hierarchy, see the topic Data Access Object Hierarchy in DAO Help.

In MFC, the DBEngine object is not exposed directly via an MFC class. Instead, all access to the underlying DAO database engine object is through a set of static member functions in class **CDaoWorkspace**. These member functions provide access to database engine properties that you can set or get to configure your database sessions. You can access the database engine through any workspace object, whether MFC creates the object implicitly or you create it explicitly. In the majority of situations, you will not need to set these properties. You can rely on the defaults instead.

Database Engine Collections

DAO's DBEngine object houses two important collections used with MFC:

- Workspaces
- Errors

The DBEngine's Workspaces Collection

The Workspaces collection contains all open DAO workspace objects that you have explicitly appended to the collection. See the article DAO Collections: Obtaining Information About DAO Objects for a discussion of how to use the Workspaces collection.

The DBEngine's Errors Collection

The Errors collection contains one DAO error object for each error returned by the most recent DAO operation. In most error situations, particularly when you are working with a Microsoft Jet (.MDB) database, the collection contains one object. If you are using an ODBC data source, it is likely that the collection might contain more than one error object. In MFC, all DAO errors are translated into thrown exceptions of type **CDaoException**. See class **CDaoException** and the article Exceptions: Database Exceptions for a discussion of how to work with MFC's DAO exceptions.

Initializing and Uninitializing the Database Engine

MFC loads a single instance of the DAO DBEngine object, housed in a DLL, per application. Thus your database engine sessions are limited to your application. Your workspaces are not available to other applications or users.

Initializing the Database Engine

MFC initializes the database engine, beginning your database engine session, the first time your application creates or opens a workspace, either implicitly or explicitly. For more information about explicit and implicit workspaces, see the article DAO Workspace.

Uninitializing the Database Engine

MFC uninitializes the database engine, ending your database engine session, when your application terminates.

See Also   DAO: Where Is..., DAO Workspace, DAO Workspace: Accessing Properties of the Database Engine

DAO Workspace: Accessing Properties of the Database Engine

If you need to get or set any of the properties of the database engine behind your workspaces, you'll need a **CDaoWorkspace** object whose static member functions provide access to those properties.

▶ **To access properties of the database engine**

1 Construct a **CDaoWorkspace** object, or use a pointer to one provided by a **CDaoRecordset** or **CDaoDatabase** object.

2 Call any of the workspace's static member functions. You do not need to call **Open** or **Create** to call these member functions.

Accessing Database Engine Properties

Table 1 describes the **CDaoWorkspace** member functions that relate to database engine properties:

Table 1   Workspace Member Functions for Database Engine Access

•DAO property	Member functions	Description
Version	**GetVersion**	Get the version number of the Microsoft Jet database file.
DefaultPassword	**SetDefaultPassword**	Specify the default password that the database engine uses when you create new workspaces without specifying a password. Setting this property is optional. You can instead require that new workspaces supply a password.
DefaultUser	**SetDefaultUser**	Specify the default user name that the database engine uses when you create new workspaces without specifying a user name. As with **SetDefaultPassword**, setting this property is optional.
LoginTimeout	**GetLoginTimeout**, **SetLoginTimeout**	Specify the number of seconds to wait before an ODBC connection attempt times out. DAO sets a default, so setting this property is optional.
IniPath	**GetIniPath, SetIniPath**	Specify a Windows registry key under which are stored application-specific options relating to special settings for the database engine. Setting this property is optional and not often needed.

CDaoWorkspace also supplies member functions for compacting (or copying) a Microsoft Jet (.MDB) database and for attempting to repair a corrupt .MDB database file. See **CDaoWorkspace::CompactDatabase** and **CDaoWorkspace::RepairDatabase**.

More Information About These Properties

For more information, see the the DAO Help topics for the named properties in Table 1. Topic names are of the form: "*propertyname* Property." For example, the topic for the Version property is Version Property. See also the **CDaoWorkspace** member functions listed and the article DAO Workspace: Accessing Properties of the Database Engine.

See Also   DAO: Where Is..., DAO Workspace, DAO Workspace: The Database Engine

DAO Workspace: Managing Transactions

This article explains the MFC facilities available for managing transactions and refers you to additional information in DAO Help. For general transaction information in DAO, see the topic BeginTrans, CommitTrans, Rollback Methods in DAO Help.

Topics covered include:

- Transaction: defined
- Transaction spaces
- Transaction example
- Additional reading about transactions

Transaction: Defined

A transaction is a series of changes made to a database's data and/or schema. Mark the beginning of a transaction by calling the **BeginTrans** member function of class **CDaoWorkspace**. Commit the transaction using the **CommitTrans** member function, or undo all your changes since **BeginTrans** using the **Rollback** member function.

The key idea of transactions is that the operation is "atomic"—a group of related smaller operations must all succeed for the whole operation to succeed. If one small operation fails, the whole operation fails.

There is an implicit transaction while action queries are running. If a query doesn't complete for any reason, it is automatically rolled back. Transactions are optional and can be nested up to five levels. (This is in contrast to ODBC, which does not permit nested transactions.) Transactions increase the speed of data changing operations and enable changes to be reversed easily.

The "current transaction" consists of all changes made to a recordset object after you last called the **BeginTrans** member function and before you call the **Rollback** or **CommitTrans** member functions.

Transaction Spaces

The workspace object defines a transaction space. Transactions are global to the workspace in which they occur. They affect all open databases, recordsets, and querydefs in the same workspace. If you have several open recordsets and/or databases in a workspace, each call to **BeginTrans**, **CommitTrans**, and **Rollback** applies to all of the objects.

For example, suppose you have have called **BeginTrans** for a workspace and you begin updates through two recordsets that belong to database objects in the same workspace. If you call **CommitTrans** or **RollBack** in the workspace, the call affects both recordsets, even if they are open on different databases.

If this transaction model is not what you need, you can open separate transaction spaces by opening separate workspaces. Create a new **CDaoWorkspace** object for each separate transaction space. For more information, see the article DAO Workspace: Opening a Separate Transaction Space.

Transaction Example

The following example illustrates transactions by using two recordsets to delete a student's enrollment from a school registration database. First it removes the student from all classes in which the student is enrolled. Then it removes the student's master record, after which, the student no longer exists in the database.

The **Delete** calls in both recordsets must succeed, so a transaction is required.

Important The example shown illustrates correct transaction procedure, but for the illustrated case this is not the most efficient way to do the job. For details, see the discussion in Efficiency Considerations for This Example.

The example assumes the existence of:

- m_dbStudentReg, a document data member that contains a **CDaoDatabase** object already open on the database.

- m_rsStudentSet, a document data member that contains a recordset object based on class CStudentSet, derived from **CDaoRecordset**. This recordset returns all enrolled students.

- CEnrollmentSet, a second **CDaoRecordset**-derived class. This recordset, as written by ClassWizard, returns all students enrolled in all classes. The example code "filters" the recordset to return only the records representing classes in which the specified student is enrolled.

The example modifies the default SQL string defined with ClassWizard before opening the recordset. The modification filters the records with a student ID passed in as a parameter.

```
BOOL CEnrollDoc::RemoveStudent(CString strStudentID)
{
    // Construct a recordset for courses student is in
    CEnrollmentSet rsEnrollmentSet( &m_dbStudentReg );

    // Define the SQL string for the recordset to
    // Filter records with the SQL keyword WHERE
    CString strSQL = rsEnrollmentSet.GetDefautlSQL( ) +
                "WHERE [Student ID] = " + strStudentID;
    try
    {
        // Open the recordset using
        // the modified SQL string
        rsEnrollmentSet.Open( dbOpenDynaset, strSQL );

        // Start the transaction
        m_dbStudentReg.m_pWorkspace->BeginTrans( );

        // Remove the student from all classes the
        // student is enrolled in
        while ( !rsEnrollmentSet.IsEOF( ) )
        {
            rsEnrollmentSet.Delete( );
            rsEnrollmentSet.MoveNext( );
        }
        // Delete the student's master record
        m_rsStudentSet.Delete( );

        // Commit the transaction
        m_dbStudentReg.m_pWorkspace->CommitTrans( );
    }
    catch(CDaoException* e)
    {
        m_dbStudentReg.m_pWorkspace->Rollback( );
        AfxMessageBox( "Failed to remove student." );
        e->Delete( );
        return FALSE;
    }
    m_rsStudentSet.Close( );
}
```

For information about the **try/catch** exception handling shown here, see the article Exceptions: Database Exceptions and the **CDaoException** class.

Efficiency Considerations for This Example

The transaction example shown in Transaction Example shows you how to do transactions. But in some cases, as in deleting records, transactions may not be the efficient way to go. In fact, there are two more efficient approaches to deleting the student record along with all related records for that student:

- Use cascade deletes

If the student registration database defines a relation between the STUDENT and ENROLLMENT tables with the cascade delete attribute set, you can delete a single student record in the STUDENT table and let cascade deletes remove all related records in the ENROLLMENT table.

For information about cacade deletes, see the topic Relation Object in DAO Help. Relations in MFC are discussed under class **CDaoDatabase** in the *Class Library Reference*.

- Use a bulk query

A bulk query would delete all records in any tables you specify that contain the student ID for the student you want to delete.

The query's SQL statement looks like this:

```
DELETE FROM STUDENT,ENROLLMENT WHERE STUDENT.StudentID =
ENROLLMENT.StudentID AND StudentID = strStudentID
```

The expression "STUDENT.StudentID = ENROLLMENT.StudentID" "joins" the tables on the StudentID field. The expression "StudentID = strStudentID" finds those records in the join that have the particular student ID in strStudentID. The SQL deletes those records.

Transactions do have their role to play, of course. The point is that you should use the best approach for the particular task.

Additional Reading About Transactions

For more information about transactions, see the following topics in DAO Help:

- BeginTrans, CommitTrans, Rollback Methods
- CreateWorkspace Method
- BOF, EOF Properties
- IsolateODBCTrans Property

In the *Class Library Reference*, see: **CDaoWorkspace**, especially the **BeginTrans**, **CommitTrans**, **Rollback**, and **SetIsolateODBCTrans** member functions.

Also see **CDaoRecordset**, especially the **AddNew**, **Edit**, **Update**, **Delete**, **IsBOF**, and **IsEOF** member functions.

See Also   DAO: Where Is..., DAO Recordset

DAO Workspace: Opening a Separate Transaction Space

A workspace defines a single transaction space for all databases open within it. This means that if you begin a transaction in a workspace, then update several recordsets on several databases in the workspace, and then commit or roll back the transaction, the commitment or rollback applies to all of the databases.

Sometimes, however, you need to separate one set of transactions—applying to database A—from another set—applying to database B.

▶ To open a separate transaction space

1 Construct a new **CDaoWorkspace** object.

2 Call the workspace object's **Create** member function. Specify a unique name in the *lpszName* parameter to make this workspace distinct from the default workspace or any other workspaces. Each workspace you create explicitly has a different name.

3 Open one or more databases in the new workspace.

4 Run transactions on the new workspace.

Transactions on the new workspace will be distinct from those on other workspaces. For related information about ODBC data sources, see the article DAO External: Working with External Data Sources and see **CDaoWorkspace::SetIsolateODBCTrans**.

For a general discussion of using transactions, see the article DAO Workspace: Managing Transactions. That article also leads you to topics in DAO Help.

See Also   DAO: Where Is..., DAO Workspace: Managing Transactions, DAO: Creating, Opening, and Closing DAO Objects

Database

For a general overview of the MFC database classes, see Chapter 7, Working with Databases. That discussion covers both the Open Database Connectivity (ODBC) classes and the newer Data Access Object (DAO) classes.

See Also Database Overview, Data Source (ODBC)

Database Overview

MFC supports two different kinds of database access:

- Access via Data Access Objects (DAO) and the Microsoft Jet database engine
- Access via Open Database Connectivity (ODBC) and an ODBC driver

Both of these supply abstractions that simplify working with databases, complete with the speed, power, and flexibility of C++. Both integrate your data access work with the MFC application framework.

This article explains the differences between DAO and ODBC and provides information to help you choose which kind of data access to use. Topics include:

- What are DAO and ODBC?
- What Is the MFC database programming model?
- DAO or ODBC?
- Calling DAO or ODBC directly
- Database definition and manipulation
- More information about the DAO and ODBC classes

What Are DAO and ODBC?

DAO is familiar to database programmers using Microsoft Access Basic or Microsoft Visual Basic. DAO uses the Microsoft Jet database engine to provide a set of data access objects: database objects, tabledef and querydef objects, recordset objects, and others. DAO is optimally useful for working with .MDB files like those created by Microsoft Access, but you can also access ODBC data sources through DAO and the Microsoft Jet database engine.

ODBC provides an application programming interface (API) which different database vendors implement via ODBC drivers specific to a particular database management system (DBMS). Your program uses this API to call the ODBC Driver Manager, which passes the calls to the appropriate driver. The driver, in turn, interacts with the DBMS using Structured Query Language (SQL).

Both DAO and ODBC give you the ability to write applications that are independent of any particular DBMS.

What Is the MFC Database Programming Model?

MFC provides a database programming model that is very similar to the model used in Microsoft Access Basic and Microsoft Visual Basic. The model is also very similar whether you are using DAO or ODBC. While MFC's implementations of DAO and ODBC are quite different underneath, the similar interfaces make it relatively easy to port your applications from one to the other, particularly from ODBC to DAO. (For information about porting from ODBC to DAO, see Technical Note 55 under MFC Technical Notes in Books Online.)

In the MFC programming model, using DAO or ODBC, you work with a database object for each open database. The database object represents your connection to the database. You make queries and updates via recordset objects. DAO provides additional objects, for working with table structure, saving queries for reuse, and so on, described later. MFC supplies classes for each of these objects: one set of classes for DAO and another set for ODBC.

DAO or ODBC?

Which set of MFC classes should you use? This depends on your needs:

- Use the ODBC classes if you are working strictly with ODBC data sources, particularly in client/server situations, where the MFC ODBC classes provide better performance.

- Use the DAO classes if you are working primarily with Microsoft Jet (.MDB) databases or with other database formats that the Microsoft Jet database engine can read directly. For a list of these, see Databases You Can Access with DAO.

One reason for choosing the DAO classes is that they provide a richer data access model, with support for Data Definition Language (DDL) as well as Data Manipulation Language (DML). For details, see Database Definition and Manipulation.

Note The introduction of DAO does not foretell the end of ODBC. As a major part of the Microsoft Windows Open Standards Architecture (WOSA), ODBC is here for the long run. DAO is optimized around the Microsoft Jet database engine, but you can still access ODBC and other external data sources via that engine, and the distinct ODBC API and the MFC classes based on it are still available and still have their role to play in your selection of database tools.

Since DAO also supports access via ODBC (through the Microsoft Jet database engine), your primary reasons for choosing the DAO classes over the ODBC classes are:

- Better performance in some cases, particularly when using Microsoft Jet (.MDB) databases.

- Compatibility with the ODBC classes and with Microsoft Access Basic and Microsoft Visual Basic.
- DAO gives you access to validation rules.
- DAO lets you specify relations between tables.

Table 1 summarizes the key differences to help you choose:

Table 1   Choosing Between MFC's DAO and ODBC Classes

	DAO Classes	ODBC Classes
Access .MDB files	Yes	Yes
Access ODBC data sources	Yes	Yes
Available for 16 Bit	No	Yes
Available for 32 Bit	Yes	Yes
Database compaction	Yes	No
Database engine support	Microsoft Jet database engine	Target DBMS
DDL support	Yes	Only via direct ODBC calls
DML support	Yes	Yes
Nature of the MFC implementation	"Wrapper" of DAO core functions	Simplified abstraction rather than a "wrapper" of the ODBC API
Optimal for	.MDB files (Microsoft Access)	Any DBMS for which you have a driver, especially in client/server situations
Transaction support	Per "workspace" or, for ODBC data, per database	Per database

Keep in mind that the capabilities of ODBC drivers vary. See the ODBC *Programmer's Reference* and the help file for your ODBC driver for more information. For information about using ODBC via DAO, see the article DAO External: Working with External Data Sources.

If you are working with ODBC databases rather than Microsoft Jet (.MDB) databases, you might want to use the ODBC classes and avoid the overhead of DAO.

What Data Sources Can You Access with DAO and ODBC?

Both sets of MFC classes let you access a wide variety of data sources and make it possible to write applications that are independent of the data source.

Databases You Can Access with DAO

Using DAO and the MFC DAO classes, you can access the following sources of data:

- Databases using the Microsoft Jet database engine, created with Microsoft Access or Microsoft Visual Basic, versions 1.x, 2.x, and 3.0 of the database engine
- Installable ISAM databases, including:

- Microsoft FoxPro, versions 2.0, 2.5, and 2.6. Able to import/export data to and from version 3.0, but can't create objects
- dBASE III, dBASE IV, and dBASE 5.0
- Paradox, versions 3.x, 4.x, and 5.x

- Open Database Connectivity (ODBC) databases, including but not limited to Microsoft SQL Server, SYBASE® SQL Server, and ORACLE® Server. To access an ODBC database, you must have an appropriate ODBC driver for the database you wish to access. See the article ODBC Driver List for a list of ODBC drivers included in this version of Visual C++ and for information about obtaining additional drivers.
- Microsoft Excel, versions 3.0, 4.0, 5.0, and 7.0 worksheets
- Lotus WKS, WK1, WK3, and WK4 spreadsheets
- Text files

DAO is best used with databases that the Microsoft Jet database engine can read. That includes all of the above except ODBC data sources. Best performance is with Microsoft Jet (.MDB) databases. Attaching external tables, especially in ODBC data sources, to an .MDB database is more efficient than opening the external database directly via the MFC DAO classes without attaching. For more information on external data sources, see the article DAO External: Working with External Data Sources.

Databases You Can Access with ODBC

Using ODBC and the MFC ODBC classes, you can access any data source, local or remote, for which the user of your application has an ODBC driver. Both 16-bit and 32-bit ODBC drivers are available for a wide range of data sources, including those listed under Databases You Can Access with DAO. If you're working with a Microsoft Jet (.MDB) database, it's more efficient to use the DAO classes than the Microsoft Access ODBC driver.

Calling DAO or ODBC Directly

As usual in MFC, if you need finer control, you can call DAO or ODBC directly in addition to accessing them through the classes. MFC attempts to simplify programming for Windows, but it also stays out of your way if you need access to the underlying APIs.

Database Definition and Manipulation

The MFC DAO classes support two kinds of access to databases:

- Data definition language (DDL) You can create and delete databases, create and delete tables, define table fields and indexes, and take other actions that affect the structure of your database.

- Data manipulation language (DML) You can run queries, add, delete, and edit records, and otherwise manipulate the content of your database.

The MFC ODBC classes support only DML, but you can call ODBC API functions directly to carry out DDL tasks.

More Information About the DAO and ODBC Classes

Because the implementations are quite different, the documentation for these sets of classes is almost completely compartmentalized. MFC DAO documentaion is separate from MFC ODBC documentation. Visual C++ also supplies both the DAO and ODBC SDK documentation. Table 2 leads you to the next article you should read if you're just beginning to study the MFC DAO classes or the MFC ODBC classes.

Table 2 Further Reading About DAO and ODBC in MFC

For more information about...	See...
The MFC DAO classes	DAO and MFC
The MFC ODBC classes	ODBC and MFC

Tip From any topic in the MFC DAO documentation, you can click the See Also button in the topic window. One topic always available in the See Also list is the topic DAO: Where Is..., which helps you quickly locate the information you seek.

MFC Database Documentation

The MFC documentation for DAO and ODBC classes consists of the components listed in Table 3.

Table 3 MFC Database Documentation

For documentation on...	See...
DAO database tutorial	Chapter 34, Data Access Objects (DAO) Tutorial, in *Tutorials*
ODBC database tutorial	Chapter 30, Creating a Database Application, in *Tutorials*
Classes for both DAO and ODBC	The class name in the *Class Library Reference*
Global functions and macros for both	The function or macro name in the *Class Library Reference*
Encyclopedia articles on programming with the MFC DAO classes	The article DAO and MFC
Encyclopedia articles on programming with the MFC ODBC classes	The article ODBC and MFC
Technical notes for both	MFC Technical Notes, under MFC Technical Notes in Books Online. See the InfoViewer in the Project Workspace window.
Sample applications	MFC Samples, under Samples in Books Online.

MFC Documentation and DAO Documentation

Throughout the MFC documentation for the MFC DAO classes, you'll find links to topics in the DAO SDK documentation, which is included in Books Online. Because MFC essentially "wraps" DAO, the documentation strategy is to:

- Focus in the MFC documents on MFC and how it differs from the underlying DAO implementation.

- Point you to the DAO SDK Help topics for the underlying details. These cross references are always worded as "topic *X* in DAO Help."

A few things to keep in mind as you use this cross-connected documentation:

- The connections are one-way, from MFC to DAO SDK Help, but in Books Online you can always use the Go Back button in the topic window to move from DAO topics to MFC topics.

- MFC sometimes does things differently from the way DAO does them, and MFC doesn't wrap all of DAO. For example, MFC doesn't supply objects for DAO's security functionality. Differences are pointed out in the articles where relevant.

- Examples in the primary DAO SDK documentation supplied in Books Online are written in the Basic programming language, not C++. (But the DAO SDK supplies a set of C++ examples that don't use MFC.) You might have to do some translating when you are browsing topics in DAO SDK Help via Books Online. For guidance, see the examples that appear in these encyclopedia articles and the MFC DAO sample applications, listed under Samples/MFC Samples/Databases (ODBC and DAO) in the InfoViewer in the Project Workspace window.

In Part 1 of *Programming with MFC*, see Chapter 7, Working with Databases, for additional implementation about your DAO or ODBC installation.

MFC Documentation and ODBC Documentation

The MFC documentation for the MFC ODBC classes is organized differently. The MFC ODBC classes supply a high-level abstraction that rests on ODBC rather than a "wrapper" of the ODBC API. The two documentation sets are thus less intimately connected than are the MFC and DAO documentation sets. The ODBC documentation uses the C language, which is much closer to C++ than is Basic.

See Also   DAO: Where Is..., DAO and MFC, ODBC and MFC, Data Access Objects (DAO), ODBC

Data Objects and Data Sources (OLE)

When you perform a data transfer, by using either the Clipboard or drag and drop, the data has a source and a destination. One application provides the data for copying and another application accepts it for pasting. Each side of the transfer needs to perform different operations on the same data for the transfer to succeed. The

Microsoft Foundation Class Library (MFC) provides two classes that represent each side of this transfer:

- Data sources (as implemented by **COleDataSource** objects) represent the source side of the data transfer. They are created by the source application when data is to be copied to the Clipboard, or when data is provided for a drag-and-drop operation.

- Data objects (as implemented by **COleDataObject** objects) represent the destination side of the data transfer. They are created when the destination application has data dropped into it, or when it is asked to perform a paste operation from the Clipboard.

The following articles explain how to use data objects and data sources in your applications. This information applies to both container and server applications, because both may be called upon to copy and paste data.

- Data Objects and Data Sources: Creation and Destruction
- Data Objects and Data Sources: Manipulation

See Also   Drag and Drop, Clipboard

In the *Class Library Reference*: **COleDataObject**, **COleDataSource**

Data Objects and Data Sources: Creation and Destruction

As explained in the article Data Objects and Data Sources (OLE), data objects and data sources represent both sides of a data transfer. This article explains when to create and destroy these objects and sources to perform your data transfers properly. Topics include:

- Creating data objects
- Destroying data objects
- Creating data sources
- Destroying data sources

Creating Data Objects

Data objects are used by the destination application—either the client or the server. A data object in the destination application is one end of a connection between the source application and the destination application. A data object in the destination application is used to access and interact with the data in the data source.

There are two common situations where a data object is needed. The first is when data is dropped in your application using drag and drop. The second is when Paste or Paste Special is chosen from the Edit Menu.

In a drag-and-drop situation, you do not need to create a data object. A pointer to an existing data object will be passed to your **OnDrop** function. This data object is created by the framework as part of the drag-and-drop operation and will also be destroyed by it. This is not always the case when pasting is done by another method. For more information, see Destroying Data Objects.

If the application is performing a paste or paste special operation, you should create a **COleDataObject** object and call its **AttachClipboard** member function. This associates the data object with the data on the Clipboard. You can then use this data object in your paste function.

For an example of how this is done, see the **DoPasteItem** function in the MAINVIEW.CPP file that is part of the MFC OLE sample OCLIENT. OCLIENT implements a function that performs all paste operations and calls **DoPasteItem** from its **OnDrop**, **OnPaste**, and **OnPasteLink** functions. Because **OnDrop** has a pointer to a data object passed to it, it passes the pointer on to **DoPasteItem**. **OnPaste** and **OnPasteLink** pass **NULL** for this parameter, telling **DoPasteItem** to create a data object and attach it to the Clipboard. This scheme separates your paste code so you only have to debug it in one place, but you can still use it for both kinds of paste operations.

Destroying Data Objects

If you follow the scheme described in Creating Data Objects, destroying them is a trivial aspect of data transfers. The data object that was created in your paste function will be destroyed when your paste function returns.

If you follow another method of handling paste operations, make sure the data object is destroyed after your paste operation is complete. Until the data object is destroyed, it will be impossible for any application to successfully copy data to the Clipboard.

Creating Data Sources

Data sources are used by the source of the data transfer—which can be either the client or the server side of the data transfer. A data source in the source application is one end of a connection between the source application and the destination application. A data object in the destination application is used to interact with the data in the data source.

Data sources are created when an application needs to copy data to the Clipboard. A typical scenario runs like this:

1. The user selects some data.

2. The user chooses Copy (or Cut) from the Edit menu or begins a drag-and-drop operation.

3. Depending on the design of the program, the application creates either a **COleDataSource** object or an object from a class derived from **COleDataSource**.

4. The selected data is inserted into the data source by calling one of the functions in the **COleDataSource::CacheData** or **COleDataSource::DelayRenderData** groups.

5. The application calls the **SetClipboard** member function (or the **DoDragDrop** member function if this is a drag-and-drop operation) belonging to the object created in step 3.

6. If this is a Cut operation or **DoDragDrop** returns **DROPEFFECT_MOVE**, the data selected in step 1 is deleted from the document.

This scenario is implemented by the MFC OLE samples OCLIENT and HIERSVR. Look at the source for each application's **CView**-derived class for all but the **GetClipboardData** and **OnGetClipboardData** functions. These two functions are in either the **COleClientItem** or **COleServerItem**-derived class implementations. These sample programs provide a good example of how to implement these concepts.

One other situation in which you might want to create a **COleDataSource** object occurs if you are modifying the default behavior of a drag-and-drop operation. For more information, see the Drag and Drop: Customizing article.

Destroying Data Sources

Data sources must be destroyed by the application currently responsible for them. In situations where you hand the data source to OLE, such as calling **COleDataSource::SetClipboard**, you do not have to worry about destroying it because it will be destroyed by OLE. If you do not hand your data source to OLE, then you are responsible for destroying it, as with any typical C++ object.

See Also   Data Objects and Data Sources: Manipulation

In the *Class Library Reference*: **COleDataObject**, **COleDataSource**

Data Objects and Data Sources: Manipulation

After a data object or data source has been created, you can perform a number of common operations on the data, such as inserting and removing data, enumerating the formats the data is in, and more. This article describes the techniques necessary to complete the most common operations. Topics include:

- Inserting data into a data source
- Determining the formats available in a data object
- Retrieving data from a data object

Inserting Data into a Data Source

How data is inserted into a data source depends on whether the data is supplied immediately or on demand, and in which medium it is supplied. The possibilities are as follows:

Supplying Data Immediately (Immediate Rendering)

- Call **COleDataSource::CacheGlobalData** repeatedly for every Clipboard format in which you are supplying data. Pass the Clipboard format to be used, a handle to the memory containing the data and, optionally, a **FORMATETC** structure describing the data.

  −or−

- If you want to work directly with **STGMEDIUM** structures, you call **COleDataSource::CacheData** instead of **COleDataSource::CacheGlobalData** in the option above.

Supplying Data on Demand (Delayed Rendering)

This is an advanced topic.

- Call **COleDataSource::DelayRenderData** repeatedly for every Clipboard format in which you are supplying data. Pass the Clipboard format to be used and, optionally, a **FORMATETC** structure describing the data. When the data is requested, the framework will call **COleDataSource::OnRenderData**, which you must override.

  −or−

- If you use a **CFile** object to supply the data, call **COleDataSource::DelayRenderFileData** instead of **COleDataSource::DelayRenderData** in the option above. When the data is requested, the framework will call **COleDataSource::OnRenderFileData**, which you must override.

Determining the Formats Available in a Data Object

Before an application allows the user to paste data into it, it needs to know if there are formats on the Clipboard that it can handle. To do this, your application should do the following:

1. Create a **COleDataObject** object and a **FORMATETC** structure.

2. Call the data object's **AttachClipboard** member function to associate the data object with the data on the Clipboard.

3. Do one of the following:

   - Call the data object's **IsDataAvailable** member function if there are only one or two formats you need. This will save you time in cases where the data on the Clipboard supports significantly more formats than your application.

     −or−

   - Call the data object's **BeginEnumFormats** member function to start enumerating the formats available on the Clipboard. Then call **GetNextFormat** until the Clipboard returns a format your application supports or there are no more formats.

If you are using **ON_UPDATE_COMMAND_UI**, you can now enable the Paste and, possibly, Paste Special items on the Edit menu. To do this, call either **CMenu::EnableMenuItem** or **CCmdUI::Enable**. For more information on what container applications should do with menu items and when, see the Menus and Resources: Container Additions article.

Retrieving Data from a Data Object

Once you have decided on a data format, all that's left is to retrieve the data from the data object. To do this, the user decides where he or she wants to put the data, and the application calls the appropriate function. The data will be available in one of the following mediums:

Medium	Function to call
Global Memory (**HGLOBAL**)	**COleDataObject::GetGlobalData**
File (**CFile**)	**COleDataObject::GetFileData**
STGMEDIUM structure (**IStorage**)	**COleDataObject::GetData**

Commonly, the medium will be specified along with its Clipboard format. For example, a **CF_EMBEDDEDSTRUCT** object is always in an **IStorage** medium which requires an **STGMEDIUM** structure; therefore, you would use **GetData** because it is the only one of these functions that can accept an **STGMEDIUM** structure.

For cases where the Clipboard format is in an **IStream** or **HGLOBAL** medium, the framework can provide a **CFile** pointer that references the data. The application can then use file read to get the data much as it might import data from a file. Essentially, this is the client-side interface to the **OnRenderData** and **OnRenderFileData** routines in the data source.

The data can then be inserted into your document just as you would handle any other data in the same format.

See Also Clipboard, Drag and Drop

In the *Class Library Reference*: **COleDataObject**, **COleDataSource**

Data Source (ODBC)

This article applies to the MFC ODBC classes. For information about the MFC DAO classes, see the article Data Access Objects (DAO).

In database terms, a data source is a specific set of data, the information required to access that data, and the location of the data source, which can be described using a data-source name. To work with class **CDatabase**, the data source must be one that you have configured through Open Database Connectivity (ODBC) Administrator. Examples of data sources include a remote database running on Microsoft SQL

Server across a network, or a Microsoft Access file in a local directory. From your application, you can access any data source for which you have an ODBC driver.

You can have one or more data sources active in your application at one time, each represented by a **CDatabase** object. You can also have multiple simultaneous connections to any data source. You can connect to remote as well as to local data sources, depending on the drivers you have installed and the capabilities of your ODBC drivers. For more information about data sources and ODBC Administrator, see the articles ODBC and ODBC Administrator.

The following articles explain more about data sources:

- Data Source: Managing Connections (ODBC)
- Data Source: Determining the Schema of the Data Source (ODBC)

See Also In the *Class Library Reference*: **CDatabase**

Data Source: Managing Connections (ODBC)

This article applies to the MFC ODBC classes. For information about the MFC DAO classes, see the article Data Access Objects (DAO).

This article explains:

- How to configure a data source.
- How a multiuser environment affects a data source and its recordsets.
- Why you generalize a connection string to a data source.
- How to connect to a data source.
- How to disconnect from a data source.
- How to reuse a **CDatabase** object.

Connecting to a data source means establishing communications with a DBMS in order to access the data. When you connect to a data source from an application through an ODBC driver, the driver makes the connection for you, either locally or across a network.

You can connect to any data source for which you have an ODBC driver. Users of your application must also have the same ODBC driver for their data source. For more information about redistributing ODBC drivers, see Redistributing ODBC Components to Your Customers in the article ODBC.

Configuring a Data Source

ODBC Administrator is used to configure your data sources. You can also use ODBC Administrator after installation to add or remove data sources. When you create applications, you can either direct your users to the ODBC Administrator to let them add data sources, or you can build this functionality into your application by making direct ODBC installation calls. For more information, see the Setup DLL Function

Reference chapter in the ODBC *Programmer's Reference*, the article ODBC Administrator, and the online ODBC API Reference help system.

Working in a Multiuser Environment

If multiple users are connected to a data source, they can change data while you are manipulating it in your recordsets. Similarly, your changes may affect other users' recordsets. For more information about how your updates affect other users, and how their updates affect you, see the articles Recordset: How Recordsets Update Records (ODBC) and Transaction (ODBC).

Generalizing the Connection String

ClassWizard uses a default connection string to establish a connection to a data source. You use this connection to view tables and columns while you are developing your application. However, this default connection string may not be appropriate for your users' connections to the data source through your application. For example, their data source and the path to its location may be different from the one used in developing your application. In that case, you should re-implement the **CRecordset::GetDefaultConnect** member function in a more generic fashion and discard ClassWizard's implementation. For example, use one of the following approaches:

- Register and manage the connect strings by using ODBC Administrator.

- Remove the data-source name completely. The framework supplies "ODBC" as the data source and ODBC will display a dialog box asking for the data-source name, and any other required connection information.

- Supply the data-source name only. ODBC will ask for the user ID and password, if required. For example, before generalizing, the connection string looks like this:

```
CString CApp1Set::GetDefaultConnect()
{
    return "ODBC;DSN=afx;UID=sa;PWD=Fred;";
}
```

To generalize it, rewrite **GetDefaultConnect** so that it returns one of the following values:

```
// Most general case. User must select data source and
// supply user and password
    return "ODBC;";
// User and password required
    return "ODBC;DSN=mydb;";
// Password required
    return "ODBC;DSN=mydb;UID=sa;";
// On most systems, will connect to server w/o any queries to user
    return "ODBC;DSN=mydb;UID=sa;PWD=Fred;";
```

Connecting to a Specific Data Source

To connect to a specific data source, your data source must already have been configured with ODBC Administrator.

▶ **To connect to a specific data source**

1 Construct a **CDatabase** object.

2 Call its **Open** member function.

For more information about how to specify the data source if it is something other than the one you specified with ClassWizard, see **CDatabase::Open** in the *Class Library Reference*.

Disconnecting from a Data Source

You must close any open recordsets before calling the **Close** member function of **CDatabase**. In recordsets associated with the **CDatabase** object you want to close, any pending **AddNew** or **Edit** statements are canceled, and all pending transactions are rolled back.

▶ **To disconnect from a data source**

1 Call the **CDatabase** object's **Close** member function.

2 Destroy the object unless you want to reuse it.

Reusing a CDatabase Object

You can reuse a **CDatabase** object after disconnecting from it, whether you use it to reconnect to the same data source or to connect to a different data source.

▶ **To reuse a CDatabase object**

1 Close the object's original connection.

2 Instead of destroying the object, call its **Open** member function again.

See Also Data Source: Determining the Schema of the Data Source (ODBC)

In the *Class Library Reference*: **CRecordset**, **CDatabase::Open**, **CDatabase::Close**

Data Source: Determining the Schema of the Data Source (ODBC)

This article applies to the MFC ODBC classes. For information about the MFC DAO classes, see the article Data Access Objects (DAO).

To set up data members in your **CRecordset** objects, you need to know the schema of the data source to which you are connecting. Determining the schema of a data source involves obtaining a list of the tables in the data source, a list of the columns in each table, the data type of each column, and the existence of any indexes.

▶ **To determine the schema of a data source**

- See the MFC Database samples CATALOG and DYNABIND, which use the ODBC API functions **::SQLTables** and **::SQLColumns**.

See Also   Data Source (ODBC), Data Source: Managing Connections (ODBC)

Date and Time

This set of articles describe how to use MFC to support various ways of working with dates and times.

Several different ways of working with dates and times are supported by MFC. These include:

- General-purpose time classes. The **CTime** and **CTimeSpan** classes encapsulate most of the functionality associated with the ANSI-standard time library, which is declared in TIME.H.

- Support for system clock. With MFC version 3.0, support was added to **CTime** for the Win32 **SYSTEMTIME** and **FILETIME** data types.

- Support for the OLE Automation **DATE** data type. **DATE** supports date, time, and date/time values. The **COleDateTime** and **COleDateTimeSpan** classes encapsulate this functionality. They work with the **COleVariant** class using in OLE Automation support.

For more information, see one or more of the following articles:

- Date and Time: General-Purpose Classes
- Date and Time: SYSTEMTIME Support
- Date and Time: OLE Automation Support

Date and Time: General-Purpose Classes

This article describes how to take advantage of the class library general-purpose services related to date and time management. Procedures described include:

- Getting the current time
- Calculating elapsed time
- Formatting a string representation of a date/time

The **CTime** class provides a way to represent date and time information easily. The **CTimeSpan** class represents elapsed time, such as the difference between two **CTime** objects.

Note   CTime objects can be used to represent dates between January 1, 1970, and February 5, 2036. CTime objects have a resolution of 1 second. CTime is based on the **time_t** data type, defined in the *Run-Time Library Reference*.

Current Time: General Purpose Classes

The following procedure shows how to create a **CTime** object and initialize it with the current time.

▶ **To get the current time**

1 Allocate a **CTime** object, as follows:

```
CTime theTime;
```

Note Uninitialized **CTime** objects are not initialized to a valid time.

2 Call the **CTime::GetCurrentTime** function to get the current time from the operating system. This function returns a **CTime** object that can be used to set the value of **CTime**, as follows:

```
theTime = CTime::GetCurrentTime();
```

Since **GetCurrentTime** is a static member function from the **CTime** class, you must qualify its name with the name of the class and the scope resolution operator (::), `CTime::GetCurrentTime()`.

Of course, the two steps outlined previously could be combined into a single program statement as follows:

```
CTime theTime = CTime::GetCurrentTime();
```

Elapsed Time: General-Purpose Classes

The following procedure shows how to calculate the difference between two **CTime** objects and get a **CTimeSpan** result.

▶ **To calculate elapsed time**

• Use the **CTime** and **CTimeSpan** objects to calculate the elapsed time, as follows:

```
CTime startTime = CTime::GetCurrentTime();

// ... perform time-consuming task ...

CTime endTime = CTime::GetCurrentTime();

CTimeSpan elapsedTime = endTime - startTime;
```

Once you have calculated `elapsedTime`, you can use the member functions of **CTimeSpan** to extract the components of the elapsed-time value.

Formatting Time Values: General-Purpose Classes

▶ **To format a string representation of a time or elapsed time**

• Use the **Format** member function from either the **CTime** or **CTimeSpan** classes to create a character string representation of the time or elapsed time, as shown by the following example.

```
CTime t( 1991, 3, 19, 22, 15, 0 );
// 10:15PM March 19, 1991

CString s = t.Format( "%A, %B %d, %Y" );
// s == "Tuesday, March 19, 1991"
```

See Also   Date and Time, Date and Time: SYSTEMTIME Support, Date and Time: OLE Automation Support

In the *Class Library Reference*: **CTime**, **CTimeSpan**

Date and Time: SYSTEMTIME Support

The **CTime** class has constructors that accept system and file times from Win32. If you use **CTime** objects for these purposes, you must modify their initialization accordingly, as described in this article.

MFC still provides **CTime** constructors that take time arguments of the MS-DOS style, but, with MFC version 3.0, the **CTime** class also supports a constructor that takes a Win32 **SYSTEMTIME** structure and another that takes a Win32 **FILETIME** structure.

The new **CTime** constructors are:

- **CTime(const SYSTEMTIME&** *sysTime* **);**
- **CTime(const FILETIME&** *fileTime* **);**

The *fileTime* parameter is a reference to a Win32 **FILETIME** structure, which represents time as a 64-bit value, a more convenient format for internal storage than a **SYSTEMTIME** structure and the format used by Win32 to represent the time of file creation.

If your code contains a **CTime** object initialized with the system time, you should use the **SYSTEMTIME** constructor in Win32.

You most likely will not use **CTime FILETIME** initialization directly. If you use a **CFile** object to manipulate a file, **CFile::GetStatus** retrieves the file timestamp for you via a **CTime** object initialized with a **FILETIME** structure.

See Also   Date and Time, Date and Time: OLE Automation Support, Date and Time: General-Purpose Classes

Date and Time: OLE Automation Support

This article describes how to take advantage of the class library services related to date and time management. Procedures described include:

- Getting the current time
- Calculating elapsed time
- Formatting a string representation of a date/time

The **COleDateTime** class provides a way to represent date and time information. It provides finer granularity and a greater range than the **CTime** class. The **COleDateTimeSpan** class represents elapsed time, such as the difference between two **COleDateTime** objects.

The **COleDateTime** and **COleDateTimeSpan** classes are designed to be used with the **COleVariant** class used in OLE Automation. However, these classes are indeed general-purpose. They can be used wherever you want to manipulate date and time values. The **COleDateTime** class has a greater range of values and finer granularity than the **CTime** class. However, it requires more storage per object than **CTime**. There are also some special considerations when working with the underlying **DATE** type. See the following section, The DATE Type, for more details on the implementation of **DATE**.

Note **COleDateTime** objects can be used to represent dates between January 1, 100, and December 31, 9999. **COleDateTime** objects are floating point values, with an approximate resolution of 1 millisecond. **COleDateTime** is based on the **DATE** data type, defined in the OLE documentation. The actual implementation of **DATE** extends beyond these bounds. The **COleDateTime** implementation imposes these bounds to facilitate working with the class.

The DATE Type

The **DATE** type is implemented using an 8-byte floating-point number. Days are represented by whole number increments starting with 30 December 1899, midnight as time zero. Hour values are expressed as the absolute value of the fractional part of the number. The following table illustrates this.

Date and time	Representation
30 December 1899, midnight	0.00
1 January 1900, midnight	2.00
4 January 1900, midnight	5.00
4 January 1900, 6 AM	5.25
4 January 1900, noon	5.50
4 January 1900, 9 PM	5.875

So, the **DATE** date type, and also the **COleDateTime** class, represent dates and times as a classic number line.

However, there are discontinuities for dates before 30 December 1899. See the following table for an illustration.

Date and time	Representation
30 December 1899, midnight	0.00
29 December 1899, midnight	-1.00
18 December 1899, midnight	-12.00
18 December 1899, 6 AM	-12.25

Date and time	Representation
18 December 1899, noon	-12.50
18 December 1899, 6 PM	-12.75
19 December 1899, midnight	-11.00

Current Time: OLE Automation Classes

The following procedure shows how to create a **COleDateTime** object and initialize it with the current time.

▶ **To get the current time**

1 Create a **COleDateTime** object.

2 Call **GetCurrentTime**.

```
COleDateTime timeNow;
timeNow = COleDateTime::GetCurrentTime();
```

Elapsed Time: OLE Automation Classes

This procedure shows how to calculate the difference between two **CTime** objects and get a **CTimeSpan** result.

▶ **To calculate elapsed time**

1 Create two **COleDateTime** objects.

2 Set one of the **COleDateTime** objects to the current time.

3 Perform some time-consuming task.

4 Set the other **COleDateTime** object to the current time.

5 Take the difference between the two times.

```
COleDateTime timeStart, timeEnd;
timeStart = COleDateTime::GetCurrentTime();
// ... perform time-consuming task
timeEnd = COleDateTime::GetCurrentTime();
COleDateTimeSpan spanElapsed = timeEnd - timeStart;
```

Formatting Time: OLE Automation Classes

▶ **To format an time**

- Use the **Format** member function of either **COleDateTime** or **COleDateTimeSpan** to create a character string representing the time or elapsed time.

```
COleDateTime time(70, 12, 18, 17, 30, 0);
// 18 December 1970, 5:30 PM
CString s = time.Format(VAR_DATEVAUEONLY);
// s contains the date formatted based on
// the current national language specifications
// (locale ID). The time portion is ignored for
// formatting purposes in this case.
```

See Also Date and Time, Date and Time: General-Purpose Classes, Date and Time: SYSTEMTIME Support

In the *Class Library Reference*: **COleDateTime**, **COleDateTimeSpan**, **COleVariant**

DBCS

Double-byte character set encoding—a form of Multibyte Character Set (MBCS) encoding in which characters are always either one or two bytes wide. MFC and Visual C++ support both DBCS and Unicode applications.

For information on using DBCS with MFC, see Chapter 13 in *Programming Techniques*.

DBMS

Database Management System.

If you're using the MFC ODBC classes, see the article Data Source (ODBC). If you're using the MFC DAO classes, see the article Data Access Objects (DAO).

Debugging

The Microsoft Foundation Class Library (MFC) and Visual C++ help you debug your applications in a variety of ways. This article presents a few useful general debugging techniques and refers you to other articles on related debugging topics.

For information about using the Visual C++ debugger, see Chapter 17, Using the Debugger, in the *Visual C++ User's Guide*.

Following are several techniques for debugging your MFC application:

- Before you start a debugging session (or as soon as possible after you start), arrange the debugger and the program you are debugging on the screen so that neither overlaps the other. Otherwise, there may be situations in which the debugger completely obscures the program being debugged.

- Turn on Multi-App Debugging from the TRACER application when you are debugging an application and one or more DLLs. The Multi-App Debugging option prefixes each trace statement with the name of the application that generated it. TRACER can be found in the BIN directory, and an icon for it is installed in the Microsoft Visual C++ program group with the name "MFC Tracer."

- If you have trouble setting breakpoints with the debugger, you can hard-code them into your application with the following statement:

```
DebugBreak( );
```

which is platform independent. For MFC applications, you can also use:

```
AfxDebugBreak( );
```

This does an

```
_asm int 3
```

in Intel® versions and calls **DebugBreak** on other platforms. The advantage (on Intel) is that you break in source code rather than in kernel code.

Be sure to remove these statements when building release-mode applications or include them under **#ifdef _DEBUG**.

- If you run into limitations with the Visual C++ debugger, you can always use **TRACE** statements and the TRACER application. Activating the Multi-App Debugging option in TRACER can be very useful in tracking the order of events.

  Note For Win32s®, you use "remote debugging"—the debugger is hosted on Windows NT, and the debuggee runs on another machine and is controlled through the serial port.

For additional information specific to MFC debugging, see the following articles:

- Diagnostics
- Debugging OLE Applications

Debugging OLE Applications

OLE applications perform a number of tasks outside of the programmer's direct control. Communication between DLLs, usage counts on objects, and Clipboard operations are just a few of the areas where you may encounter unexpected behavior. Usually when this happens, your first step is to track down the source of the problem. The difficulty with OLE applications is that it isn't always obvious how to debug a particular problem. This series of articles describes techniques you can use to track down problems, some of which are unique to OLE applications. It also introduces you to the special tools and testing aids available to help you write solid OLE applications.

Debugging OLE applications begins with the same general debugging techniques you use in other kinds of applications. For more information, see the article Debugging.

Tip When you're debugging an OLE server and container, start up two instances of Visual C++, load the server and container projects, set appropriate breakpoints in each, and debug. When the container makes a call into the server that hits a breakpoint, the container will wait until the server code returns (that is, until you finish debugging it). You can also trace into calls that go across process boundaries. For more information on tracing into these calls, see Debugging an OLE Application in Chapter 17 of the *Visual C++ User's Guide*.

For more detailed information on debugging containers and servers, and for information on the tools available in Visual C++, see the following articles:

Debugging OLE Applications: Containers

This article briefly discusses an issue unique to OLE container applications. Debugging a container application is very similar to debugging a standard, non-OLE MFC program, except when you attempt to debug an event that generates a callback (such as dragging data over the container application). In this case, you must set a breakpoint in the callback function.

Note The Visual C++ debugger supports stepping across and into OLE containers and servers. This includes the ability to step across OLE Remote Procedure Calls (LRPC). For more information, see Debugging an OLE Application in Chapter 17 of the *Visual C++ User's Guide*.

See Also Debugging OLE Applications: Servers

Debugging OLE Applications: Servers

Debugging OLE server applications poses a unique set of problems that are not always easy to solve. This article details debugging tasks that might not behave the way you would expect when debugging a server application. Topics include:

- Starting to debug the server
- Debugging containers and servers simultaneously
- Debugging an SDI server

Starting to Debug the Server

If you do not have debugging information for your container application, or do not need to see symbolic information for the container, starting to debug the server application is a three-step process:

1. Start debugging the server as a normal application.

2. Set breakpoints as desired.

3. Start the container application from Program Manager or File Manager.

For information on viewing symbolic information for both the container and the server, see Debugging Containers and Servers Simultaneously.

Debugging Containers and Servers Simultaneously

To debug both a container and a server at the same time, start a separate session of Visual C++ for each. That is, run multiple instances of Visual C++, one for the container and one for the server. See the Tip in the article Debugging OLE Applications.

Debugging an SDI Server

If you are debugging an SDI server application, you should set the Program Arguments line of the Debug Options dialog box to "/Embedding" or "/Automation" so the debugger can launch the server application as though it were launched from a container. Starting the container from Program Manager or File Manager will then cause the container to use the instance of the server started in the debugger.

See Also   Debugging OLE Applications: Tools

Debugging OLE Applications: Tools

Visual C++ supplies several tools that can help you find problems in your OLE applications. This article briefly summarizes the purpose of each tool. The tools include:

- Test applications
- Viewers and Spy programs
- Installing OLE development tools

Test Applications

Test applications allow you to test various types of OLE applications against existing OLE applications. Visual C++ and the OLE SDK provide a number of samples to use for testing. These include:

Container and Server   CL32TEST and SR32TEST are applications you can use to test your OLE applications. Both CL32TEST and SR32TEST are full-featured OLE applications and allow testing particular OLE API calls. This can be helpful in reproducing a series of events, one call at a time.

Outline Series   This series of applications shows how to convert a non-OLE application to an OLE server and container.

Microsoft Foundation Class Samples   The MFC OLE samples OCLIENT, SUPERPAD, and HIERSVR, as well as the MFC Tutorials CONTAINER and SCRIBBLE (Step 7), are also available to test your applications against. Full source code for these samples is included. CONTAINER and SCRIBBLE are fully explained in *Tutorials*.

The CL32TEST and SR32TEST tools are not installed on your hard disk. You can find them in the BIN directory on the Visual C++ CD-ROM.

Viewers and Spy Programs

Viewers and spy programs allow you to examine objects and events on your computer and in memory.

OLE2Viewer   OLE2VW32 displays the OLE objects installed on your computer and the interfaces they support. It also allows you to edit the registry and look at type libraries.

IDataObject Viewer   DOBJVIEW displays the list of data formats offered by OLE data objects created by the Clipboard or drag-and-drop operations.

Running Object Table Viewer   IROTVIEW displays information about OLE objects currently existing in memory.

Docfile Viewer   DFVIEW displays the contents of a small compound file. The executable for DFVIEW is not on the Visual C++ CD-ROM. However, the source files for the SDK OLE sample DFVIEW are on the Visual C++ CD-ROM. To use DFVIEW, you must get the source code for this sample and build it.

Installing OLE Development Tools

Unless you installed the OLE development tools during the initial setup, the tools such as OLE2VW32, DOBJVIEW, and IROTVIEW will not be available on your system. You can install them after the initial installation by running the Setup program again. Alternately, you can run them directly from the Visual C++ CD-ROM.

To install the OLE development tools on your system, use the Custom installation option and select Tools from the VC++ Setup Menu. Then, select OLE Development Tools from the Tools Menu. After the installation program runs, you can add the tool icons to your VC++ program group using the instructions in your system documentation.

Diagnostics

The Microsoft Foundation Class Library (MFC) contains many diagnostic features to help debug your program during development. These features, especially those that track memory allocations, will slow down your program. Others, such as assertion testing, will cause your program to halt when erroneous conditions are encountered.

In a retail product, slow performance and program interruption are clearly unacceptable. For this reason, MFC provides a method for turning the debugging and diagnostic features on or off. When you are developing your program, you typically build a Debug version of your program and link with the Debug version of MFC. Once the program is completed and debugged, you build a Release version and link with the Release version of MFC.

Note   Before you can use many of the MFC diagnostic features, you must enable diagnostic tracing by setting the **afxTraceEnabled** flag and customizing the **afxTraceFlags** to the level of detail you would like to see in trace messages. The easiest way to make these settings is with the TRACER.EXE utility.

Open the Microsoft Visual C++ program group and double-click the MFC Tracer icon. For more information, see Technical Note 7 under MFC Technical Notes in Books Online.

The following articles describe the debugging and diagnostic features of the class library:

- Diagnostics: Debugging Features
- Diagnostics: Detecting Memory Leaks
- Diagnostics: Dumping All Objects
- Diagnostics: Tracking Memory Allocations

Diagnostics: Debugging Features

The following features are included for all classes derived from **CObject** in the Debug version of the Microsoft Foundation Class Library (MFC):

- **Dump** member function to dump object contents to debugging output

  See the articles Diagnostics: Dumping Object Contents and Diagnostics: Dumping All Objects.

- Trace output to print or display debugging output to evaluate argument validity

  See the article Diagnostics: The TRACE Macro.

- Assertions and **AssertValid** member function

  See the article Diagnostics: Checking Object Validity.

- Memory diagnostics to detect memory leaks

  See the article Diagnostics: Detecting Memory Leaks.

- **DEBUG_NEW** macro to show where objects were allocated

  See the article Diagnostics: Tracking Memory Allocations.

▶ **To enable the debugging features**

1 Compile with the symbol **_DEBUG** defined. This is typically done by passing the **/D_DEBUG** flag on the compiler command line. To accomplish this in Visual C++, choose the Debug target in the Set Default Project Configuration box on the Project toolbar. When you define the **_DEBUG** symbol, sections of code delimited by **#ifdef _DEBUG** / **#endif** are compiled.

2 Link with the Debug versions of MFC. Setting the Debug option in Visual C++ ensures linking with the Debug libraries. The Debug versions of the library have a "D" at the end of the library name. The Debug version of MFC is named NAFXCWD.LIB, and the Release version (non-debug) is named NAFXCW.LIB.

Note Pragmas in the MFC header files will automatically link the correct version of MFC. You don't need to explicitly specify the MFC library in Visual C++. Thus this step 2 is informational only. For more information, see the article Library Versions.

Diagnostics: Dumping Object Contents

This article explains how to get a diagnostic dump of the contents of your objects.

When deriving a class from **CObject**, you have the option to override the Dump member function and write a textual representation of the object's member variables to a dump context which is similar to an I/O stream. Like an I/O stream, you can use the insertion (<<) operator to send data to a **CDumpContext**.

You do not have to override **Dump** when you derive a class from **CObject.** However, if you use other diagnostic features for debugging, providing the capability for dumping an object and viewing its contents is very helpful and highly recommended.

Note Before you can dump objects, you must enable diagnostic tracing so you can see the results of your dump in the debugger. See the Note in the article Diagnostics.

▶ **To override the Dump member function**

1 Call the base class version of **Dump** to dump the contents of a base class object.

2 Write a textual description and value for each member variable of your derived class.

The declaration of the Dump function in the class declaration looks like:

```
class CPerson : public CObject
{
public:
#ifdef _DEBUG
    virtual void Dump( CDumpContext& dc ) const;
#endif

    CString m_firstName;
    CString m_lastName;
    // etc. ...
};
```

Note Since object dumping only makes sense when you are debugging your program, the declaration of the Dump function is bracketed with an **#ifdef _DEBUG** / **#endif** block.

In the following example from an implementation file for the class CPerson, the Dump function's first statement calls the **Dump** member function for its base class. It then writes a short description of each member variable along with the member's value to the diagnostic stream.

```
#ifdef _DEBUG
void CPerson::Dump( CDumpContext& dc ) const
{
    // call base class function first
    CObject::Dump( dc );

    // now do the stuff for our specific class
    dc << "last name: " << m_lastName << "\n"
        << "first name: " << m_firstName << "\n";
}
#endif
```

Note Again, notice that the definition of the Dump function is bracketed by **#ifdef _DEBUG /
#endif** directives. If you refer to **afxDump** in a program linked with the nondebug libraries, you
will get unresolved externals errors at link time.

▶ **To send Dump output to afxDump**

• You must supply a **CDumpContext** argument to specify where the dump output
   will go when you call the Dump function for an object. MFC supplies a predefined
   CDumpContext object named **afxDump** that you will normally use for routine
   object dumping. The following example shows how to use **afxDump**:

```
CPerson pMyPerson = new CPerson;
// set some fields of the CPerson object...
//...
// now dump the contents
#ifdef _DEBUG
pMyPerson->Dump( afxDump );
#endif
```

In Windows NT, **afxDump** output is sent to the debugger, if present. Otherwise,
you will not get any **afxDump** output.

Note **afxDump** is defined only in the Debug version of MFC.

See Also Diagnostics: The TRACE Macro

Diagnostics: The TRACE Macro

This article explains how to use the **TRACE** macro during development to print or
display debugging messages from a program. **TRACE** prints a string argument to
your debugger.

Note With 32-bit MFC, the only way to get debug output is via the debugger.

The **TRACE** macro can handle a variable number of arguments, similar to the way
printf operates. Following are examples of different ways to use **TRACE** macros:

```
int x = 1;
int y = 16;
float z = 32.0;
TRACE( "This is a TRACE statement\n" );
```

```
TRACE( "The value of x is %d\n", x );

TRACE( "x = %d and y = %d\n", x, y );

TRACE( "x = %d and y = %x and z = %f\n", x, y, z );
```

The **TRACE** macro is active only in the Debug version of the class library. After a program has been debugged, you can build a Release version to deactivate all **TRACE** calls in the program.

Tip When debugging Unicode, the **TRACE0**, **TRACE1**, **TRACE2**, and **TRACE3** macros are easier to use because the **_T** macro is not needed.

For important information on the **TRACE** macro, see Macros and Globals in the *Class Library Reference* and Technical Note 7 under MFC Technical Notes in Books Online.

See Also Diagnostics: The ASSERT Macro

Diagnostics: The ASSERT Macro

This article explains how to check assumptions made by your functions, using the **ASSERT** macro.

Note As of MFC version 4.0, MFC uses the same assertion mechanisms as the C Run-time Library. This means that the message format has changed somewhat.

For more information on C run-time library macros, see Using Macros for Verification and Reporting, ASSERT, ASSERTE Macros, and _RPT, _RPTF Macros in Chapter 4, Debug Version of the C Run-Time Library, in the *Run-Time Library Reference*.

The most typical use of the **ASSERT** macro is to identify program errors during development. The argument given to **ASSERT** should be chosen so that it holds true only if the program is operating as intended. The macro evaluates the **ASSERT** argument and, if the argument expression is false (0), alerts the user and halts program execution. No action is taken if the argument is true (nonzero).

When an assertion fails, a message box appears with the following text:

```
assertion failed in file <name> in line <num>
Abort Retry Ignore
```

where <name> is the name of the source file and <num> is the line number of the assertion that failed.

If you choose Abort, program execution terminates. If you choose Ignore, program execution continues. It is possible to break into the debugger after an **ASSERT** by choosing the Retry button. Neither Abort nor Ignore will activate a debugger, so they provide no way to examine the call stack.

If you are running under the debugger and choose Retry, a call to **AfxDebugBreak** embedded in the code causes a break into the debugger. At this point, you can examine the call stack. In the Visual C++ debugger, you can do this by choosing the Call Stack command on the Debug menu. If you have enabled "Just-in-Time debugging" this will work even if the application is not being debugged. For more information about Just-in-Time debugging, see Chapter 17, Using the Debugger, in the *Visual C++ User's Guide*.

The following example shows how the **ASSERT** macro could be used to check the validity of a function's return value:

```
int x = SomeFunc(y);
ASSERT(x >= 0);   // Assertion fails if x is negative
```

ASSERT can also be used in combination with the **IsKindOf** function to provide extra checking for function arguments, such as in the following example. (For a discussion of the **IsKindOf** function, see the article CObject Class: Accessing Run-Time Class Information.)

```
ASSERT( pObject1->IsKindOf( RUNTIME_CLASS( CPerson ) ) );
```

The liberal use of assertions throughout your programs can catch errors during development. A good rule of thumb is that you should write assertions for any assumptions you make. For example, if you assume that an argument is not **NULL**, use an assertion statement to check for that condition.

The **ASSERT** macro will catch program errors only when you are using the Debug version of the Microsoft Foundation Class Library during development. It will be turned off (and produce no code) when you build your program with the Release version of the library.

Note The expression argument to **ASSERT** will not be evaluated in the Release version of your program. If you want the expression to be evaluated in both debug and release environments, use the **VERIFY** macro instead of **ASSERT**. In Debug versions, **VERIFY** is the same as **ASSERT**. In release environments, **VERIFY** evaluates the expression argument but does not check the result.

See Also Diagnostics: Checking Object Validity

Diagnostics: Checking Object Validity

This article explains how to check the internal consistency of the objects in your application. Topics include:

- Using the **ASSERT_VALID** macro
- Overriding the **AssertValid** function

Using the ASSERT_VALID Macro

Use the **ASSERT_VALID** macro to perform a run-time check of an object's internal consistency. The class of that object should override the **AssertValid** function of **CObject** as described in Overriding the AssertValid Function. The **ASSERT_VALID** macro is a more robust way of accomplishing:

```
pObject->AssertValid();
```

Like the **ASSERT** macro, **ASSERT_VALID** is turned on in the Debug version of your program, but turned off in the Release version.

Overriding the AssertValid Function

The **AssertValid** member function is provided in **CObject** to allow run-time checks of an object's internal state. **AssertValid** typically performs assertions on all the object's member variables to see if they contain valid values. For example, **AssertValid** can check that all pointer member variables are not **NULL**. If the object is invalid, **AssertValid** halts the program.

Although you are not required to override **AssertValid** when you derive your class from **CObject**, you can make your class safer and more reliable by doing so. The following example shows how to declare the **AssertValid** function in the class declaration:

```
class CPerson : public CObject
{
protected:
    CString m_strName;
    float   m_salary;
public:
#ifdef _DEBUG
    virtual void AssertValid() const;    // Override
#endif
    // ...
};
```

When you override AssertValid, first call **AssertValid** for the base class. Then use the **ASSERT** macro to check the validity of the members unique to your derived class, as shown by the following example:

```
#ifdef _DEBUG
void CPerson::AssertValid()
{
    // call inherited AssertValid first
    CObject::AssertValid();

    // check CPerson members...
    ASSERT( !m_strName.IsEmpty()); // Must have a name
    ASSERT( m_salary > 0 ); // Must have an income
}
#endif
```

If any of the member variables of your class store objects, you can use the
ASSERT_VALID macro to test their internal validity (if their classes override
AssertValid). The following example shows how this is done.

Consider a class CMyData, which stores a **CObList** in one of its member variables.
The **CObList** variable, m_DataList, stores a collection of CPerson objects. An
abbreviated declaration of CMyData looks like this:

```
class CMyData : public CObject
{
    // Constructor and other members ...
    protected:
        CObList* m_pDataList;
    // Other declarations ...
    public:
#ifdef _DEBUG
        virtual void AssertValid( ) const; // Override
#endif
    // Etc. ...
};
```

The **AssertValid** override in CMyData looks like this:

```
#ifdef _DEBUG
void CMyData::AssertValid( )
{
    // Call inherited AssertValid
    CObject::AssertValid( );
    // Check validity of CMyData members
    ASSERT_VALID( m_pDataList );
    // ...
}
#endif
```

CMyData uses the **AssertValid** mechanism to add validity tests for the objects stored
in its data member to the validity test of the CMyData object itself. The overriding
AssertValid of CMyData invokes the **ASSERT_VALID** macro for its own
m_pDataList member variable.

The chain of validity testing might stop at this level, but in this case class **CObList**
overrides **AssertValid** too, and the **ASSERT_VALID** macro causes it to be called.
This override performs additional validity testing on the internal state of the list. If an
assertion failure occurs, diagnostic messages are printed, and the program halts.

Thus a validity test on a CMyData object leads to additional validity tests for the
internal states of the stored **CObList** list object. With a little more work, the validity
tests could include the CPerson objects stored in the list as well. You could derive a
class CPersonList from **CObList** and override **AssertValid**. In the override, you
would call **CObject::AssertValid** and then iterate through the list, calling
AssertValid on each CPerson object stored in the list. The CPerson class shown at
the beginning of this section already overrides **AssertValid**.

This is a powerful mechanism when you build for debugging, and when you subsequently build for release, the mechanism is turned off automatically.

Users of an `AssertValid` function of a given class should be aware of the limitations of this function. A triggered assertion indicates that the object is definitely bad and execution will halt. However, a lack of assertion only indicates that no problem was found, but the object isn't guaranteed to be good.

Diagnostics: Detecting Memory Leaks

This article explains the facilities that MFC provides for detecting memory leaks. Topics include:

- Memory diagnostics
- Detecting a memory leak
- Dumping memory statistics

Note As of MFC version 4.0, MFC uses the same debug heap and memory allocator as the C Run-Time Library. For more information, see Chapter 4, Debug Version of the C Run-Time Library, in the Run-*Time Library Reference*.

A memory leak occurs when you allocate memory on the heap and never deallocate that memory to make it available for reuse, or if you mistakenly use memory that has already been allocated. This is a particular problem for programs that are intended to run for extended periods. In a long-lived program, even a small incremental memory leak can compound itself; eventually all available memory resources are exhausted and the program crashes. Traditionally, memory leaks have been very hard to detect.

The Microsoft Foundation Class Library (MFC) provides classes and functions you can use to detect memory leaks during development. Basically, these functions take a snapshot of all memory blocks before and after a particular set of operations. You can use these results to determine if all memory blocks allocated during the operation have been deallocated.

Note MFC automatically dumps all leaked objects when your program exits.

The size or length of the operation you choose to bracket with these diagnostic functions is arbitrary. It can be as small as a single program statement, or it can span the entry and exit from the entire program. Either way, these functions allow you to detect memory leaks and identify which memory blocks have not been deallocated properly.

Memory Diagnostics

Before you can use the memory diagnostics facilities, you must enable diagnostic tracing. See the Note at the end of the article Diagnostics as well as the rest of this discussion.

▶ **To enable or disable memory diagnostics**

- Call the global function **AfxEnableMemoryTracking** to enable or disable the diagnostic memory allocator. Since memory diagnostics are on by default in the Debug library, you will typically use this function to temporarily turn them off, which increases program execution speed and reduces diagnostic output.

▶ **To select specific memory diagnostic features with afxMemDF**

- If you want more precise control over the memory diagnostic features, you can selectively turn individual memory diagnostic features on and off by setting the value of the MFC global variable **afxMemDF**. This variable can have the following values as specified by the enumerated type **AfxMemDF**:

Value	Meaning
allocMemDF	Turn on diagnostic memory allocator (default).
delayFreeMemDF	Delay freeing memory when calling **delete** or **free** until program exits. This will cause your program to allocate the maximum possible amount of memory.
checkAlwaysMemDF	Call **AfxCheckMemory** every time memory is allocated or freed.

These values can be used in combination by performing a logical-OR operation, as shown here:

```
afxMemDF |= delayFreeMemDF | checkAlwaysMemDF;
```

Detecting a Memory Leak

The following instructions and example show you how to detect a memory leak.

▶ **To detect a memory leak**

1 Create a **CMemoryState** object and call the **Checkpoint** member function to get the initial snapshot of memory.

2 After you perform the memory allocation and deallocation operations, create another **CMemoryState** object and call **Checkpoint** for that object to get a current snapshot of memory usage.

3 Create a third **CMemoryState** object, call the **Difference** member function, and supply the previous two **CMemoryState** objects as arguments. The return value for the **Difference** function will be nonzero if there is any difference between the two specified memory states, indicating that some memory blocks have not been deallocated.

The following example shows how to check for memory leaks:

```
// Declare the variables needed
#ifdef _DEBUG
    CMemoryState oldMemState, newMemState, diffMemState;
    oldMemState.Checkpoint();
#endif
```

```
    // do your memory allocations and deallocations...
    CString s = "This is a frame variable";
    // the next object is a heap object
    CPerson* p = new CPerson( "Smith", "Alan", "581-0215" );

#ifdef _DEBUG
    newMemState.Checkpoint();
    if( diffMemState.Difference( oldMemState, newMemState ) )
    {
        TRACE( "Memory leaked!\n" );
    }
#endif
```

Notice that the memory-checking statements are bracketed by **#ifdef _DEBUG /
#endif** blocks so that they are only compiled in Debug versions of your program.

Dumping Memory Statistics

The **CMemoryState** member function **Difference** determines the difference between
two memory-state objects. It detects any objects that were not deallocated from the
heap between the beginning and end memory-state snapshots.

▶ **To dump memory statistics**

- The following example (continuing the example from the previous section) shows
  how to call **DumpStatistics** to get information about the objects that have not been
  deallocated:

```
if( diffMemState.Difference( oldMemState, newMemState ) )
{
    TRACE( "Memory leaked!\n" );
    diffMemState.DumpStatistics();
}
```

A sample dump from the example above is shown here:

```
0 bytes in 0 Free Blocks
22 bytes in 1 Object Blocks
45 bytes in 4 Non-Object Blocks
Largest number used: 67 bytes
Total allocations: 67 bytes
```

- The first line describes the number of blocks whose deallocation was delayed if
  afxMemDF was set to **delayFreeMemDF**. For a description of **afxMemDF**,
  see the procedure "To select specific memory diagnostic features with
  afxMemDF" presented under Memory Diagnostics.

- The second line describes how many objects remain allocated on the heap.

- The third line describes how many non-object blocks (arrays or structures
  allocated with **new**) were allocated on the heap and not deallocated.

- The fourth line gives the maximum memory used by your program at any one time.
- The last line lists the total amount of memory used by your program.

See Also   Diagnostics: Dumping All Objects, Diagnostics: Tracking Memory Allocations

In the *Class Library Reference*: **AfxEnableMemoryTracking, CMemoryState**

Diagnostics: Dumping All Objects

This article explains how to obtain a diagnostic dump of all objects in your program. Topics include:

- Performing an object dump
- Interpreting an object dump

For information on dumping C run-time objects, see Using the Debug Heap and **_CrtSetDbgFlag** in Chapter 4, Debug Version of the C Run-Time Library, in the *Run-Time Library Reference*.

DumpAllObjectsSince dumps out a description of all objects detected on the heap that have not been deallocated. As the name implies, **DumpAllObjectsSince** dumps all objects allocated since the last **Checkpoint**. However, if no **Checkpoint** has taken place, all objects and non-objects currently in memory are dumped.

Note   Before you can use MFC object dumping, you must enable diagnostic tracing. See the Note in the article Diagnostics.

Performing an Object Dump

▶ **To dump all objects**

- Expanding on the example shown in Detecting a Memory Leak in the article Diagnostics: Detecting Memory Leaks, the following code dumps all objects that have not been deallocated when a memory leak is detected:

```
if( diffMemState.Difference( oldMemState, newMemState ) )
{
    TRACE( "Memory leaked!\n" );
    diffMemState.DumpAllObjectsSince();
}
```

A sample dump from the preceding example is shown here:

```
Dumping objects ->

{5} strcore.cpp(80) : non-object block at $00A7521A, 9 bytes long
{4} strcore.cpp(80) : non-object block at $00A751F8, 5 bytes long
{3} strcore.cpp(80) : non-object block at $00A751D6, 6 bytes long
{2} a CPerson at $51A4
```

```
Last Name: Smith
First Name: Alan
Phone #: 581-0215

{1} strcore.cpp(80) : non-object block at $00A7516E, 25 bytes long
```

The numbers in braces at the beginning of most lines specify the order in which the objects were allocated. The most recently allocated object is displayed first. You can use these ordering numbers to help identify allocated objects.

To set a breakpoint when a particular allocation occurs, first start your application in the debugger. Set the global variable **_afxBreakAlloc** to the number in braces discussed earlier. This will set a conditional breakpoint in your application that will trigger when the allocation you specify is being made. Looking at the call stack at this point will tell you the path your program took to get to the specified allocation.

The C run-time library has a similar function, **_CrtSetBreakAlloc**, that you can use for C run-time allocations.

Interpreting an Object Dump

The preceding dump comes from the memory checkpoint example introduced in Detecting a Memory Leak in the article Diagnostics: Detecting Memory Leaks. Remember that there were only two explicit allocations in that program—one on the frame and one on the heap:

```
// do your memory allocations and deallocations ...
CString s = "This is a frame variable";
// the next object is a heap object
CPerson* p = new CPerson( "Smith", "Alan", "581-0215" );
```

Start with the CPerson object; its constructor takes three arguments that are pointers to **char**. The constructor uses these arguments to initialize **CString** member variables for the CPerson class. In the memory dump, you can see the CPerson object listed along with three non-object blocks (3, 4, and 5) that hold the characters for the **CString** member variables. These memory blocks will be deleted when the destructor for the CPerson object is invoked.

Block number 2 represents the CPerson object itself. After the CPerson address listing, the contents of the object are displayed. This is a result of **DumpAllObjectsSince** calling the Dump member function for the CPerson object.

You can guess that block number 1 is associated with the **CString** frame variable because of its sequence number and its size, which match the number of characters in the frame **CString** variable. The allocations associated with frame variables are automatically deallocated when the frame variable goes out of scope.

In general, you shouldn't worry about heap objects associated with frame variables because they are automatically deallocated when the frame variables go out of scope.

In fact, you should position your calls to **Checkpoint** so that they are outside the scope of frame variables to avoid clutter in your memory diagnostic dumps. For example, place scope brackets around the previous allocation code, as shown here:

```
oldMemState.Checkpoint();
{
    // do your memory allocations and deallocations ...
    CString s = "This is a frame variable";
    // the next object is a heap object
    CPerson* p = new CPerson( "Smith", "Alan", "581-0215" );
}
newMemState.Checkpoint();
```

With the scope brackets in place, the memory dump for this example is as follows:

```
Dumping objects ->

{5} strcore.cpp(80) : non-object block at $00A7521A, 9 bytes long
{4} strcore.cpp(80) : non-object block at $00A751F8, 5 bytes long
{3} strcore.cpp(80) : non-object block at $00A751D6, 6 bytes long
{2} a CPerson at $51A4

Last Name: Smith
First Name: Alan
Phone #: 581-0215
```

Notice that some allocations are objects (such as CPerson) and some are non-object allocations. "Non-object allocations" are allocations for objects not derived from **CObject** or allocations of primitive C types such as **char**, **int**, or **long**. If the **CObject-**derived class allocates additional space, such as for internal buffers, those objects will show both object and non-object allocations.

Notice that the memory block associated with the **CString** frame variable has been deallocated automatically and does not show up as a memory leak. The automatic deallocation associated with scoping rules takes care of most memory leaks associated with frame variables.

For objects allocated on the heap, however, you must explicitly delete the object to prevent a memory leak. To clean up the last memory leak in the previous example, you can delete the CPerson object allocated on the heap, as follows:

```
{
    // do your memory allocations and deallocations ...
    CString s = "This is a frame variable";
    // the next object is a heap object
    CPerson* p = new CPerson( "Smith", "Alan", "581-0215" );
    delete p;
}
```

See Also   Diagnostics: Detecting Memory Leaks

In the *Run-Time Library Reference*:   **_CrtMemDumpAllObjectsSince**

Diagnostics: Tracking Memory Allocations

The Microsoft Foundation Class Library (MFC) defines the macro **DEBUG_NEW** to assist you in locating memory leaks. You can use **DEBUG_NEW** everywhere in your program that you would ordinarily use the **new** operator.

Note As of MFC version 4.0, MFC uses the same debug heap and memory allocator as the C Run-Time Library. For more information, see Chapter 4, Debug Version of the C Run-Time Library, in the *Run-Time Library Reference*.

When you compile a Debug version of your program, **DEBUG_NEW** keeps track of the filename and line number for each object that it allocates. Then, when you call **DumpAllObjectsSince**, as described in the article Diagnostics: Dumping All Objects, each object allocated with **DEBUG_NEW** will be shown with the file and line number where it was allocated, thus allowing you to pinpoint the sources of memory leaks.

When you compile a Release version of your program, **DEBUG_NEW** resolves to a simple **new** operation without the filename and line number information. Thus, you pay no speed penalty in the Release version of your program.

▶ **To use DEBUG_NEW**

- Define a macro in your source files that replaces **new** with **DEBUG_NEW**, as shown here:

  ```
  #define new DEBUG_NEW
  ```

  Note While the framework uses **DEBUG_NEW** in debug builds, your code does not. You must enable this feature as shown in this procedure.

  You can then use **new** for all heap allocations. The preprocessor will substitute **DEBUG_NEW** when compiling your code. In the Debug version of the library, **DEBUG_NEW** will create debugging information for each heap block. In the Release version, **DEBUG_NEW** will resolve to a standard memory allocation without the extra debugging information.

Note You must place the **#define** statement after all statements that use the **IMPLEMENT_DYNCREATE** or **IMPLEMENT_SERIAL** macros in your source module, or you will get a compile-time error.

See Also Diagnostics: Detecting Memory Leaks

Dialog Boxes in OLE

While a user runs an OLE-enabled application, there are times when the application needs information from the user in order to carry out the operation. The MFC OLE classes provide a number of dialog boxes to gather the required information. This article lists the tasks handled by the OLE dialog boxes and the classes needed to display those dialog boxes. For full details on OLE dialog boxes and the structures used to customize their behavior, see the *Class Library Reference* and see the *User Interface Dialog Help* (OLE2UI.HLP) file included with the OLE SDK.

Insert Object This dialog box allows the user to insert newly created or existing objects into the compound document. It also allows the user to choose to display the item as an icon and enables the Change Icon command button. Display this dialog box when the user chooses Insert Object from the Edit menu. Use the **COleInsertDialog** class to display this dialog box.

Paste Special This dialog box allows the user to control the format used when pasting data into a compound document. The user can choose the format of the data, whether to embed or link the data, and whether to display it as an icon. Display this dialog box when the user chooses Paste Special from the Edit menu. Use the **COlePasteSpecialDialog** class to display this dialog box.

Change Icon This dialog box allows the user to select which icon is displayed to represent the linked or embedded item. Display this dialog box when the user chooses Change Icon from the Edit menu or chooses the Change Icon button in either the Paste Special or Convert dialog boxes. Also display it when the user opens the Insert Object dialog box and chooses Display as Icon. Use the **COleChangeIconDialog** class to display this dialog box.

Convert This dialog box allows the user to change the type of an embedded or linked item. For example, if you have embedded a metafile in a compound document and later want to use another application to modify the embedded metafile, you can use the Convert dialog box. This dialog box is usually displayed by choosing *item type* Object from the Edit menu and then, on the cascading menu, choosing Convert. Use the **COleConvertDialog** class to display this dialog box. For an example, run the MFC OLE sample OCLIENT.

Edit Links or Update Links The Edit Links dialog box allows the user to change information about the source of a linked object. The Update Links dialog box verifies the sources of all the linked items in the current dialog box and displays the Edit Links dialog box if necessary. Display the Edit Links dialog box when the user chooses Links from the Edit menu. The Update Links dialog box is usually displayed when a compound document is first opened. Use either the **COleLinksDialog** or the **COleUpdateDialog** class depending on which dialog box you want to display.

Server Busy or Server Not Responding The Server Busy dialog box is displayed when the user attempts to activate an item and the server is currently unable to handle the request, usually because the server is in use by another user or task. The Server Not Responding dialog box is displayed if the server does not respond to the activation request at all. These dialog boxes are displayed via **COleMessageFilter**, based on an implementation of the OLE interface **IMessageFilter**, and the user can decide whether to attempt the activation request again. Use the **COleBusyDialog** class to display this dialog box.

Document/View Architecture

For general information, see Chapter 1, Using the Classes to Write Applications for Windows, and Chapter 3, Working with Frame Windows, Documents, and Views.

See Also MFC: Using Database Classes with Documents and Views, MFC: Using Database Classes Without Documents and Views

Drag and Drop (OLE)

The drag-and-drop feature of OLE is primarily a shortcut for copying and pasting data. When you use the Clipboard to copy or paste data, a number of steps are required. You select the data, choose Cut or Copy from the Edit menu, move to the destination file, window or application, place the cursor in the desired location, and choose Paste from the Edit menu.

OLE drag and drop is different from File Manager's drag-and-drop mechanism, which can only handle filenames and is designed specifically to pass filenames to applications. OLE drag and drop is much more general. It allows you to drag and drop any data that could also be placed on the Clipboard.

When you use OLE drag and drop, you remove two steps from the process. You select the data from the source window (the "drop source"), drag it to the desired destination (the "drop target"), and drop it by releasing the mouse button. The operation eliminates the need for menus and is quicker than the copy/paste sequence. The only requirement is that both the drop source and drop target must be open and at least partially visible on the screen.

Using OLE drag and drop, data can be transferred from one location to another within a document, between different documents, or between applications. It can be implemented in either a container or a server application, and any application can be a drop source, a drop target, or both. If an application has both drop-source and drop-target support implemented, drag and drop is enabled between child windows, or within one window. This feature can make your application much easier to use.

If you only want to use the drag-and-drop capabilities of OLE, see the article Drag and Drop: Customizing. You can use the techniques explained in that article to make non-OLE applications drop sources. The article Drag and Drop: Implementing a Drop Target describes how to implement drop-target support for both OLE and non-OLE applications. It will also be helpful to to examine the MFC OLE samples OCLIENT and HIERSVR.

If you have not read the Data Objects and Data Sources (OLE) family of articles, you may want to do so now. These articles explain the fundamentals of data transfer, and how to implement it in your applications.

For more information about drag and drop, see the following articles:

- Drag and Drop: Implementing a Drop Source

- Drag and Drop: Implementing a Drop Target

- Drag and Drop: Customizing

See Also Data Objects and Data Sources (OLE)

Drag and Drop: Implementing a Drop Source

This article explains how to get your application to provide data to a drag-and-drop operation.

Basic implementation of a drop source is relatively simple. The first step is to determine what events begin a drag operation. Recommended user interface guidelines define the beginning of a drag operation as the selection of data and a **WM_LBUTTONDOWN** event occurring on a point inside the selected data. The MFC OLE samples OCLIENT and HIERSVR follow these guidelines.

If your application is a container and the selected data is a linked or an embedded object of type **COleClientItem**, call its **DoDragDrop** member function. Otherwise, construct a **COleDataSource** object, initialize it with the selection, and call the data source object's **DoDragDrop** member function. If your application is a server, use **COleServerItem::DoDragDrop**. For information about customizing standard drag-and-drop behavior, see the article Drag and Drop: Customizing.

If **DoDragDrop** returns **DROPEFFECT_MOVE**, you should delete the source data from the source document immediately. No other return value from **DoDragDrop** has any effect on a drop source.

See Also Drag and Drop: Implementing a Drop Target, Drag and Drop: Customizing, Data Objects and Data Sources: Creation and Destruction, Data Objects and Data Sources: Manipulation

In the *Class Library Reference*: **COleDataSource::DoDragDrop**, **COleClientItem::DoDragDrop**, **CView::OnDragLeave**

Drag and Drop: Implementing a Drop Target

This article outlines how to make your application a drop target. Implementing a drop target takes slightly more work than implementing a drop source, but it's still relatively simple. These techniques also apply to non-OLE applications.

▶ **To implement a drop target**

1 Add a member variable to each view in the application that you want to be a drop target. This member variable must be of type **COleDropTarget** or a class derived from it.

2 From your view class's function that handles the **WM_CREATE** message (typically **OnCreate**), call the new member variable's **Register** member function. **Revoke** will be called automatically for you when your view is destroyed.

3 Override the following functions. If you want the same behavior throughout your application, override these functions in your view class. If you want to modify behavior in isolated cases or want to enable dropping on non-**CView** windows, override these functions in your **COleDropTarget**-derived class.

Override	To allow
OnDragEnter	Drop operations to occur in the window. Called when the cursor first enters the window.
OnDragLeave	Special behavior when the drag operation leaves the specified window.
OnDragOver	Drop operations to occur in the window. Called when the cursor is being dragged across the window.

Override	To allow
OnDrop	Handling of data being dropped into the specified window.
OnScrollBy	Special behavior for when scrolling is necessary in the target window.

See the MAINVIEW.CPP file that is part of the MFC OLE sample OCLIENT for an example of how these functions work together.

See Also   Drag and Drop: Implementing a Drop Source, Data Objects and Data Sources: Creation and Destruction, Data Objects and Data Sources: Manipulation

In the *Class Library Reference*: **COleDropTarget**

Drag and Drop: Customizing

The default implementation of the drag-and-drop feature is sufficient for most applications. However, some applications may require that this standard behavior be changed. This article explains the steps necessary to change these defaults. In addition, you can use this technique to establish applications that do not support compound documents as drop sources.

If you are customizing standard OLE drag-and-drop behavior, or you have a non-OLE application, you must create a **COleDataSource** object to contain the data. When the user starts a drag-and-drop operation, your code should call the **DoDragDrop** function from this object instead of from other classes that support drag-and-drop operations.

Optionally, you can create a **COleDropSource** object to control the drop and override some of its functions depending on the type of behavior you want to change. This drop-source object is then passed to **COleDataSource::DoDragDrop** to change the default behavior of these functions. These different options allow a great deal of flexibility in how you support drag-and-drop operations in your application. For more information about data sources, see the article Data Objects and Data Sources (OLE).

You can override the following functions to customize drag-and-drop operations:

Override	To customize
OnBeginDrag	How dragging is initiated after you call **DoDragDrop**.
GiveFeedback	Visual feedback, such as cursor appearance, for different drop results.
QueryContinueDrag	The termination of a drag-and-drop operation. This function enables you to check modifier key states during the drag operation.

See Also Drag and Drop: Implementing a Drop Source

In the *Class Library Reference*: **COleDropSource**, **COleDataSource**

Driver Manager, ODBC

See the article ODBC.

Driver, ODBC

For information on drivers in general, see the article ODBC.

For a list of ODBC drivers included in this version of Visual C++ and for information about obtaining additional drivers, see the article ODBC Driver List.

Drop Source

See the article Drag and Drop: Implementing a Drop Source.

Drop Target

See the article Drag and Drop: Implementing a Drop Target.

Dynamic-Link Libraries (DLLs)

A "dynamic-link library" (DLL) is a binary file that acts as a shared library of functions that can be used simultaneously by multiple applications. DLLs are used for a variety of reasons, primarily for either:

- Sharing common code between different executable files.

    −or−

- Breaking an application into separate components, thus allowing easy upgrades.

The Microsoft Foundation Class Library (MFC) supports three different DLL development scenarios:

- Building a regular DLL that statically links MFC.
- Building a regular DLL that dynamically links MFC.
- Building an extension DDL. These always dynamically link MFC.

This article describes:

- Regular DLLs, Statically Linked
- Regular DLLs, Dynamically Linked
- Extension DLLs, Dynamically Linked
- Other DLL Topics

Note In Visual C++ version 4.0, the term "USRDLL" is obsolete. In earlier versions, USRDLL described DLLs that used MFC internally, but typically export functions using the standard "C" interface. USRDLLs could be used by either MFC or non-MFC applications. In version 4.0, such DLLs are called "Regular DLLs." Regular DLLs, Statically Linked to MFC have the same characteristics as the former USRDLL.

Regular DLLs, Statically Linked

Use AppWizard to create a starting point for a Regular DLL that statically links MFC. In MFC AppWizard (DLL) Step 1 of 1, select Regular DLL With MFC Statically Linked. For more information on this type of DLL, see the article DLLs: Building and Using the Static Link Version of the Regular DLL.

If your DLL is statically linked to MFC, functions in your DLL can be called by any Win32 application, as well as by programs that also use MFC. Before version 4.0 of MFC, USRDLLs provided this type of functionality. Special variants of the MFC static link libraries were used when building USRDLLs. These variants no longer exist. To create your statically linked Regular DLL, use the standard MFC static link libraries, which are named according to the convention described in the article DLLs: Naming Conventions.

In Visual C++ version 4.0, you can now dynamically link your Regular DLL to a shared MFC DLL. By dynamically linking to the MFC DLL, you can share the class library between multiple executable files to save disk and memory usage. For more information about this type of DLL, see the section Regular DLLs, Dynamically Linked, also, see the article DLLs: Building and Using the Shared Version of the Regular DLL.

Regular DLLs, Dynamically Linked

Use AppWizard to create a starting point for a Regular DLL that dynamically links MFC. In MFC AppWizard (DLL) Step 1 of 1, select Regular DLL Using Shared MFC DLL. For more information on this type of DLL, see the article DLLs: Building and Using the Shared Version of the Regular DLL.

If your Regular DLL is dynamically linked to the shared MFC DLL, functions in your DLL can be called by any Win32 application, as well as by programs that also use MFC.

The MFC libraries needed to build this type of DLL follow the naming convention described in the article DLLs: Naming Conventions.

If you are building a C++ extension to MFC and wish to put it in a DLL, you must create an Extension DLL. For more information about Extension DLLs, see the section Extension DLLs, Dynamically Linked and the article DLLs: Building and Using an Extension DLL.

Extension DLLs, Dynamically Linked

Use AppWizard to create a starting point for an Extension DLL. In MFC AppWizard (DLL) Step 1 of 1, select MFC Extension DLL (Using Shared MFC DLL). For more information on this type of DLL, see the article DLLs: Building and Using an Extension DLL.

Before version 4.0 of MFC, this type of DLL was called an AFXDLL. AFXDLL refers to the _**AFXDLL** preprocessor symbol that is defined when building the DLL.

By dynamically linking to the AFXDLL, your DLL can derive new custom classes from MFC in the shared DLL, and then offer this "extended" version of MFC to applications that call your DLL. A DLL built and used in this manner is called an "Extension DLL." Note that functions in an Extension DLL can only be called by MFC applications that also dynamically link to MFC. To create a DLL that dynamically links MFC and can be called by non-MFC applications, see the section Regular DLLs, Dynamically Linked, and the article DLLs: Building and Using the Shared Version of the Regular DLL.

The import libraries for the shared version of MFC are named according to the convention described in the article DLLs: Naming Conventions. Visual C++ supplies prebuilt versions of the MFC DLLs, plus a number of non-MFC DLLs that you can use and distribute with your applications. These are documented in REDISTRB.WRI, which is found in the REDIST directory on the Visual C++ CD-ROM.

Other DLL Topics

The remaining articles in this group explain how to build and use each version of the MFC DLLs and how to follow the library naming convention:

- DLLs: Using the Shared AFXDLL Version of MFC
- DLLs: Building and Using an Extension DLL
- DLLs: Building and Using the Static Link Version of the Regular DLL
- DLLs: Building and Using the Shared Version of the Regular DLL
- DLLs: Programming Tips
- DLLs: Naming Conventions
- DLLs: Redistribution

For more information, also see Creating DLLs for Win32 in Chapter 4 of *Programming Techniques*, and Dynamic-Link Libraries in the Win32 SDK.

DLLs: Using the Shared AFXDLL Version of MFC

This article describes the AFXDLL shared version of MFC, and when and how to use it in your applications. For additional information on using this shared DLL version of MFC with your DLL, see the articles DLLs: Building and Using the Shared Version of the Regular DLL and DLLs: Building and Using an Extension DLL.

The entire Microsoft Foundation Class Library (MFC) is provided in a set of redistributable DLLs. This enables applications to access MFC functionality by dynamically linking to these DLLs. This architecture is particularly useful in two situations: sharing the class library between multiple executable files to save disk space and memory usage and building MFC Extension DLLs.

If you are building an application that consists of multiple executable files, all of which are written using MFC, you can save a significant amount of disk and memory space by using this shared version of the class library. The only disadvantage is that you must distribute the shared DLL MFCx0.DLL (or another similar file) with your application. See the article DLLs: Naming Conventions for a complete list of MFC DLLs.

Note Applications created with AppWizard will use this shared DLL version of MFC by default.

If you are building an extension to MFC and wish to put it in a DLL, you must use the AFXDLL version of the class library. See the article DLLs: Building and Using an Extension DLL.

Using the Shared AFXDLL with Your Application

Any application that uses the shared AFXDLL version of MFC must be an MFC application—the application must have a **CWinApp**-derived object.

In addition, you must choose Use MFC In A Shared DLL. AppWizard sets this option for you if you choose Use MFC In A Shared DLL when creating an AppWizard executable. You can change this option on the General tab in the Project Settings dialog box.

Rebuilding the Shared AFXDLL

The AFXDLL version of MFC can be rebuilt. Normally this would be done only if you modify the MFC source code, or if you need to build MFC with special compiler options. For information on how to do this, see the README.TXT and MAKEFILE files in the MFC\SRC directory. If you modify and rebuild the AFXDLL version of MFC, you must rename the newly built DLL to something other than MFCx0.DLL to reflect that it has been modified. Otherwise, applications that depend on this DLL could stop functioning correctly.

For more information, also see Creating DLLs for Win32, in Chapter 4 of *Programming Techniques*, and Dynamic-Link Libraries in the Win32 SDK.

See Also   DLLs: Naming Conventions

DLLs: Building and Using an Extension DLL

An MFC Extension DLL is a DLL that typically implements reusable classes derived from the existing Microsoft Foundation Class Library classes. Extension DLLs can also be used for passing MFC-derived objects between the application and the DLL. This article describes how to build and use these DLLs. Topics include:

- Building an extension DLL
- Exporting classes without using decorated names
- Exporting symbols by ordinal
- Calling an extension DLL from your application

An MFC extension DLL uses a shared version of MFC in the same way an application uses the shared AFXDLL version of MFC, as described in the article DLLs: Using the Shared AFXDLL Version of MFC, with a few additional considerations:

- It does not have a **CWinApp**-derived object.

- It calls **AfxInitExtensionModule** in its **DllMain** function. The return value of this function should be checked. If a zero value is returned from **AfxInitExtensionModule**, return 0 from your **DllMain** function.

- It will create a **CDynLinkLibrary** object during initialization if the extension DLL wishes to export **CRuntimeClass** objects or resources to the application.

For an example of a DLL that fulfills the basic requirements of an extension DLL, see the MFC Advanced Concepts sample DLLHUSK. In particular, look at the TESTDLL1.CPP and TESTDLL2.CPP files.

Building an Extension DLL

To create an Extension DLL, do the following:

- When creating a new project, choose MFC AppWizard (DLL) as your target type.
- In AppWizard, select Extension DLL (Using Shared MFC DLL).

In response, AppWizard sets the option Use MFC In A Shared DLL. You can change this option on the General tab of the Project Settings dialog box.

When you create your extension DLL, you must also create a C++ header file (.H) and a definitions file (.DEF) for the DLL so applications can access its contents. There are two methods for creating these two files. The first method exports entire classes without requiring decorated names for that class in the .DEF file. The second method requires putting decorated names in a .DEF file. This latter method is more efficient as you can export the symbols by ordinal. MFC uses this method.

Exporting Classes Without Using Decorated Names

In the header file for your DLL, add the **AFX_EXT_CLASS** keyword to the declaration of your class as follows:

```
class AFX_EXT_CLASS CMyClass : public CDocument
{
// <body of class>
};
```

This allows you to export entire classes without placing the decorated names for all that class's symbols in the .DEF file. This method is used by the MFC Advanced Concepts sample DLLHUSK.

Exporting Symbols by Ordinal

This method requires that you place the decorated names for all external symbols in your .DEF file. This is more efficient, but is useful if you want to export only a small percentage of the symbols in the DLL.

To use this method, place the following code at the beginning and end of your header file:

```
#undef AFX_DATA
#define AFX_DATA AFX_EXT_DATA
// <body of your header file>
#undef AFX_DATA
#define AFX_DATA
```

These four lines ensure that your code will be compiled correctly for an extension DLL. Leaving out these four lines may cause your DLL to either compile or link incorrectly.

For information on how to export symbols from your extension DLL, see Creating DLLs for Win32, in Chapter 4 of *Programming Techniques*.

Calling an Extension DLL from Your Application

Applications that use MFC Extension DLLs have the same restrictions as applications that use the AFXDLL version of MFC: they must be an MFC application containing a **CWinApp**-derived object.

To build an application that uses an MFC Extension DLL, you must choose Use MFC In A Shared DLL. AppWizard sets this option for you if you choose Use MFC In A Shared DLL when creating an AppWizard executable. You can change this option on the General tab in the Project Settings dialog box.

After you have either run AppWizard or made the necessary change to your project, add the import library for the Extension DLL to your list of libraries to link with in the Object/Library Modules edit box on the Linker tab in the Project Settings dialog box. Make sure you put the debug version of the import library in the debug settings and the release version in the release settings.

The only other change you must make is to add the include file for the DLL to any source files that use the DLL.

For more information, also see Dynamic-Link Libraries in the Win32 SDK.

See Also   DLLs: Naming Conventions

DLLs: Building and Using the Static Link Version of the Regular DLL

Note   In Visual C++ version 4.0, the term "USRDLL" is obsolete. In earlier versions, USRDLL described DLLs that used MFC internally, but typically exported functions using the standard "C" interface. USRDLLs could be used by either MFC or non-MFC applications. In version 4.0, such DLLs are called "Regular DLLs." Regular DLLs, statically linked to MFC have the same characteristics as the former USRDLL.

This article explains how to build a DLL that statically links MFC and how to use it from your application.

A Regular DLL can be called by any Win32 application. Symbols are usually exported from a Regular DLL using the standard "C" interface. The declaration of a function exported from a static link Regular DLL would look something like this:

```
extern "C" EXPORT YourExportedFunction( );
```

Building a DLL Using the Static Link Regular DLL Version of MFC

To create a DLL that statically links to MFC, do the following:

- When creating a new project, choose MFC AppWizard (DLL) as your target type.

- In AppWizard, select Regular DLL With MFC Statically Linked.

In response, AppWizard sets the option Use MFC In A Static Library. You can change this option on the General tab of the Project Settings dialog box.

A DLL that is statically linked to MFC cannot also dynamically link to the shared MFC DLLs.

For more information about dynamically linking a DLL to the MFC, see the articles DLLs: Building and Using the Shared Version of the Regular DLL and Extension DLLs, Dynamically Linked.

Calling a DLL that is Statically Linked to the Static Link Version of MFC

A DLL that is statically linked to MFC is dynamically bound to an application just like any other DLL. You must add the import library of the DLL to the list of libraries you link with the application. Or, you can dynamically link to the DLL by calling **LoadLibrary** (see the Win32 SDK) from your application.

When you build your DLL, Visual C++ also builds an import library for you. This library has the same base name as your DLL, but has the extension .LIB. When you wish to implicitly link with your DLL, add the import library to the Object/Library Modules edit box on the Linker tab in the Project Settings dialog box.

For more information, also see Creating DLLs for Win32, in Chapter 4 of *Programming Techniques*, and Dynamic-Link Libraries in the Win32 SDK.

See Also   DLLs: Naming Conventions

DLLs: Building and Using the Shared Version of the Regular DLL

In Visual C++ version 4.0, you can now dynamically link your Regular DLL to a shared version of MFC. In earlier versions of MFC, a DLL that dynamically linked MFC had to be an Extension DLL and, therefore, could only be called by MFC applications. This article explains how to build a Regular DLL that dynamically links to the shared MFC DLLs and how to use it from your application.

The entire Microsoft Foundation Class Library (MFC) is provided in a set of redistributable DLLs. This enables applications to access MFC functionality by dynamically linking to these DLLs. This architecture is particularly useful for sharing the class library between multiple executable files to save disk space and minimize memory usage.

If you are building an application that consists of multiple executable files, either written using MFC or Win32, you can save a significant amount of disk and memory space by using this shared version of the class library. The only disadvantage is that you must distribute the shared DLLs MFCx0.DLL and MSVCRTx0.DLL (or similar files) with your application. See the article DLLs: Naming Conventions for a complete list of MFC DLL libraries.

If you intend to create extensions to MFC and offer them in your DLL, you must create an Extension DLL. For more information about Extension DLLs, see DLLs: Building and Using an Extension DLL.

Note The only difference between a DLL that statically links to MFC and one that dynamically links to MFC in this fashion is that they use different versions of the MFC implementation. They both still expose a "C" interface and can be called from any application, that is, either MFC or non-MFC applications.

Building a DLL Using the Shared Regular DLL Version of MFC

To create a Regular DLL that dynamically links to MFC, do the following:

- When creating a new project, choose MFC AppWizard (DLL) as your target type.
- In AppWizard, select Regular DLL Using MFC DLL.

In response, AppWizard sets the option Use MFC In A Shared DLL. You can change this option on the General tab of the Project Settings dialog box.

Calling a DLL that is Dynamically Linked to the Shared Regular DLL Version of MFC

After you have either run AppWizard or made the necessary change to your project, add the import library for the DLL to your list of libraries to link with in the Object/Library Modules edit box on the Linker tab in the Project Settings dialog box. Make sure you put the debug version of the import library in the debug settings and the release version in the release settings. The only other change you must make is to add the include file for the DLL to any source files that use the DLL.

For more information, also see Creating DLLs for Win32, in Chapter 4 of *Programming Techniques*, and Dynamic-Link Libraries in the Win32 SDK.

See Also DLLs: Naming Conventions, DLLs: Using the Shared AFXDLL Version of
MFC, DLLs: Building and Using an Extension DLL.

DLLs: Programming Tips

This article covers topics specific to writing and using DLLs with MFC. You should
read Chapter 4, Creating DLLs for Win32, in *Programming Techniques* before
reading this article. The topics in this article build on information in that chapter.
Topics include:

- Initialization and termination

- OLE and DLLs

- OLE automation in a DLL

- Multithreading and DLLs

- Passing object pointers between applications and extension DLLs

- DLL sample programs

Initialization and Termination

The only special initialization case that you should be aware of is that MFC
Extension DLLs need to do two things in their **DllMain** function:

- Call **AfxInitExtensionModule** and check the return value.

- Create a **CDynLinkLibrary** object if the DLL will be exporting **CRuntimeClass**
  objects or has its own custom resources.

Note In Visual C++ version 4.0, the terminology "USRDLL" is obsolete. In version 4.0, create
a Regular DLL that statically links MFC to obtain the same functionality.

DLLs statically linked to MFC should perform their initialization and termination
tasks in the same location as an MFC application: in **InitInstance** and **ExitInstance**.

OLE and DLLs

OLE allows object servers to be completely implemented inside a DLL. This type of
server is called an "in-proc server." MFC does not completely support in-proc servers
for all the features of visual editing, mainly because OLE does not provide a way for a
server to hook into the container's main message loop. MFC requires access to the
container application's message loop to handle accelerator keys and idle-time
processing.

If you are writing an OLE Automation server and your server has no user interface,
you can make your server an in-proc server and put it completely into a DLL.

For more information, see the article Automation Servers.

OLE Automation in a DLL

When you choose the OLE Automation option in AppWizard, the wizard provides you with the following:

- A starter object description language (.ODL) file

- An include directive in the STDAFX.H file for AFXOLE.H

- An implementation of the **DllGetClassObject** function, which calls the **AfxDllGetClassObject** function

- An implementation of the **DllCanUnloadNow** function, which calls the **AfxDllCanUnloadNow** function

- An implementation of the **DllRegisterServer** function, which calls the **COleObjectFactory::UpdateRegistryAll** function

Multithreading and DLLs

Note In Visual C++ version 4.0, the terminology "USRDLL" is obsolete. In version 4.0, create a Regular DLL that statically links MFC to obtain the same functionality.

A Regular DLL should keep track of multiple threads by calling **TlsAlloc** and **TlsGetValue** (see the Win32 SDK) in its **InitInstance** function. This method allows the DLL to keep track of thread-specific data without worrying about what code was executed before the DLL was loaded. For more information on thread local storage (TLS) see Chapter 43, Processes and Threads, in the Win32 SDK.

Extension DLLs have another method available to handle multithreading in addition to the Regular DLL method. The DLL can handle the **DLL_THREAD_ATTACH** and **DLL_THREAD_DETACH** cases in its **DllMain** function. These cases are passed to **DllMain** when threads attach and detach from the DLL. Calling **::TlsAlloc** when a DLL is attaching allows the DLL to maintain TLS indices for every thread attached to the DLL.

A sample initialization function that handles these cases is included in Section 50.2.5, Using Thread Local Storage in a Dynamic-Link Library, in the Win32 SDK. (The sample actually names the function **LibMain**, but MFC requires that this function be named **DllMain**.)

Passing Object Pointers Between Applications and Extension DLLs

If you need to pass an MFC or MFC-derived object pointer to or from an MFC DLL, the DLL should be an Extension DLL. The member functions associated with the passed object exist in the module where the object was created. Since these functions are properly exported when using the shared DLL version of MFC, you can freely pass MFC or MFC-derived object pointers between an application and the Extension DLLs it loads.

DLL Sample Programs

Two MFC Advanced Concepts samples dealing with DLLs are included with Visual C++:

DLLHUSK   Demonstrates how to write, build, and use Extension DLLs.

DLLTRACE   Demonstrates how to write, build, and use Regular DLLs.

Examining the source code and makefiles for these samples can give you pointers for building your DLLs.

For more information, also see Creating DLLs for Win32, in Chapter 4 of *Programming Techniques*, and Dynamic-Link Libraries in the Win32 SDK.

See Also   Multithreading, OLE Overview, Dynamic-Link Libraries (DLLs).

DLLs: Naming Conventions

The DLLs and libraries included in MFC version 4.0 follow a structured naming convention. This makes it easier to know which DLL or library you should be using for which purpose. The naming convention for libraries is fully described in the article Library Versions. This article describes the naming conventions for files required to build and use DLLs with MFC version 4.0.

The AFXDLL version of MFC comes in a number of different forms. These forms are named according to the convention MFC[O|D|N]x0[U][D].DLL (where x is the MFC version number) as detailed in Table 1. The import libraries needed to build applications or extension DLLs that use these DLLs have the same base name as the DLL but have a .LIB extension.

Table 1   AFXDLL Naming Convention

DLL	Description
MFCx0.DLL	MFC DLL, ANSI Release version
MFCx0U.DLL	MFC DLL, Unicode Release version
MFCx0D.DLL	MFC DLL, ANSI Debug version
MFCx0UD.DLL	MFC DLL, Unicode Debug version
MFCOx0D.DLL	MFC DLL for OLE, ANSI Debug version
MFCOx0UD.DLL	MFC DLL for OLE, Unicode Debug version
MFCDx0D.DLL	MFC DLL for database, ANSI Debug version
MFCDx0UD.DLL	MFC DLL for database, Unicode Debug version
MFCNx0D.DLL	MFC DLL for network, ANSI Debug version
MFCNx0UD.DLL	MFC DLL for network, Unicode Debug version
MFCSx0.LIB	MFC DLL, statically linked code, Release version
MFCSx0D.LIB	MFC DLL, statically linked code, Debug version

Note The OLE control DLLs OC[D]x0[U][D].DLL are gone. OLE control support is now included in the MFC DLL listed in the table above.

Note The MFCSx0[D].LIB libraries are used in conjunction with the DLL versions of MFC. These library files contain code that must be statically linked in the application or DLL.

If you are dynamically linking to the AFXDLL version of MFC, whether it is from an application or from an extension DLL, you must include MFC40.DLL with your product. If you require Unicode support in your application, include MFC40U.DLL instead.

Note The MFC40.DLL and MFC40U.DLL Retail version of the DLLs contain OLE, database, and network support in a single DLL. The Debug version maintains separate DLLs for these functional areas.

Note In Visual C++ version 4.0, the terminology "USRDLL" is obsolete. In version 4.0, create a Regular DLL that statically links MFC to obtain the same functionality.

If you are statically linking your DLL to MFC, you must link it with one of the static MFC libraries. These versions are named according to the convention [N|U]AFXCW[D].LIB as listed in Table 2.

Table 2   Static Link Regular DLL Naming Conventions

DLL	Description
NAFXCW.LIB	MFC Static Link Library, Release version
NAFXCWD.LIB	MFC Static Link Library, Debug version
UAFXCW.LIB	MFC Static Link Library with Unicode support, Release version
UAFXCWD.LIB	MFC Static Link Library with Unicode support, Debug version

Note In earlier version of MFC (before version 4.0), there were special DLL variants of the libraries with names in the form [N|U]AFXDW[D].LIB. These variants no longer exist. Use the versions listed in the table above.

For a list of DLLs included with Visual C++ version 4.0 that can be distributed with your applications, see the file REDISTRB.WRI in the REDIST directory on the Visual C++ CD.

See Also   Library Versions

DLLs: Redistribution

Applications built with Microsoft Visual C++ may require a number of supporting dynamic-link libraries (DLLs), depending on the way the application was built. The conditions under which you may or may not redistribute these files are described in the separate License Agreement included in the Visual C++ product. This article details the DLLs that must be redistributed with different types of applications. The article covers:

- Categories of redistributable files
- Version checking of redistributable files
- MFC/other DLL files
- ODBC files

All Visual C++ redistributable files are located in REDIST on the Visual C++ version 4.0 CD. These files are not installed by Visual C++ Setup in a separate directory on your hard disk. However, depending on the setup options you choose, Visual C++ Setup may install some of these files in your Windows System directory. When you redistribute any of these files, you should copy them from the CD to your own distribution disk image, rather than from your hard disk, to make sure you are redistributing the correct version of the files.

Categories of Redistributable Files

Redistributable files may be categorized as follows:

- MFC/Other DLL files
- ODBC Files

Tables 1 and 2 list the files and gives a brief description of each.

Table 1   MFC/Other Files

File	Description
\ANSI\CTL3D32.DLL	3D controls support DLL for ANSI (use with Win32s)
CTL3D32.DLL	3D controls support DLL
MFCx0.DLL	MFC core code (MBCS-enabled)
MFCx0U.DLL	MFC core code (Unicode-enabled)
MSVCRTx0.DLL	Shared DLL version of C-runtime

Table 2   32-bit ODBC Files

File	Description
_BOOTSTP.EXE	Used by ODBC setup
MSSETUP.EX	Used by ODBC setup
_MSSETUP.EXE	ODBC setup (same as SETUP.EXE)
CTL3D32.DLL	3D controls support (required by ODBC)
DS16GT.DLL	ODBC driver setup 16-bit generic thunk DLL
DS32GT.DLL	ODBC driver setup 32-bit generic thunk DLL
INSTCAT.SQL	SQL server stored procedures
MSVCRT40.DLL	See Caution below
MSVCRT10.DLL	Used by ODBC setup
ODBC.INF	File list for the ODBC installer

Table 2   32-bit ODBC Files *(cont.)*

File	Description
ODBC16GT.DLL	ODBC 16-bit generic thunk DLL 16-bit
ODBC32GT.DLL	ODBC 32-bit generic thunk DLL 32-bit
ODBC32.DLL	32-bit ODBC driver manager
ODBCCP32.CPL	32-bit ODBC control panel component
ODBCCP32.DLL	32-bit ODBC installer/administrator
ODBCCR32.DLL	32-bit ODBC cursor library
ODBCINST.HLP	ODBC 2.0 help file
ODBCINT.DLL	ODBC error messages and dialog boxes
SETUP.EXE	ODBC setup (run after MSVC 4.0 setup)
SETUP.LST	ODBC setup (same as SETUP.EXE)

Caution   MSVCRTx0.DLL has the same name in Win32s and Visual C++ 4.0 They are different files and you must redistribute the proper matching file for the intended target (Win32 or Win32s).

In addition, you must also redistribute DLLs to support specific OBDC drivers. The SQL Server drivers are listed in Table 3. See ODBCJET.HLP in the REDIST directory for the supporting files for other ODBC data sources, such as .MDB and .DBF files.

Table 3   SQL Server ODBC Files

File	Description
CTL3D32.DLL	3D controls support (required by ODBC)
DBNMPNTW.DLL	32-bit SQL Server named-pipes network library
DRVSSRVR.HLP	32-bit SQL Server driver help file
SQLSRV32.DLL	32-bit SQL Server ODBC driver file

Note   There are separate components needed for Win32s. These are found in the \WIN32S\ODBC and \WIN32S\REDIST directories.

Version Checking of Redistributable Files

Because other applications may redistribute earlier or later versions of the same files as redistributed with your application, it is important that you install newer versions of the files over older versions on your user's system, but not older versions over newer versions. Typically, version checking is the responsibility of your setup program. If you do not have a setup program for your main application, then your application must manually check the version when installing the redistributable files on your user's system.

The programmatic technique for version checking varies, depending on which category of file you are redistributing. Briefly, the version checking techniques are as follows:

- For the MFC DLLs, use the version checking APIs available as a standard part of the Win32 API. For more information, see Chapter 80, File Installation Library, in the Win32 SDK documentation.

- For the ODBC files, see Chapter 19, Installing ODBC Software, and Chapter 20, Configuring Data Sources, in the *ODBC Programmer's Reference*.

MFC/Other DLL Files

You can link your application with the MFC library either statically or dynamically. For information on dynamically linking your application to the MFC library, see the article Dynamic-Link Libraries (DLLs).

If you dynamically link your application to the MFC library, you will, at a minimum, need to redistribute MFCx0[U].DLL and MSVCRTx0.DLL, where *x* is the version number. MFCx0[U].DLL includes all of the basic framework classes. All MFC DLLs use the shared version of the C run-time library; thus MSVCRTx0.DLL is required. If your application uses the MFC database classes, such as **CRecordset** and **CRecordView**, you will need to redistribute ODBC and any ODBC drivers that your application uses.

If you redistribute any of these MFC DLLs, be sure you distribute the retail version rather than the debug version. Debug versions of the DLLs may <u>not</u> be redistributed. (Debug versions of the MFC DLLs have a trailing "D" in their file names, such as in MFCx0D.DLL).

If you modify MFC in any way, you must rename the modified MFC DLL so that it will not conflict with the MFC DLL that might be installed by other MFC applications on your user's system. *This is not a recommended procedure*. For more information, see Technical Note 33 under MFC in Books Online.

ODBC Files

Use the ODBC Installer DLL to install the ODBC files on your user's system from your application's setup program. The redistributable files include the ODBC Driver Manager and the various ODBC drivers included in REDIST.

For information on using the ODBC Installer DLL, and other important information about installing ODBC files, see Chapter 19, Installing ODBC Software, and Chapter 20, Configuring Data Sources, in the *ODBC Programmer's Reference*.

See Also   Dynamic-Link Libraries (DLLs)

Dynaset

This article describes dynasets and discusses their availability.

Note This article applies to the MFC ODBC classes, including **CRecordset**. For information about dynasets in the DAO classes, see class **CDaoRecordset**. With DAO, you can open dynaset-type recordsets.

A "dynaset" is a recordset with dynamic properties. During its lifetime, a recordset object in dynaset mode (usually called simply a "dynaset") stays synchronized with the data source in the following way. In a multiuser environment, other users may edit or delete records that are in your dynaset or add records to the table your dynaset represents. Records your application adds to or deletes from the recordset are reflected in your dynaset. Records that other users add to the table will not be reflected in your dynaset until you rebuild the dynaset by calling its **Requery** member function. When other users delete records, MFC code skips over the deletions in your recordset. Other users' editing changes to existing records are reflected in your dynaset as soon as you scroll to the affected record.

Similarly, edits you make to records in a dynaset are reflected in dynasets in use by other users. Records you add are not reflected in other users' dynasets until they requery their dynasets. Records you delete are marked as "deleted" in other users' recordsets. If you have multiple connections to the same database (multiple **CDatabase** objects), recordsets associated with those connections have the same status as the recordsets of other users.

Dynasets are most valuable when data must be dynamic, as, for example, in an airline reservation system.

Important To use dynasets, you must have an ODBC driver for your data source that supports dynasets, and the ODBC cursor library must not be loaded. See Availability of Dynasets.

To specify that a recordset is a dynaset, pass **CRecordset::dynaset** as the first parameter to the **Open** member function of your recordset object.

Note For updatable dynasets, your ODBC driver must support either positioned update statements or the **::SQLSetPos** ODBC API function. If both are supported, MFC uses **::SQLSetPos** for efficiency.

Availability of Dynasets

The MFC database classes support dynasets if the following requirements are met:

- The ODBC cursor library DLL must not be in use for this data source.

  If the cursor library is used, it masks some functionality of the underlying ODBC driver that is necessary for dynaset support. If you want to use dynasets (and your ODBC driver has the functionality required for dynasets, as described in the rest of this section), you can cause MFC not to load the cursor library when you create a **CDatabase** object. For more information, see the article ODBC and the **Open** member function of class **CDatabase**.

In ODBC terminology, dynasets and snapshots are referred to as "cursors." A cursor is a mechanism used for keeping track of its position in a recordset. For more information about cursors, see the ODBC SDK *Programmer's Reference*.

- The ODBC driver for your data source must support keyset-driven cursors.

  Keyset-driven cursors manage data from a table by getting and storing a set of keys. The keys are used to obtain current data from the table when the user scrolls onto a particular record. To determine whether your driver provides this support, call the **::SQLGetInfo** ODBC API function with the **SQL_SCROLL_OPTIONS** parameter.

  If you try to open a dynaset without keyset support, you get a **CDBException** with the return code value **AFX_SQL_ERROR_DYNASET_NOT_SUPPORTED**.

- The ODBC driver for your data source must support extended fetching.

  "Extended fetching" is the ability to scroll backward as well as forward over the resulting records of your SQL query. To determine whether your driver supports this ability, call the **::SQLGetFunctions** ODBC API function with the **SQL_API_SQLEXTENDEDFETCH** parameter.

If you want updatable dynasets (or snapshots, for that matter), your ODBC driver must also support either:

- The **::SQLSetPos** ODBC API function.

  –or–

- Positioned updates.

The **::SQLSetPos** function allows MFC to update the data source without sending SQL statements. If this support is available, MFC uses it in preference to making updates via SQL. To determine whether your driver supports **::SQLSetPos**, call **::SQLGetInfo** with the **SQL_POS_OPERATIONS** parameter.

Positioned updates use SQL syntax (of the form **WHERE CURRENT OF** <cursorname>) to identify a particular row in the table on the data source. To determine whether your driver supports positioned updates, call **::SQLGetInfo** with the **SQL_POSITIONED_STATEMENTS** parameter.

Generally, MFC dynasets (but not forward-only recordsets) require an ODBC driver with level 2 API conformance. If the driver for your data source conforms to the level 1 API set, you can still use both updatable and read-only snapshots and forward-only recordsets, but not dynasets. However, a level 1 driver can support dynasets if it supports extended fetching and keyset-driven cursors. For more information about ODBC conformance levels, see the article ODBC.

Note If you want to use both snapshots and dynasets, you must base them on two different **CDatabase** objects (two different connections).

Unlike snapshots, which use intermediate storage maintained by the ODBC cursor library, dynasets fetch a record directly from the data source as soon as you scroll to it. This keeps the records originally selected by the dynaset synchronized with the data source.

See the article ODBC Driver List for a list of ODBC drivers included in this version of Visual C++ and for information about obtaining additional drivers.

Embedded OLE Item

See the article Activation.

Events

OLE controls use events to notify a container that something has happened to the control. Common examples of events include clicks on the control, data entered using the keyboard, and changes in the control's state. When these actions occur, the control fires an event, to alert the container.

MFC supports two kinds of events: stock and custom. Stock events are those events that class **COleControl** handles automatically. For a complete list of stock events, see the article Events: Adding Stock Events to an OLE Control. Custom events allow a control the ability to notify the container when an action specific to that control occurs. Some examples would be a change in the internal state of a control or receipt of a certain window message.

For your control to properly fire events, your control class must map each event of the control to a member function that should be called when the related event occurs. This mapping mechanism (called an "event map") centralizes information about the event and allows ClassWizard to easily access and manipulate the control's events. This event map is declared by the following macro, located in the header (.H) file of the control class declaration:

```
DECLARE_EVENT_MAP()
```

Figure 1 shows the OLE Events tab in ClassWizard. You use this tab to add custom and stock events.

Figure 1   The OLE Events Tab

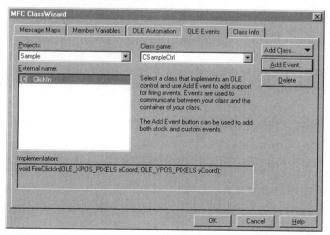

Once the event map has been declared, it must be defined in your control's implementation (.CPP) file. The following lines of code define the event map, allowing your control to fire specific events:

```
BEGIN_EVENT_MAP(CSampleCtrl, COleControl)
//{{AFX_EVENT_MAP(CSampleCtrl)
...
//}}AFX_EVENT_MAP
END_EVENT_MAP()
```

If you use ControlWizard to create the project, it automatically adds these lines. If you do not use ControlWizard, you must add these lines manually.

With ClassWizard, you can add stock events supported by class **COleControl** or custom events that you define. For each new event, ClassWizard automatically adds the proper entry to the control's event map and the control's .ODL file.

Note When an event is fired, a limit of 15 parameters can be passed to the recipient. This limitation is due to the MFC implementation of the **IDispatch** interface.

Two other articles discuss events in detail:

- Events: Adding Stock Events to an OLE Control
- Events: Adding Custom Events to an OLE Control

See Also OLE Controls, Methods

In the *Class Library Reference*: **COleControl**

Events: Adding Stock Events to an OLE Control

Stock events differ from custom events in that they are automatically fired by class **COleControl**. **COleControl** contains predefined member functions that fire events resulting from common actions. Some common actions implemented by **COleControl** include single- and double-clicks on the control, keyboard events, and changes in the state of the mouse buttons. Event map entries for stock events are always preceded by the **EVENT_STOCK** prefix.

Stock Events Supported by ClassWizard

The **COleControl** class provides nine stock events, listed in Table 1. You can specify the events you want in your control in the OLE Events tab in ClassWizard.

Table 1 Stock Events

Event	Firing function	Comments
Click	**void FireClick( )**	Fired when the control captures the mouse, any **BUTTONUP** (left, middle, or right) message is received, and the button is released over the control. The stock MouseDown and MouseUp events occur before this event.
		Event map entry: **EVENT_STOCK_CLICK( )**
DblClick	**void FireDblClick( )**	Similar to Click but fired when a **BUTTONDBLCLK** message is received.
		Event map entry: **EVENT_STOCK_DBLCLICK( )**
Error	**void FireError(SCODE** *scode*, **LPCSTR** *lpszDescription*, **UINT** *nHelpID* = **0**)	Fired when an error occurs within your OLE control outside of the scope of a method call or property access.
		Event map entry: **EVENT_STOCK_ERROR( )**
KeyDown	**void FireKeyDown(short** *nChar*, **short** *nShiftState*)	Fired when a **WM_SYSKEYDOWN** or **WM_KEYDOWN** message is received.
		Event map entry: **EVENT_STOCK_KEYDOWN( )**
KeyPress	**void FireKeyPress(short*** *pnChar*)	Fired when a **WM_CHAR** message is received.
		Event map entry: **EVENT_STOCK_KEYPRESS( )**
KeyUp	**void FireKeyUp(short** *nChar*, **short** *nShiftState*)	Fired when a **WM_SYSKEYUP** or **WM_KEYUP** message is received.
		Event map entry: **EVENT_STOCK_KEYUP( )**
MouseDown	**void FireMouseDown(short** *nButton*, **short** *nShiftState*, **float** *x*, **float** *y*)	Fired if any **BUTTONDOWN** (left, middle, or right) is received. The mouse is captured immediately before this event is fired.
		Event map entry: **EVENT_STOCK_MOUSEDOWN( )**
MouseMove	**void FireMouseMove(short** *nButton*, **short** *nShiftState*, **float** *x*, **float** *y*)	Fired when a **WM_MOUSEMOVE** message is received.
		Event map entry: **EVENT_STOCK_MOUSEMOVE( )**
MouseUp	**void FireMouseUp(short** *nButton*, **short** *nShiftState*, **float** *x*, **float** *y*)	Fired if any **BUTTONUP** (left, middle, or right) is received. The mouse capture is released before this event is fired.
		Event map entry: **EVENT_STOCK_MOUSEUP( )**

Adding a Stock Event Using ClassWizard

Adding stock events requires less work than adding custom events because the firing of the actual event is handled automatically by the base class, **COleControl**. The following procedure adds a stock event to a control that was developed using ControlWizard. The event, called KeyPress, fires when a key is pressed and the control is active. This procedure can also be used to add other stock events. Simply substitute the desired stock event name for KeyPress.

▶ **To add the KeyPress stock event using ClassWizard**

1 Load your control's project.

2 From the View menu, choose ClassWizard.

3 Choose the OLE Events tab.

4 Choose the name of your control class from the Class Name box.

5 Choose the Add Event button.

6 From the External Name box, select KeyPress.

7 Choose OK.

8 Choose OK again to confirm your choices and exit ClassWizard.

ClassWizard Changes for Stock Events

Because stock events are handled by the control's base class, ClassWizard does not change your class declaration in any way; it simply adds the event to the control's event map and makes an entry in its .ODL file. The following line is added to the control's event map, located in the control class implementation (.CPP) file:

```
EVENT_STOCK_KEYPRESS()
```

Adding this code fires a KeyPress event when a **WM_CHAR** message is received and the control is active. The KeyPress event can be fired at other times by calling its firing function (for example, `FireKeyPress`) from within the control code.

ClassWizard adds the following line of code to the control's .ODL file:

```
[id(DISPID_KEYPRESS)] void KeyPress(short* KeyAscii);
```

This line associates the KeyPress event with its standard dispatch ID and allows the container to anticipate the KeyPress event.

See Also   OLE Controls, Methods

In the *Class Library Reference*: **COleControl**

Events: Adding Custom Events to an OLE Control

Custom events differ from stock events in that they are not automatically fired by class **COleControl**. A custom event recognizes a certain action, determined by the control developer, as an event. The event map entries for custom events are represented by the **EVENT_CUSTOM** macro. The following section implements a custom event for an OLE control project that was created using ControlWizard.

Adding a Custom Event with ClassWizard

The following procedure adds a specific custom event, ClickIn. You can use this procedure to add other custom events. Simply substitute your custom event name and its parameters for the ClickIn event name and parameters.

▶ **To add the ClickIn custom event using ClassWizard**

1 Load your control's project.

2 From the View menu, choose ClassWizard.

3 Choose the OLE Events tab.

4 Choose the name of the control class from the Class Name box.

5 Choose the Add Event button.

   ClassWizard displays the Add Event dialog box, as illustrated in Figure 1.

6 In the External Name box, type `ClickIn`.

7 In the Internal Name box, type the name of the event's firing function. For this example, use the default value provided by ClassWizard (`FireClickIn`).

8 Add a parameter, called `xCoord` (type `OLE_XPOS_PIXELS`), using the grid control.

9 Add a second parameter, called `yCoord` (type `OLE_YPOS_PIXELS`), using the grid control.

10 Choose OK to close the Add Event box.

11 Choose OK again to confirm your choices and close ClassWizard.

ClassWizard Changes for Custom Events

When you add a custom event, ClassWizard makes changes to the control class .H, .CPP, and .ODL files. The following code samples are specific to the ClickIn event.

The following lines are added to the header (.H) file of your control class:

```
void FireClickIn(OLE_XPOS_PIXELS xCoord, OLE_YPOS_PIXELS yCoord)
    {FireEvent(eventidClickIn,EVENT_PARAM(VTS_XPOS_PIXELS  VTS_YPOS_PIXELS), xCoord,
yCoord);}
```

This code declares an inline function called `FireClickIn` that calls **COleControl::FireEvent** with the ClickIn event and parameters you defined using ClassWizard.

In addition, the following line is added to the event map for the control, located in the implementation (.CPP) file of your control class:

```
EVENT_CUSTOM("ClickIn", FireClickIn, VTS_XPOS_PIXELS  VTS_YPOS_PIXELS)
```

This code maps the event ClickIn to the inline function `FireClickIn`, passing the parameters you defined using ClassWizard.

Finally, the following line is added to your control's .ODL file:

```
[id(1)] void ClickIn(OLE_XPOS_PIXELS xCoord, OLE_YPOS_PIXELS yCoord);
```

This line assigns the ClickIn event a specific ID number, taken from the event's position in the ClassWizard event list. The entry in the event list allows a container to anticipate the event. For example, it might provide handler code to be executed when the event is fired.

Calling FireClickIn

Now that you have added the ClickIn custom event using ClassWizard, you must decide when this event is to be fired. You do this by calling `FireClickIn` when the appropriate action occurs. For this discussion, the control uses the `InCircle` function inside a **WM_LBUTTONDOWN** message handler to fire the ClickIn event when a user clicks inside a circular or elliptical region. The following procedure adds the **WM_LBUTTONDOWN** handler.

▶ **To add a message handler with ClassWizard**

1 Load your control's project.

2 From the View menu, choose ClassWizard.

3 Choose the Message Maps tab.

4 In the Object IDs box, select the control class name. In this case, CSampleCtrl.

5 From the Messages box, select the message you would like to handle. For this example, select WM_LBUTTONDOWN.

6 Choose the Add Function button to add the handler function to your application.

7 Choose the Edit Code button to jump to the location of the message handler, or the OK button to confirm your choice.

The following code sample calls the InCircle function every time the left mouse button is clicked within the control window. This sample can be found in the **WM_LBUTTONDOWN** handler in Responding to Mouse Events in Chapter 24 of *Tutorials*. For more information on this function, see Hit Testing, also in Chapter 24:

```
void CSampleCtrl::OnLButtonDown(UINT nFlags, CPoint point)
{
    if (InCircle(point))
        FireClickIn(point.x, point.y);

    COleControl::OnLButtonDown(nFlags, point);
}
```

Note When ClassWizard creates message handlers for mouse button actions, a call to the same message handler of the base class is automatically added. Do not remove this call. If your control uses any of the stock mouse messages, the message handlers in the base class must be called to ensure that mouse capture is handled properly.

In the following example, the event fires only when the click occurs inside a circular or elliptical region within the control. To achieve this behavior, you can place the `InCircle` function, taken from Hit Testing of *Tutorials*, in your control's implementation (.CPP) file:

```
BOOL CSampleCtrl::InCircle(CPoint& point)
{
    CRect rc;
    GetClientRect(rc);
    // Determine radii
    double a = (rc.right - rc.left) / 2;
    double b = (rc.bottom - rc.top) / 2;

    // Determine x, y
    double x = point.x - (rc.left + rc.right) / 2;
    double y = point.y - (rc.top + rc.bottom) / 2;

    // Apply ellipse formula
    return ((x * x) / (a * a) + (y * y) / (b * b) <= 1);
}
```

You will also need to add the following declaration of the `InCircle` function to your control's header (.H) file:

```
BOOL InCircle( CPoint& point );
```

Custom Events with Stock Names

You can create custom events with the same name as stock events, however you can not implement both in the same control. For example, you might want to create a custom event called Click that does not fire when the stock event Click would normally fire. You could then fire the Click event at any time by calling its firing function.

The following procedure adds a custom Click event.

▶ **To add a custom event that uses a stock event name**

1 Load your control's project.

2 From the View menu, choose ClassWizard.

3 Choose the OLE Events tab.

4 Choose the Add Event button.

5 From the External Name box, select a stock event name. For this example, select Click.

6 Under the Implementation group, select Custom.

7 Choose OK.

8 Choose OK again to confirm your choices and exit ClassWizard.

9 Call `FireClick` at appropriate places in your code.

See Also   OLE Controls, Methods

In the *Class Library Reference*: **COleControl**

Exceptions

This article explains the exception-handling mechanisms available in MFC. Two mechanisms are available:

- C++ exceptions, available in MFC version 3.0 and later
- The MFC exception macros, available in MFC versions 1.0 and later

If you're writing a new application using MFC, you should use the C++ mechanism. You can use the macro-based mechanism if your existing application already uses that mechanism extensively.

You can readily convert existing code to use C++ exceptions instead of the MFC exception macros. Advantages of converting your code and guidelines for doing so are described in the article Exceptions: Converting from MFC Exception Macros.

If you have already developed an application using the MFC exception macros, you can continue using the MFC exception macros in your existing code, while using C++ exceptions in your new code. The article Exceptions: Changes to Exception Macros in Version 3.0 gives guidelines for doing so.

Note   To enable C++ exception handling in your code, select Enable Exception Handling in the C++ Language category of the C/C++ tab of the Project Settings dialog box, or use the /GX compiler option. The default is /GX-, which disables exception handling.

This article covers the following topics:

- When to use exceptions
- MFC exception support
- Further reading about exceptions

When to Use Exceptions

Three categories of outcomes can occur when a function is called during program execution: normal execution, erroneous execution, or abnormal execution. Each category is described below.

- Normal execution

  The function may execute normally and return. Some functions return a result code to the caller, which indicates the outcome of the function. The possible result codes are strictly defined for the function and represent the range of possible outcomes of the function. The result code can indicate success or failure or can even indicate a particular type of failure that is within the normal range of expectations. For example, a file-status function can return a code that indicates that the file does not exist. Note that the term "error code" is not used since a result code represents one of many expected outcomes.

- Erroneous execution

  The caller makes some mistake in passing arguments to the function or calls the function in an inappropriate context. This situation causes an error, and it should be detected by an assertion during program development. (For more information on assertions, see the article Diagnostics: The ASSERT Macro.)

- Abnormal execution

  Abnormal execution includes situations where conditions outside the program's control are influencing the outcome of the function, such as low memory or I/O errors. Abnormal situations should be handled by catching and throwing exceptions.

Using exceptions is especially appropriate for the third category: abnormal execution.

MFC Exception Support

Whether you use the C++ exceptions directly or use the MFC exception macros, you will use **CException** or **CException**-derived objects that may be thrown by the framework or by your application.

MFC provides several predefined kinds of exceptions:

Exception class	Meaning
CMemoryException	Out-of-memory
CFileException	File exception
CArchiveException	Archive/Serialization exception
CNotSupportedException	Response to request for unsupported service
CResourceException	Windows resource allocation exception
CDaoException	Database exceptions (DAO classes)
CDBException	Database exceptions (ODBC classes)
COleException	OLE exceptions
COleDispatchException	OLE dispatch (automation) exceptions
CUserException	Exception that alerts the user with a message box, then throws a generic **CException**

For a description of each MFC function and the exceptions that can possibly be thrown by that function, see the *Class Library Reference*.

Note MFC supports both C++ exceptions and the MFC exception macros. MFC does not directly support Windows NT structured exception handlers (SEH) as discussed in Chapter 8, Structured Exception Handling in *Programming Techniques*.

Further Reading About Exceptions

The following articles explain using the class library for exception handing:

- Exceptions: Catching and Deleting Exceptions
- Exceptions: Examining Exception Contents
- Exceptions: Freeing Objects in Exceptions
- Exceptions: Throwing Exceptions from Your Own Functions
- Exceptions: Database Exceptions
- Exceptions: OLE Exceptions

The following articles compare the MFC exception macros and the C++ exception keywords and explain how you can adapt your code:

- Exceptions: Changes to Exception Macros in Version 3.0
- Exceptions: Converting from MFC Exception Macros
- Exceptions: Using MFC Macros and C++ Exceptions

See Also   In the *Class Library Reference*: **CException**

Exceptions: Changes to Exception Macros in Version 3.0

This is an advanced topic.

In MFC version 3.0 and later, the exception-handling macros have been changed to use C++ exceptions. This article tells how those changes can affect the behavior of existing code that uses the macros.

This article covers the following topics:

- Exception types and the CATCH macro
- Re-throwing exceptions

Exception Types and the CATCH Macro

In earlier versions of MFC, the **CATCH** macro uses MFC run-time type information to determine an exception's type; the exception's type is determined, in other words, at the catch site. With C++ exceptions, however, the exception's type is always determined at the throw site by the type of the exception object that is thrown. This will cause incompatibilities in the rare case in which the type of the pointer to the thrown object differs from the type of the thrown object.

The following example illustrates the consequence of this difference between MFC version 3.0 and earlier versions:

```
TRY
{
    THROW( (CException*) new CCustomException() );
}
CATCH( CCustomException, e )
{
    TRACE( "MFC 2.x will land here\n" );
}
AND_CATCH( CException, e )
{
    TRACE( "MFC 3.0 will land here\n" );
}
END_CATCH
```

This code behaves differently in version 3.0 because control always passes to the first catch block with a matching exception-declaration. The result of the throw expression

```
THROW((CException*)new CCustomException());
```

is thrown as a **CException*** even though it is constructed as a **CCustomException**. The **CATCH** macro in MFC versions 2.5 and earlier uses **CObject::IsKindOf** to test the type at run time. Because the expression

```
e->IsKindOf( RUNTIME_CLASS( CException ) )
```

is true, the first catch block catches the exception. In version 3.0, which uses C++ exceptions to implement many of the exception-handling macros, the second catch block matches the thrown **CException**.

Code like this is not common. It usually appears when an exception object is passed to another function that accepts a generic **CException***, performs "pre-throw" processing, and finally throws the exception.

To work around this problem, move the throw expression from the function to the calling code and throw an exception of the actual type known to the compiler at the time the exception is generated.

Re-Throwing Exceptions

A catch block cannot throw the same exception pointer that it caught.

For example, this code was valid in previous versions, but will have unexpected results with version 3.0:

```
TRY
{
    // Do something to throw an exception.
}
CATCH( CSomeException, e )
{
    THROW( e );     // Wrong. Use THROW_LAST() instead
}
END_TRY
```

Using **THROW** in the catch block causes the pointer e to be deleted, so that the outer catch site will receive an invalid pointer. Use **THROW_LAST** to re-throw e.

See Also   Exceptions: Catching and Deleting Exceptions

Exceptions: Catching and Deleting Exceptions

The following instructions and examples show you how to catch and delete exceptions. For more information on the **try**, **catch**, and **throw** keywords, see Chapter 7, C++ Exception Handling, in *Programming Techniques*.

Your exception handlers must delete exception objects they handle, because failure to delete the exception causes a memory leak whenever that code catches an exception.

Your **catch** block must delete an exception when:

- The **catch** block throws a new exception.

  Of course, you must not delete the exception if you throw the same exception again:
  ```
  catch(CException* e)
  {
      if (m_bThrowExceptionAgain)
          throw; // Do not delete e
  }
  ```

- Execution returns from within the **catch** block.

Note   When deleting a **CException**, use the **Delete** member function to delete the exception. Do not use the **delete** keyword, since it can fail if the exception is not on the heap.

▶ To catch and delete exceptions

- Use the **try** keyword to set up a **try** block. Execute any program statements that might throw an exception within a **try** block.

  Use the **catch** keyword to set up a **catch** block. Place exception-handling code in a **catch** block. The code in the **catch** block is executed only if the code within the **try** block throws an exception of the type specified in the **catch** statement.

  The following skeleton shows how **try** and **catch** blocks are normally arranged:
  ```
  // Normal program statements
  ...

  try
  {
      // Execute some code that might throw an exception.
  }
  catch( CException* e )
  {
      // Handle the exception here.
      // "e" contains information about the exception.
  ```

```
        e->Delete();
}

// Other normal program statements
...
```

When an exception is thrown, control passes to the first **catch** block whose exception-declaration matches the type of the exception. You can selectively handle different types of exceptions with sequential **catch** blocks as listed below:

```
try
{
    // Execute some code that might throw an exception.
}
catch( CMemoryException* e )
{
    // Handle the out-of-memory exception here.
}
catch( CFileException* e )
{
    // Handle the file exceptions here.
}
catch( CException* e )
{
    // Handle all other types of exceptions here.
}
```

See Also   Exceptions: Converting from MFC Exception Macros

Exceptions: Converting from MFC Exception Macros

This is an advanced topic.

This article explains how to convert existing code written with Microsoft Foundation Class macros—**TRY**, **CATCH**, **THROW**, and so on—to use the C++ exception-handling keywords **try**, **catch**, and **throw**. Topics include:

- Conversion advantages
- Converting code with exception macros to use C++ exceptions

Advantages of Converting

You probably do not need to convert existing code, although you should be aware of differences between the macro implementations in MFC version 3.0 and the implementations in earlier versions. These differences and subsequent changes in code behavior are discussed in Exceptions: Changes to Exception Macros in Version 3.0.

The principal advantages of converting are:

- Code that uses the C++ exception-handling keywords compiles to a slightly smaller .EXE or .DLL.
- The C++ exception-handling keywords are more versatile: they can handle exceptions of any data type that can be copied (**int**, **float**, **char**, and so on), whereas the macros handle exceptions only of class **CException** and classes derived from it.

The major difference between the macros and the keywords is that code using the macros "automatically" deletes a caught exception when the exception goes out of scope. Code using the keywords does not, so you must explicitly delete a caught exception. For more information, see the article Exceptions: Catching and Deleting Exceptions.

Another difference is syntax. The syntax for macros and keywords differs in three respects:

1. Macro arguments and exception declarations:

    A **CATCH** macro invocation has the following syntax:

    CATCH(*exception_class*, *exception_object_pointer_name*)

    Notice the comma between the class name and the object pointer name.

    The exception declaration for the **catch** keyword uses this syntax:

    catch(*exception_type exception_name*)

    This exception declaration statement indicates the type of exception the catch block handles.

2. Delimitation of catch blocks:

    With the macros, the **CATCH** macro (with its arguments) begins the first catch block; the **AND_CATCH** macro begins subsequent catch blocks; and the **END_CATCH** macro terminates the sequence of catch blocks.

    With the keywords, the **catch** keyword (with its exception declaration) begins each catch block. There is no counterpart to the **END_CATCH** macro; the catch block ends with its closing brace.

3. The throw expression:

    The macros use **THROW_LAST** to re-throw the current exception. The **throw** keyword, with no argument, has the same effect.

Doing the Conversion

▶ **To convert code using macros to use the C++ exception-handling keywords**

1 Locate all occurrences of the MFC macros **TRY**, **CATCH**, **AND_CATCH**, **END_CATCH**, **THROW**, and **THROW_LAST**.

2 Replace or delete all occurrences of the macros:

For this macro:	Perform this action:
TRY	Replace with **try**
CATCH	Replace with **catch**
AND_CATCH	Replace with **catch**
END_CATCH	Delete
THROW	Replace with **throw**
THROW_LAST	Replace with **throw**

3 Modify the macro arguments so that they form valid exception declarations.

For example, change

```
CATCH( CException, e )
```

to

```
catch( CException* e )
```

4 Modify the code in the catch blocks so that it deletes exception objects as necessary. For more information, see the article Exceptions: Catching and Deleting Exceptions.

Here is an example of exception-handling code using MFC exception macros. Note that because the code in the following example uses the macros, the exception e is deleted automatically:

```
TRY
{
    // Do something to throw an exception.
}
CATCH(CException, e)
{
    if (m_bPassExceptionsUp)
        THROW_LAST();

    if (m_bReturnFromThisFunction)
        return;

    // Not necessary to delete the exception e.
}
END_CATCH
```

The code in the next example uses the C++ exception keywords, so the exception must be explicitly deleted:

```
try
{
    // Do something to throw an exception.
}
catch(CException* e)
{
    if (m_bPassExceptionsUp)
        throw;

    if (m_bThrowDifferentException)
    {
        e->Delete();
        throw new CMyOtherException;
    }

    if (m_bReturnFromThisFunction)
    {
        e->Delete();
        return;
    }

    e->Delete();
}
```

See Also Exceptions: Using MFC Macros and C++ Exceptions

Exceptions: Using MFC Macros and C++ Exceptions

This article discusses considerations for writing code that uses both the MFC exception-handling macros and the C++ exception-handling keywords.

This article covers the following topics:

- Mixing exception keywords and macros
- Try blocks inside catch blocks

Mixing Exception Keywords and Macros

You can mix MFC exception macros and C++ exception keywords in the same program. But you cannot mix MFC macros with C++ exception keywords in the same block because the macros delete exception objects automatically when they go out of scope, whereas code using the exception-handling keywords does not. For more information, see the article Exceptions: Catching and Deleting Exceptions.

The main difference between the macros and the keywords is that the macros "automatically" delete a caught exception when the exception goes out of scope. Code using the keywords does not do so; exceptions caught in a catch block must be explicitly deleted. Mixing macros and C++ exception keywords can cause memory leaks when an exception object is not deleted, or heap corruption when an exception is deleted twice.

The following code, for example, invalidates the exception pointer:

```
TRY
{
    TRY
    {
        // Do something to throw an exception.
    }
    CATCH(CException, e)  // The "inner" catch block
    {
        throw;  // Invalid attempt to throw exception
                // to the outer catch block below.
    }
    END_CATCH
}
CATCH(CException, e)  // The "outer" catch block
{
    // Pointer e is invalid because
    // it was deleted in the inner catch block.
}
END_CATCH
```

The problem occurs because e is deleted when execution passes out of the "inner" **CATCH** block. Using the **THROW_LAST** macro instead of the **THROW** statement will cause the "outer" **CATCH** block to receive a valid pointer:

```
TRY
{
    TRY
    {
        // Do something to throw an exception.
    }
    CATCH(CException, e)  // The "inner" catch block
    {
        THROW_LAST() // Throw exception to the outer catch block below.
    }
    END_CATCH
}
CATCH(CException, e)  // The "outer" catch block
{
    // Pointer e is valid because
    // THROW_LAST() was used.
}
END_CATCH
```

Try Blocks Inside Catch Blocks

You cannot re-throw the current exception from within a **try** block that is inside a **CATCH** block. The following example is invalid:

```
TRY
{
    // Do something to throw an exception.
}
CATCH(CException, e)
{
    try
    {
        throw;  // Wrong.  Causes e (the exception
                // being thrown) to be deleted.
    }
}
END_CATCH
```

See Also Exceptions: Examining Exception Contents

Exceptions: Examining Exception Contents

Although a **catch** block's argument can be of almost any data type, the MFC functions throw exceptions of types derived from the class **CException**. To catch an exception thrown by an MFC function, then, you write a **catch** block whose argument is a pointer to a **CException** object (or an object derived from **CException**, such as **CMemoryException**). Depending on the exact type of the exception, you can examine the data members of the exception object to gather information about the specific cause of the exception.

For example, the **CFileException** type has the **m_cause** data member, which contains an enumerated type that specifies the cause of the file exception. Some examples of the possible return values are **CFileException::fileNotFound** and **CFileException::readOnly**.

The following example shows how to examine the contents of a **CFileException**. Other exception types can be examined in a similar way.

```
try
{
    // Do something to throw a file exception.
}
catch( CFileException* theException )
{
    if( theException->m_cause == CFileException::fileNotFound )
        TRACE( "File not found\n" );
    theException->Delete();
}
```

See Also Exceptions: Freeing Objects in Exceptions, Exceptions: Catching and Deleting Exceptions

Exceptions: Freeing Objects in Exceptions

This article explains the need and the method of freeing objects when an exception occurs. Topics include:

- Handling the exception locally

- Throwing exceptions after destroying objects

Exceptions thrown by the framework or by your application interrupt normal program flow. Thus, it is very important to keep close track of objects so that you can properly dispose of them in case an exception is thrown.

There are two primary methods to do this.

- Handle exceptions locally using the **try** and **catch** keywords, then destroy all objects with one statement.

- Destroy any object in the **catch** block before throwing the exception outside the block for further handling.

These two approaches are illustrated below as solutions to the following problematic example:

```
void SomeFunc()        // Problematic code
{
    CPerson* myPerson = new CPerson;

    // Do something that might throw an exception.
    myPerson->SomeFunc();

    // Now destroy the object before exiting.
    delete myPerson;
}
```

As written above, myPerson will not be deleted if an exception is thrown by SomeFunc. Execution jumps directly to the next outer exception handler, bypassing the normal function exit and the code that deletes the object. The pointer to the object goes out of scope when the exception leaves the function, and the memory occupied by the object will never be recovered as long as the program is running. This is a memory leak; it would be detected by using the memory diagnostics.

Handling the Exception Locally

The **try**/**catch** paradigm provides a defensive programming method for avoiding memory leaks and ensuring that your objects are destroyed when exceptions occur. For instance, the example shown earlier in this article could be rewritten as follows:

```
void SomeFunc()
{
    CPerson* myPerson = new CPerson;

    try
    {
        // Do something that might throw an exception.
        myPerson->SomeFunc();
    }
    catch( CException* e )
```

```
    {
        // Handle the exception locally
        e->Delete();
    }

    // Now destroy the object before exiting.
    delete myPerson;
}
```

This new example sets up an exception handler to catch the exception and handle it locally. It then exits the function normally and destroys the object. The important aspect of this example is that a context to catch the exception is established with the **try**/**catch** blocks. Without a local exception frame, the function would never know that an exception had been thrown and would not have the chance to exit normally and destroy the object.

Throwing Exceptions After Destroying Objects

Another way to handle exceptions is to pass them on to the next outer exception-handling context. In your **catch** block, you can do some cleanup of your locally allocated objects and then throw the exception on for further processing.

The throwing function may or may not need to deallocate heap objects. If the function always deallocates the heap object before returning in the normal case, then the function should also deallocate the heap object before throwing the exception. On the other hand, if the function does not normally deallocate the object before returning in the normal case, then you must decided on a case-by-case basis whether the heap object should be deallocated.

The following example shows how locally allocated objects can be cleaned up:

```
void SomeFunc()
{
    CPerson* myPerson = new CPerson;

    try
    {
        // Do something that might throw an exception.
        myPerson->SomeFunc();
    }
    catch( CException, e )
    {
        // Destroy the object before passing exception on.
        delete myPerson;
        // Throw the exception to the next handler.
        throw;
    }

    // On normal exits, destroy the object.
    delete myPerson;
}
```

The exception mechanism automatically deallocates frame objects; the destructor of the frame object is also called.

If you call functions that can throw exceptions, you can use **try/catch** blocks to make sure that you catch the exceptions and have a chance to destroy any objects you have created. In particular, be aware that many MFC functions can throw exceptions.

See Also   Exceptions: Catching and Deleting Exceptions

Exceptions: Throwing Exceptions from Your Own Functions

It is possible to use the MFC exception-handling paradigm solely to catch exceptions thrown by functions in MFC or other libraries. In addition to catching exceptions thrown by library code, you can throw exceptions from your own code if you are writing functions that can encounter exceptional conditions.

When an exception is thrown, execution of the current function is aborted and jumps directly to the **catch** block of the innermost exception frame. The exception mechanism bypasses the normal exit path from a function. Therefore, you must be sure to delete those memory blocks that would be deleted in a normal exit.

▶ **To throw an exception**

- Use one of the MFC helper functions, such as **AfxThrowMemoryException**. These functions throw a preallocated exception object of the appropriate type.

  In the following example, a function tries to allocate two memory blocks and throws an exception if either allocation fails:

  ```
  {
      char* p1 = (char*)malloc( SIZE_FIRST );
      if( p1 == NULL )
          AfxThrowMemoryException();
      char* p2 = (char*)malloc( SIZE_SECOND );
      if( p2 == NULL )
      {
          free( p1 );
          AfxThrowMemoryException();
      }

      // ... Do something with allocated blocks ...

      // In normal exit, both blocks are deleted.
      free( p1 );
      free( p2 );
  }
  ```

  If the first allocation fails, you can simply throw the memory exception. If the first allocation is successful but the second one fails, you must free the first allocation block before throwing the exception. If both allocations succeed, then you can proceed normally and free the blocks when exiting the function.

−or−

- Use a user-defined exception to indicate a problem condition. You can throw an item of any type, even an entire class, as your exception.

This example attempts to play a sound through a wave device and throws an exception if there is a failure.

```
#define WAVE_ERROR -5
{
    // This Win32 API returns 0 if the sound cannot be played.
    // Throw an integer constant if it fails.
    if( sndPlaySound("SIREN.WAV", SND_ASYNC) )
        throw WAVE_ERROR;
}
```

Note MFC's default handling of exceptions applies only to pointers to **CException** objects (and objects of **CException**-derived classes). The example above bypasses MFC's exception mechanism.

See Also Exceptions: Exceptions in Constructors

Exceptions: Exceptions in Constructors

When throwing an exception in a constructor, clean up whatever objects and memory allocations you have made prior to throwing the exception, as explained in Exceptions: Throwing Exceptions from Your Own Functions.

Throwing an exception in a constructor is tricky, however, because the memory for the object itself has already been allocated by the time the constructor is called. There is no simple way to deallocate the memory occupied by the object from within the constructor for that object. Thus, you will find that throwing an exception in a constructor will result in the object remaining allocated. For a discussion of how to detect objects in your program that have not been deallocated, see the article Diagnostics: Detecting Memory Leaks.

If you are performing operations in your constructor that can fail, it might be a better idea to put those operations into a separate initialization function rather than throwing an exception in the constructor. That way, you can safely construct the object and get a valid pointer to it. Then, you can call the initialization function for the object. If the initialization function fails, you can delete the object directly.

See Also Exceptions: Freeing Objects in Exceptions

Exceptions: Database Exceptions

This article explains how to handle database exceptions. Most of the material in this article applies whether you are working with the MFC classes for Open Database

Connectivity (ODBC) or the MFC classes for Data Access Objects (DAO). Material specific to one or the other model is explicitly marked. Topics include:

- Approaches to exception handling
- A database exception-handling example

Approaches to Exception Handling

The approach is the same whether you are working with DAO or ODBC.

You should always write exception handlers to handle exceptional conditions.

The most pragmatic approach to catching database exceptions is to test your application with exception scenarios. Determine the likely exceptions that might occur for an operation in your code, and force the exception to occur. Then examine the trace output to see what exception is thrown, or examine the returned error information in the debugger. This lets you know which return codes you'll see for the exception scenarios you are using.

Error Codes Used for ODBC Exceptions

In addition to return codes defined by the framework, which have names of the form **AFX_SQL_ERROR_XXX**, some **CDBExceptions** are based on ODBC return codes. The return codes for such exceptions have names of the form **SQL_ERROR_XXX**.

The return codes—both framework-defined and ODBC-defined—that the database classes can return are documented under the **m_nRetCode** data member of class **CDBException**. Additional information about return codes defined by ODBC is available in the ODBC SDK *Programmer's Reference*.

Error Codes Used for DAO Exceptions

For DAO exceptions, more information is typically available. You can access error information through three data members of a caught **CDaoException** object:

m_pErrorInfo contains a pointer to a **CDaoErrorInfo** object that encapsulates error information in DAO's collection of error objects associated with the database.

m_nAfxDaoError contains an extended error code from the MFC DAO classes. These error codes, which have names of the form **AFX_DAO_ERROR_XXX**, are documented under the data member in **CDaoException**.

m_scode contains an OLE **SCODE** from DAO, if applicable. You'll seldom need to work with this error code, however. Usually more information is available in the other two data members. See the data member for more about **SCODE** values.

Additional information about DAO errors, the DAO Error object type, and the DAO Errors collection is available under class **CDaoException** and in the topics Trappable Data Access Errors and Error Object, Errors Collection in DAO Help.

A Database Exception-Handling Example

The following example attempts to construct a **CRecordset**-derived object on the
heap with the **new** operator, and then open the recordset (for an ODBC data source).
For a similar example for the DAO classes, see DAO Exception Example below.

ODBC Exception Example

The **Open** member function could throw an exception (of type **CDBException** for the
ODBC classes), so this code brackets the **Open** call with a **try** block. The subsequent
catch block will catch a **CDBException**. You could examine the exception object
itself, called e, but in this case it's enough to know that the attempt to create a
recordset has failed. The **catch** block displays a message box and cleans up by
deleting the recordset object.

```
CRecordset* CSectionView::OnGetRecordset()
{
    if ( m_pSet != NULL )
        return m_pSet;          // Recordset already allocated

    m_pSet = new CSectionSet( NULL );
    try
    {
        m_pSet->Open( );
    }
    catch( CDBException* e )
    {
        AfxMessageBox( e->m_strError,
                    MB_ICONEXCLAMATION );
        // Delete the incomplete recordset object
        delete m_pSet;
        m_pSet = NULL;
        e->Delete();
    }
    return m_pSet;
}
```

DAO Exception Example

The DAO example is similar to the example for ODBC, but you can typically retrieve
more kinds of information. The following code also attempts to open a recordset. If
that attempt throws an exception, you can examine a data member of the exception
object for error information. As with the previous ODBC example, it's probably
enough to know that the attempt to create a recordset failed.

```
CDaoRecordset* CSectionView::OnGetRecordset()
{
    if ( m_pSet != NULL )
        return m_pSet;  // Recordset already allocated

    m_pSet = new CSectionSet( NULL );
    try
    {
```

```
        m_pSet->Open( );
    }
    catch( CDaoException* e )
    {
        AfxMessageBox(
                e->m_pErrorInfo->m_strDescription,
                MB_ICONEXCLAMATION );
        // Delete the incomplete recordset object
        delete m_pSet;
        m_pSet = NULL;
        e->Delete( );
    }
    return m_pSet;
}
```

This code gets an error message string from the **m_pErrorInfo** member of the exception object. MFC fills this member when it throws the exception.

For a discussion of the error information returned by a **CDaoException** object, see classes **CDaoException** and **CDaoErrorInfo**.

When you are working with Microsoft Jet (.MDB) databases, and in most cases when you are working with ODBC, there will be only one error object. In the rare case when you are using ODBC and there are multiple errors, you can loop through DAO's Errors collection based on the number of errors returned by **CDaoException::GetErrorCount**. Each time through the loop, call **CDaoException::GetErrorInfo** to refill the **m_pErrorInfo** data member.

See Also   Exceptions: OLE Exceptions

In the *Class Library Reference*: **CDBException**, **CDaoException**

Exceptions: OLE Exceptions

The techniques and facilities for handling exceptions in OLE are the same as those for handling other exceptions. For further information on exception handling, see the article Exceptions.

All exception objects are derived from the abstract base class **CException**. MFC provides two classes for handling OLE exceptions:

- **COleException**   For handling general OLE exceptions.
- **COleDispatchException**   For generating and handling OLE dispatch (automation) exceptions.

The difference between these two classes is the amount of information they provide and where they are used. **COleException** has a public data member that contains the OLE status code for the exception. **COleDispatchException** supplies more information, including the following:

- An application-specific error code

- An error description, such as "Disk full"
- A help context that your application can use to provide additional information for the user
- The name of your application's help file
- The name of the application that generated the exception

COleDispatchException provides more information so that it can be used with products like Microsoft Visual Basic. The verbal error description can be used in a message box or other notification; the help information can be used to help the user respond to the conditions that caused the exception.

Two global functions correspond to the two OLE exception classes: **AfxThrowOleException** and **AfxThrowOleDispatchException**. Use them to throw general OLE exceptions and OLE dispatch exceptions, respectively.

See Also   In the *Class Library Reference*: **COleException**, **COleDispatchException**

Frequently Asked Questions (FAQ) About MFC

This group of articles highlights questions that Microsoft Product Support Services (PSS) has received frequently from users of MFC. Each question below is followed by the title of an article that answers the question.

How do I update the text of a pane in a status bar? See FAQ: Updating the Text of a Status-Bar Pane.

What are the user interface guidelines? See FAQ: The User Interface Guidelines for Microsoft Windows.

How do I change the styles of a window that is created by the framework? See FAQ: Changing the Styles of a Window Created by MFC.

How do I perform background processing in an MFC application? See FAQ: Background Processing in an MFC Application.

How do I create an ODBC data source from my program? See FAQ: Programmatically Configuring an ODBC Data Source.

How do I create a table in an ODBC data source? See FAQ: Programmatically Creating a Table in an ODBC Data Source.

Note Future editions of the Visual C++ documentation will move some of these articles into appropriate parts of the encyclopedia and add new FAQ articles.

FAQ: Updating the Text of a Status-Bar Pane

This article explains how to change the text that appears in one of the panes of an MFC status bar. A status bar—a window object of class **CStatusBar**—contains several "panes." Each pane is a rectangular area of the status bar that you can use to display information. For example, many applications display the status of the CAPS LOCK, NUM LOCK, and other keys in the rightmost panes. Applications also often display informative text in the leftmost pane (pane 0), sometimes called the "message pane." For example, the default MFC status bar uses the message pane to display a string explaining the currently selected menu item or toolbar button. Figure 1 shows a status bar from an AppWizard-created MFC application:

Figure 1   An MFC Status Bar

Save the active document	CAP NUM SCRL

By default, MFC does not enable a **CStatusBar** pane when it creates the pane. To activate a pane, you must use the **ON_UPDATE_COMMAND_UI** macro for each pane on the status bar and update the panes. Because panes do not send

WM_COMMAND messages (they aren't like toolbar buttons), you can't use ClassWizard to create an update handler to activate a pane; you must type the code manually.

For example, suppose one pane has ID_INDICATOR_PAGE as its command identifier and that it contains the current page number in a document. The following procedure describes how to create a new pane in the status bar.

▶ **To make a new pane**

1 Define the pane's command ID.

Open the ResourceView in the Project Workspace window. Open the Symbol Browser with the Resource Symbols command on the View menu, and click New. Type a command ID name: for example, ID_INDICATOR_PAGE. Specify a value for the ID, or accept the value suggested by the Symbol Browser. For example, for ID_INDICATOR_PAGE, accept the default value. Close the Symbol Browser.

2 Define a default string to display in the pane.

With the ResourceView open, double-click String Table in the window that lists resource types for your application. With the String Table editor open, choose New String from the Insert menu. In the String Properties window, select your pane's command ID (for example, ID_INDICATOR_PAGE) and type a default string value, such as "Page   ". Close the string editor. (You need a default string to avoid a compiler error.)

3 Add the pane to the **indicators** array.

In file MAINFRM.CPP, locate the **indicators** array. This array lists command IDs for all of the status bar's indicators, in order from left to right. At the appropriate point in the array, enter your pane's command ID, as shown here for ID_INDICATOR_PAGE:

```
static UINT BASED_CODE indicators[] =
{
    ID_SEPARATOR,                 // status line indicator
    ID_INDICATOR_CAPS,
    ID_INDICATOR_NUM,
    ID_INDICATOR_SCRL,
    ID_INDICATOR_PAGE,
};
```

The recommended way to display text in a pane is to call the **SetText** member function of class **CCmdUI** in an update handler function for the pane. For example, you might want to set up an integer variable m_nPage that contains the current page number and use **SetText** to set the pane's text to a string version of that number.

Note   The **SetText** approach is recommended. It is possible to attack this task at a slightly lower level by calling the **CStatusBar** member function **SetPaneText**. Even so, you still need an update handler. Without such a handler for the pane, MFC automatically disables the pane, erasing its content.

The following procedure shows how to use an update handler function to display text in a pane.

▶ To make a pane display text

1 Add a command update handler for the command.

You can't use ClassWizard to write a handler for a status bar pane, so manually add a prototype for the handler, as shown here for ID_INDICATOR_PAGE (in MAINFRM.H):

```
afx_msg void OnUpdatePage(CCmdUI *pCmdUI);
```

In the appropriate .CPP file, add the handler's definition, as shown here for ID_INDICATOR_PAGE (in MAINFRM.CPP):

```
void CMainFrame::OnUpdatePage(CCmdUI *pCmdUI)
{
    pCmdUI->Enable();
}
```

In the appropriate message map, add the **ON_UPDATE_COMMAND_UI** macro (outside the "{{AFX" comments), as shown here for ID_INDICATOR_PAGE (in MAINFRM.CPP):

```
ON_UPDATE_COMMAND_UI(ID_INDICATOR_PAGE, OnUpdatePage)
```

2 Add code to the handler to display your text.

For ID_INDICATOR_PAGE, expand the OnUpdatePage handler from step 1 above, adding the last three lines:

```
void CMainFrame::OnUpdatePage(CCmdUI *pCmdUI)
{
    pCmdUI->Enable();
    CString strPage;
    strPage.Format( "Page %d", m_nPage );
    pCmdUI->SetText( strPage );
}
```

Once you define the value of the m_nPage member variable (of class CMainFrame), this technique causes the page number to appear in the pane during idle processing in the same manner that the application updates other indicators. If m_nPage changes, the display changes during the next idle loop.

See Also In Chapter 2: How to Update User-Interface Objects

In the *Class Library Reference*: **CStatusBar**

FAQ: The User Interface Guidelines for Microsoft Windows

Most first-class applications for the Microsoft Windows operating system share a familiar and consistent user interface. This improves the usability of the application because the user is not forced to relearn common operations. For example, a user who regularly prints documents from Microsoft Word intuitively looks for a Print option on the File menu when confronted with the task of printing in an unfamiliar application.

Microsoft suggests guidelines that help you use the standard Windows user interface objects and environment in a consistent manner. The book *The Windows Interface: An Application Design Guide* is available from Microsoft Press; it contains a chapter on overall principles and methodology along with specific guidelines for keyboard input, windows, menus, and so on.

The Microsoft Foundation Class Library (MFC), and especially the skeleton applications created with AppWizard, provide a good starting point to develop an application that conforms to the published guidelines. These tools ease the process of developing an application that has the "look and feel" expected by experienced users of the Windows environment.

MFC was designed to support the published user interface guidelines. Overriding the default behavior in derived classes tends to be more difficult than working with the default behavior of MFC. Adding to the default behavior is relatively simple.

FAQ: Changing the Styles of a Window Created by MFC

In its version of the **WinMain** function, MFC registers several standard window classes for you. Because you don't normally edit MFC's **WinMain**, that function gives you no opportunity to change the MFC default window styles. This article explains how you can change the styles of such a preregistered window class in an existing application.

Changing Styles in a New MFC Application

If you're using Visual C++ 2.0 or later, you can change the default window styles in AppWizard when you create your application. In AppWizard's Advanced Options dialog box, choose the Main Frame tab (to change styles for your main frame window) or the MDI Child Frame tab (to change styles for MDI child windows). For either window type, you can specify its frame thickness (thick or thin) and any of the following:

- Whether the window has Minimize or Maximize controls.

- Whether the window appears initially minimized, maximized, or neither.

For main frame windows, you can also specify whether the window has a System Menu. For MDI child windows, you can specify whether the window supports splitter panes.

Changing Styles in an Existing Application

If you're using a version of Visual C++ prior to version 2.0 or changing window attributes in an existing application, follow the instructions in the rest of this article instead.

To change the default window attributes used by a framework application created with AppWizard, override the window's **PreCreateWindow** virtual member function. **PreCreateWindow** allows an application to access the creation process normally managed internally by the **CDocTemplate** class. The framework calls **PreCreateWindow** just prior to creating the window. By modifying the **CREATESTRUCT** parameter to **PreCreateWindow**, your application can change the attributes used to create the window.

The CTRLBARS sample application, provided with MFC version 3.0 and later, demonstrates this technique for changing window attributes. Depending on what your application changes in **PreCreateWindow**, it may be necessary to call the base class implementation of the function. You can access the source code for the MFC General sample CTRLBARS using Sample help.

The following discussion covers the SDI case and the MDI case.

The SDI Case

In a single document interface (SDI) application, the default window style in the framework is a combination of the **WS_OVERLAPPEDWINDOW** and **FWS_ADDTOTITLE** styles. **FWS_ADDTOTITLE** is an MFC-specific style that instructs the framework to add the document title to the window's caption. To change the window attributes in an SDI application, override the **PreCreateWindow** function in your class derived from **CFrameWnd** (which AppWizard names CMainFrame). For example:

```
BOOL CMainFrame::PreCreateWindow(CREATESTRUCT& cs)
{
    // Create a window without min/max buttons or sizable border
    cs.style = WS_OVERLAPPED | WS_SYSMENU | WS_BORDER;

    // Size the window to 1/3 screen size and center it
    cs.cy = ::GetSystemMetrics(SM_CYSCREEN) / 3;
    cs.cx = ::GetSystemMetrics(SM_CXSCREEN) / 3;
    cs.y = ((cs.cy * 3) - cs.cy) / 2;
    cs.x = ((cs.cx * 3) - cs.cx) / 2;

    // Call the base-class version
    return CFrameWnd::PreCreateWindow(cs);
}
```

This code creates a main frame window without Minimize and Maximize buttons and without a sizable border. The window is initially centered on the screen.

The MDI Case

A little more work is required to change the window style of a child window in a multiple document interface (MDI) application. By default, an MDI application created with AppWizard uses the default **CMDIChildWnd** class defined in MFC. To change the window style of an MDI child window, you must derive a new class from **CMDIChildWnd** and replace all references to **CMDIChildWnd** in your project with references to the new class. Most likely, the only reference to **CMDIChildWnd** in the application is located in your application's `InitInstance` member function.

The default window style used in an MDI application is a combination of the **WS_CHILD**, **WS_OVERLAPPEDWINDOW**, and **FWS_ADDTOTITLE** styles. To change the window attributes of an MDI application's child windows, override the **PreCreateWindow** function in your class derived from **CMDIChildWnd**. For example:

```
BOOL CMyChildWnd::PreCreateWindow(CREATESTRUCT& cs)
{
    // Create a child window without the maximize button
    cs.style &= ~WS_MAXIMIZEBOX;

    // Call the base-class version
    return CMDIChildWnd::PreCreateWindow(cs);
}
```

This code creates MDI child windows without a maximize button.

See Also In the *Class Library Reference*: **CWnd::PreCreateWindow**

FAQ: Background Processing in an MFC Application

Many applications perform lengthy processing "in the background." Sometimes performance considerations dictate using multithreading for such work. Threads involve extra development overhead, so they are not recommended for simple tasks like the idle-time work that MFC does in the **OnIdle** function. This article focuses on idle processing. For more information about multithreading, see the article Multithreading.

Some kinds of background processing are appropriately done during intervals that the user is not otherwise interacting with the application. In an application developed for the Microsoft Windows operating system, an application can perform idle-time processing by splitting a lengthy process into many small fragments. After processing each fragment, the application yields execution control to Windows using a **PeekMessage** loop.

This article explains two ways to do idle processing in your application:

- Using **PeekMessage** in MFC's main message loop

- Embedding another **PeekMessage** loop somewhere else in the application

PeekMessage in the MFC Message Loop

In an application developed with MFC, the main message loop in the **CWinThread** class contains a message loop that calls the **PeekMessage** member function. This loop also calls the **OnIdle** member function of **CWinThread** between messages. An application can process messages in this idle time by overriding the **OnIdle** function.

Note Run, PeekMessage, OnIdle, and certain other member functions are now members of class **CWinThread** rather than of class **CWinApp**. **CWinApp** is derived from **CWinThread**.

For more information about performing idle processing in the **OnIdle** function, see the documentation for **OnIdle** in the *Class Library Reference*.

PeekMessage Elsewhere in Your Application

Another method for performing idle processing in an application involves embedding a message loop in one of your functions. This message loop is very similar to MFC's main message loop, found in the **Run** member function of class **CWinThread**. So such a loop in an application developed with MFC must perform many of the same functions as the main message loop. The following code fragment demonstrates writing a message loop that is compatible with MFC:

```
while ( bDoingBackgroundProcessing )
{
    while ( ::PeekMessage( &msg, NULL, 0, 0, PM_NOREMOVE ) )
    {
        if ( !PumpMessage( ) )
        {
            bDoingBackgroundProcessing = FALSE;
            ::PostQuitMessage( );
            break;
        }
    }
    // let MFC do its idle processing
    LONG lIdle = 0;
    while ( AfxGetApp()->OnIdle(lIdle++ ) )
        ;
    // Perform some background processing here
    // using another call to OnIdle
}
```

This code, embedded in some function, loops as long as there is idle processing to do. Within that loop, a nested loop repeatedly calls **PeekMessage**. As long as that call returns a nonzero value, the loop calls **CWinThread::PumpMessage** to perform normal message translation and dispatching. Although **PumpMessage** is undocumented, you can examine its source code in the THRDCORE.CPP file in MFC\SRC relative to your Visual C++ installation.

Once the inner loop ends, the outer loop performs idle processing with one or more calls to **OnIdle**. The first call is for MFC's purposes. You can make additional calls to **OnIdle** to do your own background work.

For more information about performing background processing in the **OnIdle** function, see **OnIdle** in the *Class Library Reference.*

See Also   In the *Class Library Reference*: **CWinApp::OnIdle**

In the *Win32 Programmer's Reference*: **::PeekMessage**

FAQ: Programmatically Configuring an ODBC Data Source

This article explains how you can configure ODBC (Open Database Connectivity) data source names programmatically. This gives you flexibility to access data without forcing the user to explicitly use the ODBC Administrator or other programs to specify the names of data sources.

Typically, a user runs the ODBC Administrator program to create a data source, provided that the associated database management system (DBMS) supports this operation.

When creating a Microsoft Access ODBC data source through the ODBC Administrator program, you are given two choices: you can select an existing .MDB file or you can create a new .MDB file. There is no programmatic way of creating the .MDB file from your MFC ODBC application. Therefore, if your application requires that you place data into a Microsoft Access data source (.MDB file), you most likely will want to have an empty .MDB file that you can use or copy whenever you need it.

However, many DBMSs allow programmatic data source creation. Some data sources, such as FoxPro, maintain a directory specification for databases. That is, a directory is the data source and each table within the data source is stored in a separate file (in the case of dBASE or FoxPro, each table is a .DBF file). Drivers for other ODBC databases, such as Microsoft Access and SQL Server, require that some specific criteria be satisfied before a data source can be established. For example, when using the SQL Server ODBC driver you need to have established a SQL Server.

SQLConfigDataSource Example

The following example uses the **::SQLConfigDataSource** ODBC API function to create a new Excel data source called "New Excel Data Source":

```
SQLConfigDataSource(NULL,ODBC_ADD_DSN, "Excel Files (*.xls)",
                "DSN=New Excel Data Source\0"
                "Description=New Excel Data Source\0"
                "FileType=Excel\0"
                "DataDirectory=C:\\EXCELDIR\0"
                "MaxScanRows=20\0");
```

Note that the data source is actually a directory (C:\EXCELDIR); this directory must exist. The Excel driver uses directories as its data sources, and files as the individual tables (one table per .XLS file).

For additional information on creating tables, see the article FAQ: Programmatically Creating a Table in an ODBC Data Source.

The information below discusses the parameters that need to be passed to the **::SQLConfigDataSource** ODBC API function. To use **::SQLConfigDataSource**, you must include the ODBCINST.H header file and use the ODBCINST.LIB import library. Also, ODBCCP32.DLL must be in the path at run time (or ODBCINST.DLL for 16 bit).

You can create an ODBC data source name using the ODBC Administrator program or a similar utility. However, sometimes it is desirable to create a data source name directly from your application to obtain access without requiring the user to run a separate utility.

The ODBC Administrator (typically installed in the Windows Control Panel) creates a new data source by putting entries in the Windows registry (or, for 16 bit, in the ODBC.INI file). The ODBC Driver Manager queries this file to obtain the required information about the data source. It's important to know what information needs to be placed in the registry because you'll need to supply it with the call to **::SQLConfigDataSource**.

Although this information could be written directly to the registry without using **::SQLConfigDataSource**, any application that does so is relying on the current technique that the Driver Manager uses to maintain its data. If a later revision to the ODBC Driver Manager implements record keeping about data sources in a different way, then any application that uses this technique would be broken. It is generally advisable to use an API function when one is provided. For example, your code is portable from 16 bit to 32 bit if you use the **::SQLConfigDataSource** function, as the function will correctly write to the ODBC.INI file or to the registry.

SQLConfigDataSource Parameters

The following explains the parameters of the **::SQLConfigDataSource** function. Much of the information is taken from the ODBC API *Programmer's Reference* supplied with Visual C++ version 1.5 and later.

Function Prototype
BOOL SQLConfigDataSource(HWND *hwndParent*,**UINT** *fRequest*, **LPCSTR** *lpszDriver*, **LPCSTR** *lpszAttributes*)**;**

Parameters and Usage
hwndParent   The window specified as the owner of any dialog boxes that either the ODBC Driver Manager or the specific ODBC driver creates to obtain additional information from the user about the new data source. If the *lpszAttributes* parameter

doesn't supply enough information, a dialog box appears. The *hwndParent* parameter may be **NULL**; see the ODBC *Programmer's Reference* for details.

lpszDriver The driver description. This is the name presented to users rather than the physical driver name (the DLL).

lpszAttributes List of attributes in the form "keyname=value". These strings are separated by null terminators with two consecutive null terminators at the end of the list. These attributes are primarily default driver-specific entries, which go into the registry for the new data source. One important key that is not mentioned in the ODBC API reference for this function is "DSN" ("data source name"), which specifies the name of the new data source. The rest of the entries are specific to the driver for the new data source. Often it is not necessary to supply all of the entries because the driver can prompt the user with dialog boxes for the new values. (Set *hwndParent* to **NULL** to cause this.) You might want to explicitly supply default values so that the user is not prompted.

▶ To determine the description of a driver for the lpszDriver parameter using the ODBC Administrator program

1 Run the ODBC Administrator program.

2 Choose Add.

This will give you a list of installed drivers and their descriptions. It is this description that you use as the *lpszDriver* parameter. Note that you use the entire description—for example, "Excel Files (*.xls)"—including the file extension and parentheses if they exist in the description.

As an alternative, you can examine the registry (or, for 16 bit, the file ODBCINST.INI), which contains a list of all driver entries and descriptions under the registry key "ODBC Drivers" (or the section [ODBC Drivers] in ODBCINST.INI).

One way to find the keynames and values for the *lpszAttributes* parameter is to examine the ODBC.INI file for an already configured data source (perhaps one that has been configured by the ODBC Administrator program):

▶ To find keynames and values for the lpszAttributes parameter

1 Run the Windows registry editor (or, for 16 bit, open the ODBC.INI file).

2 Find the ODBC data sources information.

- For 32 bit, find the key HKEY_CURRENT_USER\Software\ODBC\ODBC.INI\ODBC Data Sources in the left-hand pane.

  The right-hand pane lists entries of the form: "pub: REG_SZ:<*data source name*>", where <*data source name*> is a data source that has already been configured with the desired settings for the driver you intend to use. Select the data source you want, for example SQL Server. The items following the string "pub:" are, in order, the keyname and value you want to use in your *lpszAttributes* parameter.

–or–

- For 16 bit, find the section in the ODBC.INI file marked by [*<data source name>*].

    The lines following this line will be of the form "keyname=value". These are exactly the entries you will want to use in your *lpszAttributes* parameter.

You might also want to examine the documentation for the specific driver you are going to use. You can find useful information in the online help for the driver, which you can access by running the ODBC Administrator. These help files are usually placed in the WINDOWS\SYSTEM directory for Windows NT, Windows 3.1, or Windows 95.

▶ **To obtain online help for your ODBC driver**

1 Run ODBC Adminstrator.

2 Choose Add.

3 Select the driver name.

4 Choose OK.

When ODBC Administrator displays the information for creating a new data source for that particular driver, select Help. This opens the help file for that particular driver, which generally contains important information concerning the use of the driver.

For related information, see the ODBC *Programmer's Reference*: Chapter 24, Installer DLL Function Reference.

See Also   FAQ: Programmatically Creating a Table in an ODBC Data Source

FAQ: Programmatically Creating a Table in an ODBC Data Source

This article explains how to create a table for your data source, using the **ExecuteSQL** member function of class **CDatabase**, passing the function a string that contains a **CREATE TABLE** SQL statement.

For general information about ODBC data sources in MFC, see the article Data Source (ODBC). The article FAQ: Programmatically Configuring an ODBC Data Source describes creating data sources.

Once you have the data source established, you can easily create tables using the **ExecuteSQL** member function and the **CREATE TABLE** SQL statement. For example, if you had a **CDatabase** object called myDB, you could use the following MFC code to create a table:

```
myDB.ExecuteSQL("CREATE TABLE OFFICES (OfficeID TEXT(4)" ",
                    OfficeName TEXT(10))");
```

The code above creates a table called "OFFICES" in the Microsoft Access data source connection maintained by myDB; the table contains two fields "OfficeID" and "OfficeName." For more information about creating tables as well as primary keys and indexes for them, see Appendix C in the ODBC *Programmer's Reference.*

Note   The field types specified in the **CREATE TABLE** SQL statement may vary according to the ODBC driver that you are using. For example, the Btrieve® ODBC driver requires "STRING" in place of the "TEXT" type shown in the **CREATE TABLE** statement above. The Microsoft Query program (distributed with Visual C++ 1.5) is one way to discover what field types are available for a data source. In MS Query, select File, choose Table_Definition, select a table from a data source, and look at the type shown in the "Type" combo box. Appendix C in the ODBC *Programmer's Reference* describes the supported SQL syntax. SQL syntax also exists to create indexes.

See Also   FAQ: Programmatically Configuring an ODBC Data Source, Data Source (ODBC)

Field

A single item of data in a record, such as a phone number field in a customer record.

See the articles Recordset (ODBC) and DAO Recordset.

Files

In the Microsoft Foundation Class Library (MFC), class **CFile** handles normal file I/O operations. This article explains how to open and close files as well as read and write data to those files. It also discusses file status operations. For a description of how to use the object-based serialization features of MFC as an alternative way of reading and writing data in files, see the article Serialization (Object Persistence).

Note When you use MFC **CDocument** objects, the framework does much of the serialization work for you. In particular, the framework creates and uses the **CFile** object. You only have to write code in your override of the **Serialize** member function of class **CDocument**.

The **CFile** class provides an interface for general-purpose binary file operations. The **CStdioFile** and **CMemFile** classes are derived from **CFile** to supply more specialized file services.

This article covers the following topics:

- Opening files
- Reading and writing files
- Closing files
- Accessing file status

Opening Files

In MFC, the most common way to open a file is a two-stage process.

▶ **To open a file**

1 Create the file object without specifying a path or permission flags.

You usually create a file object by declaring a **CFile** variable on the stack frame.

2 Call the **Open** member function for the file object, supplying a path and permission flags.

The return value for **Open** will be nonzero if the file was opened successfully or 0 if the specified file could not be opened. The **Open** member function is prototyped as follows:

```
virtual BOOL Open( LPCTSTR lpszFileName, UINT nOpenFlags,
CFileException* pError = NULL );
```

The open flags specify which permissions, such as read-only, you want for the file. The possible flag values are defined as enumerated constants within the **CFile** class, so they are qualified with "**CFile::,**" as in **CFile::modeRead**. Use the **CFile::modeCreate** flag if you want to create the file.

The following example shows how to create a new file with read/write permission (replacing any previous file with the same path):

```
char* pszFileName = "c:\\test\\myfile.dat";
CFile myFile;
CFileException fileException;

if ( !myFile.Open( pszFileName, CFile::modeCreate |
        CFile::modeReadWrite ), &fileException )
{
    TRACE( "Can't open file %s, error = %u\n",
        pszFileName, fileException.m_cause );
}
```

Note This example creates and opens a file. If there are problems, the **Open** call can return a **CFileException** object in its last parameter, as shown here. The **TRACE** macro prints both the filename and a code indicating the reason for failure. You can call the **AfxThrowFileException** function if you require more detailed error reporting.

Reading and Writing Files

If you've used the C run-time library file-handling functions, MFC reading and writing operations will appear familiar. This section describes reading directly from and writing directly to a **CFile** object. You can also do buffered file I/O with the **CArchive** class.

▶ **To read from and write to the file**

- Use the **Read** and **Write** member functions to read and write data in the file.

    –or–

- The **Seek** member function is also available for moving to a specific offset within the file.

Read takes a pointer to a buffer and the number of bytes to read and returns the actual number of bytes that were read. If the required number of bytes could not be read because end-of-file (EOF) is reached, the actual number of bytes read is returned. If any read error occurs, an exception is thrown. **Write** is similar to **Read**, but the number of bytes written is not returned. If a write error occurs, including not writing all the bytes specified, an exception is thrown. If you have a valid **CFile** object, you can read from it or write to it as shown in the following example:

```
char        szBuffer[256];
UINT        nActual = 0;
CFile myFile;
```

```
myFile.Write( szBuffer, sizeof( szBuffer ) );
myFile.Seek( 0, CFile::begin );
nActual = myFile.Read( szBuffer, sizeof( szBuffer ) );
```

Note You should normally carry out input/output operations within a **try/catch** exception handling block. For more information, see the article Exceptions.

Closing Files

As usual in I/O operations, once you finish with a file, you must close it.

▶ **To close a file**

- Use the **Close** member function. This function closes the file-system file and flushes buffers if necessary.

If you allocated the **CFile** object on the frame (as in the examples shown earlier in this article), the object will automatically be closed and then destroyed when it goes out of scope. Note that deleting the **CFile** object does not delete the physical file in the file system.

Accessing File Status

CFile also supports getting file status, including whether the file exists, creation and modification dates and times, logical size, and path.

▶ **To get file status**

- Use the **CFile** class to get and set information about a file. One useful application is to use the **CFile** static member function **GetStatus** to determine if a file exists. **GetStatus** returns 0 if the specified file does not exist.

Thus, you could use the result of **GetStatus** to determine whether to use the **CFile::modeCreate** flag when opening a file, as shown by the following example:

```
CFile theFile;
char* szFileName = "c:\\test\\myfile.dat";
BOOL bOpenOK;

CFileStatus status;
if( CFile::GetStatus( szFileName, status ) )
{
    // Open the file without the Create flag
    bOpenOK = theFile.Open( szFileName,
                    CFile::modeWrite );
}
else
{
    // Open the file with the Create flag
    bOpenOK = theFile.Open( szFileName,
                    CFile::modeCreate | CFile::modeWrite );
}
```

See Also   Serialization (Object Persistence)

In the *Class Library Reference*: **CFile**

Find

Unlike the MFC DAO database classes, the MFC ODBC recordset class does not have a **Find** member function. For information about how to find records in an ODBC recordset, see the article Recordset: Scrolling (ODBC). For information about finding records with DAO, see **CDaoRecordset::Find**.

Forms

For information about form-based data-access programs, see the article Record Views.

For information about MFC support for form-based programs in general, see classes **CRecordView**, **CDaoRecordView**, **CDialog**, and **CFormView** in the *Class Library Reference*.

Framework

The Microsoft Foundation Class Library (MFC) is frequently referred to as "the framework" or "application framework." For an introduction and general information about the framework, see Part 1 of this book and the Scribble tutorial, Chapters 2 through 11 in *Tutorials*.

For further reading, see the article MFC.

See Also   CObject Class, MFC: Using Database Classes with Documents and Views, MFC: Using Database Classes Without Documents and Views

Help

This group of articles describes support provided by the Microsoft Foundation Class Library (MFC) for context-senstive Windows Help for your applications.

Applications written for Windows usually provide context-sensitive Help, allowing the user to get help on a particular window, dialog box, command, or toolbar button. MFC makes it simple to add context-sensitive Help to your application.

The user can access Help in the following ways:

- Pressing the F1 key

  The user can press the F1 key from an active window, dialog box, or message box, or with a menu item or toolbar button selected, to invoke a Help topic relevant to the selected item. For menu items, help is summoned for the item currently highlighted.

  Note You can define a key other than F1 for Help, but it is common among Windows applications to use F1.

- Entering Help mode

  From within an active application, the user can press SHIFT+F1 or click on the Help toolbar button to put the application into "Help mode."

  In Help mode, the mouse cursor changes to an arrow with a question mark. While the application is in this mode, the user can click any window, dialog box, message box, menu item, or toolbar button to summon help specific to the item. Help mode ends when Help is displayed. Pressing ESC or switching away from the application and back also ends Help mode.

- Using the Help menu

  Most applications provide help support through one or more menu items. For instance, most Windows applications include a Help menu item that invokes the application's Help file when chosen. Additional items on the Help menu might, for example, display a Search dialog.

This article presents an overview of the MFC help subsystem, in the following topics:

- Components of Help
- Help-menu support
- More precise context-sensitivity
- Help support tools
- Authoring and compiling Help

The following additional articles explain MFC help support in more detail:

- Help: F1 and SHIFT+F1 Help
- Help: OLE Support for Help
- Help: Message-Map Support
- Help: The Help Project File
- Help: The MAKEHM and MAKEHELP.BAT Tools
- Help: CPropertySheet and CPropertyPage
- Help: Authoring Help Topics

For a detailed example, see Chapter 11 in *Tutorials*. For additional technical information, see Technical Note 28 under MFC in Books Online.

Components of Help

The help subsystem in the MFC framework has the following components, many of which are supplied by AppWizard when you choose its Context-Sensitive Help option:

- A Help drop-down menu with several commands. For a new MDI application, there are two copies of this menu: one for an application with no open documents and one for each type of document that uses its own menu structure. AppWizard supplies these menus.

- Several message-map entries in your **CWinApp**-derived application class. These entries bind F1 and SHIFT+F1 commands to their respective command handlers. AppWizard supplies these message-map entries.

- Message handlers for F1 and SHIFT+F1. Class **CWinApp** supplies these handlers, and AppWizard supplies the message-map entries for them.

- The **CWinApp::WinHelp** member function, which calls the Windows Help program.

- Additional AppWizard support for help, including several help-related files. The files include skeleton .RTF files that contain help entries for the common elements of the Windows user interface, such as the File and Edit menus. You can edit these files to revise the supplied text and add your own application-specific help information.

- A mechanism and tool for mapping resource and command IDs in your application to "help contexts" in Windows Help. The MAKEHM tool is introduced in Using MAKEHM and MAKEHELP.BAT.

Help-Menu Support

The framework implements a Help Topics item in the Help menu. This item displays the table of contents for Help.

For a description of this support and its effect on the message map in your application class, see the article Help: Message-Map Support.

More Precise Context-Sensitivity

F1 help and SHIFT+F1 help are activated based on help context IDs. The standard help implementation in the framework can obtain a help context from a window, dialog box, message box, menu item, or toolbar button. If you need more precise control over this mechanism, you can override parts of the mechanism.

For additional information, see Technical Note 28 under MFC in Books Online.

Help Support Tools

You will use three main tools to develop your application's Help system: AppWizard, MAKEHM, and the Windows Help Compiler. You also need an editor, such as Microsoft Word for Windows, that can edit rich text format (.RTF) files. You can use the Visual C++ bitmap editor to create bitmaps to include in your Help files.

Note You can upgrade your Help Project files to a 4.0 format with the Windows 4.0 Help compiler. This gives you access to the Windows 4.0 Help Workshop, a graphical help authoring environment with many useful features. If you're planning on porting your applications to other platforms, first ensure that those platforms have a compiler that's compatible with the 4.0 Help Project file before upgrading.

Choosing the Help Option in AppWizard

AppWizard is your first tool for implementing context-sensitive Help. Check the Context-Sensitive Help checkbox in AppWizard. AppWizard then provides the message-map entries in your **CWinApp**-derived class that connect the whole help mechanism, adds a menu item to the Help menu, and adds a button to the toolbar resource that the user can press to invoke Help mode.

AppWizard also creates a set of skeletal starter files, as shown in Table 1.

Table 1   AppWizard-Supplied Help Files

File	Description
MAKEHELP.BAT	A batch file that manages help ID mapping and calls the Help Compiler.
HLP\\<project>.HPJ	A Windows Help project file that the Windows Help Compiler uses.
HLP\\<project>.CNT	A file containing the information needed to create the Help Contents screen.
HLP*.BMP	Various bitmap files used with the supplied Help files.
HLP*.RTF	Help files in .RTF format that contain starter help for the application components supplied by the framework.

The MAKEHELP.BAT file is in your project directory. The .BMP, .RTF, .CNT, and Help project file (.HPJ) are in an HLP subdirectory that AppWizard creates in your project directory.

You can edit these files as described in Authoring and Compiling Help to fill in application-specific help information.

Using MAKEHM and MAKEHELP.BAT

Once you've created an AppWizard application with help support, you can build help simply by choosing Build <project> from the Build menu in Developer Studio. This runs MAKEHELP.BAT to compile the .HPJ file and create an .HLP file. (You can also run MAKEHELP.BAT from the command line.)

The first thing that MAKEHELP.BAT does is call the MAKEHM tool. MAKEHM reads your project's RESOURCE.H file and creates a help mapping (.HM) file. This .HM file defines help-context IDs corresponding to the resource IDs in your RESOURCE.H file, so that each dialog, menu item, or other resource has a help-context ID associated with it.

Your project's .HPJ file contains a statement in its [MAP] section that includes your project's .HM file, as well as the standard .HM file included with MFC. The Help Compiler uses the help-context IDs in these .HM files to determine which Help topic is associated with each dialog, menu item, or other resource.

Whenever you add new resources to your project, you must add new Help topics for those resources to your .RTF files and then recompile your Help file. For more information, see Compiling Your Help Files.

After MAKEHELP.BAT runs the MAKEHM tool, it then calls the Windows Help Compiler to create the .HLP file. The Help Compiler creates the .HLP file in your application's main source code directory. If a WINDEBUG and/or WINREL subdirectory already exists, the MAKEHELP.BAT tool also copies the .HLP file to that subdirectory. This is useful because when you run either the Debug or Release version of your application, it will expect to find the .HLP file in the same directory as the debug or release executable file.

If you build a Debug or Release version of the application after you have already run MAKEHELP.BAT, and you don't need or care to rebuild the .HLP file, copy the .HLP file manually from the application source directory to the WINDEBUG or WINREL subdirectory.

If you add new resources for which you wish to implement help contexts, run MAKEHELP.BAT again by compiling the .HPJ from either the command line or from within Developer Studio.

Authoring and Compiling Help

For details about authoring and compiling Windows Help, see the *Help Compiler User's Guide*.

Figure 1 shows the general process for creating a Help system for your application.

Figure 1   Preparing Help Files

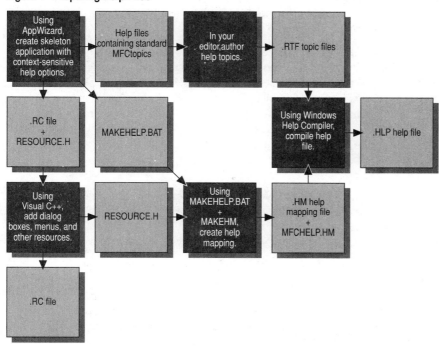

For an example of preparing Help files, see Chapter 11 in *Tutorials*.

See Also   Help: F1 and SHIFT+F1 Help

Help: F1 and SHIFT+F1 Help

This article describes the two forms of context-sensitive Windows Help supported by MFC.

F1 Help opens help on a topic associated with the currently selected item in your application. MFC supplies F1 help for windows, dialog boxes, message boxes, menus, and toolbar buttons.

SHIFT+F1 Help invokes a special "Help mode" in which the cursor turns into a Help cursor. The user can then select a visible object in the user interface, such as a menu item, toolbar button, or window. This opens help on a topic that describes the selected item.

F1 Help Support

The framework implements F1 help for windows, dialog boxes, message boxes, menus, and toolbar buttons. If the cursor is over a window, dialog box, or message box when the user presses the F1 key, the framework opens Windows Help for that window. If a menu item is highlighted, the framework opens Windows Help for that menu item. And if a toolbar button has been pressed (but the mouse not released yet), the framework opens Windows Help for that toolbar button when the user presses F1. (With extra work, you can implement F1 help for other things.)

When the user presses the F1 key, the framework processes the keystroke as a help request as follows, using a variation on the normal command routing. Pressing F1 causes a **WM_COMMAND** message to be sent for the **ID_HELP** command. If the application supports help, this command is mapped to the **OnHelp** message handler of class **CWinApp** and is routed directly there. **OnHelp** uses the ID of the current frame window or dialog box to determine the appropriate Help topic to display. If no specific Help topic is found, **OnHelp** displays the default Help topic.

SHIFT+F1 Help Support

If the user presses SHIFT+F1 or clicks on the Help toolbar button at any time that the application is active, the framework puts the application into Help mode and changes the cursor to a Help cursor (arrow + question mark). The next thing the user clicks determines what help context the framework opens in Windows Help.

When the user presses SHIFT+F1 or clicks on the Help toolbar button, the framework routes the command **ID_CONTEXT_HELP** through the normal command routing. The command is mapped to the **CWinApp** member function **OnContextHelp**, which captures the mouse, changes the cursor to a Help cursor, and puts the application into Help mode. The Help cursor is maintained as long as the application is in Help mode but reverts to a normal arrow cursor if it is not over the application that is in Help mode. Activating a different application cancels Help mode in the original application. While in Help mode, the application determines what object the user clicks and calls the **CWinApp** member function **WinHelp** with the appropriate context, determined from the object clicked upon. Once an object has been selected, Help mode ends and the cursor is restored to the normal arrow.

Note For information about how context-sensitive Help is managed in OLE applications, see the article Help: OLE Support for Help.

For more information, see Technical Note 28 under MFC Technical Notes in Books Online.

See Also Help: Message-Map Support

Help: OLE Support for Help

This article describes the requirements for Help support in OLE visual editing applications.

For SHIFT+F1 support, some special coordination is required between OLE containers and in-place active servers. When the user chooses to activate SHIFT+F1 Help mode, both applications need to enter the mode. Whichever application first gets the message to enter the mode notifies the other application. Then either application is prepared to respond when the user clicks the mouse on an item for which he or she wants help. Likewise, when the user terminates Help mode, the application that gets the message first notifies the other application. Note that MFC automatically handles this notification process between the container and the in-place server.

Caution Neither the container nor the server can enter SHIFT+F1 help mode unless the other application also supports the mode.

For F1 help support, by contrast, whichever application gets the message when F1 is pressed handles the help request.

See Also Help: Message-Map Support

Help: Message-Map Support

AppWizard adds a new menu command to the two Help menus: Help Topics. Support for this command and for F1 and SHIFT+F1 help is provided through the message map. Topics covered in this article include:

- Help commands in the message map
- About the Help commands
- Completing your application's Help

Help Commands in the Message Map

To support the Help Topics menu item, F1 help, and SHIFT+F1 help, AppWizard adds four entries to the message map for your **CFrameWnd**-derived or **CMDIFrameWnd**-derived class. This message map is in the MainFrm.cpp file, and the relevant message map entries are located below the `// Global help commands` comment.

After you run AppWizard, choosing the Context-Sensitive Help option, the message map for class CMainFrame will look like the following for an MDI application:

```
// CMainFrame

BEGIN_MESSAGE_MAP(CMainFrame, CMDIFrameWnd)
    //{{AFX_MSG_MAP(CMainFrame)

    // NOTE - the ClassWizard will add and remove mapping macros here.
    //  DO NOT EDIT what you see in these blocks of generated code !
    ON_WM_CREATE()
    //}}AFX_MSG_MAP
    // Global help commands
    ON_COMMAND(ID_HELP_FINDER, CMDIFrameWnd::OnHelpFinder)
    ON_COMMAND(ID_HELP, CMDIFrameWnd::OnHelp)
    ON_COMMAND(ID_CONTEXT_HELP, CMDIFrameWnd::OnContextHelp)
    ON_COMMAND(ID_DEFAULT_HELP, CMDIFrameWnd::OnHelpFinder)
END_MESSAGE_MAP()
```

For an SDI application, references to **CMDIFrameWnd** in this code are replaced by references to **CFrameWnd**.

About the Help Commands

The four help-related message-map entries follow the `// Global help commands` comment Table 1 explains the purpose of each command ID used in these entries.

Table 1   Help-Related Command IDs

Command ID	Purpose
ID_HELP_FINDER	Responds to the Help Topics item on the Help menu by displaying the Windows Contents screen.
ID_HELP	Responds to F1 by displaying a specific topic in Windows Help.
ID_CONTEXT_HELP	Responds to SHIFT+F1 by putting the application into Help mode.
ID_DEFAULT_HELP	Used when a specific help context cannot be found.

Notice that all of these commands are mapped to member functions of class **CMDIFrameWnd** (in the case of an MDI application); or to **CFrameWnd** (in the case of an SDI application). Unlike most of the other commands you place into the message map, these have handler functions predefined by the class library. Making the message-map entry enables the command.

The application's accelerator table defines F1 for **ID_HELP** and SHIFT+F1 for **ID_CONTEXT_HELP**. You can change the keys used for these help functions by using Visual C++ to change the key values in the accelerator table.

When the user chooses a Help menu command (or uses one of the context-sensitive Help techniques described in F1 Help Support and SHIFT+F1 Help Support in the article Help: F1 and SHIFT+F1 Help), the framework calls the **CWinApp::WinHelp** member function. This action, in turn, starts the Windows Help program and passes context information to it.

Completing Your Application's Help

Once you have used AppWizard to provide the generic help support, you can complete the help for your application by doing the following:

1. Add application-specific user-interface elements.

   Use Developer Studio to create your application's dialog boxes, menus, and other resources.

2. Write application-specific Help topics.

   Starting with the .RTF files supplied by AppWizard in your project's HLP subdirectory, remove topics that don't apply to your application, edit the remaining material, and add new topics for the menu commands, dialog boxes, toolbar buttons, and so on, that you added to your program. Each Help topic requires a help context ID; the help context is the same as the resource ID with an "H" added to the beginning. For example, if your application's RESOURCE.H file contains the resource ID ID_PEN_WIDTHS, write a topic with the help-context ID HID_PEN_WIDTHS.

This mapping between the resource ID and the help-context ID is established by the MAKEHM tool. Note that the .RTF file refers the context ID as a string, while the application and the framework refer to the context ID as a number. The article Help: Authoring Help Topics describes the process of mapping these IDs to Help topics and writing the topics in your .RTF files.

3. Compile Help.

   If you want to compile your application help from the command line instead of from within Developer's Studio, the Windows Help Compiler and MAKEHM.EXE must be in your path statement. To ensure that this is the case (and to set other relevant environment variables for a specific build target) you may want to run the VCVARS32 batch file. In general, it's a good idea to run VCVARS32 prior to running build tools such as MAKEHELP from the command line.

   Note By default AppWizard generates the Help Project files in Windows 3.1 format. When you use the VC++ tools to compile your Help Project, the result is a system compatible with either Windows 3.1 or 4.0. If porting your applications to other environments is not an issue, you can also easily convert your Help Project to the 4.0 format. For more information, see Upgrading Your Help Project File to Windows 95.

▶ **To run VCVARS32.BAT**

- At the command line, type:

      VCVARS32 [*target*]

  where target is one of the following: x86, m68k, mppc.

▶ **To compile your Help files from the command line**

1 At the command line, change to the root directory of your Help Project.

   AppWizard copies MAKEHELP.BAT to this directory by default.

2 Type MAKEHELP and press ENTER.

   The MAKEHM tools creates a .HM file and the Windows Help compiler generates your application help (.HLP) file.

▶ **To compile your Help files from within the Developer Studio**

1 From the Build pane of the Project workspace, select your Help Project (.HPJ) file. (You needn't open the file, but it must remain selected while you perform the next step.)

2 From the Build menu, choose Compile.

This calls MAKEHELP.BAT, which in turn calls the following two programs:

- MAKEHM.EXE, a program that generates your context-sensitive topic IDs, and

- Windows Help Compiler, which builds your .HLP file.

See Also   Example Help Contexts

Help: The Help Project File

This article describes the Help Project (.HPJ) file that AppWizard creates for you.

The Help Project file provides information used by the Windows Help Compiler. You can view the .HPJ file using the Microsoft Help Workshop (HCW.EXE); you can also use a text editor. Following is the .HPJ file for the Scribble sample application. When you create your project with AppWizard and choose the Context-Sensitive Help option, your application's .HPJ file will look similar:

```
[OPTIONS]
CONTENTS=new_index
TITLE=Scribble Application Help
COMPRESS=true
WARNING=2
REPORT=Yes
BMROOT=..,.
ROOT=..,.

[FILES]
afxcore.rtf
afxprint.rtf

...

[ALIAS]
HIDR_MAINFRAME = main_index
HIDR_SCRIBBTYPE = HIDR_DOC1TYPE
HIDD_ABOUTBOX = HID_APP_ABOUT

HID_HT_SIZE = HID_SC_SIZE
HID_HT_HSCROLL = scrollbars
HID_HT_VSCROLL = scrollbars
HID_HT_MINBUTTON = HID_SC_MINIMIZE
HID_HT_MAXBUTTON = HID_SC_MAXIMIZE
AFX_HIDP_INVALID_FILENAME   = AFX_HIDP_default
AFX_HIDP_FAILED_TO_OPEN_DOC = AFX_HIDP_default

...

[MAP]
#include <C:\MSDEV\MFC\include\afxhelp.hm>
#include <hlp\scribble.hm>
```

This file lists options used by the Windows Help Compiler, the topic files with the .RTF extension to be used for the help build, bitmap files to be included in the build, equivalencies between context strings, mapping files, and more.

Of particular interest is the [MAP] section, which in this example points to two included files with the .HM (help mapping) extension.

Note Keep in mind when you name your .HPJ file that the name cannot contain spaces. Including a space in the file name causes help to compile incorrectly.

The article Help: The MAKEHM and MAKEHELP.BAT Tools explains more about help-context mapping. For more information about Windows Help project files, see the *Tools User's Guide* for Microsoft Win32.

See Also Help: The MAKEHM and MAKEHELP.BAT Tools

Help: The MAKEHM and MAKEHELP.BAT Tools

This article describes the tools you use to map help context IDs in your application which maps to Help topics in your Help file. Topics covered include:

- Help context IDs
- Preferred resource ID prefixes
- Example help contexts
- Running the tools

In Windows Help, a "help context" consists of a string and an ID number. The help context string is what the help text author uses to identify Help topics. The help context ID number is what the programmer associates with each resource. The context strings and ID numbers are mapped together in the [MAP] section of the .HPJ file. When your application calls Windows Help, Windows Help uses the context ID your application passes to locate and display the Help topic denoted by that context. At run time, the framework manages supplying the appropriate help context ID.

To facilitate relating the windows, dialog boxes, and commands in your application to Windows Help contexts, MFC provides the MAKEHM.EXE tool, which creates the information used in the [MAP] section of the .HPJ file.

AppWizard creates a MAKEHELP.BAT file that you'll use, directly or indirectly, to compile your help. MAKEHELP.BAT calls MAKEHM.EXE and then calls the Windows Help Compiler.

Help Context IDs

When you use Visual C++ to create dialog-template resources, menu commands, and the like, Visual C++ writes **#define** statements in a file named RESOURCE.H. For example, there might be **#define** statements for such symbols as IDD_MY_DIALOG and ID_PEN_WIDTHS.

The following illustrates the resource IDs that Visual C++ creates in your RESOURCE.H file and the help context IDs that the MAKEHM tool creates. IDs in RESOURCE.H like

```
#define IDD_MY_DIALOG    2000
#define ID_MY_COMMAND     150
```

would be translated by MAKEHM into

```
HIDD_MY_DIALOG      0x207d0
HID_MY_COMMAND      0x10096
```

Dialog-box IDs are translated to values beginning at 0x20000. Command and resource IDs are translated to values beginning at 0x10000. That is, the framework reserves specific ranges of values for different kinds of objects. For details, see the contents of MAKEHELP.BAT and Technical Note 28 under MFC Technical Notes in Books Online.

This format is compatible with the Help Compiler, which maps context IDs (the numbers on the right side) to context strings (the symbols on the left). Use these context strings in the .RTF Help files to identify topics.

For more information about how Visual C++ adds symbols to RESOURCE.H and how you can view and manipulate them with the Visual C++ Symbol Browser, see Browsing Through Symbols, in the *Visual C++ User's Guide*.

Preferred Resource ID Prefixes

To facilitate using MAKEHELP.BAT and MAKEHM, observe the conventions in specifying IDs for your resource objects, as shown in Table 1. It is important that different kinds of resource objects have different ID prefixes.

Table 1   Preferred Resource ID Naming Conventions

Predefined ID	Object
IDP_	Message-box prompt
IDD_	Dialog-box ID
ID_	Toolbar or menu command (**IDM_** is okay too)
IDR_	Frame-related resources
IDW_	Control bar

For example, here's a call to the MAKEHM tool in the MAKEHELP.BAT file for the Scribble tutorial application:

```
makehm IDD_,HIDD_,0x20000 resource.h >> hlp\scribble.hm
```

MAKEHELP.BAT expects dialog resources to be named with **IDD_** prefixes. The corresponding help contexts will be named with **HIDD_** prefixes.

Note   The Scribble tutorial teaches MFC programming techniques. See *Tutorials*.

Use the **IDS_** prefix for normal string resources, and do not write Help topics for
them. For string resources used in message boxes, use the **IDP_** prefix and write Help
topics for them so the user can get context-sensitive Help by pressing F1 while the
message box is displayed.

Example Help Contexts

As your application grows, you'll define a number of new IDs (symbols). For
example, the following lists the RESOURCE.H file for the Scribble application after
Step 6 of the tutorial:

```
//{{NO_DEPENDENCIES}}
// Visual C++ generated include file.
// Used by SCRIBBLE.RC
//
#define IDD_ABOUTBOX            100
#define IDR_MAINFRAME           128
#define IDR_SCRIBBTYPE          129
#define IDD_PEN_WIDTHS          131
#define IDC_THIN_PEN_WIDTH      1000
#define IDC_THICK_PEN_WIDTH     1001
#define IDC_DEFAULT_PEN_WIDTHS  1002
#define ID_PEN_THICK_OR_THIN    32771
#define ID_PEN_WIDTHS           32772
```

Symbols defined for the Scribble tutorial include IDR_SCRIBBTYPE (Scribble's menus
and other application-specific resources), IDD_PEN_WIDTHS (a Pen Widths dialog box),
ID_PEN_THICK_OR_THIN (a Thick Line command), and so on. Notice that one Scribble
command, **ID_EDIT_CLEAR_ALL**, doesn't appear in RESOURCE.H because it's
predefined ID in the class library. AppWizard will already have generated a Help
topic for it in the .RTF files it created to get you started.

MAKEHM maps these symbols to Windows Help contexts when you run
MAKEHELP.BAT. The following excerpt from a MAKEHELP.BAT file for the
Scribble tutorial shows how MAKEHELP.BAT calls MAKEHM:

```
...
echo // Commands (ID_* and IDM_*) >>hlp\scribble.hm
makehm ID_,HID_,0x10000 IDM_,HIDM_,0x10000 resource.h >>hlp\scribble.hm
echo. >>hlp\scribble.hm
echo // Prompts (IDP_*) >>hlp\scribble.hm
makehm IDP_,HIDP_,0x30000 resource.h >>hlp\scribble.hm
echo. >>hlp\scribble.hm
echo // Resources (IDR_*) >>hlp\scribble.hm
makehm IDR_,HIDR_,0x20000 resource.h >>hlp\scribble.hm
.
.
.
REM -- Make help for Project SCRIBBLE
...
start /wait hcrtf -x "hlp\scribble.hpj"
echo.
```

After you run MAKEHELP.BAT, the SCRIBBLE.HM file looks like the following:

```
// MAKEHELP.BAT generated Help Map file.  Used by SCRIBBLE.HPJ.

// Commands (ID_* and IDM_*)
HID_PEN_THICK_OR_THIN          0x18003
HID_PEN_WIDTHS                 0x18004

// Prompts (IDP_*)

// Resources (IDR_*)
HIDR_MAINFRAME                 0x20080
HIDR_SCRIBBTYPE                0x20081

// Dialogs (IDD_*)
HIDD_ABOUTBOX                  0x20064
HIDD_PEN_WIDTHS                0x20083

// Frame Controls (IDW_*)
```

This file contains help contexts for two commands, two resources (menus and other application resources), and two dialog boxes.

Running the Tools

When you build the .HPJ file from within Developer Studio, or when you run MAKEHELP.BAT from the command line, MAKEHELP.BAT calls the MAKEHM tool to map the **#define** statements in RESOURCE.H to Windows Help strings in an .HM file. The MAKEHM tool collects **#define** statements from RESOURCE.H and uses the command-line parameters passed to MAKEHM to map defined symbols to help strings in a .HM file. For the example IDs in the previous paragraph, it would create help strings such as HIDD_MY_DIALOG and HID_PEN_WIDTHS. These context strings are formed by prefixing an "H" to the symbol found in RESOURCE.H. MAKEHM also maps the ID's numeric value to a corresponding number for the help context. An example is shown in Example Help Contexts.

When MAKEHELP.BAT runs the Windows Help Compiler, the compiler uses the .HM files pointed to by the .HPJ file to set up the help contexts in your new Help file. Once you finish compiling your .HLP file, you can use it from your application.

See Also   Help: Authoring Help Topics

Help: CPropertySheet and CPropertyPage

Objects of class **CPropertySheet** represent property sheets, also called tab dialog boxes. A property sheet consists of a **CPropertySheet** object and one or more **CPropertyPage** objects. A property sheet is displayed by the framework as a window with a set of tab indices, with which the user selects the current page, and an area for the currently selected page.

Using Help

Help in **CPropertySheet** is supported by the F1 key and the Help button only. The Help button appears in the application framework by default. No intervention by the user is necessary. When the user adds the help information for each of the pages inside the property sheet, the help mechanism automatically displays the help for that page when the Help button is clicked.

You can deactivate the Help button capability by modifying **m_psh** in the property sheet object as follows:

```
mySheet.m_psh->dwFlags &= ~(PSH_HASHELP)
```

You can activate the Help button again with the following:

```
mySheet.m_psh->dwFlags |= PSH_HASHELP
```

The **m_psh** flag in **CPropertyPage** determines if the Help button of the property sheet (the parent of the property page) is enabled or disabled.

See Also   In the *Class Library Reference*: **CPropertyPage**, **CPropertySheet**

Help: Authoring Help Topics

The framework manages navigation from application user interfaces to help contexts. Implementing further navigation within the Help file is the domain of help authoring rather than programming. The purpose of this article is to describe the general process of authoring and editing Help topic files. Topics covered include:

- Editing the starter .RTF files
- Help topics in the .RTF file
- Topic examples
- Compiling and testing your Help file

Editing the Help topics for any application is too big a task to work through in just one article; however a few examples will help you get started. The examples in this article were edited with Microsoft Word for Windows, but you can use any application that can edit rich text format (.RTF) files. To make the following discussion concrete, the examples are drawn from the Scribble tutorial program, presented in Chapters 2 through 12 of *Tutorials*. If you want to see how Help is prepared for Scribble, look at Adding Context-Sensitive Help, in that book.

When you run AppWizard to start the Scribble tutorial, the wizard creates not only source code files but also a set of files in rich text format (.RTF) containing starter Help topics for many of the user-interface elements that Scribble will have, including its menu commands. To complete a Help file for Scribble, follow the steps outlined in this group of Help articles. Then edit the .RTF files to fill in help material that AppWizard couldn't supply.

You can easily upgrade your Help project files to a 4.0 format with the Windows 4.0 Help compiler included with Visual C++ version 4.0. This gives you access to the Windows 4.0 Help Workshop, a graphical help authoring environment with many useful features. Before you port any of your applications to other platforms, you must make sure that those platforms have a compiler that's compatible with the 4.0 Help project file before upgrading.

The discussion in the rest of this article takes you through part of that process to illustrate the techniques and to point out some guidelines and tips. Scribble is used here merely as an example.

Editing the Starter .RTF Files

The .RTF files that AppWizard creates for an application—such as Scribble— contain starter Help topics for many elements of the Windows user interface. Some of them are fairly complete, while others are skeletal and must be filled out.

If you want to customize the Help topics supplied by AppWizard, you must do the following, using all of the .RTF files in your project's HLP subdirectory (for example, \MYSCRIB\HLP):

- Globally replace the placeholder string "<<YourApp>>" in the .RTF files with the name of the application: for example, replace "<<YourApp>>" with "Scribble".

- From the Help topics, remove any references to menu items absent in your application. Add any additional menu items to the .CNT file, which contains the information needed to create the Help Contents screen.

   For example, file PEN.RTF contains a topic for the Edit Links command, which Scribble doesn't support.

- Replace the directives in the Help topics with your own information. These directives are bracketed by << and >> symbols.

   Notice that because the class library predefines **ID_EDIT_CLEAR_ALL**, Scribble's file PEN.RTF already contains a Help topic for the Clear All command added to the Edit menu in the Scribble tutorial. However, the skeletal directive for such commands, "<< Write application-specific help here. >>," needs to be replaced with a real description.

- Add topics for new commands and dialog boxes.

   Examine the listing of RESOURCE.H in Example Help Contexts in the article Help: The MAKEHM and MAKEHELP.BAT Tools. It lists the following Help topics (as seen in Scribble):

   - Two resource-related HIDs (**HIDR_**), for menus and related resources

   - Two dialog-box HIDs (**HIDD_**), for the About and Pen Widths dialog boxes

   - Two command HIDs (**HID_**), for the Thick Line and Pen Widths commands

In the Scribble tutorial, the Pen Widths dialog box is new, so new Help topics are needed for the dialog box and for two new commands. (The About dialog box is created by AppWizard, so it already has a topic in PEN.RTF.)

Help Topics in the .RTF File

Help topics in an .RTF file are separated by hard page breaks. Each topic has a name and a "footnote" symbol (#).

The footnote symbol (#) identifies a context string in the .RTF file as a "jump" or a "popup". When the user clicks on a hot-link to a context string, a jump takes the user to another topic screen in the Help system, while a popup displays a small popup window containing extra information.

Other possible footnote symbols identify keywords for searching (K) and topic names ($). For more information, see the *Tools User's Guide* in the Win32 SDK. If you're using Word for Windows for .RTF files, you can examine the file PEN.RTF with hidden text displayed.

Topic Examples

To illustrate the process of adding topics, this section shows the structure needed for a user to jump from the main contents screen in Help to a screen showing general information about the new Pen menu, and from there to screens that describe the Scribble tutorial application's two Pen menu commands. These items are added to the PEN.RTF file.

The Main Contents Screen

Figure 1 shows the Help topic for the main contents screen as it appears in Microsoft Word for Windows (with hidden text displayed). The screen contains entries for six menus: File, Edit, View, Pen, Window, and Help. The Pen menu is Scribble-specific, so this jump has been added. The others are created by AppWizard.

Figure 1   The Main Contents Screen in PEN.RTF

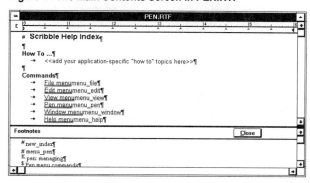

Each of the menu names on this screen is a "hot spot" that links to another topic. By clicking this hot spot, the user can jump to another screen in the Help system. If you examine this screen in the PEN.RTF file using Word for Windows, you see that the menu names—such as "Pen Menu"— are formatted with double underlining. (This might be represented differently by another RTF editor.) Each menu name is followed immediately by a context name formatted as hidden text. For the Pen menu, this text reads "menu_pen."

The Pen Menu Screen

Figure 2 shows the text in PEN.RTF for a Help screen about the Pen Menu topic. The upper part of the figure shows the text of the file; the lower part shows footnote text. All formatting and hidden text are displayed.

Figure 2   The Pen Menu Topic in the PEN.RTF File

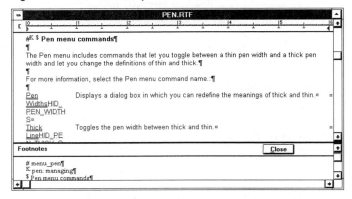

The topic screen begins with a hard page break. The next line shows the footnote character, #, followed by the title to be displayed on the user's screen, "Pen menu commands." The rest of the screen contains descriptive text and two more hot spots for jumping to screens about the individual menu items.

The footnote text associated with the # footnote for the Pen menu is "menu_pen," which is the help context; jumps to this screen of the Help system must specifiy this help context.

Setting up this screen requires entering the hard page break and the footnote, then writing the text. In Word for Windows, for example, you use the Break command on the Insert menu to enter a hard page break. Then you use the Footnote entry on the Insert menu to specify a footnote with the special footnote character #.

Next, type the footnote text in the footnote window. Finally, type the descriptive text and format the hot-links.

A hot-link consist of the two parts:

- Visible text, such as "Pen Widths," formatted as double underlined, to designate how the hot-link looks onscreen.
- Hidden text, such as "pen_widths," to designate the help context of the destination topic.

In the RTF files that AppWizard supplies, tables (as in Word for Windows) are used to present groups of jumps, but help authors are not required to use tables.

A Screen for a Menu Item

Figure 3 shows a screen for the Pen Widths and Thick Line menu items.

Figure 3   The Pen Widths and Thick Line Topics in the PEN.RTF File

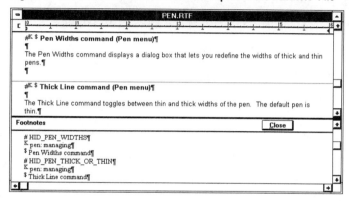

The screen is set up similarly to its parent screen for the Pen menu as a whole. Notice the text used for the footnotes in the lower part of Figure 3.

Compiling and Testing Your Help File

Once your Help authoring is finished, you can compile your Help file. If you're trying out the techniques described in these articles, perhaps by working through the Scribble tutorial in *Tutorials*, and you've chosen to author the application's Help files, use the following procedure to see the results.

▶ **To compile and test the application's Help**

Use one of the following methods to compile Help:

- Run MAKEHELP.BAT from the command line.

  –or–

- Compile the Help project (.HPJ) file from within Developer Studio.

▶ **To compile your Help files from the command line**

1 At the command line, change to the root directory of your Help project.

  AppWizard copies MAKEHELP.BAT to this directory by default.

2 Type MAKEHELP and press ENTER.

The Windows Help compiler generates your application Help (.HLP) file.

▶ To compile your Help files from within Developer Studio

1 From the FileView pane of the Project workspace window, select your Help project (.HPJ) file. (You needn't open the file; but it must remain selected while you perform the next step.)

2 From the Build menu, choose Compile.

This calls MAKEHELP.BAT, which in turn calls the Windows Help Compiler. As the compiler runs, it prints a row of dots in the Visual C++ output window, displaying any errors in the help build process.

See Also   Help: The Help Project File, Help: The MAKEHM and MAKEHELP.BAT Tools

In-Place Activation

See the article Servers: Implementing In-Place Frame Windows.

In-Place Editing

See the article Servers: Implementing In-Place Frame Windows.

Library Versions

This article provides information on available versions of the MFC. Topics covered include:

- Automatic linking of MFC library version
- Library naming conventions
- AFXDLL versions
- Dynamic-Link Library (DLL) support

Automatic Linking of MFC Library Version

In versions of MFC prior to version 3.0 (prior to Visual C++ version 2.0), you had to manually specify the correct version of the MFC library in the input list of libraries for the linker. With MFC version 3.0 and later, it is no longer necessary to manually specify the version of the MFC library. Instead, the MFC header files automatically determine the correct version of the MFC library, based on values defined with **#define**, such as **_DEBUG** or **_UNICODE**. The MFC header files add "/defaultlib" directives instructing the linker to link in a specific version of the MFC library.

For example, the following code fragment from the AFX.H header file instructs the linker to link in either the NAFXCWD.LIB or NAFXCW.LIB version of MFC, depending on whether you are using the debug version of MFC:

```
...
#ifndef _UNICODE
    #ifdef _DEBUG
        #pragma comment(lib, "nafxcwd.lib")
    #else
        #pragma comment(lib, "nafxcw.lib")
    #endif
#else
    #ifdef _DEBUG
        #pragma comment(lib, "uafxcwd.lib")
    #else
        #pragma comment(lib, "uafxcw.lib")
    #endif
#endif...
```

MFC header files also link in all required libraries, including MFC libraries, Win32 libraries, OLE libraries, OLE libraries built from samples, ODBC libraries, and so on. The Win32 libraries include KERNEL32.LIB, USER32.LIB, and GDI32.LIB.

Library Naming Conventions

Object-code libraries for MFC use the following naming conventions. The library names have the form *u*AFX*c*W*d*.LIB

where the letters shown in italic lowercase are placeholders for specifiers whose meanings are shown in Table 1:

Table 1 Library Naming Conventions

Specifier	Values and meanings
u	ANSI (N) or Unicode (U)
c	Type of program to create: C=all
d	Debug or Release: D=Debug; omit specifier for Release

The default is to build a debug Windows ANSI application for the Intel® platform: NAFXCWD.LIB. All libraries—listed in Table 2—are included prebuilt in the MFC\LIB directory on the Visual C++ CD-ROM.

Table 2 Static Library Versions

Library	Description
NAFXCW.LIB	Release version
NAFXCWD.LIB	Debug version (default)
UAFXCW.LIB	Release version with Unicode support
UAFXCWD.LIB	Debug version with Unicode support

Note If you need to build a library version, see the README.TXT file in \MFC\SRC directory. This file describes using the supplied MAKEFILE with NMAKE.

AFXDLL Versions

Instead of building your application by statically linking to the MFC object-code libraries, you can build your application to use one of the AFXDLL libraries—which contain MFC in a DLL that multiple running applications can share. For a table of AFXDLL names, see the article DLLs: Naming Conventions.

Note By default, AppWizard creates an AFXDLL project. To use static linking of MFC code instead, set the Use MFC in a static library option in AppWizard.

Dynamic-Link Library Support

The NAFXDWD.LIB and NAFXDW.LIB libraries create your project as a dynamic-link library, called a "Regular DLL," (formerly a "USRDLL") that can be used with applications not built with the class library. Don't confuse this DLL support with MFCx0.DLL and MFCx0D.DLL (known as AFXDLL), which contain the entire 32-bit class library in a DLL. For more information, see the article Dynamic-Link Libraries (DLLs). For a table of DLL names, see the article DLLs: Naming Conventions.

See Also Dynamic-Link Libraries (DLLs)

Linked OLE Item

See the article Activation.

Mail API

See MAPI and MAPI Support in MFC.

MAPI

This article describes MAPI, the Microsoft Messaging Application Programming Interface for client message application developers. MFC supplies support for a subset of MAPI in class **CDocument** but does not encapsulate the entire API. For more information, see MAPI Support in MFC.

MAPI is a set of functions that mail-enabled and mail-aware applications use to create, manipulate, transfer, and store mail messages. It gives application developers the tools to define the purpose and content of mail messages, and gives them flexibility in their management of stored mail messages. MAPI also provides a common interface that application developers can use to create mail-enabled and mail-aware applications independent of the underlying messaging system.

Messaging clients provide a human interface for interaction with the Microsoft Windows Messaging System (WMS). This interaction typically includes requesting services from MAPI-compliant providers such as message stores and address books.

For more information about MAPI, see the following MAPI Software Development Kit (SDK) documents: the *Client Developer's Guide* and the *Provider Developer's Guide*.

See Also   MAPI Support in MFC

In the *Class Library Reference*: **CDocument::OnFileSendMail**, **CDocument::OnUpdateFileSendMail, COleDocument::OnFileSendMail**

MAPI Support in MFC

MFC supplies support for a subset of the Microsoft Messaging Application Program Interface (MAPI) in class **CDocument**. Specifically, **CDocument** has member functions that determine whether mail support is present on the end-user's machine and, if so, enable a Send Mail command whose standard command ID is **ID_FILE_SEND_MAIL**. The MFC handler function for this command allows the user to send a document via electronic mail.

Tip   Although MFC does not encapsulate the entire MAPI function set, you can still call MAPI functions directly, just as you can call Win32 API functions directly from MFC programs.

Providing the Send Mail command in your application is very easy. MFC provides the implementation to package a document (that is, a **CDocument**-derived object) as an attachment and send it as mail. This attachment is equivalent to a File Save command that saves (serializes) the document's contents to the mail message. This implementation calls upon the mail client on the user's machine to give the user the opportunity to address the mail and to add subject and message text to the mail message. Users see their familiar mail application's user interface. This functionality is supplied by two **CDocument** member functions: **OnFileSendMail** and **OnUpdateFileSendMail**.

MAPI needs to read the file to send the attachment. If the application keeps its data file open during an **OnFileSendMail** function call, the file needs to be opened with a share mode that allows multiple processes to access the file.

Note An overriding version of **OnFileSendMail** for class **COleDocument** correctly handles compound documents.

▶ **To implement a Send Mail command with MFC**

1 Use the Visual C++ menu editor to add a menu item whose command ID is **ID_FILE_SEND_MAIL**.

This command ID is provided by the framework in AFXRES.H. The command can be added to any menu, but it is usually added to the File menu.

2 Manually add the following to your document's message map:

```
ON_COMMAND(ID_FILE_SEND_MAIL, OnFileSendMail)
ON_UPDATE_COMMAND_UI(ID_FILE_SEND_MAIL, OnUpdateFileSendMail)
```

Place the new lines outside of the special "//{{AFX" comments.

Note This message map works for a document derived from either **CDocument** or **COleDocument**—it picks up the correct base class in either case, even though the message map is in your derived document class.

3 Build your application.

If mail support is available, MFC enables your menu item with **OnUpdateFileSendMail** and subsequently processes the command with **OnFileSendMail**. If mail support is not available, MFC automatically removes your menu item so the user will not see it.

Tip Rather than manually adding message map entries as described above, you can use ClassWizard to add them, although the method is indirect. To use ClassWizard, add an OnFileSendMail command handler and an OnUpdateFileSendMail command update handler as you normally would. This gives you two empty handlers which effectively override the **OnFileSendMail** and **OnUpdateFileSendMail** handlers in **CDocument**, which contain the MAPI implementations. To use those implementations, call the base-class versions of **OnFileSendMail** and **OnUpdateFileSendMail** in your new handlers. While this approach works, manually adding the message map entries, as described in the procedure above, is quicker and more direct.

Note also that AppWizard lets you select an option that adds MAPI support directly to your new MFC application. If you use that option, you can skip steps 1 and 2 above.

See Also MAPI

In the *Class Library Reference*: **CDocument::OnFileSendMail**,
CDocument::OnUpdateFileSendMail, **COleDocument::OnFileSendMail**

Managing the State Data of MFC Modules

This article discusses the state data of MFC modules and how this state is updated
when the flow of execution (the path code takes through an application when
executing) enters and leaves a module. Switching module states with the
AFX_MANAGE_STATE and **METHOD_PROLOGUE** macros is also discussed.

Note The term "module" here refers to an executable program, or to a DLL (or set of DLLs)
that operate independently of the rest of the application, but uses a shared copy of the MFC
DLL. An OLE control is a typical example of a module.

As shown in Figure 1, MFC has state data for each mocule used in an application.
Examples of this data include: Windows instance handles (used for loading
resources), pointers to the current **CWinApp** and **CWinThread** objects of an
application, OLE module reference counts, and a variety of maps that maintain the
connections between Windows object handles and corresponding instances of MFC
objects. However, when an application uses multiple modules, the state data of each
module is not application-wide. Rather, each module has its own private copy of the
MFC's state data.

Figure 1   State Data of a Single Module (Application).

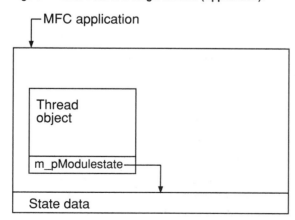

A module's state data is contained in a structure, and is always via a pointer to that
structure. When the flow of execution enters a particular module (as shown in Figure
2), that module's state must be the "current" or "effective" state. Therefore, each
thread object has a pointer to the effective state structure of that application. Keeping
this pointer updated at all times is vital to managing the application's global state and

maintaining the integrity of each module's state. Incorrect management of the global state can lead to unpredictable application behaviour.

Figure 2   State Data of Multiple Modules

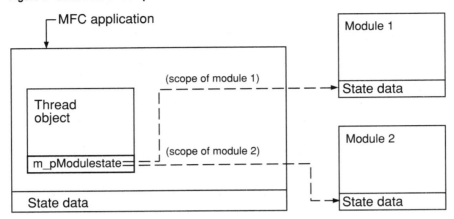

In other words, each module is responsible for correctly switching between module states at all of its entry points. An "entry point" is any place where the flow of execution can enter the module's code. Entry points include:

- Exported functions in a DLL

- Member functions of OLE/COM interfaces

- Window procedures

Exported DLL Function Entry Points

For exported functions of a DLL, use the **AFX_MANAGE_STATE** macro to maintain the proper global state when switching from the DLL module to the calling application's DLL.

When called, this macro sets *pModuleState*, a parameter of type **AFX_MODULE_STATE***, as the effective module state for the remainder of the containing scope of the function. Upon leaving the scope containing the macro, the previous effective module state is automatically restored.

This switching is achieved by constructing an instance of a class on the stack. In its constructor, this class obtains a pointer to the current module state and stores it in a member variable, and then sets *pModuleState* as the new effective module state. In its destructor, this class restores the pointer stored in its member variable as the effective module state.

OLE/COM Interface Entry Points

For member functions of an OLE/COM interface, use the **METHOD_PROLOGUE** macro to maintain the proper global state when calling methods of an exported interface.

Typically, member functions of interfaces implemented by **CCmdTarget**-derived objects already use this macro to provide automatic initialization of the *pThis* pointer. For additional information, see Technical Note 38, MFC/OLE IUnknown Implementation, under MFC Technical Notes in Books Online.

The portion of the macro concerned with managing the global state is equivalent to the following expression:

```
AFX_MANAGE_STATE( pThis->m_pModuleState )
```

In this expression, *m_pModuleState* is assumed to be a member variable of the containing object. It is implemented by the **CCmdTarget** base class, and is initialized to the appropriate value by **COleObjectFactory**, when the object is instantiated.

Window Procedure Entry Points

To protect MFC window procedures, a module static links with a special window procedure implementation. The linkage occurs automatically when the module is linked with MFC. This window procedure uses the **AFX_MANAGE_STATE** macro to properly set the effective module state, then it calls **AfxWndProc**, which in turn delegates to the **WindowProc** member function of the appropriate **CWnd**-derived object.

MBCS

Multibyte Character Set encoding. In Visual C++, MBCS support is limited to double byte character set (DBCS) encoding. MFC supports both DBCS and Unicode.

For information about using DBCS with MFC, see Chapter 13, Developing for International Markets, in *Programming Techniques*.

Memory Management

This group of articles describes how to take advantage of the general-purpose services of the MFC related to memory management. Memory allocation can be divided into two main categories: frame allocations and heap allocations.

One main difference between the two allocation techniques is that with frame allocation you typically work with the actual memory block itself, whereas with heap allocation you are always given a pointer to the memory block. Another major difference between the two schemes is that frame objects are automatically deleted, while heap objects must be explicitly deleted by the programmer.

The following articles describe how to use the capabilities of C and C++ to accomplish memory allocations on the frame and on the heap:

- Memory Management: Frame Allocation
- Memory Management: Heap Allocation
- Memory Management: Memory Allocation on the Frame and on the Heap
- Memory Management: Resizable Memory Blocks

The third article above demonstrates MFC memory allocation techniques.

Memory Management: Frame Allocation

Allocation on the frame takes its name from the "stack frame" that is set up whenever a function is called. The stack frame is an area of memory that temporarily holds the arguments to the function as well as any variables that are defined local to the function. Frame variables are often called "automatic" variables because the compiler automatically allocates the space for them.

There are two key characteristics of frame allocations. First, when you define a local variable, enough space is allocated on the stack frame to hold the entire variable, even if it is a large array or data structure. Second, frame variables are automatically deleted when they go out of scope:

```
void MyFunction( )
{
    // Local object created on the stack
    CString strName;
    ...
    // Object goes out of scope and is deleted as function ends
}
```

For local function variables, this scope transition happens when the function exits, but the scope of a frame variable can be smaller than a function if nested braces are used. This automatic deletion of frame variables is very important. In the case of simple primitive types (such as **int** or **byte**), arrays, or data structures, the automatic deletion simply reclaims the memory used by the variable. Since the variable has gone out of scope, it cannot be accessed anyway. In the case of C++ objects, however, the process of automatic deletion is a bit more complicated.

When an object is defined as a frame variable, its constructor is automatically invoked at the point where the definition is encountered. When the object goes out of scope, its destructor is automatically invoked before the memory for the object is reclaimed. This automatic construction and destruction can be very handy, but you must be aware of the automatic calls, especially to the destructor.

The key advantage of allocating objects on the frame is that they are automatically deleted. When you allocate your objects on the frame, you don't have to worry about forgotten objects causing memory leaks. (For details on memory leaks, see the article Diagnostics: Detecting Memory Leaks.) A disadvantage of frame allocation is that frame variables cannot be used outside their scope. Another factor in choosing frame allocation versus heap allocation is that for large structures and objects, it is often better to use the heap instead of the stack for storage since stack space is often limited.

Memory Management: Heap Allocation

The heap is reserved for the memory allocation needs of the program. It is an area apart from the program code and from the stack. Typical C programs use the functions **malloc** and **free** to allocate and deallocate heap memory. The Debug version of the provides modified versions of the C++ built-in operators **new** and **delete** to allocate and deallocate objects in heap memory.

When you use **new** and **delete** instead of **malloc** and **free**, you are able to take advantage of the class library's memory-management debugging enhancements, which can be useful in detecting memory leaks. When you build your program with the Release version of the , the standard versions of the **new** and **delete** operators provide an efficient way to allocate and deallocate memory (the Release version of the does not provide modified versions of these operators).

Note that the total size of objects allocated on the heap is limited only by your system's available virtual memory.

Memory Management: Allocation on the Frame and on the Heap

This article describes how MFC performs frame allocations and heap allocations for each of the three typical kinds of memory allocations:

- An array of bytes
- A data structure
- An object

Allocation of an Array of Bytes

▶ **To allocate an array of bytes on the frame**

- Define the array as shown by the following code. The array is automatically deleted and its memory reclaimed when the array variable exits its scope.

```
{
    const int BUFF_SIZE = 128;

    // Allocate on the frame
    char myCharArray[BUFF_SIZE];
    int myIntArray[BUFF_SIZE];
    // Reclaimed when exiting scope
}
```

▶ **To allocate an array of bytes (or any primitive data type) on the heap**

- Use the **new** operator with the array syntax shown in this example:

```
const int BUFF_SIZE = 128;

// Allocate on the heap
char* myCharArray = new char[BUFF_SIZE];
int* myIntArray = new int[BUFF_SIZE];
```

▶ **To deallocate the arrays from the heap**

- Use the **delete** operator as follows:

```
delete [] myCharArray;
delete [] myIntArray;
```

Allocation of a Data Structure

▶ **To allocate a data structure on the frame**

- Define the structure variable as follows:

```
struct MyStructType {...};
void SomeFunc(void)
{
    // Frame allocation
    MyStructType myStruct;

    // Use the struct
    myStruct.topScore = 297;

    // Reclaimed when exiting scope
}
```

The memory occupied by the structure is reclaimed when it exits its scope.

▶ **To allocate data structures on the heap**

• Use **new** to allocate data structures on the heap and **delete** to deallocate them, as shown by the following examples:

```
// Heap allocation
MyStructType* myStruct = new MyStructType;

// Use the struct through the pointer ...
myStruct->topScore = 297;

delete myStruct;
```

Allocation of an Object

▶ **To allocate an object on the frame**

• Declare the object as follows:

```
{
    CPerson myPerson;      // Automatic constructor call here

    myPerson.SomeMemberFunction();      // Use the object
}
```

The destructor for the object is automatically invoked when the object exits its scope.

▶ **To allocate an object on the heap**

• Use the **new** operator, which returns a pointer to the object, to allocate objects on the heap. Use the **delete** operator to delete them.

The following heap and frame examples assume that the CPerson constructor takes no arguments.

```
// Automatic constructor call here
CPerson* myPerson = new CPerson;

myPerson->SomeMemberFunction();        // Use the object

delete myPerson;                       // Destructor invoked during delete
```

If the argument for the CPerson constructor is a pointer to **char**, the statement for frame allocation is:

```
CPerson myPerson( "Joe Smith" );
```

The statement for heap allocation is:

```
CPerson* MyPerson = new CPerson( "Joe Smith" );
```

Memory Management: Resizable Memory Blocks

The **new** and **delete** operators, described in the article Memory Management: Allocation on the Frame and on the Heap, are good for allocating and deallocating fixed-size memory blocks and objects. Occasionally, your application may need resizable memory blocks. You must use the standard C run-time library functions **malloc**, **realloc**, and **free** to manage resizable memory blocks on the heap.

Important   Mixing the **new** and **delete** operators with the resizable memory-allocation functions on the same memory block will result in corrupted memory in the Debug version of the . You should not use **realloc** on a memory block allocated with **new**. Likewise, you should not allocate a memory block with the **new** operator and delete it with **free**, or use the **delete** operator on a block of memory allocated with **malloc**.

Menus and Resources

This group of articles explains the use of menus and resources in MFC OLE document applications.

OLE visual editing places additional requirements on the menu and other resources provided by OLE document applications because there are a number of modes in which both container and server (component) applications can be started and used. For example, a full-server application can run in any of these three modes:

- Stand-alone
- In place, for editing an item within the context of a container
- Open, for editing an item outside the context of its container, often in a separate window

This requires three separate menu layouts, one for each possible mode of the application. Accelerator tables are also necessary for each new mode. A container application may or may not support in-place activation; if it does, it needs a new menu structure and associated accelerator tables.

In-place activation requires that the container and server applications must negotiate for menu, toolbar, and status bar space. All resources must be designed with this in mind. The article Menus and Resources: Menu Merging covers this topic in detail.

Because of these issues, OLE document applications created with AppWizard can have up to four separate menus and accelerator table resources. These are used for the following reasons:

Resource name	Use
IDR_MAINFRAME	Used in an MDI application if no file is open, or in an SDI application regardless of open files. This is the standard menu used in non-OLE applications.
IDR_<project>TYPE	Used in an MDI application if files are open. Used when an application is running stand-alone. This is the standard menu used in non-OLE applications.
IDR_<project>TYPE_SRVR_IP	Used by the server or container when an object is open in place.
IDR_<project>TYPE_SRVR_EMB	Used by a server application if an object is opened without using in-place activation.

Each of these resource names represents a menu and, usually, an accelerator table. A similar scheme should be used in MFC applications that are not created with AppWizard.

The following articles discuss topics related to containers, servers, and the menu merging necessary to implement in-place activation:

- Menus and Resources: Container Additions

- Menus and Resources: Server Additions

- Menus and Resources: Menu Merging

Menus and Resources: Container Additions

This article explains the changes that need to be made to the menus and other resources in a visual editing container application. In container applications, two types of changes need to be made: modifications to existing resources to support OLE visual editing and addition of new resources used for in-place activation. If you use AppWizard to create your container application, these steps will be done for you, but they may require some customization.

If you don't use AppWizard, you may want to look at OCLIENT.RC, the resource script for the OCLIENT sample application, to see how these changes are implemented. See the MFC OLE sample OCLIENT.

Topics covered in this article include:

- Container menu additions
- Accelerator table additions
- String table additions

Container Menu Additions

You must add a number of items to the Edit menu:

Item	Purpose
Insert New Object...	Opens the OLE Insert Object dialog box to insert a linked or embedded item into the document.
Paste Link	Pastes a link to the item on the Clipboard into the document.
OLE Verb	Calls the selected item's primary verb. The text of this menu item changes to reflect the primary verb of the selected item.
Links...	Opens the OLE Edit Links dialog box to change existing linked items.

In addition to the changes listed in this article, your source file must include AFXOLECL.RC, which is required for the implementation. Insert New Object is the only required menu addition. Other items can be added, but these listed are the most common.

You must create a new menu for your container application if you want to support in-place activation of contained items. This menu consists of the same File menu and Window pop-up menus used when files are open, but it has two separators placed between them. These separators are used to indicate where the server (component) item (application) should place its menus when activated in place. For more information on this menu-merging technique, see the article Menus and Resources: Menu Merging.

Container Application Accelerator Table Additions

Small changes to a container application's accelerator table resources are necessary if you are supporting in-place activation. The first change allows the user to press the escape key (ESC) to cancel the in-place editing mode. Add the following entry to the main accelerator table:

ID	Key	Type
ID_CANCEL_EDIT_CNTR	**VK_ESCAPE**	**VIRTKEY**

The second change is to create a new accelerator table that corresponds to the new menu resource created for in-place activation. This table has entries for the File and Window menus in addition to the **VK_ESCAPE** entry above. The following example is the accelerator table created for in-place activation in the MFC Container Tutorial:

ID	Key	Type
ID_FILE_NEW	CTRL + N	VIRTKEY
ID_FILE_OPEN	CTRL + O	VIRTKEY
ID_FILE_SAVE	CTRL + S	VIRTKEY
ID_FILE_PRINT	CTRL + P	VIRTKEY
ID_NEXT_PANE	VK_F6	VIRTKEY
ID_PREV_PANE	SHIFT + VK_F6	VIRTKEY
ID_CANCEL_EDIT_CNTR	VK_ESCAPE	VIRTKEY

String Table Additions for Container Applications

Most of the changes to string tables for container applications correspond to the additional menu items mentioned in Container Menu Additions. They supply the text displayed in the status bar when each menu item is displayed. As an example, here are the string-table entries AppWizard generates:

ID	String
IDP_OLE_INIT_FAILED	OLE initialization failed. Make sure that the OLE libraries are the correct version.
IDP_FAILED_TO_CREATE	Failed to create object. Make sure that the object is entered in the system registry.

See Also   Menus and Resources: Server Additions

Menus and Resources: Server Additions

This article explains the changes that need to be made to the menus and other resources in a visual editing server (component) application. A server application requires many additions to the menu structure and other resources because it can be started in one of three modes: stand-alone, embedded, or in place. As described in the Menus and Resources article, there are a maximum of four sets of menus. All four are used for an MDI full-server application, while only three are used for a mini-server. AppWizard will create the menu layout necessary for the type of server you want. Some customization may be necessary.

If you don't use AppWizard, you may want to look at HIERSVR.RC, the resource script for the MFC sample application HIERSVR, to see how these changes are implemented.

Topics covered in this article include:

- Server menu additions
- Accelerator table additions
- String table additions
- Mini-Server additions

Server Menu Additions

Server (component) applications must have menu resources added to support OLE visual editing. The menus used when the application is run in stand-alone mode do not have to be changed, but you must add two new menu resources before building the application; one to support in-place activation and one to support the server being fully open. Both menu resources are used by full- and mini-server applications.

- To support in-place activation, you must create a menu resource that is very similar to the menu resource used when run in stand-alone mode. The difference in this menu is that the File and Window items (and any other menu items that deal with the application, and not the data) are missing. The container application will supply these menu items. For more information on, and an example of, this menu-merging technique, see the article Menus and Resources: Menu Merging.

- To support fully open activation, you must create a menu resource nearly identical to the menu resource used when run in stand-alone mode. The only modification to this menu resource is that some items are reworded to reflect the fact that the server is operating on an item embedded in a compound document. For example, in Step 7 of the Scribble tutorial, when the application is open in-place, the Save command on the File menu changes to Save Copy As.

In addition to the changes listed in this article, your resource file needs to include AFXOLESV.RC, which is required for the implementation. This file is in the MFC\INCLUDE subdirectory.

Server Application Accelerator Table Additions

Two new accelerator table resources must be added to server applications; they correspond directly to the new menu resources described above. The first accelerator table is used when the server application is activated in place. It consists of all the entries in the view's accelerator table except those tied to the File and Window menus.

The second table is nearly an exact copy of the view's accelerator table. Any differences parallel changes made in the fully open menu mentioned in Server Menu Additions.

For an example of these accelerator table changes, compare the **IDR_HIERSVRTYPE_SRVR_IP** and **IDR_HIERSVRTYPE_SRVR_EMB** accelerator tables with **IDR_MAINFRAME** in the HIERSVR.RC file included in the

MFC OLE sample HIERSVR. The File and Window accelerators are missing from the in-place table and exact copies of them are in the embedded table.

String Table Additions for Server Applications

Only one string table addition is necessary in a server application—a string to signify that the OLE initialization failed. As an example, here is the string-table entry AppWizard generates:

ID	String
IDP_OLE_INIT_FAILED	OLE initialization failed. Make sure that the OLE libraries are the correct version.

Mini-Server Additions

The same additions apply for mini-servers as those listed above for full-servers. Because a mini-server can't be run in stand-alone mode, its main menu is much smaller. The main menu created by AppWizard has only a File menu, containing only the items Exit and About. Embedded and in-place menus and accelerators for mini-servers are exactly the same as those for full-servers.

See Also   Menus and Resources: Menu Merging

Menus and Resources: Menu Merging

This article details the steps necessary for OLE document applications to handle visual editing and in-place activation properly. In-place activation poses a challenge for both container and server (component) applications. The user remains in the same frame window (within the context of the container document), but is actually running another application, the server. This requires coordination between the resources of the container and server applications.

Topics covered in this article include:

- Menu layouts
- Toolbars and status bars

Menu Layouts

The first step is to coordinate menu layouts.

For more information, see Menu Creation in the Win32 SDK.

Container applications should create a new menu to be used only when embedded items are activated in place. At the minimum, this menu should consist of the following, in the order listed:

1. File menu identical to the one used when files are open. (Usually no other menu items are placed before the next item.)
2. Two consecutive separators.

3. Window menu identical to the one used when files are open (only if the container application in an MDI application). Some applications may have other menus, such as an Options menu, that belong in this group that remains on the menu when an embedded item is activated in place.

Note There may be other menus which affect the view of the container document, such as Zoom. These "Container" menus appear between the two separators in this menu resource.

Server (component) applications should also create a new menu specifically for in-place activation. It should be like the menu used when files are open, but without menu items, such as File and Window that manipulate the server document instead of the data. Typically, this menu consists of the following:

1. Edit menu identical to the one used when files are open.

2. Separator.

3. Object editing menus, such as the Pen menu in the Scribble tutorial application.

4. Separator.

5. Help menu.

For an example, take a look at the layout of some sample in-place menus for a container and a server. The details of each menu item have been removed to make the example clearer. The container's in-place menu has the following entries:

```
IDR_CONTAINERTYPE_CNTR_IP MENU PRELOAD DISCARDABLE
BEGIN
    POPUP "&File C1"
    MENUITEM SEPARATOR
    POPUP "&Zoom C2"
    MENUITEM SEPARATOR
    POPUP "&Options C3"
    POPUP "&Window C3"
END
```

The consecutive separators indicate where the first part of the server's menu should go. Now look at the server's in-place menu:

```
IDR_SERVERTYPE_SRVR_IP MENU PRELOAD DISCARDABLE
BEGIN
    POPUP "&Edit S1"
    MENUITEM SEPARATOR
    POPUP "&Format S2"
    MENUITEM SEPARATOR
    POPUP "&Help S3"
END
```

The separators here indicate where the second group of container menu items should go. The resulting menu structure when an object from this server is activated in place inside this container looks like this:

```
BEGIN
    POPUP "&File C1"
    POPUP "&Edit S1"
    POPUP "&Zoom C2"
    POPUP "&Format S2"
    POPUP "&Options C3
    POPUP "&Window C3"
    POPUP "&Help S3"
END
```

As you can see, the separators have been replaced with the different groups of each application's menu.

Accelerator tables associated with the in-place menu should also be supplied by the server application. The container will incorporate them into its own accelerator tables.

When an embedded item is activated in place, the framework loads the in-place menu. It then asks the server application for its menu for in-place activation and inserts it where the separators are. This is how the menus combine. You get menus from the container for operating on the file and window placement, and you get menus from the server for operating on the item.

Toolbars and Status Bars

Server applications should create a new toolbar and store its bitmap in a separate file. AppWizard-generated applications store this bitmap in a file called ITOOLBAR.BMP. The new toolbar replaces the container application's toolbar when your server's item is activated in place, and should contain the same items as your normal toolbar, but remove icons representing items on the File and Window menus.

This toolbar is loaded in your **COleIPFrameWnd**-derived class, created for you by AppWizard. The status bar is handled by the container application. For more information on the implementation of in-place frame windows, see the article Servers: Implementing a Server.

See Also   Activation, Servers, Containers

Message Map

The MFC uses a mechanism called the "message map" to route Windows messages and commands to the windows, documents, views, and other objects in an MFC application. Message maps map Windows messages; commands from menus, toolbar buttons, and accelerators; and control-notification messages.

The standard Windows message loop is encapsulated in the **Run** member function of class **CWinApp**. The message loop gets messages representing mouse clicks, keystrokes, and other events from Windows and dispatches them to particular windows or other "command targets." Each object derived from class **CCmdTarget**, including objects derived from class **CWnd**, has a message map. This includes windows, dialog boxes, documents, views, threads, and the application itself.

Message maps connect messages to message handler functions, or "handlers," in the target object. For example, a **WM_LBUTTONDOWN** message might be mapped to an **OnLButtonDown** handler function in a view object. When the message is received, the message map calls the handler function.

Message maps, command targets, message handlers, and other components of the message-handling architecture of MFC are described in detail in Chapter 2, Working with Messages and Commands.

See Also   Message Map: Ranges of Messages

In the *Class Library Reference*: **CCmdTarget**

Message Map: Ranges of Messages

This article explains how to map a range of messages to a single message handler function (instead of mapping one message to only one function).

There are times when you need to process more than one message or control notification in exactly the same way. At such times, you might wish to map all of the messages to a single handler function. Message-map ranges allow you to do this for a contiguous range of messages:

- You can map ranges of command IDs to:
  - A command handler function.
  - A command update handler function.
- You can map control-notification messages for a range of control IDs to a message handler function.

Topics covered in this article include:

- Writing the message-map entry
- Declaring the handler function
- Example for a range of command IDs
- Example for a range of control IDs

Important   ClassWizard does not support message-map ranges, so you must write the message-map entries and handler function declarations yourself, as described in this article.

Writing the Message-Map Entry

In the .CPP file, add your message-map entry, as shown in the following example:

```
...
BEGIN_MESSAGE_MAP(CMyApp, CWinApp)
    //{{AFX_MSG_MAP(CMyApp)
    ...
        ON_COMMAND_RANGE(ID_MYCMD_ONE, ID_MYCMD_TEN, OnDoSomething)
    //}}AFX_MSG_MAP
END_MESSAGE_MAP( )
...
```

The message-map entry consists of the following items:

- The message-map range macro:
  - **ON_COMMAND_RANGE**
  - **ON_UPDATE_COMMAND_UI_RANGE**
  - **ON_CONTROL_RANGE**
- Parameters to the macro:

  The first two macros take three parameters:
  - The command ID that starts the range
  - The command ID that ends the range
  - The name of the message handler function

  The range of command IDs must be contiguous.

  The third macro, **ON_CONTROL_RANGE**, takes an additional first parameter: a control-notification message, such as **EN_CHANGE**.

Declaring the Handler Function

In the .H file, add your handler function declaration outside the //{{AFX_MSG comment brackets. The following code shows how this might look, as shown in the next-to-last line below:

```
// Generated message-map functions
protected:
    //{{AFX_MSG(CMyView)
        ...
    //}}AFX_MSG
    afx_msg void OnDoSomething( UINT nID );
    DECLARE_MESSAGE_MAP()
```

Handler functions for single commands normally take no parameters. Handler functions for message-map ranges require an extra parameter, *nID*, of type **UINT**. This parameter is the first parameter. The extra parameter accommodates the extra command ID needed to specify which command the user actually chose.

Example for a Range of Command IDs

When might you use ranges? One example is in handling commands like the Zoom command in the MFC OLE sample HIERSVR. This command zooms the view, scaling it between 25% and 300% of its normal size. HIERSVR's view class uses a range to handle the Zoom commands with a message-map entry resembling this:

```
ON_COMMAND_RANGE(ID_VIEW_ZOOM25, ID_VIEW_ZOOM300, OnZoom)
```

When you write the message-map entry, you specify:

- Two command IDs, beginning and ending a contiguous range.

  Here they're ID_VIEW_ZOOM25 and ID_VIEW_ZOOM300.
- The name of the handler function for the commands.

  Here it's OnZoom.

The function declaration would resemble this:

```
afx_msg void OnZoom(UINT nID);
```

The case of update handler functions is similar, and likely to be more widely useful. It's quite common to write **ON_UPDATE_COMMAND_UI** handlers for a number of commands and find yourself writing, or copying, the same code over and over. The solution is to map a range of command IDs to one update handler function using the **ON_UPDATE_COMMAND_UI_RANGE** macro. The command IDs must form a contiguous range. For an example, see the **OnUpdateZoom** handler and its **ON_UPDATE_COMMAND_UI_RANGE** message-map entry in the HIERSVR sample's view class.

Example for a Range of Control IDs

Another interesting case is mapping control-notification messages for a range of control IDs to a single handler. Suppose the user can click any of 10 buttons. To map all 10 buttons to one handler, your message-map entry would look like this:

```
ON_CONTROL_RANGE(BN_CLICKED, IDC_BUTTON1, IDC_BUTTON10, OnButtonClicked)
```

To write the **ON_CONTROL_RANGE** macro in your message map, specify:

- A particular control-notification message.

  Here it's **BN_CLICKED**.
- The control ID values associated with the contiguous range of controls.

  Here these are IDC_BUTTON1 and IDC_BUTTON10.
- The name of the message handler function.

  Here it's OnButtonClicked.

When you write the handler function, specify the extra **UINT** parameter, as shown in the following:

```
...
void CMyDialog::OnButtonClicked( UINT nID )
{
    int nButton = nID - IDC_BUTTON1;
    ASSERT( nButton >= 0 && nButton < 10 );
    // ...
}
```

The OnButtonClicked handler for a single **BN_CLICKED** message takes no parameters. The same handler for a range of buttons takes one **UINT**. The extra parameter allows for identifying the particular control responsible for generating the **BN_CLICKED** message.

The code shown in the example is typical: converting the value passed to an **int** within the message range and asserting that this is the case. Then you might take some different action depending on which button was clicked.

Methods

An OLE control fires events to communicate between itself and its control container. A container can also communicate with a control by means of methods and properties. Methods and properties provide an exported interface for use by other applications, such as OLE Automation clients and OLE control containers. For more information on OLE control properties, see the article Properties.

Methods are similar in usage and purpose to the member functions of a C++ class. There are two types of methods your control can implement: stock and custom. Similar to stock events, stock methods are those methods for which **COleControl** provides an implementation. For more information on stock methods, see the article Methods: Adding Stock Methods to an OLE Control. Custom methods, defined by the developer, allow additional customization of the control. For more information, see the article Methods: Adding Custom Methods to an OLE Control.

The Microsoft Foundation Class Library (MFC) implements a mechanism that allows your control to support stock and custom methods. The first part is class **COleControl**. Derived from **CWnd**, **COleControl** member functions support stock methods that are common to all OLE controls. The second part of this mechanism is the dispatch map. A dispatch map is similar to a message map; however, instead of mapping a function to a Windows message ID, a dispatch map maps virtual member functions to IDispatch IDS.

For a control to properly support various methods, its class must declare a dispatch map. This is accomplished by the following line of code located in control class header (.H) file:

```
DECLARE_DISPATCH_MAP()
```

The main purpose of the dispatch map is to establish the relationship between the method names used by an external caller (such as the container) and the member functions of the control's class that implement the methods. Once the dispatch map has been declared, it needs to be defined in the control's implementation (.CPP) file. The following lines of code define the dispatch map:

```
BEGIN_DISPATCH_MAP(CSampleCtrl, COleControl)
    //{{AFX_DISPATCH_MAP(CSampleCtrl)
    ...
    //}}AFX_DISPATCH_MAP
END_DISPATCH_MAP()
```

If ControlWizard was used to create the project, these lines were added automatically. If ControlWizard was not used, you must add these lines manually. The two comment lines allow ClassWizard to automatically insert macros into the dispatch map.

The following articles discuss Methods in detail:

- Methods: Adding Stock Methods to an OLE Control
- Methods: Adding Custom Methods to an OLE Control
- Methods: Returning Error Codes From a Method

Methods: Adding Stock Methods to an OLE Control

A stock method differs from a custom method in that it is already implemented by class **COleControl**. For example, **COleControl** contains a predefined member function supports the Refresh method for your control. The dispatch map entry for this stock method is **DISP_STOCKFUNC_REFRESH**.

COleControl supports two stock methods: DoClick and Refresh. Refresh is invoked by the control's user to immediately update the control's appearance; DoClick is invoked to fire the control's Click event.

Method	Dispatch Map Entry	Comment
DoClick	**DISP_STOCKPROP_DOCLICK( )**	Fires a Click event.
Refresh	**DISP_STOCKPROP_REFRESH( )**	Immediately updates the control's appearance.

Adding a Stock Method Using ClassWizard

Adding a stock method is simple using ClassWizard. The following procedure demonstrates adding the Refresh method to a control created using ControlWizard.

▶ **To add the stock Refresh method using ClassWizard**

1 Load your control's project.

2 From the View menu, choose ClassWizard.

3 Choose the OLE Automation tab.

4 Choose the Add Method button.

5 Choose the control class in the Class Name box.

6 In the External Name box, select Refresh.

7 Choose the OK button.

8 Choose the OK button to confirm your choices and close ClassWizard.

ClassWizard Changes for Stock Methods

Because the stock Refresh method is supported by the control's base class, ClassWizard does not change the control's class declaration in any way; it simply adds an entry for the method to the control's dispatch map and to its .ODL file. The following line is added to the control's dispatch map, located in its implementation (.CPP) file:

```
DISP_STOCKFUNC_REFRESH( )
```

This makes the Refresh method available to the control's users.

The following line is added to the control's .ODL file:

```
[id(DISPID_REFRESH)] void Refresh();
```

This line assigns the Refresh method a specific ID number.

Methods: Adding Custom Methods to an OLE Control

Custom methods differ from stock methods in that they are not already implemented by **COleControl**. You must supply the implementation for each custom method you add to your control.

An OLE control user can call a custom method at any time to perform control-specific actions. The dispatch map entry for custom methods is of the form **DISP_FUNCTION**.

Adding a Custom Method With ClassWizard

The following procedure demonstrates adding the custom method PtInCircle to an OLE control's skeleton code. PtInCircle determines whether the coordinates passed to the control are inside or outside the circle. This same procedure can also be used to add other custom methods. Simply substitute your custom method name and its parameters for the PtInCircle method name and parameters. (This example uses the `InCircle` function from the article Events. For more information on this function, see the article Events: Adding Custom Events to an OLE Control.)

▶ **To add the PtInCircle custom method using ClassWizard**

1 Load the control's project.

2 From the View menu, choose ClassWizard.

3 Choose the OLE Automation tab.

4 Choose the control's class from the Class Name box.

5 Choose the Add Method button.

6 In the External Name box, type `PtInCircle`.

7 In the Internal Name box, type the name of the method's internal function or use the default value provided by ClassWizard (in this case, `PtInCircle`).

8 From the Return Type box, select BOOL for the method's return type.

9 Using the grid control, add a parameter, called xCoord (type `OLE_XPOS_PIXELS`).

10 Using the grid control, add a second parameter, called yCoord (type `OLE_YPOS_PIXELS`).

11 Choose the OK button to close the Add Method dialog box.

12 Choose the OK button to confirm your choices and close ClassWizard.

Figure 1 shows the Add Method dialog box of ClassWizard.

Figure 1   The Add Method Dialog Box

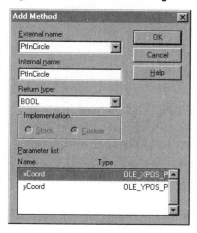

ClassWizard Changes for Custom Methods

When you add a custom method, ClassWizard makes some changes to the control class header (.H) and implementation (.CPP) files. The following line is added to the dispatch map declaration in the control class header (.H) file:

```
afx_msg BOOL PtInCircle(long xCoord, long yCoord);
```

This code declares a dispatch method handler called PtinCircle. This function can be called by the control user using the external name PtInCircle.

The following line is added to the control's .ODL file:

```
[id(1)] boolean PtInCircle(OLE_XPOS_PIXELS xCoord, OLE_YPOS_PIXELS yCoords);
```

This line assigns the PtInCircle method a specific ID number, taken from the method's position in ClassWizard's methods and properties list. Because ClassWizard was used to add the custom method, the entry for it was added automatically to the project's .ODL file.

In addition, the following line, located in the implementation (.CPP) file of the control class, is added to the control's dispatch map:

```
DISP_FUNCTION(CSampleCtrl, "PtInCircle", PtInCircle, VT_BOOL, VTS_I4 VTS_I4)
```

The **DISP_FUNCTION** macro maps the method PtInCircle to the control's handler function, PtInCircle, declares the return type to be **BOOL**, and declares two parameters of type **short** to be passed to PtInCircle.

Finally, ClassWizard adds the stub function CSampleCtrl::PtinCircle to the bottom of the control's implementation (.CPP) file. For PtinCircle to function as stated previously, it must be modified as follows:

```
BOOL CSampleCtrl::PtInCircle(short xCoord, short yCoord)
{
    return InCircle(CPoint(xCoord, yCoord));
}
```

Methods: Returning Error Codes From a Method

This article describes how to return error codes from an OLE control method.

To indicate that an error has occurred within a method, you should use the **COleControl::ThrowError** member function, which takes an **SCODE** (status code) as a parameter. You can use a predefined **SCODE** or define one of your own.

Note ThrowError is meant to be used only as a means of returning an error from within a property's Get or Set function or an automation Method. These are the only times that the appropriate exception handler will be present on the stack.

Helper functions exist for the most common predefined **SCODE**s, such as **COleControl::SetNotSupported**, **COleControl::GetNotSupported**, and **COleControl::SetNotPermitted**.

For a list of predefined **SCODE**s and instructions on defining custom **SCODE**s, see the section Handling Errors in Your OLE Control in OLE Controls: Advanced Topics.

For more information on reporting exceptions in other areas of your code, see **COleControl::FireError** and the section Handling Errors in Your OLE Control in OLE Controls: Advanced Topics.

MFC

The Microsoft Foundation Class Library (MFC) is an "application framework" (often called the "framework" in this documentation) for writing applications for Microsoft Windows and other platforms that support the Win32 API. The framework is implemented as a group of C++ classes, many of which represent common objects such as documents, windows, dialog boxes, toolbars, and so on.

This article presents an overview of MFC, and lists articles describing various components of MFC and MFC tools, and articles describing changes from previous versions of MFC.

For an Overview of MFC

Part 1 of *Programming with MFC* presents an overview of MFC:

- Chapter 1, Using the Classes to Write Applications for Windows
- Chapter 2, Working with Messages and Commands
- Chapter 3, Working with Frame Windows, Documents, and Views
- Chapter 4, Working with Dialog Boxes, Controls, and Control Bars

- Chapter 5, Working with OLE
- Chapter 6, Developing OLE Controls
- Chapter 7, Working with Databases
- Chapter 8, Using the General-Purpose Classes

Encyclopedia Articles About Aspects of MFC

The following main articles explain specific areas in more detail. Some articles describe how a component or feature of MFC works. Others describe how to carry out a procedure in programming with MFC. Each of these articles is typically the "main" article in a group of related "child" articles.

- AppWizard
- ClassWizard
- Clipboard
- CObject Class
- Collections
- COMMON.RES Sample Resources
- Database Overview
- Date and Time
- Debugging
- Diagnostics
- Dynamic-Link Libraries (DLLs)
- Exceptions
- Files
- Help
- Library Versions
- Memory Management
- Message Map
- Multithreading
- OLE Controls
- OLE Overview
- Printing
- Property Sheets
- Serialization (Object Persistence)
- Strings

- Toolbars
- Tools for MFC Programming

If MFC is new to you, begin with the overview. If you need information in a specific area, refer to a related article. You can also access specific topics easily using the search capabilities in Books Online.

Differences from Other Versions of MFC

For details about how this version of MFC has changed from previous versions, and for information about porting your applications from previous versions of MFC to this version, see the following articles:

- MFC: Changes from MFC Versions 3.0 and 3.1
- MFC: Changes from MFC Versions 2.0 and 2.5
- MFC: Changes from MFC Version 2.0 32-Bit Edition
- MFC: Features No Longer Available
- MFC: 32-Bit Programming Issues
- MFC: Porting MFC Applications to 32 Bit
- MFC: Porting Tips
- MFC: Using the MFC Source Files

MFC: Changes from MFC Versions 3.0 and 3.1

You may be upgrading to version 4.0 of the Microsoft Foundation Class Library from either MFC version 3.0 or 3.1. Version 3.0 was released with Visual C++ version 2.0. MFC version 3.1 was a subscription release with Visual C++ version 2.1.

Note The changes described here also apply to MFC version 3.2, released with Visual C++ version 2.2.

This and related articles cover the following topics:

- MFC: Windows 95 Support
- MFC: Win32 Features in MFC
- MFC: OLE Control Container Support
- MFC: Data Access Objects (DAO) Support
- MFC: OLE and Other Enhancements in MFC Version 4.0

Changes not covered in the related articles, but discussed in this article, include:

- New view classes
- Other new classes in version 4.0
- A new toolbar resource type

- Enhancements to CFile and CFileException
- Previously undocumented MFC functions now documented

New View Classes

MFC has added three new **CView**-derived classes:

- **CListView**   A view based on a **CListCtrl** object. Simplifies use of the list control with MFC's document-view architecture.
- **CTreeView**   A view based on a **CTreeCtrl** object. Simplifies use of the tree control with MFC's document-view architecture.
- **CRichEditView**   A view based on a **CRichEditCtrl** object. Simplifies creating simple text editors with rich formatting.

The MFC database sample DAOVIEW illustrates **CListView** and **CTreeView**. The MFC OLE sample WORDPAD illustrates **CRichEditView**. You can access the code for these samples through Samples in Books Online.

Other New Classes in Version 4.0

Other new classes in MFC version 4.0 include:

- Classes for working with OLE **VARIANT** data: **COleVariant**, **COleDateTime**, **COleCurrency**; see the article MFC: OLE and Other Enhancements in MFC Version 4.0
- Encapsulation of the Windows wait cursor: **CWaitCursor**
- New common dialog box classes: **CPageSetupDialog** and **COlePropertiesDialog**; see the article MFC: Windows 95 Support
- New Windows common control classes; see the article MFC: Windows 95 Support
- Synchronization classes for multithreaded programming: **CSyncObject**, **CSemaphore**, **CCriticalSection**, **CMutex**, **CEvent**, **CSingleLock**, **CMultiLock**; see the article MFC: Win32 Features in MFC
- New **CListBox**-derived classes: **CCheckListBox** and **CDragListBox**; see the article MFC: Windows 95 Support

A New Toolbar Resource Type

MFC version 4.0 adds a new resource type, **RT_TOOLBAR**. The Visual C++ toolbar editor uses **RT_TOOLBAR** to edit toolbars directly. You can load toolbars more easily now, using only a single call to **CToolbar::LoadToolbar**. For more information, see the article Toolbars and Chapter 11, Using the Toolbar Editor, in the *Visual C++ User's Guide*.

Enhancements to CFile and CFileException

Classes **CFile** and **CFileException** have been enhanced to make it easier to retrieve human-readable error messages and to display error messages. The **GetErrorMessage** and **ReportError** member functions allow you to provide error messages to your users without knowing the specific type of **CException**.

Previously Undocumented MFC Functions Now Documented

Over 100 previously undocumented class member functions have now been documented in the *Class Library Reference*. These members formerly appeared below the // Implementation comment in their classes and so were not documented. The purpose in choosing these member functions was to document "implementation" APIs that:

- Aren't likely to change in the future, based on a track record of several versions of MFC.

- Are useful enough that you might want to call them (but often couldn't because they were declared as implementation details, subject to change).

Check your favorite classes for new members.

See Also   MFC, MFC: Changes from MFC Versions 2.0 and 2.5, MFC: Changes from MFC Version 2.0 32-Bit Edition, MFC: Features No Longer Available

MFC: Windows 95 Support

This article describes how MFC version 4.0 supports programming for Windows 95.

The most important change is that MFC version 4.0 fully supports programming for Microsoft Windows 95. Your MFC applications can run on either Windows 95 or Windows NT version 3.51. Under each environment, your applications have the appropriate visual look.

Here are the key features for Windows 95:

- New common control classes
- New implementations for control bar and property sheet classes
- Rich edit classes
- Other new controls
- New common dialogs
- Ability to easily customize the File Open dialog box

For tutorial information about many of these Windows 95 features, see Adding Windows 95 Functionality in *Tutorials*.

New Common Control Classes

MFC supplies classes for new Win32 common controls, including the rich edit control. These controls are available under Windows 95, Windows NT version 3.51 or later, and Win32s version 1.3. They supplement Windows common controls such as list boxes, edit controls, and combo boxes. Most of the new control classes were released in beta quality with MFC version 3.1; version 4.0 supplies them in finished form and includes controls not released with version 3.1. Here are the controls:

CAnimateCtrl   A window that displays successive frames of an Audio Video Interleaved (AVI) clip during a lengthy operation.

CHeaderCtrl   A resizable button that appears above a column of text, allowing the user to display more or less information in the column.

CHotKeyCtrl   A window that enables the user to create a hot key. A "hot key" is a key combination that the user can press to perform an action quickly.

CImageList   A collection of images used to efficiently manage large sets of icons or bitmaps.

CListCtrl   A window that displays a collection of items each consisting of an icon and a label.

CProgressCtrl   (Also known as a "progress bar control.") A window that an application can use to indicate the progress of a lengthy operation.

CRichEditCtrl   A window in which the user can enter and edit text with character and paragraph formatting. The control can include embedded OLE objects. See Rich Edit Classes for related information.

CSliderCtrl   (Also known as a "trackbar.") A window containing a slider and optional tick marks that sends notification messages to indicate changes in its position.

CSpinButtonCtrl   (Also known as an "up-down control.") A pair of arrow buttons that the user can click to increment or decrement a value, such as a scroll position or a number displayed in a companion control.

CStatusBarCtrl   A horizontal window in a parent window in which an application can display various kinds of status information. This control resembles the MFC **CStatusBar** class.

CTabCtrl   Analogous to the dividers in a notebook or the labels in a file cabinet. By using a tab control, an application can define multiple pages for the same area of a window or dialog box. (See also MFC class **CPropertySheet**.)

CToolBarCtrl   A window that contains one or more command-generating buttons. This control resembles the MFC **CToolBar** class.

CToolTipCtrl   A small pop-up window that displays a single line of text describing the purpose of a toolbar button or other tool in an application.

CTreeCtrl   (Also known as a "tree view control.") A window that displays a hierarchical list of items, such as the headings in a document, the entries in an index, or the files and directories on a disk. Each item consists of a label and an optional bitmapped image, and each item can have a list of subitems associated with it.

For additional programming information about these classes, see Technical Note 60 under MFC in Books Online.

New Implementations for Control Bar and Property Sheet Classes

The following MFC classes have been reimplemented using some of the new Windows common controls listed earlier in this article:

CToolBar Now uses the toolbar control represented by class **CToolBarCtrl**. Class **COldToolBar** provides the previous implementation for backward compatibility so that you can continue to use your customizations from the previous versions of MFC. See the MFC sample DOCTOOL. You can access the source code under Samples in Books Online.

Tool Tips Now uses the tooltip control represented by class **CToolTipCtrl**.

CStatusBar Now uses the status bar control represented by class **CStatusBarCtrl**. Class **COldStatusBar** provides the previous implementation for backward compatibility so that you can continue to use your customizations from the previous version of MFC.

CPropertySheet and **CPropertyPage** Now use the Win32 property sheet API.

In addition, enhancements to class **CControlBar**, the base class for **CToolBar**, **CStatusBar**, and **CDialogBar**, let your users resize toolbars in the same way you can resize the toolbars in Visual C++ and many other Microsoft applications.

Rich Edit Classes

In addition to a class that encapsulates the rich edit text control, MFC supplies related classes to complement the control and enhance its use for building text editors. These new classes are listed below. The new classes integrate a rich edit control with the MFC document/view architecture.

CRichEditDoc Maintains a list of OLE client items and works with a **CRichEditView**.

CRichEditView Maintains the text and its formatting characteristics and works with a **CRichEditDoc**.

CRichEditCntrItem Provides container-side access to the OLE client items stored in a **CRichEditDoc**.

Other New Controls

Other new MFC classes provide specialized list box controls:

CDragListBox A list box control in which you can drag items to produce orderings other than alphabetical.

CCheckListBox A list box control in which the strings are preceded by check boxes. For an example, see the Custom Options dialog box in Visual C++ Setup.

New Common Dialogs

There are several new classes for common dialog boxes. OLE dialog boxes now use the OLEDLG.DLL file supplied by the system. All common dialog classes are now derived from **CCommonDialog**.

CPageSetupDialog Encapsulates the services provided by the Windows common OLE Page Setup dialog box with additional support for setting and modifying print margins. This class is designed to take the place of the Print Setup dialog box.

COlePropertiesDialog Encapsulates the Windows common OLE Object Properties dialog box. Common OLE Object Properties dialog boxes provide an easy way to display and modify the properties of an OLE document item in a manner consistent with Windows standards.

Ability to Easily Customize the File Open Dialog Box

Class **CFileDialog** includes new member functions for customizing the File Open dialog box. For example, you can add your own controls to the dialog box.

See Also MFC, MFC: Changes from MFC Versions 2.0 and 2.5, MFC: Changes from MFC Version 2.0 32-Bit Edition, MFC: Features No Longer Available

MFC: Win32 Features in MFC

New Win32 features in MFC version 4.0 include:

- Classes for the new Windows common controls on Windows 95, Windows NT version 3.51, and Win32s version 1.3. See New Common Control Classes.

- Classes for new common dialogs. See New Common Dialogs.

- Win32 synchronization objects for multithreaded programming.

Win32 Synchronization Objects

Multithreaded programs often require synchronizing access to shared resources by different concurrent threads. To manage synchronization, MFC supplies a new base class, **CSyncObject**, and several derived objects that represent common synchronization techniques.

CSyncObject Provides functionality common to the derived synchronization objects in Win32. Support includes **Lock** and **Unlock** as virtual abstract operations that derived classes override.

Classes derived from **CSyncObject**:

CSemaphore Represents a "semaphore"—a synchronization object that allows a limited number of threads in one or more processes to access a resource. A

CSemaphore object maintains a count of the number of threads currently accessing a specified resource.

CCriticalSection Represents a "critical section"—a synchronization object that allows one thread at a time to access a resource or section of code.

CMutex Represents a "mutex" (for "mutually exclusive")—a synchronization object that allows one thread mutually exclusive access to a resource.

CEvent Represents an "event"—a synchronization object that allows one thread to notify another that an event has occurred. Events are useful when a thread needs to know when to perform its task.

Other synchronization objects not derived from **CSyncObject**:

CSingleLock Represents the access control mechanism used in controlling access to a resource in a multithreaded program. Used with **CSemaphore**, **CMutex**, **CCriticalSection**, and **CEvent** objects.

CMultiLock Similar to **CSingleLock**, but used when there are multiple objects that you could use at one time.

See Also   MFC, MFC: Changes from MFC Versions 2.0 and 2.5, MFC: Changes from MFC Version 2.0 32-Bit Edition, MFC: Features No Longer Available, Multithreading

MFC: OLE Control Container Support

This article describes support in MFC version 4.0 for OLE control containers.

MFC now integrates the OLE Controls Development Kit (CDK) with the rest of MFC and supplies complete OLE control container support.

With the OLE new controls container, you need not understand all the details of using OLE container applications. Support is now based on the **CWnd** class, which allows you to create both the container and the control sides. In MFC version 4.0, an OLE control becomes a special kind of child window, with **CWnd** functions, including **CWnd::CreateControl**, which dynamically creates an OLE control rather than an ordinary window.

Other OLE controls support includes creation from a dialog template, preloaded OCX files for better performance, and transparent keyboard translation in **IsDialogMessage**.

The Visual C++ dialog editor supports placing OLE controls in a dialog template resource.

OLE controls now use the same run-time library and debug heap as the core of MFC.

See Also   MFC, MFC: Changes from MFC Versions 2.0 and 2.5, MFC: Changes from MFC Version 2.0 32-Bit Edition, MFC: Features No Longer Available, OLE Controls

MFC: Data Access Objects (DAO) Support

This article describes a new set of MFC classes for database programming.

MFC now supplies two different sets of classes for database programming. Besides the existing classes based on Open Database Connectivity (ODBC), MFC supplies classes based on Data Access Objects (DAO).

As an alternative to the MFC ODBC database classes, the MFC DAO classes use the Microsoft Jet database engine to provide a set of data access objects: database objects, tabledef and querydef objects, recordset objects, and others. You can use DAO for working with .MDB files like those created by Microsoft Access. You can also access a number of installable Indexed Sequential Access Methods (ISAMs) and ODBC data sources through DAO.

Classes now available using DAO include:

CDaoDatabase   Manages a connection to a database.

CDaoQueryDef   Manages saving queries in a database for reuse.

CDaoRecordset   Manages a result set, a set of records returned by a query.

CDaoTabledef   Manages manipulating or viewing the structure of a table in a database.

CDaoWorkspace   Manages transactions and access to properties of the database engine.

CDaoRecordView   Lets you view the contents of a recordset in a **CFormView**-derived object.

See Also   MFC, MFC: Changes from MFC Versions 2.0 and 2.5, MFC: Changes from MFC Version 2.0 32-Bit Edition, MFC: Features No Longer Available, Database Overview

MFC: OLE and Other Enhancements in MFC Version 4.0

This article describes enhancements to MFC's OLE support in version 4.0 and other MFC enhancements, including DLL improvements. Topics include:

- OLE enhancements in MFC version 4.0
- Other enhancements in MFC version 4.0

OLE Enhancements in MFC Version 4.0

- MFC version 4.0 no longer uses MFCANS32.DLL. Unicode™/ANSI translation is now done within MFC. Performance increases by a factor of 10 in some cases.
- New classes provided as part of the OLE enhancements include:

- **COleVariant**   Encapsulates the **VARIANT** data type from OLE. MFC uses **COleVariant** to pass variable-type parameters in the OLE classes and in the DAO database classes.

- **COleDateTime**   Encapsulates a date and time value. **COleDateTime** has a wider range of dates than **CTime**.

- **COleCurrency**   Encapsulates a currency value.

- OLEDLG.DLL replaces MFCUIx32.DLL.

See the article OLE Overview for general information about using OLE.

Other Enhancements in MFC Version 4.0

New features include:

- MFC DLLs
- Better static linking support
- **CString** reference counting
- Integration of the CDK with MFC
- Message reflection
- Debug memory allocation

MFC DLLs

- MFC DLLs are tuned for a significant reduction in the working set. This results in MFC applications that use less memory.

- The **_USRDLL** option has been removed.

- A new DLL model is now available. Generic DLLs can use MFC DLLs, including DLLs with "C" and MFC inproc servers.

See the article Dynamic-Link Libraries (DLLs).

Better Static Linking Support

- Static linking encourges simplified distributions instead of code sharing, and you can now build an application that is fully statically linked.

- **CWinApp::Enable3dControlsStatic** is available, allowing you to efficiently use statically linked dialog boxes and windows whose controls have a three dimensional appearance.

CString Reference Counts

CString data is reference counted, reducing redundant copy-constructor calls for enhanced efficiency in returning **CString** objects.

Integration of the CDK with MFC

Many features of the OLE Control Development Kit (CDK) are now available in core MFC, including connection maps, custom "verbs" in message maps, and OLE automation "type library" support. For information, see the article OLE Controls.

Message Reflection

Message reflection lets you handle messages for a control, such as **WM_CTLCOLOR, WM_COMMAND**, and **WM_NOTIFY**, within the control itself. This makes the control more self-contained and portable. The mechanism works with Windows common controls as well as with OLE controls.

Message reflection lets you reuse your **CWnd** derived classes more readily. Message reflection works via **CWnd::OnChildNotify**, using special **ON_XXX_REFLECT** message map entries such as **ON_CTLCOLOR_REFLECT** and **ON_CONTROL_REFLECT.**

Debug Memory Allocation

The MFC debug allocator has been moved to C-runtime, which fixes problems associated with different allocators, and checks on **malloc/free/realloc** as a side-effect.

See Chapter 4, Debug Version of the C Run-Time Library, in the *Run-Time Library Reference.*

See Also   MFC, MFC: Changes from MFC Versions 2.0 and 2.5, MFC: Changes from MFC Version 2.0 32-Bit Edition, MFC: Features No Longer Available

MFC: Changes from MFC Versions 2.0 and 2.5

You may be upgrading to version 3.0 of the Microsoft Foundation Class Library from one of the previous 16-bit versions: either MFC version 2.0 or 2.5, which are part of Visual C++ versions 1.0 and 1.5, respectively.

This article covers the following topics:

- Upgrading from MFC version 2.5
- Upgrading from MFC version 2.0

Upgrading from MFC Version 2.5

- Support for 32-bit programming.

  MFC version 3.0 targets Win32 platforms, including Intel Win32s, Windows NT, and Windows 95, as well as MIPS® Windows NT and the Macintosh®. The same MFC code works for all of the different targets.

- Extended Win32 API coverage.

  The coverage includes new GDI functionality such as Beziers and Paths and a number of other Win32 "USER" APIs.

- Support for C++ exceptions.

  MFC uses C++ exceptions. The MFC exception handling macros are also provided for backward compatibility and compiler portability.

- Collection classes based on C++ templates.

  These classes make it easier to derive your own type-safe collection classes.

- Support for creating property sheets, also referred to as "tab dialog boxes," in your programs.

  You can create property sheets containing tabs like those found in Microsoft Word for Windows version 6.0 and Visual C++. This support is in classes **CPropertyPage** and **CPropertySheet**.

- Support for creating "dockable" tool bars in your programs.

  You can create toolbars that the user can drag to various parts of the main frame window. API member functions for dockable toolbars are in classes **CToolBar** and **CFrameWnd**.

- Support for "tool tips" like those in Microsoft Excel.

  When the user moves the mouse over a toolbar button in your application, a small box is shown on top of the button to describe the action that would be performed.

- Support for Unicode and Double-Byte Character Sets (DBCS).

  Your applications can be more easily internationalized using Unicode or DBCS strings.

- Support for 3D controls.

  Simply call **CWinApp::Enable3dControls** from your `InitInstance` function to get a three-dimensional appearance in your dialog boxes.

- Support for frame windows with thin caption bars, such as those used for Visual C++ property windows.

  See class **CMiniFrameWnd** in the *Class Library Reference*.

- Message-map support for ranges of command IDs and control IDs.

  For example, you can map a range of command IDs to a single message handler.

- New **CString** member functions, such as **Format**, which resembles the **sprintf** run-time function.

- Automatic linking of the correct version of the MFC library and any other required libraries, such as the Win32 libraries, OLE libraries, or ODBC libraries.

Upgrading from MFC Version 2.0

If you're upgrading from version 2.0, you get the following support in addition to the features listed under Upgrading from MFC Version 2.5:

- Support for OLE.

MFC OLE classes make it easier to write OLE visual editing servers and containers and to implement OLE Automation in your applications. See Chapter 5, Working with OLE, and the article OLE Overview.

- Support for data access with Open Database Connectivity (ODBC).

MFC database classes help you manipulate data in databases for which you have the appropriate 32-bit ODBC driver. See Chapter 7, Working with Databases, and the article Database Overview.

To complete your picture of what's new in this version, also see the article MFC: Changes from MFC Version 2.0 32-Bit Edition.

See Also Dynamic-Link Libraries (DLLs), MFC: 32-Bit Programming Issues, Toolbars: Docking and Floating, Toolbars: Tool Tips, Strings: Unicode and Multibyte Character Set (MBCS) Support, Property Sheets, Collections, Exceptions, Message Map: Ranges of Messages

In *Programming Techniques*: Chapter 13, Developing for International Markets

MFC: Changes from MFC Version 2.0 32-Bit Edition

This article discusses changes in version 3.0 of the Microsoft Foundation Class Library for users of the 32-bit version of MFC version 2.0 (sometimes called MFC version 2.1), which is part of Visual C++ 1.0 32-Bit Edition. Changes include:

- Full support for writing multithreaded applications.

You can use MFC functionality in both the primary thread of execution and in secondary threads.

- Support for OLE.

MFC OLE classes make it easier to write OLE servers and containers and to implement OLE Automation in your applications. See Chapter 5, Working with OLE, and the article OLE Overview.

- Support for data access with Open Database Connectivity (ODBC).

MFC database classes help you manipulate data in databases for which you have the appropriate 32-bit ODBC driver. See Chapter 7, Working with Databases, and the article Database Overview.

- Support for MFC packaged in a shared DLL, called AFXDLL.

To use AFXDLL, a set of DLLs that contains the entire 32-bit Microsoft Foundation Class Library, use "/D_AFXDLL" in your compiler options and one of the "MFC30" DLLs in your linker options.

Using AFXDLL results in smaller executable files than statically linking the class library with your application. This is particularly useful if you have several applications that run at the same time; they can share the DLL.

AFXDLL is the default when you create an MFC application with AppWizard.

- **WIN32_LEAN_AND_MEAN**.

  To improve build times and reduce the size of your application's precompiled header, MFC defines the symbol **WIN32_LEAN_AND_MEAN**. This definition lists a group of less commonly used header files that MFC does not automatically include through including AFXWIN.H.

  To see the list of header files specifically excluded from MFC builds, look at the definition of **WIN32_LEAN_AND_MEAN** in WINDOWS.H. If you need the definitions provided by any of those files, you must explicitly include the appropriate file yourself.

  WIN32_LEAN_AND_MEAN was not defined in MFC version 2.1, and all of the extra headers were included.

For a more detailed accounting of these differences, see the article MFC: 32-Bit Programming Issues. To complete your picture of what's new in this version, see the article MFC: Changes from MFC Versions 2.0 and 2.5.

See Also   MFC: Changes from MFC Versions 2.0 and 2.5, Multithreading, Dynamic-Link Libraries (DLLs), Library Versions, MFC: 32-Bit Programming Issues, OLE Overview, Database Overview

MFC: Features No Longer Available

This article describes features of MFC that are not available in this Win32 version. These include:

- VBX controls (not supported on 32-bit platforms).

- Microsoft Windows for Pen Computing classes (not supported under Windows NT).

- The **UnrealizeObject** function has been deleted in Win32.

  Since calls to **CGdiObject::UnrealizeObject** are common in programs written for Windows version 3.*x*, yet are now unnecessary, this member function is retained for backward compatibility. It now always returns a nonzero value, without making an underlying Win32 function call. Calls to **CGdiObject::UnrealizeObject** should not be made in new Win32 programs and should be removed from existing programs eventually.

- The **QueryAbort** function has been deleted in Win32; the **CDC::QueryAbort** member function has also been deleted.

  If your program needs this functionality, you should create a member function that calls your `AbortProc` callback function directly.

- The console library variants, NAFXCR.LIB and NAFXCRD.LIB, are no longer available.

You should now link with NAFXCW.LIB or NAFXCWD.LIB with no loss in capability or content from projects that previously used NAFXCR.LIB or NAFXCRD.LIB.

See Also MFC: Changes from MFC Version 2.0 32-Bit Edition, MFC: Changes from MFC Versions 2.0 and 2.5

MFC: 32-Bit Programming Issues

This article summarizes issues that arise when programming in the 32-bit environment.

Version 3.0 and later of the Microsoft Foundation Class Library (MFC) uses the Win32 application programming interface (API). Many of the Win32 API functions are encapsulated in MFC class member functions. However, one of the fundamental tenets of programming with MFC is that you can always make direct calls to the Windows API.

Issues include:

- Applications created with the 32-bit version of MFC version 3.0 can run on Windows NT, Windows version 3.1 (using Win32s), and other Win32 platforms. To write portable applications, you must avoid using Win32 API functions that are not supported on all of your target platforms.

  (OLE applications on Windows NT require Windows NT version 3.5 or later.)

- Visual C++ version 2.0 cannot load and save executable (.EXE) files, compiled resource script (.RES) files, or dynamic-link libraries, and it does not directly support new Win32 resource types (the message table resource type or Unicode strings in resources).

- Differences between the 16-bit versions of MFC and version 3.0 (32-bit) are:

  - The packing of *lParam* and *wParam* in the **CWnd** members **OnCommand** and **OnParentNotify** has changed from 16-bit MFC. For more information, see Changing Message Handlers in the article MFC: Porting Tips.

  - The **CTime** class has constructors that accept system and file times from Win32. For more information, see the article Date and Time: SYSTEMTIME Support.

  - The class library provides new member functions that wrap many Win32 API functions, including many Win32 GDI functions.

  - Class **CWinThread** supports multithreaded programming. For more information, see the article Multithreading.

  - Most of the class library is enabled for Unicode and for Double-Byte Character Set (DBCS) programming. The database classes are the exception. This enabling means that many class member functions now take character and string parameters of types based on type **TCHAR**. For more information, see Chapter 13 in *Programming Techniques*.

- The 32-bit MFC static link and dynamic-link libraries are named differently from the 16-bit libraries. See the article Library Versions.

Some features of the class library are no longer available in the 32-bit environment. See the article MFC: Features No Longer Available.

See Also   MFC: Porting MFC Applications to 32-Bit, MFC: Porting Tips

MFC: Porting MFC Applications to 32-Bit

This article describes how to port a 16-bit MFC application to 32-bit. For more general information on writing 32-bit applications, see the article MFC: 32-Bit Programming Issues.

Well-written MFC 2.0 and 2.5 applications that don't use 16-bit features (such as VBX controls, inline assembler, 16-bit ints, or Win32 API functions) can usually be migrated to Win32 with no changes.

This article describes:

- A porting procedure.
- General tips for porting to Win32.

Porting Procedure

The following procedure uses the same top-down approach advocated in Chapter 1, Porting 16-Bit Code to 32-Bit Windows, of *Programming Techniques*.

▶ **To port a 16-bit framework application to 32 bits**

1 Import your application files into a new Visual C++ project.

   Simply open your old project. Projects created with Visual C++ versions 1.0 and 1.5 are converted automatically to version 2.0 format.

2 Remove VBX controls.

   VBX controls are not supported in a 32-bit application. Thus, the **CVBControl** class, the **AfxRegisterVBEvent**, **AfxGetPict**, **AfxSetPict**, and **AfxReferencePict** global functions, and the **ON_VBXEVENT** macro are unavailable with Win32. If you use VBX controls in your application, you must replace them with standard Windows controls, redesigning your application as necessary.

3 Remove Windows for Pens extensions.

   The 32-bit version of MFC does not currently include the **CHEdit** and **CBEdit** classes, which implement 16-bit extensions for Windows for Pens. Thus, if your existing application supports pen extensions, it will not compile as a 32-bit application. If you want to run with Win32, you will need to substitute another form of user input, most likely keyboard input, for the pen class input.

4 Replace difficult-to-port code, such as assembly-language functions and MS-DOS calls, with stubs.

Win32 is designed to be portable, and your applications should follow suit. If your 16-bit application makes calls to an assembly-language module, you should rewrite it in C or C++ if possible. Otherwise, you will be faced with rewriting the assembly-language portion for each hardware platform that can run Win32.

If you've used any MS-DOS services for file I/O, including those used by Windows version 3.x, you will have to rewrite the code using the new Win32 file I/O set that replaces these services. If you've used the **CFile** class for file I/O, you are shielded from this change because **CFile** uses the new function calls even though its member function interface remains unchanged.

If you need to write custom file I/O functions, see the Win32 Software Development Kit documentation for more information.

5 Build your application with Visual C++ version 2.0 and note any 32-bit related problems.

6 Use the information in General Tips for Porting to Win32 to fix any problems. Rebuild until the main body of your program is running correctly.

7 Implement each function you stubbed in step 4 with portable code until the entire application runs correctly.

8 Remove MFC libraries from the link input list.

Let the MFC header files automatically link in the correct version of MFC, as described in the article Library Versions.

Note If you want your application to support Unicode, follow the guidelines in Chapter 13, Developing for International Markets, in *Programming Techniques*.

General Tips for Porting to Win32

Moving to 32 bits means changing from a 16-bit segmented architecture to a 32-bit flat address space. What will this change in architecture mean when you port your existing 16-bit application? Different memory models, near and far pointers, and the limitations of 64K segments do not exist under Win32.

Certain fundamental Windows parameters also change in Win32:

- Handles to windows and to GDI objects such as pens, brushes, and menus are now 32 bits wide.

- System metrics have changed (screen dimensions and colors are now 32-bit values), and thus many graphics and other functions have changed.

- A **WPARAM** is now 32 bits wide, which means that message packing and window procedures change.

- The **WinMain** function parameters have changed (this is handled for you in the **CWinApp** class).

For more general information about porting to Win32, see Chapter 1, Porting 16-Bit Code to 32-Bit Windows, in *Programming Techniques*.

See Also MFC: 32-Bit Programming Issues, MFC: Porting Tips

MFC: Porting Tips

This article gives tips for porting your application from 16-bit to 32-bit.

Although most of the changes in Windows parameters are handled for you within the framework, there are some changes you will have to make manually. They are described in this article, which covers:

- Changing message handlers
- Using the collection classes

The **CTime** class has also changed. See the article Date and Time: SYSTEMTIME Support.

Changing Message Handlers

Window handles in the Win32 API are now 32-bit values; consequently, the **WPARAM** type has been widened from 16 to 32 bits to accommodate this change. This widening often necessitates repacking the values carried by the *wParam* and *lParam* parameters.

A 16-bit application, written for Windows without using the framework, requires a considerable amount of code rewriting to port successfully to 32-bit. Each window procedure declaration must be modified, as well as the message-handling code within the procedure.

The class library accommodates most of these changes internally. The framework hides the window procedure from you, unpacks *wParam* and *lParam*, and passes the properly unpacked values to you in message handlers. The only two instances that require your attention are functions that override the **CWnd::OnCommand** and **CWnd::OnParentNotify** message handlers, where the framework passes *wParam* or *lParam* directly from Windows to you.

The framework also unpacks the *wParam* and *lParam* values associated with a **WM_COMMAND** message to implement message-map entries. The framework properly unpacks the values as appropriate for Windows version 3.*x* or Win32 with no attention from you.

CWnd::OnCommand Changes

If your application overrides **OnCommand**, check the code carefully and modify it so that it unpacks *wParam* and *lParam* correctly. Your 16-bit override of **OnCommand** may compile successfully, but will not execute correctly.

When the framework receives a **WM_COMMAND** message, it calls the **CWnd::OnCommand** member function with the following arguments:

virtual BOOL OnCommand(WPARAM *wParam*, **LPARAM** *lParam* **);**

A command ID, a control handle, and a notification message can be packed in *wParam* and *lParam*, depending on the circumstances of the call.

You don't need to change the way you extract the command ID; it is packed the same way in both environments. You can extract it this way:

```
UINT nID = LOWORD(wParam);
```

You extract the remaining two values in this way in the 16-bit framework:

```
HWND hWndCtrl = (HWND)LOWORD(lParam);      //Control handle
int nCode = HIWORD(lParam);                //Notification code
```

You extract them this way in the 32-bit framework:

```
HWND hWndCtrl = (HWND)lParam;              //Control handle
int nCode = HIWORD(wParam);                //Notification code
```

In both the 16-bit and 32-bit versions, if the **OnCommand** message is from an accelerator, the value retrieved in nCode is 1. If the message is from a menu, the value in nCode is 0.

CWnd::OnParentNotify Changes

As with **OnCommand**, carefully check any code in your application that overrides **OnParentNotify** and modify it so that it unpacks values from *lParam* correctly. Your 16-bit override of **OnParentNotify** will compile successfully, but will not execute correctly.

The framework calls the **CWnd::OnParentNotify** member function with the following arguments:

afx_msg void OnParentNotify(UINT *message*, **LPARAM** *lParam* **);**

The **OnParentNotify** member function is called for the parent of a child window in two cases: when the mouse is clicked over a child window, and when a child window is created or destroyed.

When the *message* parameter is equal to **WM_CREATE** or **WM_DESTROY**, the framework's 16-bit packing of *lParam* puts the child window handle in the low-order word and the identifier of the child window in the high-order word. For the 32-bit framework, the child window handle has been widened and now takes up all of *lParam*; the child window identifier is unavailable.

If your Win32 code in **OnParentNotify** requires the child ID, retrieve it like this:

```
CWnd* pChild = FromHandle( (HWND)lParam );
int nID = pChild->GetDlgCtrlID();
```

In this example, **FromHandle** returns the **CWnd** object attached to the child window handle. The **GetDlgCtrlID** member function returns the child window ID. You could also retrieve the child ID by passing the child handle directly to the Windows

GetDlgCtrlID function, but the code above also retrieves a pointer to the child **CWnd** object.

The pointer returned in pChild is temporary and should not be stored for use beyond the scope of **OnParentNotify**.

Using the Collection Classes

With Windows version 3.*x*, the **CObArray** class and all related array collection classes are constrained by 16-bit memory models and must fit within a single 64K segment.

With Win32, the number of elements that can fit within a framework array collection is limited only by the amount of available memory. The maximum number of collection elements is the largest possible value of a **UINT**, which is much larger than a typical computer's memory. The increase in maximum collection size should have little effect upon your code because a framework collection simply throws a **CMemoryException** when it reaches its memory limit in both the 16-bit version and the 32-bit version of the framework.

See Also   MFC: 32-Bit Programming Issues, MFC: Porting MFC Applications to 32-Bit, Date and Time: SYSTEMTIME Support

MFC: Using Database Classes with Documents and Views

You can use the MFC database classes—DAO or ODBC—with or without the document/view architecture. This article emphasizes working with documents and views. It explains:

- How to write a form-based application using a **CRecordView** or **CDaoRecordView** object as the main view on your document.

- How to use recordset objects in your documents and views.

- Other considerations.

For alternatives, see the article MFC: Using Database Classes Without Documents and Views.

Writing a Form-Based Application

Many data-access applications are based on forms. The user interface is a form containing controls in which the user examines, enters, or edits data. To make your application form-based, use class **CRecordView** or **CDaoRecordView**. You can specify **CRecordView** or **CDaoRecordView** for your view class when you run AppWizard, or you can use ClassWizard later to create a **CRecordView**-derived or **CDaoRecordview**-derived class.

In a form-based application, each record view object stores a pointer to a **CRecordset** or **CDaoRecordset** object. The framework's record field exchange (RFX) mechanism exchanges data between the recordset and the data source. The dialog data exchange (DDX) mechanism exchanges data between the field data members of the recordset object and the controls on the form. **CRecordView** or **CDaoRecordView** also provides default command handler functions for navigating from record to record on the form.

▸ **To create a form-based application with AppWizard**

- See the article AppWizard: Database Support.

▸ **To add a database form to your application with ClassWizard**

- See the article ClassWizard: Creating a Database Form.

For a full discussion of forms, see the article Record Views. For an example of an application with multiple record views on a database, see the MFC tutorial sample ENROLL, Step 4. The step is not covered in the tutorial, but you can examine the code.

Using Recordsets in Documents and Views

Many simple form-based applications don't need "documents." If your application is more complex, you'll probably want to use a document as a proxy for the database, storing a **CDatabase** or **CDaoDatabase** object that connects to the data source. Form-based applications usually store a pointer to a recordset object in the view. Other kinds of database applications store recordsets and **CDatabase** or **CDaoDatabase** objects in the document. Here are some possibilities for using documents in database applications:

- If you're accessing a recordset in a local context, create **CRecordset** or **CDaoRecordset** objects locally in member functions of the document or the view, as needed.

  Declare a recordset object as a local variable in a function. Pass **NULL** to the constructor, which causes the framework to create and open a temporary **CDatabase** or **CDaoDatabase** object for you. As an alternative, pass a pointer to a **CDatabase** or **CDaoDatabase** object. Use the recordset within the function and let it be destroyed automatically when the function exits.

  When you pass **NULL** to a recordset constructor, the framework uses information returned by the recordset's **GetDefaultConnect** member function to create a **CDatabase** or **CDaoDatabase** object and open it. The wizards implement **GetDefaultConnect** for you.

- If you're accessing a recordset during the lifetime of your document, embed one or more **CRecordset** or **CDaoRecordset** objects in your document.

  Construct the recordset objects either when you initialize the document or as needed. You might write a function that returns a pointer to the recordset if it already exists, or constructs and opens the recordset if it doesn't exist yet. Close, delete, and re-create the recordset as needed, or call its **Requery** member function to refresh the records.

- If you're accessing a data source during the lifetime of your document, embed a **CDatabase** or **CDaoDatabase** object or store a pointer to a **CDatabase** or **CDaoDatabase** object in it.

  The **CDatabase** or **CDaoDatabase** object manages a connection to your data source. The object is constructed automatically during document construction, and you call its **Open** member function when you initialize the document. When you construct recordset objects in document member functions, you pass a pointer to the document's **CDatabase** or **CDaoDatabase** object. This associates each recordset with its data source. The database object is usually destroyed when the document closes. The recordset objects are typically destroyed when they exit the scope of a function.

Other Factors

Form-based applications often do not have any use for the framework's document serialization mechanism, so you might want to remove, disable, or replace the New and Open commands on the File menu. See the article Serialization: Serialization vs. Database Input/Output.

You might also want to make use of the many user-interface possibilities that the framework can support. For example, you could use multiple **CRecordView** or **CDaoRecordView** objects in a splitter window, open multiple recordsets in different multiple document interface (MDI) child windows, and so on.

You might want to implement printing of whatever is in your view—whether it's a form implemented with **CRecordView** or **CDaoRecordView** or something else. As classes derived from **CFormView**, **CRecordView** and **CDaoRecordView** don't support printing, but you can override the **OnPrint** member function. For more information, see class **CFormView**, and see the MFC General sample VIEWEX.

You might not want to use documents and views at all. In that case, see the article MFC: Using Database Classes Without Documents and Views.

See Also Serialization: Serialization vs. Database Input/Output

MFC: Using Database Classes Without Documents and Views

Although in many cases you will want to use the framework's document/view architecture in your database applications, sometimes you might not want to use them. This article explains:

- When you don't need to use document/view functionality such as document serialization.

- AppWizard options to support applications without serialization and without document-related File menu commands such as New, Open, Save, and Save As.

- How to work with an application that uses a minimal document.

- How to structure an application with no document or view.

When You Don't Need Documents

For some applications, there is a distinct concept of a "document." These applications typically load all or most of a file from storage into memory with a File Open command. They write the updated file back to storage all at once with a File Save or Save As command. What the user sees is a data file.

Some categories of applications, however, don't require a document. Database applications operate in terms of "transactions." The application selects records from a database and presents them to the user, often one at a time. What the user sees is usually a single current record, which may be the only one in memory.

If your application doesn't require a document for storing data, you can dispense with some or all of the framework's document/view architecture. How much you dispense with depends on the approach you prefer. You might:

- Use a minimal document as a place to store a connection to your data source but dispense with normal document features such as serialization. This is advantageous especially when you want several views of the data and would like to synchronize all of the views, updating them all at once and so on.

- Use a frame window, into which you draw directly, rather than using a view. Omit the document. Store any data or data connections in the frame-window object.

AppWizard Options for Documents and Views

If you use AppWizard to create your application, all of the database options produce applications with documents and views. Some of the options provide documents and views without document functionality you won't need for your database application. Table 1 shows the kinds of document/view support for each option.

Table 1   AppWizard Options for Documents and Views

Option	View	Document
None (no database support).	Derived from **CView**.	Full document support including serialization and New, Open, Save, and Save As commands on the File menu.
Only include header files.	Derived from **CView**.	Same. You can store **CDatabase** or **CDaoDatabase** and/or **CRecordset** or **CDaoRecordset** objects in your document or your view.

Table 1 AppWizard Options for Documents and Views *(cont.)*

Option	View	Document
A database view, without file support.	Derived from **CRecordView** or **CDaoRecordView**.	Document does not support serialization or the New, Open, Save, and Save As commands. You can use it to store your **CRecordset** or **CDaoRecordset** and to coordinate multiple views.
Both a database view and file support.	Derived from **CRecordView** or **CDaoRecordView**.	Full document support, including serialization and document-related File menu commands. Use serialization for special purposes, such as storing user profile information.

For a discussion of using the AppWizard options "A database view, without file support" and "Both a database view and file support," see Applications with Minimal Documents.

For a discussion of writing applications with no document, see Applications with No Document.

For a discussion of alternatives to serialization, and alternative uses for serialization, see the article Serialization: Serialization vs. Database Input/Output.

Applications with Minimal Documents

AppWizard has two options that support form-based data-access applications. Each option creates a **CRecordView**-or **CDaoRecordView** derived view class and a document. They differ in what they leave out of the document.

A Document Without File Support

Select the AppWizard database option "A database view, without file support" if you don't need document serialization. The document still serves the following useful purposes:

- It's a convenient place to store a **CRecordset** or **CDaoRecordset**.

  This usage parallels ordinary document concepts: the document "stores" the data —or, in this case, a set of records—and the view is a view of the document.

- If your application presents multiple views (such as multiple record views), a document supports coordinating the views.

  If multiple views show the same data, you can use the **CDocument::UpdateAllViews** member function to coordinate updates to all views when any view changes the data.

You'll usually use this option for simple form-based applications such as the Enroll tutorial application. AppWizard supports a convenient structure for such applications automatically.

A Document with File Support

Select the AppWizard database option "Both a database view and file support" when you have an alternative use for the document-related File menu commands and document serialization. For the data-access portion of your program, you can use the document in the same way as described in A Document Without File Support. You can use the document's serialization capability, for example, to read and write a serialized user profile document that stores the user's preferences or other useful information. For more ideas, see the article Serialization: Serialization vs. Database Input/Output.

AppWizard supports this option, but you must write the code that serializes the document. Store the serialized information in document data members.

Applications with No Document

You might sometimes want to write an application that uses neither documents nor views. Without documents, you store your data (such as a **CRecordset** or **CDaoRecordset** object) in your frame-window class or your application class. Any additional requirements depend on whether the application presents a user interface.

Database Support with a User Interface

If you have a user interface (other than, say, a console command-line interface), your application draws directly into the frame window's client area rather than into a view. Such an application doesn't use **CRecordView**, **CDaoRecordView**, **CFormView**, or **CDialog** for its main user interface (but it will normally use **CDialog** for ordinary dialogs).

Writing Applications Without Documents

Applications without documents resemble applications written with the Microsoft Foundation Class Library version 1.0. AppWizard doesn't support creating this kind of application, so you must write your own **CWinApp**-derived class and, if needed, also create a **CFrameWnd** or **CMDIFrameWnd** class. Override **CWinApp::InitInstance** and declare an application object as

```
CYourNameApp NEAR theApp;
```

The framework still supplies the message-map mechanism and many other features.

Database Support Separate from the User Interface

Some applications need either no user interface or only a minimal one. For example, suppose you're writing:

- An intermediate data-access object that other applications (clients) call for special processing of data between the application and the data source.

- An application that processes data without user intervention, such as an application that moves data from one database format to another, or one that does calculations and performs batch updates.

Because there is no document that owns the **CRecordset** or **CDaoRecordset** object, you'll probably want to store it as an embedded data member in your **CWinApp**-derived application class. Alternatives include:

- Not keeping a permanent **CRecordset** or **CDaoRecordset** object at all. You can pass **NULL** to your recordset class constructors. In that case, the framework creates a temporary **CDatabase** or **CDaoDatabase** object using the information in the recordset's **GetDefaultConnect** member function. This is the most likely alternative approach.

- Making the **CRecordset** or **CDaoRecordset** object a global variable. This variable should be a pointer to a recordset object that you create dynamically in your **CWinApp::InitInstance** override. (This avoids attempting to construct the object before the framework is initialized.)

- Using recordset objects as you would within the context of a document or a view. Create recordsets in the member functions of your application or frame-window objects.

See Also   Serialization: Serialization vs. Database Input/Output

MFC: Using the MFC Source Files

Full source code is supplied with the Microsoft Foundation Class Library (MFC). Header files (.H) are in the MFC\INCLUDE directory; implementation files (.CPP) are in the MFC\SRC directory.

Note   The MFC\SRC directory contains a makefile you can use with NMAKE to build MFC library versions, including a browse version. A browse version of MFC is useful for tracing through the calling structure of MFC itself. The file README.TXT in that directory explains how to use this makefile.

This article explains the conventions that MFC uses to comment the various parts of each class, what these comments mean, and what you should expect to find in each section. ClassWizard and AppWizard use similar conventions for the classes they create for you, and you will probably find these conventions useful for your own code.

You might be familiar with the **public**, **protected**, and **private** C++ keywords. When looking at the MFC header files, you'll find that each class may have several of each of these. For example, public member variables and functions might be under more than one **public** keyword. This is because MFC separates member variables and functions based on their use, not by the type of access allowed. MFC uses **private** sparingly—even items considered implementation details are generally protected and many times are public. Even though access to the implementation details is discouraged, MFC leaves the decision to you.

In both the MFC source files and the files that AppWizard creates, you will find comments like these within class declarations (usually in this order):

```
// Constructors
// Attributes
// Operations
// Overridables
// Implementation
```

Topics covered in this article include:

- An example of the comments

- The // Implementation comment

- The // Constructors comment

- The // Attributes comment

- The // Operations comment

- The // Overridables comment

An Example of the Comments

The following partial listing of class **CStdioFile** uses most of the comments:

```
class CStdioFile : public CFile
{
    DECLARE_DYNAMIC(CStdioFile)

public:
// Constructors
    CStdioFile();
...

// Attributes
    FILE* m_pStream;      // stdio FILE
...

// Operations
    virtual void WriteString(LPCTSTR lpsz);
...
    virtual LPTSTR ReadString(LPTSTR lpsz, UINT nMax);
...

// Implementation
public:
...
};
```

These comments consistently mark sections of the class declaration that contain similar kinds of class members. Keep in mind that these are MFC conventions, not hard and fast rules.

The // **Implementation Comment**

The most important section is the // Implementation section.

This section houses all implementation details. Both member variables and member functions can appear in this section. Everything below this line could change in a future release of MFC. Unless you can't avoid it, you should not rely on details below the // Implementation line. In addition, members declared below the implementation line are not documented, although some implementation is discussed in technical notes. Overrides of virtual functions in the base class reside in this section, regardless of which section the base class function is defined in, since the fact that a function overrides the base class implementation is considered an implementation detail. Typically these members are protected, but not always.

Notice from the **CStdioFile** listing under An Example of the Comments that members declared below the // Implementation comment may be declared as **public**, **protected**, or **private**. The point is that you should only use these members with caution, because they might change in the future. Declaring a group of members as **public** may be necessary for the class library implementation to work correctly. However, this does not imply that you may safely use the members so declared.

Note You may find comments of the remaining types either above or below the // Implementation comment. In either case, they describe the kinds of members declared below them. If they occur below the // Implementation comment, you should assume that the members might change in future versions of MFC.

The // **Constructors Comment**

This section declares constructors (in the C++ sense) as well as any initialization functions required to really use the object. For example, **CWnd::Create** is in the constructors section because before you use the **CWnd** object it must be "fully constructed" by first calling the C++ constructor and then calling the **Create** function. Typically these members are public.

CStdioFile has three constructors, one of which is shown in the listing under An Example of the Comments.

The // **Attributes Comment**

This section contains the public attributes (or properties) of the object. Typically these are member variables, or Get/Set functions. The "Get" and "Set" functions may or may not be virtual. The "Get" functions are usually **const**, since in most cases they don't have side effects. These members are normally public; protected and private attributes are typically found in the implementation section.

In the sample listing from class **CStdioFile**, under An Example of the Comments, the list includes one member variable, **m_pStream**. Class **CDC** lists nearly 20 members under this comment.

Note Large classes, such as **CDC** and **CWnd**, may have so many members that simply listing all of the attributes in one group would not add much to clarity. In such cases, the class library uses other comments as headings to further delineate the members. For example, **CDC** uses `// Device-Context Functions`, `// Drawing Tool Functions`, `// Drawing Attribute Functions`, and more. Groups that represent attributes will follow the usual syntax described above. Many of the OLE classes have an implementation section called `// Interface Maps`.

The // Operations Comment

This section contains member functions that you can call on the object to make it do things or perform actions (perform operations). These functions are typically non-**const** since they usually have side effects. They may be virtual or nonvirtual depending on the needs of the class. Typically these members are public.

In the sample listing from class **CStdioFile**, under An Example of the Comments, the list includes two member functions under this comment: **ReadString** and **WriteString**.

As with attributes, operations may be further subdivided.

The // Overridables Comment

This section contains virtual functions that you can override in a derived class when you need to modify the base class behavior. They are usually named starting with "On", although it is not strictly necessary. Functions here are designed to be overridden, and often implement or provide some sort of "callback" or "hook." Typically these members are protected.

In MFC itself, pure virtual functions are always placed in this section. A pure virtual function in C++ is one of the form:

```
virtual void OnDraw( ) = 0;
```

In the sample listing from class **CStdioFile**, under An Example of the Comments, the list includes no overridables section. Class **CDocument**, on the other hand, lists approximately 10 overridable member functions.

In some classes, you may also see the comment `// Advanced Overridables`. These are functions that only advanced programmers should attempt to override. You will probably never need to override them.

Note The conventions described in this article also work well, in general, for OLE Automation methods and properties. Automation methods are similar to MFC operations. Automation properties are similar to MFC attributes. Automation events (supported for OLE controls) are similar to MFC overridable member functions.

Multithreading

The Microsoft Foundation Class Library (MFC) provides support for multithreaded applications. This article describes what processes and threads are, and MFC's approach to multithreading.

A "process" is an executing instance of an application. For example, when you double-click the Notepad icon, you start a process that runs Notepad.

A "thread" is a path of execution within a process. When you start Notepad, the operating system creates a process and begins executing the primary thread of that process. When this thread terminates, so does the process. This primary thread is supplied to the operating system by the startup code in the form of a function address. Usually, it is the address of the **main** or **WinMain** function that is supplied.

You can create additional threads in your application if you wish. You may want to do this to handle background or maintenance tasks when you don't want the user to wait for them to complete. All threads in MFC applications are represented by **CWinThread** objects. In most situations, you don't even have to explicitly create these objects; instead call the framework helper function **AfxBeginThread**, which creates the **CWinThread** object for you.

MFC distinguishes two types of threads: user-interface threads and worker threads. User-interface threads are commonly used to handle user input and respond to events and messages generated by the user. Worker threads are commonly used to complete tasks, such as recalculation, that do not require user input. The Win32 API does not distinguish between types of threads; it just needs to know the thread's starting address so it can begin to execute the thread. MFC handles user-interface threads specially by supplying a message pump for events in the user interface. **CWinApp** is an example of a user-interface thread object, as it derives from **CWinThread** and handles events and messages generated by the user.

Special attention should be given to situations where more than one thread may require access to the same object. The article Multithreading: Programming Tips describes techniques you can use to get around problems that may arise in these situations. The article Multithreading: How to Use the Synchronization Classes describes how to use the classes that are available to synchronize access from multiple threads to a single object.

Writing and debugging multithreaded programming is inherently a complicated and tricky undertaking, as you must ensure that objects are not accessed by more than one thread at a time. The articles in the Multithreading group do not teach the basics of multithreaded programming, only how to use MFC in your multithreaded program. The multithreaded MFC samples included in Visual C++ illustrate a few multithreaded programming techniques and Win32 APIs not encompassed by MFC, but are only intended to be a starting point.

For more information on how the operating system handles processes and threads, see Chapter 43, Processes and Threads, in the *Win32 Programmer's Reference, Volume 2.*

To gain an understanding of how to write a multithreaded program, you should refer to a book such as Jeffrey Richter's *Advanced Windows NT* (Microsoft Press, 1994).

For more details on MFC multithreading support, see the following articles:

- Multithreading: Creating User-Interface Threads
- Multithreading: Creating Worker Threads
- Multithreading: How to Use the Synchronization Classes
- Multithreading: Terminating Threads
- Multithreading: Programming Tips
- Multithreading: When to Use the Synchronization Classes

Multithreading: Creating User-Interface Threads

A user-interface thread is commonly used to handle user input and respond to user events independently of threads executing other portions of the application. The main application thread (provided in your **CWinApp**-derived class) is already created and started for you. This article describes the steps necessary to create additional user-interface threads.

The first thing you must do when creating a user-interface thread is derive a class from **CWinThread**. You must declare and implement this class using the **DECLARE_DYNCREATE** and **IMPLEMENT_DYNCREATE** macros. This class must override some functions, and can override others. These functions and what they should do are presented in Table 1.

Table 1 Functions to Override When Creating a User-Interface Thread

Function name	Purpose
ExitInstance	Perform cleanup when thread terminates. Usually overridden.
InitInstance	Perform thread instance initialization. Must be overridden.
OnIdle	Perform thread-specific idle-time processing. Not usually overridden.
PreTranslateMessage	Filter messages before they are dispatched to **TranslateMessage** and **DispatchMessage**. Not usually overridden.

Table 1 Functions to Override When Creating a User-Interface Thread *(cont.)*

Function name	Purpose
ProcessWndProcException	Intercept unhandled exceptions thrown by the thread's message and command handlers. Not usually overridden.
Run	Controlling function for the thread. Contains the message pump. Rarely overridden.

MFC provides two versions of **AfxBeginThread** through parameter overloading: one for user-interface threads and the other for worker threads. To start your user-interface thread, call **AfxBeginThread** providing the following information:

- The **RUNTIME_CLASS** of the class you derived from **CWinThread**.

- (Optionally) The desired priority level. The default is normal priority. For more information on the available priority levels, see **::SetThreadPriority** in the *Win32 Programmer's Reference, Volume 4*.

- (Optionally) The desired stack size for the thread. The default is the same size stack as the creating thread.

- (Optionally) **CREATE_SUSPENDED** if you want the thread to be created in a suspended state. The default is 0, or start the thread normally.

- (Optionally) The desired security attributes. The default is the same access as the parent thread. For more information on the format of this security information, see **SECURITY_ATTRIBUTES** in the *Win32 Programmer's Reference, Volume 5*.

AfxBeginThread does most of the work for you. It creates a new object of your class, initializes it with the information you supply, and calls **CWinThread::CreateThread** to start executing the thread. Checks are made throughout the procedure to make sure all objects are deallocated properly should any part of the creation fail.

See Also Multithreading: Terminating Threads, Multithreading: Creating Worker Threads

In the *Class Library Reference*: **CWinThread**

In the *Win32 Programmer's Reference, Volume 2*: Chapter 43, Processes and Threads

Multithreading: Creating Worker Threads

A worker thread is commonly used to handle background tasks that the user shouldn't have to wait for to continue using your application. Tasks such as recalculation and background printing are good examples of worker threads. This article details the steps necessary to create a worker thread. Topics include:

- Starting the thread

- Implementing the controlling function

- Example

Creating a worker thread is a relatively simple task. Only two steps are required to get your thread running: implementing the controlling function and starting the thread. It is not necessary to derive a class from **CWinThread**. You can if you need a special version of **CWinThread**, but it is not required for most simple worker threads. You can use **CWinThread** without modification.

Starting the Thread

There are two overloaded versions of **AfxBeginThread**: one for user-interface threads and one for worker threads. To begin execution of your worker thread, call **AfxBeginThread** providing the following information:

- The address of the controlling function.

- The parameter to be passed to the controlling function.

- (Optionally) The desired priority of the thread. The default is normal priority. For more information on the available priority levels, see **::SetThreadPriority** in the *Win32 Programmer's Reference, Volume 4.*

- (Optionally) The desired stack size for the thread. The default is the same size stack as the creating thread.

- (Optionally) **CREATE_SUSPENDED** if you want the thread to be created in a suspended state. The default is 0, or start the thread normally.

- (Optionally) The desired security attributes. The default is the same access as the parent thread. For more information on the format of this security information, see **SECURITY_ATTRIBUTES** in the *Win32 Programmer's Reference, Volume 5.*

AfxBeginThread creates and initializes a **CWinThread** object for you, starts it, and returns its address so you can refer to it later. Checks are made throughout the procedure to make sure all objects are deallocated properly should any part of the creation fail.

Implementing the Controlling Function

The controlling function defines the thread. When this function is entered, the thread starts, and when it exits, the thread terminates. This function should have the following prototype:

```
UINT MyControllingFunction( LPVOID pParam );
```

The parameter is a single 32-bit value. The value the function receives in this parameter is the value that was passed to the constructor when the thread object was created. The controlling function can interpret this value in any manner it chooses. It can be treated as a scalar value, or a pointer to a structure containing multiple parameters, or it can be ignored. If the parameter refers to a structure, the structure can be used not only to pass data from the caller to the thread, but also to pass data back from the thread to the caller. If you use such a structure to pass data back to the caller, the thread will need to notify the caller when the results are ready. For information on communicating from the worker thread to the caller, see the article Multithreading: Programming Tips.

When the function terminates, it should return a **DWORD** value indicating the reason for termination. Typically, this exit code is 0 to indicate success with other values indicating different types of errors. This is purely implementation dependent. Some threads may maintain usage counts of objects, and return the current number of uses of that object. To see how applications can retrieve this value, see the article Multithreading: Terminating Threads.

There are some restrictions on what you can do in a multithreaded program written with the Microsoft Foundation Class Library. For descriptions of these restrictions and other tips on using threads, see the article Multithreading: Programming Tips.

Controlling Function Example

This example shows how to define a controlling function and use it from another portion of the program.

```
DWORD MyThreadProc( LPVOID pParam )
{
    CMyObject* pObject = (CMyObject*)pParam;

    if (pObject == NULL ||
        !pObject->IsKindOf(RUNTIME_CLASS(CMyObject)))
    return -1;  // illegal parameter

    // do something with 'pObject'

    return 0;   // thread completed successfully
}

// inside a different function in the program
.
.
.
pNewObject = new CMyObject;
AfxBeginThread(MyThreadProc, pNewObject);
.
.
.
```

See Also   Multithreading: Creating User-Interface Threads, Multithreading: Terminating Threads, Multithreading: Programming Tips

Multithreading: How to Use the Synchronization Classes

Synchronizing resource access between threads is a common problem when writing multithreaded applications. Having two or more threads simultaneously access the same data can lead to undesirable and unpredictable results. For example, one thread could be updating the contents of a structure while another thread is reading the contents of the same structure. It is unknown what data the reading thread will receive; the old data, the newly written data, or possibly a mixture of both. MFC provides a number of synchronization and synchronization access classes to aid in solving this problem. This article explains the classes available and how to use them to create thread-safe classes in a typical multithreaded application.

A typical multithreaded application has a class that represents a resource to be shared among threads. A properly designed, fully thread-safe class does not require you to call any synchronization functions. Everything is handled internally to the class, allowing you to worry about how to best use the class, not about how it might get corrupted. The best technique for creating a fully thread-safe class is to merge the synchronization class into the resource class. Merging the synchronization classes into the shared class is a straightforward process.

As an example, take an application that maintains a linked-list of accounts. This application allows up to three accounts to be examined in separate windows, but only one can be updated at any particular time. When an account is updated, the updated data is sent over the network to a data archive.

This example application uses all three types of synchronization classes. Since it allows up to three accounts to be examined at one time, it uses **CSemaphore** to limit access to three view objects. When an attempt to view a fourth account occurs, the application either waits until one of the first three windows closes or it fails. When an account is updated, the application uses **CCriticalSection** to ensure that only one account is updated at a time. After the update succeeds, it signals **CEvent**, which releases a thread waiting for the event to be signaled. This thread sends the new data to the data archive.

Designing a Thread-Safe Class

To make a class fully thread-safe, first add the appropriate synchronization class to the shared classes as a data member. In the previous account-management example, a **CSemaphore** data member would be added to the view class, a **CCriticalSection** data member would be added to the linked-list class, and a **CEvent** data member would be added to the data storage class.

Next, add synchronization calls to the appropriate member functions of each thread-safe class. This means that all member functions that modify the data in the class or access a controlled resource should create either a **CSingleLock** or **CMultiLock** object and call that object's **Lock** function. When the lock object goes out of scope and is destroyed, **Unlock** is called for you by the object's destructor, releasing the resource. Of course, you can call **Unlock** directly if you wish.

Designing your thread-safe class in this fashion allows it to be used in a multithreaded application as easily as a non-thread-safe class, but with complete safety. Encapsulating the synchronization object and synchronization access object into the resource's class provides all the benefits of fully thread-safe programming without the drawback of maintaining synchronization code.

The drawbacks to this approach are that the class will be slightly slower than the same class without the synchronization objects added. Also, if there is a chance that more than one thread may delete the object, the merged approach may not always work. In this situation, it is better to maintain separate synchronization objects.

For example code that uses the synchronization classes, see the MFC sample programs MTGDI and MUTEXES. These and other MFC sample programs can be found under Samples in Books Online.

For information on determining which synchronization class to use in different situations, see the article Multithreading: When to Use the Synchronization Classes. For more information on synchronization, see Chapter 44, Synchronization, in the *Microsoft Win32 Programmer's Reference, Volume 2*. For more information on multithreading support in MFC, see the article Multithreading.

See Also Multithreading: When to Use the Synchronization Classes

Multithreading: Terminating Threads

Two normal situations cause a thread to terminate: the controlling function exits or the thread should not be allowed to run to completion. If a word processor used a thread for background printing, the controlling function would terminate normally if printing completed successfully. Should the user wish to cancel the printing, however, the background printing thread would have to be terminated prematurely. This article explains both how to implement each situation and how to get the exit code of a thread after it terminates.

Normal Thread Termination

For a worker thread, normal thread termination is simple: exit the controlling function and return a value that signifies the reason for termination. You can use either the **AfxEndThread** function or a **return** statement. Typically, 0 signifies successful completion, but that is up to you.

For a user-interface thread, the process is just as simple: from within the user-interface thread, call **::PostQuitMessage** in the *Win32 Programmer's Reference, Volume 4*. The only parameter that **::PostQuitMessage** takes is the exit code of the thread. As for worker threads, 0 typically signifies successful completion.

Premature Thread Termination

Terminating a thread prematurely is almost as simple: call **AfxEndThread** from within the thread. Pass the desired exit code as the only parameter. This stops execution of the thread, deallocates the thread's stack, detaches all DLLs attached to the thread, and deletes the thread object from memory.

AfxEndThread must be called from within the thread to be terminated. If you want to terminate a thread from another thread, you must set up a communication method between the two threads.

Retrieving the Exit Code of a Thread

To get the exit code of either the worker or the user-interface thread, call the **::GetExitCodeThread** function. For more information about this function, see the *Win32 Programmer's Reference, Volume 3*. This function takes the handle to the thread (stored in the m_hThread data member of **CWinThread** objects) and the address of a **DWORD**.

If the thread is still active, **::GetExitCodeThread** will place **STILL_ACTIVE** in the supplied **DWORD** address; otherwise, the exit code is placed in this address.

Retrieving the exit code of **CWinThread** objects takes an extra step. By default, when a **CWinThread** thread terminates, the thread object is deleted. This means that you cannot access the m_hThread data member since the **CWinThread** object no longer exists. To avoid this situation, do one of the following two things:

- Set the m_bAutoDelete data member to **FALSE**. This allows the **CWinThread** object to survive after the thread has been terminated. You can then access the m_hThread data member after the thread has been terminated. If you use this technique, however, you are responsible for destroying the **CWinThread** object as the framework will not automatically delete it for you. This is the preferred method.

  –or–

- Store the thread's handle separately. After the thread is created, copy its m_hThread data member (using **::DuplicateHandle**) to another variable and access it through that variable. This way the object is deleted automatically upon termination and you can still find out why the thread terminated. Be careful that the thread does not terminate before you can duplicate the handle. The safest way to do this is to pass **CREATE_SUSPENDED** to **AfxBeginThread**, store the handle, and then resume the thread by calling **ResumeThread**.

Either method allows you to determine why a **CWinThread** object terminated.

See Also In the *Class Library Reference*: **CWinThread**, **AfxEndThread**

In the *Run-Time Library Reference*: **_endthreadex**, **_beginthreadex**

In the *Win32 Programmer's Reference, Volume 3*: **::GetExitCodeThread**, **::ExitThread**

Multithreading: Programming Tips

Multithreaded applications require stricter care than single-threaded applications when accessing data. Since there are multiple, independent paths of execution in use simultaneously in multithreaded applications, either the algorithms, the data, or both must be aware that data could be used by more than one thread at a time. This article explains techniques for avoiding potential problems when programming multithreaded applications with the Microsoft Foundation Class Library (MFC).

Accessing Objects from Multiple Threads

For size and performance reasons, MFC objects are not thread safe at the object level, only at the class level. This means that you can have two separate threads manipulating two different **CString** objects, but not two threads manipulating the same **CString** object. If you absolutely must have multiple threads manipulating the same object, protect such access with appropriate Win32 synchronization mechanisms, such as critical sections. For more information on critical sections and other related objects, see Chapter 44, Synchronization, in the *Win32 Programmer's Reference, Volume 2*.

The class library uses critical sections internally to protect global data structures, such as those used by the debug memory allocator.

Accessing MFC Objects from Non-MFC Threads

If you have a multithreaded application that creates a thread in a way other than using a **CWinThread** object, you cannot access other MFC objects from that thread. In other words, if you want to access any MFC object from a secondary thread, you must create that thread with one of the methods described in the Multithreading: Creating User-Interface Threads or Multithreading: Creating Worker Threads articles. These methods are the only ones that allow the class library to initialize the internal variables necessary to handle multithreaded applications.

Windows Handle Maps

As a general rule, a thread can only access MFC objects that it created. This is because temporary and permanent Windows handle maps are kept in thread local storage to ensure protection from simultaneous access from multiple threads. For example, a worker thread cannot perform a calculation and then call a document's **UpdateAllViews** member function to have the windows that contain views on the new data modified. This will have no effect at all, since the map from **CWnd** objects to **HWND**s is local to the primary thread. What this means is that one thread may have a mapping from a Windows handle to a C++ object, but another thread may map that same handle to a different C++ object. Changes made in one thread would not be reflected in the other.

There are several ways around this problem. The first is to pass individual handles (such as an **HWND**) rather than C++ objects to the worker thread. The worker thread then adds these objects to its temporary map by calling the appropriate **FromHandle** member function. You could also add the object to the thread's permanent map by calling **Attach**, but this should only be done if you are guaranteed that the object will exist longer than the thread.

Another method is to create new user-defined messages corresponding to the different tasks your worker threads will be performing and post these messages to the application's main window using **::PostMessage**. This method of communication is similar to two different applications conversing except that both threads are executing in the same address space.

For more information on handle maps, see Technical Note 3 under MFC in Books Online. For more information on thread local storage, see sections 43.1.7, Thread Local Storage, and 43.2.4, Using Thread Local Storage, in the *Win32 Programmer's Reference, Volume 2*.

Communicating Between Threads

MFC provides a number of classes that allow threads to synchronize access to objects to maintain thread safety. Usage of these classes is described in the articles Multithreading: How to Use the Synchronization Classes and Multithreading: When to Use the Synchronization Classes. More information on these objects can be found in Chapter 44, Synchronization, in the *Win32 Programmer's Reference, Volume 2*.

See Also In the *Class Library Reference*: **CWinThread**

Multithreading: When to Use the Synchronization Classes

The six multithreaded classes provided with MFC fall into two categories: synchronization objects (**CSyncObject**, **CSemaphore**, **CMutex**, **CCriticalSection**, and **CEvent**) and synchronization access objects (**CMultiLock** and **CSingleLock**).

Synchronization classes are used when access to a resource must be controlled to ensure integrity of the resource. Synchronization access classes are used to gain access to these controlled resources. This article describes when to use each class.

To determine which synchronization class you should use, ask the following series of questions:

1. Does the application have to wait for something to happen before it can access the resource (for example, data must be received from a communications port before it can be written to a file)?

    If yes, use **CEvent**.

2. Can more than one thread within the same application access this resource at one time (for example, your application allows up to five windows with views on the same document)?

    If yes, use **CSemaphore**.

3. Can more than one application use this resource (for example, the resource is in a DLL)?

    If yes, use **CMutex**.

    If no, use **CCriticalSection**.

CSyncObject is never used directly. It is the base class for the other four synchronization classes.

As an example, take an application that maintains a linked-list of accounts. This application allows up to three accounts to be examined in separate windows, but only one can be updated at any particular time. When an account is updated, the updated data is sent over the network to a data archive.

This example application uses all three types of synchronization classes. Since it allows up to three accounts to be examined at one time, it uses **CSemaphore** to limit access to three view objects. When an attempt to view a fourth account occurs, the application either waits until one of the first three windows close or it fails. When an account is updated, the application uses **CCriticalSection** to ensure that only one account is updated at a time. After the update succeeds, it signals **CEvent**, which releases a thread waiting for the event to be signaled. This thread sends the new data to the data archive.

Choosing which synchronization access class to use is even simpler. If your application is concerned with accessing a single controlled resource only, use **CSingleLock**. If it needs access to any one of a number of controlled resources, use **CMultiLock**. In the earlier example, **CSingleLock** would have been used, as in each case only one resource was needed at any particular time.

For example code that uses the synchronization classes, see the MFC sample programs MTGDI and MUTEXES. These and other MFC sample programs can be found under Samples in Books Online.

For information on how the synchronization classes are used, see the article Multithreading: How to Use the Synchronization Classes. For more information on synchronization, see Chapter 44, Synchronization, in the *Microsoft Win32 Programmer's Reference, Volume 2*. For more information on multithreading support in MFC, see the article Multithreading.

See Also   Multithreading: How to Use the Synchronization Classes

ODBC

In addition to an overview of Open Database Connectivity (ODBC), this article explains:

- How ODBC works with the database classes.
- How ODBC drivers work with dynasets.
- What ODBC components you need to redistribute with your applications.

You will also want to read the related article ODBC: The ODBC Cursor Library.

Note ODBC data sources are accessible through the MFC ODBC classes, as described in this article, or through the MFC Data Access Object (DAO) classes. For information about the DAO classes, see the article Database Overview.

Note The MFC ODBC classes now support Unicode.

ODBC is a call-level interface that allows applications to access data in any database for which there is an ODBC driver. Using ODBC, you can create database applications with access to any database for which your end-user has an ODBC driver. ODBC provides an API that allows your application to be independent of the source database management system (DBMS).

ODBC is the database portion of the Microsoft Windows Open Services Architecture (WOSA), an interface which allows Windows-based desktop applications to connect to multiple computing environments without rewriting the application for each platform.

The following are components of ODBC:

- ODBC API

  A library of function calls, a set of error codes, and a standard Structured Query Language (SQL) syntax for accessing data on DBMSs.

- ODBC Driver Manager

  A dynamic-link library (ODBC32.DLL) that loads ODBC database drivers on behalf of an application. This DLL is transparent to your application.

- ODBC database drivers

  One or more DLLs that process ODBC function calls for specific DBMSs.

- ODBC Cursor Library

  A dynamic-link library (ODBCCR32.DLL) that resides between the ODBC Driver Manager and the drivers and handles scrolling through the data.

- ODBC Administrator

A tool used for configuring a DBMS to make it available as a data source for an application.

An application achieves independence from DBMSs by working through an ODBC driver written specifically for a DBMS rather than working directly with the DBMS. The driver translates the calls into commands its DBMS can use, simplifying the developer's work, and making it available for a wide range of data sources.

The database classes support any data source for which you have an ODBC driver. This might, for example, include a relational database, an Indexed Sequential Access Method (ISAM) database, a Microsoft Excel spreadsheet, or a text file. The ODBC drivers manage the connections to the data source, and SQL is used to select records from the database.

See the article ODBC Driver List for a list of ODBC drivers included in this version of Visual C++ and for information about obtaining additional drivers.

Parts of the ODBC Software Development Kit (SDK) are included with this product. For more information on ODBC, see the ODBC SDK *Programmer's Reference*, and the ODBC API Reference Help system.

ODBC and the Database Classes

The MFC ODBC database classes encapsulate the ODBC API function calls you would normally make yourself in the member functions of the **CDatabase** and **CRecordset** classes. For example, the complex ODBC call sequences, binding of returned records to storage locations, handling of error conditions, and other operations are managed for you by the database classes. As a result, you use a considerably simpler class interface to manipulate records through a recordset object.

Note ODBC data sources are accessible through the MFC ODBC classes, as described in this article, or through the MFC Data Access Object (DAO) classes. For information about the DAO classes, see the article Database Overview.

Although the database classes encapsulate ODBC functionality, they do not provide a one-to-one mapping of ODBC API functions. The database classes provide a higher level of abstraction, modeled after data-access objects found in Microsoft Access and Microsoft Visual Basic. For more information, see What Is the MFC Database Programming Model?.

ODBC Driver Requirements for Dynasets

In the MFC ODBC database classes, dynasets are recordsets with dynamic properties —they remain synchronized with the data source in certain ways. MFC dynasets (but not forward-only recordsets) require an ODBC driver with Level 2 API conformance. If the driver for your data source conforms to the Level 1 API set, you can still use both updatable and read-only snapshots and forward-only recordsets, but not dynasets. However, a Level 1 driver can support dynasets if it supports extended fetch and keyset-driven cursors.

In ODBC terminology, dynasets and snapshots are referred to as "cursors." A cursor is a mechanism used for keeping track of its position in a recordset. For more information about driver requirements for dynasets, see the article Dynaset. For more information about cursors, see the ODBC SDK *Programmer's Reference*.

Note For updatable recordsets, your ODBC driver must support either positioned update statements or the **::SQLSetPos** ODBC API function. If both are supported, MFC uses **::SQLSetPos** for efficiency. Alternatively, for snapshots, you can use the cursor library, which provides the required support for updatable snapshots (static cursors and positioned update statements).

Redistributing ODBC Components to Your Customers

If you incorporate the functionality of the ODBC Setup and ODBC Administrator programs into your application, you must also distribute to your users the files which run these programs. These ODBC files reside in the REDIST directory of the Visual C++ version 4.0 CD-ROM. The REDISTRB.WRI file and the license agreement both contain the list of ODBC files that you may redistribute.

Consult the documentation for any ODBC drivers you plan to ship. You'll need to determine which DLLs and other files to ship.

In addition, you need to include one other file in most cases. The ODBCCR32.DLL is the ODBC Cursor Library. This library gives Level 1 drivers the capability of forward and backward scrolling. It also provides the capability of supporting snapshots. For more information on the ODBC Cursor Library, see the article ODBC: The ODBC Cursor Library.

The following articles provide more information on using ODBC with the database classes:

- ODBC: The ODBC Cursor Library
- ODBC: Configuring an ODBC Data Source
- ODBC: Calling ODBC API Functions Directly

See Also ODBC Administrator

ODBC: The ODBC Cursor Library

This article describes the ODBC Cursor Library and explains how to use it. Topics include:

- The Cursor Library and Level 1 ODBC drivers
- Positioned updates and timestamp columns
- Using the Cursor Library

The ODBC Cursor Library is a dynamic-link library (DLL) that resides between the ODBC Driver Manager and the driver. In ODBC terms, a driver maintains a "cursor" to keep track of its position in the recordset. The cursor marks the position in the recordset to which you have already scrolled — the current record.

The Cursor Library and Level 1 ODBC Drivers

The ODBC Cursor Library gives Level 1 drivers the following new capabilities:

- Forward and backward scrolling. Level 2 drivers don't need the cursor library because they are already scrollable.

- Support for snapshots. The cursor library manages a buffer containing the snapshot's records. This buffer reflects your program's deletions and edits to records but not the additions, deletions, or edits of other users, so the snapshot is only as current as the cursor library's buffer. The buffer also does not reflect your own additions until you call **Requery**. Dynasets do not use the cursor library.

The cursor library will give you snapshots (static cursors) even if they are not normally supported by your driver. If your driver already supports static cursors, you don't need to load the cursor library to get snapshot support. If you do use the cursor library, you can use only snapshots and forward-only recordsets. If your driver supports dynasets (KEYSET_DRIVEN cursors) and you want to use them, you must not use the cursor library. If you want to use both snapshots and dynasets, you must base them on two different **CDatabase** objects (two different connections) unless your driver supports both.

Positioned Updates and Timestamp Columns

Note ODBC data sources are accessible through the MFC ODBC classes, as described in this article, or through the MFC Data Access Object (DAO) classes. For information about the DAO classes, see the article Database Overview.

Note If your ODBC driver supports **SQLSetPos**, which MFC uses if available, this topic does not apply to you.

Most Level 1 drivers do not support positioned updates. Such drivers rely on the cursor library to emulate the capabilities of Level 2 drivers in this regard. The cursor library emulates positioned update support by doing a searched update on the unchanging fields.

In some cases, a recordset may contain a timestamp column as one of those unchanging fields. Two issues arise in using MFC recordsets with tables that contain timestamp columns.

The first issue concerns updatable snapshots on tables with timestamp columns. If the table to which your snapshot is bound contains a timestamp column, you should call **Requery** after you call **Edit** and **Update**. If not, you may not be able to edit the same record again. When you call **Edit** and then **Update**, the record is written to the data source and the timestamp column is updated. If you don't call **Requery**, the timestamp value for the record in your snapshot no longer matches the corresponding timestamp on the data source. When you try to update the record again, the data source may disallow the update because of the mismatch.

The second issue concerns limitations of class **CTime** when used with the **RFX_Date** function to transfer time and date information to or from a table. Processing the **CTime** object imposes some overhead in the form of extra intermediate processing during the data transfer. The date range of **CTime** objects may also be too limiting for some applications. A new version of the **RFX_Date** function takes an ODBC **TIMESTAMP_STRUCT** parameter instead of a **CTime** object. For more information, see **RFX_Date** in Macros and Globals in the *Class Library Reference*.

Using the Cursor Library

When you connect to a data source—by calling **CDatabase::Open**—you can specify whether to use the cursor library for the data source. If you will be creating snapshots on that data source, specify **TRUE** for the **bUseCursorLib** parameter to **Open** (or rely on the default value of **TRUE**). However, if your ODBC driver supports dynasets and you want to open dynasets on the data source, the cursor library must not be used (it masks some driver functionality needed for dynasets). In that case, specify **FALSE** for the **bUseCursorLib** parameter.

ODBC: Configuring an ODBC Data Source

To use a data source with an application you've developed, you must use ODBC Administrator to configure it. ODBC Administrator keeps track of available data sources and their connection information in the Windows registry. You use ODBC Administrator to add, modify, and delete data sources in the Data Sources dialog box, and to add and delete ODBC drivers.

Note This information applies when you use MFC Data Access Object (DAO) classes for ODBC access as well as when you use MFC ODBC classes.

ODBC Administrator is automatically installed with the Microsoft Foundation Class Library database support. For more information about the ODBC Administrator program, see the article ODBC Administrator and the online ODBC API Reference help system.

Technical Note 48, available under MFC in Books Online, describes how to write ODBC Setup and Administration programs for MFC database applications.

See Also ODBC: Calling ODBC API Functions Directly

ODBC: Calling ODBC API Functions Directly

Note ODBC data sources are accessible through the MFC ODBC classes, as described in this article, or through the MFC Data Access Object (DAO) classes. For information about the DAO classes, see the article Database Overview.

The database classes provide a simpler interface to a data source than does ODBC. As a result, the classes don't encapsulate all of the ODBC API. For any functionality that falls outside the abilities of the classes, you must call ODBC API functions directly. For example, you must call the ODBC catalog functions (**::SQLColumns**, **::SQLProcedures**, **::SQLTables**, and others) directly. Samples of direct ODBC function calls used with the classes can be found in the MFC Database sample CATALOG.

To call an ODBC API function directly, you must take the same steps you'd take if you were making the calls without the framework. You must:

- Allocate storage for any results the call returns.

- Pass an ODBC **HDBC** or **HSTMT** handle, depending on the parameter signature of the function.

   Member variables **CDatabase::m_hdbc** and **CRecordset::m_hstmt** are available so that you do not need to allocate and initialize these yourself.

- Perhaps call additional ODBC functions to prepare for or follow up the main call.

- Deallocate storage when you finish.

For more information about these steps, see the ODBC SDK *Programmer's Reference*.

In addition to these steps, you need to take extra steps to check function return values, assure that your program isn't waiting for an asynchronous call to finish, and so on. You can simplify these last steps by using the **AFX_SQL_ASYNC** and **AFX_SQL_SYNC** macros. See Macros and Globals in the *Class Library Reference* for information.

See Also   ODBC

ODBC Administrator

ODBC Administrator is used to register and configure the data sources available to you either locally or across a network. ClassWizard uses information supplied by ODBC Administrator to create code in your applications that connects your users to data sources.

Note   This information applies to ODBC data sources set up for use with either the MFC ODBC classes or the MFC Data Access Object (DAO) classes. To use an ODBC data source, you must register and configure it.

You must use ODBC Administrator to add and remove data sources. Depending on the ODBC driver, you can also create new data sources.

During Setup, you select the ODBC drivers you want to install. You can later install additional drivers that ship with Visual C++ using the Visual C++ Setup program.

Note ODBC Administrator is installed during Setup. If you chose Custom Installation and did not select any ODBC drivers in the "Database Options" dailog box, you need to run Setup again to install the necessary files.

If you want to install ODBC drivers that do not ship with Visual C++, you must run the setup program that accompanies the driver.

▶ **To install ODBC drivers that ship with Visual C++**

Note This procedure assumes that you have already installed VC++ and are rerunning Setup to add the ODBC drivers that ship with VC++.

1 Run Setup from your Visual C++ distribution CD.

This displays the opening dialog box in the Setup program.

2 Click Next on each dialog box until you reach the Installation Options dialog box. Select the Custom radio button and click Next.

3 Clear all of the check boxes on the Microsoft Visual C++ Setup dialog box except the Database Options check box. Click the Details push button to display the Database Options dialog box.

4 Clear the Microsoft Data Access Objects check box, check the Microsoft ODBC Drivers check box, and click the Details button.

This displays the Microsoft ODBC Drivers dialog box.

5 Select the drivers you want to install, then click OK twice.

6 Click Next on the remaining dialog boxes to begin the installation. Setup notifies you when the installation is complete.

Once the drivers are installed, you can configure the data source using the ODBC Administrator. You will find the ODBC icon in the Control Panel. For information about configuring a data source with ODBC Administrator, see the ODBC *SDK Programmer's Reference*.

See Also Data Source (ODBC)

ODBC Driver List

Visual C++ version 4.0 provides ODBC drivers for the following databases:

- SQL Server
- Microsoft Access
- Microsoft FoxPro
- Microsoft Excel
- dBASE
- Paradox
- Text files

For information about ODBC drivers available from Microsoft and other companies, including the ODBC Driver Pack, contact Microsoft Customer Service. You can reach Customer Service by calling 1-800-426-9400. Outside the United States and Canada, please contact your local Microsoft Subsidiary.

ODBC and MFC

Important To use the MFC database classes for targeting a Win32 platform (such as Windows NT), you must have the 32-bit ODBC driver for your data source. Some drivers are included with Visual C++; others can be obtained from Microsoft and other vendors. For more information, see the article ODBC Driver List.

This article introduces the main concepts of the Microsoft Foundation Class Library's ODBC-based database classes and provides an overview of how the classes work together. (For information about using the MFC DAO classes instead, see the article DAO and MFC.) Topics covered in this article include:

- Connecting to a data source
- Selecting and manipulating records
- Displaying and manipulating data in a form
- Working with documents and views
- Access to ODBC and SQL
- Further reading about the MFC ODBC classes

The MFC database classes based on ODBC are designed to provide access to any database for which an ODBC driver is available. Because the classes use ODBC, your application can access data in many different data formats and different local/remote configurations. You do not have to write special-case code to handle different database management systems (DBMSs). As long as your users have an appropriate 32-bit ODBC driver for the data they wish to access, they can use your program to manipulate data in tables stored there.

Connecting to a Data Source

An ODBC data source is a specific set of data, the information required to access that data, and the location of the data source, which can be described using a data-source name. From your program's point of view, the data source includes the data, the DBMS, the network (if any), and ODBC.

To access data provided by a data source, your program must first establish a connection to the data source. All data access is managed through that connection.

Data-source connections are encapsulated by class **CDatabase**. Once a **CDatabase** object is connected to a data source, you can:

- Construct recordsets, which select records from tables or queries.

- Manage transaction, batching updates so all are "committed" to the data source at once (or the whole transaction is "rolled back" so the data source is unchanged)—if the data source supports the required level of transactions.

- Directly execute Structured Query Language (SQL) statements.

When you finish working with a data-source connection, you close the **CDatabase** object and either destroy it or reuse it for a new connection. For more information about data-source connections, see the article Data Source (ODBC).

Selecting and Manipulating Records

Normally when you select records from a data source using an SQL **SELECT** statement, you get a "result set"—a set of records from a table or a query. With the database classes, you use a "recordset" object to select and access the result set. This is an object of an application-specific class that you derive from class **CRecordset**. When you define a recordset class, you specify the data source to associate it with, the table to use, and the columns of the table. Either ClassWizard or AppWizard creates a class with a connection to a specific data source. The wizards write the **GetDefaultSQL** member function of class **CRecordset** to return the table name. For more information on using the wizards to create recordset classes, see the articles AppWizard: Database Support and ClassWizard: Database Support.

Using a **CRecordset** object at run time, you can:

- Examine the data fields of the current record.

- Filter or sort the recordset.

- Customize the default SQL **SELECT** statement.

- Scroll through the selected records.

- Add, update, or delete records (if both the data source and the recordset are updatable).

- Test whether the recordset allows requerying, and refresh the recordset's contents.

When you finish using the recordset object, you close and destroy it. For more information about recordsets, see the article Recordset (ODBC).

Displaying and Manipulating Data in a Form

Many data-access applications select data and display it in fields in a form. The database class **CRecordView** gives you a **CFormView** object directly connected to a recordset object. The record view uses dialog data exchange (DDX) to move the values of the fields of the current record from the recordset to the controls on the form, and to move updated information back to the recordset. The recordset, in turn, uses record field exchange (RFX) to move data between its field data members and the corresponding columns in a table on the data source.

You can use AppWizard or ClassWizard to create the record view class and its associated recordset class in conjunction.

The record view and its recordset are destroyed when you close the document. For more information about record views, see the article Record Views. For more information about RFX, see the article Record Field Exchange (RFX).

Working with Documents and Views

The Microsoft Foundation Class Library relies on a document/view architecture for many of its features. Typically a document stores your data, and a view displays it within the client area of a frame window and manages user interaction with the data. The view communicates with the document to obtain and update the data. You can use the database classes with the framework or without it.

For more information about using database classes in the framework, see the article MFC: Using Database Classes with Documents and Views.

By default, AppWizard creates a skeleton application with no database support. But you can select options to include minimal database support or more complete form-based support. For more information about AppWizard options, see the article AppWizard: Database Support.

You can also use the database classes without using the full document/view architecture. For more information, see the article MFC: Using Database Classes Without Documents and Views.

Access to ODBC and SQL

Just as the Microsoft Foundation Class Library encapsulates many Windows API calls but still lets you call any Windows API function directly, the database classes give you the same flexibility with regard to the ODBC API. While the database classes shield you from much of the complexity of ODBC, you can call ODBC API functions directly from anywhere in your program.

Similarly, the database classes shield you from having to work much with SQL, but you can use SQL directly if you wish. You can customize recordset objects by passing a custom SQL statement (or setting portions of the default statement) when you open the recordset. You can also make SQL calls directly using the **ExecuteSQL** member function of class **CDatabase**.

Further Reading About the MFC ODBC Classes

The following articles further explain the concepts and techniques introduced in this article:

- AppWizard: Database Support
- ClassWizard: Database Support
- Data Source (ODBC)

- Dynaset
- Exceptions: Database Exceptions
- MFC: Using Database Classes with Documents and Views
- MFC: Using Database Classes Without Documents and Views
- ODBC
- ODBC Administrator
- Record Field Exchange (RFX)
- Recordset (ODBC)
- Record Views
- Serialization: Serialization vs. Database Input/Output
- Snapshot
- SQL
- Transaction (ODBC)

A good place to begin your reading is with the article Recordset (ODBC).

In the *Class Library Reference* see **CDatabase**, **CRecordset**, **CRecordView**, **CFieldExchange**, **CDBException**

In *Tutorials* see the ODBC-based database tutorial in Chapters 30 through 33. Chapter 30 is titled Creating a Database Application.

See Also   Database Overview

OLE Control Containers

An OLE control container is a container that fully supports OLE controls and can incorporate them into its own windows or dialogs. An OLE control is a reusable software element that you can use in many development projects. Controls allow your application's user to access databases, monitor data, and make various selections within your applications. For more information on OLE Controls, see the article OLE Controls.

Control containers typically take two forms in a project:

- Dialogs and dialog-like windows such as form views, where an OLE control is used somewhere in the dialog box.

- Windows in an application, where an OLE control is used in a toolbar, or other location in the user window.

The OLE control container interacts with the control via exposed methods and properties. These methods and properties, which can be accessed and modified by the control container, are accessed through a wrapper class in the OLE control container project. The embedded OLE control can also interact with the container by firing events to notify the container that an action has occurred. The control container can choose to act upon these notifications or not.

Additional articles discuss several topics, from creating an OLE control container project to basic implementation issues related to OLE control containers built with Visual C++ 4.0:

- OLE Control Containers: Using AppWizard to Create a Container Application
- OLE Control Containers: Manually Enabling OLE Control Containment
- OLE Control Container: Inserting a Control into a Control Container Application
- OLE Control Containers: Connecting an OLE Control to a Member Variable
- OLE Control Containers: Handling Events from an OLE Control
- OLE Control Containers: Viewing and Modifying Control Properties
- OLE Control Containers: Programming OLE Controls in an OLE Control Container
- OLE Control Containers: Using Controls in a Non-Dialog Container

For more information about using OLE controls in a dialog box, see Using OLE Controls in a Dialog Box in Chapter 6 of the *Visual C++ User's Guide*.

For a list of articles that explain the details of developing OLE controls using Visual C++ and the MFC OLE control classes, see OLE Controls. The articles are grouped by functional categories.

See Also OLE Controls

OLE Control Containers: Using AppWizard to Create a Container Application

You can use AppWizard to create a control container application that can support one or more OLE controls. For more information on AppWizard, see the article AppWizard.

▶ **To create an application with support for control containters**

1 From the File menu, choose New.

The New dialog box appears.

2 Select Project Workspace and choose OK.

The New Workspace dialog box appears.

3 In the Project Name box, type a name for your container.

4 In the Type list box, make sure MFC AppWizard (exe) is selected.

5 If necessary, use the Location box to specify a different root directory for the your project files.

6 In the platforms box, if any check boxes other than Win32 are selected, clear them. OLE controls are not supported on Macintosh platforms.

7 Click the Create button.

AppWizard creates the project directory, and the MFC AppWizard-Step 1 dialog box appears.

8 In Step 1, choose an application type. For this example, choose Dialog-based.

9 Click the Next button.

10 In Step 2, choose OLE Controls for the type of OLE support. (If you chose a Single Document Interface (SDI) or Multiple Document Interface (MDI) application type in Step 1, this will be Step 3.)

11 Click the Finish button to complete your project choices.

The New Project Information dialog box appears, summarizing the settings and features AppWizard will generate for you when it creates your project.

12 Click the OK button in the New Project Information dialog box.

AppWizard creates all necessary files, and opens the project.

See Also AppWizard, Containers

OLE Control Containers: Manually Enabling OLE Control Containment

If you did not enable OLE control support when you used AppWizard to generate your application, you will have to add this support manually. This article describes the process for manually adding OLE control containment to an existing OLE container application. If you know in advance that you want OLE control support in your OLE container, see the article OLE Control Containers: Using AppWizard to Create a Container Application. In addition, you can use the Component Gallery OLE Control Containment component to automatically add control containment to your application.

Note This article uses a dialog-based OLE control container project named Container and an embedded control named Circ2 as examples in the procedures and code.

To support OLE controls, you must add one line of code to two of your project's files.

- Modify your main dialog's InitInstance function (found in CONTAINER.CPP) by making a call to **AfxEnableControlContainer**, as in the following example:

```
// CContainerApp initialization

BOOL CContainerApp::InitInstance()
{
    AfxEnableControlContainer();
...
}
```

- Add the following to your project's STDAFX.H header file:

```
#include <Afxdisp.h>
```

After you have completed these steps, rebuild your project by choosing Build from the Build menu.

OLE Control Containers: Inserting a Control into a Control Container Application

For information on this topic, see the section Inserting an OLE Control Into a Project, in the article OLE Control Containers: Programming OLE Controls in an OLE Control Container.

OLE Control Containers: Connecting an OLE Control to a Member Variable

For information on this topic, see the section Adding a Member Variable to a Project, in the article OLE Control Containers: Programming OLE Controls in an OLE Control Container.

OLE Control Containers: Handling Events from an OLE Control

This article discusses using ClassWizard to install event handlers for OLE controls in an OLE control container. The event handlers are used to receive notifications (from the control) of certain events and perform some action in response.

Note This article uses a dialog-based OLE control container project named Container and an embedded control named Circ2 as examples in the procedures and code.

Using the Message Maps tab in ClassWizard, you can create a map of events that can occur in your OLE control container application. This map, called an "event sink map," is created and maintained by ClassWizard when you add event handlers to the control container class. Each event handler, implemented with an event map entry, maps a specific event to a container event handler member function. This event handler function is called when the specified event is fired by the OLE control object.

For more information on event sink maps, see Event Sink Maps in the *Class Library Reference*.

▶ **To create a event handler function**

  1 From the View menu, choose ClassWizard.

  2 Choose the Message Maps tab.

  3 In the Class Name box, select the dialog box class that contains the OLE control. For this example, use CContainerDlg.

  4 In the Object IDs box, select the control ID of the embedded OLE control. For this example, use IDC_CIRC2CTRL1.

    The Messages box displays a list of events that can be fired by the embedded OLE control. Any member function shown in bold already has handler functions assigned to it.

  5 Select the message you want the application to handle. For this example, select ClickIn.

  6 Click the Add Function button.

    A suggested name for the handler function appears in the Member Functions box. For this example, use the suggested name.

7 Click OK to close the Add Function dialog box.

8 Click the Edit Code button to jump to the event handler code in the implementation (.CPP) file of `CContainerDlg` or Close to close ClassWizard.

Event Handler Modifications to the Project

When you use ClassWizard to add event handlers, an event sink map is declared and defined in your project. The following statements are added to the control .CPP file the first time an event handler is added. This code declares an event sink map for the dialog box class (in this case, `CContainerDlg`):

```
BEGIN_EVENTSINK_MAP(CContainerDlg, CDialog)
    //{{AFX_EVENTSINK_MAP(CContainerDlg)
    //}}AFX_EVENTSINK_MAP
END_EVENTSINK_MAP()
```

As you use ClassWizard to add events, an event map entry (**ON_EVENT**) is added to the event sink map and an event handler function is added to the container's implementation (.CPP) file.

The following example declares an event handler, called `OnClickInCirc2Ctrl`, for the Circ2 control's ClickIn event:

```
BEGIN_EVENTSINK_MAP(CContainerDlg, CDialog)
    //{{AFX_EVENTSINK_MAP(CContainerDlg)
    ON_EVENT(CContainerDlg, IDC_CIRC2CTRL1, 1 /*
ClickIn */, OnClickInCirc2ctrl, VTS_I4 VTS_I4)
    //}}AFX_EVENTSINK_MAP
END_EVENTSINK_MAP()
```

In addition, the following template is added to the `CContainerDlg` class implementation (.CPP) file for the event handler member function:

```
void CContainerDlg::OnClickInCirc2ctrl1()
{
    // TODO: Add your control notification handler code here

}
```

For more information on event sink macros, see Event Sink Maps in the *Class Library Reference*.

OLE Control Containers: Viewing and Modifying Control Properties

When you insert an OLE control into a project it is useful to view and change the properties supported by the OLE control. This article discusses how to use the Visual C++ resource editor to do this.

If your OLE container application uses embedded controls, you can view and modify the control's properties while in the resource editor. You can also use the resource editor to set property values during design time. The resource editor then automatically saves these values in the project's resource file. Any instance of the control will then have its properties initialized to these values.

This procedure assumes that you have used Component Gallery to insert a control into your project. For information on this topic, see the section Inserting an OLE Control Into a Project, in the article OLE Control Containers: Programming OLE Controls in an OLE Control Container.

The first step in viewing the control's properties is to add an instance of the control to the project's dialog template.

▶ **To add a control to the dialog template**

1 In the Project Workspace window, load your OLE control container project into the developer environment. For this example, use the Container project.

2 Click the ResourceView button in the Project Workspace window.

3 Open the Dialog folder.

4 Open your main dialog box template.

5 From the Controls toolbar, choose the control icon.

6 Click a spot within the dialog box area to insert the control.

Once you have added the control to the dialog box, double-click on the control to bring up the control Properties dialog box. Use this dialog box to modify and test new properties immediately.

OLE Control Containers: Programming OLE Controls in an OLE Control Container

This article describes the process for accessing the exposed methods and properties of embedded OLE controls. Basically, you will follow these steps:

1. Insert an OLE control into the OLE container project using Component Gallery.

2. Define a member variable (or other form of access) of the same type as the OLE control wrapper class.

3. Program the OLE control using predefined member functions of the wrapper class.

For this discussion, a dialog-based project (named Container), with OLE control support, was created with AppWizard and the Circ2 sample control, Circ2, will be added to the resulting project.

Inserting an OLE Control into the OLE Container Project

Before you can access an OLE control from an OLE container application, you must use Component Gallery to add the OLE control to the container application.

▶ **To add an OLE control to the OLE container project**

1 From the Insert menu, choose Component.

The Component Gallery dialog box appears.

2 Select the OLE Controls tab.

3 Select the control you want by clicking the OLE control icon in the Component Gallery window.

4 Click the Insert button.

The Confirm Classes dialog box appears. This dialog box lists the class (or classes) that will be generated for each inserted control. It also lists the class name, header, and implementation files; which can be modified. (In the case of Container and Circ2, only one class is generated.)

5 Click the OK button to accept the class generated by Component Gallery.

6 Click the Close button to close Component Gallery

An icon representing each control installed appears on the dialog editor Controls toolbar.

Once you complete this procedure, the class generated by Component Gallery, referred to as a wrapper class, is added to your project. This class (in this example, `CCirc2`) is used as an interface between the control container, Container, and the embedded control, Circ2.

Once the Circ2 control is inserted in to the project, insert an instance of the Circ2 control into the application's main dialog box.

▶ **To add the Circ2 control to the dialog template**

1 Load the OLE control container project into Developer Studio. For this example, use the Container project.

2 Click the ResourceView button in the Project Workspace window.

3 Open the Dialog folder.

4 Double-click the main dialog box template. For this example, use IDD_CONTAINER_DIALOG.

5 Choose the Circ2 control icon from the Controls toolbar.

6 Click a spot within the dialog box to insert the Circ2 control.

7 From the File menu, choose Save All to save all modifications to the dialog box template.

Modifications to the project

To enable the Container application to access the Circ2 control, Component Gallery automatically adds the wrapper class (`CCirc2`) implementation file (.CPP) to the Container project and the wrapper class header (.H) file to the dialog box implementation file:

```
//{{AFX_INCLUDES(CContainerDlg)
#include "circ2.h"
//}}AFX_INCLUDES
// ContainerDlg.cpp : implementation file
//
```

The Wrapper Class Header (.H) File

To get and set properties (and invoke methods) for the Circ2 control, the `CCirc2` wrapper class provides a declaration of all exposed methods and properties. In the example, these declarations are found in CIRC2.H. The following sample is the portion of class `CCirc2` that defines the exposed interfaces of the OLE control:

```
class CCirc2 : public CWnd
{
...
// Attributes
public:
    OLE_COLOR GetBackColor();
    void SetBackColor(OLE_COLOR);
    BOOL GetCircleShape();
    void SetCircleShape(BOOL);
    short GetCircleOffset();
    void SetCircleOffset(short);
    unsigned long GetFlashColor();
    void SetFlashColor(unsigned long);
    BSTR GetCaption();
    void SetCaption(LPCTSTR);
    LPFONTDISP GetFont();
    void SetFont(LPFONTDISP);
    OLE_COLOR GetForeColor();
    void SetForeColor(OLE_COLOR);
    CString GetNote();
    void SetNote(LPCTSTR);

// Operations
public:
    void AboutBox();
};
```

These functions can then be called from other of the application's procedures using normal C++ syntax. For more information on using this member function set to access the control's methods and properties, see the section Programming the OLE Control.

Adding a Member Variable to a Project

Now that the OLE control has been added to the project and embedded in a dialog box container, it can be accessed by other parts of the project. The easiest way to access the control is to create a member variable of the dialog class, `CContainerDlg`, that is of the same type as the wrapper class added to the project by Component Gallery. You can then use the member variable to access the embedded control at any time.

Note This is not the only way to access an embedded control from within a container class, but for the purposes of this article it is sufficient.

▶ **Adding a member variable to the dialog class**

1 Load your OLE container project. (For this example, use Container.)

2 From the View menu, choose ClassWizard.

3 Choose the Member Variables tab.

4 From the Class Name drop-down list box, select the main dialog class. For this example, use CContainerDlg.

5 From the Control IDs drop-down list box, select the control ID of the embedded OLE control. For this example, use IDC_CIRC2CTRL1.

6 Click the Add Variable button.

The Add Member Variable dialog box appears.

7 In the Member Variable edit box enter a name.

For this example, use m_circ2ctl.

8 From the Category drop-down list box, select Control.

The Type edit box automatically contains the name of the control wrapper class.

Note Additional entries in the Category drop-down list box are for exposed properties of the OLE control.

9 Click OK to close the Add Member Variables dialog box.

10 Click OK to accept your choices and exit ClassWizard.

Member Variable Modifications to the Project

When ClassWizard adds the `m_circ2ctl` member variable to the project, it also adds the following lines to the the header file (.H) of the `CContainerDlg` class:

```
class CContainerDlg : public CDialog
{
// Construction
public:
    CContainerDlg(CWnd* pParent = NULL);   // standard constructor

// Dialog Data
    //{{AFX_DATA(CContainerDlg)
    enum { IDD = IDD_CONTAINER_DIALOG };
    CCirc2  m_circ2ctl;
    //}}AFX_DATA
};
```

In addition, ClassWizard adds a **DDX_Control** call to the `CContainerDlg`'s implementation of `DoDataExchange`:

```
DDX_Control(pDX, IDC_CIRC2CTRL1, m_circ2ctl);
```

Programming the OLE Control

At this point, you have inserted the OLE control into your dialog template and created a member variable for it. You can now use common C++ syntax to access the properties and methods of the embedded control.

As noted (in The Wrapper Class Header (.H) File), the header file (.H) for the CCirc2 wrapper class, in this case CIRC2.H, contains a listing of member functions that you can use to get and set any exposed property value. Member functions for exposed methods are also available.

A common place to modify the control's properties is in the OnInitDialog member function of the main dialog class. This function is called just before the dialog box appears and is used to initialize its contents, including any of its controls.

The following code example uses the m_circ2ctl member variable to modify the Caption and CircleShape properties of the embedded Circ2 control:

```
BOOL CContainerDlg::OnInitDialog()
{
    CDialog::OnInitDialog();

    // Add "About..." menu item to system menu.

    // IDM_ABOUTBOX must be in the system command range.
    ASSERT((IDM_ABOUTBOX & 0xFFF0) == IDM_ABOUTBOX);
    ASSERT(IDM_ABOUTBOX < 0xF000);

    CMenu* pSysMenu = GetSystemMenu(FALSE);
    CString strAboutMenu;
    strAboutMenu.LoadString(IDS_ABOUTBOX);
    if (!strAboutMenu.IsEmpty())
    {
        pSysMenu->AppendMenu(MF_SEPARATOR);
        pSysMenu->AppendMenu(MF_STRING, IDM_ABOUTBOX, strAboutMenu);
    }

    m_circ2ctl.SetCaption(_T("Circ 2 Control"));
    if( !m_circ2ctl.GetCircleShape())
        m_circ2ctl.SetCircleShape(TRUE);

    return TRUE;  // return TRUE  unless you set the focus to a control
}
```

OLE Control Containers: Using Controls in a Non-Dialog Container

In some applications, such as an SDI or MDI appplication, you will want to embed a control in a window of the application. The **Create** member function of the wrapper class, inserted by Component Gallery, can create an instance of the control dynamically, without the need of a dialog box.

The **Create** member function has the following parameters:

lpszWindowName A pointer to the text to be displayed in the control's Text or Caption property (if any).

dwStyle Windows styles. For a complete list, see **CWnd::CreateControl**.

rect Specifies the control's size and position.

pParentWnd Specifies the control's parent window, usually a **CDialog**. It must not be **NULL**.

nID Specifies the control ID and can be used by the container to refer to the control.

One example of using this function to dynamically create an OLE control would be in a form view of an SDI application. You could then create an instance of the control in the **WM_CREATE** handler of the application.

For this example, CMyView is the main view class, CCirc2 is the wrapper class, and CIRC2.H is the header (.H) file of the wrapper class.

Implementing this feature is a four-step process:

1. Insert CIRC2.H in CMYVIEW.H, just before the CMyView class definition:

   ```
   #include "circ2.h"
   ```

2. Add a member variable (of type CCirc2) to the protected section of the CMyView class definition located in CMYVIEW.H:

   ```
   class CMyView : public CView
   {
   ...
   protected:

   CCirc2 m_myCtl;
   ...
   };
   ```

3. Add a **WM_CREATE** message handler to class CMyView.

4. In the handler function, CMyView::OnCreate, make a call to the control's Create function using the **this** pointer as the parent window:

```
int CMyView::OnCreate(LPCREATESTRUCT lpCreateStruct)
{
    if (MyView::OnCreate(lpCreateStruct) == -1)
        return -1;

// ****** Add your code below this line ********** //

    m_myCtl.Create(NULL, WS_VISIBLE,
        CRect(50,50,100,100), this, 0);
    m_myCtl.SetCaption(_T("Control created"));

// ****** Add your code above this line ********** //

    return 0;
}
```

Rebuild the project. A Circ2 control will be created dynamically whenever the application's view is created.

OLE Controls

An OLE control is a reusable software component that supports a wide variety of OLE functionality and can be customized to fit many software needs. These controls can be developed for many uses, such as database access, data monitoring, or graphing. Besides their portability, OLE controls support features previously not available to custom controls, such as compatibility with existing OLE containers and the ability to integrate their menus with the OLE container menus. In addition, an OLE control fully supports OLE Automation, which allows the control to expose writable properties and a set of methods that can be called by the control user.

An OLE control is implemented as an in-process server (typically a small object) that can be used in any OLE container. Note that the full functionality of an OLE control is available only when used within an OLE container designed to be aware of OLE controls. Currently, Microsoft FoxPro 3.0, Microsoft Access 2.0, Microsoft Visual Basic 4.0, and OLE containers built with MFC in Visual C++ version 4.0 fully support OLE controls. This container type, hereafter referred to as a control container, is able to operate an OLE control by using the control's properties and methods, and receives notifications from the OLE control in the form of events. Figure 1 demonstrates this interaction.

Figure 1 Interaction Between an OLE Control Container and an OLE Control

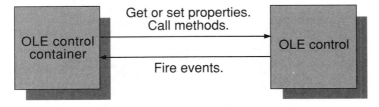

Basic Components of an OLE control

An OLE control uses several programmatic elements to interact efficiently with a control container and with the user. These are class **COleControl**, a set of event-firing functions, and a dispatch map.

Every OLE control object you develop inherits a powerful set of features from its MFC base class, **COleControl**. These features include OLE document object functionality, in-place activation, and OLE Automation logic. **COleControl** also provides the control object with the same functionality as an MFC window object, plus the ability to fire events.

Because the control class derives from **COleControl**, it inherits the capability to send messages, called "events," to the control container when certain conditions are met. Events are used to notify the control container when something important happens in the control. You can send additional information about an event to the control container by attaching parameters to the event. For more information about OLE control events, see the article Events.

The final element is a dispatch map, which is used to expose a set of functions (called methods) and attributes (called properties) to the control user. Properties allow the control container or the control user to manipulate the control in various ways. The user can change the appearance of the control, change certain values of the control, or make requests of the control, such as accessing a specific piece of data that the control maintains. This interface is determined by the control developer and is defined using ClassWizard. For more information on OLE control methods and properties, see the articles Methods and Properties.

Interaction Between Controls and OLE Control Containers

When a control is used within a control container, it uses two mechanisms to communicate: it exposes properties and methods, and it fires events. Figure 2 demonstrates how these two mechanisms are implemented.

Figure 2   Communication Between an OLE Control Container and an OLE Control

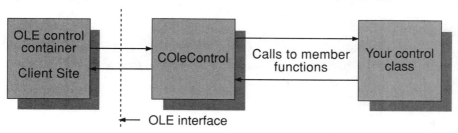

Figure 2 also illustrates how other OLE interfaces (besides automation and events) are handled by controls.

All of a control's communication with the container is performed by **COleControl**. To handle some of the container's requests, **COleControl** will call member functions that are implemented in the control class. All methods and some properties are handled in this way. Your control's class can also initiate communication with the container by calling member functions of **COleControl**. Events are fired in this manner.

Active and Inactive States of an OLE control

During execution, a control is always in one of two states: active or inactive. When inactive, the control does not have an active window visible on the screen and, therefore, has limited capabilities. For example, the control cannot respond to mouse clicks or keystrokes. However, the control container is still able to notify the control in certain cases, such as when a request is made for painting.

When a control becomes active, it is able to interact fully with the control container, the user, and Windows. Figure 3 demonstrates the paths of communication between the OLE control, the control container, and the operating system.

Figure 3   Windows Message Processing in an OLE Control (When Active)

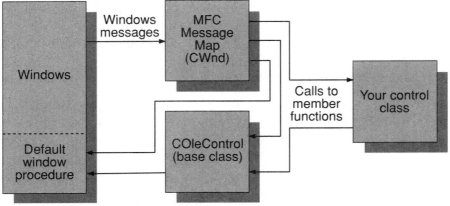

Serialization

The ability to serialize data, sometimes referred to as persistence, allows the control to write the value of its properties to persistent storage. Controls can then be re-created by reading the object's state from the storage.

Note that a control is not responsible for obtaining access to the storage medium. Instead, the control's container is responsible for providing the control with a storage medium to use at the appropriate times. For more information on serialization, see the article OLE Controls: Serializing.

Further Reading

The articles listed below explain the details of developing OLE controls using Visual C++ and the MFC OLE control classes. The articles are listed in functional categories.

Articles about the OLE control development process

- OLE ControlWizard
- OLE Control Wizard: How Control Wizard Works
- OLE ControlWizard: Files Created

Articles about events, methods, and properties of OLE controls

- Events
- Events: Adding Stock Events to an OLE Control

- Events: Adding Custom Events to an OLE Control
- Methods
- Methods: Adding Stock Methods to an OLE Control
- Methods: Adding Custom Methods to an OLE Control
- Methods: Returning Error Codes From a Method
- Properties
- Properties: Adding Stock Properties
- Properties: Adding Custom Properties
- Properties: Advanced Implementation
- Properties: Accessing Ambient Properties

Articles about user-interface aspects of OLE controls

- OLE Controls: Painting an OLE Control
- OLE Controls: Property Pages
- OLE Controls: Adding Another Custom Property Page
- OLE Controls: Using Stock Property Pages
- OLE Controls: Using Fonts in an OLE Control
- OLE Controls: Using Pictures in an OLE Control

Articles about advanced topics of OLE controls

- OLE Controls: Advanced Topics
- OLE Controls: Distributing OLE Controls
- OLE Controls: Licensing an OLE Control
- OLE Controls: Localizing an OLE Control
- OLE Controls: Serializing
- OLE Controls: Subclassing a Windows Control

Other articles regarding OLE controls

- OLE Controls: Using Data Binding in an OLE Control
- OLE Controls: Adding an OLE Control to an Existing CDK Project
- OLE Controls: VBX Control Migration
- OLE Controls: Converting a CDK Project to a Visual C++ Project

See Also   Chapter 5, Developing OLE Controls; Test Container

OLE Controls: Painting an OLE Control

This article describes the OLE control painting process and how you can alter paint code to optimize the process.

Examples in this article are from a control created by ControlWizard with default settings. For more information on creating a skeleton control application using ControlWizard, see the article OLE ControlWizard.

The following topics are covered:

- The overall process for painting a control and the code created by ControlWizard to support painting
- How to optimize the painting process
- How to paint your control using metafiles

The Painting Process of an OLE Control

When OLE controls are initially displayed or are redrawn, they follow a painting process similar to other applications developed using MFC, with one important distinction: OLE controls can be in an active or an inactive state.

An active control is represented in an OLE control container by a child window. Like other windows, it is responsible for painting itself when a **WM_PAINT** message is received. The control's base class, **COleControl**, handles this message in its **OnPaint** function. This default implementation calls the OnDraw function of your control.

An inactive control is painted differently. When the control is inactive, its window is either invisible or nonexistent, so it can not receive a paint message. Instead, the control container directly calls the OnDraw function of the control. This differs from an active control's painting process in that the **OnPaint** member function is never called.

As discussed in the preceding paragraphs, how an OLE control is updated depends on the state of the control. However, because the framework calls the OnDraw member function in both cases, you add the majority of your painting code in this member function.

The OnDraw member function handles control painting. When a control is inactive, the control container calls OnDraw, passing the device context of the control container and the coordinates of the rectangular area occupied by the control.

The rectangle passed by the framework to the OnDraw member function contains the area occupied by the control. If the control is active, the upper-left corner is (0, 0) and the device context passed is for the child window that contains the control. If the control is inactive, the upper-left coordinate is not necessarily (0, 0) and the device context passed is for the control container containing the control.

Note It is important that your modifications to OnDraw do not depend on the rectangle's upper-left point being equal to (0, 0) and that you draw only inside the rectangle passed to OnDraw. Unexpected results can occur if you draw beyond the rectangle's area.

The default implementation provided by ControlWizard in the control implementation file (.CPP), shown below, paints the rectangle with a white brush and fills the ellipse with the current background color.

```
void CSampleCtrl::OnDraw( CDC* pdc, const CRect& rcBounds, const CRect& rcInvalid )
{
    pdc->FillRect( rcBounds,
        CBrush::FromHandle((HBRUSH)GetStockObject(WHITE_BRUSH)));
    pdc->Ellipse( rcBounds );
}
```

Note When painting a control, you should not make assumptions about the state of the device context that is passed as the *pdc* parameter to the OnDraw function. Occasionally the device context is supplied by the container application and will not necessarily be initialized to the default state. In particular, you should explicitly select the pens, brushes, colors, fonts, and other resources that your drawing code depends upon.

Optimizing Your Paint Code

Once the control is successfully painting itself, the next step is to optimize the OnDraw function.

The default implementation of OLE control painting simply paints the entire control area. This is sufficient for simple controls, but in many cases repainting the control would be faster if only the portion that needed updating was repainted, instead of the entire control.

The OnDraw function provides an easy method of optimization by passing rcInvalid, the rectangular area of the control that needs redrawing. Use this area, usually smaller than the entire control area, to speed up the painting process.

Painting Your Control Using Metafiles

In most cases the pdc parameter to the OnDraw function points to a screen device context (DC). However, when printing images of the control or during a print preview session, the DC received for rendering is a special type called a "metafile DC". Unlike a screen DC, which immediately handles requests sent to it, a metafile DC stores requests to be played back at a later time. Some container applications, such as Microsoft Access 2.0, may also choose to render the control image using a metafile DC when in design mode.

Drawing requests can be made by the container through two interface functions: **IViewObject::Draw** (this function can also be called for non-metafile drawing) and **IDataObject::GetData**. When a metafile DC is passed as one of the parameters, the MFC framework makes a call to **COleControl::OnDrawMetafile**. Because this is a virtual member function, override this function in the control class to do any special processing. The default behavior calls **COleControl::OnDraw**.

To make sure the control can be drawn in both screen and metafile device contexts, you must use only member functions that are supported in both a screen and a metafile DC. Be aware that the coordinate system may not be measured in pixels.

Because the default implementation of **OnDrawMetafile** calls the control's OnDraw function, use only member functions that are suitable for both a metafile and a screen device context, unless you override **OnDrawMetafile**. The following lists the subset of **CDC** member functions that can be used in both a metafile and a screen device context. For more information on these functions, see class **CDC** in the *Class Library Reference*.

Arc	**Pie**	**SetMapMode**
Chord	**Polygon**	**SetMapperFlags**
Ellipse	**Polyline**	**SetPixel**
Escape	**PolyPolygon**	**SetPolyFillMode**
BitBlt	**RealizePalette**	**SetROP2**
ExcludeClipRect	**RestoreDC**	**SetStretchBltMode**
ExtTextOut	**RoundRect**	**SetTextColor**
FloodFill	**SaveDC**	**SetTextJustification**
IntersectClipRect	**ScaleViewportExt**	**SetViewportExt**
LineTo	**ScaleWindowExt**	**SetViewportOrg**
MoveTo	**SelectClipRgn**	**SetWindowExt**
OffsetClipRgn	**SelectObject**	**SetWindowOrg**
OffsetViewportOrg	**SelectPalette**	**StretchBlt**
OffsetWindowOrg	**SetBkColor**	**TextOut**
PatBlt	**SetBkMode**	

In addition to **CDC** member functions, there are several other functions that are compatible in a metafile DC. These include **CPalette::AnimatePalette**, **CFont::CreateFontIndirect**, and three member functions of **CBrush**: **CreateBrushIndirect**, **CreateDIBPatternBrush**, and **CreatePatternBrush**.

Another point to consider when using a metafile DC is that the coordinate system may not be measured in pixels. For this reason, all your drawing code should be adjusted to fit in the rectangle passed to OnDraw in the *rcBounds* parameter. This prevents accidental painting outside the control because *rcBounds* represents the size of the control's window.

Once you have implemented metafile rendering for the control, use Test Container to test the metafile.

▶ **To test the control's metafile using Test Container**

1 From the Tools menu, choose OLE Control Test Container.

2 From the Test Container Edit menu, choose Insert OLE Control.

3 In the Insert OLE Control dialog box, select the desired control and choose OK.

The control will appear in Test container.

4 From the Edit menu, choose Draw Metafile.

A separate window appears in which the metafile is displayed. You can change the size of this window to see how scaling affects the control's metafile. You can close this window at any time.

See Also   In the Circle Sample tutorial of *Tutorials*: Painting the Control

OLE Controls: Property Pages

Property pages allow an OLE control user to view and change OLE control properties. These properties are accessed by invoking a control properties dialog box, which contains one or more property pages that provide a customized, graphical interface for viewing and editing the control properties.

OLE control property pages are displayed in two ways:

- When the control's "Properties" verb (**OLEIVERB_PROPERTIES**) is invoked, the control opens a modal property dialog box that contains the control's property pages.

- The container can display its own modeless dialog box that shows the property pages of the selected control.

The properties dialog box (illustrated in Figure 1) consists of an area for displaying the current property page, tabs for switching between property pages, and a collection of buttons that perform common tasks such as closing the property page dialog, canceling any changes made, or immediately applying any changes to the OLE control.

Figure 1   A Properties Dialog Box

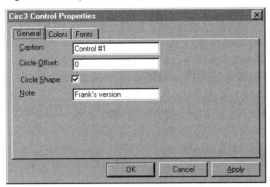

This article covers basic topics related to using property pages in an OLE control. These include:

- Implementing the default property page for an OLE control
- Adding controls to a property page
- Customizing the **DoDataExchange** function

For more information on using property pages in an OLE control, see the following articles:

- OLE Controls: Adding Another Custom Property Page
- OLE Controls: Using Stock Property Pages

For more information on using property sheets in an MFC application other than an OLE control, see the article Property Sheets.

Implementing the Default Property Page

If you use ControlWizard to create your control project, ControlWizard provides a default property page class for the control derived from **COlePropertyPage**. Initially, this property page is blank, but you can add any dialog box control or set of controls to it. Because ControlWizard only creates one property page class by default, additional property page classes (also derived from **COlePropertyPage**) must be created using ClassWizard. For more information on this procedure, see OLE Controls: Adding Another Custom Property Page.

Implementing a property page (in this case, the default) is a three step process:

▶ **To implement a property page**

1 Add a **CPropertyPage**-derived class to the control project. If the project was created using ControlWizard (as in this case), the default property page class already exists.

2 Use the dialog editor to add any controls to the property page template.

3 Customize the `DoDataExchange` function of the control to exchange values between the property page control and the OLE control.

For example purposes, the following procedures use a simple control (named "Sample"). Sample was created using ControlWizard and contains only the stock Caption property.

Adding Controls to a Property Page

► **To add controls to a property page**

1 Open the project's .RC file icon to load your project's resources.

2 Double-click the Dialog directory icon.

3 Open the IDD_PROPPAGE_SAMPLE dialog box.

ControlWizard appends the name of the project to the end of the dialog ID. In this case, Sample.

4 Click the desired control on the Control Palette and drag and drop it into the dialog box area.

For this example, a text label control "Caption :" and an edit box control with an IDC_CAPTION identifier are sufficient.

5 Click the Save button on the Toolbar to save your changes.

Now that the user interface has been modified, you need to link the edit box with the Caption property. This is done in the following section by editing the `CSamplePropPage::DoDataExchange` function.

Customizing the DoDataExchange Function

Your property page `DoDataExchange` function allows you to link property page values with the actual values of properties in the control. To establish links, you must map the appropriate property page fields to their respective control properties.

These mappings are implemented using the property page **DDP_** functions. The **DDP_** functions work in a manner similar to the **DDX_** functions used in standard MFC dialogs, with one exception. In addition to the reference to a member variable, **DDP_** functions take the name of the control property. The following is a typical entry in the `DoDataExchange` function for a property page.

```
DDP_Text(pDX, IDC_CAPTION, m_caption, _T("Caption"));
```

This function associates the property page's `m_caption` member variable with the Caption property of the control.

Once you have the property page control inserted, you need to establish a link between the property page control, `IDC_CAPTION`, and the actual control property, Caption.

For more information on this procedure, see Linking Controls with Properties in Chapter 27 of *Tutorials*.

DDP functions are available for other dialog control types, such as check boxes, radio buttons, and list boxes. Table 1 lists the entire set of property page **DDP_** functions and their purposes:

Table 1   Property Page Functions

Function Name	Use this function to link ...
DDP_CBIndex	The selected string's index in a combo box with a control property.
DDP_CBString	The selected string in a combo box with a control property. The selected string can begin with the same letters as the property's value but need not match it fully.
DDP_CBStringExact	The selected string in a combo box with a control property. The selected string and the property's string value must match exactly.
DDP_Check	A check box with a control property.
DDP_LBIndex	The selected string's index in a list box with a control property.
DDP_LBString	The selected string in a list box with a control property. The selected string can begin with the same letters as the property's value but need not match it fully.
DDP_LBStringExact	The selected string in a list box with a control property. The selected string and the property's string value must match exactly.
DDP_Radio	A radio button with a control property.
DDP_Text	Text with a control property.

See Also   In the *Class Library Reference*: **COlePropertyPage**

OLE Controls: Adding Another Custom Property Page

Ocasionally, an OLE control will have more properties than can reasonably fit on one property page. In this case, you can add property pages to the OLE control to display these properties.

This article discusses adding new property pages to an OLE control that already has at least one property page. For more information on adding stock property pages (font, picture, or color), see the article OLE Controls: Using Stock Property Pages.

The following procedures use a sample OLE control framework created by ControlWizard. Therefore, the class names and identifiers are unique only to this example.

For more information on using property pages in an OLE control, see the following articles:

- OLE Controls: Property Pages
- OLE Controls: Using Stock Property Pages

Note It is strongly recommended that new property pages adhere to the size standard for OLE control property pages. The stock picture and color property pages measure 250x62 dialog units (DLUs). The standard font property page is 250x110 DLUs. The default property page created by ControlWizard uses the 250x62 DLU standard.

▶ **To create another property page**

1 Load the workspace of the control project you want to add a property page to.

2 From the Project Workspace window, double-click on the .RC file icon to open the project's resource file.

3 From the Insert menu, choose Resource.

4 Double-click on the dialog resource type to create a new dialog resource.

This example uses `IDD_PROPPAGE_NEWPAGE`.

5 Delete the OK and Cancel button controls.

6 From the Dialog Properties dialog box, select the Styles tab.

7 From the Style box, select Child.

8 From the Border box, select None.

Make sure that the Titlebar and Visible options are not checked.

9 Save the project's .RC file.

10 Open ClassWizard.

11 In the Class Name box, type a name for the new dialog class.

In this example, `CAddtlPropPage`.

12 Type in the names for your implementation and header files, or accept the default names.

13 From the Class Type box, select COlePropertyPage.

14 From the ClassResources box, select IDD_PROPPAGE_NEWPAGE.

15 Click Create to create the class.

16 Choose OK to close ClassWizard.

To allow the control's users access to this new property page, make the following changes to the control's property page IDs macro section (found in the control implementation file):

```
BEGIN_PROPPAGEIDS(CSampleCtrl, 2)
    PROPPAGEID(CMyPropPage::guid)
    PROPPAGEID(CAddtlPropPage::guid)
...
END_PROPPAGEIDS(CSampleCtrl)
```

Note that you must increase the second parameter of the **BEGIN_PROPPAGEIDS** macro (the property page count) from 1 to 2.

You must also modify the control implementation file (.CPP) file to include the header (.H) file of the new property page class.

The next step involves creating two new string resources that will provide a type name and a caption for the new property page.

▶ **To add new string resources to a property page**

1 Load the workspace of the control project you wish to add a property page to.

2 From the Project Workspace window, double-click on the .RC file icon to open the project's resource file.

3 Select an existing entry in the string table.

4 From the Resource menu, choose New String.

5 Enter a new string ID in the ID edit box.

For example purposes, we've used IDS_SAMPLE_ADDPAGE for the type name of the new property page.

6 Type a new string in the Caption box. For example, "Additional Property Page."

7 Repeat steps 4 and 5 using IDS_SAMPLE_ADDPPG_CAPTION for the ID and "Additional Property Page" for the caption.

8 In the .CPP file of your new property page class (in this example, CAddtlPropPage) modify the CAddtlPropPage::CAddtlPropPageFactory::UpdateRegistry so that IDS_SAMPLE_ADDPAGE is passed by **AfxOleRegisterPropertyPageClass**, as in the following example:

```
BOOL CAddtlPropPage::CAddtlPropPageFactory::UpdateRegistry(BOOL
    bRegister)
{
    if (bRegister)
        return AfxOleRegisterPropertyPageClass(AfxGetInstanceHandle(),
                    m_clsid, IDS_SAMPLE_ADDPAGE);
    else
        return AfxOleUnregisterClass(m_clsid, NULL);
}
```

9 Modify the constructor of CAddtlPropPage so that IDS_SAMPLE_ADDPPG_CAPTION is passed to the **COlePropertyPage** constructor, as follows:

```
CAddtlPropPage::CAddtlPropPage() :
// ****** Add your code below this line ********** //
    COlePropertyPage(IDD,  IDS_SAMPLE_ADDPPG_CAPTION)
// ****** Add your code above this line ********** //
{
    //{{AFX_DATA_INIT(CAddtlPropPage)
    // NOTE: ClassWizard will add member initialization here
    //    DO NOT EDIT what you see in these blocks of generated code !
    //}}AFX_DATA_INIT
}
```

After you have made the necessary modifications rebuild your project and use Test Container to test the new property page. For more information on testing an OLE control with Test Container, see Test Container.

OLE Controls: Using Stock Property Pages

This article discusses the stock property pages available for OLE controls and how to use them.

For more information on using property pages in an OLE control, see the following articles:

- OLE Controls: Property Pages

- OLE Controls: Adding Another Custom Property Page

MFC provides three stock property pages for use with OLE controls: **CLSID_CColorPropPage**, **CLSID_CFontPropPage**, and **CLSID_CPicturePropPage**. These pages display a user interface for stock color, font, and picture properties, respectively.

To incorporate these property pages into a control, add their IDs to the code that initializes the control's array of property page IDs. In the following example, this code, located in the control implementation file (.CPP), initializes the array to contain all three stock property pages and the default property page (named `CMyPropPage` in this example):

```
BEGIN_PROPPAGEIDS( CSampleCtrl, 4 )
    PROPPAGEID( CMyPropPage::guid )
    PROPPAGEID( CLSID_CFontPropPage )
    PROPPAGEID( CLSID_CColorPropPage )
    PROPPAGEID( CLSID_CPicturePropPage )
END_PROPPAGEIDS(CSampleCtrl)
```

Note that the count of property pages, in the **BEGIN_PROPPAGEIDS** macro, is 4. This represents the number of property pages supported by the OLE control.

After these modifications have been made, rebuild your project. Your control now has property pages for the font, picture, and color properties.

Note If the control stock property pages cannot be accessed, it may be because the MFC DLL (MFCx0.DLL) has not been properly registered with the current operating system. This usually results from installing Visual C++ under an operating system different from the one currently running.

If your stock property pages are not visible (see Note above), register the DLL by running REGSVR32.EXE from the command line with the path name to the DLL. For example, REGSVR32 C:\WINDOWS\SYSTEM\MFCx0.DLL, for Windows and REGSVR32 C:\NT\SYSTEM32\MFCx0.DLL, for NT.

See Also Properties: Adding Stock Properties

OLE Controls: Using Fonts in an OLE Control

If your OLE control displays text, you can allow the control user to change the text appearance by changing a font property. Font properties are implemented as font objects and can be one of two types: stock or custom. Stock Font properties are preimplemented font properties that you can add using ClassWizard. Custom Font properties are not preimplemented and the control developer determines the property's behavior and usage.

This article covers the following topics:

- Using the stock Font property
- Using custom font properties in your control

Using the Stock Font Property

Stock Font properties are preimplemented by the class **COleControl**. In addition, a standard Font property page is also available, allowing the user to change various attributes of the font object, such as its name, size, and style.

Access the font object through the **GetFont**, **SetFont**, and **InternalGetFont** functions of **COleControl**. The control user will access the font object via the GetFont and SetFont functions in the same manner as any other Get/Set property. When access to the font object is required from within a control, use the **InternalGetFont** function.

As discussed in Properties, adding stock properties is easy with ClassWizard's OLE Automation page. You choose the Font property, and ClassWizard automatically inserts the stock Font entry into the control's dispatch map.

▶ **To add the stock Font property using ClassWizard**

1 With your control project open, open ClassWizard by choosing ClassWizard from the View menu.

2 Choose the OLE Automation tab.

3 Click the Add Property button.

4 In the External Name box, select Font.

5 Click the OK button.

6 Click the OK button to confirm your choices and close ClassWizard.

ClassWizard adds the following line to the control's dispatch map, located in the control class implementation file:

```
DISP_STOCKPROP_FONT()
```

In addition, ClassWizard adds the following line to the control .ODL file:

```
[id(DISPID_FONT), bindable] IFontDisp* Font;
```

The stock Caption property is an example of a text property that can be drawn using the stock Font property information. Adding the stock Caption property to the control uses steps similar to those used for the stock Font property.

▶ **To add the stock Caption property using ClassWizard**

1 With your control project open, open ClassWizard by choosing ClassWizard from the View menu.

2 Choose the OLE Automation tab.

3 Click the Add Property button.

4 In the External Name box, select Caption.

5 Click the OK button.

6 Click the OK button to confirm your choices and close ClassWizard.

ClassWizard adds the following line to the control's dispatch map, located in the control class implementation file:

```
DISP_STOCKPROP_CAPTION()
```

Modifying the OnDraw Function

The default implementation of OnDraw uses the Windows system font for all text displayed in the control. This means that you must modify the OnDraw code by selecting the font object into the device context. To do this, call **COleControl::SelectStockFont** and pass the control's device context, as shown in the following example:

```
void CSampleCtrl::OnDraw( CDC* pdc, const CRect& rcBounds, const CRect& rcInvalid)
{
    CFont* pOldFont;
    TEXTMETRIC tm;
     const CString& strCaption = InternalGetText();

    pOldFont = SelectStockFont( pdc );
    pdc->FillRect(rcBounds, CBrush::FromHandle(
     (HBRUSH )GetStockObject(WHITE_BRUSH)));
    pdc->Ellipse(rcBounds);
    pdc->GetTextMetrics(&tm);
    pdc->SetTextAlign(TA_CENTER | TA_TOP);
    pdc->ExtTextOut((rcBounds.left + rcBounds.right) / 2,
     (rcBounds.top + rcBounds.bottom - tm.tmHeight) / 2,
     ETO_CLIPPED, rcBounds, strCaption, strCaption.GetLength(),
     NULL);

    pdc->SelectObject(pOldFont);
}
```

Once the OnDraw function has been modified to use the font object, any text within the control is displayed with characteristics from the control's stock Font property.

Using Custom Font Properties in Your Control

In addition to the stock Font property, the OLE control can have custom Font properties. To add a custom font property you must:

- Use ClassWizard to implement the custom Font property
- Process standard font change notifications
- Implement a new Font notification interface

Implementing a Custom Font Property

To implement a custom Font property, you use ClassWizard to add the property and then make some modifications to the code. The following sections describe how to add the custom HeadingFont property to the Sample control.

Adding a Custom Font Property

▶ **To add a custom font property**

1 With your control project open, open ClassWizard by choosing ClassWizard from the View menu.

2 Open ClassWizard.

3 Choose the OLE Automation tab.

4 Click the Add Property button.

5 In the External Name box, type a name for the property. For this example, use HeadingFont.

6 From the Implementation box, select Get/Set Methods.

7 From the Return Type box, select LPFONTDISP for the property's type.

8 Click the OK button.

9 Click the OK button to confirm your choices and close ClassWizard.

ClassWizard will create the code to add the HeadingFont custom property to the CSampleCtrl class and the SAMPLE.ODL file. Since HeadingFont is a Get/Set property type, ClassWizard modifies the CSampleCtrl class's dispatch map to include a **DISP_PROPERTY_EX** macro entry:

```
BEGIN_DISPATCH_MAP(CSampleCtrl, COleControl)
//{{AFX_DISPATCH_MAP(CSampleCtrl)
DISP_PROPERTY_EX(CSampleCtrl, "HeadingFont", GetHeadingFont,
    SetHeadingFont, VT_DISPATCH)
//}}AFX_DISPATCH_MAP
END_DISPATCH_MAP()
```

The **DISP_PROPERTY_EX** macro associates the HeadingFont property name with its corresponding CSampleCtrl class Get and Set methods, GetHeadingFont and SetHeadingFont. The type of the property value is also specified; in this case, **VT_DISPATCH**.

ClassWizard also adds a declaration in the control header file (.H) for the
`GetHeadingFont` and `SetHeadingFont` functions and adds their function templates in
the control implementation file (.CPP):

```
LPDISPATCH CSampleCtrl::GetHeadingFont()
{
 // TODO: Add your property handler here
 return NULL;
}

void CSampleCtrl::SetHeadingFont(LPDISPATCH newValue)
{
 // TODO: Add your property handler here
 SetModifiedFlag();
}
```

Finally, ClassWizard modifies the control .ODL file by adding an entry for the
`HeadingFont` property:

```
[id(1)] IDispatch* HeadingFont;
```

Modifications to the Control Code

Now that you have added the `HeadingFont` property to the control, you must make
some changes to the control header and implementation files to fully support the new
property.

In the control header file (.H), add the following declaration of a protected member
variable:

```
protected:

CFontHolder m_fontHeading;
```

In the control implementation file (.CPP), do the following:

- Initialize `m_fontHeading` in the control constructor.

  ```
  CSampleCtrl::CSampleCtrl( ) : m_fontHeading( &m_xFontNotification )
  {
      // [...body of constructor...]
  }
  ```

- Declare a static **FONTDESC** structure containing default attributes of the font.

  ```
  static const FONTDESC _fontdescHeading =
    { sizeof(FONTDESC), OLESTR("MS Sans Serif"), FONTSIZE( 12 ),
  FW_BOLD,
        ANSI_CHARSET, FALSE, FALSE, FALSE };
  ```

- In the control `DoPropExchange` member function, add a call to the **PX_Font**
  function. This provides initialization and persistence for your custom Font
  property.

```
void CSampleCtrl::DoPropExchange(CPropExchange* pPX)
{
    COleControl::DoPropExchange(pPX);

    // [...other PX_ function calls...]
    PX_Font(pPX, _T("HeadingFont"), m_fontHeading, &_fontdescHeading);
}
```

- Finish implementing the control `GetHeadingFont` member function.

```
LPFONTDISP CSampleCtrl::GetHeadingFont( )
{
    return m_fontHeading.GetFontDispatch( );
}
```

- Finish implementing the control `SetHeadingFont` member function.

```
void CSampleControl::SetHeadingFont( LPFONTDISP newValue )
{
    m_fontHeading.InitializeFont( &_fontdescHeading, newValue);
    OnFontChanged();    //notify any changes
    SetModifiedFlag( );
}
```

- Modify the control `OnDraw` member function to define a variable to hold the previously selected font.

```
CFont* pOldHeadingFont;
```

- Modify the control `OnDraw` member function to select the custom font into the device context by adding the following line wherever the font is to be used.

```
pOldHeadingFont = SelectFontObject(pdc, m_fontHeading);
```

- Modify the control `OnDraw` member function to select the previous font back into the device context by adding the following line after the font has been used.

```
pdc->SelectObject(pOldHeadingFont);
```

After the custom Font property has been implemented, the standard Font property page should be implemented, allowing control users to change the control's current font. To add the property page ID for the standard Font property page, insert the following line after the **BEGIN_PROPPAGEIDS** macro:

```
PROPPAGEID(CLSID_CFontPropPage)
```

You must also increment the count parameter of your **BEGIN_PROPPAGEIDS** macro by one. The following line illustrates this:

```
BEGIN_PROPPAGEIDS(CSampleCtrl, 2)
```

After these changes have been made, rebuild the entire project to incorporate the additional functionality.

Processing Font Notifications

In most cases the control needs to know when the characteristics of the font object have been modified. Each font object is capable of providing notifications when it changes by calling a member function of the **IFontNotification** interface, implemented by **COleControl**.

If the control uses the stock Font property, its notifications are handled by the **OnFontChanged** member function of **COleControl**. When you add custom font properties, you can have them use the same implementation. In the example in the previous section, this was accomplished by passing **&m_xFontNotification** when initializing the **m_fontHeading** member variable.

Figure 1   Implementing Multiple Font Object Interfaces

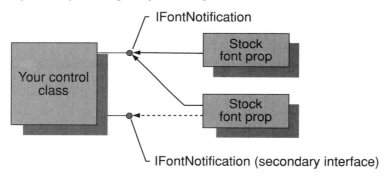

The solid lines in Figure 1 show that both font objects are using the same implementation of **IFontNotification**. This could cause problems if you wanted to distinguish which font changed.

One way to distinguish between the control's font object notifications is to create a separate implementation of the **IFontNotification** interface for each font object in the control. This technique allows you to optimize your drawing code by updating only the string, or strings, that use the recently modified font. The following sections demonstrate the steps necessary to implement separate notification interfaces for a second Font property. The second font property is assumed to be the HeadingFont property that was added in the previous section.

Implementing a New Font Notification Interface

To distinguish between the notifications of two or more fonts, a new notification interface must be implemented for each font used in the control. The following sections describe how to implement a new font notification interface by modifying the control header and implementation files.

Additions to the Header File

In the control header file (.H), add the following lines to the class declaration:

```
protected:
BEGIN_INTERFACE_PART(HeadingFontNotify, IPropertyNotifySink)
INIT_INTERFACE_PART(CSampleCtrl, HeadingFontNotify)
      STDMETHOD(OnRequestEdit)(DISPID);
      STDMETHOD(OnChanged)(DISPID);
   END_INTERFACE_PART(HeadingFontNotify)
```

This creates an implementation of the **IPropertyNotifySink** interface called
HeadingFontNotify. This new interface contains a method called OnChanged.

Additions to the Implementation File

In the code that initializes the heading font (in the control constructor), change
&m_xFontNotification to &m_xHeadingFontNotify. Then add the following code:

```
STDMETHODIMP_(ULONG) CSampleCtrl::XHeadingFontNotify::AddRef( )
{
    METHOD_MANAGE_STATE(CSampleCtrl, HeadingFontNotify)
    return 1;
}
STDMETHODIMP_(ULONG) CSampleCtrl::XHeadingFontNotify::Release( )
{
    METHOD_MANAGE_STATE(CSampleCtrl, HeadingFontNotify)
    return 0;
}


STDMETHODIMP CSampleCtrl::XHeadingFontNotify::QueryInterface( REFIID iid,
    LPVOID FAR* ppvObj )
{
    METHOD_MANAGE_STATE( CSampleCtrl, HeadingFontNotify )
    if( IsEqualIID( iid, IID_IUnknown ) ||
        IsEqualIID( iid, IID_IPropertyNotifySink))
    {
     *ppvObj= this;
     AddRef( );
     return NOERROR;
    }
    return ResultFromScode(E_NOINTERFACE);
}


STDMETHODIMP CSampleCtrl::XHeadingFontNotify::OnChanged(DISPID)
{
    METHOD_MANAGE_STATE( CSampleCtrl, HeadingFontNotify )
    pThis->InvalidateControl( );
    return NOERROR;
}


STDMETHODIMP CSampleCtrl::XHeadingFontNotify::OnRequestEdit(DISPID)
{
    return NOERROR;
}
```

The AddRef and Release methods in the **IPropertyNotifySink** interface keep track of the reference count for the OLE control object. When the control obtains access to interface pointer, the control calls AddRef to increment the reference count. When the control is finished with the pointer, it calls Release, in much the same way that **GlobalFree** might be called to free a global memory block. When the reference count for this interface goes to zero, the interface implementation can be freed. In this example, the QueryInterface function returns a pointer to a **IPropertyNotifySink** interface on a particular object. This function allows an OLE control to query an object to determine what interfaces it supports.

After these changes have been made to your project, you should rebuild the project and use Test Container to test the interface.

See Also   OLE Controls: Using Pictures in an OLE Control, OLE Controls: Using Stock Property Pages

OLE Controls: Using Pictures in an OLE Control

This article describes the common Picture type and how to implement it in your OLE control. Topics include:

- Overview of custom Picture properties
- Implementing a custom Picture property in your OLE control

Overview of Custom Picture Properties

A Picture type is one of a group of types common to all OLE controls. The Picture type handles metafiles, bitmaps, or icons and allows the user to specify a picture to be displayed in an OLE control. Custom Picture properties are implemented using a picture object and Get/Set functions that allow the control user access to the Picture property. Control users access the custom Picture property using the stock Picture property page.

In addition to the standard Picture type, Font and Color types are also available. For more information on using the standard Font type in your OLE control, see the article OLE Controls: Using Fonts in an OLE Control.

The OLE control classes provide several components you can use to implement the Picture property within the control. These components include:

- The **CPictureHolder** class.

  This class provides easy access to the picture object and functionality for the item displayed by the custom Picture property.

- Support for properties of type **LPPICTUREDISP**, implemented with Get/Set functions.

  Using ClassWizard you can quickly add a custom property, or properties, that supports the Picture type. For more information on adding OLE control properties with ClassWizard, see the article Properties.

- A property page that manipulates a control's Picture property or properties.

  This property page is part of a group of stock property pages available to OLE controls. For more information on OLE control property pages, see the article OLE Controls: Using Stock Property Pages

Implementing a Custom Picture Property in Your OLE Control

When you have completed the steps outlined in this section, the control can display pictures chosen by its user. The user can change the displayed picture using a property page that shows the current picture and has a Browse button that allows the user to the select different pictures.

A custom Picture property is implemented using a process similar to that used for implementing other properties, the main difference being that the custom property must support a Picture type. Because the item of the Picture property must be drawn by the OLE control, a number of additions and modifications must be made to the property before it can be fully implemented.

To implement a custom Picture property, you must do the following:

- Add code to your control project.

  A standard Picture property page ID, a data member of type **CPictureHolder**, and a custom property of type **LPPICTUREDISP** with a Get/Set implementation must be added.

- Modify several functions in your control class.

  These modifications will be made to several functions that are responsible for the drawing of your OLE control.

Additions to Your Control Project

To add the property page ID for the standard Picture property page, insert the following line after the **BEGIN_PROPPAGEIDS** macro in the control implementation file (.CPP):

```
PROPPAGEID(CLSID_CPicturePropPage)
```

You must also increment the count parameter of your **BEGIN_PROPPAGEIDS** macro by one. The following line illustrates this:

```
BEGIN_PROPPAGEIDS(CSampleCtrl, 2)
```

To add the **CPictureHolder** data member to the control class, insert the following line under the protected section of the control class declaration in the control header file (.H):

```
CPictureHolder    m_pic;
```

It is not necessary to name your data member m_pic; any name will suffice.

Next, add a custom property that supports a Picture type:

▶ To add a custom picture property using ClassWizard

1 With your control project open, open ClassWizard by choosing ClassWizard from the View menu.

2 Choose the OLE Automation tab.

3 Click the Add Property button.

4 In the External Name box, type the property name. For example purposes, `ControlPicture` is used in this procedure.

5 Under Implementation, select Get/Set Methods.

6 From the Return Type box, select LPPICTUREDISP for the property type.

7 Type unique names for your Get and Set Functions or accept the default names. (In this example, the default names, `GetControlPicture` and `SetControlPicture`, are used.)

8 Click the OK button to close the Add Property dialog box.

9 Click the OK button to confirm your choices and close ClassWizard.

ClassWizard adds the following code between the dispatch map comments in the control header (.H) file:

```
afx_msg LPPICTUREDISP GetControlPicture();
afx_msg void SetControlPicture(LPPICTUREDISP newValue);
```

In addition, the following code was inserted in the dispatch map of the control implementation (.CPP) file:

```
DISP_PROPERTY_EX(CSampleCtrl, "ControlPicture", GetControlPicture, SetControlPicture,
    VT_PICTURE)
```

ClassWizard also adds the following two stub functions in the control implementation file:

```
LPPICTUREDISP CSampleCtrl::GetControlPicture()
{
    // TODO: Add your property handler here

    return NULL;
}


void CSampleCtrl::SetControlPicture(LPPICTUREDISP newValue)
{
    // TODO: Add your property handler here

    SetModifiedFlag();
}
```

Note Your control class and function names might differ from the example above.

Modifications to Your Control Project

Once you have made the necessary additions to your control project, you need to modify several functions that affect the rendering of your OLE control. These functions, OnResetState, OnDraw, and the Get/Set functions of a custom Picture property, are located in the control implementation file. (Note that in this example the control class is called CSampleCtrl, the **CPictureHolder** data member is called m_pic, and the custom picture property name is ControlPicture.)

In the control OnResetState function, add the following optional line after the call to **COleControl::OnResetState**:

```
m_pic.CreateEmpty();
```

This sets the control's picture to a blank picture.

You need to make a call to **CPictureHolder::Render**, in the control OnDraw function, to draw the picture properly. Modify your function to resemble the following example:

```
void CSampleCtrl::OnDraw(
    CDC* pdc, const CRect& rcBounds, const CRect& rcInvalid)
{
// ****** Add your code below this line ********** //
    m_pic.Render(pdc, rcBounds, rcBounds);
}
```

In the Get function of the control's custom picture property, add the following line:

```
return m_pic.GetPictureDispatch();
```

In the Set function of the control's custom Picture property, add the following lines:

```
m_pic.SetPictureDispatch(newValue);
InvalidateControl();
```

Note Your class and function names might differ from the example above.

After you complete the modifications, rebuild your project to incorporate the new functionality of the custom Picture property and use Test Container to test the new property.

See Also OLE Controls: Using Fonts in an OLE Control, OLE Controls: Property Pages

OLE Controls: Advanced Topics

This article covers advanced topics related to developing OLE controls. These include:

- Using database classes in OLE controls
- Implementing a parameterized property
- Handling errors in your OLE control
- Handling special keys in the control

Using Database Classes in OLE Controls

Because the OLE control classes are part of the class library, you can apply the same procedures and rules for using database classes in a standard MFC application to developing OLE controls that use the MFC database classes.

For a general overview of the MFC database classes, see Chapter 7, Working with Databases and the following, Database Overview. The article introduces both the MFC ODBC and the MFC DAO classes.

Implementing a Parameterized Property

A parameterized property (sometimes called an property array) is a method for exposing a homogeneous collection of values as a single property of the control. For example, you can use a parameterized property to expose an array or a dictionary as a property. In Visual Basic, such a property is accessed using array notation:

```
x = obj.ArrayProp(2, 3)      ' gets element of 2D array
obj.ArrayProp(2, 3) = 7      ' sets element of 2D array
```

Use the OLE Automation tab of ClassWizard to implement a parameterized property. ClassWizard implements the property by adding a pair of Get/Set functions that allow the control user to access the property using the above notation or in the standard fashion.

Similar to methods and properties, parameterized properties also have a limit to the number of parameters allowed. In the case of parameterized properties, the limit is 15 parameters (with one parameter reserved for storing the property value).

The following procedure adds a parameterized property, called Array, which can be accessed as a two-dimensional array of integers.

▶ **To add a parameterized property using ClassWizard**

1 Load your control project.

2 From the Browse menu, choose ClassWizard.

3 Choose the OLE Automation tab.

4 Click the Add Property button.

5 In the External Name box, type `Array`.

6 Under Implementation, select Get/Set Methods.

7 From the Type box, select short for the property's type.

8 In the Get Function and Set Function boxes type unique names for your Get and Set Functions or accept the default names.

9 Using the grid control, add a parameter, called row (type short).

10 Using the grid control, add a second parameter, called column (type short).

11 Click the OK button to confirm your choices and close ClassWizard.

Changes Made by ClassWizard

When you add a custom property, ClassWizard makes changes to the control class header (.H) and the implementation (.CPP) files.

The following lines are added to the control class .H file:

```
afx_msg short GetArray(short row, short column);
afx_msg void SetArray(short row, short column, short nNewValue);
```

This code declares two functions called `GetArray` and `SetArray` that allow the user to request a specific row and column when accessing the property.

In addition, ClassWizard adds the following lines the control dispatch map , located in the control class implementation (.CPP) file:

```
DISP_PROPERTY_PARAM(CSampleCtrl, "Array", GetArray, SetArray, VT_I2,
        VTS_I2 VTS_I2)
```

Finally, the implementations of the `GetArray` and `SetArray` functions are added to the end of the .CPP file. In most cases, you will modify the Get function to return the value of the property. The Set function will usually contain code that should execute, either before or after the property changes.

For this property to be useful, you could declare a two-dimensional array member variable in the control class, of type **short**, to store values for the parameterized property. You could then modify the Get function to return the value stored at the proper row and column, as indicated by the parameters, and modify the Set function to update the value referenced by the row and column parameters.

Handling Errors in Your OLE Control

If error conditions occur in the control, you may need to report the error to the control container. There are two methods for reporting errors, depending on the situation in which the error occurs. If the error occurs within a property's Get or Set function, or within the implementation of an OLE Automation method, the control should call **COleControl::ThrowError**, which signals the control user that an error has occurred. If the error occurs at any other time, the control should call **COleControl::FireError**, which fires a stock Error event.

To indicate the kind of error that has occurred, the control must pass an error code to **ThrowError** or **FireError**. An error code is an OLE status code, which has a 32-bit value. When possible, choose an error code from the standard set of codes defined in the OLECTL.H header file. Table 1 summarizes these codes.

Table 1 OLE Control Error Codes

Error	Description
CTL_E_ILLEGALFUNCTIONCALL	Illegal function call
CTL_E_OVERFLOW	Overflow
CTL_E_OUTOFMEMORY	Out of memory
CTL_E_DIVISIONBYZERO	Division by zero
CTL_E_OUTOFSTRINGSPACE	Out of string space
CTL_E_OUTOFSTACKSPACE	Out of stack space
CTL_E_BADFILENAMEORNUMBER	Bad file name or number
CTL_E_FILENOTFOUND	File not found
CTL_E_BADFILEMODE	Bad file mode
CTL_E_FILEALREADYOPEN	File already open
CTL_E_DEVICEIOERROR	Device I/O error
CTL_E_FILEALREADYEXISTS	File already exists
CTL_E_BADRECORDLENGTH	Bad record length
CTL_E_DISKFULL	Disk full
CTL_E_BADRECORDNUMBER	Bad record number
CTL_E_BADFILENAME	Bad file name
CTL_E_TOOMANYFILES	Too many files
CTL_E_DEVICEUNAVAILABLE	Device unavailable
CTL_E_PERMISSIONDENIED	Permission denied
CTL_E_DISKNOTREADY	Disk not ready
CTL_E_PATHFILEACCESSERROR	Path/file access error
CTL_E_PATHNOTFOUND	Path not found
CTL_E_INVALIDPATTERNSTRING	Invalid pattern string
CTL_E_INVALIDUSEOFNULL	Invalid use of NULL
CTL_E_INVALIDFILEFORMAT	Invalid file format
CTL_E_INVALIDPROPERTYVALUE	Invalid property value
CTL_E_INVALIDPROPERTYARRAYINDEX	Invalid property array index
CTL_E_SETNOTSUPPORTEDATRUNTIME	Set not supported at run time
CTL_E_SETNOTSUPPORTED	Set not supported (read-only property)
CTL_E_NEEDPROPERTYARRAYINDEX	Need property array index
CTL_E_SETNOTPERMITTED	Set not permitted
CTL_E_GETNOTSUPPORTEDATRUNTIME	Get not supported at run time

Table 1   OLE Control Error Codes *(cont.)*

Error	Description
CTL_E_GETNOTSUPPORTED	Get not supported (write-only property)
CTL_E_PROPERTYNOTFOUND	Property not found
CTL_E_INVALIDCLIPBOARDFORMAT	Invalid clipboard format
CTL_E_INVALIDPICTURE	Invalid picture
CTL_E_PRINTERERROR	Printer error
CTL_E_CANTSAVEFILETOTEMP	Can't save file to TEMP
CTL_E_SEARCHTEXTNOTFOUND	Search text not found
CTL_E_REPLACEMENTSTOOLONG	Replacements too long

If necessary, use the **CUSTOM_CTL_SCODE** macro to define a custom error code for a condition that is not covered by one of the standard codes. The parameter for this macro should be an integer between 1000 and 32767, inclusive. For example:

```
#define MYCTL_E_SPECIALERROR CUSTOM_CTL_SCODE(1000)
```

If you are creating an OLE control to replace an existing VBX control, define your OLE control error codes with the same numeric values the VBX control uses to ensure that the error codes are compatible.

Handling Special Keys in Your Control

In some cases you may want to handle certain keystroke combinations in a special way; for example, insert a new line when the ENTER key is pressed in a multiline text box control or move between a group of edit controls when a directional key ID pressed.

If the base class of your OLE control is **COleControl**, you can override **CWnd::PreTranslateMessage** to handle messages before the container receives them. When using this technique, always return **TRUE** if you handle the message in your override of **PreTranslateMessage**.

The following code example demonstrates a possible way of handling any messages related to the directional keys.

```
BOOL CSampleControl::PreTranslateMessage(LPMSG lpmsg)
{
    BOOL bHandleNow = FALSE;

    switch (lpmsg->message)
    {
    case WM_KEYDOWN:
        switch (lpmsg->wParam)
        {
        case VK_UP:
        case VK_DOWN:
        case VK_LEFT:
```

```
            case VK_RIGHT:
                bHandleNow = TRUE;
                break;
        }
        if (bHandleNow)
            OnKeyDown(lpmsg->wParam, LOWORD(lpmsg
                ->lParam), HIWORD(lpmsg->lParam));
        break;
    }
    return bHandleNow;
}
```

For more information on handling keyboard interfaces for an OLE control, see the Keyboard Interface topic of the OLE Control Architecture Specification, which is found only in Books Online.

OLE Controls: Distributing OLE Controls

This article discusses several issues related to redistributing OLE controls:

- ANSI or Unicode control versions
- Installing the control and its components
- Registering the OLE control
- List of redistributable files

ANSI or Unicode Control Versions

You must decide whether to ship an ANSI or Unicode version of the control, or both. This decision is based on portability factors inherent in ANSI and Unicode character sets.

ANSI controls, which work on all Win32 operating systems, allow for maximum portability between the various Win32 operating systems. Unicode controls work on only Windows NT (version 3.51 or later), but not on Windows 95. If portability is your primary concern, you should ship ANSI controls. If your controls will run only on Windows NT, you can ship Unicode controls. You could also choose to ship both and have your application install the version most appropriate for the user's operating system.

Installing OLE Controls and Redistributable DLLs

The setup program you provide with your OLE controls should create a special subdirectory of the Windows directory and install the controls' .OCX files in it.

Tip Use the Windows **GetWindowsDirectory** API in your setup program to obtain the name of the Windows directory.

You may want to derive the subdirectory name from the name of your company or product.

The setup program must install the necessary redistributable DLL files in the Windows system directory. If any of the DLLs are already present on the user's machine, the setup program should compare their versions with the versions you are installing. Only reinstall a file if its version number is higher than the file already installed.

Because OLE controls can be used only in OLE container applications, there is no need to distribute the full set of OLE DLLs with your controls. You can assume that the containing application (or the operating system itself) has the standard OLE DLLs installed.

Registering Controls

Before a control can be used, appropriate entries must be created for it in the Windows registration database. Some OLE control containers provide a menu item for users to register new controls, but this feature may not be available in all containers. Therefore, you may want your setup program to register the controls when they are installed. Visual C++ includes a redistributable program, REGSVR32.EXE, which can be used to register controls. Just pass the complete path and filename of the control .OCX file as an argument to REGSVR32. The MFC OLE Controls sample REGSVR provides the source code for REGSVR32.EXE. This sample illustrates one method for performing the registration task and can be used as a guide to writing your own registration routine.

If you prefer, you can write your setup program to register the control directly instead.

Use the **LoadLibrary** Windows API to load the control DLL. Next, use **GetProcAddress** to obtain the address of the "DllRegisterServer" function. Finally, call the DllRegisterServer function. The following code sample demonstrates one possible method, where hLib stores the handle of the control library, and lpDllEntryPoint stores the address of the "DllRegisterServer" function.

```
HINSTANCE hLib = LoadLibrary(pszDllName);

if (hLib < (HINSTANCE)HINSTANCE_ERROR)
{
 DisplayMessage(IDS_LOADLIBFAILED, pszDllName); //unable to load DLL
 iReturn = FAIL_LOAD;                    //unable to load DLL
}

// Find the entry point.
(FARPROC&)lpDllEntryPoint = GetProcAddress(hLib,
    _T("DllRegisterServer"));
if (lpDllEntryPoint != NULL)
 (*lpDllEntryPoint)();
else
    //unable to locate entry point
```

The advantage of registering the control directly is that you don't need to invoke and load a separate process (namely, REGSVR32), lessening installation time. In addition, because registration is an internal process, the setup program can handle errors and unforeseen situations better than an external process can.

Note Before your setup program installs an OLE control, it should call **OleInitialize**. When your setup program is finished, call **OleUnitialize**. This ensures that the OLE system DLLs are in the proper state for registering an OLE control.

When you install and register a control, you should also register OLEPRO32.DLL. Use the same procedure for registering this DLL as you did for your .OCX file. Perform this registration step only if you need to install OLEPRO32.DLL. If the DLL is installed already, you should assume that it has been registered.

If your control uses one of the stock property pages, you should also register MFCx0.DLL. Unlike OLEPRO32.DLL, you should always register this DLL, even if it is already installed.

List of Redistributable Files

This section lists the files you may redistribute with your OLE control. The conditions under which you may or may not redistribute these files are described in the License Agreement included in the product. Visual C++ Setup may install some of these files on your development machine, depending on the options you chose during Setup. When you redistribute any of these files, you should copy them from the Visual C++ CD to your distribution medium. This ensures that you are redistributing the correct version of the files. Table 1 lists files that must be redistributed with your OLE control.

Table 1   Redistributable Files

File	Description
MFCx0.DLL	MFC DLL (ANSI)
MFCx0U.DLL	MFC DLL (Unicode)
MSVCRTx0.DLL	C run-time libraries
OLEPRO32.DLL	OLE property frame and standard types support
REGSVR32.EXE	Control registration utility

OLE Controls: Licensing an OLE Control

Licensing support, an optional feature of OLE controls, allows you to control who is able to use or distribute the control.

This article discusses the following topics:

- Overview of OLE control licensing
- Creating a licensed control
- Licensing support
- Customizing the licensing of an OLE control

OLE controls that implement licensing allow you, as the control developer, to determine how other people will use the OLE control. You provide the control purchaser with the control and .LIC file, with the agreement that the purchaser may distribute the control, but not the .LIC file, with an application that uses the control. This prevents users of that application from writing new applications that use the control, without first licensing the control from you.

Overview of OLE Control Licensing

To provide licensing support for OLE controls, the **COleObjectFactory** class provides an implementation for several functions in the **IClassFactory2** interface: **IClassFactory2::RequestLicKey**, **IClassFactory2::GetLicInfo**, and **IClassFactory2::CreateInstanceLic**. When the container application developer makes a request to create an instance of the control, a call to **GetLicInfo** is made to verify that the control .LIC file is present. If the control is licensed, an instance of the control can be created and placed in the container. After the developer has finished constructing the container application, another function call, this time to **RequestLicKey**, is made. This function returns a license key (a simple character string) to the container application. The returned key is then embedded in the application.

Figure 1 demonstrates the license verification of an OLE control that will be used during the development of a container application. As mentioned previously, the container application developer must have the proper .LIC file installed on the development machine to create an instance of the control.

Figure 1   Verification of a Licensed OLE Control During Development

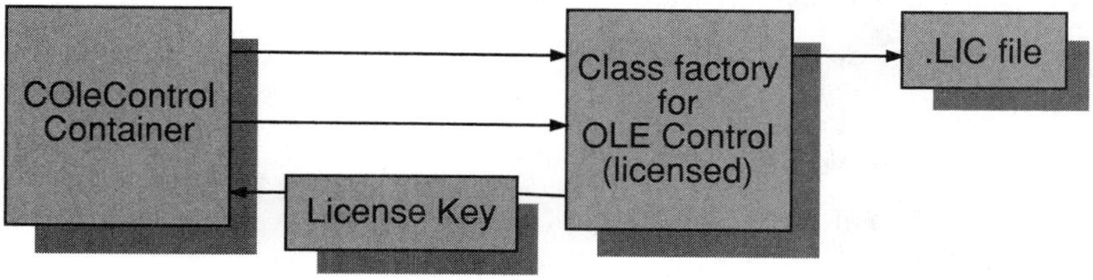

The next process, shown in Figure 2, occurs when the end-user runs the container application.

When the application is started, an instance of the control usually needs to be created. The container accomplishes this by making a call to **CreateInstanceLic**, passing the embedded license key as a parameter. A string comparison is then made between the embedded license key and the control's own copy of the license key. If the match is successful, an instance of the control is created and the application continues to execute normally. Note that the .LIC file need not be present on the control user's machine.

Figure 2   Verification of a Licensed OLE Control During Execution

Control licensing consists of two basic components: (1) specific code in the control implementation DLL and (2) the license file. The code is composed of two (or possibly three) function calls and a character string, hereafter referred to as a "license string", containing a copyright notice. These calls and the license string are found in the control implementation (.CPP) file. The license file, generated by ControlWizard, is a text file with a copyright statement. It is named using the project name with an .LIC extension, for example SAMPLE.LIC. A licensed control must be accompanied by the license file if design-time use is needed.

Creating a Licensed Control

When you use ControlWizard to create the control framework, it is easy to include licensing support. When the Enforce License option is selected, ControlWizard adds code to the control class to support licensing. The code consists of functions that use a key and license file for license verification. These functions also can be modified to customize the control licensing. For more information on license customization, see Customizing the Licensing of an OLE Control later in this article.

▶ **To add support for licensing with ControlWizard**

1 From the File menu, choose New.

The New dialog box appears.

2 In the New box, select Project Workspace.

The New box allows selection of various file types.

3 Click OK.

The New Workspace dialog box appears.

4 In the Name box, type a project name.

A directory for the new project is added to the currently specified workspace directory structure. ControlWizard uses the name that you specify in the Project Name box to derive default names for most of the files and classes it creates for the control project.

5 In the Type list box, select OLE ControlWizard

6 In the first dialog box, choose Yes for License Validation.

7 Select any other options for your project.

8 Choose Finish to confirm your project choices.

The New Project Information dialog box appears.

9 Click OK to have ControlWizard generate the OLE control framework.

ControlWizard now generates an OLE control framework that includes basic licensing support. For a detailed explanation of the licensing code, see the next topic, Licensing Support.

Licensing Support

When you use ControlWizard to add licensing support to an OLE control, ControlWizard adds code that declares and implements the licensing capability is added to the control header and implementation files. This code is composed of a **VerifyUserLicense** member function and a **GetLicenseKey** member function, which override the default implementations found in **COleObjectFactory** . These functions retrieve and verify the control license.

Note A third member function, **VerifyLicenseKey** is not generated by ControlWizard, but can be overidden to customize the license key verification behavior.

These member functions are:

- **VerifyUserLicense**

   Verifies that the control allows design-time usage by checking the system for the presence of the control license file. This function is called by the framework as part of processing **IClassFactory2::GetLicInfo** and **IClassFactory::CreateInstanceLic**.

- **GetLicenseKey**

   Requests a unique key from the control DLL. This key is embedded in the container application and used later, in conjunction with **VerifyLicenseKey**, to create an instance of the control. This function is called by the framework as part of processing **IClassFactory2::RequestLicKey**.

- **VerifyLicenseKey**

   Verifies that the embedded key and the control's unique key are the same. This allows the container to create an instance of the control for its use. This function is called by the framework as part of processing **IClassFactory2::CreateInstanceLic** and can be overridden to provide customized verification of the license key. The default implementation performs a string comparison. For more information, see Customizing the Licensing of an OLE Control, later in this article.

Header File Modifications

ControlWizard places the following code in the control header file. In this example, two member functions of `CSampleCtrl`'s object `factory` are declared, one that verifies the presence of the control .LIC file and another that retrieves the license key to be used in the application containing the control:

```
BEGIN_OLEFACTORY(CSampleCtrl)          // Class factory and guid
    virtual BOOL VerifyUserLicense();
    virtual BOOL GetLicenseKey(DWORD, BSTR FAR*);
END_OLEFACTORY(CSampleCtrl)
```

Implementation File Modifications

ControlWizard places the following two statements in the control implementation file to declare the license filename and license string:

```
static const TCHAR BASED_CODE _szLicFileName[] =
    _T("License.lic");

static const WCHAR BASED_CODE _szLicString[] =
    L"Copyright (c) 1995 ";
```

Note If you modify **szLicString** in any way, you must also modify the first line in the control .LIC file or licensing will not function properly.

ControlWizard places the following code in the control implementation file to define the control class' VerifyUserLicense and GetLicenseKey functions:

```
/////////////////////////////////////////////////////////////////////////////
// CLicenseCtrl::CLicenseCtrlFactory::VerifyUserLicense
// Checks for existence of a user license

BOOL CLicenseCtrl::CLicenseCtrlFactory::VerifyUserLicense()
{
    return AfxVerifyLicFile(AfxGetInstanceHandle(),
_szLicFileName, _szLicString);
}

/////////////////////////////////////////////////////////////////////////////
// CLicenseCtrl::CLicenseCtrlFactory::GetLicenseKey -
// Returns a runtime licensing key

BOOL CLicenseCtrl::CLicenseCtrlFactory::GetLicenseKey(DWORD dwReserved,
    BSTR FAR* pbstrKey)
{
    if (pbstrKey == NULL)
        return FALSE;

    *pbstrKey = SysAllocString(_szLicString);
    return (*pbstrKey != NULL);
}
```

Finally, ControlWizard modifies the control project .ODL file. The **licensed** keyword is added to the class information section of the control, as in the following example:

```
[ uuid(A728C248-BD2C-11CE-88F9-00AA00339DC7),
version(1.0), helpstring("Sample OLE Custom Control
module"), control ]
library SAMPLELib
```

Customizing the Licensing of an OLE Control

Because **VerifyUserLicense**, **GetLicenseKey**, and **VerifyLicenseKey** are declared as virtual member functions of the control factory class, you can customize the control's licensing behavior.

For example, you can provide several levels of licensing for the control by overriding the **VerifyUserLicense** and/or **VerifyLicenseKey** member functions. Inside this function you could adjust which properties and/or methods are exposed to the user according to the license level you detected.

You can also add code to the **VerifyLicenseKey** function that provides a customized method forinforming the user that control creation has failed. For instance, in your **VerifyLicenseKey** member function you could display a message box stating that the control failed to initialize and why.

Note Another way to customize OLE control license verification, is to check the registration database for a specific registry key, instead of calling **AfxVerifyLicFile**. For an example of the default implementation, see the Implementation File Modifications section of this article.

See Also OLE ControlWizard

OLE Controls: Localizing an OLE Control

This article discusses procedures for localizing OLE control interfaces.

If you want to adapt an OLE control to an international market, you may want to localize the control. Windows supports several languages in addition to the default English, including German, French, and Swedish. This can present problems for the control if its interface is in English only.

In general, OLE controls should always base their locale on the ambient LocaleID property. There are three ways to do this:

- Load resources, always on demand, based on the current value of the ambient LocaleID property. The MFC OLE Controls sample LOCALIZE uses this strategy.

- Load resources when the first control is instanced, based on the ambient LocaleID property, and use these resources for all other instances. This article demonstrates this strategy.

  Note This will not work correctly in some cases, if future instances have different locales.

- Use the **OnAmbientChanged** notification function to dynamically load the proper resources for the container's locale.

  Note This will work for the control, but the run-time DLL will not dynamically update its own resources when the ambient LocaleID property changes. In addition, run-time DLLs for OLE controls use the thread locale to determine the locale for its resources.

The rest of this article describes two localizing strategies. The first strategy localizes the control's programmability interface (names of properties, methods, and events). The second strategy localizes the control's user interface, using the container's ambient LocaleID property. For a demonstration of control localization, see the MFC OLE Controls sample LOCALIZE.

Localizing the Control's Programmability Interface

When localizing the control's programmability interface (the interface used by programmers writing applications that use your control), you must create a modified version of the control .ODL file (a script for building the control type library) for each language you intend to support. This is the only place you need to localize the control property names.

When you develop a localized control, you should include the locale ID as an attribute at the type library level. For example, if you want to provide a type library with French localized property names, make a copy of your SAMPLE.ODL file, and call it SAMPLEFR.ODL. Add a locale ID attribute to the file (the locale ID for French is 0x040c), similar to the following:

```
[ uuid(xxxxxxxx-xxxx-xxxx-xxxx-xxxxxxxxxxxx), version(1.0), lcid(0x040c) ]
library Sample
```

Change the property names in SAMPLEFR.ODL to their French equivalents, and then use MKTYPLIB.EXE to produce the French type library, SAMPLEFR.TLB.

To create multiple localized type libraries you can add any localized .ODL files to the project and they will be built automatically.

▶ To add an .ODL file to your OLE control project

1 From the Insert menu, choose Source Files.

The Insert Project Files dialog box appears.

2 If necessary, select the drive and directory to view.

3 Add each file using one of the following methods:

- Select the .ODL file in the File Name list and choose Add.

– or–

- Double-click the the .ODL file in the File Name list.

4 Close the Insert Project Files dialog box when you have added all necessary .ODL files.

Because the files have been added to the project they will be built when the rest of the project is built. The localized type libraries are located in the current OLE control project directory.

Within your code, the internal property names (usually in English) are always used and are never localized. This includes the control dispatch map, the property exchange functions, and your property page data exchange code.

Only one type library (.TLB) file may be bound into the resources of the control implementation (.OCX) file. This is usually the version with the standardized (typically, English) names. To ship a localized version of your control you need to ship the .OCX (which has already been bound to the default .TLB version) and the .TLB for the appropriate locale. This means that only the .OCX is needed for English versions, since the correct .TLB has already been bound to it. For other locales, the localized type library also must be shipped with the .OCX.

To ensure that clients of your control can find the localized type library, register your locale-specific .TLB file(s) under the TypeLib section of the Windows system registry. The third parameter (normally optional) of the **AfxOleRegisterTypeLib** function is provided for this purpose. The following example registers a French type library for an OLE control:

```
STDAPI DllRegisterServer(void)
{
    AFX_MANAGE_STATE(_afxModuleAddrThis);

    if (!AfxOleRegisterTypeLib(AfxGetInstanceHandle(), _tlid))
        return ResultFromScode(SELFREG_E_TYPELIB);
    AfxOleRegisterTypeLib(AfxGetInstanceHandle(), _tlid,
        _T("samplefr.tlb"))
    if (!COleObjectFactoryEx::UpdateRegistryAll(TRUE))
        return ResultFromScode(SELFREG_E_CLASS);

    return NOERROR;
}
```

When your control is registered, the **AfxOleRegisterTypeLib** function automatically looks for the specified .TLB file in the same directory as the control and registers it in the Windows registration database. If the .TLB file isn't found, the function has no effect.

Localizing the Control's User Interface

To localize a control's user interface, place all of the control's user-visible resources (such as property pages and error messages) into language-specific resource DLLs. You then can use the container's ambient LocaleID property to select the appropriate DLL for the user's locale.

The following code example demonstrates one approach to locate and load the resource DLL for a specific locale. This member function, called GetLocalizedResourceHandle for this example, can be a member function of your OLE control class:

```
HINSTANCE CSampleCtrl::GetLocalizedResourceHandle(LCID lcid)
{
    LPCTSTR lpszResDll;
    HINSTANCE hResHandle = NULL;
    LANGID lang = LANGIDFROMLCID(lcid);
    switch (PRIMARYLANGID(lang))
    {
    case LANG_ENGLISH:
        lpszResDll = "myctlen.dll";
        break;

    case LANG_FRENCH:
        lpszResDll = "myctlfr.dll";
        break;

    case LANG_GERMAN:
        lpszResDll = "myctlde.dll";
        break;

    case 0:
    default:
        lpszResDll = NULL;
```

```
    }

    if (lpszResDll != NULL)
        hResHandle = LoadLibrary(lpszResDll);
#ifndef _WIN32
        if(hResHandle <= HINSTANCE_ERROR)
            hResHandle = NULL;
#endif

    return hResHandle;
}
```

Note that the sublanguage ID could be checked in each case of the switch statement, to provide more specialized localization (for example, local dialects of German). For a demonstration of this function, see the GetResourceHandle function in the MFC OLE Controls sample LOCALIZE.

When the control first loads itself into a container, it can call **COleControl::AmbientLocaleID** to retrieve the locale ID. The control can then pass the returned locale ID value to the GetLocalizedResourceHandle function, which loads the proper resource library. The control should pass the resulting handle, if any, to **AfxSetResourceHandle**:

```
m_hResDll = GetLocalizedResourceHandle( AmbientLocaleID() );
if (m_hResDll != NULL)
    AfxSetResourceHandle(m_hResDll);
```

Place the code sample above into a member function of the control, such as an override of **COleControl::OnSetClientSite**. In addition, m_hResDLL should be a member variable of the control class.

You can use similar logic for localizing a control's property page. To localize the property page, add code similar to the following sample to your property page's implementation file (in an override of **COlePropertyPage::OnSetPageSite**):

```
LPPROPERTYPAGESITE pSite;
LCID lcid = 0;
if((pSite = GetPageSite()) != NULL)
    pSite->GetLocaleID(&lcid);
HINSTANCE hResource = GetLocalizedResourceHandle(lcid);
HINSTANCE hResourceSave = NULL;

if (hResource != NULL)
{
    hResourceSave = AfxGetResourceHandle();
    AfxSetResourceHandle(hResource);
}

// Load dialog template and caption string.
COlePropertyPage::OnSetPageSite( );

if (hResource != NULL)
    AfxSetResourceHandle(hResourceSave);
```

OLE Controls: Serializing

This article discusses how to serialize an OLE control. Serialization is the process of reading from or writing to a persistent storage medium, such as a disk file. The Microsoft Foundation Class Library (MFC) provides built-in support for serialization in class **CObject**. **COleControl** extends this support to OLE controls through the use of a property exchange mechanism

Serialization for OLE controls is implemented by overriding **COleControl::DoPropExchange**. This function, called during the loading and saving of the control object, stores all properties implemented with a member variable or a member variable with change notification.

The following topics cover the main issues related to serializing an OLE control:

- Implementing DoPropExchange to serialize your control object

- Customizing the serialization process

- Implementing version support

Implementing the DoPropExchange Function

When you use ControlWizard to generate the control project, several default handler functions are automatically added to the control class, including the default implementation of **COleControl::DoPropExchange**. The following example shows the code added to classes created with ControlWizard:

```
void CSampleCtrl::DoPropExchange( CPropExchange* pPX)
{
    ExchangeVersion(pPX, MAKELONG(_wVerMinor, _wVerMajor));
    COleControl::DoPropExchange(pPX);

    // TODO: Call PX_ functions for each persistent custom property.
}
```

If you want to make a property persistent, modify DoPropExchange by adding a call to the property exchange function. The following example demonstrates the serialization of a custom boolean CircleShape property:

```
void CSampleCtrl::DoPropExchange(CPropExchange* pPX)
{
    ExchangeVersion(pPX, MAKELONG(_wVerMinor, _wVerMajor));
    COleControl::DoPropExchange(pPX);

    PX_Bool(pPX, "CircleShape", m_bCircleShape, TRUE);
}
```

The following table lists the possible property exchange functions you can use to serialize the control's properties:

Property Exchange Functions	Purpose
PX_Blob( )	Serializes a type Binary Large Object (BLOB) data property.
PX_Bool( )	Serializes a type Boolean property.
PX_Color( )	Serializes a type color property.
PX_Currency( )	Serializes a type **CY** (currency) property.
PX_Double( )	Serializes a type **double** property.
PX_Font( )	Serializes a Font type property.
PX_Float( )	Serializes a type **float** property.
PX_IUnknown( )	Serializes a property of type **LPUNKNOWN**.
PX_Long( )	Serializes a type **long** property.
PX_Picture( )	Serializes a type Picture property.
PX_Short( )	Serializes a type **short** property.
PX_String( )	Serializes a type **CString** property.
PX_ULong( )	Serializes a type **ULONG** property.
PX_UShort( )	Serializes a type **USHORT** property.

For more information on these property exchange functions, see Persistence of OLE Controls in the *Class Library Reference*.

Customizing the Default Behavior of DoPropExchange

The default implementation of **DoPropertyExchange** (as shown in the previous topic) makes a call to base class **COleControl**. This serializes the set of properties automatically supported by **COleControl**, which uses more storage space than serializing only the custom properties of the control. Removing this call allows your object to serialize only those properties you consider important. Any stock property states the control has implemented will not be serialized when saving or loading the control object unless you explicitly add **PX_** calls for them.

Implementing Version Support

Version support enables a revised OLE control to add new persistent properties, and still be able to detect and load the persistent state created by an earlier version of the control. To make a control's version available as part of the its persistent data, call **COleControl::ExchangeVersion** in the control's DoPropExchange function. This call is automatically inserted if the OLE control was created using ControlWizard. It can be removed if version support is not desired. However, the cost in control size is very small (4 bytes) for the added flexibility that version support provides.

If the control was not created with ControlWizard, add a call to **COleControl::ExchangeVersion** by inserting the following line at the beginning of your DoPropExchange function (before the call to **COleControl::DoPropExchange**):

```
void CSampleCtrl::DoPropExchange(CPropExchange* pPX)
{
 ExchangeVersion(pPX, MAKELONG(_wVerMinor, _wVerMajor));
 COleControl::DoPropExchange(pPX);
 ...
}
```

You can use any **DWORD** as the version number. Projects generated by ControlWizard use **_wVerMinor** and **_wVerMajor** as the default. These are global constants defined in the implementation file of the project's OLE control class. Within the remainder of your DoPropExchange function, you can call **CPropExchange::GetVersion** at any time to retrieve the version you are saving or retrieving.

In the following example, version 1 of this sample control has only a "ReleaseDate" property. Version 2 adds an "OriginalDate" property. If the control is instructed to load the persistent state from the old version, it initializes the member variable for the new property to a default value.

```
void CSampleCtrl::DoPropExchange(CPropExchange* pPX)
{
    ExchangeVersion(pPX, MAKELONG(_wVerMinor, _wVerMajor));
    COleControl::DoPropExchange(pPX);
    PX_Long(pPX, "ReleaseDate", m_releaseDate);
    if (pPX->GetVersion() >= MAKELONG(0, 2))
    {
        PX_Long(pPX, "OriginalDate", m_originalDate);
    }
    else
    {
        if (pPX->IsLoading())
            m_originalDate = 0;
    }
}
```

By default, a control "converts" old data to the latest format. For example, if version 2 of a control loads data that was saved by version 1, it will write the version 2 format when it is saved again. If you want the control to save data in the format last read, pass **FALSE** as a third parameter when calling **ExchangeVersion**. This third parameter is optional and is **TRUE** by default.

OLE Controls: Subclassing a Windows Control

This article describes the process for subclassing a common Windows control to create an OLE control. Subclassing an existing Windows control is a quick way to develop an OLE control. The new control will have the abilities of the subclassed Windows control, such as painting and responding to mouse clicks. The MFC OLE Controls sample BUTTON is an example of subclassing a Windows control.

To subclass a Windows control, complete the following tasks:

- Override the **IsSubclassedControl** and **PreCreateWindow** member functions of **COleControl**.

- Modify the **OnDraw** member function.

- Handle any OLE control messages (OCM) reflected to the control.

Note Much of this work is done for you by ControlWizard if you select the Subclass Windows Control option in the Control Options dialog box.

Overriding IsSubclassedControl and PreCreateWindow

To override **PreCreateWindow** and **IsSubclassedControl**, add the following lines of code to the **protected** section of the control class declaration:

```
BOOL PreCreateWindow( CREATESTRUCT& cs );
BOOL IsSubclassedControl( );
```

In the control implementation file (.CPP), add the following lines of code to implement the two overridden functions:

```
BOOL CSampleCtrl::PreCreateWindow( CREATESTRUCT& cs )
{
    cs.lpszClass = _T("BUTTON");
    return COleControl::PreCreateWindow(cs);
}
BOOL CSampleCtrl::IsSubclassedControl( )
{
    return TRUE;
}
```

Notice that, in this example, the Windows button control is specified in **PreCreateWindow**. However, any of the standard Windows controls can be subclassed. For more information on standard Windows controls, see Controls.

When subclassing a Windows control, you may want to specify particular window style (**WS_**) or extended window style (**WS_EX_**) flags to be used in creating the control's window. You can set values for these parameters in the **PreCreateWindow** member function by modifying the **cs.style** and the **cs.dwExStyle** structure fields. Modifications to these fields should be made using an **OR** operation, to preserve the default flags that are set by class **COleControl**. For example, if the control is subclassing the BUTTON control and you want the control to appear as a checkbox, insert the following line of code into the implementation of `CSampleCtrl::PreCreateWindow`, before the return statement:

```
cs.style |= BS_CHECKBOX;
```

This operation adds the **BS_CHECKBOX** style flag, while leaving the default style flag (**WS_CHILD**) of class **COleControl** intact.

Modifying the OnDraw Member Function

If you want your subclassed control to keep the same appearance as the corresponding Windows control, the `OnDraw` member function for the control should contain only a call to the **DoSuperclassPaint** member function, as in the following example:

```
void CSampleCtrl::OnDraw( CDC* pdc, const CRect& rcBounds,
    const CRect& rcInvalid )
{
DoSuperclassPaint( pdc, rcBounds );
}
```

The **DoSuperclassPaint** member function, implemented by **COleControl**, uses the window procedure of the Windows control to draw the control in the specified device context, within the bounding rectangle. This makes the control visible even when it is not active.

Note   The **DoSuperclassPaint** member function will work only with those control types that allow a device context to be passed as the **wParam** of a **WM_PAINT** message, such as **SCROLLBAR** and **BUTTON**. For controls that do not support this behavior, you will have to provide your own code to properly display an inactive control.

Handling Reflected Window Messages

Windows controls typically send certain window messages to their parent window. Some of these messages, such as **WM_COMMAND**, provide notification of an action by the user. Others, such as **WM_CTLCOLOR**, are used to obtain information from the parent window. An OLE control usually communicates with the parent window by other means. Notifications are communicated by firing events, and information about the control container is obtained by accessing the container's ambient properties. Because these communication techniques exist, OLE control containers are not expected to process any window messages sent by the control.

To prevent the container from receiving the window messages sent by a subclassed Windows control, **COleControl** creates an extra window to serve as the control's parent. This extra window, called a "reflector", is created only for an OLE control that subclasses a Windows control and has the same size and position as the control window. The reflector window intercepts certain window messages and sends them back to the control. The control, in its window procedure, can then process these reflected messages by taking actions appropriate for an OLE control (for example, firing an event).

Table 1 shows the messages that are intercepted and the corresponding messages that the reflector window sends:

Table 1 Reflected Windows Messages

Message sent by control	Message reflected to control
WM_COMMAND	OCM_COMMAND
WM_CTLCOLOR	OCM_CTLCOLOR
WM_DRAWITEM	OCM_DRAWITEM
WM_MEASUREITEM	OCM_MEASUREITEM
WM_DELETEITEM	OCM_DELETEITEM
WM_VKEYTOITEM	OCM_VKEYTOITEM
WM_CHARTOITEM	OCM_CHARTOITEM
WM_COMPAREITEM	OCM_COMPAREITEM
WM_HSCROLL	OCM_HSCROLL
WM_VSCROLL	OCM_VSCROLL
WM_NOTIFY	OCM_NOTIFY
WM_PARENTNOTIFY	OCM_PARENTNOTIFY

Note If the control runs on a Win32 system, there are several types of **WM_CTLCOLOR** messages it may receive instead of **WM_CTLCOLOR**. For more information, see **WM_CTLCOLORBTN**, **WM_CTLCOLORDLG**, **WM_CTLCOLOREDIT**, **WM_CTLCOLORLISTBOX**, **WM_CTLCOLORMSGBOX**, **WM_CTLCOLORSCROLLBAR**, **WM_CTLCOLORSTATIC**.

An OLE control container may be designed to perform message reflection itself, eliminating the need for **COleControl** to create the reflector window and reducing the run-time overhead for a subclassed Windows control. **COleControl** detects whether the container supports this capability by checking for a MessageReflect ambient property with a value of **TRUE**.

To handle a reflected window message, you need to add an entry to the control message map and implement a handler function. Because reflected messages are not part of the standard set of messages defined by Windows, ClassWizard does not support adding such message handlers. However, it is not difficult to add a handler manually.

To add a message handler for a reflected window message manually do the following:

- In the control class .H file, declare a handler function. The function should have a return type of **LRESULT** and two parameters, with types **WPARAM** and **LPARAM**, respectively. For example:

```
class CSampleCtrl : public COleControl
{
 protected:
    LRESULT OnOcmCommand( WPARAM wParam, LPARAM lParam );
...
}
```

- In the control class .CPP file, add an **ON_MESSAGE** entry to the message map. The parameters of this entry should be the message identifier and the name of the handler function. For example:

```
BEGIN_MESSAGE_MAP(CSampleCtrl, COleControl)
    //{{AFX_MSG_MAP(CSampleCtrl)
    ...
    ON_MESSAGE(OCM_COMMAND, OnOcmCommand)
    ...
    //}}AFX_MSG_MAP
END_MESSAGE_MAP()
```

- Also in the .CPP file, implement the **OnOcmCommand** member function to process the reflected message. The **wParam** and **lParam** parameters are the same as those of the original window message.

For an example of how reflected messages are processed, refer to the MFC OLE Controls sample BUTTON. It demonstrates an **OnOcmCommand** handler that detects the **BN_CLICKED** notification code and responds by firing a Click event.

OLE Controls: Using Data Binding in an OLE Control

One of the more powerful uses of OLE controls is "data binding," which allows a property of the control to "bind" with a specific field in a database. When this control property is modified by the control user, the control notifies the database that the value has changed and requests that the record field be updated. The database then notifies the control of the success or failure of the request.

This article covers the control side of your task. Implementing the data binding interactions with the database is the responsibility of the control container. How you manage the database interactions in your container is beyond the scope of this documentation. How you prepare the control for data binding is explained in the rest of this article.

This article covers the following topics:

- How data binding works
- Defining a bindable property

How Data Binding Works

Data binding allows a database entry, such as a record field, to be linked to a property of an OLE control. This control is typically used in a form view and provides a visual interface to the current record state. Figure 1 shows a conceptual representation of this linkage. In this example, the OLE control is an edit box which has bound its Text property to the Name field of a record. When modifications are made to the control's Text property, these changes are communicated to the database.

Figure 1   Conceptual Diagram of a Data Bound Control

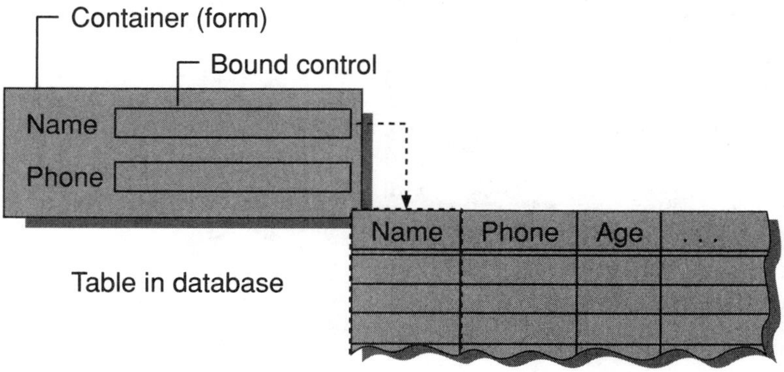

When an OLE control property is bound, the developer must make sure that the control is able to send notifications to the database when the property changes. The notification is sent to an interface provided by the control container, which processes it and returns the database's response to the control.

The **COleControl** class provides two member functions that make data binding an easy process to implement. The first function, **BoundPropertyRequestEdit** is used to request permission to change the property value. **BoundPropertyChanged**, the second function, is called after the property value has been successfully changed.

Defining a Bindable Property

If the control was created using ControlWizard, data binding is automatically enabled. Once you have successfully compiled your OLE control, you can use ClassWizard to incorporate data binding. ClassWizard allows you to choose which properties to make bindable and provides several options of binding.

Binding option	Description
Sends OnRequestEdit	The property requests permission from the database before modifying the value.
Visible to the End User	The container displays the property in a property binding dialog.
Default Bindable Property	Makes the bindable property the control container's default choice.

The following procedure demonstrates adding a text property to an existing control that subclasses an edit box. This property can then be bound to a record field. Figure 2 shows the Data Binding dialog box.

Figure 2 The Data Binding Dialog Box

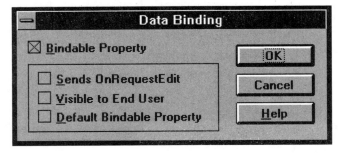

▶ **To add a bound property using ClassWizard**

1 Load your control project.

2 From the Browse menu, choose ClassWizard.

3 Choose the OLE Automation tab.

4 Click the Add Property button.

5 In the External Name box, type the external name of the property. For this example, use RecordName.

6 Under Implementation, select Get/Set Methods.

Note Data binding is not supported for properties implemented as member variables.

7 From the Return Type box, select the property's type. For this example, select BSTR.

8 Type unique names for your Get and Set Functions or accept the default names.

9 Click the OK button to confirm your choices and close the Add Property dialog box.

10 Click the Data Binding button.

11 Set the Bindable Property check box.

12 Set any other data binding options you desire.

Click the OK button to confirm your choices and close the Data Binding dialog box.

13 Click the OK button to confirm your choices and close ClassWizard.

After completing this process you will have a property called RecordName that can be bound to a string-valued field in a database.

Code Changes Related to Data Bound Property

Implementing a bound property requires code changes in some of the control project files.

The following code is added to the control declaration file (.H) between the dispatch map comments:

```
afx_msg BSTR GetRecordName( );
afx_msg void SetRecordName( LPCTSTR lpszNewValue );
```

In addition, changes will be made to the control implementation file. The following sample shows what would be added if you followed the example in the procedure:

```
BSTR CSampleCtrl::GetRecordName()
{
    CString strResult;
    // TODO: Add your property handler here

    return strResult.AllocSysString();
}

void CSampleCtrl::SetRecordName(LPCTSTR lpszNewValue)
{
    // TODO: Add your property handler here

    SetModifiedFlag( );
}
```

To fully implement the control data binding you have to modify the `GetRecordName` and `SetRecordName` functions. For example, in the `SetRecordName` function, you would make a call to **BoundPropertyRequestEdit** to obtain permission to change the value of the bound property. If it was successful, you would save the new value and handle any other actions needed before notifying the container that the property has changed. This notification would be done by calling **BoundPropertyChanged**. The following code sample demonstrates this:

```
void CSampleCtrl::SetRecordName( LPCTSTR lpszNewValue )
{
 if( !BoundPropertyRequestEdit( dispidRecordName) )
   SetNotPermitted( );
//TODO: Actually set property value.
 BoundPropertyChanged( dispidRecordName);
 SetModifiedFlag( );

}
```

OLE Controls: Adding an OLE Control to an Existing CDK Project

This article provides step-by-step instructions for combining two existing OLE control projects into an existing OLE Custom Control Developer's Kit (CDK) project. For clarity, the first control project is named *Proj1*; the second is named *Proj2*. After you have successfully completed this procedure, you will need to follow the steps detailed in the article OLE Controls: Converting a CDK Project to a Visual C++ Project to use this project with Visual C++ 4.0.

To protect the original code from becoming corrupted, you should work with the two controls in a separate directory. For example purposes, we've named the directory COMBINED. It is also recommended that you use Developer Studio for modifying and saving project files.

To successfully add an OLE control to an existing CDK project, you must:

- Collect all relevant .H, .CPP, .PPG, and .RC files .
- Combine both .ODL files into one .ODL file.
- Modify the PROJ2.MAK makefile.
- Combine the resources of both controls.
- Build the resultant project.

Collecting Implementation Files

The *Proj1* and *Proj2* directories both contain files that you can simply copy to the COMBINED directory with no changes. These files are used mainly to initialize the DLL and provide basic implementation of the control classes. You should copy the following files into the COMBINED directory:

- STDAFX.H, STDAFX.CPP

- *PROJ2*.RC, RESOURCE.H

- *PROJ2*CTL.BMP, *PROJ2*.ICO

- *PROJ1*.H

- *PROJ2*.H, *PROJ2*.CPP

- *PROJ1*CTL.H, *PROJ1*CTL.CPP

- *PROJ1*PPG.H, *PROJ1*PPG.CPP

- *PROJ2*CTL.H, *PROJ2*CTL.CPP

- *PROJ2*PPG.H, *PROJ2*PPG.CPP

- *PROJ2*.DEF

There are two other files, used as templates, that must be copied to the COMBINED directory:

- *PROJ2*.MAK

  In a following section, this makefile will be modified to include the necessary files from *PROJ1*.

- *PROJ2*.ODL

  This file will eventually contain both the *Proj1* and *Proj2* OLE control interfaces.

Merging the .ODL Files

Because there are two controls in the project, you will have to merge *PROJ1*.ODL into *PROJ2*.ODL. The .ODL file contains definitions for interfaces, so you need copy only those interfaces unique to *Proj1* and insert them into the *PROJ2*.ODL file.

▶ **To merge PROJ1.ODL with PROJ2.ODL**

1 From the PROJ1 .ODL file, copy the lines that are in the same position as the lines indicated in the following .ODL file:

```
//
// Type Library for Proj1.DLL
//
    #include <otldisp.h>
    [ uuid(A7A91CE8-B974-101A-8077-00AA00339DC7), version(1.0),
      helpstring("PROJ1 OLE Control module") ]
    library Proj1
    {
    importlib("stdole.tlb");
    importlib("stdtype.tlb");

// ****** Copy code below this line ********** //
        [ uuid(A7A91CE6-B974-101A-8077-00AA00339DC7),
          helpstring("Dispatch interface for PROJ1 Control") ]
        dispinterface IProj1Ctrl
        {
```

```
              properties:
                  //{{AFX_ODL_PROP(CProj1Ctrl)
                  //}}AFX_ODL_PROP

              methods:
              //{{AFX_ODL_METHOD(CProj1Ctrl)
              //}}AFX_ODL_METHOD

          };

          [ uuid(A7A91CE7-B974-101A-8077-00AA00339DC7),
            helpstring("Event interface for PROJ1 Control") ]
          dispinterface IProj1CtrlEvents
          {
              properties:
                  //  Event interface has no properties

              methods:
                  //{{AFX_ODL_EVENT(CProj1Ctrl)
                  //}}AFX_ODL_EVENT
          };
// ****** Copy code above this line ********** //
//   Class information for CProj1Ctrl

      [ uuid(003256C3-AA78-11CE-8C98-00AA00339DC7),
        helpstring("Proj1 Control"), control ]
      coclass Proj1
      {
          [default] dispinterface _DProj1;
          [default, source] dispinterface
            _DProj1Events;
      };
};
```

2 Paste the code that you copied in the example above into *PROJ2*.ODL, just prior to the last closing brace.

Modifying the Proj2 Makefile

Now that you have moved the needed files from *Proj1* to the COMBINED directory you need to incorporate them into the *Proj2* makefile.

Note If *PROJ2*.MAK is an external makefile you will need to edit it directly to add the new files from *Proj1*.

▶ **To incorporate Proj1 files into the Proj2 makefile**

1 From the File menu, choose Open.

The Open dialog box appears.

2 Select the drive and directory containing the project workspace that you want to open.

For this example select the COMBINED directory and choose the *Proj2* project.

3 From the Insert menu, choose Files.

4 From the Insert Project Files dialog box, select *PROJ1*CTL.CPP.

5 Click the Add button.

6 Repeat Steps 3 and 4 for *PROJ1*PPG.CPP.

7 Choose Close to save changes to the makefile and to close the Insert Project Files dialog box.

Combining the Resources of Both Controls

The last modification required before building the project is to add the resources from *PROJ1*.RC to *PROJ2*.RC. This is easily done because you can drag and drop resources from one project into another.

▶ **To add resources from Proj1 to Proj2**

1 From the File menu, choose Open.

The Open dialog box appears.

2 Select the drive and directory containing the project workspace that you want to open.

For this example select the COMBINED directory and choose the *Proj2* project.

3 Double-click the .RC file icon to open *PROJ2*'s resources.

4 From the File menu, choose Open.

5 Select PROJ1.RC from the PROJ1 directory.

6 Click OK to close the Open dialog box.

7 Drag and drop the bitmap, icon, string resources, and property pages from *Proj1* into *Proj2*. Be sure to hold down the CTRL key so the resources are copied and not moved.

For an example of a similar procedure, see Adding Help to Scribble After the Fact in Chapter 11 of *Tutorials*.

8 After you have added the resources, save the changes by choosing the Save toolbar button.

Building the New Project

After completing the preceding steps, you can build the new project as you would any OLE control project. Once the project has been successfully built, register the controls. You can then use Test Container, or another container application, to test your OLE control. For more information on this procedure, see the article Test Container.

Please note that the .CLW file for *Proj2* needs to be rebuilt to include the new classes added from the PROJ1 project.

▶ **To rebuild your .CLW file**

1 From the File menu, choose Open.

The Open dialog box appears.

2 Select the drive and directory containing the project workspace that you want to open.

For this example select the COMBINED directory and choose the *Proj2* project.

3 Double-click the .RC file icon to open the control resources.

4 Click the ClassWizard button on the App Studio toolbar.

A dialog box will appear, stating that your project's .CLW file does not exist.

5 Choose Yes to select the source files to be used.

6 Click OK to select all files in the project and rebuild the .CLW file.

ClassWizard will now open with all classes from *Proj2* loaded and accessible.

OLE Controls: VBX Control Migration

VBX control migration was only available through the VBX template tool, a part of the ControlWizard found in version 1.x of the CDK. Because this tool was removed from the ControlWizard shipped with Visual C++ 4.0, migrating existing VBX controls demands version 1.x of the CDK. The only option for VBX migration using VC ++ 4.0 is to create a framework from ControlWizard and manually port the entire code base of the VBX control into the OLE control framework.

As stated above, developers with existing VBX controls can use the VBX template tool, found in the CDK ControlWizard, to convert existing VBX controls to the OLE control format.

The VBX template tool helps you migrate your VBX custom control to an OLE control. The template tool uses model information in the .VBX file and creates a Visual C++ project file, as well as source code files for creating the OLE control. These files can be compiled and linked to produce a working framework for the OLE control.

Once this framework is built and tested, the next step is to take code from your VBX source files and place it in the appropriate areas of the generated OLE source files. The transplanted code will probably require some degree of modification to work in the new source code files.

This article explains:

• Preparing your .VBX source code files for conversion

• Using the VBX template tool

- What gets converted
- Building and testing the framework of your OLE control
- Where to go from here

If you want to port your OLE control framework to Visual C++ 4.0, see the article OLE Controls: Converting a CDK Project to a Visual C++ Project.

Preparing the VBX Custom Control

For the VBX template tool to properly translate the VBX control, you must expose the VBX control model information to the template builder, using the **VBGetModelInfo** function. If your VBX source code does not already define this function, first define a **MODELINFO** structure containing a specific Visual Basic version number, and a **NULL**-terminated array of **MODEL** structures. The MFC OLE Controls sample CIRC3 defines the **MODELINFO** structure as follows:

```
LPMODEL modellistCircle[] =
    {
    &modelCircle,
    NULL
    };
```

Note Remember to NULL-terminate the array of model pointers.

```
MODELINFO modelinfoCircle =
    {
    VB_VERSION,       // VB version being used
    modellistCircle   // MODEL list
    };
```

Note If your .VBX file provides different models to support earlier versions, you should create similar **MODELINFO** structures to point to those models. The CIRC3 custom control, for example, also defines ModelinfoCircle_VB1 and ModelinfoCircle_VB2 structures.

Once you have defined the **MODELINFO** structure(s), you can define the **VBGetModelInfo** function, as an export, in your source code. The MFC OLE Controls sample CIRC3 defines the function:

```
LPMODELINFO FAR PASCAL _export VBGetModelInfo
(
    USHORT usVersion
)
{
    if (usVersion <= VB100_VERSION)
        return &modelinfoCircle_Vb1;

    if (usVersion <= VB200_VERSION)
        return &modelinfoCircle_Vb2;
    else
        return &modelinfoCircle;
}
```

Once this function is defined, rebuild your VBX control before using the template tool.

Running the VBX Template Tool

After your VBX control has been built with the **VBGetModelInfo** function, as described in the previous topic, you are ready to run the VBX template tool.

As mentioned before, you must be using the ControlWizard that shipped with version 1.x of the CDK. The template tool is not available with Visual C++ 4.0.

If you only need to use the ControlWizard shipped with version 1.x of the CDK, you can copy two files from the distribution CD. These two files, CTLWZLIB.DLL and MFCCTLWZ.EXE, can be found in the MSVCCDK directory of the Visual C++ Version 1.52 CD.

▶ **To run the VBX template tool**

1 Start ControlWizard by running MFCCTLWZ.EXE from the DOS command prompt, File Manager, or Windows Explorer.

2 When the ControlWizard dialog box appears, change to the desired drive and directory and enter a project name. ControlWizard automatically creates a new subdirectory with the same name as the project.

3 Click the Control Options button. When the Control Options dialog box appears, choose the Use VBX Control as Template check box.

4 Click the Select VBX Control button.

5 When the Use VBX Control as Template dialog box appears, enter the .VBX file name, including the drive and directory path. Alternatively, you can use the Browse button to locate and select your .VBX file. All control names defined in the .VBX file are displayed in the control name drop down list. Select the desired control name from the drop down list.

   Note If you select a .VBX file that does not properly export the model information (as described in the Note in Preparing the VBX Custom Control), Visual C++ may crash at this point.

6 Click OK twice to close the Use VBX Control as Template dialog box and the Control Options dialog box. Click OK from ControlWizard to prepare to create the template.

7 When the New Control Information dialog appears, a summary of the generated files is displayed. Click the Create button to create all the files for the OLE control.

8 When the VBX template tool is finished, your project directory should contain the following files (the files listed here assume the VBX example control, CIRC3.VBX, was used as the project):

   • CIRC3.CLW

- CIRC3.CPP
- CIRC332.DEF
- CIRC3.DEF
- CIRC3.H
- CIRC3.ICO
- CIRC3.MAK
- CIRC332.MAK
- MAKEFILE
- CIRC3.ODL
- CIRC3.RC
- CIRC3.RC2
- CIRC3CTL.BMP
- CIRC3CTL.CPP
- CIRC3CTL.H
- CIRC3PPG.CPP
- CIRC3PPG.H
- README.TXT
- RESOURCE.H
- STDAFX.CPP
- STDAFX.H

In addition, a subdirectory for the Type library file is created. If you are using the 16-bit version of the CDK, it is called TLB16. If you are using the 32-bit version of the CDK, it is called OBJDU.

The README.TXT file contains a summary description of each file created by the VBX template tool. These files are all that is required to build a complete working framework of the new OLE control.

What Gets Converted

The template generated by the VBX template tool is similar to the "blank" template that is generated when you use ControlWizard to create a new control, with the following differences:

Stock Properties and Events

ControlWizard converts most of the standard properties and events in your .VBX to fully implemented stock properties and events in the template's source code.

Stock properties supported by the VBX template tool include:

- BorderStyle
- Enabled
- Font
- Caption
- Text
- ForeColor
- BackColor
- hWnd

Stock events supported by the VBX template tool include:

- Click
- DblClick
- KeyDown
- KeyPress
- KeyUp
- MouseDown
- MouseMove
- MouseUp

Note A number properties not mentioned above that were formerly "standard" in the .VBX Control model are automatically supported by OLE as standard "extender" properties (e.g., Left, Top, Height, Width); therefore these properties are not needed in an OLE control ,and are not converted by the VBX template tool.

Currently Unimplemented Properties and Events

Stock properties of the VBX model not supported:

- DragIcon
- DragMode
- MouseCursor
- MousePointer

Stock events of the VBX model not supported:

- DragDrop
- DragOver
- LinkOpen
- LinkClose
- LinkError

- LinkNotify

Custom Properties and Events

Custom properties and events in your VBX are provided in the template as stub functions. In order to make these properties and events functional, you must port the implementation code from your VBX source files into the appropriate files in the new control template. These places are indicated by similar comments in the template's source code files:

```
// TODO: Initialize your control's instance data here.
```

Building and Testing the OLE Control Framework

After ControlWizard generates the basic framework for your VBX control, you should build and test the control to familiarize yourself with OLE control behavior. The following sections describe this process and demonstrate how to use Test Container to test your new OLE control.

Creating the Type Library for the OLE Control

Note that the following information only applies if you are using the 16-bit version of Visual C++. If you are using the 32-bit version of Visual C++, the type library is automatically generated by the control makefile.

Before you can compile and link the control template, you must create a type library, used by control containers that use your control. This will be based on the information contained in the Object Description Library (.ODL) file created by the porting tool.

▶ **To create the type library**

1 Load the project make file that you generated by running the VBX template tool.

2 From the Tools menu, choose Make TypeLib. MKTYPLIB.EXE creates a type library based on the .ODL file in the project. After building successfully, MKTYPLIB automatically adds the resulting *.TLB file to your project. The information in this .TLB file will be built into your .DLL as a resource.

Compiling, Linking, and Registering the OLE Control Framework

Note that the following information only applies if you are using the 16-bit version of Visual C++.

After creating the Type Library, you can build the framework control by choosing Build from the Visual C++ Project menu.

When the project has built successfully, you must register the new control before you can test it. Choose Register Control from the Tools menu. A message box appears, indicating that the control was successfully registered.

Testing the OLE Control Framework

For procedures on testing your OLE control framework, see the article Test Container.

Where to Go From Here

When you are satisfied that the control framework is working properly, the next step is to port the implementation of your OLE control's custom properties and events from your VBX source code to the new control's source code files. To do this, use ClassWizard and the implementation guidelines in the OLE Controls articles. Remember to back up your files frequently and to use Test Container to test each new block of code as you go.

Once the VBX control is ported to a CDK project you could port the CDK project to Visaul C++ 4.0 by following the steps given in the article OLE Controls: Converting a CDK Project to a Visual C++ Project.

See Also   OLE Controls: Converting a CDK Project to a Visual C++ Project

OLE Controls: Converting a CDK Project to a Visual C++ Project

This article discusses converting existing OLE Custom Control Developer's Kit (CDK) projects (versions 1.0 and 1.1) to Visual C++ 4.0 projects. Because the support for OLE controls has been fully integrated into MFC, there are several changes that need to be made to an existing project before the control can be successfully built.

In summary, the necessary changes are:

- Remove all references to the OCS30 libraries.
- Remove **RESIDENTNAME** from the module definition (.DEF) file.
- Delete the contents of the project's output directories and TLB16 directory.

For demonstration purposes, this article converts a project named SAMPLE32.

▶ To remove all references to the OCS30 libraries

1 In Visual C++, open the control's 32-bit project file, in this case, SAMPLE32.MAK.

2 From the Build menu, choose the Settings command.

The Project Settings dialog box will appear.

3 Choose the Link tab.

4 Select the first target in the Settings For list box. In this case, Win32 ANSI Debug (SAMPLE.OCX).

5 In the Object/Library Modules text box, delete any library name of the form "OCS30*.LIB." For example, when the Win32 ANSI Debug target is selected, delete the library name "OCS30D.LIB."

6 Repeat steps 4 and 5 for each target in the Settings For list box.

7 Click the OK button to accept the changes and dismiss the dialog.

▶ To remove RESIDENTNAME from the module definition file

1 In Visual C++, open the control's 32-bit module definition file, in this case, SAMPLE32.DEF.

2 Delete each occurrence of the string `RESIDENTNAME` from the file. There are typically four occurrences of this string.

For example, the following line of code:

```
DllCanUnloadNow       @1 RESIDENTNAME
```

should be changed to:

```
DllCanUnloadNow       @1
```

3 From the File menu, choose Save.

The final step is to remove any existing directories and project files from earlier builds.This ensures a clean build with the new project settings.

▶ **To delete the contents of the project's output directories and the TLB16 subdirectory**

- From the DOS command prompt, File Manager, or Windows Explorer delete the directories named "TLB16", "OBJ32", "OBJD32", "OBJU32" and "OBJDU32" from the project directory.

ANSI/Unicode Changes

One of the changes that occurred between the original release of the CDK and its integration into VC ++ 4.0, was the removal of the MFCANS32 DLL. This DLL was responsible for the ANSI/Unicode translation layer used for Unicode-based OLE interfaces with an ANSI-targeted control. If your control supported licensing, it was affected by this change.

In order for your control to function properly, you will need to make some code changes to the control implementation (.CPP) files.

- If your control supports licensing, change the declaration of the license string, found in the control implementation (.CPP) file, to the following:

```
static const OLECHAR BASED_CODE _szLicString[] =
OLESTR("Licensed Control Copyright (c) 1994-1995 My Corporation");
```

- Every direct call to the OLE API that passes a string as a parameter must first convert the string, by making a call to **MultiByteToWideChar**, and then passing the result to the **SysAllocString** function. The following example first translates a string constant and then calls the function **SysAllocString** directly:

```
char szMyString[] = "Licensed Control Copyright (c) 1994-1995 My
Corporation";  //a multi-byte string

BSTR strWide;  //wide string passed to OLE function
WCHAR szwMyWideString[80];
MultiByteToWideChar(CP_ACP, 0, szMyString, _tcslen(szMyString),
szwMyWideString, 80);

strWide = SysAllocString(szwMyWideString);
```

See Also   OLE Controls, OLE ControlWizard

OLE ControlWizard

OLE ControlWizard (hereafter referred to as ControlWizard) is a custom AppWizard that can be used to create the framework of an OLE control project.

You use ControlWizard to create a set of starter files for an OLE control. This set includes all the files necessary to build the control, including source and header files, resource files, a module-definition file, a project file, an object description language file, and so on. Starter files generated by ControlWizard are compatible with ClassWizard, and you can then use ClassWizard to define the control's events, properties, and methods, some of which have been already implemented in MFC.

Creating a project with ControlWizard provides a large amount of built-in functionality. This includes code to draw the control, serialize data, and define dispatch, event, and message maps that you expand later in the development cycle.

To further investigate ControlWizard use and capabilities, you can create and build a simple OLE control, similar to the MFC OLE Controls sample CIRCLE, found in Chapter 20, Creating the Circle Control, in *Tutorials*.

The following articles provide additional information about ControlWizard:

- OLE ControlWizard: How ControlWizard Works
- OLE ControlWizard: Files Created

OLE ControlWizard: How ControlWizard Works

ControlWizard is launched from either the New Workspace dialog box or the Insert Project dialog box. Once started, ControlWizard displays a series of dialog boxes listing options for OLE control features. You select options by cycling through the dialog boxes, forwards or backwards. You can change the options at any time before you create the control.

When the user finishes running ControlWizard, the New Project Information dialog box displays information about the control to be created, such as its name, the names of the control classes, the names of the files that make up the project, and the control's features. Once you are satisfied with the proposed project, click the OK button to create the project files. For more information about the project files, see the article OLE ControlWizard: Files Created.

When ControlWizard finishes creating an OLE control project, it automatically opens in the development environment.

▶ **To create a new project and an OLE control**

1 Start Visual C++.

2 From the File menu, choose New.

The New dialog box appears.

3 In the New box, select Project Workspace.

The New box allows selection of various file types.

4 Click OK.

The New Workspace dialog box appears.

5 In the Name box, type a project name.

A directory for the new project is added to the currently specified workspace directory structure. ControlWizard uses the name that you specify in the Project Name box to derive default names for most of the files and classes it creates for the control project.

6 In the Type list box, select OLE ControlWizard

7 Specify the target Platforms for this project.

Use the list box provided to select any of the available platforms.

Note Win32 is the default platform. To select other platforms, the associated cross-development edition of Visual C++ must be installed.

8 In the Location box, specify the path of a new workspace. A workspace will be created if you specify one that does not exist.

−or−

Use the Browse button to select a drive and a directory.

9 Choose Create.

Microsoft Developer Studio creates a workspace and/or inserts a project into a workspace. With the workspace structure created, ControlWizard displays the various options of the control project. For more information on projects and workspaces, see Chapter 2, Working with Projects, in the *Visual C++ User's Guide*.

Project Options

The following options are available in the Project Options dialog box, the first dialog box ControlWizard displays:

Number of Controls ControlWizard can generate up to 99 separate controls per project. Each control has a control class and a property page class. For more information about these control classes, see Control Options.

License Validation ControlWizard inserts several functions and generates a separate .LIC file that supports licensing for the control. For more information on licensing, see OLE Controls: Licensing an OLE Control.

Generate Source Comments ControlWizard inserts comments in the source and header files that guide you in writing your control. The comments indicate where you need to add your own code. This option is enabled by default.

Context Sensitive Help ControlWizard generates a set of help files that are used to provide context-sensitive Help. Help support requires using the Help compiler, which is provided with Visual C++.

Figure 1 shows the Project Options dialog box.

Figure 1 The Project Options Dialog Box

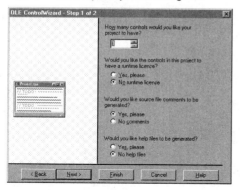

Control Options

The Control Options dialog box, the second displayed by ControlWizard, allows you to specify certain options for each control in your project. Use the Control Name drop-down list box to choose the control whose options you wish to modify. For more information on the Edit Names button, see Edit Names Dialog Box in this article.

Activates when visible   Indicates to the control container that the control prefers to be activated automatically when it is visible. The container is not required to support this request.

Invisible at runtime   Indicates to the control container that it should be invisible when the container is operating in "run time" mode. When the container is in "design time" mode, the control will be visible. Some containers may ignore the Invisible at runtime option. In such containers, the control will be visible at all times.

Available in "Insert Object" dialog   Enabling this option, disabled by default, makes the control appear in the Insert Object dialog of every OLE container application. Since some OLE containers are not "control-aware," they may not provide a way to activate controls with the mouse. Therefore, this option also adds an "Edit" verb to the control's set of available verbs.

If you initially create the control with this option disabled, and later decide to enable it in your code, remember to also add an Edit verb in the control message map. The Edit verb entry should look like this:

```
ON_OLEVERB(AFX_IDS_VERB_EDIT, OnEdit)
```

Has an "About" box   Creates a standard About box for the control.

Acts as a simple frame control   Allows the control to behave as a simple frame. For more information, see New MiscStatus Bits and "Simple Frame" Containment of Controls in Books Online and **COleControl::EnableSimpleFrame** in *Class Library Reference*.

Subclassing a Windows control   Use this drop-down combo box to subclass common Windows controls, such as buttons, scrollbars, and edit controls.

Figure 2 shows the Control Options dialog box.

Figure 2   The Control Options Dialog Box

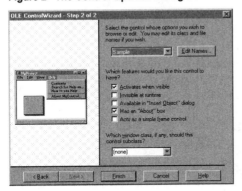

Edit Names Dialog Box

ControlWizard uses the project name you specify in the Project Name dialog box to name the control's classes and files. The Edit Names dialog box, accessed by clicking the Edit Names button in the Control Options dialog box, allows you to modify some of the assigned names. Names you can change include the Short name (base name of the class), the Type name (the name exposed to the control user), and the Type ID (the ID of the OLE control class).

The following discussion assumes that the project name is *PROJNAME*.

Note   Modifying the short name of the control class will automatically updates the values of the edit boxes for various parts of a selected class.

Below the Short Name edit box there are two groups of edit box controls: Control and Property Page.

Control
This is the main control class. You can change the values for class name, header file, implementation file, type name, and Type ID.

Property Page
This is the control property page class. The property page allows the control user to view and modify the control's properties. You can change the values for class name, header file, implementation file, type name, and Type ID.

Figure 3 shows the Edit Names dialog box.

Figure 3   The Edit Names Dialog Box

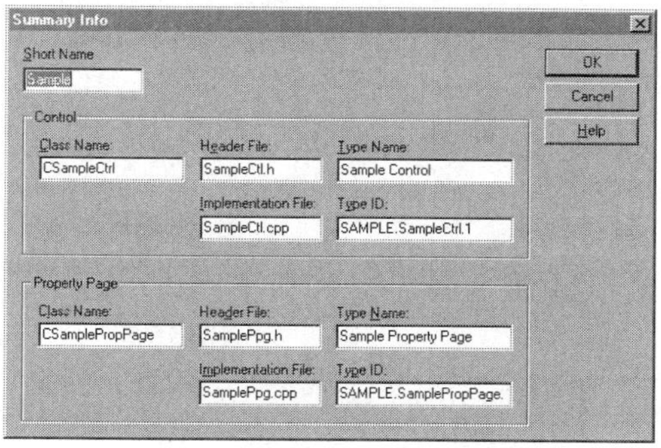

Toolbar Bitmap Support

When you use ControlWizard to generate the framework for the control, it creates a default bitmap as part of the project. Containers take this image and place it as a button in a toolbox (for example, Visual Basic's toolbox) or toolbar. When you have finished developing your control, you should use the Visual C++ resource editor to modify this bitmap to more accurately represent the control's purpose . See Modifying The Control Bitmap in Chapter 20 of *Tutorials* for instructions on modifying the toolbar bitmap.

Note   Unlike VBX controls, the OLE control bitmap shouldn't include borders, beveled edges, or margins around the edge. The bitmap should also have a light-gray background, which is the standard for toolbox bitmaps.

OLE ControlWizard: Files Created

ControlWizard creates a core set of files for every control. Additional files are created if context-sensitive Help or license validation options are checked in the Project Options dialog. This article first describes the core files every control must have, and then describes additional files that implement other project options.

ControlWizard uses the project name you specified in the Name box to derive filenames and class names. In the following descriptions, where the full project name is used in the filename, *PROJNAME* is used as a placeholder for the name you specified.

Note   The name substitutions indicated in these filenames might not apply if you have used the Edit Names dialog box to alter any of them.

Standard ControlWizard Files

This section describes the categories of standard files created by ControlWizard, grouped by function. ControlWizard also creates a file named README.TXT (located in the parent directory of the control project) that describes each file in your project using the actual filenames created by ControlWizard.

Project and Makefiles

PROJNAME.MAK   This is the project file used within the development environment. It is also compatible with NMAKE, which is shipped with Visual C++.

PROJNAME.CLW   This file is used by ClassWizard to store information about the classes in your project

PROJNAME.ODL   This file contains the Object Description Language source code for the control type library. This file is used by Visual C++ to generate a type library. The generated library exposes the control's interface to other OLE Automation clients.

Resource and Module-Definition Files

PROJNAME.RC, RESOURCE.H   This is the resource file for the project and its header file. The resource file contains a bitmap for use in a palette or toolbar, a dialog box used by the property page, and a default "About" box.

PROJNAME.ICO   This is the icon file for the generic OLE control. This icon is used in the About box.

*PROJNAME*CTL.BMP   This file is used to represent your OLE control in a toolbar or palette. This bitmap is included in the project's resource file.

PROJNAME.DEF   This is the module-definition file for the project. It provides the name and description of the control, as well as the size of the run-time heap.

Control Source and Header Files

PROJNAME.H   This is the main include file for the OLE control DLL. It derives the `CPrjnameApp` class from **CWinApp** and declares an `InitInstance` member function.

PROJNAME.CPP   This file creates an instance of `CProjNameApp`. The member function `CProjNameApp::InitInstance` registers the control's object factory with OLE by calling **COleObjectFactory::RegisterAll** and makes a call to **AfxOLEControlInit**. In addition, the member function `CProjNameApp::ExitInstance` is used to unload the control from memory with a call to **AfxOleControlTerm**.

This file also registers and unregisters the control in the Windows registration database by implementing the **DllRegisterServer** and **DllUnregisterServer** functions.

*PROJNAME*CTL.H, *PROJNAME*CTL.CPP   These files declare and implement the `CProjnameCtrl` class. `CProjnameCtrl` is derived from **COleControl**, and skeleton implementation of some member functions are defined that initialize, draw, and serialize (load and save) the control. Message, event, and dispatch maps are also defined.

*PROJNAME*PPG.H, *PROJNAME*PPG.CPP   These files declare and implement the `CProjnamePropPage` class. `CProjnamePropPage` is derived from **COlePropertyPage** and a skeleton member function, `DoDataExchange`, is provided to implement data exchange and validation.

Precompiled Header and Types Files

STDAFX.H, STDAFX.CPP   These files are used to build a precompiled header (PCH) file named STDAFX.PCH and a precompiled types (PCT) file named STDAFX.OBJ.

Files Added By Options

Help support provides a number of files that implement context-sensitive Help. These files are contained in the parent directory and HLP subdirectory of the project. License validation provides a .LIC file contained in the top-level directory of the project.

Help Option

MAKEHELP.BAT   This batch file (located in the parent directory) is used to create the help file *PROJNAME*.HLP for your OLE control.

PROJNAME.HPJ   This file (located in the parent directory) is the Help project file used by the Help compiler to create your OLE control's Help file.

PROJNAME.RTF   This Help file (located in the HLP subdirectory) contains template topics that you can edit and information on customizing your .HPJ file.

BULLET.BMP   This bitmap is used by standard Help file topics to represent bulleted lists.

License Option

PROJNAME.LIC   This is the user license file. This file must be present in the same directory as the control DLL to allow an instance of the control to be created in a design-time environment. Typically, you will distribute this file with your control, but your customers will not distribute it.

For more information on providing licensing support for your control, see the article OLE Controls: Licensing an OLE Control.

Now that you are familiar with the files created by ControlWizard, several articles discuss important topics that you can use to enhance the usability and performance of your OLE control.

- The Events articles discusses stock and custom events, including how events are implemented and how to add events using ClassWizard.

- The Methods and Properties articles discuss stock and custom properties and methods. These articles explain how properties and methods are implemented using MFC and how to use ClassWizard to add stock and custom properties and methods.

OLE Overview

OLE is a mechanism that allows users to create and edit documents containing items or "objects" created by multiple applications.

Note OLE was originally an acronym for Object Linking and Embedding. However, it is now referred to simply as OLE.

OLE documents, historically called "compound documents," seamlessly integrate various types of data, or "components." Sound clips, spreadsheets, and bitmaps are typical examples of components found in OLE documents. Supporting OLE in your application allows your users to use OLE documents without worrying about switching between the different applications; OLE does the switching for you.

You use a "container application" to create compound documents and a "server application" or "component application" to create the items within the container document. Any application you write can be a container, a server, or both.

OLE incorporates many different concepts that all work toward the goal of seamless interaction between applications. These areas include the following:

Linking and Embedding Linking and Embedding are the two methods for storing items inside a OLE document that were created in another application. For general information on the differences between the two, see the article OLE Overview: Linking and Embedding article. For more detailed information, see the articles Containers and Servers.

In-Place Activation Activating an embedded item in the context of the container document is called "in-place activation" or "visual editing." The container application's interface changes to incorporate the features of the component application that created the embedded item. Linked items are never activated "in-place" because the actual data for the item is contained in a separate file, out of the context of the application containing the link. For more information on in-place activation, see the article Activation.

Note Linking and embedding and in-place activation provide the main features of OLE visual editing.

Automation OLE Automation allows one application to drive another application. The driving application is known as an "automation client" or "automation controller," and the application being driven is known as an "automation server" or "automation component." For more information on automation, see the articles Automation Clients and Automation Servers.

Compound Files Compound files provide a standard file format that simplifies structured storing of compound documents for OLE applications. Within a compound file, "storages" have many features of directories and "streams" have many features of files. This technology is also called "structured storage." For more information on compound files, see the article Containers: Compound Files.

Uniform Data Transfer   Uniform Data Transfer (UDT) is a set of interfaces that allow data to be sent and received in a standard fashion, regardless of the actual method chosen to transfer the data. UDT forms the basis for data transfers by drag and drop. UDT now serves as the basis for existing Windows data transfer, such as the Clipboard and dynamic data exchange (DDE). For more information on UDT, see the article Data Objects and Data Sources (OLE).

Drag and Drop   Drag and drop is an easy-to-use, direct-manipulation technique to transfer data between applications, between windows within an application, or even within a single window in an application. The data to be transferred is simply selected and dragged to the desired destination. For more information on drag and drop, see the article Drag and Drop.

Component Object Model   The Component Object Model (COM) provides the infrastructure used when OLE objects communicate with each other. The MFC OLE classes simplify COM for the programmer. For more information about COM, see Chapter 1 in the *OLE 2 Programmer's Reference, Volume 1*.

Some of the more important general OLE topics are covered in the following articles:

- OLE Overview: Linking and Embedding
- OLE Overview: Containers and Servers
- OLE Overview: Implementation Strategies
- OLE Overview: Microsoft Foundation Class Library Implementation

For information about handling context-sensitive Help in OLE applications, see the article Help: OLE Support for Help.

For general OLE information not found in the above articles, see the *OLE 2 Programmer's Reference, Volume 1*. Another good source of information is Kraig Brockschmidt's book *Inside OLE 2* (Microsoft Press, 1994).

OLE Overview: Linking and Embedding

This article defines the OLE terms "linking" and "embedding."

Using the Paste command in a container application can create an "embedded component" or "embedded item." The source data for an embedded item is stored as part of the OLE document that contains it. In this way, a document file for a word processor document can contain not only text, but also bitmaps, graphs, formulas, or any other type of data.

OLE provides another way to incorporate data from another application: creating a "linked component" or "linked item" or simply "link." The steps for creating a linked item are similar to those for creating an embedded item, except that you use the Paste

Link command instead of the Paste command. Unlike an embedded component, a linked component stores a path to the original data, which is often in a separate file.

For example, if you are working in a word processor document and create a linked item to some spreadsheet cells, the data for the linked item is stored in the original spreadsheet document. The word processor document contains only the information specifying where the item can be found; that is, it contains a link to the original spreadsheet document. When you double-click the cells, the spreadsheet application is launched and the original spreadsheet document is loaded from where it was stored.

Every OLE item, whether embedded or linked, has a type associated with it based on the application that created it. For example, a Microsoft Paintbrush item is one type of item, while a Microsoft Excel item is another type. However, some applications can create more than one item type; for example, Microsoft Excel can create worksheet items, chart items, and macrosheet items. Each of these items can be uniquely identified by the system using a "Class Identifier" or **CLSID**.

For more information on the kind of data stored in embedded and linked items, see the *OLE 2 Programmer's Reference, Volume 1*.

See Also   OLE Overview: Containers and Servers, Containers: Client Items, Servers: Server Items

OLE Overview: Containers and Servers

This article explains and defines container and server applications.

A "container application" is an application that can incorporate embedded or linked items into its own documents. The documents managed by a container application must be able to store and display OLE document components as well as the data created by the application itself. A container application must also allow users to insert new items or edit existing items by activating server applications when necessary. The user-interface requirements of a container application are listed in the article Containers: User-Interface Issues.

A "server application" or "component application" is an application that can create OLE document components for use by container applications. Server applications usually support copying their data to the Clipboard or drag and drop so that a container application can insert the data as an embedded or linked item. An application can be both a container and a server.

Most servers are stand-alone applications or "full-servers"; they can either be run as stand-alone applications or can be launched by a container application. A "mini-server" is a special type of server application that can be launched only by a container; it cannot be run as a stand-alone application. Microsoft Draw and Microsoft Graph servers are examples of mini-servers.

Containers and servers do not communicate directly. Instead, they communicate through the OLE system DLLs. These DLLs provide functions that containers and servers call, and the containers and servers provide callback functions that the DLLs call.

Using this means of communication, a container doesn't need to know the implementation details of the server application. It allows a container to accept items created by any server without having to define the types of servers with which it can work. As a result, the user of a container application can take advantage of future applications and data formats. As long as these new applications are OLE servers, a compound document will be able to incorporate items created by those applications.

See Also   OLE Overview: Microsoft Foundation Class Library Implementation, Containers, Servers, Containers: Client Items, Servers: Server Items

OLE Overview: Implementation Strategies

Depending on your application, there are four possible implementation strategies for adding OLE support:

- You are writing a new application.

  This situation usually requires the least work. You simply run AppWizard and select OLE options to create a skeleton application. For information on the OLE options in AppWizard and what they do, see the article AppWizard: OLE Support.

- You have a program written with the Microsoft Foundation Class Library version 2.0 or higher that does not support OLE.

  Create a new application with AppWizard as above, then copy and paste the code from the new application into your existing application. This will work for servers, containers, or automated applications. See the MFC Tutorial sample, SCRIBBLE, Step 7 for an example of this strategy.

- You have a Microsoft Foundation Class Library program that implements OLE version 1.0 support.

  See Technical Note 41 under MFC in Books Online for this conversion strategy.

- You have an application that was not written using the Microsoft Foundation classes and that may or may not have implemented OLE support.

  This situation requires the most work. One approach is to create a new application, as in the first strategy, then copy and paste your existing code into it. If your existing code is written in C, you may need to modify it so it can compile as C++ code. If your C code calls the Windows API, you do not have to change it to use the Microsoft Foundation classes. This approach likely will require some restructuring of your program to support the document/view architecture used by versions 2.0 and higher of the Microsoft Foundation classes. For more information on this architecture, see Technical Note 25 under MFC in Books Online.

Once you have decided on a strategy, you should either read the Containers or Servers family of articles (depending on the type of application you are writing), or examine the sample programs, or both. The MFC OLE samples OCLIENT and HIERSVR show how to implement the various aspects of containers and servers, respectively. At various points throughout this encyclopedia, you will be referred to certain functions in these samples as examples of the techniques being discussed. The sample programs may be found under Samples in Books Online.

See Also   Containers: Implementing a Container, Servers: Implementing a Server, AppWizard: OLE Support

OLE Overview: Microsoft Foundation Class Library Implementation

Because of the size and complexity of the raw OLE API, calling it directly to write OLE applications can be very time-consuming. The goal of the Microsoft Foundation Class Library implementation of OLE is to reduce the amount of work you have to do to write full-featured, OLE-capable applications.

This article explains the parts of the OLE API that have *not* been implemented inside MFC. The discussion also explains how what is implemented maps to the OLE 2 SDK.

Portions of OLE Not Implemented by the Class Library

There are a few interfaces and features of OLE not directly provided by MFC. If you want to use these features, you can call the OLE API directly.

IMoniker Interface   The **IMoniker** interface is implemented by the class library (for example, the **COleServerItem** class), but is not exposed to the programmer. For more information about this interface, see Chapter 8 in the *OLE 2 Programmer's Reference, Volume 1*.

IUnknown and IMarshal Interfaces   The **IUnknown** interface is implemented by the class library, but is not exposed to the programmer. The **IMarshal** interface is not implemented by the class library, but is used internally. OLE Automation servers built using the class library already have marshalling capabilities built in. For more information about these interfaces, see Chapter 5 in the *OLE 2 Programmer's Reference, Volume 1*.

Docfiles (Compound Files)   Compound files are partially supported by the class library. None of the functions that directly manipulate compound files beyond creation are supported. MFC uses class **COleFileStream** to support manpulation of streams with standard file functions. For more information, see the article Containers: Compound Files.

In-Process Servers and Object Handlers   In-process servers and object handlers allow implementing visual editing data or full component object model (COM) objects in a DLL. To do this, you can implement your DLL by calling the OLE

API directly. However, if you are writing an OLE Automation server and your server has no user interface, you can use AppWizard to make your server an in-process server and put it completely into a DLL. For more information about these topics, see the article Automation Servers and see Chapters 1 and 5 in the *OLE 2 Programmer's Reference, Volume 1*.

Tip The easiest way to implement an OLE Automation server is to place it in a DLL. MFC supports this approach.

For detailed information on how the Microsoft Foundation OLE classes implement OLE interfaces, see Technical Notes 38, 39, and 40 under MFC in Books Online.

See Also OLE Overview: Implementation Strategies, OLE Overview

Porting

See the articles MFC: Porting MFC Applications to 32-Bit and MFC: Porting Tips.

Additional information is available in the following locations:

- In *Programming Techniques*: Chapter 1, Porting 16-Bit Code to 32-Bit Windows.
- Under MFC in Books Online: Technical Note 19, Updating Existing MFC Applications to MFC 3.0. This note describes migration to MFC version 2.0 and above.
- In the *MFC Migration Guide*. The *MFC Migration Guide*, which documents the MFC Migration Kit, describes how to migrate applications written for Windows in C to C++, using MFC. The *MFC Migration Guide* and the MFC Migration Kit are available in the MFCKIT directory on the Visual C++ CD-ROM disc. The *MFC Migration Guide* is not available in Books Online.
- Under Key Visual C++ Topics/Programming Topics/Porting in the InfoView pane of the Microsoft Developer Studio Workspace window.

Print Preview

See the article Printing.

See Also   Printing: The Print Preview Architecture

Printing

This group of articles explains how printing is implemented in the Microsoft Foundation Class Library (MFC) and how to take advantage of the printing architecture already built into the framework. The articles also explain how MFC supports easy implementation of print preview functionality and how you can use and modify that functionality.

Microsoft Windows implements device-independent display. In MFC, this means that the same drawing calls, in the OnDraw member function of your view class, are responsible for drawing on the display and on other devices, such as printers. For print preview, the target device is a simulated printer output to the display.

Your Role in Printing vs. the Framework's Role

Your view class has the following responsibilities:

- Inform the framework how many pages are in the document.
- When asked to print a specified page, draw that portion of the document.

- Allocate and deallocate any fonts or other graphics device interface (GDI) resources needed for printing.

- If necessary, send any escape codes needed to change the printer mode before printing a given page; for example, to change the printing orientation on a per-page basis.

The framework's responsibilities are as follows:

- Display the Print dialog box.

- Create a **CDC** object for the printer.

- Call the **StartDoc** and **EndDoc** member functions of the **CDC** object.

- Repeatedly call the **StartPage** member function of the **CDC** object, inform the view class which page should be printed, and call the **EndPage** member function of the **CDC** object.

- Call overridable functions in the view at the appropriate times.

The following articles discuss how the framework supports printing and print preview:

- Printing: How Default Printing Is Done

- Printing: Multipage Documents

- Printing: Headers and Footers

- Printing: Allocating GDI Resources

- Printing: The Print Preview Architecture

See Also In *Tutorials*: Chapter 10, Enhancing Printing

Printing: How Default Printing Is Done

This article explains the default printing process in Windows in terms of the MFC framework.

In MFC applications, the view class has a member function named OnDraw which contains all the drawing code. OnDraw takes a pointer to a **CDC** object as a parameter. That **CDC** object represents the device context to receive the image produced by OnDraw. When the window displaying the document receives a **WM_PAINT** message, the framework calls OnDraw and passes it a device context for the screen (a **CPaintDC** object, to be specific). Accordingly, OnDraw's output goes to the screen.

In programming for Windows, sending output to the printer is very similar to sending output to the screen. This is because the Windows graphics device interface (GDI) is hardware-independent; you can use the same GDI functions for screen display or for printing simply by using the appropriate device context. If the **CDC** object that OnDraw receives represents the printer, OnDraw's output goes to the printer.

This explains how MFC applications can perform simple printing without requiring extra effort on your part. The framework takes care of displaying the Print dialog box and creating a device context for the printer. When the user selects the Print command from the File menu, the view passes this device context to `OnDraw`, which draws the document on the printer.

However, there are some significant differences between printing and screen display. When you print, you have to divide the document into distinct pages and display them one at a time, rather than display whatever portion is visible in a window. As a corollary, you have to be aware of the size of the paper (whether it's letter size, legal size, or an envelope). You may want to print in different orientations, such as landscape or portrait mode. The Microsoft Foundation Class Library can't predict how your application will handle these issues, so it provides a protocol for you to add these capabilities.

That protocol is described in the article Printing: Multipage Documents.

See Also   In the *Class Library Reference*: **CDC**

Printing: Multipage Documents

This article describes the Windows printing protocol and explains how to print documents that contain more than one page. The article covers the following topics:

- Printing protocol
- Overriding view class functions
- Pagination
- Printer pages vs. document pages
- Print-time pagination

The Printing Protocol

To print a multipage document, the framework and view interact in the following manner. First the framework displays the Print dialog box, creates a device context for the printer, and calls the **StartDoc** member function of the **CDC** object. Then, for each page of the document, the framework calls the **StartPage** member function of the **CDC** object, instructs the view object to print the page, and then calls the **EndPage** member function. If the printer mode must be changed before starting a particular page, the view object sends the appropriate escape code by calling the **Escape** member function of the **CDC** object. When the entire document has been printed, the framework calls the **EndDoc** member function.

Overriding View Class Functions

The **CView** class defines several member functions that are called by the framework during printing. By overriding these functions in your view class, you provide the connections between the framework's printing logic and your view class's printing logic. Table 1 lists these member functions.

Table 1   CView's Overridable Functions for Printing

Name	Reason for overriding
OnPreparePrinting	To insert values in the Print dialog box, especially the length of the document
OnBeginPrinting	To allocate fonts or other GDI resources
OnPrepareDC	To adjust attributes of the device context for a given page, or to do print-time pagination
OnPrint	To print a given page
OnEndPrinting	To deallocate GDI resources

You can do printing-related processing in other functions as well, but these functions are the ones that drive the printing process.

Figure 1 illustrates the steps involved in the printing process and shows where each of **CView**'s printing member functions are called. The rest of this article explains most of these steps in more detail. Additional parts of the printing process are described in the article Printing: Allocating GDI Resources.

Figure 1   The Printing Loop

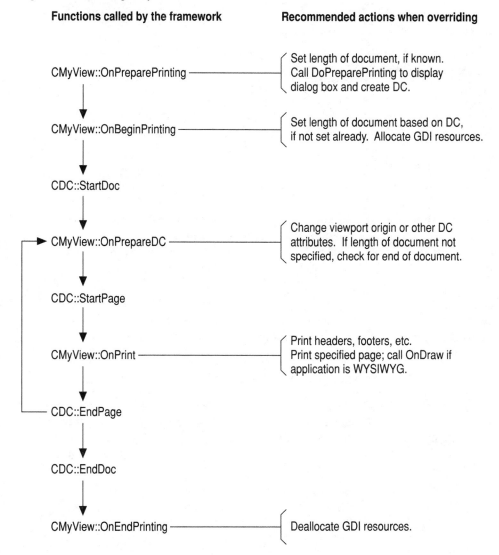

Functions called by the framework	Recommended actions when overriding
CMyView::OnPreparePrinting	Set length of document, if known. Call DoPreparePrinting to display dialog box and create DC.
CMyView::OnBeginPrinting	Set length of document based on DC, if not set already. Allocate GDI resources.
CDC::StartDoc	
CMyView::OnPrepareDC	Change viewport origin or other DC attributes. If length of document not specified, check for end of document.
CDC::StartPage	
CMyView::OnPrint	Print headers, footers, etc. Print specified page; call OnDraw if application is WYSIWYG.
CDC::EndPage	
CDC::EndDoc	
CMyView::OnEndPrinting	Deallocate GDI resources.

Pagination

The framework stores much of the information about a print job in a **CPrintInfo** structure. Several of the values in **CPrintInfo** pertain to pagination; these values are accessible as shown in Table 2.

Table 2   Page Number Information Stored in CPrintInfo

Member variable or function name(s)	Page number referenced
GetMinPage / SetMinPage	First page of document
GetMaxPage / SetMaxPage	Last page of document
GetFromPage	First page to be printed
GetToPage	Last page to be printed
m_nCurPage	Page currently being printing

Page numbers start at 1; that is, the first page is numbered 1, not 0. For more information about these and other members of **CPrintInfo**, see the *Class Library Reference*.

At the beginning of the printing process, the framework calls the view's **OnPreparePrinting** member function, passing a pointer to a **CPrintInfo** structure. AppWizard provides an implementation of **OnPreparePrinting** that calls **DoPreparePrinting**, another member function of **CView**. **DoPreparePrinting** is the function that displays the Print dialog box and creates a printer device context.

At this point the application doesn't know how many pages are in the document; it uses the default values 1 and 0xFFFF for the numbers of the first and last page of the document. If you know how many pages your document has, override **OnPreparePrinting** and call **SetMaxPage** for the **CPrintInfo** structure before you send it to **DoPreparePrinting**; this lets you specify the length of your document.

DoPreparePrinting then displays the Print dialog box; when it returns, the **CPrintInfo** structure contains the values specified by the user. If the user wishes to print only a selected range of pages, he or she can specify the starting and ending page numbers in the Print dialog box; the framework retrieves these values using the **GetFromPage** and **GetToPage** functions. If the user doesn't specify a page range, the framework calls **GetMinPage** and **GetMaxPage** and uses the values returned to print the entire document.

For each page of a document to be printed, the framework calls two member functions in your view class, **OnPrepareDC** and **OnPrint**, and passes each function two parameters: a pointer to a **CDC** object and a pointer to a **CPrintInfo** structure. Each time the framework calls **OnPrepareDC** and **OnPrint**, it passes a different value in the **m_nCurPage** member of the **CPrintInfo** structure. In this way the framework tells the view which page should be printed.

The **OnPrepareDC** member function is also used for screen display; it makes adjustments to the device context before drawing takes place. **OnPrepareDC** serves a similar role in printing, but there are a couple of differences: first, the **CDC** object represents a printer device context instead of a screen device context, and second, a **CPrintInfo** object is passed as a second parameter. (This parameter is **NULL** when **OnPrepareDC** is called for screen display.) Override **OnPrepareDC** to make adjustments to the device context based on which page is being printed; for example, you can move the viewport origin and the clipping region to ensure that the appropriate portion of the document gets printed.

The **OnPrint** member function performs the actual printing of the page. The article Printing: How Default Printing Is Done shows how the framework calls **OnDraw** with a printer device context to perform printing. More precisely, the framework calls **OnPrint** with a **CPrintInfo** structure and a device context, and **OnPrint** passes the device context to **OnDraw**. Override **OnPrint** to perform any rendering that should be done only during printing and not for screen display; for example, to print headers or footers (see the article Printing: Headers and Footers for more information). Then call **OnDraw** from the override of **OnDraw** to do the rendering common to both screen display and printing.

The fact that **OnDraw** does the rendering for both screen display and printing means that your application is WYSIWYG: "What you see is what you get." However, suppose you aren't writing a WYSIWYG application. For example, consider a text editor that uses a bold font for printing but displays control codes to indicate bold text on the screen. In such a situation, you use **OnDraw** strictly for screen display. When you override **OnPrint**, substitute the call to **OnDraw** with a call to a separate drawing function. That function draws the document the way it appears on paper, using the attributes that you don't display on the screen.

Printer Pages vs. Document Pages

When you refer to page numbers, it's sometimes necessary to distinguish between the printer's concept of a page and a document's concept of a page. From the point of view of the printer, a page is one sheet of paper. However, one sheet of paper doesn't necessarily equal one page of the document. For example, if you're printing a newsletter, where the sheets are to be folded, one sheet of paper might contain both the first and last pages of the document, side by side. Similarly, if you're printing a spreadsheet, the document doesn't consist of pages at all; instead, one sheet of paper might contain rows 1 through 20, columns 6 through 10.

All the page numbers in the **CPrintInfo** structure refer to printer pages. The framework calls **OnPrepareDC** and **OnPrint** once for each sheet of paper that will pass through the printer. When you override the **OnPreparePrinting** function to specify the length of the document, you must use printer pages. If there is a one-to-one correspondence (that is, one printer page equals one document page), then this is easy. If, on the other hand, document pages and printer pages do not directly correspond, you must translate between them. For example, consider printing a spreadsheet. When overriding **OnPreparePrinting**, you must calculate how many sheets of paper will be required to print the entire spreadsheet and then use that value when calling the **SetMaxPage** member function of **CPrintInfo**. Similarly, when overriding **OnPrepareDC**, you must translate **m_nCurPage** into the range of rows and columns that will appear on that particular sheet and then adjust the viewport origin accordingly.

Print-Time Pagination

In some situations, your view class may not know in advance how long the document is until it has actually been printed. For example, suppose your application isn't WYSIWYG, so a document's length on the screen doesn't correspond to its length when printed.

This causes a problem when you override **OnPreparePrinting** for your view class: you can't pass a value to the **SetMaxPage** function of the **CPrintInfo** structure, because you don't know the length of a document. If the user doesn't specify a page number to stop at using the Print dialog box, the framework doesn't know when to stop the print loop. The only way to determine when to stop the print loop is to print out the document and see when it ends; your view class must check for the end of the document while it is being printed, and then inform the framework when the end is reached.

The framework relies on your view class's **OnPrepareDC** function to tell it when to stop. After each call to **OnPrepareDC**, the framework checks a member of the **CPrintInfo** structure called **m_bContinuePrinting**. Its default value is **TRUE**; as long as it remains so, the framework continues the print loop. If it is set to **FALSE**, the framework stops. To perform print-time pagination, override **OnPrepareDC** to check whether the end of the document has been reached, and set **m_bContinuePrinting** to **FALSE** when it has.

The default implementation of **OnPrepareDC** sets **m_bContinuePrinting** to **FALSE** if the current page is greater than 1. This means that if the length of the document wasn't specified, the framework assumes the document is one page long. One consequence of this is that you must be careful if you call the base class version of **OnPrepareDC**; do not assume that **m_bContinuePrinting** will be **TRUE** after calling the base class version.

See Also Printing: Headers and Footers, Printing: Allocating GDI Resources

In the *Class Library Reference*: **CView**, **CDC**

Printing: Headers and Footers

This article explains how to add headers and footers to a printed document.

When you look at a document on the screen, the name of the document and your current location in the document are commonly displayed in a title bar and a status bar. When looking at a printed copy of a document, it's useful to have the name and page number shown in a header or footer. This is a common way in which even WYSIWYG programs differ in how they perform printing and screen display.

The **OnPrint** member function is the appropriate place to print headers or footers because it is called for each page, and because it is called only for printing, not for screen display. You can define a separate function to print a header or footer, and pass it the printer device context from **OnPrint**. You may need to adjust the window origin or extent before calling **OnDraw** to avoid having the body of the page overlap the header or footer. You might also have to modify **OnDraw** because the amount of the document that fits on the page could be reduced.

One way to compensate for the area taken by the header or footer is to use the **m_rectDraw** member of **CPrintInfo**. Each time a page is printed, this member is initialized with the usable area of the page. If you print a header or footer before printing the body of the page, you can reduce the size of the rectangle stored in **m_rectDraw** to account for the area taken by the header or footer. Then **OnPrint** can refer to **m_rectDraw** to find out how much area remains for printing the body of the page.

You cannot print a header, or anything else, from **OnPrepareDC**, because it is called before the **StartPage** member function of **CDC** has been called. At that point, the printer device context is considered to be at a page boundary. You can perform printing only from the **OnPrint** member function.

See Also   Printing: Multipage Documents, Printing: Allocating GDI Resources

Printing: Allocating GDI Resources

This article explains how to allocate and deallocate the Windows graphics device interface (GDI) objects needed for printing.

Suppose you need to use certain fonts, pens, or other GDI objects for printing, but not for screen display. Because of the memory they require, it's inefficient to allocate these objects when the application starts up. When the application isn't printing a document, that memory might be needed for other purposes. It's better to allocate them when printing begins, and then delete them when printing ends.

To allocate these GDI objects, override the **OnBeginPrinting** member function. This function is well suited to this purpose for two reasons: the framework calls this function once at the beginning of each print job and, unlike **OnPreparePrinting**, this function has access to the **CDC** object representing the printer device driver. You can store these objects for use during the print job by defining member variables in your view class that point to GDI objects (for example, **CFont *** members, and so on).

To use the GDI objects you've created, select them into the printer device context in the **OnPrint** member function. If you need different GDI objects for different pages of the document, you can examine the **m_nCurPage** member of the **CPrintInfo** structure and select the GDI object accordingly. If you need a GDI object for several consecutive pages, Windows requires that you select it into the device context each time **OnPrint** is called.

To deallocate these GDI objects, override the **OnEndPrinting** member function. The framework calls this function at the end of each print job, giving you the opportunity to deallocate printing-specific GDI objects before the application returns to other tasks.

See Also   Printing: How Default Printing Is Done

Printing: The Print Preview Architecture

This article explains how the MFC framework implements print preview functionality. Topics covered include:

- The print preview process
- Modifying print preview

Print preview is somewhat different from screen display and printing because, instead of directly drawing an image on a device, the application must simulate the printer using the screen. To accommodate this, the Microsoft Foundation Class Library defines a special class derived from **CDC**, called **CPreviewDC**. All **CDC** objects contain two device contexts, but usually they are identical. In a **CPreviewDC** object, they are different: the first represents the printer being simulated, and the second represents the screen on which output is actually displayed.

The Print Preview Process

When the user selects the Print Preview command from the File menu, the framework creates a **CPreviewDC** object. Whenever your application performs an operation that sets a characteristic of the printer device context, the framework also performs a similar operation on the screen device context. For example, if your application selects a font for printing, the framework selects a font for screen display that simulates the printer font. Whenever your application would send output to the printer, the framework instead sends the output to the screen.

Print preview also differs from printing in the order that each draws the pages of a document. During printing, the framework continues a print loop until a certain range of pages has been rendered. During print preview, one or two pages are displayed at any time, and then the application waits; no further pages are displayed until the user responds. During print preview, the application must also respond to **WM_PAINT** messages, just as it does during ordinary screen display.

The **OnPreparePrinting** function is called when preview mode is invoked, just as it is at the beginning of a print job. The **CPrintInfo** structure passed to the function contains several members whose values you can set to adjust certain characteristics of the print preview operation. For example, you can set the **m_nNumPreviewPages** member to specify whether you want to preview the document in one-page or two-page mode.

Modifying Print Preview

You can modify the behavior and appearance of print preview in a number of ways rather easily. For example, you can, among other things:

- Cause the print preview window to display a scroll bar for easy access to any page of the document.

- Cause print preview to maintain the user's position in the document by beginning its display at the current page.

- Cause different initialization to be performed for print preview and printing.

- Cause print preview to display page numbers in your own formats.

If you know how long the document is and call **SetMaxPage** with the appropriate value, the framework can use this information in preview mode as well as during printing. Once the framework knows the length of the document, it can provide the preview window with a scroll bar, allowing the user to page back and forth through the document in preview mode. If you haven't set the length of the document, the framework cannot position the scroll box to indicate the current position, so the framework doesn't add a scroll bar. In this case, the user must use the Next Page and Previous Page buttons on the preview window's control bar to page through the document.

For print preview, you may find it useful to assign a value to the **m_nCurPage** member of **CPrintInfo**, even though you would never do so for ordinary printing. During ordinary printing, this member carries information from the framework to your view class; this is how the framework tells the view which page should be printed.

By contrast, when print preview mode is started, the **m_nCurPage** member carries information in the opposite direction: from the view to the framework. The framework uses the value of this member to determine which page should be previewed first. The default value of this member is 1, so the first page of the document is displayed initially. You can override **OnPreparePrinting** to set this member to the number of the page being viewed at the time the Print Preview command was invoked. This way, the application maintains the user's current position when moving from normal display mode to print preview mode.

Sometimes you may want **OnPreparePrinting** to perform different initialization depending on whether it is called for a print job or for print preview. You can determine this by examining the **m_bPreview** member variable in the **CPrintInfo** structure; this member is set to **TRUE** when print preview is invoked.

The **CPrintInfo** structure also contains a member named **m_strPageDesc**, which is used to format the strings displayed at the bottom of the screen in single-page and multiple-page modes. By default these strings are of the form "Page *n*" and "Pages *n - m*," but you can modify **m_strPageDesc** from within **OnPreparePrinting** and set the strings to something more elaborate. See **CPrintInfo** in the *Class Library Reference* for more information.

See Also Printing

In the *Class Library Reference*: **CView, CDC**

Properties

An OLE control fires events to communicate with its control container. The container, in return, uses methods and properties to communicate with the control. Methods and properties are similar in use and purpose, respectively, to member functions and member variables of a C++ class. Properties are data members, of the OLE control, which are exposed to any container. Properties provide an interface for applications that contain OLE controls, such as OLE Automation clients and OLE control containers.

For more information on OLE control methods, see the article Methods.

OLE controls can implement both stock and custom methods and properties. Class **COleControl** provides an implementation for stock properties. (For a complete list of stock properties, see the article Properties: Adding Stock Properties.) Custom properties, defined by the developer, add specialized capabilities to an OLE control. For more information, see Properties: Adding Custom Properties.

Both custom and stock properties, like methods, are supported by a mechanism that consists of a dispatch map that handles properties and methods and existing member functions of the **COleControl** class. In addition, these properties can have parameters that the developer uses to pass extra information to the control.

The following articles discuss OLE control properties in more detail:

- Properties: Adding Stock Properties
- Properties: Adding Custom Properties
- Properties: Advanced Implementation
- Properties: Accessing Ambient Properties

Properties: Adding Stock Properties

Stock properties differ from custom properties in that they are already implemented by the class **COleControl**. **COleControl** contains predefined member functions that support common properties for the control. Some common properties include the control's caption and the foreground and background colors. For information on other stock properties, see Stock Properties Supported by ClassWizard later in this article. The dispatch map entries for stock properties are always prefixed by **DISP_STOCKPROP**.

This article describes how to to add a stock property (in this case, Caption) to an OLE control using ClassWizard and explains the resulting code modifications. Topics include:

- Using ClassWizard to add a stock property

- ClassWizard changes for stock properties
- Stock properties supported by ClassWizard
- Stock properties and notification
- Color properties

Note Visual Basic custom (VBX) controls typically have properties such as Top, Left, Width, Height, Align, Tag, Name, TabIndex, TabStop, and Parent. OLE control containers, however, are responsible for implementing these control properties and therefore OLE controls should not support these properties.

Using ClassWizard to Add a Stock Property

Adding stock properties requires less code than adding custom properties because support for the property is automatically handled by **COleControl**. The following procedure demonstrates adding the stock Caption property to an OLE control framework. This same procedure can also be used to add other stock properties. Simply substitute the desired stock property name for Caption.

▶ **To add the stock Caption property using ClassWizard**

1 Load your control's project.

2 From the View menu, choose ClassWizard.

3 Choose the OLE Automation tab.

4 Choose the control's class from the Class name combo box.

5 Choose the Add Property button.

6 In the External Name box, select Caption.

   Note that in the Implementation group, Stock is automatically selected.

7 Choose the OK button to close the Add Property dialog box.

8 Choose the OK button to confirm your choices and close ClassWizard.

ClassWizard Changes for Stock Properties

Because **COleControl** supports stock properties, ClassWizard does not change the class declaration in any way; it simply adds the property to the dispatch map. ClassWizard adds the following line to the dispatch map of the control, which is located in the implementation (.CPP) file:

```
DISP_STOCKPROP_CAPTION( )
```

The following line is added to your control's Object Description (.ODL) file:

```
[id(DISPID_CAPTION), bindable, requestedit] BSTR Caption;
```

This line assigns the Caption property a specific ID. Notice that the property is bindable and will request permission from the database before modifying the value.

This makes the Caption property available to users of your control. To use the value of a stock property, access a member variable or member function of the **COleControl** base class. For more information on these member variables and member functions, see Stock Properties Supported by ClassWizard.

Stock Properties Supported by ClassWizard

The **COleControl** class provides nine stock properties. You can specify the properties you want in the control in the OLE Automation tab of the MFC ClassWizard dialog box.

Property	Dispatch map entry	How to access value
Appearance	DISP_STOCKPROP_APPEARANCE( )	Value accessible as **m_sAppearance**.
BackColor	DISP_STOCKPROP_BACKCOLOR( )	Value accessible by calling **GetBackColor**.
BorderStyle	DISP_STOCKPROP_BORDERSTYLE( )	Value accessible as **m_sBorderStyle**.
Caption	DISP_STOCKPROP_CAPTION( )	Value accessible by calling **InternalGetText**.
Enabled	DISP_STOCKPROP_ENABLED( )	Value accessible as **m_bEnabled**.
Font	DISP_STOCKPROP_FONT( )	See the article OLE Controls: Using Fonts in an OLE Control for usage.
ForeColor	DISP_STOCKPROP_FORECOLOR( )	Value accessible by calling **GetForeColor**.
hWnd	DISP_STOCKPROP_HWND( )	Value accessible as **m_hWnd**.
Text	DISP_STOCKPROP_TEXT( )	Value accessible by calling **InternalGetText**. This property is the same as **Caption**, except for the property name.

Stock Properties and Notification

Most of the stock properties have notification functions that can be overridden. For example, whenever the **BackColor** property is changed, the **OnBackColorChanged** function (a member function of the control class) is called. The default implementation (in **COleControl**) calls **InvalidateControl**. Override this function if you want to take additional actions in response to this situation.

Color Properties

You can use the stock **ForeColor** and **BackColor** properties, or your own custom color properties, when painting the control. To use a color property, call the **COleControl::TranslateColor** member function. The parameters of this function are the value of the color property and an optional palette handle. The return value is a **COLORREF** value that can be passed to GDI functions, such as **SetTextColor** and **CreateSolidBrush**.

The color values for the stock **ForeColor** and **BackColor** properties are accessed by calling either the **GetForeColor** or the **GetBackColor** function, respectively.

The following example demonstrates using these two color properties when painting a control. It initializes a temporary **COLORREF** variable and a **CBrush** object with calls to **TranslateColor**: one using the **ForeColor** property and the other using the **BackColor** property. A temporary **CBrush** object is then used to paint the control's rectangle, and the text color is set using the **ForeColor** property.

```
CBrush bkBrush(TranslateColor(GetBackColor()));
COLORREF clrFore = TranslateColor(GetForeColor());
pdc->FillRect( rcBounds, &bkbrush );
pdc->SetTextColor( clrFore );
pdc->DrawText( InternalGetText(), -1, rcBounds, DT_SINGLELINE | DT_CENTER |
    DT_VCENTER );
```

See Also   Properties, Methods

In the *Class Library Reference*: **COleControl**

Properties: Adding Custom Properties

Custom properties differ from stock properties in that they are not already implemented by the **COleControl** class. A custom property is used to expose a certain state or appearance of an OLE control to a programmer using the control.

This article describes how to add a custom property to the OLE control using ClassWizard and explains the resulting code modifications. Topics include:

- Using ClassWizard to add a custom property
- ClassWizard changes for custom properties

Custom properties come in four varieties of implementation: Member Variable, Member Variable with Notification, Get/Set Methods, and Parameterized.

- Member Variable Implementation

  This implementation represents the property's state as a member variable in the control class. Use the Member Variable implementation when it is not important to know when the property value changes. Of the three types, this implementation creates the least amount of support code for the property. The dispatch map entry macro for member variable implementation is **DISP_PROPERTY**. For a detailed example of this implementation, see Chapter 24, Adding Special Effects, in *Tutorials*.

- Member Variable with Notification Implementation

  This implementation consists of a member variable and a notification function created by ClassWizard. The notification function is automatically called by the framework after the property value changes. Use the Member Variable with Notification implementation when you need to be notified after a property value has changed. This implementation creates some overhead because it requires a function call. The dispatch map entry macro for this implementation is **DISP_PROPERTY_NOTIFY**. For a detailed example of this implementation, see Chapter 22, Adding a Custom Notification Property, in *Tutorials*.

- Get/Set Methods Implementation

This implementation consists of a pair of member functions in the control class. The Get/Set Methods implementation automatically calls the Get member function when the control's user requests the current value of the property and the Set member function when the control's user requests that the property be changed. Use this implementation when you need to compute the value of a property during run time, validate a value passed by the control's user before changing the actual property, or implement a read- or write-only property type. The dispatch map entry macro for this implementation is **DISP_PROPERTY_EX**. The following section, Using ClassWizard to Add a Custom Property, uses the CircleOffset custom property to demonstrate this implementation.

- Parameterized Implementation

  Parameterized implementation is supported by ClassWizard. A parameterized property (sometimes called a property array) can be used to access a set of values through a single property of your control. The dispatch map entry macro for this implementation is **DISP_PROPERTY_PARAM**. For more information on implementing this type, see Implementing a Parameterized Property in the article OLE Controls: Advanced Topics.

Using ClassWizard to Add a Custom Property

The following procedure demonstrates adding a custom property, CircleOffset, which uses the Get/Set Methods implementation. The CircleOffset custom property allows the control's user to offset the circle from the center of the control's bounding rectangle. The procedure for adding custom properties with an implementation other than Get/Set Methods is very similar.

This same procedure can also be used to add other custom properties you desire. Simply substitute your custom property name for the CircleOffset property name and parameters.

▶ **To add the CircleOffset custom property using ClassWizard**

1 Load your control's project.

2 From the View menu, choose ClassWizard.

3 Choose the OLE Automation tab.

4 Choose the control's class from the Class name combo box.

5 Choose the Add Property button.

6 In the External Name box, type **CircleOffset**.

7 Under Implementation, select Get/Set Methods.

8 From the Type box, select short for the property's type.

9 Type unique names for your Get and Set Functions, or accept the default names.

10 Choose the OK button to close the Add Property dialog box.

11 Choose the OK button to confirm your choices and close ClassWizard.

ClassWizard Changes for Custom Properties

When you add the CircleOffset custom property, ClassWizard makes changes to the header (.H) and the implementation (.CPP) files of the control class.

The following lines are added to the .H file to declare two functions called `GetCircleOffset` and `SetCircleOffset`:

```
afx_msg short GetCircleOffset( );
afx_msg void SetCircleOffset(short nNewValue);
```

The following line is added to your control's .ODL file:

```
[id(1)] short CircleOffset;
```

This line assigns the CircleOffset property a specific ID number, taken from the method's position in the methods and properties list of ClassWizard.

In addition, the following line is added to the dispatch map (in the .CPP file of the control class) to map the CircleOffset property to the control's two handler functions:

```
DISP_PROPERTY_EX(CSampleCtrl,"CircleOffset",
    GetCircleOffset, SetCircleOffset, VT_I2)
```

Finally, the implementations of the `GetCircleOffset` and `SetCircleOffset` functions are added to the end of the control's .CPP file. In most cases, you will modify the Get function to return the value of the property. The Set function will usually contain code that should be executed either before or after the property changes.

```
void CFooCtrl::SetCircleOffset(short nNewValue)
{
    // TODO: Add your property handler here
    SetModifiedFlag();
}
```

Note that ClassWizard automatically adds a call, to **SetModifiedFlag**, to the body of the Set function. Calling this function marks the control as modified. If a control has been modified, its new state will be saved when the container is saved. This function should be called whenever a property, saved as part of the control's persistent state, changes value.

For a detailed implementation of the CircleOffset property, see Chapter 23, Adding a Custom Get/Set Property, in *Tutorials*.

See Also Properties, Methods

In the *Class Library Reference*: **COleControl**

Properties: Advanced Implementation

This article describes topics related to implementing advanced properties in an OLE control:

- Read-only and write-only properties
- Returning error codes from a property

Read-only and Write-only Properties

ClassWizard provides a quick and easy method to implement read-only or write-only properties for the control.

▶ **To implement a read-only or write-only property**

1 Load the control project.

2 From the View menu, choose ClassWizard.

3 Choose the OLE Automation tab.

4 Choose the control's class from the Class name combo box.

5 Choose the Add Property button.

6 In the External Name box, type the name of your property.

7 Under Implementation, select Get/Set Methods.

8 From the Type box, select the proper type for the property.

9 If you want a read-only property, clear the Set function name specified by ClassWizard. If you want a write-only property, clear the Get function name.

10 Choose the OK button to close the Add Property dialog box.

11 Choose the OK button to confirm your choices and close ClassWizard.

When you do this, ClassWizard inserts the function **SetNotSupported** or **GetNotSupported** in the dispatch map entry in place of a normal Set or Get function.

If you want to change an existing property to be read- or write-only, you can edit the dispatch map manually and remove the unnecessary Set or Get function from the control class.

If you want a property to be conditionally read-only or write-only (for example, only when your control is operating in a particular mode), you can provide the Set or Get function, as normal, and call the **SetNotSupported** or **GetNotSupported** function where appropriate. For example:

```
void CSampleCtrl::SetMyProperty( short propVal )
{
    if ( m_bReadOnlyMode )  // some control-specific state
        SetNotSupported( );
    else
        m_ipropVal = propVal;  // set property as normal
}
```

This code sample calls **SetNotSupported** if the m_bReadOnlyMode data member is **TRUE**. If **FALSE**, then the property is set to the new value.

Returning Error Codes From a Property

To indicate that an error has occurred while attempting to get or set a property, use the **COleControl::ThrowError** function, which takes an **SCODE** (status code) as a parameter. You can use a predefined **SCODE** or define one of your own. For a list of predefined **SCODE**s and instructions for defining custom **SCODE**s, see Handling Errors in Your OLE Control in the article OLE Controls: Advanced Topics.

Helper functions exist for the most common predefined **SCODE**s, such as **COleControl::SetNotSupported**, **COleControl::GetNotSupported**, and **COleControl::SetNotPermitted**.

Note **ThrowError** is meant to be used only as a means of returning an error from within a property's Get or Set function or an automation method. These are the only times that the appropriate exception handler will be present on the stack.

For more information on reporting exceptions in other areas of the code, see **COleControl::FireError** and the section Handling Errors in Your OLE Control in the article OLE Controls: Advanced Topics.

See Also Properties, Methods

In the *Class Library Reference*: **COleControl**

Properties: Accessing Ambient Properties

This article discusses how an OLE control can access the ambient properties of its control container.

A control can obtain information about its container by accessing the container's "ambient properties." These properties expose visual characteristics, such as the container's background color, the current font used by the container, and operational characteristics, such as whether the container is currently in "user" mode or "designer" mode. A control can use ambient properties to tailor its appearance and behavior to the particular container in which it is embedded. However, a control should never assume that its container will support any particular ambient property. In fact, some containers may not support any ambient properties at all. In the absence of an ambient property, a control should assume a reasonable default value.

To access an ambient property, make a call to **COleControl::GetAmbientProperty**. This function expects the dispatch ID for the ambient property as the first parameter (the file OLECTL.H defines dispatch IDs for the standard set of ambient properties).

The parameters of the **GetAmbientProperty** function are the dispatch ID, a variant tag indicating the expected property type, and a pointer to memory where the value should be returned. The type of data to which this pointer refers will vary depending on the variant tag. The function returns **TRUE** if the container supports the property, otherwise it returns **FALSE**.

The following code example obtains the value of the ambient property called "UserMode." If the property is not supported by the container, a default value of **TRUE** is assumed:

```
BOOL bUserMode;
if( !GetAmbientProperty( DISPID_AMBIENT_USERMODE,
    VT_BOOL, &bUserMode ) )
    bUserMode = TRUE;
```

For your convenience, **COleControl** supplies helper functions that access many of the commonly used ambient properties and return appropriate defaults when the properties are not available. These helper functions are as follows:

- **COleControl::AmbientBackColor**

- **AmbientDisplayName**

- **AmbientFont**

Note Caller must call **Release( )** on the returned font.

- **AmbientForeColor**

- **AmbientLocaleID**

- **AmbientScaleUnits**

- **AmbientTextAlign**

- **AmbientUserMode**

- **AmbientUIDead**

- **AmbientShowHatching**

- **AmbientShowGrabHandles**

If the value of an ambient property changes (through some action of the container), the **OnAmbientPropertyChanged** member function of the control is called. Override this member function to handle such a notification. The parameter for **OnAmbientPropertyChanged** is the dispatch ID of the affected ambient property. The value of this dispatch ID may be **DISPID_UNKNOWN**, which indicates that one or more ambient properties have changed, but information about which properties were affected is unavailable.

Property Sheets

The Microsoft Foundation Class Library (MFC) contains support for property sheets, also known as "tab dialog boxes." This article explains how and when to use property sheets in your MFC applications. Topics include:

- Using property sheets in your application
- Adding controls to a property sheet

A property sheet is a special kind of dialog box that is generally used to modify the attributes of some external object, such as the current selection in a view. The property sheet has three main parts: the containing dialog box, one or more property pages shown one at a time, and a tab at the top of each page that the user clicks to select that page. Property sheets are useful for situations where you have a number of similar groups of settings or options to change. An example of a property sheet is the Project Settings dialog box in Microsoft Developer Studio. In this case, there are a number of different groups of options that need to be set. The property sheet allows a large amount of information to be grouped in an easily understood fashion.

Using Property Sheets in Your Application

To use a property sheet in your application, complete the following steps:

1. Create a dialog template resource for each property page. Keep in mind that the user may be switching from one page to another, so lay out each page as consistently as possible.

   The dialog templates for all pages do not have to be the same size. The framework uses the size of the largest page to determine how much space to allocate in the property sheet for the property pages.

   When you create the dialog template resource for a property page, you must specify the following styles in the Dialog Properties property sheet:

   - Set the Caption edit box on the General page to the text you wish to appear in the tab for this page.
   - Set the Style list box on the Styles page to Child.
   - Set the Border list box on the Styles page to Thin.
   - Ensure that the Titlebar check box on the Styles page is checked.
   - Ensure that the Disabled check box on the More Styles page is checked.

2. Use ClassWizard to create a **CPropertyPage**-derived class corresponding to each property page dialog template. To do this, choose ClassWizard from the View menu while the focus is on a particular property page dialog box. Choose **CPropertyPage** as the base class in ClassWizard.

3. Using ClassWizard, create member variables to hold the values for this property page. The process for adding member variables to a property page is exactly the same as adding member variables to a dialog box, since a property page is a specialized dialog box.

4. Construct a **CPropertySheet** object in your source code. Usually, you construct the **CPropertySheet** object in the handler for the command that displays the property sheet. This object represents the entire property sheet. If you create a modal property sheet with the **DoModal** function, the framework supplies three pushbuttons by default: OK, Cancel, and Apply. The framework creates no pushbuttons for modeless property sheets created with the **Create** function. You do not need to derive a class from **CPropertySheet** unless you want to either add other controls (such as a preview window) or display a modeless property sheet. This step is necessary for modeless property sheets since they do not contain any default controls that could be used to close the property sheet.

5. For each page to be added to the property sheet, do the following:

   - Construct one object for each **CPropertyPage**-derived class that you created using ClassWizard earlier in this process.

   - Call **CPropertySheet::AddPage** for each page.

   Typically, the object that creates the **CPropertySheet** also creates the **CPropertyPage** objects in this step. However, if you implement a **CPropertySheet**-derived class, you can embed the **CPropertyPage** objects in the **CPropertySheet** object and call **AddPage** for each page from the **CPropertySheet**-derived class constructor. **AddPage** adds the **CPropertyPage** object to the property sheet's list of pages but does not actually create the window for that page. Therefore, it is not necessary to wait until creation of the property sheet window to call **AddPage**; you can call **AddPage** from the property sheet's constructor.

6. Call **CPropertySheet::DoModal** or **Create** to display the property sheet. Call **DoModal** to create a property sheet as a modal dialog box. Call **Create** to create the property sheet as a modeless dialog box.

7. Exchange data between property pages and the owner of the property sheet. This is explained in the article Property Sheets: Exchanging Data.

For an example of how to use property sheets, see the MFC General sample PROPDLG.

Adding Controls to a Property Sheet

By default, a property sheet allocates window area for the property pages, the tab index, and the OK, Cancel, and Apply buttons. (A modeless property sheet does not have the OK, Cancel, and Apply buttons.) You can add other controls to the property sheet. For example, you can add a preview window to the right of the property page area, to show the user what the current settings would look like if applied to an external object.

You can add controls to the property sheet dialog in the **OnCreate** handler. Accommodating additional controls usually requires expanding the size of the property sheet dialog. After calling the base class **CPropertySheet::OnCreate**, call **GetWindowRect** to get the width and height of the currently allocated property sheet window, expand the rectangle's dimensions, and call **MoveWindow** to change the size of the property sheet window.

For more information on property sheets, see the following articles:

- Property Sheets: Exchanging Data
- Property Sheets: Creating a Modeless Property Sheet
- Property Sheets: Handling the Apply Button

See Also   In the *Class Library Reference*: **CPropertyPage**, **CPropertySheet**

Property Sheets: Exchanging Data

As with most dialog boxes, the exchange of data between the property sheet and the application is one of the most important functions of the property sheet. This article describes how to accomplish this task.

Exchanging data with a property sheet is actually a matter of exchanging data with the individual property pages of the property sheet. The procedure for exchanging data with a property page is the same as for exchanging data with a dialog box, since a **CPropertyPage** object is just a specialized **CDialog** object. The procedure takes advantage of the framework's dialog data exchange (DDX) facility, which exchanges data between controls in a dialog box and member variables of the dialog box object.

The important difference between exchanging data with a property sheet and with a normal dialog box is that the property sheet has multiple pages, so you must exchange data with all the pages in the property sheet. For more information on DDX, see Dialog Data Exchange and Validation in Chapter 4.

The following example illustrates exchanging data between a view and two pages of a property sheet:

```
void CMyView::DoModalPropertySheet()
{
    CPropertySheet propsheet;
    CMyFirstPage pageFirst; // derived from CPropertyPage
    CMySecondPage pageSecond; // derived from CPropertyPage

    // Move member data from the view (or from the currently
    // selected object in the view, for example).
    pageFirst.m_nMember1 = m_nMember1;
    pageFirst.m_nMember2 = m_nMember2;

    pageSecond.m_strMember3 = m_strMember3;
    pageSecond.m_strMember4 = m_strMember4;

    propsheet.AddPage(&pageFirst);
    propsheet.AddPage(&pageSecond);

    if (propsheeet.DoModal() == IDOK)
    {
        m_nMember1 = pageFirst.m_nMember1;
        m_nMember2 = pageFirst.m_nMember2;
        m_nMember3 = pageSecond.m_strMember1;
        m_nMember4 = pageSecond.m_strMember2;
        GetDocument()->SetModifiedFlag();
        GetDocument()->UpdateAllViews(NULL);
    }
}
```

See Also   Property Sheets

Property Sheets: Creating a Modeless Property Sheet

Normally, the property sheets you create will be modal. When using a modal property sheet, the user must close the property sheet before using any other part of the application. This article describes methods you can use to create a modeless property sheet that allows the user to keep the property sheet open while using other parts of the application.

To display a property sheet as a modeless dialog box instead of as a modal dialog box, call **CPropertySheet::Create** instead of **DoModal**. However, there are some extra tasks that you must implement to support a modeless property sheet.

One of the additional tasks is exchanging data between the property sheet and the external object it is modifying when the property sheet is open. This is generally the same task as for standard modeless dialog boxes. Part of this task is implementing a channel of communication between the modeless property sheet and the external object to which the property settings apply. This implementation is far easier if you derive a class from **CPropertySheet** for your modeless property sheet. This article assumes you have done so.

One method for communicating between the modeless property sheet and the external object (the current selection in a view, for example) is to define a pointer from the property sheet to the external object. Define a function (called something like SetMyExternalObject) in the **CPropertySheet**-derived class to change the pointer whenever the focus changes from one external object to another. The SetMyExternalObject function needs to reset the settings for each property page to reflect the newly selected external object. To accomplish this, the SetMyExternalObject function must be able to access the **CPropertyPage** objects belonging to the **CPropertySheet** class.

The most convenient way to provide access to property pages within a property sheet is to embed the **CPropertyPage** objects in the **CPropertySheet**-derived object. Embedding **CPropertyPage** objects in the **CPropertySheet**-derived object differs from the typical design for modal dialog boxes, where the owner of the property sheet creates the **CPropertyPage** objects and passes them to the property sheet via **CPropertySheet::AddPage**.

There are many user-interface alternatives for determining when the settings of the modeless property sheet should be applied to an external object. One alternative is to apply the settings of the current property page whenever the user changes any value. Another alternative is to provide an Apply button, which allows the user to accumulate changes in the property pages before committing them to the external object. For information on ways to handle the Apply button, see the article Property Sheets: Handling the Apply Button.

See Also   Property Sheets, Property Sheets: Exchanging Data, Life Cycle of a Dialog Box (in Chapter 4)

Property Sheets: Handling the Apply Button

Property sheets have a capability that standard dialog boxes do not: they allow the user to apply changes they have made before closing the property sheet. This is done using the Apply button. This article discusses methods you can use to properly implement this feature.

Modal dialog boxes usually apply the settings to an external object when the user clicks OK to close the dialog box. The same is true for a property sheet: when the user clicks OK, the new settings in the property sheet take effect.

However, you may want to allow the user to save settings without having to close the property sheet dialog box. This is the function of the Apply button. The Apply button applies the current settings in all of the property pages to the external object, as opposed to applying only the current settings of the currently active page.

By default, the Apply button is always disabled. You must write code to enable the Apply button at the appropriate times, and you must write code to implement the effect of Apply, as explained below.

If you do not wish to offer the Apply functionality to the user, it is not necessary to remove the Apply button. You can leave it disabled, as will be common among applications that use standard property sheet support available in future versions of Windows.

To report a page as being modified and enable the Apply button, call **CPropertyPage::SetModified(TRUE)**. If any of the pages report being modified, the Apply button will remain enabled, regardless of whether the currently active page has been modified.

You should call **CPropertyPage::SetModified** whenever the user changes any settings in the page. One way to detect when a user changes a setting in the page is to implement change notification handlers for each of the controls in the property page, such as **EN_CHANGE** or **BN_CLICKED**.

To implement the effect of the Apply button, the property sheet must tell its owner, or some other external object in the application, to apply the current settings in the property pages. At the same time, the property sheet should disable the Apply button by calling **CPropertyPage::SetModified(FALSE)** for all pages that applied their modifications to the external object.

For an example of this process, see the MFC General sample PROPDLG.

See Also   Property Sheets

Record

A record is a collection of data about a single entity, such as an account or a customer, stored in a table (a "row" of the table). A record consists of a group of contiguous columns (sometimes called fields) that contain data of various types. A set of records selected from a data source—often called a "result set" in database terms—is called a "recordset" in MFC. See the articles Recordset (ODBC)or DAO Recordset for more details.

Record Field Exchange (RFX)

The MFC database classes automate moving data between the data source and a recordset using a mechanism called "record field exchange" (RFX). RFX is similar to dialog data exchange (DDX). Moving data between a data source and the field data members of a recordset requires multiple calls to the recordset's **DoFieldExchange** function and considerable interaction between the framework and ODBC. The RFX mechanism is type-safe and saves you the work of calling ODBC functions such as **::SQLBindCol**. (For more information about DDX, see Chapter 14, Working with Classes, in the *Visual C++ User's Guide*.)

RFX is mostly transparent to you. If you declare your recordset classes with AppWizard or ClassWizard, RFX is built into them automatically. All recordset classes are derived from the base class **CRecordset** supplied by the framework. AppWizard lets you create an initial recordset class. ClassWizard lets you add other recordset classes as you need them. You use ClassWizard to map recordset field data members to table columns on the data source. For more information and examples, see the article ClassWizard: Creating a Recordset Class.

You must manually add a small amount of RFX code in three cases—when you want to:

- Use parameterized queries. See the article Recordset: Parameterizing a Recordset (ODBC).

- Perform joins—using one recordset for columns from two or more tables. See the article Recordset: Performing a Join (ODBC).

- Bind data columns dynamically. This is less common than parameterization. See the article Recordset: Dynamically Binding Data Columns (ODBC).

If you need a more advanced understanding of RFX, see the article Record Field Exchange: How RFX Works.

The following articles explain the details of using recordset objects:

- Record Field Exchange: Using RFX
- Record Field Exchange: Using the RFX Functions

- Record Field Exchange: How RFX Works

See Also Recordset (ODBC), ClassWizard: Creating a Recordset Class, AppWizard: Database Support

In the *Class Library Reference*: **CRecordset**

Record Field Exchange: Using RFX

This article explains what you do to use RFX in relation to what the framework does. The related article, Record Field Exchange: Working with the Wizard Code, continues the discussion. That article introduces the main components of RFX and explains the code that AppWizard and ClassWizard write to support RFX and how you might want to modify the wizard code.

Writing calls to the RFX functions in your **DoFieldExchange** override is explained in the article Record Field Exchange: Using the RFX Functions.

Table 1 shows your role in relation to what the framework does for you.

Table 1 Using RFX: You and the Framework

You...	The framework...
Declare your recordset classes with ClassWizard. Specify names and data types of field data members.	ClassWizard derives a **CRecordset** class and writes a **DoFieldExchange** override for you, including an RFX function call for each field data member.
(Optional) Manually add any needed parameter data members to the class. Manually add an RFX function call to **DoFieldExchange** for each parameter data member, add a call to **CFieldExchange::SetFieldType** for the group of parameters, and specify the total number of parameters in **m_nParams**. See Recordset: Parameterizing a Recordset (ODBC).	
(Optional) Manually bind additional columns to field data members. Manually increment **m_nFields**. See Recordset: Dynamically Binding Data Columns (ODBC).	

Table 1   Using RFX: You and the Framework *(cont.)*

You...	The framework...
Construct an object of your recordset class. Before using the object, set the values of its parameter data members, if any.	For efficiency, the framework prebinds the parameters, using ODBC. When you pass parameter values, the framework passes them to the data source. Only the parameter values are sent for requeries, unless the sort and/or filter strings have changed.
Open a recordset object using **CRecordset::Open**.	Executes the recordset's query, binds columns to field data members of the recordset, and calls **DoFieldExchange** to exchange data between the first selected record and the recordset's field data members.
Scroll in the recordset using **CRecordset::Move** or a menu or toolbar command.	Calls **DoFieldExchange** to transfer data to the field data members from the new current record.
Add, update, and delete records.	Calls **DoFieldExchange** to transfer data to the data source.

See Also   Record Field Exchange: How RFX Works, Recordset: Obtaining SUMs and Other Aggregate Results (ODBC)

In the *Class Library Reference*: **CRecordset**, **CFieldExchange**, Macros and Globals

Record Field Exchange: Working with the Wizard Code

This article explains the code that AppWizard and ClassWizard write to support RFX and how you might want to alter that code.

When you create a recordset class with ClassWizard (or with AppWizard), the wizard writes the following RFX-related elements for you, based on the data source, table, and column choices you make in the wizard:

- Declarations of the recordset field data members in the recordset class.
- An override of **CRecordset::DoFieldExchange**.
- Initialization of recordset field data members in the recordset class constructor.

The Field Data Member Declarations

The wizards write a recordset class declaration in an .H file that resembles the following for class CSections:

```
class CSections : public CRecordset
{
public:
    CSections(CDatabase* pDatabase);
    CSections::~CSections();

// Field/Param Data
    //{{AFX_FIELD(CSections, CRecordset)
    CString m_strCourseID;
    CString m_strInstructorID;
    CString m_strRoomNo;
    CString m_strSchedule;
    CString m_strSectionNo;
    //}}AFX_FIELD

// Implementation
protected:
    virtual CString GetDefaultConnect();  // Default connection string
    virtual CString GetDefaultSQL();    // Default SQL for Recordset
    virtual void DoFieldExchange(CFieldExchange* pFX);  // RFX support
    DECLARE_DYNAMIC(CSections)
};
```

Notice the following key features about the class above:

- Special "//{{AFX_FIELD" comments that bracket the field data member declarations. ClassWizard uses these to update your source file.

- The wizard overrides the **DoFieldExchange** member function of class **CRecordset**.

Caution   Never edit the code inside "//{{AFX" brackets. Always use ClassWizard. If you add parameter data members or new field data members that you bind yourself, add them outside the brackets.

The DoFieldExchange Override

DoFieldExchange is the heart of RFX. The framework calls **DoFieldExchange** any time it needs to move data either from data source to recordset or from recordset to data source. **DoFieldExchange** also supports obtaining information about field data members through the **IsFieldDirty** and **IsFieldNull** member functions.

The following **DoFieldExchange** override is for the CSections class. ClassWizard writes the function in the .CPP file for your recordset class.

```
void CSections::DoFieldExchange(CFieldExchange* pFX)
{
    //{{AFX_FIELD_MAP(CSections)
    pFX->SetFieldType(CFieldExchange::outputColumn);
    RFX_Text(pFX, "CourseID", m_strCourseID);
    RFX_Text(pFX, "InstructorID", m_strInstructorID);
    RFX_Text(pFX, "RoomNo", m_strRoomNo);
```

```
    RFX_Text(pFX, "Schedule", m_strSchedule);
    RFX_Text(pFX, "SectionNo", m_strSectionNo);
    //}}AFX_FIELD_MAP
}
```

Notice the following key features of the function:

- The special "//{{AFX_FIELD_MAP" comments. ClassWizard uses these to update your source file. This section of the function is called the "field map."

- A call to **CFieldExchange::SetFieldType**, through the *pFX* pointer. This call specifies that all RFX function calls up to the end of **DoFieldExchange** or the next call to **SetFieldType** are "output columns." See **CFieldExchange::SetFieldType** in the *Class Library Reference* for more information.

- Several calls to the **RFX_Text** global function—one per field data member (all of which are **CString** variables in the example). These calls specify the relationship between a column name on the data source and a field data member. The RFX functions do the actual data transfer. The class library supplies RFX functions for all of the common data types. For more information about RFX functions, see the article Record Field Exchange: Using the RFX Functions.

    Note The order of the columns in your result set must match the order of the RFX function calls in `DoFieldExchange`.

- The *pFX* pointer to a **CFieldExchange** object that the framework passes when it calls **DoFieldExchange**. The **CFieldExchange** object specifies the operation that **DoFieldExchange** is to perform, the direction of transfer, and other context information.

The Recordset Constructor

The recordset constructor that the wizards write contains two things related to RFX:

- An initialization for each field data member.

- An initialization for the **m_nFields** data member, which contains the number of field data members.

The constructor for the `CSections` recordset example looks like this:

```
CSections::CSections(CDatabase* pdb)
    : CRecordset(pdb)
{
    //{{AFX_FIELD_INIT(CSections)
    m_strCourseID = "";
    m_strInstructorID = "";
    m_strRoomNo = "";
    m_strSchedule = "";
    m_strSectionNo = "";
    m_nFields = 5;
    //}}AFX_FIELD_INIT
}
```

Important If you add any field data members manually, as you might if you bind new columns dynamically, you must increment **m_nFields**. Do so with another line of code outside the "//{{AFX_FIELD_INIT" brackets:

```
m_nFields += 3;
```

This is the code for adding three new fields. If you add any parameter data members, you must initialize the **m_nParams** data member, which contains the number of parameter data members. Put the **m_nParams** initialization outside the brackets.

See Also Record Field Exchange: Using the RFX Functions

Record Field Exchange: Using the RFX Functions

This article explains how to use the RFX function calls that make up the body of your **DoFieldExchange** override.

The RFX global functions exchange data between columns on the data source and field data members in your recordset. Normally you use ClassWizard to write the RFX function calls in your recordset's **DoFieldExchange** member function. This article describes the functions briefly and shows the data types for which RFX functions are available. Technical Note 43 under MFC in Books Online describes how to write your own RFX functions for additional data types.

RFX Function Syntax

Each RFX function takes three parameters (and some take an optional fourth or fifth parameter):

- A pointer to a **CFieldExchange** object. You simply pass along the *pFX* pointer passed to **DoFieldExchange**.

- The name of the column as it appears on the data source.

- The name of the corresponding field data member or parameter data member in the recordset class.

- (Optional) In some of the functions, the maximum length of the string or array being transferred. This defaults to 255 bytes, but you might want to change it. The maximum size is based on the maximum size of a **CString** object—**INT_MAX** (2,147,483,647) bytes—but you will probably encounter driver limits before that size.

- (Optional) In the **RFX_Text** function, you sometimes use a fifth parameter to specify the data type of a column.

For more information, see the RFX functions under Macros and Globals in the *Class Library Reference*. For an example of when you might make special use of the parameters, see the article Recordset: Obtaining SUMs and Other Aggregate Results (ODBC).

RFX Data Types

The class library supplies RFX functions for transferring many different data types between the data source and your recordsets. The following list summarizes the RFX functions by data type. In cases where you must write your own RFX function calls, select from these functions by data type.

Function	Data Type
RFX_Bool	BOOL
RFX_Byte	BYTE
RFX_Binary	CByteArray
RFX_Double	double
RFX_Single	float
RFX_Int	int
RFX_Long	long
RFX_LongBinary	CLongBinary
RFX_Text	CString
RFX_Date	CTime

For more information, see the RFX function documentation under Macros and Globals in the *Class Library Reference*. For information about how C++ data types map to SQL data types, see Table 1 in the article SQL: SQL and C++ Data Types (ODBC).

See Also   Record Field Exchange: How RFX Works, Recordset: Parameterizing a Recordset (ODBC), Recordset: Dynamically Binding Data Columns (ODBC), Recordset: Obtaining SUMs and Other Aggregate Results (ODBC)

In the *Class Library Reference*: **CRecordset, CFieldExchange**

Record Field Exchange: How RFX Works

This article explains the RFX process. This is a fairly advanced topic, covering:

- RFX and the recordset
- The RFX process

RFX and the Recordset

The recordset object's field data members, taken together, constitute an "edit buffer" that holds the selected columns of one record. When the recordset is first opened and is about to read the first record, RFX binds (associates) each selected column to the address of the appropriate field data member. When the recordset updates a record, RFX calls ODBC API functions to send an SQL **UPDATE** or **INSERT** statement to the driver. RFX uses its knowledge of the field data members to specify the columns to write.

The framework backs up the edit buffer at certain stages so it can restore its contents if necessary. RFX backs up the edit buffer before adding a new record and before editing an existing record. It restores the edit buffer in some cases—for example, after an **Update** call following **AddNew**, but not if you abandon a newly changed edit buffer by, for example, moving to another record before calling **Update**.

Besides exchanging data between the data source and the recordset's field data members, RFX manages binding parameters. When the recordset is opened, any parameter data members are bound in the order of the "?" placeholders in the SQL statement that **CRecordset::Open** constructs. For more information, see the article Recordset: Parameterizing a Recordset (ODBC).

Your recordset class's override of **DoFieldExchange** does all the work, moving data in both directions. Like dialog data exchange (DDX), RFX needs information about the data members of your class. ClassWizard provides the necessary information by writing a recordset-specific implementation of **DoFieldExchange** for you, based on the field data member names and data types you specify with the wizard.

The Record Field Exchange Process

This section describes the sequence of RFX events as a recordset object is opened and as you add, update, and delete records. Table 1 in the article Record Field Exchange: Using RFX shows the process at a high level, illustrating operations as a recordset is opened. Table 1 and Table 2 in this article show the process as RFX processes a **Move** command in the recordset and as RFX manages an update. During these processes, **DoFieldExchange** is called to perform many different operations. The **m_nOperation** data member of the **CFieldExchange** object determines which operation is requested. You might find it helpful to read the articles Recordset: How Recordsets Select Records (ODBC) and Recordset: How Recordsets Update Records (ODBC) before you read this material.

RFX: Initial Binding of Columns and Parameters

The following RFX activities occur, in the order shown, when you call a recordset object's **Open** member function:

- If the recordset has parameter data members, the framework calls **DoFieldExchange** to "bind" the parameters to parameter placeholders in the recordset's SQL statement string. A data type-dependent representation of the value of the parameter is used for each placeholder found in the **SELECT** statement. This occurs after the SQL statement is "prepared" but before it is executed. (For information about statement preparation, see the **::SQLPrepare** function in the ODBC *Programmer's Reference*.)

- The framework calls **DoFieldExchange** a second time to bind the values of selected columns to corresponding field data members in the recordset. This establishes the recordset object as an edit buffer containing the columns of the first record.

- The recordset executes the SQL statement and the data source selects the first record. The record's columns are loaded into the recordset's field data members.

Table 1 shows the sequence of RFX operations when you open a recordset.

Table 1   Sequence of RFX Operations During Recordset Open

Your operation	DoFieldExchange operation	Database/SQL operation
1. Open recordset.		
	2. Build an SQL statement.	
		3. Send the SQL.
	4. Bind parameter data member(s).	
	5. Bind field data member(s) to column(s).	
		6. ODBC does the move and fills in the data.
	7. Fix up the data for C++.	

Recordsets use ODBC's "prepared execution" to allow for fast requerying with the same SQL statement. For more information about prepared execution, see the ODBC SDK *Programmer's Reference*.

RFX: Scrolling

When you scroll from one record to another, the framework calls **DoFieldExchange** to replace the values previously stored in the field data members with values for the new record.

Table 2 shows the sequence of RFX operations when the user moves from record to record.

Table 2   Sequence of RFX Operations During Scrolling

Your operation	DoFieldExchange operation	Database/SQL operation
1. Call **MoveNext** or one of the other Move functions.		
		2. ODBC does the move and fills in the data.
	3. Fix up the data for C++.	

RFX: Adding New Records and Editing Existing Records

If you add a new record, the recordset operates as an edit buffer to build up the contents of the new record. As with adding records, editing records involves changing the values of the recordset's field data members. From the RFX perspective, the sequence is as follows:

1. Your call to the recordset's **AddNew** or **Edit** member function causes RFX to store the current edit buffer so it can be restored later.

2. **AddNew** or **Edit** prepares the fields in the edit buffer so RFX can detect changed field data members.

   Since a new record has no previous values to compare new ones with, **AddNew** sets the value of each field data member to a **PSEUDO_NULL** value. Later, when you call **Update**, RFX compares each data member's value with the **PSEUDO_NULL** value; if there's a difference, the data member has been set. (**PSEUDO_NULL** is not the same thing as a record column with a true Null value; nor is either the same as C++ **NULL**.)

   Unlike the **Update** call for **AddNew**, the **Update** call for **Edit** compares updated values with previously stored values rather than using **PSEUDO_NULL**. The difference is that **AddNew** has no previous stored values for comparison.

3. You directly set the values of field data members whose values you want to edit or that you want filled for a new record. (This can include calling **SetFieldNull**.)

4. Your call to **Update** checks for changed field data members, as described in step 2 (see Table 2). If none have changed, **Update** returns 0. If some field data members have changed, **Update** prepares and executes an SQL **INSERT** statement that contains values for all updated fields in the record.

5. For **AddNew**, **Update** concludes by restoring the previously stored values of the record that was current before the **AddNew** call. For **Edit**, the new, edited values remain in place.

Table 3 shows the sequence of RFX operations when you add a new record or edit an existing record.

Table 3   Sequence of RFX Operations During AddNew and Edit

Your operation	DoFieldExchange operation	Database/SQL operation
1. Call **AddNew** or **Edit**.		
	2. Back up the edit buffer.	
	3. For **AddNew**, mark field data members as "clean" and Null.	
4. Assign values to recordset field data members.		
5. Call **Update**.		
	6. Check for changed fields.	
	7. Build SQL **INSERT** statement for **AddNew** or **UPDATE** statement for **Edit**.	
		8. Send the SQL.
	9. For **AddNew**, restore the edit buffer to its backed-up contents. For **Edit**, delete the backup.	

RFX: Deleting Existing Records

When you delete a record, RFX sets all the fields to **NULL** as a reminder that the record is deleted and you must move off it. You won't need any other RFX sequence information.

See Also   ClassWizard

In the *Class Library Reference*: **CFieldExchange**, **CRecordset::DoFieldExchange**, Macros and Globals

Recordset (ODBC)

This article applies to the MFC ODBC classes. For DAO recordsets, see the article DAO Recordset.

A **CRecordset** object represents a set of records selected from a data source. The records can be from:

- A table
- A query
- A stored procedure that accesses one or more tables

An example of a recordset based on a table is "all customers," which accesses a Customer table. An example of a query is "all invoices for Joe Smith." An example of a recordset based on a stored procedure (sometimes called a predefined query) is "all of the delinquent accounts," which invokes a stored procedure in the back-end database. A recordset can join two or more tables from the same data source, but not from different data sources.

Note Some ODBC drivers support "views" of the database. A view in this sense is a query originally created with the SQL **CREATE VIEW** statement. AppWizard and ClassWizard don't currently support views, but it is possible to code this support yourself.

Recordset Capabilities

All recordset objects share the following capabilities:

- If the data source is not read-only, you can specify that your recordset be updatable, appendable, or read-only. If the recordset is updatable, you can choose either pessimistic or optimistic locking methods, provided the driver supplies the appropriate locking support. If the data source is read-only, the recordset will be read-only.
- You can call member functions to scroll through the selected records.
- You can filter the records to constrain which records are selected from those available.
- You can sort the records in ascending or descending order, based on one or more columns.
- You can parameterize the recordset in order to qualify the recordset selection at run time.

Snapshots and Dynasets

There are two principal kinds of recordsets: snapshots and dynasets, both supported by class **CRecordset**. Each shares the common characteristics of all recordsets, but each also extends the common functionality in its own specialized way. Snapshots provide a static view of the data and are useful for reports and other situations in which you want a view of the data as it existed at a particular time. Dynasets provide a dynamic view of the data and are necessary if you want records to reflect updates made by other users or via other recordsets in your own application (without having to "requery" or "refresh" the recordset, except that you must requery to see records added by other users). Both can be updatable or read-only.

CRecordset also allows for a third kind of recordset, a "forward-only recordset." If you do both of the following

- Pass the option **CRecordset::forwardOnly** as the *nOpenType* parameter of the **Open** member function

- Pass **CRecordset::readOnly** as the *dwOptions* parameter to **Open**

you get a recordset that doesn't allow updates or backward scrolling. Use this kind of recordset for less program overhead when you don't need backward scrolling. For example, you might use a forward-only recordset to migrate data from one data source to another, where you only need to move through the data in a forward direction.

Important   For information about ODBC driver requirements for dynaset support, see the article ODBC. For a list of ODBC drivers included in this version of Visual C++ and for information about obtaining additional drivers, see the article ODBC Driver List.

Your Recordsets

For every distinct table, view, or stored procedure you wish to access, you must define a class derived from **CRecordset**, normally with the help of ClassWizard. (The exception is a database join, in which one recordset represents columns from two or more tables.) When you declare a recordset class with ClassWizard, you also enable the record field exchange (RFX) mechanism. RFX simplifies transfer of data from the data source into your recordset and from your recordset to the data source, much as the dialog data exchange (DDX) mechanism does.

A recordset object gives you access to all the selected records. You scroll through the multiple selected records using **CRecordset** member functions, such as **MoveNext** and **MovePrev**. At the same time, a recordset object represents only one of the selected records, the "current record." You can examine the fields of the current record by declaring recordset class member variables that correspond to columns of the table or of the records that result from the database query. ClassWizard helps you declare these recordset class data members. You update a record by scrolling to it— making it the current record—and changing the values of these data members. For details about recordset data members, see the article Recordset: Architecture (ODBC).

The articles listed below explain the details of using recordset objects. The articles are listed in functional categories and a natural browse order to permit sequential reading.

Articles about the mechanics of opening, reading, and closing recordsets

- Recordset: Architecture (ODBC)
- Recordset: Declaring a Class for a Table (ODBC)
- Recordset: Creating and Closing Recordsets (ODBC)
- Recordset: Scrolling (ODBC)
- Recordset: Filtering Records (ODBC)
- Recordset: Sorting Records (ODBC)
- Recordset: Parameterizing a Recordset (ODBC)

Articles about the mechanics of modifying recordsets

- Recordset: Adding, Updating, and Deleting Records (ODBC)
- Recordset: Locking Records (ODBC)
- Recordset: Requerying a Recordset (ODBC)

Articles about somewhat more advanced techniques

- Recordset: Performing a Join (ODBC)
- Recordset: Declaring a Class for a Predefined Query (ODBC)
- Recordset: Dynamically Binding Data Columns (ODBC)
- Recordset: Working with Large Data Items (ODBC)
- Recordset: Obtaining SUMs and Other Aggregate Results (ODBC)

Articles about how recordsets work

- Recordset: How Recordsets Select Records (ODBC)
- Recordset: How Recordsets Update Records (ODBC)

See Also   Recordset: Declaring a Class for a Table (ODBC), ClassWizard: Creating a Recordset Class, Record Field Exchange (RFX), Transaction (ODBC)

Recordset: Architecture (ODBC)

This article applies to the MFC ODBC classes. For DAO recordsets, see the article DAO Recordset.

This article describes the data members that comprise the architecture of a recordset object:

- Field data members

- Parameter data members

- **m_nFields** and **m_nParams** data members

A Sample Class

When you use ClassWizard to declare a recordset class derived from **CRecordset**, the resulting class has the general structure shown in the following simple class:

```
class CCourse : CRecordset
{
    //{{AFX_FIELD(CCourse, CRecordset)
    CString m_strCourseID;
    CString m_strCourseTitle;
    //}}AFX_FIELD
    CString m_strIDParam;
};
```

At the beginning of the class, ClassWizard writes a set of field data members. When you create the class with ClassWizard, you must specify one or more field data members. If the class is parameterized, as the sample class is (with the data member m_strIDParam), you must manually add parameter data members. ClassWizard doesn't support adding parameters to a class.

Field Data Members

The most important members of your recordset class are the field data members. For each column you select from the data source, the class contains a data member of the appropriate data type for that column. For example, the sample class shown at the beginning of this article has two field data members, both of type **CString**, called m_strCourseID and m_strCourseTitle.

When the recordset selects a set of records, the framework automatically "binds" the columns of the current record (after the **Open** call, the first record is current) to the field data members of the object. That is, the framework uses the appropriate field data member as a buffer in which to store the contents of a record column.

As the user scrolls to a new record, the framework uses the field data members to represent the current record. The framework refreshes the field data members, replacing the previous record's values. The field data members are also used for updating the current record and for adding new records. As part of the process of updating a record, you specify the update values by assigning values directly to the appropriate field data member(s).

Parameter Data Members

If the class is "parameterized," it has one or more parameter data members. A parameterized class lets you base a recordset query on information obtained or calculated at run time.

Note You must manually place these data members outside the "//{{AFX_FIELD" comment brackets.

Typically, the parameter helps narrow the selection, as in the following example. Based on the sample class at the beginning of this article, the recordset object might execute the following SQL statement:

```
SELECT CourseID, CourseTitle FROM Course WHERE CourseID = ?
```

The "?" is a placeholder for a parameter value that you supply at run time. When you construct the recordset and set its m_strIDParam data member to "MATH101", the effective SQL statement for the recordset becomes:

```
SELECT CourseID, CourseTitle FROM Course WHERE CourseID = MATH101
```

By defining parameter data members, you tell the framework about parameters in the SQL string. The framework binds the parameter, which lets ODBC know where to get values to substitute for the placeholder. In the example, the resulting recordset contains only the record from the Course table with a CourseID column whose value is "MATH101". All specified columns of this record are selected. You can specify as many parameters (and placeholders) as you need.

Note MFC does nothing itself with the parameters—in particular, it doesn't perform a text substitution. Instead, MFC tells ODBC where to get the parameter; ODBC retrieves the data and performs the necessary parameterization.

Important The order of parameters is important. For details about this and more information about parameters, see the article Recordset: Parameterizing a Recordset (ODBC).

Using m_nFields and m_nParams

When ClassWizard writes a constructor for your class, it also initializes the **m_nFields** data member, which specifies the number of field data members in the class. If you add any parameters to your class, you must also add an initialization for the **m_nParams** data member, which specifies the number of parameter data members. The framework uses these values to work with the data members.

For more information and examples, see the article Record Field Exchange: Using RFX.

See Also Recordset: Declaring a Class for a Table (ODBC), Record Field Exchange

Recordset: Declaring a Class for a Table (ODBC)

This article applies to the MFC ODBC classes. For DAO recordsets, see the article DAO Recordset.

The most common recordset class opens a single table. To declare a recordset class for a single table, use ClassWizard. In ClassWizard, choose each column you want by naming a corresponding recordset field data member. See the article ClassWizard: Creating a Recordset Class.

Other uses for recordsets include:

- Joining two or more tables.
- Containing the results of a predefined query.

See Also Recordset: Creating and Closing Recordsets (ODBC), Recordset: Declaring a Class for a Predefined Query (ODBC), Recordset: Performing a Join (ODBC)

Recordset: Creating and Closing Recordsets (ODBC)

This article applies to the MFC ODBC classes. For DAO recordsets, see the article DAO Recordset.

To use a recordset, you must construct a recordset object, then call its **Open** member function to run the recordset's query and select records. When you finish with the recordset, you must close and destroy the object.

This article explains:

- When and how to create a recordset object.
- When and how you can qualify the recordset's behavior by parameterizing, filtering, sorting, or locking it.
- When and how to close a recordset object.

Creating Recordsets at Run Time

Before you can create recordset objects in your program, you must write application-specific recordset classes. For more information on this preliminary step, see the article ClassWizard: Creating a Recordset Class.

Open a dynaset or snapshot object when you need to select records from a data source. The type of object to create depends on what you need to do with the data in your application and on what your ODBC driver supports. For more information, see the articles Dynaset and Snapshot.

▶ **To open a recordset**

1 Construct an object of your **CRecordset**-derived class.

   You can construct the object on the heap or on the stack frame of a function.

2 Optionally modify the default recordset behavior. For the available options, see Setting Recordset Options.

3 Call the object's **Open** member function.

In the constructor, pass a pointer to a **CDatabase** object, or pass **NULL** to use a temporary database object that the framework will construct and open based on the connection string returned by the **GetDefaultConnect** member function. The **CDatabase** object may or may not already be connected to a data source.

The call to **Open** uses SQL to select records from the data source. The first record selected (if any) is the "current record." The values of this record's fields are stored in the recordset object's field data members. If any records were selected, both the **IsBOF** and **IsEOF** member functions return 0.

In your **Open** call, you can:

- Specify whether the recordset is a dynaset or snapshot. Recordsets open as snapshots by default. Or you can specify a forward-only recordset, which allows only forward scrolling, one record at a time.

  By default, a recordset uses the default type stored in the **CRecordset** data member **m_nDefaultType**. AppWizard or ClassWizard writes code to initialize **m_nDefaultType** to the recordset type you choose in the wizard. Rather than accepting this default, you can substitute another recordset type.

- Specify a string to replace the default SQL **SELECT** statement that the recordset constructs.

- Specify whether the recordset is read-only or append-only. Recordsets allow full updating by default, but you can limit that to adding new records only or you can disallow all updates.

The following example shows how to open a read-only snapshot object, of class CStudentSet, an application-specific class:

```
// Construct the snapshot object
CStudentSet rsStudent( NULL );
// Set options if desired, then open the recordset
if(!rsStudent.Open(CRecordset::snapshot, NULL, CRecordset::readOnly))
    return FALSE;
// Use the snapshot to operate on its records...
```

After you call **Open**, use the member functions and data members of the object to work with the records. In some cases, you may want to "requery" or "refresh" the recordset to include changes that have occurred on the data source. See the article Recordset: Requerying a Recordset (ODBC).

Tip The connect string you use during development might not be the same connect string that your eventual users need. For ideas about generalizing your application in this regard, see the article Data Source: Managing Connections (ODBC).

Setting Recordset Options

After you construct your recordset object but before you call **Open** to select records, you may want to set some options to control the recordset's behavior. For all recordsets, you can:

- Specify a filter to constrain record selection.
- Specify a sort order for the records.
- Specify parameters so you can select records using information obtained or calculated at run time.

You can also set the following option if conditions are right:

- If the recordset is updatable and supports locking options, specify the locking method used for updates.

Important To affect record selection, you must set these options before you call the **Open** member function.

Closing a Recordset

When you finish with your recordset, you must dispose of it and deallocate its memory.

▶ **To close a recordset**

1 Call its **Close** member function.

2 Destroy the recordset object.

  If you declared it on the stack frame of a function, the object is destroyed automatically when the object goes out of scope. Otherwise, use the **delete** operator.

Close frees the recordset's **HSTMT** handle. It doesn't destroy the C++ object.

See Also Recordset: Scrolling (ODBC), Recordset: Adding, Updating, and Deleting Records (ODBC), Dynaset, Snapshot

Recordset: Scrolling (ODBC)

This article applies to the MFC ODBC classes. For DAO recordsets, see the article DAO Recordset.

After you select records, you need to access each record to display it or to use it for calculations, report writing, and so on. Scrolling lets you move from record to record within your recordset.

This article explains:

- How to scroll from one record to another in a recordset.

- Under what circumstances scrolling is and is not supported.

Scrolling from One Record to Another

Recordsets provide several member functions you can use to "scroll" or move from one record to the next, previous, first, or last record, or move *n* records relative to the current position. You can also test whether you have scrolled beyond the first or the last record.

To determine whether scrolling is possible in your recordset, call the **CanScroll** member function of class **CRecordset**.

▶ **To scroll**

- Forward one record: call the **MoveNext** member function.

- Backward one record: call the **MovePrev** member function.

- To the first record in the recordset: call the **MoveFirst** member function.

- To the last record in the recordset: call the **MoveLast** member function.

- *N* records relative to the current position: call the **Move** member function.

▶ **To test for the end or the beginning of the recordset**

- Have you scrolled past the last record? Call the **IsEOF** member function.

- Have you scrolled past the first record (moving backward)? Call the **IsBOF** member function.

For example, the following code uses **IsBOF** and **IsEOF** to detect the limits of a recordset as the code scrolls through it in both directions.

```
// Open a snapshot; first record is current
CEnrollmentSet rsEnrollmentSet( NULL );
rsEnrollmentSet.Open( );
// Deal with empty recordset
if( rsEnrollmentSet.IsEOF( ) )
    return FALSE;
// Scroll to the end of the snapshot
while ( !rsEnrollmentSet.IsEOF( ) )
    rsEnrollmentSet.MoveNext( );
// Past last record, so no record is current
// Move to the last record
rsEnrollmentSet.MoveLast( );
// Scroll to beginning of the snapshot
while( !rsEnrollmentSet.IsBOF( ) )
    rsEnrollmentSet.MovePrev( );
// Past first record, so no record is current
rsEnrollmentSet.MoveFirst( );
// First record (if any) is current again
```

IsEOF returns a nonzero value if the recordset is positioned past the last record. **IsBOF** returns a nonzero value if the recordset is positioned past the first record (before all records). In either case, there is no current record to operate on. If you call **MovePrev** when **IsBOF** is already true, or call **MoveNext** when **IsEOF** is already true, the framework throws a **CDBException**.

Tip In the general case, where records may be deleted by you or by other users (other recordsets), check that both **IsEOF** and **IsBOF** return a nonzero value to detect an empty recordset.

When Scrolling Is Supported

As originally designed, SQL provided only forward scrolling, but ODBC extends scrolling capabilities. The available level of support for scrolling depends on the ODBC driver(s) your application will work with, your driver's ODBC API conformance level, and whether the ODBC Cursor Library is loaded into memory. For more information, see the articles ODBC and ODBC: The ODBC Cursor Library.

Tip You can control whether the cursor library is used. See the *bUseCursorLib* parameter to **CDatabase::Open**.

Note Unlike Microsoft Access and Microsoft Visual Basic, the MFC database classes don't provide a set of **Find** functions for locating the next (or previous) record that meets specified criteria.

See Also Recordset: Filtering Records (ODBC)

Recordset: Filtering Records (ODBC)

This article applies to the MFC ODBC classes. For DAO recordsets, see the article DAO Recordset.

This article explains how to "filter" a recordset so that it selects only a particular subset of the available records. For example, you might want to select only the class sections for a particular course, such as MATH101. A filter is a "search condition" defined by the contents of an SQL **WHERE** clause. When the framework appends it to the recordset's SQL statement, the **WHERE** clause constrains the selection.

You must establish a recordset object's filter after you construct the object but before you call its **Open** member function (or before you call the **Requery** member function for an existing recordset object whose **Open** member function has been called previously).

▶ To specify a filter for a recordset object

1 Construct a new recordset object (or prepare to call **Requery** for an existing object).

2 Set the value of the object's **m_strFilter** data member.

   The filter is a null-terminated string. It contains the contents of the SQL **WHERE** clause but not the keyword **WHERE**. For example, use

```
m_pSet->m_strFilter = "CourseID = 'MATH101'";
```

not

```
m_pSet->m_strFilter = "WHERE CourseID = 'MATH101'";
```

Note The literal string "MATH101" is shown with single quotation marks above. In the ODBC SQL specification, single quotes are used to denote a character string literal. Check your ODBC driver documentation for the quoting requirements of your DBMS in this situation. This syntax is also discussed further near the end of this article.

3 Set any other options you need, such as sort order, locking mode, or parameters. Specifying a parameter is especially useful. For information on parameterizing your filter, see the article Recordset: Parameterizing a Recordset (ODBC).

4 Call **Open** for the new object (or **Requery** for a previously opened object).

Tip Using parameters in your filter is potentially the most efficient method for retrieving records.

Tip Recordset filters are useful for joining tables and for using parameters based on information obtained or calculated at run time.

The recordset selects only those records that meet the search condition you specified. For example, to specify the course filter described above (assuming a variable strCourseID currently set, for instance, to "MATH101"), do the following:

```
// Using the recordset pointed to by m_pSet
// Set the filter
m_pSet->m_strFilter = "CourseID = " + strCourseID;
// Run the query with the filter in place
if( m_pSet->Open( snapshot, NULL, CRecordset::readOnly ) )
    // Use the recordset
```

The recordset contains records for all class sections for MATH101.

Notice how the filter string was set in the example above, using a string variable. This is the typical usage. But suppose you wanted to specify the literal value 100 for the course ID. The following code shows how to set the filter string correctly with a literal value:

```
m_strFilter = "StudentID = '100'";   // correct
```

Note the use of single quote characters; if you set the filter string directly, the filter string is *not*:

```
m_strFilter = "StudentID = 100";   // incorrrect for some drivers
```

The quoting shown above conforms to the ODBC specification, but some DBMSs may require other quote characters. For more information, see the article SQL: Customizing Your Recordset's SQL Statement (ODBC).

Note If you choose to override the recordset's default SQL string by passing your own SQL string to **Open**, you should not set a filter if your custom string has a **WHERE** clause. For more information about overriding the default SQL, see the article SQL: Customizing Your Recordset's SQL Statement (ODBC).

See Also Recordset: Sorting Records (ODBC), Recordset: How Recordsets Select Records (ODBC), Recordset: Parameterizing a Recordset (ODBC), Recordset: How Recordsets Update Records (ODBC), Recordset: Locking Records (ODBC)

Recordset: Sorting Records (ODBC)

This article applies to the MFC ODBC classes. For DAO recordsets, see the article DAO Recordset.

This article explains how to sort your recordset. You can specify one or more columns on which to base the sort, and you can specify ascending or descending order (**ASC** or **DESC**; **ASC** is the default) for each specified column. For example, if you specify two columns, the records are sorted first on the first column named, then on the second column named. An SQL **ORDER BY** clause defines a sort. When the framework appends the **ORDER BY** clause to the recordset's SQL query, the clause controls the selection's ordering.

You must establish a recordset's sort order after you construct the object but before you call its **Open** member function (or before you call the **Requery** member function for an existing recordset object whose **Open** member function has been called previously).

▸ **To specify a sort order for a recordset object**

1 Construct a new recordset object (or prepare to call **Requery** for an existing one).

2 Set the value of the object's **m_strSort** data member.

The sort is a null-terminated string. It contains the contents of the **ORDER BY** clause but not the keyword **ORDER BY**. For example, use:

```
recordset.m_strSort = "LastName DESC, FirstName DESC";
```

not

```
recordset.m_strSort = "ORDER BY LastName DESC, FirstName DESC";
```

3 Set any other options you need, such as a filter, locking mode, or parameters.

4 Call **Open** for the new object (or **Requery** for an existing object).

The selected records are ordered as specified. For example, to sort a set of student records in descending order by last name, then first name, do the following:

```
// Construct the recordset
CStudentSet rsStudent( NULL );
// Set the sort
rsStudent.m_strSort = "LastName DESC, FirstName DESC";
// Run the query with the sort in place
rsStudent.Open( );
```

The recordset contains all of the student records, sorted in descending order (Z to A) by last name, then by first name.

Note If you choose to override the recordset's default SQL string by passing your own SQL string to **Open**, do not set a sort if your custom string has an **ORDER BY** clause.

See Also Recordset: Parameterizing a Recordset (ODBC), Recordset: Filtering Records (ODBC)

Recordset: Parameterizing a Recordset (ODBC)

This article applies to the MFC ODBC classes. For DAO recordsets, see the article DAO Recordset.

Sometimes you'd like to be able to select records at run time, using information you've calculated or obtained from your end-user. Recordset parameters let you accomplish that goal.

This article explains:

- The purpose of a parameterized recordset.

- When and why you might want to parameterize a recordset.

- How to declare parameter data members in your recordset class.

- How to pass parameter information to a recordset object at run time.

Parameterized Recordsets

A parameterized recordset lets you pass parameter information at run time. This has two valuable effects:

- It may result in better execution speed.

- It lets you build a query at run time, based on information not available to you at design time, such as information obtained from your user or calculated at run time.

When you call **Open** to run the query, the recordset uses the parameter information to complete its **SQL SELECT** statement. You can parameterize any recordset.

When to Use Parameters

Typical uses for parameters include:

- Passing run-time arguments to a predefined query.

To pass parameters to a stored procedure, you must specify a complete custom ODBC **CALL** statement—with parameter placeholders—when you call **Open**, overriding the recordset's default SQL statement. See **CRecordset::Open** in the *Class Library Reference* and the articles SQL: Customizing Your Recordset's SQL Statement (ODBC) and Recordset: Declaring a Class for a Predefined Query (ODBC).

- Efficiently performing numerous requeries with different parameter information.

  For example, each time your end-user looks up information for a particular student in the student registration database, you can specify the student's name or ID as a parameter obtained from the user. Then, when you call your recordset's **Requery** member function, the query selects only that student's record.

  Your recordset's filter string, stored in **m_strFilter**, might look like this:

  ```
  "StudentID = ?"
  ```

  Suppose you obtain the student ID in the variable `strInputID`. When you set a parameter to `strInputID` (for example, the student ID 100) the value of the variable is bound to the parameter placeholder represented by the "?" in the filter string.

  Assign the parameter value as follows:

  ```
  strInputID = "100";
  ...
  m_strParam = strInputID;
  ```

  Note that you would *not* want to set up a filter string this way:

  ```
  m_strFilter = "StudentID = 100";   // 100 is incorrectly quoted
                                     // for some drivers
  ```

  For a discussion of how to use quotes correctly for filter strings, see the article Recordset: Filtering Records (ODBC).

  The parameter value is different each time you requery the recordset for a new student ID.

  Tip Using a parameter is more efficient than simply a filter. For a parameterized recordset, the database must process an SQL **SELECT** statement only once. For a filtered recordset without parameters, the **SELECT** statement must be processed each time you **Requery** with a new filter value.

For more information about filters, see the article Recordset: Filtering Records (ODBC).

Parameterizing Your Recordset Class

Before you create your recordset class, determine what parameters you need, what their data types are, and how the recordset will use them.

▶ **To parameterize a recordset class**

1 Run ClassWizard and create the class. See the article ClassWizard: Creating a Recordset Class.

2 Specify field data members for the recordset's columns.

3 After ClassWizard writes the class to a file in your project, go to the .H file and manually add one or more parameter data members to the class declaration. The addition might look something like the following example, part of a snapshot class designed to answer the query "Which students are in the senior class?"

```
class CStudentSet : public CRecordset
{
// Field/Param Data
    //{{AFX_FIELD(CStudentSet, CRecordset)
    CString m_strFirstName;
    CString m_strLastName;
    CString m_strStudentID;
    CString m_strGradYear;
    //}}AFX_FIELD
    CString m_strGradYrParam;
};
```

ClassWizard writes field data members inside the "//{{AFX_FIELD" comment brackets. You add your parameter data members outside the comment brackets. The convention is to append the word "Param" to each name.

4 Modify the **DoFieldExchange** member function definition in the .CPP file. Add an RFX function call for each parameter data member you added to the class. For information on writing your RFX functions, see the article Record Field Exchange: How RFX Works. Precede the RFX calls for the parameters with a single call to

```
pFX->SetFieldType( CFieldExchange::param );
// RFX calls for parameter data members
```

5 In the constructor of your recordset class, increment the count of parameters, **m_nParams**.

For information, see The Recordset Constructor in the article Record Field Exchange: Working with the Wizard Code.

6 When you write the code that creates a recordset object of this class, place a "?" (question mark) symbol in each place in your SQL statement string(s) where a parameter is to be replaced.

At run time, "?" placeholders are filled, in order, by the parameter values you pass. The first parameter data member set after the **SetFieldType** call replaces the first "?" in the SQL string, the second parameter data member replaces the second "?", and so on.

Important Parameter order is important: the order of RFX calls for parameters in your `DoFieldExchange` function must match the order of the parameter placeholders in your SQL string.

Tip The most likely string to work with is the string you specify (if any) for the class's **m_strFilter** data member, but some ODBC drivers may allow parameters in other SQL clauses.

Passing Parameter Values at Run Time

You must specify parameter values before you call **Open** (for a new recordset object) or **Requery** (for an existing one).

▶ **To pass parameter values to a recordset object at run time**

1 Construct the recordset object.

2 Prepare a string or strings, such as the **m_strFilter** string, containing the SQL statement, or part(s) of it. Put "?" placeholders where the parameter information is to go.

3 Assign a run-time parameter value to each parameter data member of the object.

4 Call the **Open** member function (or **Requery**, for an existing recordset).

For example, suppose you want to specify a filter string for your recordset using information obtained at run time. Assume you have constructed a recordset of class `CStudentSet` earlier—called `rsStudents`—and now want to requery it for a particular kind of student information.

```
// Set up a filter string with parameter placeholders
rsStudents.m_strFilter = "GradYear <= ?";
// Obtain or calculate parameter values to pass--simply assigned here
CString strGradYear = GetCurrentAcademicYear( );
// Assign the values to parameter data members
rsStudents.m_strGradYrParam = strGradYear;
// Run the query
if( !rsStudents.Requery( ) )
    return FALSE;
```

The recordset contains records for those students whose records meet the conditions specified by the filter, which was constructed from run-time parameters. In this case, the recordset contains records for all senior students.

Note If needed, you can set the value of a parameter data member to Null, using **SetFieldNull**. You can likewise check whether a parameter data member is Null, using **IsFieldNull**.

See Also Recordset: Adding, Updating, and Deleting Records (ODBC), Recordset: Filtering Records (ODBC), Recordset: How Recordsets Select Records (ODBC)

Recordset: Adding, Updating, and Deleting Records (ODBC)

This article applies to the MFC ODBC classes. For DAO recordsets, see the article DAO Recordset.

Note You can now add records in bulk more efficiently. For information, see the article **Recordset: Adding Records in Bulk (ODBC)**.

Updatable snapshots and dynasets allow you to add, edit (update), and delete records. This article explains:

- How to determine whether your recordset is updatable.
- How to add a new record.
- How to edit an existing record.
- How to delete a record.

For more information about how updates are carried out and how your updates appear to other users, see the article Recordset: How Recordsets Update Records (ODBC). Normally, when you add, edit, or delete a record, the recordset changes the data source immediately. You can instead batch groups of related updates into "transactions." If a transaction is in progress, the update doesn't become final until you "commit" the transaction. This allows you to "take back" or "roll back" the changes. For information about transactions, see the article Transaction (ODBC).

Table 1 summarizes the options available for recordsets with different update characteristics.

Table 1   Recordset Read/Update Options

Type	Read	Edit records	Delete records	Add new (append)
read-only	Y	N	N	N
append-only	Y	N	N	Y
fully updatable	Y	Y	Y	Y

Determining Whether Your Recordset is Updatable

A recordset object is updatable if the data source is updatable, and you opened the recordset as updatable. Its updatability also depends on the SQL statement you use, the capabilities of your ODBC driver, and whether the ODBC Cursor Library is in memory or not. You can't update a read-only recordset or data source.

▶ **To determine whether your recordset is updatable**

- Call the recordset object's **CanUpdate** member function.

   CanUpdate returns a nonzero value if the recordset is updatable.

By default, recordsets are fully updatable (you can perform **AddNew**, **Edit**, and **Delete** operations). But you can also use the **appendOnly** option to open updatable recordsets. A recordset opened this way allows only the addition of new records with **AddNew**. You can't edit or delete existing records. You can test whether a recordset is open only for appending by calling the **CanAppend** member function. **CanAppend** returns a nonzero value if the recordset is either fully updatable or open only for appending.

The following code shows how you might use **CanUpdate** for a recordset object called rsStudentSet:

```
if( !rsStudentSet.Open( ) )
    return FALSE;
if( !rsStudentSet.CanUpdate( ) )
{
    AfxMessageBox( "Unable to update the Student recordset." );
    return;
}
```

Caution When you prepare to update a recordset by calling **Update**, take care that your recordset includes all columns making up the primary key of the table (or all of the columns of any unique index on the table). In some cases, the framework can use only the columns selected in your recordset to identify which record in your table to update. Without all the necessary columns, multiple records may be updated in the table, possibly damaging the referential integrity of the table. In this case, the framework will throw exceptions when you call **Update**.

Adding a Record to a Recordset

You can add new records to a recordset if its **CanAppend** member function returns a nonzero value.

▶ **To add a new record to a recordset**

1 Make sure the recordset is appendable.

2 Call the recordset object's **AddNew** member function.

   AddNew prepares the recordset to act as an edit buffer. All field data members are set to the special value Null and marked as unchanged so only changed ("dirty") values will be written to the data source when you call **Update**.

3 Set the values of the new record's field data members.

   Assign values to the field data members. Those you don't assign will not be written to the data source.

4 Call the recordset object's **Update** member function.

   Update completes the addition by writing the new record to the data source. For what happens if you fail to call **Update**, see the article Recordset: How Recordsets Update Records (ODBC).

For information about how adding records works and about when added records are visible in your recordset, see the article Recordset: How AddNew, Edit, and Delete Work (ODBC).

The following example shows how to add a new record:

```
if( !rsStudent.Open( ) )
    return FALSE;
if( !rsStudent.CanAppend( ) )
    return FALSE;                      // no field values were set
rsStudent.AddNew( );
rsStudent.m_strName = strName;
rsStudent.m_strCity = strCity;
rsStudent.m_strStreet = strStreet;
if( !rsStudent.Update( ) )
{
    AfxMessageBox( "Record not added; no field values were set." );
    return FALSE;
}
```

For additional information, see Adding a Record in the article Recordset: How AddNew, Edit, and Delete Work.

Tip To cancel an **AddNew** or **Edit** call, simply make another call to **AddNew** or **Edit** or call **Move** with the **AFX_MOVE_REFRESH** parameter. Data members will be reset to their previous values and you will still be in **Edit** or **Add** mode.

Editing a Record in a Recordset

You can edit existing records if your recordset's **CanUpdate** member function returns a nonzero value.

▶ **To edit an existing record in a recordset**

1 Make sure the recordset is updatable.

2 Scroll to the record you want to update.

3 Call the recordset object's **Edit** member function.

   Edit prepares the recordset to act as an edit buffer. All field data members are marked so that the recordset can tell later whether they were changed. The new values for changed field data members are written to the data source when you call **Update**.

4 Set the values of the new record's field data members.

   Assign values to the field data members. Those you don't assign values will remain unchanged.

5 Call the recordset object's **Update** member function.

   Update completes the edit by writing the changed record to the data source. For what happens if you fail to call **Update**, see the article Recordset: How Recordsets Update Records (ODBC).

After you edit a record, the edited record remains the current record.

The following example shows an **Edit** operation. It assumes the user has moved to a record he or she wants to edit.

```
rsStudent.Edit( );
rsStudent.m_strStreet = strNewStreet;
rsStudent.m_strCity = strNewCity;
rsStudent.m_strState = strNewState;
rsStudent.m_strPostalCode = strNewPostalCode;
if( !rsStudent.Update( ) )
{
    AfxMessageBox( "Record not updated; no field values were set." );
    return FALSE;
}
```

For more information, see Editing an Existing Record in the article Recordset: How AddNew, Edit, and Delete Work.

Tip To cancel an **AddNew** or **Edit** call, simply make another call to **AddNew** or **Edit** or call **Move** with the **AFX_MOVE_REFRESH** parameter. Data members will be reset to their previous values and you will still be in **Edit** or **Add** mode.

Deleting a Record from a Recordset

You can delete records if your recordset's **CanUpdate** member function returns a nonzero value.

▶ **To delete a record**

1 Make sure the recordset is updatable.

2 Scroll to the record you want to update.

3 Call the recordset object's **Delete** member function.

Delete immediately marks the record as deleted, both in the recordset and on the data source.

Unlike **AddNew** and **Edit**, **Delete** has no corresponding **Update** call.

4 Scroll to another record.

Important After a **Delete** call, there is no current record and **IsDeleted** returns a nonzero value. An error occurs if you call **Delete** again, or another update operation, before you scroll to another record. Once you have scrolled off the record, MFC will skip over that record the next time you scroll to it.

The following example shows a **Delete** operation. It assumes the user has moved to a record he or she wants to delete. After **Delete** is called, it's important to move to a new record.

```
rsStudent.Delete( );
rsStudent.MoveNext( );
```

For more information about the effects of the **AddNew**, **Edit**, and **Delete** member functions, see the article Recordset: How Recordsets Update Records (ODBC).

See Also　Recordset: Locking Records (ODBC)

Recordset: Adding Records in Bulk (ODBC)

This article applies to the MFC ODBC classes. For DAO recordsets, see the article DAO Recordset.

The MFC **CRecordset** class has a new optimization (in both 16- and 32-bit versions) that improves efficiency when you're adding new records in bulk to a table.

A new option for the *dwOptions* parameter to the **CRecordset::Open** member function, **optimizeBulkAdd**, improves performance when you're adding multiple records consecutively without calling **Requery** or **Close**. Only those fields that are "dirty" prior to the first **Update** call are marked as "dirty" for subsequent **AddNew/Update** calls.

If you are using the database classes to take advantage of the **::SQLSetPos** ODBC API function for adding, editing, and deleting records, this optimization is unnecessary.

If the ODBC Cursor Library is loaded or the ODBC driver doesn't support adding, editing, and deleting via **::SQLSetPos**, this optimization should improve bulk add performance. To turn on this optimization, set the *dwOptions* parameter in the **Open** call for your recordset to :

```
appendOnly | optimizeBulkAdd
```

See Also　Recordset: Adding, Updating, and Deleting Records (ODBC), Recordset: Locking Records (ODBC)

Recordset: Locking Records (ODBC)

This article applies to the MFC ODBC classes. For DAO recordsets, see the article DAO Recordset.

This article explains:

- The kinds of record locking available.
- How to lock records in your recordset during updates.

When you use a recordset to update a record on the data source, your application can lock the record so no other user can update the record at the same time. The state of a record updated by two users at "the same time" is undefined unless the system can guarantee that two users can't update a record simultaneously.

Record-Locking Modes

The database classes provide two record-locking modes:

- Optimistic locking (the default)
- Pessimistic locking

Updating a record occurs in three steps:

1. You begin the operation by calling the **Edit** member function.
2. You change the appropriate fields of the current record.
3. You end the operation—and normally commit the update—by calling the **Update** member function.

Optimistic locking locks the record on the data source only during the **Update** call. If you use optimistic locking in a multiuser environment, the application should handle an **Update** failure condition. Pessimistic locking locks the record as soon as you call **Edit** and doesn't release it until you call **Update** (failures are indicated via the **CDBException** mechanism, not by a value of **FALSE** returned by **Update**). Pessimistic locking has a potential performance penalty for other users, since concurrent access to the same record may have to wait until completion of your application's **Update** process.

Locking Records in Your Recordset

If you want to change a recordset object's locking mode from the default, you must change the mode before you call **Edit**.

▶ **To change the current locking mode for your recordset**

- Call the **SetLockingMode** member function, specifying either **CRecordset::pessimistic** or **CRecordset::optimistic**.

The new locking mode remains in effect until you change it again or the recordset is closed.

Note   Relatively few ODBC drivers currently support pessimistic locking.

See Also   Recordset: Performing a Join (ODBC), Recordset: Adding, Updating, and Deleting Records (ODBC)

Recordset: Performing a Join (ODBC)

This article applies to the MFC ODBC classes. For DAO recordsets, see the article DAO Recordset.

This article explains:

- What a join is.
- How to perform a join of multiple tables.

What a Join Is

The join operation—a common data-access task—lets you work with data from more than one table using a single recordset object. Joining two or more tables yields a recordset that can contain columns from each table, but appears as a single table to your application. Sometimes the join uses all columns from all tables, but sometimes the SQL **SELECT** clause in a join uses only some of the columns from each table. The database classes support read-only joins but not updatable joins.

The key to a join operation is one or more columns that the tables have in common. For example, suppose there is a "CourseID" column in both the Course table and the Section table for an application such as the ENROLL tutorial. In the Course table, the CourseID column contains a unique ID value for each possible course. In the Section table, the CourseID column probably doesn't contain unique values, since each course usually has more than one section.

To select records containing columns from joined tables, you need the following items:

- A table list containing the names of all tables being joined.
- A column list containing the names of all participating columns. Columns with the same name but from different tables are qualified by the table name.
- A filter (SQL **WHERE** clause) that specifies the column(s) on which the tables are joined. This filter takes the form "Table1.KeyCol = Table2.KeyCol" and actually accomplishes the join. For the ENROLL example above, the filter is:

```
Course.CourseID = Section.CourseID
```

Performing the Join

The following procedure shows a join of two tables but can apply to joins of any number of tables (all on the same data source). The procedure involves first binding columns from multiple tables with ClassWizard, then directly modifying source code to complete the join.

Binding the Table Columns

▶ **To bind columns from both tables to a single recordset**

1 Use ClassWizard to create a recordset class for the join. In ClassWizard choose Data Sources to open the Data Sources dialog box and bind columns from the first table to recordset field data members.

See the article ClassWizard: Creating a Recordset Class.

2 Choose ClassWizard's Update Columns button to open the Data Sources dialog box a second time.

3 Select a data source and choose OK to close the Data Sources dialog box.

4 In the Tables dialog box, select the name of the second table and choose OK to close the dialog box.

5 Bind columns from the second table to additional recordset field data members.

If any column names from the second table duplicate column names from the first table, be sure to give the corresponding recordset field data members unique names. For example, if you're joining Instructor and Section tables, each table might contain a column named RoomNo; you might bind one column to `m_strInstrOffice` and the other to `m_strClassRoom`.

6 Close ClassWizard.

Modifying the Source Files

Once you create the recordset class with ClassWizard, you must customize two parts of the class code. First, edit the class's table list, then qualify any columns with the same name but from different tables. You'll need to edit the calls in your `DoFieldExchange` override to insert table names.

For example, the student registration database for the MFC Tutorial sample ENROLL contains Instructor and Section tables. The Instructor table contains the following columns:

- InstructorID
- Name
- RoomNo (the instructor's office)

The Section table contains the following columns:

- InstructorID
- Schedule
- RoomNo (where the class is held)
- SectionNo
- CourseID
- Capacity (maximum size of the section)

▶ To modify the recordset's table list

- Rewrite the recordset's `GetDefaultSQL` member function to return a string containing a comma-delimited list of table names.

For example, if your `CJoinSet` recordset joins a Course table to a Section table, you should rewrite your `GetDefaultSQL` function to look something like this:

```
CString CJoinSet::GetDefaultSQL()
{
    return "SECTION, INSTRUCTOR";
}
```

Tip As an alternative, you can pass a string containing a comma-delimited list of table names in the *lpszSQL* parameter when you call the recordset's **Open** member function. The string has the same form as the string returned in the example above.

▶ **To qualify columns with the same name from different tables**

- Edit the RFX function calls in the recordset's **DoFieldExchange** member function.

  For each duplicate column name, edit the second parameter in the RFX call to prefix a table name to the column name already there. Separate the table name and the column name with a period.

For example, because `CJoinSet` binds a `RoomNo` column from each table, you must modify the two RFX calls for these columns as shown in the following code:

```
void CJoinSet::DoFieldExchange(CFieldExchange* pFX)
{
    //{{AFX_FIELD_MAP(CJoinSet)
    SetFieldType(pFX, CFieldExchange::outputColumn);
    RFX_Text(pFX, "Section.RoomNo", m_strClassRoom);
    RFX_Text(pFX, "Instructor.RoomNo", m_strInstructorOffice);
    // ...
    //}}AFX_FIELD_MAP
}
```

In the second parameter of each RFX function call above, the name `RoomNo` is prefixed by the table name. The two items are separated by a period.

Setting the Join Conditions with a Filter

When you construct a `CJoinSet` object in your program, set its filter to specify which columns constitute the join. Then call the recordset's **Open** member function as shown in the following example, which joins the Instructor and Section tables on their common InstructorID column:

```
CJoinSet ssJoin( NULL );
ssJoin.m_strFilter = "Instructor.InstructorID = Section.InstructorID";
if( !ssJoin.Open( ) )
    return FALSE;        // recordset could not be opened
```

The filter supplies the connection between two columns that makes it possible to view two tables as if they were one.

You can join more than two tables in the same way by equating multiple pairs of columns, each pair joined by the SQL keyword **AND**.

See Also Recordset: Declaring a Class for a Predefined Query (ODBC), Recordset: Declaring a Class for a Table (ODBC), Recordset: Requerying a Recordset (ODBC)

Recordset: Declaring a Class for a Predefined Query (ODBC)

This article applies to the MFC ODBC classes. For DAO recordsets, see the article DAO Recordset.

This article explains how to create a recordset class for a predefined query (sometimes called a "stored procedure," as in Microsoft SQL Server).

Some database management systems (DBMSs) allow you to create a predefined query and call it from your programs like a function. The query has a name, may or may not take parameters, and may or may not return records. The procedure in this article describes how to call a predefined query that returns records (and perhaps takes parameters).

The database classes don't support updating predefined queries. The difference between a snapshot predefined query and a dynaset predefined query is not updatability but whether changes made by other users (or other recordsets in your program) are visible in your recordset.

Tip You don't need a recordset to call a predefined query that doesn't return records. Prepare the SQL statement as described below, but execute it by calling the **CDatabase** member function **ExecuteSQL**.

You can create a single recordset class to manage calling a predefined query, but you must do some of the work yourself. ClassWizard doesn't support creating a class specifically for this purpose.

▶ **To create a class for calling a predefined query (stored procedure)**

1 Use ClassWizard to create a recordset class for the table that contributes the most columns returned by the query. This gives you a head start.

2 Manually add field data members for any columns of any tables that the query returns but that ClassWizard didn't create for you. Add them outside the "//{{AFX_FIELD" comments.

For example, if the query returns three columns each from two additional tables, add six field data members (of the appropriate data types) to the class.

3 Manually add RFX function calls in the DoFieldExchange member function of the class, one corresponding to the data type of each added field data member.

Add these function calls outside the "//{{AFX_FIELD_MAP" comments. Immediately before these RFX calls, call **SetFieldType**, as shown here:

```
pFX->SetFieldType( CFieldExchange::outputColumn );
```

Note You must know the data types and the order of columns returned in the result set. The order of RFX function calls in DoFieldExchange must match the order of result set columns.

4 Manually add initializations for the new field data members in the recordset class constructor.

You must also increment the initialization value for the **m_nFields** data member. ClassWizard writes the initialization, but it only covers the field data members it adds for you. Put the increment statement outside the comment brackets. For example:

```
m_nFields += 6;
//{{AFX_FIELD(CDelinquents, CRecordset)
...
//}}AFX_FIELD
```

Some data types shouldn't be initialized here—for example, **CLongBinary** or byte arrays.

5 If the query takes parameters, add a parameter data member for each parameter, an RFX function call for each, and an initialization for each.

6 You must increment **m_nParams** for each added parameter, as you did **m_nFields** for added fields in step 4 above. See the article Recordset: Parameterizing a Recordset (ODBC) for details.

7 Manually write an SQL statement string with the following form:

```
{CALL proc-name [(? [, ?]...)]}
```

where **CALL** is an ODBC keyword, *proc-name* is the name of the query as it is known on the data source, and the "?" items are placeholders for the parameter values you supply to the recordset at run time (if any). The following example prepares a placeholder for one parameter:

```
CString mySQL = "{CALL Delinquent_Accts (?)}";
```

8 In the code that opens the recordset, first set the values of the recordset's parameter data members, then call the **Open** member function, passing your SQL string for the *lpszSQL* parameter. Or, instead, replace the string returned by the `GetDefaultSQL` member function in your class.

The following examples illustrate the procedure for calling a predefined query, named `Delinquent_Accts`, which takes one parameter for a sales district number. This query returns three columns: `Acct_No`, `L_Name`, `Phone`. All columns are from the Customers table.

The recordset below specifies field data members for the columns the query returns and a parameter for the sales district number requested at run time.

```
class CDelinquents : public CRecordset
{
// Field/Param Data
    //{{AFX_FIELD(CDelinquents, CRecordset)
    LONG m_lAcct_No;
    CString m_strL_Name;
    CString m_strPhone;
    //}}AFX_FIELD
    LONG m_lDistParam;
    // ...
};
```

This class declaration is as ClassWizard writes it, except for the m_lDistParam member added manually outside the "//{{AFX_FIELD" comment. Other members below the comments aren't shown here.

The next example shows the initializations for the data members in the CDelinquents constructor. You add the two lines outside the comment brackets.

```
CDelinquents::CDelinquents(CDatabase* pdb)
    : CRecordset(pdb)
{
    //{{AFX_FIELD_INIT(CDelinquents)
    m_lAcct_No = 0;
    m_strL_Name = "";
    m_strPhone = "";
    m_nFields = 3;
    //}}AFX_FIELD_INIT
    m_nParams = 1;
    m_lDistParam = 0;
}
```

Note the initializations for **m_nFields** and **m_nParams**. ClassWizard initializes **m_nFields**; you initialize **m_nParams**.

The next example shows the RFX functions in CDelinquents::DoFieldExchange:

```
void CDelinquents::DoFieldExchange(CFieldExchange* pFX)
{
//{{AFX_FIELD_MAP(CDelinquents)
    pFX->SetFieldType(CFieldExchange::outputColumn);
    RFX_Long(pFX, "Acct_No", m_lAcct_No);
    RFX_Text(pFX, "L_Name", m_strL_Name);
    RFX_Text(pFX, "Phone", m_strPhone);
//}}AFX_FIELD_MAP
    pFX->SetFieldType(CFieldExchange::param);
    RFX_Long(pFX, "Dist_No", m_lDistParam);
}
```

Besides making the RFX calls for the three returned columns, this code manages binding the parameter you pass at run time. The parameter is keyed to the Dist_No (district number) column.

The next example shows how to set up the SQL string and how to use it to open the recordset.

```
// Construct a CDelinquents recordset object
CDelinquents rsDel( NULL );
CString strSQL = "{CALL Delinquent_Accts (?)}"
// Specify a parameter value (obtained earlier from the user)
rsDel.m_lDistParam = lDistrict;
// Open the recordset and run the query
if( rsDel.Open( CRecordset::snapshot, strSQL ) )
    // Use the recordset ...
```

This code constructs a snapshot, passes it a parameter obtained earlier from the user, and calls the predefined query. When the query runs, it returns records for the specified sales district. Each record contains columns for the account number, customer's last name, and customer's phone number.

Tip You might want to handle a return value (output parameter) from a stored procedure. The MFC database classes don't support output parameters, but see the **::SQLProcedures** example code in the ODBC *Programmer's Reference* for information.

See Also Recordset: Requerying a Recordset (ODBC), Recordset: Declaring a Class for a Table (ODBC), Recordset: Performing a Join (ODBC)

Recordset: Requerying a Recordset (ODBC)

This article applies to the MFC ODBC classes. For DAO recordsets, see the article DAO Recordset.

This article explains how you can use a recordset object to "requery"—refresh—itself from the database, and when you might want to do that with the **Requery** member function.

The principal reasons for requerying a recordset are to:

- Bring the recordset up to date with respect to records added by you or by other users and records deleted by other users (those you delete are already reflected in the recordset).

- Refresh the recordset based on changing parameter values.

Bringing the Recordset Up to Date

Frequently you will want to requery your recordset object to bring it up to date. In a multiuser database environment, other users can make changes to the data during the life of your recordset. For more information about when your recordset reflects changes made by other users and when other users' recordsets reflect your changes, see the articles Recordset: How Recordsets Update Records (ODBC) and Dynaset.

Requerying Based on New Parameters

Another frequent—and equally important—use of **Requery** is to select a new set of records based on changing parameter values. For example, Step 2 in the ENROLL tutorial application illustrates using a combo box in a record view to select from a list of all available college courses. When the user selects a different course from the combo box, ENROLL requeries a Section table to select only those class sections for the course the user chose in the combo box. See the `CSectionForm::OnSelendokCourseList` member function in Requerying the CSectionSet Recordset in *Tutorials*.

Tip Query speed is probably significantly faster if you call **Requery** with changing parameter values than if you call **Open** again.

Requerying Dynasets vs. Snapshots

Because dynasets are meant to present a set of records with dynamic, up-to-date data, you'll want to requery dynasets often if you want to reflect other users' additions. Snapshots, on the other hand, are useful because you can safely rely on their static contents while you prepare reports, calculate totals, and so on. Still, you may sometimes want to requery a snapshot as well. In a multiuser environment, snapshot data may lose synchronization with the data source as other users change the database.

▶ **To requery a recordset object**

- Call the **Requery** member function of the object.

Alternatively, you can simply close and reopen the original recordset. In either case, the new recordset represents the current state of the data source.

For an example, see the article Record Views: Filling a List Box from a Second Recordset.

Tip To optimize **Requery** performance, avoid changing the recordset's filter or sort. Change only the parameter value before calling **Requery**.

If the **Requery** call fails, you can retry the call; otherwise, your application should terminate gracefully. A call to **Requery** or **Open** might fail for any of a number of reasons. Perhaps a network error occurs; or, during the call, after the existing data is released but before the new data is obtained, another user might get exclusive access; or the table on which your recordset depends could be deleted.

See Also Recordset: Dynamically Binding Data Columns (ODBC), Recordset: Creating and Closing Recordsets (ODBC)

Recordset: Dynamically Binding Data Columns (ODBC)

This article applies to the MFC ODBC classes. For DAO recordsets, see the article DAO Recordset.

Recordsets manage binding table columns that you specify at design time, but there are cases when you may want to bind columns that were unknown to you at design time. This article explains:

- When you might want to bind columns dynamically to a recordset.

- How to bind columns dynamically at run time.

When You Might Bind Columns Dynamically

At design time, ClassWizard creates recordset classes based on the known tables and columns on your data source. Databases can change between when you design them and later when your application uses those tables and columns at run time. You or another user might add or drop a table or add or drop columns from a table that your application's recordset relies upon. This probably isn't a concern for all data-access applications, but if it is for yours, how can you cope with changes in the database schema, other than by redesigning and recompiling? The purpose of this article is to answer that question.

This article describes the most common case in which you might bind columns dynamically—having begun with a recordset based on a known database schema, you want to handle additional columns at run time. The article further assumes that the additional columns map to **CString** field data members, the most common case, although suggestions are supplied to help you manage other data types.

With a small amount of extra code, you can:

- Determine what columns are available at run time.

- Bind additional columns to your recordset dynamically, at run time.

Your recordset still contains data members for the columns you knew about at design time. It also contains a small amount of extra code that dynamically determines whether any new columns have been added to your target table and, if so, binds these new columns to dynamically allocated storage (rather than to recordset data members).

This article doesn't cover other dynamic binding cases, such as dropped tables or columns. For those, you'll need to use ODBC API calls more directly. See the ODBC *Programmer's Reference*.

Example code for this article comes from the MFC Database samples DYNABIND and CATALOG.

How to Bind Columns Dynamically

To bind columns dynamically in a case like that of the DYNABIND example, you must know (or be able to determine) the names of the additional columns. You must also allocate storage for the additional field data members, specify their names and their types, and specify the number of columns you're adding.

The following discussion mentions two different recordsets. The first is the "main recordset" that selects records from the target table. The second is a special "column recordset" used to get information about the columns in your target table.

The General Process

At the most general level, you follow these steps:

1. Construct your main recordset object.

   Optionally, pass a pointer to an open **CDatabase** object, or be able to supply connection information to the column recordset in some other way.

2. Take steps to add columns dynamically.

   See the process described in Adding the Columns below.

3. Open your main recordset.

   The recordset selects records and uses record field exchange (RFX) to bind both the "static" columns (those mapped to recordset field data members) and the dynamic columns (mapped to extra storage that you allocate).

Adding the Columns

Dynamically binding added columns at run time requires the following steps:

1. Determine at run time what columns are in the target table. Extract from that information a list of the columns that have been added to the table since your recordset class was designed.

   A good approach is to use a "column recordset" class designed to query the data source for column information for the target table—such as column name, data type, and so on. The MFC Database sample CATALOG provides a recordset class called CColumns that you can use to build a list of the new columns' names.

2. Provide storage for the new field data members. Your main recordset class doesn't have field data members for unknown columns, so you must provide a place to store the names, result values, and possibly data type information (if the columns are of different data types).

   One approach is to build one or more dynamic lists: one for the new columns' names, another for their result values, and a third for their data types (if necessary). These lists, particularly the value list, provide the information and the necessary storage for binding. Figure 1 illustrates building the lists.

Figure 1   Building Lists of Columns to Bind Dynamically

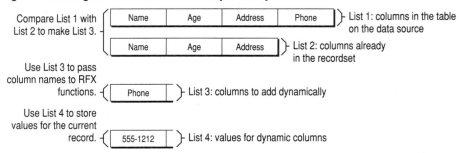

3. Add an RFX function call in your main recordset's `DoFieldExchange` function for each added column. These RFX calls do the work of fetching a record, including the additional columns, and binding the columns to recordset data members or to your dynamically supplied storage for them.

   One approach is to add a loop to your main recordset's `DoFieldExchange` function that loops through your list of new columns, calling the appropriate RFX function for each column in the list. On each RFX call, pass a column name from the column name list and a storage location in the corresponding member of the result value list.

Lists of Columns

The four lists you need to work with are named as follows throughout this article:

Current-Table-Columns (List 1 in Figure 1)   A list of the columns currently in the table on the data source. This list may or may not match the list of columns currently bound in your recordset.

Bound-Recordset-Columns (List 2 in Figure 1)   A list of the columns bound in your recordset (usually set up with ClassWizard). These columns already have RFX statements in your `DoFieldExchange` function.

Columns-To-Bind-Dynamically (List 3 in Figure 1)   A list of columns in the table but not in your recordset. These are the columns you want to bind dynamically.

Dynamic-Column-Values (List 4 in Figure 1)   A list containing storage for the values retrieved from the columns you bind dynamically. Elements of this list correspond to those in Columns-to-Bind-Dynamically, one to one.

Building Your Lists

With a general strategy in mind, you can turn to the details. The procedures in the rest of this article show you how to build the lists shown in Lists of Columns. The procedures guide you through:

- Determining the columns in your table at run time

- Determining the names of columns not in your recordset

- Providing dynamic storage for columns newly added to the table
- Dynamically adding RFX calls for new columns

Determining the Columns in Your Table at Run Time

First, build Current-Table-Columns (as in Figure 1): a list of the columns in the table on the data source.

▶ **To determine the columns in a table at run time (Current-Table-Columns)**

1 Borrow the files COLUMNST.H/.CPP from the MFC Database sample CATALOG. Add the .CPP file to your project and include the .H file as needed.

2 At run time, construct a "column recordset" object of class `CColumn`, passing a pointer to an open **CDatabase** object.

3 Before you call **Open**, set one or more of the column recordset's parameters. The following table describes what these parameters specify.

Parameter	Description
`m_strQualifierParam`	Identifies the database containing the table for ODBC. You usually don't need to specify this value.
`m_strOwnerParam`	Identifies the person who created the target table.
`m_strTableNameParam`	Identifies the target table by name.
`m_strColumnNameParam`	Identifies a specific column by name.

In most cases, you need only the table name, although some data sources might require the owner name as well, and others might require even more information. In addition to table name, use the column name parameter if you need information for only a single column in the table. For information about these parameters, see **::SQLColumns** in the ODBC SDK *Programmer's Reference*.

4 Call **Open** for the column recordset.

The recordset returns a record for each column in the specified table (unless you specify **m_strColumnNameParam**).

5 Construct Current-Table-Columns, a collection object that can hold **CString** objects.

For example, you might use a **CStringList**.

6 Scroll through the object's records, loading column names into Current-Table-Columns as you go.

This procedure results in a collection object that contains the names of all columns in a specified table. For example, Figure 1 shows Current-Table-Columns (List 1) with four elements. The last element is "Phone." For descriptions of the lists, see Lists of Columns.

Determining Which Table Columns Are Not in Your Recordset

Next, build a list (Bound-Recordset-Columns, as in List 2 in Figure 1) that contains a list of the columns already bound in your main recordset. Then build a list (Columns-to-Bind-Dynamically, derived from Current-Table-Columns and Bound-Recordset-Columns) that contains column names that are in the table on the data source but not in your main recordset.

▶ **To determine the names of columns not in the recordset (Columns-to-Bind-Dynamically)**

1 Build a list (Bound-Recordset-Columns) of the columns already bound in your main recordset.

One approach is to create Bound-Recordset-Columns at design time. You can visually examine the RFX function calls in the recordset's `DoFieldExchange` function to get these names. Then set up your list as an array initialized with the names.

For example, Figure 1 shows Bound-Recordset-Columns (List 2) with three elements. Bound-Recordset-Columns is missing the Phone column shown in Current-Table-Columns (List 1).

2 Compare Current-Table-Columns and Bound-Recordset-Columns to build a list (Columns-to-Bind-Dynamically) of the columns not already bound in your main recordset.

One approach is to loop through your list of columns in the table at run time (Current-Table-Columns) and your list of columns already bound in your recordset (Bound-Recordset-Columns) in parallel. Into Columns-to-Bind-Dynamically put any names in Current-Table-Columns that don't appear in Bound-Recordset-Columns.

For example, Figure 1 shows Columns-to-Bind-Dynamically (List 3) with one element: the Phone column found in Current-Table-Columns (List 1) but not in Bound-Recordset-Columns (List 2).

3 Build a list of Dynamic-Column-Values (as in List 4 in Figure 1) in which to store the data values corresponding to each column name stored in your list of columns to bind dynamically (Columns-to-Bind-Dynamically).

The elements of this list play the role of new recordset field data members. They are the storage locations to which the dynamic columns are bound. For descriptions of the lists, see Lists of Columns.

Providing Storage for the New Columns

Next, set up storage locations for the columns to be bound dynamically. The idea is to provide a list element in which to store each column's value. These storage locations parallel the recordset member variables, which store the normally bound columns.

▶ **To provide dynamic storage for new columns (Dynamic-Column-Values)**

- Build Dynamic-Column-Values, parallel to Columns-to-Bind-Dynamically, to contain the value of the data in each column.

  For example, Figure 1 shows Dynamic-Column-Values (List 4) with one element: a **CString** object containing the actual phone number for the current record: "555-1212".

  In the most common case, Dynamic-Column-Values has elements of type **CString**. If you're dealing with columns of varying data types, you'll need a list that can contain elements of a variety of types.

The result of the preceding procedures is two main lists: Columns-to-Bind-Dynamically containing the names of columns and Dynamic-Column-Values containing the values in the columns for the current record.

Tip If the new columns aren't all of the same data type, you might want an extra parallel list containing items that somehow define the type of each corresponding element in the column list. (You can use the values **AFX_RFX_BOOL**, **AFX_RFX_BYTE**, and so on, for this if you wish. These constants are defined in AFXDB.H.) Choose a list type based on how you represent the column data types.

Adding RFX Calls to Bind the Columns

Finally, arrange for the dynamic binding to occur by placing RFX calls for the new columns in your `DoFieldExchange` function.

▶ **To dynamically add RFX calls for new columns**

- In your main recordset's `DoFieldExchange` member function, add code that loops through your list of new columns (Columns-to-Bind-Dynamically). In each loop, extract a column name from Columns-to-Bind-Dynamically and a result value for the column from Dynamic-Column-Values. Pass these items to an RFX function call appropriate to the data type of the column. For descriptions of the lists, see Lists of Columns.

In the common case, in your **RFX_Text** function calls you extract **CString** objects from the lists, as in the following lines of code, where Columns-to-Bind-Dynamically is a **CStringList** called `m_listName` and Dynamic-Column-Values is a **CStringList** called `m_listValue`:

```
RFX_Text( pFX,
            m_listName.GetNext( posName ),
            m_listValue.GetNext( posValue ));
```

For an example of such a loop added to `DoFieldExchange`, see `CSections::DoFieldExchange` in the file SECTIONS.CPP in the MFC Database sample DYNABIND. For more information about RFX functions, see Macros and Globals in the *Class Library Reference*.

Tip If the new columns are of different data types, use a switch statement in your loop to call the appropriate RFX function for each type.

When the framework calls `DoFieldExchange` during the **Open** process to bind columns to the recordset, the RFX calls for the static columns bind those columns. Then your loop repeatedly calls RFX functions for the dynamic columns.

See the complete source code in the MFC Database sample DYNABIND.

See Also Recordset: Working with Large Data Items (ODBC)

Recordset: Working with Large Data Items (ODBC)

This article applies to both the MFC ODBC classes and the MFC DAO classes.

Note If you're using the MFC DAO classes, manage your large data items with class **CByteArray** rather than class **CLongBinary**.

Suppose your database can store large pieces of data, such as bitmaps (employee photographs, maps, pictures of products, OLE objects, and so on). This kind of data is often referred to as a Binary Large Object (or BLOB) because:

- Each field value is large.
- Unlike numbers and other simple data types, it has no predictable size.
- The data is formless from the perspective of your program.

This article explains what support the database classes provide for working with such objects.

Managing Large Objects

Recordsets have two ways to solve the special difficulty of managing binary large objects. You can use class **CByteArray**, or you can use class **CLongBinary**. In general, **CByteArray** is the preferred way to manage large binary data.

CByteArray requires more overhead than **CLongBinary** but is more capable, as described in The CByteArray Class, following. **CLongBinary** is described briefly in The CLongBinary Class later in this chapter.

For detailed information about using **CByteArray** to work with large data items, see Technical Note 45.

The CByteArray Class

CByteArray is one of the MFC collection classes. A **CByteArray** object stores a dynamic array of bytes—the array can grow if needed. The class provides fast access by index, as with built-in C++ arrays. **CByteArray** objects can be serialized and dumped for diagnostic purposes. The class supplies member functions for getting and setting specified bytes, inserting and appending bytes, and removing one byte or all bytes. These facilities make parsing the binary data easier. For example, if the binary object is an OLE object, you might have to work through some header bytes to reach the actual object.

Using CByteArray in Recordsets

By giving a field data member of your recordset the type **CByteArray**, you provide a fixed base from which RFX can manage the transfer of such an object between your recordset and the data source and through which you can manipulate the data inside the object. RFX needs a specific site for retrieved data, and you need a way to access the underlying data.

For detailed information about using **CByteArray** to work with large data items, see Technical Note 45.

The CLongBinary Class

A **CLongBinary** object is a simple shell around an **HGLOBAL** handle to a block of storage allocated on the heap. When it binds a table column containing a binary large object, RFX allocates the **HGLOBAL** handle when it needs to transfer the data to the recordset and stores the handle in the **CLongBinary** field of the recordset.

In turn, you use the **HGLOBAL** handle, **m_hData**, to work with the data itself, operating on it as you would on any handle data. This is where **CByteArray** adds capabilities.

Caution **CLongBinary** objects can't be used as parameters in function calls. In addition, their implementation, which calls **::SQLGetData**, necessarily slows scrolling performance for a scrollable snapshot. This may also be true when you use an **::SQLGetData** call yourself to retrieve dynamic schema columns.

See Also Recordset: Obtaining SUMs and Other Aggregate Results (ODBC), Record Field Exchange

Recordset: Obtaining SUMs and Other Aggregate Results (ODBC)

This article applies to the MFC ODBC classes. For DAO recordsets, see the article DAO Recordset.

This article explains how to obtain aggregate results using the following SQL keywords:

- **SUM** Calculates the total of the values in a column with a numeric data type.
- **MIN** Extracts the smallest value in a column with a numeric data type.
- **MAX** Extracts the largest value in a column with a numeric data type.
- **AVG** Calculates an average value of all the values in a column with a numeric data type.

- **COUNT**   Counts the number of records in a column of any data type.

You use these SQL functions to obtain statistical information about the records in a data source rather than to extract records from the data source. The recordset that is created usually consists of a single record (if all columns are aggregates) that contains a value. (There might be more than one record if you used a **GROUP BY** clause.) This value is the result of the calculation or extraction performed by the SQL function.

Tip   To add an SQL **GROUP BY** clause (and possibly a **HAVING** clause) to your SQL statement, append it to the end of **m_strFilter**. For example:

```
m_strFilter = "sales > 10 GROUP BY SALESPERSON_ID";
```

You can limit the number of records you use to obtain aggregate results by filtering and sorting the columns.

Caution   Some aggregation operators return a different data type from the column(s) over which they are aggregating.

- **SUM** and **AVG** may return the next larger data type (for example, calling with **int** returns **LONG** or **double**).

- **COUNT** usually returns **LONG** regardless of target column type.

- **MAX** and **MIN** return the same data type as the columns they calculate.

For example, ClassWizard creates `long m_lSales` to accommodate a Sales column, but you'll need to replace this with a `double m_dblSumSales` data member to accommodate the aggregate result. See the example that follows.

▶ **To obtain an aggregate result for a recordset**

1 Create a recordset containing the column(s) from which you want to obtain aggregate results.

2 Modify the DoFieldExchange function for the recordset. Replace the string representing the column name (the second argument of the RFX function call(s)) with a string representing the aggregation function on the column. For example, replace

```
RFX_Long(pFX, "Sales", m_lSales);
```

with

```
RFX_Double(pFX, "Sum(Sales)", m_dblSumSales)
```

3 Open the recordset. The result of the aggregation operation will be left in `m_dblSumSales`.

Note ClassWizard actually assigns data member names without Hungarian prefixes. For example, the wizard would produce `m_Sales` for a Sales column, rather than the `m_lSales` name used earlier for illustration.

If you're using a **CRecordView** class to view the data, you'll have to change the DDX function call to display the new data member value; in this case, changing it from

```
DDX_FieldText(pDX, IDC_SUMSALES, m_pSet->m_lSales, m_pSet);
```

to

```
DDX_FieldText(pDX, IDC_SUMSALES, m_pSet->m_dblSumSales, m_pSet);
```

See Also Recordset: How Recordsets Select Records (ODBC)

Recordset: How Recordsets Select Records (ODBC)

This article applies to the MFC ODBC classes. For DAO recordsets, see the article DAO Recordset.

This article explains:

- Your role and your options in selecting records.
- How a recordset constructs its SQL statement and selects records.
- What you can do to customize the selection.

Recordsets select records from a data source through an ODBC driver by sending SQL statements to the driver. The SQL sent depends on how you design and open your recordset class.

Your Options in Selecting Records

Table 1 shows your options in selecting records.

Table 1 How and When You Can Affect a Recordset

When you ...	You can ...
Declare your recordset class with ClassWizard...	Specify which table to select from.
	Specify which columns to include.
	See ClassWizard: Creating a Recordset Class.
Complete your recordset class implementation...	Override member functions such as **OnSetOptions** (advanced) to set application-specific options or to change defaults. Specify parameter data members if you want a parameterized recordset.

Table 1   How and When You Can Affect a Recordset *(cont.)*

When you ...	You can ...
Construct a recordset object (before you call **Open**) and then...	Specify a search condition (possibly compound) for use in a **WHERE** clause that filters the records. See Recordset: Filtering Records (ODBC).
	Specify a sort order for use in an **ORDER BY** clause that sorts the records. See Recordset: Sorting Records (ODBC).
	Specify parameter values for any parameters you added to the class. See Recordset: Parameterizing a Recordset (ODBC).
Run the recordset's query by calling **Open**...	Specify a custom SQL string to replace the default SQL string set up by ClassWizard. See **CRecordset::Open** in the *Class Library Reference* and SQL: Customizing Your Recordset's SQL Statement (ODBC).
Call **Requery** to requery the recordset with the latest values on the data source...	Specify new parameters, filter, or sort. See Recordset: Requerying a Recordset (ODBC).

How a Recordset Constructs Its SQL Statement

When you call a recordset object's **Open** member function, **Open** constructs an SQL statement using some or all of the following ingredients:

- The *lpszSQL* parameter passed to **Open**. If not **NULL**, this parameter specifies a custom SQL string, or part of one. The framework parses the string. If the string is an SQL **SELECT** statement or an ODBC **CALL** statement, the framework uses the string as the recordset's SQL statement. If the string does not begin with "SELECT" or "{CALL", the framework uses what's supplied to construct an SQL **FROM** clause.

- The string returned by **GetDefaultSQL**. By default, this is the name of the table you specified for the recordset in ClassWizard, but you can change what the function returns. The framework calls **GetDefaultSQL**—if the string doesn't begin with "SELECT" or "{CALL", it is assumed to be a table name, which is used to construct an SQL string.

- The field data members of the recordset, which are to be bound to specific columns of the table. The framework binds record columns to the addresses of these members, using them as buffers. The framework determines the correlation of field data members to table columns from the RFX function calls in the recordset's **DoFieldExchange** member function.

- The filter for the recordset, if any, contained in the **m_strFilter** data member. The framework uses this string to construct an SQL **WHERE** clause.

- The sort order for the recordset, if any, contained in the **m_strSort** data member. The framework uses this string to construct an SQL **ORDER BY** clause.

  Tip To use the SQL **GROUP BY** clause (and possibly the **HAVING** clause), append the clause(s) to the end of your filter string.

- The values of any parameter data members you specify for the class. You set parameter values just before you call **Open** or **Requery**. The framework binds the parameter values to "?" placeholders in the SQL string. At compile time, you specify the string with placeholders; at run time, the framework fills in the details based on the parameter values you pass.

Open constructs an SQL **SELECT** statement from these ingredients. See Customizing the Selection for details about how the framework uses the ingredients.

After constructing the statement, **Open** sends the SQL to the ODBC Driver Manager (and the ODBC Cursor Library if it is in memory), which sends it on to the ODBC driver for the specific DBMS. The driver communicates with the DBMS to carry out the selection on the data source and fetches the first record. The framework loads the record into the field data members of the recordset.

You can use a combination of these techniques to open tables and to construct a query based on a join of multiple tables. With additional customization, you can call predefined queries (stored procedures), select table columns not known at design time and bind them to recordset fields, or perform most other data-access tasks. Tasks you can't accomplish by customizing recordsets can still be accomplished by calling ODBC API functions or directly executing SQL statements with **CDatabase::ExecuteSQL**.

Customizing the Selection

Besides supplying a filter, a sort order, or parameters, you can take the following actions to customize your recordset's selection:

- Pass a custom SQL string in *lpszSQL* when you call **Open** for the recordset. Anything you pass in *lpsqSQL* takes precedence over what the **GetDefaultSQL** member function returns.

  See the article SQL: Customizing Your Recordset's SQL Statement (ODBC). That article describes the kinds of SQL statements (or partial statements) you can pass to **Open** and what the framework does with them.

  Note If the custom string you pass does not begin with "SELECT" or "{CALL", MFC assumes it contains a table name. This also applies to the next bulleted item below.

- Alter the string that ClassWizard writes in your recordset's **GetDefaultSQL** member function. Edit the function's code to change what it returns. By default, ClassWizard writes a **GetDefaultSQL** function that returns a single table name.

  You can have **GetDefaultSQL** return any of the items that you can pass in the *lpszSQL* parameter to **Open**. If you don't pass a custom SQL string in *lpszSQL*, the framework uses the string that **GetDefaultSQL** returns. At a minimum, **GetDefaultSQL** must return a single table name. But you can have it return multiple table names, a full **SELECT** statement, an ODBC **CALL** statement, and so on. For a list of what you can pass to *lpszSQL*—or have **GetDefaultSQL** return —see the article SQL: Customizing Your Recordset's SQL Statement (ODBC).

If you're performing a join of two or more tables, rewrite **GetDefaultSQL** to customize the table list used in the SQL **FROM** clause. See the article Recordset: Performing a Join (ODBC).

- Manually bind additional field data members, perhaps based on information you obtain about the schema of your data source at run time. You add field data members to the recordset class, RFX function calls for them to the **DoFieldExchange** member function, and initializations of the data members in the class constructor.

  See the article Recordset: Dynamically Binding Data Columns (ODBC).

- Override recordset member functions, such as **OnSetOptions**, to set application-specific options or to override defaults.

If you want to base the recordset on a complex SQL statement, you'll need to use some combination of these customization techniques. For example, perhaps you want to use SQL clauses and keywords not directly supported by recordsets, or perhaps you're joining multiple tables.

See Also Recordset: How Recordsets Update Records (ODBC), ODBC, SQL, Recordset: Filtering Records (ODBC), Recordset: Sorting Records (ODBC), Recordset: Locking Records (ODBC)

Recordset: How Recordsets Update Records (ODBC)

This article applies to the MFC ODBC classes. For DAO recordsets, see the article DAO Recordset.

Besides their ability to select records from a data source, recordsets can (optionally) update or delete the selected records or add new records. Three factors determine a recordset's updatability: whether the connected data source is updatable, the options you specify when you create a recordset object, and the SQL that is created.

Note The SQL upon which your **CRecordset** object is based can affect your recordset's updatability. For example, if your SQL contains a join or a **GROUP BY** clause, MFC sets the updatability to **FALSE**.

This article explains:

- Your role in recordset updating and what the framework does for you.
- The recordset as an "edit buffer" and the differences between dynasets and snapshots.

The article Recordset: How AddNew, Edit, and Delete Work (ODBC) describes the actions of these functions from the point of view of the recordset.

The article Recordset: More About Updates (ODBC) completes the recordset update story by explaining how transactions affect updates, how closing a recordset or scrolling affects updates in progress, and how your updates interact with the updates of other users.

Your Role in Recordset Updating

Table 1 shows your role in using recordsets to add, edit, or delete records, along with what the framework does for you.

Table 1   Recordset Updating: You and the Framework

You...	The framework...
Determine whether the data source is updatable (or appendable).	Supplies **CDatabase** member functions for testing the data source's updatability or appendability.
Open an updatable recordset (of any type).	
Determine whether the recordset is updatable by calling **CRecordset** update functions such as **CanUpdate** or **CanAppend**.	
Call recordset member functions to add, edit, and delete records.	Manages the mechanics of exchanging data between your recordset object and the data source.
Optionally, use transactions to control the update process.	Supplies **CDatabase** member functions to support transactions.

For more information about transactions, see the article Transaction (ODBC).

The Edit Buffer

Taken collectively, the field data members of a recordset serve as an "edit buffer" that contains one record—the current record. Update operations use this buffer to operate on the current record.

- When you add a record, the edit buffer is used to build a new record. When you finish adding the record, the record that was previously current becomes current again.

- When you update (edit) a record, the edit buffer is used to set the field data members of the recordset to new values. When you finish updating, the updated record is still current.

When you call **AddNew** or **Edit**, the current record is stored so it can be restored later as needed. When you call **Delete**, the current record is not stored but is marked as deleted, and you must scroll to another record.

Note The edit buffer plays no role in record deletion. When you delete the current record, the record is marked as deleted, and the recordset is "not on a record" until you scroll to a different record.

Dynasets and Snapshots

Dynasets refresh a record's contents as you scroll to the record. Snapshots are static representations of the records, so a record's contents are not refreshed unless you call **Requery**. To use all the functionality of dynasets, you must be working with an ODBC driver that conforms to the correct level of ODBC API support. For more information, see the articles ODBC and Dynaset.

See Also Recordset: How AddNew, Edit, and Delete Work (ODBC)

Recordset: How AddNew, Edit, and Delete Work (ODBC)

This article applies to the MFC ODBC classes. For DAO recordsets, see the article DAO Recordset.

This article explains how the **AddNew**, **Edit**, and **Delete** member functions of class **CRecordset** work. Topics covered include:

- How adding records works
- Visibility of added records
- How editing records works
- How deleting records works

As a supplement, you might want to read the article Record Field Exchange: How RFX Works, which describes the corresponding role of RFX in update operations.

Adding a Record

Adding a new record to a recordset involves calling the recordset's **AddNew** member function, setting the values of the new record's field data members, and calling the **Update** member function to write the record to the data source.

As a precondition for calling **AddNew**, the recordset must not have been opened as read-only. The **CanUpdate** and **CanAppend** member functions let you determine these conditions.

When you call **AddNew**:

1. The record in the edit buffer is stored, so its contents can be restored if the operation is canceled.

2. The field data members are flagged so it will be possible to detect changes in them later. The field data members are also marked "clean" (unchanged) and set to a Null.

After you call **AddNew**, the edit buffer represents a new, empty record, ready to be filled in with values. To do this, you manually set the values by assigning to them. Instead of specifying an actual data value for a field, you can call **SetFieldNull** to specify the value Null.

To commit your changes, you call **Update**.

When you call **Update** for the new record:

- If your ODBC driver supports the **::SQLSetPos** ODBC API function, MFC uses the function to add the record on the data source. With **::SQLSetPos**, MFC can add a record more efficiently because it doesn't have to construct and process an SQL statement.

  –or–

- If **::SQLSetPos** can't be used, MFC does the following:

1. If no changes are detected, **Update** does nothing and returns 0.

2. If there are changes, **Update** constructs an SQL **INSERT** statement. The columns represented by all dirty field data members are listed in the **INSERT** statement. To force a column to be included, call the **SetFieldDirty** member function:

   ```
   SetFieldDirty( &m_dataMember, TRUE );
   ```

3. **Update** commits the new record—the **INSERT** statement is executed and the record is committed to the table on the data source (and the recordset, if not a snapshot) unless a transaction is in progress (see How Transactions Affect Updates in the article Recordset: More About Updates).

4. The stored record is restored to the edit buffer. The record that was current before the **AddNew** call is current again regardless of whether the **INSERT** statement was successfully executed.

Tip For complete control of a new record, take the following approach: (a) set the values of any fields that will have values; (b) explicitly set any fields that will remain Null by calling **SetFieldNull** with a pointer to the field and the parameter **TRUE** (the default). If you want to ensure that a field is not written to the data source, call **SetFieldDirty** with a pointer to the field and the parameter **FALSE**, and do not modify the field's value. To determine whether a field is allowed to be Null, call **IsFieldNullable**.

Tip *Advanced*: To detect when recordset data members change value, MFC uses a **PSEUDO_NULL** value appropriate to each data type that you can store in a recordset. If you must explicitly set a field to the **PSEUDO_NULL** value and the field happens already to be marked Null, you must also call **SetFieldNull**, passing the address of the field in the first parameter and **FALSE** in the second parameter.

Visibility of Added Records

When is an added record visible to your recordset? Added records sometimes show up and sometimes aren't visible, depending on two things:

- What your driver is capable of
- What the framework can take advantage of

If your ODBC driver supports the **::SQLSetPos** ODBC API function, MFC uses the function to add records. With **::SQLSetPos**, added records are visible to any updatable MFC recordset. Without support for the function, added records are not visible, and you must call **Requery** to see them. Using **::SQLSetPos** is also more efficient.

Editing an Existing Record

Editing an existing record in a recordset involves scrolling to the record, calling the recordset's **Edit** member function, setting the values of the new record's field data members, and calling the **Update** member function to write the changed record to the data source.

As a precondition for calling **Edit**, the recordset must be updatable and on a record. The **CanUpdate** and **IsDeleted** member functions let you determine these conditions. The current record also must not already have been deleted, and there must be records in the recordset (both **IsBOF** and **IsEOF** return 0).

When you call **Edit**, the record in the edit buffer (the current record) is stored. The stored record's values are later used to detect whether any fields have changed.

After you call **Edit**, the edit buffer still represents the current record but is now ready to accept changes to the field data members. To change the record, you manually set the values of any field data members you want to edit. Instead of specifying an actual data value for a field, you can call **SetFieldNull** to specify the value Null. To commit your changes, you call **Update**.

Tip To get out of **AddNew** or **Edit** mode, call **Move** with the parameter **AFX_MOVE_REFRESH**.

As a precondition for calling **Update**, the recordset must not be empty and the current record must not have been deleted. **IsBOF**, **IsEOF**, and **IsDeleted** should all return 0.

When you call **Update** for the edited record:

- If your ODBC driver supports the **::SQLSetPos** ODBC API function, MFC uses the function to update the record on the data source. With **::SQLSetPos**, the driver compares your edit buffer with the corresponding record on the server, updating the record on the server if the two are different. With **::SQLSetPos**, MFC can update a record more efficiently because it doesn't have to construct and process an SQL statement.

−or−

- If **::SQLSetPos** can't be used, MFC does the following:

1. If there have been no changes, **Update** does nothing and returns 0.

2. If there are changes, **Update** constructs an SQL **UPDATE** statement. The columns listed in the **UPDATE** statement are based on the field data members that have changed.

3. **Update** commits the changes—executes the **UPDATE** statement—and the record is changed on the data source, but not committed if a transaction is in progress (see the article Transaction: Performing a Transaction in a Recordset (ODBC) for details about how the transaction affects the update). ODBC keeps a copy of the record, which also changes.

4. Unlike the process for **AddNew**, the **Edit** process does not restore the stored record. The edited record remains in place as the current record.

Caution   When you prepare to update a recordset by calling **Update**, take care that your recordset includes all columns making up the primary key of the table (or all of the columns of any unique index on the table, or enough columns to uniquely identify the row). In some cases, the framework can use only the columns selected in your recordset to identify which record in your table to update. Without all the necessary columns, multiple records may be updated in the table. In this case, the framework will throw exceptions when you call **Update**.

Tip   If you call **AddNew** or **Edit** after having called either function previously but before you call **Update**, the edit buffer is refreshed with the stored record, replacing the new or edited record in progress. This behavior gives you a way to abort an **AddNew** or **Edit** and begin a new one: if you determine that the record-in-progress is faulty, simply call **Edit** or **AddNew** again.

Deleting a Record

Deleting a record from a recordset involves scrolling to the record and calling the recordset's **Delete** member function. Unlike **AddNew** and **Edit**, **Delete** does not require a matching call to **Update**.

As a precondition for calling **Delete**, the recordset must be updatable and it must be on a record. The **CanUpdate**, **IsBOF**, **IsEOF**, and **IsDeleted** member functions let you determine these conditions.

When you call **Delete**:

- If your ODBC driver supports the **::SQLSetPos** ODBC API function, MFC uses the function to delete the record on the data source. Using **::SQLSetPos** is usually more efficient than using SQL.

  –or–

- If **::SQLSetPos** can't be used, MFC does the following:

1. The current record in the edit buffer is not backed up as in **AddNew** and **Edit**.

2. **Delete** constructs an SQL **DELETE** statement that will remove the record.

   The current record in the edit buffer is not stored as in **AddNew** and **Edit**.

3. **Delete** commits the deletion—executes the **DELETE** statement. The record is marked deleted on the data source and, if the record is a snapshot, in ODBC.

4. The deleted record's values are still in the field data members of the recordset, but the field data members are marked Null and the recordset's **IsDeleted** member function will return a nonzero value.

Important After deleting a record, you should scroll to another record to refill the edit buffer with the new record's data. It's an error to call **Delete** again, or to call **Edit**.

For information about the SQL statements used in update operations, see the article SQL.

See Also Recordset: More About Updates (ODBC), Record Field Exchange

Recordset: More About Updates (ODBC)

This article applies to the MFC ODBC classes. For DAO recordsets, see the article DAO Recordset.

This article explains:

- How other operations, such as transactions, affect updates.

- Your updates and those of other users.

- More about the **Update** and **Delete** member functions.

How Other Operations Affect Updates

Your updates are affected by transactions in effect at the time of the update, by closing the recordset before completing a transaction, and by scrolling before completing a transaction.

How Transactions Affect Updates

Beyond understanding how **AddNew**, **Edit**, and **Delete** work, it's important to understand how the **BeginTrans**, **CommitTrans**, and **Rollback** member functions of **CDatabase** work with the update functions of **CRecordset**.

By default, calls to **AddNew** and **Edit** affect the data source immediately when you call **Update**. **Delete** calls take effect immediately. But you can establish a transaction and execute a batch of such calls. The updates are not permanent until you commit them. If you change your mind, you can roll back the transaction instead of committing it.

Tip The MFC transaction model is, by design, rather restrictive. If it is too restrictive for your application, see Technical Note 47 under MFC in Books Online.

For more information about transactions, see the article Transaction (ODBC).

How Closing the Recordset Affects Updates

If you close a recordset, or its associated **CDatabase** object, with a transaction in progress (you haven't called **CommitTrans** or **Rollback**), the transaction is rolled back automatically. How Rollback Affects Transactions in the article Transaction: How Transactions Affects Updates (ODBC) describes the effect this has on **AddNew**, **Edit**, or **Delete** operations in progress.

How Scrolling Affects Updates

When you scroll in a recordset, the edit buffer is filled with each new current record (the previous record is not stored first). Scrolling skips over records previously deleted. If you scroll after an **AddNew** or **Edit** call without calling **Update**, **CommitTrans**, or **Rollback** first, any changes are lost (with no warning to you) as a new record is brought into the edit buffer. The edit buffer is filled with the record scrolled to, the stored record is freed, and no change occurs on the data source. This applies to both **AddNew** and **Edit**.

Your Updates and the Updates of Other Users

When you use a recordset to update data, your updates affect other users. Similarly, the updates of other users during the lifetime of your recordset affect you.

In a multiuser environment, other users can open recordsets that contain some of the same records you have selected in your recordset. Changes to a record before you retrieve it are reflected in your recordset. Dynasets retrieve a record each time you scroll to it, so dynasets reflect changes each time you scroll to a record. Snapshots retrieve a record the first time you scroll to it, so snapshots reflect only those changes that occur before you scroll to the record initially.

Records added by other users after you open the recordset don't show up in your recordset unless you requery. If your recordset is a dynaset, edits to existing records by other users do show up in your dynaset when you scroll to the affected record. If your recordset is a snapshot, edits don't show up until you requery the snapshot. If you want to see records added or deleted by other users in your snapshot, or records added by other users in your dynaset, call **Requery** to rebuild the recordset. (Note that the deletions of other users show up in your dynaset.) You may also call **Requery** to see records you add, but not to see your deletions.

Tip To force caching of an entire snapshot at once, call **MoveLast** immediately after you open the snapshot. Then call **MoveFirst** to begin working with the records. **MoveLast** is equivalent to scrolling over all the records, but it retrieves them all at once. Note, however, that this can lower performance and may not be required for some drivers.

The effects of your updates on other users are similar to their effects on you.

More About Update and Delete

This section provides additional information to help you work with **Update** and **Delete**.

Update Success and Failure

If **Update** succeeds, the **AddNew** or **Edit** mode ends. To begin an **AddNew** or **Edit** mode again, call **AddNew** or **Edit**.

If **Update** fails (returns **FALSE** or throws an exception), you remain in **AddNew** or **Edit** mode, depending on which function you called last. You can then do one of the following:

- Modify a field data member and try the **Update** again.

- Call **AddNew** to reset the field data members to Null, set the values of the field data members, then call **Update** again.

- Call **Edit** to reload the values that were in the recordset before the first call to **AddNew** or **Edit**, then set the values of the field data members, then call **Update** again. After a successful **Update** call (except after an **AddNew** call), the field data members retain their new values.

- Call **Move** (including **Move** with a parameter of **AFX_MOVE_REFRESH**, or 0), which flushes any changes and ends any **AddNew** or **Edit** mode in effect.

Update and Delete

This section applies to both **Update** and **Delete**.

On an **Update** or **Delete** operation, one and only one record should be updated. That record is the current record, which corresponds to the data values in the fields of the recordset. If for some reason no records are affected or more than one record is affected, an exception is thrown containing one of the following **RETCODE** values:

- **AFX_SQL_ERROR_NO_ROWS_AFFECTED**

- **AFX_SQL_ERROR_MULTIPLE_ROWS_AFFECTED**

When these exceptions are thrown, you remain in the **AddNew** or **Edit** state you were in when you called **Update** or **Delete**. Here are the most common scenarios in which you would see these exceptions. You're most likely to see:

- **AFX_SQL_ERROR_NO_ROWS_AFFECTED** when you're using optimistic locking mode and another user has modified the record in a way that prevents the framework from identifying the correct record to update or delete.

- **AFX_SQL_ERROR_MULTIPLE_ROWS_AFFECTED** when the table you're updating has no primary key or unique index, and you don't have enough columns in the recordset to uniquely identify a table row.

See Also   Recordset: How Recordsets Select Records (ODBC), Record Field Exchange, Transaction (ODBC), SQL, Exceptions: Database Exceptions

Record Views

To support form-based data-access applications, the class library provides class **CRecordView** and class **CDaoRecordView**. A "record view" is a form view object whose controls are mapped directly to the field data members of a recordset object (and indirectly to the corresponding columns in a query result or table on the data source). Like their base class **CFormView**, **CRecordView** and **CDaoRecordView** are based on a dialog template resource.

The material in this group of articles applies to both the ODBC-based and the DAO-based classes. Use **CRecordView** for ODBC and **CDaoRecordView** for DAO.

Topics covered in this article include:

- Uses for database forms
- Features of class record view classes
- Data exchange for record views
- Your role in working with a record view
- Designing and creating a record view

Form Uses

Forms are useful for a variety of data-access tasks:

- Data entry
- Read-only examination of data
- Updating data

Features of Record View Classes

You can do form-based data-access programming with class **CFormView**, but **CRecordView** and **CDaoRecordView** are generally better classes to derive from. In addition to their **CFormView** features, **CRecordView** and **CDaoRecordView**:

- Provide dialog data exchange (DDX) between the form controls and the associated recordset object.
- Handle Move First, Move Next, Move Previous, and Move Last commands for navigating through the records in the associated recordset object.
- Update changes to the current record when the user moves to another record.

For more information about navigation, see the article Record Views: Supporting Navigation in a Record View.

Data Exchange for Record Views

When you use ClassWizard to map the controls in a record view's dialog template resource to the fields of a recordset, the framework manages exchanging data in both directions—from recordset to controls and from controls to recordset. Using the DDX mechanism means you don't have to write the code to transfer data back and forth yourself. Make a few connections in ClassWizard and you're done.

DDX for record views works in conjunction with:

- RFX for recordsets of class **CRecordset** (ODBC)

- DFX for recordsets of class **CDaoRecordset** (DAO)

Although they differ in implementation, at the interface level RFX and DFX are very similar data exchange mechanisms. The DAO version, DFX, is modeled closely on the earlier ODBC version, RFX. If you know how to use RFX, you know how to use DFX.

RFX and DFX move data between the current record of the data source and the field data members of a recordset object. DDX moves the data from the field data members to the controls in the form. This combination fills the form controls initially and as the user moves from record to record. It can also move updated data back to the recordset and then the data source.

Figure 1 shows the relationship between DDX and RFX (or DFX) for record views.

Figure 1   Dialog Data Exchange and Record Field Exchange

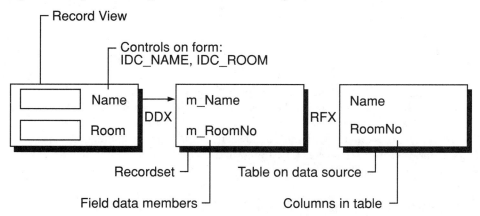

For more information about DDX, see Chapter 14, Working with Classes, in the *Visual C++ User's Guide*. For more information about RFX, see the article Record Field Exchange (RFX). For more information about DFX, see the article DAO Record Field Exchange (DFX).

Your Role in Working with a Record View

Table 1 shows what you typically must do to work with a record view and what the framework does for you.

Table 1   Working with a Record View: You and the Framework

You...	The framework...
Use the Visual C++ dialog editor to design the form.	The dialog editor makes it easy to create a dialog template resource with controls.
Use ClassWizard to create classes derived from **CRecordView** and **CRecordset** or from **CDaoRecordView** and **CDaoRecordset**.	ClassWizard writes the classes for you.
Use ClassWizard to map record view controls to recordset field data members.	Provides DDX between the controls and the recordset fields.
	Provides default command handlers for Move First, Move Last, Move Next, and Move Previous commands from menus or toolbar buttons.
	Updates changes to the data source.
[Optional] Write code to fill list boxes or combo boxes or other controls with data from a second recordset.	
[Optional] Write code for any special validations.	
[Optional] Write code to add or delete records.	

Form-based programming is only one approach to working with a database. For information on applications using some other user interface, or no user interface, see the articles MFC: Using Database Classes with Documents and Views and MFC: Using Database Classes Without Documents and Views. For alternative approaches to displaying database records, see classes **CListView** and **CTreeView** as well as the MFC Database sample DAOVIEW.

Designing and Creating a Record View

You can create your record view class with either AppWizard or ClassWizard. If you use AppWizard, the wizard creates the record view class and a dialog template resource for it (without controls). You must use the Visual C++ dialog editor to add controls to the dialog template resource. On the other hand, if you use ClassWizard, you must first create the dialog template resource in the dialog editor, then open ClassWizard and create the record view class.

This information applies to both **CRecordView** and **CDaoRecordView**.

▶ **To create your record view with AppWizard**

- See the article AppWizard: Database Support.

▶ **To design your form**

- See Chapter 6, Using the Dialog Editor, in the *Visual C++ User's Guide*.

▶ **To create your record view class with ClassWizard**

- See the article ClassWizard: Creating a Database Form.

Tip For an example of an application with multiple record views on a database, see the ENROLL tutorial application, Step 4. The step is described in MFC Tutorial sample ENROLL.

The following articles explain additional details of using record views:

- Record Views: Supporting Navigation in a Record View
- Record Views: Using a Record View
- Record Views: Filling a List Box from a Second Recordset

See Also Record Views: Supporting Navigation in a Record View, AppWizard: Database Support, ClassWizard: Creating a Database Form, ClassWizard: Mapping Form Controls to Recordset Fields, Recordset (ODBC)

Record Views: Supporting Navigation in a Record View

This article explains how to support movement from record to record in your record view. The article covers:

- Command handling for record scrolling commands.
- User-interface update handlers for scrolling commands.

The information in this article applies to both **CRecordView** (ODBC) and **CDaoRecordView** (DAO).

Command Handlers for Record Scrolling

Classes **CRecordView** and **CDaoRecordView** provide default command handling for the following standard commands:

- **ID_RECORD_MOVE_FIRST**
- **ID_RECORD_MOVE_LAST**
- **ID_RECORD_MOVE_NEXT**
- **ID_RECORD_MOVE_PREV**

The **OnMove** member function of classes **CRecordView** and **CDaoRecordView** provides default command handling for all four commands, which move from record to record. As these commands are issued, RFX (or DFX) loads the new record into the recordset's fields and DDX moves the values into the record form's controls. (For information about RFX, see the article Record Field Exchange (RFX).) For information about DFX, see the article DAO Record Field Exchange (DFX).

Important Be sure to use these standard command IDs for any user-interface objects associated with the standard record navigation commands.

User-Interface Updating for Record Views

CRecordView and **CDaoRecordView** also provide default user-interface update handlers for the navigation commands. These handlers automate enabling and disabling the user-interface objects—menu items and toolbar buttons. AppWizard supplies standard menus and, if you choose the AppWizard "Dockable Toolbar" option, a set of toolbar buttons for the commands. If you create a record view class with ClassWizard, you may want to add similar user-interface objects to your application.

▶ **To create menu resources with the menu editor**

* Using the information in Chapter 7, Using the Menu Editor, in the *Visual C++ User's Guide*, create your own menu with the same four commands.

▶ **To create toolbar buttons with the graphics editor**

* Using the information in Chapter 11, Using the Toolbar Editor, in the *Visual C++ User's Guide*, edit the toolbar resource to add toolbar buttons for your record navigation commands.

For an example of these steps, see Chapter 10, Constructing the User Interface, in *Tutorials*.

See Also Record Views: Using a Record View

Record Views: Using a Record View

This article explains how you might commonly customize the default code for record views that the wizard writes for you. Typically, you'll want to constrain the record selection with a filter or parameters, perhaps sort the records, or customize the SQL statement.

This information applies both to **CRecordView** (ODBC) and **CDaoRecordView** (DAO).

Using **CRecordView** or **CDaoRecordView** is much the same as using **CFormView**. The basic approach is to use the record view to display and perhaps update the records of a single recordset. Beyond that, you might want to use other recordsets as well, as discussed in the article Record Views: Filling a List Box from a Second Recordset.

Record View Code Created by AppWizard

ClassWizard (or AppWizard) overrides the view's **OnInitialUpdate** and **OnGetRecordset** member functions. After the framework creates the frame window, document, and view, it calls `OnInitialUpdate` to initialize the view. `OnInitialUpdate` obtains a pointer to the recordset from the document. A call to the base class **CView::OnInitialUpdate** function opens the recordset. The following code shows this process for a CRecordView—the code for a **CDaoRecordView** is similar:

```
void CSectionForm::OnInitialUpdate()
{
    m_pSet = &GetDocument()->m_sectionSet;
    CRecordView::OnInitialUpdate();
}
```

When the recordset opens, it selects records. **CRecordset::Open** or **CDaoRecordset::Open** makes the first record the current record, and DDX moves data from the recordset's field data members to the corresponding form controls in the view. For more information about RFX, see the article Record Field Exchange (RFX). For more information about DFX, see the article DAO Record Field Exchange (DFX). For more information about DDX, see Chapter 14, Working with Classes, in the *Visual C++ User's Guide*. For details of the document/view creation process, see Chapter 1, Using the Classes to Write Applications for Windows, in this book.

Important   You should give your end users the capability to "refresh" the record view controls from the recordset. Without this capability, if a user changes a control's value to an illegal value, he or she could be permanently stuck on the current record. To refresh the controls, you call the **CWnd** member function **UpdateData** with a parameter of **FALSE**. For an example, see Step 3 in the ENROLL tutorial—look at the `OnRecordAdd` member function in file SECTFORM.CPP. The tutorial begins in Chapter 30, Creating a Database Application, in *Tutorials*.

Changes You Might Make to the Default Code

ClassWizard writes a recordset class for you that simply selects all records in a single table. You'll often want to modify that behavior in one or more of the following ways:

- Set a filter and/or a sort order for the recordset. Do this in `OnInitialUpdate` after the recordset object is constructed but before its **Open** member function is called. See the articles Recordset: Filtering Records (ODBC) and Recordset: Sorting Records (ODBC) for details. For DAO, see the article DAO Queries: Filtering and Parameterizing Queries. For an example, see the `OnInitialUpdate` member function in the file SECTFORM.CPP in the MFC Tutorial sample ENROLL, Step 2.

- Parameterize the recordset. Specify the actual run-time parameter value after the filter. See the article Recordset: Parameterizing a Recordset (ODBC) or DAO Queries: Filtering and Parameterizing Queries for details.

- Pass a customized SQL string to the **Open** member function. For a discussion of what you can accomplish with this technique:

- For ODBC, see the article SQL: Customizing Your Recordset's SQL Statement (ODBC).

- For DAO, see the article DAO Queries.

See Also   Record Views: Filling a List Box from a Second Recordset

Record Views: Filling a List Box from a Second Recordset

By default, a record view is associated with a single recordset object, whose fields are mapped to the record view's controls. Sometimes you will want to put a list box or combo box control in your record view and fill it with values from a second recordset object. The user can use the list box to select a new category of information to display in the record view. This article explains how and when to do that.

Tip   Be aware that filling a combo box or list box from a data source might be slow. Take precautions against trying to fill a control from a recordset with a large number of records.

For example, the ENROLL tutorial in *Tutorials* uses a **CRecordView**, CSectionForm, to display information about sections of college courses. (For DAO tutorial purposes, follow the ODBC ENROLL tutorial except for Step 1.) ENROLL binds the form's controls to the field data members of a recordset of class CSectionSet. CSectionForm's combo box control is filled from a second recordset of class CCourseSet that contains a record for each course offered at the school. When the user selects a new course in the combo box, the record view requeries the CSectionSet recordset to get the sections for the selected course. See the MFC Tutorial sample ENROLL. Step 2 adds the combo box.

The model for this article, then, consists of a primary recordset that fills the controls of your form, while a secondary recordset fills a list box or combo box. Selecting a string from the list box causes your program to requery the primary recordset based on what was selected. The procedure below uses a combo box but applies equally to a list box.

▶ **To fill a list box or combo box from a second recordset**

1 Create the recordset object (**CRecordset** for ODBC, **CDaoRecordset** for DAO).

2 Obtain a pointer to the **CComboBox** object for the combo box control.

3 Empty the combo box of any previous contents.

4 Move through all records in the recordset, calling **CComboBox::AddString** for each string from the current record you want to add to the combo box.

5 Initialize the selection in the combo box.

The code in the `OnInitialUpdate` member function of class `CSectionForm` in the MFC Tutorial sample ENROLL illustrates the procedure. The following excerpt shows how the combo box is filled by extracting a course ID value from each record in the recordset pointed to by `pCourses`. (The code for DAO is quite similar.)

```
void CSectionForm::OnInitialUpdate()
{
    // ...

    // Fill the combo box with all of the courses
    CENROLLDoc* pDoc = GetDocument();
    if (!pDoc->m_courseSet.Open())
        return;

    // ...

    m_ctlCourseList.ResetContent();
    if (pDoc->m_courseSet.IsOpen())
    {
        while (!pDoc->m_courseSet.IsEOF() )
        {
            m_ctlCourseList.AddString(
                pDoc->m_courseSet.m_CourseID);
            pDoc->m_courseSet.MoveNext();
        }
    }
    m_ctlCourseList.SetCurSel(0);
}
```

This function uses a second recordset, `m_courseSet`, which contains a record for each course offered, and a **CComboBox** control, `m_ctlCourseList`, which is stored in the record view class.

The function gets `m_courseSet` from the document and opens it. Then it empties `m_ctlCourseList` and scrolls through `m_courseSet`. For each record, the function calls the combo box's **AddString** member function to add the course ID value from the record. Finally, the code sets the combo box's selection.

Registration

When a user wants to insert an OLE item into an application, OLE presents a list of object types to choose from. OLE gets this list from the system registration database, which contains information provided by all server applications. When a server registers itself, the entries it puts into the system registration database describe each type of object it supplies, file extensions, and the path to itself, among other information.

The framework and the OLE system DLLs use this registry to determine what types of OLE items are available on the system. The OLE system DLLs also use this registry to determine how to launch a server application when a linked or embedded object is activated.

This article describes what each server application needs to do when it is installed and each time it is executed.

For detailed information about the system registration database and the format of the .REG files used to update it, see the *OLE 2 Programmer's Reference, Volume 1*.

Server Installation

When you first install your server application, it should register all the types of OLE items that it supports. You can also have the server update the system registration database every time it executes as a stand-alone application. This keeps the registration database up-to-date if the server's executable file is moved.

Note MFC applications generated by AppWizard automatically register themselves when they are run as stand-alone applications.

If you want to register your application during installation, use the REGEDIT.EXE program. (In Windows 95, REGEDIT is in the Windows directory. In Windows NT, it is in the Windows System32 directory.) If you include a setup program with your application, you should have the setup program run "REGEDIT /S *appname*.REG". (The /S flag indicates "silent" operation; that is, do not display the dialog box reporting successful completion of the command.) Otherwise, instruct the user to run REGEDIT manually.

Important The REG file created by AppWizard does not include the complete path for the executable. Your installation program must either modify the .REG file to include the complete path to the executable or modify the PATH environment variable to include the installation directory.

REGEDIT merges the contents of the .REG text file into the registration database. To actually verify the database or to repair it, use the registry editor. Exercise care to avoid deleting essential OLE entries. (In Windows 95, the registry editor is REGEDIT.EXE. In Windows NT, it is REGEDT32.EXE.)

Server Initialization

When you create a server application with AppWizard, the wizard completes all initialization tasks for you automatically. This section describes what you must do if you write a server application manually.

When a server application is launched by a container application, the OLE system DLLs add the "/Embedding" option to the server's command line. A server application's behavior differs depending on whether it was launched by a container, so the first thing an application should do when it begins execution is check for the

"/Embedding" or "-Embedding" option on the command line. If this switch exists, you should load a different set of resources that show the server as being either in-place active or fully open. For more information, see the article Menus and Resources: Server Additions.

Your server application should also call its **CWinApp::RunEmbedded** function to parse the command line. If it returns a nonzero value, the application should not show its window because it has been run from a container application, not as a stand-alone application. This function updates the server's entry in the system registration database and calls the **RegisterAll** member function for you, performing instance registration.

When your server application is starting, you must ensure that it can perform instance registration. Instance registration does not add an entry to the registration database. Instead, it informs the OLE system DLLs that the server is active and ready to receive requests from containers. Perform instance registration of the server by calling the **ConnectTemplate** member function defined by **COleTemplateServer**. This connects the **CDocTemplate** object to the **COleTemplateServer** object.

The **ConnectTemplate** function takes three parameters: the server's **CLSID**, a pointer to the **CDocTemplate** object, and a flag indicating whether the server supports multiple instances. A mini-server must be able to support multiple instances; that is, it must be possible for multiple instances of the server to run simultaneously, one for each container. Consequently, you should pass **TRUE** for this flag when launching a mini-server.

If you are writing a mini-server, by definition it will always be launched by a container. You should still parse the command line to check for the "/Embedding" option. The absence of this option on the command line means that the user has tried to launch the mini-server as a stand-alone application. If this occurs, you should register the server with the system registration database and then display a message box informing the user to launch the mini-server from a container application.

See Also Servers

In the *Class Library Reference*: **CWinApp::RunAutomated**, **CWinApp::RunEmbedded**, **COleTemplateServer**

Result Set

If you're using the MFC ODBC classes, see the article Recordset (ODBC). If you're using the MFC DAO classes, see the article DAO: Recordset.

RFX

If you're using the MFC ODBC classes, see the article Record Field Exchange (RFX). The MFC DAO classes have a similar mechanism called DFX. See the article DAO Record Field Exchange (DFX).

Rollback

If you're using the MFC ODBC classes, see the article Transaction (ODBC). If you're using the MFC DAO classes, see the article DAO Workspace: Managing Transactions.

Schema

A database schema describes the current structure of the tables and database views in the database. In general, ClassWizard assumes that the schema for the table(s) accessed by a recordset will not change, but the database classes can deal with some schema changes, such as adding, reordering, or deleting unbound columns. If a table changes, you can "refresh" your recordset for the table using ClassWizard's Update Columns button and then recompile your application.

You can also supplement the code ClassWizard produces to deal with a database whose schema is not entirely known at compile time. For more information, see the article Recordset: Dynamically Binding Data Columns (ODBC).

To determine schema information with the MFC DAO classes, see the article DAO Tabledef: Examining a Database Schema at Run Time.

See Also SQL, Recordset (ODBC), ClassWizard

Serialization (Object Persistence)

This article explains the serialization mechanism provided in the Microsoft Foundation Class Library (MFC) to allow objects to persist between runs of your program.

"Serialization" is the process of writing or reading an object to or from a persistent storage medium, such as a disk file. MFC supplies built-in support for serialization in the class **CObject**. Thus, all classes derived from **CObject** can take advantage of **CObject**'s serialization protocol.

The basic idea of serialization is that an object should be able to write its current state, usually indicated by the value of its member variables, to persistent storage. Later, the object can be re-created by reading, or deserializing, the object's state from the storage. Serialization handles all the details of object pointers and circular references to objects that are used when you serialize an object. A key point is that the object itself is responsible for reading and writing its own state. Thus, for a class to be serializable, it must implement the basic serialization operations. As shown in the Serialization group of articles, it is easy to add this functionality to a class.

MFC uses an object of the **CArchive** class as an intermediary between the object to be serialized and the storage medium. This object is always associated with a **CFile** object, from which it obtains the necessary information for serialization, including the filename and whether the requested operation is a read or write. The object that performs a serialization operation can use the **CArchive** object without regard to the nature of the storage medium.

A **CArchive** object uses overloaded insertion (<<) and extraction (>>) operators to perform writing and reading operations. For more information, see Storing and Loading CObjects via an Archive in the article Serialization: Serializing an Object.

Note Do not confuse the **CArchive** class with general-purpose iostream classes, which are for formatted text only. The **CArchive** class is for binary-format serialized objects.

The following articles cover the two main tasks required for serialization:

- Serialization: Making a Serializable Class
- Serialization: Serializing an Object

The article Serialization: Serialization vs. Database Input/Output is part of the group of articles on database topics. The article describes when serialization is an appropriate input/output technique in database applications.

Serialization: Making a Serializable Class

Five main steps are required to make a class serializable. They are listed below and explained in the following sections:

1. Deriving your class from CObject (or from some class derived from **CObject**).
2. Using the **DECLARE_SERIAL** macro in the class declaration.
3. Overriding the **Serialize** member function.
4. Defining a constructor that takes no arguments.
5. Using the **IMPLEMENT_SERIAL** macro in the implementation file for your class.

If you call **Serialize** directly rather than through the >> and << operators of **CArchive**, the last three steps are not required for serialization.

Deriving Your Class from CObject and Using the DECLARE_SERIAL Macro

The basic serialization protocol and functionality are defined in the **CObject** class. By deriving your class from **CObject** (or from a class derived from **CObject**), as shown in the following declaration of class CPerson, you gain access to the serialization protocol and functionality of **CObject**.

The **DECLARE_SERIAL** macro is required in the declaration of classes that will support serialization, as shown here:

```
class CPerson : public CObject
{
    DECLARE_SERIAL( CPerson )
    // rest of declaration follows...
};
```

Overriding the Serialize Member Function

The **Serialize** member function, which is defined in the **CObject** class, is responsible for actually serializing the data necessary to capture an object's current state. The **Serialize** function has a **CArchive** argument that it uses to read and write the object data. The **CArchive** object has a member function, **IsStoring**, which indicates whether **Serialize** is storing (writing data) or loading (reading data). Using the results of **IsStoring** as a guide, you either insert your object's data in the **CArchive** object with the insertion operator (<<) or extract data with the extraction operator (>>).

Consider a class that is derived from **CObject** and has two new member variables, of types **CString** and **WORD**. The following class declaration fragment shows the new member variables and the declaration for the overridden **Serialize** member function:

```
class CPerson : public CObject
{
public:
    DECLARE_SERIAL( CPerson, )
    // empty constructor is necessary
    CPerson(){};

    CString m_name;
    WORD    m_number;

    void Serialize( CArchive& archive );

    // rest of class declaration
};
```

▶ **To override the Serialize member function**

1 Call your base class version of **Serialize** to make sure that the inherited portion of the object is serialized.

2 Insert or extract the member variables specific to your class.

The insertion and extraction operators interact with the archive class to read and write the data. The following example shows how to implement **Serialize** for the CPerson class declared above:

```
void CPerson::Serialize( CArchive& archive )
{
    // call base class function first
    // base class is CObject in this case
    CObject::Serialize( archive );

    // now do the stuff for our specific class
    if( archive.IsStoring() )
        archive << m_name << m_number;
    else
        archive >> m_name >> m_number;
}
```

You can also use the **CArchive::Read** and **CArchive::Write** member functions to read and write large amounts of untyped data.

Defining a Constructor with No Arguments

MFC requires a default constructor when it re-creates your objects as they are deserialized (loaded from disk). The deserialization process will fill in all member variables with the values required to re-create the object.

This constructor can be declared public, protected, or private. If you make it protected or private, you ensure that it will only be used by the serialization functions. The constructor must put the object in a state that allows it to be safely deleted if necessary.

Note If you forget to define a constructor with no arguments in a class that uses the **DECLARE_SERIAL** and **IMPLEMENT_SERIAL** macros, you will get a "no default constructor available" compiler warning on the line where the **IMPLEMENT_SERIAL** macro is used.

Using the IMPLEMENT_SERIAL Macro in the Implementation File

The **IMPLEMENT_SERIAL** macro is used to define the various functions needed when you derive a serializable class from **CObject**. You use this macro in the implementation file (.CPP) for your class. The first two arguments to the macro are the name of the class and the name of its immediate base class.

The third argument to this macro is a schema number. The schema number is essentially a version number for objects of the class. Use an integer greater than or equal to 0 for the schema number. (Don't confuse this schema number with database terminology.)

The MFC serialization code checks the schema number when reading objects into memory. If the schema number of the object on disk does not match the schema number of the class in memory, the library will throw a **CArchiveException**, preventing your program from reading an incorrect version of the object.

If you want your Serialize member function to be able to read multiple versions— that is, files written with different versions of the application—you can use the value **VERSIONABLE_SCHEMA** as an argument to the **DECLARE_SERIAL** macro. For usage information and an example, see the **GetObjectSchema** member function of class **CArchive**.

The following example shows how to use **IMPLEMENT_SERIAL** for a class, CPerson, that is derived from **CObject**:

```
IMPLEMENT_SERIAL( CPerson, CObject, 1 )
```

Once you have a serializable class, you can serialize objects of the class, as discussed in the article Serialization: Serializing an Object.

See Also In the *Class Library Reference*: **CArchive**

Serialization: Serializing an Object

The article Serialization: Making a Serializable Class shows how to make a class serializable. Once you have a serializable class, you can serialize objects of that class to and from a file via a **CArchive** object. This article explains:

- What a **CArchive** object is.
- Two ways to create a **CArchive**.
- How to use the **CArchive** << and >> operators.
- Storing and loading **CObjects** via an archive.

You can let the framework create the archive for your serializable document or explicitly create the **CArchive** object yourself. You can transfer data between a file and your serializable object by using the << and >> operators for **CArchive** or, in some cases, by calling the Serialize function of a **CObject**-derived class.

What Is a CArchive Object

A **CArchive** object provides a type-safe buffering mechanism for writing or reading serializable objects to or from a **CFile** object. Usually the **CFile** object represents a disk file; however, it can also be a memory file (**CSharedFile** object), perhaps representing the Clipboard.

A given **CArchive** object either stores (writes, serializes) data or loads (reads, deserializes) data, but never both. The life of a **CArchive** object is limited to one pass through writing objects to a file or reading objects from a file. Thus, two successively created **CArchive** objects are required to serialize data to a file and then deserialize it back from the file.

When an archive stores objects to a file, the archive attaches the **CRuntimeClass** name to the objects. Then, when another archive loads objects from a file to memory, the **CObject**-derived objects are dynamically reconstructed based on the **CRuntimeClass** of the objects. A given object may be referenced more than once as it is written to the file by the storing archive. The loading archive, however, will reconstruct the object only once. The details about how an archive attaches **CRuntimeClass** information to objects and reconstructs objects, taking into account possible multiple references, are described in Technical Note 2 under MFC in Books Online.

As data is serialized to an archive, the archive accumulates the data until its buffer is full. Then the archive writes its buffer to the **CFile** object pointed to by the **CArchive** object. Similarly, as you read data from an archive, it reads data from the file to its buffer and then from the buffer to your deserialized object. This buffering reduces the number of times a hard disk is physically read, thus improving your application's performance.

Two Ways to Create a CArchive Object

There are two ways to create a **CArchive** object:

- Implicit creation of a **CArchive** object via the framework
- Explicit creation of a **CArchive** object

Implicit Creation of a CArchive Object via the Framework

The most common, and easiest, way is to let the framework create a **CArchive** object for your document on behalf of the Save, Save As, and Open commands on the File menu.

Here is what the framework does when the user of your application issues the Save As command from the File menu:

1. Presents the Save As dialog box and gets the filename from the user.

2. Opens the file named by the user as a **CFile** object.

3. Creates a **CArchive** object that points to this **CFile** object. In creating the **CArchive** object, the framework sets the mode to "store" (write, serialize), as opposed to "load" (read, deserialize).

4. Calls the Serialize function defined in your **CDocument**-derived class, passing it a reference to the **CArchive** object.

Your document's Serialize function then writes data to the **CArchive** object, as explained shortly. Upon return from your Serialize function, the framework destroys the **CArchive** object and then the **CFile** object.

Thus, if you let the framework create the **CArchive** object for your document, all you have to do is implement the document's Serialize function that writes and reads to and from the archive. You also have to implement Serialize for any **CObject**-derived objects that the document's Serialize function in turn serializes directly or indirectly.

Explicit Creation of a CArchive Object

Besides serializing a document via the framework, there are other occasions when you may need a **CArchive** object. For example, you might want to serialize data to and from the Clipboard, represented by a **CSharedFile** object. Or, you may want to use a user interface for saving a file that is different from the one offered by the framework. In this case, you can explicitly create a **CArchive** object. You do this the same way the framework does, using the following procedure.

▶ **To explicitly create a CArchive object**

1 Construct a **CFile** object or an object derived from **CFile**.

2 Pass the **CFile** object to the constructor for **CArchive**, as shown in the following example:

```
CFile theFile;
theFile.Open(..., CFile::modeWrite);
CArchive archive(&theFile, CArchive::store);
```

The second argument to the **CArchive** constructor is an enumerated value that specifies whether the archive will be used for storing or loading data to or from the file. The `Serialize` function of an object checks this state by calling the **IsStoring** function for the archive object.

When you are finished storing or loading data to or from the **CArchive** object, close it. Although the **CArchive** (and **CFile**) objects will automatically close the archive (and file), it is good practice to explicitly do so since it makes recovery from errors easier. For more information about error handling, see the article Exceptions: Catching and Deleting Exceptions.

▶ **To close the CArchive object**

- The following example illustrates how to close the **CArchive** object:

```
archive.Close();
theFile.Close();
```

Using the CArchive << and >> Operators

CArchive provides << and >> operators for writing and reading simple data types as well as **CObject**s to and from a file.

▶ **To store an object in a file via an archive**

- The following example shows how to store an object in a file via an archive:

```
CArchive ar(&theFile, CArchive::store);
WORD wEmployeeID;
...
ar << wEmployeeID;
```

▶ **To load an object from a value previously stored in a file**

- The following example shows how to load an object from a value previously stored in a file:

```
CArchive ar(&theFile, CArchive::load);
WORD wEmployeeID;
...
ar >> wEmployeeID;
```

Usually, you store and load data to and from a file via an archive in the `Serialize` functions of **CObject**-derived classes, which you must have declared with the **DECLARE_SERIALIZE** macro. A reference to a **CArchive** object is passed to your `Serialize` function. You call the **IsLoading** function of the **CArchive** object to determine whether the `Serialize` function has been called to load data from the file or store data to the file.

The `Serialize` function of a serializable **CObject**-derived class typically has the following form:

```
void CPerson::Serialize(CArchive& ar)
{
    CObject::Serialize(ar);
    if (ar.IsStoring())
    {
        // TODO:  add storing code here
    }
    else
    {
    // TODO:  add loading code here
    }
}
```

The above code template is exactly the same as the one AppWizard creates for the `Serialize` function of the document (a class derived from **CDocument**). This code template helps you write code that is easier to review, because the storing code and the loading code should always be parallel, as in the following example:

```
void CPerson:Serialize(CArchive& ar)
{
    if (ar.IsStoring())
    {
        ar << m_strName;
        ar << m_wAge;
    }
    else
    {
        ar >> m_strName;
        ar >> m_wAge;
    }
}
```

The library defines **<<** and **>>** operators for **CArchive** as the first operand and the following data types and class types as the second operand:

CObject*	**SIZE** and **CSize**	**float**
WORD	**CString**	**POINT** and **CPoint**
DWORD	**BYTE**	**RECT** and **CRect**
double	**LONG**	**CTime** and **CTimeSpan**

Note Storing and loading **CObject**s via an archive requires extra consideration. For more information see Storing and Loading CObjects via an Archive below.

The **CArchive** **<<** and **>>** operators always return a reference to the **CArchive** object, which is the first operand. This enables you to chain the operators, as illustrated in the following example:

```
BYTE bSomeByte;
WORD wSomeWord;
DWORD wSomeDoubleWord;
...
ar << bSomeByte << wSomeWord << wSomeDoubleWord;
```

Storing and Loading CObjects via an Archive

Storing and loading **CObject**s via an archive requires extra consideration. In certain cases, you should call the Serialize function of the object, where the **CArchive** object is a parameter of the Serialize call, as opposed to using the << or >> operator of the **CArchive**. The important fact to keep in mind is that the **CArchive** >> operator constructs the **CObject** in memory based on **CRuntimeClass** information previously written to the file by the storing archive.

Therefore, whether you use the **CArchive** << and >> operators, versus calling Serialize, depends on whether you *need* the loading archive to dynamically reconstruct the object based on previously stored **CRuntimeClass** information. Use the Serialize function in the following cases:

- When deserializing the object, you know the exact class of the object beforehand.

- When deserializing the object, you already have memory allocated for it.

Caution If you load the object using the Serialize function, you must also store the object using the Serialize function. Don't store using the **CArchive** << operator and then load using the Serialize function, or store using the Serialize function and then load using **CArchive** >> operator.

The following example illustrates the cases:

```
class CMyObject : public CObject
{
    // ...Member functions
    CMyObject();
    virtual void Serialize( CArchive& ar );

// Implementation
protected:
    DECLARE_SERIAL( CMyObject )
};

class COtherObject : public CObject
{
    // ...Member functions
    COtherObject();
    virtual void Serialize( CArchive& ar );
```

```
// Implementation
protected:
    DECLARE_SERIAL( COtherObject )
};

class CCompoundObject : public CObject
{
    // ...Member functions
    CCompoundObject();
    virtual void Serialize( CArchive& ar );

// Implementation
protected:
    CMyObject m_myob;       // Embedded object
    COtherObject* m_pOther;     // Object allocated in constructor
    CObject* m_pObDyn;      // Dynamically allocated object
    //..Other member data and implementation

    DECLARE_SERIAL( CCompoundObject )
};

CCompoundObject::CCompoundObject()
{
    m_pOther = new COtherObject; // Exact type known and object already
                //allocated.
    m_pObDyn = NULL;    // Will be allocated in another member function
                // if needed, could be a derived class object.
}

void CCompundObject::Serialize( CArchive& ar )
{
    CObject::Serialize( ar );     // Always call base class Serialize.
    m_myob.Serialize( ar );    // Call Serialize on embedded member.
    m_pOther->Serialize( ar );     // Call Serialize on objects of known
                exact type.

    // Serialize dynamic members and other raw data
    if ( ar.IsStoring() )
    {
        ar << m_pObDyn;
        // Store other members
    }
    else
    {
        ar >> m_pObDyn; // Polymorphic reconstruction of persistent
                // object
                //load other members
    }
}
```

In summary, if your serializable class defines an embedded **CObject** as a member,
you should *not* use the **CArchive** << and >> operators for that object, but should call
the Serialize function instead. Also, if your serializable class defines a pointer to a

CObject (or an object derived from **CObject**) as a member, but constructs this other object in its own constructor, you should also call `Serialize`.

See Also   In the *Class Library Reference*: **CArchive**

Serialization: Serialization vs. Database Input/Output

This article explains when to use document objects and serialization for file-based input/output (I/O) and when other I/O techniques are appropriate—because the application reads and writes data on a per-transaction basis, as in database applications. If you don't use serialization, you also won't need the File Open, Save, and Save As commands. Topics covered include:

- Deciding how your application will handle input/output
- Handling the File menu in database applications

Deciding How to Handle Input/Output

Whether you use file-based I/O or not depends on how you respond to the questions in the following decision tree, which begins with the question:

Does the primary data in your application reside in a disk file?

1. Yes, the primary data resides in a disk file.

   Does the application read the whole file into memory on File Open and write the whole file back to disk on File Save?

2. Yes—this is the default MFC document case.

   Use **CDocument** serialization.

3. No—this is typically the case of transaction-based updating of the file.

   The MFC Advanced Concepts sample CHKBOOK is an example of this case. You update the file on a per-transaction basis and don't need **CDocument** serialization.

4. No, the primary data doesn't reside in a disk file.

   Does the data reside in an ODBC data source?

5. Yes, the data resides in an ODBC data source.

   Use MFC's database support. The standard MFC implementation for this case includes a **CDocument** object that stores a **CDatabase** object, as discussed in the article Database Overview. The application might also read and write an auxiliary file—the purpose of the AppWizard "both a database view and file support" option. In this case, you'd use serialization for the auxiliary file.

6. No, the data doesn't reside in an ODBC data source.

   Examples of this case: the data resides in a non-ODBC DBMS; the data is read via some other mechanism, such as OLE or DDE.

In such cases, you won't use serialization, and your application won't have Open and Save menu items. You might still want to use a **CDocument** as a "home base," just as an MFC ODBC application uses the document to store **CRecordset** objects. But you won't use the framework's default File Open/Save document serialization.

To support the Open, Save, and Save As commands on the File menu, the framework provides document serialization. Serialization reads and writes data, including objects derived from class **CObject**, to permanent storage, normally a disk file. Serialization is easy to use and serves many of your needs, but it may be inappropriate in many data-access applications. Data-access applications typically update data on a "per-transaction" basis. They update the records affected by the transaction rather than reading and writing a whole data file at once.

For general information about serialization, see the article Serialization (Object Persistence). For information on MFC sample programs, such as CHKBOOK, see Samples in Books Online.

The File Menu in an MFC Database Application

If you create an MFC database application and don't use serialization, how should you interpret the Open, Close, Save, and Save As commands on the File menu? While there are no style guidelines for this question, here are a few suggestions:

- Eliminate the File menu's Open command entirely.

- Interpret the Open command as "open database" and show the user a list of data sources your application recognizes.

- Interpret the Open command as, perhaps, "open profile." Retain Open for opening a serialized file, but use the file to store a serialized document containing "user profile" information, such as the user's preferences, including his or her login ID (optionally excluding the password) and the data source he or she most recently worked with.

AppWizard supports creating an application with no document-related File menu commands. Select the "A database view, without file support" option on the database options page.

To interpret a File menu command in a special way, you must override one or more command handlers, mostly in your **CWinApp**-derived class. For example, if you completely override **OnFileOpen** (which implements the **ID_FILE_OPEN** command) to mean "open database":

- Don't call the base class version of **OnFileOpen**, since you're completely replacing the framework's default implementation of the command.

- Use the handler instead to display a dialog box listing data sources. You can display such a dialog by calling **CDatabase::Open** with the parameter **NULL**.

This opens an ODBC dialog box that displays all available data sources on the user's machine.

- Because database applications typically don't save a whole document, you'll probably want to remove the Save and Save As implementations unless you use a serialized document to store profile information. Otherwise, you might implement the Save command as, for example, "commit transaction." See Technical Note 22 under MFC in Books Online for more information about overriding these commands.

Servers

A "server application" (or component application) creates OLE items (or components) for use by container applications. A "visual editing server application" also supports visual editing or in-place activation. Another form of OLE server is an automation server. Some server applications only support the creation of embedded items; others support the creation of both embedded and linked items. Some support linking only, although this is rare. All server applications must support activation by container applications when the user wants to edit an item. An application can be both a container and a server; that is, it can both incorporate data into its documents, and create data that can be incorporated as items into other applications' documents.

A "mini-server" is a special type of server application that can only be launched by a container. Microsoft Draw and Microsoft Graph are examples of mini-servers. A mini-server does not store documents as files on disk; instead, it reads its documents from and writes them to items in documents belonging to containers. As a result, a mini-server only supports embedding, not linking.

A "full-server" can be run either as a stand-alone application or launched by a container application. A full-server can store documents as files on disk. It can support embedding only, both embedding and linking, or only linking. The user of a container application can create an embedded item by choosing the Cut or Copy command in the server and the Paste command in the container. A linked item is created by choosing the Copy command in the server and the Paste Link command in the container. Alternately, the user can create an embedded or linked item using the Insert Object dialog box.

Table 1 summarizes characteristics of different types of servers:

Table 1   Server Characteristics

Type of server	Supports multiple instances	Items per document	Documents per instance
Mini-server	Yes	1	1
SDI full-server	Yes	1 (if linking is supported, 1 or more)	1
MDI full-server	No (not required)	1 (if linking is supported, 1 or more)	0 or more

A server application should support multiple containers simultaneously, in the event that more than one container wants to edit an embedded or linked item. If the server is an SDI application (or a mini-server with a dialog box interface), multiple instances of the server must be able to run simultaneously. This allows a separate instance of the application to handle each container request.

If the server is an MDI application, it can simply create a new MDI child window each time a container needs to edit an item. In this way, a single instance of the application can support multiple containers.

Your server application must tell the OLE system DLLs what to do if one instance of the server is already running when another container requests its services: whether it should launch a new instance of the server or direct all containers' requests to one instance of the server.

For more details on servers, see the following articles:

- Servers: Implementing a Server
- Servers: Implementing Server Documents
- Servers: Implementing In-Place Frame Windows
- Servers: Server Items
- Servers: User-Interface Issues

See Also Containers, Containers: Advanced Features, Menus and Resources, Registration, Automation Servers

Servers: Implementing a Server

This article explains the code AppWizard creates for a visual editing server application. If you are not using AppWizard, this article lists the areas where you must write code to implement a server application.

If you are using AppWizard to create a new server application, AppWizard provides a significant amount of server-specific code for you. If you are adding visual editing server functionality to an existing application, you must duplicate the code that AppWizard would have provided before adding the rest of the necessary server code.

The server code that AppWizard provides falls into several categories:

- Defining server resources:
  - The menu resource used when the server is editing an embedded item in its own window.
  - The menu and toolbar resources used when the server is active in place.

  For more information on these resources, see the article Menus and Resources: Server Additions.

- Defining an item class derived from **COleServerItem**. For further details on server items, see the article Servers: Server Items.

- Changing the base class of the document class to **COleServerDoc**. For further details, see the article Servers: Implementing Server Documents.

- Defining a frame-window class derived from **COleIPFrameWnd**. For further details, see the article Servers: Implementing In-Place Frame Windows.

- Creating an entry for the server application in the Windows registration database and registering the new instance of the server with the OLE system. For information on this topic, see the article Registration.

- Initializing and launching the server application. For information on this topic, see the article Registration.

For more information, see **COleServerItem**, **COleServerDoc**, and **COleIPFrameWnd** in the *Class Library Reference*.

See Also   Containers, Menus and Resources, Registration

Servers: Implementing Server Documents

This article explains the steps you must take to successfully implement a server document if you did not specify the OLE Server option in AppWizard.

▶ **To define a server document class**

1 Derive your document class from **COleServerDoc** instead of **CDocument**.

2 Create a server item class derived from **COleServerItem**.

3 Implement the **OnGetEmbeddedItem** member function of your server document class.

OnGetEmbeddedItem is called when the user of a container application creates or edits an embedded item. It should return an item representing the entire document. This should be an object of your **COleServerItem**-derived class.

4 Override the **Serialize** member function to serialize the contents of the document. You do not need to serialize the list of server items unless you are using them to represent the native data in your document. For more information, see Implementing Server Items in the article Servers: Server Items.

When a server document is created, the framework automatically registers the document with the OLE system DLLs. This allows the DLLs to identify the server documents.

For more information, see **COleServerItem** and **COleServerDoc** in the *Class Library Reference*.

See Also   Servers: Server Items, Servers: Implementing a Server, Servers: Implementing In-Place Frame Windows

Servers: Implementing In-Place Frame Windows

This article explains what you must do to implement in-place frame windows in your visual editing server application if you do not use AppWizard to create your server application. In place of following the procedure outlined in this article, you could use an existing in-place frame-window class from either an AppWizard-generated application or a sample provided with Visual C++.

▶ **To declare an in-place frame-window class**

1 Derive an in-place frame-window class from **COleIPFrameWnd**.

- Use the **DECLARE_DYNCREATE** macro in your class header file.

- Use the **IMPLEMENT_DYNCREATE** macro in your class implementation (.CPP) file. This allows objects of this class to be created by the framework.

2 Declare a **COleResizeBar** member in the frame-window class. This is needed if you want to support in-place resizing in server applications.

Declare an **OnCreate** message handler (using ClassWizard); call **Create** for your **COleResizeBar** member, if you've defined it.

3 If you have a toolbar, declare a **CToolBar** member in the frame-window class.

Override the **OnCreateControlBars** member function to create a toolbar when the server is active in place. For example:

```
BOOL CInPlaceFrame::OnCreateControlBars
    (CWnd* pWndFrame, CWnd* pWndDoc)
{
    // create toolbar on client's frame window
    if (!m_wndToolBar.Create(pWndFrame) ||
        !m_wndToolBar.LoadToolBar(IDR_PROJ_SRVR_IP))
    {
        TRACE("Failed to create toolbar\n");
        return FALSE;
    }

    // set this window as owner, so messages are
    // delivered to proper app
    m_wndToolBar.SetOwner(this);

    // enable docking for the toolbar
    m_wndToolBar.EnableDocking(CBRS_ALIGN_ANY);
    pWndFrame->EnableDocking(CBRS_ALIGN_ANY);
    pWndFrame->DockControlBar(&m_wndToolBar);

    // enable tooltips for the toolbar
    m_wndToolBar.SetBarStyle(CBRS_TOOLTIPS |
        CBRS_FLYBY | m_wndToolBar.GetBarStyle());

    return TRUE;
}
```

See the discussion of this code following step 5.

4 Include the header file for this in-place frame-window class in your main .CPP file.

5 In **InitInstance** for your application class, call the **SetServerInfo** function of the document template object to specify the resources and in-place frame window to be used in open and in-place editing.

The series of function calls in the **if** statement creates the toolbar from the resources the server provided. At this point, the toolbar is part of the container's window hierarchy. Because this toolbar is derived from **CToolBar**, it will pass its messages to its owner, the container application's frame window, unless you change the owner. That is why the call to **SetOwner** is necessary. This call changes the window where commands are sent to be the server's in-place frame window, causing the messages to be passed to the server. This allows the server to react to operations on the toolbar that it provides.

The ID for the toolbar bitmap should be the same as the other in-place resources defined in your server application. See the article Menus and Resources: Server Additions for details.

For more information, see the **COleIPFrameWnd**, **COleResizeBar**, and **CDocTemplate::SetServerInfo** entries in the *Class Library Reference*.

See Also   Servers: Implementing a Server, Servers: Implementing Server Documents, Servers: Server Items

Servers: Server Items

When a container launches a server so that a user can edit an embedded or linked OLE item, the server application creates a "server item." The server item, which is an object of a class derived from **COleServerItem**, provides an interface between the server document and the container application.

The **COleServerItem** class defines several overridable member functions that are called by OLE, usually in response to requests from the container. Server items can represent part of the server document or the entire document. When an OLE item is embedded in the container document, the server item represents the entire server document. When the OLE item is linked, the server item can represent a part of the server document or the whole document, depending on whether the link is to a part or to the whole.

In the HIERSVR sample, for example, the server-item class, **CServerItem**, has a member that is a pointer to an object of the class **CServerNode**. The **CServerNode** object is a node in the HIERSVR application's document, which is a tree. When the **CServerNode** object is the root node, the **CServerItem** object represents the whole document. When the **CServerNode** object is a child node, the **CServerItem** object represents a part of the document. See the MFC OLE sample HIERSVR for an example of this interaction.

Implementing Server Items

If you use AppWizard to produce "starter" code for your application, all you have to do to include server items in your starter code is to choose one of the server options from the OLE Options page. If you're adding server items to an existing application, perform the following steps:

▶ **To implement a server item**

1 Derive a class from **COleServerItem**.

2 In your derived class, override the **OnDraw** member function.

The framework calls **OnDraw** to render the OLE item into a metafile; the container application uses this metafile to render the item. Your application's view class also has an **OnDraw** member function, which is used to render the item when the server application is active.

3 Implement an override of **OnGetEmbeddedItem** for your server-document class. For further information, see the article Servers: Implementing Server Documents and the MFC OLE sample HIERSVR in Books Online.

4 Implement your server-item class's **OnGetExtent** member function. The framework calls this function to retrieve the size of the item; the default implementation does nothing.

A Tip for Server-Item Architecture

As noted in Implementing Server Items, server applications must be able to render items both in the server's view and in a metafile used by the container application. In the Microsoft Foundation Class Library's application architecture, the view class's **OnDraw** member function renders the item when it is being edited (see **CView::OnDraw** in the *Class Library Reference*); the server item's **OnDraw** renders the item into a metafile in all other cases (see **COleServerItem::OnDraw**).

You can avoid duplication of code by writing helper functions in your server-document class and calling them from the **OnDraw** functions in your view and server-item classes. The MFC OLE sample HIERSVR uses this strategy: the functions **CServerView::OnDraw** and **CServerItem::OnDraw** both call **CServerDoc::DrawTree** to render the item.

The view and the item both have **OnDraw** member functions because they draw under different conditions. The view must take into account such factors as zooming, selection size and extent, clipping, and user-interface elements such as scroll bars. The server item, on the other hand, always draws the entire OLE object.

For more information, see the **CView::OnDraw**, **COleServerItem**, **COleServerItem::OnDraw**, and **COleServerDoc::OnGetEmbeddedItem** entries in the *Class Library Reference*.

Servers: User-Interface Issues

A server application has a number of features that must be added to the user interface to supply OLE items to container applications. For further information on the menus and additional resources that need to be added to a server application, see the article Menus and Resources: Server Additions.

See Also　Menus and Resources

Snapshot

A snapshot is a recordset that reflects a static view of the data as it existed at the time the snapshot was created. Once you open the snapshot and move to all the records, the set of records it contains and their values don't change until you rebuild the snapshot by calling **Requery**.

Note　This article applies to the MFC ODBC classes. If you're using the MFC DAO classes instead of the MFC ODBC classes, see **CDaoRecordset::Open** for a description of snapshot-type recordsets. Also see the article DAO Recordset: Creating Recordsets.

You can create updatable or read-only snapshots with the database classes. Unlike a dynaset, an updatable snapshot doesn't reflect changes to record values made by other users but does reflect updates and deletions made by your program. Records added to a snapshot don't become visible to the snapshot until you call **Requery**.

Tip　A snapshot is an ODBC "static cursor." Static cursors don't actually get a row of data until you scroll to that record. To ensure that all records are immediately retrieved, you can scroll to the end of your recordset, then scroll to the first record you're interested in. Note, however, that scrolling to the end entails extra overhead and can lower performance.

Snapshots are most valuable when you need the data to remain fixed during your operations, as when you're generating a report or performing calculations. Even so, the data source can diverge considerably from your snapshot, so you may want to rebuild it from time to time.

Snapshot support is based on the ODBC Cursor Library, which provides static cursors and positioned updates (needed for updatability) for any Level 1 driver. The cursor library DLL must be loaded in memory for this support. By default, the cursor library is loaded when you construct a **CDatabase** object and call its **Open** member function. (If you are using dynasets instead of snapshots, you'll want to cause the cursor library *not* to be loaded.)

Snapshots are available only if the ODBC Cursor Library was loaded when the **CDatabase** object was constructed or the ODBC driver you're using supports static cursors.

Important　For some ODBC drivers, snapshots (static cursors) may not be updatable. Check your driver documentation for cursor types supported and the concurrency types they support.

To guarantee updatable snapshots, make sure you load the cursor library into memory when you create a **CDatabase** object. See the article ODBC: The ODBC Cursor Library.

Note If you want to use both snapshots and dynasets, you must base them on two different **CDatabase** objects (two different connections).

For more information about the properties snapshots share with all recordsets, see the article Recordset (ODBC). For more information about ODBC and snapshots, including the ODBC Cursor Library, see the article ODBC.

SQL

Structured Query Language (SQL) is a way to communicate with a relational database that lets you define, query, modify, and control the data. Using SQL syntax, you can construct a statement that extracts records according to criteria you specify.

Note This information applies to the MFC ODBC classes. If you're working with the MFC DAO classes, see the topic Comparison of Microsoft Jet Database Engine SQL and ANSI SQL in DAO Help.

SQL statements begin with a keyword "verb" such as **CREATE** or **SELECT**. It is a very powerful language; a single statement can affect an entire table.

Many versions of SQL exist, each developed with a particular DBMS in mind. The MFC database classes recognize a set of SQL statements that corresponds to the X/Open and SQL Access Group Common Applications Environment (CAE) SQL draft specification (1991). For details on the syntax of these statements, see Appendix C in the ODBC SDK *Programmer's Reference*.

This article explains:

- The relationship between ODBC and SQL.
- The most common SQL keywords used by the database classes.
- How the database classes use SQL.

Open Database Connectivity (ODBC)

The database classes are implemented with ODBC, which uses SQL in a call-level interface rather than embedding SQL commands in the code. ODBC uses SQL to communicate with a data source through ODBC drivers. These drivers interpret the SQL and translate it, if necessary, for use with a particular database format, such as Microsoft Access. For more information about how ODBC uses SQL, see the article ODBC and the ODBC SDK *Programmer's Reference*.

The Database Classes

The database classes are designed to let you manipulate and update data in an existing data source. ClassWizard and the database classes construct most of the SQL statements for you.

The database classes use a portion of SQL known as the Data Manipulation Language (DML). These commands let you work with all or part of the data source, add new records, edit records, and delete records. Table 1 lists the most common SQL keywords and the ways the database classes use them.

Table 1   Some Common SQL Keywords

SQL keyword	ClassWizard and database classes use it ...
SELECT	To identify which tables and columns in the data source are to be used.
WHERE	To apply a filter which narrows the selection.
ORDER BY	To apply a sort order to the recordset.
INSERT	To add new records to a recordset.
DELETE	To delete records from a recordset.
UPDATE	To modify the fields of a record.

In addition, the database classes recognize ODBC **CALL** statements, which you can use to call a predefined query (or stored procedure) on some data sources. The ODBC database driver interprets these statements and substitutes the command appropriate for each DBMS.

Note   Not all DBMSs support **CALL** statements.

If the classes cannot recognize a user-supplied statement in **CRecordset::Open**, it is interpreted as a table name.

For an explanation of how the framework constructs SQL statements, see the articles Recordset: How Recordsets Select Records (ODBC) and SQL: Customizing Your Recordset's SQL Statement (ODBC).

SQL databases use data types similar to those used in C and C++. For a discussion of these similarities, see the article SQL: SQL and C++ Data Types (ODBC).

You can find more information about SQL, including a list of supported SQL statements, data types, SQL core grammar, and a reading list of recommended publications about SQL, in the ODBC SDK *Programmer's Reference*.

How the Database Classes Use SQL

The recordsets you derive from the database classes use ODBC to communicate with a data source, and ODBC retrieves records from the data source by sending SQL statements. This article explains the relationship between the database classes and SQL.

A recordset constructs an SQL statement by building up the pieces of an SQL statement into a **CString**. The string is constructed as a **SELECT** statement, which returns a set of records.

When the recordset calls ODBC to send an SQL statement to the data source, the ODBC Driver Manager passes the statement to the ODBC driver, and the driver sends it to the underlying DBMS. The DBMS returns a result set of records, and the ODBC driver returns the records to the application. The database classes let your program access the result set in a type-safe C++ class derived from **CRecordset**.

The following articles provide more information about how the database classes use SQL:

- SQL: Customizing Your Recordset's SQL Statement (ODBC)
- SQL: SQL and C++ Data Types (ODBC)
- SQL: Making Direct SQL Calls (ODBC)

See Also   ODBC

SQL: Customizing Your Recordset's SQL Statement (ODBC)

Note   This information applies to the MFC ODBC classes. If you're working with the MFC DAO classes, see the topic Comparison of Microsoft Jet Database Engine SQL and ANSI SQL in DAO Help.

This article explains:

- How the framework constructs an SQL statement.
- How to override the SQL statement.

SQL Statement Construction

Your recordset bases record selection primarily on an SQL **SELECT** statement. When you declare your class with ClassWizard, the wizard writes an overriding version of the **GetDefaultSQL** member function that looks something like this (for a recordset class called CAuthors).

```
CString CAuthors::GetDefaultSQL()
{
    return "AUTHORS";
}
```

By default, this override returns the table name you specified with ClassWizard—in the example, the table name is "AUTHORS." When you later call the recordset's **Open** member function, **Open** constructs a final **SELECT** statement of the form:

```
SELECT rfx-field-list FROM table-name [WHERE m_strFilter]
    [ORDER BY m_strSort]
```

where `table-name` is obtained by calling **GetDefaultSQL** and `rfx-field-list` is obtained from the RFX function calls in **DoFieldExchange**. This is what you get for a **SELECT** statement unless you replace it with an overriding version at run time, although you can also modify the default statement with parameters or a filter.

Important If you specify a column name that contains (or could contain) spaces, you must enclose the name in square brackets. For example, the name "First Name" should be "[First Name]".

To override the default **SELECT** statement, pass a string containing a complete **SELECT** statement when you call **Open**. Instead of constructing its own default string, the recordset uses the string you supply. If your replacement statement contains a **WHERE** clause, don't specify a filter in **m_strFilter** because you would then have two filter statements. If your replacement statement contains an **ORDER BY** clause, don't specify a sort in **m_strSort** so that you will not have two sort statements.

Caution In the ENROLL tutorial application, filter strings typically use a parameter placeholder, "?", rather than assigning a specific literal value, such as "MATH101", at compile time. If you do use literal strings in your filters (or other parts of the SQL statement), you may have to "quote" such strings with a DBMS-specific "literal prefix" and "literal suffix" character (or characters). For example, the code in the ENROLL tutorial uses a single quote character to bracket the value assigned as the filter, "MATH101". You may also encounter special syntactic requirements for operations such as outer joins, depending on your DBMS. Use ODBC functions to obtain this information from your driver for the DBMS. For example, call **::SQLGetTypeInfo** for a particular data type, such as **SQL_VARCHAR**, to request the **LITERAL_PREFIX** and **LITERAL_SUFFIX** characters. If you are writing database-independent code, see Appendix C in the ODBC *Programmer's Reference* for detailed syntax information.

A recordset object "constructs" the SQL statement that it uses to select records unless you pass a custom SQL statement. How this is done depends mainly on the value you pass in the *lpszSQL* parameter of the **Open** member function.

The general form of an SQL **SELECT** statement is:

```
SELECT [ALL | DISTINCT] column-list FROM table-list
    [WHERE search-condition][ORDER BY column-list [ASC | DESC]]
```

One way to add the **DISTINCT** keyword to your recordset's SQL statement is to embed the keyword in the first RFX function call in **DoFieldExchange**. For example:

```
...
    RFX_Text(pFX, "DISTINCT CourseID", m_strCourseID);
...
```

Warning	Use this technique only with a recordset opened as read-only.

Overriding the SQL Statement

Table 1 shows the possibilities for the *lpszSQL* parameter to **Open**. The cases in the table are explained following the table.

Table 1   The *lpszSQL* Parameter and the SQL String Constructed

Case	What you pass in *lpszSQL*	The resulting SELECT statement
1	**NULL**	**SELECT** *rfx-field-list* **FROM** *table-name*
		CRecordset::Open calls **GetDefaultSQL** to get the table name. The resulting string is one of Cases 2 through 5, depending on what **GetDefaultSQL** returns.
2	A table name	**SELECT** *rfx-field-list* **FROM** *table-name*
		The field list is taken from the RFX statements in **DoFieldExchange**. If **m_strFilter** and **m_strSort** are not empty, adds the **WHERE** and/or **ORDER BY** clauses.
3 *	A complete **SELECT** statement but without a **WHERE** or **ORDER BY** clause	As passed. If **m_strFilter** and **m_strSort** are not empty, adds the **WHERE** and/or **ORDER BY** clauses.
4 *	A complete **SELECT** statement with a **WHERE** and/or **ORDER BY** clause	As passed. **m_strFilter** and/or **m_strSort** must remain empty, or two filter and/or sort statements will be produced.
5 *	A call to a stored procedure	As passed.

*   **m_nFields** must be less than or equal to the number of columns specified in the **SELECT** statement. The data type of each column specified in the **SELECT** statement must be the same as the data type of the corresponding RFX output column.

Case 1   *lpszSQL* = NULL

The recordset selection depends on what **GetDefaultSQL** returns when **CRecordset::Open** calls it. Cases 2 through 5 describe the possible strings.

Case 2   *lpszSQL* = a Table Name

The recordset uses record field exchange (RFX) to build the column list from the column names provided in the RFX function calls in the recordset class's override of **DoFieldExchange**. If you used ClassWizard to declare your recordset class, this case has the same result as Case 1 (provided that you pass the same table name you specified in ClassWizard). If you don't use ClassWizard to write your class, this is the simplest way to construct the SQL statement.

The following example constructs an SQL statement that selects records from the MFC tutorial sample ENROLL. When the framework calls the **GetDefaultSQL** member function, the function returns the name of the table, SECTION.

```
CString CEnrollSet::GetDefaultSQL()
{
    return "SECTION";
}
```

To obtain the names of the columns for the SQL **SELECT** statement, the framework calls the **DoFieldExchange** member function.

```
void CEnrollSet::DoFieldExchange(CFieldExchange* pFX)
{
    pFX->SetFieldType(CFieldExchange::outputColumn);
    //{{AFX_FIELD_MAP(CEnrollSet)
    RFX_Text(pFX, "CourseID", m_strCourseID);
    RFX_Text(pFX, "InstructorID", m_strInstructorID);
    RFX_Text(pFX, "RoomNo", m_strRoomNo);
    RFX_Text(pFX, "Schedule", m_strSchedule);
    RFX_Text(pFX, "SectionNo", m_strSectionNo);
    //}}AFX_FIELD_MAP
}
```

When complete, the SQL statement looks like this:

```
SELECT CourseID, InstructorID, RoomNo, Schedule, SectionNo
    FROM SECTION
```

Case 3 *lpszSQL* = a SELECT/FROM Statement

You specify the column list by hand rather than relying on RFX to construct it automatically. You might want to do this when:

- You want to specify the **DISTINCT** keyword following **SELECT**.

  Your column list should match the column names and types in the same order as they are listed in **DoFieldExchange**.

- You have reason to manually retrieve column values using the ODBC function **::SQLGetData** rather than relying on RFX to bind and retrieve columns for you.

  You might, for example, want to accommodate new columns a customer of your application added to the database tables after the application was distributed. You need to add these extra field data members not known at the time you declared the class with ClassWizard.

  Your column list should match the column names and types in the same order as they are listed in **DoFieldExchange**, followed by the names of the manually bound columns. The MFC Database sample CATALOG provides classes called **CTable** and **CColumn** which you can use to retrieve column information from the data source. For more information, see the article Recordset: Dynamically Binding Data Columns (ODBC) and CATALOG in Books Online.

- You want to join tables by specifying multiple tables in the **FROM** clause.

For information and an example, see the article Recordset: Performing a Join (ODBC).

Case 4   *IpszSQL* = SELECT/FROM Plus WHERE and/or ORDER BY

You specify everything: the column list (based on the RFX calls in **DoFieldExchange**), the table list, and the contents of a **WHERE** and/or an **ORDER BY** clause. If you specify your **WHERE** and/or **ORDER BY** clauses this way, be sure not to use **m_strFilter** and/or **m_strSort**.

Case 5   *IpszSQL* = a Stored Procedure Call

If you need to call a predefined query (such as a stored procedure in a Microsoft SQL Server database), you must write a **CALL** statement in the string you pass to *IpszSQL*. ClassWizard doesn't support declaring a recordset class for calling a predefined query. Not all predefined queries return records.

If a predefined query doesn't return records, you can use the **CDatabase** member function **ExecuteSQL** directly. For a predefined query that does return records, you must also manually write the RFX calls in **DoFieldExchange** for any columns the procedure returns. The RFX calls must be in the same order, and return the same types, as the predefined query. For more information, see the article Recordset: Declaring a Class for a Predefined Query (ODBC).

See Also   SQL: SQL and C++ Data Types (ODBC), SQL: Making Direct SQL Calls (ODBC)

SQL: SQL and C++ Data Types (ODBC)

Note   This information applies to the MFC ODBC classes. If you're working with the MFC DAO classes, see the topic Comparison of Microsoft Jet Database Engine SQL and ANSI SQL in DAO Help.

Table 1 maps ANSI SQL data types to C++ data types. This augments the C language information given in Appendix D of the ODBC SDK *Programmer's Reference*. ClassWizard manages most data-type mapping for you. If you don't use ClassWizard, you can use the mapping information to help you write the field exchange code manually.

Table 1   ANSI SQL Data Types Mapped to C++ Data Types

ANSI SQL data type	C++ data type
CHAR	**CString**
DECIMAL	**CString** [1]
SMALLINT	**int**
REAL	**float**
INTEGER	**long**
FLOAT	**double**

Table 1   ANSI SQL Data Types Mapped to C++ Data Types *(cont.)*

ANSI SQL data type	C++ data type
DOUBLE	double
NUMERIC	CString [1]
VARCHAR	CString
LONGVARCHAR	CLongBinary, CString [2]
BIT	BOOL
TINYINT	BYTE
BIGINT	CString [1]
BINARY	CByteArray
VARBINARY	CByteArray
LONGVARBINARY	CLongBinary, CByteArray [3]
DATE	CTime, CString
TIME	CTime, CString
TIMESTAMP	CTime, CString

[1] ANSI **DECIMAL** and **NUMERIC** map to **CString** because **SQL_C_CHAR** is the default ODBC transfer type.

[2] Character data beyond 255 characters is truncated by default when mapped to **CString**. You can extend the truncation length by explicitly setting the *nMaxLength* argument of **RFX_Text**.

[3] Binary data beyond 255 characters is truncated by default when mapped to **CByteArray**. You can extend the truncation length by explicitly setting the *nMaxLength* argument of **RFX_Binary**.

See Also   SQL: Making Direct SQL Calls (ODBC)

SQL: Making Direct SQL Calls (ODBC)

Note   This information applies to the MFC ODBC classes. If you're working with the MFC DAO classes, see the topic Comparison of Microsoft Jet Database Engine SQL and ANSI SQL in DAO Help.

This article explains:

- When to use direct SQL calls.
- How you make direct SQL calls to the data source.

When to Call SQL Directly

To create new tables, drop tables, alter existing tables, create indexes, and perform other SQL functions which change the data source schema, you must issue an SQL statement directly to the data source using Database Definition Language (DDL). When you use ClassWizard to create a recordset for a table — at design time — you can choose which columns of the table to represent in the recordset. This doesn't allow for columns you or another user of the data source add to the table later, after your program has been compiled. The database classes don't support DDL directly, but you can still write code to bind a new column to your recordset dynamically, at run time. For information on how to do this binding, see the article Recordset: Dynamically Binding Data Columns (ODBC).

You can use the DBMS itself to alter the schema, or another tool which lets you perform DDL functions.

You can also use ODBC function calls for sending SQL statements, such as calling a predefined query (stored procedure) that doesn't return records.

Making Direct SQL Function Calls

You can directly execute an SQL call using a **CDatabase** object. Set up your SQL statement string (usually in a **CString**) and pass it to the **ExecuteSQL** member function of your **CDatabase** object. If you use ODBC function calls to send an SQL statement that normally returns records, the records are ignored. For more information, see the member function **CDatabase::ExecuteSQL** of class **CDatabase** in the *Class Library Reference*.

See Also   In the *Class Library Reference*: **CDatabase::ExecuteSQL**

Stored Procedure

A predefined query stored in a data source and activated by an ODBC CALL statement.

If you're using the MFC ODBC classes, see the articles Recordset: Declaring a Class for a Table (ODBC) and SQL: Making Direct SQL Calls (ODBC). If you're using the MFC DAO classes, see the article DAO Querydef: Using QueryDefs.

Strings

This article describes the general-pupose services that the class library provides related to string manipulation. Topics covered in this article include:

- Unicode and MBCS provide portability
- CStrings and const char pointers
- CString reference counting

The **CString** class provides support for manipulating strings. It is intended to replace and extend the functionality normally provided by the C run-time library string package. The **CString** class supplies member functions and operators for simplified string handling, similar to those found in Basic. The class also provides constructors and operators for constructing, assigning, and comparing **CStrings** and standard C++ string data types. Because **CString** is not derived from **CObject**, you can use **CString** objects independently of most of the Microsoft Foundation Class Library (MFC).

CString objects follow "value semantics." A **CString** object represents a unique value. Think of a **CString** as an actual string, not as a pointer to a string.

A **CString** object represents a sequence of a variable number of characters. **CString** objects can be thought of as arrays of characters.

Unicode and MBCS Provide Portability

With MFC version 3.0 and later, MFC, including **CString**, is enabled for both Unicode and Multibyte Character Sets (MBCS). This support makes it easier for you to write portable applications that you can build for either Unicode or ANSI characters. To enable this portability, each character in a **CString** object is of type **TCHAR**, which is defined as **wchar_t** if you define the symbol **_UNICODE** when you build your application, or as **char** if not. A **wchar_t** character is 16 bits wide. (Unicode is available only under Windows NT.) MBCS is enabled if you build with the symbol **_MBCS** defined. MFC itself is built with either the **_MBCS** symbol (for the NAFX libraries) or the **_UNICODE** symbol (for the UAFX libraries) defined.

Note The **CString** examples in this and the accompanying articles on strings show literal strings properly formatted for Unicode portability, using the _T macro, which translates the literal string to the form

```
L"literal string"
```

which the compiler treats as a Unicode string. For example, the following code:

```
CString strName = _T("Name");
```

is translated as a Unicode string if **_UNICODE** is defined or as an ANSI string if not. For more information, see the article Strings: Unicode and Multibyte Character Set (MBCS) Support.

A **CString** object can store up to **INT_MAX** (2,147,483,647) characters. The **TCHAR** data type is used to get or set individual characters inside a **CString** object. Unlike character arrays, the **CString** class has a built-in memory allocation capability. This allows **CString** objects to automatically grow as needed (that is, you don't have to worry about growing a **CString** object to fit longer strings).

CStrings and const char Pointers

A **CString** object also can act like a literal C-style string (an **LPCTSTR**, which is the same as **const char*** if not under Unicode). The **LPCTSTR** conversion operator allows **CString** objects to be freely substituted for character pointers in function calls. The **CString(LPCTSTR** *lpsz* **)** constructor allows character pointers to be substituted for **CString** objects.

No attempt is made to fold **CString** objects. If you make two **CString** objects containing Chicago, for example, the characters in Chicago are stored in two places. (This may not be true of future versions of MFC, so you should not depend on it.)

Tips   Use the **GetBuffer** and **ReleaseBuffer** member functions when you need to directly access a **CString** as a nonconstant pointer to a character (**LPTSTR** instead of a **const** character pointer, **LPCTSTR**).

Use the **AllocSysString** and **SetSysString** member functions to allocate and set **BSTR** objects used in OLE Automation.

Where possible, allocate **CString** objects on the frame rather than on the heap. This saves memory and simplifies parameter passing.

The **CString** class is not implemented as a Microsoft Foundation Class Library collection class, although **CString** objects can certainly be stored as elements in collections.

CString Reference Counting

As of MFC version 4.0, when **CString** objects are copied, MFC increments a reference count rather than copying the data. This makes passing parameters by value and returning **CString** objects by value more efficient. These operations cause the copy constructor to be called, sometimes more than once. Incrementing a reference count reduces that overhead for these common operations and makes using **CString** a more attractive option.

As each copy is destroyed, the reference count in the original object is decremented. The original **CString** object is not destroyed until its reference count is reduced to zero.

You can use the **CString** member functions **LockBuffer** and **UnlockBuffer** to disable or enable reference counting.

Further Reading About Strings

The following articles provide more information about **CString**:

- Strings: Basic CString Operations
- Strings: CString Semantics
- Strings: CString Operations Relating to C-Style Strings
- Strings: CString Exception Cleanup
- Strings: CString Argument Passing
- Strings: Unicode and Multibyte Character Set (MBCS) Support

See Also   In the *Class Library Reference*: **CString**

Strings: Basic CString Operations

This article explains basic **CString** operations, including:

- Creating CString objects from standard C literal strings

- Accessing individual characters in a CString
- Concatenating two CString objects
- Comparing CString objects

The **CString** class provides member functions and overloaded operators that duplicate and, in some cases, surpass the string services of the C run-time libraries (for example, **strcat**). This article describes some of the main operations of the **CString** class.

Creating CString Objects from Standard C Literal Strings

You can assign C-style literal strings to a **CString** just as you can assign one **CString** object to another:

- Assign the value of a C literal string to a **CString** object:

```
CString myString = "This is a test";
```

- Assign the value of one **CString** to another **CString** object:

```
CString oldString = "This is a test";
CString newString = oldString;
```

The contents of a **CString** object are copied when one **CString** object is assigned to another. Thus, the two strings do not share a reference to the actual characters that make up the string. For more information on using **CString** objects as values, see the article Strings: CString Semantics.

Tip To write your application so that it can be compiled for Unicode or for ANSI, code literal strings using the **_T** macro. For more information, see the article Strings: Unicode and Multibyte Character Set (MBCS) Support.

Accessing Individual Characters in a CString

You can access individual characters within a **CString** object with the **GetAt** and **SetAt** member functions. You can also use the array element, or subscript, operator ([ ]) instead of **GetAt** to get individual characters (this is similar to accessing array elements by index, as in standard C-style strings). Index values for **CString** characters are zero-based.

Concatenating Two CString Objects

To concatenate two **CString** objects, use the concatenation operators (+ or +=) as follows:

```
CString s1 = "This ";         //Cascading concatenation
s1 += "is a ";
CString s2 = "test";
CString message = s1 + "big " + s2;
//Message contains "This is a big test".
```

At least one of the arguments to the concatenation operators (+ or +=) must be a **CString** object, but you can use a constant character string (such as `"big"`) or a **char** (such as `'x'`) for the other argument.

Comparing CString Objects

The **Compare** member function and the == operator for **CString** are equivalent. **Compare**, **operator==**, and **CompareNoCase** are MBCS- and Unicode-aware; **CompareNoCase** is also case insensitive. The **Collate** member function of **CString** is locale-sensitive and is often slower than **Compare**. **Collate** should be used only where it is necessary to abide by the sorting rules as specified by the current locale.

The following list shows the available **CString** comparison functions and their equivalent Unicode/MBCS-portable functions in the C run-time library:

CString function	MBCS function	Unicode function
Compare	**_mbscmp**	**wcscmp**
CompareNoCase	**_mbsicmp**	**_wcsicmp**
Collate	**strcoll**	**wcscoll**

The **CString** class overrides the relational operators (<, <=, >=, >, ==, and !=). You can compare two **CStrings** using these operators, as shown here:

```
CString s1( "Tom" );
CString s2( "Jerry" );
if( s1 < s2 )
    ...
```

Strings: CString Semantics

Even though **CString** objects are dynamically growable objects, they act like built-in primitive types and simple classes. Each **CString** object represents a unique value. **CString** objects should be thought of as the actual strings rather than as pointers to strings.

The most obvious consequence of using **CString** objects as values is that the string contents are copied when you assign one **CString** to another. Thus, even though two **CString** objects may represent the same sequence of characters, they do not share those characters. Each **CString** has its own copy of the character data. When you modify one **CString** object, the copied **CString** object is not modified, as shown by the following example:

```
CString s1, s2;
s1 = s2 = "hi there";

if( s1 == s2 )              // TRUE - they are equal
    ...

s1.MakeUpper();         // Does not modify s2
if( s2[0] == 'h' )         // TRUE - s2 is still "hi there"
```

Notice in the example that the two **CString** objects are considered to be "equal" because they represent the same character string. The **CString** class overloads the equality operator (==) to compare two **CString** objects based on their value (contents) rather than their identity (address).

Strings: CString Operations Relating to C-Style Strings

It is often useful to manipulate the contents of a **CString** object as if it were a C-style null-terminated string. This article covers the following topics:

- Converting to C-style null-terminated strings
- Working with standard run-time library string functions
- Modifying **CString** contents directly
- Using **CString** objects with variable argument functions
- Specifying **CString** formal parameters

Converting to C-Style Null-Terminated Strings

Consider the following two cases:

- In the simplest case, you can cast a **CString** object to be an **LPCTSTR**. The LPCTSTR type conversion operator returns a pointer to a read-only C-style null-terminated string from a **CString** object.

  The pointer returned by **LPCTSTR** points into the data area used by the **CString**. If the **CString** goes out of scope and is automatically deleted or something else changes the contents of the **CString**, the **LPCTSTR** pointer will no longer be valid. Treat the string to which the pointer points as being temporary.

- You can use **CString** functions, such as **SetAt**, to modify individual characters in the string object. However, if you need a copy of a **CString** object's characters that you can modify directly, use **strcpy** (or the Unicode/MBCS-portable **_tcscpy**) to copy the **CString** object into a separate buffer where the characters can be safely modified, as shown by the following example:

```
CString theString( "This is a test" );
LPCTSTR lpsz = new TCHAR[theString.GetLength()+1];
strcpy( lpsz, theString );
//... modify lpsz as much as you want
```

Note The second argument to **strcpy** (or the Unicode/MBCS-portable **_tcscpy**) is either a **const wchar_t*** (Unicode) or a **const char*** (ANSI). The example above passes a **CString** for this argument. The C++ compiler automatically applies the conversion function defined for the **CString** class that converts a **CString** to an **LPCTSTR**. The ability to define casting operations from one type to another is one of the most useful features of C++.

Working with Standard Run-Time Library String Functions

In most situations, you should be able to find **CString** member functions to perform any string operation for which you might consider using the standard C run-time library string functions, such as **strcmp** (or the Unicode/MBCS-portable **_tcscmp**).

If you need to use the C run-time string functions, you can use the techniques described in Converting to C-Style Null-Terminated Strings to copy the **CString** object to an equivalent C-style string buffer, perform your operations on the buffer, and then assign the resulting C-style string back to a **CString** object.

Modifying CString Contents Directly

In most situations, you should use **CString** member functions to modify the contents of a **CString** object or to convert the **CString** to a C-style character string.

However, there are certain situations, such as working with operating-system functions that require a character buffer, where it is advantageous to directly modify the **CString** contents.

The **GetBuffer** and **ReleaseBuffer** member functions allow you to gain access to the internal character buffer of a **CString** object and modify it directly. The following steps show how to use these functions for this purpose:

1. Call **GetBuffer** for a **CString** object, specifying the length of the buffer you require.

2. Use the pointer returned by **GetBuffer** to write characters directly into the **CString** object.

3. Call **ReleaseBuffer** for the **CString** object to update all the internal **CString** state information (such as the length of the string). After modifying a **CString** object's contents directly, you must call **ReleaseBuffer** before calling any other **CString** member functions.

Using CString Objects with Variable Argument Functions

Some C functions take a variable number of arguments. A notable example is **printf**. Because of the way this kind of function is declared, the compiler cannot be sure of the type of the arguments and cannot determine which conversion operation to perform on the argument. Therefore, it is essential that you use an explicit type cast when passing a **CString** object to a function that takes a variable number of arguments.

▶ **To use a CString object in a variable argument function**

- Explicitly cast the **CString** to an **LPCTSTR** string, as shown here:

```
CString kindOfFruit = "bananas";
int     howmany = 25;
printf( "You have %d %s\n", howmany, (LPCTSTR)kindOfFruit );
```

Specifying CString Formal Parameters

For most functions that need a string argument, it is best to specify the formal parameter in the function prototype as a **const** pointer to a character (**LPCTSTR**) instead of a **CString**. When a formal parameter is specified as a **const** pointer to a character, you can pass either a pointer to a **TCHAR** array, a literal string ["hi there"], or a **CString** object. The **CString** object will be automatically converted to an **LPCTSTR**. Any place you can use an **LPCTSTR**, you can also use a **CString** object.

You can also specify a formal parameter as a constant string reference (that is, **const CString&**) if the argument will not be modified. Drop the **const** modifier if the string will be modified by the function. If a default null value is desired, initialize it to the null string [""], as shown below:

```
void AddCustomer( const CString& name,
                  const CString& address,
                  const CString& comment = "" );
```

For most function results, you can simply return a **CString** object by value.

See Also   Strings: CString Argument Passing

In the *Class Library Reference*: **CString**

Strings: CString Exception Cleanup

In previous versions of MFC, it was important that you clean up **CString** objects after use. With MFC version 3.0 and later, explicit cleanup is no longer necessary.

Under the C++ exception handling mechanism that MFC now uses, you don't have to worry about cleanup after an exception. For a description of how C++ "unwinds" the stack after an exception is caught, see Chapter 7, C++ Exception Handling, in *Programming Techniques*. Even if you use the MFC **TRY/CATCH** macros instead of the C++ keywords **try** and **catch**, MFC uses the C++ exception mechanism underneath, so you still don't need to clean up explicitly.

See Also   Exceptions

Strings: CString Argument Passing

This article explains how to pass **CString** objects to functions and how to return **CString** objects from functions.

Argument-Passing Conventions

When you define a class interface, you must determine the argument-passing convention for your member functions. There are some standard rules for passing and returning **CString** objects. If you follow the rules described in Strings as Function Inputs and Strings as Function Outputs, you will have efficient, correct code.

Strings as Function Inputs

If a string is an input to a function, in most cases it is best to declare the string function parameter as **LPCTSTR**. Convert to a **CString** object as necessary within the function using constructors and assignment operators. If the string contents are to be changed by a function, declare the parameter as a nonconstant **CString** reference (**CString&**).

Strings as Function Outputs

Normally you can return **CString** objects from functions since **CString** objects follow value semantics like primitive types. To return a read-only string, use a constant **CString** reference (**const CString&**). The following example illustrates the use of **CString** parameters and return types:

```
class CName : public CObject
{
private:
    CString m_firstName;
    char m_middleInit;
    CString m_lastName;
public:
    CName() {}
    void SetData( LPCTSTR fn, const char mi, LPCTSTR ln )
    {
        m_firstName = fn;
        m_middleInit = mi;
        m_lastName = ln;
    }
    void GetData( CString& cfn, char mi, CString& cln )
    {
        cfn = m_firstName;
        mi = m_middleInit;
        cln = m_lastName;
    }
    CString GetLastName()
    {
        return m_lastName;
    }
};
...
CName name;
CString last, first;
TCHAR middle;
name.SetData( "John", 'Q', "Public" );
ASSERT( name.GetLastName() == "Public" );
name.GetData( first, middle, last );
ASSERT( ( first == "John" ) && ( last == "Public" ) );
...
```

Strings: Unicode and Multibyte Character Set (MBCS) Support

Some international markets use languages, such as Japanese and Chinese, with large character sets. To support programming for these markets, the Microsoft Foundation Class Library (MFC) is enabled for two different approaches to handling large character sets:

- Unicode
- Multibyte Character Sets (MBCS)

MFC Support for Unicode Strings

The entire class library (except the database classes) is conditionally enabled for Unicode characters and strings. In particular, class **CString** is Unicode-enabled.

CString is based on the **TCHAR** data type. If the symbol **_UNICODE** is defined for a build of your program, **TCHAR** is defined as type **wchar_t**, a 16-bit character encoding type; otherwise, it is defined as **char**, the normal 8-bit character encoding. Under Unicode, then, **CString**s are composed of 16-bit characters. Without Unicode, they are composed of characters of type **char**.

To complete the Unicode picture for your application, you must also:

- Use the **_T** macro to conditionally code literal strings to be portable to Unicode.
- When you pass strings, pay attention to whether function arguments require a length in characters or a length in bytes. The difference is important if you're using Unicode strings.
- Use portable versions of the C run-time string-handling functions.
- Use the following data types for characters and character pointers:

    TCHAR   Where you would use **char**.

    LPTSTR   Where you would use **char***.

    LPCTSTR   Where you would use **const char***. **CString** provides the **operator LPCTSTR** to convert between **CString** and **LPCTSTR**.

CString also supplies Unicode-aware constructors, assignment operators, and comparison operators.

For more information on Unicode programming, see Chapter 13, Developing for International Markets, in *Programming Techniques*. The *Run-Time Library Reference* defines portable versions of all of its string-handling functions. See the category Internationalization in Chapter 1 of that book.

MFC Support for MBCS Strings

The class library is also enabled for multibyte character sets (except for the database classes)—specifically for double-byte character sets (DBCS).

Note The version of ODBC shipped with Visual C++ version 2.0 is not MBCS enabled. Subsequent versions of ODBC will be MBCS enabled (specifically DBCS enabled).

Under this scheme, a character can be either one or two bytes wide. If it is two bytes wide, its first byte is a special "lead byte," chosen from a particular range depending on which code page is in use. Taken together, the lead and "trail bytes" specify a unique character encoding.

If the symbol **_MBCS** is defined for a build of your program, type **TCHAR**, on which **CString** is based, maps to **char**. It's up to you to determine which bytes in a **CString** are lead bytes and which are trail bytes. The C run-time library supplies functions to help you determine this.

Under DBCS, a given string can contain all single-byte ANSI characters, all double-byte characters, or a mixture of the two. These possibilities require special care in parsing strings, including **CString** objects.

Note Unicode string serialization in MFC can read both Unicode and MBCS strings regardless of which version of the application you are running. Because of this, your data files are portable between Unicode and MBCS versions of your program.

CString member functions use special "generic text" versions of the C run-time functions they call, or they use Unicode-aware functions such as **lstrlen** or **lstrcpy**. Thus, for example, if a **CString** function would normally call **strcmp**, it calls the corresponding generic-text function **_tcscmp** instead. Depending on how the symbols **_MBCS** and **_UNICODE** are defined, **_tcscmp** maps as follows:

_MBCS defined   **_mbscmp**

_UNICODE defined   **wcscmp**

Neither symbol defined   **strcmp**

Note **_MBCS** and **_UNICODE** are mutually exclusive symbols.

Generic-text function mappings for all of the run-time string-handling routines are detailed in the *Run-Time Library Reference*. See the category Internationalization.

Similarly, **CString** member functions are implemented using "generic" data type mappings. To enable both MBCS and Unicode, MFC uses **TCHAR** for **char**, **LPTSTR** for **char***, and **LPCTSTR** for **const char***. These result in the correct mappings for either MBCS or Unicode.

For more information about MFC support for MBCS (DBCS), see Chapter 13, Developing for International Markets, in *Programming Techniques*.

Structured Query Language

See the article SQL.

Table

A table is the fundamental structure of a relational database management system. It is typically a data structure composed of records (rows) and fields (columns) with data stored in each cell formed by the record and field intersection.

A table in a database for which there is an ODBC driver can be accessed via a **CRecordset** object. The recordset object can select some or all of the records, and some or all of the columns.

See Also   Record, Recordset (ODBC)

Test Container

The Test Container application, shipped with Visual C++, is an OLE control container for testing OLE controls. Test Container allows the control developer to test the control's functionality by changing its properties, invoking its methods, and firing its events. In addition, Test Container can display logs of data-binding notifications and also provides facilities for testing an OLE control's persistence functionality: you can save properties to a stream or to substorage, reload them, and examine the stored stream data. For more information on using Test Container, see the Test Container help.

This article discusses how to:

- Test your OLE control using Test Container and the integrated debugger
- Test the events, methods, and properties of an OLE control

Testing Your OLE Control Using Test Container

Because OLE controls are implemented as system DLLs, they cannot be run as stand-alone applications. In order to interact with the control (in this case debug it), a calling application is needed. The Test Container application can fill this role. The integrated debugger will use Test Container as the test harness for the OLE control. Once Test Container is running you can begin the debugging process for your control.

Note   In addition to Test Container, Microsoft FoxPro® 3.0, Microsoft Access, Microsoft Visual Basic® 4.0, and OLE containers built with the MFC class library in Visual C++ version 4.0 fully support OLE controls.

▶ To test your control using the integrated debugger

1 Load your control's project.

2 Ensure that the OLE control has been built as a debug version with symbolic debugging information.

3 From the Build menu, choose Settings.

The Project Settings dialog box appears.

4 Select the Debug tab.

5 Type the name of the executable program which calls the OLE control DLL in your project in the Executable for debug session box.

For this example, the Test Container application TSTCON32.EXE (shipped with Visual C++) will be used. It is found in the BIN directory of your installation.

6 Choose OK.

The information is now stored with your project.

After completing this procedure, Test Container automatically starts when you begin a debugging session of your control. Begin a debugging session by choosing the Go command from the Debug submenu of the Build menu (or press F5).

When you first start debugging your control, a message box appears stating that no debug information is available for the Test Container. You can safely ignore this by choosing the OK button. You can now step through your code, set breakpoints, or perform other debugging techniques.

Testing the Events, Methods, and Properties of an OLE Control

Once an OLE control has been successfully compiled and linked, you can immediately test the functionality of the OLE control using the Test Container.

▶ **To test your OLE control**

1 From the Tools menu of Visual C++, choose OLE Control Test Container.

2 From the Edit menu of Test Container, choose Insert OLE Control.

3 In the Insert OLE Control dialog box, select the desired control and choose OK. The control will appear in the control container.

Note If your control is not listed in the Insert OLE Control dialog box, make sure you have registered it with the Register Controls command from the File menu of Test Container.

At this point you can test your control's properties or events.

▶ **To test properties**

1 From the Edit menu, choose the *xxxx* Control Object command, where *xxxx* represents your control's name.

2 Modify the value of a property on the property page.

3 Click the Apply button to apply the new value to the *xxxx* control.

The property now contains the new value.

▶ **To test events**

1 From the View menu, choose the Event Log command.

2 Perform an action that causes the control to fire an event.

The event will appear in the Event Log window.

After you have finished testing your control, close the Test Container by choosing the Close command on the File menu, or double-click the system menu button.

See Also   OLE Controls

Toolbars

The toolbar family of articles describes MFC toolbars and how to create and use them. This article gives an overview of the features available. Topics covered include:

- Toolbar: definition
- Docking and floating toolbars
- Tool tips
- The **CToolBar** class
- Further reading about toolbars

Toolbar: Definition

A toolbar is a form of control bar—a child window that can contain buttons, edit boxes, check boxes, or other kinds of Windows controls. Some kinds of control bars, such as dialog bars, can contain a wide variety of controls, but a toolbar contains a row of button images. These buttons can behave like pushbuttons, check boxes, or radio buttons.

Docking and Floating Toolbars

Toolbars are usually aligned to the top of a frame window, but a toolbar in an application created with the Microsoft Foundation Class Library (MFC) can, if you choose, be "docked" to any side (or sides) of its parent window that you specify. MFC toolbars can also be made to "float" in draggable "mini-frame windows," and users can now resize floating toolbars. You can also create a floating palette that cannot be docked. See the article Toolbars: Docking and Floating.

Tool Tips

You can also have your toolbars show "tool tips" as the user moves the mouse over the toolbar buttons. A tool tip is a small popup window that appears near a toolbar button to explain its purpose to the user.

The CToolBar Class

You manage your application's toolbars via class **CToolBar**. As of MFC version 4.0, **CToolBar** has been reimplemented to use the toolbar common control available under Windows 95 and Windows NT version 3.51 or later.

This reimplementation results in less MFC code for toolbars, because MFC makes use of operating system support. The reimplementation also improves capability. You can use **CToolBar** member functions to manipulate toolbars, or you can obtain a reference to the underlying **CToolBarCtrl** object and call its member functions for toolbar customization and additional functionality.

Tip If you have invested heavily in the older MFC implementation of **CToolBar**, that support is still available. See the article Toolbars: Using Your Old Toolbars.

Also see the MFC General sample DOCKTOOL.

For Further Reading About Toolbars

For information about docking and floating toolbars and about tool tips, see the following articles:

- Toolbars: Fundamentals
- Toolbars: Docking and Floating
- Toolbars: Tool Tips
- Toolbars: Working with the Toolbar Control
- Toolbars: Using Your Old Toolbars

In the *Class Library Reference*, see classes **CToolBar**, **CControlBar**, and **CToolBarCtrl**.

For example code, see the MFC General sample DOCKTOOL in Books Online.

See Also   Toolbars: Fundamentals, Toolbars: Docking and Floating, Toolbars: Tool Tips, Toolbars: Working with the Toolbar Control, Toolbars: Using Your Old Toolbars

Toolbars: Fundamentals

This article describes the fundamental MFC implementation that lets you add a default toolbar to your application by selecting an option in AppWizard. Topics covered include:

- The AppWizard Toolbar Option
- The Toolbar in Code
- Editing the Toolbar Resource
- Multiple Toolbars

The AppWizard Toolbar Option

To get a single toolbar with default buttons, select the Dockable Toolbar option on the AppWizard Step 4 of 6 page. This adds code to your application that:

- Creates the toolbar object.
- Manages the toolbar, including its ability to dock or to float.

The Toolbar in Code

The toolbar object is a **CToolBar** object declared as a data member of your application's **CMainFrame** class. In other words, the toolbar object is embedded in the main frame window object. This means that MFC creates the toolbar when it creates the frame window and destroys the toolbar when it destroys the frame window. The following partial class declaration, for a multiple document interface (MDI) application, shows data members for an embedded toolbar and an embedded status bar. It also shows the override of the **OnCreate** member function.

```
class CMainFrame : public CMDIFrameWnd
{
    // ...

// Implementation
    // ...

protected:  // control bar embedded members
    CStatusBar  m_wndStatusBar;
    CToolBar    m_wndToolBar;

// Generated message map functions
protected:
    //{{AFX_MSG(CMainFrame)
    afx_msg int OnCreate(LPCREATESTRUCT lpCreateStruct);
        // NOTE - the ClassWizard will add and remove member functions here.
        // DO NOT EDIT what you see in these blocks of
        // generated code!
    //}}AFX_MSG
    DECLARE_MESSAGE_MAP()
};
```

Toolbar creation occurs in **CMainFrame::OnCreate**. MFC calls **OnCreate** after creating the Windows window for the frame but before the frame window becomes visible. The default **OnCreate** that AppWizard generates does the following toolbar tasks:

1. Calls the **CToolBar** object's **Create** member function to create the underlying **CToolBarCtrl** object.

2. Calls **LoadToolBar** to load the toolbar resource information.

3. Calls functions to enable docking, floating, and tool tips. For details about these calls, see the article Toolbars: Docking and Floating.

Note The MFC General sample DOCKTOOL includes illustrations of both old and new MFC toolbars. The toolbars that use **COldToolbar** require calls in step 2 to **LoadBitmap** (rather than **LoadToolBar**) and to **SetButtons**. The new toolbars require calls to **LoadToolBar**. Samples are available under MFC, under Samples in Books Online.

The docking, floating, and tool tips calls are optional. You can remove those lines from **OnCreate** if you prefer. The result is a toolbar that remains fixed, unable to float or redock and unable to display tool tips.

Editing the Toolbar Resource

The default toolbar you get with AppWizard is based on an **RT_TOOLBAR** custom resource, introduced in MFC version 4.0. You can edit this resource with the Visual C++ toolbar editor. The editor lets you easily add, delete, and rearrange buttons. It contains a graphical editor for the buttons that is very similar to the general graphics editor in Visual C++. If you edited toolbars in previous versions of Visual C++, you'll find the task much easier now.

To connect a toolbar button to a command, you give the button a command ID, such as ID_MYCOMMAND. Specify the command ID in the button's property page in the toolbar editor. Then use ClassWizard to create a handler function for the command.

New **CToolBar** member functions work with the **RT_TOOLBAR** resource. **LoadToolBar** now takes the place of **LoadBitmap** to load the bitmap of the toolbar button images, and **SetButtons** to set the button styles and connect buttons with bitmap images.

For details about the Visual C++ toolbar editor, see Chapter 11, Using the Toolbar Editor, in the *Visual C++ User's Guide*.

Multiple Toolbars

AppWizard gives you one toolbar. If you want more, you need to model your code for the additional toolbars on the code for the first one.

If you want to display a toolbar as the result of a command, you'll need to:

- Create a new toolbar resource with the toolbar editor and load it in **OnCreate** with the **LoadToolbar** member function.

- Embed a new **CToolBar** object in your main frame window class.

- Make the appropriate function calls in **OnCreate** to dock or float the toolbar, set its styles, and so on.

See Also Toolbars, Toolbars: Docking and Floating, Toolbars: Tool Tips, Toolbars: Working with the Toolbar Control, Toolbars: Using Your Old Toolbars

Toolbars: Docking and Floating

The Microsoft Foundation Class Library supports dockable toolbars. A dockable toolbar can be attached, or "docked," to any side of its parent window, or it can be "floated" in its own mini-frame window. This article explains how to use dockable toolbars in your applications.

If you use AppWizard to generate the skeleton of your application, you are asked to choose whether you want dockable toolbars. By default, AppWizard generates the code that performs the three actions necessary to place a dockable toolbar in your application:

- Enable docking for the frame window.
- Enable docking for the toolbar.
- Dock the toolbar to the frame window.

If any of these steps are missing, your application will display a standard toolbar. The last two steps must be performed for each dockable toolbar in your application.

Other topics covered in this article include:

- Floating the toolbar
- Dynamically resizing the toolbar
- Setting wrap positions for a fixed-style toolbar

See the MFC General sample DOCKTOOL for examples.

Enabling Docking in a Frame Window

To dock toolbars to a frame window, the frame window (or destination) must be enabled to allow docking. This is done using the **CFrameWnd::EnableDocking** function, which takes one **DWORD** parameter that is a set of style bits indicating which side of the frame window accepts docking. If a toolbar is about to be docked and there are multiple sides that it could be docked to, the sides indicated in the parameter passed to **EnableDocking** are used in the following order: top, bottom, left, right. If you want to be able to dock control bars anywhere, pass **CBRS_ALIGN_ANY** to **EnableDocking**.

Enabling Docking for a Toolbar

After you have prepared the destination for docking, you must prepare the toolbar (or source) in a similar fashion. Call **CControlBar::EnableDocking** for each toolbar you want to dock, specifying the destination sides to which the toolbar should dock. If none of the sides specified in the call to **CControlBar::EnableDocking** match the sides enabled for docking in the frame window, the toolbar cannot dock—it will float. Once it has been floated, it remains a floating toolbar, unable to dock to the frame window.

If the effect you want is a permanently floating palette, call **EnableDocking** with a parameter of 0. Then call **CFrameWnd::FloatControlBar**. The toolbar remains floating, permanently unable to dock anywhere.

Docking the Toolbar

To actually dock the toolbar to the frame window, you must call **CFrameWnd::DockControlBar**. This is normally called by the framework when the user attempts to drop the toolbar on a side of the frame window that allows docking.

In addition, you can call this function at any time to dock control bars to the frame window. This is normally done during initialization. More than one toolbar can be docked to a particular side of the frame window.

Floating the Toolbar

Detaching a dockable toolbar from the frame window is called "floating" the toolbar. Call **CFrameWnd::FloatControlBar** to do this. Specify the toolbar to be floated, the point where it should be placed, and an alignment style that determines whether the floating toolbar is horizontal or vertical.

This function is normally called when a user drags a toolbar off its docked location and drops it in a location where docking is not enabled. This can be anywhere inside or outside the frame window. As with **DockControlBar**, this function can also be called during initialization.

The MFC implementation of dockable toolbars does not provide some of the extended features found in some applications that support dockable toolbars. Features such as customizable toolbars are not provided.

Dynamically Resizing the Toolbar

As of Visual C++ version 4.0, you can make it possible for users of your application to resize floating toolbars dynamically. Typically, a toolbar has a long, linear shape, displayed horizontally. But you can change the toolbar's orientation and its shape. For example, when the user docks a toolbar against one of the vertical sides of the frame window, the shape changes to a vertical layout. It's also possible to reshape the toolbar into a rectangle with multiple rows of buttons.

You can:

- Specify dynamic sizing as a toolbar characteristic.
- Specify fixed sizing as a toolbar characteristic.

To provide this support, there are two new toolbar styles for use in your calls to the **CToolBar::Create** member function. They are

- **CBRS_SIZE_DYNAMIC**   Control bar is dynamic.
- **CBRS_SIZE_FIXED**   Control bar is fixed.

The size dynamic style lets your user resize the toolbar while it is floating, but not while it is docked. The toolbar "wraps" where needed to change shape as the user drags its edges.

The size fixed style preserves the wrap states of a toolbar, fixing the position of the buttons in each column. Your application's user can't change the shape of the toolbar. The toolbar wraps at designated places, such as the locations of separators between the buttons. It maintains this shape whether the toolbar is docked or floating. The effect is a fixed palette with multiple columns of buttons.

You can also use **CToolBar::GetButtonStyle** to return a state and style for buttons on your toolbars. A button's style determines how the button appears and how it responds to user input; the state tells whether the button is in a wrapped state.

Setting Wrap Positions for a Fixed-Style Toolbar

For a toolbar with the size fixed style, you need to designate toolbar button indexes at which the toolbar will wrap. The following code shows how to do this in your main frame window's OnCreate override:

```
// Get the style of the first button separator
UINT nStyle = m_wndToolBar->GetButtonStyle( 3 );
// Augment the state for wrapping
nStyle |= TBBS_WRAPPED;
m_wndToolBar->SetButtonStyle( 3, nStyle );

// Do the same for other wrap locations ...

// Set the bar style to size fixed
m_wndToolBar->SetBarStyle(m_wndToolBar->GetBarStyle() |
        CBRS_TOOLTIPS | CBRS_FLYBY | CBRS_SIZE_FIXED);

// Call docking/floating functions as needed ...
```

The MFC General sample DOCKTOOL shows how to use member functions of classes **CControlBar** and **CToolBar** to manage dynamic layout of a toolbar. See the file EDITBAR.CPP in DOCKTOOL.

See Also Toolbars: Fundamentals, Toolbars, Toolbars: Tool Tips, Toolbars: Working with the Toolbar Control, Toolbars: Using Your Old Toolbars

Toolbars: Tool Tips

Tool tips are the tiny popup windows that present short descriptions of a toolbar button's purpose when you position the mouse over a button for a period of time. When you create an application with AppWizard that has a toolbar, tool tip support is provided for you. This article explains both the tool tip support created by AppWizard and how to add tool tip support to your application.

Activating Tool Tips

To activate tool tips in your application, you must do two things:

- Add the **CBRS_TOOLTIPS** style to the other styles (such as **WS_CHILD**, **WS_VISIBLE**, and other **CBRS_** styles) passed as the dwStyle parameter to the **CToolBar::Create** function or in **SetBarStyle**.

- As described in the procedure below, append the toolbar tip text, separated by a newline character ('\n'), to the string resource containing the command-line prompt for the toolbar command. The string resource shares the ID of the toolbar button.

▶ **To add the tool tip text**

1 While you are editing the toolbar in the toolbar editor, open the Toolbar Button Properties window for a given button.

2 In the Prompt box, specify the text you want to appear in the tool tip for that button.

Note Setting the text as a button property in the toolbar editor replaces the former procedure, in which you had to open and edit the string resource.

If a control bar with tool tips enabled has child controls placed on it, the control bar will display a tool tip for every child control on the control bar as long as it meets the following criteria:

- The ID of the control is not −1.

- The string-table entry with the same ID as the child control in the resource file has a tool tip string.

Fly By Status Bar Updates

A feature related to tool tips is "fly by" status bar updating. By default, the message on the status bar only describes a particular toolbar button when the button is activated. By including **CBRS_FLYBY** in your list of styles passed to **CToolBar::Create**, you can have these messages updated when the mouse cursor passes over the toolbar without actually activating the button.

See Also Toolbars: Fundamentals, Toolbars: Docking and Floating, Toolbars, Toolbars: Working with the Toolbar Control, Toolbars: Using Your Old Toolbars

Toolbars: Working with the Toolbar Control

This article explains how you can access the **CToolBarCtrl** object underlying a **CToolBar** for greater control over your toolbars. This is an advanced topic.

▶ **To access the toolbar common control underlying your CToolBar object**

- Call **CToolBar::GetToolBarCtrl**.

GetToolBarCtrl returns a reference to a **CToolBarCtrl** object. You can use the reference to call member functions of the toolbar control class.

Caution While calling **CToolBarCtrl Get** functions is safe, use caution if you call the **Set** functions. This is an advanced topic. Normally you shouldn't need to access the underlying toolbar control.

For general information about using Windows common controls, see Common Controls in the Windows 95 SDK *Programmer's Reference*.

For more information about **CToolBarCtrl**, see CToolBarCtrl: Handling Tool Tip Notifications and CToolBarCtrl: Handling Customization Notifications.

See Also Toolbars: Fundamentals, Toolbars: Docking and Floating, Toolbars: Tool Tips, Toolbars, Toolbars: Using Your Old Toolbars

Toolbars: Using Your Old Toolbars

If you have used previous versions of Visual C++ to create customized toolbars, the new implementation of class **CToolBar** could cause you problems.

So that you don't have to give up your old toolbars to use the new functionality, the old implementation is still supported. The older implementation of class **CToolBar** is now available in class **COldToolBar**.

▶ To use the older implementation

1 Replace occurrences of "CToolBar" in your code with "COldToolBar".

2 As documentation for **COldToolBar**, see the documentation for **CToolBar** in a version of MFC earlier than version 4.0.

As demonstrated in the MFC General sample DOCKTOOL, you can use old-style toolbars alongside new toolbars in your application. However, you can't edit old-style toolbars with the toolbar resource editor.

The older implementation of class **CToolBar** is now available in the OLDBARS sample program. For information on how to use that code in your own application, see the sample abstract for OLDBARS.

The DOCKTOOL sample does not use the old-style toolbars, only the new-style toolbars.

See Also Toolbars: Fundamentals, Toolbars: Docking and Floating, Toolbars: Tool Tips, Toolbars: Working with the Toolbar Control, Toolbars

Tools for MFC Programming

Visual C++ supplies a number of tools that help you build applications for Windows using the Microsoft Foundation Class Library (MFC). These tools include:

- AppWizard
- Resource editors
- ClassWizard
- New tools, including ClassView, a toolbar editor, the WizardBar, and Component Gallery

The final topic in this article, Using the Tools To Create an Application, highlights the roles of these tools in combination. Other articles explore the details of each wizard. The *Visual C++ User's Guide* details the resource editors in Chapters 5 through 13.

AppWizard Creates Skeleton Code

AppWizard creates the starter files for a new application. The starter files consist of C++ source files, resource files, header files, and a project file. They include the code necessary to implement basic features for applications for Windows. These basic features include such things as window management, a basic menu structure, and basic menu commands. They also include skeleton code for features that you need to implement for your specific application. In the course of developing your application, you add the code required to flesh out the skeleton fully. For instance, you need to add code that loads a file for your application properly, or saves a document in the appropriate file format on disk. AppWizard marks these locations in the source files it creates as "// TODO" comments.

Resource Editors Create Resources

Visual C++ has a number of integrated editors for various kinds of Windows resources. These include menus, dialogs, string tables, accelerator tables, version resources, and graphical objects, such as icons, cursors, and bitmaps.

AppWizard creates an .RC file containing basic resources: standard menus, an About dialog box, a string table containing predefined strings, and so on. Other files contain a default icon, a version resource, and, if you choose the option to include an initial toolbar, a bitmap containing images for toolbar buttons.

As you program, you'll usually need to add more menus, additional dialog boxes, new strings and accelerators, and so on. Typically, you invoke the appropriate editor to create or edit these resources. In some cases, such as menus, toolbar buttons, and dialog boxes, you first create the resource, specifying its ID, then use ClassWizard to connect the resource to code.

ClassWizard Fills Out Implementation Details

ClassWizard allows you to create new classes or member functions and variables to implement the details of your application's operation. It also works with the resource editors to implement user-interface objects, such as dialog boxes, in your application.

You use the resource editors to create these user-interface objects. You then use ClassWizard to generate functions and message maps for each user-interface object. For example, you might use the dialog editor to create an edit control in a dialog box. Later, in ClassWizard, you can create a class member function to handle input to the edit box and the member variables to validate and store the entered information. You can also use ClassWizard to connect a menu command or a toolbar button to the dialog box to display it.

Using the Tools To Create an Application

The development phase of any Windows-based application typically includes a number of passes, involving editing source and resource files, building the project, and testing and debugging. Because these activities are iterative and interwoven during a normal development cycle, they don't follow one another in a strict sequential order.

The following steps, nonetheless, describe the general procedure for beginning application development using AppWizard, ClassWizard, and the Visual C++ resource editors.

▶ **To use the tools together**

1 Choose the File New command and select Project Workspace and then select the MFC AppWizard project type. Use AppWizard to select the location for your project and the characteristics of your project.

2 Use ClassWizard to create classes, member functions, and member variables for the skeleton code in your application. ClassWizard also displays the locations in the source files where you need to add code specific to your implementation.

3 Use the Visual C++ resource editors to create resources for your application.

4 Use ClassWizard to create the classes and member functions to handle those resources.

5 Build the application with the Build command on the Build menu.

New Tools in Visual C++ version 4.0

With Visual C++ version 4.0, the following new tools are available to make your MFC programming easier:

ClassView pane in the Project Workspace window   Switch from BuildView to ClassView to InfoView. In ClassView, view your project in terms of classes, not files. In BuildView, view your project in terms of familiar files. In InfoView, view the documentation, now compatible with the Microsoft Developer Network and completely integrated with the IDE.

WizardBar   At the top of your source code windows in the Visual C++ source code editor, the WizardBar makes it easy to bind Windows message and commands to handlers, to open the include file for a source module, and to navigate to code.

Toolbar Editor and RT_TOOLBAR resource type   Support now includes a new toolbar resource type and a new version of class **CToolBar** based on the toolbar control available in Windows 95 and Windows NT version 3.51. Visual C++ supplies a toolbar editor in the IDE. Creating dockable, floating toolbars is easier than ever.

Component Gallery   Store reusable components—our own or from third-party vendors. Add them to your projects almost seamlessly.

See Also   AppWizard, ClassWizard

Trackers

The **CRectTracker** class provides a user interface between rectangular items in your application and your user by providing a variety of display styles. These styles include: solid, hatched, or dashed borders; a hatched pattern that covers the item; and resize handles that can be located on the outside or inside of a border. Trackers are often used in conjunction with OLE items, that is, objects derived from **COleClientItem**. The tracker rectangles give visual cues on the current status of the item.

The MFC OLE sample OCLIENT demonstrates a common interface using trackers and OLE client items from the viewpoint of a container application. For a demonstration of the different styles and abilities of a tracker object, see the MFC general sample TRACKER.

For more information on implementing trackers in your OLE application, see the following article:

- Trackers: Implementing Trackers in Your OLE Application

See Also   Trackers: Implementing Trackers in Your OLE Application

In the *Class Library Reference*: **COleClientItem**, **CRectTracker**

Trackers: Implementing Trackers in Your OLE Application

Trackers provide a graphical interface to enable users to interact with OLE client items. By using different tracker styles, OLE client items can be displayed with hatched borders, resize handles, or a variety of other visual effects. This article describes:

- Tracking and how to implement it in your code.
- The rubber-band effect and trackers.

The article also covers the use of styles with trackers.

This article makes several references to the MFC OLE sample OCLIENT. This sample is described in the Samples documentation.

How to Implement Tracking in Your Code

To track an OLE item, you must handle certain events related to the item, such as clicking the item or updating the view of the document. In all cases, it is sufficient to declare a temporary **CRectTracker** object and manipulate the item by means of this object.

When a user selects an item or inserts an object with a menu command, you must initialize the tracker with the proper styles to represent the state of the OLE item. Table 1 outlines the convention used by the OCLIENT sample. For more information on these styles, see **CRectTracker** in the *Class Library Reference*.

Table 1   Container Styles and State of the OLE Item

Style displayed	State of OLE item
Dotted border	Item is linked
Solid border	Item is embedded in your document
Resize handles	Item is currently selected
Hatched border	Item is currently in-place active
Hatching pattern overlays item	Item's server is open

You can handle this initialization easily using a procedure that checks the state of the OLE item and sets the appropriate styles. The SetupTracker function found in the OCLIENT sample demonstrates tracker initialization. The parameters for this function are the address of the tracker, *pTracker*; a pointer to the client item that is related to the tracker, *pItem*; and a pointer to a rectangle, *pTrueRect*. For a more complete example of this function, see the MFC OLE sample OCLIENT.

The SetupTracker code example below presents a single function; lines of the function are interspersed with discussion of the function's features:

```
void CMainView::SetupTracker( CRectTracker* pTracker,
  CRectItem* pItem, CRect* pTrueRect )
{
```

The tracker is initialized by setting the minimum size and clearing the style of the tracker.

```
pTracker->m_sizeMin.cx = 8;
pTracker->m_sizeMin.cy = 8;

pTracker->m_nStyle = 0;
```

The following code sample checks to see whether the item is currently selected and whether the item is linked to the document or embedded in it. Resize handles located on the inside of the border are added to the style, indicating that the item is currently selected. If the item is linked to your document, the dotted border style is used. A solid border is used if the item is embedded.

```
if ( pItem == m_pSelection )
  pTracker->m_nStyle |= CRectTracker::resizeInside;

if ( pItem->GetType( ) == OT_LINK )
  pTracker->m_nStyle |= CRectTracker::dottedLine;
else
  pTracker->m_nStyle |= CRectTracker::solidLine;
```

The following code overlays the item with a hatched pattern if the item is currently open.

```
if ( pItem->GetItemState( ) ==
     COleClientItem::openState ||
     pItem->GetItemState( ) ==
     COleClientItem::activeUIState )
  pTracker->m_nStyle |= CRectTracker::hatchInside;
}
```

You can then call this function whenever the tracker has to be displayed. For example, call this function from the **OnDraw** function of your view class. This updates the tracker's appearance whenever the view is repainted. For a complete example, see the **CMainView::OnDraw** function of the MFC OLE sample OCLIENT.

Events will occur in your application that require tracker code, such as resizing, moving, or hit detecting. These actions usually indicate that an attempt is being made to grab or move the item. In these cases you will need to decide what was grabbed: a resize handle or a portion of the border between resize handles. The **OnLButtonDown** message handler is a good place to test the position of the mouse in relation to the item. Make a call to **CRectTracker::HitTest**. If the test returns something besides **CRectTracker::hitOutside**, the item is being resized or moved. Therefore, you should make a call to the **Track** member function. See the **CMainView::OnLButtonDown** function located in the MFC OLE sample OCLIENT for a complete example.

The **CRectTracker** class provides several different cursor shapes used to indicate whether a move, resize, or drag operation is taking place. To handle this event, check to see whether the item currently under the mouse is selected. If it is, make a call to **CRectTracker::SetCursor**, or call the default handler. The following example is from the MFC OLE sample OCLIENT:

```
BOOL CMainView::OnSetCursor( CWnd* pWnd, UINT nHitTest,
  UINT message )
{
  if ( pWnd == this && m_pSelection != NULL )
  {
    // give the tracker for the selection a chance
    CRectTracker tracker;
    SetupTracker( &tracker, m_pSelection );
    if ( tracker.SetCursor( this, nHitTest ))
      return TRUE;
  }
  return CScrollView::OnSetCursor( pWnd,
    nHitTest, message );
}
```

Rubber-Banding and Trackers

Another feature supplied with trackers is the "rubber-band" selection, which allows a user to select multiple OLE items by dragging a sizing rectangle around the items to be selected. When the user releases the left mouse button, items within the region selected by the user are selected and can be manipulated by the user. For instance, the user might drag or drop the selection into another container application.

Implementing this feature requires some additional code in your application's **WM_LBUTTONDOWN** handler function.

The following code sample implements rubber-band selection and additional features and is taken from the **WM_LBUTTONDOWN** handler function of MFC General sample TRACKER.

```
if (pDoc->m_tracker.HitTest(point) < 0)
{
  // just to demonstrate CRectTracker::TrackRubberBand
  CRectTracker tracker;
  if (tracker.TrackRubberBand(this, point,
    pDoc->m_bAllowInvert))
  {
    MessageBeep(0); // beep indicates TRUE

    // see if rubber band intersects with the doc's tracker
    CRect rectT;
    // so intersect rect works
    tracker.m_rect.NormalizeRect();
    if (rectT.IntersectRect(tracker.m_rect,
      pDoc->m_tracker.m_rect))
    {
    // if so, put resize handles on it (i.e. select it)
      if (pDoc->m_tracker.m_nStyle &
        CRectTracker::resizeInside)
      {
      // swap from resize inside to resize outside for effect
        pDoc->m_tracker.m_nStyle &=
          ~CRectTracker::resizeInside;
```

```
    pDoc->m_tracker.m_nStyle |=
      CRectTracker::resizeOutside;
  }
  else
  {
  // just use inside resize handles on first time
    pDoc->m_tracker.m_nStyle &=
      ~CRectTracker::resizeOutside;
    pDoc->m_tracker.m_nStyle |=
      CRectTracker::resizeInside;
  }
  pDoc->SetModifiedFlag();
  pDoc->UpdateAllViews(NULL,
    (LPARAM)(LPCRECT)rectSave);
  pDoc->UpdateAllViews(NULL);
    }
  }
}
```

If you want to allow reversible orientation of the tracker during rubber-banding, you should call **CRectTracker::TrackRubberBand** with the third parameter set to **TRUE**. Remember that allowing reversible orientation will sometimes cause **CRectTracker::m_rect** to become inverted. This can be corrected by a call to **CRect::NormalizeRect**.

See Also Containers: Client Items, Drag and Drop: Customizing

In the *Class Library Reference*: **CRectTracker**

Transaction (ODBC)

A transaction is a way to "batch" a series of updates to a data source so that all are committed at once, or none are committed if you roll back the transaction. If you do not use a transaction, changes to the data source are committed automatically rather than committed on demand.

Note This article applies to the MFC ODBC classes. If you're working with the MFC DAO classes, see the article DAO Workspace: Managing Transactions.

Note Not all ODBC database drivers support transactions to the level required by the database classes. Call the **CanTransact** member function of your **CDatabase** or **CRecordset** object to determine whether your driver supports transactions for a given database. **CanTransact** tells you whether transaction support on the data source is sufficient for the database classes; it does not tell you whether the data source provides full transaction support. For more information about required transaction levels and the MFC transaction model, see Technical Note 47 under MFC in Books Online.

Calls to the **AddNew** and **Edit** member functions of a **CRecordset** object affect the data source immediately when you call **Update**. **Delete** calls also take effect immediately. In contrast, you can use a transaction consisting of multiple calls to

AddNew, **Edit**, **Update**, and **Delete**, which are performed but not committed until you call **CommitTrans** explicitly. By establishing a transaction, you can execute a series of such calls while retaining the ability to roll them back. If a critical resource is unavailable or some other condition prevents the entire transaction from being completed, you can roll back the transaction instead of committing it. In that case, none of the changes belonging to the transaction affect the data source.

Note Besides affecting your recordset, transactions affect SQL statements that you execute directly as long as you use the ODBC **HDBC** associated with your **CDatabase** object or an ODBC **HSTMT** based on that **HDBC**.

Transactions are particularly useful when you have multiple records that must be simultaneously updated. In this case, you want to avoid a half-completed transaction, such as might happen if an exception were thrown before the last update was made. Grouping such updates into a transaction allows a recovery (rollback) from the changes, and returns the records to the pretransaction state. For example, if a bank transfers money from account A to account B, both the withdrawal from A and the deposit to B must succeed to process the funds correctly, or the whole transaction must fail.

In the database classes, you perform transactions through **CDatabase** objects. A **CDatabase** object represents a connection to a data source, and one or more recordsets associated with that **CDatabase** object operate on tables of the database through recordset member functions.

Note Only one level of transactions is supported; you cannot nest transactions, nor can a transaction span multiple database objects.

Note The MFC transaction model, which is recordset-centered, requires that the cursor be preserved on commit and on rollback. If this requirement is too restrictive for your application, see Technical Note 47 under MFC in Books Online.

The following articles provide more information about how transactions are performed:

- Transaction: Performing a Transaction in a Recordset (ODBC)
- Transaction: How Transactions Affect Updates (ODBC)

See Also In the *Class Library Reference*: **CDatabase**, **CRecordset**

Transaction: Performing a Transaction in a Recordset (ODBC)

This article explains how to perform a transaction in a recordset.

Note Only one level of transactions is supported; you cannot nest transactions.

► **To perform a transaction in a recordset**

1 Call the **CDatabase** object's **BeginTrans** member function.

2 Call the **AddNew/Update**, **Edit/Update**, and **Delete** member functions of one or more recordset objects of the same database as many times as needed. See the article Recordset: Adding, Updating, and Deleting Records (ODBC).

3 Finally, call the **CDatabase** object's **CommitTrans** member function. Or, if an error occurs in one of the updates, or you decide to cancel the changes, call its **Rollback** member function.

The following example uses two recordsets to delete a student's enrollment from a school registration database, removing the student from all classes in which the student is enrolled. The **Delete** calls in both recordsets must succeed, so a transaction is required. The example assumes the existence of m_dbStudentReg, a member variable of type **CDatabase** already connected to the data source, and the recordset classes CEnrollmentSet and CStudentSet. The strStudentID function contains a value obtained from the user.

```
BOOL CEnrollDoc::RemoveStudent(CString strStudentID)
{
    // remove student from all the classes student is enrolled in
    CEnrollmentSet  rsEnrollmentSet(&m_dbStudentReg);
    rsEnrollmentSet.m_strFilter = "StudentID = " + strStudentID;
    if ( !rsEnrollmentSet.Open(CRecordset::dynaset) )
        return FALSE;
    CStudentSet  rsStudentSet(&m_dbStudentReg);
    rsStudentSet.m_strFilter = "StudentID = " + strStudentID;
    if ( !rsStudentSet.Open(CRecordset::dynaset) )
        return FALSE;
    if ( !m_dbStudentReg.BeginTrans())
        return FALSE;
    TRY
    {
        while (!rsEnrollmentSet.IsEOF())
        {
            rsEnrollmentSet.Delete();
            rsEnrollmentSet.MoveNext();
        }

        // delete the student record
        rsStudentSet.Delete();

        m_dbStudentReg.CommitTrans();
    }
    CATCH_ALL(e)
    {
        m_dbStudentReg.Rollback();
        return FALSE;
    }
    return TRUE;
}
```

Warning Calling **BeginTrans** again without calling **CommitTrans** or **Rollback** is an error.

See Also Transaction: How Transactions Affect Updates (ODBC)

In the *Class Library Reference*: **CDatabase, CRecordset**

Transaction: How Transactions Affect Updates (ODBC)

Updates to the data source are managed during transactions through the use of an "edit buffer" (the same method used outside of transactions). The field data members of a recordset collectively serve as an edit buffer that contains the current record, which the recordset backs up temporarily during an **AddNew** or **Edit**. During a **Delete** operation, the current record is not backed up within a transaction. For more information about the edit buffer and how updates store the current record, see the article Recordset: How Recordsets Update Records (ODBC).

During transactions, **AddNew**, **Edit**, and **Delete** operations can be committed or rolled back. The effects of **CommitTrans** and **Rollback** may cause the current record to not be restored to the edit buffer. To make sure that the current record is properly restored, it is important to understand how the **CommitTrans** and **Rollback** member functions of **CDatabase** work with the update functions of **CRecordset**.

How CommitTrans Affects Updates

Table 1 explains the effects of **CommitTrans** on transactions.

Table 1   How CommitTrans Affects Updates

Operation	Status of data source
AddNew and **Update**, then **CommitTrans**	New record added to data source.
AddNew (without **Update**), then **CommitTrans**	New record is lost. Record not added to data source.
Edit and **Update**, then **CommitTrans**	Edits committed to data source.
Edit (without **Update**), then **CommitTrans**	Edits to the record are lost. Record remains unchanged on the data source.
Delete then **CommitTrans**	Records deleted from data source.

How Rollback Affects Transactions

Table 2 explains the effects of **Rollback** on transactions.

Table 2   How Rollback Affects Transactions

Operation	Status of current record	You must also:	Status of data source
AddNew and **Update**, then **Rollback**	Content of the current record is stored temporarily to make room for new record. New record is entered into edit buffer. After **Update** is called, the current record is restored to the edit buffer.		Addition to data source made by **Update** is reversed.
AddNew (without **Update**), then **Rollback**	Content of the current record is stored temporarily to make room for new record. Edit buffer contains new record.	Call **AddNew** again to restore the edit buffer to an empty, new record. Or call **Move**(0) to restore the old values to the edit buffer.	Because **Update** was not called, there were no changes made to the data source.
Edit and **Update**, then **Rollback**	An unedited version of the current record is stored temporarily. Edits are made to the content of the edit buffer. After **Update** is called, the unedited version of the record is still temporarily stored.	*Dynaset*: Scroll off the current record then back to restore the unedited version of the record to the edit buffer. *Snapshot*: Call **Requery** to refresh the recordset from the data source.	Changes to data source made by **Update** are reversed.
Edit (without **Update**), then **Rollback**	An unedited version of the current record is stored temporarily. Edits are made to the content of the edit buffer.	Call **Edit** again to restore the unedited version of the record to the edit buffer.	Because **Update** was not called, there were no changes made to the data source.
Delete then **Rollback**	Content of the current record is deleted.	Call **Requery** to restore the content of the current record from the data source.	Deletion of data from data source is reversed.

See Also   Transaction (ODBC), Transaction: Performing a Transaction in a Recordset (ODBC)

In the *Class Library Reference*: **CDatabase**, **CRecordset**

Type Library

See the article Automation Clients: Using Type Libraries.

Unicode

On Windows NT platforms, MFC supports the Unicode standard for encoding wide characters.

For information on using Unicode with MFC, see Chapter 13, Developing for International Markets, in *Programming Techniques*.

Verbs, OLE

See the article Activation: Verbs.

Visual Editing

See the article Servers: Implementing In-Place Frame Windows.

Windows Sockets in MFC: Overview

MFC supplies two models for writing network communications programs with Windows Sockets, embodied in two MFC classes. This article describes these models and further details MFC sockets support. A "socket" is an endpoint of communication —an object through which your application communicates with other Windows Sockets applications across a network.

This article describes:

- Sockets programming models.
- MFC socket samples and Windows Sockets DLLs.
- Windows sockets articles.

For background information on Windows Sockets, including a detailed explanation of the socket concept, see the article Windows Sockets: Background.

Sockets Programming Models

The two MFC Windows Sockets programming models are supported by the following classes:

- **CAsyncSocket**

   This class encapsulates the Windows Sockets API. **CAsyncSocket** is for programmers who know network programming and want the flexibility of programming directly to the sockets API but also want the convenience of callback functions for notification of network events. Other than packaging sockets in object-oriented form for use in C++, the only additional abstraction this class supplies is converting certain socket-related Windows messages into callbacks. (See the article Windows Sockets: Socket Notifications.)

- **CSocket**

   This class, derived from **CAsyncSocket**, supplies a higher-level abstraction for working with sockets via an MFC **CArchive** object. Using a socket with an archive greatly resembles using MFC's file serialization protocol. This makes it easier to use than the **CAsyncSocket** model. **CSocket** inherits many member functions from **CAsyncSocket** that encapsulate Windows Sockets APIs; you will have to use some of these functions and understand sockets programming generally. But **CSocket** manages many aspects of the communication that you would have to do yourself using either the raw API or class **CAsyncSocket**. Most important, **CSocket** provides blocking (with background processing of Windows messages), which is essential to the synchronous operation of **CArchive**.

Creating and using **CSocket** and **CAsyncSocket** objects is described in the articles Windows Sockets: Using Sockets with Archives and Windows Sockets: Using Class CAsyncSocket.

MFC Socket Samples and Windows Sockets DLLs

Visual C++ supplies the CHATTER and CHATSRVR sample applications to illustrate the client/server model, which is the most common model. CHATTER is the client; CHATSRVR is the server. These samples make good templates for writing your own clients and servers. You can access the source code for the MFC Advanced Concepts samples CHATTER and CHATSRVR under Samples in Books Online.

The Microsoft Windows NT operating system supplies the Windows Sockets dynamic link libraries (DLLs). Visual C++ supplies the appropriate header files and libraries and the Windows Sockets specification. The specification is available in Books Online under Win32.

Note   Under Windows NT, Windows Sockets support for 16-bit applications is based on WINSOCK.DLL. For 32-bit applications, the support is in WSOCK32.DLL. The APIs provided are identical except that the 32-bit versions have parameters widened to 32 bits. Under Win32, thread safety is supplied.

ClassWizard does not support creating classes derived from the MFC Windows Sockets classes.

Windows Sockets Articles

For detailed information about Windows Sockets and their implementation in MFC, see the following articles:

- Windows Sockets: Background
- Windows Sockets: Stream Sockets
- Windows Sockets: Datagram Sockets
- Windows Sockets: Using Sockets with Archives
- Windows Sockets: Sequence of Operations
- Windows Sockets: Example of Sockets Using Archives
- Windows Sockets: How Sockets with Archives Work
- Windows Sockets: Using Class CAsyncSocket
- Windows Sockets: Deriving from Socket Classes
- Windows Sockets: Socket Notifications
- Windows Sockets: Blocking
- Windows Sockets: Byte Ordering
- Windows Sockets: Converting Strings

- Windows Sockets: Ports and Socket Addresses

See Also   In the *Class Library Reference*: **CAsyncSocket**, **CSocket**, **CArchive**

Samples: CHATTER, CHATSRVR

Windows Sockets: Background

This article explains the nature and purpose of Windows Sockets. The article also:

- Defines the term "socket."
- Describes the SOCKET handle data type.
- Describes uses for sockets.

The Windows Sockets specification defines a binary-compatible network programming interface for Microsoft Windows. Windows Sockets are based on the UNIX® sockets implementation in the Berkeley Software Distribution (BSD, release 4.3) from the University of California at Berkeley. The specification includes both BSD-style socket routines and extensions specific to Windows. Using Windows Sockets permits your application to communicate across any network that conforms to the Windows Sockets API. On Win32, Windows Sockets provide for thread safety.

Many network software vendors support Windows Sockets under network protocols including Transmission Control Protocol/Internet Protocol (TCP/IP), Xerox® Network System (XNS), Digital Equipment Corporation's DECNet™ protocol, Novell® Corporation's Internet Packet Exchange/Sequenced Packed Exchange (IPX/SPX), and others. Although the present Windows Sockets specification defines the sockets abstraction for TCP/IP, any network protocol can comply with Windows Sockets by supplying its own version of the dynamic link library (DLL) that implements Windows Sockets. Examples of commercial applications written with Windows Sockets include X Window servers, terminal emulators, and electronic mail systems.

Note   Keep in mind that the purpose of Windows Sockets is to abstract away the underlying network so you don't have to be knowledgeable about that network and so your application can run on any network that supports sockets. Consequently, this documentation doesn't discuss the details of network protocols.

The Microsoft Foundation Class Library (MFC) supports programming with the Windows Sockets API by supplying two classes. One of these classes, **CSocket**, provides a high level of abstraction to simplify your network communications programming. For more information about MFC socket support, see Windows Sockets in MFC: Overview.

The Windows Sockets specification, Windows Sockets: An Open Interface for Network Computing Under Microsoft Windows, now at version 1.1, was developed as an open networking standard by a large group of individuals and corporations in the TCP/IP community and is freely available for use. The sockets programming model supports one "communication domain" currently, using the Internet Protocol Suite. The specification is available in Books Online under Win32.

Tip Because sockets use the Internet Protocol Suite, they are the preferred route for applications that support Internet communications on the "information highway."

Definition of a Socket

A socket is a communication endpoint—an object through which a Windows Sockets application sends or receives packets of data across a network. A socket has a type and is associated with a running process, and it may have a name. Currently, sockets generally exchange data only with other sockets in the same "communication domain," which uses the Internet Protocol Suite.

Both kinds of sockets are bi-directional: they are data flows that can be communicated in both directions simultaneously (full-duplex).

Two socket types are available:

- Stream sockets

  Stream sockets provide for a data flow without record boundaries—a stream of bytes. Streams are guaranteed to be delivered and to be correctly sequenced and unduplicated.

- Datagram sockets

  Datagram sockets support a record-oriented data flow that is not guaranteed to be delivered and may not be sequenced as sent or unduplicated.

"Sequenced" means that packets are delivered in the order sent. "Unduplicated" means that you get a particular packet only once.

Note Under some network protocols, such as XNS, streams can be record-oriented—streams of records rather than streams of bytes. Under the more common TCP/IP protocol, however, streams are byte streams. Windows Sockets provides a level of abstraction independent of the underlying protocol.

For information about these types and which kind of socket to use in which situations, see the articles Windows Sockets: Stream Sockets and Windows Sockets: Datagram Sockets.

The SOCKET Data Type

Each MFC socket object encapsulates a handle to a Windows Sockets object. The data type of this handle is **SOCKET**. A **SOCKET** handle is analogous to the **HWND** for a window. MFC socket classes provide operations on the encapsulated handle.

The **SOCKET** data type is described in detail in Books Online under Win32. See the topic Socket Data Type and Error Values under Windows Sockets.

Uses for Sockets

Sockets are highly useful in at least three communications contexts:

- Client/Server models

- Peer-to-peer scenarios, such as chat applications

- Making remote procedure calls (RPC) by having the receiving application interpret a message as a function call

Tip The ideal case for using MFC sockets is when you're writing both ends of the communication: using MFC at both ends. For more information on this topic, including how to manage the case when you're communicating with non-MFC applications, see the article Windows Sockets: Byte Ordering.

For more information, see Windows Sockets Specification: **ntohs**, **ntohl**, **htons**, **htonl**.

See Also Windows Sockets in MFC: Overview, Windows Sockets: Using Sockets with Archives, Windows Sockets: Example of Sockets Using Archives, Windows Sockets: Using Class CAsyncSocket, Windows Sockets: Stream Sockets, Windows Sockets: Datagram Sockets

Samples: CHATTER, CHATSRVR

Windows Sockets: Stream Sockets

This article describes stream sockets, one of the two Windows Socket types available. (The other type is the datagram socket.)

Stream sockets provide for a data flow without record boundaries—a stream of bytes that can be bi-directional (the application is full-duplex: it can both transmit and receive through the socket). Streams can be relied upon to deliver sequenced, unduplicated data. ("Sequenced" means that packets are delivered in the order sent. "Unduplicated" means that you get a particular packet only once.) Receipt of stream messages is guaranteed, and streams are well-suited to handling large amounts of data.

The network transport layer may break up or group data into packets of reasonable size. The **CSocket** class will handle the packing and unpacking for you.

Streams are based on explicit connections: socket A requests a connection to socket B; socket B accepts or rejects the connection request.

A telephone call provides a good analogy for a stream: under normal circumstances, the receiving party hears what you say in the order that you say it, without duplication or loss. Stream sockets are appropriate, for example, for implementations such as the File Transfer Protocol (FTP), which facilitates transferring ASCII or binary files of arbitrary size.

Stream sockets are preferable to datagram sockets when the data must be guaranteed to arrive and when data size is large. For more information about stream sockets, see the Windows Sockets specification. The specification is available in Books Online under Win32.

The MFC Advanced Concepts samples CHATTER and CHATSRVR use stream sockets. These samples might have been designed to use a datagram socket for broadcasting to all receiving sockets on the network. The present design is superior because (a) the broadcast model is subject to network flood (or "storm") problems, (b) the client-server model adopted subsequently is more efficient, (c) the stream model supplies reliable data transfer, where the datagram model does not, and (d) the final model takes advantage of the ability to communicate between Unicode and ANSI socket applications that class **CArchive** lends to class **CSocket**.

Important   If you use class **CSocket**, you must use a stream. An MFC assertion fails if you specify the socket type as **SOCK_DGRAM**.

For source code and information about MFC samples, see MFC Samples under Samples in Books Online.

See Also   Windows Sockets: Datagram Sockets, Windows Sockets: Background

Samples: CHATTER, CHATSRVR

Windows Sockets: Datagram Sockets

This article describes datagram sockets, one of the two Windows Socket types available. (The other type is the stream socket.)

Datagram sockets support a bi-directional data flow that is not guaranteed to be sequenced or unduplicated. Datagrams also are not guaranteed to be reliable; they can fail to arrive. Datagram data may arrive out of order and possibly duplicated, but record boundaries in the data are preserved, as long as the records are smaller than the receiver's internal size limit. You are responsible for managing sequencing and reliability. (Reliability tends to be good on local area networks (LANs) but less so on wide area networks (WANs), such as the Internet.)

Datagrams are "connectionless"—no explicit connection is established; you send a datagram message to a specified socket and you can receive messages from a specified socket.

An example of a datagram socket is an application that keeps system clocks on the network synchronized. This illustrates an additional capability of datagram sockets in at least some settings: broadcasting messages to a large number of network addresses.

Datagram sockets are better than stream sockets for record-oriented data. For more information about datagram sockets, see the Windows Sockets specification. The specification is available in Books Online under Win32.

See Also   Windows Sockets: Stream Sockets, Windows Sockets: Background

Windows Sockets: Using Sockets with Archives

This article describes the Csocket programming model. Class **CSocket** supplies socket support at a higher level of abstraction than does class **CAsyncSocket**. **CSocket** uses a version of the MFC serialization protocol to pass data to and from a socket object via an MFC **CArchive** object. **CSocket** provides blocking (while managing background processing of Windows messages) and gives you access to **CArchive**, which manages many aspects of the communication that you would have to do yourself using either the raw API or class **CAsyncSocket**.

Tip You can use class **CSocket** by itself, as a more convenient version of **CAsyncSocket**, but the simplest programming model is to use **CSocket** with a **CArchive** object.

For additional information about how the implementation of sockets with archives works, see the article Windows Sockets: How Sockets with Archives Work. For example code, see the articles Windows Sockets: Sequence of Operations and Windows Sockets: Example of Sockets Using Archives. For information about some of the functionality you can gain by deriving your own classes from the sockets classes, see the article Windows Sockets: Deriving from Socket Classes.

Caution If you are writing an MFC client program to communicate with established (non-MFC) servers, don't send C++ objects via the archive. Unless the server is an MFC application that understands the kinds of objects you want to send, it won't be able to receive and deserialize your objects. For related material on the subject of communicating with non-MFC applications, also see the article Windows Sockets: Byte Ordering.

The CSocket Programming Model

Using a **CSocket** object involves creating and associating together several MFC class objects. In the procedure below, each step is taken by both the server socket and the client socket, except for step 3, in which each socket type requires a different action.

Tip At run time, the server application usually starts first in order to be ready and "listening" when the client application seeks a connection. If the server is not ready when the client tries to connect, you typically require the user application to try connecting again later.

▶ **To set up communication between a server socket and a client socket**

1 Construct a **CSocket** object.

2 Use the object to create the underlying **SOCKET** handle.

For a **CSocket** client object, you should normally use the default parameters to **Create**, unless you need a datagram socket. For a **CSocket** server object, you must specify a port in the **Create** call.

Note **CArchive** doesn't work with datagram sockets. If you want to use **CSocket** for a datagram socket, you must use the class as you would **CAsyncSocket**—without an archive. Because datagrams are unreliable (not guaranteed to arrive and may be repeated or out of sequence), they aren't compatible with serialization via an archive. You expect a serialization operation to complete reliably and in sequence. If you try to use **CSocket** with a **CArchive** object for a datagram, an MFC assertion fails.

3 If the socket is a client, call **CAsyncSocket::Connect** to connect the socket object to a server socket.

–or–

If the socket is a server, call **CAsyncSocket::Listen** to begin listening for connect attempts from a client. Upon receiving a connection request, accept it by calling **CAsyncSocket::Accept**.

Note The **Accept** member function takes a reference to a new, empty **CSocket** object as its parameter. You must construct this object before you call **Accept**. Keep in mind that if this socket object goes out of scope, the connection closes. Do not call **Create** for this new socket object.

4 Create a **CSocketFile** object, associating the **CSocket** object with it.

5 Create a **CArchive** object for either loading (receiving) or storing (sending) data. The archive is associated with the **CSocketFile** object.

Keep in mind that **CArchive** doesn't work with datagram sockets.

6 Use the **CArchive** object to pass data between the client and server sockets.

Keep in mind that a **CArchive** object moves data in one direction only: either for loading (receiving) or storing (sending). In some cases, you'll use two **CArchive** objects, one for sending data, the other for receiving acknowledgements.

After accepting a connection and setting up the archive, you can perform such tasks as validating passwords.

7 Destroy the archive, socket file, and socket objects.

Note Class **CArchive** supplies the **IsBufferEmpty** member function specifically for use with class **CSocket**. If the buffer contains multiple data messages, for example, you need to loop until all of them are read and the buffer is cleared. Otherwise, your next notification that there is data to be received may be indefinitely delayed. Use **IsBufferEmpty** to assure that you retrieve all data. For examples of using **IsBufferEmpty**, see the CHATSRVR sample application. For source code and information about MFC samples, see MFC Samples under Samples in Books Online.

The article Windows Sockets: Sequence of Operations illustrates both sides of this process with example code.

See Also Windows Sockets: Example of Sockets Using Archives, Windows Sockets: Stream Sockets, Windows Sockets: Datagram Sockets

In the *Class Library Reference*: **CSocket, CAsyncSocket, CSocketFile, CArchive, CSocket::Create**

Samples: CHATTER, CHATSRVR

Windows Sockets: Sequence of Operations

This article illustrates, side by side, the sequence of operations for a server socket and a client socket. Because the sockets use **CArchive** objects, they are necessarily stream sockets.

Sequence of Operations for a Stream Socket Communication

Up to the point of constructing a **CSocketFile** object, the following sequence is accurate (with a few parameter differences) for both **CAsyncSocket** and **CSocket**. From that point on, the sequence is strictly for **CSocket**. Table 1 illustrates the sequence of operations for setting up communication between a client and a server.

Table 1   Setting Up Communication Between a Server and a Client

Server	Client
`// construct a socket` `CSocket sockSrvr;`	`// construct a socket` `CSocket sockClient;`
`// create the SOCKET` `sockSrvr.Create(nPort);`[1,2]	`// create the SOCKET` `sockClient.Create( );`[2]
`// start listening` `sockSrvr.Listen( );`	

	`// seek a connection`
	`sockClient.Connect(strAddr,`
	`nPort);`[3,4]

`// construct a new, empty socket` `CSocket sockRecv;`	
`// accept connection` `sockSrvr.Accept( sockRecv );`[5]	
`// construct file object` `CSocketFile file(&sockRecv);`	`// construct file object` `CSocketFile file(&sockClient);`

`// construct an archive`
`CArchive arIn(&file,`
`    CArchive::load);`
	`// construct an archive`
	`CArchive arIn(&file,`
	`    CArchive::load);`

—or—	—or—
`CArchive arOut(&file,` `    CArchive::store);`	`CArchive arOut(&file,` `    CArchive::store);`
—or Both—	—or Both—

Table 1   Setting Up Communication Between a Server and a Client *(cont.)*

Server	Client
`// use the archive to pass data:`	`// use the archive to pass data:`
`arIn >> dwValue;`	`arIn >> dwValue;`
–or–	–or–
`arOut << dwValue;`[6]	`arOut << dwValue;`[6]

[1]   Where *nPort* is a port number. See Windows Sockets: Ports and Socket Addresses for details about ports.

[2]   The server must always specify a port so clients can connect. The **Create** call sometimes also specifies an address. On the client side, use the default parameters, which ask MFC to use any available port.

[3]   Where *nPort* is a port number and *strAddr* is a machine address or an Internet Protocol (IP) address.

[4]   Machine addresses can take several forms: "ftp.microsoft.com", "ucsd.edu". IP addresses use the "dotted number" form "127.54.67.32". The **Connect** function checks to see if the address is a dotted number (although it doesn't check to ensure the number is a valid machine on the network). If not, **Connect** assumes a machine name of one of the other forms.

[5]   When you call **Accept** on the server side, you pass a reference to a new socket object. You must construct this object first, but do not call **Create** for it. Keep in mind that if this socket object goes out of scope, the connection closes. MFC connects the new object to a **SOCKET** handle. You can construct the socket on the stack, as shown, or on the heap.

[6]   The archive and the socket file are closed when they go out of scope. The socket object's destructor also calls the **Close** member function for the socket object when the object goes out of scope or is deleted.

Additional Notes About the Sequence

The sequence of calls shown in Table 1 is for a stream socket. Datagram sockets, which are connectionless, don't require the **CAsyncSocket::Connect**, **Listen**, and **Accept** calls (although you can optionally use **Connect**). Instead, if you're using class **CAsyncSocket**, datagram sockets use the **CAsyncSocket::SendTo** and **ReceiveFrom** member functions. (If you use **Connect** with a datagram socket, you use **Send** and **Receive**.) Because **CArchive** doesn't work with datagrams, don't use **CSocket** with an archive if the socket is a datagram.

CSocketFile doesn't support all of **CFile**'s functionality; **CFile** members such as **Seek**, which make no sense for a socket communication, are unavailable. Because of this, some default MFC **Serialize** functions aren't compatible with **CSocketFile**. This is particularly true of the **CEditView** class. You should not try to serialize **CEditView** data through a **CArchive** object attached to a **CSocketFile** object using **CEditView::SerializeRaw**; use **CEditView::Serialize** instead (not documented). The **SerializeRaw** function expects the file object to have functions, such as **Seek**, that **CSocketFile** does not support.

See Also   Windows Sockets: Using Sockets with Archives, Windows Sockets: Using Class CAsyncSocket, Windows Sockets: Ports and Socket Addresses, Windows Sockets: Stream Sockets, Windows Sockets: Datagram Sockets

In the *Class Library Reference*: **CSocket**, **CAsyncSocket::Create**,
CAsyncSocket::Listen, **CAsyncSocket::Connect**, **CAsyncSocket::Accept**,
CAsyncSocket::Close, **CSocketFile**, **CEditView::SerializeRaw**

Samples: CHATTER, CHATSRVR

Windows Sockets: Example of Sockets Using Archives

This article presents an example of using class **CSocket**. The example employs
CArchive objects to serialize data via a socket. Note that this is not document
serialization to or from a file.

The following example illustrates how you use the archive to send and receive data
via **CSocket** objects. The example is designed so that two instances of the application
(on the same machine or on different machines on the network) exchange data. One
instance sends data, which the other instance receives and acknowledges. Either
application can initiate an exchange—either can act as server or as client to the other
application. The following function is defined in the application's view class:

```
void CBlabberView::PacketSerialize(long nPackets, CArchive& arData,
                                   CArchive& arAck)
{
    if (arData.IsStoring())
    {
        CString strText;

        for(int p = 0; p < nPackets; p++)
        {
            BYTE bValue = (BYTE)(rand()%256);
            WORD nCopies = (WORD)(rand()%32000);

            // send header information
            arData << bValue << nCopies;
            for(int c = 0; c < nCopies; c++)
            {
                // send data
                arData << bValue;
            }

            Text.Format("Received Packet %d of %d
                (Value=%d,Copies=%d)",p,nPackets,(int)bValue,nCopies);

            // send receipt string
            arData << strText;
            arData.Flush();

            // receive acknowledgment
            arAck >> strText;
            // display it
            DisplayMessage(strText);
        }
    }
```

```
        else
        {
            CString strText;
            BYTE bCheck;
            WORD nCopies;

            for(int p = 0; p < nPackets; p++)
            {
                // receive header information
                arData >> bCheck >> nCopies;
                for(int c = 0; c < nCopies; c++)
                {
                    // receive data
                    arData >> bValue;
                    if (nCheck != bValue)
                        AfxMessageBox("Packet Failure");
                }
            }

            // receive receipt string and display it
            arData >> strText;
            DisplayMessage(strText);

            Text.Format("Sent Packet %d of %d
                (Value=%d,Copies=%d)",p,nPackets,(int)bValue,nCopies);

            // send acknowledgment
            arAck << strText;
            arAck.Flush();
        }
    }
```

The most important thing about this example is that its structure parallels that of an
MFC **Serialize** function. The PacketSerialize member function consists of an **if**
statement with an **else** clause. The function receives two **CArchive** references as
parameters: *arData* and *arAck*. If the *arData* archive object is set for storing
(sending), the **if** branch executes; otherwise, if *arData* is set for loading (receiving)
the function takes the **else** branch. For more information about serialization in MFC,
see the article Serialization.

Note The *arAck* archive object is assumed to be the opposite of *arData*. If *arData* is for
sending, *arAck* receives, and vice versa.

For sending, the example function loops for a specified number of times, each time
generating some random data for demonstration purposes. Your application would
obtain real data from some source, such as a file. The *arData* archive's insertion
operator (<<) is used to send a stream of three consecutive chunks of data:

- A "header" that specifies the nature of the data (in this case, the value of the
  bValue variable and how many copies will be sent).

  Both items are generated randomly for this example.

- The specified number of copies of the data.

  The inner **for** loop sends `bValue` the specified number of times.

- A string called `strText` that the receiver displays to its user.

For receiving, the function operates similarly, except that it uses the archive's extraction operator (>>) to get data from the archive. The receiving application verifies the data it receives, displays the final "Received" message, then sends back a message that says "Sent" for the sending application to display.

Don't be confused by the word "Received" in the message sent in the `strText` variable. In this communications model, it's for display at the other end of the communication, so it specifies to the receiving user that a certain number of packets of data have been received. The receiver replies with a similar string that says "Sent" —for display on the original sender's screen. Receipt of both strings indicates that successful communication has occurred.

Caution If you are writing an MFC client program to communicate with established (non-MFC) servers, don't send C++ objects via the archive. Unless the server is an MFC application that understands the kinds of objects you want to send, it won't be able to receive and deserialize your objects. An example in the article Windows Sockets: Byte Ordering shows a communication of this type.

For more information, see Windows Sockets Specification: **htonl, htons, ntohl, ntohs**

See Also Serialization, Windows Sockets: Deriving from Socket Classes, Windows Sockets: How Sockets with Archives Work, Windows Sockets in MFC: Overview, Windows Sockets: Background

In the *Class Library Reference*: **CSocket, CArchive, CArchive::IsStoring, CArchive::operator<<, CArchive::operator>>, CString::Format, CArchive::Flush, CObject::Serialize**

Samples: CHATTER, CHATSRVR

Windows Sockets: How Sockets with Archives Work

This article explains how a **CSocket** object, a **CSocketFile** object, and a **CArchive** object are combined to simplify sending and receiving data via a Windows socket.

The article Windows Sockets: Example of Sockets Using Archives presents the `PacketSerialize` function. The archive object in the `PacketSerialize` example works much like an archive object passed to an MFC **Serialize** function. The essential difference is that for sockets, the archive is attached not to a standard **CFile** object (typically associated with a disk file) but to a **CSocketFile** object. Rather than connecting to a disk file, the **CSocketFile** object connects to a **CSocket** object.

A **CArchive** object manages a buffer. When the buffer of a storing (sending) archive is full, an associated **CFile** object writes out the buffer's contents. Flushing the buffer of an archive attached to a socket is equivalent to sending a message. When the buffer of a loading (receiving) archive is full, the **CFile** object stops reading until the buffer is available again.

Class **CSocketFile** derives from **CFile**, but it doesn't support **CFile** member functions such as the positioning functions (**Seek**, **GetLength**, **SetLength**, and so on), the locking functions (**LockRange**, **UnlockRange**), or the **GetPosition** function. All the **CSocketFile** object must do is write or read sequences of bytes to or from the associated **CSocket** object. Because a file is not involved, operations such as **Seek** and **GetPosition** make no sense. **CSocketFile** is derived from **CFile**, so it would normally inherit all of these member functions. To prevent this, the unsupported **CFile** member functions are overridden in **CSocketFile** to throw a **CNotSupportedException**.

The **CSocketFile** object calls member functions of its **CSocket** object to send or receive data.

Figure 1 shows the relationships among these objects on both sides of the communication.

Figure 1   CArchive, CSocketFile, and CSocket

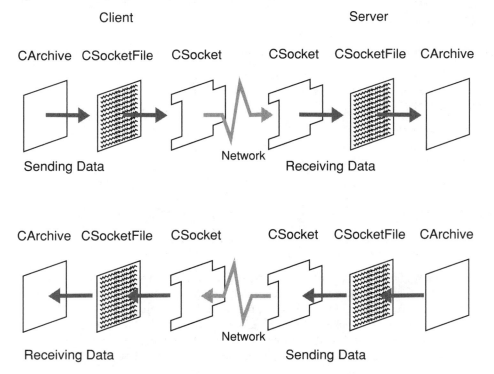

The purpose of this apparent complexity is to shield you from the necessity of managing the details of the socket yourself. You simply create the socket, the file, and the archive, then begin sending or receiving data by inserting it to the archive or extracting it from the archive. **CArchive**, **CSocketFile**, and **CSocket** manage the details behind the scenes.

A **CSocket** object is actually a two-state object: sometimes asynchronous (the usual state) and sometimes synchronous. In its asynchronous state, a socket can receive asynchronous notifications from the framework. But during an operation such as receiving or sending data the socket becomes synchronous. This means the socket will receive no further asynchronous notifications until the synchronous operation has completed. Because it switches modes, you can, for example, do something like the following:

```
CMySocket::OnReceive( )
{
    // ...
    ar >> str;
    // ...
}
```

If **CSocket** were not implemented as a two-state object, it might be possible to receive additional notifications for the same kind of event while you were processing a previous notification. For example, you might get an `OnReceive` notification while processing an `OnReceive`. In the code fragment above, extracting `str` from the archive might lead to recursion. By switching states, **CSocket** prevents recursion by preventing additional notifications. The general rule is: no notifications within notifications.

The CHATTER and CHATSRVR sample applications illustrate such usage. For source code and information about MFC samples, see MFC Samples under Samples in Books Online.

Note A **CSocketFile** can also be used as a (limited) file without a **CArchive** object. By default, the **CSocketFile** constructor's *bArchiveCompatible* parameter is **TRUE**. This specifies that the file object is for use with an archive. To use the file object without an archive, pass **FALSE** in the *bArchiveCompatible* parameter.

In its "archive compatible" mode, a **CSocketFile** object provides better performance and reduces the danger of a "deadlock." A deadlock occurs when both the sending and receiving sockets are waiting on each other, or waiting for a common resource. This situation might occur if the **CArchive** object worked with the **CSocketFile** the way it does with a **CFile** object. With **CFile**, the archive can assume that if it receives fewer bytes than it requested, the end of file has been reached. With **CSocketFile**, however, data is message based; the buffer can contain multiple messages, so receiving fewer than the number of bytes requested does not imply end of file. The application doesn't block in this case as it might with **CFile**, and it can continue reading messages from the buffer until the buffer is empty. The **IsBufferEmpty** function in **CArchive** is useful for monitoring the state of the archive's buffer in such a case.

See Also   Windows Sockets: Using Sockets with Archives, Windows Sockets: Example of Sockets Using Archives

In the *Class Library Reference*: **CSocket**, **CSocketFile**, **CArchive**, **CObject::Serialize**, **CFile**, **CNotSupportedException**, **CArchive::IsBufferEmpty**

Samples: CHATTER, CHATSRVR

Windows Sockets: Using Class CAsyncSocket

This article explains how to use class **CAsyncSocket**. Be aware that this class encapsulates the Windows Sockets API at a very low level. **CAsyncSocket** is for use by programmers who know network communications in detail but want the convenience of callbacks for notification of network events. Based on this assumption, this article provides only basic instruction. You should probably consider using **CAsyncSocket** if you want Windows Sockets' ease of dealing with multiple network protocols in an MFC application but don't want to sacrifice flexibility. You might also feel that you can get better efficiency by programming the communications more directly yourself than you could using the more general alternative model of class **CSocket**.

CAsyncSocket is documented in the *Class Library Reference*. Visual C++ also supplies the Windows Sockets specification, located in Books Online under Win32. The details are left to you. Visual C++ does not supply a sample application for **CAsyncSocket**.

If you aren't highly knowledgeable about network communications and want a simple solution that shields you from most of the details, use class **CSocket** with a **CArchive** object. See the article Windows Sockets: Using Sockets with Archives.

This article covers:

- Creating and using a **CAsyncSocket** object.
- Your responsibilities with CAsyncSocket.

Creating and Using a CAsyncSocket Object

▶ **To use CAsyncSocket**

1 Construct a **CAsyncSocket** object and use the object to create the underlying **SOCKET** handle.

Creation of a socket follows the MFC pattern of two-stage construction.

For example:

```
CAsyncSocket sock;
sock.Create( );     // Use the default parameters
```

−or−

```
CAsyncSocket* pSocket = new CAsyncSocket;
int nPort = 27;
pSocket->Create( nPort, SOCK_DGRAM );
```

The first constructor above creates a **CAsyncSocket** object on the stack. The second constructor creates a **CAsyncSocket** on the heap. The first **Create** call above uses the default parameters to create a stream socket. The second **Create** call creates a datagram socket with a specified port and address. (You can use either **Create** version with either construction method.)

The parameters to **Create** are:

- A "port": a short integer.

  For a server socket, you must specify a port. For a client socket, you'll typically accept the default value for this parameter, which lets Windows Sockets select a port.

- A socket type: **SOCK_STREAM** (the default) or **SOCK_DGRAM**.

- A socket "address," such as "ftp.microsoft.com" or "128.56.22.8".

  This is your Internet Protocol (IP) address on the network. You'll probably always rely on the default value for this parameter.

The terms "port" and "socket address" are explained in the article Windows Sockets: Ports and Socket Addresses.

2 If the socket is a client, connect the socket object to a server socket, using **CAsyncSocket::Connect**.

–or–

If the socket is a server, set the socket to begin listening (with **CAsyncSocket::Listen**) for connect attempts from a client. Upon receiving a connection request, accept it with **CAsyncSocket::Accept**.

After accepting a connection, you can perform such tasks as validating passwords.

Note The **Accept** member function takes a reference to a new, empty **CSocket** object as its parameter. You must construct this object before you call **Accept**. Keep in mind that if this socket object goes out of scope, the connection closes. Do not call **Create** for this new socket object. For an example, see the article Windows Sockets: Sequence of Operations.

3 Carry out communications with other sockets by calling the **CAsyncSocket** object's member functions that encapsulate the Windows Sockets API functions.

See the Windows Sockets specification and class **CAsyncSocket** in the *Class Library Reference*.

4 Destroy the **CAsyncSocket** object.

If you created the socket object on the stack, its destructor is called when the containing function goes out of scope. If you created the socket object on the heap, using the **new** operator, you are responsible for using the **delete** operator to destroy the object.

The destructor calls the object's **Close** member function before destroying the object.

For an example of this sequence in code (actually for a **CSocket** object), see the article Windows Sockets: Sequence of Operations.

Your Responsibilities with CAsyncSocket

When you create an object of class **CAsyncSocket**, the object encapsulates a Windows **SOCKET** handle and supplies operations on that handle. When you use **CAsyncSocket**, you must deal with all of the issues you might face if using the API directly. For example:

- "Blocking" scenarios
- Byte order differences between the sending and receiving machines
- Converting between Unicode and multibyte character set (MBCS) strings

For definitions of these terms and additional information, see the articles Windows Sockets: Blocking, Windows Sockets: Byte Ordering, Windows Sockets: Converting Strings.

Despite these issues, class **CAsycnSocket** may be the right choice for you if your application requires all the flexibility and control you can get. If not, you should consider using class **CSocket** instead. **CSocket** hides a lot of detail from you: it pumps Windows messages during blocking calls and gives you access to **CArchive**, which manages byte order differences and string conversion for you.

See Also Windows Sockets: Background, Windows Sockets: Using Sockets with Archives, Windows Sockets: Blocking, Windows Sockets: Byte Ordering, Windows Sockets: Converting Strings, Windows Sockets: Sequence of Operations, Windows Sockets: Ports and Socket Addresses, Windows Sockets: Stream Sockets, Windows Sockets: Datagram Sockets

In the *Class Library Reference*: **CAsyncSocket, CAsyncSocket::Create, CAsyncSocket::Connect, CAsyncSocket::Listen, CAsyncSocket::Accept**

Samples: CHATTER, CHATSRVR

Windows Sockets: Deriving from Socket Classes

This article describes some of the functionality you can gain by deriving your own class from one of the socket classes.

You can derive your own socket classes from either **CAsyncSocket** or **CSocket** to add your own functionality. In particular, these classes supply a number of virtual member functions that you can override. These functions include **OnReceive**, **OnSend**, **OnAccept**, **OnConnect**, and **OnClose**. You can override the functions in your derived socket class to take advantage of the notifications they provide when network events occur. The framework calls these notification callback functions to notify you of important socket events, such as the receipt of data that you can begin reading. For more information about notification functions, see Windows Sockets: Socket Notifications. For an illustration of overriding the notification functions, see the CHATTER and CHATSRVR sample applications. For source code and information about MFC samples, see MFC Samples under Samples in Books Online.

Additionally, class **CSocket** supplies the **OnMessagePending** member function (an advanced overridable). MFC calls this function while the socket is pumping Windows-based messages. You can override **OnMessagePending** to look for particular messages from Windows and respond to them.

The default version of **OnMessagePending** supplied in class **CSocket** examines the message queue for **WM_PAINT** messages while waiting for a blocking call to complete. It dispatches paint messages in order to improve display quality. Aside from doing something useful, this illustrates one way you might override the function yourself. As another example, consider using **OnMessagePending** for the following task. Suppose you display a modeless dialog box while waiting for a network transaction to complete. The dialog box contains a Cancel button that the user can use to cancel blocking transactions that take too long. Your `OnMessagePending` override might pump messages related to this modeless dialog box.

In your `OnMessagePending` override, return either **TRUE** or the return from a call to the base-class version of **OnMessagePending**. Call the base-class version if it performs work that you still want done.

See Also   Windows Sockets: Socket Notifications, Windows Sockets: Using Sockets with Archives, Windows Sockets: Using Class CAsyncSocket, Windows Sockets: Blocking, Windows Sockets: Byte Ordering, Windows Sockets: Converting Strings

In the *Class Library Reference*: **CAsyncSocket, CSocket, CAsyncSocket::OnReceive, CAsyncSocket::OnSend, CAsyncSocket::OnAccept, CAsyncSocket::OnConnect, CAsyncSocket::OnClose, CSocket::OnMessagePending**

Samples: CHATTER, CHATSRVR

Windows Sockets: Socket Notifications

This article describes the notification functions in the socket classes. These member functions are callback functions that the framework calls to notify your socket object of important events. The notification functions are:

- **OnReceive**: Notifies this socket that there is data in the buffer for it to retrieve by calling **Receive**.

- **OnSend**: Notifies this socket that it can now send data by calling **Send**.

- **OnAccept**: Notifies this listening socket that it can accept pending connection requests by calling **Accept**.

- **OnConnect**: Notifies this connecting socket that its connection attempt completed: perhaps successfully or perhaps in error.
- **OnClose**: Notifies this socket that the socket it is connected to has closed.

Note An additional notification function is **OnOutOfBandData**. This notification tells the receiving socket that the sending socket has "out-of-band" data to send. Out-of-band data is a logically independent channel associated with each pair of connected stream sockets. The out-of-band channel is typically used to send "urgent" data. MFC supports out-of-band data. Advanced users working with class **CAsyncSocket** might need to use the out-of-band channel, but users of class **CSocket** are discouraged from using it. The easier way is to create a second socket for passing such data. For more information about out-of-band data, see the Windows Sockets specification, available in Books Online under Win32.

If you derive from class **CAsyncSocket**, you must override the notification functions for those network events of interest to your application. If you derive a class from class **CSocket**, it's your choice whether to override the notification functions of interest. You can also use **CSocket** itself, in which case the notification functions default to doing nothing.

These functions are overridable callback functions. **CAsyncSocket** and **CSocket** convert messages to notifications, but you must implement how the notification functions respond if you wish to use them. The notification functions are called at the time your socket is notified of an event of interest, such as the presence of data to be read.

MFC calls the notification functions to let you customize your socket's behavior at the time it is notified. For example, you might call **Receive** from your **OnReceive** notification function. That is, on being notified that there is data to read, you call **Receive** to read it. This approach isn't necessary, but it is a valid scenario. As an alternative, you might use your notification function to track progress, print **TRACE** messages, and so on.

You can take advantage of these notifications by overriding the notification functions in a derived socket class and providing an implementation. For an example implementation, see the notification function overrides in the MFC Advanced Concepts samples CHATTER and CHATSRVR.

During an operation such as receiving or sending data, a **CSocket** object becomes synchronous. During the synchronous state, any notifications meant for other sockets are queued while the current socket waits for the notification it wants. (For example, during a **Receive** call, the socket wants a notification to read.) Once the socket completes its synchronous operation and becomes asynchronous again, other sockets can begin receiving the queued notifications.

Important In **CSocket**, the **OnSend** and **OnConnect** notification functions are never called. To send data, you simply call **Send**, which won't return until all the data has been sent. The use of the notification to complete this task is an MFC implementation detail for **CSocket**. For connections, you simply call **Connect**, which will return when the connection is completed (either successfully or in error). How connection notifications are handled is also an MFC implementation detail.

For details about each notification function see the function under class **CAsyncSocket** in the *Class Library Reference*. For source code and information about MFC samples, see MFC Samples under Samples in Books Online.

See Also Windows Sockets: Using Class CAsyncSocket, Windows Sockets: Deriving from Socket Classes, Windows Sockets: How Sockets with Archives Work, Windows Sockets: Blocking, Windows Sockets: Byte Ordering, Windows Sockets: Converting Strings

In the *Class Library Reference*: **CAsyncSocket::OnReceive, CAsyncSocket::OnSend, CAsyncSocket::OnAccept, CAsyncSocket::OnConnect, CAsyncSocket::OnClose, CAsyncSocket::OnOutOfBandData, CSocket, CAsyncSocket**

Samples: CHATTER, CHATSRVR

Windows Sockets: Blocking

This article and two companion articles explain several issues in Windows Sockets programming. This article covers blocking. The other issues are covered in the articles: Windows Sockets: Byte Ordering and Windows Sockets: Converting Strings.

If you use or derive from class **CAsyncSocket**, you will need to manage these issues yourself. If you use or derive from class **CSocket**, MFC manages them for you.

Blocking

A socket can be in "blocking mode" or "nonblocking mode." The functions of sockets in blocking (or synchronous) mode do not return until they can complete their action. This is called blocking because the socket whose function was called can't do anything—is blocked—until the call returns. A call to the **Receive** member function, for example, might take an arbitrarily long time to complete as it waits for the sending application to send (this is if you are using **CSocket**, or using **CAsyncSocket** with blocking). If a **CAsyncSocket** object is in nonblocking mode (operating asynchronously), the call returns immediately and the current error code, retrievable with the **GetLastError** member function, is **WSAEWOULDBLOCK**, indicating that the call would have blocked had it not returned immediately because of the mode. (**CSocket** never returns **WSAEWOULDBLOCK**. The class manages blocking for you.)

The behavior of sockets is different under Windows 95 and Windows NT than under Windows 3.1 (16 bit). Unlike Windows 3.1, both Windows 95 and Windows NT use preemptive multitasking and provide multithreading. Under these 32-bit operating systems, you can put your sockets in separate worker threads. A socket in a thread can block without interfering with other activities in your application and without spending compute time on the blocking. For information on multithreaded programming, see the article Multithreading.

Note In multithreaded applications, you can use the blocking nature of **CSocket** to simplify your program's design without affecting the responsiveness of the user interface. By handling user interactions in the main thread and **CSocket** processing in alternate threads, you can separate these logical operations. In an application that is not multithreaded, these two activities must be combined and handled as a single thread, which usually means using **CAsyncSocket** so you can handle communications requests on demand, or overriding **CSocket::OnMessagePending** to handle user actions during lengthy synchronous activity.

The rest of this discussion is for programmers targeting Windows 3.1.

Normally, if you're using **CAsyncSocket**, you should avoid using blocking operations and operate asynchronously instead. In asynchronous operations, from the point at which you receive a **WSAEWOULDBLOCK** error code after calling **Receive**, for example, you wait until your **OnReceive** member function is called to notify you that you can read again. Asynchronous calls are made by calling back your socket's appropriate callback notification function, such as **OnReceive**.

Under Windows, blocking calls are considered bad practice. By default, **CAsyncSocket** supports asynchronous calls, and you must manage the blocking yourself using callback notifications. Class **CSocket**, on the other hand, is synchronous. It pumps Windows messages and manages blocking for you.

For more information about blocking, see the Windows Sockets specification. For more information about "On" functions, see the articles Windows Sockets: Socket Notifications and Windows Sockets: Deriving from Socket Classes.

See Also Windows Sockets: Using Class CAsyncSocket, Windows Sockets: Converting Strings, Windows Sockets: Using Sockets with Archives, Windows Sockets: Background, Windows Sockets: Stream Sockets, Windows Sockets: Datagram Sockets

In the *Class Library Reference*: **CAsyncSocket, CSocket, CAsyncSocket::OnReceive, CAsyncSocket::OnSend**

Samples: CHATTER, CHATSRVR

Windows Sockets: Byte Ordering

This article and two companion articles explain several issues in Windows Sockets programming. This article covers byte ordering. The other issues are covered in the articles: Windows Sockets: Blocking and Windows Sockets: Converting Strings.

If you use or derive from class **CAsyncSocket**, you will need to manage these issues yourself. If you use or derive from class **CSocket**, MFC manages them for you.

Byte Ordering

Different machine architectures sometimes store data using different byte orders. For example, Intel-based machines store data in the reverse order of Macintosh (Motorola) machines. Intel's byte order, called "little-Endian," is also the reverse of the network standard "big-Endian" order. Table 1 explains these terms.

Table 1   Big- and Little-Endian Byte Ordering

Byte ordering	Meaning
Big-Endian	The most significant byte is on the left end of a word.
Little-Endian	The most significant byte is on the right end of a word.

Typically, you don't have to worry about byte-order conversion for data that you send and receive over the network, but there are situations in which you must convert byte orders.

When You Must Convert Byte Orders

You need to convert byte orders in the following situations:

- You're passing information that needs to be interpreted by the network, as opposed to the data you're sending to another machine. For example, you might pass ports and addresses, which the network must understand.

- The server application with which you're communicating is not an MFC application (and you don't have source code for it). This calls for byte order conversions if the two machines don't share the same byte ordering.

When You Don't Have to Convert Byte Orders

You can avoid the work of converting byte orders in the following situations:

- The machines on both ends can agree not to swap bytes, and both machines use the same byte order.

- The server you're communicating with is an MFC application.

- You have source code for the server you're communicating with, so you can tell explicitly whether you must convert byte orders or not.

- You can port the server to MFC.

  This is fairly easy to do, and the result is usually smaller, faster code. For information, see the MFC Migration Kit, which is included with Visual C++.

Working with **CAsyncSocket**, you must manage any necessary byte-order conversions yourself. Windows Sockets standardizes the "big-Endian" byte-order model and provides functions to convert between this order and others. **CArchive**, however, which you use with **CSocket**, uses the opposite ("little-Endian") order—but **CArchive** takes care of the details of byte-order conversions for you. By using this standard ordering in your applications, or using Windows Sockets byte-order conversion functions, you can make your code more portable.

The ideal case for using MFC sockets is when you're writing both ends of the communication: using MFC at both ends. If you're writing an application that will communicate with non-MFC applications, such as an FTP server, you'll probably need to manage byte-swapping yourself before you pass data to the archive object, using the Windows Sockets conversion routines, **ntohs**, **ntohl**, **htons**, and **htonl**. An example of these functions used in communicating with a non-MFC application appears later in this article.

Note   When the other end of the communication is not an MFC application, you also must avoid streaming C++ objects derived from **CObject** into your archive because the receiver will not be able to handle them. See the Caution in the article Windows Sockets: Using Sockets with Archives.

For more information about byte orders, see the Windows Sockets specification, available in Books Online under Win32.

A Byte-Order Conversion Example

The following example shows a serialization function for a **CSocket** object that uses an archive. It also illustrates using the byte-order conversion functions in the Windows Sockets API.

This example presents a scenario in which you are writing a client that communicates with a non-MFC server application for which you have no access to the source code. In this scenario, you must assume that the non-MFC server uses standard network byte order. In contrast, your MFC client application uses a **CArchive** object with a **CSocket** object, and **CArchive** uses "little-Endian" byte order, the opposite of the network standard.

Suppose the non-MFC server with which you plan to communicate has an established protocol for a message packet like the following:

```
struct Message
{
    long MagicNumber;
    unsigned short Command;
    short Param1;
    long Param2;
};
```

In MFC terms, this would be expressed as follows:

```
struct Message
{
    long m_lMagicNumber;
    short m_nCommand;
    short m_nParam1;
    long m_lParam2;

    void Serialize( CArchive& ar );
};
```

In C++, a **struct** is essentially the same thing as a class. The Message structure can have member functions, such as the Serialize member function declared above. The Serialize member function might look like this:

```
void Message::Serialize(CArchive& ar)
{
    if (ar.IsStoring())
    {
        ar << (DWORD)htonl(m_lMagicNumber);
        ar << (WORD)htons(m_nCommand);
        ar << (WORD)htons(m_nParam1);
        ar << (DWORD)htonl(m_lParam2);
    }
    else
    {
        WORD w;
        DWORD dw;
        ar >> dw;
        m_lMagicNumber = ntohl((long)dw);
        ar >> w ;
        m_nCommand = ntohs((short)w);
        ar >> w;
        m_nParam1 = ntohs((short)w);
        ar >> dw;
        m_lParam2 = ntohl((long)dw);
    }
}
```

This example calls for byte-order conversions of data because there is a clear mismatch between the byte ordering of the non-MFC server application on one end and the **CArchive** used in your MFC client application on the other end. The example illustrates several of the byte-order conversion functions that Windows Sockets supplies. Table 2 describes these functions.

Table 2 Windows Sockets Byte-Order Conversion Functions

Function	Purpose
ntohs	Convert a 16-bit quantity from network byte order to host byte order (Big-Endian to Little-Endian).
ntohl	Convert a 32-bit quantity from network byte order to host byte order (Big-Endian to Little-Endian).
htons	Convert a 16-bit quantity from host byte order to network byte order (Little-Endian to Big-Endian).
htonl	Convert a 32-bit quantity from host byte order to network byte order (Little-Endian to Big-Endian).

Another point of this example is that when the socket application on the other end of the communication is a non-MFC application, you must avoid doing something like the following:

```
ar << pMsg;
```

where `pMsg` is a pointer to a C++ object derived from class **CObject**. This will send extra MFC information associated with objects and the server won't understand it, as it would if it were an MFC application.

See Also   Windows Sockets: Using Class CAsyncSocket, Windows Sockets: Blocking, Windows Sockets: Converting Strings, Windows Sockets: Using Sockets with Archives, Windows Sockets: Background, Windows Sockets: Stream Sockets, Windows Sockets: Datagram Sockets

In the *Class Library Reference*: **CAsyncSocket**, **CSocket**

Samples: CHATTER, CHATSRVR

Windows Sockets: Converting Strings

This article and two companion articles explain several issues in Windows Sockets programming. This article covers converting strings. The other issues are covered in the articles: Windows Sockets: Blocking and Windows Sockets: Byte Ordering.

If you use or derive from class **CAsyncSocket**, you will need to manage these issues yourself. If you use or derive from class **CSocket**, MFC manages them for you.

Converting Strings

If you communicate between applications that use strings stored in different wide-character formats, such as Unicode or multibyte character sets (MBCS), or between one of these and an application using ANSI character strings, you must manage the conversions yourself under **CAsyncSocket**. The **CArchive** object used with a **CSocket** object manages this conversion for you via the capabilities of class **CString**. For more information, see the Windows Sockets specification, located in Books Online under Win32.

See Also   Windows Sockets: Using Class CAsyncSocket, Windows Sockets: Blocking, Windows Sockets: Byte Ordering, Windows Sockets: Using Sockets with Archives, Windows Sockets: Background, Windows Sockets: Stream Sockets, Windows Sockets: Datagram Sockets

In the *Class Library Reference*: **CAsyncSocket**, **CSocket**

Samples: CHATTER, CHATSRVR

Windows Sockets: Ports and Socket Addresses

This article explains the terms "port" and "address" as used with Windows Sockets.

Port

A port identifies a unique process for which a service can be provided. In the present context, a port is associated with an application that supports Windows Sockets. The idea is to identify each Windows Sockets application uniquely so you can have more than one Windows Sockets application running on a machine at the same time.

Certain ports are reserved for common services, such as FTP. You should avoid using those ports unless you are providing that kind of service. The Windows Sockets specification details these reserved ports. The file WINSOCK.H also lists them.

To let the Windows Sockets DLL select a usable port for you, pass 0 as the port value. MFC selects a port value greater than 1,024 decimal. You can retrieve the port value that MFC selected by calling the **CAsyncSocket::GetSockName** member function.

Socket Address

Each socket object is associated with an Internet Protocol (IP) address on the network. Typically, the address is a machine name, such as "ftp.microsoft.com", or a dotted number, such as "128.56.22.8".

When you seek to create a socket, you typically don't need to specify your own address.

Important It's possible that your machine has multiple network cards (or your application might someday run on such a machine), each representing a different network. If so, you might need to give an address to specify which network card the socket will use. This is certain to be an advanced usage and a possible portability issue.

See Also Windows Sockets: Using Class CAsyncSocket, Windows Sockets: Using Sockets with Archives, Windows Sockets: How Sockets with Archives Work, Windows Sockets: Stream Sockets, Windows Sockets: Datagram Sockets

In the *Class Library Reference*: **CAsyncSocket::GetSockName**

Samples: CHATTER, CHATSRVR

Wizards

See the articles AppWizard and ClassWizard.

Index

W

Contributors to *Programming with MFC*

Gail Brown, Editor

Ted Chiang, Writer

Frank Crockett, Writer

Sam Dawson, Index Editor

Mike Eddy, Production

David Adam Edelstein, Art Director

Jocelyn Garner, Writer

Kate Harper, Proofreader

Dan Jinguji, Writer

Paul Johns, Writer

Eric Landes, Writer

Sibyl Lundy, Writer

Robert Reynolds, Illustrator

Chuck Sphar, Writer

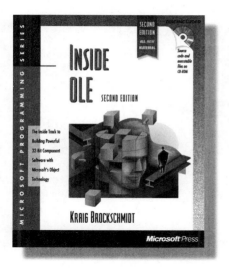

ISBN 1-55615-843-2, 1232 pages, $49.95 ($67.95 Canada)

OLE is a unified and extensible environment of object-based services with the overall purpose of enabling rich integration between components. As Microsoft's object technology, it represents major innovations in object-based programming, making it possible to create applications and software components with unprecedented capabilities. But with this power come additional complexity and new programming paradigms.

INSIDE OLE provides both a clear tutorial and a strong set of example programs, giving you the tools to incorporate OLE into your own development projects. Written by a member of the Microsoft® OLE team, this book truly gives you the insider's perspective on the power of OLE for creating the next generation of innovative software.

INSIDE OLE provides detailed coverage and reference material on:

- **OLE and object fundamentals:** Objects and interfaces, connectable objects, custom components and the Component Object Model, and Local/Remote Transparency

- **Storage and naming technologies:** Structured storage and compound files, persistent objects, and naming and binding

- **Data transfer, viewing, and caching:** Uniform Data Transfer, viewable objects, data caching, OLE Clipboard, and OLE Drag and Drop

- **OLE Automation and OLE Properties:** Automation controllers; property pages, changes, and persistence

- **OLE Documents:** OLE Documents and embedding containers, OLE Documents and local embedding servers, in-process object handlers and servers, linking containers, and in-place activation (visual editing) for containers and objects

- **OLE Controls and the future of OLE:** OLE Controls, future enhancements, and component software

VALUABLE INFORMATION INCLUDED ON CD!

CD includes 75 source code examples (more than 100,000 lines of code) that demonstrate how to create components and how to integrate OLE features into applications.

System Requirements
32-Bit Platforms: Windows® 95 or Windows NT™ 3.51 and Visual C++™ 2.0 or later (Win32™ SDK required for some samples). 16-Bit Platforms: Windows 3.1 or later and Visual C++ 1.51 or later (some samples are 32-bit only and will not work with 16-bit Windows).

If you're interested in fully exploring and understanding OLE and component software, there's no better source than INSIDE OLE.

Microsoft·Press

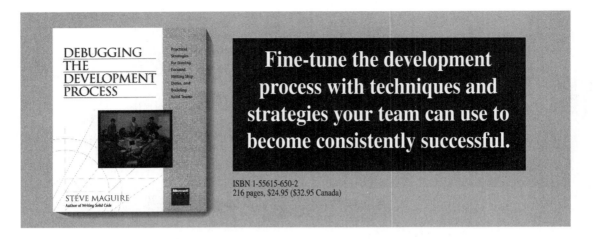

Fine-tune the development process with techniques and strategies your team can use to become consistently successful.

ISBN 1-55615-650-2
216 pages, $24.95 ($32.95 Canada)

In this eagerly awaited companion to the award winning, bestselling *Writing Solid Code*, Steve Maguire describes the sometimes controversial but always effective practices that enable his software teams at Microsoft to develop high-quality software—on schedule.

With the refreshing candor reviewers admired in *Writing Solid Code*, Maguire talks about what did and what didn't work at Microsoft and tells you:

- How to energize software teams to work effectively
- How to deliver on schedule and without overwork
- How to pull twice the value out of everything you do
- How to get your team going on a creative roll

If you're part of a development team, this book is for you. Once you've read it, you'll want to give it to your manager, your peers, and your friends.

More Ways to Smooth Software Development with the *Programming Practices Series* from Microsoft Press

Code Complete
Steve McConnell
ISBN 1-55615-484-4
880 pages
$35.00 ($44.95 Canada)

Debugging the Development Process
Steve Maguire
ISBN 1-55615-650-2
216 pages
$24.95 ($32.95 Canada)

Writing Solid Code
Steve Maguire
ISBN 1-55615-551-4
288 pages
$24.95 ($32.95 Canada)

Microsoft Press

Programming Techniques

Microsoft® Visual C++™

Development System for Windows® 95 and Windows NT™
Version 4

Microsoft Corporation

ISBN 1-55615-921-8

Contents

Chapter 6   Templates   75

Chapter 7   C++ Exception Handling   83

Chapter 11   Programming with Mixed Languages   129

Chapter 12   Advanced Profiling   145

Figures and Tables

Figures

Tables

Introduction

The Windows® 95 and Windows NT™ operating systems provide many new challenges for programmers. You may need to port Windows 3.*x* applications, or want to explore new areas of functionality provided by Windows 95 and Windows NT.

Visual C++™ is designed to make these new features easy to use. The product includes language elements that support areas of functionality such as templates, exception handling, DLLs, and multithread applications.

Programming Techniques is a guide to these advanced language features. Most are directly relevant to services provided by Windows 95 and Windows NT, or are at least different from Windows 3.*x*. Therefore, most of the chapters in this manual deal with porting or use of advanced features for Windows 95 and Windows NT.

Development Strategies for Win32

Windows 95 and Windows NT are complete operating systems, not just graphical user interfaces (GUI), so you can use either one to run simple console applications. In fact, you can use any technique described in this manual without writing for a graphical user interface, as long as no GUI objects are involved. The rest of this section describes how to approach development when porting a traditional program for Windows®, which does involve GUI objects such as window handles, window procedures, and messages.

You can begin using Visual C++ without using new areas of functionality. Instead, you can concentrate on adapting code for Windows 3.*x* to compile and run correctly with Windows 95 or Windows NT. (Chapters 1–4 contain information on porting issues for applications written for Windows and the new programming model for DLLs.) However, you may want to start using new features that are most useful to your application. For example, you can use threads if your application has many operations that would be best handled as background tasks.

Note The term Win32® is used in this manual to refer to the *common* feature-set and architecture of the Win32 API. Certain features are not supported by some implementations of the Win32 API (such as multithread operations not supported by Win32s®).

Using this Manual

To understand the basic use of Visual C++, you should refer to other manuals in this documentation set. Despite its name, *Programming Techniques* does not attempt to teach the basics of C, C++, or programming in Windows. Instead, it covers advanced topics.

However, the first few chapters may be immediately useful if you port existing applications from Windows 3.*x*. The order of information in the manual reflects the different ways you can use it. The following table suggests which chapters you should turn to for various topics.

To do this	Refer to chapters
Port 16-bit applications to Win32®	1–3
Create a 32-bit DLL	4
Create a multithread application	5
Use new language features of Visual C++	6–8
Learn about advanced topics, such as new calling conventions, programming with assembly language or mixed languages, advanced profiling, and developing for international markets	9–13

Note For information on Microsoft product support, see "Using Microsoft Support Services" in the PSS.HLP file.

CHAPTER 1

Porting 16-Bit Code to 32-Bit Windows

This chapter describes how to create a 32-bit version of an application written for Windows 3.*x* in C, and how to make the code portable *between* versions of Windows. Portable code can be recompiled as a 16-bit application or a 32-bit application.

Overview of 32-Bit Programming

The 32-bit API was designed to minimize the impact on existing code so that 16-bit applications could be adapted as easily as possible. However, some changes were mandated by the larger address space. Pointers are all 32 bits wide and no longer **near** or **far**, and your code cannot make assumptions based on segmented memory.

Items which have increased to 32 bits include:

- Window handles
- Handles to other objects, such as pens, brushes, and menus
- Graphics coordinates

These size differences are generally resolved in WINDOWS.H or by the C language, but some changes to source code are necessary. Because the different sizes can change the way information is packed in some message parameters, you must rewrite code that handles these messages. The larger size of graphics coordinates also affects a number of function calls.

Some source code changes are required because Win32 uses higher-level mechanisms for certain operations, such as MS-DOS calls. With these mechanisms, the 32-bit API is adaptable to many platforms, and it supports powerful new features such as multiple threads of execution.

Although Windows 3.*x* and Win32 were designed to be as compatible as possible, you may need to carefully review large amounts of source code. Where do you start? The top-down approach is recommended:

1. Compile the application for 32 bits, and note the compiler-generated errors.

2. Replace complex procedures that are difficult to port, and procedures written in assembly language, with stub procedures (which do nothing except return).

3. Fix errors in the main portion of the application, using the techniques described in this chapter.

4. Individually fill each stub procedure with portable code after the main portion of the application compiles and runs correctly.

Using PORTTOOL to Automate Porting

You can use the PORTTOOL utility (PORTTOOL.EXE) to port applications more easily. This utility finds locations in your code, such as references to certain API functions and messages, that are likely to need revision.

Use the following steps to start using the PORTTOOL utility:

1. Run PORTTOOL and load a Windows 3.x source file.

2. From the Search menu, select the SearchAPI option to search for problematic API functions and messages.

When a problem is found, a dialog box is displayed specifying the message or function and suggesting what change is needed. Although the porting tool is not intended to replace your primary editor, it does have basic editing capabilities (such as Cut, Paste, and Search).

PORTTOOL uses settings in the file PORT.INI to determine what items to look for. This file is based on the "Summary of API and Message Differences" table on page 17.

Note The source code for the PORTTOOL utility is in the following directory: \MSDEV\SAMPLES\SDK\SDKTOOLS\PORTTOOL. You can examine this code to better understand how PORTTOOL works, or modify it and rebuild it for your own needs. An executable file version of the PORTTOOL utility is included in the \MSDEV\BIN directory.

Porting Applications

The following sections describe general areas of code you need to modify when porting a 16-bit application to Win32. These areas include the following:

- Window procedure declarations
- Near and far type declarations
- Data types
- Messages
- Calls to API functions
- WinMain function

If your application uses advanced techniques, such as manipulating the WIN.INI file, focus, and mouse capture, you may need to consult the section "Special Considerations for Advanced Applications" on page 14.

Revising the Window Procedure Declaration

To port a Windows 3.*x* application, you must revise the declaration of the window procedure. The following is a declaration of a window procedure for a Windows 3.*x* application.

```
LONG FAR PASCAL MainWndProc(  HWND hWnd,
    unsigned message,
    WORD wParam,
    LONG lParam)
```

To revise the declaration for Win32, replace the data types used in Windows 3.*x* as shown in Table 1.1. The following code can be compiled as a 32-bit application, but it can still be used to compile 16-bit applications as before:

```
LRESULT CALLBACK MainWndProc(  HWND hWnd,
    UINT message,
    WPARAM wParam,
    LPARAM lParam)
```

Table 1.1 summarizes the changes to the declaration noted in the previous example.

Table 1.1   Changes to the Window Procedure Declaration

Windows 3.x	Win32 (portable code)	Reason for changing
FAR PASCAL	**CALLBACK**	**CALLBACK** is guaranteed to use whatever calling convention is appropriate for windows and dialog procedures.
unsigned	**UINT**	Meaning is the same, but **UINT** guarantees portability for future platforms.
WORD	**WPARAM**	**WORD** is always 16 bits. The **WPARAM** type grows to 32 bits.
LONG	**LPARAM**	Meaning is the same, but **LPARAM** guarantees portability for future platforms.

A significant difference between the Windows 3.*x* declaration and the portable version involves the *wParam* parameter, which grows to 32 bits under Win32. Therefore, replacing the **WORD** type with **WPARAM** is critical. The **WPARAM** type varies with the operating system, as does **UINT**: these types are 16 bits wide under Windows 3.*x* and 32 bits wide under Win32.

The other changes shown in Table 1.1 are recommended for code clarity and portability. For example, **WPARAM** and **LPARAM** are automatically defined to be the correct types for message parameters, and **CALLBACK** will always be the correct declaration for window procedures.

A 32-bit *wParam* message parameter combined with the addresses and handles that grow to 32 bits, means that some messages must be repacked, as described in "Handling 32-Bit Messages" below.

Removing Near and Far Type Declarations

Win32 does not distinguish between near and far addresses. Because the types **NEAR** and **FAR** are defined in WINDEF.H, they are automatically handled by the include file, which redefines them as empty strings for Win32. Thus, **NEAR** and **FAR** are ignored. A convenient solution is to use the /D command-line option to replace the keywords by empty strings. For example:

```
/D_near=   /D_far= /D__near=   /D__far=
```

Using Proper Data Types

Windows 3.*x* source code often uses the type **WORD** interchangeably with types such as **HWND** and **HANDLE**. For example, the type cast **(WORD)** might be used to cast a data type to a handle:

```
hWnd = (WORD) SendMessage( hWnd, WM_GETMDIACTIVATE, 0, 0 );
```

This code compiles Windows 3.*x* applications correctly because both the **WORD** type and handles are 16 bits. But the code produces errors when compiled for Win32 because handles (such as **HWND** types) grow to 32 bits while the **WORD** type is still 16 bits.

Examine each occurrence of **WORD** casts and data definitions in your code, and revise as follows:

- If a variable or expression is to hold a handle, replace **WORD** with **HWND**, **HPEN**, **HINSTANCE**, or another handle type.

- If a variable or expression is a graphics coordinate or some other integer value that grows from 16 to 32 bits, replace **WORD** with **UINT**, and **short** with **int.**

- Continue to use the **WORD** type only if the data type needs to be 16 bits for all versions of Windows (usually because it is a function argument or structure member).

In the portable version of the previous example, the **(WORD)** cast is replaced by **(HWND)**:

```
hWnd = (HWND) SendMessage( hWnd, WM_GETMDIACTIVATE, 0, 0 );
```

In general, it is best to use the most specific type possible. Avoid using a generic handle type such as **HANDLE**, and use a more specific type such as **HPEN**. You should also define specific types for application-specific objects you create.

Handling 32-Bit Messages

Handles grow to 32 bits under Win32, so they can no longer be combined with other information and still fit into a 32-bit parameter (*lParam*). The handle now occupies all of *lParam*, so information formerly in the high or low word of *lParam* must now move to *wParam*.

Because the *wParam* message parameter also grows to 32 bits, it can hold the information that can no longer be held in *lParam*.

Figure 1.1 illustrates how the parameter sizes change, and how information is repacked for WM_COMMAND, one of the messages affected.

Figure 1.1   Parameter Sizes

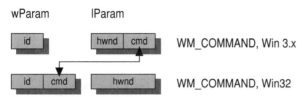

Extracting Data from Messages with Portable Code

The cleanest way to handle a repacked message is to revise your code so that it extracts needed information and stores it in local variables. This localizes message-packing issues to a few lines of your code.

For example, you can use the following code to handle the WM_COMMAND message:

```
case WM_COMMAND:
  id = LOWORD(wParam);
  hwndChild = (HWND)(UINT)lParam;
  cmd = HIWORD(wParam);
```

Summary of Windows Messages Affected

Use Table 1.2 to reference the packing of Windows messages affected by porting.

Except for WM_CTLCOLOR, each message in Table 1.2 lists both 16-bit Windows packing and Win32 packing for messages.

Table 1.2   Windows Messages Affected by Porting

Message	Windows	wParam	lParam
WM_ACTIVATE	16-bit	state	fMinimized, hwnd
	Win32	state, fMinimized	hwnd (32 bits)
WM_CHARTOITEM	16-bit	char	pos, hwnd
	Win32	char, pos	hwnd (32 bits)
WM_COMMAND	16-bit	id	hwnd, cmd
	Win32	id, cmd	hwnd (32 bits)

Table 1.2 Windows Messages Affected by Porting *(continued)*

Message	Windows	wParam	lParam
WM_CTLCOLOR	16-bit	hdc	hwnd, type
WM_CTLCOLOR*type*[1]	Win32	hdc (32 bits)	hwnd (32 bits)
WM_MENUSELECT	16-bit	cmd	flags, hMenu
	Win32	cmd, flags	hMenu (32 bits)
WM_MDIACTIVATE	16-bit	fActivate	hwndDeactivate, hwndActivate
	Win32	hwndActivate (32 bits)	hwndDeactivate (32 bits)
WM_MDISETMENU	16-bit	0	hMenuFrame, hMenuWindow
	Win32	hMenuFrame (32 bits)	hMenuWindow (32 bits)
WM_MENUCHAR	16-bit	char	hMenu, fMenu
	Win32	char, fMenu	hMenu (32 bits)
WM_PARENTNOTIFY	16-bit	msg	id, hwndChild
	Win32	msg, id	hwndChild (32 bits)
WM_VKEYTOITEM	16-bit	code	item, hwnd
	Win32	code, item	hwnd (32 bits)
EM_GETSEL	16-bit	0	0
(returns wStart, wEnd)	Win32	0 or lpdwStart	0 or lpdwEnd
EM_LINESCROLL	16-bit	0	nLinesVert, nLinesHorz
	Win32	mLinesHorz (32 bits)	nLinesVert (32 bits)
EM_SETSEL	16-bit	0	wStart, wEnd
	Win32	wStart (32 bits)	wEnd (32 bits)
WM_HSCROLL,	16-bit	code	pos, hwnd
WM_VSCROLL	Win32	code, pos	hwnd (32 bits)

[1] Under Win32, WM_CTLCOLOR is replaced by a series of messages, each corresponding to a different type. To write portable code, use **#ifdef** statements to handle this difference.

Summary of DDE Messages Affected

DDE messages are packed differently for Win32 and Windows 3.*x*., as shown in Table 1.3.

Table 1.3   DDE Messages Affected by Porting

Message	Windows	wParam	lParam
WM_DDE_ACK (posted form only)	16-bit	hwnd	wStatus, aItem or wStatus, hCommands
	Win32	hwnd (32 bits)	hDDEAck (see following paragraph)
WM_DDE_ADVISE	16-bit	hwnd	hOptions, aItem
	Win32	hwnd (32 bits)	hDDEAdvise (see following paragraph)
WM_DDE_DATA	16-bit	hwnd	hData, aItem
	Win32	hwnd (32 bits)	hDDEData (see following paragraph)
WM_DDE_POKE	16-bit	hwnd	hData, aItem
	Win32	hwnd (32 bits)	hDDEPoke (see following paragraph)

Because of storage limitations, some of the information is stored in a structure, which is accessed through the handle in *lParam*. You can use the following API functions to extract information from these structures: **PackDDElParam**, **UnPackDDElParam**, and **FreeDDElParam**.

For information on how to use these structures and API functions, consult the Win32 API reference.

Adjusting Calls to API Functions

Most of your source code is not affected by differences between the APIs of Windows 3.*x* and Win32. The underlying definitions in WINDOWS.H automatically adjust data to the correct size. But you may need to revise code if you call API functions in any of the following categories:

- Graphics functions
- Functions accessing "extra" window data
- MS-DOS system calls
- Far-pointer functions
- Functions getting list and combo box contents

Graphics Functions

Most of the Windows 3.*x* API functions that must be replaced return packed x- and y-coordinates.

In Windows 3.*x*, the x- and y-coordinates are 16 bits each and are packed into the 32-bit (**DWORD**) function return value, the largest valid size. In Win32, the coordinates are 32 bits each, totaling 64 bits, and are thus too large to fit into a single return value. Each Windows 3.*x* function is replaced by a Win32 function with the same name, but with an **Ex** suffix added. The **Ex** functions pass the x- and y-coordinates using an additional parameter instead of a return value. Both Win32 and Windows 3.*x* support these new functions.

The problematic graphics functions fall into two groups. The first group, functions that set coordinates, are shown in the following table with the Win32 versions.

Windows 3.x function	Portable version of function
MoveTo	**MoveToEx**
OffsetViewportOrg	**OffsetViewportOrgEx**
OffsetWindowOrg	**OffsetWindowOrgEx**
ScaleViewportExt	**ScaleViewportExtEx**
ScaleWindowExt	**ScaleWindowExtEx**
SetBitmapDimension	**SetBitmapDimensionEx**
SetMetaFileBits	**SetMetaFileBitsEx**
SetViewportExt	**SetViewportExtEx**
SetWindowExt	**SetWindowExtEx**
SetWindowOrg	**SetWindowOrgEx**

Each of the functions in the first column returns a value, although application code frequently ignores it. However, even if you do not care about the return value, you must replace the old function call with the new form. The old functions are not supported under Win32.

Each **Ex** function includes an additional parameter that points to a location to receive data. After the function call, this data provides the same information as the corresponding function's return value. If you do not need this information, you can pass **NULL** to this parameter.

Under Windows 3.*x*, a call to the **MoveTo** function can be written as follows:

```
MoveTo( hDC, x, y );
```

In the portable version supported by both versions of Windows, the call to **MoveTo** is rewritten as follows. Note that the information returned by **MoveTo** under Windows 3.*x* is still ignored:

```
MoveToEx( hDC, x, y, NULL );
```

As a general rule, pass **NULL** as the last parameter unless you need to use the x- and y-coordinates returned by the Windows 3.*x* version. In the latter case, use the procedure outlined in the next few paragraphs for the **Get** functions.

The second group consists of functions in which the application code normally does use the return value. They are listed in the following table.

Windows 3.x function	Portable version of function
GetAspectRatioFilter	GetAspectRatioFilterEx
GetBitmapDimension	GetBitmapDimensionEx
GetBrushOrg	GetBrushOrgEx
GetCurrentPosition	GetCurrentPositionEx
GetTextExtent	GetTextExtentPoint
GetTextExtentEx	GetTextExtentExPoint
GetViewportExt	GetViewportExtEx
GetViewportOrg	GetViewportOrgEx
GetWindowExt	GetWindowExtEx
GetWindowOrg	GetWindowOrgEx

The **GetTextExtent** function uses the **Point** suffix because there is already a Windows 3.1 extended function **GetTextExtentEx**. Therefore, the **Point** suffix is added to the functions **GetTextExtent** and **GetTextExtentEx**, to name the portable versions for each.

As with the first group of functions, each **Ex** (and **Point**) version adds an additional parameter: a pointer to a **POINT** or **SIZE** structure to receive x- and y-coordinates. Because this structure is always the appropriate size for the environment, you can write portable code by:

- Declaring a local variable of type **POINT** or **SIZE**, as appropriate.
- Passing a pointer to this structure as the last parameter to the function.
- Calling the function. The function responds by filling the structure with the appropriate information.

For example, the Windows 3.*x* version call to **GetTextExtent** extracts the x- and y-coordinates from a **DWORD** return value (stored in a temporary variable, dwXY):

```
DWORD   dwXY;

dwXY = GetTextExtent( hDC, szLabel, strlen( szLabel ) );
rect.left = 0; rect.bottom = 0;
rect.right = LOWORD(dwXY);
rect.top = HIWORD(dwXY);
InvertRect( hDC, &rect );
```

The portable version passes a pointer to a temporary **SIZE** structure, and then it extracts data from the structure:

```
SIZE sizeRect;

GetTextExtentPoint( hDC, szLabel1, strlen( szLabel1 ), &sizeRect );
rect.left = 0; rect.bottom = 0;
rect.right = sizeRect.cx;
rect.top = sizeRect.cy;
InvertRect( hDC, &rect );
```

Functions That Access the Extra Window Data

The functions described in this section manipulate the "extra" data area of a window structure. This structure can contain system information and user-defined data. You specify the size of this data area by using the **cbClsExtra** and **cbWndExtra** members of the **WNDCLASS** structure when you register the window class.

The following Windows 3.*x* functions get or set 16 bits during each call: **GetClassWord**, **GetWindowWord**, **SetClassWord**, and **SetWindowWord**.

In Win32, each of these system-information items grows to 32 bits. Therefore, in Win32, you would use the following functions which access 32 bits at a time: **GetClassLong**, **GetWindowLong**, **SetClassLong**, and **SetWindowLong**.

Each of these functions takes two parameters: a window handle and an offset into the data area. These offsets differ depending on whether you are compiling for Windows 3.*x* or Win32.

The index values specifying these offsets correspond to each other as follows:

Windows 3.x	Win32 (nonportable)
GCW_CURSOR	GCL_CURSOR
GCW_HBRBACKGROUND	GCL_HBRBACKGROUND
GCW_HICON	GCL_HICON
GWW_HINSTANCE	GWL_HINSTANCE
GWW_HWNDPARENT	GWL_HWNDPARENT
GWW_ID	GWL_ID
GWW_USERDATA	GWL_USERDATA

In the case of **GWW_HWNDPARENT**, you can avoid calls to **GetWindowLong** and **GetWindowWord**, and instead use a single call to a new API function, **GetParent**. This API function returns a handle of the appropriate size. The following example illustrates a call to **GetParent** that has the same results as the **#ifdef** statements shown in the previous example:

```
hwndParent = GetParent( hWnd );
```

Remember that offsets may change for private data that you store in the window structure. You should review this code carefully and recalculate offsets for Win32, noting that some data types, such as handles, increase in size.

Porting MS-DOS System Calls

The **DOS3Call** API function in Windows 3.x must be called from assembly language. It is typically used to perform file I/O. In Win32, you should replace assembly language code that calls **DOS3Call** with the appropriate Win32 file I/O calls. Other (non-file) INT 21H functions should be replaced with the portable Windows API call as shown in the following table.

INT 21H subfunction	MS-DOS operation	Win32 API equivalent
0EH	Select Disk	**SetCurrentDirectory**
19H	Get Current Disk	**GetCurrentDirectory**
2AH	Get Date	**GetDateAndTime**
2BH	Set Date	**SetDateAndTime**
2CH	Get Time	**GetDateAndTime**
2DH	Set Time	**SetDateAndTime**
36H	Get Disk Free Space	**GetDiskFreeSpace**
39H	Create Directory	**CreateDirectory**
3AH	Remove Directory	**RemoveDirectory**
3BH	Set Current Directory	**SetCurrentDirectory**
3CH	Create Handle	**CreateFile**
3DH	Open Handle	**CreateFile**
3EH	Close Handle	**CloseHandle**
3FH	Read Handle	**ReadFile**
40H	Write Handle	**WriteFile**
41H	Delete File	**DeleteFile**
42H	Move File Pointer	**SetFilePointer**
43H	Get File Attributes	**GetAttributesFile**
43H	Set File Attributes	**SetAttributesFile**
47H	Get Current Directory	**GetCurrentDirectory**
4EH	Find First File	**FindFirstFile**
4FH	Find Next File	**FindNextFile**
56H	Change Directory Entry	**MoveFile**
57H	Get Date/Time of File	**GetDateAndTimeFile**
57H	Set Date/Time of File	**SetDataAndTimeFile**
59H	Get Extended Error	**GetLastError**
5AH	Create Unique File	**GetTempFileName**
5BH	Create New File	**CreateFile**
5CH	Lock	**LockFile**
5CH	Unlock	**UnlockFile**
67H	Set Handle Count	**SetHandleCount**

File Operations

You may need to increase the size of fixed-length buffers for filenames and environment strings. Windows 95 and Windows NT support filenames of up to 256 characters, rather than the 8.3 format supported by MS-DOS. You can make code more portable by allocating longer buffers or by using dynamic memory allocation. If you want to conserve memory under Windows 3.*x*, you can use **#ifdef** statements to allocate buffers of the proper length for the environment. You can also use macros such as _MAX_PATH and _MAX_FNAME, defined in STDLIB.H.

Windows 95 and Windows NT require stricter use of file open and close operations than Windows 3.*x*. There are some combinations of open and close functions (for example, mixing **_open** with **_lclose**) that may work in code for Windows 3.*x*, but require revision to work correctly with Windows 95 and Windows NT.

You may also need to make changes in low-level file I/O. In porting Windows 3.*x* code, some developers change from using the Windows API file I/O functions (such as **_lopen** and **_lread**) to using the C run-time low-level I/O functions (such as **_open** and **_read**). All versions of the Windows API support only binary mode, not text mode, but the C run-time calls use text mode by default. Therefore, when changing from the Windows file I/O to the C run-time versions, open files in binary mode by doing one of the following:

- Link with BINMODE.OBJ, which changes the default mode for all file-open operations.
- Open the individual files with _O_BINARY flag set.
- Use **setmode** to change an open file to _O_BINARY.

Far-Pointer Functions

Windows 3.*x* provides functions for memory and file manipulation using far pointers, which have the form **_f***xxxx*. In Win32, these functions are replaced by similarly-named functions of the form *xxxx*, because there is no need for far pointers in Win32. (The **_f** prefix is dropped from the name.)

The WINDOWSX.H file defines the **_f***xxxx* function names so that in Win32, the **_f***xxxx* function names are equated to corresponding functions that are still supported. This means that as long as you include WINDOWSX.H, you don't have to rewrite calls to these functions. Some of the definitions are:

```
#define _fmemcpy    memcpy
#define _fstrcpy    strcpy
#define _fstrcmp    strcmp
#define _fstrcat    strcat
```

Functions Getting List and Combo Box Contents

The Win32 API contains two new functions, shown in the following table, that provide an improved means of extracting list and combo box contents. In each case, you use the portable version of the function to specify a buffer size for a string that receives the information.

Windows 3.x function	Portable version of the function
DlgDirSelect	**DlgDirSelectEx**
DlgDirSelectComboBox	**DlgDirSelectComboBoxEx**

For example, Windows 3.x code might contain the following function call:

```
DlgDirSelect( hDlg, lpString, nIDListBox );
```

This line of code should be replaced by the following call to **DlgDirSelectEx**:

```
DlgDirSelectEx( hDlg, lpString, strlen(lpString), nIDListBox );
```

Revising the WinMain Function

You need to revise the **WinMain** function if either of the following is true:

- Your application needs to know when another instance of the application is running, or

- You need to access the command line.

Otherwise, the code in this function generally needs no change.

The parameter list for **WinMain** is the same for Win32 and Windows 3.x:

```
int PASCAL WinMain(hInstance, hPrevInstance, lpCmdLine, nCmdShow)
```

Note that under Win32, the *hPrevInstance* parameter is always passed NULL (see the next section, "Initializing Instances"). As with 16-bit Windows 3.x, the *lpCmdLine* parameter points to a string containing the entire command line.

Initializing Instances

The *hPrevInstance* parameter is always passed NULL in Win32. This causes each instance of an application to act as though it were the only instance running. The application must register the window class, and it cannot access data used by other instances, except through standard interprocess communication techniques such as shared memory or DDE. Calls to **GetInstanceData** must be replaced with these techniques.

Before registering a window class, source code for Windows 3.x normally tests *hPrevInstance* to see whether another instance of the application is already running. This code needs no change, because under Win32, it will always register the window class.

Some applications must know whether other instances are running. Sometimes this is because data sharing is required. More frequently, it is because only one instance of the application should run at a time. Examples of this latter case include Control Panel and Task Manager.

Applications cannot use *hPrevInstance* to test for previous instances under Win32. An alternative method must be used, such as creating a unique named pipe, creating or testing for a named semaphore, broadcasting a unique message, or calling **FindWindow**.

Special Considerations for Advanced Applications

Additional revisions may sometimes be necessary for applications that use advanced API calls or coding tricks. If your application is fairly complex, you should scan this section to make sure that you don't need to make additional changes.

Revising Advanced API Calls

Applications may need further revision if they use API calls dealing with any of the following: accessing .INI files, setting focus and active window, capturing the mouse, and sharing graphical objects.

Profile Strings and .INI Files

Although Windows 95, Windows NT, and Win32s are all examples of Win32, Windows 95 and Windows NT have some features not present in Win32s.

Windows 3.*x* applications can access .INI files directly. In Windows 95 and Windows NT, however, such code doesn't work because the information in .INI files is replaced by a registration database. This database offers some advantages, including security controls that prevent an application from corrupting system information, error logging, remote software updating, and remote administration of workstation software.

You can write portable code by using the profile API supported by Windows 3.*x* and all versions of Win32, including Windows 95 and Windows NT. Call the **GetProfileString** and **WriteProfileString** API functions instead of accessing .INI files directly. These functions use whichever underlying mechanism (.INI file or registration database) is supported by the environment you are compiling for.

Focus, Mouse Capture, and Localized Input

Windows 95 and Windows NT differ from Windows 3.*x* in that each thread of execution has its own message pump. This change affects window focus and mouse capture.

Window Focus

In Win32, each thread of execution can set or get the focus only to windows created by the current thread. This prevents applications from interfering with each other. One application's delay in responding cannot cause other applications to suspend their response to user actions, as often happens in Windows 3.*x*.

Consequently, the following API functions work differently under Win32:

GetActiveWindow(VOID)	**SetActiveWindow(HWND)**
GetCapture(VOID)	**SetCapture(HWND)**
GetFocus(VOID)	**SetFocus(HWND)**
ReleaseCapture(VOID)	

The **Get** functions in the preceding list can now return NULL, which could not happen in Windows 3.*x*. Therefore, it's important to test the return value of **GetFocus** before using it. Instead of returning the window handle of another thread, the function returns NULL. For example, you call **GetFocus** and another thread has the focus. Note that it's possible for a call to **GetFocus** to return NULL even though an earlier call to **SetFocus** successfully set the focus. Similar considerations apply to **GetCapture** and **GetActiveWindow**.

The **Set** functions can only specify a window created by the current thread. If you attempt to pass a window handle created by another thread, the call to the **Set** function fails.

Mouse Capture

Mouse capture is also affected by the Windows 95 and Windows NT localized input queues. If the mouse is captured on mouse down, the window capturing the mouse receives mouse input until the mouse button is released, as in Windows 3.*x*. But if the mouse is captured while the mouse button is up, the window receives mouse input only as long as the mouse is over that window or another window created by the same thread.

Shared Graphical Objects

Win32 applications run in separate address spaces. Graphical objects are specific to the application and cannot be manipulated by other processes as in Windows 3.*x*. A handle to a bitmap passed to another process cannot be used because the original process retains ownership.

Each process should create its own pens and brushes. A cooperative process may access the bitmap data in shared memory (by way of standard interprocess communications) and create its own copy of the bitmap. Bitmap alterations must be communicated between the cooperative processes by way of interprocess communication, such as DDE.

Win32 adds an explicit ownership transfer API function for graphical objects to explicitly allow cooperative applications to share graphical objects.

Solving Problems Due to C Coding Techniques

Some portability problems can be caused by coding techniques that do not translate successfully to other memory models and processors. You can avoid these problems by not using segmented memory. The header files will then handle standard pointers and manage memory correctly.

Memory and Pointers

To be portable, source code must avoid any techniques that rely on the 16-bit *segment*:*offset* address structure, because all pointers are 32 bits in size under Win32 and use flat rather than segmented memory.

This difference in pointer structure is usually not a problem unless the code uses **HIWORD**, **LOWORD**, or similar macros to manipulate portions of the pointer.

For example, in Windows 3.*x*, memory is allocated to align on a segment boundary, which makes memory allocation functions return a pointer with an offset of 0x0000. The following code exploits this fact to run successfully under Windows 3.*x*:

```
ptr2 = ptr1 = malloc();              // ptr2 = xxxx:0000
LOWORD( ptr2 ) = index * elementsize; // Place offset of array element
                                     //    into ptr2 low word
```

Such code does not work properly under Win32. But standard pointer constructs, such as the following, always result in portable code:

```
ptr1 = malloc();        // Set ptr1 to start of memory block
ptr2 = &ptr1[i];        // Place offset of array element
```

Here are some other guidelines for dealing with pointers:

- All pointers, including those that access the local heap, are 32 bits under Win32.

- Addresses never wrap, as they can with the low word in segmented addressing. For example, in Windows 3.*x*, an address can wrap from 1000:FFFF to 1000:0000.

- Structures that hold near pointers in Windows 3.*x* must be revised because all pointers are 32 bits in Win32. This may affect code that uses constants to access structure members, and it may also affect alignment.

Structure Alignment

Applications should generally align structure members at addresses that are "natural" for the data type and the processor involved. For example, a 4-byte data member should have an address that is a multiple of four.

This principle is especially important when you write code for porting to multiple processors. A misaligned 4-byte data member, which is on an address that is not a multiple of four, causes a performance penalty with an 80386 processor and a hardware exception with a MIPS® RISC processor. In the latter case, although the system handles the exception, the performance penalty is significantly greater.

The following guidelines ensure proper alignment for processors targeted by Win32:

Type	Alignment
char	Align on byte boundaries
short (16-bit)	Align on even byte boundaries
int and **long** (32-bit)	Align on 32-bit boundaries
float	Align on 32-bit boundaries
double	Align on 64-bit boundaries
structures	Largest alignment requirement of any member
unions	Alignment requirement of the first member

The compiler automatically aligns data in accordance with these requirements, inserting padding in structures up to the limit (default pack size) specified by the /Zp option or **#pragma pack**. For example, /Zp2 permits up to 1 byte of padding, /Zp4 permits up to 3 bytes of padding, and so on. The default pack size for Windows 3.*x* is 2, whereas the default for Win32 is 8. As a consequence:

- If you have specified a packing limit with /Zp or **#pragma pack**, you may not get the proper alignment (the default value) for Win32.

- The different default setting for Win32 can impact your source code by changing the offsets of some structure members. Examine your code closely to see whether you have hard-coded these offsets, or whether your code makes assumptions based on a certain default pack size.

Ranges and Promotions

Occurrences of **int**, **unsigned**, and **unsigned int** indicate potential portability problems because size and range are not constant. Data that would not exceed its range in Win32 could exceed range in Windows 3.*x*. Sign extension also works differently, so exercise caution in performing bitwise manipulation of this data.

Source code that relies on wrapping often presents portability problems and should be avoided. For example, a loop should not rely on an **unsigned** variable wrapping at 65535 (the maximum value in Windows 3.*x*) back down to 0.

Summary of API and Message Differences

Table 1.4 provides a complete list of API calls and messages that require implementation changes for Win32.

Table 1.4   API and Message Implementation Changes for Win32

API/Message	Support	Comments
AccessResource	Dropped	No Win32 API equivalent (resource API in progress)
AddFontResource	Enhanced	Must use string, not handle, for filename
AllocDSToCSAlias	Dropped	No Win32 API equivalent

Table 1.4 API and Message Implementation Changes for Win32 *(continued)*

API/Message	Support	Comments
AllocResource	Dropped	No Win32 API equivalent (resource API in progress)
AllocSelector	Dropped	No Win32 API equivalent
ChangeSelector	Dropped	No Win32 API equivalent
CloseComm	Dropped	Replaced by **CloseFile**
CloseSound	Dropped	Replaced by multimedia sound support
CountVoiceNotes	Dropped	Replaced by multimedia sound support
DeviceCapabilities	Dropped	Replaced by portable **DeviceCapabilitiesEx**
DeviceMode	Dropped	Replaced by portable **DeviceModeEx**
DlgDirSelect	Dropped	Replaced by portable **DlgDirSelectEx**
DlgDirSelectComboBox	Dropped	Replaced by portable **DlgDirSelectComboBoxEx**
DOS3Call	Dropped	Replaced by named, portable Win32 API
ExtDeviceMode	Dropped	Replaced by portable **ExtDeviceModeEx**
FlushComm	Dropped	Replaced by **PurgeComm**
FreeSelector	Dropped	No Win32 API equivalent
GetAspectRatioFilter	Dropped	Replaced by portable **GetAspectRatioFilterEx**
GetBitmapDimension	Dropped	Replaced by portable **GetBitmapDimensionEx**
GetBrushOrg	Dropped	Replaced by portable **GetBrushOrgEx**
GetClassWord	Enhanced	Use **GetClassLong** for values that grow to 32 bits in Win32
GetCodeHandle	Dropped	No Win32 API equivalent
GetCodeInfo	Dropped	No Win32 API equivalent
GetCommError	Dropped	Replaced by **GetCommState**
GetCurrentPDB	Dropped	No Win32 API equivalent
GetCurrentPosition	Dropped	Replaced by portable **GetCurrentPositionEx**
GetEnvironment	Dropped	No Win32 API equivalent
GetInstanceData	Dropped	No equivalent; use alternative supported IPC mechanism
GetKBCodePage	Dropped	No Win32 API equivalent
GetMetaFileBits	Dropped	Replaced by portable **GetMetaFileBitsEx**
GetModuleUsage	Enhanced	Always returns 1 on Win32
GetTempDrive	Dropped	Not applicable to Win32

Table 1.4   API and Message Implementation Changes for Win32 *(continued)*

API/Message	Support	Comments
GetTextExtent	Dropped	Replaced by portable **GetTextExtentPoint**
GetTextExtentEx	Dropped	Replaced by portable **GetTextExtentExPoint**
GetThresholdEvent	Dropped	Replaced by multimedia sound support
GetThresholdStatus	Dropped	Replaced by multimedia sound support
GetViewportExt	Dropped	Replaced by portable **GetViewportExtEx**
GetViewportOrg	Dropped	Replaced by portable **GetViewportOrgEx**
GetWindowExt	Dropped	Replaced by portable **GetWindowExtEx**
GetWindowOrg	Dropped	Replaced by portable **GetWindowOrgEx**
GetWindowWord	Enhanced	Use **GetWindowLong** for values that grow to 32 bits on Win32
GlobalDosAlloc	Dropped	No Win32 API equivalent
GlobalDosFree	Dropped	No Win32 API equivalent
GlobalPageLock	Dropped	No Win32 API equivalent
GlobalPageUnlock	Dropped	No Win32 API equivalent
LimitEMSPages	Dropped	No Win32 API equivalent
LocalNotify	Dropped	No Win32 equivalent
MoveTo	Dropped	Replaced by portable **MoveToEx**
NetBIOSCall	Dropped	Replaced by named, portable Win32 API
OffsetViewportOrg	Dropped	Replaced by portable **OffsetViewportOrgEx**
OffsetWindowOrg	Dropped	Replaced by portable **OffsetWindowOrgEx**
OpenComm	Dropped	Replaced by **OpenFile**
OpenSound	Dropped	Replaced by multimedia sound support
ProfClear	Dropped	Replaced by Win32 profile-string API
ProfFinish	Dropped	Replaced by Win32 profile-string API
ProfFlush	Dropped	Replaced by Win32 profile-string API
ProfInsChk	Dropped	Replaced by Win32 profile-string API
ProfSampRate	Dropped	Replaced by Win32 profile-string API
ProfSetup	Dropped	Replaced by Win32 profile-string API
ProfStart	Dropped	Replaced by Win32 profile-string API
ProfStop	Dropped	Replaced by Win32 profile-string API
ReadComm	Dropped	Replaced by ReadFile
RemoveFontResource	Enhanced	Must use string, not handle, for filename

Table 1.4   API and Message Implementation Changes for Win32 *(continued)*

API/Message	Support	Comments
ScaleViewportExt	Dropped	Replaced by portable **ScaleViewportExtEx**
ScaleWindowExt	Dropped	Replaced by portable **ScaleWindowExtEx**
SetBitmapDimension	Dropped	Replaced by portable **SetBitmapDimensionEx**
SetClassWord	Enhanced	Use **SetClassLong** for values that grow to 32 bits on Win32
SetCommEventMask	Dropped	Replaced by **SetCommMask**
SetEnvironment	Dropped	No Win32 API equivalent
SetMetaFileBits	Dropped	Replaced by portable **SetMetaFileBitsEx**
SetResourceHandler	Dropped	No Win32 API equivalent (resource API in progress)
SetSoundNoise	Dropped	Replaced by multimedia sound support
SetViewportExt	Dropped	Replaced by portable **SetViewportExtEx**
SetViewportOrg	Dropped	Replaced by portable **SetViewportOrgEx**
SetVoiceAccent	Dropped	Replaced by multimedia sound support
SetVoiceEnvelope	Dropped	Replaced by multimedia sound support
SetVoiceNote	Dropped	Replaced by multimedia sound support
SetVoiceQueueSize	Dropped	Replaced by multimedia sound support
SetVoiceSound	Dropped	Replaced by multimedia sound support
SetVoiceThreshold	Dropped	Replaced by multimedia sound support
SetWindowExt	Dropped	Replaced by portable **SetWindowExtEx**
SetWindowOrg	Dropped	Replaced by portable **SetWindowOrgEx**
SetWindowWord	Enhanced	Use **SetWindowLong** for values that grow to 32 bits on Win32
StartSound	Dropped	Replaced by multimedia sound support
StopSound	Dropped	Replaced by multimedia sound support
SwitchStackBack	Dropped	No Win32 API equivalent
SwitchStackTo	Dropped	No Win32 API equivalent
SyncAllVoices	Dropped	Replaced by multimedia sound support
UngetCommChar	Dropped	No Win32 equivalent
ValidateCodeSegments	Dropped	No Win32 API equivalent
ValidateFreeSpaces	Dropped	No Win32 API equivalent
WaitSoundState	Dropped	Replaced by multimedia sound support
WriteComm	Dropped	Replaced by **WriteFile**
EM_GETSEL	Enhanced	*wParam/lParam* packing changed
EM_LINESCROLL	Enhanced	*wParam/lParam* packing changed

Table 1.4   API and Message Implementation Changes for Win32 *(continued)*

API/Message	Support	Comments
EM_SETSEL	Enhanced	*wParam/lParam* packing changed
WM_ACTIVATE	Enhanced	*wParam/lParam* packing changed
WM_CHANGECBCHAIN	Enhanced	*wParam/lParam* packing changed
WM_CHARTOITEM	Enhanced	*wParam/lParam* packing changed
WM_COMMAND	Enhanced	*wParam/lParam* packing changed
WM_CTLCOLOR	Replaced	Replaced by WM_CTLCOLOR*type* messages; *wParam/lParam* packing changed
WM_DDE_ACK	Enhanced	*wParam/lParam* packing changed
WM_DDE_ADVISE	Enhanced	*wParam/lParam* packing changed
WM_DDE_DATA	Enhanced	*wParam/lParam* packing changed
WM_DDE_EXECUTE	Enhanced	*wParam/lParam* packing changed
WM_DDE_POKE	Enhanced	*wParam/lParam* packing changed
WM_HSCROLL	Enhanced	*wParam/lParam* packing changed
WM_MDIACTIVATE	Enhanced	*wParam/lParam* packing changed
WM_MDISETMENU	Enhanced	*wParam/lParam* packing changed
WM_MENUCHAR	Enhanced	*wParam/lParam* packing changed
WM_MENUSELECT	Enhanced	*wParam/lParam* packing changed
WM_PARENTNOTIFY	Enhanced	*wParam/lParam* packing changed
WM_VKEYTOITEM	Enhanced	*wParam/lParam* packing changed
WM_VSCROLL	Enhanced	*wParam/lParam* packing changed
(**WORD**)	16-bit	Check if incorrect cast of 32-bit value; **WORD** is unsigned 16-bit int
GCW_CURSOR	Dropped	Replaced by **Get|SetClassCursor**
GCW_HBRBACKGROUND	Dropped	Replaced by **Get|SetClassBrBackground**
GCW_HICON	Dropped	Replaced by **Get|SetClassIcon**
GWW_HINSTANCE	Dropped	Replaced by GWL_HINSTANCE
GWW_HWNDPARENT	Dropped	Replaced by GWL_HWNDPARENT
GWW_ID	Dropped	Replaced by GWL_ID
GWW_USERDATA	Dropped	Replaced by GWL_USERDATA
HIWORD	16-bit	Check if HIWORD target is 16-bit or 32-bit
LOWORD	16-bit	Check if LOWORD target is 16-bit or 32-bit
WndProc	Widened	Define Window procedures: **WndProc** (**HWND** hwnd, **UINT** msg, **UINT** *wParam*, **UINT** *lParam*)

Table 1.4 API and Message Implementation Changes for Win32 *(continued)*

API/Message	Support	Comments
wndproc	Widened	Define Window procedures: **WndProc** (**HWND** hwnd, **UINT** msg, **UINT** *wParam*, **UINT** *lParam*)
DCB	Enhanced	Changes to bit fields and additional structure members
MAKEPOINT	Dropped	Replaced by LONG2POINT

Handling Messages with Portable Macros

Instead of taking the case-by-case approach shown in Chapter 1, "Porting 16-Bit Code to 32-Bit Windows," you can use message-cracking macros to write message handlers similar to those you would write when using Microsoft Foundation Classes. These message handlers use the same parameter list regardless of operating system, thereby solving message-packing issues. This chapter describes these and other macros defined in WINDOWSX.H (or WINDOWSX.H16 in the case of 16-bit applications).

Using Message Crackers

Message crackers are a set of macros that extract useful information from the *wParam* and *lParam* parameters of a message and hide the details of how information is packed.

Using message crackers initially requires that you revise some of your code. Message crackers also have a minor impact on performance by involving an additional function call. However, they offer the following advantages:

- Portability. Message crackers free you from packing issues and guarantee proper extraction of information, regardless of which environment you're compiling for.

- Readability. With message crackers, you can understand source code because message parameters are translated into data with meaningful names.

- Ease of use. In addition to decoding *wParam* and *lParam*, message crackers place message-handling code in separate functions. Instead of a long **switch** statement, you have a separate handler for each message.

Overview of Message Crackers

You use message crackers in your code by writing a separate message handler function for each message. Then you use a macro to call each of those functions from within your window procedure.

Use of message crackers for all messages is recommended, but you can optionally combine code that uses message crackers for some messages with code that responds directly to other messages.

Note To use message crackers, make sure you include the file WINDOWSX.H (or WINDOWSX.H16, in the case of 16-bit applications).

Suppose you have a message, WM_THIS. The code to handle this message would look like this:

```
LRESULT CALLBACK My_WndProc( HWND hwnd, UINT msg, UINT wParam, LONG lParam )
.
.
.
switch( msg ) {
    case WM_THIS:
        // Place code to handle message here
```

To use message crackers, write a message handler, then call it from the **switch** statement. Suppose that there are two pieces of information contained in the WM_THIS message: *thisHdc* and *thisData*. Message crackers unpack this information from *wParam* and *lParam*, and pass it as parameters to your message handler, MyWnd_OnThis, as depicted in Figure 2.1.

Figure 2.1 Passing Parameters to Message Handlers with Message Crackers

```
switch( msg ) {
    case WM_THIS:
        return HANDLE_WM_THIS( hwnd, wParam, lParam, MyWnd_OnThis );


BOOL MyWnd_OnThis( HWND hwnd, HDC thisHdc, WORD thisData )
{
// Place code to handle message here
}
```

Note that the parameters to MyWnd_OnThis (after *hwnd*, which is always the first parameter) consist of information directly usable by your code: *thisHdc* and *thisData*. The macro HANDLE_WM_THIS translates *wParam* and *lParam* into *thisHdc* and *thisData* as it makes the function call.

The following general steps summarize how to use message crackers:

- Declare a prototype for each message-handling function.

- In the window procedure, call the message handler. Use either a message decoder (such as HANDLE_WM_CREATE) or the HANDLE_MSG macro.

- Write the message handler. Use a message forwarder such as FORWARD_WM_CREATE to call the default message procedure.

Declaring Message-Handler Prototypes

To use message crackers, first declare a prototype for the message handling function ("message handler" for short). Although you can give your message handlers any name you want, a recommended convention is:

*WndClass_***On***Msg*

in which *WndClass* is the name of the window class, and *Msg* is the name of the message in mixed case, with the "WM" dropped. For example, the following code contains prototypes for functions handling WM_CREATE, WM_PAINT, and WM_MOUSEMOVE:

```
BOOL MyWnd_OnCreate( HWND hwnd, CREATESTRUCT FAR* lpCreateStruct );
void MyWnd_OnPaint( HWND hwnd );
void MyWnd_OnMouseMove( HWND hwnd, int x, int y, UINT keyFlags );
```

The first parameter to each function is always *hwnd*, which is a handle to the window that received the message. The rest of the parameters vary; each message handler has its own customized parameter list. To declare the appropriate parameters for a message, see the corresponding definitions in WINDOWSX.H.

Calling the Message Handler

In your window procedure, you call a message handler by using a message-decoder macro such as HANDLE_WM_CREATE or HANDLE_WM_PAINT. The general form for using these macros is:

case *msg***:**
> **return HANDLE_***msg* **(hwnd, wParam, lP aram,** *handler* **);**

You should always return the value of the macro, even if no return value is expected and the corresponding message handler has **void** return type.

For example, you could place the following macros in your code:

```
switch( msg ) {
    case WM_CREATE:
        return HANDLE_WM_CREATE( hwnd, wParam, lParam, MyWnd_OnCreate );
    case WM_PAINT:
        return HANDLE_WM_PAINT( hwnd, wParam, lParam, MyWnd_OnPaint );
    case WM_MOUSEMOVE:
        return HANDLE_WM_MOUSEMOVE( hwnd, wParam, lParam,
                                    MyWnd_OnMouseMove );
    .
    .
    .
```

Alternatively, you can use the generic HANDLE_MSG macro, which generates the same code as the previous example, but saves space:

```
switch( msg ) {
    HANDLE_MSG( hwnd, WM_CREATE, MyWnd_OnCreate );
```

```
        HANDLE_MSG( hwnd, WM_PAINT, MyWnd_OnPaint );
        HANDLE_MSG( hwnd, WM_MOUSEMOVE, MyWnd_OnMouseMove );
        .
        .
        .
```

HANDLE_MSG assumes that you use the names *wParam* and *lParam* in the window procedure parameter list. You cannot use this macro if you have given these parameters other names.

Writing the Message Handler

In the message-handling function, you respond to the message using parameters that have been translated from *wParam* and *lParam* and passed to the function. In the following example, *lpCreateStruct* is an example of a parameter translated from *wParam* and *lParam*:

```
BOOL MyCls_OnCreate(HWND hwnd, CREATESTRUCT FAR* lpCreateStruct)
{
    // Place message-handling code here

    return FORWARD_WM_CREATE(hwnd, lpCreateStruct, DefWindowProc);
}
```

Message-handling code often finishes by calling **DefWindowProc** or some other default message procedure. You make this function call by using a "message forwarder," which uses the following form:

return FORWARD_*msg***(** *parmlist***,** *defaultMsgProc* **);**

The *parmlist* is the same list of parameters in the message handler, and *defaultMsgProc* is the default message procedure, typically **DefWindowProc**. The message forwarder repacks the information in the parameter list into the appropriate *wParam/lParam* format (depending on target environment) and forwards the message to the default message procedure.

Putting it Together: An Example

In the following example, several message handlers are used in a window procedure to show where the various prototypes and macros fit into the code.

The header file, MYAPP.H, consists of function prototypes, including prototypes for the message handlers. Note how each message handler has its own parameter list, which is customized to represent the information packed in the corresponding message:

```
// MYAPP.H

// Window procedure prototype

LRESULT CALLBACK MyWnd_WndProc(HWND hwnd, UINT msg, WPARAM wParam, LPARAM lParam);
```

```
// Default message handler

#define MyWnd_DefProc    DefWindowProc

// MyWnd class message handler functions, declared in a .h file:
//
void MyWnd_OnMouseMove(HWND hwnd, int x, int y, UINT keyFlags);
void MyWnd_OnLButtonDown(HWND hwnd, BOOL fDoubleClick, int x, int y, UINT keyFlags);
void MyWnd_OnLButtonUp(HWND hwnd, int x, int y, UINT keyFlags);
```

The rest of the code in this example is in MYAPP.C, which contains the window
procedure and the individual message handlers. With message crackers, the function
of the window procedure is principally to route each message to the appropriate
handler.

Both the WM_LBUTTONDOWN and WM_LBUTTONDBLCLK messages map to
the MyWnd_OnLButtonDown procedure. This mapping is one of the special cases of
message handling described in the next section.

```
// MYAPP.C   ------------------------------------------------------------------

// MyWnd window procedure implementation.
//
LRESULT CALLBACK MyWnd_WndProc(HWND hwnd, UINT msg, WPARAM wParam, LPARAM lParam)
{
    switch (msg)
    {
        HANDLE_MSG(hwnd, WM_MOUSEMOVE,MyWnd_OnMouseMove);
        HANDLE_MSG(hwnd, WM_LBUTTONDOWN, MyWnd_OnLButtonDown);
        HANDLE_MSG(hwnd, WM_LBUTTONDBLCLK, MyWnd_OnLButtonDown);
        HANDLE_MSG(hwnd, WM_LBUTTONUP, MyWnd_OnLButtonUp);
    default:
        return MyWnd_DefProc(hwnd, msg, wParam, lParam);
    }
}


// Message handler function implementations:
//
void MyWnd_OnMouseMove(HWND hwnd, int x, int y, UINT keyFlags)
{
    .
    .
    .
    return FORWARD_WM_MOUSEMOVE( hwnd, x, y, keyFlags, MyWnd_DefProc);
}

void MyWnd_OnLButtonDown(HWND hwnd, BOOL fDoubleClick, int x, int y, UINT keyFlags)
{
    .
    .
    .
    return FORWARD_WM_LBUTTONDOWN( hwnd, fDoubleClick, x, y, keyFlags, MyWnd_DefProc);
}
```

27

```
void MyWnd_OnLButtonUp(HWND hwnd, int x, int y, UINT keyFlags)
{
    .
    .
    .
    return FORWARD_WM_LBUTTONUP( hwnd, x, y, keyFlags, MyWnd_DefProc);
}
```

Note that the symbol `MyWnd_DefProc` is defined to represent **DefWindowProc** to make code more reusable. This approach assumes you have a similar definition in each application. For example, in an MDI child control procedure, you would have this definition:

```
#define MyWnd_DefProc    DefMDIChildProc
```

If you then copied your message handler to the MDI procedure, you would only need to change the prefix in `MyWnd_DefProc` to make the copied code work correctly. Conversely, if your code used the explicit call to **DefWindowProc**, it could create a bug that would be difficult to find when copied to the MDI code.

Handling Special Cases of Messages

As a general rule, there is one set of message crackers for each message: a message decoder and a message forwarder. Another rule is that each message handler you write should return the same value that your code would normally return for that message. The following messages present exceptions to these rules.

Message handler	Comment
OnCreate, OnNCCreate	**BOOL** return type: returns TRUE if there are no errors. If FALSE is returned, a window will not be created.
OnKey	Handles both key up and key down messages. The extra parameter *fDown* indicates whether the key is down or up.
OnLButtonDown, OnRButtonDown	Handles both click (button down) and double-click messages. The extra parameter *fDoubleClick* indicates whether the message received is a double-click message.
OnChar	This handler is passed only by character, and not the virtual key or key flags information.

Writing Message Crackers for User-Defined Messages

You can use message crackers with window messages that you define, but you must write your own macros. The easiest way to do this is to copy and modify existing macros from WINDOWSX.H.

To understand how to write these macros, consider some of the message crackers defined in WINDOWSX.H:

```
/* BOOL Cls_OnCreate(HWND hwnd, CREATESTRUCT FAR* lpCreateStruct) */

#define HANDLE_WM_CREATE(hwnd, wParam, lParam, fn) \
    ((fn)(hwnd, (CREATESTRUCT FAR*)lParam) ? 0L : (LRESULT)-1L)

#define FORWARD_WM_CREATE(hwnd, lpCreateStruct, fn) \
    (BOOL)(DWORD)(fn)(hwnd, WM_CREATE, 0, (LPARAM)lpCreateStruct)
```

The message decoder (**HANDLE**_*msg*) should be defined as a function call, (fn), followed by *hwnd* and other parameters derived from *wParam* and *lParam*. The message forwarder (**FORWARD**_*msg*) performs the reverse operation on the parameters, putting information back together to restore *wParam* and *lParam* before making the function call (fn). Each of these macros must cast the return value so that the correct type is returned.

When calling the message crackers you write, be careful about variable message values. If your message value is a constant (such as WM_USER+100), you can use HANDLE_MSG with the message in a **switch** statement. However, if the message is registered with **RegisterWindowMessage**, it assigns a number at run time. In this situation, you can't use HANDLE_MSG, because variables cannot be used as **case** values. You must handle the message separately, in an **if** statement:

```
// In MyWnd class initialization code:
//
UINT WM_NEWMESSAGE= 0;

WM_NEWMESSAGE= RegisterWindowMessage("WM_NEWMESSAGE");
    .
    .
    .
// In MyWnd_WndProc(): window procedure:
//
LRESULT CALLBACK MyWnd_WndProc(HWND hwnd, WORD msg, WPARAM wParam,
                        LPARAM lParam)
{
    if (msg == WM_NEWMESSAGE)
        HANDLE_WM_NEWMESSAGE(hwnd, wParam, lParam, MyWnd_OnNewMessage);

    switch (msg)
    {
        HANDLE_MSG(hwnd, WM_MOUSEMOVE, MyWnd_OnMouseMove);
        .
        .
        .
    }
}
```

Adapting Message Crackers for Special Cases

Generally, you can use message crackers with all types of application code. However, certain situations require modifications in coding style.

The next few sections show how to adapt message-cracker coding techniques for dialog procedures, window subclassing, and window instance data.

Dialog Procedures

Dialog procedures return a **BOOL** value to indicate whether the message was processed. (Window procedures, in contrast, return a **LONG** value rather than a **BOOL**.) Therefore, to adapt a message cracker to dialog-procedure code, you must call the message handler and cast the value to **BOOL**.

Because you have to insert the **(BOOL)** cast, you can't use HANDLE_MSG. You must invoke the message-decoder macro explicitly. Here's an example that shows how you would use message crackers in a dialog procedure:

```
BOOL MyDlg_OnInitDialog(HWND hwndDlg, HWND hwndFocus, LPARAM lParam);
void MyDlg_OnCommand(HWND hwnd, int id, HWND hwndCtl, UINT codeNotify);

BOOL CALLBACK MyDlg_DlgProc(HWND hwndDlg, UINT msg, WPARAM wParam, LPARAM lParam)
{
    switch (msg)
    {
    //
    // Since HANDLE_WM_INITDIALOG returns an LRESULT,
    // we must cast it to a BOOL before returning.
    //
    case WM_INITDIALOG:
        return (BOOL)HANDLE_WM_INITDIALOG(hwndDlg, wParam, lParam, MyDlg_OnInitDialog);

    case WM_COMMAND:
        HANDLE_WM_COMMAND(hwndDlg, wParam, lParam, MyDlg_OnCommand);
        return TRUE;
        break;

    default:
        return FALSE;
    }
}
```

Window Subclassing

When you use message crackers with a subclassed window procedure, the strategy described earlier for using message forwarders does not work. Recall that this strategy involves the following macro call:

return FORWARD_*msg*(*parmlist*, *defaultMsgProc*);

This use of a message forwarder (**FORWARD**_*msg*) calls *defaultMsgProc* directly. But in a subclassed window procedure, you must call the window procedure of the superclass by using the API function **CallWindowProc**. The problem is that **FORWARD**_*msg* calls *defaultMsgProc* with four parameters, but **CallWindowProc** needs five parameters.

The solution is to write an intermediate procedure. For example, the intermediate procedure could be named test_DefProc:

```
        FORWARD_WM_CHAR(hwnd, ch, cRepeat, test_DefProc);
```

The test_DefProc function calls **CallWindowProc** and prepends the address of the superclass function (in this case, test_lpfnwpDefProc) to the parameter list:

```
LRESULT test_DefProc( HWND hwnd, UINT msg, WPARAM wParam, LPARAM lParam)
{
    return CallWindowProc(test_lpfnwpDefProc, hwnd, msg, wParam,
lParam);
}
```

You need to write one such procedure for each subclassed window in your application. Each time you use a message forwarder, you give this intermediate procedure as the function address instead of **DefWindowProc**. The following example code shows the complete context:

```
// Global variable that holds the previous window proc address of
// the subclassed window:
//
WNDPROC test_lpfnwpDefProc = NULL;

// Code fragment to subclass a window and store previous wndproc value:
//
void Subclasstest(HWND hwndtest)
{
    extern HINSTANCE g_hinsttest;    // Global application instance handle

    // SubclassWindow() is a macro API that calls SetWindowLong()
    // as appropriate to change the window proc of hwndtest.
    //
    test_lpfnwpDefProc = SubclassWindow(hwndtest,
        (WNDPROC)MakeProcInstance( (FARPROC)test_WndProc, g_hinsttest));
    .
    .
    .
}

// Default message handler function
//
// This function invokes the superclasses' window procedure.  It
// must be declared with the same signature as any window proc,
// so it can be used with the FORWARD_WM_* macros.
//
```

```
LRESULT test_DefProc( HWND hwnd, UINT msg, WPARAM wParam, LPARAM lParam)
{
    return CallWindowProc(test_lpfnwpDefProc, hwnd, msg, wParam, lParam);
}
// test window procedure.  Everything here is the same as in the
// normal non-subclassed case: the differences are encapsulated in
// test_DefProc.
//
LRESULT CALLBACK test_WndProc(HWND hwnd, UINT msg, WPARAM wParam, LPARAM lParam)
{
    switch (msg)
    {
        HANDLE_MSG(hwnd, WM_CHAR, test_OnChar);
        .
        .
        .
    default:
        //
        // Be sure to call test_DefProc(), NOT DefWindowProc()!
        //
        return test_DefProc(hwnd, msg, wParam, lParam);
    }
}

// Message handlers
//
void test_OnChar(HWND hwnd, UINT ch, int cRepeat)
{
    if (ch == testvalue)
    {
        // handle it here
    }
    else
    {
        // Forward the message on to test_DefProc
        //
        FORWARD_WM_CHAR(hwnd, ch, cRepeat, test_DefProc);
    }
}
```

Window Instance Data

It is common for a window to keep user-declared state variables (or "instance data") in a separate data structure allocated by the application. You associate this data structure with its corresponding window by storing a pointer to the structure in a specially named window property or in a window word (allocated by setting the **cbWndExtra** field of the WNDCLASS structure when the class is registered).

You can adapt message crackers to work with this use of instance data. Place the *hwnd* of the window in the first member of the structure. Then, in the message decoders (**HANDLE_msg** macros), pass the address of the structure instead of the *hwnd*. The message handler now gets a pointer to the structure instead of the *hwnd*, but it can access the *hwnd* through indirection. You may need to rewrite some of the message handler to make it use indirection to access the window handle.

The following example illustrates this technique:

```
// Window instance data structure.  Must include window handle field.
//
typedef struct _test
{
    HWND hwnd;
    int otherStuff;
} test;

// "test" window class was registered with cbWndExtra = sizeof(test*), so we
// can use a window word to store back pointer.  Window properties can also
// be used.
//
// These macros get and set the pointer to the instance data corresponding to the
// window.  Use GetWindowWord or GetWindowLong as appropriate based on the default
// size of data pointers.
//
#ifdef _WIN32
#define test_GetPtr(hwnd)         (test*)GetWindowLong((hwnd), 0)
#define test_SetPtr(hwnd, ptest)  (test*)SetWindowLong((hwnd), 0, (LONG)(ptest))
#else
#define test_GetPtr(hwnd)         (test*)GetWindowWord((hwnd), 0)
#define test_SetPtr(hwnd, ptest)  (test*)SetWindowWord((hwnd), 0, (WORD)(ptest))
#endif


// Default message handler

#define test_DefProc DefWindowProc

// Message handler functions, declared with a test* as their first argument,
// rather than an HWND.  Other than that, their signature is identical to
// that shown in WINDOWSX.H.
//
BOOL test_OnCreate(test* ptest, CREATESTRUCT FAR* lpcs);
void test_OnPaint(test* ptest);
//
// Code to register the test window class:
//
BOOL test_Init(HINSTANCE hinst)
{
    WNDCLASS cls;

    cls.hCursor        = ...;
    cls.hIcon          = ...;
    cls.lpszMenuName   = ...;
    cls.hInstance      = hinst;
    cls.lpszClassName  = "test";
    cls.hbrBackground  = ...;
    cls.lpfnWndProc    = test_WndProc;
    cls.style          = CS_DBLCLKS;
```

```
        cls.cbWndExtra       = sizeof(test*);  // room for instance data ptr
        cls.cbClsExtra       = 0;

        return RegisterClass(&cls);
}

// The window proc for class "test".  This demonstrates how instance data is
// attached to a window and passed to the message handler functions.
//
LRESULT CALLBACK test_WndProc(HWND hwnd, UINT msg, WPARAM wParam, LPARAM lParam)
{
        test* ptest = test_GetPtr(hwnd);

        if (ptest == NULL)
        {
        // If we're creating the window, try to allocate it.
        //
            if (msg == WM_NCCREATE)
            {
            // Create the instance data structure, set up the hwnd backpointer
            // field, and associate it with the window.
            //
            ptest = (test*)LocalAlloc(LMEM_FIXED | LMEM_ZEROINIT, sizeof(test));

            // If an error occurred, return 0L to fail the CreateWindow call.
            // This will cause CreateWindow() to return NULL.
            //
            if (ptest == NULL)
                return 0L;
            ptest->hwnd = hwnd;
            test_SetPtr(hwnd, ptest);

            // NOTE: the rest of the test structure should be initialized
            // inside Template_OnCreate() (or Template_OnNCCreate()).  Further
            // creation data may be accessed through the CREATESTRUCT FAR* parameter.
            //
            }
            else
            {
            // It turns out WM_NCCREATE is NOT necessarily the first message
            // received by a top-level window (WM_GETMINMAXINFO is).
            // Pass messages that precede WM_NCCREATE on through to
            // test_DefProc
            //
            return test_DefProc(hwnd, msg, wParam, lParam);
            }
        }

        if (msg == WM_NCDESTROY)
        {
            LocalFree((HLOCAL)ptest);
            ptest = NULL;
            test_SetPtr(hwnd, NULL);
        }
```

```
switch (msg)
{
HANDLE_MSG(ptest, WM_CREATE, test_OnCreate);
HANDLE_MSG(ptest, WM_PAINT, test_OnPaint);
...

default:
    return test_DefProc(hwnd, msg, wParam, lParam);
}
}
```

Using Control Message Functions

The role of the control message API functions is the opposite of message crackers: instead of handling messages sent to your window, they send messages to other windows (controls).

Each of the control message functions packs parameters into the appropriate *wParam/lParam* format and then calls **SendMessage**. These functions offer the same portability advantages as message crackers; they free you from having to know how the current operating system packs *wParam* and *lParam*.

The function calls also improve code readability and support better type checking. When used with the STRICT enhancements, the control message functions help prevent incorrect passing of message parameters.

To see how the control message functions work, first look at the following source code, which makes two calls to **SendMessage** to print all the lines in an edit control:

```
void PrintLines(HWND hwndEdit, WHND hwndDisplay)
{
    int line;
    int lineLast = (int)SendMessage(hwndEdit, EM_GETLINECOUNT, 0, 0L);

    for (line = 0; line < lineLast; line++)
    {
        int cch;
        char ach[80];

        *((LPINT)ach) = sizeof(ach);
        cch = (int)SendMessage(hwndEdit, EM_GETLINE,
                line, (LONG)(LPSTR)ach);

        PrintInWindow(ach, hwndDisplay);
    }
}
```

The following source code uses two control message functions, **Edit_GetLineCount** and **Edit_GetLine**, to perform the same task. This version of the code is shorter, easier to read, doesn't generate compiler warnings, and doesn't have any nonportable casts:

```
void PrintLines(HWND hwndEdit, WHND hwndDisplay)
{
    int line;
    int lineLast = Edit_GetLineCount(hwndEdit);

    for (line = 0; line < lineLast; line++)
    {
        int cch;
        char ach[80];

        cch = Edit_GetLine(hwndEdit, line, ach, sizeof(ach));

        PrintInWindow(ach, hwndDisplay);
    }
}
```

The control message API functions are listed in Table 2.1. For more information, refer to the macro definitions in WINDOWSX.H and the documentation for the corresponding window message.

Table 2.1 Control Message API Functions

Control group	Functions
Static Text Controls:	**Static_Enable**(*hwnd*, *fEnable*)
	Static_GetIcon(*hwnd*, *hIcon*)
	Static_GetText(*hwnd*, *lpch*, *cchMax*)
	Static_GetTextLength(*hwnd*)
	Static_SetIcon(*hwnd*, *hIcon*)
	Static_SetText(*hwnd*, *lpsz*)
Button Controls:	**Button_Enable**(*hwnd*, *fEnable*)
	Button_GetCheck(*hwnd*)
	Button_GetState(*hwnd*)
	Button_GetText(*hwnd*, *lpch*, *cchMax*)
	Button_GetTextLength(*hwnd*)
	Button_SetCheck(*hwnd*, *check*)
	Button_SetState(*hwnd*, *state*)
	Button_SetStyle(*hwnd*, *style*, *fRedraw*)
	Button_SetText(*hwnd*, *lpsz*)
Edit Controls:	**Edit_CanUndo**(*hwnd*)
	Edit_EmptyUndoBuffer(*hwnd*)
	Edit_Enable(*hwnd*, *fEnable*)
	Edit_FmtLines(*hwnd*, *fAddEOL*)

Table 2.1   Control Message API Functions *(continued)*

Control group	Functions
Edit Controls:	**Edit_GetFirstVisible**(*hwnd*)
	Edit_GetHandle(*hwnd*)
	Edit_GetLine(*hwnd, line, lpch, cchMax*)
	Edit_GetLineCount(*hwnd*)
	Edit_GetModify(*hwnd*)
	Edit_GetRect(*hwnd, lprc*)
	Edit_GetSel(*hwnd*)
	Edit_GetText(*hwnd, lpch, cchMax*)
	Edit_GetTextLength(*hwnd*)
	Edit_LimitText(*hwnd, cchMax*)
	Edit_LineFromChar(*hwnd, ich*)
	Edit_LineIndex(*hwnd, line*)
	Edit_LineLength(*hwnd, line*)
	Edit_ReplaceSel(*hwnd, lpszReplace*)
	Edit_Scroll(*hwnd, dv, dh*)
	Edit_SetHandle(*hwnd, h*)
	Edit_SetModify(*hwnd, fModified*)
	Edit_SetPasswordChar(*hwnd, ch*)
	Edit_SetRect(*hwnd, lprc*)
	Edit_SetRectNoPaint(*hwnd, lprc*)
	Edit_SetSel(*hwnd, ichStart, ichEnd*)
	Edit_SetTabStops(*hwnd, cTabs, lpTabs*)
	Edit_SetText(*hwnd, lpsz*)
	Edit_SetWordBreak(*hwnd, lpfnWordBreak*)
	Edit_Undo(*hwnd*)
Scroll Bar Controls:	**ScrollBar_Enable**(*hwnd, flags*)
	ScrollBar_GetPos(*hwnd*)
	ScrollBar_GetRange(*hwnd, lpposMin, lpposMax*)
	ScrollBar_SetPos(*hwnd, pos, fRedraw*)
	ScrollBar_SetRange(*hwnd, posMin, posMax, fRedraw*)
	ScrollBar_Show(*hwnd, fShow*)
List Box Controls:	**ListBox_AddFile**(*hwnd, lpszFilename*)
	ListBox_AddItemData(*hwnd, data*)
	ListBox_AddString(*hwnd, lpsz*)
	ListBox_DeleteString(*hwnd, index*)

Table 2.1 Control Message API Functions *(continued)*

Control group	Functions
List Box Controls:	**ListBox_Dir**(*hwnd*, *attrs*, *lpszFileSpec*)
	ListBox_Enable(*hwnd*, *fEnable*)
	ListBox_FindItemData(*hwnd*, *indexStart*, *data*)
	ListBox_FindString(*hwnd*, *indexStart*, *lpszFind*)
	ListBox_GetAnchorIndex(*hwnd*)
	ListBox_GetCaretIndex(*hwnd*)
	ListBox_GetCount(*hwnd*)
	ListBox_GetCurSel(*hwnd*)
	ListBox_GetHorizontalExtent(*hwnd*)
	ListBox_GetItemData(*hwnd*, *index*)
	ListBox_GetItemHeight(*hwnd*, *index*)[1]
	ListBox_GetItemRect(*hwnd*, *index*, *lprc*)
	ListBox_GetSel(*hwnd*, *index*)
	ListBox_GetSelCount(*hwnd*)
	ListBox_GetSelItems(*hwnd*, *cItems*, *lpIndices*)
	ListBox_GetText(*hwnd*, *index*, *lpszBuffer*)
	ListBox_GetTextLen(*hwnd*, *index*)
	ListBox_GetTopIndex(*hwnd*)
	ListBox_InsertItemData(*hwnd*, *lpsz*, *index*)
	ListBox_InsertString(*hwnd*, *lpsz*, *index*)
	ListBox_ResetContent(*hwnd*)
	ListBox_SelectItemData(*hwnd*, *indexStart*, *data*)
	ListBox_SelectString(*hwnd*, *indexStart*, *lpszFind*)
	ListBox_SelItemRange(*hwnd*, *fSelect*, *first*, *last*)
	ListBox_SetAnchorIndex(*hwnd*, *index*)
	ListBox_SetCaretIndex(*hwnd*, *index*)
	ListBox_SetColumnWidth(*hwnd*, *cxColumn*)
	ListBox_SetCurSel(*hwnd*, *index*)
	ListBox_SetHorizontalExtent(*hwnd*, *cxExtent*)
	ListBox_SetItemData(*hwnd*, *index*, *data*)
	ListBox_SetItemHeight(*hwnd*, *index*, *cy*)[1]
	ListBox_SetSel(*hwnd*, *fSelect*, *index*)
	ListBox_SetTabStops(*hwnd*, *cTabs*, *lpTabs*)
	ListBox_SetTopIndex(*hwnd*, *indexTop*)
Combo Box Controls:	**ComboBox_AddItemData**(*hwnd*, *data*)
	ComboBox_AddString(*hwnd*, *lpsz*)

Table 2.1   Control Message API Functions *(continued)*

Control group	Functions
Combo Box Controls:	**ComboBox_DeleteString**(*hwnd*, *index*)
	ComboBox_Dir(*hwnd*, *attrs*, *lpszFileSpec*)
	ComboBox_Enable(*hwnd*, *fEnable*)
	ComboBox_FindItemData(*hwnd*, *indexStart*, *data*)
	ComboBox_FindString(*hwnd*, *indexStart*, *lpszFind*)
	ComboBox_GetCount(*hwnd*)
	ComboBox_GetCurSel(*hwnd*)
	ComboBox_GetDroppedControlRect(*hwnd*, *lprc*)[1]
	ComboBox_GetDroppedState(*hwnd*)[1]
	ComboBox_GetEditSel(*hwnd*)
	ComboBox_GetExtendedUI(*hwnd*)[1]
	ComboBox_GetItemData(*hwnd*, *index*)
	ComboBox_GetItemHeight(*hwnd*)
	ComboBox_GetLBText(*hwnd*, *index*, *lpszBuffer*)
	ComboBox_GetLBTextLen(*hwnd*, *index*)
	ComboBox_GetText(*hwnd*, *lpch*, *cchMax*)
	ComboBox_GetTextLength(*hwnd*)
	ComboBox_InsertItemData(*hwnd*, *index*, *data*)
	ComboBox_InsertString(*hwnd*, *index*, *lpsz*)
	ComboBox_LimitText(*hwnd*, *cchLimit*)
	ComboBox_ResetContent(*hwnd*)
	ComboBox_SelectItemData(*hwnd*, *indexStart*, *data*)
	ComboBox_SelectString(*hwnd*, *indexStart*, *lpszSelect*)
	ComboBox_SetCurSel(*hwnd*, *index*)
	ComboBox_SetEditSel(*hwnd*, *ichStart*, *ichEnd*)
	ComboBox_SetExtendedUI(*hwnd*, *flags*)[1]
	ComboBox_SetItemData(*hwnd*, *index*, *data*)
	ComboBox_SetItemHeight(*hwnd*, *cyItem*)[1]
	ComboBox_SetText(*hwnd*, *lpsz*)
	ComboBox_ShowDropdown(*hwnd*, *fShow*)

[1] Supported only for Win32, not for Windows 3.*x*. These APIs are not available if you define the symbol WINVER as equal to 0x0300, on the command line or with a **#define** statement.

WINDOWS.H and STRICT Type Checking

The WINDOWS.H file contains definitions, macros, and structures to help you write source code that is portable between versions of Microsoft Windows. Some of the WINDOWS.H features are enabled when you define the STRICT symbol in the Project Settings dialog box, on the command line, or in a makefile. This chapter explains the advantages of STRICT features and how using them affects the writing of code.

New Types and Macros

Chapter 1, "Porting 16-Bit Code to 32-Bit Windows," introduced some new standard types for programming in Windows. The old types, such as **FAR PASCAL** for declaring window procedures, may work in existing code but are not guaranteed to work in all future versions of Windows. Therefore, you should convert your code to use the new standards wherever appropriate.

General Data Types

The following table summarizes the new standard types defined in WINDOWS.H. These types are polymorphic (they can contain different kinds of data) and are generally useful throughout applications. Other new types, handles, and function pointers also are introduced in following sections.

Typedef	Description
WINAPI	Use in place of **FAR PASCAL** in API declarations. If you are writing a DLL with exported API entry points, you can use this for your own APIs.
CALLBACK	Use in place of **FAR PASCAL** in application callback routines such as window procedures and dialog procedures.
LPCSTR	Same as **LPSTR**, except used for read-only string pointers. Defined as (**const char FAR***).

Typedef	Description
UINT	Portable unsigned integer type whose size is determined by host environment (32 bits for Windows NT and Windows 95). Synonym for **unsigned int**. Used in place of **WORD** except in the rare cases where a 16-bit unsigned quantity is desired even on 32-bit platforms.
LRESULT	Type used for return value of window procedures.
LPARAM	Type used for declaration of lParam, the fourth parameter of a windows procedure.
WPARAM	Type used for declaration of wParam, the third parameter of a windows procedure (a polymorphic data type).
LPVOID	Generic pointer type, equivalent to (**void ***). Should be used instead of **LPSTR**.

Utility Macros

WINDOWS.H provides a series of utility macros that are useful for working with the types listed in the previous section, "General Data Types." The utility macros listed in the following table help create and extract data from these types. The **FIELDOFFSET** macro is particularly useful when you need to give the numeric offset of a structure member as an argument.

Utility	Description
MAKELPARAM(*low*, *high*)	Combines two 16-bit quantities into an **LPARAM**.
MAKELRESULT(*low*, *high*)	Combines two 16-bit quantities into an **LRESULT**.
MAKELP(*sel*, *off*)	Combines a selector and an offset into a **FAR VOID*** pointer. Useful only for Windows 3.*x*.
SELECTOROF(*lp*)	Extracts the selector part of a far pointer. Returns a **UINT**. Useful only for Windows 3.*x*.
OFFSETOF(*lp*)	Extracts the offset part of a far pointer. Returns a **UINT**. Useful only for Windows 3.*x*.
FIELDOFFSET(*type*, *field*)	Calculates the offset of a member of a data structure. The *type* is the type of structure, and *field* is the name of the structure member or field.

New Handle Types

In addition to the existing Windows handle types such as **HWND**, **HDC**, **HBRUSH**, and so on, WINDOWS.H defines the following new handle types. They are particularly important if STRICT type checking is enabled, but you can use them even if you do not define STRICT.

Handle	Description
HINSTANCE	Instance handle type
HMODULE	Module handle type
HBITMAP	Bitmap handle type
HLOCAL	Local handle type
HGLOBAL	Global handle type
HTASK	Task handle type
HFILE	File handle type
HRSRC	Resource handle type
HGDIOBJ	Generic GDI object handle type (except HMETAFILE)
HMETAFILE	Metafile handle type
HDWP	**DeferWindowPos( )** handle
HACCEL	Accelerator table handle
HDRVR	Driver handle

Using STRICT to Improve Type Checking

When you define the STRICT symbol, you enable features that require more care in declaring and using types. This helps you write more portable code. This extra care will also reduce your debugging time. Enabling STRICT redefines certain data types so that the compiler won't permit assignment from one type to another without an explicit cast. This is especially helpful with Windows code. Errors in passing data types are reported at compile time instead of causing fatal errors at run time.

When STRICT is defined, WINDOWS.H type definitions change as follows:

- Specific handle types are defined to be mutually exclusive; for example, you won't be able to pass an **HWND** where an **HDC** type argument is required. Without STRICT, all handles are defined as integers, so the compiler doesn't prevent you from using one type of handle where another type is expected.

- All callback function types (dialog procedures, window procedures, and hook procedures) are defined with full prototypes. This prevents you from declaring callback functions with incorrect parameter lists.

- Parameter and return value types that should use a generic pointer are declared correctly as **LPVOID** instead of as **LPSTR** or another pointer type.

- The **COMSTAT** structure is declared according to the ANSI standard.

Enabling STRICT Type Checking

To enable STRICT type checking, define the symbol name "STRICT." Open the Project Settings dialog box, select the C/C++ tab, select General in the Category box, and type **STRICT** in the Preprocessor Definitions box. You can also specify this definition on the command line or in a makefile by giving /DSTRICT as a compiler option.

To define STRICT on a file-by-file basis (supported by C but not C++ as explained in the note that follows), insert a **#define** statement before including WINDOWS.H in files where you want to enable STRICT:

```
#define STRICT
#include WINDOWS.H
```

For best results, you should also set the warning level for error messages to at least /W3. This is always advisable with applications for Windows, because a coding practice that causes a warning (for example, passing the wrong number of parameters) usually causes a fatal error at run time if it is not corrected.

Note If you are writing a C++ application, you don't have the option of applying STRICT to only some of your source files. Because of the way C++ "type-safe linking" works, mixing STRICT and non-STRICT source files in your application can cause linking errors.

Making Your Application STRICT Compliant

Some source code that in the past compiled successfully might produce error messages when you enable STRICT type checking. The following sections describe the minimal requirements for making your code compile when STRICT is enabled. Additional steps are recommended, especially if you want to produce portable code. These are covered in the section "Using STRICT Type Checking" on page 46.

General Requirements

The principal requirement is that you must declare correct handle types and function pointers instead of relying on more general types such as **unsigned int** and **FARPROC**. You cannot use one handle type where another is expected. This also means that you may have to change function declarations and use more type casts.

For best results, the generic **HANDLE** type should be used only when necessary. Consult "New Types and Macros" on page 41 for a list of new specific handle types.

Using Function Pointers

Always declare function pointers with the proper function type (such as **DLGPROC** or **WNDPROC**) rather than **FARPROC**. You'll need to cast function pointers to and from the proper function type when using **MakeProcInstance**, **FreeProcInstance**, and other functions that take or return a **FARPROC**, as shown in the following code:

```
BOOL CALLBACK DlgProc(HWND hwnd, UINT msg, WPARAM wParam,
                            LPARAM lParam);
DLGPROC lpfnDlg;

lpfnDlg = (DLGPROC)MakeProcInstance((FARPROC)DlgProc, hinst);
...
FreeProcInstance((FARPROC)lpfnDlg);
```

Declaring Functions Within Your Application

Make sure all application functions are declared. Placing all function declarations in an include file is recommended because you can easily scan your declarations and look for parameter and return types that should be changed.

If you use the /Zg compiler option to create header files for your functions, remember that you'll get different results depending on whether you have enabled STRICT type checking. With STRICT disabled, all handle types generate the same base type (**unsigned short** in Windows 3.*x*). With STRICT enabled, they generate base types such as **HWND __near *** or **HDC __near ***. To avoid conflict, you need to recreate the header file each time you disable, enable STRICT, or edit the header file to use the types **HWND**, **HDC**, **HANDLE**, and so on, instead of the base types.

Any API function declarations that you copied from WINDOWS.H into your source code may have changed, and your local declaration may be out of date. Remove your local declaration.

Functions That Require Casts

Some API functions have generic return types or parameters. For example, a function like **SendMessage** returns data that may be any number of types, depending on the context. When you see any of these functions in your source code, make sure that you use the correct type cast and that it is as specific as possible.

The following table summarizes these functions.

API Function	Comment
LocalLock	Cast result to the proper kind of data pointer.
GlobalLock	Cast result to the proper kind of data pointer.
GetWindowWord	Cast result to appropriate data type.
GetWindowLong	Cast result to appropriate data type.
SetWindowWord	Cast argument as it is passed to function.
SetWindowLong	Cast argument as it is passed to function.
SendMessage	Cast result to appropriate data type; cast to **UINT** before casting to a handle type.
DefWindowProc	See comment for **SendMessage**.
SendDlgItemMsg	See comment for **SendMessage**.

When you call **SendMessage**, **DefWindowProc**, or **SendDlgItemMessage**, you should first cast the result to type **UINT**. You need to take similar steps for any API function that returns **LRESULT** or **LONG,** where the result contains a handle. This is necessary for writing portable code because the size of a handle is either 16 bits or 32 bits, depending on the version of Windows. The **(UINT)** cast ensures proper conversion. The following code shows an example in which **SendMessage** returns a handle to a brush:

```
HBRUSH hbr;

hbr = (HBRUSH)(UINT)SendMessage(hwnd, WM_CTLCOLOR, ..., ...);
```

The CreateWindow Function

The **CreateWindow** and **CreateWindowEx** *hmenu* parameter is sometimes used to pass an integer control ID. In this case, you must cast this to an **HMENU** type:

```
HWND hwnd;
int id;

hwnd = CreateWindow("Button", "Ok", BS_PUSHBUTTON,
        x, y, cx, cy, hwndParent,
        (HMENU)id,       // Cast required here
        hinst,
        NULL);
```

Using STRICT Type Checking

To get the most benefit from STRICT type checking, there are additional guidelines you should follow. Your code will be more portable in future versions of Windows if you make the following changes:

Change	To
HANDLE	A specific handle such as **HINSTANCE, HMODULE, HGLOBAL, HLOCAL,** and so on
WORD	**UINT,** except where you want a 16-bit value even when the platform is 32 bits
WORD	**WPARAM,** where *wParam* is declared
LONG	**LPARAM** or **LRESULT** as appropriate

Anytime you need an integer data type, you should declare it as **UINT** except where a 16-bit value is specifically required (as in a structure or parameter). Even if a variable never exceeds the range of a 16-bit integer, it can be more efficiently handled by the processor if it is 32 bits.

The types **WPARAM, LPARAM, LRESULT,** and **void *** are "polymorphic data types." They hold different kinds of data at different times, even when STRICT type checking is enabled. To get the benefit of type checking, you should cast values of these types as soon as possible. Note that message crackers (as well as the Microsoft Foundation Classes) automatically recast *wParam* and *lParam* for you in a portable way.

Take special care to distinguish **HMODULE** and **HINSTANCE** types. Even with STRICT enabled, they are defined as the same base type. Most kernel module management functions use **HINSTANCE** types, but there are a few API functions that return or accept only **HMODULE** types.

Accessing the New COMSTAT Structure

The Windows 3.x declaration of the **COMSTAT** structure is not compatible with ANSI standards. WINDOWS.H now defines the **COMSTAT** structure, for compatibility with ANSI compilers, so that the /W4 option does not issue warnings.

To support backward compatibility of source code, WINDOWS.H does not use the new structure definition unless the version of Windows (as indicated by WINVER) is 3.x or later, or if STRICT is defined. When you enable STRICT, the presumption is that you are trying to write portable code. Therefore, WINDOWS.H uses the new **COMSTAT** structure for all versions of Windows if STRICT is enabled.

The new structure definition replaces the bit fields with flags which access bits in a single field, named **status**, as shown in the following table. Each flag turns on a different bit.

Windows 3.x field name	Flag accessing the status field
fCtsHold	CSTF_CTSHOLD
fDsrHold	CSTF_DSRHOLD
fEof	CSTF_EOF
fRlsdHold	CSTF_RLSDHOLD
fTxim	CSTF_TXIM
fXoffHold	CSTF_XOFFHOLD
fXoffSent	CSTF_XOFFSENT

If your code accesses any of these status fields, you need to change your code as appropriate. For example, suppose you have the following code written for Windows 3.x:

```
if (comstat.fEof || fCondition)
    comstat.fCtsHold = TRUE;
    comstat.fTxim = FALSE;
```

This code should be replaced by code that accesses individual bits of the **status** field by using flags. Note the use of bitwise operators:

```
if ((comstat.status & CSTF_EOF) || fCondition)
    comstat.status |= CSTF_CTSHOLD;
    comstat.status &= ~CSTF_TXIM;
```

Interpreting Error Messages Affected by STRICT

Enabling STRICT type checking may affect the kind of error messages you receive. With STRICT enabled, all handle types are defined as pointer types. When you incorrectly use these types (for example, passing an **int** where an **HDC** is expected), you will get warning messages referring to errors in pointer indirection.

STRICT also requires that **FARPROC** function pointers be recast as more specific function pointer types such as **DLGPROC**. However, **MakeProcInstance** and **FreeProcInstance** still work with the **FARPROC** type. If you do not cast between **FARPROC** and the appropriate function pointer type, the compiler will warn about an error in function parameter lists.

Note that using **MakeProcInstance** is useful for portability, if you want to use the same source to compile for Windows 3.*x*. Under Win32, however, **MakeProcInstance** performs no operation, but returns the function name.

CHAPTER 4

Creating DLLs for Win32

Microsoft Visual C++ offers full support for creating dynamic-link libraries (DLLs) as well as applications. Technically, a DLL is an executable file, but it usually functions as a library for applications. Multiple applications can access the contents of a single copy of a DLL in memory.

The compiler supports placement of data symbols and C++ objects in DLLs and in functions. The compiler's run-time library initializes global C++ objects as needed.

The compiler, run-time library, and Microsoft Foundation Class Library (MFC) support DLL creation in other important ways as well. If you are porting DLL source code written for Windows 3.*x*, you may need to revise it as described in this chapter. If you are building a DLL using MFC, read the article "Dynamic Link Libraries (DLLs)" in *Programming with the Microsoft Foundation Class Library* after reading this chapter. It contains information specific to building DLLs with MFC.

This chapter covers the following topics:

- Overview of differences
- Run-time library behavior
- The **DllMain** function
- The **dllexport** and **dllimport** attributes
- Exporting C++ functions
- Building the DLL
- Special issues with DLLs

Overview of Differences

If you have built 16-bit DLLs for Windows 3.*x*, you should find that building DLLs for Windows 95 and Windows NT is more convenient. The compiler offers more direct support, which can save you several steps in DLL creation. The specific differences are:

- There is no separate startup module. The DLL startup sequence is handled directly by C/C++ run-time library code linked into your DLL.

- The run-time library code initializes any static non-local C++ objects by calling the appropriate constructors. (Each process gets its own copy of all the DLL's static data, including objects.)

- Other initialization and termination are handled through the single user-defined function, **DllMain**. You can write or choose not to include this function.

You import and export symbols directly in your source code. Using the **dllexport** attribute (similar to **__export** in Windows 3.*x*) saves you from having to use a separate module-definition file. Using **dllimport** improves efficiency and enables you to import data and objects as well as code.

- The timing of calls to routines registered with **atexit** can differ.

The most fundamental difference is that code from the C/C++ run-time library is linked into your DLL (or linked at run time if you are using the DLL version of the run-time library), which minimizes some coding problems. The run-time library code calls the constructors and destructors as appropriate for static, non-local C++ objects in the DLL.

The run-time code also calls the user-defined **DllMain** function for both initialization and termination, so that you have an opportunity to allocate or release additional resources, as needed. These calls are made in four situations: process attach, process detach, thread attach, and thread detach. If you don't need initialization or termination, you can omit **DllMain** from source code.

The rest of this chapter describes how to build a DLL, and how to write a **DllMain** function and use the **dllexport** and **dllimport** attributes.

Run-Time Library Behavior

As explained in the previous section, the C/C++ run-time library code performs the DLL startup sequence, eliminating the need for a separate module; it also calls constructors and destructors as appropriate for global C++ objects.

For example, in the following DLL source code, Equus and Sugar are two static, non-local objects of class CHorse, defined in HORSES.H. There is no function in source code that contains calls to a constructor function for CHorse or to the destructor function, because these objects are defined outside of any function. Therefore, calls to these constructors and destructors must be performed by the run-time code. (The run-time library code for applications also performs this function.)

```
#include "horses.h"

CHorse   Equus( ARABIAN, MALE );
CHorse   Sugar( THOROUGHBRED, FEMALE );

BOOL     WINAPI   DllMain (HANDLE hInst,
                           ULONG ul_reason_for_call,
                           LPVOID lpReserved)
...
```

Each time a new process attempts to use the DLL, the operating system creates a separate copy of the DLL's data: this is called *process attach*. The run-time library code for the DLL calls the constructors for all the global objects, if any, and then calls your **DllMain** function with process attach selected. The opposite situation is process detach: the run-time library code calls **DllMain** with process detach selected and then calls a list of termination functions including **atexit** functions, destructors for the global objects, and destructors for the **static** objects. Note that the order of events in process attach is the reverse of that in process detach.

The run-time library code is also called during thread attach and thread detach (explained later in this chapter), but the run-time code does no initialization or termination on its own.

The DllMain Function

Unlike Windows 3.*x* DLLs, Windows 95 and Windows NT call one function, **DllMain**, for both initialization and termination. It also makes calls on both a per-process and per-thread basis, so several initialization calls can be made if a process is multithreaded. The function is optional; if you don't provide it in source code, the compiler links its own version, which does nothing but return TRUE.

If you are building a DLL with MFC, **DllMain** may need to perform additional tasks. For more information, see the article "DLLs: Initialization and Termination" in *Programming with the Microsoft Foundation Class Library*.

DllMain uses the **WINAPI** convention and three parameters. The following code shows the first line in a **DllMain** definition:

```
BOOL     WINAPI   DllMain (HANDLE hInst,
                           ULONG ul_reason_for_call,
                           LPVOID lpReserved)
```

The function returns TRUE (1) to indicate success. If, during per-process initialization, the function returns zero, the system cancels the process.

The *ul_reason_for_call* parameter indicates the reason **DllMain** was called: initialization or termination, for a process or a thread. The following table describes the meaning of the four possible values.

Value of *ul_reason_for_call*	Description
DLL_PROCESS_ATTACH	A new process is attempting to access the DLL; one thread is assumed.
DLL_THREAD_ATTACH	A new thread of an existing process is attempting to access the DLL; this call is made beginning with the *second thread* of a process attaching to the DLL.
DLL_PROCESS_DETACH	A process is detaching from the DLL.
DLL_THREAD_DETACH	One of the additional threads (not the first thread) of a process is detaching from the DLL.

The *lpReserved* parameter is reserved for the system's use and should not be manipulated by your source code.

Windows 3.*x* DLL initialization functions are passed the following information:

- The DLL's instance handle
- The DLL's data segment (DS)
- The heap size specified in the DLL's .DEF file
- The command line

Win32 DLL initialization functions are passed the following information:

- The *hModule* parameter, a module handle.
- The *ul_reason_for_call* parameter, an enumerated type that indicates which of four reasons the **LibMain** procedure is being called: process attach, thread attach, thread detach, or process detach.
- The *lpReserved* parameter, which is unused.

The following code presents a basic skeleton showing what the definition of **DllMain** might look like:

```
BOOL APIENTRY DllMain( HANDLE hModule,
                       DWORD ul_reason_for_call,
                       LPVOID lpReserved )
{
    switch( ul_reason_for_call ) {
    case DLL_PROCESS_ATTACH:
    ...
    case DLL_THREAD_ATTACH:
    ...
    case DLL_THREAD_DETACH:
    ...
    case DLL_PROCESS_DETACH:
    ...
    }
    return TRUE;
}
```

The Win32 module handle has the same purpose as the Windows 3.*x* instance handle. Otherwise, Win32 DLL initialization functions do not include the parameters for Windows 3.*x* initialization, as described in the following table.

Parameter	Comment
DLL data segment	Not needed in Win32; memory model is flat, not segmented.
Size of DLL's local heap	All calls to local memory management functions operate on the default heap.
Pointer to command line	The command line can be obtained through a call to the **GetCommandLine** API function.

The dllimport and dllexport Attributes

The DLL model for Win32 is different from that for Windows 3.*x*. To write the most efficient DLL code and to make the transition as smooth as possible, use the **dllexport** and **dllimport** import attributes.

As you write a DLL, you can use **dllexport** to declare that a symbol (function, data, or object) is being exported to applications and other DLLs. The compiler produces the most efficient code as a result, and you no longer need a module-definition (.DEF) file to export your symbols.

When you create header files for use with your DLLs, you should include **dllimport** declarations for each symbol, so applications properly declare each DLL symbol to be used. The DLL users still need an import library, but use of **dllimport** produces more efficient code. Also, **dllimport** must be used to import data items and objects.

Because they are attributes and not keywords, **dllexport** and **dllimport** must be used in conjunction with the __**declspec** keyword. The following procedure is recommended:

1. Use the __**declspec** keyword, along with **dllexport** and **dllimport**, to define import and export macros for your source code.

2. Use these macros you've defined to declare symbols as export or import.

For more information on **dllexport** and **dllimport**, see "The dllexport and dllimport Attributes" in Appendix B of the *C++ Language Reference*.

The __declspec Keyword

The Visual C++ language (including C source modules) uses the __**declspec** keyword to extend storage class attributes. Storage class determines how a given symbol is accessed by the compiler. For example, **static**, a storage class attribute in standard C/C++, specifies that a variable is not stored on the stack.

This version of Visual C++ defines four extended storage class attributes: **dllexport**, **dllimport**, **thread**, and **naked**. These are not supported directly as keywords. Instead, these Microsoft-specific extended class storage attributes are used with **__declspec** to reduce the number of reserved words. This chapter introduces the **dllexport** and **dllimport** attributes. Chapter 5 discusses the **thread** attribute, and Chapter 9 discusses the **naked** attribute.

The syntax for using **__declspec** is:

__declspec(*attribute* **)** *variable-declaration*

For example, the following definition exports an integer, using **dllexport** as the attribute:

```
__declspec( dllexport ) int SumInterest = 0;
```

Exporting Symbols

The use of **dllexport** (when used with **__declspec** as explained in the previous section) replaces the **__export** keyword supported in Windows 3.*x*. To port DLL source code, you should replace each instance of **__export**. The **dllexport** attribute eliminates the need for a .DEF file.

To export symbols, the recommended approach is to define a macro for **__declspec(dllexport)** and then use the macro with each symbol:

```
#define DllExport   __declspec( dllexport )

DllExport   int i = 10;       // Definition, because initialized
DllExport   int j;            // Definition, because of DllExport
DllExport   void func();      // Declaration
```

With uninitialized data, **dllexport** causes the statement to be a definition unless it is combined with **extern**, in which case it is a declaration. The difference is important: a definition tells the compiler to create a symbol; a declaration informs the compiler that the symbol is created somewhere else. Thus, in the previous example, j is defined rather than declared, because of **DllExport**. The nature of the other two statements is already clear from syntax.

When you combine the **extern** keyword with **dllexport**, it tells the compiler that the symbol is defined and exported by the DLL, but not necessarily in this source-code module. For example, the following is a data declaration, not definition:

```
extern  DllExport  j;         // Symbol j is declared
```

It should be clear that exporting a symbol is inconsistent with automatic ("stack" or "local") storage class. Therefore, the following code produces an error, because it attempts to export a symbol Sum defined on the stack:

```
void func()
{
b   DllExport   int Sum;      // Error: cannot export local variable
```

However, the following code compiles correctly because Sum is only declared, not defined, within the function. This code enables Sum to be used within the scope of func, but the code does not create it:

```
void func()
{
    extern   DllExport   int   Sum;     // Ok, because extern means Sum
                                        //  is defined in another
                                        //  module of this DLL.
```

Importing Symbols

A program that uses public symbols defined by a DLL is said to *import* them. Windows 3.*x* required only the use of an import library, normally supplied by the DLL author, to handle the mechanics of importing. In Win32, the DLL user must still link with the import library, but needs to use **dllimport** as well.

As a DLL author, you should accommodate this requirement by using **dllimport** in the header files you supply. If you don't, DLL users can still access DLL functions, but their code will be less efficient, and they will not have access to DLL public data symbols and objects.

To import symbols, the recommended approach is to define a macro for **__declspec(dllimport)** and then use the macro to declare each imported symbol:

```
#define DllImport   __declspec( dllimport )

DllImport   int     j;
DllImport   voidfunc();
```

The **dllimport** attribute must be used in a declaration, not a definition, because you obviously cannot define a new symbol and at the same time import it from another program. You also cannot declare an imported symbol as **static**, which implies that the symbol is defined in the current module.

```
DllImport   int  j = 2;     // Error: initialization implies definition

void func()
{
    static DllImport int  i;  // Error: static
```

It is valid to give the same symbol both the **dllexport** and **dllimport** attributes. This could happen if you are sharing header files between different programs. Otherwise, it should not happen. When both attributes are used, the **dllexport** attribute takes precedence:

```
DllImport   int     i;
DllExport   int     i;   // Warning issued, but dllexport takes
                         //  precedence
```

If you are compiling your program as a C language module, you cannot use the address of an imported symbol to initialize a global or static variable. However, in

C++, you can use the address of an imported symbol to initialize any variable or object.

Exporting C++ Functions

If you have functions in a DLL written in C++ that you want to access from a C language module, you will probably want to declare these functions with C linkage instead of C++ linkage. Unless otherwise specified, the C++ compiler uses C++ type-safe naming (also known as name decoration) and C++ calling conventions, which can be difficult to call from C.

To specify C linkage, specify extern "C" for your function declarations, for example:

```
extern "C" __declspec( dllexport ) int MyFunc(long parm1);
```

For more information on linkage specification, see "Linkage Specifications" in Chapter 6 of the *C++ Language Reference*.

Importing and Exporting Inline Functions

Imported functions can be defined as inline. The effect is roughly the same as defining a standard function inline; calls to the function are expanded into inline code, much like a macro. This is principally useful as a way of supporting C++ classes in a DLL that may inline some of their member functions for efficiency.

One feature of an imported inline function is that in C++, you can take its address. The compiler returns the address of the copy of the inline function residing in the DLL. Another feature of imported inline functions is that unlike global imported data, you can initialize static local data of the imported function.

You should exercise care when providing imported inline functions, because they can create the possibility of version conflicts. An inline function gets expanded into the application code; therefore, if you later rewrite the function, it does not get updated unless the application itself is recompiled. (Normally, DLL functions can be updated without rebuilding the applications that use them.)

Building the DLL

There are two categories of compiler options you should know about when you build a DLL. The /LD option causes the compiler to build a DLL instead of an application. You can select it automatically by using the Visual C++ environment to build a DLL, or by specifying /LD on the command line. The other options that can affect building of a DLL are /MD, /MT, and /ML, which select run-time library type.

Using Visual C++ to Build DLLs

To build a DLL from within the Visual C++ environment, make sure that you select "Dynamic-link library" as the initial project type when you create a new project workspace. Visual C++ uses a dialog box to offer a choice of project types when you choose Workspace from the New dialog box (File menu).

To debug a DLL, you must run an application that calls your DLL. Choose the Settings command from the Build menu. In the Project Settings dialog box, select the Debug tab. In the Executable For Debug Session box, specify which application to run while debugging.

The /LD Option

The Visual C++ environment automatically sets the /LD option when you choose "Dynamic-link library" as the project type. You can also specify /LD directly when using the command line to invoke the compiler.

When the /LD option is specified, the compiler passes the –DLL option to the linker, causing a DLL to be built. The compiler also does the following:

- Looks for the **DllMain** function in the source code.

- Links with DLL startup code that performs some initialization for you.

- Produces an import library to be linked to applications that call your DLL.

- Interprets /Fe as naming a DLL rather than an EXE file; the default program name becomes *basename*.DLL instead of *basename*.EXE.

- Changes default for C run-time library support, as explained in the next section.

Multithread Support and /M Options

The /MD, /ML, and /MT options determine whether the program being built has single-thread support, multithread support, or uses a dynamic-link version of the run-time library (MSVCRT40.DLL). The following table shows the purpose of each option.

Option	Links to
/MD	MSVCRT40.DLL, a dynamic-link library that is multithread aware
/ML	Single-thread-aware library (default for applications)
/MT	Multithread-aware library (default for DLLs)

It is usually best to use the /MD or /MT option when building a DLL. These options support multithread applications. When you specify /ML, your DLL will work reliably only when called by single-thread applications. A multithread application that calls a DLL without multithread awareness is likely to fail. Therefore, don't specify /ML unless you know that it will be used only by single-thread applications.

The compiler chooses /MT by default when you build a DLL.

Note that deciding whether to use MSVCRT40.DLL and whether to build an application or DLL are largely independent choices. You could, for example, choose to build an application that uses the DLL version of the run-time library (/MD);

conversely, you could build a DLL that is statically linked to the C run-time library (/MT or /ML).

Special Issues with DLLs

The following sections discuss issues that occur occasionally in special situations: mutual DLL imports and the effect of dynamic loading on thread-local storage. You can write a simple DLL without worrying about these issues. However, if you use any of these features, it is helpful to be aware of the issues.

Mutual Imports

Exporting or importing to another executable file presents complications when the imports are mutual (or "circular"). For example, two DLLs import symbols from each other, similar to mutually-recursive functions.

The problem with mutually-importing executable files (usually DLLs) is that neither can be built without building the other first. Each build process requires, as input, an import library produced by the *other* build process.

The solution is to use the LIB utility with the /DEF option, which produces an import library without building the executable file. Using this utility, you can build all the import libraries you need, no matter how many DLLs are involved or how complicated the dependencies are.

The general solution is:

1. Take each DLL in turn. (Any order is feasible, although some orders are more optimal.) If all the needed import libraries exist and are current, run LINK to build the executable file (DLL). This produces an import library. Otherwise, run LIB to produce an import library.

   Running LIB with the /DEF option produces an additional file with an .EXP extension. The .EXP file must be used later to build the executable file.

2. After using either LINK or LIB to build all the import libraries, go back and run LINK to build any executable files that were not built in the previous step. Note that the corresponding .EXP file must be specified on the LINK line.

   If you had run the LIB utility earlier to produce an import library for DLL1, LIB produced the file DLL1.EXP as well. You must use DLL1.EXP as input to LINK when building DLL1.DLL.

Figure 4.1 illustrates a solution for two mutually-importing DLLs, DLL1 and DLL2. The first step is to run LIB, with the /DEF option set, on DLL1. This step produces DLL1.LIB, an import library, and DLL1.EXP. The import library is used to build DLL2, which in turn produces an import library for DLL2's symbols. The final step builds DLL1, by using DLL1.EXP and DLL2.LIB as input. Note that an .EXP file for DLL2 is *not* necessary, because LIB was not used to build DLL2's import library.

Figure 4.1   Linking Two DLLs with Mutual Imports

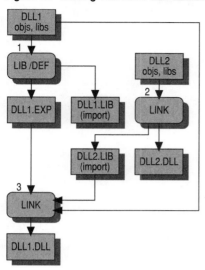

For more information on the LIB utility and the /DEF option, see Chapter 30, "LIB Reference," in the *Visual C++ User's Guide*.

DLL Loading and Thread-Local Storage

An executable file loads a DLL in one of two ways: statically or dynamically. The exported contents of a DLL are *always* dynamically bound, regardless of how it is loaded. Furthermore, these mechanisms are not mutually exclusive, as one application can statically load a DLL and another can attach to it dynamically. A statically-loaded DLL is "static" only in the sense that an application sets up imports to it at build time.

- Static loading is the standard mechanism, invoked when a program is built with import libraries referring to the DLL. When the application builder is relatively sure that a particular DLL will be used, this method is most efficient because symbols can be accessed with the **dllimport** attribute.

- Dynamic loading attaches to a DLL specified at run time. This mechanism uses **LoadLibrary** and other API functions such as **GetProcAddress**, bypassing use of imports. Use this technique when you don't know at build time whether a DLL will be accessed. This way the DLL is not initialized until it is accessed.

If a DLL declares static-extent data as __**declspec(thread)**, it can cause a protection fault if dynamically loaded. After the DLL is loaded with **LoadLibrary**, it causes system failure whenever the code references this data. (Static-extent data includes both global and local **static** items.)

Therefore, when you create a DLL, you should either avoid this use of thread-local storage, or inform DLL users about potential pitfalls, in case they attempt dynamic loading.

Creating Multithread Applications for Win32

Microsoft Visual C++ provides support for creating multithread applications with 32-bit versions of Microsoft Windows: Windows NT and Windows 95. You should consider using more than one thread if your application needs to manage multiple activities, such as simultaneous keyboard and mouse input. One thread can process keyboard input while a second thread filters mouse activities. A third thread can update the display screen based on data from the mouse and keyboard threads. At the same time, other threads can access disk files or get data from a communications port.

With Visual C++, there are two ways to program with multiple threads: use the Microsoft Foundation Class library (MFC) or the C run-time library and the Win32 API. For information on creating multithread applications with MFC, read the "Multithreading" articles in *Programming with the Microsoft Foundation Class Library* after reading this chapter.

This chapter explains the features in Visual C++ that support the creation of multithread programs.

Note Win32s does not support multithreading. Calls to the Win32 APIs and C run-time library functions mentioned in this chapter will return an error.

Multithread Programs

A thread is basically a path of execution through a program. It is also the smallest unit of execution that Win32 schedules. A thread consists of a stack, the state of the CPU registers, and an entry in the execution list of the system scheduler. Each thread shares all of the process's resources.

A process consists of one or more threads and the code, data, and other resources of a program in memory. Typical program resources are open files, semaphores, and dynamically allocated memory. A program executes when the system scheduler gives one of its threads execution control. The scheduler determines which threads should run and when they should run. Threads of lower priority may have to wait while higher priority threads complete their tasks. On multiprocessor machines, the scheduler can move individual threads to different processors to "balance" the CPU load.

Each thread in a process operates independently. Unless you make them visible to each other, the threads execute individually and are unaware of the of other threads in a process. Threads sharing common resources, however, must coordinate their work by using semaphores or another method of interprocess communication. See "Writing a Multithread Program" on page 68 for more information about synchronizing threads.

Library Support

If one thread is suspended by the Win32 scheduler while executing the **printf** function, one of the program's other threads might start executing. If the second thread also calls **printf**, data might be corrupted. To avoid this, access to static data used by the function must be restricted to one thread at a time.

You do not need to serialize access to stack-based (automatic) variables because each thread has a different stack. Therefore, a function that uses only automatic (stack) variables is reentrant. The standard C run-time libraries, such as LIBCE, have a limited number of reentrant functions. A multithread program needing to use C run-time library functions that are normally not reentrant should be built with the multithread library LIBCMT.LIB.

The Multithread C Libraries: LIBCMT.LIB and MSVCRT.LIB

The support library LIBCMT.LIB is a reentrant library for creating multithread programs. The MSVCRT.LIB library, which calls code in the shared MSVCRT40.DLL, is also reentrant. When your application calls functions in these libraries, the following rules may apply:

All library calls must use the C (**__cdecl**) calling convention; programs compiled using other calling conventions (such as **__fastcall** or **__stdcall**) must use the standard include files for the run-time library functions they call.

- Variables passed to library functions must be passed by value or cast to a pointer.

Programs built with LIBCMT.LIB do not share C run-time library code or data with any dynamic-link libraries they call.

Alternatives to LIBCMT.LIB and MSVCRT.LIB

If you build a multithread program without using LIBCMT.LIB, you must do the following:

- Use the standard C libraries and limit library calls to the set of reentrant functions.

- Use the Win32 API thread management functions, such as **CreateThread**.

- Provide your own synchronization for functions that are not reentrant by using Win32 services such as semaphores and the **EnterCriticalSection** and **LeaveCriticalSection** functions.

Warning   The multithread library LIBCMT.LIB includes the **_beginthread** and **_endthread** functions. The **_beginthread** function performs initialization without which many C run-time functions will fail. You must use **_beginthread** instead of **CreateThread** in C programs built with LIBCMT.LIB if you intend to call C run-time functions.

The Multithread Libraries Compile Option

To build a multithread application that uses the C run-time libraries, you must tell the compiler to use a special version of the libraries (LIBCMT.LIB). To select these libraries, first choose Settings from the Visual C++ Build menu, then choose the C/C++ tab in the Project Settings dialog box. Select Code Generation from the Category drop-down list box. From the Use Run-Time Library drop-down box, select Multithreaded. Choose OK to return to editing.

From the command line, the Multithread Library compiler option (/MT) is the best way to build a multithread program with LIBCMT.LIB. This option, which is automatically set when you specify a multithreaded application when creating a new project, embeds the LIBCMT library name in the object file.

Include Files

The Microsoft Visual C++ include files contain conditional sections for multithread applications using LIBCMT.LIB. To compile your application with the appropriate definitions, you can:

- Compile with the Multithread Library compiler option described in the previous section.

- Define the symbolic constant **_MT** in your source file or on the command line with the /D option.

Standard include files declare C run-time library functions as they are implemented in the libraries. If you used the Maximum Optimization (/Ox) or Register Calling Convention (/Gr) option, the compiler assumes that all functions should be called using the register calling convention. The run-time library functions were compiled using the C calling convention, and the declarations in the standard include files tell the compiler to generate correct external references to these functions.

See "Compiling and Linking" on page 70 for examples of how to use the **_MT** constant.

C Run-Time Library Functions for Thread Control

All Win32 programs have at least one thread. Any thread can create additional threads. A thread can complete its work quickly and then terminate, or it can stay active for the life of the program.

The LIBCMT and MSVCRT C run-time libraries provide two functions for thread creation and termination: the **_beginthread** and **_endthread** functions.

The **_beginthread** function creates a new thread and returns a thread identifier if the operation is successful. The thread terminates automatically if it completes execution, or it can terminate itself with a call to **_endthread**.

Warning If you are going to call C run-time routines from a program built with LIBCMT.LIB, you must start your threads with the **_beginthread** function. Do not use the Win32 functions **ExitThread** and **CreateThread**. Using **SuspendThread** can lead to a deadlock when more than one thread is blocked waiting for the suspended thread to complete its access to a C run-time data structure.

The _beginthread Function

The **_beginthread** function creates a new thread. A thread shares the code and data segments of a process with other threads in the process, but has its own unique register values, stack space, and current instruction address. The system gives CPU time to each thread, so that all threads in a process can execute concurrently. You can find a complete description of **_beginthread** and its arguments in the *Run-Time Library Reference*.

The **_beginthread** function is similar to the **CreateThread** function in the Win32 API but has these differences:

- The **_beginthread** function lets you pass multiple arguments to the thread.

- The **_beginthread** function initializes certain C run-time library variables. This is important only if you use the C run-time library in your threads.

- **CreateThread** provides control over security attributes. You can use this function to start a thread in a suspended state.

The **_beginthread** function returns a handle to the new thread if successful or –1 if there was an error.

The _endthread Function

The **_endthread** function terminates a thread created by **_beginthread**. Threads terminate automatically when they finish. The **_endthread** function is useful for conditional termination from within a thread. A thread dedicated to communications processing, for example, can quit if it is unable to get control of the communications port. You can find a complete description of **_endthread** in the *Run-Time Library Reference*.

Sample Multithread C Program

BOUNCE.C is a sample multithread program that creates a new thread each time the letter 'a' or 'A' is entered at the keyboard. Each thread bounces a "happy face" of a different color around the screen. Up to 32 threads can be created. The program's normal termination occurs when 'q' or 'Q' is entered. See "Compiling and Linking" on page 70 for details on compiling and linking BOUNCE.C.

```c
/*  Bounce - Creates a new thread each time the letter 'a' is typed.
 *  Each thread bounces a happy face of a different color around the screen.
 *  All threads are terminated when the letter 'Q' is entered.
 *
 *  This program requires the multithread library. For example, compile
 *  with the following command line:
 *      CL /MT BOUNCE.C
 */

#include <windows.h>
#include <stdlib.h>
#include <string.h>
#include <stdio.h>
#include <conio.h>
#include <process.h>

#define MAX_THREADS  32

/* getrandom returns a random number between min and max, which must be in
 * integer range.
 */
#define getrandom( min, max ) ((rand() % (int)(((max) + 1) - (min))) + (min))

void main( void );                      /* Thread 1: main */
void KbdFunc( void  );                  /* Keyboard input, thread dispatch */
void BounceProc( char * MyID );         /* Threads 2 to n: display */
void ClearScreen( void );               /* Screen clear */
void ShutDown( void );                  /* Program shutdown */
void WriteTitle( int ThreadNum );       /* Display title bar information */

HANDLE   hConsoleOut;                   /* Handle to the console */
HANDLE   hRunMutex;                     /* "Keep Running" mutex */
HANDLE   hScreenMutex;                  /* "Screen update" mutex   */
int      ThreadNr;                      /* Number of threads started */
CONSOLE_SCREEN_BUFFER_INFO csbiInfo;    /* Console information */

void main()                             /* Thread One */
{
    /* Get display screen information & clear the screen.*/
    hConsoleOut = GetStdHandle( STD_OUTPUT_HANDLE );
    GetConsoleScreenBufferInfo( hConsoleOut, &csbiInfo );
    ClearScreen();
    WriteTitle( 0 );
```

```
    /* Create the mutexes and reset thread count. */
    hScreenMutex = CreateMutex( NULL, FALSE, NULL );    /* Cleared */
    hRunMutex = CreateMutex( NULL, TRUE, NULL );        /* Set */
    ThreadNr = 0;

    /* Start waiting for keyboard input to dispatch threads or exit. */
    KbdFunc();

    /* All threads done. Clean up handles. */
    CloseHandle( hScreenMutex );
    CloseHandle( hRunMutex );
    CloseHandle( hConsoleOut );
}

void ShutDown( void )                    /* Shut down threads */
{
    while ( ThreadNr > 0 )
    {
        /* Tell thread to die and record its death. */
        ReleaseMutex( hRunMutex );
        ThreadNr--;
    }
    /* Clean up display when done */
    WaitForSingleObject( hScreenMutex, INFINITE );
    ClearScreen();
}

void KbdFunc( void )                     /* Dispatch and count threads. */
{
    int        KeyInfo;

    do
    {
        KeyInfo = _getch();
        if( tolower( KeyInfo ) == 'a' && ThreadNr < MAX_THREADS )
        {
            ThreadNr++;
            _beginthread( BounceProc, 0, &ThreadNr );
            WriteTitle( ThreadNr );
        }
    } while( tolower( KeyInfo ) != 'q' );

    ShutDown();
}

void BounceProc( char *MyID )
{
    char       MyCell, OldCell;
    WORD       MyAttrib, OldAttrib;
    char       BlankCell = 0x20;
    COORD      Coords, Delta;
    COORD      Old = {0,0};
    DWORD      Dummy;
```

```
/* Generate update increments and initial display coordinates. */
    srand( (unsigned) *MyID * 3 );
    Coords.X = getrandom( 0, csbiInfo.dwSize.X - 1 );
    Coords.Y = getrandom( 0, csbiInfo.dwSize.Y - 1 );
    Delta.X = getrandom( -3, 3 );
    Delta.Y = getrandom( -3, 3 );

    /* Set up "happy face" & generate color attribute from thread number.*/
    if( *MyID > 16)
        MyCell = 0x01;                      /* outline face */
    else
        MyCell = 0x02;                      /* solid face */
    MyAttrib =  *MyID & 0x0F;               /* force black background */

    do
    {
        /* Wait for display to be available, then lock it. */
        WaitForSingleObject( hScreenMutex, INFINITE );

        /* If we still occupy the old screen position, blank it out. */
        ReadConsoleOutputCharacter( hConsoleOut, &OldCell, 1, Old, &Dummy );
        ReadConsoleOutputAttribute( hConsoleOut, &OldAttrib, 1, Old, &Dummy );
        if (( OldCell == MyCell ) && (OldAttrib == MyAttrib))
            WriteConsoleOutputCharacter( hConsoleOut, &BlankCell, 1, Old, &Dummy );

        /* Draw new face, then clear screen lock */
        WriteConsoleOutputCharacter( hConsoleOut, &MyCell, 1, Coords, &Dummy );
        WriteConsoleOutputAttribute( hConsoleOut, &MyAttrib, 1, Coords, &Dummy );
        ReleaseMutex( hScreenMutex );

        /* Increment the coordinates for next placement of the block. */
        Old.X = Coords.X;
        Old.Y = Coords.Y;
        Coords.X += Delta.X;
        Coords.Y += Delta.Y;

        /* If we are about to go off the screen, reverse direction */
        if( Coords.X < 0 || Coords.X >= csbiInfo.dwSize.X )
        {
            Delta.X = -Delta.X;
            Beep( 400, 50 );
        }
        if( Coords.Y < 0 || Coords.Y > csbiInfo.dwSize.Y )
        {
            Delta.Y = -Delta.Y;
            Beep( 600, 50 );
        }
    }
    /* Repeat while RunMutex is still taken. */
    while ( WaitForSingleObject( hRunMutex, 75L ) == WAIT_TIMEOUT );

}
```

```
void WriteTitle( int ThreadNum )
{
    char    NThreadMsg[80];

    sprintf( NThreadMsg, "Threads running: %02d.  Press 'A' to start a thread,'Q' to
quit.", ThreadNum );
    SetConsoleTitle( NThreadMsg );
}

void ClearScreen( void )
{
    DWORD   dummy;
    COORD   Home = { 0, 0 };
    FillConsoleOutputCharacter( hConsoleOut, ' ', csbiInfo.dwSize.X *
csbiInfo.dwSize.Y, Home, &dummy );
}
```

Writing a Multithread Program

When you write a program with multiple threads, you must coordinate their behavior and use of the program's resources. You must also make sure that each thread receives its own stack.

Sharing Common Resources

Each thread has its own stack and its own copy of the CPU registers. Other resources, such as files, static data, and heap memory, are shared by all threads in the process. Threads using these common resources must be synchronized. Win32 provides several ways to synchronize resources, including semaphores, critical sections, events, and mutexes.

When multiple threads are accessing static data, your program must provide for possible resource conflicts. Consider a program where one thread updates a static data structure containing x,y coordinates for items to be displayed by another thread. If the update thread alters the x coordinate and is preempted before it can change the y coordinate, the display thread may be scheduled before the y coordinate is updated. The item would be displayed at the wrong location. You can avoid this problem by using semaphores to control access to the structure.

A mutex (short for *mut*ual *ex*clusion) is a way of communicating among threads or processes that are executing asynchronously of one another. This communication is usually used to coordinate the activities of multiple threads or processes, typically by controlling access to a shared resource by "locking" and "unlocking" the resource. To solve this x,y coordinate update problem, the update thread would set a mutex indicating that the data structure is in use before performing the update. It would clear the mutex after both coordinates had been processed. The display thread must wait for the mutex to be clear before updating the display. This process of waiting for a mutex is often called "blocking" on a mutex because the process is blocked and cannot continue until the mutex clears.

The BOUNCE.C program shown in the previous section uses a mutex named ScreenMutex to coordinate screen updates. Each time one of the display threads is ready to write to the screen, it calls **WaitForSingleObject** with the handle to ScreenMutex and constant **INFINITE** to indicate that the **WaitForSingleObject** call should block on the mutex and not time out. If ScreenMutex is clear, the wait function sets the mutex so other threads cannot interfere with the display and continues executing the thread. Otherwise, the thread blocks until the mutex clears. When the thread completes the display update, it releases the mutex by calling **ReleaseMutex**.

Screen displays and static data are only two of the resources requiring careful management. For example, your program may have multiple threads accessing the same file. Because another thread may have moved the file pointer, each thread must reset the file pointer before reading or writing. In addition, each thread must make sure that it is not preempted between the time it positions the pointer and the time it accesses the file. These threads should use a semaphore to coordinate access to the file by bracketing each file access with **WaitForSingleObject** and **ReleaseMutex** calls. The following code fragment illustrates this technique:

```
HANDLE    hIOMutex= CreateMutex (NULL, FALSE, NULL);

WaitForSingleObject( hIOMutex, INFINITE );
fseek( fp, desired_position, 0L );
fwrite( data, sizeof( data ), 1, fp );
ReleaseMutex( hIOMutex);
```

Thread Stacks

All of an application's default stack space is allocated to the first thread of execution, which is known as thread 1. As a result, you must specify how much memory to allocate for a separate stack for each additional thread your program needs. The operating system will allocate additional stack space for the thread, if necessary, but you must specify a default value.

The first argument in the **_beginthread** call is a pointer to the **BounceProc** function, which will execute the threads. The second argument specifies the default stack size for the thread. The last argument is an ID number that is passed to **BounceProc**. **BounceProc** uses the ID number to seed the random number generator and to select the thread's color attribute and display character.

Threads that make calls to the C run-time library or to the Win32 API must allow sufficient stack space for the library and API functions they call. The C **printf** function requires more than 500 bytes of stack space, and you should have 2K of stack space available when calling Win32 API routines.

Because each thread has its own stack, you can avoid potential collisions over data items by using as little static data as possible. Design your program to use automatic stack variables for all data that can be private to a thread. The only global variables in the BOUNCE.C program are either mutexes or variables that never change after they are initialized.

Win32 also provides Thread-Local Storage (TLS) to store per-thread data. See "Thread Local Storage" on page 71 for more information.

Compiling and Linking

The steps for compiling and linking the multithread program BOUNCE.C using the Visual C++ environment are:

1. Create a new project. Choose Console Application from the Type list.

2. Add the file containing the C source code to the project.

3. From the Build menu, choose Settings. In the Project Settings dialog box, choose the C/C++ tab. Select Code Generation from the Category drop-down list box. From the Use Run-Time Library drop-down box, select Multithreaded. Choose OK.

4. Build the project by choosing Build from the Build menu.

The steps for compiling and linking the multithread program BOUNCE.C from the command line are:

1. Ensure that the Win32 library files and LIBCMT.LIB are in the directory specified in your LIB environment variable.

2. Compile and link the program with the CL command-line option /MT:

```
CL /MT BOUNCE.C
```

3. If you choose not to use the /MT option, you must take these steps:

   • Define the _MT symbol before including header files. You can do this by specifying /D _MT on the command line.

   • Specify the multithread library and suppress default library selection.

The multithread include files are used when you define the symbolic constant _MT. You can do this with the CL command line option /D _MT or within the C source file before any include statements, as follows:

```
#define _MT
#include <stdlib.h>
```

Avoiding Problem Areas

There are several problems you might encounter in creating, linking, or executing a multithread C program. Some of the more common ones are described here.

Problem	Probable cause
You get a message box showing that your program caused a protection violation.	Many Win32 programming errors cause protection violations. A common cause of protection violations is the indirect assignment of data to null pointers. This results in your program trying to access memory that does not "belong" to it, so a protection violation is issued.
	An easy way to detect the cause of a protection violation is to compile your program with debugging information, and then run it through the debugger in the Visual C++ environment. When the protection fault occurs, Windows transfers control to the debugger, and the cursor is positioned on the line that caused the problem.
Your program generates numerous compile and link errors.	If you attempt to compile and link a multithread program without defining the symbolic constant _MT, many of the definitions required for the multithread library will be missing. If you are using the Visual C++ development environment, make sure that the Project Settings dialog box specifies multithread libraries. From the command line, define _MT to CL with /MT or /D _MT, or use #define _MT in your program.
	You can eliminate many potential problems by setting the compiler's warning level to one of its highest values and heeding the warning messages. By using the level 3 or level 4 warning level options, you can detect unintentional data conversions, missing function prototypes, and use of non-ANSI features.

Thread Local Storage (TLS)

Thread Local Storage (TLS) is the method by which each thread in a given multi-threaded process may allocate locations in which to store thread-specific data. Dynamically bound (run-time) thread-specific data is supported by way of the TLS API (**TlsAlloc**, **TlsGetValue**, **TlsSetValue**, **TlsFree**). Win32 and the Visual C++ compiler now support statically bound (load-time) per-thread data in addition to the existing API implementation.

API Implementation

Thread Local Storage is implemented through the Win32 API layer as well as the compiler. For details, see the Win32 API documentation for **TlsAlloc**, **TlsGetValue**, **TlsSetValue**, and **TlsFree**.

The Visual C++ compiler includes a keyword to make thread local storage operations more automatic, rather than through the API layer. This syntax is described in the next section, "Compiler Implementation."

Compiler Implementation

To support TLS, a new attribute, **thread**, has been added to the C and C++ languages and is supported by the Visual C++ compiler. This attribute is an extended storage class modifier, as described in the previous section. Use the **__declspec** keyword to declare a **thread** variable. For example, the following code declares an integer thread local variable and initializes it with a value:

```
__declspec( thread ) int tls_i = 1;
```

Rules and Limitations for TLS

The following guidelines must be observed when declaring statically-bound thread local objects and variables:

- The **thread** attribute can be applied only to data declarations and definitions. It cannot be used on function declarations or definitions. For example, the following code will generate a compiler error:

```
#define Thread  __declspec( thread )
Thread void func();     // This will generate an error.
```

- The **thread** modifier may be specified only on data items with **static** extent. This includes global data objects (both **static** and **extern**), local static objects, and static data members of C++ classes. Automatic data objects may not be declared with the **thread** attribute. The following code will generate compiler errors:

```
#define Thread  __declspec( thread )
void func1()
{
    Thread int tls_i;          // This will generate an error.
}

int func2( Thread int tls_i )  // This will generate an error.
{
    return tls_i;
}
```

- The declarations and the definition of a thread local object must all specify the **thread** attribute. For example, the following code will generate an error:

```
#define Thread  __declspec( thread )
extern int tls_i;        // This will generate an error, since the
int Thread tls_i;        // declaration and definition differ.
```

- The **thread** attribute cannot be used as a type modifier. For example, the following code will generate a compiler error:

```
char __declspec( thread ) *ch;        // Error
```

- C++ classes cannot use the **thread** attribute. However, C++ class objects may be instantiated with the **thread** attribute. For example, the following code will generate a compiler error:

```
#define Thread   __declspec( thread )
class Thread C        // Error: classes cannot be declared Thread.
{
// Code
};
C CObject;
```

Because the declaration of C++ objects that utilize the **thread** attribute is permitted, the following two examples are semantically equivalent:

```
#define Thread   __declspec( thread )
Thread class B
{
// Code
} BObject;             // OK--BObject is declared thread local.

class B
{
// Code
};
Thread B BObject;      // OK--BObject is declared thread local.
```

- Because C++ objects with constructors and destructors (as well as any object that utilizes some form of initialization semantics) may be allocated as thread local objects, an associated initialization routine (such as the constructor) is called to initialize that object. For example:

```
class tlsClass
{
    private:
        int x;
    public:
        tlsClass() { x = 1; } ;
        ~tlsClass();
}

__declspec( thread ) tlsClass tlsObject;
extern int func();
__declspec( thread ) int y = func();
```

In this case, data or objects initialized by the `func` routine do not necessarily belong to the same thread into which `tlsObject` is instantiated.

- The address of a thread local object is not considered constant, and any expression involving such an address is not considered a constant expression. In standard C, the effect of this is to forbid the use of the address of a thread local variable as an initializer for an object or pointer. For example, the following code will be flagged as an error by the C compiler:

```
#define Thread   __declspec( thread )
Thread int tls_i;
int *p = &tls_i;      //This will generate an error in C.
```

This restriction does not apply in C++, however. Because C++ permits dynamic initialization of all objects, you can initialize an object with an expression that uses the address of a thread local variable. This is accomplished in the same way as the construction of thread local objects. For example, the code shown previously will not generate an error when compiled as a C++ source file. Note that the address of a thread local variable is only valid as long as the thread in which the address was taken still exists.

- Standard C permits the initialization of an object or variable with an expression involving a reference to itself, but only for objects of non-static extent. Although C++ normally permits such dynamic initialization of objects with an expression involving a reference to itself, this type of initialization is not permitted with thread local objects. For example:

```
#define Thread   __declspec( thread )
Thread int tls_i = tls_i;            // Error in C and C++
int j = j;                           // OK in C++, error in C
Thread int tls_i = sizeof( tls_i )   // Legal in C and C++
```

Note that a **sizeof** expression that includes the object being initialized does not constitute a reference to itself, and is legal in both C and C++.

C++ does not allow such dynamic initialization of thread data because of possible future enhancements to the thread local storage facility.

If a DLL declares any non-local data or object as **__declspec**(thread), it can cause a protection fault if dynamically loaded. After the DLL is loaded with **LoadLibrary**, it causes system failure whenever the code references the non-local **__declspec**(**thread**) data. Because the global variable space for a thread is allocated at run time, the size of this space is based on a calculation of the requirements of the application plus the requirements of all of the DLLs that are statically linked. When you use **LoadLibrary**, there is no way to extend this space to allow for the thread local variables declared with **__declspec**(**thread**). Use the TLS APIs, such as **TlsAlloc**, in your DLL to allocate TLS if the DLL might be loaded with **LoadLibrary**.

For Further Information

You can find more information on:

- Creating multithreaded programs using MFC in *Programming with the Microsoft Foundation Class Library*.

- C run-time functions in *Run-Time Library Reference*.

- Win32 APIs covering threads and synchronization in *Win32 Programmer's Reference*.

Templates

Templates enable you to define a family of functions or classes that can operate on different types of information. This chapter describes the Microsoft implementation of C++ templates, which is based on the ISO WG21/ANSI X3J16 working papers towards the evolving standard for C++.

For more information on templates, see Chapter 6, "Declarations," in the *C++ Language Reference*.

What Are Templates?

Templates are a mechanism for generating functions and classes based on type parameters (templates are sometimes called "parameterized types"). By using templates, you can design a single class that operates on data of many types, instead of having to create a separate class for each type.

For example, to create a type-safe function that returns the minimum of two parameters without using templates, you would have to write a set of overloaded functions like this:

```
// min for ints
int min( int a, int b )
    return ( a < b ) ? a : b;

// min for longs
long min( long a, long b )
    return ( a < b ) ? a : b;

// min for chars
char min( char a, char b )
    return ( a < b ) ? a : b;

//etc...
```

By using templates you can reduce this duplication to a single templated function:

```
template <class T> T min( T a, T b )
    return ( a < b ) ? a : b;
```

Templates can significantly reduce source code size and increase code flexibility without reducing type safety.

Working with Function Templates

With function templates, you can specify a set of functions that are based on the same code, but act on different types or classes. For example:

```
template <class T> void MySwap( T& a, T& b )
{
    T c( a );
    a = b; b = c;
}
```

This code defines a family of functions that swap their parameters. From this template you can generate functions that will swap not only **int** and **long** types, but also user-defined types. `MySwap` will even swap classes if the class's copy constructor and assignment operator are properly defined.

In addition, the function template will prevent you from swapping objects of different types, since the compiler knows the types of the a and b parameters at compile time. Note that all of the template parameters inside the angle brackets must be used as parameters for the templated function.

You call a templated function as you would a nontemplated function; no special syntax is needed. For example:

```
int i, j;
char k;
MySwap( i, j );     //OK
MySwap( i, k );     //Error, different types.
```

Function Template Instantiation

When a templated function is first called for each type, the compiler creates an "instantiation," a specialized version of the templated function for the type. This instantiation will be called every time the function is used for the type. If you have several identical instantiations, even in different modules, only one copy of the instantiation will end up in the executable.

Standard type conversions are not applied to templated functions. Instead, the compiler first looks for an "exact match" for the parameters supplied. If this fails, it tries to create a new instantiation to create an "exact match." Finally, the compiler attempts to apply overloading resolution to find a match for the parameters. If this fails, the compiler generates an error.

Microsoft Specific→

Trivial type conversions, but not promotions, are applied when trying to match template types. This behavior is disabled by turning on "Disable Language Extensions" (/Za) C++ compiler option.

END Microsoft Specific

Function Template Overrides

With a templated function, you can define special behavior for a specific type by providing a non-templated function for that type. For example:

```
void MySwap( double a, double b);
```

This declaration enables you to define a different function for **double** variables. Like other non-templated functions, standard type conversions (such as promoting a variable of type **float** to **double**) are applied.

Working with Class Templates

You can use class templates to create a family of classes that operate on a type.

```
template <class T, int i> class TempClass
{
public:
    TempClass( void );
    ~TempClass( void );
    int MemberSet( T a, int b );
private:
    T Tarray[i];
    int arraysize;
};
```

In this example, the templated class uses two parameters, a type T and an int i. The T parameter can be passed any type, including structures and classes. The i parameter has to be passed an integer constant. Since i is a constant defined at compile time, you can define a member array of size i using a standard automatic array declaration.

Unlike function templates, you do not need to use all template parameters in the definition of a templated class.

Members of Template Classes

Members of classes are defined slightly differently than those of nontemplated classes. Continuing the preceding example:

```
template <class T, int i>
    int TempClass< T, i >::MemberSet( T a, int b )
    {
        if( ( b >= 0 ) && (b < i) )
        {
            Tarray[b++] = a;
            return sizeof( a );
        }
        else
            return -1;
    }
```

Constructors and Destructors

Although constructors and destructors reference the name of the templated class twice, the template parameters should be referenced only once in the fully specified name.

```
template <class T, int i>
TempClass< T, i >::TempClass( void )
{
    TRACE( "TempClass created.\n" );
}

template <class T, int i>
TempClass< T, i >::~TempClass( void )
{
    TRACE( "TempClass destroyed.\n" );
}
```

Class Template Instantiation

Unlike function templates, when instantiating a class template, you must explicitly instantiate the class by giving the parameters for the templated class. To create an instance of TempClass:

```
TempClass< float, 6 > test1;      // OK
TempClass< char, items++ > test2; // Error, second parameter
                                  // must be constant.
```

No code is generated for a templated class (or function) until it is instantiated. Moreover, member functions are instantiated only if they are called. This can cause problems if you are building a library with templates for other users. See "Explicit Instantiation" in Chapter 6 of the *C++ Language Reference* for more information.

Angle Bracket Placement

Bad placement of angle brackets (<>) causes many template syntax errors. Make sure that you use proper spacing and parentheses to distinguish angle brackets from operators such as >> and ->. For example:

```
TempClass< float, a > b ? a : b > test1;
```

should be rewritten as

```
TempClass< float, (a > b ? a : b) > test1;
```

Similarly, pay extra attention when using macros that use angle brackets as template arguments.

When Should You Use Templates?

Templates are often used to:

- Create a type-safe collection class (for example, a stack) that can operate on data of any type.
- Add extra type checking for functions that would otherwise take **void** pointers.
- Encapsulate groups of operator overrides to modify type behavior (such as smart pointers).

Most of these uses can be implemented without templates; however templates offer several advantages:

- Templates are easier to write. You create only one generic version of your class or function instead of manually creating specializations.
- Templates can be easier to understand, since they can provide a straightforward way of abstracting type information.
- Templates are type safe. Since the types that templates act upon are known at compile-time, the compiler can perform type checking before errors occur.

Templates vs. Macros

In many ways, templates work like preprocessor macros, replacing the templated variable with the given type. However, there are many differences between a macro like this:

```
#define min(i, j) (((i) < (j)) ? (i) : (j))
```

and a template:

```
template<class T> T min (T i, T j) { return ((i < j) ? i : j) }
```

Here are some problems with the macro:

- There is no way for the compiler to verify that the macro parameters are of compatible types. The macro is expanded without any special type checking.
- The i and j parameters are evaluated twice. For example, if either parameter has a postincremented variable, the increment is performed two times.

- Since macros are expanded by the preprocessor, compiler error messages will refer to the expanded macro, rather than the macro definition itself. Also the macro will show up in expanded form during debugging.

Templates vs. Void Pointers

Many functions that are now implemented with void pointers can be implemented with templates. Void pointers are often used to allow functions to operate on data of an unknown type. When using void pointers, the compiler cannot distinguish types, so it cannot perform type checking or type-specific behavior such as using type-specific operators, operator overloading, or constructors and destructors.

With templates, you can create functions and classes that operate on typed data. The type looks abstracted in the template definition. However, at compile-time the compiler creates a separate version of the function for each specified type. This enables the compiler to treat templated classes and functions as if they acted on specific types. Templates can also improve coding clarity, since you don't need to create special cases for complex types such as structures.

Collection Classes

Templates are a good way of implementing collection classes. Version 4.0 of the Microsoft Foundation Class Library uses templates to implement six new collection classes: **CArray**, **CMap**, **CList**, **CTypedPtrArray**, **CTypedPtrList**, and **CTypedPtrMap**. For information on these classes, see the *Class Library Reference*. For additional information on using and customizing these classes, see the "Collections" articles in *Programming with the Microsoft Foundation Class Library*.

The MyStack collection is a simple implementation of a stack. The two template parameters, T and i, specify the type of elements in the stack and the maximum number of that item in the stack. The push and pop member functions add and remove items on the stack, with the stack growing from the bottom of the stack.

```
template <class T, int i> class MyStack
{
    T StackBuffer[i];
    int cItems;
public:
    void MyStack( void ) : cItems( i ) {};
    void push( const T item );
    T pop( void );
};

template <class T, int i> void MyStack< T, i >::push( const T item )
{
    if( cItems > 0 )
     StackBuffer[--cItems] = item;
```

```
        else
         throw "Stack overflow error.";
        return;
}

template <class T, int i> T MyStack< T, i >::pop( void )
{
        if( cItems < i )
         return StackBuffer[cItems++]
        else

         throw "Stack underflow error.";
}
```

Smart Pointers

C++ allows you to create "smart pointer" classes that encapsulate pointers and override pointer operators to add new functionality to pointer operations. Templates allow you to create generic wrappers to encapsulate pointers of almost any type.

The following code outlines a simple reference count garbage collector. The template class Ptr<T> implements a garbage collecting pointer to any class derived from RefCount.

```
class RefCount {
        int crefs;
public:
        RefCount(void) { crefs = 0; }
        void upcount(void) { ++crefs; }
        void downcount(void) { if (--crefs == 0) delete this; }
};

class Sample : public RefCount {
public:
        void doSomething(void) { TRACE("Did something\n");}
};

template <class T> class Ptr {
        T* p;
public:
        Ptr(T* p_) : p(p_) { p->upcount(); }
        ~Ptr(void) { p->downcount(); }
        operator T*(void) { return p; }
        T& operator*(void) { return *p; }
        T* operator->(void) { return p; }
        Ptr& operator=(T* p_) {
                p->upcount(); p = p_; p->downcount(); return *this;
        }
};
```

```
int main() {
    Ptr<Sample> p  = new Sample; // sample #1
    Ptr<Sample> p2 = new Sample; // sample #2
    p = p2; // #1 has 0 refs, so it is destroyed; #2 has two refs
    p->doSomething();
    return 0;
    // As p2 and p go out of scope, their destructors call
    // downcount. The cref variable of #2 goes to 0, so #2 is
    // destroyed
}
```

Classes RefCount and Ptr<T> together provide a simple garbage collection solution for any class that can afford the int per instance overhead to inherit from RefCount. Note that the primary benefit of using a parametric class like Ptr<T> instead of a more generic class like Ptr is that the former is completely type-safe. The preceding code ensures that a Ptr<T> can be used almost anywhere a T* is used; in contrast, a generic Ptr would only provide implicit conversions to void*.

For example, if this class is used to create and manipulate garbage collected files, symbols, strings, and so forth. From the class template Ptr<T>, the compiler will create template classes Ptr<File>, Ptr<Symbol>, Ptr<String>, and so on, and their member functions: Ptr<File>::~Ptr(), Ptr<File>::operator File*(), Ptr<String>::~Ptr(), Ptr<String>::operator String*(), and so on.

C++ Exception Handling

The C++ language provides built-in support for handling anomalous situations, known as "exceptions," which may occur during the execution of your program. With C++ exception handling, your program can communicate unexpected events to a higher execution context that is better able to recover from such abnormal events. These exceptions are handled by code which is outside the normal flow of control.

Note In this chapter, the terms "structured exception handling" and "structured exception" (or "C exception") refer exclusively to the Win32 structured exception handling mechanism provided by Windows 95 and Windows NT. All other references to exception handling (or "C++ exception") refer to the C++ exception handling mechanism.

Unlike the Win32 structured exception handling mechanism, the language itself provides support for C++ exception handling. This chapter describes the Microsoft implementation of C++ exception handling, which is based on the ISO WG21/ANSI X3J16 working papers towards the evolving standard for C++.

Exception Handling Overview

For C++ programs, you should use C++ exception handling rather than structured exception handling. While structured exception handling works in C++ programs, you can ensure that your code is more portable by using C++ exception handling. The C++ exception handling mechanism is more flexible, in that it can handle exceptions of any type. C exceptions are always of type **unsigned int**.

In C++, the process of raising an exception is called "throwing" an exception. A designated exception handler then "catches" the thrown exception.

To enable C++ exception handling in your code, open the Project Settings dialog box, select the C/C++ tab, select C++ Language in the Category box, and select Enable Exception Handling; or use the /GX compiler option. The default is /GX-, which disables exception handling unwind semantics.

Note Version 4.0 of the Microsoft Foundation Class Library, which is included with Visual C++, uses the C++ exception handling mechanism. Although you are encouraged to use C++

exception handling in new code, version 4.0 retains the macros from previous versions of MFC so that old code will not be broken. The macros and the new mechanism can be combined, as well. For information on mixing macros and C++ exception handling and on converting old code to use the new mechanism, see the articles "Exceptions: Macros and C++," and "Exceptions: Converting from MFC Exception Macros," in *Programming with the Microsoft Foundation Class Library.*

Exception Handling Syntax

The structure for C++ exception handling is represented by the following syntax:

Syntax

try-block :
    try *compound-statement handler-list*

handler-list :
    *handler handler-list*_{opt}

handler :
    catch (*exception-declaration*) *compound-statement*

exception-declaration :
    type-specifier-list declarator
    type-specifier-list abstract-declarator
    type-specifier-list
    . . .

throw-expression :
    throw *assignment-expression*_{opt}

The *compound-statement* after the **try** clause is the guarded section of code. The *throw-expression* throws an exception. The *compound-statement* after the **catch** clause is the exception handler, and catches the exception thrown by the **throw**-expression. The *exception-declaration* statement after the **catch** clause indicates the type of exception the clause handles. The type can be any valid data type, including a C++ class.

If the exception-declaration statement is an ellipsis (...), the catch clause handles any type of exception, including C exceptions as well as system-generated and application-generated exceptions. This includes exceptions such as memory protection, divide-by-zero, and floating-point violations. An ellipsis catch handler must be the last handler for its try block.

The operand of **throw** is syntactically similar to the operand of a **return** statement.

Microsoft Specific →

Microsoft C++ does not support the function exception specification mechanism, as described in section 15.4 of the ANSI C++ draft.

END Microsoft Specific

Type-Safe Exception Handling

C++ exception handling supports type-safe exception handlers. C exceptions are always identified by an **unsigned int**. With C++ exception handling, you can specify that exceptions of a particular type (including C++ objects) are caught by a handler that matches the type of the exception being thrown.

How It Works

Exceptions are typically thrown inside a guarded section of code known as a **try** block. Directly below the **try** block are a series of associated **catch** handlers. The C++ exception handling model is known as "non-resumable." Once the flow of program control has left the **try** block, it never returns to that block.

For example, this program detects failure of a memory allocation operation using the **new** operator. If **new** is successful, the **catch** handler is never executed:

```
#include <iostream.h>

int main()
{
    char *buf;
    try
    {
        buf = new char[512];
        if( buf == 0 )
            throw "Memory allocation failure!";
    }
    catch( char * str )
    {
        cout << "Exception raised: " << str << endl;
    }
    // ...
    return 0;
}
```

The operand of the **throw** expression specifies that an exception of type char * is being thrown. It is handled by a **catch** handler that expresses the ability to catch an exception of type char *. In the event of a memory allocation failure, this is the output from the preceding example:

```
Exception raised: Memory allocation failure!
```

If no exception is thrown during execution of a **try** block, the **catch** clause(s) that follow the **try** block are not executed. Execution continues at the statement after the last **catch** clause following the **try** block in which the exception was thrown. Control can only enter a **catch** handler through a thrown exception; never via a **goto** statement or a **case** label in a **switch** statement.

C++ Exceptions

The real power of C++ exception handling lies not only in its ability to deal with exceptions of varying types, but also in its ability to automatically call destructor functions during stack unwinding for all local objects constructed before the exception was thrown.

The context which exists between the **throw** site and the **catch** handler is referred to as the "exception stack frame." This frame may contain objects with destructor semantics. If an exception is thrown during execution of the guarded section or in any routine the guarded section calls (directly or indirectly), an exception object is created from the object created by the **throw** operand. (This implies that a copy constructor may be involved.) At this point, the compiler looks for a **catch** clause in a higher execution context that can handle an exception of the type thrown, or a **catch** handler that can handle any type of exception. The **catch** handlers are examined in order of their appearance following the **try** block. If no appropriate handler is found, the next dynamically enclosing **try** block is examined. This process continues until the outermost enclosing **try** block is examined.

If a matching handler is still not found, or if an exception occurs while unwinding, but before the handler gets control, the predefined run-time function **terminate** is called. If an exception occurs after throwing the exception, but before the unwind begins, the **terminate** function is called. You can install a custom termination function to handle such situations. See "Unhandled Exceptions" on page 89 for more information.

The following example demonstrates C++ exception handling using classes with destructor semantics. It declares two C++ classes; one (class CTest) for defining the exception object itself, and the second (class CDtorDemo) for demonstrating the destruction of a separate frame object during stack unwinding:

```
#include <iostream.h>

void MyFunc( void );

class CTest
{
public:
    CTest(){};
    ~CTest(){};
    const char *ShowReason() const { return "Exception in CTest class."; }

};

class CDtorDemo
{
public:
    CDtorDemo();
    ~CDtorDemo();
};
```

```
CDtorDemo::CDtorDemo()
{
    cout << "Constructing CDtorDemo." << endl;
}

CDtorDemo::~CDtorDemo()
{
    cout << "Destructing CDtorDemo." << endl;
}

void MyFunc()
{

    CDtorDemo D;
    cout<< "In MyFunc(). Throwing CTest exception." << endl;
    throw CTest();
}

int main()
{
    cout << "In main." << endl;
    try
    {
        cout << "In try block, calling MyFunc()." << endl;
        MyFunc();
    }
    catch( CTest E )
    {
        cout << "In catch handler." << endl;
        cout << "Caught CTest exception type: ";
        cout << E.ShowReason() << endl;
    }
    catch( char *str )
    {
        cout << "Caught some other exception: " << str << endl;
    }
    cout << "Back in main. Execution resumes here." << endl;
    return 0;

}
```

If a matching **catch** handler is found, and it catches by value, its formal parameter is initialized by copying the exception object. If it catches by reference, the parameter is initialized to refer to the exception object. After the formal parameter is initialized, the process of "unwinding the stack" begins. This involves the destruction of all automatic objects that were constructed (but not yet destructed) between the beginning of the **try** block associated with the **catch** handler and the exception's throw site. Destruction occurs in reverse order of construction. The **catch** handler is executed and the program resumes execution following the last handler (that is, the first statement or construct which is not a **catch** handler).

This is the output from the preceding example:

```
In main.
In try block, calling MyFunc().
Constructing CDtorDemo.
In MyFunc(). Throwing CTest exception.
Destructing CDtorDemo.
In catch handler.
Caught CTest exception type: Exception in CTest class.
Back in main. Execution resumes here.
```

Note the declaration of the exception parameter in both **catch** handlers:

```
catch( CTest E )
{ // ... }
catch( char *str )
{ // ... }
```

You do not need to declare this parameter; in many cases it may be sufficient to notify the handler that a particular type of exception has occurred. However, if you do not declare an exception object in the exception declaration, you will not have access to the object in the **catch** handler clause. For example:

```
catch( CTest )
{
    // No access to a CTest exception object in this handler.
}
```

A **throw** expression with no operand re-throws the exception currently being handled. Such an expression should appear only in a **catch** handler or in a function called from within a **catch** handler. The re-thrown exception object is the original exception object (not a copy). For example:

```
try
{
    throw CSomeOtherException();
}
catch(...)        // Handle all exceptions
{
    // Respond (perhaps only partially) to exception
    //...

    throw;        // Pass exception to some other handler
}
```

Catchable Types

Because C++ enables you to throw exceptions of any type, you need to determine which **catch** handlers can catch an exception of a specific class type. A C++ exception can be caught by a **catch** handler that specifies the same type as the thrown exception, or by a handler that can catch any type of exception. An exception can also be caught by a **catch** handler that uses a reference to the same type as the thrown exception.

If the type of thrown exception is a class, which also has a base class (or classes), it can be caught by handlers that accept base classes of the exception's type, as well as references to bases of the exception's type. Note that when an exception is caught by a reference, it is bound to the actual thrown exception object; otherwise, it is a copy (much the same as an argument to a function).

When an exception is thrown, it may be caught by the following types of **catch** handlers:

- A handler that can accept any type (using the ellipsis syntax).

- A handler that accepts the same type as the exception object; since it is a copy, **const** and **volatile** modifiers are ignored.

- A handler that accepts a reference to the same type as the exception object.

- A handler that accepts a reference to a **const** or **volatile** form of the same type as the exception object.

- A handler that accepts a base class of the same type as the exception object; since it is a copy, **const** and **volatile** modifiers are ignored. The **catch** handler for a base class must not precede the **catch** handler for the derived class.

- A handler that accepts a reference to a base class of the same type as the exception object.

- A handler that accepts a reference to a **const** or **volatile** form of a base class of the same type as the exception object.

- A handler that accepts a pointer to which a thrown pointer object can be converted via standard pointer conversion rules.

Unhandled Exceptions

If a matching **catch** handler (or ellipsis **catch** handler) cannot be found for the current exception, the predefined **terminate** run-time function is called. (You can also explicitly call **terminate** in any of your handlers.) The default action of **terminate** is to call **abort**. If you want **terminate** to call some other function in your program before exiting the application, call the **set_terminate** function with the name of the function to be called as its single argument. You can call **set_terminate** at any point in your program. The **terminate** routine always calls the last function given as an argument to **set_terminate**.

The following example code throws a char * exception, but does not contain a handler designated to catch exceptions of type char *. The call to **set_terminate** instructs **terminate** to call term_func:

```
#include <eh.h>        // For function prototypes
#include <iostream.h>
#include <process.h>
```

```
void term_func()
{
    //...
    cout << "term_func was called by terminate." << endl;
    exit( -1 );
}
int main()
{
    try
    {
        // ...
        set_terminate( term_func );
        // ...
        throw "Out of memory!"; // No catch handler for this exception
    }
    catch( int )
    {
        cout << "Integer exception raised." << endl;
    }
    return 0;
}
```

After performing any desired cleanup tasks, the term_func function should terminate the program or current thread, ideally by calling exit. If it doesn't, and instead returns to its caller, abort is called.

Order of Handlers

The order in which **catch** handlers appear is significant, because handlers for a given **try** block are examined in order of their appearance. For example, it is an error to place the handler for a base class before the handler for a derived class. Once a matching **catch** handler is found, subsequent handlers are not examined. As a result, an ellipsis **catch** handler must be the last handler for its **try** block. For example:

```
// ...
try
{
    // ...
}
catch( ... )
{
    // Handle exception here.
}
// Error: the next two handlers are never examined.
catch( const char * str )
{
    cout << "Caught exception: " << str << endl;
}
catch( CExcptClass E )
{
    // Handle CExcptClass exception here.
}
```

In this example, the ellipsis **catch** handler is the only handler that is examined.

Mixing C and C++ Exceptions

If you want to write more portable code, using structured exception handling in a C++ program is not recommended. However, you may sometimes want to mix C and C++ source code, and need some facility for handling both kinds of exceptions. Because a structured exception handler has no concept of objects or typed exceptions, it cannot handle exceptions thrown by C++ code; however, C++ **catch** handlers can handle C exceptions. As such, C++ exception handling syntax (**try**, **throw**, **catch**) is not accepted by the C compiler, but structured exception handling syntax (**__try**, **__except**, **__finally**) is supported by the C++ compiler.

If you mix C and C++ exceptions, note the following:

1. C++ exceptions and C exceptions cannot be mixed within the same function.

2. Termination handlers (**__finally** blocks) are always executed, even during unwinding after an exception is thrown.

3. C++ exception handling can catch and preserve unwind semantics in all modules compiled with the /GX compiler option (this option enables unwind semantics).

4. There may be some situations in which destructor functions are not called for all objects. For example, if a C exception occurs while attempting to make a function call through an uninitialized function pointer, and that function takes as parameters objects that were constructed before the call, those objects will not have their destructors called during stack unwind.

Using setjmp/longjmp

Do not use **setjmp** and **longjmp** in C++ programs; these functions do not support C++ object semantics. Also, using these functions in C++ programs may degrade performance by preventing optimization on local variables. Use the C++ exception handling **try/catch** constructs instead.

If you do use **setjmp/longjmp** in a C++ program, the interaction between these functions and C++ exception handling requires that you include SETJMP.H or SETJMPEX.H. Destructors for local objets will be called during the stack unwind if you compile with the /GX option (Enable Exception Handling). Also, if you intend your code to be portable, do not rely on correct destruction of frame-based objects when executing a non-local goto using a call to **longjmp**.

Exception Handling Differences

The major difference between structured exception handling and C++ exception handling is that the C++ exception handling model deals in types, while the C structured exception handling model deals with exceptions of one type; specifically, **unsigned int**. That is, C exceptions are identified by an unsigned integer value, whereas C++ exceptions are identified by data type. When an exception is raised in C, each possible handler executes a filter, which examines the C exception context and determines whether to accept the exception, pass it to some other handler, or ignore it. When an exception is thrown in C++, it may be of any type.

A second difference is that the C structured exception handling model is referred to as "asynchronous," in that exceptions occur secondary to the normal flow of control. The C++ exception handling mechanism is fully "synchronous," which means that exceptions occur only when they are thrown.

If a C exception is raised in a C++ program, it can be handled by a structured exception handler with its associated filter, or by a C++ **catch** handler, whichever is dynamically nearest to the exception context. For example, the following C++ program raises a C exception inside a C++ **try** context:

```
#include <iostream.h>

void SEHFunc( void );

int main()
{
    try
    {
        SEHFunc();
    }
    catch( ... )
    {
        cout << "Caught a C exception."<< endl;
    }
    return 0;
}
void SEHFunc()
{
    __try
    {
        int x, y = 0;
        x = 5 / y;
    }
    __finally
    {
        cout << "In finally." << endl;
    }
}
```

This is the output from the preceding example:

```
In finally.
Caught a C exception.
```

C Exception Wrapper Class

In a simple example like this, the C exception can be caught only by an ellipsis (...) **catch** handler. No information about the type or nature of the exception is communicated to the handler. While this method works, in some cases you may need to define a transformation between the two exception handling models so that each C exception is associated with a specific class. To do this, you can define a C exception "wrapper" class, which can be used or derived from to attribute a specific class type to a C exception. By doing so, each C exception can be handled by a C++ **catch** handler in more discrete ways than the preceding example.

Your wrapper class might have an interface consisting of some member functions that determine the value of the exception, and for accessing the extended exception context information provided by the C exception model. You might also want to define a default constructor and a constructor that accepts an unsigned int argument (to provide for the underlying C exception representation), and a bitwise copy constructor. The following is a possible implementation of a C exception wrapper class:

```
class SE_Exception
{
private:
    unsigned int nSE;
protected:
    SE_Exception( unsigned int n ) : nSE( n ) {}
public:
    SE_Exception() {}
    SE_Exception( SE_Exception& ) {}
    ~SE_Exception() {}
    unsigned int getSeNumber() { return nSE; }
};
```

To use this class, you install a custom C exception translator function which is called by the internal exception handling mechanism each time a C exception is thrown. Within your translator function, you can throw any typed exception (perhaps an SE_Exception type, or a class type derived from SE_Exception), which can be caught by an appropriate matching C++ **catch** handler. The translator function can simply return, which indicates that it did not handle the exception. If the translator function itself raises a C exception, **terminate** is called.

To specify a custom translation function, call the **_set_se_translator** function with the name of your translation function as its single argument. The translator function that you write is called once for each function invocation on the stack that has **try** blocks. There is no default translator function; if you do not specify one by calling **_set_se_translator**, the C exception can only be caught by an ellipsis **catch** handler.

For example, the following code installs a custom translation function, then raises a C exception which is wrapped by the SE_Exception class:

```
#include <stdio.h>
#include <eh.h>
#include <windows.h>

class SE_Exception {
private:
    unsigned int nSE;
```

```
protected:
    SE_Exception(unsigned int n) : nSE(n) {}
public:
    SE_Exception() {}
    SE_Exception( SE_Exception& ) {}
    ~SE_Exception() {}
    unsigned int getSeNumber() { return nSE; }
};

void SEFunc(void);
void trans_func( unsigned, _EXCEPTION_POINTERS*);

int main()
{
    _set_se_translator( trans_func );
    try
    {
        SEFunc();
    }
    catch( SE_Exception e )
    {
        printf( "Caught a __try exception with SE_Exception.\n" );
        printf( "nSE = 0x%x\n", e.getSeNumber() );
    }
    return 0;
}
void SEFunc()
{
    __try
    {
        int x, y=0;
        x = 5 / y;
    }
    __finally
    {
        printf( "In finally\n" );
    }
}
void trans_func( unsigned int u, _EXCEPTION_POINTERS* pExp )
{
    printf( "In trans_func.\n" );
    throw SE_Exception( u );
}
```

Exception Handling Overhead

There is a certain amount of extra overhead associated with the C++ exception
handling mechanism, which may increase the size of executable files and slow
program execution time. The /GX compiler option enables C++ exception handling
and unwind semantics. If you are not using C++ exception handling in your program
and you want to eliminate the associated overhead, you can use the /GX- compiler

option to turn off exception handling and unwind semantics. Note that /GX‑ is the default.

Due to the nature of exception handling and the extra overhead involved, exceptions should be used only to signal the occurrence of unusual or unanticipated program events. Exception handlers should not be used to redirect the program's normal flow of control. For example, an exception should not be thrown in cases of potential logic or user input errors, such as the overflow of an array boundary. In these cases, simply returning an error code may be cleaner and more concise. Judicious use of exception handling constructs makes your program easier to maintain, and your code more readable.

For more information about C++ exception handling, see the *C++ Annotated Reference Manual* by Margaret Ellis and Bjarne Stroustrup.

CHAPTER 8

Structured Exception Handling

Windows 95 and Windows NT support a robust approach to handling exceptions, called structured exception handling, which involves cooperation of the operating system but also has direct support in the programming language.

You can write more reliable code with structured exception handling. You can ensure that resources, such as memory blocks and files, are properly closed in the event of unexpected termination. You can also handle specific problems, such as insufficient memory, with concise, structured code that doesn't rely on **goto** statements or elaborate testing of return codes.

Note This chapter describes structured exception handling for the C programming language. Although structured exception handling can also be used with C++, the new C++ exception handling method should be used for C++ programs. See "Using Structured Exception Handling with C++" on page 108 for information on special considerations. For more information on C++ exception handling, see Chapter 7, "C++ Exception Handling" on page 83.

Overview of Structured Exception Handling

An "exception" is an event that is unexpected or disrupts the ability of the process to proceed normally. Exceptions can be detected by both hardware and software. Hardware exceptions include dividing by zero and overflow of a numeric type. Software exceptions include those you detect and signal to the system by calling the **RaiseException** function, and special situations detected by Windows 95 and Windows NT.

How Structured Exception Handling Works

The traditional approach to exception handling involves passing error codes: one function detects an error and passes an error code to its caller. This process may continue through many levels, until the error is communicated to the function that can properly respond to the error. If there is a weak link in the chain of function calls, the whole procedure fails.

Structured exception handling avoids this propagation of error codes. Its distinctive feature is that after an exception handler is installed, it can handle the exception no matter how many other functions are called. Thus, function A can handle an exception raised inside a function called by A.

Exception Handlers and Termination Handlers

The previous section used the term "exception handlers" in a generic sense, but there are actually two kinds:

- Exception handlers, which can respond to or dismiss the exception
- Termination handlers, which are called when an exception causes termination inside a block of code

These two types of handlers are distinct, yet they are closely related through a process called "unwinding the stack." When an exception occurs, Windows 95 and Windows NT look for the most recently installed exception handler that is currently active. The handler can do one of three things:

- Pass control to other handlers (fail to recognize the exception).
- Recognize but dismiss the exception.
- Recognize and handle the exception.

The exception handler that recognizes the exception may not be in the function that was running when the exception occurred. In some cases it may be in a function much higher on the stack. The currently running function, as well as all functions on the stack frame, are terminated. During this process, the stack is "unwound": local variables of terminated functions, unless they are **static**, are cleared from the stack.

As it unwinds the stack, the operating system calls any termination handlers you've written for each function. Use of a termination handler gives you a chance to clean up resources that otherwise would remain open due to abnormal termination. If you've entered a critical section, you can exit in the termination handler. If the program is going to shut down, you can perform other housekeeping tasks such as closing and removing temporary files.

Writing an Exception Handler

Exception handlers are typically used to respond to specific errors. You can use the exception-handling syntax to filter out all exceptions other than those you know how to handle. Other exceptions should be passed to other handlers (possibly in the run-time library or the operating system) written to look for those specific exceptions.

Syntax of Exception Handlers

The structure for C exception handlers is shown in the following syntax:

__try {
  statement-block-1
}
__except (*filter*) **{**
  statement-block-2
}

The statements in *statement-block-1* are executed unconditionally. During execution of *statement-block-1*, the exception handler defined by *filter* and *statement-block-2* is active (it becomes the current exception handler).

If an exception occurs during execution of *statement-block-1*, including any function called directly or indirectly, the system gives control to the current exception handler —unless a handler with higher precedence takes control.

For example, in the following code, the first exception is handled by the outer block, because it is outside the scope of the inner __**try** block. The second exception is handled by the inner block, which takes precedence.

```
__try {
    float x, y=0;
    x = 5 / y;         // This exception handled by outer block
    __try {
        x = 0;
        y = 27 / x; // This exception handled by inner block
    }
    __except( GetExceptionCode() == STATUS_FLOATING_DIVIDE_BY_ZERO) {
        printf("handled by inner block");
    }
}
__except( GetExceptionCode() == STATUS_FLOATING_DIVIDE_BY_ZERO ) {
    printf( "handled by outer block" );
}
```

This code shows an example of nested exception handlers. Note that calling a function that has a **try-except** block has the same effect as nesting; the **try-except** block in the most recently called function takes precedence.

When an exception handler takes control, the system first evaluates the *filter*. One of the powerful features of structured exception handling is that although *filter* is evaluated out of normal program sequence (often during execution of another function), *filter* can refer to local variables within its scope just as any C expression. After *filter* is evaluated, the next action depends on the value returned.

Value of filter	Description
EXCEPTION_CONTINUE_SEARCH (0)	Passes control to exception handler with next highest precedence. The handler has declined to recognize the exception.
EXCEPTION_CONTINUE_EXECUTION(–1)	Dismisses exception, and continues execution at the location where the exception was raised.
EXCEPTION_EXECUTE_HANDLER (1)	Handles exception by executing statements in *statement-block-2*. Execution then falls through to the end of this statement block.

If the value of *filter* is EXCEPTION_EXECUTE_HANDLER, execution does not resume where the exception was raised, but falls through to the end of *statement-block-2* after it is executed. All blocks and function calls nested inside *statement-block-1* are terminated before *statement-block-2* is entered.

Writing an Exception Filter

You can handle an exception either by jumping to the level of the exception handler or by continuing execution. Instead of using *statement-block-2* to handle the exception and falling through, you can use *filter* to clean up the problem and then, by returning –1, resume normal flow without clearing the stack.

Note Some exceptions cannot be continued. If *filter* evaluates to –1 for such an exception, the system raises a new exception. When you call **RaiseException**, you determine whether the exception will continue.

For example, the following code uses a function call in the *filter* expression: this function handles the problem and then returns –1 to resume normal flow of control:

```
main ()
{
    int Eval_Exception( void );

    __try {
    ...
    }
    __except ( Eval_Exception( GetExceptionCode( ))) {
        // No code; this block never executed.
    }
...
}

int Eval_Exception ( int n_except )
{
    if ( n_except != STATUS_INTEGER_OVERFLOW &&
        n_except != STATUS_FLOATING_OVERFLOW )     // Pass on most
        return EXCEPTION_CONTINUE_SEARCH;              //  exceptions
```

```
    // Execute some code to clean up problem

    ResetVars( 0 );     // ResetVars -- example function to initialize
                        //  data to 0
    return EXCEPTION_CONTINUE_EXECUTION;
}
```

It's a good idea to use a function call in the *filter* expression whenever *filter* needs to do anything complex. Evaluating the expression causes execution of the function, in this case, Eval_Exception.

Note the use of **GetExceptionCode** to determine the exception. You must call this function inside the filter itself. Eval_Exception cannot call **GetExceptionCode**, but it must have the exception code passed to it.

This handler passes control to another handler unless the exception is an integer or floating-point overflow. If it is, the handler calls a function (ResetVars is only an example, not an API function) to reset some global variables. *Statement-block-2*, which in this example is empty, can never be executed because Eval_Exception never returns EXCEPTION_EXECUTE_HANDLER (1).

Using a function call is a good general-purpose technique for dealing with complex filter expressions. Two other C language features that are useful are:

- The conditional operator
- The comma operator

The conditional operator is frequently useful, because it can be used to check for a specific return code and then return one of two different values. For example, the filter in the following code recognizes the exception only if the exception is STATUS_INTEGER_OVERFLOW:

```
__except( GetExceptionCode() == STATUS_INTEGER_OVERFLOW ? 1 : 0 ) {
```

The purpose of the conditional operator in this case is mainly to provide clarity, because the following code produces the same results:

```
__except( GetExceptionCode() == STATUS_INTEGER_OVERFLOW ) {
```

The conditional operator is more useful in situations where you might want the filter to evaluate to –1, EXCEPTION_CONTINUE_EXECUTION.

Another useful C language feature is the comma operator, which enables you to perform multiple, independent operations inside a single expression. The effect is roughly that of executing multiple statements and then returning the value of the last expression. For example, the following code stores the exception code in a variable and then tests it:

```
__except( nCode = GetExceptionCode(), nCode == STATUS_INTEGER_OVERFLOW )
```

Raising Software Exceptions

Some of the most common sources of program errors are not flagged as exceptions by the system. For example, if you attempt to allocate a memory block but there is insufficient memory, the run-time or API function does not raise an exception but returns an error code.

However, you can treat any condition as an exception by detecting that condition in your code and then reporting it by calling the **RaiseException** function. By flagging errors this way, you can bring the advantages of structured exception handling to any kind of run-time error.

To use structured exception handling with errors you:

- Define your own exception code for the event.
- Call **RaiseException** when you detect a problem.
- Use exception-handling filters to test for the exception code you defined.

The WINERROR.H file shows the format for exception codes. To make sure that you do not define a code that conflicts with an existing exception code, set the third most significant bit to 1. The four most-significant bits should be set as shown in the following table.

Bits	Recommended binary setting	Description
31–30	11	These two bits describe the basic status of the code: 11 = error, 00 = success, 01 = informational, 10 = warning.
29	1	Client bit. Set to 1 for user-defined codes.
28	0	Reserved bit. (Leave set to 0.)

You can set the first two bits to a setting other than 11 binary if you want, although the "error" setting is appropriate for most exceptions. The important thing to remember is to set bits 29 and 28 as shown in the table.

The resulting error code should therefore have the highest four bits set to hexadecimal E. For example, the following definitions define exception codes that do not conflict with any Windows 95 or Windows NT exception codes. (You may, however, need to check which codes are used by third-party DLLs.)

```
#define STATUS_INSUFFICIENT_MEM      0xE0000001
#define STATUS_FILE_BAD_FORMAT       0xE0000002
```

After you have defined an exception code, you can use it to raise an exception. For example, the following code raises the STATUS_INSUFFICIENT_MEM exception in response to a memory allocation problem:

```
lpstr = _malloc( nBufferSize );
if (lpstr == NULL)
    RaiseException( STATUS_INSUFFICIENT_MEM, 0, 0, 0);
```

If you want to simply raise an exception, you can set the last three parameters to 0. The three last parameters are useful for passing additional information and setting a flag that prevents handlers from continuing execution. See the *Win32 Programmer's Reference* for more information on the **RaiseException** function.

In your exception-handling filters, you can then test for the codes you've defined. For example:

```
__try {
    ...
}
__except (GetExceptionCode() == STATUS_INSUFFICIENT_MEM ||
        GetExceptionCode() == STATUS_FILE_BAD_FORMAT )
```

Hardware Exceptions

Most of the standard exceptions recognized by the operating system are hardware-defined exceptions. Windows 95 and Windows NT recognize a few low-level software exceptions, but these are usually best handled by the operating system.

Windows NT maps the hardware errors of different processors to the exception codes in this section. In some cases, a processor may generate only a subset of these exceptions. Windows NT preprocesses information about the exception and issues the appropriate exception code.

The hardware exceptions recognized by Windows NT are summarized in the following table:

Exception code	Cause of exception
STATUS_ACCESS_VIOLATION	Reading or writing to an inaccessible memory location.
STATUS_BREAKPOINT	Encountering a hardware-defined breakpoint; used only by debuggers.
STATUS_DATATYPE_MISALIGNMENT	Reading or writing to data at an address that is not properly aligned; for example, 16-bit entities must be aligned on 2-byte boundaries. (Not applicable to Intel 80x86 processors.)
STATUS_FLOATING_DIVIDE_BY_ZERO	Dividing floating-point type by 0.0.
STATUS_FLOATING_OVERFLOW	Exceeding maximum positive exponent of floating-point type.
STATUS_FLOATING_UNDERFLOW	Exceeding magnitude of lowest negative exponent of floating-point type.

Exception code	Cause of exception
STATUS_FLOATING_RESEVERED_OPERAND	Using a reserved floating-point format (invalid use of format).
STATUS_ILLEGAL_INSTRUCTION	Attempting to execute an instruction code not defined by the processor.
STATUS_PRIVILEGED_INSTRUCTION	Executing an instruction not allowed in current machine mode.
STATUS_INTEGER_DIVIDE_BY_ZERO	Dividing an integer type by 0.
STATUS_INTEGER_OVERFLOW	Attempting an operation that exceeds the range of the integer.
STATUS_SINGLE_STEP	Executing one instruction in single-step mode; used only by debuggers.

Many of the exceptions listed in this table are intended to be handled by debuggers, the operating system, or other low-level code. With the exception of integer and floating-point errors, your code should not handle these errors. Thus, you should usually use the exception-handling filter to ignore exceptions (evaluate to 0). Otherwise, you may prevent lower-level mechanisms from responding appropriately.

You can, however, take appropriate precautions against the potential effect of these low-level errors by writing termination handlers as described later in this chapter.

Restrictions on Exception Handlers

The principal limitation to using exception handlers in code is that you cannot use a **goto** statement to jump into a **__try** statement block. Instead, you must enter the statement block through normal flow of control. You can jump out of a **__try** statement block and nest exception handlers as you choose.

You also cannot nest an exception handler or termination handler inside an **__except** block.

Writing a Termination Handler

Unlike an exception handler, a termination handler is always executed, regardless of whether the protected block of code terminated normally. The sole purpose of the termination handler should be to ensure that resources, such as memory, handles, and files, are properly closed regardless of how a section of code finishes executing.

Syntax of Termination Handlers

The structure of a termination handler is shown in the following syntax:

__try {
  statement-block-1
}
__finally {
  statement-block-2
}

The statements in *statement-block-1* are executed unconditionally. The statements in *statement-block-2* are always executed, in one of two ways:

- If *statement-block-1* finishes execution normally, *statement-block-2* is then executed.

- If *statement-block-1* is prematurely terminated for any reason, including a jump out of the block, the system executes *statement-block-2* as a part of the process of unwinding the stack.

In the second case, the **AbnormalTermination** function returns TRUE if called from within *statement-block-2*; otherwise, it returns FALSE.

If *statement-block-1* was abnormally terminated, the termination handler is executed as a part of the process of unwinding the stack. If control jumps outside of several blocks of code at once, the system clears the stack frame for each block of code or function exited, starting with the lowest (most deeply-nested) stack frame. As each frame is cleared, the system executes its termination handler.

For example, suppose a series of function calls links function A to function D, as shown in Figure 8.1. Each function has one termination handler. If an exception is raised in function D and handled in A, the termination handlers are called in this order as the system unwinds the stack: D, C, B.

Figure 8.1   Order of Termination-Handler Execution

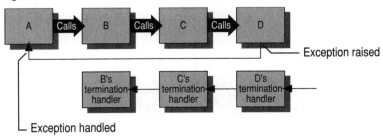

Cleaning up Resources

During termination-handler execution, you may not know which resources are actually allocated before the termination handler was called. It is possible that the __try statement block was interrupted before all resources were allocated, so that not all resources were opened.

Therefore, to be safe, you should check to see which resources are actually open before proceeding with termination-handling cleanup. A recommended procedure is to:

1. Initialize handles to NULL.

2. In the __try statement block, allocate resources. Handles are set to positive values as the resource is allocated.

3. In the __finally statement block, release each resource whose corresponding handle or flag variable is nonzero or not NULL.

For example, the following code uses a termination handler to close three files and a memory block that were allocated in the __try statement block. Before cleaning up a resource, the code first checks to see if the resource was allocated.

```
void    FileOps()
{
   FILE *fp1, *fp2, *fp3;
   LPVOID  lpvoid;

   lpvoid = fp1 = fp2 = fp3 = NULL;
   __try {
       lpvoid = malloc( BUFFERSIZE );
       fp1 = fopen( "ADDRESS.DAT", "w+" );
       fp2 = fopen( "NAMES.DAT", "w+" );
       fp3 = fopen( "CARS.DAT", "w+" );
       .
       .
       .

   }
   __finally {
       if ( fp1 ) fclose( fp1 );
       if ( fp2 ) fclose( fp2 );
       if ( fp3 ) fclose( fp3 );
       if ( lpvoid ) free( lpvoid );
   }
}
```

Timing of Exception Handling: A Summary

A termination handler is executed no matter how the __try statement block is terminated. Causes include jumping out of the __try block, a **longjmp** statement that transfers control out of the block, and unwinding the stack due to exception handling.

Note   Visual C++ supports two forms of the **setjmp** and **longjmp** statements. The fast version bypasses termination handling but is more efficient. To use this version, include the file SETJMP.H. The other version supports termination handling as described in the previous paragraph. To use this version, include the file SETJMPEX.H. The increase in performance of the fast version depends on hardware configuration.

The operating system executes all termination handlers in the proper order before any other code can be executed, including the body of an exception handler.

When the cause for interruption is an exception, the system must first execute the filter portion of one or more exception handlers before deciding what to terminate. The order of events is:

1. An exception is raised.

2. The system looks at the hierarchy of active exception handlers and executes the filter of the handler with highest precedence; this is the exception handler most recently installed and most deeply nested, in terms of blocks and function calls.

3. If this filter passes control (returns 0), the process continues until a filter is found that does not pass control.

4. If this filter returns −1, execution continues where the exception was raised, and no termination takes place.

5. If the filter returns 1, the following events occur:

   - The system unwinds the stack, clearing all stack frames between the currently executing code (where the exception was raised) and the stack frame that contains the exception handler gaining control.

   - As the stack is unwound, each termination handler on the stack is executed.

   - The exception handler itself is executed.

   - Control passes to the line of code after the end of this exception handler.

Restrictions on Termination Handlers

You cannot use a **goto** statement to jump into a **__try** statement block or a **__finally** statement block. Instead, you must enter the statement block through normal flow of control. (You can, however, jump out of a **__try** statement block.) Also, you cannot nest an exception handler or termination handler inside a **__finally** block.

In addition, some kinds of code permitted in a termination handler produce questionable results, so you should use them with caution, if at all. One is a **goto** statement that jumps out of a **__finally** statement block. If the block is executing as part of normal termination, nothing unusual happens. But if the system is unwinding the stack, that unwinding stops, and the current function gains control as if there were no abnormal termination.

A **return** statement inside a **__finally** statement block presents roughly the same situation. Control returns to the immediate caller of the function containing the termination handler. If the system was unwinding the stack, this process is halted, and the program proceeds as if there had been no exception raised.

Using Structured Exception Handling with C++

Structured exception handling described in this chapter works with both C and C++ source files. However, it is not specifically designed for C++ and is not recommended. You can ensure that your code is more portable by using C++ exception handling. Also, the C++ exception handling mechanism is more flexible, in that it can handle exceptions of any type.

Microsoft C++ now supports the C++ exception handling model, based on the ISO WG21/ANSI X3J16 working papers towards the evolving standard for C++. This mechanism automatically handles destruction of local objects during stack unwind. If you are writing fault-tolerant C++ code, and you want to implement exception handling, it is strongly recommended that you use C++ exception handling, rather than structured exception handling. (Note that while the C++ compiler supports structured exception handling constructs as described in this chapter, the standard C compiler does not support the C++ exception handling syntax.) For detailed information about C++ exception handling, see Chapter 7, "C++ Exception Handling," Chapter 5, "Statements," in the *C++ Language Reference*, and the *Annotated C++ Reference Manual* by Margaret Ellis and Bjarne Stroustrup.

Using Calling Conventions

The Visual C/C++ compiler provides several ways to call internal and external functions. The information in this chapter can help you debug your program and link your code with assembly-language routines.

This chapter covers the differences between the calling conventions, how arguments are passed, and how values are returned by functions. It also discusses naked function calls, an advanced feature that enables you to write your own prolog and epilog code.

Argument Passing and Naming Conventions

All arguments are widened to 32 bits when they are passed. Return values are also widened to 32 bits and returned in the EAX register, except for 8-byte structures, which are returned in the EDX:EAX register pair. Larger structures are returned in the EAX register as pointers to hidden return structures. Parameters are pushed onto the stack from right to left.

The compiler generates prolog and epilog code to save and restore the ESI, EDI, EBX, and EBP registers, if they are used in the function.

Note For information on how to define your own function prolog and epilog code see "Naked Function Calls" on page 113.

The following calling conventions are supported by the Visual C/C++ compiler.

Keyword	Stack clean-up	Parameter passing
__cdecl	Caller	Pushes parameters on the stack, in reverse order (right to left)
__stdcall	Callee	Pushes parameters on the stack, in reverse order (right to left)
__fastcall	Callee	Stored in registers, then pushed on stack
thiscall (not a keyword)	Callee	Pushed on stack; **this** pointer stored in ECX

_ _cdecl

This is the default calling convention for C and C++ programs. Because the stack is cleaned up by the caller, it can do **vararg** functions. The _ _**cdecl** calling convention creates larger executables than _ _**stdcall**, because it requires each function call to include stack clean-up code. The following list shows the implementation of this calling convention:

Element	Implementation
Argument-passing order	Right to left
Stack-maintenance responsibility	Calling function pops the arguments from the stack.
Name-decoration convention	Underscore character (_) is prefixed to names
Case-translation convention	No case translation performed

Note For more information on decorated names, see Appendix A, "Decorated Names," in the *Visual C++ User's Guide*.

The /Gd compiler option forces the _ _**cdecl** calling convention.

_ _stdcall

The _ _**stdcall** calling convention is used to call Win32 API functions. The callee cleans the stack, so the compiler makes **vararg** functions _ _**cdecl**. Functions that use this calling convention require a function prototype. The following list shows the implementation of this calling convention.

Element	Implementation
Argument-passing order	Right to left
Argument-passing convention	By value, unless a pointer or reference type is passed
Stack-maintenance responsibility	Called function pops its own arguments from the stack
Name-decoration convention	An underscore (_) is prefixed to the name. The name is followed by the at-sign (@) character, followed by the number of bytes (in decimal) in the argument list. Therefore, the function declared as `int func( int a, double b )` is decorated as follows: `_func@12`
Case-translation convention	None

The /Gz compiler options specifies _ _**stdcall** for all functions not explicitly declared with a different calling convention.

Functions declared using the _ _**stdcall** modifier return values the same way as functions declared using _ _**cdecl**.

_ _fastcall

The **_ _fastcall** calling convention specifies that arguments to functions are to be passed in registers, when possible. The following list shows the implementation of this calling convention.

Element	Implementation
Argument-passing order	The first two DWORD or smaller arguments are passed in ECX and EDX registers; all other arguments are passed right to left.
Stack-maintenance responsibility	Called function pops the arguments from the stack.
Name-decoration convention	At sign (@) is prefixed to names; an at sign @ followed by the number of bytes (in decimal) in the parameter list is suffixed to names.
Case-translation convention	No case translation performed.
Return-value conventions	Identical to **_ _cdecl**.

Note Future compiler versions may use different registers to store parameters.

Using the /Gr compiler option causes each function in the module to compile as fastcall unless the function is declared with a conflicting attribute, or the name of the function is `main`.

thiscall

This is the default calling convention used by C++ member functions that do not use variable arguments. The callee cleans the stack, so the compiler makes **vararg** functions **_ _cdecl**, and pushes the **this** pointer on the stack last. The *thiscall* calling convention cannot be explicitly specified in a program, because *thiscall* is not a keyword.

All function arguments are pushed on the stack. Because this calling convention applies only to C++, there is no C name decoration scheme.

Obsolete Calling Conventions

The **_ _pascal**, **_ _fortran**, and **_ _syscall** calling conventions are no longer supported. You can emulate their functionality by using one of the supported calling conventions and appropriate linker options.

WINDOWS.H now supports the **WINAPI** macro, which translates to the appropriate calling convention for the target. Use **WINAPI** where you previously used **PASCAL** or **_ _far _ _pascal**.

Calling Example: Function Prototype and Call

The following example shows the results of making a function call using various calling conventions.

This example is based on the following function skeleton. Replace *calltype* with the appropriate calling convention.

```
void    calltype MyFunc( char c, short s, int i, double f );
.
.
.
void    MyFunc( char c, short s, int i, double f )
    {
    .
    .
    .
    }
.
.
.
MyFunc ('x', 12, 8192, 2.7183);
```

Results

__cdecl

The C decorated function name is "_MyFunc."

Figure 9.1 The __cdecl calling convention

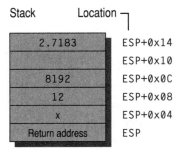

Stack	Location
2.7183	ESP+0x14
	ESP+0x10
8192	ESP+0x0C
12	ESP+0x08
x	ESP+0x04
Return address	ESP

Registers

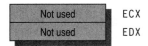

Not used	ECX
Not used	EDX

__stdcall and thiscall

The C decorated name (__**stdcall**) is "_MyFunc@20." The C++ decorated name is proprietary.

Figure 9.2   The __stdcall and thiscall calling conventions

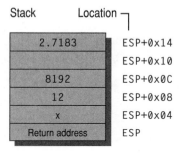

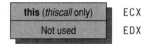

__fastcall

The C decorated name (__**stdcall**) is "@MyFunc@20." The C++ decorated name is proprietary.

Figure 9.3   The __fastcall calling convention

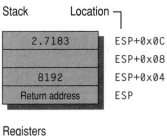

Naked Function Calls

Functions declared with the **naked** attribute are emitted without prolog or epilog code, enabling you to write your own custom prolog/epilog sequences using inline assembler. Naked functions are provided as an advanced feature. They enable you to declare a function that is being called from a context other than C/C++, and thus make different assumptions about where parameters are, or which registers are preserved. Examples include routines such as MS-DOS interrupt handlers. This feature is particularly useful for writers of virtual device drivers (VxDs).

Syntax

Because the **naked** attribute is not a type modifier, naked functions use the extended attribute syntax, as described previously. For example, the following code defines a function with the **naked** attribute:

```
__declspec( naked ) int func( formal_parameters )
{
    // Function body
}
```

Or, alternatively:

```
#define Naked    __declspec( naked )
Naked int func( formal_parameters )
{
    // Function body
}
```

The **naked** modifier affects only the nature of the compiler's code generation for the function's prolog and epilog sequences. It does not affect the code that is generated for calling such functions. Thus, the **naked** attribute is not considered part of the function's type. As such, function pointers cannot have the **naked** attribute. Furthermore, the **naked** attribute has no meaning when applied to a data definition. Any attempt to apply it to a data definition will generate a compiler error. For example, the following code samples will generate errors:

```
__declspec( naked ) int i;  // Error--naked attribute not permitted on
                            // data declarations.

extern __declspec( naked ) int i;   // Error--naked attribute not
                                    // permitted on data declarations.
```

The **naked** attribute is relevant only to the definition of the function. Thus it cannot be specified on the function's prototype. The following declaration will generate a compiler error:

```
__declspec( naked ) int func();  // Error--naked attribute not permitted
                                 // on function declarations.
```

A new symbolic argument for use in the inline assembler block of function prolog code is provided by the compiler. This symbol, **__LOCAL_SIZE**, is used to allocate space for local variables on the stack frame in your custom prolog code. This constant contains a value determined by the compiler, and it represents the number of bytes of local variables.

__LOCAL_SIZE includes all user-defined locals as well as compiler-generated temporary variables. __LOCAL_SIZE may be used as an immediate operand or in an expression. For example:

```
mov     eax, __LOCAL_SIZE           /* Immediate operand */
mov     eax, __LOCAL_SIZE + 4       /* Expression */
mov     eax, [ebp - __LOCAL_SIZE]   /* Expression */
```

Rules and Limitations for Naked Functions

The following rules and limitations apply to naked functions:

- The **return** statement is not permitted.

- Structured Exception Handling constructs are not permitted because they must unwind across the stack frame.

- For the same reason, any form of **setjmp** is prohibited.

- Use of the **_alloca** function is prohibited.

- To ensure that no initialization code for local variables appears before the prolog sequence, initialized local variables are not permitted at function scope. In particular, the declaration of C++ objects is not permitted at function scope. There may, however, be initialized data in a nested scope.

- Frame pointer optimization (the /Oy compiler option) is not recommended, but it is automatically suppressed for a naked function.

- You cannot declare C++ class objects at the function lexical scope. You can, however, declare objects in a nested block.

Naked Function Example

The following is a minimal example of a naked function containing custom prolog and epilog sequences:

```
__declspec ( naked ) func()
{
    int i;
    int j;

    _asm
        {
        push ebp
        mov     ebp, esp
        sub     esp, __LOCAL_SIZE
        }
```

```
/* C and/or _asm code */

_asm
    {
    mov     esp, ebp
    pop     ebp
    ret
    }
}
```

Floating Point Coprocessor

If you are writing assembly routines for the floating point coprocessor, you must preserve the floating point control word and clean the coprocessor stack unless you are returning a **float** or **double** value (which your function should return in ST(0)).

CHAPTER 10

Using the Inline Assembler

This chapter explains how to use the Visual C/C++ inline assembler with Intel x86-series compatible processors (such as the AMD386 and the i486™). Assembly language serves many purposes, such as improving program speed, reducing memory needs, and controlling hardware. You can use the inline assembler to embed assembly-language instructions directly in your C and C++ source programs without extra assembly and link steps. The inline assembler is built into the compiler—you don't need a separate assembler such as the Microsoft Macro Assembler (MASM).

Advantages of Inline Assembly

Because the inline assembler doesn't require separate assembly and link steps, it is more convenient than a separate assembler. Inline assembly code can use any C variable or function name that is in scope, so it is easy to integrate it with your program's C code. Because the assembly code can be mixed inline with C or C++ statements, it can do tasks that are cumbersome or impossible in C or C++.

The uses of inline assembly include:

- Writing functions in assembly language.
- Spot-optimizing speed-critical sections of code.
- Making direct hardware access for device drivers.
- Writing prolog and epilog code for "naked" calls.

Inline assembly is a special-purpose tool. If you plan to port an application to different machines, you'll probably want to place machine-specific code in a separate module. Because the inline assembler doesn't support all of MASM's macro and data directives, you may find it more convenient to use MASM for such modules.

The _ _asm Keyword

The **_ _asm** keyword invokes the inline assembler and can appear wherever a C or C++ statement is legal. It cannot appear by itself. It must be followed by an assembly instruction, a group of instructions enclosed in braces, or, at the very least, an empty pair of braces. The term "__asm block" here refers to any instruction or group of instructions, whether or not in braces.

The following code fragment is a simple __asm block enclosed in braces:

```
__asm
{
   mov al, 2
   mov dx, 0xD007
   out al, dx
}
```

Alternatively, you can put __asm in front of each assembly instruction:

```
__asm mov al, 2
__asm mov dx, 0xD007
__asm out al, dx
```

Because the __asm keyword is a statement separator, you can also put assembly instructions on the same line:

```
__asm mov al, 2    __asm mov dx, 0xD007    __asm out al, dx
```

All three examples generate the same code, but the first style (enclosing the __asm block in braces) has some advantages. The braces clearly separate assembly code from C or C++ code and avoid needless repetition of the __asm keyword. Braces can also prevent ambiguities. If you want to put a C or C++ statement on the same line as an __asm block, you must enclose the block in braces. Without the braces, the compiler cannot tell where assembly code stops and C or C++ statements begin. Finally, because the text in braces has the same format as ordinary MASM text, you can easily cut and paste text from existing MASM source files.

The braces enclosing an __asm block don't affect variable scope, as do braces in C and C++. You can also nest __asm blocks; nesting does not affect variable scope.

Using Assembly Language in __asm Blocks

The inline assembler has much in common with other assemblers. For example, it accepts any expression that is legal in MASM. This section describes the use of assembly-language features in __asm blocks.

Instruction Set

The inline assembler supports the full instruction set of the Intel 486 processor. Additional instructions supported by the target processor can be created with the _emit instruction. See "The _emit Pseudoinstruction" on page 120 for more information.

MASM Expressions

Inline assembly code can use any MASM expression, which is any combination of operands and operators that evaluates to a single value or address.

Data Directives and Operators

Although an __asm block can reference C or C++ data types and objects, it cannot define data objects with MASM directives or operators. Specifically, you cannot use the definition directives **DB**, **DW**, **DD**, **DQ**, **DT**, and **DF**, or the operators **DUP** or **THIS**. MASM structures and records are also unavailable. The inline assembler doesn't accept the directives **STRUC**, **RECORD**, **WIDTH**, or **MASK**.

EVEN and ALIGN Directives

Although the inline assembler doesn't support most MASM directives, it does support **EVEN** and **ALIGN**. These directives put **NOP** (no operation) instructions in the assembly code as needed to align labels to specific boundaries. This makes instruction-fetch operations more efficient for some processors.

MASM Macro Directives

The inline assembler is not a macro assembler. You cannot use MASM macro directives (**MACRO**, **REPT**, **IRC**, **IRP**, and **ENDM**) or macro operators (<>, !, **&**, %, and **.TYPE**). An __asm block can use C preprocessor directives, however. See "Using C or C++ in __asm Blocks" on page 121 for more information.

Segment References

You must refer to segments by register rather than by name (the segment name _TEXT is invalid, for instance). Segment overrides must use the register explicitly, as in ES:[BX].

Type and Variable Sizes

The **LENGTH**, **SIZE**, and **TYPE** operators have a limited meaning in inline assembly. They cannot be used at all with the **DUP** operator (because you cannot define data with MASM directives or operators). But you can use them to find the size of C or C++ variables or types:

- The **LENGTH** operator can return the number of elements in an array. It returns the value 1 for non-array variables.

- The **SIZE** operator can return the size of a C or C++ variable. A variable's size is the product of its **LENGTH** and **TYPE**.

- The **TYPE** operator can return the size of a C or C++ type or variable. If the variable is an array, **TYPE** returns the size of a single element of the array.

For example, if your program has an 8-element **int** array,

```
int arr[8];
```

the following C and assembly expressions yield the size of arr and its elements.

__asm	C	Size
LENGTH arr	**sizeof**(arr)/**sizeof**(arr[0])	8
SIZE arr	**sizeof**(arr)	16
TYPE arr	**sizeof**(arr[0])	2

Assembly-Language Comments

Instructions in an __**asm** block can use assembly-language comments:

```
__asm mov ax, offset buff ; Load address of buff
```

Because C macros expand into a single logical line, avoid using assembly-language comments in macros. (See "Defining __**asm** Blocks as C Macros" on page 127.) An __**asm** block can also contain C-style comments; for more information, see "Using C or C++ in __**asm** Blocks" on page 121.

The _emit Pseudoinstruction

The _**emit** pseudoinstruction is similar to the **DB** directive of MASM. You use _**emit** to define a single immediate byte at the current location in the current text segment. However, _**emit** can define only one byte at a time, and it can only define bytes in the text segment. It uses the same syntax as the **INT** instruction.

The following fragment places the given bytes into the code:

```
#define randasm __asm _emit 0x4A __asm _emit 0x43 __asm _emit 0x4B
    .
    .
    .
__asm {
    randasm
    }
```

Debugging and Listings

Programs containing inline assembly code can be debugged with a source-level debugger if you compile with the /Zi option.

Within the debugger, you can set breakpoints on both C or C++ and assembly-language lines. If you enable mixed assembly and source mode, you can display both the source and disassembled form of the assembly code.

Note that putting multiple assembly instructions or source language statements on one line can hamper debugging. In source mode, you can use the debugger to set breakpoints on a single line but not on individual statements on the same line. The same principle applies to an **__asm** block defined as a C macro, which expands to a single logical line.

If you create a mixed source and assembly listing with the /Fc compiler option, the listing contains both the source and assembly forms of each assembly-language line. Macros are not expanded in listings, but they are expanded during compilation.

Using C or C++ in _ _asm Blocks

Because inline assembly instructions can be mixed with C or C++ statements, they can refer to C or C++ variables by name and use many other elements of those languages.

An **__asm** block can use the following language elements:

- Symbols, including labels and variable and function names
- Constants, including symbolic constants and **enum** members
- Macros and preprocessor directives
- Comments (both /* */ and //)
- Type names (wherever a MASM type would be legal)
- **typedef** names, generally used with operators such as **PTR** and **TYPE** or to specify structure or union members

Within an **__asm** block, you can specify integer constants with either C notation or assembler radix notation (0x100 and 100h are equivalent, for example). This allows you to define (using **#define**) a constant in C and then use it in both C or C++ and assembly portions of the program. You can also specify constants in octal by preceding them with a 0. For example, 0777 specifies an octal constant.

Using Operators

An **__asm** block cannot use C or C++ specific operators, such as the **<<** operator. However, operators shared by C and MASM, such as the * operator, are interpreted as assembly-language operators. For instance, outside an **__asm** block, square brackets ([ ]) are interpreted as enclosing array subscripts, which C automatically scales to the size of an element in the array. Inside an **__asm** block, they are seen as the MASM index operator, which yields an unscaled byte offset from any data object or label (not just an array). The following code illustrates the difference:

```
int array[10];

__asm mov array[6], bx ;  Store BX at array+6 (not scaled)

array[6] = 0;            /* Store 0 at array+12 (scaled) */
```

The first reference to array is not scaled, but the second is. Note that you can use the **TYPE** operator to achieve scaling based on a constant. For example, the following statements are equivalent:

```
__asm mov array[6 * TYPE int], 0 ; Store 0 at array + 12

array[6] = 0;                     /* Store 0 at array + 12 */
```

Using C or C++ Symbols

An __**asm** block can refer to any C or C++ symbol in scope where the block appears. (C and C++ symbols are variable names, function names, and labels; that is, names that aren't symbolic constants or **enum** members. You cannot call C++ member functions.)

A few restrictions apply to the use of C and C++ symbols:

- Each assembly-language statement can contain only one C or C++ symbol. Multiple symbols can appear in the same assembly instruction only with **LENGTH**, **TYPE**, and **SIZE** expressions.

- Functions referenced in an __**asm** block must be declared (prototyped) earlier in the program. Otherwise, the compiler cannot distinguish between function names and labels in the __**asm** block.

- An __**asm** block cannot use any C or C++ symbols with the same spelling as MASM reserved words (regardless of case). MASM reserved words include instruction names such as **PUSH** and register names such as SI.

- Structure and union tags are not recognized in __**asm** blocks.

Accessing C or C++ Data

A great convenience of inline assembly is the ability to refer to C or C++ variables by name. An __**asm** block can refer to any symbols, including variable names, that are in scope where the block appears. For instance, if the C variable var is in scope, the instruction

```
__asm mov eax, var
```

stores the value of var in EAX.

If a class, structure, or union member has a unique name, an __**asm** block can refer to it using only the member name, without specifying the variable or **typedef** name before the period (.) operator. If the member name is not unique, however, you must place a variable or **typedef** name immediately before the period operator. For example, the following structure types share same_name as their member name:

```
struct first_type
{
    char *weasel;
    int same_name;
};
```

```
struct second_type
{
    int wonton;
    long same_name;
};
```

If you declare variables with the types

```
struct first_type hal;
struct second_type oat;
```

all references to the member same_name must use the variable name because same_name is not unique. But the member weasel has a unique name, so you can refer to it using only its member name:

```
__asm
{
    mov ebx, OFFSET hal
    mov ecx, [ebx]hal.same_name ; Must use 'hal'
    mov esi, [ebx].weasel       ; Can omit 'hal'
}
```

Note that omitting the variable name is merely a coding convenience. The same assembly instructions are generated whether or not the variable name is present.

You can access data members in C++ without regard to access restrictions. However, you cannot call member functions.

Writing Functions

If you write a function with inline assembly code, it's easy to pass arguments to the function and return a value from it. The following examples compare a function first written for a separate assembler and then rewritten for the inline assembler. The function, called power2, receives two parameters, multiplying the first parameter by 2 to the power of the second parameter. Written for a separate assembler, the function might look like this:

```
; POWER.ASM
; Compute the power of an integer
;
        PUBLIC _power2
_TEXT SEGMENT WORD PUBLIC 'CODE'
_power2 PROC

        push ebp        ; Save EBP
        mov ebp, esp    ; Move ESP into EBP so we can refer
                        ;    to arguments on the stack
        mov eax, [ebp+4] ; Get first argument
        mov ecx, [ebp+6] ; Get second argument
        shl eax, cl     ; EAX = EAX * ( 2 ^ CL )
        pop ebp         ; Restore EBP
        ret             ; Return with sum in EAX
```

```
_power2 ENDP
_TEXT   ENDS
        END
```

Since it's written for a separate assembler, the function requires a separate source file and assembly and link steps. C and C++ function arguments are usually passed on the stack, so this version of the power2 function accesses its arguments by their positions on the stack. (Note that the **MODEL** directive, available in MASM and some other assemblers, also allows you to access stack arguments and local stack variables by name.)

The POWER2.C program writes the power2 function with inline assembly code:

```
/* POWER2.C */
#include <stdio.h>

int power2( int num, int power );

void main( void )
{
   printf( "3 times 2 to the power of 5 is %d\n", \
           power2( 3, 5) );
}
int power2( int num, int power )
{
   __asm
   {
      mov eax, num    ; Get first argument
      mov ecx, power  ; Get second argument
      shl eax, cl     ; EAX = EAX * ( 2 to the power of CL )
   }
   /* Return with result in EAX */
}
```

The inline version of the power2 function refers to its arguments by name and appears in the same source file as the rest of the program. This version also requires fewer assembly instructions.

Because the inline version of power2 doesn't execute a C **return** statement, it causes a harmless warning if you compile at warning level 2 or higher. The function does return a value, but the compiler cannot tell that in the absence of a **return** statement. You can use **#pragma warning** to disable the generation of this warning.

Using and Preserving Registers

In general, you should not assume that a register will have a given value when an __asm block begins. An __asm block inherits whatever register values happen to result from the normal flow of control.

If you use the __fastcall calling convention, the compiler passes function arguments in registers instead of on the stack. This can create problems in functions with __asm blocks because a function has no way to tell which parameter is in which register. If the function happens to receive a parameter in EAX and immediately stores something else in EAX, the original parameter is lost. In addition, you must preserve the ECX register in any function declared with __fastcall.

To avoid such register conflicts, don't use the __fastcall convention for functions that contain an __asm block. If you specify the __fastcall convention globally with the /Gr compiler option, declare every function containing an __asm block with __cdecl or __stdcall. (The __cdecl attribute tells the compiler to use the C calling convention for that function.) If you are not compiling with /Gr, avoid declaring the function with the __fastcall attribute.

As you may have noticed in the POWER2.C example in "Writing Functions" on page 123, the power2 function doesn't preserve the value in the EAX register. When you write a function in assembly language, you don't need to preserve the EAX, EBX, ECX, EDX, ES, and flags registers. However, you should preserve any other registers you use (EDI, ESI, DS, SS, SP, and BP).

Note If your inline assembly code changes the direction flag using the STD or CLD instructions, you must restore the flag to its original value.

Assembly instructions that appear inline with C or C++ statements are free to alter the EAX, EBX, ECX, and EDX registers. C and C++ don't expect these registers to be maintained between statements, so you don't need to preserve them. The same is true of the ESI and EDI registers, with some exceptions (see "Optimizing" on page 128). You should preserve the ESP and EBP registers unless you have some reason to change them—to switch stacks, for example.

Jumping to Labels

Like an ordinary C or C++ label, a label in an __asm block has scope throughout the function in which it is defined (not only in the block). Both assembly instructions and **goto** statements can jump to labels inside or outside the __asm block.

Labels defined in __asm blocks are not case sensitive; both **goto** statements and assembly instructions can refer to those labels without regard to case. C and C++ labels are case sensitive only when used by **goto** statements. Assembly instructions can jump to a C or C++ label without regard to case.

The following do-nothing code shows all the permutations:

```
void func( void )
{
    goto C_Dest;   /* Legal: correct case   */
    goto c_dest;   /* Error: incorrect case */

    goto A_Dest;   /* Legal: correct case   */
    goto a_dest;   /* Legal: incorrect case */
```

```
    __asm
    {
        jmp C_Dest ; Legal: correct case
        jmp c_dest ; Legal: incorrect case

        jmp A_Dest ; Legal: correct case
        jmp a_dest ; Legal: incorrect case

        a_dest:     ; __asm label
    }

    C_Dest:         /* C label */
    return;
}
```

Don't use C library function names as labels in **__asm** blocks. For instance, you might be tempted to use exit as a label, as follows:

```
; BAD TECHNIQUE: using library function name as label
jne exit
    .
    .
    .
exit:
    ; More __asm code follows
```

Because **exit** is the name of a C library function, this code might cause a jump to the **exit** function instead of to the desired location.

As in MASM programs, the dollar symbol (**$**) serves as the current location counter. It is a label for the instruction currently being assembled. In **__asm** blocks, its main use is to make long conditional jumps:

```
jne $+5 ; next instruction is 5 bytes long
jmp farlabel
; $+5
    .
    .
    .
farlabel:
```

Calling C Functions

An **__asm** block can call C functions, including C library routines. The following example calls the **printf** library routine:

```
#include <stdio.h>

char format[] = "%s %s\n";
char hello[] = "Hello";
char world[] = "world";
```

```
void main( void )
{
    __asm
    {
        mov   eax, offset world
        push eax
        mov   eax, offset hello
        push eax
        mov   eax, offset format
        push eax
        call printf
    }
}
```

Because function arguments are passed on the stack, you simply push the needed arguments—string pointers, in the previous example—before calling the function. The arguments are pushed in reverse order, so they come off the stack in the desired order. To emulate the C statement

```
printf( format, hello, world );
```

the example pushes pointers to world, hello, and format, in that order, and then calls **printf**.

Calling C++ Functions

An **__asm** block can call only global C++ functions that are not overloaded. If you call an overloaded global C++ function or a C++ member function, the compiler issues an error.

You can also call any functions declared with **extern "C"** linkage. This allows an **__asm** block within a C++ program to call the C library functions, because all the standard header files declare the library functions to have **extern "C"** linkage.

Defining _ _asm Blocks as C Macros

C macros offer a convenient way to insert assembly code into your source code, but they demand extra care because a macro expands into a single logical line. To create trouble-free macros, follow these rules:

- Enclose the **__asm** block in braces.
- Put the **__asm** keyword in front of each assembly instruction.
- Use old-style C comments (/* comment */) instead of assembly-style comments (; comment) or single-line C comments (// comment).

To illustrate, the following example defines a simple macro:

```
#define PORTIO __asm        \
/* Port output */           \
{                           \
    __asm mov al, 2         \
    __asm mov dx, 0xD007    \
    __asm out al, dx        \
}
```

At first glance, the last three **__asm** keywords seem superfluous. They are needed, however, because the macro expands into a single line:

```
__asm /* Port output */ { __asm mov al, 2  __asm mov dx, 0xD007 __asm out al, dx }
```

The third and fourth **__asm** keywords are needed as statement separators. The only statement separators recognized in **__asm** blocks are the newline character and **__asm** keyword. Because a block defined as a macro is one logical line, you must separate each instruction with **__asm**.

The braces are essential as well. If you omit them, the compiler can be confused by C or C++ statements on the same line to the right of the macro invocation. Without the closing brace, the compiler cannot tell where assembly code stops, and it sees C or C++ statements after the **__asm** block as assembly instructions.

Assembly-style comments that start with a semicolon (;) continue to the end of the line. This causes problems in macros because the compiler ignores everything after the comment, all the way to the end of the logical line. The same is true of single-line C or C++ comments (// comment). To prevent errors, use old-style C comments (/* comment */) in **__asm** blocks defined as macros.

An **__asm** block written as a C macro can take arguments. Unlike an ordinary C macro, however, an **__asm** macro cannot return a value. So you cannot use such macros in C or C++ expressions.

Be careful not to invoke macros of this type indiscriminately. For instance, invoking an assembly-language macro in a function declared with the **__fastcall** convention may cause unexpected results. (See "Using and Preserving Registers" on page 124.)

Optimizing

The presence of an **__asm** block in a function affects optimization in several ways. First, the compiler doesn't try to optimize the **__asm** block itself. What you write in assembly language is exactly what you get. Second, the presence of an **__asm** block affects register variable storage. The compiler avoids putting variables in registers across an **__asm** block if the register's contents would be changed by the **__asm** block. Finally, some other function-wide optimizations will be affected by the inclusion of assembly language in a function.

Programming with Mixed Languages

Mixed-language programming is the process of building programs in which the source code is written in two or more languages. Although mixed-language programming presents some additional challenges, it is worthwhile because it enables you to call existing code that may be written in another language.

Microsoft provides 32-bit versions of C, C++, MASM, and Fortran, and mixed-language programming is possible between all these languages. Mixed-language programming for Win32 is not the same as for 16-bit environments, but in many respects it is simpler. This chapter describes important mixed-language programming considerations.

Overview of Mixed-Language Issues

This section reviews basic concepts of mixed-language programming, and introduces relevant new Win32 features. For example, the __**stdcall** keyword replaces the **fortran** and **pascal** keywords in C modules. Another important aspect of Win32 is that all addresses are the same size, simplifying pass by reference. Thus, you may want to review this section even if you have written mixed-language programs extensively for MS-DOS.

Mixed-language programming is possible with Microsoft languages because each language implements functions, subroutines, and procedures in approximately the same way. Table 11.1 shows how different kinds of routines from each language equate to each other. For example, a C main program could call an external **void** function, which is actually implemented as a Fortran subroutine.

Table 11.1 Language Equivalents for Calls to Routines

Language	Call with return value	Call with no return value
Assembly language	Procedure	Procedure
C and C++	function	(**void**) function
Fortran	**FUNCTION**	**SUBROUTINE**

In this chapter, the term "routine" refers to functions, subroutines, and procedures from different languages. This definition does not include macros or inline functions, which are not implemented using the stack.

There are some important differences in the way languages implement these routines, however. This chapter presents a series of keywords, attributes, and techniques to reconcile these differences, which fall into three categories:

- Adjusting calling conventions
- Adjusting naming conventions
- Passing by value or by reference

In addition, you need to reconcile differences in the way individual data types (strings, arrays, common blocks, and so on) may be treated. This important and complex topic is discussed in the last section.

Adjusting Calling Conventions

The calling convention determines how a program makes a call and where the parameters are passed. In a single-language program, calling conventions are nearly always correct, because there is one default for all modules and because header files enforce consistency between the caller and the called routine. In a mixed-language program, different languages cannot share the same header files. It's easy to link Fortran and C modules that use different calling conventions, and the error isn't apparent until the bad call is made at run time, causing immediate program failure. Therefore, you should check calling conventions carefully for each mixed-language call.

Table 11.2 summarizes how C and Fortran calling conventions work.

Table 11.2   C and Fortran Calling Conventions

Calling convention	Parameter passing	Stack cleared by
C/C++	Pushes parameters on the stack, in reverse order (right to left)	Caller
Fortran (__stdcall)	Pushes parameters on the stack, in reverse order (right to left)	Called function

In C and C++ modules, you can specify the Fortran calling convention by using the __stdcall keyword in a function prototype or definition. The __stdcall convention is also used by window procedures and API functions. For example, the following C language prototype sets up a function call to a subroutine using the Fortran calling convention:

```
extern void __stdcall fortran_routine (int n);
```

Instead of changing the calling convention of the C code, you can adjust the Fortran source code by using the **C** attribute, enclosed in brackets ([ ]). For example, the following declaration assumes the subroutine is called with the C calling convention:

```
SUBROUTINE CALLED_FROM_C [C] (A)
INTEGER*4 A
```

It should be clear that calling conventions need only agree between individual calls and the called routines, and that the conventions must be the same: both caller and called routine must use the C/C++ convention or both must use the __**stdcall** convention (the Fortran default).

Note   In programs written for the graphical user interface of Windows, **PASCAL**, **WINAPI**, and **CALLBACK** are all defined with __**stdcall**. But the C language default is still **cdecl**.

Table 11.3 summarizes how to specify calling conventions. You can always specify calling conventions explicitly rather than relying on the default, which is a good technique for mixed-language programming.

Table 11.3   Specifying Calling Conventions

Language	C calling convention	Fortran calling convention
C/C++	**cdecl** (default)	__**stdcall**
Fortran	**C** attribute	**STDCALL** attribute (default)

Adjusting Naming Conventions

The naming convention determines how a language alters a symbol name as it places the name in an .OBJ file. This is an issue for external data symbols shared between modules as well as external routines. Parameter names are never affected. The reasons for altering the name include case sensitivity or lack thereof, type decoration, and other issues. Note that you can always see exactly how a name has been placed in an .OBJ file by using the DUMPBIN utility with the /SYMBOLS option. If naming conventions are not reconciled, the program cannot successfully link. You will receive an "unresolved external" error.

Naming conventions are closely related to calling conventions because the keywords that specify calling conventions affect naming conventions as well. However, C/C++ preserves case sensitivity in its symbol tables and Fortran does not, which can necessitate some additional work on your part. Fortunately, you can use the Fortran **ALIAS** attribute to resolve any discrepancy in names.

Table 11.4 summarizes how C, Fortran, and C++ handle public names.

Table 11.4 Naming Conventions in C, Fortran, and C++

Language	Name translated as	Case of name in .OBJ file
C, **cdecl** (default)	_name	Mixed case preserved
C, __**stdcall**	_name@nn	Mixed case preserved
Fortran [C]	_name	All lowercase
Fortran [STDCALL]	_name@nn	All lowercase
Fortran default	_name@nn	All uppercase
C++	_name@@decoration	Mixed case preserved

In Table 11.4, *nn* represents the stack space, in decimal notation, occupied by parameters. For example, assume a function is declared in C as

```
extern int __stdcall Sum_Up( int a, int b, int c );
```

Each integer occupies 4 bytes, so the symbol name placed in the .OBJ file is:

```
_Sum_Up@12
```

Case sensitivity can present a problem. The 32-bit linker always distinguishes case. The strategy you use to handle a discrepancy due to case depends on whether the situation involves:

- Calls from C to Fortran, where Fortran cannot be recompiled
- Symbol names that are all lowercase
- Mixed-case names

C Calls Using Fortran Names

If you call a Fortran routine from C and cannot recompile the Fortran code, and if the routine uses Fortran defaults, then you must use an all-uppercase name to make the call. Use of the __**stdcall** convention is not enough, because __**stdcall** (unlike the **fortran** keyword in 16-bit code) always preserves case. Fortran generates all-uppercase names by default and the C code must match it.

For example, this prototype sets up a call to a Fortran function `ffarctan`:

```
extern float __stdcall FFARCTAN( float angle );
```

All-Lowercase Names

If the name of the routine appears as all lowercase in C, then naming conventions are automatically correct when the **C** or **STDCALL** attribute is applied to the Fortran declaration. Any case may be used in the Fortran source code, including mixed case; the **C** and **STDCALL** attributes change the name to all lowercase. Note that this is a way in which **STDCALL** differs from the Fortran default behavior.

Mixed-Case Names

If the name of the routine appears as mixed-case in C, and you cannot change the name, you can only resolve naming conflicts by using the Fortran **ALIAS** attribute. **ALIAS** is required in this situation so that Fortran will generate mixed-case names.

To use the **ALIAS** attribute, place the name in quotation marks exactly as it is to appear in the .OBJ file. For example, suppose you are calling a C function that has the following prototype:

```
extern void My_Proc (int i);
```

The Fortran call to this function should be declared with the following **INTERFACE** block:

```
INTERFACE TO SUBROUTINE My_Proc [C, ALIAS:'_My_Proc'] (I)
INTEGER*4 I
END
```

Note   When using the **__stdcall** convention, both Fortran and C should calculate parameter-space size by rounding each parameter upward to multiples of four (because it is more efficient to keep the stack-pointer aligned on 4-byte boundaries). Thus, the function Print_Nums which is passed a byte, a short, and a long integer should be translated as _Print_Nums@12. However, there is an early version of 32-bit Fortran that translates this as _Print_Nums@7, not rounding upward. To correct the discrepancy, use the **ALIAS** attribute.

Passing By Value or By Reference

Each individual parameter can be passed by value or by reference (which places the address of the parameter on the stack). In Fortran, C, and C++, all addresses are the same size (4 bytes), so there is no passing by near or far reference. You need to make sure that for every call, the calling program and the called routine agree on how each parameter is passed. Otherwise, the called routine receives bad data.

The C/C++ technique for passing parameters is always the same, regardless of calling convention: all parameters are passed by value, except for arrays, which are translated into the address of the first member. To pass data by reference, pass a pointer to it.

The Fortran technique for passing parameters changes depending on the calling convention specified. By default, Fortran passes all data by reference (except the hidden length argument of strings, which is a special case). If the **C** or **STDCALL** attribute is used, the default changes to passing all data by value.

In Fortran, use the **VALUE** and **REFERENCE** attributes to specify pass by value or pass by reference. In mixed-language programming, it is a good idea to always specify passing technique explicitly rather than relying on defaults. For example, the following C declaration sets up a call to a Fortran subroutine:

```
extern void __stdcall TESTPROC( int ValParm, int *RefParm );
```

In the following example, the definition of TESTPROC in Fortran declares how each parameter is passed. The **REFERENCE** attribute is not strictly necessary in this example, but using it is a good idea, in case you later change the calling convention.

```
SUBROUTINE TESTPROC( VALPARM, REFPARM )
INTEGER*4 VALPARM [VALUE]
INTEGER*4 REFPARM [REFERENCE]
END
```

Table 11.5 summarizes parameter-passing defaults. Note that an array name in C is equated to its starting address. Therefore arrays are passed by reference. To pass an array by value, declare a structure with the array as its only member.

Table 11.5 C/C++ and Fortran Defaults for Passing Parameters

Language	By value	By reference
C/C++	*variable*	* *variable*
Fortran	*variable* [**VALUE**]	*variable* [**REFERENCE**], or *variable*
Fortran [C or STDCALL]	*variable* [**VALUE**], or *variable*	*variable* [**REFERENCE**]
C/C++ arrays	**struct** { *type* } *variable*	*variable*

C Calls to Fortran

This section applies the principles in the section "Overview of Mixed-Language Issues" to a typical case involving one function call and one subroutine call from C to Fortran. Default conventions are assumed for Fortran, so adjustments are made to the C code.

The C main program uses the **__stdcall** keyword to call the Fortran routines with the correct calling convention. The C source must use all-uppercase names for the routines, because this Fortran code does not use the **C**, **STDCALL**, or **ALIAS** attributes. Finally, pass by value and pass by reference are specified explicitly, though pass by reference would have been assumed by default for Fortran.

```
/*      File CMAIN.C    */

#include <stdio.h>

extern int __stdcall FACT (int n);
extern void __stdcall PYTHAGORAS (float a, float b, float *c);

main()
{
    float c;
    printf("Factorial of 7 is: %d\n", FACT(7));
    PYTHAGORAS (30, 40, &c);
    printf("Hypotenuse if sides 30, 40 is: %f\n", c);
}
```

```
C    File FORSUBS.FOR
C
     INTEGER*4 FUNCTION Fact (n)
     INTEGER*4 n [VALUE]
     INTEGER*4 i, amt
     amt = 1
     DO i = 1, n
       amt = amt * i
     END DO
     Fact = amt
     END

     SUBROUTINE Pythagoras (a, b, c)
     REAL*4 a [VALUE]
     REAL*4 b [VALUE]
     REAL*4 c [REFERENCE]
     c = SQRT (a * a + b * b)
     END
```

Fortran Calls to C

This section applies the principles in the section "Overview of Mixed-Language Issues" to a typical case involving one function call and one subroutine call from Fortran to C. Default conventions are assumed for C, so adjustments are made to the Fortran code. The example in this section is the converse of that in the previous section.

The Fortran main program uses the **C** attribute to call the C functions with the correct calling convention. The **C** attribute causes Fortran to generate all-lowercase names, so the **ALIAS** attribute must be used to preserve mixed case. Finally, pass by value and pass by reference are specified explicitly, though pass by value would have been assumed because of the **C** attribute.

```
C    File FORMAIN.FOR
C
     INTERFACE TO INTEGER*4 FUNCTION Fact [C,ALIAS:'_Fact'] (n)
     INTEGER*4 n [VALUE]
     END

     INTERFACE TO SUBROUTINE Pythagoras [C,ALIAS:'_Pythagoras'] (a,b,c)
     REAL*4 a [VALUE]
     REAL*4 b [VALUE]
     REAL*4 c [REFERENCE]
     END

     INTEGER*4 Fact
     REAL*4 c
     WRITE (*,*) 'Factorial of 7 is ', Fact (7)
     CALL Pythagoras (30, 40, c)
     WRITE (*,*) 'Hypotenuse if sides 30, 40 is ', c
     END
```

```
/*  File CSUBS.C  */

#include <math.h>

int Fact( int n )
{
    if (n > 1)
        return( n * Fact( n - 1 ));
    return 1;
}

void Pythagoras( float a, float b, float *c)
{
    *c = sqrt( a * a + b * b );
}
```

Building the Mixed-Language Program

In Win32, the choice of libraries is much simpler than it is in 16-bit environments. Consequently, it is easier to build a mixed-language program. To link C and Fortran modules, use the Fortran linker; the linker should find the correct default libraries.

For example, the simple console applications featured in the previous sections require no special options. The CMAIN application can be created with the following commands:

```
cl /c cmain.c
fl32 cmain.obj forsubs.for
```

The FORMAIN application can be created with the following commands:

```
cl /c csubs.c
fl32 formain.for cmain.obj
```

Multithread applications should have full multithread support, so if you use LIBFMT.LIB, make sure that LIBCMT.LIB is specified as a default library as well.

Mixed-Language Programming with C++

C++ uses the same calling convention and parameter-passing techniques as C, but naming conventions are different because of C++ decoration of external symbols. The **extern "C"** syntax makes it possible for a C++ module to share data and routines with other languages, by causing C++ to drop name decoration.

The following example declares prn as an external function using the C naming convention. This declaration appears in C++ source code.

```
extern "C"
{
    void prn();
}
```

To call functions written in Fortran (or MASM), declare the function as you would in C and use a **"C"** linkage specification. For example, to call the Fortran function FACT from C++, declare it as follows:

```
extern "C" { int __stdcall FACT( int n ); }
```

The **extern "C"** syntax can be used to adjust a call from C++ to other languages, or to change the naming convention of C++ routines called from other languages. However, **extern "C"** can only be used from within C++. If the C++ code does not use **extern "C"** and cannot be changed, you can call C++ routines only by determining the name decoration and generating it from the other language. You can always determine the decoration by using the DUMPBIN utility. Use this approach only as a last resort, because the decoration scheme is not guaranteed to remain the same between versions.

Use of **extern "C"** has some restrictions:

- You cannot declare a member function with **extern "C"**.

- You can specify **extern "C"** for only one instance of an overloaded function; all other instances of an overloaded function have C++ linkage.

For more information on the **extern "C"** linkage specification, see "Linkage Specifications" in chapter 6 of the *C++ Language Reference*.

Handling Data Types

Even when you've reconciled calling conventions, naming conventions, and parameter passing technique (pass by value or pass by reference), it is still possible to pass data incorrectly, because each language has different ways of handling data types. The following sections describe how to pass each type of data between languages.

Numeric Data Types

Normally, passing numeric data does not present a problem. The most important thing to keep in mind when passing numeric types is that in Win32, the C **int** type is 4 bytes, not 2 bytes, and therefore is equivalent to the Fortran **INTEGER*4** type. The **COMPLEX** type is a special case and is discussed in a later section. Table 11.6 summarizes equivalent numeric data types for Fortran, MASM, and C/C++.

Table 11.6   Equivalent Fortran, MASM, and C/C++ Numeric Data Types

Fortran	MASM	C/C++
CHARACTER*1	**BYTE**	**unsigned char**
INTEGER*1	**SBYTE**	**char**
(none)	**WORD**	**unsigned short**

Table 11.6 Equivalent Fortran, MASM, and C/C++ Numeric Data Types *(continued)*

Fortran	MASM	C/C++
INTEGER*2	**SWORD**	**short**
(none)	**DWORD**	**unsigned long, unsigned int**
INTEGER, INTEGER*4	**SDWORD**	**long, int**
REAL, REAL*4	**REAL4**	**float**
DOUBLE PRECISION, REAL*8	**REAL8**	**double**

If a C program passes an unsigned data type to a Fortran routine, the routine can accept the argument as the equivalent signed data type, but you should be careful that the range of the signed type is not exceeded.

Pointers (Address Variables)

In Fortran, you use the **LOC** function to extract the address of a variable. (In Win32, all addresses are 4 bytes, so there is no separate **LOCFAR** function as for 16-bit environments.) Because Fortran does not have a pointer type, the result of the **LOC** function must be stored in an **INTEGER*4** variable or passed as a parameter of type **INTEGER*4**. Generally, a pointer should be passed by value.

Passing a pointer by value is equivalent to passing what it points to by reference. In the following example, the two subroutine calls push identical data on the stack, and in each case the C routine called should expect an address. The two functions require different parameter declarations.

```
INTERFACE TO SUBROUTINE pass_addr1 [C] (addr_data)
REAL*8 addr_data [REFERENCE]
END

INTERFACE TO SUBROUTINE pass_addr2 [C] (addr_data)
INTEGER*4 addr_data [VALUE]
END


REAL*8 x
INTEGER*4 ptr
CALL pass_addr1 (x)
ptr = LOC(x)
CALL pass_addr2 (ptr)
```

Declaring and Indexing Arrays

Each language varies in the way that arrays are declared and indexed. Array indexing is a source-level consideration and involves no difference in the underlying data. There are two differences in the way elements are indexed by each language:

- The value of the lower array bound is different.

  By default, Fortran indexes the first element of an array as 1. C and C++ index it as 0. Fortran subscripts should therefore be 1 higher. (Fortran also provides the option of specifying another integer lower bound.)

- C varies subscripts in row-major order, Fortran in column-major order.

The differences in how subscripts are varied only affect arrays with more than one dimension. With row-major order (C and C++), the rightmost dimension changes fastest. With column-major order (Fortran), the leftmost dimension changes fastest. Thus, in C, the first four elements of an array declared as X[3][3] are

X[0][0]   X[0][1]   X[0][2]   X[1][0]

In Fortran, the four elements are

X(1,1)   X(2,1)   X(3,1)   X(1,2)

The preceding C and Fortran arrays illustrate the difference between row-major and column-major order, and also the difference in the assumed lower bound between C and Fortran. Table 11.7 shows equivalencies for array declarations in each language. In this table, r is the number of elements of the row dimension (which changes the slowest), and c is the number of elements of the column dimension (which changes the fastest).

Table 11.7 Equivalent Array Declarations

Language	Array declaration	Array reference
C/C++	*type x[r][c]*, or **struct** { *type x[r][c];* } *x* [1]	*x[r][c]*
Fortran	*type x(c, r)*	*x(c+1, r+1)*

[1] Use a structure to pass an array by value in C and C++.

The order of indexing extends to any number of dimensions you declare. For example, the C declaration

int arr1[2][10][15][20];

is equivalent to the Fortran declaration

INTEGER*2 ARR1(20, 15, 10, 2)

The constants used in a C array declaration represent dimensions, not upper bounds as they do in other languages. Therefore, the last element in the C array declared as int arr[5][5] is arr[4][4], not arr[5][5].

The following code provides a complete example, showing how arrays are passed as arguments to a routine.

```
C     File FORARRS.FOR
C

      INTERFACE TO SUBROUTINE Pass_Arr [C,ALIAS:'_Pass_Arr'] ( Array )
      INTEGER*4 Array( 10, 10 )
      END

      INTEGER*4 Arr( 10, 10 )
      CALL Pass_Arr( Arr )
      write (*,*) 'Array values: ', Arr(1, 10), Arr(2, 10)
      END

/*     File CF.C   */

#include <stdio.h>

void Pass_Arr ( int arr[10][10] )
{
    arr[9][0] = 10;
    arr[9][1] = 20;
}
```

Character Strings

In Win32, Fortran by default passes a hidden length argument for strings. This argument is easily accessible to other languages, unlike the string-length information passed in 16-bit versions of Fortran. The hidden length argument consists of an unsigned 4-byte integer, always passed by value, immediately following the character string argument.

For example, if a Fortran program sets up the following call to a routine, Pass_Str, implemented in C:

```
      INTERFACE TO SUBROUTINE Pass_Str (string)
      CHARACTER*(*) string
      END
```

Then the C routine must expect two arguments:

```
void __stdcall PASS_STR (char *string, unsigned int length_arg )
```

Another important difference is in the format of the strings themselves. C strings are null-terminated. For example, given the following assignment:

```
Char *cstring="C text string";
```

The string data is stored as shown in the following figure.

Fortran strings are not null-terminated, and they are padded with blank spaces when assigned string data that is shorter than the declared length. For example, given the following assignment:

```
CHARACTER*14 forstring
DATA FORSTRING /"Fortran STRING'/
```

The string data is stored as follows. Note that if the string were any longer, it would be padded with trailing blanks.

A more efficient approach, wherever possible, is to adopt C string behavior. When the **C** or **STDCALL** attribute is applied to a routine, Fortran does not pass a hidden length argument. Furthermore, you can use the C-string feature to assign null-terminated string data in Fortran, as follows:

```
CHARACTER*20 forstring
DATA forstring /'This is a string'C/
```

The string variable, forstring, can then be passed to a C routine. If the **C** or **STDCALL** attribute is used, Fortran passes forstring just as C does: pushing the address of a null-terminated string onto the stack, with no hidden length argument.

Note   Fortran functions of type **CHARACTER*(*)** place a hidden string argument at the beginning of the parameter list; this may include both string address and length, as appropriate. C functions that implement such a call from Fortran must declare this hidden string argument explicitly and use it to return a value. However, you are more likely to avoid errors by not using character-string return types. Use subroutines whenever possible.

The following example demonstrates how a Fortran main program calls a C function that translates a string to all-uppercase. Because the string is passed by reference, there is no need to use a string return type. Note that the **C** attribute stops Fortran from passing a hidden string-length argument, and the **DATA** statement uses a "C" to specify null termination.

```
C     File FORMAIN.FOR
C
      INTERFACE TO SUBROUTINE Ucase [C,ALIAS:'_Ucase'] (text)
      CHARACTER*(*) text [REFERENCE]
      END

      CHARACTER*40 forstring
      DATA forstring /'This is a sample string.'C/
      WRITE (*, *) forstring
      CALL Ucase (forstring)
      WRITE (*, *) forstring
      END
```

```
/*      File CSTR.C    */

#include <ctype.h>

void Ucase( char *string )
{
    char *ptr;

    for (ptr = string; *ptr; ptr++)
        *ptr = toupper( *ptr );
}
```

This use of C strings is usually the best approach, because most C library functions, as well as API functions, assume null-termination. However, if you use C to write string-manipulation functions, it is a good idea to translate null-terminated strings back into blank-padded strings after the C function returns. The following code performs this operation:

```
      SUBROUTINE Fix_C_Str (text, length)
      CHARACTER*(*) text
      INTEGER*4 length

      INTEGER*4 i

C  Find the first null ('\0')

      i = 1
      DO WHILE ((i .LE. length) .AND. (text(i:i) .NE. '\0'))
        i = i + 1
      END DO

C  Pad with blanks to the end of the string

      DO WHILE (i .LE. length)
        text (i:i) = ' '
      END DO
      END
```

Structures, COMPLEX, and LOGICAL Types

The Fortran structure variable, defined with the **STRUCTURE** keyword and declared with the **RECORD** statement, is equivalent to C **struct** declarations. You can pass structures by value or by reference. Be careful, however, about the effect of structure alignment if you are going to share structures.

C, C++, and MASM do not directly implement the Fortran types **COMPLEX*8** and **COMPLEX*16**. However, you can write structures that are equivalent. The type **COMPLEX*8** has two fields, both of which are 4-byte floating-point numbers; the first contains the real-number component, and the second contains the imaginary-number component. The type **COMPLEX** is equivalent to the type **COMPLEX*8**. The type **COMPLEX*16** is similar to **COMPLEX*8**. The only difference is that each field of **COMPLEX*16** contains an 8-byte floating-point number.

Note   Fortran functions of type **COMPLEX** place a hidden **COMPLEX** argument at the beginning of the parameter list. C functions that implement such a call from Fortran must declare this argument explicitly, and use it to return a value. The C return type should be **void**.

Here are the C/C++ structure definitions for the Fortran **COMPLEX** types.

```
struct complex8 {
    float    real, imag;
};

struct complex16 {
    double   real, imag;
};
```

A Fortran **LOGICAL*2** is stored as a 1-byte indicator value (1=true, 0=false) followed by one unused byte. A Fortran **LOGICAL*4** is stored as a 1-byte indicator value followed by three unused bytes. The type **LOGICAL** is equivalent to **LOGICAL*4**.

To pass or receive a Fortran **LOGICAL** type, use an integer. Note that only the low byte is tested or used by Fortran.

The C++ **class** type has the same layout as the corresponding C **struct** type, unless the class defines virtual functions or has base classes. Classes that lack those features can be passed in the same way as C structures.

Common Blocks

You can pass individual members of a Fortran common block in an argument list, just as you can any data item. However, you can also give a different language module access to the entire common block.

C or C++ modules can reference the items of a common block by first declaring a structure with fields that correspond to the common-block variables. Having defined a structure with the appropriate fields, the C or C++ module must then connect with the common block. The next two sections present methods for gaining access to common blocks.

Passing the Address of a Common Block

To pass the address of a common block, simply pass the address of the first variable in the block. (In other words, pass the first variable by reference.) The receiving C or C++ module should expect to receive a structure by reference.

In the following example, the C function initcb receives the address of the variable N, which it considers to be a pointer to a structure with three fields:

```
C       Fortran SOURCE CODE
C
        COMMON /CBLOCK/N, X, Y
        INTEGER*4 N
        REAL*8    X, Y
    .
    .
    .
        CALL INITCB( N )
```

```
/* C source code */

struct block_type
{
    long   n;
    double x;
    double y;
};

initcb( struct block_type * block_hed )
{
    block_hed->n = 1;
    block_hed->x = 10.0;
    block_hed->y = 20.0;
}
```

Accessing Common Blocks Directly

You can access Fortran common blocks directly by defining a structure with the appropriate fields and then declaring the structure as an external data symbol. For example, the following code defines a structure named CBLOCK, which the C code can use to directly access items in the Fortran common block named CBLOCK:

```
struct block_type
{
    int    n;
    double x;
    double y;
};

extern struct block_type CBLOCK;
```

CHAPTER 12

Advanced Profiling

The Microsoft 32-Bit Source Profiler is a powerful analysis tool for examining the run-time behavior of your programs. You can use information generated by the profiler to identify which sections of code work efficiently and which need to be examined more carefully. (For basic information on the profiler, see Chapter 18, "Profiling Code," in the *Visual C++ User's Guide*.)

Note For complete syntax and command-line options for PREP, PROFILE and PLIST see Chapter 29, "Profiler Reference," in the *Visual C++ User's Guide*.

Combining PROFILE Sessions

With the profiler's modular design, you can make several profiling runs without having to run PREP each time (see Figure 12.1). After PREP has created .PBI and .PBT files, you can reuse these files with PROFILE to create multiple .PBO files. You can then merge the .PBO files using the PREP /IO command-line option with multiple .PBO files. The Visual C++ Profile dialog box contains a Merge option button that automates this process.

Figure 12.1 Combining PROFILE Sessions

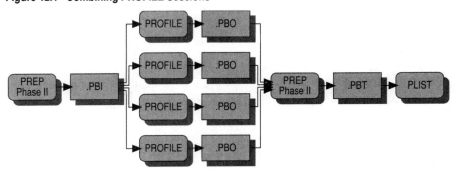

Using the Profile Dialog Box Merge Option

The .PBI, .PBO, and .PBT files for your project are generated the first time you run PROFILE. After that, you can use the Merge option button in the Profile dialog box (shown in Figure 12.2). PROFILE executes each time you choose the Merge button, and PREP Phase II adds the result to the existing .PBT file. PLIST prints the cumulative results each time the profiled program exits.

Figure 12.2 Profile dialog box

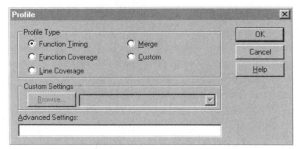

Using Batch Files

If you use the Merge button, you will get a PLIST report each time you invoke PROFILE. If, instead, you need a single PLIST report from multiple profile runs, you must write and execute a batch file like this:

```
PREP /LV myprog.exe myfuncs.dll
PROFILE /O myprog1 myprog.exe
PROFILE /O myprog2 myprog.exe
PROFILE /O myprog3 myprog.exe
PREP /IT myprog /IO myprog1 /IO myprog2 /IO myprog3 /OT myprog
PLIST myprog >myprog.out
```

Or, alternatively, because PREP Phase II adds data to an existing .PBT file:

```
PREP /LV myprog.exe myfuncs.dll
PROFILE myprog
PREP /M myprog
PROFILE myprog
PREP /M myprog
PROFILE myprog
PREP /M myprog
PLIST myprog >myprog.out
```

Note You can merge only eight .PBO files from the command line with each PREP invocation. To overcome this limitation, use PREP Phase II to merge groups of .PBO files into .PBT files. Then, merge the resulting .PBT files to yield a single .PBT file that contains statistics from the constituent .PBO files.

You cannot merge .PBO or .PBT files from different .PBI files. PREP can combine information only from profiling sessions that use the same .EXE and .PBI files (and therefore have identical profiling characteristics). You cannot, for example, merge the results of a timing session with the results of a coverage session.

Reusing .PBT and .PBI Files

For a large program, it can take a lot of time for PREP to create .PBT and .PBI files from scratch. You must rebuild these files if you change your source code or the profiling method, but you can reuse the files if you only need another profile run with different program input data. Just copy the .PBT file after the initial Phase I PREP run. The .PBI file is never changed, so you don't need to copy it.

Profiling Dynamic-Link Libraries

Profiling a dynamic-link library (DLL) is similar to profiling an .EXE file. When you profile a DLL, you follow the same steps and use the same commands that you would for an .EXE file. The same profiling rules that apply to .EXE files (such as the need to include debugging information and to supply a .MAP file) apply to DLLs.

For function profiling, the DLL is typically renamed with an _LL extension, but the .EXE file looks for a file with a .DLL extension when it executes. Therefore the prepared DLL must be renamed prior to profiling.

The following batch file (PROFDLL.BAT) profiles a DLL with the assumption that the .EXE file has not been prepared for profiling:

```
COPY %1.dll save
PREP /OM %1.dll
COPY %1._ll %1.dll
PROFILE /I %1 /O %1 %2 %3 %4 %5 %6
COPY save %1.dll
PREP /M %1
PLIST %1
```

Note The preceding batch generates a message warning you that the main program has not been prepared for profiling.

If you had a main program HEARTS.EXE that used a DLL called CARDS.DLL, and you wanted to profile only CARDS.DLL, you would run the preceding batch as:

```
PROFDLL cards hearts
```

Profiling Multiple .DLL and .EXE Files

The profiler can profile several DLLs and their calling executable file in a single profiler run. With phase I PREP command-line options, you can specify more than one .DLL or .EXE.

The following commands demonstrate how to profile an executable file and two DLLs from the command line:

```
PREP /OM /FC wingame.exe aliens.dll hiscore.dll
PROFILE wingame.exe
PREP /M  wingame
PLIST wingame >wingame.out
```

The first line causes PREP to create WINGAME.PBI and WINGAME.PBT files that include information on WINGAME.EXE, ALIENS.DLL, and HISCORE.DLL. The next line causes PROFILE to run WINGAME.EXE (actually WINGAME._XE, as generated by PREP Phase I). During the execution of WINGAME, PROFILE collects statistics for WINGAME.EXE as well as ALIENS.DLL and HISCORE.DLL, if they are called. The final two lines process the information from the profiling session and store the results in WINGAME.OUT.

Program Statistics vs. Module Statistics

PLIST reports always start with a "Program Statistics" section followed by a "Module Statistics" section. If there are several DLLs involved, as in the previous example, there is one "Module Statistics" section per .EXE or .DLL. The "Program Statistics" section lists totals for the entire program, including DLLs. Total time includes time in functions and modules not being profiled.

Profiling Inlined Code

If you specify, the Visual C++ compiler will perform inlining, which replaces a function call with an actual copy of the code. Profiling inlined code requires special attention.

Function Profiling for Inlined Functions

Because inlined functions don't generate .MAP file entries or CALL instructions, the profiler cannot tell when the computer is executing one of these functions. The time, hit, and coverage data will be attributed to the "calling" function.

Note In many cases there are .MAP file entries for "inlined" functions because the functions are not necessarily inlined everywhere in the application. Take this into account when you analyze profiler results.

Line Profiling for Inlined Functions

The profiler can provide line-level hit count and coverage information for inlined functions. Be sure to include the source lines in the Phase I PREP command-line options, just as you would include source lines in the calling program.

Profiling Win32 Console Applications

Win32 console applications do not use the graphical user interface; they run from the command line, often doing console input/output. You can easily use the profiler with these applications. If the application does do console I/O, you should run the profiling batch from the command prompt rather than from the Profile dialog box.

Profiling Multithreaded Applications

For multithreaded applications, profiler behavior depends on the profiling method.

For line counting and line coverage, the profiler does not discriminate among threads. The hit counts encompass all the program's threads.

For function timing, function counting, and function coverage, profiling is thread-dependent. You can profile an individual thread by (1) declaring the thread's main function as the starting function (PREP /SF option), and (2) including all functions in the program (don't use the PREP/EXC option).

The profile results will be difficult to interpret if you do not specify a starting function, if you specify a starting function that is called from multiple threads, or if you don't include all functions.

Profiling on a "Quiet" Computer

For maximum profiler accuracy, close as many other applications as possible during profiling. In particular, do not run programs such as electronic mail that execute at random intervals. If you have a network connection, you might want to disconnect it as well, since networks can cause differences in profile results.

Miscellaneous Profiler Restrictions

Function-level profiling works only with ordinary functions that return with the stack pointer unchanged. Profiling should be turned off for functions that change the stack pointer or store the return address for later use. The profiler automatically turns off profiling for the functions **alloca** and **setjmp**. If you write your own similar functions, you must write them in assembly language. By default, assembly-language functions are excluded from profiling. Do not use these functions with the PREP /INC option.

CHAPTER 13

Developing for International Markets

An important aspect of developing applications for international markets is the adequate representation of local character sets. The ASCII character set defines characters in the range 0x00 to 0x7F. There are other character sets, primarily European, that define the characters within the range 0x00 to 0x7F identically to the ASCII character set and also define an extended character set from 0x80 to 0xFF. Thus an 8-bit, single-byte–character set (SBCS) is sufficient to represent the ASCII character set as well as the character sets for many European languages. However, some non-European character sets, such as Japanese Kanji, include many more characters than can be represented in a single-byte coding scheme, and therefore require multibyte-character set (MBCS) encoding.

This chapter describes the Visual C++ support for extended character sets, and focuses on writing portable code that can be built for several different character sets.

Unicode and MBCS

The Microsoft Foundation Class Library (MFC), the C run-time library for Visual C++, and the Visual C++ development environment are enabled to assist your international programming:

- Support for the Unicode standard on Windows NT.

- Unicode is a 16-bit character encoding, providing enough encodings for all languages. All ASCII characters are included in Unicode as "widened" characters.

  Note The Unicode standard is not supported on Windows 95.

- Support for a form of Multibyte Character Set (MBCS) called Double Byte Character Set (DBCS) on all platforms.

  DBCS characters are composed of one or two bytes. Some ranges of bytes are set aside for use as "lead bytes." A lead byte specifies that it and the following "trail byte" comprise a single two-byte-wide character. You must keep track of which bytes are lead bytes. In a particular multibyte-character set, the lead bytes fall within a certain range, as do the trail bytes. When these ranges overlap, it may be necessary to evaluate the context to determine whether a given byte is functioning as a lead byte or a trail byte.

- Support for tools that simplify MBCS programming of applications written for international markets.

  When run on an MBCS-enabled version of the Windows NT operating system, the Visual C++ development system—including the integrated source code editor, debugger, and command line tools—is completely MBCS-enabled. For more information, see "MBCS Support in Visual C++" on page 159.

Note In this documentation, "MBCS" is used to describe all non-Unicode support for wide characters. In Visual C++, MBCS always means DBCS. Character sets wider than two bytes are not supported.

By definition, the ASCII character set is a subset of all multibyte-character sets. In many multibyte character sets, each character in the range 0x00–0x7F is identical to the character that has the same value in the ASCII character set. For example, in both ASCII and MBCS character strings, the one-byte **NULL** character ('\0') has value 0x00 and indicates the terminating null character.

International Enabling

Most traditional C and C++ code makes assumptions about character and string manipulation that do not work well for international applications. While both MFC and the run-time library support Unicode or MBCS, there is still work for you to do. To guide you, this section explains the meaning of "international enabling" in Visual C++:

- Both Unicode and MBCS are enabled by means of portable data types in MFC function parameter lists and return types. These types are conditionally defined in the appropriate ways, depending on whether your build defines the symbol _UNICODE or the symbol _MBCS (which means DBCS). Different variants of the MFC libraries are automatically linked with your application, depending on which of these two symbols your build defines.

- Class library code uses portable run-time functions and other means to ensure correct Unicode or MBCS behavior.

- You still must handle certain kinds of internationalization tasks in your code:

  - Use the same portable run-time functions that make MFC portable under either environment.

  - Make literal strings and characters portable under either environment using the _T macro. For more information, see "Generic-Text Mappings in TCHAR.H" on page 164.

  - Take precautions when parsing strings under MBCS. These precautions are not needed under Unicode. For more information, see "MBCS Programming Tips" on page 160.

- Take care if you mix ANSI (8-bit) and Unicode (16-bit) characters in your application. It's possible to use ANSI characters in some parts of your program and Unicode characters in others, but you cannot mix them in the same string.

- Don't "hard-code" strings in your application. Instead, make them STRINGTABLE resources by adding them to the application's .RC file. Your application can then be localized without requiring source code changes or recompilation. For more information on STRINGTABLE resources, see "Multiline Statements" in the *Visual C++ User's Guide*.

Note   European and MBCS character sets have some characters, such as accented letters, with character codes greater than 0x80. Since most code uses signed characters, these characters greater than 0x80 are sign extended when converted to **int**. This is a problem for array indexing because the sign-extended characters, being negative, will index outside the array.

Languages that use MBCS, such as Japanese, are also unique. Since a character may consist of one or two bytes, you should always manipulate both bytes at the same time.

Internationalization Strategies

Depending on your target operating system(s) and markets, you have several internationalization strategies:

- Your application uses Unicode and therefore runs on Windows NT (but not on Windows 95).

  You use Unicode-specific programming techniques and all characters are 16 bits wide (although you can use ANSI characters in some parts of your program for special purposes). The C run-time library provides functions, macros, and data types for Unicode-only programming. MFC is fully Unicode-enabled.

- Your application uses MBCS and can be run on any Win32 platform.

  You use MBCS-specific programming techniques. Strings can contain single-byte characters, double-byte characters, or both. The C run-time library provides functions, macros, and data types for MBCS-only programming. MFC is fully MBCS-enabled.

- The source code for your application is written for complete portability—by recompiling with the symbol **_UNICODE** or the symbol **_MBCS** defined, you can produce versions that use either. For more information, see "Generic-Text Mappings in TCHAR.H" on page 164.

  You use fully portable C run-time functions, macros, and data types. MFC's flexibility supports any of these strategies.

The remainder of this chapter focuses on writing completely portable code that you can build as Unicode or as MBCS.

Locales and Code Pages

A "locale" reflects the local conventions and language for a particular geographical region. A given language may be spoken in more than one country; for example, Portuguese is spoken in Brazil as well as Portugal. Conversely, a country may have more than one official language. For example, Canada has two: English and French. Thus, Canada has two distinct locales: Canadian-English and Canadian-French. Some locale-dependent categories include the formatting of dates and the display format for monetary values.

The language determines the text and data formatting conventions, while the country determines the national conventions. Every language has a unique mapping, represented by "code pages," which includes characters other than those in the alphabet (such as punctuation marks and numbers). A code page is a character set and is related to the current locale and language. As such, a locale is a unique combination of language, country, and code page. The code page setting can determine the locale setting and can be changed at run-time by calling the **setlocale** run-time function.

Different languages may use different code pages. For example, the ANSI code page 1252 is used for American English and most European languages, and the ANSI code page 932 is used for Japanese Kanji. Virtually all code pages share the ASCII character set for the lowest 128 characters (0x00 to 0x7F).

Any single-byte code page can be represented in a table (with 256 entries) as a mapping of byte values to characters (including numbers and punctuation marks), or glyphs. Any multibyte code page can also be represented as a very large table (with 64K entries) of double-byte values to characters. In practice, however, they are usually represented as a table for the first 256 (single-byte) characters and as ranges for the double-byte values.

The C run-time library has two types of internal code pages: locale and multibyte. You can change the current code page during program execution (see the documentation for the **setlocale** and **_setmbcp** functions). Also, the run-time library may obtain and use the value of the operating system code page. In Windows NT, the operating system code page is the "system default ANSI" code page. This code page is constant for the duration of the program's execution.

When the locale code page changes, the behavior of the locale-dependent set of functions changes to that dictated by the chosen code page. By default, all locale-dependent functions begin execution with a locale code page unique to the "C" locale. You can change the internal locale code page (as well as other locale-specific properties) by calling the **setlocale** function. A call to **setlocale**(LC_ALL, "") will set the locale to that indicated by the operating system's default code page.

Similarly, when the multibyte code page changes, the behavior of the multibyte functions changes to that dictated by the chosen code page. By default, all multibyte functions begin execution with a multibyte code page corresponding to the operating system's default code page. You can change the internal multibyte code page by calling the **setmbcp** function.

The C run-time function **setlocale** sets, changes, or queries some or all of the current program's locale information. The **_wsetlocale** routine is a wide-character version of **setlocale**; the arguments and return values of **_wsetlocale** are wide-character strings. For more information, see the documentation for **setlocale** in the *Run-Time Library Reference*.

Benefits of Character Set Portability

You can benefit from using MFC and C run-time portability features even if you don't currently intend to internationalize your application:

- Coding portably makes your code base flexible. You can later move it easily to Unicode or MBCS.

- Using Unicode makes your applications for Windows NT more efficient. Windows NT uses Unicode, so non-Unicode strings passed to and from the operating system must be translated, incurring overhead.

- Using MBCS enables you to support international markets on Win32 platforms other than Windows NT, such as Windows 95.

Support for Unicode

A "wide character" is a two-byte multilingual character code. Any character used in modern computing worldwide, including technical symbols and special publishing characters, can be represented according to the Unicode specification as a wide character. Because each wide character is always represented in a fixed size of 16 bits, using wide characters simplifies programming with international character sets.

A wide-character string is represented as a **wchar_t[]** array and is pointed to by a **wchar_t*** pointer. Any ASCII character can be represented as a wide character by prefixing the letter L to the character. For example, L'\0' is the terminating wide (16-bit) **NULL** character. Similarly, any ASCII string literal can be represented as a wide-character string literal by prefixing the letter L to the ASCII literal (L"Hello").

Generally, wide characters take more space in memory than multibyte characters but are faster to process. In addition, only one locale can be represented at a time in multibyte encoding, whereas all character sets in the world are represented simultaneously by the Unicode representation.

The MFC framework is Unicode-enabled throughout, except for the database classes. (ODBC is not Unicode enabled.) MFC accomplishes Unicode enabling by using "portable" macros throughout, as shown in Table 13.1:

Table 13.1 Portable Data Types in MFC

Non-portable Data Type(s)	Replaced by This Macro
char	_TCHAR
char*, LPSTR (Win32 data type)	LPTSTR
const char*, LPCSTR (Win32 data type)	LPCTSTR

Class **CString** uses **_TCHAR** as its base and provides constructors and operators for easy conversions. Most string operations for Unicode can be written by using the same logic used for handling the Windows ANSI character set, except that the basic unit of operation is a 16-bit character instead of an 8-bit byte. Unlike working with multibyte character sets (MBCS), you do not have to (and should not) treat a Unicode character as if it were two distinct bytes.

Support for Using wmain

Microsoft Specific →

Visual C++ supports defining a **wmain** function and passing wide-character arguments to your Unicode application. You declare formal parameters to **wmain** using a format similar to **main**. You can then pass wide-character arguments and, optionally, a wide-character environment pointer to the program. The *argv* and *envp* parameters to **wmain** are of type **wchar_t***. For example:

wmain(int *argc*, **wchar_t** **argv*[ ], **wchar_t** **envp*[ ])

Note MFC Unicode applications use **wWinMain** as the entry point. In this case, **CWinApp::m_lpCmdLine** is a Unicode string. Be sure to set **wWinMainCRTStartup** as the Entry Point symbol in the Output category of the Link tab in the Project Settings dialog box.

If your program uses a **main** function, the multibyte-character environment is created by the run-time library at program startup. A wide-character copy of the environment is created only when needed (for example, by a call to the **_wgetenv** or **_wputenv** functions). On the first call to **_wputenv**, or on the first call to **_wgetenv** if an MBCS environment already exists, a corresponding wide-character string environment is created. The environment is then pointed to by the **_wenviron** global variable, which is a wide-character version of the **_environ** global variable. At this point, two copies of the environment (MBCS and Unicode) exist simultaneously and are maintained by the run-time system throughout the life of the program.

Similarly, if your program uses a **wmain** function, a wide-character environment is created at program startup and is pointed to by the **_wenviron** global variable. An MBCS (ASCII) environment is created on the first call to **_putenv** or **getenv**, and is pointed to by the **_environ** global variable.

END Microsoft Specific

Unicode Programming Summary

To take advantage of the MFC and C run-time support for Unicode, you need to:

- Define _UNICODE.

  Define the symbol **_UNICODE** before you build your program.

- Specify entry point.

  In the Output category of the Link tab in the Project Settings dialog box, set the Entry Point Symbol to **wWinMainCRTStartup**.

- Use "portable" run-time functions and types.

  Use the proper C run-time functions for Unicode string handling. You can use the **wcs** family of functions, but you may prefer the fully "portable" (internationally enabled) **_TCHAR** macros. These macros are all prefixed with **_tcs**; they substitute, one for one, for the **str** family of functions. These functions are described in detail in the "Internationalization" section in Chapter 1 of the *Run-Time Library Reference*. For more information, see "Generic-Text Mappings in TCHAR.H" on page 164.

  Use **_TCHAR** and the related portable data types described in "Support for Unicode" on page 155.

- Handle literal strings properly.

  The Visual C++ compiler interprets a literal string coded as

  ```
  L"this is a literal string"
  ```

  to mean a string of Unicode characters. You can use the same prefix for literal characters. Use the **_T** macro to code literal strings generically, so they compile as Unicode strings under Unicode or as ANSI strings (including MBCS) without Unicode. For example, instead of:

  ```
  pWnd->SetWindowText( "Hello" );
  ```

  use:

  ```
  pWnd->SetWindowText( _T("Hello") );
  ```

- With **_UNICODE** defined, **_T** translates the literal string to the L-prefixed form; otherwise, **_T** translates the string without the L prefix.

 Tip   The _T macro is identical to the **_TEXT** macro.

- Be careful passing string lengths to functions.

  Some functions want the number of characters in a string; others want the number of bytes. For example, if **_UNICODE** is defined, the following call to a **CArchive** object will not work (str is a **CString**):

  ```
  archive.Write( str, str.GetLength( ) );    // invalid
  ```

In a Unicode application, the length gives you the number of characters but not the correct number of bytes, since each character is two bytes wide. Instead, you must use:

```
archive.Write( str, str.GetLength( ) * sizeof( _TCHAR ) );    // valid
```

which specifies the correct number of bytes to write.

However, MFC member functions that are character-oriented, rather than byte-oriented, work without this extra coding:

```
pDC->TextOut( str, str.GetLength( ) );
```

CDC::TextOut takes a number of characters, not a number of bytes.

To summarize, MFC and the run-time library provide the following support for Unicode programming under Windows NT:

- Except for database class member functions, all MFC functions are Unicode enabled, including **CString**. **CString** also provides Unicode/ANSI conversion functions.

- The run-time library supplies Unicode versions of all string-handling functions. (The run-time library also supplies "portable" versions suitable for Unicode or for MBCS. These are the **_tcs** macros.)

- TCHAR.H supplies portable data types and the **_T** macro for translating literal strings and characters. See "Generic-Text Mappings in TCHAR.H" on page 164.

- The run-time library provides a wide-character version of **main**. Use **wmain** to make your application "Unicode aware."

Support for Multibyte Character Sets (MBCS)

For platforms used in markets whose languages use large character sets, the best alternative to Unicode is MBCS. MFC supports MBCS by using "internationalizable" data types and C run-time functions. You should do the same in your code.

Under MBCS, characters are encoded in either one or two bytes. In two-byte characters, the first, or "lead-byte," signals that both it and the following byte are to be interpreted as one character. The first byte comes from a range of codes reserved for use as lead bytes. Which ranges of bytes can be lead bytes depends on the code page in use. For example, Japanese code page 932 uses the range 0x81 through 0x9F as lead bytes, but Korean code page 949 uses a different range.

Consider all of the following in your MBCS programming:

MBCS characters in the environment   MBCS characters can appear in strings such as file and directory names.

Editing operations   Editing operations in MBCS applications should operate on characters, not bytes. The caret should not split a character, the RIGHT ARROW key should move right one character, and so on. Delete should delete a character; Undo should reinsert it.

String handling   In an application that uses MBCS, string handling poses special problems. Characters of both widths are mixed in a single string; therefore you must remember to check for lead bytes.

Run-time library support   The C run-time library and MFC support single-byte, MBCS, and Unicode programming. Single-byte strings are processed with the *str* family of run-time functions; MBCS strings are processed with corresponding *_mbs* functions; and Unicode strings are processed with corresponding *wcs* functions. MFC class member function implementations use portable run-time functions that map, under the right circumstances, to the normal *str* family of functions, the MBCS functions, or the Unicode functions, as described in "MBCS/Unicode portability."

MBCS/Unicode portability   Using the header file TCHAR.H, you can build single-byte, MBCS, and Unicode applications from the same sources. TCHAR.H defines macros prefixed with *_tcs*, which map to *str*, *_mbs*, or *wcs* functions as appropriate. To build MBCS, define the symbol **_MBCS**. To build Unicode, define the symbol **_UNICODE**. By default, **_MBCS** is defined for MFC applications. For more information, see "Generic-Text Mappings in TCHAR.H" on page 164.

Note   Behavior is undefined if you define both **_UNICODE** and **_MBCS**.

The MBCTYPE.H and MBSTRING.H header files define MBCS-specific functions and macros, which you may need in some cases. For example, **_ismbblead** tells you whether a specific byte in a string is a lead byte.

MBCS Support in Visual C++

When run on an MBCS-enabled version of the Windows 95 or Windows NT operating system, the Visual C++ development system, including the integrated source code editor, debugger, and command line tools, is completely MBCS-enabled. Visual C++ will accept double-byte characters wherever it is appropriate to do so. This includes path names and filenames in dialog boxes, and text entries in the Visual C++ resource editor (for example, static text in the dialog editor, and static text entries in the icon editor). In addition, the preprocessor recognizes some double-byte directives—for example, filenames in **#include** statements, and as arguments to the **code_seg** and **data_seg** pragmas. In the source code editor, double-byte characters in comments and string literals are accepted, although not in C/C++ language elements (such as variable names).

Support for the Input Method Editor (IME)

Applications written for Far East markets that use MBCS (for example, Japan) normally support the Windows IME for entering both single- and double-byte characters. The Visual C++ development environment contains full support for the IME.

Japanese keyboards do not directly support Kanji characters. The IME converts a phonetic string, entered in one of the other Japanese alphabets, Romaji, Katakana, or Hiragana, into its possible Kanji representations. If there is ambiguity, you can select from several alternate possibilities. Once you have selected the intended Kanji character, the IME passes two **WM_CHAR** messages to the controlling application.

The IME, activated by the ALT+` key combination, appears as a set of buttons (an indicator) and a conversion window. The application positions the window at the text insertion point. The application must handle **WM_MOVE** and **WM_SIZE** messages by repositioning the conversion window to conform to the new location or size of the target window.

If you want users of your application to have the ability to enter Kanji characters, the application must handle Windows IME messages. For more information on IME programming, see the *Internationalization Handbook for Software Design*, in the Microsoft Development Library.

Visual C++ Debugger

The Visual C++ debugger provides the ability to set breakpoints on IME messages. In addition, the memory window can display double-byte characters.

Command-Line Tools

The Visual C++ command-line tools, including the compiler, NMAKE, and the resource compiler (RC.EXE), are MBCS-enabled. You can use the resource compiler's /c option to change the default code page when compiling your application's resources.

To change the default locale at source code compile time, use the **setlocale** pragma.

Graphical Tools

The Visual C++ Windows-based tools, such as Spy++ and the resource editing tools, fully support IME strings.

MBCS Programming Tips

This section supplies tips for successful multibyte character set (MBCS) programming. The advice applies to MFC applications and applications written without MFC. Topics include:

- General MBCS programming advice
- Incrementing and decrementing pointers
- Byte indices
- Last character in a string

- Character assignment
- Character comparison
- Buffer overflow

General MBCS Programming Advice

Use the following tips:

- For flexibility, use run-time macros such as **_tcschr** and **_tcscpy** when possible. For more information, see "Generic-Text Mappings in TCHAR.H" on page 164.

- Use the C run-time **_getmbcp** function to get information about the current code page.

- Do not reuse string resources. Depending on the target language, a given string may have a different meaning when translated. For example, "File" on the application's main menu might translate differently than the string "File" in a dialog box. If you need to use more than one string with the same name, use different string IDs for each.

- You may want to find out whether or not your application is running on an MBCS-enabled operating system. To do so, set a flag at program startup; do not rely on API calls.

- When designing dialog boxes, allow approximately 30% extra space at the end of static text controls, to allow for MBCS translation.

- Be careful when selecting fonts for your application, since some fonts are not available on all systems. For example, the Japanese version of Windows NT does not support the Helvetica font.

- When designing your application, decide which strings can or cannot be localized. If in doubt, assume that any given string will be localized. As such, do not mix strings that can be localized with those that cannot.

Incrementing and Decrementing Pointers

Use the following tips:

- Point to lead bytes, not trail bytes. It is usually unsafe to have a pointer to a trail byte. It's usually safest to scan a string forward rather than in reverse.

- There are pointer increment/decrement functions and macros available which move over a whole character:

```
sz1++;
```

becomes

```
sz1 = _mbsinc( sz1 );
```

The **_mbsinc** and **_mbsdec** functions correctly increment and decrement in *character* units, regardless of the character size.

- For decrements, you need a pointer to the head of the string, as in the following:

```
sz2--;
```

becomes

```
sz2 = _mbsdec( sz2Head, sz2 );
```

Alternatively, your "head" pointer could be to a valid character in the string, such that

```
sz2Head < sz2
```

You must have a pointer to a known valid lead byte.

- You may want to maintain a pointer to the previous character for faster calls to **_mbsdec**.

Byte Indices

Use the following tips:

- Working with a bytewise index into a string presents problems similar to those posed by pointer manipulation. Consider this example, which scans a string for a backslash character:

```
while ( rgch[ i ] != '\\' )
    i++;
```

This may index a trail byte, not a lead byte, and thus it may not point to a *character*.

- Use the **_mbslen** function to solve the preceding problem:

```
while ( rgch[ i ] != '\\' )
    i += _mbslen( rgch + i );
```

This correctly indexes to a lead byte, hence to a *character*. The **_mbslen** function determines the size of a character (one or two bytes).

The Last Character in a String

Use the following tips:

- Trail byte ranges overlap the ASCII character set in many cases. You can safely use bytewise scans for any control characters (less than 32).

- Consider the following line of code, which might be checking to see if the last character in a string is a backslash character:

```
if ( sz[ strlen( sz ) - 1 ] == '\\' )     // Is last character a '\'?
    // . . .
```

Since **strlen** is not "MBCS-aware," it will return the number of bytes, not the number of characters, in a multibyte string. Also, note that in some code pages (932, for example), '\' (0x5c) is a valid trail byte (sz is a C string).

One possible solution is to rewrite the code this way:

```
char *pLast;
pLast = _mbsrchr( sz, '\\' );      // find last occurence of '\' in sz
if ( pLast && ( *_mbsinc( pLast ) == '\0' ) )
    // . . .
```

This code uses the MBCS functions **_mbsrchr** and **_mbsinc**. Since these functions are MBCS-aware, they can distinguish between a '\' character and a trail byte '\'. The code performs some action if the last character in the string is a null ('\0').

Character Assignment

Consider the following example, in which the **while** loop scans a string, copying all characters except 'X' into another string:

```
while( *sz2 )
{
    if( *sz2 != 'X' )
        *sz1++ = *sz2;
    else
        sz2++;
}
```

The code copies the byte at sz2 to the location pointed to by sz1, then increments sz1 to receive the next byte. But if the next character in sz2 is a double-byte character, the assignment to sz1 will copy only the first byte. The following code uses a portable function to copy the character safely and another to increment sz1 and sz2 correctly:

```
while( *sz2 )
{
    if( *sz2 != 'X' )
    {
        _mbscpy( sz1, sz2 );
        sz1 = _mbsinc( sz1 );
    }
    else
        sz2 = _mbsinc( sz2 );
}
```

Character Comparison

Use the following tips:

- Comparing a known lead byte with an ASCII character works correctly:

  ```
  if( *sz1 == 'A' )
  ```

- Comparing two unknown characters requires the use of one of the macros defined in MBSTRING.H:

  ```
  if( !_mbccmp( sz1, sz2) )
  ```

This ensures that both bytes of a double-byte character are compared for equality.

Buffer Overflow

Varying character sizes can cause problems when you put characters into a buffer. Consider the following code, which copies characters from a string, sz, into a buffer, rgch:

```
cb = 0;
while( cb < sizeof( rgch ) )
    rgch[ cb++ ] = *sz++;
```

The question is: was the last byte copied a lead byte? The following does not solve the problem because it can potentially overflow the buffer:

```
cb = 0;
while( cb < sizeof( rgch ) )
{
    _mbccpy( rgch + cb, sz );
    cb += _mbclen( sz );
    sz = _mbsinc( sz );
}
```

The **_mbccpy** call attempts to do the right thing—copy the full character, whether it's one or two bytes. But it doesn't take into account that the last character copied may not fit the buffer if the character is two bytes wide. The correct solution is:

```
cb = 0;
while( (cb + _mbclen( sz )) <= sizeof( rgch ) )
{
    _mbccpy( rgch + cb, sz );
    cb += _mbclen( sz );
    sz = _mbsinc( sz );
}
```

This code tests for possible buffer overflow in the loop test, using **_mbclen** to test the size of the current character pointed to by sz. By making a call to the **_mbsnbcpy** function, you can replace the code in the **while** loop with a single line of code. For example:

```
cb = 0;
while( (cb + _mbclen( sz )) <= sizeof( rgch ) )
{
    _mbsnbcpy( rgch, sz, sizeof( rgch ) );
}
```

Generic-Text Mappings in TCHAR.H

To simplify transporting code for international use, the Microsoft run-time library provides Microsoft-specific "generic-text" mappings for many data types, routines, and other objects. You can use these mappings, which are defined in TCHAR.H, to write generic code that can be compiled for single byte, multibyte, or Unicode, depending on a manifest constant you define using a **#define** statement. Generic-text mappings are Microsoft extensions that are not ANSI compatible.

Using the header file TCHAR.H, you can build single-byte, MBCS, and Unicode applications from the same sources. TCHAR.H defines macros prefixed with **_tcs**, which, with the correct preprocessor definitions, map to **str**, **_mbs**, or **wcs** functions as appropriate. To build MBCS, define the symbol **_MBCS**. To build Unicode, define the symbol **_UNICODE**. To build a single-byte application, define neither (the default). By default, **_MBCS** is defined for MFC applications.

The **_TCHAR** data type is defined conditionally in TCHAR.H. If the symbol **_UNICODE** is defined for your build, **_TCHAR** is defined as **wchar_t**; otherwise, for single-byte and MBCS builds, it is defined as **char**. (**wchar_t**, the basic Unicode wide character data type, is the 16-bit counterpart to an 8-bit signed **char**.) For international applications, use the **_tcs** family of functions, which operate in **_TCHAR** units, not bytes. For example, **_tcsncpy** copies *n* **_TCHAR**s, not *n* bytes.

Because some SBCS string-handling functions take (signed) **char*** parameters, a type mismatch compiler warning will result when **_MBCS** is defined. There are three ways to avoid this warning, listed in order of efficiency:

1. Use the "type-safe" inline function thunks in TCHAR.H. This is the default behavior.

2. Use the "direct" macros in TCHAR.H by defining **_MB_MAP_DIRECT** on the command line. If you do this, you must manually match types. This is the fastest method, but is not type-safe.

3. Use the "type-safe" statically-linked library function thunks in TCHAR.H. To do so, define the constant **_NO_INLINING** on the command line. This is the slowest method, but the most type-safe.

Table 13.2   Preprocessor Directives for Generic-Text Mappings

# define	Compiled Version	Example
_UNICODE	Unicode (wide-character)	**_tcsrev** maps to **_wcsrev**
_MBCS	Multibyte-character	**_tcsrev** maps to **_mbsrev**
None (the default: neither **_UNICODE** nor **_MBCS** defined)	SBCS (ASCII)	**_tcsrev** maps to **strrev**

For example, the generic-text function **_tcsrev**, defined in TCHAR.H, maps to **_mbsrev** if you defined **_MBCS** in your program, or to **_wcsrev** if you defined **_UNICODE**. Otherwise **_tcsrev** maps to **strrev**. Other data type mappings are provided in TCHAR.H for programming convenience, but **_TCHAR** is the most useful.

Table 13.3 Generic-Text Data Type Mappings

Generic-Text Data Type Name	SBCS (_UNICODE, _MBCS Not Defined)	_MBCS Defined	_UNICODE Defined
_TCHAR	char	char	wchar_t
_TINT	int	int	wint_t
_TSCHAR	signed char	signed char	wchar_t
_TUCHAR	unsigned char	unsigned char	wchar_t
_TXCHAR	char	unsigned char	wchar_t
_T or **_TEXT**	No effect (removed by preprocessor)	No effect (removed by preprocessor)	**L** (converts following character or string to its Unicode counterpart)

For a complete list of generic-text mappings of routines, variables, and other objects, see Appendix B, "Generic-Text Mappings," in the *Run-Time Library Reference*.

Note Do not use the **str** family of functions with Unicode strings, which are likely to contain embedded null bytes. Similarly, do not use the **wcs** family of functions with MBCS (or SBCS) strings.

The following code fragments illustrate the use of **_TCHAR** and **_tcsrev** for mapping to the MBCS, Unicode, and SBCS models.

```
_TCHAR *RetVal, *szString;
RetVal = _tcsrev(szString);
```

If **_MBCS** has been defined, the preprocessor maps this fragment to the code:

```
char *RetVal, *szString;
RetVal = _mbsrev(szString);
```

If **_UNICODE** has been defined, the preprocessor maps this fragment to the code:

```
wchar_t *RetVal, *szString;
RetVal = _wcsrev(szString);
```

If neither **_MBCS** nor **_UNICODE** has been defined, the preprocessor maps the fragment to single-byte ASCII code:

```
char *RetVal, *szString;
RetVal = strrev(szString);
```

Thus you can write, maintain, and compile a single source code file to run with routines that are specific to any of the three kinds of character sets.

Using TCHAR.H Data Types with _MBCS Code

When the manifest constant **_MBCS** is defined, a given generic-text routine maps to one of the following kinds of routines:

- An SBCS routine that handles multibyte bytes, characters, and strings appropriately. In this case, the string arguments are expected to be of type **char***. For example, **_tprintf** maps to **printf**; the string arguments to **printf** are of type **char***. If you use the **_TCHAR** generic-text data type for your string types, the formal and actual parameter types for **printf** match because **_TCHAR*** maps to **char***.

- An MBCS-specific routine. In this case, the string arguments are expected to be of type **unsigned char***. For example, **_tcsrev** maps to **_mbsrev**, which expects and returns a string of type **unsigned char***. If you use the **_TCHAR** generic-text data type for your string types, there is a potential type conflict because **_TCHAR** maps to type **char**.

Following are three solutions for preventing this type conflict (and the C compiler warnings or C++ compiler errors that would result).

- Use the default behavior. TCHAR.H provides generic-text routine prototypes for routines in the run-time libraries, as in the following example.

```
char * _tcsrev( char *);
```

  In the default case, the prototype for **_tcsrev** maps to **_mbsrev** through a thunk in LIBC.LIB. This changes the types of the **_mbsrev** incoming parameters and outgoing return value from **_TCHAR *** (that is, **char ***) to **unsigned char ***. This method ensures type matching when you are using **_TCHAR**, but it is relatively slow due to the function call overhead.

- Use function inlining by incorporating the following preprocessor statement in your code.

```
#define _USE_INLINING
```

  This method causes an inline function thunk, provided in TCHAR.H, to map the generic-text routine directly to the appropriate MBCS routine. The following code excerpt from TCHAR.H provides an example of how this is done.

```
__inline char *_tcsrev(char *_s1)
{return (char *)_mbsrev((unsigned char *)_s1);}
```

  If you can use inlining, this is the best solution, because it guarantees type matching and has no additional time cost.

- Use "direct mapping" by incorporating the following preprocessor statement in your code.

```
#define _MB_MAP_DIRECT
```

This approach provides a fast alternative if you do not want to use the default behavior or cannot use inlining. It causes the generic-text routine to be mapped by a macro directly to the MBCS version of the routine, as in the following example from TCHAR.H.

```
#define _tcschr _mbschr
```

When you take this approach, you must be careful to ensure use of appropriate data types for string arguments and string return values. You can use type casting to ensure proper type matching or you can use the **_TXCHAR** generic-text data type. **_TXCHAR** maps to type **char** in SBCS code but maps to type **unsigned char** in MBCS code. For more information about generic-text macros, see Appendix B, "Generic-Text Mappings," in the *Run-Time Library Reference*.

For More Information

For more information on developing for international markets, see the following:

- In the *Run-Time Library Reference*: "Internationalization."

- In the *Win32 Programmer's Reference, Volume 2*: "String Manipulation and Unicode."

- In *Advanced Windows NT*, Microsoft Press, 1994, by Jeffrey Richter: Chapter 11, "Unicode."

- "The Unicode™ Standard: Worldwide Character Encoding," Version 1.0, Volumes 1 and 2, Addison-Wesley, 1992.

Index

Contributors to *Programming Techniques*

Richard Carlson, Index Editor

Pat Fenn, Production

Roger Haight, Editor

Jonathan Kagle, Writer

Seth Manheim, Writer

Chuck Sphar, Writer

David Adam Edelstein, Art Director

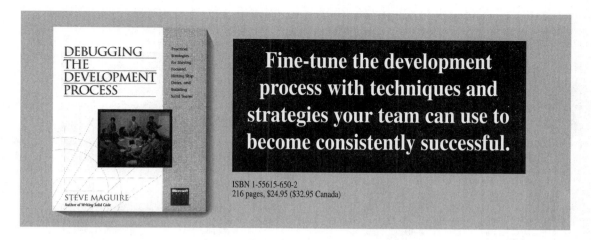

Fine-tune the development process with techniques and strategies your team can use to become consistently successful.

ISBN 1-55615-650-2
216 pages, $24.95 ($32.95 Canada)

In this eagerly awaited companion to the award winning, bestselling *Writing Solid Code*, Steve Maguire describes the sometimes controversial but always effective practices that enable his software teams at Microsoft to develop high-quality software—on schedule.

With the refreshing candor reviewers admired in *Writing Solid Code*, Maguire talks about what did and what didn't work at Microsoft and tells you:

- How to energize software teams to work effectively
- How to deliver on schedule and without overwork
- How to pull twice the value out of everything you do
- How to get your team going on a creative roll

If you're part of a development team, this book is for you. Once you've read it, you'll want to give it to your manager, your peers, and your friends.

More Ways to Smooth Software Development
with the *Programming Practices Series*
from Microsoft Press

Code Complete	Debugging the	Writing Solid Code
Steve McConnell	Development Process	Steve Maguire
ISBN 1-55615-484-4	Steve Maguire	ISBN 1-55615-551-4
880 pages	ISBN 1-55615-650-2	288 pages
$35.00 ($44.95 Canada)	216 pages	$24.95 ($32.95 Canada)
	$24.95 ($32.95 Canada)	

Microsoft Press